Lecture Notes in Artificial Intelligence 9648

Subseries of Lecture Notes in Computer Science

More information about this series at http://www.springer.com/series/1244

Francisco Martínez-Álvarez · Alicia Troncoso
Héctor Quintián · Emilio Corchado (Eds.)

Hybrid Artificial Intelligent Systems

11th International Conference, HAIS 2016
Seville, Spain, April 18–20, 2016
Proceedings

 Springer

Editors
Francisco Martínez-Álvarez
Universidad Pablo de Olavide
Sevilla
Spain

Héctor Quintián
University of Salamanca
Salamanca
Spain

Alicia Troncoso
Universidad Pablo de Olavide
Sevilla
Spain

Emilio Corchado
University of Salamanca
Salamanca
Spain

ISSN 0302-9743   ISSN 1611-3349   (electronic)
Lecture Notes in Artificial Intelligence
ISBN 978-3-319-32033-5   ISBN 978-3-319-32034-2   (eBook)
DOI 10.1007/978-3-319-32034-2

Library of Congress Control Number: 2016934675

LNCS Sublibrary: SL7 – Artificial Intelligence

Printed on acid-free paper

This Springer imprint is published by Springer Nature
The registered company is Springer International Publishing AG Switzerland

Preface

This volume of *Lecture Notes in Artificial Intelligence* (LNAI) includes the papers accepted for presentation at HAIS 2016 – the 11th International Conference on Hybrid Artificial Intelligence Systems – held in the beautiful city of Seville, Spain, in April 2016.

The International Conference on Hybrid Artificial Intelligence Systems has become a unique, established, and broad interdisciplinary forum for researchers an practitioners who are involved in developing and applying symbolic and sub-symbolic techniques aimed at the construction of highly robust and reliable problem-solving techniques and at bringing the most relevant achievements in this field.

Hybridization of intelligent techniques, coming from different computational intelligence areas, has become popular because of the growing awareness that such combinations frequently perform better than individual techniques such as neurocomputing, fuzzy systems, rough sets, evolutionary algorithms, agents and multiagent systems, etc.

Practical experience has indicated that hybrid intelligence techniques might be helpful for solving some of the challenging real-world problems. In a hybrid intelligence system, a synergistic combination of multiple techniques is used to build an efficient solution to deal with a particular problem. This is, thus, the setting of the HAIS conference series, and its increasing success is the proof of the vitality of this exciting field.

HAIS 2016 received more than 150 technical submissions. After a rigorous peer-review process, the international Program Committee selected 63 papers, which are published in this conference proceedings.

The selection of papers was extremely rigorous in order to maintain the high quality of the conference and we would like to thank the Program Committee for their hard work in the reviewing process. This process is very important to the creation of a conference of high standard and the HAIS conference would not exist without their help.

The large number of submissions is certainly not only to testimony to the vitality and attractiveness of the field but an indicator of the interest in the HAIS conferences themselves.

HAIS 2016 enjoyed outstanding keynote speeches by distinguished guest speakers: Prof. João Gama – University of Porto (Portugal); Prof. Bogusław Cyganek – Visiting Professor at Wroclaw University of Technology (Poland) and Associate Professor at AGH University of Science and Technology (Poland); and Prof. Richard Duro – University of A Coruña (Spain).

Moreover, HAIS 2016 has teamed up with *Neurocomputing* (Elsevier), *BioData Mining* (BioMed Central), and the *Logic Journal of the IGPL* (Oxford Journals) for a set of special issues including selected papers from HAIS 2016.

Particular thanks also go to the conference's main sponsors, ENGINE — European Research Centre of Network Intelligence for Innovation Enhancement (http://engine. pwr.edu.pl) sponsored by EC under FP7Coordination and Support Action (Grant Agreement Number 316097), IEEE — Spanish Section, IEEE Systems, Man and Cybernetics — Spanish Chapter, Universidad Pablo de Olavide, University of Salamanca, and The International Federation for Computational Logic, who jointly contributed in an active and constructive manner to the success of this initiative.

We would like to thank Alfred Hofmann and Anna Kramer from Springer for their help and collaboration during this demanding publication project.

April 2016

Francisco Martínez-Álvarez
Alicia Troncoso
Héctor Quintián
Emilio Corchado

Organization

General Chair

Emilio Corchado — University of Salamanca, Spain

Local Chairs

Francisco Martínez-Álvarez — Pablo de Olavide University of Seville, Spain

Alicia Troncoso Lora — Pablo de Olavide University of Seville, Spain

International Advisory Committee

Ajith Abraham	Machine Intelligence Research Labs, Europe
Antonio Bahamonde	University of Oviedo, Spain
Andre de Carvalho	University of São Paulo, Brazil
Sung-Bae Cho	Yonsei University, Korea
Juan M. Corchado	University of Salamanca, Spain
José R. Dorronsoro	Autonomous University of Madrid, Spain
Michael Gabbay	Kings College London, UK
Ali A. Ghorbani	UNB, Canada
Mark A. Girolami	University of Glasgow, UK
Manuel Graña	University of País Vasco, Spain
Petro Gopych	Universal Power Systems USA-Ukraine LLC, Ukraine
Jon G. Hall	The Open University, UK
Francisco Herrera	University of Granada, Spain
César Hervás-Martínez	University of Córdoba, Spain
Tom Heskes	Radboud University Nijmegen, The Netherlands
Dusan Husek	Academy of Sciences of the Czech Republic, Czech Republic
Lakhmi Jain	University of South Australia, Australia
Samuel Kaski	Helsinki University of Technology, Finland
Daniel A. Keim	University Konstanz, Germany
Isidro Laso	D.G. Information Society and Media, European Commission
Marios Polycarpou	University of Cyprus, Cyprus
Witold Pedrycz	University of Alberta, Canada
Václav Snášel	VSB-Technical University of Ostrava, Czech Republic
Xin Yao	University of Birmingham, UK
Hujun Yin	University of Manchester, UK
Michał Woźniak	Wroclaw University of Technology, Poland

Aditya Ghose	University of Wollongong, Australia
Ashraf Saad	Armstrong Atlantic State University, USA
Fanny Klett	German Workforce Advanced Distributed Learning Partnership Laboratory, Germany
Paulo Novais	Universidade do Minho, Portugal
Rajkumar Roy	The EPSRC Centre for Innovative Manufacturing in Through-life Engineering Services, UK
Amy Neustein	Linguistic Technology Systems, USA
Jaydip Sen	Innovation Lab, Tata Consultancy Services Ltd., India

Program Committee

Emilio Corchado	University of Salamanca, Spain (PC Chair)
Francisco Martínez-Álvarez	University Pablo de Olavide, Spain (PC Chair)
Alicia Troncoso	University Pablo de Olavide, Spain (PC Chair)
Abdel-Badeeh Salem	Ain Shams University, Egypt
Aboul Ella Hassanien	Cairo University, Egypt
Adolfo R. De Soto	University of Leon, Spain
Albert Cano	University of Cordoba, Spain
Alberto Fernandez	Rey Juan Carlos University, Spain
Alfredo Cuzzocrea	ICAR-CNR and University of Calabria, Italy
Álvaro Herrero	University of Burgos, Spain
Amelia Zafra Gómez	University of Cordoba, Spain
Ana Madureira	Instituto Politécnico do Porto, Portugal
Ana M. Bernardos	Universidad Politécnica de Madrid, Spain
Anca Andreica	Babes-Bolyai University, Romania
Andreea Vescan	Babes-Bolyai University, Cluj-Napoca, Romania
Andres Ortiz	University of Malaga, Spain
Antonio Dourado	University of Coimbra, Portugal
Antonio Morales-Esteban	University of Seville, Spain
Antonio D. Masegosa	University of Deusto, Spain
Arkadiusz Grzybowski	Wrocław University of Technology, Poland
Arkadiusz Kowalski	Wrocław University of Technology, Poland
Barna Laszlo Iantovics	Petru Maior University of Tg. Mures, Romania
Bogdan Trawinski	Wroclaw University of Technology, Poland
Bozena Skolud	Silesian University of Technology, Poland
Bruno Baruque	University of Burgos, Spain
Camelia Pintea	Technical University of Cluj-Napoca North and University Baia-Mare, Romania
Carlos Carrascosa	Universidad Politecnica de Valencia, Spain
Carlos Laorden	University of Deusto, Spain
Carlos Pereira	ISEC, Portugal
Cezary Grabowik	Silesian Technical University, Poland
Cristina Rubio-Escudero	University of Seville, Spain

Damian Krenczyk	Silesian University of Technology, Poland
Dario Landa-Silva	The University of Nottingham, UK
David Iclanzan	Sapientia — Hungarian Science University of Transylvania, Romania
Diego P. Ruiz	University of Granada, Spain
Dragan Simic	University of Novi Sad, Serbia
Dragos Horvath	University of Strasbourg, France
Eiji Uchino	Yamaguchi University, Japan
Eneko Osaba	University of Deusto, Spain
Enrique Onieva	University of Deusto, Spain
Eva Volna	Univerzity of Ostrava, Czech Republic
Fabrício Olivetti De França	Universidade Federal do ABC — UFABC, Brazil
Fawad Hassan	Pakistan Institute of Engineering and Applied Sciences, Pakistan
Federico Divina	Pablo de Olavide University, Spain
Fermin Segovia	University of Granada, Spain
Fidel Aznar	Universidad de Alicante, Spain
George Papakostas	EMT Institute of Technology, Greece
Georgios Dounias	University of the Aegean, Greece
Giancarlo Mauri	University of Milano-Bicocca, Italy
Giorgio Fumera	University of Cagliari, Italy
Gloria Cerasela Crisan	University of Bacau, Romania
Gonzalo A. Aranda-Corral	Universidad de Huelva, Spain
Gualberto Asencio-Cortés	Pablo de Olavide University, Spain
Guiomar Corral	Universitat Ramon Llull — La Salle, Spain
Hais Conference	University of Salamanca, Spain
Héctor Quintián	University of Salamanca, Spain
Henrietta Toman	University of Debrecen, Hungary
Ignacio Turias	Universidad de Cádiz, Spain
Ingo R. Keck	Dublin Institute of Technology, Ireland
Ioannis Hatzilygeroudis	University of Patras, Greece
Irene Diaz	University of Oviedo, Spain
Isabel Barbancho	Universidad of Málaga, Spain
Isabel Nepomuceno	University of Seville, Spain
Iskander Sánchez-Rola	University of Deusto, Spain
Javier Bajo	Universidad Politécnica de Madrid, Spain
Javier De Lope	Universidad Politécnica de Madrid, Spain
Javier Sedano	Instituto Tecnológico de Castilla y León, Spain
Jorge García-Gutiérrez	University of Seville, Spain
Jorge Reyes	NT2 Labs, Chile
Jose Dorronsoro	Universidad Autnoma de Madrid, Spain
Jose Garcia-Rodriguez	University of Alicante, Spain

Jose Alfredo Ferreira Costa	UFRN – Universidade Federal do Rio Grande do Norte, Brazil
Jose Luis Calvo-Rolle	University of A Coruña, Spain
José Luis Verdegay	Universidad de Granada, Spain
Jose M. Molina	Universidad Carlos III de Madrid, Spain
Jose Manuel Lopez-Guede	University of the Basque Country, Spain
José María Armingol	Universidad Carlos III de Madrid, Spain
José María Luna	University of Cordoba, Spain
José María Luna Romera	University of Seville, Spain
José Ramón Villar	University of Oviedo, Spain
Jose-Ramon Cano De Amo	University of Jaen, Spain
Joses Ranilla	University of Oviedo, Spain
Juan Pavón	Universidad Complutense de Madrid, Spain
Juan Humberto Sossa Azuela	National Polytechnic Institute, Mexico
Juan J. Flores	Universidad Michoacana de San Nicolas de Hidalgo, Mexico
Julio Ponce	Universidad Autónoma de Aguascalientes, Mexico
Khawaja Asim	Pakistan Institute of Engineering and Applied Sciences, Pakistan
Krzysztof Kalinowski	Silesian University of Technology, Poland
Lauro Snidaro	University of Udine, Italy
Lenka Lhotska	Czech Technical University in Prague, Czech Republic
Leocadio G. Casado	University of Almeria, Spain
Manuel Grana	University of the Basque Country, Spain
Maria Guijarro	Universidad Complutense de Madrid, Spain
María Martínez Ballesteros	University of Seville, Spain
Mario Koeppen	Kyushu Institute of Technology, Japan
Martin Macas	Czech Technical University in Prague, Czech Republic
Matjaz Gams	Jozef Stefan Institute, Slovenia
Miguel García Torres	Universidad Pablo de Olavide, Spain
Miguel Ángel Veganzones	GIPSA-lab, Grenoble INP, France
Miroslav Bursa	Czech Technical University in Prague, Czech Republic
Mohammed Chadli	University of Picardie Jules Verne, France
Oscar Fontenla-Romero	University of A Coruña, Spain
Ozgur Koray Sahingoz	Turkish Air Force Academy, Turkey
Paula M. Castro	University of A Coruña, Spain
Paulo Novais	University of Minho, Portugal
Pavel Brandstetter	VSB-Technical University of Ostrava, Czech Republic
Pedro López	Universidad de Deusto, Spain
Peter Rockett	University of Sheffield, UK
Petrica Claudiu Pop	North University of Baia Mare, Romania

Rafael Alcala	University of Granada, Spain
Ramon Rizo	Universidad de Alicante, Spain
Ricardo Del Olmo	Universidad de Burgos, Spain
Ricardo L. Talavera-Llames	University Pablo de Olavide, Spain
Robert Burduk	Wroclaw University of Technology, Poland
Rodolfo Zunino	University of Genoa, Italy
Roman Senkerik	TBU in Zlin, Czech Republic
Rubén Fuentes-Fernández	Universidad Complutense de Madrid, Spain
Rubén Pérez-Chacón	Pablo de Olavide University, Spain
Sean Holden	University of Cambridge, UK
Sebastián Ventura	University of Cordoba, Spain
Stella Heras	Universitat Politècnica de València, Spain
Theodore Pachidis	Kavala Institute of Technology, Greece
Tomasz Kajdanowicz	Wroclaw University of Technology, Poland
Urszula Stanczyk	Silesian University of Technology, Poland
Waldemar Małopolski	Cracow University of Technology, Poland
Wiesław Chmielnicki	Jagiellonian University, Poland
Yannis Marinakis	Technical University of Crete, Greece
Yusuke Nojima	Osaka Prefecture University, Japan
Zuzana Oplatkova	Tomas Bata University in Zlin, Czech Republic

Organizing Committee

Francisco Martínez-Álvarez	Pablo de Olavide University of Seville, Spain
Alicia Troncoso Lora	Pablo de Olavide University of Seville, Spain
Jesús S. Aguilar Ruiz	Pablo de Olavide University of Seville, Spain
Raúl Giráldez Rojo	Pablo de Olavide University of Seville, Spain
Roberto Ruiz Sánchez	Pablo de Olavide University of Seville, Spain
Gualberto Asencio Cortés	Pablo de Olavide University of Seville, Spain
Francisco Javier Gil Cumbreras	Pablo de Olavide University of Seville, Spain
Francisco Javier Duque Pintor	Pablo de Olavide University of Seville, Spain
Miguel Ángel Montero Navarro	Pablo de Olavide University of Seville, Spain
María Martínez Ballesteros	University of Seville, Spain
Cristina Rubio Escudero	University of Seville, Spain
Jorge García Gutiérrez	University of Seville, Spain
José C. Riquelme Santos	University of Seville, Spain
Emilio Corchado	University of Salamanca, Spain
Héctor Quintián	University of Salamanca, Spain

Contents

Data Mining and Knowledge Discovery

Screening a Case Base for Stroke Disease Detection 3
José Neves, Nuno Gonçalves, Ruben Oliveira, Sabino Gomes,
João Neves, Joaquim Macedo, António Abelha, César Analide,
José Machado, Manuel Filipe Santos, and Henrique Vicente

SemSynX: Flexible Similarity Analysis of XML Data via Semantic
and Syntactic Heterogeneity/Homogeneity Detection 14
Jesús M. Almendros-Jiménez and Alfredo Cuzzocrea

Towards Automatic Composition of Multicomponent Predictive Systems 27
Manuel Martin Salvador, Marcin Budka, and Bogdan Gabrys

LiCord: Language Independent Content Word Finder 40
Md-Mizanur Rahoman, Tetsuya Nasukawa, Hiroshi Kanayama,
and Ryutaro Ichise

Mining Correlated High-Utility Itemsets Using the Bond Measure. 53
Philippe Fournier-Viger, Jerry Chun-Wei Lin, Tai Dinh,
and Hoai Bac Le

An HMM-Based Multi-view Co-training Framework for Single-View Text
Corpora 66
Eva Lorenzo Iglesias, Adrián Seara Vieira, and Lourdes Borrajo Diz

Does Sentiment Analysis Help in Bayesian Spam Filtering? 79
Enaitz Ezpeleta, Urko Zurutuza, and José María Gómez Hidalgo

A Context-Aware Keyboard Generator for Smartphone Using Random
Forest and Rule-Based System 91
Sang-Muk Jo and Sung-Bae Cho

Privacy Preserving Data Mining for Deliberative Consultations. 102
Piotr Andruszkiewicz

Feature Selection Using Approximate Multivariate Markov Blankets 114
Rafael Arias-Michel, Miguel García-Torres, Christian Schaerer,
and Federico Divina

Student Performance Prediction Applying Missing Data Imputation
in Electrical Engineering Studies Degree   126
Concepción Crespo-Turrado, José Luis Casteleiro-Roca,
Fernando Sánchez-Lasheras, José Antonio López-Vázquez,
Francisco Javier de Cos Juez, José Luis Calvo-Rolle,
and Emilio Corchado

Accuracy Increase on Evolving Product Unit Neural Networks via Feature
Subset Selection   136
Antonio J. Tallón-Ballesteros, José C. Riquelme, and Roberto Ruiz

Time Series

Rainfall Prediction: A Deep Learning Approach   151
Emilcy Hernández, Victor Sanchez-Anguix, Vicente Julian,
Javier Palanca, and Néstor Duque

Time Series Representation by a Novel Hybrid Segmentation Algorithm   163
Antonio Manuel Durán-Rosal, Pedro Antonio Gutiérrez-Peña,
Francisco José Martínez-Estudillo, and César Hervás-Martínez

A Nearest Neighbours-Based Algorithm for Big Time Series Data
Forecasting.   174
Ricardo L. Talavera-Llames, Rubén Pérez-Chacón,
María Martínez-Ballesteros, Alicia Troncoso,
and Francisco Martínez-Álvarez

Active Learning Classifier for Streaming Data   186
Michał Woźniak, Bogusław Cyganek, Andrzej Kasprzak,
Paweł Ksieniewicz, and Krzysztof Walkowiak

Bio-inspired Models and Evolutionary Computation

Application of Genetic Algorithms and Heuristic Techniques for the
Identification and Classification of the Information Used by a Recipe
Recommender.   201
Cristian Peñaranda, Soledad Valero, Vicente Julian, and Javier Palanca

A New Visualization Tool in Many-Objective Optimization Problems   213
Roozbeh Haghnazar Koochaksaraei, Rasul Enayatifar,
and Frederico Gadelha Guimarães

A Novel Adaptive Genetic Algorithm for Mobility Management in Cellular
Networks   225
Zakaria Abd El Moiz Dahi, Chaker Mezioud, and Enrique Alba

Bio-Inspired Algorithms and Preferences for Multi-objective Problems   238
Daniel Cinalli, Luis Martí, Nayat Sanchez-Pi,
and Ana Cristina Bicharra Garcia

Assessment of Multi-Objective Optimization Algorithms for Parametric
Identification of a Li-Ion Battery Model.   250
Yuviny Echevarría, Luciano Sánchez, and Cecilio Blanco

Comparing ACO Approaches in Epilepsy Seizures   261
Paula Vergara, José R. Villar, Enrique de la Cal, Manuel Menéndez,
and Javier Sedano

Estimating the Maximum Power Delivered by Concentrating Photovoltaics
Technology Through Atmospheric Conditions Using a Differential
Evolution Approach   273
Cristobal J. Carmona, F. Pulgar, Antonio Jesús Rivera-Rivas,
Maria Jose del Jesus, and J. Aguilera

A Hybrid Bio-inspired ELECTRE Approach for Decision Making
in Purchasing Agricultural Equipment   283
Dragan Simić, Jovana Gajić, Vladimir Ilin, Vasa Svirčević,
and Svetlana Simić

Learning Algorithms

Evaluating the Difficulty of Instances of the Travelling Salesman Problem in
the Nearby of the Optimal Solution Based on Random Walk Exploration   299
Miguel Cárdenas-Montes

A Nearest Hyperrectangle Monotonic Learning Method   311
Javier García, José-Ramón Cano, and Salvador García

Knowledge Modeling by ELM in RL for SRHT Problem.   323
Jose Manuel Lopez-Guede, Asier Garmendia, and Manuel Graña

Can Metalearning Be Applied to Transfer on Heterogeneous Datasets?   332
Catarina Félix, Carlos Soares, and Alípio Jorge

Smart Sketchpad: Using Machine Learning to Provide Contextually
Relevant Examples to Artists   344
Michael Fischer and Monica Lam

An Analysis of the Hardness of Novel TSP Iberian Instances   353
Gloria Cerasela Crişan, Camelia-M. Pintea, Petrică Pop,
and Oliviu Matei

A Data Structure to Speed-Up Machine Learning Algorithms on Massive
Datasets... 365
  Francisco Padillo, J.M. Luna, Alberto Cano, and Sebastián Ventura

A Sensory Control System for Adjusting Group Emotion Using Bayesian
Networks and Reinforcement Learning 377
  Jun-Ho Kim, Ki-Hoon Kim, and Sung-Bae Cho

Video and Image

Identification of Plant Textures in Agricultural Images by Principal
Component Analysis... 391
  *Martín Montalvo, María Guijarro, José Miguel Guerrero,
  and Ángela Ribeiro*

Automatic Image-Based Method for Quantitative Analysis of
Photosynthetic Cell Cultures..................................... 402
  Alzbeta Vlachynska, Jan Cerveny, Vratislav Cmiel, and Tomas Turecek

Fall Detection Using Body-Worn Accelerometer and Depth Maps Acquired
by Active Camera... 414
  Michal Kepski and Bogdan Kwolek

Classification of Melanoma Presence and Thickness Based
on Computational Image Analysis................................ 427
  *Javier Sánchez-Monedero, Aurora Sáez, María Pérez-Ortiz,
  Pedro Antonio Gutiérrez, and Cesar Hervás-Martínez*

Classification and Cluster Analysis

Solution to Data Imbalance Problem in Application Layer Anomaly
Detection Systems... 441
  Rafał Kozik and Michał Choraś

Ordinal Evolutionary Artificial Neural Networks for Solving an Imbalanced
Liver Transplantation Problem 451
  *Manuel Dorado-Moreno, María Pérez-Ortiz,
  María Dolores Ayllón-Terán, Pedro Antonio Gutiérrez,
  and Cesar Hervás-Martínez*

A Fuzzy-Based Approach for the Multilevel Component Selection Problem ... 463
  Andreea Vescan and Camelia Şerban

A Clustering-Based Method for Team Formation in Learning Environments ... 475
  *Marta Guijarro-Mata-García, Maria Guijarro,
  and Rubén Fuentes-Fernández*

R Ultimate Multilabel Dataset Repository.   487
  Francisco Charte, David Charte, Antonio Rivera, María José del Jesus,
  and Francisco Herrera

On the Impact of Dataset Complexity and Sampling Strategy in Multilabel
Classifiers Performance   500
  Francisco Charte, Antonio Rivera, María José del Jesus,
  and Francisco Herrera

Managing Monotonicity in Classification by a Pruned AdaBoost.   512
  Sergio González, Francisco Herrera, and Salvador García

Model Selection for Financial Distress Prediction by Aggregating TOPSIS
and PROMETHEE Rankings   524
  Vicente García, Ana I. Marqués, L. Cleofas-Sánchez,
  and José Salvador Sánchez

Combining k-Nearest Neighbor and Centroid Neighbor Classifier for Fast
and Robust Classification.   536
  Wiesław Chmielnicki

A First Study on the Use of Boosting for Class Noise Reparation   549
  Pablo Morales Álvarez, Julián Luengo, and Francisco Herrera

Ensemble of HOSVD Generated Tensor Subspace Classifiers with Optimal
Tensor Flattening Directions.   560
  Bogusław Cyganek, Michał Woźniak, and Dariusz Jankowski

Applications

Evaluation of Decision Trees Algorithms for Position Reconstruction
in Argon Dark Matter Experiment.   575
  Miguel Cárdenas-Montes, Bárbara Montes, Roberto Santorelli,
  and Luciano Romero, on behalf of Argon Dark Matter Collaboration

A Preliminary Study of the Suitability of Deep Learning to Improve
LiDAR-Derived Biomass Estimation   588
  Jorge García-Gutiérrez, Eduardo González-Ferreiro,
  Daniel Mateos-García, and José C. Riquelme-Santos

Fisher Score-Based Feature Selection for Ordinal Classification:
A Social Survey on Subjective Well-Being.   597
  María Pérez-Ortiz, Mercedes Torres-Jiménez, Pedro Antonio Gutiérrez,
  Javier Sánchez-Monedero, and César Hervás-Martínez

A Soft Computing Approach to Optimize the Clarification Process in
Wastewater Treatment   609
   Marina Corral Bobadilla, Roberto Fernandez Martinez,
   Ruben Lostado Lorza, Fatima Somovilla Gomez,
   and Eliseo P. Vergara Gonzalez

A Proposed Methodology for Setting the Finite Element Models Based
on Healthy Human Intervertebral Lumbar Discs   621
   Fatima Somovilla Gomez, Ruben Lostado Lorza,
   Roberto Fernandez Martinez, Marina Corral Bobadilla,
   and Ruben Escribano Garcia

Passivity Based Control of Cyber Physical Systems Under Zero-Dynamics
Attack   634
   Fawad Hassan, Naeem Iqbal, Francisco Martínez-Álvarez,
   and Khawaja M. Asim

The Multivariate Entropy Triangle and Applications   647
   Francisco José Valverde-Albacete and Carmen Peláez-Moreno

Motivational Engine with Sub-goal Identification in Neuroevolution Based
Cognitive Robotics   659
   Rodrigo Salgado, Abraham Prieto, Pilar Caamaño, Francisco Bellas,
   and Richard J. Duro

Bioinformatics

TRIQ: A Comprehensive Evaluation Measure for Triclustering Algorithms. . .   673
   David Gutiérrez-Avilés and Cristina Rubio-Escudero

Biclustering of Gene Expression Data Based on *SimUI* Semantic Similarity
Measure.   685
   Juan A. Nepomuceno, Alicia Troncoso,
   Isabel A. Nepomuceno-Chamorro, and Jesús S. Aguilar–Ruiz

Discovery of Genes Implied in Cancer by Genetic Algorithms
and Association Rules   694
   Alejandro Sánchez Medina, Alberto Gil Pichardo,
   Jose Manuel García-Heredia, and María Martínez-Ballesteros

Extending Probabilistic Encoding for Discovering Biclusters in Gene
Expression Data   706
   Francisco Javier Gil-Cumbreras, Raúl Giráldez,
   and Jesús S. Aguilar-Ruiz

Hybrid Intelligent Systems for Data Mining and Applications

A Hybrid Approach to Closeness in the Framework of Order of Magnitude
Qualitative Reasoning   721
   Alfredo Burrieza, Emilio Muñoz-Velasco, and Manuel Ojeda-Aciego

Hybrid Algorithm for Floor Detection Using GSM Signals in Indoor
Localisation Task   730
   Marcin Luckner and Rafał Górak

Hybrid Optimization Method Applied to Adaptive Splitting and Selection
Algorithm   742
   Pedro Lopez-Garcia, Michał Woźniak, Enrique Onieva,
   and Asier Perallos

Hybrid Intelligent Model for Fault Detection of a Lithium Iron Phosphate
Power Cell Used in Electric Vehicles   751
   Héctor Quintián, José-Luis Casteleiro-Roca,
   Francisco Javier Perez-Castelo, José Luis Calvo-Rolle,
   and Emilio Corchado

Author Index   763

Data Mining and Knowledge Discovery

Screening a Case Base for Stroke Disease Detection

José Neves[1(✉)], Nuno Gonçalves[2], Ruben Oliveira[2], Sabino Gomes[2],
João Neves[3], Joaquim Macedo[1], António Abelha[1], César Analide[1],
José Machado[1], Manuel Filipe Santos[1], and Henrique Vicente[1,4]

[1] Centro Algoritmi, Universidade do Minho, Braga, Portugal
{jneves,macedo,abelha,analide,jmac}@di.uminho.pt,
mfs@dsi.uminho.pt
[2] Departamento de Informática, Universidade do Minho, Braga, Portugal
{pg24168,pg24166}@alunos.uminho.pt,
sabinogomes.antonio@gmail.com
[3] Drs. Nicolas and Asp, Dubai, United Arab Emirates
joaocpneves@gmail.com
[4] Departamento de Química, Escola de Ciências e Tecnologia,
Universidade de Évora, Évora, Portugal
hvicente@uevora.pt

Abstract. Stroke stands for one of the most frequent causes of death, without distinguishing age or genders. Despite representing an expressive mortality figure, the disease also causes long-term disabilities with a huge recovery time, which goes in parallel with costs. However, stroke and health diseases may also be prevented considering illness evidence. Therefore, the present work will start with the development of a decision support system to assess stroke risk, centered on a formal framework based on Logic Programming for knowledge representation and reasoning, complemented with a Case Based Reasoning (CBR) approach to computing. Indeed, and in order to target practically the CBR cycle, a normalization and an optimization phases were introduced, and clustering methods were used, then reducing the search space and enhancing the cases retrieval one. On the other hand, and aiming at an improvement of the CBR theoretical basis, the predicates` attributes were normalized to the interval $0...1$, and the extensions of the predicates that match the universe of discourse were rewritten, and set not only in terms of an evaluation of its Quality-of-Information (QoI), but also in terms of an assessment of a Degree-of-Confidence (DoC), a measure of one's confidence that they fit into a given interval, taking into account their domains, i.e., each predicate attribute will be given in terms of a pair (QoI, DoC), a simple and elegant way to represent data or knowledge of the type incomplete, self-contradictory, or even unknown.

Keywords: Stroke Disease · Logic Programming · Knowledge Representation and Reasoning · Case Based Reasoning · Similarity Analysis

© Springer International Publishing Switzerland 2016
F. Martínez-Álvarez et al. (Eds.): HAIS 2016, LNAI 9648, pp. 3–13, 2016.
DOI: 10.1007/978-3-319-32034-2_1

1 Introduction

Stroke stands for a blood supply interruption that occurs in the brain, once a blood vessel is blocked, causing an ischaemic hit or bursts, leading to a hemorrhagic blow. Being a major factor related with mortality, this disease is closely followed with the main purpose of preventing it from happen, once, when diagnosed, it becomes less hazardous and more treatable, comparing with similar ones [1]. However, there are several factors associated with stroke, which transport a higher probability of occurrence, and may lead to such a happening. Some of these risk factors can be avoid or controlled, like high blood pressure [1, 2], cigarette smoking [2, 3], diabetes mellitus [4, 5], high blood cholesterol [6, 7], or the absence of physical activity [8, 9].

Despite these causes there are those who cannot be controlled, such as age (older people have more tendency to stroke [2, 10]), and gender (stroke is more common in men than in women, and the mere fact of having suffered a previous stroke represents an increased risk not controlled by any means [2, 11]), ethnicity [10, 11], among others. In this work it will be emphasized the prediction of a giving event, according to a historical dataset, under a Case Based Reasoning (CBR) approach to computing [12, 13]. Indeed, CBR provides the ability of solving new problems by reusing knowledge acquired from past experiences [12], i.e., CBR is used especially when similar cases have similar terms and solutions, even when they have different backgrounds [13]. Indeed, its use may be found in different arenas, namely in The Law, Online Dispute Resolution [14, 15] or Medicine [16, 17], just to name a few.

It must be also highlighted that up to present CBR systems have been unable to deal with incomplete, self-contradictory, or even unknown information. As a matter of fact the approach to CBR presented in this work will be a generic one and will have a focus on such a setting. It brings to evidence that the first step to be tackled is related with the construction of the Case Base. Thus, a normalization and optimization phases were introduced and clustering methods were used to distinguish and aggregate collections of historical data, in order to reduce the search space that speeds up the retrieve stage and all associated computational processes.

The article develops along five sections. In a former one a brief introduction to the problem is made. Then the proposed approach to knowledge representation and reasoning is introduced. In the third and fourth sections it is assumed a case study and presented a solution to the problem. Finally, in the last section the most relevant conclusions are described and possible directions for future work are outlined.

2 Knowledge Representation and Reasoning

Many approaches to knowledge representation and reasoning have been proposed using the Logic Programming (LP) paradigm, namely in the area of Model Theory [18, 19], and Proof Theory [20, 21]. In this work it is followed the proof theoretical approach in terms of an extension to LP. An Extended Logic Program is a finite set of clauses in the form:

{

$\quad p \leftarrow p_1, \cdots, p_n, not\ q_1, \cdots, not\ q_m$

$\quad ?\ (p_1, \cdots, p_n, not\ q_1, \cdots, not\ q_m)\ (n, m \geq 0)$

$\quad exception_{p_1}\ \ldots\ exception_{p_j}\ (j \leq m, n)$

$\}$ :: $scoring_{value}$

where "?" is a domain atom denoting falsity, the p_i, q_j, and p are classical ground literals, i.e., either positive atoms or atoms preceded by the classical negation sign $\neg$ [20]. Under this formalism, every program is associated with a set of abducibles [18, 19], given here in the form of exceptions to the extensions of the predicates that make the program. The term $scoring_{value}$ stands for the relative weight of the extension of a specific *predicate* with respect to the extensions of the peers ones that make the overall program.

In order to evaluate the knowledge that stems from a logic program, an assessment of the *Quality-of-Information (QoI)*, given by a truth-value in the interval [0, 1], inclusive in dynamic environments aiming at decision-making purposes, is set [22, 23]. Indeed, the objective is to build a quantification process of *QoI* and measure one's Degree of Confidence (*DoC*) that the argument values or attributes of the terms that make the extension of a given predicate with relation to their domains fit into a given interval [24]. Thus, the universe of discourse is engendered according to the information presented in the extensions of a given set of predicates, according to productions of the type:

$$predicate_i - \bigcup_{1 \leq j \leq m} clause_j((QoI_{x_1}, DoC_{x_1}), \cdots, (QoI_{x_m}, DoC_{x_m})) :: QoI_i :: DoC_i \quad (1)$$

where ∪ and m stand, respectively, for *set union* and the *cardinality* of the extension of *predicate$_i$*. QoI_i and DoC_i stand for themselves [24].

3   A Case Study

As a case study, consider a database given in terms of the extensions of the relations (or tables) depicted in Fig. 1, which stand for a situation where one has to manage information about stroke predisposing detection. The tables include features obtained by both objective and subjective methods, i.e., the physicians will fill the tables that are related to the *Stroke Predisposing* one while executing the health check. The clinics may populate some issues, others may be perceived by additional exams.

Under this scenario some incomplete and/or default data is also available. For instance, the *Triglycerides* in case 2 is unknown, while the *Risk Factors* range in the interval [0, 1]. In *Previous Stroke Episode* column 0 (zero) and 1 (one) denote, respectively, *nonoccurrence* and *occurrence*. In *Lifestyle Habits* and *Risk Factors* tables 0 (zero) and 1 (one) denote, respectively, *yes* and *no*. The values presented in the *Lifestyle Habits* and *Risk Factors* columns of *Stroke Predisposing* table are the sum of the correspondent table values, ranging between [0, 6] and [0, 4], respectively. The *Descriptions* column stands for free text fields that allow for the registration of relevant patient features.

Applying the rewritten algorithm presented in [24], to all the fields that make the knowledge base for *Stroke Predisposing* (Fig. 1), excluding of such a process the *Description* one, and looking to the *DoCs* values obtained in this manner, it is possible to set the arguments of the predicate referred to below, that also denotes the objective function with respect to the problem under analyze.

$$stroke : Age, P_{revious}S_{troke}E_{pisodes}, B_{lood}S_{ystolic}P_{ressure}, Chol_{esterol_{LDL}},$$
$$Chol_{esterol_{HDL}}, Trigly_{cerides}, L_{ifestyle}H_{abits}, R_{isk}F_{actors} \rightarrow \{0, 1\}$$

where 0 (zero) and 1 (one) denote, respectively, the truth values *false* and *true*.

Exemplifying the application of the rewritten algorithm presented in [24], in relation to the term that presents the feature vector $Age = 69$, $P_{revious}\ S_{troke}\ E_{pisodes} = 1$, $S_{ystolic}\ B_{lood}\ P_{ressure} = \perp$, $Chol_{esterolLDL} = 131$, $Chol_{esterolHDL} = 49$, $Trigly_{cerides} = 200$, $L_{ifestyle}\ H_{abits} = 4$, $R_{isk}\ F_{actors} = [1, 2]$, one may have:

Patients' Information							
#	Age	Gender	Previous Stroke Episode	Systolic Blood Pressure	Cholesterol (LDL)	Cholesterol (HDL)	Triglycerides	Description
1	63	F	1	122	132	45	192	Description 1
2	32	M	0	120	$\perp$	$\perp$	$\perp$	Description 2
...	...	...	...	...	...	...	...	...
n	41	M	0	115	104	68	135	Description n

Stroke (Predisposing)								
#	Age	Previous Stroke Episode	Systolic Blood Pressure	Cholesterol (LDL)	Cholesterol (HDL)	Triglycerides	Lifestyle Habits	Risk Factors	Description
1	63	1	122	132	45	192	3	[2, 3]	Description 1
2	32	0	120	$\perp$	$\perp$	$\perp$	4	[0, 1]	Description 2
...	...	...	...	...	...	...	...	...	...
n	41	0	115	104	68	135	6	0	Description n

Lifestyle Habits						
#	No Smoking	Exercise	Breakfast	Vegetables/Fruit	Low Salt	Low Sugar
1	1	0	1	1	0	0
2	1	0	1	1	1	0
...	...	...	...	...	...	...
n	1	1	1	1	1	1

Risk Factors				
#	Diabetes	Obesity	Hypertension	Long-term Medicaments
1	1	0	1	$\perp$
2	0	0	0	$\perp$
...	...	...	...	...
n	0	0	0	0

Fig. 1. A fragment of the knowledge base for Stroke Predisposing Diagnosis.

Begin, (DoCs evaluation),

The predicate's extension that maps the Universe-of-Discourse for the term under observation is set ←

{

$\neg\, stroke\, \big((QoI_{Age}, DoC_{Age}),\, \cdots, (QoI_{SBP}, DoC_{SBP}),\, \cdots, (QoI_{RF}, DoC_{RF})\big)$

$\leftarrow not\, stroke\, \big((QoI_{Age}, DoC_{Age}),\, \cdots, (QoI_{SBP}, DoC_{SBP}),\, \cdots, (QoI_{RF}, DoC_{RF})\big)$

$stroke\, \underbrace{\big((1_{69}, DoC_{69}),\, \cdots, (1_{\perp}, DoC_{\perp}),\, \cdots, (1_{[1,2]}, DoC_{[1,2]})\big)}_{attribute's\ values}\ ::1::DoC$

$\underbrace{[22,95]\quad\cdots\quad [70,200]\quad\cdots\quad [0,4]}_{attribute's\ domains}$

}:: 1

The attribute's values ranges are rewritten ←

{

$\neg\, stroke\, \big((QoI_{Age}, DoC_{Age}),\, \cdots, (QoI_{SBP}, DoC_{SBP}),\, \cdots, (QoI_{RF}, DoC_{RF})\big)$

$\leftarrow not\, stroke\, \big((QoI_{Age}, DoC_{Age}),\, \cdots, (QoI_{SBP}, DoC_{SBP}),\, \cdots, (QoI_{RF}, DoC_{RF})\big)$

$stroke\, \underbrace{\big((1_{[69,69]}, DoC_{[69,69]}),\, \cdots, (1_{[70,200]}, DoC_{[70,200]}),\, \cdots, (1_{[1,2]}, DoC_{[1,2]})\big)}_{attribute's\ values}$

$::1::DoC$

$\underbrace{[22,95]\qquad\cdots\qquad [70,200]\qquad\cdots\qquad [0,4]}_{attribute's\ domains}$

}:: 1

The attribute's boundaries are set to the interval [0,1] ←

{

$\neg\, stroke\, \big((QoI_{Age}, DoC_{Age}),\, \cdots, (QoI_{SBP}, DoC_{SBP}),\, \cdots, (QoI_{RF}, DoC_{RF})\big)$

$\leftarrow not\, stroke\, \big((QoI_{Age}, DoC_{Age}),\, \cdots, (QoI_{SBP}, DoC_{SBP}),\, \cdots, (QoI_{RF}, DoC_{RF})\big)$

$stroke\, \underbrace{\big((1_{[0.64,0.64]}, DoC_{[0.64,0.64]}),\, \cdots, (1_{[0,1]}, DoC_{[0,1]}),\, \cdots, (1_{[0.25,0.5]}, DoC_{[0.25,0.5]})\big)}_{attribute's\ values\ once\ normalized}$

$::1::DoC$

$\underbrace{[0,1]\qquad\cdots\qquad [0,1]\qquad\cdots\qquad [0,1]}_{attribute's\ domains\ once\ normalized}$

}:: 1

The DoC's values are evaluated ←

$\{$

$\neg\, stroke\, \big((QoI_{Age}, DoC_{Age}),\, \cdots, (QoI_{SBP}, DoC_{SBP}),\, \cdots, (QoI_{RF}, DoC_{RF})\big)$

$\quad\quad \leftarrow not\, stroke\, \big((QoI_{Age}, DoC_{Age}),\, \cdots, (QoI_{SBP}, DoC_{SBP}),\, \cdots, (QoI_{RF}, DoC_{RF})\big)$

$stroke\, \underbrace{((1,\,1),\quad\quad\cdots,\quad\quad (1,\,0),\quad\quad\cdots,\quad\quad (1,\,0.97))}_{attribute's\ quality-of-information\ and\ respective\ confidence\ values}\, ::\, 1\, ::\, 0.89$

$\underbrace{[0.64, 0.64]\quad\cdots\quad\quad [0,1]\quad\quad\cdots\quad\quad [0.25, 0.5]}_{attribute's\ values\ ranges\ once\ normalized}$

$\underbrace{[0,1]\quad\quad\cdots\quad\quad [0,1]\quad\quad\cdots\quad\quad [0,1]}_{attribute's\ domains\ once\ normalized}$

$\}$ :: 1

End.

It is now possible to represent the normalized case repository in a graphic form, showing each case in the Cartesian plane in terms of its *QoI* and *DoC* (Fig. 2). Furthermore, the retrieval stage can be improved by reducing the search space, using data mining techniques, like clustering, in order to obtain different groups to identify the one(s) that are more closed to the *New Case*, which is represented as a square in Fig. 2.

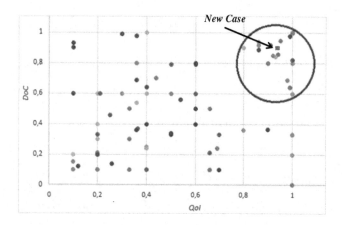

Fig. 2. A case's set split into clusters.

4 Case Based Reasoning

CBR methodology for problem solving stands for an act of finding and justifying the solution to a given problem based on the consideration of similar past ones, by repro-cessing and/or adapting their data or knowledge [12]. In *CBR – the cases –* are stored in a *Case-Base*, and those cases that are similar (or close) to a new one are used in the problem solving process. The typical CBR cycle presents the mechanism that should be followed to have a consistent model. In fact, it is an iterative process since the solution must be tested and adapted while the result of applying that solution is inconclusive. In the final stage the case is learned and the knowledge base is updated with the new case [12, 13]. Despite promising results, the current CBR systems are neither complete nor adaptable enough for all domains. In some cases, the user is required to follow the similarity method defined by the system, even if it does not fit into their needs [25]. Moreover, other problems may be highlighted. On the one hand, the existent CBR systems have limitations related to the capability of dealing with unknown, incomplete and self-contradictory information. On the other hand, an important feature that often is discarded is the ability to compare strings. In some domains strings are important to describe a situation, a problem or even an event [12, 25].

Contrasting with other problem solving methodologies (e.g., those that use *Decision Trees* or *Artificial Neural Networks*), relatively little work is done offline. Undeniably, in almost all the situations, the work is performed at query time. The main difference between this new approach and the typical CBR one relies on the fact that not only all the cases have their arguments set in the interval [0, 1] but it also allows for the handling of incomplete, unknown, or even self-contradictory data or knowledge [25]. The classic CBR cycle was changed in order to include a normalization phase aiming to enhance the retrieve process (Fig. 3). The Case-Base will be given in terms of triples that follow the pattern:

$$Case = \{ <Raw_{case}, Normalized_{case}, Description_{case} > \}$$

where Raw_{case} and $Normalized_{case}$ stand for themselves, and $Description_{case}$ is made on a set of strings or even in free text, which may be analyzed with string similarity algorithms.

When confronted with a new case, (Fig. 4), the system is able to retrieve all cases that meet such a structure and optimize such a population, i.e., it considers the attributes DoC's value of each case or of their optimized counterparts when analysing similarities among them. Thus, under the occurrence of a new case, the goal is to find similar cases in the CaseBase. Having this in mind, the reductive algorithm given in [24] is applied to the new case, with the results:

$$\underbrace{stroke_{new}((1,1),(1,1),(1,1),(1,1),(1,1),(1,1),(1,1),(1,0.87)) :: 1 :: 0.98}_{new\ case}$$

After the normalization process, the new case is compared with every retrieved case from the cluster using a similarity function, *sim*, given in terms of the average of the modulus of the arithmetic difference between the arguments of the each case of the retrieved cluster and those of their counterparts in the problem (once *Description* stands for free text, its analysis is excluded at this stage). Thus, one may get:

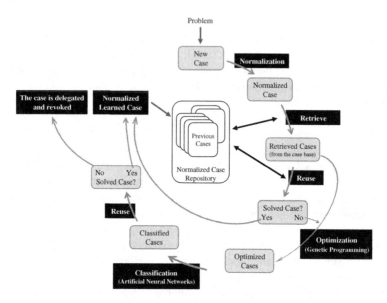

Fig. 3. The extended CBR cycle [25].

$$stroke_1\big((1,1),(1,1),(1,0),(1,1),(1,1),(1,1),(1,\ 1),(1,\ 0.97)\big) :: 1 :: 0.89$$
$$stroke_2\big((1,1),(1,1),(1,1),(1,0),(1,1),(1,1),,(1,0.8),(1,0.92)\big) :: 1 :: 0.84$$
$$\vdots$$
$$\underbrace{stroke_j\big((1,1),(1,1),(1,0),(1,1),(1,1),(1,1),(1,\ 1),(1,\ 0.96)\big) :: 1 :: 0.87}_{normalized\ cases\ from\ retrieved\ cluster}$$

$$stroke_{new\to1}^{DoC} = \frac{\|1-1\|+\|1-1\|+\|1-0\|+\|1-1\|+\|1-1\|+\ \|1-1\|+\|1-1\|+\|0.87-0.97\|}{8} = 0.14$$

where $stroke_{new\to1}^{DoC}$ denotes the dissimilarities between $stroke_{new}^{DoC}$ and the $stroke_1^{DoC}$. It was assumed that every attribute has equal weight. Thus, the similarity for $stroke_{new\to1}^{DoC}$ is $1 - 0.14 = 0.86$. With respect to *QoI* the procedure is similar returning $stroke_{new\to1}^{QoI} = 1$.

#	Age	PSE	SBP	Cholesterol (LDL)	Cholesterol (HDL)	Triglycerides	Lifestyle Habits	Risk Factors	Description
new	58	1	115	102	67	149	6	[0, 2]	new description

Stroke (Predisposing)

Fig. 4. The *new case* characteristics and description.

Descriptions will be compared using String Similarity Algorithms in order to get a similarity measure between them. It is then necessary to compare the description of the new case with the descriptions of the cases stored in the repository (in this study the strategy used was the Dice Coefficient one [26]):

$$stroke_{new \to 1}^{Description} = 0.78$$

With these values we are able to get the final similarity function, *sim*:

$$sim\_stroke_{new \to 1} = \frac{0.86 + 1 + 0.78}{3} = 0.88$$

These procedures should be applied to the remaining cases of the retrieved cluster in order to obtain the most similar ones, which may stand for the possible solutions to the problem.

5 Conclusions

In order to target the CBR cycle theoretically and practically, the Decision Support System presented in this work to assess stroke predisposing risk, is centred on a formal framework based on Logic Programming for Knowledge Representation and Reasoning, complemented with a CBR approach to computing that caters for the handling of incomplete, unknown, or even self-contradictory data or knowledge. Under this approach the cases' retrieval and optimization phases were heightened and the time spent on those tasks shortened in 18.7 %, when compared with existing systems, being its accuracy around 89 %. The proposed method also allows for the analysis of free text attributes using *String Similarities Algorithms*, which fulfils a gap that is present in almost all *CBR* software tools. Additionally, under this approach, the user may define the weights of the cases' attributes on-the-fly, letting him/her to choose the most appropriate strategy to address the problem (i.e., it gives the user the possibility to narrow the search space for similar cases at runtime).

Acknowledgments. This work has been supported by FCT – Fundação para a Ciência e Tecnologia within the Project Scope UID/CEC/00319/2013.

References

1. Go, A.S., Mozaffarian, D., Roger, V.L., Benjamin, E.J., Berry, J.D., Blaha, M.J., Dai, S., Ford, E.S., Fox, C.S., Franco, S., Fullerton, H.J., Gillespie, C., Hailpern, S.M., Heit, J.A., Howard, V.J., Huffman, M.D., Judd, S.E., Kissela, B.M., Kittner, S.J., Lackland, D.T., Lichtman, J.H., Lisabeth, L.D., Mackey, R.H., Magid, D.J., Marcus, G.M., Marelli, A., Matchar, D.B., McGuire, D.K., Mohler 3rd, E.R., Moy, C.S., Mussolino, M.E., Neumar, R.W., Nichol, G., Pandey, D.K., Paynter, N.P., Reeves, M.J., Sorlie, P.D., Stein, J., Towfighi, A., Turan, T.N., Virani, S.S., Wong, N.D., Woo, D., Turner, M.B.: On behalf of the american heart association statistics committee and stroke statistics subcommittee: heart disease and stroke statistics — 2014 update: a report from the american heart association. Circulation **129**, e28–e292 (2014)
2. Lindgren, A.: Risk factors. In: Norrving, B. (ed.) Oxford Textbook of Stroke and Cerebrovascular Disease, pp. 9–18. Oxford University Press, Oxford (2014)

3. Shah, R.S., Cole, J.W.: Smoking and stroke: the more you smoke the more you stroke. Expert Rev. Cardiovasc. Ther. **8**, 917–932 (2010)
4. Hopper, I., Billah, B., Skiba, M., Krum, H.: Prevention of diabetes and reduction in major cardiovascular events in studies of subjects with prediabetes: meta-analysis of randomised controlled clinical trials. Eur. J. Cardiovasc. Prev. Rehabil. **18**, 813–823 (2011)
5. Khoury, J.C., Kleindorfer, D., Alwell, K., Moomaw, C.J., Woo, D., Adeoye, O., Flaherty, M.L., Khatri, P., Ferioli, S., Broderick, J.P., Kissela, B.M.: Diabetes mellitus: a risk factor for ischemic stroke in a large biracial population. Stroke **44**, 1500–1504 (2013)
6. Amarenco, P., Labreuche, J., Touboul, P.: High-density lipoprotein-cholesterol and risk of stroke and carotid atherosclerosis: a systematic review. Atherosclerosis **196**, 489–496 (2008)
7. Zhang, Y., Tuomilehto, J., Jousilahti, P., Wang, Y., Antikainen, R., Hu, G.: Total and high-density lipoprotein cholesterol and stroke risk. Stroke **43**, 1768–1774 (2012)
8. Grau, A.J., Barth, C., Geletneky, B., Ling, P., Palm, F., Lichy, C., Becher, H., Buggle, F.: Association between recent sports activity, sports activity in young adulthood, and stroke. Stroke **40**, 426–431 (2009)
9. McDonnell, M.N., Hillier, S.L., Hooker, S.P., Le, A., Judd, S.E., Howard, V.J.: Physical activity frequency and risk of incident stroke in a national US study of blacks and whites. Stroke **44**, 2519–2524 (2013)
10. Sealy-Jefferson, S., Wing, J.J., Sánchez, B.N., Brown, D.L., Meurer, W.J., Smith, M.A., Morgenstern, L.B., Lisabeth, L.D.: Age- and ethnic-specific sex differences in stroke risk. Gend. Med. **9**, 121–128 (2012)
11. Kissela, B.M., Khoury, J.C., Alwell, K., Moomaw, C.J., Woo, D., Adeoye, O., Flaherty, M. L., Khatri, P., Ferioli, S., De Los Rios La Rosa, F., Broderick, J.P., Kleindorfer, D.O.: Age at stroke: temporal trends in stroke incidence in a large, biracial population. Neurology **79**, 1781–1787 (2012)
12. Aamodt, A., Plaza, E.: Case-based reasoning: foundational issues, methodological variations, and system approaches. AI Communications **7**, 39–59 (1994)
13. Balke, T., Novais, P., Andrade, F., Eymann, T.: From real-world regulations to concrete norms for software agents – a case-based reasoning approach. In: Poblet, M., Schild, U., Zeleznikow, J. (eds.) Proceedings of the Workshop on Legal and Negotiation Decision Support Systems (LDSS 2009), pp. 13–28. Huygens Editorial, Barcelona (2009)
14. Carneiro, D., Novais, P., Andrade, F., Zeleznikow, J., Neves, J.: Using case-based reasoning to support alternative dispute resolution. In: de Leon F. de Carvalho, A.P., Rodríguez-González, S., De Paz Santana, J.F., Corchado Rodríguez, J.M. (eds.) Distributed Computing and Artificial Intelligence. AISC, vol. 79, pp. 123–130. Springer, Heidelberg (2010)
15. Carneiro, D., Novais, P., Andrade, F., Zeleznikow, J., Neves, J.: Using case-based reasoning and principled negotiation to provide decision support for dispute resolution. Knowl. Inf. Syst. **36**, 789–826 (2013)
16. Guessoum, S., Laskri, M.T., Lieber, J.: Respidiag: a case-based reasoning system for the diagnosis of chronic obstructive pulmonary disease. Expert Syst. Appl. **41**, 267–273 (2014)
17. Ping, X.-O., Tseng, Y.-J., Lin, Y.-P., Chiu, H.-J., Feipei Lai, F., Liang, J.-D., Huang, G.-T., Yang, P.-M.: A multiple measurements case-based reasoning method for predicting recurrent status of liver cancer patients. Comput. Ind. **69**, 12–21 (2015)
18. Kakas, A., Kowalski, R., Toni, F.: The role of abduction in logic programming. In: Gabbay, D., Hogger, C., Robinson, I. (eds.) Handbook of Logic in Artificial Intelligence and Logic Programming, vol. 5, pp. 235–324. Oxford University Press, Oxford (1998)
19. Pereira, L.M., Anh, H.T.: Evolution prospection. In: Nakamatsu, K., P-W, G., Jain, L.C., Howlett, R.J. (eds.) New Advances in Intelligent Decision Technologies. SCI, vol. 199, pp. 51–63. Springer, Heidelberg (2009)

20. Neves, J.: A logic interpreter to handle time and negation in logic databases. In: Muller, R., Pottmyer, J. (eds.) Proceedings of the 1984 annual conference of the ACM on the 5th Generation Challenge, pp. 50–54. Association for Computing Machinery, New York (1984)
21. Neves, J., Machado, J., Analide, C., Abelha, A., Brito, L.: The halt condition in genetic programming. In: Neves, J., Santos, M.F., Machado, J.M. (eds.) EPIA 2007. LNCS (LNAI), vol. 4874, pp. 160–169. Springer, Heidelberg (2007)
22. Lucas, P.: Quality checking of medical guidelines through logical abduction. In: Coenen, F., Preece, A., Mackintosh, A. (eds.) Research and Developments in Intelligent Systems XX, pp. 309–321. Springer, London (2003)
23. Machado J., Abelha A., Novais P., Neves J., Neves J.: Quality of service in healthcare units. In Bertelle, C., Ayesh, A. (eds.) Proceedings of the ESM 2008, pp. 291–298. Eurosis – ETI Publication, Ghent (2008)
24. Fernandes, F., Vicente, H., Abelha, A., Machado, J., Novais, P., Neves J.: Artificial neural networks in diabetes control. In: Proceedings of the 2015 Science and Information Conference (SAI 2015), pp. 362–370. IEEE Edition (2015)
25. Neves J., Vicente, H.: A quantum approach to case-based reasoning (in Preparation)
26. Dice, L.R.: Measures of the amount of ecologic association between species. Ecology **26**, 297–302 (1945)

SemSynX: Flexible Similarity Analysis of XML Data via Semantic and Syntactic Heterogeneity/Homogeneity Detection

Jesús M. Almendros-Jiménez[1]([⊠]) and Alfredo Cuzzocrea[2]

[1] Informatics Department, University of Almería, Almería, Spain
jalmen@ual.es

[2] DIA Department, University of Trieste and ICAR-CNR, Trieste, Italy
alfredo.cuzzocrea@dia.units.it

Abstract. In this paper we introduce and experimentally assess SemSynX, *a novel technique for supporting similarity analysis of XML data via semantic and syntactic heterogeneity/homogeneity detection.* Given two *XML trees*, SemSynX retrieves a list of semantic and syntactic heterogeneity/homogeneity matches of objects (i.e., elements, values, tags, attributes) occurring in certain paths of the trees. A *local score* that takes into account the path and value similarity is given for each heterogeneity/homogeneity found. A *global score* that summarizes the number of equal matches as well as the local scores globally is also provided. The proposed technique is highly *customizable*, and it permits the specification of *thresholds* for the requested *degree of similarity* for paths and values as well as for the *degree of relevance* for path and value matching. It thus makes possible to "adjust" the similarity analysis depending on the nature of the input XML trees. SemSynX has been implemented in terms of a *XQuery library*, as to enhance interoperability with other XML processing tools. To complete our analytical contributions, a comprehensive experimental assessment and evaluation of SemSynX over several classes of XML documents is provided.

1 Introduction

Data fusion [4,8] is a research topic of increasing interest, mainly motivated by the need of accessing multiple data sources in an integrated way. This requirement is becoming harder and harder in novel emerging contexts, such as challenging *Cloud Computing environments* (e.g. [19]), where Cloud entities not only need to *exchange data* but also to *combine data,* for a wide spectrum on advanced applications. Without loss of generality, the main data-fusion's goal is to provide users with a *complete and concise view* of all the existent data (including *data objects* and *data entities*). "Concise" means that no object is represented twice and with so-called contradictions (e.g., [9]). "Complete" means that no object is forgotten in the final (integrated/fused) result.

Semantic and syntactic heterogeneity can be found in data sources and detecting them is the major goal of the *data-fusion research initiative* [4,8].

© Springer International Publishing Switzerland 2016
F. Martínez-Álvarez et al. (Eds.): HAIS 2016, LNAI 9648, pp. 14–26, 2016.
DOI: 10.1007/978-3-319-32034-2_2

In this respect, *schema matching* [23] and *duplicate detection* [27] are two well-studied mechanisms. In addition to this, *data-conflict detection* and *data repairing/cleaning* strategies have been proposed in the data-fusion research area (see [4,12,13,15,29] as some authoritative examples) in order to deal with semantic heterogeneity, while syntactic heterogeneity has been typically addressed by *schema matching approaches* (e.g., [9]). Data heterogeneity has also been investigated via using *Ontologies* [21,22], whose main functionality is that of supporting semantics-based description of data sources. In this research area, *approximate data instance matching* [14] aims at providing a measure of *data similarity*, which is later exploited to identify multiple instances of real-word (data) objects based on suitable *distance functions*. *XML data clustering* [1,2,25] is also tightly connected to the data-instance matching problem, and the general goal here consists in classifying target XML documents in groups of similar content. Applications of XML similarity also include *data warehousing version control* (e.g., [11]) and *change management* (e.g., [24]).

In order to be able of integrating data from multiple sources, a typical strategy consists in, first, identifying (data) objects to be integrated (usually, by means of unique keys), and, secondly, mixing attributes in the integrated data repository. Nevertheless, attributes of a certain object can have different names, even representing the same concept, or they can have the same names, even representing so-called *conflicting values* (e.g., [9]). In the first case, an *attribute name mapping* is required, while in the second one, a *conflict resolution strategy* is adopted. Strategies for conflict resolution range from the *most-frequent value* and the *most-trusted source* selection to more intuitive *date-based* selection. Also, values represented as strings can be compared via applying well-known *string comparison algorithms* (e.g., [18,28]).

In our research, we focus on *XML data* specially, for which several data fusion strategies have been proposed (e.g., [8,12,16,21,26]). XML data require specific mechanisms for data fusion since they are semi-structured data represented by *tagged trees* where leaf nodes have textual content. *Graph-based data*, e.g. *RDF data*, are also subject of recently-proposed targeted data fusion mechanisms (e.g., [5,20,30]), and they expose several "touching points" with the related XML data fusion research area. It is also significant to highlight that, in the semi-structured context (both XML and RDF data), conflicts of attribute values are more sophisticate since the same real-world (data) objects can be represented using different tree/graph structures. This makes the investigated problem harder.

Following the so-delineated research area, in this paper we introduce and experimentally assess **SemSynX**, *a novel technique for supporting similarity analysis of XML data via detecting semantic and syntactic heterogeneity/homogeneity matches of objects* (i.e., elements, values, tags, attributes) *occurring in certain paths of the two (XML) trees* that model the input data sources. SemSynX retrieves a list of similarity/dissimilarity matches found in the target objects as well as a measure of similarity of the XML trees expressed by a *score*. A *local score* that takes into account path and value similarity is provided for each heterogeneity/homogeneity found. A *global score* that summarizes the number of equal matches as well as the local scores is also provided. Such a list of similarity/dissimilarity matches is suitable to support *automatic definition of schema mapping* and *conflicting strategies* of the target XML data. In addition to this, SemSynX is highly *customizable,* and it permits the specification of *thresholds* for the required *degree of similarity* for paths and values as well as for the *degree of relevance* for path and value matching, hence finally it makes possible to "adjust" the comparison of input XML trees depending on the nature of the trees themselves. Furthermore, in order to improve matching in some specialized scenarios, *selection of paths* to be matched between documents is supported, while assigning suitable *weights* to selected paths. *Semantics-based approach* has also been adopted in order to *compare label content,* thus introducing more precision during the matching of similar items characterized by a specific semantics. We complete our analytical contributions by means of a comprehensive experimental assessment and evaluation of SemSynX over several classes of XML documents. A preliminary version of this paper appears in [3].

1.1   On the Innovativeness of the SemSynX Proposal

By analyzing active literature, we recognize that several studies on how to match string values exist, but there is a general lack of methods supporting the definition of *similarity functions* that work on "specific cases". Since SemSynX aims at offering a high degree of parametrization, our strategy is assigning a proper similarity function to each label. As an alternative to this, a *naive* strategy would assign similarity functions to types, indeed, but semantics of labels of the same type can vary one from another. As an example, labels of type Integer can represent the age of a person, the number of children as well as the population of a city, alternatively. Therefore, we would "lost" the specific semantics of the XML element. In order to avoid this, we would aim at semantically enriching meta-data of target documents (i.e., *DTD* or *XML Schemas*) with similarity functions. Unfortunately, neither DTD nor XML Schemas provide mechanisms for expressing semantics of element. As a consequence, our strategy embedded in SemSynX has been that of attaching a suitable *XML template* to each XML document, being this template capable of providing semantics to labels, and enabling a more fine-grained comparison of labels according to their semantics.

As far as we know, SemSynX is the first technique that fully-provides semantics-based similarity analysis of XML documents. All this confers highly *flexibility* to our proposed similarity analysis framework, with powerful benefits in the context of large-scale management of XML data over Clouds (e.g., [19]).

2   Running Example

Figures 1 and 2 show two example XML trees, namely $T_{X,1}$ and $T_{X,2}$, respectively, where two objects modeling books, i.e. "*XML in a Nutshell*" and "*XML Pocket Reference*", are represented in *both* XML trees. The first tree, $T_{X,1}$, includes the XML elements year, isbn, author, title, edition, price and

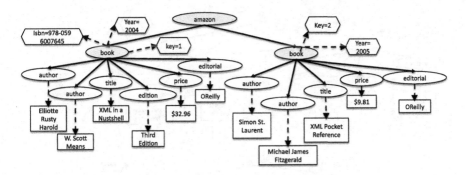

Fig. 1. Example XML document $T_{X,1}$

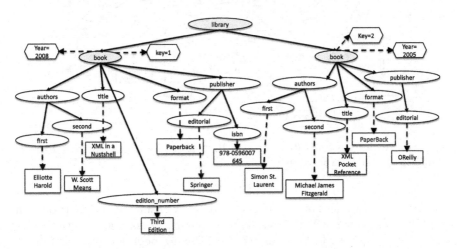

Fig. 2. Example XML document $T_{X,2}$

editorial, while the second tree, $T_{X,2}$, also includes, beyond the same previous $T_{X,1}$'s elements except price, the element format. However, looking in more details, the representation of the *same* data objects (i.e., the two books) are different in the target XML trees. In fact, $T_{X,1}$ models isbn as an attribute, while $T_{X,2}$ makes use of an element to this end. Also, $T_{X,1}$ makes use of the element author to model authors, while elements first, second, and so forth, are used in $T_{X,2}$ as enclosed under the element authors to this end. Additionally, editorial is used in $T_{X,2}$ as sub-element of publisher, which also includes the element isbn, while editorial is under book in $T_{X,1}$. As regards conflicts, edition is used in $T_{X,1}$ and edition_number in $T_{X,2}$ to represent the same concept. Finally, year and editorial for the data object "*XML in a Nutshell*" have different values for both XML trees $T_{X,1}$ and $T_{X,2}$.

As highlighted in Sect. 1, the goal of SemSynX is to automatically discover similarity/dissimilarity matches in the target XML trees, by setting as input parameters the following two parameters: (*i*) paths of objects to be

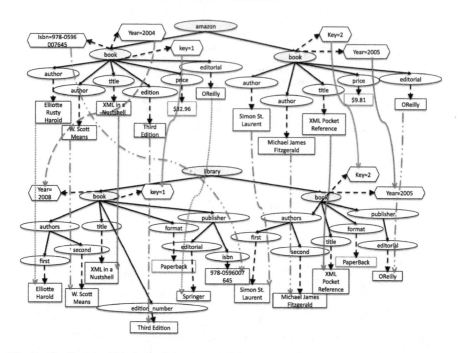

Fig. 3. Similarities/Dissimilarities detected by SemSynX for the XML trees $T_{X,1}$ and $T_{X,2}$ of Figs. 1 and 2, respectively

analyzed, and (*ii*) names of keys of such objects[1] Consider again the two example XML trees shown in Figs. 1 and 2, respectively. Here, objects paths are set as $P_{X,1}$:/amazon/book for $T_{X,1}$ and $P_{X,2}$:/library/book for $T_{X,2}$; key names are set as the attribute key which is associated to both books of $T_{X,1}$ and $T_{X,2}$. The similarities/dissimilarities of $T_{X,1}$ and $T_{X,2}$ of Figs. 1 and 2, respectively, detected by SemSynX are finally shown in Fig. 3. Here, full arrows model similarities, while dashed arrows model dissimilarities.

The SemSynX running example shown in Fig. 3, and focusing on *both* similarities and dissimilarities of XML trees $T_{X,1}$ and $T_{X,2}$ of Figs. 1 and 2, respectively, provides the following similarity/dissimilarity analysis. First, exact matches exist, for both paths and values. This is the case of title of both $T_{X,1}$ and $T_{X,2}$ and year in the $T_{X,2}$. Special cases of exact matching are those exchanging attributes by tags. This is the case of isbn in $T_{X,1}$. Weaker matching are those in which the value is the same while the path is different. This is the case of the second element author (i.e., "*W. Scott Means*") and edition in $T_{X,1}$, and both author and editorial in $T_{X,2}$. Paths are different in two cases: tag changing (in edition of $T_{X,1}$), tag removing/adding (in the second element author of $T_{X,1}$, i.e. "*W. Scott Means*", and both author and editorial of $T_{X,2}$). Other weaker

---

[1] The use of keys is not mandatory in our approach, but keys are used in the running example to guide similarity search.

matching are those in which the path is the same but value is different. This is the case of year in $T_{X,1}$. The weakest matching are those in which paths are similar and values are not equal or are similar. This is the case of the first author (i.e., "*Elliotte Rusty Harold*") and editorial in $T_{X,1}$. Finally, two elements can be considered as "new" in $T_{X,1}$ and $T_{X,2}$: price and format, respectively.

The motivating example has clearly shown the potentialities and the flexibility of our proposed technique SemSynX in dealing with XML data similarity (and dissimilarity) detection that is perfectly suitable with the requirements posed by modern Cloud Computing environments (e.g., [19]), since the same detection task can also be easily deployed on top of Cloud infrastructures.

3 The SemSynX Approach

In this Section, we provide the details and the proof-of-concept of SemSynX, our proposed XML data similarity analysis technique.

SemSynX is based on the analysis of similarity of both paths and values, where similarity is measured by means of a score. From Sect. 1, recall that both a local and a global score is provided. In the case of paths, the local score represents the number of equal matches as well as the number of changes made, i.e. the number of tags that have been removed, added and changed. It is finally obtained as the percentage of tags that occur in the same order in both compared paths. In the case of values, the local score is provided by a similarity function, which is defined by the user (e.g., the Levenshtein's distance [18]). SemSynX offers a wide repertoire of string comparison functions and semantics-based functions (see Sect. 4), but others can be still defined by user for supporting every particular matching case that is of interest for the target similarity analysis.

SemSynX enables the specification of the following thresholds and weights:

1. **Equality Threshold:** Cut value at which the content of labels is considered equal. Content of labels are compared by means of a user-defined similarity function that reports a value between 0 and 1, and, depending on the type of content, users can establish a suitable equality threshold. In the case of non-exact matching, relaxing equality threshold is required.
2. **Similarity Threshold:** Cut value at which the content of labels is considered similar. Users are allowed to establish a similarity threshold for content of labels. Relaxing similarity threshold for matching of close-values is ensured.
3. **Path Threshold:** Cut value at which paths are considered equal. The user can specify a threshold based on which paths are considered equal or different. High thresholds ensure similarity in structure of XML elements, while low thresholds permit XML elements of varying in structure. Paths are thus classified into similar paths or *new paths.*
4. **Path Weight:** Degree of relevance of paths. Higher relevance of paths rather than values' relevance requires similar structure.
5. **Value Weight:** Degree of relevance of values. Higher relevance of values rather than paths' relevance requires similar content.

6. **Main Path Weight:** Degree of relevance of *main paths*. SemSynX makes it possible to select paths of each document to be compared. This functionality turns to be useful in order to remove non-relevant paths as well as paths that user know in advance as being different. Selected paths are called "main paths", while *secondary paths* are similar paths not selected by the user. The user can assign more relevance to main paths, but leaving some weight to secondary paths as well as new paths.

7. **Secondary Path Weight:** Degree of relevance of secondary paths. Low weight to secondary paths involves in assigning more relevance to main paths, while high weight to secondary paths makes it possible to debug the matching. Whenever increasing weight of secondary paths, the global score is considerably higher, and the selection of main paths is not successful.

8. **New Path Weight:** Degree of relevance of new paths. By assigning more relevance to new paths, distinct elements can be detected.

These model concepts characterize SemSynX as a flexible XML similarity analysis technique. Indeed, the main advantage of SemSynX over state-of-the-art approaches is represented by the ability of customizing path and value similarity via the so-called "degree of similarity" (see Sect. 1) as well as specifying thresholds and weights for path and value similarity as to support the desired degree of similarity. Also, the flexibility provided by SemSynX is higher than the one of other comparative approaches because it works with user-defined similarity functions ranging from string-based comparison to semantics-based comparison (see Sect. 4) for each type of XML element, and it enables the selection of main, secondary and new paths, as well assigning weights to such paths in a proportional manner.

3.1 XML Data Similarity Analysis in SemSynX

By combining the above concepts, SemSynX distinguishes the following cases of XML data similarity analysis, which represent the core of the proposed technique. The cases referred in the following description are still related to the running example provided in Sect. 2.

1. Equal Value and Equal Tag/Attribute. This is the best matching. Both value and tag/attribute match. This is the case, for instance, of title in both books *"XML in a Nutshell"* and *"XML Pocket Reference"* (of both XML trees $T_{X,1}$ and $T_{X,2}$), and editorial in the second book *"XML Pocket Reference"* (of both XML trees $T_{X,1}$ and $T_{X,2}$). Nevertheless, the semantic of equality can be customized by a threshold over which values are considered equal. A small change in any of the element title can be accepted as exact match, depending on the threshold. Equal tag/attribute does not mean equality of paths. For instance, depending on the path threshold, editorial can be rejected since $P_{X,3}$:/amazon/book/editorial and $P_{X,4}$:/amazon/book/publisher/editorial are corresponding paths in both documents. In particular, when the threshold is over 0.75, similarity of `editorial` is no longer detected. Change of an attribute for a tag is also allowed. This is the case of `isbn` in the first book "*XML in a Nutshell*" (of both XML trees $T_{X,1}$ and $T_{X,2}$).

2. Similar Value and Equal Tag/Attribute. Here, tags are equal but values are similar. This is the case of the first author name of the first book "*XML in a Nutshell*" (of both XML trees $T_{X,1}$ and $T_{X,2}$). Obviously, detecting similarity versus equality for values depends on the specified threshold. The value of `year` in the first book "*XML in a Nutshell*" of $T_{X,1}$ is 2004, while the value of `year` in the first book "*XML in a Nutshell*" of $T_{X,2}$ is 2008. Thanks to user-defined similarity functions, in our approach `Integer` values can be specifically handled. For instance, the user can define a similarity function that consider 2004 and 2008 as similar or distinct. Moreover, equality and similarity thresholds play a relevant role in this case. Change of an attribute for a tag is also allowed.

3. Distinct Value and Equal Tag/Attribute. This is one case of conflict, also exposing semantic dissimilarity. The tag is equal but the content is distinct. The value has to be neither equal nor similar according to the defined threshold. This is the case of `editorial` in the first book "*XML in a Nutshell*" (of both XML trees $T_{X,1}$ and $T_{X,2}$). Again, equality of tags does not mean equality of paths. Change of an attribute for a tag is also allowed.

4. Equal Value and Distinct Tag/Attribute. This is another case of conflict, also exposing syntactic dissimilarity. The value is the same but the tag is distinct. Again, detecting this case depends on the defined threshold. This is the case of `edition` and `edition_number` of the first book "*XML in a Nutshell*" (of both XML trees $T_{X,1}$ and $T_{X,2}$). Tags are compared as strings, and thus `edition` is `edition_number` are distinct. Change of an attribute for a tag is also allowed.

5. Similar Value and Distinct Tag/Attribute. This is, again, a syntactic disagreement. This case is not reported in the running example. Change of an attribute for a tag is also allowed.

6. Distinct Value and Tag/Attribute. This is the worst case which also means that a new element has been found in the compared XML tress. This is the case of `price` (in the second book "*XML Pocket Reference*" of $T_{X,1}$) and `format` (in the second book "*XML Pocket Reference*" of $T_{X,2}$). The value has to be neither equal nor similar according to the required threshold.

As result of the XML similarity analysis provided by `SemSynX`, a list of agreements/disagreements is retrieved, being the list itself represented as a XML document. This XML document makes use of tags for describing the kind of similarity (dissimilarity, respectively) for each element detected by the target analysis, as well as the path to such element and its content, by also reporting the similarity (local) score. A global score is also reported on the top of the document, and counts of agreements and disagreements are shown. In particular, the global score is computed in a *proportional manner* by taking into account weights assigned to main, secondary and new paths.

Figure 4 shows the final similarity analysis provided by `SemSynX` for the first book "*XML Pocket Reference*" of the running examples, having fixed: 0.5 as value

```
<result global_score="0.5336309523809524"
dissimilar="2" similar="8">
  <new>
    <path>library/book</path>
    <subpath>book/format</subpath></new>
  <new>
    <path>amazon/book</path>
    <subpath>book/price</subpath></new>
  <EqValueandDistinctLabel score="0.52380952380952381">
    <item>
      <content>Elliotte Harold</content>
      <path>book/authors/first</path></item>
    <item>
      <content>Elliotte Rusty Harold</content>
      <path>book/author</path></item>
  </EqValueandDistinctLabel>
  <EqValueandDistinctLabel score="0.666666666666666666">
    <item>
      <content>W. Scott Means</content>
      <path>book/authors/second</path></item>
    <item>
      <content>W. Scott Means</content>
      <path>book/author</path></item>
  </EqValueandDistinctLabel>
  <EqValueandDistinctLabel score="0.75">
    <item>
      <content>Third Edition</content>
      <path>book/edition_number</path></item>
    <item>
      <content>Third Edition</content>
      <path>book/edition</path></item>
  </EqValueandDistinctLabel>
  <EqLabelandContent score="1">
    <item>
      <path>book/title</path>
      <content>XML in a Nutshell</content></item>
```
```
  <item>
    <path>book/title</path>
    <content>XML in a Nutshell</content></item>
  </EqLabelandContent>
  <EqLabelandDistinctValue score="0.395833333333333334">
    <item>
      <path>book/publisher/editorial</path>
      <content>Springer</content></item>
    <item>
      <path>book/editorial</path>
      <content>OReilly</content></item>
  </EqLabelandDistinctValue>
  <EqAttributeandDistinctValue score="0.5">
    <item>
      <path>book</path>
      <attribute>year</attribute>
      <content>2008</content></item>
    <item>
      <path>book</path>
      <attribute>year</attribute>
      <content>2004</content></item>
  </EqAttributeandDistinctValue>
  <EqAttributeandContent score="1">
    <item>
      <path>book</path>
      <attribute>key</attribute>
      <content>1</content></item>
    <item>
      <path>book</path>
      <attribute>key</attribute>
      <content>1</content></item>
  </EqAttributeandContent>
  <EqAttributeLabelandContent score="0.5">
    <item>
      <path>book</path>
      <attribute>isbn</attribute></item>
    <path>book/publisher/isbn</path>
    <content>978-0596007645</content></item>
  </EqAttributeLabelandContent>
</result>
```

Fig. 4. Similarity analysis provided by **SemSynX** for the first book "*XML pocket reference*" of the running example

Table 1. Retrieved Scores and Thresholds

ThEq	ThSim	ThP	RV	RP	Score	Diss	Sim
1	1	1	1	1	0,178	11	3
1	1	0,75	1	1	0,178	11	3
1	1	0,5	1	1	0,303	7	5
1	1	0,25	1	1	0,392	5	6
1	1	0	1	1	0,437	4	11
0,75	0,5	0	1	1	0,437	4	7
0,5	0,25	0	1	1	0,533	2	8

(a) Running Example

Documents	ThEq	ThSim	ThP	RV	RP	Score	Diss	Sim
Ex1-Ex2	1	1	1	1	1	0,090	10	1
Ex1-Ex2	1	1	0.5	1	1	0,583	2	5
Ex1-Ex2	1	1	0.25	1	1	0,784	0	6
Ex1-Ex2	1	1	0.25	5	1	0,928	0	6
Ex1-Ex3	1	1	1	1	1	0,703	0	6
Ex1-Ex3	0,5	0,25	1	1	1	0,703	0	6
Ex1-Ex3	0,5	0,25	1	1	5	0,910	0	6

(b) Documents of Figure 5

equality threshold, 0.25 as value similarity threshold, and 0.0 as path similarity threshold, respectively. All the paths have considered relevant here, and the Levenshtein's distance function [18] has been considered for all the elements.

4   Experimental Results

In this Section, we propose the experimental assessment and analysis of **SemSynX** over several classes of XML documents. The final goal of this assessment is to show the evident improvements obtained by customizing the similarity analysis by means of several thresholds, relevance measures, selection of paths and user-defined similarity functions. It should be noted that this special feature

```
                              <example>
                              <member id="1">
                              <personal_info>                   *
<example>                     <name>                            <example>
<member id="1">               <familyname>Smith</familyname>    <member id="1">
<familyname>Smith</familyname> <firstname>John</firstname>       <familyname>Smith </familyname>
<firstname>John</firstname>   </name>                           <firstname>J.</firstname>
<age>67</age>                 <age>67</age>                     <age>67 years</age>
<address>Fifth avenue</address> <postal_address>                <address>
<city>NY</city>               <street>Fifth avenue</street>     767 Fifth Avenue, 3rd Floor</address>
</member>                     <city>NY</city>                   <city>New York, NY 10153</city>
</example>                    </postal_address>                 </member>
                             </personal_info>                  </example>
                             </member>
                             </example>

         Example 1                        Example 2                         Example 3
```

Fig. 5. Synthetic XML documents

represents one of the main advantages of SemSynX over state-of-the-art approaches (see Sect. 3).

As synthetic XML documents, we considered instances with different characteristics (see Sect. 3), in order to stress the flexible properties of SemSynX. Hence, we considered both XML documents of the running example (see Figs. 1 and 2) and XML documents shown in Fig. 5. We then set different values of thresholds, according to our main XML similarity analysis asset (see Sect. 3). Table 1 shows the retrieved results. In more details, in the case of the running example, where we compared the XML document $T_{X,1}$ (see Fig. 1) and the XML document $T_{X,2}$ (see Fig. 2), Table 1(a) reports the retrieved results. Here, when thresholds are strong (i.e., 1.0), the similarity global score is 0.178 and the rate of similar/dissimilar elements is 3/11, which appears to be too low. By decreasing the path similarity threshold from 1.0 to 0.0, a score of 0.437 and a rate of 11/4 are obtained. Let us remark that decreasing the path similarity threshold from 0.25 to 0.0 causes that paths with similarity under 25 % are also compared. In order to improve similarity scores, equality and similarity thresholds for values must be decreased from 1.0 to 0.75 and 0.5 and from 1.0 to 0.5 and 0.25, respectively, thus obtaining rates of similar/dissimilar elements equal to 7/4 and 8/2, respectively. The last case provides a score equal to 0.533 that represents more than 50 % of similarity and 2 distinct elements over 8 similar elements in total, which is the expected result from the user point of view.

In the case of the example XML documents shown in Fig. 5, we compared have been taken in order to compare the document *Example 1*, named as $D_{X,1}$, against two documents *Example 2*, named as $D_{X,2}$, and *Example 3*, named as $D_{X,3}$, respectively. In the first case, i.e. the comparison of $D_{X,1}$ against $D_{X,2}$, it follows that $D_{X,2}$ is similar to $D_{X,1}$ in content but dissimilar in structure. Thus, we hope to find best scores when path comparisons are relaxed (see Sect. 3). As shown in Table 1(b), by decreasing path similarity threshold to 0.25 and conferring 5 times more relevance to value similarity, even when value equality and similarity remain fixed, the score is improved up to more than 92 % of similarity. In the second case, i.e. the comparison of $D_{X,1}$ against $D_{X,3}$, it follows that $D_{X,3}$ is similar to $D_{X,1}$ in structure but dissimilar in content. As shown in Table 1(b), by decreasing equality and similarity thresholds to 0.5 and 0.25, respectively, and conferring 5 times more relevance to paths, the score is improved up to more than 91 % of similarity. Let us remark that, in all the cases, the rate of similarity/dissimilarity is equal to 6/0.

In summary, our experimental assessment and analysis has shown that similarity analysis of XML documents greatly depends on the thresholds and relevance required for path and value similarity, and, depending on the structure/content of the documents (i.e., depending on the nature of the documents themselves), thresholds, relevance, selected paths and user-defined similarity functions play a key role. This completely proofs the powerful flexibility of the proposed XML similarity analysis technique SemSynX.

5   Conclusions and Future Work

In this paper, we have introduced and experimentally assessed SemSynX, a XML similarity analysis technique whose main benefits can be summarized by three main concepts: customization, flexibility and interoperability. The proposed technique retrieves the list of agreement/disagreement matches of two input XML documents, also determining suitable local and global similarity scores. SemSynX is fully customizable, thus enabling the specification of thresholds for path and value equality/similarity. Also, it makes possible to confer more relevance to paths versus values, and vice-versa, according to a proportional approach, as well as selection of paths and similarity functions. Finally, we have provided an experimental assessment and analysis of SemSynX against several classes of XML documents. The tool has been implemented as an XQuery library.

As future work we plan to move the attention on the following research lines. Firstly, incorporating within SemSynX a more sophisticated notion of path similarity. On one hand, path order as well as path duplicates are not still considered in path similarity analysis. On the other hand, asymmetric comparison (i.e., electing a master XML document) should be addressed in future efforts. Secondly, the thresholding technique will be extended. A possible improvement can be introduced by considering *distinct thresholds* for each type of tag. Thirdly, a very interesting future extension is represented by considering RDF data as target data format. This opens an interesting research line where trees are replaced by graphs. Providing similarity scores for RDF graphs enables comparison and fusion of *Semantic Web Data*. Lastly, considering *adaptiveness features* (e.g., [6,7]), *knowledge representation techniques* (e.g., [10]), and *uncertainty in data* (e.g., [17]) are open research problems to be considered in future, and suitable characteristics of SemSynX should deal with those accordingly.

Acknowledgments. This work was funded by the EU ERDF and the Spanish Ministry of Economy and Competitiveness (MINECO) under Project TIN2013-44742-C4-4-R as well as by the Andalusian Regional Government under Project P10-TIC-6114.

References

1. Aïtelhadj, A., Boughanem, M., Mezghiche, M., Souam, F.: Using structural similarity for clustering XML documents. Knowl. Inf. Syst. **32**(1), 109–139 (2012)
2. Algergawy, A., Mesiti, M., Nayak, R., Saake, G.: XML data clustering: an overview. ACM Comput. Surv. (CSUR) **43**(4), 25 (2011)
3. Almendros-Jiménez, J.M., Cuzzocrea, A.: Towards flexible similarity analysis of XML data. In: On the Move to Meaningful Internet Systems: OTM 2015 Workshops, Rhodes, Greece, 26–30 October 2015, pp. 573–576 (2015)
4. Bleiholder, J., Naumann, F.: Data fusion. ACM Comput. Surv. (CSUR) **41**(1), 1 (2008)
5. Bryl, V., Bizer, C., Isele, R., Verlic, M., Hong, S.G., Jang, S., Yi, M.Y., Choi, K.-S.: Interlinking and knowledge fusion. In: Auer, S., Bryl, V., Tramp, S. (eds.) Linked Open Data. LNCS, vol. 8661, pp. 70–89. Springer, Heidelberg (2014)
6. Cannataro, M., Cuzzocrea, A., Mastroianni, C., Ortale, R., Pugliese, A.: Modeling adaptive hypermedia with an object-oriented approach and XML. In: Proceedings of the Second International Workshop on Web Dynamics, pp. 35–44 (2002)
7. Cannataro, M., Cuzzocrea, A., Pugliese, A., Bucci, V.P.: A probabilistic approach to model adaptive hypermedia systems. In: Proceedings of the First International Workshop for Web Dynamics, pp. 12–30 (2001)
8. Cecchin, F., de Aguiar Ciferri, C.D., Hara, C.S.: XML data fusion. In: Bach Pedersen, T., Mohania, M.K., Tjoa, A.M. (eds.) DAWAK 2010. LNCS, vol. 6263, pp. 297–308. Springer, Heidelberg (2010)
9. Costa, G., Cuzzocrea, A., Manco, G., Ortale, R.: Data de-duplication: a review. In: Biba, M., Xhafa, F. (eds.) Learning Structure and Schemas from Documents. SCI, vol. 375, pp. 385–412. Springer, Heidelberg (2011)
10. Cuzzocrea, A.: Combining multidimensional user models and knowledge representation and management techniques for making web services knowledge-aware. Web Intell. Agent Syst. **4**(3), 289–312 (2006)
11. Cuzzocrea, A., Puglisi, P.L.: Record linkage in data warehousing: state-of-the-art analysis and research perspectives. In: Database and Expert Systems Applications, DEXA 2011, International Workshops, Toulouse, France, August 29 – September 2 2011, pp. 121–125 (2011)
12. Do Nascimento, A.M., Hara, C.S.: A model for XML instance level integration. In: Proceedings of the 23rd Brazilian Symposium on Databases, pp. 46–60. Sociedade Brasileira de Computação (2008)
13. Dong, X.L., Naumann, F.: Data fusion: resolving data conflicts for integration. Proc. VLDB Endowment **2**(2), 1654–1655 (2009)
14. Dorneles, C.F., Gonçalves, R., dos Santos Mello, R.: Approximate data instance matching: a survey. Knowl. Inf. Syst. **27**(1), 1–21 (2011)
15. Geerts, F., Mecca, G., Papotti, P., Santoro, D.: Mapping and cleaning. In: IEEE 30th International Conference on Data Engineering (ICDE 2014), pp. 232–243. IEEE (2014)
16. Hara, C.S., de Aguiar Ciferri, C.D., Ciferri, R.R.: Incremental data fusion based on provenance information. In: Tannen, V., Wong, L., Libkin, L., Fan, W., Tan, W.-C., Fourman, M. (eds.) Buneman Festschrift 2013. LNCS, vol. 8000, pp. 339–365. Springer, Heidelberg (2013)
17. Leung, C.K.-S., Cuzzocrea, A., Jiang, F.: Discovering frequent patterns from uncertain data streams with time-fading and landmark models. T. Large-Scale Data-Knowl. Centered Syst. **8**, 174–196 (2013)

18. Levenshtein, V.I.: Binary codes capable of correcting deletions, insertions and reversals. In: Soviet physics doklady, vol. 10, p. 707 (1966)
19. Lung, C.-H., Sanaullah, M., Cao, Y., Majumdar, S.: Design and performance evaluation of cloud-based XML publish/subscribe services. In: IEEE International Conference on Services Computing, SCC 2014, Anchorage, AK, USA, June 27 – July 2 2014, pp. 583–589 (2014)
20. Mendes, P.N., Mühleisen, H., Bizer, C.: Sieve: linked data quality assessment and fusion. In: Proceedings of the Joint EDBT/ICDT 2012 Workshops, pp. 116–123. ACM (2012)
21. Milano, D., Scannapieco, M., Catarci, T.: Using ontologies for XML data cleaning. In: Meersman, R., Tari, Z. (eds.) OTM-WS 2005. LNCS, vol. 3762, pp. 562–571. Springer, Heidelberg (2005)
22. Oliveira, P., de Fatima Rodrigues, M., Henriques, P.R.: An ontology-based approach for data cleaning. In: ICIQ, pp. 307–320 (2006)
23. Rahm, E., Bernstein, P.A.: A survey of approaches to automatic schema matching. VLDB J. **10**(4), 334–350 (2001)
24. Sundaram, S., Kumar, S.: Madria.: a change detection system for unordered XML data using a relational model. Data Knowl. Eng. **72**, 257–284 (2012)
25. Tekli, J., Chbeir, R., Yetongnon, K.: An overview on XML similarity: background, current trends and future directions. Comput. Sci. Rev. **3**(3), 151–173 (2009)
26. Weis, M., Manolescu, I.: Declarative XML data cleaning with XClean. In: Krogstie, J., Opdahl, A.L., Sindre, G. (eds.) CAiSE 2007 and WES 2007. LNCS, vol. 4495, pp. 96–110. Springer, Heidelberg (2007)
27. Weis, M., Naumann, F.: Detecting duplicates in complex XML data. In: Proceedings of the 22nd International Conference on Data Engineering, ICDE 2006, pp. 109–109. IEEE (2006)
28. Winkler, W.E.: The state of record linkage and current research problems. In: Statistical Research Division, US Census Bureau (1999)
29. Yaguinuma, C.A., Afonso, G.F., Ferraz, V., Borges, S., Santos, M.T.: A fuzzy ontology-based semantic data integration system. J. Inf. Knowl. Manage. **10**(03), 285–299 (2011)
30. Zhang, D., Song, T., He, J., Shi, X., Dong, Y.: A similarity-oriented RDF graph matching algorithm for ranking linked data. In: 2012 IEEE 12th International Conference on Computer and Information Technology (CIT), pp. 427–434. IEEE (2012)

Towards Automatic Composition of Multicomponent Predictive Systems

Manuel Martin Salvador[✉], Marcin Budka, and Bogdan Gabrys

Data Science Institute, Bournemouth University, Poole, UK
{msalvador,mbudka,bgabrys}@bournemouth.ac.uk

Abstract. Automatic composition and parametrisation of multicomponent predictive systems (MCPSs) consisting of chains of data transformation steps is a challenging task. In this paper we propose and describe an extension to the Auto-WEKA software which now allows to compose and optimise such flexible MCPSs by using a sequence of WEKA methods. In the experimental analysis we focus on examining the impact of significantly extending the search space by incorporating additional hyperparameters of the models, on the quality of the found solutions. In a range of extensive experiments three different optimisation strategies are used to automatically compose MCPSs on 21 publicly available datasets. A comparison with previous work indicates that extending the search space improves the classification accuracy in the majority of the cases. The diversity of the found MCPSs are also an indication that fully and automatically exploiting different combinations of data cleaning and preprocessing techniques is possible and highly beneficial for different predictive models. This can have a big impact on high quality predictive models development, maintenance and scalability aspects needed in modern application and deployment scenarios.

Keywords: KDD process · CASH problem · Bayesian optimisation · Data mining and decision support systems · Data preprocessing

1 Introduction

Performance of data-driven predictive models heavily relies on the quality and quantity of data used to build them. However, in real applications, even if data is abundant, it is also often imperfect and considerable effort needs to be invested into a labour-intensive task of cleaning and preprocessing such data in preparation for subsequent modelling. Some authors claim that these tasks can account for as much as 60–80 % of total time spent on development of a predictive model [1,2]. Therefore, approaches and practical techniques that allow to reduce this effort by at least partially automating some of the data preparation steps, can potentially transform the way in which predictive models are typically built.

In many scenarios one needs to sequentially apply multiple preprocessing methods to the same data (e.g. outlier detection → missing value imputation →

© Springer International Publishing Switzerland 2016
F. Martínez-Álvarez et al. (Eds.): HAIS 2016, LNAI 9648, pp. 27–39, 2016.
DOI: 10.1007/978-3-319-32034-2_3

dimensionality reduction), effectively forming a preprocessing chain. Composition of a preprocessing chain is a challenging problem that has been addressed in different fields (e.g. clinical data [3,4], historical documents [5] and process industry [6]). Despite these works attempting to be as abstract as possible, the frameworks they propose are optimised for a particular case study. Hence their underlying approaches are lacking in the context of cross-domain generalisation, and potentially require additional manual work to improve the results.

After the data has been pre-processed in an appropriate way, the next step in a data mining process is modelling. Similarly to preprocessing, this step can also be very time-consuming, requiring evaluation of multiple alternative models. Hence automatic model selection has been attempted in different ways, e.g. active testing [7], meta-learning [8] and information theory [9]. A common theme in the literature is comparison of different models using data always pre-processed in the same way. However, some models may perform better if they are built using data specifically pre-processed with a particular model type in mind.

Hyper-parameter optimisation is an additional step which is usually performed after the model has been selected (see e.g. [10–12]). However, the problem is in fact very similar to model selection since different parametrisations of the same model (e.g. different kernels in an SVM, different structures of a neural network) can be treated as different models. Therefore it makes sense to approach both model and hyper-parameter selection problems jointly. The Combined Algorithm Selection and Hyper-parameter optimisation (CASH) problem was presented in [13]. A limitation of that study was the use of only two native types of attributes (i.e. numerical and categorical). This paper extends the approach presented in [13] to support complex categorical attributes, which consists of a WEKA class and therefore can contain additional hyper-parameters.

We refer to a sequence of preprocessing steps followed by a machine learning model as a multicomponent predictive system (MCPS). The motivation for automating composition of MCPS is twofold. In the first instance it will help to reduce the amount of time spent on such activities and therefore allow to dedicate the human expertise to other tasks. The second motivation is to achieve better results than a human expert could, given a limited amount of time. The number of possible methods and hyperparameter combinations increases exponentially with the number of components in an MCPS and in majority of cases it is not computationally feasible to evaluate all of them.

This paper is organised as follows. The next section reviews previous work in automating the CASH problem and available software. Section 3 describes multicomponent predictive systems and the challenges related to automation of their composition. In Sect. 4, our contributions to Auto-WEKA software, now allowing to optimise additional hyperparameters, are presented. The methodology used to automate MCPS composition is discussed in Sect. 5 followed by the results in Sect. 6, and conclusions in Sect. 7.

2   Related Work

The Combined Algorithm Selection and Hyper-parameter configuration (CASH) problem [13] consists of finding the best combination of learning algorithm A^* and hyperparameters λ^* that optimise an objective function $\mathcal{L}$ (e.g. Eq. 1 minimises the k-fold cross-validation error) for a given dataset $\mathcal{D}$. Formally, CASH problem is given by:

$$A^*_{\lambda^*} \in \underset{A^{(j)} \in \mathcal{A}, \lambda \in \Lambda^{(j)}}{\operatorname{argmin}} \frac{1}{k} \sum_{i=1}^{k} \mathcal{L}(A^{(j)}_{\lambda}, \mathcal{D}^{(i)}_{train}, \mathcal{D}^{(i)}_{valid}) \tag{1}$$

where $\mathcal{A} = \{A^{(1)}, \ldots, A^{(k)}\}$ is a set of algorithms with associated hyperparameter spaces $\Lambda^{(1)}, \ldots, \Lambda^{(k)}$. The loss function $\mathcal{L}$ takes as arguments an algorithm configuration A_{λ} (i.e. an instance of a learning algorithm and hyperparameters), a training set $\mathcal{D}_{train}$ and a validation set $\mathcal{D}_{valid}$.

The CASH problem can be approached in different ways. One example is grid search – an exhaustive search over all the possible combinations of discretized parameters. Such technique can however be computationally prohibitive in large search spaces or with big datasets. Instead, a simpler mechanism like random search, where the search space is randomly explored in a limited amount of time, has been shown to be more effective in high-dimensional spaces [12].

A promising approach that is gaining popularity in the last years is Bayesian optimization [14]. In particular, Sequential Model-Based Optimization (SMBO) [15] is a framework that incrementally builds a regression model using instances formed of an algorithm configuration λ and its predictive performance c. Such a model is then used to explore promising candidate configurations.

Examples of SMBO methods are SMAC (Sequential Model-based Algorithm Configuration [15]) and TPE (Tree-structure Parzen Estimation [16]). SMAC models $p(c|\lambda)$ using a random forest, while TPE maintains separate models for $p(c)$ and $p(\lambda|c)$. Both methods support continuous, categorical and conditional attributes (i.e. attributes whose presence in the optimisation problem depend on the values of some other attributes – e.g. Gaussian kernel width parameter in SVM is only present if SVM is using Gaussian kernels).

Two other methods falling into the same category are ROAR (Random Online Aggressive Racing [15]) which randomly selects the set of candidates instead of using a regression model, and Spearmint [17] which uses Gaussian processes to model $p(c|\lambda)$ similarly to SMAC. However, due to their limitations (it has been shown that SMAC outperforms ROAR [15], while Spearmint does not support conditional attributes) we are not using these methods in this study.

Currently available software tools supporting SMBO methods are:

– SMAC[1] [15] tool, which includes both SMAC and ROAR methods.
– Hyperopt[2] [16] is a Python library including random search and TPE.

---

[1] http://www.cs.ubc.ca/labs/beta/Projects/SMAC.
[2] https://github.com/hyperopt/hyperopt.

- HPOLib[3] [18] is a wrapper for SMAC, TPE and Spearmint methods.
- Auto-Sklearn[4] [19] uses HPOLib and meta-learning to automate the selection of scikit-learn methods.
- Auto-WEKA[5] [13] allows to use either SMAC or TPE to automatically select and optimise 39 classifiers and 24 possible feature selection methods included in WEKA[6].

3   MCPS Description

A multicomponent predictive system can be represented as a directed acyclic graph, where the vertices correspond to data transformations and the edges represent the flow of data between the components. In this study we focus on MCPSs of the $F = \langle f_1, ..., f_N \rangle$ form, which as shown in Fig. 1, are directed linear graphs of length N. The components f_1 to f_{N-1} are preprocessing methods while component f_N is either a predictive model or an ensemble of models. Although post-processing methods can also be included as additional components, without the loss of generality, we are not investigating such MCPSs here.

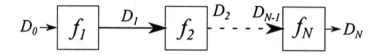

Fig. 1. N-component predictive system

The ith component is a function $D_i = f_i(D_{i-1})$ that takes a data frame D_{i-1} as input and returns a data frame D_i. Such data frames can have any size and contain any type of data (e.g. continuous or categorical). However, values of a single column are assumed to be of identical type.

The connection between components must be consistent, i.e. output of component f_n must be compatible with the input of f_{n+1}. For example, if component f_{n+1} cannot handle missing values, output from f_n should not contain any.

Typically, the first component receives the raw data as input, and the last component returns the predictions (i.e. a label in case of classification problems or a continuous value in regression problems). The number of components in an MCPS can vary from 1 (i.e. when no preprocessing is used) to $N \in \mathbb{N}_{>1}$. Some flows in OpenML experiments repository[7] contain up to 7 components, while data mining tools like RapidMiner or Knime allow building even longer flows.

---

[3] https://github.com/automl/hpolib.
[4] https://github.com/mfeurer/auto-sklearn.
[5] http://www.cs.ubc.ca/labs/beta/Projects/autoweka.
[6] An open-source data mining package developed at the University of Waikato.
[7] http://openml.org.

An MCPS can be seen as a type of workflow that can be found in platforms like Taverna[8]. However, we prefer to avoid such generic term in this paper in order to highlight the predictive nature of this type of systems.

Building an MCPS is typically a manual process. Even though some efforts are being made to automate such process (see e.g. [20] for a survey), a reliable fully automated approach is still far from being available.

The main reason that makes MCPS composition a challenging problem is the potentially huge size of the search space. To begin with, the undetermined number of components can make the flow very simple or very complex. Secondly, we do not know a priori the order in which the components have to be connected. Also, the type of each hyper-parameter can be either continuous, categorical or conditional. Therefore, defining a range for each of the hyperparameters is an additional problem in itself.

The search space size can be reduced by applying constraints like limiting the number of components, restricting the list of methods using meta-learning [21], prior knowledge [22] or surrogates [23].

In this paper we use the predictive performance as a single optimisation objective. We note however, that some problems may require to optimise several objectives at the same time (e.g. error rate, model complexity and runtime [24]).

4   Contribution to Auto-WEKA

Auto-WEKA is a software developed by Thornton et al. [13] which allows algorithm selection and hyper-parameter optimisation both in regression and classification problems. The current Auto-WEKA version is 0.5 and it provides an interface for a CASH problem, where the search space is defined by WEKA predictors and feature selection methods. Available optimisation strategies are SMAC and TPE.

We have developed a new feature consisting of automatic expansion of WEKA classes during the creation of the search space. That is, if a hyper-parameter is a category formed of several WEKA classes, Auto-WEKA will now add the hyperparameters of such class recursively. For example, the kernel of an SVM classifier can be either NormalizedPolyKernel, PolyKernel, Puk, or RBFKernel; and each of them contains different hyperparameters.

While the space restriction does not allow us to include more implementation details, all the scripts for the analysis of the extended Auto-WEKA results such as the creation of plots and tables have been also released in our repository[9].

5   Methodology

The three main characteristics which define a CASH problem are: (a) the search space, (b) the objective function and (c) the optimisation algorithm.

In this study we have considered two search spaces:

---

[8] http://www.taverna.org.uk.

[9] https://github.com/dsibournemouth/autoweka.

- PREV: This is the search space used in [13] where predictors and meta-predictors (which take outputs from one or more base predictive models as their input) were considered (756 hyperparameters). Feature selection is also performed as a preprocessing step before the optimisation process (30 hyper-parameters). We use it as a baseline.
- NEW: This search space only includes predictors and meta-predictors. In contrast with PREV space, no preprocessing steps are involved. Instead, we take into account that a categorical hyperparameter can be either simple or complex (i.e. when it contains WEKA classes). In the latter case, we increase the search space by adding recursively the hyperparameters of each method belonging to such complex parameter (e.g. the 'DecisionTable' predictor contains a complex hyperparameter whose values are three different types of search methods with further hyperparameters). That extension increases the search space to 1186 hyperparameters.

Table 1. Datasets, number of continuous attributes, number of categorical attributes, number of classes, number of instances, and percentage of missing values.

Dataset	Cont	Disc	Class	Train	Test	%Miss
abalone	7	1	28	2924	1253	0
amazon	10000	0	50	1050	450	0
car	0	6	4	1210	518	0
cifar10	3072	0	10	50000	10000	0
cifar10small	3072	0	10	10000	10000	0
convex	784	0	2	8000	50000	0
dexter	20000	0	2	420	180	0
dorothea	100000	0	2	805	345	0
germancredit	7	13	2	700	300	0
gisette	5000	0	2	4900	2100	0
kddcup09app	192	38	2	35000	15000	69.47
krvskp	0	36	2	2238	958	0
madelon	500	0	2	1820	780	0
mnist	784	0	10	12000	50000	0
mnistrot	784	0	10	12000	50000	0
secom	590	0	2	1097	470	4.58
semeion	256	0	10	1116	477	0
shuttle	9	0	7	43500	14500	0
waveform	40	0	3	3500	1500	0
wineqw	11	0	11	3429	1469	0
yeast	8	0	10	1039	445	0

The objective function guides the optimisation process. Since the datasets we use in our experiments are intended for classification, we have chosen to minimise the classification error averaged over 10 cross-validation folds.

Two SMBO strategies (SMAC and TPE) have been compared against two baselines (WEKA-Def and random search). The following experimental scenarios have been devised:

- WEKA-Def: All the predictors and meta-predictors are run using WEKA's default hyperparameter values. Filters are not included in this strategy, although some predictors may perform specific preprocessing steps as part of their default behaviour.
- Random search: The whole search space is randomly explored allowing 30 CPU-hours for the process.
- SMAC and TPE: An initial configuration is randomly selected and then the optimiser is run for 30 CPU-hours to explore the search space in an intelligent way, allowing for comparison with the random search.

In order to compare our results with the ones presented in [13] we have replicated the experimental settings as closely as possible. We have evaluated different optimisation strategies over 21 well-known datasets representing classification tasks (see Table 1). For each strategy we performed 25 runs with different random seeds and a 30 CPU-hours optimisation time limit. In case a configuration exceeds 30 min or 3 GB of RAM to evaluate, it is stopped and not considered further. Once the optimisation process has finished, the returned configuration is used to build a model using the whole training set and produce predictions over the testing set.

6   Results and Discussion

Classification performance for each dataset are presented in Tables 2 and 3, which show the 10-fold cross-validation error and the test error achieved by each strategy, respectively. Random search, SMAC and TPE results have been calculated using the mean of 100,000 bootstrap samples (i.e. randomly selecting 4 out of the 25 runs and keeping the one with the lowest cross-validation error in order to simulate a 4-core CPU), while only the lowest errors are reported for WEKA-Def. PREV columns contain the values reported in [13], while NEW columns contain the results of the strategies using extended search space investigated in this paper. An upward arrow indicates an improvement when using extended search space (NEW) in comparison to previous results (PREV) reported in [13]. Boldfaced values indicate the lowest classification error for each dataset.

Table 2. 10-fold Cross Validation error (% missclassification). An upward arrow indicates an improvement with respect to PREV space. Boldfaced values indicate the lowest classification error for each dataset.

Dataset	WEKA-DEF	RANDOM		SMAC		TPE	
	PREV = NEW	PREV	NEW	PREV	NEW	PREV	NEW
abalone	73.33	72.03	72.53	**71.71**	72.21	72.14	72.01 ↑
amazon	43.94	59.85	45.72 ↑	47.34	**39.57** ↑	50.26	40.27 ↑
car	2.71	0.53	0.47 ↑	0.61	0.38 ↑	0.91	**0.21** ↑
cifar10	65.54	69.46	58.89 ↑	62.36	56.44 ↑	67.73	**55.59** ↑
cifar10small	66.59	67.33	60.45 ↑	58.84	57.90 ↑	58.41	**56.56** ↑
convex	28.68	33.31	25.02 ↑	25.93	**21.88** ↑	28.56	23.19 ↑
dexter	10.20	10.06	7.54 ↑	**5.66**	6.42	9.83	6.19 ↑
dorothea	6.03	8.11	6.25 ↑	**5.62**	5.95	6.81	5.92 ↑
germancredit	22.45	20.15	21.31	**17.87**	19.65	21.56	19.88 ↑
gisette	3.62	4.84	2.30 ↑	2.43	**2.21** ↑	3.55	2.35 ↑
kddcup09app	1.88	1.75	1.80	**1.70**	1.80	1.88	1.80 ↑
krvskp	0.89	0.63	0.42 ↑	0.30	**0.28** ↑	0.43	0.31 ↑
madelon	25.98	27.95	19.20 ↑	20.70	**15.61** ↑	24.25	16.03 ↑
mnist	5.12	5.05	3.78 ↑	3.75	**3.50** ↑	10.02	3.60 ↑
mnistr	66.15	68.62	58.10 ↑	57.86	**55.73** ↑	73.09	57.17 ↑
secom	6.25	5.27	5.85	**5.24**	6.01	6.21	5.85 ↑
semeion	6.52	6.06	4.82 ↑	4.78	4.48 ↑	6.76	**4.28** ↑
shuttle	0.0328	0.0345	0.0121 ↑	0.0224	0.0112 ↑	0.0251	**0.0104** ↑
waveform	12.73	12.43	12.50	**11.92**	12.33	12.55	12.43 ↑
wineqw	38.94	35.36	33.08 ↑	34.65	**32.64** ↑	35.98	32.67 ↑
yeast	39.43	38.74	37.16 ↑	35.51	36.50	**35.01**	36.17

As shown in the tables, in the majority of the cases, expanding the search space has been beneficial for finding better solutions (i.e. NEW < PREV). The potential negative impact on predictive accuracy by optimising many more parameters has not been observed. Although, we still found some cases with higher classification error (i.e. NEW > PREV).

Figure 2 compares CV error and test error for all the runs. Although both errors are in general consistent, we found some cases in which the model seems to overfit. That is the case for example in 'germancredit' and 'amazon' datasets. A possible explanation is given below, at the end of this section.

The best MCPSs found for each dataset are reported in Table 4. Each row of this table represents a sequence of data transformations and predictive models. It is not feasible to include all the hyperparameters in the table due to limited space, but they do play a crucial role in the final performance. We can see that all the MCPSs include at least one or more preprocessing steps.

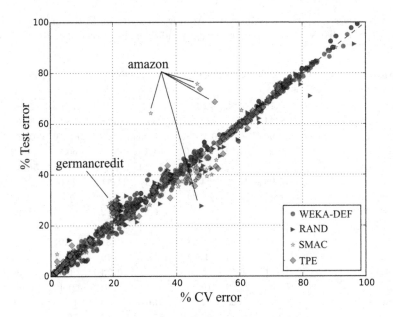

Fig. 2. CV vs Test error of all runs

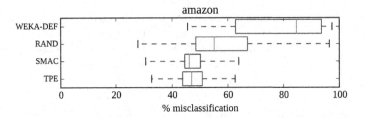

Fig. 3. Range of CV errors for 'amazon'

As shown in Table 4 the solutions found are quite diverse for different datasets but they often also vary a lot across the 25 random seed runs performed for each dataset. In order to better understand all of the observed differences in the MCPSs found we have therefore also measured the average pairwise similarity of the 25 MCPSs found for each dataset and the variance between their performances. While in this paper there is no space for full analysis or explanation of how the pairwise similarity was measured, below we have selected three interesting cases for a brief discussion:

– Low error variance and high MCPS similarity. Most of the best solutions found follow a very similar sequence of methods. Therefore similar classification performance is to be expected. For example, a repeated sequence in 'wineqw' dataset with SMAC optimisation is RandomForest (22/25) → MultiClassClassifier (8/25).

Table 3. Test error (% missclassification). An upward arrow indicates an improvement with respect to PREV space. Boldfaced values indicate the lowest classification error for each dataset.

Dataset	DEF	RANDOM		SMAC		TPE	
	PREV = NEW	PREV	NEW	PREV	NEW	PREV	NEW
abalone	73.18	74.88	**72.92** ↑	73.51	73.41 ↑	72.94	73.04
amazon	**28.44**	41.11	39.22 ↑	33.99	36.26	36.59	35.69 ↑
car	0.7700	0.0100	0.1300	0.4000	0.0526 ↑	0.1800	**0.0075** ↑
cifar10	64.27	69.72	58.23 ↑	61.15	55.54 ↑	66.01	**54.88** ↑
cifar10small	65.91	66.12	59.84 ↑	56.84	57.87	57.01	**56.41** ↑
convex	25.96	31.20	24.75 ↑	23.17	**21.31** ↑	25.59	22.62 ↑
dexter	8.89	9.18	8.29 ↑	7.49	7.31 ↑	8.89	**6.90** ↑
dorothea	6.96	5.22	5.27	6.21	**5.12** ↑	6.15	5.25 ↑
germancredit	27.33	29.03	**25.40** ↑	28.24	25.42 ↑	27.54	25.49 ↑
gisette	2.81	4.62	2.28 ↑	**2.24**	2.34	3.94	2.37 ↑
kddcup09app	1.7405	1.74	**1.72** ↑	1.7358	1.74	1.7381	1.74
krvskp	0.31	0.58	0.34 ↑	0.31	**0.23** ↑	0.54	0.36 ↑
madelon	21.38	24.29	19.10 ↑	21.56	**16.80** ↑	21.12	16.91 ↑
mnist	5.19	5.05	4.00 ↑	**3.64**	4.10	12.28	3.96 ↑
mnistr	63.14	66.4	57.16 ↑	57.04	**54.86** ↑	70.20	56.31 ↑
secom	8.09	8.03	7.88 ↑	8.01	7.87 ↑	8.10	**7.84** ↑
semeion	8.18	6.10	**4.78** ↑	5.08	5.10	8.26	4.91 ↑
shuttle	0.0138	0.0157	0.0071 ↑	0.0130	0.0070 ↑	0.0145	**0.0069** ↑
waveform	14.40	14.27	14.26 ↑	14.42	**14.17** ↑	14.23	14.34
wineqw	37.51	34.41	32.99 ↑	33.95	**32.90** ↑	33.56	32.93 ↑
yeast	40.45	43.15	37.68 ↑	40.67	**37.60** ↑	40.10	37.89 ↑

- Low error variance and low MCPS similarity. Despite having different solutions, classification performance in a group of analysed datasets does not vary much. This can mean that the classification problem is not difficult and a range of different models can perform well on it. This is for instance the case of the solutions found by using random search for the 'secom' dataset.
- High error variance and low MCPS similarity. In such cases, there are many differences between both the best MCPSs found and their classification performances. For instance, it is the case of 'amazon' dataset (with 50 different classes) for which a high error variance was observed in all of the optimisation strategies (see Fig. 3 for CV error and Fig. 2 for test error). We believe such difference likely results from a combination of difficulty of the classification task (i.e. high input dimensionality, large number of small classes) and/or an insufficient exploration from the random starting configuration in a very large search space.

Table 4. Best MCPS for each dataset and its test error. MC = Remove instances with missing class. MV = Remove/Replace instances with missing values. N2B = NominalToBinary. NOR = Normalization. DIS = Discretize. FS = Random Feature Selection. BAG = Bagging. BOOST = Boosting.

Dataset	MC	MV	N2B	NOR	DIS	FS	BAG	BOOST	Predictor	Meta-predictor	Error
abalone	•	•	•	•					MLP	RandomCommittee	71.43
amazon	•	•	•				•		SimpleLogistic	RandomSubSpace	26.67
car	•	•	•	•				•	SMO	AdaBoostM1	0.00
cifar10	•				•	•			RandomForest	MultiClassClassifier	52.28
cifar10small	•					•			RandomTree	MultiClassClassifier	54.48
convex	•				•	•		•	RandomForest	AdaBoostM1	18.47
dexter	•							•	DecisionStump	AdaBoostM1	5.00
dorothea	•				•	•			OneR	RandomSubSpace	4.64
germancredit	•	•	•				•		LogisticModelTree	Bagging	23.33
gisette	•								NaiveBayes	LWL	1.95
kddcup09app	•								ZeroR	LWL	1.67
krvskp	•							•	JRip	AdaBoostM1	0.10
madelon	•					•			REPTree	RandomSubSpace	15.64
mnist	•	•	•	•					SMO	LWL	3.28
mnistr	•				•	•			RandomForest	RandomCommittee	52.20
secom	•							•	J48	AdaBoostM1	7.66
semeion	•								NaiveBayes	LWL	3.98
shuttle	•				•	•		•	RandomForest	AdaBoostM1	0.0069
waveform	•	•	•	•		•			SMO	RandomSubSpace	14.00
wineqw	•				•	•		•	RandomForest	AdaBoostM1	32.33
yeast	•				•	•			RandomForest	Bagging	36.40

7   Conclusion and Future Work

We have shown that it is possible to automate the composition of a multicomponent predictive system. Our contribution to Auto-WEKA demonstrates that a lot of time and effort can be saved in the process of building predictive systems.

Extending the search space has led optimisation strategies to find solutions that improve the predictive performance in the majority of cases. Results have indicated that SMBO strategies perform better than random search giving the same time for optimisation in most of the cases. While we have performed optimisation for each of the datasets starting with 25 random seeds, in the future it would be interesting to investigate further how the best performance changes over time while varying the number of starting seeds.

The datasets used in the study have been chosen primarily for the purpose of comparison with previous work [13]. As it turned out, the datasets have been relatively 'clean', hence not requiring much preprocessing. In future work we will focus on datasets that require extensive preprocessing. Furthermore, the use of custom preprocessing chains will allow optimising the data that is being used to build predictive models.

In addition, it would also be valuable to investigate if using a different data partitioning like DPS [25] would make any difference in the optimisation process. We believe that it could have a considerable impact in SMAC strategy since it discards potential poor solutions early in the optimisation process based on the performance on only a few folds. In case the folds used are not representative of the overall data distribution, which as shown in [25] can happen quite often in the case of cross-validation, this can have a detrimental effect on the final solutions found.

At the moment, available SMBO methods only support single objective optimisation. However, it would be useful to find solutions that optimise more than one objective, including for instance a combination of prediction error, model complexity and running time as discussed in [24].

References

1. Pyle, D.: Data Preparation for Data Mining. Morgan Kaufmann, San Francisco (1999)
2. Linoff, G.S., Berry, M.J.A.: Data Mining Techniques: For Marketing, Sales, and Customer Relationship Management. Wiley (2011). ISBN: 978-0-470-65093-6
3. Teichmann, E., Demir, E., Chaussalet, T.: Data preparation for clinical data mining to identify patients at risk of readmission. In: IEEE 23rd International Symposium on Computer-Based Medical Systems, pp. 184–189 (2010)
4. Zhao, J., Wang, T.: A general framework for medical data mining. In: Future Information Technology and Management Engineering, pp. 163–165 (2010)
5. Messaoud, I., El Abed, H., Märgner, V., Amiri, H.: A design of a preprocessing framework for large database of historical documents. In: Proceedings of the 2011 Workshop on Historical Document Imaging and Processing, pp. 177–183 (2011)
6. Budka, M., Eastwood, M., Gabrys, B., Kadlec, P., Martin Salvador, M., Schwan, S., Tsakonas, A., Žliobaitė, I.: From sensor readings to predictions: on the process of developing practical soft sensors. In: Blockeel, H., van Leeuwen, M., Vinciotti, V. (eds.) IDA 2014. LNCS, vol. 8819, pp. 49–60. Springer, Heidelberg (2014)
7. Leite, R., Brazdil, P., Vanschoren, J.: Selecting classification algorithms with active testing. In: Perner, P. (ed.) MLDM 2012. LNCS, vol. 7376, pp. 117–131. Springer, Heidelberg (2012)
8. Lemke, C., Gabrys, B.: Meta-learning for time series forecasting and forecast combination. Neurocomputing 73(10–12), 2006–2016 (2010)
9. MacQuarrie, A., Tsai, C.L.: Regression and Time Series Model Selection. World Scientific (1998). ISBN: 978-981-02-3242-9
10. Bengio, Y.: Gradient-based optimization of hyperparameters. Neural Comput. 12(8), 1889–1900 (2000)
11. Guo, X.C., Yang, J.H., Wu, C.G., Wang, C.Y., Liang, Y.C.: A novel LS-SVMs hyper-parameter selection based on particle swarm optimization. Neurocomputing 71, 3211–3215 (2008)
12. Bergstra, J., Bengio, Y.: Random search for hyper-parameter optimization. J. Mach. Learn. Res. 13, 281–305 (2012)
13. Thornton, C., Hutter, F., Hoos, H.H., Leyton-Brown, K.: Auto-WEKA: combined selection and hyperparameter optimization of classification algorithms. In: Proceedings of the 19th ACM SIGKDD, pp. 847–855 (2013)

14. Brochu, E., Cora, V.M., de Freitas, N.: A Tutorial on Bayesian Optimization of Expensive Cost Functions with Application to Active User Modeling and Hierarchical Reinforcement Learning. Technical report, University of British Columbia, Department of Computer Science (2010)
15. Hutter, F., Hoos, H.H., Leyton-Brown, K.: Sequential model-based optimization for general algorithm configuration. In: Coello, C.A.C. (ed.) LION 2011. LNCS, vol. 6683, pp. 507–523. Springer, Heidelberg (2011)
16. Bergstra, J., Bardenet, R., Bengio, Y., Kegl, B.: Algorithms for hyper-parameter optimization. In: Advances in NIPS, vol. 24, pp. 1–9 (2011)
17. Snoek, J., Larochelle, H., Adams, R.P.: Practical bayesian optimization of machine learning algorithms. In: Advances in NIPS, vol. 25, pp. 2960–2968 (2012)
18. Eggensperger, K., Feurer, M., Hutter, F.: Towards an empirical foundation for assessing bayesian optimization of hyperparameters. In: NIPS Workshop on Bayesian Optimization in Theory and Practice, pp. 1–5 (2013)
19. Feurer, M., Klein, A., Eggensperger, K., Springenberg, J.T., Blum, M., Hutter, F.: Methods for improving bayesian optimization for AutoML. In: ICML (2015)
20. Serban, F., Vanschoren, J., Kietz, J.U., Bernstein, A.: A survey of intelligent assistants for data analysis. ACM Comput. Surv. **45**(3), 1–35 (2013)
21. Feurer, M., Springenberg, J.T., Hutter, F.: Using meta-learning to initialize bayesian optimization of hyperparameters. In: Proceedings of the Meta-Learning and Algorithm Selection Workshop at ECAI, pp. 3–10 (2014)
22. Swersky, K., Snoek, J., Adams, R.P.: Multi-task bayesian optimization. In: Advances in NIPS, vol. 26, pp. 2004–2012 (2013)
23. Eggensperger, K., Hutter, F., Hoos, H.H., Leyton-brown, K.: Efficient benchmarking of hyperparameter optimizers via surrogates background: hyperparameter optimization. In: Proceedings of the 29th AAAI Conference on Artificial Intelligence, pp. 1114–1120 (2012)
24. Al-Jubouri, B., Gabrys, B.: Multicriteria approaches for predictive model generation: a comparative experimental study. In: IEEE Symposium on Computational Intelligence in Multi-Criteria Decision-Making, pp. 64–71 (2014)
25. Budka, M., Gabrys, B.: Density-preserving sampling: robust and efficient alternative to cross-validation for error estimation. IEEE Trans. Neural Netw. Learn. Syst. **24**(1), 22–34 (2013)

LiCord: Language Independent Content Word Finder

Md-Mizanur Rahoman[1(✉)], Tetsuya Nasukawa[2], Hiroshi Kanayama[2],
and Ryutaro Ichise[1,3]

[1] SOKENDAI (The Graduate University for Advanced Studies), Hayama, Japan
mizan@nii.ac.jp
[2] IBM Research – Tokyo, Tokyo, Japan
{nasukawa,hkana}@jp.ibm.com
[3] National Institute of Informatics, Tokyo, Japan
ichise@nii.ac.jp

Abstract. Content Words (CWs) are important segments of the text. In text mining, we utilize them for various purposes such as topic identification, document summarization, question answering etc. Usually, the identification of CWs requires various language dependent tools. However, such tools are not available for many languages and developing of them for all languages is costly. On the other hand, because of recent growth of text contents in various languages, language independent text mining carries great potentiality. To mine text automatically, the language tool independent CWs finding is a requirement. In this research, we devise a framework that identifies text segments into CWs in a language independent way. We identify some structural features that relate text segments into CWs. We devise the features over a large text corpus and apply machine learning-based classification that classifies the segments into CWs. The proposed framework only uses large text corpus and some training examples, apart from these, it does not require any language specific tool. We conduct experiments of our framework for three different languages: English, Vietnamese and Indonesian, and found that it works with more than 83 % accuracy.

Keywords: Content words · Language independent · Word segmentation

1 Introduction

Content Words (CWs) are words that belongs to nouns, most verbs, adjectives, and adverbs that refer to some object, action, or characteristic. Usually CWs are the meaning holding part of a sentence and carry independent meaning. Moreover, CWs are also open-words i.e., new words can be introduced as CWs [18]. For example, for a sentence "Toyota Motor Corporation is a Japanese automotive manufacturer headquartered in Toyota, Aichi, Japan", we can devise following CWs { "Toyota Motor Corporation", "Japanese Automotive Manufacturer", "headquartered", "Toyota", "Achi, Japan"}.

© Springer International Publishing Switzerland 2016
F. Martínez-Álvarez et al. (Eds.): HAIS 2016, LNAI 9648, pp. 40–52, 2016.
DOI: 10.1007/978-3-319-32034-2_4

In text mining, CWs play diverse roles e.g., finding of (new) topic [3,9], sentiment analysis [4,14], summarization of document [7], automatic answering of questions [13] etc. Therefore, the text mining communities have developed several tools such as sentence parser, lexical resources (e.g., Wordnet), parallel corpora etc. to identify the CWs over the text. However, those tools are predominantly belong to well investigated languages such as English, German, Japanese etc. On the contrary, language tools are not available for most of the other languages and developing them for all languages are costly. Example of such languages are Vietnamese, Indonesian, Malaysian, Bangla etc. On the other hand, because of popularity of Web 2.0 [6] people from different languages are generating contents in their own languages. The good example of such language specific contents are language specific Wikipedia pages. The language specific contents are getting increased, therefore we realize that those contents are also potential to be automatically mined. Since each language dependent tool development is not feasible, language independent CWs finding is a requirement. It motivates us doing in this research. In our research, we devise a framework **Language independent Content Word Finder LiCord** that identifies text segments into CWs in a language independent way. The proposed framework only uses large text corpus and some training examples. Apart from these, it does not require any language specific tool development which differs from contemporary such researches. Therefore, the solution is relatively easy. In this research, we contribute by (i) identifying structural features of text that separates CWs from other parts of the text (described in Sect. 3.3), (ii) devising a supervised machine learning model that classifies segment of the text into CWs (described in Sect. 3.4), and (iii) developing and evaluating the system (described in Sect. 4).

The remainder of this paper is organized as follows. Section 2 introduces work related to this study. In Sect. 3 we describe the proposed framework in details. In Sect. 4 we describe experiments implementing the proposal and discuss our results. Finally, Sect. 5 concludes our study.

2   Related Work

The finding of CWs is an active research field in the natural language processing communities because CWs support other NLP researches. However, the finding of CWs in a language independent way research is relatively new. Usually to find CWs over the text, first we need to find word segments and then identify the segments into CWs. By relating the above two points with our research, we will first discuss the researches that deal with word segmentation for low language tool supported languages. Then, we will discuss the researches that deal with the CWs identification for multiple languages.

The word segmentation research over low language tool supported languages mainly evolves with parallel corpora − large corpus of translated text for more than one languages. The parallel corpora dependent research technique was initiated by Yarowsky et al. [20]. However, the parallel corpora usually hold noises which later researchers handled by incorporating filtering rules such as research done by Wang et al. [17], or introducing various constraints such as work done by Wisniewski et al. [16,19]. But the parallel corpora are not readily available for all languages. Moreover, building of them is not easy.

On the other hand, the CWs identification research over multiple languages mainly evolves with multi-lingual Named Entity (NE) recognition or text summarization [5,7,8]. Such researches also found in different business solutions e.g., Nasukawa et al., in their framework TAKMI [9] and Gamon et al., in their framework Plus [3] investigated to find CWs from large review text. However, these works are based upon language tools, therefore they are not suitable for CWs finding over low language tool support languages.

In our research, we want to devise a framework that will not require parallel corpora, or any new tool development for a language. Rather, we will automatically exploit sentence structural morphology and calculate some features which will identify CWs in a language independent way.

3   LiCord: Proposed Framework

In this section, we describe the proposed framework **LiCord** in detail. In LiCord, we use (i) *language L specific large text corpus T* – usually the corpus should be large enough so that it covers quite high number of vocabularies and sentence structures, and (ii) *language L specific training examples* – usually the examples should include various type of CWs such as nouns, named entities, verbs, adjectives, and adverbs over the T. By observing training examples over the T, we identify some structural features and learn some machine learning classification model that classifies text segments of T into CWs.

Figure 1 shows work-flow of this classification model learning. It holds four processes: (1) NGram Constructor, (2) Function Word Decider, (3) Feature Value Calculator, and (4) Classifier Learner. Here Process 1 performs text segmentation, Process 2 and 3 devise feature values for the segments, and Process 4 learns machine learning-based classification model to decide the segments into CWs. Below we describe each process in brief.

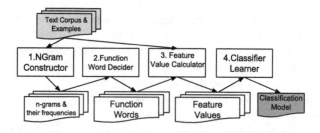

Fig. 1. Work-flow of LiCord classification learning

3.1 NGram Constructor

In NGram Constructor, we segment corpus Ŧ by word token segmenting tag such as "space" (i.e., " ") and construct word n-grams[1] $\mathcal{N}$ between size 1 and η. Niesler et al., mentioned such kind of n-grams as variable length n-grams [10]. In our description, we will use variable length n-grams as n-grams unless we want to discuss about their sizes. For each n-gram $x \in \mathcal{N}$ we also count its frequency $frq(x)$ over the Ŧ.

For example, Table 1 shows variable length n-gram of size between 1 and 3 for some exemplary corpus "Japan is an Asian country. Japan is a peaceful country". In the Table, the first column indicates variable length n-grams, and the second column shows n-grams and their frequencies. We show each n-gram and its frequency value in a square bracket (i.e., []) by putting a hyphen mark (i.e., "−") in between.

Table 1. Variable length n-grams and their frequencies for an exemplary corpus Ŧ = "Japan is an Asian country. Japan is a peaceful country".

	n-grams and frequencies over the Ŧ
size 1 n-gram (/uni-gram)	{[Japan−2], [is−2], [an−1], ..., [country−2], [a−1], ... }
size 2 n-gram (/bi-gram)	{[Japan is−2], [is an−1], ..., [Asian country−1], ...}
size 3 n-gram (/tri-gram)	{[Japan is an−1], [is an Asian−1], [an Asian country−1], ... }

3.2 Function Word Decider

In Function Word Decider, we decide language Ļ specific Function Words (FWs). Usually FWs indicate important sentence structural morphology [15]. We use them to harness these morphologies.

By definition, FWs are words that have little lexical meaning or have ambiguous meaning. In a sentence, FWs serve to express grammatical relationships with other words, or specify the attitude or mood of the speaker [15].

For English language, the FWs are well documented. Therefore, we use them directly (collected from Bunkyo Gakuin University site[2]). For a non-English language, we decide them heuristically. The basic idea of this heuristic is that usually the FWs are frequently appeared words, therefore we will search them in frequent n-grams.

To decide non-English FWs, we first pick threshold α number of top frequent n-grams from $\mathcal{N}$. Then for the top frequent α number of n-grams, we translate them into English and filter them for FWs. Algorithm 1 describe identification of FWs for a non-English language. Here function $TopFrequent(\mathcal{N}, \alpha)$ picks α number of top frequent n-grams from $\mathcal{N}$. For each n-gram $x \in X_\alpha$, function $EnglishTranslat\,ion(x)$ translates x into English and produces English translation et. Then function $Tokens(et)$ tokenize the English translation et

---

[1] In later part, we will use n-gram(s) to mean word n-gram(s).

[2] http://www2.fs.u-bunkyo.ac.jp/~gilner/wordlists.html#functionwords.

Algorithm 1. Selection of non-English FWs

Input: English Function Word set $EFWs$, n-grams $\mathcal{N}$, threshold α
Output: non-English FWs $nEFWs$
$X_\alpha \leftarrow$ ***TopFrequent*** $(\mathcal{N}, \alpha)$;
$nEFWs \leftarrow \emptyset$;
foreach $x \in X_\alpha$ **do**
   | $et \leftarrow$ ***EnglishTranslation*** (x) ;
   | $tokenSet \leftarrow$ ***Tokens*** (et) ;
   | **if** $(EFWs \cap tokenSet) \neq \emptyset$ **then**
   | ⌊ $nEFWs \leftarrow \{nEFWs \cup x\}$
return $nEFWs$

---

and produces set of tokens *tokenSet*. We decide a n-gram x is a FW if any token of *tokenSet* matches with English FWs $EFWs$. The decided FWs are returned as non-English FWs $nEFWs$. However, if an English Translation service (such as Google Translator[3]) is not available for a non-English language, we decide all the top frequent α number of n-grams as FWs.

Below we show selection of two Indonesian FWs. In Indonesian language, "yang" (="that") and "bagin dari" (="part of") are considered as two different FWs because both of them are found as first $\alpha = 1000$ frequent n-grams and some token(s) of their English translations matches with English FWs − "that" and "of" respectively.

Usually FWs are close-set words [18], therefore, unlike CWs, we need to decide FWs once only.

3.3 Feature Value Calculator

In Feature Value Calculator, we devise 15 different features for n-grams. We create the features by observing sentence structural morphology. The observation factors are as follow − (i) how frequently CWs are appeared in the whole corpus and the croups sentences [1], (ii) where CWs usually are appeared over the corpus sentences i.e., at the beginning/middle/last part of sentences [1,7], (iii) how CWs relate other words such as FWs [15], and (iv) how CWs follow punctuation marks (e.g., ",", "−", etc.) [1].

Table 2 shows features and their calculations. Here the first column shows features with their number. The second column describes how we calculate each feature value. We calculate feature values over the corpus Ŧ and sentences Ş of Ŧ. We assume that sentences will hold language specific period marks such as, "."(dot), or "|"etc. Here x is a n-gram.

We used the above features and their calculation techniques in next process and collect feature values which are used to learn classification model.

---

[3] https://translate.google.com/.

Table 2. Features and their calculations

	Feature Calculation
f_1	number of tokens in x
f_2	frequency of x over the Ŧ
f_3	number of sentences Ş that contains x
f_4	number of sentences Ş that starts with x
f_5	number of sentences Ş that ends with x
f_6	number of sentences Ş that contains x but not at the start and at the end
f_7	number of FWs contained by x
f_8	Boolean value whether the first token of x is a function word (FW) f
f_9	Boolean value whether the last token of x is a FW f
f_{10}	number of sentences Ş that simultaneously contain n-gram x and a FW f in a way that f always appears immediate left to the x
f_{11}	number of sentences Ş that simultaneously contain n-gram x and a FW f in a way that f always appears immediate right to the x
f_{12}	Boolean value whether the first token of x is a training example
f_{13}	Boolean value whether the right token of x is a training example. For one token x, first and last token are same
f_{14}	number of sentences that simultaneously contain n-gram x and a punctuation mark p in a way that p always appears immediate left to the x
f_{15}	number of sentences that simultaneously contain n-gram x and a punctuation mark p in a way that p always appears immediate right to the x

3.4   Classifier Learner

In Classifier Learner, we collect feature values for $\mathcal{N}$ (n-grams). Then we use some classification algorithm and learn classification model that predicts whether a n-gram should be CW.

However, since n-grams are huge in number, feature value calculation for them is not scalable. Moreover, randomly picking of n-grams is not enough to represent the whole corpus. Usually in the classification model learning, the whole corpus representing data is a requirement. We handle the scalability issue by dividing $\mathcal{N}$ into several n-gram sets which represent the whole corpus. Each of these sets hold n-grams with similar range frequencies. For similar range n-gram frequencies, we select some randomly picked n-grams and then devise a classification model for that range. This frequency based approach works because n-grams with similar kind of frequency values should hold similar kind of feature values.

To get frequency range based n-grams, we group n-grams for their frequency range values. If a frequency range value is i to j (i,j), we get n-grams $X_{(i,j)}$ as below

$$X_{(i,j)} = \{x \mid x \in \mathcal{N} \wedge i \leq frq(x) \leq j\}$$

Algorithm 2. Selection of frequency range based training n-grams

---

Input: Frequency range based n-grams $X_{(i,j)}$, maximum size of n-gram η,
      threshold β

Output: Frequency range based training n-grams $T_{(i,j)}$

$S_{pos} \leftarrow \{x \mid x \in X_{(i,j)} \wedge \textbf{\textit{isPos(x)}} = true\}$;

$S_{neg} \leftarrow \{x \mid x \in X_{(i,j)} \wedge \textbf{\textit{isPos(x)}} = false\}$;

$T_{(i,j)} \leftarrow \emptyset$;

for $t \leftarrow 1$ *to* η **do**

    $tmp_{pos} \leftarrow \{x \mid x \in S_{pos} \wedge \textbf{\textit{nToken(x)}} = t\}$;

    $tmp_{neg} \leftarrow \{x \mid x \in S_{neg} \wedge \textbf{\textit{nToken(x)}} = t\}$;

    $T_{(i,j)} \leftarrow \{T_{(i,j)} \cup \textbf{\textit{selRandom(tmp}}_{pos}\textbf{\textit{,}}\beta\textbf{\textit{)}}\}$;

    $T_{(i,j)} \leftarrow \{T_{(i,j)} \cup \textbf{\textit{selRandom(tmp}}_{neg}\textbf{\textit{,}}\beta\textbf{\textit{)}}\}$;

return $T_{(i,j)}$

Here x is an n-gram. We consider that no two n-grams fall into two different sets. Therefore, if two range values are (i,j) and (k,l), we constrain range values as $i \leq j < k \leq l$.

Even these frequency range based n-gram sets hold huge number of n-grams, therefore within a set, we pick them randomly. To collect training n-grams from a $X_{(i,j)}$ set, we select them for their each n-gram size positive examples and each n-gram size negative examples. Algorithm 2 shows this selection. It takes the frequency range based n-grams $X_{(i,j)}$, maximum size of n-gram η and threshold β and generates the frequency range based training n-grams $T_{(i,j)}$. Here we use three functions: $isPos(x)$, $nToken(x)$ and $selRandom(tmp, \beta)$. The function $isPos(x)$ identifies whether x belong to the example, the function $nToken(x)$ identifies number of token in x and the function $selRandom(tmp, \beta)$ randomly selects β number of elements from the set tmp. The main idea of this Algorithm is that we separate $X_{(i,j)}$ into positive and negative sets. Then, for each n-gram size 1 to η, we randomly select β number of positive and β negative examples. This kind of training set construction reduces classification bias because the training examples are representative for each token, and each kind of examples.

So, this frequency range based feature values are used to learn different classification models which later are used to classify n-grams for their respective frequency range based model. In Classifier Learner, we learn individual classification model $CM_{(i,j)}$ for frequency range based n-grams $X_{(i,j)}$. We use binary class classification algorithm to learn the classification model.

4   Experiment

We experimented on three different languages: (i) English (ii) Vietnamese (iii) Indonesian. We used language $Ł$ specific Wikipedia page contents $Ŧ$ as large text corpus. We find approximately 35 M ($1 M = 10^6$), 2 M, 1.5 M, different Wikipedia pages for English, Vietnamese, and Indonesian languages respectively. On the other hand, we use page titles of those Wikipedia pages as training examples.

Table 3. Statistics of corpus and corresponding n-grams

Language	Size of Corpus	# of n-gram
English (1/20th part of the corpus)	500 MB	170 M
Vietnamese	500 MB	108 M
Indonesian	300 MB	29 M

We consider page titles as training examples because they, by large, describe the CWs which belong to nouns, or noun phrases, or named entities, verbs, etc.

In experiments, we set $\eta = 5$. To decide FWs (function words) for non-English languages, we set $\alpha = 1000$. Moreover, to select training n-grams, we set $\beta = 2000$. Over the corpus, we used SRI Language Modeling Toolkit[4] to calculate variable length n-grams and their n-gram frequencies. Table 3 shows statistics of different language corpus and their corresponding number of variable length n-grams of size between 1 and 5.

We learned classification model for n-grams with different n-gram frequency ranges such as (1,1), (2,2), (3,4), (5,9), (10,14), (15,19) etc. For each model, we collected feature values for randomly picked 20,000 training n-grams: for each token (i.e., 1 to 5) 2000 as positive and 2000 as negative examples. In preliminary experiment, we learned classification model for two binary classification algorithms: C4.5 [11] and SVM [2] and found C4.5 performs better than SVM. Therefore, in LiCord, we decided to use C4.5-based classification model.

We experimented our proposed framework LiCord to serve two major purposes. First, we checked LiCord that whether it can identify NEs (Named Entities), and parser like parts of speeches. Second, we checked that whether LiCord can identify CWs in a language independent way.

4.1 Experiment 1

In first experiment, we checked LiCord for identification of NEs and parts of speeches. The related researches used NE annotation tool to find CWs, therefore LiCord also should find the NEs. On the other hand, parser generated nouns, verbs, adjectives, and adverbs should be included in LiCord identified CWs, therefore we verify them to know their coverage.

The Named Entities (NEs). To check whether LiCord can identify NEs, we annotated some text using LiCord and compare the annotation outputs with two NE annotators. Usually an annotator identifies some part of the text into some defined set of items. We compared LiCord with two Wikipedia title annotators: Wikifier [12] and Spotlight[5] [8]. Both the annotators identify text to Wikipedia

---

[4] http://www.speech.sri.com/projects/srilm/.

[5] More accurately DBpedia annotator, DBpedia works as structured version of Wikipedia, it can be found at http://dbpedia.org/about/.

Table 4. Comparison for LiCord with Wikifier

	Recall
Wikifier	33.33 %
LiCord	90.47 %

Table 5. Comparison for LiCord with Spotlight

	Recall
Spotlight	83.33 %
LiCord	91.66 %

Table 6. Comparison for LiCord with Parser

Language	Recall
English	92.30 %

titles. Since most of the cases the Wikipedia titles are NEs, we assume that Wikipedia annotation corresponds the NE annotation.

For some given text, LiCord can check whether some of its n-grams or text segments should be positively classified. Therefore, if Wikipedia titles are available over the text, LiCord should identify them as the positively classified n-grams. Thereby, LiCord can be considered as Wikipedia title annotator. However, this comparison can be done for English language only because the other two annotators do not support languages like Indonesian, Vietnamese.

We compared LiCord with Wikifier and Spotlight for the given text in the respective demo sites[6]. To compare LiCord with Wikifier, we used the Spotlight given demo text. Over the Spotlight given demo text, we first executed Spotlight itself which generated 21 Wikipedia titles. Then we executed Wikifier and LiCord for the the same text and measured how many Wikipedia titles are identified by both systems respectively. On the other hand, to compare LiCord with Spotlight, we used Wikifier given demo text and follow the likewise procedure with respective systems. Over the Wikifier demo given text, Wikifier generated 12 Wikipedia titles.

Tables 4 and 5 show annotation comparisons in recall values for LiCord with Wikifier, and LiCord with Spotlight. It shows, LiCord identified more number of Wikipedia titles than the other two systems. Therefore, we consider that LiCord can identify the NEs. In LiCord, we checked a large number of sentence structural features over a big corpus and then classified the n-grams with their respective frequency range based models which identified more number of Wikipedia titles than the other two systems.

The Parts of Speech. To check whether LiCord can identify parser like parts of speeches, we executed LiCord and parser on some text. Usually a parser identifies parts of speech, we collected the nouns, verbs, adjectives and adverbs for the text. Since LiCord identified CWs should hold nouns, verbs, adjectives and adverbs for the text, we compared recall values between parser output for nouns, verbs,

---

[6] http://cogcomp.cs.illinois.edu/page/demo_view/Wikifier (for the example of GoogleChina), and http://dbpediaspotlight.github.io/demo/, respectively.

adjectives and adverbs, and the LiCord identified CWs. Since English has state-of-the-art parser such as Stanford Parser[7], we experimented this for English language only.

We executed LiCord and Stanford parser on Spotlight demo given text. On Spotlight demo given text, Stanford parser generated 26 words as nouns, verbs, adjectives and adverbs, among which LiCord identified 24 of them. Table 6 shows comparison result with Stanford parser. Achieving of good recall informs that the devised structural features were effective which identified most of the required parts of speeches.

4.2   Experiment 2

In second experiment, we checked that whether LiCord can identify CWs in a language independent way. We also checked whether LiCord can maintain open-word property of CWs. Usually CWs are open-words that is new words can be introduced as CWs [18].

To check whether LiCord can identify CWs in a language independent way, we experimented LiCord over some test n-grams that belong to three different languages and checked their classification accuracy. If LiCord can classify both positive and negative test n-grams with high accuracy, we can consider that LiCord serves our research goal − the finding of CWs in a language independent way.

As discussed, the individual classification model $CM_{(i,j)}$ works over the n-grams that hold n-gram frequency between i and j. Here, the test n-grams are different from the training n-grams. For each n-gram frequency range (i, j), we randomly picked 2,000 test n-grams: 1,000 positive and 1,000 negative. In English, example of such test n-grams are "ahead of all" (size 3 n-gram), "May-ors of New York" (size 4 n-gram) etc. We executed LiCord classification model for each test n-gram. For a true classified n-gram, if it was found in Wikipedia title, we considered that the proposed framework worked correctly, otherwise it worked incorrectly. For a false classified n-gram, it works with the opposite manner.

In Table 7 we show classification accuracy (in %) over test n-grams. We present this result for n-grams with five different n-gram frequency ranges: (1,1), (2,2), (3,4), (5,9) and (10,14). We selected those ranges to grasp the evaluation results for different ranges n-grams from small to large. Here, the first column shows n-grams' frequency range. The remaining columns show test n-gram classification accuracy (in %) for English, Indonesian and Vietnamese languages respectively. Here we find that while the classification accuracy for Indonesian and Vietnamese languages was high, the classification accuracy for English language was low. Our detail observation indicates that drop of accuracy in English could come from a reason that some *false* n-grams (i.e., not found in Wikipedia titles) were classified as *true* that is they were discovered as new CWs. For example, in English, LiCord discovered "Australian Air Force Military" as a

---

[7] http://nlp.stanford.edu/software/lex-parser.shtml.

Table 7. CW finding classification accuracy % in test

Frequency Range	English	Indonesian	Vietnamese
(1,1)	76.68	90.56	90.30
(2,2)	83.00	93.20	94.15
(3,4)	84.37	94.23	94.76
(5,9)	83.87	95.89	93.97
(10,14)	87.09	96.15	94.95
Average	**83.25**	**93.80**	**93.54**

Table 8. Newly discovered CWs finding accuracy % for non-accurate classified test n-grams of Table 7

Frequency Range	English	Indonesian	Vietnamese
(1,1)	27.90	11.34	10.63
(2,2)	45.00	18.54	25.00
(3,4)	52.11	24.45	27.56
(5,9)	50.34	25.56	30.88
(10,14)	61.90	29.89	35.13
Average	**47.45**	**21.95**	**22.50**

new CW which was not appeared as Wikipedia title previously. Since Table 7 accuracy was calculated ignoring the newly discovered CWs, we examined the non-accurate classified test n-grams and checked whether they correctly identified as new CWs. To evaluate this discovery accuracy, we engage 3 native users for each languages and verified whether the discoveries were correct. We verified the result for majority voting. Table 8 shows newly discovered CWs finding accuracy (in %) for non-accurate classified test n-grams of Table 7. Here, the first column shows n-grams' frequency range for which the CWs were discovered, the remaining columns show discovery accuracy (in %) for English, Indonesian and Vietnamese languages respectively. It is seen that the discovery of CWs in English is more accurate (47.45 %) than the other languages. In our observation, we found that since English language corpus is big and hold various sentence structural morphologies, the feature value calculation were more accurate which learned more accurate classification model.

We also found that the most of the cases, when n-gram frequencies are more, the classification accuracy are higher. Moreover, we also found that the classification accuracy gets increased, if the number of tokens in n-grams are more. For example, for n-gram frequency range 10–14 in English, we achieved accuracy 81.25 %, 85.75 %, 91.49 % and 89.50 % for 2 tokens, 3 tokens, 4 tokens and 5 tokens n-grams respectively.

Anyway, as an initial evaluation, the overall accuracy was 83.25 % for all three languages which we consider a reasonable performance. Therefore, we consider that LiCord can identify CWs in a language independent way. This performance comes because LiCord checked a large number of sentence structural features which correctly generated classification models and classified n-grams into Wikipedia titles (or CWs).

5   Conclusion

CWs describe important parts of the text which have various usage over the text mining. However, their identification are mainly supported by various language dependent tools which are not available for many languages. In this research, we propose a framework that identifies CWs from a large text corpus such as Wikipedia contents. Here we outlined that how a large text corpus can be exploited to identify CWs: particularly in feature calculation and scalability handling. We also showed the experimental result and their findings. Although experiments show compelling results on non-inflectional languages, we assume that adaptation of LiCord for inflectional languages such as Turkish requires more investigation. Moreover, we also want to investigate Language like Thai that does not have clear word token segmenting tag.

References

1. Aggarwal, C.C., Zhai, C. (eds.): Mining Text Data. Springer, New York (2012)
2. Cortes, C., Vapnik, V.: Support-vector networks. Mach. Learn. **20**(3), 273–297 (1995)
3. Gamon, M., Aue, A., Corston-Oliver, S., Ringger, E.: Pulse: mining customer opinions from free text. In: Famili, A.F., Kok, J.N., Peña, J.M., Siebes, A., Feelders, A. (eds.) IDA 2005. LNCS, vol. 3646, pp. 121–132. Springer, Heidelberg (2005)
4. Kanayama, H., Nasukawa, T.: Unsupervised lexicon induction for clause-level detection of evaluations. Nat. Lang. Eng. **18**(1), 83–107 (2012)
5. Kim, S., Toutanova, K., Yu, H.: Multilingual named entity recognition using parallel data and metadata from wikipedia. In: Proceedings of the 50th Annual Meeting on Association for Computational Linguistics, pp. 694–702 (2012)
6. Lewis, D.: What is web 2.0? Crossroads **13**(1), 3–3 (2006)
7. Ma, Y., Wu, J.: Combining n-gram and dependency word pair for multi-document summarization. In: IEEE 17th International Conference on Computational Science and Engineering, pp. 27–31 (2014)
8. Mendes, P.N., Jakob, M., García-Silva, A., Bizer, C.: Dbpedia spotlight: Shedding light on the web of documents. In: Proceedings of the 7th International Conference on Semantic Systems, pp. 1–8 (2011)
9. Nasukawa, T., Nagano, T.: Text analysis and knowledge mining system. IBM Syst. J. **40**(4), 967–984 (2001)
10. Niesler, T., Woodland, P.C.: Variable-length category n-gram language models. Comput. Speech Lang. **13**(1), 99–124 (1999)
11. Quinlan, R.: C4.5: Programs for Machine Learning. Morgan Kaufmann Publishers, San Mateo (1993)
12. Ratinov, L., Roth, D., Downey, D., Anderson, M.: Local, global algorithms for disambiguation to wikipedia. In: Proceedings of the 49th Annual Meeting of the Association for Computational Linguistics: Human Language Technologies, pp. 1375–1384 (2011)
13. Shinzato, K., Shibata, T., Kawahara, D., Kurohashi, S.: Tsubaki: An open search engine infrastructure for developing information access methodology. Inf. Med. Technol. **7**(1), 354–365 (2012)
14. Zhu, X., Kiritchenko, S., Mohammad, S.M.: Sentiment analysis of short informal texts. J. Artif. Intell. Res. **50**, 723–762 (2014)
15. Volpe, A.D., Klammer, T.P., Schulz, M.R.: Analyzing English Grammar. Longman, New York (2009)
16. Tckstrm, O., Das, D., Petrov, S., McDonald, R., Nivre, J.: Token and type constraints for cross-lingual part-of-speech tagging. Trans. Assoc. Comput. Linguist. **1**, 1–12 (2013)

17. Wang, M., Manning, C.D.: Cross-lingual projected expectation regularization for weakly supervised learning. TACL **2**, 55–66 (2014)
18. Winkler, E.: Understanding Language: A Basic Course in Linguistics. Continuum, London (2007)
19. Wisniewski, G., Pécheux, N., Gahbiche-Braham, S., Yvon, F.: Cross-lingual part-of-speech tagging through ambiguous learning. In: Proceedings of the Conference on Empirical Methods in Natural Language Processing, pp. 1779–1785 (2014)
20. Yarowsky, D., Ngai, G., Wicentowski, R.: Inducing multilingual text analysis tools via robust projection across aligned corpora. In: Proceedings of the First International Conference on Human Language Technology Research, pp. 1–8 (2001)

Mining Correlated High-Utility Itemsets Using the Bond Measure

Philippe Fournier-Viger[1(✉)], Jerry Chun-Wei Lin[2], Tai Dinh[3],
and Hoai Bac Le[4]

[1] School of Natural Sciences and Humanities,
Harbin Institute of Technology Shenzhen Graduate School, Shenzhen, China
`philippe.fournier-viger@umoncton.ca`
[2] School of Computer Science and Technology,
Harbin Institute of Technology Shenzhen Graduate School, Shenzhen, China
`jerrylin@ieee.org`
[3] Faculty of Information Technology,
Ho Chi Minh City Industry and Trade College, Ho Chi Minh City, Vietnam
`duytai@fit-hitu.edu.vn`
[4] Faculty of Information Technology, University of Science,
Ho Chi Minh City, Vietnam
`lhbac@fit.hcmus.edu.vn`

Abstract. Mining high-utility itemsets (HUIs) is the task of finding the sets of items that yield a high profit in customer transaction databases. An important limitation of traditional high-utility itemset mining is that only the utility measure is used for assessing the interestingness of patterns. This leads to finding many itemsets that have a high profit but contain items that are weakly correlated. To address this issue, this paper proposes to integrate the concept of *correlation* in high-utility itemset mining to find profitable itemsets that are highly correlated, using the bond measure. An efficient algorithm named FCHM (Fast Correlated high-utility itemset Miner) is proposed to efficiently discover correlated high-utility itemsets. Experimental results show that FCHM is highly-efficient and can prune a huge amount of weakly correlated HUIs.

Keywords: High-utility itemset mining · Correlation · Bond measure · Correlated high-utility itemsets

1 Introduction

High-Utility Itemset Mining (HUIM) [3,11,12,14] is an important data mining task. Given a customer transaction database, it consists of discovering high-utility itemsets (HUIs), i.e. groups of items (itemsets) that have a high utility (e.g. yield a high profit). HUIM generalizes the problem of Frequent Itemset Mining (FIM) [1] by considering that items may appear more than once in each transaction, and that weight are associated to items to represent their relative importance, or utility (e.g. unit profit). HUIM has a wide range of applications

© Springer International Publishing Switzerland 2016
F. Martínez-Álvarez et al. (Eds.): HAIS 2016, LNAI 9648, pp. 53–65, 2016.
DOI: 10.1007/978-3-319-32034-2_5

such as website click stream analysis, cross-marketing in retail stores and bio-medical applications [11,14]. Although, numerous HUIM algorithms have been proposed [3,8,10–12,14], an important limitation of traditional HUIM algorithms is that only the utility measure is used to assess the interestingness of patterns. This leads to finding many itemsets yielding a high profit but containing items that are weakly correlated. Those itemsets are misleading or useless for taking marketing decisions. For example, consider the transaction database of a retail store. Current algorithms may find that buying a 50 inch plasma television and a pen is a high-utility itemset, because these two items have globally generated a high profit when sold together. But it would be a mistake to use this pattern to promote plasma television to people who buy pens because these two items are rarely sold together. The reason why this pattern may be a HUI despite that there is a very low correlation between pens and plasma televisions, is that plasma televisions are very expensive, and thus almost any items combined with a plasma television may be a HUI. This limitation of current HUIM algorithms is important. In the experimental section of this paper, it will be shown that often less than 1 % of the patterns found by traditional HUIM algorithms contains items that are strongly correlated. It is thus a key research problem to design algorithms for discovering HUIs having a high correlation. This paper addresses this issue by introducing the concept of correlation in high-utility itemset mining, using the bond measure [6,7]. The contributions of this paper are threefold. First, the concept of *bond* correlation used in FIM is combined with the concept of HUIs to define a new type of patterns named *correlated high-utility itemsets* (CHIs), and study their properties. Second, a novel algorithm named FCHM (Fast Correlated high-utility itemset Miner) is proposed to efficiently discover CHIs in transaction databases. The proposed algorithm integrates several strategies to discover correlated high-utility itemsets efficiently. Third, an extensive experimental evaluation is evaluate the efficiency of FCHM. Experiments results show that FCHM can be more than two orders of magnitude faster than the state-of-the-art FHM algorithm for HUIM, and in some case discover five orders of magnitude less patterns by avoiding weakly correlated HUIs.

The rest of this paper is organized as follows. Sections 2, 3, 4, and 5 respectively presents preliminaries and related work related to HUIM, the FCHM algorithm, the experimental evaluation and the conclusion.

2   Preliminaries and Related Work

The problem of HUIM is defined as follows [3,12]. Let I be a set of items (symbols). A *transaction database* is a set of transactions $D = \{T_1, T_2, ..., T_n\}$ such that for each transaction T_c, $T_c \subseteq I$ and T_c has a unique identifier c called its Tid. Each item $i \in I$ is associated with a positive number $p(i)$, called its external utility (e.g. representing the unit profit of this item). For each transaction T_c such that $i \in T_c$, a positive number $q(i, T_c)$ is called the internal utility of i (e.g. representing the purchase quantity of item i in transaction T_c). For example, consider the database of Table 1, which will be used as our running

Table 1. A transaction database

TID	Transaction
T_1	$(a,1),(b,5),(c,1),(d,3),(e,1),(f,5)$
T_2	$(b,4),(c,3),(d,3),(e,1)$
T_3	$(a,1),(c,1),(d,1)$
T_4	$(a,2),(c,6),(e,2),(g,5)$
T_5	$(b,2),(c,2),(e,1),(g,2)$

Table 2. External utility values

Item	a	b	c	d	e	f	g
Unit profit	5	2	1	2	3	1	1

example. This database contains five transactions $(T_1, T_2...T_5)$. For the sake of readability, internal utility values are shown as integer values beside each item, in transactions. For example, transaction T_4 indicates that items a, c, e and g appear in this transaction with an internal utility of respectively 2, 6, 2 and 5. Table 2 indicates that the external utility of these items are respectively 5, 1, 3 and 1.

The utility of an item i in a transaction T_c is denoted and defined as $u(i, T_c) = p(i) \times q(i, T_c)$. The utility of an itemset X (a group of items $X \subseteq I$) in a transaction T_c is denoted and defined as $u(X, T_c) = \sum_{i \in X} u(i, T_c)$. The utility of an itemset X is denoted as $u(X)$ and defined as $u(X) = \sum_{T_c \in g(X)} u(X, T_c)$, where $g(X)$ is the set of transactions containing X. For example, the utility of the itemset $\{a, c\}$ is $u(\{a, c\}) = u(a) + u(c) = u(a, T_1) + u(a, T_3) + u(a, T_4) + u(c, T_1) + u(c, T_3) + u(c, T_4) = 5+5+10+1+1+6 = 28$. The *problem of high-utility itemset mining* is to discover all high-utility itemsets. An itemset X is a *high-utility itemset* if $u(X) \geq minutil$, where *minutil* is a user-specified minimum utility threshold. For instance, if *minutil* = 30, the complete set of HUIs is $\{a, c, e\} : 31$, $\{a, b, c, d, e, f\} : 30$, $\{b, c, d\} : 34$, $\{b, c, d, e\} : 40$, $\{b, c, e\} : 37$, $\{b, d\} : 30$, $\{b, d, e\} : 36$, and $\{b, e\} : 31$, where each HUI is annotated with its utility.

HUIM algorithms such as Two-Phase [12], BAHUI [10], and UPGrowth+ [14] utilize the *Transaction-Weighted Utilization (TWU)* [12,14] measure to prune the search space. They first identify candidate high-utility itemsets by considering their TWUs. Then, in a second phase, they scan the database to calculate the exact utility of all candidates to filter those having a low utility. The TWU measure and its pruning property are defined as follows. The *transaction-weighted utilization (TWU)* of an itemset X is defined as the sum of the transaction utility of transactions containing X, i.e. $TWU(X) = \sum_{T_c \in g(X)} \sum_{x \in T_c} u(x, T_c)$. For example, the TWU of single items a, b, c, d, e, f and g are respectively 65, 61, 96, 58, 88, 30 and 38. $TWU(\{c, d\}) = TU(T_1) + TU(T_2) + TU(T_3) = 30+20+8 = 58$. The following property is used by the aforementioned algorithms to prune the search space.

Property 1 (Pruning search space using the TWU). Let X be an itemset, if $TWU(X) < minutil$, then X and its supersets are low utility [12].

A drawback of algorithms working in two phases is that they generate a huge amount of candidates. Recently, an efficient depth-first search algorithm named *HUI-Miner* [11] was proposed, which discovers HUIs using a single phase. A faster version was then proposed called FHM [3], by introducing a technique called co-occurrence pruning. It was shown that FHM can be up to 6 times faster than HUI-Miner. The FHM algorithm associates a structure named *utility-list* to each itemset [3,11]. Utility-lists allow calculating the utility of an itemset quickly by making join operations with utility-lists of shorter patterns.

Let $\succ$ be any total order on items from I. The *utility-list* $ul(X)$ of an itemset X in a database D is a set of tuples such that there is a tuple $(tid, iutil, rutil)$ for each transaction T_{tid} containing X. The *iutil* element of a tuple is the utility of X in T_{tid}. i.e., $u(X, T_{tid})$. The *rutil* element of a tuple is defined as $\sum_{i \in T_{tid} \wedge i \succ x \forall x \in X} u(i, T_{tid})$. For example, Assume that $\succ$ is the alphabetical order. The utility-list of $\{a\}$ is $\{(T_1, 5, 25), (T_3, 5, 3), (T_4, 10, 17)\}$. The utility-list of $\{a, d\}$ is $\{(T_1, 11, 3), (T_3, 7, 0)\}$.

The FHM algorithm scans the database once to create the utility-lists of itemsets containing a single item. Then, the utility-lists of larger itemsets are constructed by joining the utility-lists of smaller itemsets. The join operation for single items is performed as follows. Consider two items x, y such that $x \succ y$, and their utility-lists $ul(\{x\})$ and $ul(\{y\})$. The utility-list of $\{x, y\}$ is obtained by creating a tuple $(ex.tid, ex.iutil + ey.iutil, ey.rutil)$ for each pairs of tuples $ex \in ul(\{x\})$ and $ey \in ul(\{y\})$ such that $ex.tid = ey.tid$. The join operation for two itemsets $P \cup \{x\}$ and $P \cup \{y\}$ such that $x \succ y$ is performed as follows. Let $ul(P)$, $ul(\{x\})$ and $ul(\{y\})$ be the utility-lists of P, $\{x\}$ and $\{y\}$. The utility-list of $P \cup \{x, y\}$ is obtained by creating a tuple $(ex.tid, ex.iutil + ey.iutil - ep.iutil, ey.rutil)$ for each set of tuples $ex \in ul(\{x\})$, $ey \in ul(\{y\})$, $ep \in ul(P)$ such that $ex.tid = ey.tid = ep.tid$. The utility-list structure allows to calculate the utility-list of itemsets and prune the search space as follows.

Property 2 (Calculating the utility of an itemset using its utility-list). The utility of an itemset is the sum of *iutil* values in its utility-list [11].

Property 3 (Pruning search space using a utility-list). Let X be an itemset. Let the *extensions* of X be the itemsets that can be obtained by appending an item y to X such that $y \succ i$, $\forall i \in X$. If the sum of *iutil* and *rutil* values in $ul(X)$ is less than *minutil*, X and its extensions are low utility [11].

A key problem of current HUIM algorithms is that they may find a huge amount of itemsets containing weakly correlated items (as it will be shown in the experimental study). The solution explored in this paper is to integrate the concept of correlation as an additional constraint in high-utility itemset mining. There have been several works on mining correlated patterns in the field of frequent pattern mining, using various correlation measures such as the all-confidence [13], frequence affinity [2], coherence [5], and bond [6,7,13]. To our knowledge, only Ahmed et al. [2] and Lin et al. [9] have used measures of correlation in high-utility itemset mining by employing the measure of *frequency affinity*. In this paper, we instead rely on the *bond* measure, which has recently attracted more attention [6,7,13]. The concept of correlated itemsets based on the bond measure is defined as follows [7]: The *conjunctive support* of an itemset X in a database D is denoted as $consup(X)$ and defined as $|g(X)|$, where $|g(X)|$ is the number of transactions in $g(X)$). The *disjunctive support* of an itemset X in a database D is denoted as $dissup(X)$ and defined as $|\{T_c \in D | X \cap T_c \neq \emptyset\}|$. The *bond* of itemset X is defined as $bond(X) = consup(X)/dissup(X)$. An itemset X is said to be correlated if $bond(X) \geq minbond$, for a given user-specified $minbond$ threshold ($0 \leq minbond \leq 1$). The bond measure is anti-monotonic.

Property 4 (Anti-monotonicity of the bond measure). Let X and Y be two itemsets such that $X \subseteq Y$. It follows that $bond(X) \geq bond(Y)$ [6].

Based on the above definitions, we define the problem of mining Correlated High-utility Itemsets (CHIs) using the bond measure. **The problem of correlated high-utility itemset mining** is to discover all correlated high-utility itemsets. An itemset X is a **correlated high-utility itemset** if it is a high-utility itemset and $bond(X) \geq minbond$, where $minbond$ is a user-specified minimum bond threshold. For example, if $minutil = 30$ and $minbond = 0.5$, CHIs are: $\{b, d\}, \{b,e\}$, and $\{b, c, e\}$, having respectively a bond of 0.50, 0.75, and 0.60. Thus, three itemsets are CHIs among the seven HUIs in the running example.

3   The FCHM Algorithm

This section presents the proposed FCHM algorithm. The main procedure, which is based on the FHM [3] algorithm, and discovers all HUIs. Then, it explains how this procedure is modified to find only CHIs.

The main procedure of FCHM (Algorithm 1) takes a transaction database with utility values as input, and the *minutil* threshold. The algorithm first scans the database to calculate the TWU of each item. Then, the algorithm identifies the set I^* of all items having a TWU no less than *minutil* (other items are ignored since they cannot be part of a high-utility itemset by Property 3). The TWU values of items are then used to establish a total order $\succ$ on items, which is the order of ascending TWU values (as in [3]). A database scan is then performed. During this database scan, items in transactions are reordered according to the total order $\succ$, the utility-list of each item $i \in I^*$ is built and a structure named EUCS (Estimated Utility Co-Occurrence Structure) is built [3]. This latter structure is defined as a set of triples of the form $(a, b, c) \in I^* \times I^* \times \mathbb{R}$. A triple (a,b,c) indicates that $TWU(\{a, b\}) = c$. The EUCS can be implemented as a triangular matrix that stores these triples for all pairs of items. For example, the EUCS for the running example is shown in Fig. 1. The EUCS is useful as it stores the TWU of all pairs of items, an information that will be used for pruning the search space. For instance, the top-left cell indicates that $TWU(\{a, b\}) = 30$. Building the EUCS is very fast (it is performed with a single database scan) and occupies a small amount of memory, bounded by $|I^*| \times |I^*|$. The reader is referred to the paper about FHM [3] for more details about the construction of the EUCS and its implementation with hashmaps. After the construction of the EUCS, the depth-first search exploration of itemsets starts by calling the recursive procedure *Search* with the empty itemset $\emptyset$, the set of single items I^*, *minutil* and the EUCS structure.

Item	a	b	c	d	e	f
b	30					
c	65	61				
d	38	50	58			
e	57	61	88	50		
f	30	30	30	30	30	
g	27	11	38	0	38	0

Item	a	b	c	d	e	f
b	1					
c	3	3				
d	2	2	3			
e	2	3	4	2		
f	1	1	1	1	1	
g	1	1	2	0	2	0

Fig. 1. The EUCS   **Fig. 2.** The Bond Matrix

Algorithm 1. The FCHM algorithm

---

input : D: a transaction database, *minutil*: a user-specified threshold
output: the set of high-utility itemsets

1 Scan D to calculate the TWU of single items;
2 $I^* \leftarrow$ each item i such that $\text{TWU}(i) \geq minutil$;
3 Let $\succ$ be the total order of TWU ascending values on I^*;
4 Scan D to built the utility-list of each item $i \in I^*$ and build the $EUCS$;
5 Output each item $i \in I^*$ such that $\text{SUM}(\{i\}.utilitylist.iutils) \geq minutil$;
6 **Search** $(\emptyset, I^*, minutil, EUCS)$;

The *Search* procedure (Algorithm 2) takes as input (1) an itemset P, (2) extensions of P having the form Pz meaning that Pz was previously obtained by appending an item z to P, (3) *minutil* and (4) the EUCS. The search procedure operates as follows. For each extension Px of P, if the sum of the *iutil* values of the utility-list of Px is no less than *minutil*, then Px is a high-utility itemset and it is output (cf. Property 4). Then, if the sum of *iutil* and *rutil* values in the utility-list of Px are no less than *minutil*, it means that extensions of Px should be explored. This is performed by merging Px with all extensions Py of P such that $y \succ x$ to form extensions of the form Pxy containing $|Px| + 1$ items. The utility-list of Pxy is then constructed as in FHM by calling the *Construct* procedure to join the utility-lists of P, Px and Py. This latter procedure is the same as in FHM [3] and is thus not detailed here. Then, a recursive call to the *Search* procedure with Pxy is done to calculate its utility and explore its extension(s). Since the *Search* procedure starts from single items, it recursively explores the search space of itemsets by appending single items and it only prunes the search space based on Property 5. It can be easily seen based on Properties 1, 2 and 3 that this procedure is correct and complete to discover all high-utility itemsets.

Algorithm 2. The *Search* procedure

---

input : P: an itemset, *ExtensionsOfP*: a set of extensions of P, *minutil*: a user-specified threshold, $EUCS$: the $EUCS$ structure

output: the set of high-utility itemsets

1 **foreach** *itemset* $Px \in$ *ExtensionsOfP* **do**
2   **if** *SUM(Px.utilitylist.iutils)+SUM(Px.utilitylist.rutils)* $\geq$ *minutil* **then**
3   *ExtensionsOfPx* $\leftarrow \emptyset$;
4   **foreach** *itemset* $Py \in$ *ExtensionsOfP such that* $y \succ x$ **do**
5   **if** $\exists (x, y, c) \in EUCS$ *such that* $c \geq$ *minutil* **then**
6                  $Pxy \leftarrow Px \cup Py$;
7                  $Pxy.utilitylist \leftarrow$ Construct (P, Px, Py);
8   *ExtensionsOfPx* $\leftarrow$ *ExtensionsOfPx* $\cup Pxy$;
9   **if** *SUM(Pxy.utilitylist.iutils)* $\geq$ *minutil* **then** output Px;
10   **end**
11   **end**
12   Search $(Px,$ *ExtensionsOfPx, minutil*$)$;
13   **end**
14 **end**

We now explain how the algorithm is modified to mine only CHIs, rather than all HUIs. The modified algorithm takes *minbond* as an additional parameter. To mine only CHIs, it is important to be able to calculate the bond of any itemset efficiently. A naive approach would be to scan the database for each HUI to calculate its disjunctive support and conjunctive support, to then calculate its bond. However, this would be inefficient. A better approach, used in FCHM, is the following. A structure called *disjunctive bit vector* [7] is appended to each utility-list to efficiently calculate the disjunctive support of any itemset.

The **disjunctive bit vector** of an itemset X in a database D is denoted as $bv(X)$. It contains $|D|$ bits, where the j-th bit is set to 1 if $\exists i \in X$ such that $i \in T_i$, and is otherwise set to 0. For example, $bv(a) = 10110$, and $bv(b) = 11001$. The disjunctive bit vector of each item is created during the first database scan (Line 4 of Algorithm 1). Then, the disjunctive bit vector of any larger itemset Pxy explored by the search procedure is obtained very efficiently by performing the logical OR of the bit vectors of Px and Py. This is added before Line 1 of the utility-list construction procedure (Algorithm 3). For example, $bv(\{a, b\}) = 10110$ OR $11001 = 11111$, and thus $dissup(\{a, b\} = |11111| = 5$. An interesting observation is that the cardinality $|bv(Pxy)|$ of the disjunctive bit vector of an itemset Pxy is equal to its disjunctive support, and that the cardinality $|ul(Pxy)|$ of its utility list is equal to its conjunctive support. Thus, the bond of an itemset Pxy can be obtained using its utility-list and disjunctive bit vector, as follows.

Property 5 (Calculating the bond of an itemset using its utility-list). Let be an itemset X. The bond of X can be calculated as $|ul(X)|/|bv(X)|$, where $|ul(X)|$ is the number of elements in the utility-list of X.

Algorithm 3. The Construct procedure

---

input : P: an itemset, Px: the extension of P with an item x, Py: the
extension of P with an item y
output: the utility-list of Pxy

1 $UtilityListOfPxy \leftarrow \emptyset$;
2 **foreach** *tuple* $ex \in Px.utilitylist$ **do**
3   **if** $\exists ey \in Py.utilitylist$ *and* $ex.tid = exy.tid$ **then**
4   **if** $P.utilitylist \neq \emptyset$ **then**
5   Search element $e \in P.utilitylist$ such that $e.tid = ex.tid.$;
6        $exy \leftarrow (ex.tid, ex.iutil + ey.iutil - e.iutil, ey.rutil)$;
7   **end**
8   **else** $exy \leftarrow (ex.tid, ex.iutil + ey.iutil, ey.rutil)$;
9      $UtilityListOfPxy \leftarrow UtilityListOfPxy \cup \{exy\}$;
10   **end**
11 **end**
12 **return** $UtilityListPxy$;

Using the above property, it is possible to calculate the bond of any itemset generated by the search procedure after its utility-list has been constructed. The algorithm is modified to only output HUIs that are CHIs (having a bond no less than *minbond*). The resulting algorithm is correct and complete for mining CHIs. To improve the performance of FCHM, the next paragraphs describe four additional strategies incorporated in FCHM to more efficiently discover CHIs.

Strategy 1. Directly Outputting Single items (DOS). A first optimization is based on the observation that the bond of single items is always equal to 1. Thus, HUIs containing a single item can be directly output without calculating their bond.

Strategy 2. Pruning Supersets of Non correlated itemsets (PSN). Because the bond measure is anti-monotonic (Property 5), if the bond of an itemset Pxy is less than *minbond*, any extensions of Pxy should not be explored. Thus, Line 8 of Algorithm 1 is modified so that if $bond(Pxy) < minutil$ for an itemset Pxy, the utility-list of Pxy is not added to the set $ExtensionsOfPx$.

Strategy 3. Pruning using the Bond Matrix (PBM). The third strategy is introduced to avoid constructing the utility-list of an itemset Pxy, and prune all its extensions. During the second database scan, a novel structure named *Bond Matrix* is created to store the bond of all itemsets containing two items from I^*. The design of this structure is similar to the EUCS. The Bond Matrix is formally defined as follows. The Bond Matrix is a set of triples of the form $(a, b, c) \in I^* \times I^* \times \mathbb{R}$. A triple (a,b,c) indicates that $bond(\{a, b\}) = c$. Note that it only stores tuples of the form (a, b, c) such that $c \neq 0$. For example, the Bond Matrix for the running example is shown in Fig. 2. Then, Line 5 of Algorithm 1 is modified to add the condition that the utility-list of Pxy should only be built if $\exists (x, y, c) \in BondMatrix$ such that $c \geq minbond$. It can be easily seen that this pruning condition preserves the correctness and completeness of FCHM, because any superset of an itemset $\{x, y\}$ such that $bond(\{x, y\}) < minbond$ is not a CHIs by Property 5.

Strategy 4. Abandoning Utility-List construction early (AUL). The fourth strategy introduced in FCHM is to stop constructing the utility-list of an itemset if some specific condition is met, indicating that the itemset may not be a CHI. The strategy is based on the following novel observation:

Property 6 (Required conjunctive support for an extension Pxy). An itemset Pxy is a correlated itemset only if its conjunctive support is no less than the value $lowerBound(Pxy) = \lceil |consup(Pxy)| * minBond) \rceil$ transactions.

This property is directly derived from the definition of the bond measure, and proof is therefore omitted. Now, consider the construction of the utility-list of an itemset Pxy by the Construct procedure (Algorithm 3). As mentioned, a first modification to this procedure is to create the disjunctive bit vector of Pxy by performing the OR operation with the bit vectors of Px and Py before Line 1. This allows obtaining the value $consup(Pxy) = |bv(Pxy)|$. A second modification is to create a variable $maxSupport$ that is initialized to the conjunctive support of Px ($consup(Px) = |bv(Px)|$, before Line 1. The third modification is to the following lines, where the utility-list of Pxy is constructed by checking if each tuple in the utility-lists of Px appears in the utility-list of Py (Line 3). For each tuple not appearing in Py, the variable $maxSupport$ is decremented by 1. If $maxSupport$ is smaller than $lowerBound(Pxy)$, the construction of the utility-list of Pxy can be stopped because the conjunctive support of Pxy will not be higher than $lowerBound(Pxy)$. Thus Pxy is not a CHI by Property 6, and its extensions can also be ignored by Property 5. As it will be shown in the experiment, this strategy is very effective, and decrease execution time and memory usage by stopping utility-list construction early. A similar pruning strategy based on the utility of itemset Pxy instead of the bond measure is also integrated in FCHM. This strategy is called the LA-prune strategy and was introduced in HUP-Miner [8], and it is thus not described here.

4   Experimental Study

Experiments were performed to assess the performance of FCHM on a computer having a third generation 64 bit Core i5 processor running Windows 7, and 5 GB of free RAM. The performance of FCHM algorithm was compared with the state-of-the-art FHM algorithm HUIM. Four real-life datasets commonly used in the HUIM litterature were used: *mushroom, retail, kosarak* and *foodmart*. They represent the main types of data typically encountered in real-life scenarios (dense, sparse, and long transactions). Let $|I|$, $|D|$ and A represents the number of transactions, distinct items and average transaction length. *mushroom* is a dense dataset ($|I| = 16{,}470$, $|D| = 88{,}162$, $A = 23$). *kosarak* is a dataset that contains many long transactions ($|I| = 41{,}270$, $|D| = 990{,}000$,

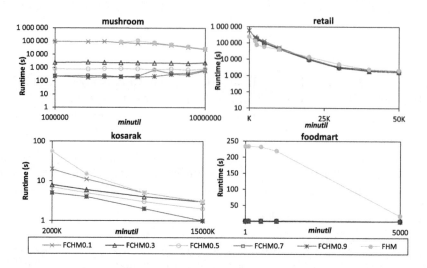

Fig. 3. Execution times

$A = 8.09$). *retail* is a sparse dataset with many different items ($|I| = 16{,}470$, $|D|$ = 88,162, $A = 10{,}30$). *foodmart* is a sparse dataset ($|I| = 1{,}559$, $|D| = 4{,}141$, A = 4.4). *foodmart* contains real external and internal utility values. For the other datasets, external utilities of items are generated between 1 and 1,000 by using a log-normal distribution and quantities of items are generated randomly between 1 and 5, as in [11,14]. The source code of algorithms and datasets can be downloaded as part of the SPMF open source data mining library [4] at http://www. philippe-fournier-viger.com/spmf/. Memory measurements were done using the Java API. FCHM was run with five different *minbond* threshold values (0.1, 0.3, 0.5, 0.7 and 0.9). Henceforth, FCHMx denotes FCHM with *minbond* = x. Algorithms were run on each dataset, while decreasing the *minutil* threshold until they became too long to execute, ran out of memory or a clear trend was observed. Figure 3 compares the execution times of FCHM and FHM. Figure 4, compares the number of CHIs and HUIs, respectively generated by these algorithms.

It can be observed that mining CHIs using FCHM can be much faster than mining HUIs. The reason is that FCHM prunes a large part of the search space using its designed pruning strategies using the bond measure. For datasets containing a huge amount of weakly correlated HUIs such as *mushroom, foodmart*, and *kosarak*, this leads to a massive performance improvement. For example, for the lowest *minutil* values and *minbond* = 0.5 on these datasets, FCHM is respectively 103, 10 and 21 times faster than FHM. In general, when *minbond* increases, the gap between the runtime of FHM and FCHM increases. For example, for *minbond* = 0.9 on *mushroom*, FCHM is 417 times faster than FHM.

A second observation is that the number of CHIs can be much less than the number of HUIs, even when using low *minbond* threshold values (see Fig. 4). For example, on *mushroom*, 3,538,181 HUIs are found for *minutil* = 3,000,000. But

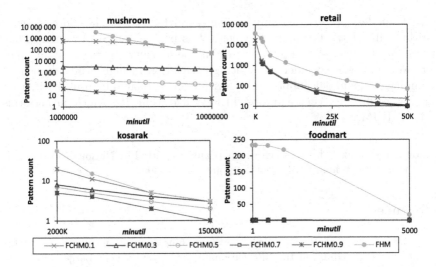

Fig. 4. Number of patterns found

only 3,186 HUIs are CHIs for *minbond* = 0.3 and only 196 for *minbond* = 0.5 (about 1 CHIs for 18,000 HUIs). Huge reduction in the number of patterns are also observed on the *foodmart* and *kosarak*. For *retail*, the reduction is less because patterns are more correlated. However, there is still from 2 to 10 times less CHIs than HUIs, depending on the *minutil* values. These overall results show that the proposed FCHM algorithm is useful as it can filter a huge amount of weakly correlated itemsets encountered in real datasets, and can run faster.

Memory consumption was also compared, although detailed results are not shown as a figure due to space limitation. It was observed that FCHM can use up to 30 times less memory than FHM depending on how the *minbond* threshold is set. For example, on *mushroom* and *minutil* = 5, 000, 000, FHM, FCHM0.9, FCHM0.7, FCHM0.5, FCHM0.3, and FCHM0.1, respectively consume 666 MB, 424 MB, 136 MB, 59 MB, 26 MB and 20 MB.

Lastly, the efficiency of the proposed PBM and AUL strategies was also assessed. Detailed results are not shown due to space limitation. But these strategies were shown to prune a huge amount of candidates for most datasets, and it greatly increases when *minbond* is increased. For example, on *mushroom* and *minutil* = 5, 000, 000, FHM, FCHM0.9, FCHM0.7, FCHM0.5, FCHM0.3, and FCHM0.1, visit 1,282,377, 536,136, 5,254, 1,160, 883, and 848 candidates.

5   Conclusion

This paper proposed an algorithm named FCHM (Fast Correlated high-utility itemset Miner) to efficiently discover correlated high-utility itemsets using the bond measure. An extensive experimental study shows that FCHM is up to two orders of magnitude faster than FHM, and can discover more than five orders of magnitude less patterns by only mining correlated HUIs. The source code of algorithms and datasets can be downloaded as part of the SPMF open source data mining library [4] at http://www.philippe-fournier-viger.com/spmf/. For future work, we will consider introducing correlation in high-utility sequential rule mining [15], and developping an algorithm for correlated high-utility itemset mining based on the recently proposed EFIM algorithm [16], which outperforms FHM for HUIM.

Acknowledgement. This research was partially supported by National Natural Science Foundation of China (NSFC) under grant No.61503092.

References

1. Agrawal, R., Srikant, R.: Fast algorithms for mining association rules in large databases. In: Proceedings of the International Conference on Very Large Databases, pp. 487–499 (1994)
2. Ahmed, C.F., Tanbeer, S.K., Jeong, B.S., Choi, H.J.: A framework for mining interesting high utility patterns with a strong frequency affinity. Inf. Sci. **181**(21), 4878–4894 (2011)
3. Fournier-Viger, P., Wu, C.-W., Zida, S., Tseng, V.S.: FHM: faster high-utility itemset mining using estimated utility co-occurrence pruning. In: Andreasen, T., Christiansen, H., Cubero, J.-C., Raś, Z.W. (eds.) ISMIS 2014. LNCS, vol. 8502, pp. 83–92. Springer, Heidelberg (2014)
4. Fournier-Viger, P., Gomariz, A., Gueniche, T., Soltani, A., Wu, C., Tseng, V.S.: SPMF: a Java Open-Source Pattern Mining Library. J. Mach. Learn. Res. **15**, 3389–3393 (2014)
5. Barsky, M., Kim, S., Weninger, T., Han, J.: Mining flipping correlations from large datasets with taxonomies. In: Proceedings of the 38th International Conference on Very Large Databases, pp. 370–381 (2012)
6. Younes, N.B., Hamrouni, T., Yahia, S.B.: Bridging conjunctive and disjunctive search spaces for mining a new concise and exact representation of correlated patterns. In: Pfahringer, B., Holmes, G., Hoffmann, A. (eds.) DS 2010. LNCS, vol. 6332, pp. 189–204. Springer, Heidelberg (2010)
7. Bouasker, S., Ben Yahia, S.: Key correlation mining by simultaneous monotone and anti-monotone constraints checking. In: Proceedings of the 30th Symposium on Applied Computing, pp. 851–856 (2015)
8. Krishnamoorthy, S.: Pruning strategies for mining high utility itemsets. Expert Syst. Appl. **42**(5), 2371–2381 (2015)
9. Lin, J.C.-W., Gan, W., Fournier-Viger, P., Hong, T.-P.: Mining discriminative high utility patterns. In: Nguyen, N.T., Trawiński, B., Fujita, H., Hong, T.-P. (eds.) ACIIDS 2016. LNCS, vol. 9622, pp. 219–229. Springer, Heidelberg (2016). doi:10.1007/978-3-662-49390-8_21
10. Song, W., Liu, Y., Li, J.: BAHUI: fast and memory efficient mining of high utility itemsets based on bitmap. Int. J. Data Warehouse. Min. **10**(1), 1–15 (2014)
11. Liu, M., Qu, J.: Mining high utility itemsets without candidate generation. In: Proceedings of the 22nd ACM International Conference on Information and Knowledge Management, pp. 55–64 (2012)

12. Liu, Y., Liao, W., Choudhary, A.K.: A two-phase algorithm for fast discovery of high utility itemsets. In: Ho, T.-B., Cheung, D., Liu, H. (eds.) PAKDD 2005. LNCS (LNAI), vol. 3518, pp. 689–695. Springer, Heidelberg (2005)
13. Soulet, A., Raissi, C., Plantevit, M., Cremilleux, B.: Mining dominant patterns in the sky. In: Proceedings of the 11th IEEE International Conference on Data Mining, pp. 655–664 (2011)
14. Tseng, V.S., Shie, B.-E., Wu, C.-W., Yu, P.S.: Efficient algorithms for mining high utility itemsets from transactional databases. IEEE Trans. Knowl. Data Eng. **25**(8), 1772–1786 (2013)
15. Zida, S., Fournier-Viger, P., Wu, C.-W., Lin, J.C.-W., Tseng, V.S.: Efficient mining of high-utility sequential rules. In: Perner, P. (ed.) MLDM 2015. LNCS, vol. 9166, pp. 157–171. Springer, Heidelberg (2015)
16. Zida, S., Fournier-Viger, P., Chun-Wei Lin, J., Wu, C.-W., Tseng, T.S.: EFIM: A highly efficient algorithm for high-utility itemset mining. In: Sidorov, G., Galicia-Haro, S.N. (eds.) MICAI 2015. LNCS, vol. 9413, pp. 530–546. Springer, Heidelberg (2015)

An HMM-Based Multi-view Co-training Framework for Single-View Text Corpora

Eva Lorenzo Iglesias, Adrián Seara Vieira, and Lourdes Borrajo Diz$^{(\boxtimes)}$

Computer Science Department,
University of Vigo, Escola Superior de Enxeñería Informática, Ourense, Spain
{eva,adrseara,lborrajo}@uvigo.es

Abstract. Multi-view algorithms such as co-training improve the accuracy of text classification because they optimize the functions to exploit different views of the same input data. However, despite being more promising than the single-view approaches, document datasets often have no natural multiple views available.

This study proposes an HMM-based algorithm to generate a new view from a standard text dataset, and a co-training framework where this view generation is applied. Given a dataset and a user classifier model as input, the goal of our framework is to improve the classifier performance by increasing the labelled document pool, taking advantage of the multi-view semi-supervised co-training algorithm.

The novel architecture was tested using two different standard text corpora: Reuters and 20 Newsgroups and a classical SVM classifier. The results obtained are promising, showing a significant increase in the efficiency of the classifier compared to a single-view approach.

Keywords: Hidden Markov Model · Text classification · Co-training · Multi-view

1 Introduction

With the rapid growth of corporate and digital databases, text classification has become one of the key techniques for handling and organizing text data. Supervised text classification algorithms usually require a large number of labelled examples to learn accurately. However, labelling can be a costly and time consuming process because it requires human effort [1,2]. Semi-supervised techniques combine both supervised and unsupervised learning to reduce the need for labelled training data. These algorithms learn a concept definition by combining a small set of labelled examples and a large set of unlabelled ones [2].

Multi-view semi-supervised algorithms are a subset of these techniques. These algorithms take advantage of datasets that have a natural separation of their features or can be described using different "kinds" of information. A prominent example are web pages, which can be classified based on their content as well as on the anchor texts of inbound hyperlinks [3].

© Springer International Publishing Switzerland 2016
F. Martínez-Álvarez et al. (Eds.): HAIS 2016, LNAI 9648, pp. 66–78, 2016.
DOI: 10.1007/978-3-319-32034-2_6

If different views of the dataset are available, then co-training [4] and other multi-view algorithms can improve classification accuracy. The co-training method is a classical algorithm in a multi-view semi-supervised learning technique that trains two independent classifiers, which provide each other with labels for unlabelled data. This algorithm tends to maximize the agreement on the predictions of the two classifiers on the labelled dataset, as well as minimize the disagreement on the predictions on the unlabelled dataset.

In contrast to single-view learning, multi-view learning algorithms introduce one function in order to model a particular view, jointly optimize all the functions to exploit different views of the same input data, and improve the learning performance [4]. However, despite being more promising than single-view approaches, document datasets often have no natural multiple views available, so that only one view may be provided to represent the data.

In this work, we propose an algorithm to generate a new view from a standard text dataset and a co-training framework where this view generation is applied. Given a dataset and a classifier model as input, the goal of our framework is to improve the classifier performance by increasing the labelled document pool, taking advantage of the multi-view semi-supervised co-training algorithm.

The remainder of the manuscript proceeds as follows. The view generation process is described in Sect. 2, and the co-training framework is presented in Sect. 3. In Sects. 4 and 5 we show the experiments and the results obtained for two different text corpora. Finally, the most relevant conclusions are collected at Sect. 6.

2   View Generation

In text classification, given a training set $T = \{(d_0, dl_0), (d_1, dl_1)...(d_n, dl_n)\}$, which consists of a set of pre-classified documents in classes (labels) dl_x, the classifiers are used to model the implicit relation between the characteristics of the document and its class (label), in order to be able to accurately classify new unlabelled documents.

To achieve this, documents need to be expressed in a format that classifying algorithms can handle. The most common approach to represent documents is the Bag-of-Words (BoW) approach [5]. In this case, every document is represented by a vector where elements describe the word frequency (number of occurrences) in that document, as shown in Fig. 1 (a). In addition, each document d_i has an attribute dl_i which has the assigned label as a value.

In order to use a multi-view algorithm like co-training, two representations or views of the documents are needed. One of main goals of this work is to generate a new view from the standard BoW approach in order to apply the co-training algorithm. Specifically, this view generation algorithm is based on Hidden Markov Models (HMMs).

In a previous study, the authors developed an HMM-based document classifier called T-HMM [6]. In this model, HMMs are used to represent sets of documents. An HMM is trained per class (label) with the documents labelled with that label. When a new document needs to be classified, the model evaluates the probability of this document being generated by each of the HMMs, and outputs the label with the maximum probability value.

The goal of the view generation process presented in this paper is to build a new view in which documents are represented by similarities to other groups of documents. Specifically, these document groups are taken from the training set of labelled documents, and a document group is created for each label. This way, each group has all the documents from the training set that share the same label. Every document in the new view is represented by similarities to each document group.

In order to calculate similarities between documents and groups, HMMs are used to represent the groups. One HMM is trained per document group, and the similarity between a document and a group is expressed with the probability of the document being generated by the HMM that represents that group.

Figure 1 shows the complete View Generation process. Firstly, each HMM is trained with a document group. The complete labelled set of the initial dataset represented by the BoW approach is used as the base of the new view. One HMM is created per label, and documents assigned with that label are used to train the HMM.

The training process of the HMMs with a document set as input is the same as that described in [6]. HMMs with the same structure as in T-HMM are used to represent each document group. The probability distributions of the HMMs are adjusted automatically depending on the content of the documents, and only two additional parameters need to be fixed to start the process: the number of stats and the generalization factor. Their corresponding values are detailed in the Experiments Section.

Once the HMMs are trained, any document d represented by a BoW approach (labelled or unlabelled) can be also represented in the new HMM view. In order to do so, the probabilities of d being generated by each HMM are calculated using the forward-backward algorithm [6,7]. Finally, the document d in the HMM view is represented by a vector with k elements, where k is the total number of labels, and each element describes the similarity of the document with the document group having the same label represented by the HMM.

Figure 2 shows an example of an HMM view generation. In this case, the documents in the initial document set can be labelled as Relevant (R) or Non-relevant (N). This is a usual scenario in multiple information retrieval systems where a document can be relevant or not to a specific topic.

Using the labelled set of documents represented by a BoW approach as input, one document group is created per label. In this case, the labelled document set is split into Relevant and Non-Relevant document groups. Afterwards, an HMM is trained for each document group using the documents from that group as input: HMM_R and HMM_N.

The new HMM view represents any document (labelled or unlabelled) by similarities to the selected document groups. In the example, each document is represented in the new view by similarities to the Relevant and Non-relevant

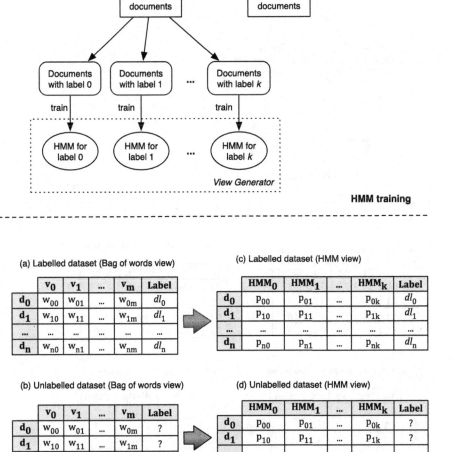

Fig. 1. Creation of the View Generator model and generation of the HMM-view. p_{ij} stands for the probability of the document i being generated by the HMM representing the label j.

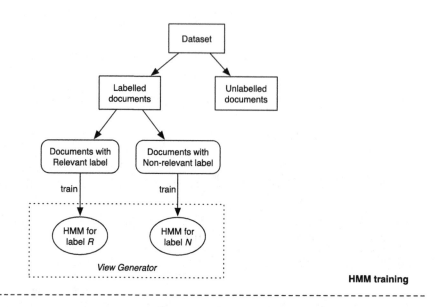

Fig. 2. Example of the creation of the View Generator model and HMM-view generation. p_{ij} stands for the probability of the document i being generated by the HMM representing the label j

document groups. Since the previously built HMMs act as the representative document group, each document d_i is expressed with a vector containing two elements: the probability of d being generated by HMM_R, and the probability of d being generated by HMM_N.

It is important to note that the label of the document that needs to be represented in the HMM view is not taken into account in the whole view generation process. Labels are only used in the training phase of the HMMs to create the document groups that share the same label.

3 Co-training with HMM View

In this study, we build a classification framework that, given a single-view dataset and a classifier provided by the user, increases the performance of the classifier by taking advantage of the multi-view classifying process using the previous view generation algorithm.

Specifically, the proposed framework integrates the classifier in a co-training algorithm using both a BoW view and an HMM view of the dataset. In co-training algorithms, one classifier is trained per view. The parameters and the classifier models can be different or the same, but a separate classifier is used for training each view. By maximizing the agreement on the predictions on the unlabelled dataset, the classifiers learn from each other to reach an optimal solution. In each iteration, the classifier on one view labels unlabelled data which are then added to the training pool of both classifiers; therefore, the information is exchanged between the learners [4].

The classic co-training scheme can be seen in Fig. 3. In each iteration, the two classifiers must reach a consensus in the classification of the unlabelled data. Once a set of unlabelled documents is assigned with a label, the documents are added to the training pool of both classifiers to start a new iteration.

Figure 4 shows the proposed co-training scheme. The HMM view is built with the BoW view and both are used in the co-training algorithm. Two instances of the classifier given by the user are created with the same parameters and each one is trained with each view (BoW view and HMM view). The iterative process follows the same structure as the classical co-training algorithm.

To improve the accuracy of the consensus between classifiers, an additional classifier is created. It is important to note that the documents labelled in this stage are included afterwards in the training pool, assuming that the assigned label is correct. This is why the precision of the consensus must be very high, since a misclassification can lead to worse results.

The proposed additional classifier is a distance-based classifier like k-NN. The choice is made based on the capacity of labelling a document with a certain level of confidence. Using a threshold, we can determine that a document is labelled with a certain level of precision. This way, the consensus in each iteration of the co-training algorithm is made between the two base classifiers and the third distance-based classifier using a threshold.

The complete specification of the proposed co-training algorithm is detailed below.

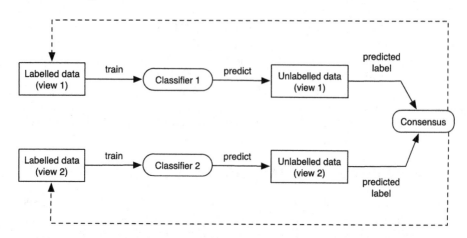

Fig. 3. Classic co-training algorithm.

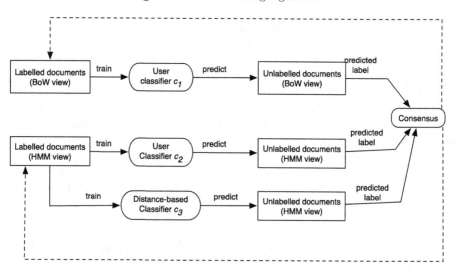

Fig. 4. Proposed co-training algorithm.

4   Experiments

The goal of the experiments is to test whether the proposed co-training algorithm improves the performance in two document corpora, Reuters and 20 Newsgroup. The collections are described below, and are used in a classification process with an SVM classifier. In order to compare the effectiveness of the proposed algorithm, the two corpora are also classified using the default single-view approach.

The first test collection is the Reuters-21578 document corpus. The document set used for this work contains the documents from the 10 top-sized categories as used in [8], ending up with a total of 8055 documents.

Data: BoW dataset, classifier model, distance-based classifier, threshold, number of iterations

Result: Trained classifier

l_1 ← Labelled portion of dataset with a BoW view;

l_2 ← Generated labelled portion of dataset with an HMM view;

u_1 ← Unlabelled portion of dataset with a BoW view;

u_2 ← Generated unlabelled portion of dataset with an HMM view;

c_1 ← Classifier model given by the user to train with the BoW view;

c_2 ← Copy of classifier model given by the user to train with the HMM view;

c_3 ← Distance-based classifier to improve the consensus;

t ← Threshold for the distance-based classifier;

k ← Number of iterations for the co-training algorithm;

s ← Number of unlabelled documents;

for $i \leftarrow 0$ **to** k **do**

> train c_1 with l_1;
>
> train c_2 with l_2;
>
> train c_3 with l_2;
>
> select s/k documents for the iteration;
>
> u_1' ← selected documents from u_1;
>
> u_2' ← selected documents from u_2;
>
> **for** *each selected document d* **do**
>
> > pl_1 ← predict label for d with c_1;
> >
> > pl_2 ← predict label for d with c_2;
> >
> > pl_3 ← predict label for d with c_3;
> >
> > cl ← confidence level for the pl_3 prediction with c_3;
> >
> > **if** *($pl_1 = pl_2 = pl_3$) and ($cl >= t$)* **then**
> >
> > > $l_1 \leftarrow l_1 \cup d$ from u_1' labelled with pl_1;
> > >
> > > $l_2 \leftarrow l_2 \cup d$ from u_2' labelled with pl_2;
> >
> > **end**
>
> **end**

end

Algorithm 1. Co-training algorithm with HMM view.

The second test collection is the 20 Newsgroups dataset. This is a collection of approximately 20,000 newsgroup documents, partitioned (nearly) evenly across 20 different newsgroups. It was originally collected by Ken Lang [9] and has become a popular dataset for experiments in text applications of machine learning techniques.

Figure 5 shows the complete experiment process for the evaluation of the proposed co-training algorithm.

Initially, the document corpora need to be pre-processed. Following the BoW approach, we format every document into a vector of feature words in which elements describe the word occurrence frequencies. All the different words that appear in the training corpus are candidates for feature words. In order to reduce the initial feature size, standard text pre-processing techniques are used. A predefined list of stopwords (common English words) is removed from the text, and a stemmer based on the Lovins stemmer [10] is applied. Finally, words occurring in fewer than ten documents of the entire training corpus are also removed.

Once the initial feature set is determined, a dataset matrix is created where rows correspond to documents and columns to feature words. The value of an element in a matrix is determined by the number of occurrences of that feature word (column) in the document (row). This value is adjusted using the TF-IDF statistic in order to measure the word relevance. The application of TF-IDF decreases the weight of terms that occur very frequently in the collection, and increases the weight of terms that occur rarely [11].

Once the pre-processing phase is finished, the corpus is randomly divided into two splits. One of them is considered the labelled set of documents and the other one the unlabelled set of documents after removing their labels. The labelled split is further divided into the Train and Test splits. The Test split contains documents that are reserved to evaluate the performance of the algorithm (see Fig. 5 (a)). Every split (Train, Test, Unlabelled) has one third of the original corpus. In the Reuters dataset, with a total of 8055 documents, each split has 2685 documents. In the 20 Newsgroups dataset, with a total of 18560 documents, each split has 6187 documents.

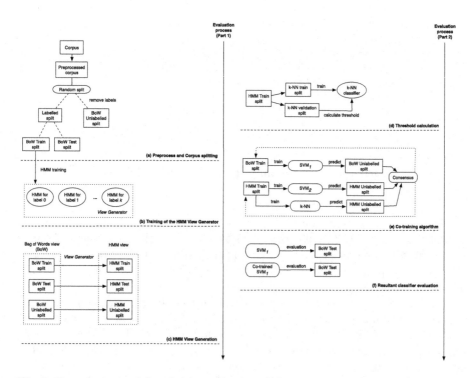

Fig. 5. Experiment workflow for the evaluation of the proposed co-training algorithms.

Using the Train split represented in the bag-of-words approach as input, the View Generator is built training one HMM per label in the corpus (Fig. 5 (b)). The parameterization of the HMM is set with a general approach. The number of states of each HMM is equal to the average number of words in the documents, and the f-factor described in [6] is set to 0.5. Once the View generator is created, it is used to generate the HMM view of each split that is originally represented with the bag-of-words view (see Fig. 5 (c)).

Before the co-training algorithm starts, the threshold for the distance-based classifier must be fixed (Fig. 5 (d)). In this experiment, the selected distance-based classifier is a k-NN with 10 neighbours. When a document is classified with this kind of classifier, the output is not only the predicted label. The classifier also outputs a vector with k elements, where k is the number of possible labels and each element describes the probability of the document having that label. With this information, an average level of confidence can be calculated using the probabilities of correctly assigned labels. In order to do so, the Train split with the HMM view is divided to train a k-NN classifier and calculate the average confidence threshold to label a new document with a validation document set.

Once the threshold is calculated, the co-training algorithm can be executed to improve the training process of a classifier given by the user. In our tests, SVM is selected as the classifier to improve (Fig. 5 (e)). The implementation of the SVM used in this case is LIBSVM [12] and the parameters are those utilized by default in the WEKA environment [13], applying a RBF kernel.

Finally, after applying the co-training algorithm, the resultant co-trained SVM is compared with a trained SVM with a single-view approach using the Test split. This entire process is repeated 50 times for each corpus in order to be able to perform a statistic test on the results.

5 Results

To evaluate the effectiveness of the model, F-measure and Kappa Statistic, evaluation measures commonly utilized in text classification and information retrieval, are used. F-measure is the weighted harmonic mean of recall and precision, and Kappa is a single metric that takes the output confusion matrix of an evaluation and reduces it into one value [14]. Kappa Statistic is interesting because it compares the accuracy of the system to the accuracy of a random system. Possible values of kappa range between -1 (random classification) and 1 (perfect classification).

Table 1 shows the results achieved. The values correspond to the average value achieved in that measure for the total of 50 executions with each method. In addition, the F-measure value corresponds to the weighted average F-measure among all the classes in the corpus. The table compares the results achieved by training the SVM with a single-view BoW approach (called Baseline) as opposed to the results achieved by training the SVM with the proposed co-training algorithm.

Furthermore, in order to demonstrate that the observed results are not just a chance effect in the estimation process, we use a statistical test that gives confidence bounds to predict the true performance from a given test set. A Student's t-test is performed on Kappa and F-measure values achieved in method and corpus.

One test is performed for each pair of collection results achieved in each method. In this case, the baseline scenario (single-view method) is compared in each corpus with the results obtained when applying the co-training algorithm. The difference in a given confidence level is checked to determine if it exceeds the confidence limit stated by a Student's distribution. If so, the *null-hypothesis* (the difference is due to chance) is rejected, proving that the application of the co-training algorithm makes a real difference in the output of the classifier. The values in brackets correspond to the t-value calculated in the comparison of the value collections. t-value gives a measure of how large the difference is between applying and not applying the co-training algorithm: higher absolute values indicate more difference.

According to the results, there is a statistical difference between the baseline and co-training methods, since the calculated t-values outrange the confidence limits. This means that the increase in the average Kappa and F-measure values using the proposed co-training algorithm is significant. The SVM classifier gets an improvement using a multi-view approach, specially in the 20 Newsgroups corpus, because the training pool has increased labelling examples from the unlabelled data, something that is not possible in a single-view approach without overfitting the model. It is important to note that the improvement achieved by using the co-training algorithm laregly depends on the corpus. The quality (in terms of information) of the unlabelled documents influences the whole process. This can be seen in the difference between the results achieved with Reuters and 20 NewsGroups.

Table 1. Results

Corpus	Kappa	F-measure
Reuters		
Baseline algorithm	0,809	0,866
Co-train algorithm	0,811 (−17,59)	0,869 (−19,13)
20 newsgroups		
Baseline algorithm	0,621	0,681
Co-train algorithm	0,667 (−42,27)	0,710 (−31,78)
p-value: 0.05		
t-value (two-tailed, 50 freedom degrees): $+/-2.009$		

6   Conclusions

In this study, we propose a co-training scheme where an HMM view is used. The proposed view generation algorithm allows any dataset and text classifier given by the user to be applied in a co-training framework and take advantage of a multi-view learning algorithm.

The experimental results show that the application of multi-view techniques improve the accuracy of the text classifiers, especially when the number of documents previously classified (used for training) is far lower than the total number of texts for classification. This is the case when accessing big text corpora as public databases (PubMed, Internet) using semi-automatic searches. As a future work, a bigger study on how different classifiers are affected by the co-training system can demonstrate its usefulness in many scenarios. This implies both the main classifier and the distance-based classifier that is used to control the confidence level of the new view.

Acknowledgements. This work has been funded from the European Union Seventh Framework Programme [FP7/REGPOT-2012-2013.1] under grant agreement n 316265, BIOCAPS, the "Platform of integration of intelligent techniques for analysis of biomedical information" project (TIN2013-47153-C3-3-R) from Spanish Ministry of Economy and Competitiveness and the [14VI05] Contract-Programme from the University of Vigo.

References

1. Blum, A., Mitchell, T.: Combining labeled and unlabeled data withco-training. In: Proceedings of the Eleventh Annual Conference on Computational Learning Theory, COLT 1998, pp. 92–100. ACM, New York (1998)
2. Matsubara, E.T., Monard, M.C., Batista, G.: Multi-view semi-supervised learning: an approach to obtain different views from text datasets. In: Proceedings of the Conference on Advances in Logic Based Intelligent Systems: Selected Papers of LAPTEC 2005, pp. 97–104. IOS Press, Amsterdam (2005)
3. Bickel, S., Scheffer, T.: Multi-view clustering. In: Proceedings of the Fourth IEEE International Conference on Data Mining, ICDM 2004, pp. 19–26. IEEE Computer Society, Washington (2004)
4. Xu, C., Taom, D., Xu, C.: A survey on multi-view learning. CoRR, abs/1304.5634 (2013)
5. Nikolaos, T., George, T.: Document classification system based on HMM word map.In: Proceedings of the 5th International Conference on Soft Computing as Transdisciplinary Science and Technology, CSTST 2008, pp. 7–12, New York, NY, USA, ACM (2008)
6. Vieira, A.S., Iglesias, E.L., Borrajo, L.: T-HMM: a novel biomedical text classifier based on hidden markov models. In: Saez-Rodriguez, J., Rocha, M.P., Fdez-Riverola, F., De Paz Santana, J.F. (eds.) PACBB 2014. Advances in Intelligent Systems and Computing, vol. 294, pp. 225–234. Springer International Publishing, Heidelberg (2014)
7. Rabiner, L.R.: A tutorial on hidden markov models and selected applications in speech recognition. Proc. IEEE **77**(2), 257–286 (1989)
8. Sebastiani, F.: Machine learning in automated text categorization. ACM Comput. Surv. **34**, 1–47 (2002)
9. Lang, K.: Newsweeder: learning to filter netnews. In: Proceedings of the Twelfth International Conference on Machine Learning, pp. 331–339 (1995)

10. Lovins, J.B.: Development of a stemming algorithm. Mech. Transl. Comput. Linguist. **11**, 22–31 (1968)
11. Baeza-Yates, R.A., Ribeiro-Neto, B.: Modern Information Retrieval. Addison-Wesley Longman, Boston (1999)
12. Chang, C., Lin, C.: LIBSVM: a library for support vector machines. ACM Trans. Intell. Syst. Technol. **2**(3), 27: 1–27: 27 (2011)
13. Sierra Araujo, B.: Aprendizaje automático: conceptos básicos y avanzados: aspectos prácticos utilizando el software Weka. Pearson Prentice Hall, Madrid (2006)
14. Viera, A.J., Garrett, J.M.: Understanding interobserver agreement: the kappa statistic. Fam. Med. **37**(5), 360–363 (2005)

Does Sentiment Analysis Help in Bayesian Spam Filtering?

Enaitz Ezpeleta[1(✉)], Urko Zurutuza[1], and José María Gómez Hidalgo[2]

[1] Electronics and Computing Department, Mondragon University,
Goiru Kalea, 2, 20500 Arrasate-Mondragón, Spain
{eezpeleta,uzurutuza}@mondragon.edu
[2] Pragsis Technologies, Manuel Tovar, 43-53, Fuencarral, 28034 Madrid, Spain
jmgomez@pragsis.com

Abstract. Unsolicited email campaigns remain as one of the biggest threats affecting millions of users per day. During the last years several techniques to detect unsolicited emails have been developed. Among all proposed automatic classification techniques, machine learning algorithms have achieved more success, obtaining detection rates up to a 96 % [1]. This work provides means to validate the assumption that being spam a commercial communication, the semantics of its contents are usually shaped with a positive meaning. We produce the polarity score of each message using sentiment classifiers, and then we compare spam filtering classifiers with and without the polarity score in terms of accuracy. This work shows that the top 10 results of Bayesian filtering classifiers have been improved, reaching to a 99.21 % of accuracy.

Keywords: Spam · Polarity · Security · Bayes · Sentiment analysis

1 Introduction

The mass mailing of unsolicited e-mails have been one of the biggest threats to Internet security for years. Spam campaigns have been used both for the sale of products such as online fraud. Researchers are investigating many approaches that try to minimize this type of malicious activity that report billionary benefits, being a booming economic sector known as black market or underground economy. The data so far are clear; thanks to the mailing of unsolicited messages, a market share sufficient to enrich a sector devoted to fraudulent activity is achieved. Different attacker communities that worked separately have multiplied their benefits while joining their efforts: new discovered vulnerabilities are sold, which are processed by exploit creators to be included in malicious web sites to spread the malware, which in turn is automatically integrated into large networks of computers, or botnets managed remotely controlled by malicious organizations, which at the end offer services such as: spam campaigns, DDoS, phishing services, a host of fraudulent activities that are generating more business opportunities.

© Springer International Publishing Switzerland 2016
F. Martínez-Álvarez et al. (Eds.): HAIS 2016, LNAI 9648, pp. 79–90, 2016.
DOI: 10.1007/978-3-319-32034-2_7

Within the spam problem, most research and products focus on improving spam classification and filtering. According to Kaspersky Lab data, the average of spam in email traffic for the year 2015 stood at 59.2 % [2].

To deal with this problem researchers started to design and develop different spam detection systems. Among others, spam filtering techniques are commonly used by both scientific and industrial communities.

This work provides means to validate the assumption that being a spam message a commercial communication, the semantics of its content should be shaped with a positive meaning. Thus, the main objective of this paper is to analyze if the polarity of the message is a useful feature for spam classification. It also aims to validate the hypothesis that polarity feature can improve the results of the typical spam filtering techniques.

On the one hand, we apply the most effective spam classification filters to a known dataset, whereby we obtain the algorithms that better classified the content into spam and ham classes. On the other hand, we analyze different settings of two sentiment classifiers: one API for diving into common natural language processing tasks and other developed by our own. Once we got the best classifiers and settings, we determine the polarity of the messages in the previous dataset, and we create new datasets adding the polarity feature per email. Then a descriptive analysis of the new dataset is carried out. Finally we apply the spam filtering classifiers that obtained the best results in the original dataset to the new ones. The main contribution of this work is that we improve spam filtering rates using the polarity.

The remainder is organized as follows. Section 2 describes the previous work conducted in the area of spam filtering techniques, natural language processing and sentiment analysis. Section 3 describes the process of the aforementioned experiments, regarding Bayesian spam filtering and email polarity classifiers. In Sect. 4, the obtained results are described, comparing Bayesian filtering results and the filtering results using the polarity of the messages. Finally, we summarize our findings and give conclusions in Sect. 5.

2 Related Work

2.1 Spam Filtering Techniques

During the last years several techniques to detect unsolicited emails have been developed [3]. Among all proposed automatic classifying techniques, machine learning algorithms have achieved more success [4]. For instance, different studies such as [5] obtained precisions up to 94.4 % using those kind of techniques.

In this work we focus on filters that are able to work with the content of the messages: content-based filters. As authors described in [6] those filters are based on analyzing the content of the emails. There are several different types of content-based spam filters such as heuristic filtering, learning-based filtering and filtering by compression.

Teli et al. presented in [7] a comparison between various existing spam detection methods including rule-based system, IP blacklist, Heuristic-based filters,

Bayesian network-based filters, white list and DNS black holes. They concluded that the most effective, accurate, and reliable spam detection method are the Bayesian based filters.

In [1] some of the content-based filtering techniques are studied and analyzed, and the Bayesian method was selected as the most effective one (classifying correctly the 96.5 % of messages). Furthermore, in [8] authors demonstrated that although more sophisticated methods have been implemented, Bayesian methods of text classification are still useful.

2.2 Sentiment Analysis

In [9] Natural Language Processing (NLP) is defined as a theoretical moti-vated range of computational techniques for analyzing and representing nat-urally occurring texts at one or more levels of linguistic analysis for the purpose of achieving human-like language processing for a range of tasks or applica-tions. As described in [10] NLP techniques are becoming more and more useful to detect and classify spam messages. Authors says that their model blocked spam messages based on the sender and the content of the text thanks to NLP techniques.

Other studies like [11] demonstrate that it is possible to create applications able to detect spam using text mining techniques. In other words, using process to extract interesting and non-trivial information or knowledge from text docu-ments. In addition, in [12] authors developed a system that integrated a semantic language model to detect opinion spam in different web pages.

While most researchers are working on opinion spam detection using NLP and/or text mining techniques, we focus on the use of NLP and text mining techniques in conjunction with Sentiment Analysis (SA) to improve the detection of spam emails.

In [13] SA or opinion mining is defined as the computational study of peo-ple's opinions, appraisals, attitudes, and emotions toward entities, individuals, issues, events, topics and their attributes. In SA NLP, text analysis and com-putational linguistics are used to identify and extract subjective information in source material. As explained in [14], the area of SA has had a huge burst of research activity during these last years, but there has been a continued interest for a while. Currently there are several research topics on opinion mining and the most important ones are explained in [13]. Among those topics we identified the document sentiment classification as a possible option for spam filtering.

The main objective of this area is classifying the positive or negative char-acter of a document [14]. In order to classify such sentiment, some researchers use supervised learning techniques, where three classes are previously defined (positive, negative and neutral) [15]. Some other authors propose the use of unsupervised learning. In unsupervised learning techniques, opinion words or phrases are the dominating indicators for sentiment classification [16].

There are several tools developed during the last years focused on NLP and sentiment analysis. One of the most used for sentiment analysis is known as SentiWordNet. It was presented in [17] and the last version, which is an improved version of the first one, was carried out by Baccianella et al. [18]. It is an enhanced lexical resource explicitly devised for supporting sentiment classification and opinion mining applications. As they explained in the paper SentiWordNet is the result of the automatic annotation of all the synsets of WordNet according to the notions of positivity, negativity, and neutrality. For instance, author in [19] used SentiWordNet for sentiment classification of reviews obtaining an accuracy of 65.85 % using term counting method.

3   Improving Spam Filtering Using Sentiment Analysis

Our study has been carried out in three different phases. In the first phase, we apply several spam filtering models with different settings to a certain dataset. Thus, we identify the best classifiers and the best settings to filter spam messages (Fig. 1).

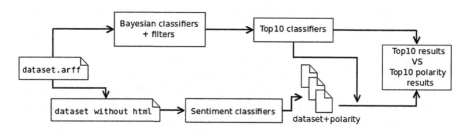

Fig. 1. Full process

As our objective is to improve the best classifiers, in the second phase we work to obtain better results than previously mentioned filters using the polarity of the messages. For that, first of all we need to determine the polarity of each email. To do so we developed our own sentiment classifier, and also used a publicly available API for NLP tasks known as TextBlob[1]. Comparing different settings of each classifier we selected the best ones, which were applied to the dataset used in the previous phase. Using the polarity of each message as new attribute, we carry out a descriptive analysis of these datasets. Finally, the best spam classifiers were applied to the new datasets and made a comparison of the results.

3.1   Bayesian Spam Filtering

Those filters, which are based on Bayes' Theorem, use Bayes logic to evaluate the header and content of an incoming e-mail message and determine the probability that it constitutes spam.

---

[1] http://textblob.readthedocs.org.

The main objective is to identify the best spam filtering classifiers and the best settings. We apply different combinations of classifiers, filters and settings to compare the results and to select the best ones.

As it is explained in Sect. 2, Bayesian classifiers are considered as the best techniques to detect and to filter spam messages. Based in this, only the next Bayesian classifiers have been used:

- Bayesian Logistic Regression.
- Complement Naive Bayes.
- DMNBtext.
- Naive Bayes Multinomial Updateable.

- Naive Bayes.
- Naive Bayes Multinomial.
- Naive Bayes Updateable.

Following a text mining process, a set of different filters have been applied to the text. Next, we detail the settings that have been used:

- A filter to convert a string to feature vector containing the words. We use the next options:
  - Words are converted to lower case.
  - A number of words to keep is defined.
  - The maximum number of words and the minimum term frequency is not enforced on a per-class basis but based on the documents in all the classes.
  - Two type of tokenizers are used:
    * One that splits the text removing the special characters.
    * And the other that removes the characters and to split a string into an n-gram with min and max grams.
  - To obtain roots of the words a stemmer based on the Lovins stemmer is used.
  - Weights:
    * IDFTransform False, TFTransform False, outputWordCounts False
    * IDFTransform False, TFTransform False, outputWordCounts True
    * IDFTransform True, TFTransform False, outputWordCounts True
- Attribute Selection: a ranker to evaluate the worth of an attribute by measuring the information gain with respect to the class is used.

At the end of this phase, the best ten settings and classifiers for spam classification have been identified. To do this selection we have use the accuracy of the classifiers, being the accuracy the percentage of testing set examples correctly classified by the classifier.

$$Accuracy = \frac{(True\ Positives\ +\ True\ Negatives)}{(Positives\ +\ Negatives)}$$

3.2 Sentiment Analysis

The objective of this phase is to carry out a sentiment classification of the dataset, in order to later add the polarity of each message as a new feature for spam detection. Later, influence of the polarity in spam filtering and classification.

First a sentiment classifier is needed, so in this task two different options have been considered: to develop our own classifier or to use an existing one. In order to obtain the best possible results, both options have been considered.

Own Sentiment Classifier. In order to design and implement a classifier, sentiment dictionaries become useful tools, so the commonly used SentiWordNet has been chosen in this case. As shown in researchers have obtained up to a 65 % of accuracy using this dictionary.

SentiWordNet is a dictionary that returns to the user the polarity of a certain word depending on its grammatical properties. Using this tool, the average polarity of the email messages have been calculated.

Five sentiment classifiers have been developed with different settings. On the one hand: *Adjective, Adverb, Verb* and *Noun*. In each classifier every word was considered to be a certain part of speech (depending on the name of the classifier), so we have obtained the polarity of those words that have that grammatical property. For instance: in the *Adjective* classifier every word was considered to be an adjective, so we have obtained the polarity of those words that can be considered as adjectives. And on the other hand, *AllPosition* classifier, which considers every part of speech per each word.

TextBlob Classifier. With the objective of comparing different results, TextBlob has been used because it provides a simple API for diving into common NLP tasks. Specifically, giving a string the sentiment analyzer function returns a float value within the range [-1.0,1.0] for the polarity.

Comparison Between Classifiers. Once the classifiers have been defined, we improve the efficiency of those classifiers by changing settings and selection thresholds. For this work, a previously tagged dataset is mandatory. One commonly used dataset is called *Movie Reviews*[2]. This dataset collects movie-review documents tagged in terms of polarity (positive or negative) or subjectivity rating. Also sentences are tagged with respect to their status or polarity. Among all these options the *polarity dataset v2.0* is used in this task, which is composed by 1,000 positive and 1,000 negative processed reviews introduced in [20]. The objective is to obtain the best accuracy classifying those reviews to find the most efficient settings and thresholds.

In the following table a comparison between the best settings and thresholds is shown. The next criteria is used to define each classifier:

- *TextBlob* means that a classifier based on Textblob library has been used.
- Some names are followed by a number. This number represent the used threshold for polarity classification. For instance, 0.1 means that every message with score higher than 0.1 has been considered to be positive, and those message with score lower than 0.1 negatives.

---

[2] http://www.cs.cornell.edu/People/pabo/movie-review-data/.

Table 1. Comparison between classifiers

Name	TP	TN	FP	FN	Accuracy
TextBlob 0.1	719	773	227	281	0.7460
TextBlob 0.05	901	467	533	99	0.6840
Adjectives	775	499	501	225	0.6370
All without verbs	798	460	540	202	0.6290
AllPositions	849	370	630	151	0.6095
Nouns	723	483	517	277	0.6030
TextBlob 0	971	229	771	29	0.6000

- "All without verbs" means that all part of speech but verb has been taken into account during the score calculation (Table 1).

Using this information the best three classifiers are selected. To decide which ones can be considered as the best classifiers, the *Accuracy* measure is used.

Descriptive Experiments. In this step several experiment have been carried out to see how sentiment analysis can affect in spam filtering.

First of all, the selected three classifiers have been applied to the dataset which is explained in the following section. This step offers an idea about the distribution of the email messages in terms of polarity. The number and the percentage of the positive and negative messages has been obtained. Moreover, this information has been used to created one file per each selected classifier, in which the polarity of each message has been added.

Then, we generate a ranking of the most important attributes based on the information gain criteria, and also by analyzing the features that better divide a *J48* classification tree node. Doing that, we preliminarily analyze how the polarity affects in terms of spam filtering.

Predictive Experiments. During this task the 10 classifiers that obtained the best results in the spam filtering experiments has been applied to the different datasets files. Those files have been created during the descriptive experiments and it consists in a certain spam dataset with the polarity of each message. So, at the end of the experiment the accuracy of the best 10 classifiers applied to the sentimentally classified messages have been obtained.

Finally, all the results are compared. Using the accuracy of each classifiers we demonstrate that the polarity of the messages can help to improve Bayesian spam filtering.

4   Experimental Results

In this Section the results obtained during the previously explained experiments are shown. To carry out those experiment the *CSDMC 2010 Spam corpus*[3] is used. In this dataset 2,949 non-spam messages and 1,378 spam messages are publicly available.

4.1   Bayesian Spam Filtering Experiment

First of all Bayesian classifiers with different settings have been applied to the *CSDMC2010* dataset. In total, 392 different combinations are analyzed. In the following table the best 10 classifiers in terms of accuracy are shown.

Table 2. Top10 Bayesian classifiers

#	Name	TP	TN	FP	FN	Accuracy
1	b.BLR.i.t.c.stwv.go.wtok	1,355	2,936	13	24	99.1451
2	b.DMNBtext.c.stwv.go.wtok	1,362	2,928	21	17	99.1220
3	b.DMNBtext.i.c.stwv.go.wtok	1,362	2,928	21	17	99.1220
4	b.DMNBtext.i.t.c.stwv.go.wtok	1,362	2,928	21	17	99.1220
5	b.DMNBtext.stwv.go.wtok	1,362	2,928	21	17	99.1220
6	b.DMNBtext.c.stwv.go.stemmer	1,360	2,927	22	19	99.0527
7	b.DMNBtext.i.c.stwv.go.stemmer	1,360	2,927	22	19	99.0527
8	b.DMNBtext.i.t.c.stwv.go.stemmer	1,360	2,927	22	19	99.0527
9	b.DMNBtext.stwv.go.stemmer	1,360	2,927	22	19	99.0527
10	b.BLR.i.t.c.stwv.go.ngtok.stemmer.igain	1,351	2,935	14	28	99.0296

In this study the objective is to improve the accuracies of the Bayesian classifier. So, we focus only on these 10 classifiers in the following steps, instead of focus on all combinations used previously.

To understand the nomenclatures used in the Table 2 a summary is presented in Table 3.

4.2   Sentiment Analysis

Descriptive Experiments. During the data exploration part, the following results are presented.

Firstly, a sentiment analysis of the dataset has been done. The polarity of each email is identified, this polarity is added to the dataset and statistics of the number of positive and negative spam or legitimate emails are extracted as it is shown in the next table. As we showed that an important number of messages

---

[3] http://csmining.org/index.php/spam-email-datasets-.html.

Table 3. Nomenclatures

	Meaning		Meaning
.b	Bayesian classifier	.stemmer	Stemmer
.BLR	BayesianLogisticRegression	.c	Idft F, tft F, outwc T
.stwv	StringToWordVector	.i.c	idft T, tft F, outwc T
.go	general options: -L -O -W 10000000	.i.t.c	idft T, tft T, outwc T
.wtok	WordTokenizer	.ngtok	NGramTokenizer 1-3
.igain	Attribute selection using InfoGainAttributeEval		

obtained score equal to 0 using *Adjective* classifier, *Adjective Plus* classifier is added in this point. It classified those emails like positive messages. So at the end of this step four different dataset are created, one per each classifier.

Table 4. Sentiment analysis of emails

	Total	Adj		Adjplus		Tb_005		Tb_01	
		P	N	P	N	P	N	P	N
Spam	1,378	913	433	945	433	1,044	332	848	516
Ham	2,949	1,103	1,831	1,118	1,831	1,934	1,009	1,419	1,514
Percentages (%)									
Spam	100	66	31	68	31	76	24	62	37
Ham	100	37	62	37	62	66	34	48	51

Analysing the data in the Table 4 it is possible to see that spam messages are more positive than non-spam or ham messages.

While this experiments gives good results, the results obtained in the rankings and in the trees were not such goods. We observed that polarity appears like a decisive attribute but not like a top one. And different results have been obtained depending on the used sentiment classifier. The best results have been obtained by the dataset analized by *Adjective* classifier. The polarity is ranked in the position 130, and is considered a bit decisive attribute in *J48* decision tree. *Adjective Plus* classifier obtains similar but worse results. And significantly worse results have been obtained by the TextBlob-based classifiers.

Predictive Experiments and Comparison. Once known that polarity can affect in spam filtering, an experiment to demonstrate the real influence are carried out. The best classifiers that appears in Table 2 are applied to the four new datasets.

Table 5. Comparing original result with the results obtained using own polarity classifiers

	Bayes			Adjective			Adjective+		
#	FP	FN	Accuracy	FP	FN	Accuracy	FP	FN	Accuracy
1	13	24	99.1451	14	22	**99.1682**	14	23	99.1451
2	21	17	99.1220	24	15	99.0989	24	15	99.0989
3	21	17	99.1220	24	15	99.0989	24	15	99.0989
4	21	17	99.1220	24	15	99.0989	24	15	99.0989
5	21	17	99.1220	24	15	99.0989	24	15	99.0989
6	22	19	99.0527	21	17	**99.1220**	22	16	**99.1220**
7	22	19	99.0527	21	17	**99.1220**	22	16	**99.1220**
8	22	19	99.0527	21	17	**99.1220**	22	16	**99.1220**
9	22	19	99.0527	21	17	**99.1220**	22	16	**99.1220**
10	14	28	99.0296	14	24	**99.1220**	15	23	**99.1220**

In the following two tables the results are displayed. In both tables the results obtained during the Bayesian filtering are shown for a proper comparison between the results.

In the first one Table 5 the original results are compared with the results obtained applying the filtering classifier to the dataset tagged by our own developed classifier.

As we can see in those first results, *Adjective* sentiment classifier is able to improve the best accuracy of Bayesian algorithms.

Table 6. Comparing original result with the results obtained using TextBlob polarity classifiers

	Bayes			TextBlob005			TextBlob01		
#	FP	FN	Accuracy	FP	FN	Accuracy	FP	FN	Accuracy
1	13	24	99.1451	13	25	99.1220	14	24	99.1220
2	21	17	99.1220	24	15	99.0989	22	12	**99.2144**
3	21	17	99.1220	24	15	99.0989	22	12	**99.2144**
4	21	17	99.1220	24	15	99.0989	22	12	**99.2144**
5	21	17	99.1220	24	15	99.0989	22	12	**99.2144**
6	22	19	99.0527	21	15	**99.1682**	22	15	99.1451
7	22	19	99.0527	21	15	**99.1682**	22	15	99.1451
8	22	19	99.0527	21	15	**99.1682**	22	15	99.1451
9	22	19	99.0527	21	15	**99.1682**	22	15	99.1451
10	14	28	99.0296	14	24	**99.1220**	14	28	99.0296

In Table 6 the original results are compared with the results obtained applying the filtering classifiers to the dataset tagged by TextBlob-based classifiers.

If we analyze these data, we can realize that polarity helps to improve the accuracy in most cases, and also that the best result obtained using Bayesian spam filtering is improved. While without polarity the best result is 99.1451 %, using the polarity feature we reached the rate of 99.2144 %.

Focusing on the results of the *TextBlob01* sentiment classifier, we see that in eight out of ten cases the accuracy is better than in the original result. And in case number 9 the same accuracy is obtained.

5 Conclusions

This work shows that the top 10 results of Bayesian filtering classifiers have been improved both generally and per each sentiment classifier.

In addition, considering that the sentiment classifier used is independent from the text, the conclusion is positive. It is supposed that the potential of a training-based one will be better.

As the main conclusions we can say that is possible to improve spam filtering classifiers adding the polarity of the messages. We have demonstrated that sentiment analysis of the emails can help to detect spam emails.

Nonetheless, in future studies we are going to try to confirm our conclusions. To do that, we are going to carry out the same experiments but with different datasets and more learning algorithms. And also it would be interesting to develop and to use a learning-based sentiment classifier calibrated with emails instead of a lexicon-based classifiers.

During following studies we will explore the possibility of using this approach per spam message types. For instance, commercial messages are positive, while other message types like Nigerian scams are negative.

Acknowledgments. This work has been partially funded by the Basque Department of Education, Language policy and Culture under the project SocialSPAM (PI_2014_1_102).

References

1. Malarvizhi, R.: Content-based spam filtering and detection algorithms-an efficient analysis & comparison 1 (2013)
2. KasperskyLab: Spam and phishing in 2015 q1 (2015). http://www.kaspersky.com/about/news/virus/2015/Spam-and-Phishing-in-Q1-New-domains-revitalize-old-spam
3. Saadat, N.: Survey on spam filtering techniques. Commun. Netw. **3**(3), 153–160 (2011)
4. Cormack, G.V.: Email spam filtering: a systematic review. Found. Trends Inf. Retrieval **1**(4), 335–455 (2007)
5. Tretyakov, K.: Machine learning techniques in spam filtering. In: Data Mining Problem-oriented Seminar, MTAT, vol. 3, pp. 60–79 (2004)

6. Sanz, E.P., Hidalgo, J.M.G., Cortizo, J.C.: Email spam filtering. Adv. Comput. **74**, 45–114 (2008)
7. Teli, S., Biradar, S.: Effective spam detection method for email. In: International Conference on Advances in Engineering & Technology (2014)
8. Eberhardt, J.J.: Bayesian spam detection. University of Minnesota, Morris Undergraduate Journal, Scholarly Horizons (2015)
9. Liddy, E.: Natural language processing (2001)
10. Giyanani, R., Desai, M.: Spam detection using natural language processing. Int. J. Comput. Sci. Res. Technol. **1**, 55–58 (2013)
11. Echeverria Briones, P.F., Altamirano Valarezo, Z.V., Pinto Astudillo, A.B., Sanchez Guerrero, J.D.C.: Text mining aplicado a la clasificación y distribución automática de correo electrónico y detección de correo spam (2009)
12. Lau, R.Y.K., Liao, S.Y., Kwok, R.C.W., Xu, K., Xia, Y., Li, Y.: Text mining and probabilistic language modeling for online review spam detection. ACM Trans. Manage. Inf. Syst. **2**(4), 25:1–25:30 (2012)
13. Liu, B., Zhang, L.: A survey of opinion mining and sentiment analysis. In: Aggarwal, C.C., Zhai, C. (eds.) Mining Text Data, pp. 415–463. Springer, New York (2012)
14. Pang, B., Lee, L.: Opinion mining and sentiment analysis. Found. Trends Inf. Retrieval **2**(1–2), 1–135 (2008)
15. Pang, B., Lee, L., Vaithyanathan, S.: Thumbs up?: sentiment classification using machine learning techniques. In: Proceedings of the ACL-02 Conference on Empirical Methods in Natural Language Processing, EMNLP 2002, Stroudsburg, PA, USA, vol. 10, pp. 79–86. Association for Computational Linguistics (2002)
16. Turney, P.D.: Thumbs up or thumbs down?: semantic orientation applied to unsupervised classification of reviews. In: Proceedings of the 40th Annual Meeting on Association for Computational Linguistics, ACL 2002, pp. 417–424. Association for Computational Linguistics, USA (2002)
17. Esuli, A., Sebastiani, F.: Sentiwordnet: a publicly available lexical resource for opinion mining. In: Proceedings of LREC, vol. 6, pp. 417–422. Citeseer (2006)
18. Baccianella, S., Esuli, A., Sebastiani, F.: Sentiwordnet 3.0: an enhanced lexical resource for sentiment analysis and opinion mining. In: LREC, vol. 10, pp. 2200–2204 (2010)
19. Ohana, B., Tierney, B.: Sentiment classification of reviews using sentiwordnet. In: 9th. IT & T Conference, p. 13 (2009)
20. Pang, B., Lee, L.: A sentimental education: sentiment analysis using subjectivity summarization based on minimum cuts. In: Proceedings of the ACL (2004)

A Context-Aware Keyboard Generator
for Smartphone Using Random Forest
and Rule-Based System

Sang-Muk Jo and Sung-Bae Cho[(✉)]

Department of Computer Science, Yonsei University, Seoul, South Korea
{sangmukjo, sbcho}@yonsei.ac.kr

Abstract. A soft keyboard is popular for inputting texts on the display of smartphone. As it is a keyboard in display, it has an advantage that can be easily changed unlike the hardware keyboard. An adaptive soft keyboard is needed as different types of people use smartphone in various situations. In this paper, we propose a hybrid system that predicts user behavior patterns using smartphone sensor log data based on random forest and generates the appropriate GUI to the predicted behavior patterns by the rules constructed from users' preference. The random forest for predicting user behavior patterns has a high generalization performance due to the ensemble of various decision trees. The GUI mapping rules are constructed according to the data collected from 210 users of different ages and genders. Experimental results with the real log data confirm that the proposed system effectively recognizes the situations and the user satisfaction is doubled compared to the conventional methods.

1 Introduction

Nowadays most of the people use smartphone every day, anywhere. Smartphone allows users to enter texts through soft keyboard, but it is difficult to input with the same performance in various situations for different purposes. Since the soft keyboard is controlled by software unlike the hardware keyboard, it can easily change the keyboard type [1] and can be entered by the gestures [2]. In this paper, we provide the users with proper GUI according to their situation by exploiting the variability of the soft keyboard. Romanoa, *et al.* made the keyboard that had the smaller number of keys and was entered by using the tap and gestures [3]. Because the QWERTY keyboard has many keys in small display, the key size in the smartphone gets very small. As the smaller number of keys allows a key to have larger region, it can reduce the wrong input. However, the new type of keyboard requires extra learning efforts as many people are familiar with the standard QWERTY keyboard.

Figure 1 is the acceleration vectors in user patterns and available soft keyboard GUI. For a particular user pattern, the acceleration vector is different from that for other patterns. Human activities can be recognized by using a classifier with acceleration data [4]. In this paper, we propose a hybrid system based on the familiar QWERTY keyboard that can be changed in the user's situations. Random forest is trained with acceleration, gyroscope, magnetic field and orientation data of smartphone. The trained

© Springer International Publishing Switzerland 2016
F. Martínez-Álvarez et al. (Eds.): HAIS 2016, LNAI 9648, pp. 91–101, 2016.
DOI: 10.1007/978-3-319-32034-2_8

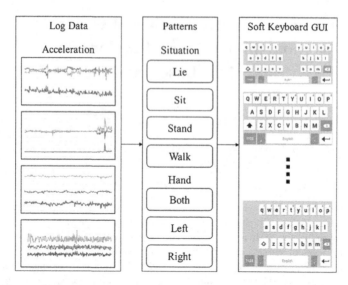

Fig. 1. The accelerometer log data for user patterns and the available soft keyboard GUIs

model predicts the user behavior patterns with which the rules generate the adaptive GUI for smartphone.

The user behavior patterns are constructed from the typing hands and the situations in which the users mainly use the smartphone. The situations include sitting, standing, lying and walking. The typing hands include both hands, left hand and right hand. The main contribution of this paper is to analyze the log data from smartphone to automatically determine the user's pattern, and generate different GUIs of the keyboard that keeps the form of the QWERTY keyboard. The GUI is determined by the keyboard layout of keys, the height of keyboard and the size of keys. The keyboard layout has the four levels such as standard form, both split form, left shifted form and right shifted form. The height of keyboard and the size of keys have three levels.

The rest of the paper is organized as follows. Section 2 presents the related works for adaptive keyboard. Section 3 describes in details the context-aware soft keyboard. Section 4 shows the experiments conducted to confirm the usefulness of the system.

2 Related Works

Researchers have studied in three aspects to improve input speed and error rate for the soft keyboard as shown in Table 1. The first aspect is to use new key arrangement rather than using QWERTY keyboard. It leads to frequent typos because of placing a lot of keys on a small screen. An alternative method is to reduce the number of keys and use gestures [3]. It changes the key arrangement to minimize the movement of the fingers during the key input [5, 6]. There are studies to change the key arrangement by placing similarly with QWERTY keyboard [5] and analyzing the words in each language [6].

Table 1. Related works for the performance improvement of soft keyboard

Authors	Description	Elements
M. Romanoa [3]	Key arrangement that reduces the number of keys and uses gestures	Key arrangement
X. Bi [5]	Optimized key arrangement that is similar with QWERTY	Key arrangement
X. Bi [6]	Key arrangement to minimize the travel distance for each language	Key arrangement
P. Sakkos [7]	Changing predicted key size by using personal dictionary	Key size
E. Rodrigues [8]	Changing predicted key GUI	Key color, key size, activation area
R. Mathieu [9]	Dynamic predicted key generation to minimize the travel distance	Dynamic key
Y. Yin [10]	Generate activation area depending on input posture and individual person	Activation area
M. Goel [11]	Coordinating activation area by using an acceleration sensor	Activation area
A. Gunawardana [12]	Setting a fixed part in activation area	Activation area
K. Hwang [13]	Word recommended by using dictionary	Additional layout for words

The second aspect is a visual alternation in the keyboard. They change the color, size and activation area of the next key predicted based on the current input sequence with the words dictionary [7–9]. Sakkos, *et al.* predicted the next word by using words in the personal dictionary constructed by the user inputs rather than words in dictionary [7]. Rodrigues, *et al.* compared three elements (key color, key size and activation area) of predicted keys [8]. Mathieu, *et al.* added new button at each corner of the predicted keys for minimizing the movement of hands [9].

The third aspect is an activation area to determine the value of the key based on the touch position on the keyboard without any visual change. Because the input in border of keys is ambiguous in touchscreen, the method determines a proper key depending on user's situations. Probability models constituted by using the user input pattern in various situations are used to determine the key [10, 11]. The models generated by using user's input posture and individual input pattern create a proper activation area [10]. The walk models generated by analyzing users' walk pattern changes the activation area [11]. Language models of predicting next keys coordinate the activation area [12].

Most of research change the keyboard based on the word dictionary. In case of using the word dictionary, time, skills and additional storage are needed to build the word dictionary. They have drawbacks to prepare word dictionaries for different languages. This paper does not use a word dictionary and provides the user with GUI of soft keyboard according to the behavior patterns. As it keeps the QWERTY keyboard, the learning efforts can be minimized.

3   Adaptive Keyboard Generator

Figure 2 shows the structure of the proposed system which consists of collecting log data, preprocessing log data, modeling random forest with log data, predicting user behavior patterns and mapping the patterns to GUI. The Latin IME is a Google open source that is running on Android [14]. The main idea is to analyze the user's behavior pattern from the log data collected with smartphone, and present a keyboard GUI appropriate to the pattern.

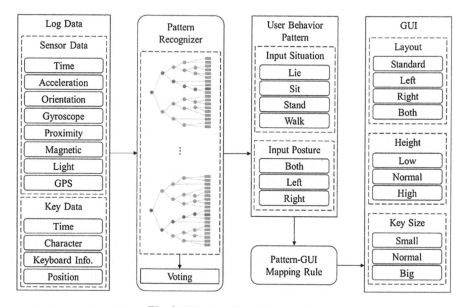

Fig. 2. The overall system structure

3.1   Data Collection

In order to recognize the user behavior patterns, the user log data were collected in smartphone. An Android application was made for collecting log data. While users enter the English sentences by using soft keyboard, the log data are collected in background. We used the English sentences proposed by Mackenzie, *et al.* [15]. Log data consist of sensor log and key log. Sensor log data such as acceleration, gyroscope, magnetic field, orientation and light are collected from smartphone sensors. Key log data such as keyboard GUI, key position, current time, intended key and entered key are collected from soft keyboard. In this paper, 150 males and 60 females participated to collect the log data. In a total of 12 different situations, the subjects selected the most appropriate GUI and entered the sentences 10 times for one situation.

3.2   Data Analysis

In the correlation matrix between the changeable elements of soft keyboard selected by users and the smartphone sensor log data, the maximum value is 0.32, indicating that there is no correlation between the sensor data and the GUI. Figure 3 is the scatterplot

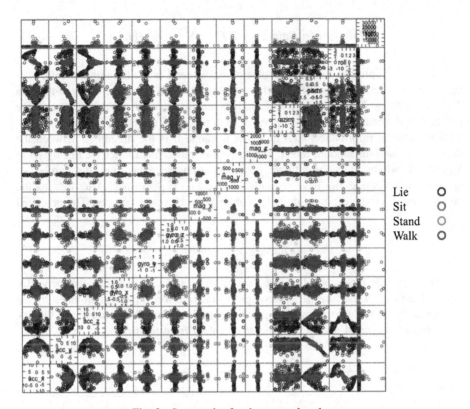

Fig. 3. Scatter plot for the sensor log data

matrices for each sensor. According to the user's situation, the points are shown in different colors. The points are separated into lying and walking in many scatterplots, whereas the points of walking, standing and sitting are overlapped.

3.3   User Behavior Pattern Recognition

Random forest is used for predicting user behavior patterns. Decision tree can be easily understood through the tree structure and achieve high accuracy with fast process. However, they are subject to get overfitting and bias to features. Random forest based on the ensemble of decision trees overcomes this problem. It makes several decision trees and votes the final result based on them. To model decision trees, the features for splitting a node are selected from a set of randomly chosen attributes [16]. As the result, the decision trees in random forest have different forms that have better generalization performance while a decision tree is dependent on training data. In this paper, the random forest gets the sensor log and key log as input and predicts the user situations and input posture.

To grow a tree in the random forest, the feature with the highest information gain is chosen at each node. The information gain for a certain feature Y,

$$Information\ Gain(Y) = I(T) - \sum_{s=1}^{S} \frac{|T_s|}{|T|} I(T_s), \tag{1}$$

is a criterion of splitting data that become purer, where T is the training log data, T_s is the log data in subset s by splitting with the feature Y, and $I(T)$ is the entropy of the data T. Random forest has the property of random feature selection. For every tree in the forest, m features are randomly selected at each node and the tree chooses the feature with the highest information gain in the m features. It is the difference between the decision tree and the random forest. The number of random attributes are mainly set to $\log_2 M + 1$, where M is the number of attributes in the data, since the number of random attributes does not have a significant effect on performance. After training the decision trees, classification is done by voting with the result of trees. The predicted class r^*,

$$r^* = \arg\max_{r \in R} \sum_{T \in F} [h(l|T) = r], \tag{2}$$

is the one with the most votes from the trees, where R is the class set, l is the log vector and T is the tree in the forest F. The output of random forest that is combined by the outputs of the multiple decision trees makes the result to generalize and reduces the risk of overfitting. Figure 4 shows the process of voting from the trees.

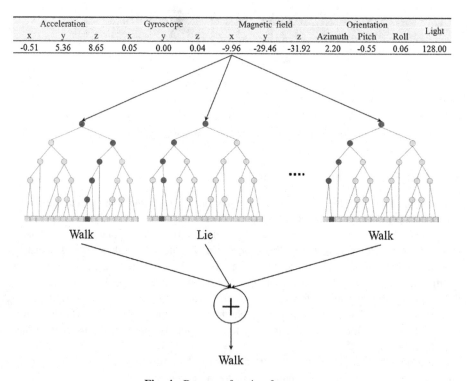

Fig. 4. Process of voting from trees

3.4 GUI Generation

Figure 5 shows the possible GUI elements. Keyboard height and key size have three levels. Layout has four levels such as standard layout, left shifted layout, right shifted layout and both split layout. Therefore, the proposed soft keyboard can have 36 (3*3*4) different GUIs. In order to map 12 user behavior patterns to 36 GUIs, we choose the best GUIs from the 36 cases.

The best GUI for each user behavior pattern is determined by the GUI that users selected most frequently in that situation: We make the rules that match the user behavior patterns to the GUIs based on the users' choice for each situation. The following rules show the result of the best GUI from the collected log data. For the key size and height, the normal size is the most frequently selected. For the keyboard layout, left-shifted is always selected for the left input posture.

The sensor log data and the key log data are preprocessed and used to predict the input posture and situation by using the random forest trained. The rules based on the number of GUIs for each user behavior pattern in different situations produce the best GUI for that situation. The rules are as follows.

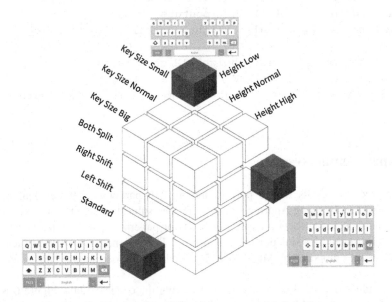

Fig. 5. The possible GUIs of the proposed soft keyboard

```
IF (situation = 'Lie') AND (posture = 'Both')
   THEN key_size='Big', height='Normal', layout='Standard'
IF (situation = 'Lie') AND (posture = 'Left')
   THEN key_size='Normal', height='Normal', layout='Left'
IF (situation = 'Lie') AND (posture = 'Right')
   THEN key_size='Big', height='Normal', layout='Standard'
IF (situation = 'Sit') AND (posture = 'Both')
   THEN key_size='Normal', height='Normal', layout='Right'
IF (situation = 'Sit') AND (posture = 'Left')
   THEN key_size='Normal', height='Normal', layout='Left'
IF (situation = 'Sit') AND (posture = 'Right')
   THEN key_size='Small', height='Low', layout='Standard'
IF (situation = 'Stand') AND (posture = 'Both')
   THEN key_size='Normal', height='Normal', layout='Standard'
IF (situation = 'Stand') AND (posture = 'Left')
   THEN key_size='Normal', height='Normal', layout='Left'
IF (situation = 'Stand') AND (posture = 'Right')
   THEN key_size='Normal', height='Normal', layout='Right'
IF (situation = 'Walk') AND (posture = 'Both')
   THEN key_size='Normal', height='Normal', layout='Right'
IF (situation = 'Walk') AND (posture = 'Left')
   THEN key_size='Small', height='High', layout='Left'
IF (situation = 'Walk') AND (posture = 'Right')
   THEN key_size='Big', height='Normal', layout='Standard'
```

4 Experimental Results

We analyzed the results for 10 persons among 210 participants for evaluating the proposed system by using Android smartphone. The subjects entered two sentences in one set and repeated ten sets for one user behavior pattern out of the total 12 patterns that are constructed by 4 situations and 3 postures. The sentences are randomly selected in 500 sentences proposed by Mackenzie [15]. In the result, one subject entered in total 240 sentences.

We conducted 10-fold cross validation by using the collected data. Figure 6 is the graphs of accuracy and AUC in the various numbers of random attributes. The bar chart represents the accuracy of random forest and the line chart represents ROC (Receiver Operating Characteristics) area of random forest. Figure 6(a) is the graph for input situations and Fig. 6(b) is the graph for input posture. The best accuracy of input situations is 81.4 % and the best accuracy of input postures is 70.0 %. Because the accuracy and AUC get lower or unchanged after 6 random attributes, and we chose the random forest with 6 random attributes while the split node is generated in trees.

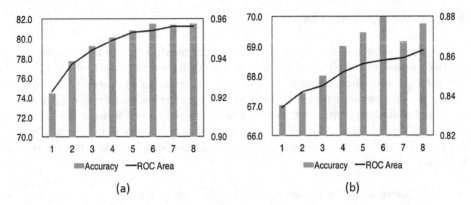

Fig. 6. Accuracy and ROC area for (a) input situation and (b) input posture

Figure 7 is the boxplot of comparison with other classification methods. The proposed random forest shows the higher accuracy than other methods. SVM has the second highest accuracy and MLP has the lowest accuracy.

We conducted the satisfaction test that the subjects chose the satisfaction of 1 to 10 scores when using the proposed keyboard and the standard keyboard. The average satisfaction of the standard keyboard was 4.7 and the satisfaction of the proposed keyboard was 8.1, which shows the significant improvement of the user satisfaction with the proposed system.

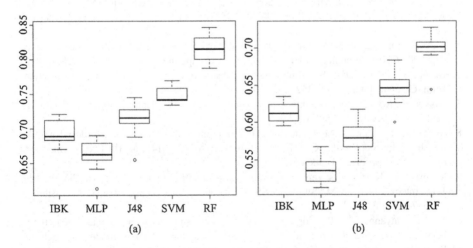

Fig. 7. Comparison of accuracies with other classification methods for (a) input situation and (b) input posture

5 Concluding Remarks

In this paper we proposed a context-aware keyboard interface that changes depending on user's situations and typing hands. Experiments with the real log data collected from 210 participants resulted in higher user satisfaction. The proposed method was used as an app for smartphone, which turned out to be acceptable because the new GUI was initialized without any extra cost. We need to investigate on performance from larger dataset with more users. Also, comparison with other techniques in the conventional approach like the use of predictive text should be conducted to show the practical usefulness of the proposed method.

Acknowledgements. This work was supported by LG Electronics, Inc.

References

1. Cheng, L., Liang, H., Wu, C., Chen, M.: iGrasp grasp-based adaptive keyboard for mobile devices. In: CHI 2013 Extended Abstracts on Human Factors in Computing Systems, pp. 2791–2792 (2013)
2. Smith, B.A., Bi, X., Zhai, S.: Optimizing touchscreen keyboards for gesture typing. In: Proceedings of the ACM CHI 2015, pp. 3365–3374 (2015)
3. Romanoa, M., Paolino, L., Tortora, G., Vitiello, G.: The tap and slide keyboard: a new interaction method for mobile device text entry. Int. J. Hum.-Comput. Interact. **20**(12), 935–945 (2014)
4. Bao, L., Intille, S.S.: Activity recognition from user-annotated acceleration data. In: Ferscha, A., Mattern, F. (eds.) PERVASIVE 2004. LNCS, vol. 3001, pp. 1–17. Springer, Heidelberg (2004)
5. Bi, X., Smith, B., Zhai, S.: Quasi-qwerty soft keyboard optimization. In: Proceedings of ACM SIGCHI Conference on Human Factors in Computing Systems, pp. 283–286 (2010)
6. Bi, X., Smith, B., Zhai, S.: Multilingual touchscreen keyboard design and optimization. Hum.-Comput. Interact. **27**, 352–382 (2012)
7. Sakkos, P., Kotsakos, D., Katakis, I., Gunopulos, D.: Anima: adaptive personalized software keyboard. arXiv:1501.05696 (2015)
8. Rodrigues, É., Carreira, M., Gonçalves, D.: Improving text-entry experience for older adults on tablets. In: Stephanidis, C., Antona, M. (eds.) UAHCI 2014, Part III. LNCS, vol. 8515, pp. 167–178. Springer, Heidelberg (2014)
9. Mathieu, R.: KeyGlasses: semi-transparent keys on soft keyboard. In: Proceedings of the 16th International ACM SIGACCESS Conference on Computers and Accessibility, pp. 347–349 (2014)
10. Yin, Y., Ouyang, T.Y., Partridge, K., Zhai, S.: Making touchscreen keyboards adaptive to keys, hand postures, and individuals – A hierarchical spatial backoff model approach. In: Proceedings of the SIGCHI Conference on Human Factors in Computing System, pp. 2775–2784. ACM (2013)
11. Goel, M., Findlater, L., Wobbrock, J.: WalkType: using accelerometer data to accommodate situational impairments in mobile touch screen text entry. In: Proceedings of ACM CHI 2012, pp. 2687–2696 (2012)

12. Gunawardana, A., Paek, T., Meek, C.: Usability guided key-target resizing for soft keyboards. In: Proceedings of International Conference on Intelligent User Interfaces, pp. 111–118. ACM (2010)
13. Hwang, K., Lee, J.: Preliminary study on soft keyboard with recommendation for mobile device. J. Inst. Webcasting Internet Telecommun. 13(6), 137–145 (2013)
14. https://android.googlesource.com/platform/packages/inputmethods/LatinIME/+/master
15. Mackenzie, I.S., Soukoreff, R.W.: Phrase sets for evaluating text entry techniques. In: Extended Abstracts of the ACM Conference on Human Factors in Computing Systems, pp. 754–755 (2003)
16. Breiman, L.: Random forests. Mach. Learn. 45(1), 5–32 (2001)

Privacy Preserving Data Mining
for Deliberative Consultations

Piotr Andruszkiewicz[✉]

Institute of Computer Science, Warsaw University of Technology, Warsaw, Poland
P.Andruszkiewicz@ii.pw.edu.pl

Abstract. In deliberative consultations, which utilise electronic surveys as a tool to obtain information from residents, preserving privacy plays an important role. In this paper investigation of a possibility of privacy preserving data mining techniques application in deliberative consultations has been conducted. Three main privacy preserving techniques; namely, heuristic-based, reconstruction-based, and cryptography-based have been analysed and a setup for online surveys performed within deliberative consultations has been proposed.

This work can be useful for designers and administrators in the assessment of the privacy risks they face with a system for deliberative consultations. It can also be used in the process of privacy preserving incorporation in such a system in order to help minimise privacy risks to users.

Keywords: Privacy preserving data mining · Deliberative consultations · Reconstruction-based technique · Cryptography-based technique · Heuristic-based technique

1 Introduction

The aim of deliberative consultations [1] is to discuss important issues with residents. One example is a deliberative consultation run by a local government in order to understand opinions of residents about a desired place of building a new high school. In the era of digital society organisers provide Internet portals that facilitate the process of gathering opinions of residents. One of the most important methods of gathering data is providing electronic surveys, especially online surveys, through which residents may give their opinions. However, in order to encourage them to participate in a survey and provide true opinions, privacy should be preserved. To this end several techniques for incorporating privacy in data mining can be employed. These methods are also helpful in statistical tasks, e.g., mean calculation, that are often used in the analysis of data collected in surveys.

This work has been supported by the National Centre for Research and Development under Grant No. IS-1/072/NCBR/2014 and the Institute of Computer Science, Warsaw University of Technology under Grant No. II/2015/DS/1.

© Springer International Publishing Switzerland 2016
F. Martínez-Álvarez et al. (Eds.): HAIS 2016, LNAI 9648, pp. 102–113, 2016.
DOI: 10.1007/978-3-319-32034-2_9

In spite of enormous diversity in privacy aspects of data mining, three main approaches can be distinguished: heuristic-based, reconstruction-based, and cryp-tography-based [2,3].

In the first approach heuristic algorithms are used to hide knowledge an organisation does not want to reveal, for instance individual values in data are changed in order to hide sensitive knowledge such as important rules in the case of association rules mining.

The reconstruction-based approach is used to incorporate privacy on an individual level by changing original individual values (for instance, users' answers) in a random way by means of a randomisation-based method and revealing only modified values.

The third approach, which is based on cryptography, uses secure multiparty computations (SMC) to carry out data mining tasks based on distributed data, that is, data possessed by different organisations that do not want to disclose their private input. Furthermore, encryption techniques which enable one to perform computations over encrypted data without being able to decrypt can be used in privacy preserving.

In this paper the use of available privacy preserving techniques in deliberative consultations is investigated. Firstly, privacy preserving data mining literature relevant to deliberative consultations is reviewed (Sect. 2). Then, privacy preserving techniques are analysed and as a result of this analysis privacy preserving technique setup suitable for deliberative consultations is proposed (Sect. 3). Finally, Sect. 4 summarises the conclusions of the study and outlines future avenues to explore.

2 Privacy Preserving Data Mining for Deliberative Consultations - Literature Review

2.1 Levels of Privacy Preserving

In privacy preserving data mining there are two levels of incorporating privacy [2], namely, aggregate level and individual level.

In the case of preserving privacy on an aggregate level, an owner of data does not want any miner to discover all or part of knowledge/relations hidden in a published data set. For instance, in the case of association rules mining, an owner does want to hide particular rules and let a miner to discover the remaining rules.

In the case of preserving privacy on an individual level, individual values of users' (objects') characteristics (values of attributes) are preserved. A miner is able to discover hidden knowledge, e.g., to build a model, however, exact objects' characteristics (e.g., true vales of an attribute *Salary*) are not provided.

2.2 Types of Data Partitioning in Privacy Preserving Data Mining

There are four types of data partitioning in privacy preserving data mining, namely, horizontally partitioned, vertically partitioned, arbitrary partitioned, and centralised. The types strictly determine the algorithms used in a given case.

Horizontally Partitioned. In the scenario with horizontally partitioned data [3], there are several sites having the same characteristics (i.e., the same attributes describing objects, e.g., residents) of different objects/people. An example of the same characteristics collected over many sites are supermarkets from the same chain that have the same product assortment and gather information about transactions of their clients. In deliberative consultations each resident can be perceived as an organisation that possesses the same characteristics about one resident, i.e., herself/himself.

Vertically Partitioned. When different information (attributes) refer to the same objects (clients) collected over many sites, data is partitioned (distributed) vertically [4]. For instance, a hospital and insurance company are gathering information about the same people from a given corporation.

Arbitrary Partitioned. The two types of data presented above can be combined together. Thus, not only can information about objects (attributes) be partitioned, but both attributes and objects can be distributed over many sites. This more generalised partitioning of data is called arbitrary partitioning [5].

Centralised. When there is only one site that collects information (all attributes for all objects), then data is not partitioned and is called centralised, i.e., stored in one database [6].

2.3   Methods of Data Modification in Privacy Preserving Data Mining

In general the modification methods are used to incorporate a desired level of privacy by distorting values of objects' characteristics. Only distorted values are revealed.

Randomisation-Based Methods. Randomisation-based methods (perturbation) are one type of the distortion methods. They are used to modify original values at random. In this scheme, only distorted values are stored in a centralised database.

A basic randomisation-based method for distorting binary attributes modifies original values in the following way:

Given a binary attribute with possible values of 0 and 1, each (original) value is kept with the probability p or flipped with the probability $1 - p$ [3]. All attributes are distorted in the same manner, however, each attribute may have a different value of the probability p. Distorted values of binary attributes create a new database and are supplied to a miner. The only information a miner gets is a distorted database and a value of probability p for each attribute.

Definition 1. A randomisation factor *is a probability that an original value of an attribute will be retained during a distortion.*

A result of a distortion process is a realisation of probabilistic function of an original database that constitutes a distorted database. A miner knows both a distorted database as well as a distorting procedure (a randomisation factor p in this scenario). However, a miner does not know an original database.

In the randomisation-based method presented above, the distortion process is applied to each item in a transaction independently. Moreover, the distortion process for a transaction T_i does not use any information about a transaction T_j, where $i \neq j$ [7]. This makes the process of distorting a true database independent for each object. Thus, collecting of all true data to distort all transactions is not necessary because each transaction can be distorted separately. Furthermore, additional distorted transactions can be added to a central distorted database at any time and a data mining process can be repeated over the whole collected distorted data.

For nominal attributes the following distortion method may be used: an original value of an attribute is kept with a probability p or changed with a probability $1-p$. Remaining nominal attributes are distorted in the same way, however, each attribute may have a different value of a probability p.

The process of changing a value will be specified in more detail. One of possible solutions is to assign the same probabilities for all values except for an original value and draw a new value, that is, for an attribute with k values, the probability for an original value is p and for other values is equal to $\frac{1-p}{k-1}$.

In general, for nominal attributes $\mathbf{P}$ matrix of retaining/changing values of an attribute [8] may be defined.

Definition 2. $\mathbf{P}$ *is a matrix of retaining/changing values of a nominal attribute of order k x k:*

$$\mathbf{P} = \begin{pmatrix} a_{1,1} & a_{1,2} & a_{1,3} & \cdots & a_{1,k} \\ a_{2,1} & a_{2,2} & a_{2,3} & \cdots & a_{2,k} \\ \vdots & \vdots & \vdots & \ddots & \vdots \\ a_{k,1} & a_{k,2} & a_{k,3} & \cdots & a_{k,k} \end{pmatrix},$$

where $a_{r,p} = Pr(v_p \to v_r)$ is a probability that a value v_p will be changed to a value v_r and the sum of all elements in each column is equal to 1.

Values of a nominal attribute are distorted according to the probabilities from $\mathbf{P}$ matrix. There is a special type of $\mathbf{P}$ matrix, where $a_{r,r} = p$ and the probabilities of changing a value of an attribute are equal. The matrix of this type for an attribute with k values will look as follows:

$$\mathbf{P} = \begin{pmatrix} p & \frac{1-p}{k-1} & \cdots & \frac{1-p}{k-1} \\ \frac{1-p}{k-1} & p & \cdots & \frac{1-p}{k-1} \\ \vdots & \vdots & \ddots & \vdots \\ \frac{1-p}{k-1} & \frac{1-p}{k-1} & \cdots & p \end{pmatrix}.$$

There are three main methods of distorting continuous attributes which do not assume any knowledge about values of attributes of other objects: the additive perturbation method [3], multiplicative perturbation [9], and the retention replacement perturbation [8].

In this method a random value drawn from a given distribution, e.g., a uniform or normal distribution, is added to an original value of an attribute. Only a modified value is revealed to an external organisation.

In the *multiplicative perturbation* an original value of an attribute is multiplied by a random value drawn from a given distribution [9]. To distort values of an object, the rotation perturbation [10] where the vector of values of attributes for a given object is multiplied by a rotation matrix can also be used. Nevertheless, when one is able to estimate the rotation matrix, it might be possible to breach the privacy [11].

In the *retention replacement perturbation* [12], an original value of an attribute is kept with a probability p and with a probability $1 - p$ an original value is replaced with an element selected from a replacing probability distribution function (pdf) on a domain of the attribute.

Blocking. A value of an attribute can be changed by replacing it with an *unknown value*, a value that does not occur in domains of attributes (often represented as '?'). Blocking replaces an original value with an unknown value instead of placing a false value, which is sometimes more desirable, e.g., for medical applications [13]. Applying this method, privacy can be preserved on both aggregate and individual levels, however, blocking is popular in hiding association rules [13,14].

Aggregation. In this method, values of an attribute are partitioned into disjoint mutually-exclusive classes which become new values of a modified attribute. A special case of aggregation is discretisation in which values of a continuous attribute are discretised into intervals. Instead of an original value, an interval in which an original value lies is provided.

Swapping. A value of an attribute for a given sample can be interchanged with a value of the same attribute for a different sample. The drawback of this method is that original values for different samples should be known to interchange values for different samples, thus swapping cannot be performed separately for each sample without knowledge about original values for other samples and original values have to be stored.

Sampling. In this method, only a sample of population is revealed. To discover hidden knowledge, the sample data should reflect relations among all data, that is, probability distribution functions of attributes should be preserved. Sampling does not modify values stored in a database, thus a data mining process is performed on real data, which eliminates the problem of building a model on distorted data [13]. Nevertheless, revealing true data, even for a few samples from a true database, may be a serious drawback in some cases, for instance, medical applications, where all true data about some patients would be revealed.

In order to avoid this drawback, that is, not to reveal true data about objects, the sample can be generated according to probability distribution functions of attributes [15].

2.4   Privacy Preserving Techniques

In privacy preserving data mining, the following three main techniques are used; namely, heuristic-based, cryptography-based, and randomisation-based.

Heuristic-Based Techniques. A selective modification of data is an NP-Hard[1] problem [2]. To address the complexity issue, heuristic algorithms can be used. This solution is especially popular in hiding given association rules [17–19]. Heuristic-based techniques are mostly used for centralised data.

Cryptography-Based Techniques. *Secure Multiparty Computation*, which is the *cryptography-based technique*, can be used to solve the following problem: two or more parties want to create a model based on their private input, but they are not willing to disclose their private data to anybody else. This problem is called *Secure Multiparty Computation* (SMC). Computations are performed in a distributed network on inputs from each participant. The assumption is that an output of a computation is correct and no more information is revealed to any participant than its own input and output. *Secure two party computation* was first investigated in [20]. Later it was generalised to secure multiparty computation in [21, 22]. *Secure multiparty computation* is used for partitioned data.

Moreover, encryption techniques which enable one to perform computations over encrypted data without being able to decrypt can be used in privacy preserving [23].

Reconstruction-Based Techniques. The idea behind *reconstruction-based techniques* is that having only data distorted by one of the randomisation-based methods, a miner reconstructs (estimates) an original distribution of attributes and based on the reconstructed (estimated) distributions builds a model of aggregated data [2]. The distorted data as well as parameters of a randomisation-based method used to distort them can be published or passed to a third party. Knowing distorted individual values and parameters of a randomisation-based method, one is able to perform data mining tasks. To this end, first original distributions of values of attributes are reconstructed (estimated) based on the distorted values and the parameters of the distortion method, and a data mining model is built based on the distorted data. The creation of a model is carried out without the need to access original individual data [8]. The reconstruction-based techniques are used for centralised and distributed data.

---

[1] The proof in the case of privacy preserving association rules mining can be found in [16].

3   Usability of Privacy Preserving Techniques in Deliberative Consultations

In this section the analysis of privacy preserving data mining in the context of deliberative consultations run by local governments is presented. Firstly different privacy preserving techniques are characterised, then the comparison of aforementioned techniques is provided.

In the analysis presented in this section focus is put on preserving privacy of data provided by users in electronic surveys, usually submitted through Internet portals used for consultations. In such surveys users usually provide numeric and nominal (categorical) data. One specific case of categorical data is binary data, e.g., yes or no answers.

In order to analyse the applicability of privacy preserving techniques to a specific domain it is necessary to verify the partitioning of data that is available. The heuristic approach to privacy preserving is designed for centralised data. The cryptography-based approach is used for the distributed data, while the reconstruction-based approach can be applied to both distributed and centralised data.

Survey data is provided by different users, usually from different locations. Thus, there are two possible types of data partition. Firstly, survey data can be perceived as horizontally partitioned; that is, each user provides values of the same attributes. Secondly, centralised scenario can be assumed. In this case data is provided by different users separately and after distortion is transferred to a server and stored.

Since the choice of privacy preserving algorithm depends on the partition of data and in the area of online surveys both types of data partition exist, all three aforementioned techniques are of interest and will be investigated below.

In the analysis of any algorithm it is important to measure its performance and accuracy.

Good performance is one of the advantages of the reconstruction-based approach compared to cryptography-based solutions [24]. Nevertheless, this technique achieves it at the cost of accuracy of the results. As the reconstruction-based approach uses individual randomised values, there is a trade-off between the level of privacy and the accuracy of the data mining results. The higher level of privacy is used, the higher is loss of accuracy of the data mining results [25].

The cryptography-based techniques do not suffer from accuracy loss, but their main drawback is high performance cost, especially when many parties are involved in the process [26]; in online surveys (surveys conducted over the Internet) each resident is treated as a separate party which leads to high performance cost.

Both the reconstruction-based and cryptography-based approaches can be used to preserve privacy on an individual level. The latter assumes that there are many information providers which need to interact to perform a data mining task. Thus, each time a data mining task is performed, information providers should be ready to interact. This is a high drawback for users participating in surveys. Cryptography-based approach also needs to interact with users submitting data within a survey each time an additional analysis is going to be performed. It would be almost impossible to gather exactly the same group of respondents more than once for consultations. The reconstruction-based approach is designed to be used for both distributed and centralised data. The distorted records can be stored in a centralised database and can be used many times in a process of building different models without interactions with information providers. Furthermore, the reconstruction-based approach enables organizations to provide data that one can use to discover hidden knowledge without revealing individual characteristics of objects. Applying reconstruction-based approach privacy preserved data can be collected and used for further analysis at any time without interactions with users. The heuristic-based approach to privacy preserving is designed to provide privacy on aggregate level; that is, hide knowledge in a data set. The goal of surveys is to gather data that will be used to discover knowledge, thus heuristic-based approach should not be used in case of online surveys and in consequence in consultations. Furthermore, deliberative consultations are meant to extract opinions and ideas about issues and not to hide them.

Table 1. Properties of reconstruction-based and cryptography-based techniques.

Property	Reconstruction-based	Cryptography-based
Privacy on an individual level	yes	yes
Privacy vs accuracy trade-off	yes	no
Needs additional interactions with users	no	yes
Fixed set of statistics	no	yes
All users at one time	no	yes
Users participate in model building	no	yes
The data set cannot be passed further	no	yes

Table 1 shows the summary of the properties of reconstruction-based and cryptography-based techniques. Heuristic-besed techniques were skipped because they were created to hide knowledge. Considering electronic surveys submitted through Internet portals, the reconstruction-based approach fits such applications better because, contrary to the cryptography-based approach, data providers do not participate in the process of building a model, i.e., they do not obtain the results or partial results of a data mining/statistical task, e.g., mean of submitted answers. Users' concerns about a possible misuse of provided data can be reduced by means of a randomisation-based method, which distorts original data and stores only distorted values in a centralised database. The distortion procedure, which modifies individual values of the object, does not depend on any information about other objects, thus it can be performed at the object site. In the case of online surveys, the distortion can be done at a user machine, which makes a randomisation-based method easy to incorporate into a web browser.

Moreover, in the reconstruction-based approach additional objects provided by new users can be added to a centralised database at any time and a data mining model can be rebuilt without the need to interact with other data providers; that is, respondents.

As the above analysis suggests that reconstruction-based technique is more suitable for electronic surveys, other interesting properties of this technique will be investigated in this section.

There are two main scenarios in privacy preserving data mining tasks conducted with the usage of the reconstruction-based technique on data distorted according to a randomisation-based method which distorts values of each attribute in a sample independently and does not use any information about other samples. In both scenarios, privacy is preserved on an individual level and data is stored in a centralised database.

These two scenarios have in common that an untrusted miner knows only a distortion procedure, its parameters and a distorted data set.

To sum up, the first scenario, that was already described, can be easily used in surveys, especially online surveys. In this scenario an original answer of a user is distorted according to a distortion procedure with known parameters and only distorted value of an answer is sent to a centralised database, where it is stored. An original answer is not stored at all. In this case, both a miner and a customer know a distorting procedure and its parameters.

Having collected distorted answers from users, a miner is able to build a model using reconstruction-based techniques and a data mining task can be repeated many times by a miner.

In this scenario a distortion procedure may be implemented in an application on a customer side that distorts a customer's answer and sends only distorted values to a central collector. This application may be built into a web browser in the case of online surveys.

Furthermore, additional distorted respondents' answers can be added to a central distorted database at any time and a data mining process can be repeated over the whole collected data.

The second scenario, that has not been discussed yet, assumes that the original (undistorted) data set is collected, and owned by an authorised organisation, e.g., a local government. Let assume that a survey was conveyed without preserving privacy and the collected data needs to be shared with a foreign untrusted organisation, for instance, when an authorised organisation hires a private company to analyse surveys. An authorised organisation distorts an original data set using a randomisation-based method and passes a distorted data set, a description of a randomisation-based method and its parameters to a foreign organisation. An original data set is not shared.

A foreign organisation knows parameters of a randomisation-based method and a distorted data set, thus it can perform a data mining task on all received data or its part. The results of a data mining/statistical task, e.g., a decision tree and additional analysis, performed by a foreign organisation can be passed to an authorised organisation. An authorised organisation can use the results to classify or cluster respondents and draw conclusions about them.

In both scenarios an untrusted miner knows only a distortion procedure, its parameters and a distorted data set. The result of a data mining/statistical task performed by an untrusted miner is a model built on an aggregate level, e.g., a classifier or calculated statistics.

In the above analysis blocking, aggregation, swapping, and sampling modification methods were omitted due to smaller level of their applicability in electronic surveys. Blocking leads to unknown values that are unwanted in surveys. Aggregation is widely used in surveys, however, it does not provide enough level of privacy [3] and cannot be assumed to be a privacy preserving method that is enough on its own. Nevertheless, the hybrid combination of aggregation and the randomisation-based method can be used. Swapping needs an access to individual values of answers that come from different users and have not been distorted. That is not the assumption that fits in surveys scenario. Sampling could be used, however, regarding the rather small number of consultation participants this method would reduce dataset size to the unaccepted level.

To sum up, the reconstruction-based technique that uses randomisation-based method is most suitable for deliberative consultations. The steps that need to be performed are as follows: get an answer from a user, distort it. For binary and nominal attributes use matrix of retaining/changing values, for continuous attributes employ additive perturbation or retention replacement. Then store data in a centralised database. Based on the distorted data create a model or calculate statistics.

4   Conclusions and Future Work

In this publication the application of privacy preserving techniques to deliberative consultations has been investigated. The focus of this publication is to find state-of-the-art privacy preserving techniques which are the most promising in the context of consultations. Those most promising techniques have been analysed and the setup for deliberative consultations has been proposed.

The results of the analysis suggest that reconstruction-based privacy preserving technique is useful for deliberative consultations and can provide adequate level of privacy in order to encourage residents to participate in surveys which makes consultations valuable.

In future works, it is planned to propose or amend the existing algorithms to create a method most suitable to deliberative consultations.

The incorporation of techniques in the system for deliberative consultations that is being under development is planned too.

It is also planned to investigate the possibility of k-anonymity application in a hybrid solution that combines aggregation, reconstruction-based technique and k-anonymity approach.

References

1. Albrecht, S.: E-consultations: a review of current practice and a proposal for opening up the process. In: Tambouris, E., Macintosh, A., Sæbø, Ø. (eds.) ePart 2012. LNCS, vol. 7444, pp. 13–24. Springer, Heidelberg (2012)
2. Li, X., Yan, Z., Zhang, P.: A review on privacy-preserving data mining. In: 14th IEEE International Conference on Computer and Information Technology, CIT 2014, Xi'an, China, 11–13 September 2014, pp. 769–774. IEEE (2014)
3. Aggarwal, C.C.: Data Mining - The Textbook. Springer, Switzerland (2015)
4. Huai, M., Huang, L., Yang, W., Li, L., Qi, M.: Privacy-preserving naive bayes classification. In: Zhang, S., Wirsing, M., Zhang, Z. (eds.) KSEM 2015. LNCS, vol. 9403, pp. 627–638. Springer, Heidelberg (2015). doi:10.1007/978-3-319-25159-2_57
5. Vaidya, J., Yu, H., Jiang, X.: Privacy-preserving svm classification. Knowl. Inf. Syst. **14**(2), 161–178 (2008)
6. Keyvanpour, M.R., Moradi, S.S.: A perturbation method based on singular value decomposition and feature selection for privacy preserving data mining. IJDWM **10**(1), 55–76 (2014)
7. Andruszkiewicz, P.: Frequent sets discovery in privacy preserving quantitative association rules mining. In: Onieva, E., Santos, I., Osaba, E., Quintian, H., Corchado, E. (eds.) HAIS 2015. LNCS, vol. 9121, pp. 3–15. Springer, Heidelberg (2015)
8. Andruszkiewicz, P.: Hierarchical combining of classifiers in privacy preserving data mining. In: Polycarpou, M., de Carvalho, A.C.P.L.F., Pan, J.-S., Woźniak, M., Quintian, H., Corchado, E. (eds.) HAIS 2014. LNCS, vol. 8480, pp. 573–584. Springer, Heidelberg (2014)
9. Chen, K., Liu, L.: A survey of multiplicative perturbation for privacy-preserving data mining, [14], pp.157–181
10. Chen, K., Liu, L.: Privacy preserving data classification with rotation perturbation. In: ICDM, pp. 589–592. IEEE Computer Society (2005)
11. Liu, K., Giannella, C.M., Kargupta, H.: An attacker's view of distance preserving maps for privacy preserving data mining. In: Fürnkranz, J., Scheffer, T., Spiliopoulou, M. (eds.) PKDD 2006. LNCS (LNAI), vol. 4213, pp. 297–308. Springer, Heidelberg (2006)
12. Agrawal, R., Srikant, R., Thomas, D.: Privacy preserving olap. In: SIGMOD 2005, Proceedings of the 2005 ACM SIGMOD International Conference on Management of Data, pp. 251–262. ACM, New York (2005)
13. Saygin, Y., Verykios, V.S., Clifton, C.: Using unknowns to prevent discovery of association rules. SIGMOD Rec. **30**(4), 45–54 (2001)
14. Aggarwal, C.C., Yu, P.S. (eds.): Privacy-Preserving Data Mining - Models and Algorithms. Advances in Database Systems, vol. 34. Springer, Heidelberg (2008)
15. Domingo-ferrer, J., Mateo-sanz, J.M.: On resampling for statistical confidentiality in contingency tables. Comput. Math. Appl. **38**, 13–32 (1999)
16. Atallah, M.J., Bertino, E., Elmagarmid, A.K., Ibrahim, M., Verykios, V.S.: Disclosure limitation of sensitive rules. In: Proceedings of the IEEE Knowledge and Data Engineering Workshop, pp. 45–52 (1999)
17. Weng, C.C., Chen, S.T., Lo, H.C.: A novel algorithm for completely hiding sensitive association rules. In: Pan, J.S., Abraham, A., Chang, C.C. (eds.) ISDA, vol. 3, pp. 202–208. IEEE Computer Society (2008)
18. Li, X., Liu, Z., Zuo, C.: Hiding association rules based on relative-non-sensitive frequent itemsets. In: Baciu, G., Wang, Y., Yao, Y., Kinsner, W., Chan, K., Zadeh, L.A. (eds.) IEEE ICCI, pp. 384–389. IEEE Computer Society (2009)

19. Modi, C.N., Rao, U.P., Patel, D.R.: An efficient solution for privacy preserving association rule mining. Int. J. Comput. Netw. Secur. **2**(5), 79–85 (2010)
20. Yao, A.C.C.: How to generate and exchange secrets (extended abstract). In: FOCS, pp. 162–167. IEEE (1986)
21. Goldreich, O., Micali, S., Wigderson, A.: How to play any mental game or a completeness theorem for protocols with honest majority. In: STOC, pp. 218–229. ACM (1987)
22. Patsakis, C., Laird, P., Clear, M., Bouroche, M., Solanas, A.: Interoperable privacy-aware e-participation within smart cities. Computer **48**(1), 52–58 (2015)
23. Gentry, C.: Fully homomorphic encryption using ideal lattices. In Mitzenmacher, M. (ed.) STOC, pp. 169–178. ACM (2009)
24. Du, W., Han, Y.S., Chen, S.: Privacy-preserving multivariate statistical analysis: linear regression and classification. In: SDM (2004)
25. Evfimievski, A., Srikant, R., Agrawal, R., Gehrke, J.: Privacy preserving mining of association rules. In: KDD 2002, Proceedings of the Eighth ACM SIGKDD International Conference on Knowledge Discovery and Data Mining, Press, pp. 217–228. ACM, New York (2002)
26. Yang, Z., Zhong, S., Wright, R.N.: Privacy-preserving classification of customer data without loss of accuracy. In: SDM (2005)

Feature Selection Using Approximate Multivariate Markov Blankets

Rafael Arias-Michel[1], Miguel García-Torres[2(✉)], Christian Schaerer[1],
and Federico Divina[2]

[1] Facultad Politécnica, Universidad Nacional de Asunción,
P.O. BOX 2111 SL, San Lorenzo, Paraguay
cshaer@pol.una.py
[2] Computer Science, Universidad Pablo de Olavide, 41013 Seville, Spain
{mgarciat,fdivina}@upo.es

Abstract. In classification tasks, feature selection has become an important research area. In general, the performance of a classifier is intrinsically affected by existence of irrelevant and redundant features. In order to find an optimal subset of features, Markov blanket discovery can be used to identify such subset. The Approximate Markov blanket (AMb) is a standard approach to induce Markov blankets from data. However, this approach considers only pairwise comparisons of features. In this paper, we introduce a multivariate approach to the AMb definition, called Approximate Multivariate Markov blanket (AMMb), which takes into account interactions among different features of a given subset. In order to test the AMMb, we consider a backward strategy similar to the Fast Correlation Based Filter (FCBF), which incorporates our proposal. The resulting algorithm, named as $FCBF_{ntc}$, is compared against the FCBF, Best First (BF) and Sequential Forward Selection (SFS) and tested on both synthetic and real-world datasets. Results show that the inclusion of interactions among features in a subset may yield smaller subsets of features without degrading the classification task.

1 Introduction

In classification problems, the *course of dimensionality* refers to the negative effect on the performance of a classifier when applying on a dataset with too many features. This is due to various reasons, e.g., the search space to explore has a too high dimensionality and that many features may be irrelevant or even redundant, introducing in this way noise in the dataset. In this context, we say that a feature is irrelevant if it does not provide any information on the class, and it is, therefore, not needed for the classification. The problem is how to identify a feature as irrelevant. Different approaches, e.g., [1,2,5,8] have addressed this problem, by considering the relevance of a feature on its contribution to the meaning of the class concept. In this context, feature relevance has arisen as a measure of the amount of relevant information that a feature may contain about the class in classification tasks.

© Springer International Publishing Switzerland 2016
F. Martínez-Álvarez et al. (Eds.): HAIS 2016, LNAI 9648, pp. 114–125, 2016.
DOI: 10.1007/978-3-319-32034-2_10

It follows that, in many cases, a preprocessing phase aimed at the selection of non-redundant and relevant features becomes necessary. Moreover, such a dimensionality reduction would be beneficial also for datasets of lower dimensionality.

Different strategies have been proposed for addressing the above mentioned problems. There are two main approaches used in feature selection: the wrapper and the filter approach [7]. In the wrapper approach, a classifier is used in order to estimate the quality of the selected features. The main advantage of such approach is that the feature selection phase benefits from the direct feedback provided by the classifier. However, the main drawback is that such methods are computationally expensive. Moreover, there is the risk of overfitting. On the other hand, strategies based on the filter approach estimate the quality of the selected features by using some estimations based on the properties of the data, without using any classifiers to this aim. Thus, filter approaches are less computationally expensive than wrapper approaches, and can deal with high-dimension datasets. This fact represents a clear advantage. However, the ausence of a classifier can imply in lower classification results.

The Fast Correlation Based Filter (FCBF) [16] approach has shown excellent performance when applied to high dimensional datasets, being able to select a set of non-redundant and informative features. In particular, this method relies on the concept of Approximate Markov blanket (AMb), proposed in [8] in order to detect redundancy and on the Symmetrical Uncertainty (SU) in order for detecting dependencies among features.

Even if the FCBF has achieved good results, it presents an important limitation: it only considers interaction that can take place between pairs of features, but does not consider interactions among different features. In this work we propose a feature selection strategy that aims at solving this limitation.

Our approach is based on the AMb, and it aims at modifying it in order to consider possible interactions that can exist among different features, and not only interactions among pairs of features. To this aim, we propose to redefine the AMb and use the SU and a normalized version of the total correlation [12,15] (NTC) as cost functions. Then, we use this definition in a variant of the FCBF algorithm denoted as $FCBF_{ntc}$. Results obtained on synthetic and real datasets confirm the effectiveness and potential of the proposed strategy.

The rest of the paper is organized as follows. In Sect. 2 we provide the basements the theoretic foundations of our proposal and a description of $FCBF_{ntc}$. The data used in this work are introduced in Sect. 3. Then, Sect. 4 provides an experimental validation of our proposal. In Sect. 5 we present the main conclusions dentifying possible future developments.

2   Theoretical Foundations

In this paper, we will use the following notation. $\mathcal{X}$ denotes the n dimensional set of features, while $x_i \in \mathcal{X}$ is used for representing its elements. $\mathcal{E}$ stands for the set of samples, and a single sample is represented by the pair (x_i, y_i)

where $y_i \in \mathcal{Y}$ is a known class label of x_i. The classification mapping F is denoted as:

$$F : \mathcal{X} \to \mathcal{Y}. \tag{1}$$

Feature selection can be formulated as the problem of finding a subset of features $\mathcal{S} \subset \mathcal{X}$ that minimizes a given cost function $J(\mathcal{X}, \mathcal{Y})$, with respect to the expression (1), i.e.:

$$\min_{x_i \in \mathcal{X},\, y_i \in \mathcal{Y}} J(x_i, y_i) \tag{2}$$

$$\text{subject to } F(x_i) = y_i. \tag{3}$$

Typically, feature selection algorithms aim at finding a set of features that minimize the cost function $J(\mathcal{X}, \mathcal{Y})$.

Several works [1,2,5,8] have made an effort for classifying the features according to the contribution to the meaning of the class concept. In this context, feature relevance has arisen as a measure of the amount of relevant information that a feature may contain about the class in classification tasks.

In this context, a feature is considered irrelevant if it contains no information about the class and therefore it is not necessary at all for the predictive task. Removing this type of features may improve the predictive model as well as the speed of the learning algorithm. In contrast relevant features are those that embodies information about the class concept. However, for minimizing the error rate it may not be necessary to select all relevant features; as a subset with the most predictive power may be sufficient. Furthermore, such subset of features may not be unique due to redundancy.

In order to identify redundant features, Holler and Sahami [8] proposed to use the concept of feature Markov blanket.

Definition 1 (Markov blanket). *Given a feature x_i, $\mathcal{M}_i \subset \mathcal{X}$ ($x_i \notin \mathcal{M}_i$) is said to be a Markov blanket for x_i iff*

$$P(\mathcal{X} - \mathcal{M}_i - \{x_i\}, \mathcal{Y} \mid x_i, \mathcal{M}_i) = P(\mathcal{X} - \mathcal{M}_i - \{x_i\}, \mathcal{Y} \mid \mathcal{M}_i). \tag{4}$$

According to this definition, a set of features $\mathcal{M}_i$ is a Markov blanket for a feature x_i if x_i is conditionally independent of $\mathcal{X} - \mathcal{M}_i - \{x_i\}$. If so, then x_i is also conditionally independent of $\mathcal{Y}$. Such condition is stronger than the conditional independence between x_i and $\mathcal{Y}$ given $\mathcal{M}_i$. It requires that $\mathcal{M}_i$ subsume not only the information that x_i has about $\mathcal{Y}$ but also about all of the other features. Therefore, given a subset $S \subseteq \mathcal{X}$, a feature $x_i \in S$ can be removed from S if we find a Markov blanket $\mathcal{M}_i$ for x_i within S. In this case we can say that x_i is a redundant feature of S and so removing it from the subset will not affect the predictive power of the classification model.

2.1 Bivariate Approach for Feature Redundancy

Redundancy is generally defined in terms of feature correlation and it is widely accepted that two features are redundant if their values are correlated. However, linear correlations may not be sufficient to detect non-linear dependencies between features. In this work we use a non-linear correlation measure based on entropy. By considering each feature as a random variable, the uncertainty about the values of a random variable (r.v.) X is measured by its entropy $H(X)$, where $H(X)$ is defined as:

$$H(X) := -\sum_i P(x_i) \log_2(P(x_i)), \qquad \forall i = 1, \ldots, n. \tag{5}$$

Given another random variable Y, the conditional entropy $H(X|Y)$ measures the uncertainty about the value of X given the value of Y and is defined as:

$$H(X|Y) := -\sum_j P(y_j) \sum_i P(x_i|y_j) \log_2(P(x_i|y_j)), \tag{6}$$

where $P(y_j)$ is the prior probability of the value y_j of Y, and $P(x_i|y_j)$ is the posterior probability of a given value x_i of variable X given the value of Y. Information Gain [13] of a given variable X with respect to variable Y (IG(Y;X)) measures the reduction in uncertainty about the value of X given the value of Y and is defined as:

$$IG(X|Y) := H(X) - H(X|Y). \tag{7}$$

Therefore IG can be used as correlation measure. For instance, given the random variables X, Y and Z, X is considered to be more correlated to Y than Z, if $IG(Y|X) > IG(Z|X)$. IG is a symmetrical measure; which is a desired property for a correlation measure. However it is biased in favor of r.v. with more values. Such values have to be normalized to ensure the values are comparable with each other. In order to do so, IG can be normalized using the corresponding entropies. To this aim, the Symmetrical Uncertainty (SU) measure can be used:

$$SU(X, Y) := 2 \left[\frac{IG(X|Y)}{H(X) + H(Y)} \right]. \tag{8}$$

SU is preferred to IG since it compensates for IG's bias and restricts its values to the range $[0, 1]$. A value of 1 indicates that X and Y are completely correlated, while a value of 0 indicates that X and Y are independent. Therefore, SU can be used as a correlation measure between features.

Based on the SU correlation measure, authors of [16] introduced the Approximate Markov blanket concept to analyze the feature redundancy:

Definition 2 (Approximate Markov blanket (AMb)). *Given two features X_i and X_j ($i \neq j$) so that $SU(X_j, \mathcal{Y}) \geq SU(X_i, \mathcal{Y})$, and given a class label set $\mathcal{Y}$ then X_j forms an approximate Markov blanket for X_i iff $SU(X_i, X_j) \geq SU(X_i, \mathcal{Y})$.*

Based on the definitions above, the authors proposed the fast correlation based filter - FCBF - algorithm, whose pseudocode is the following:

Algorithm 1. FCBF

Input: $S(X_1, X_2, \ldots, X_N, \mathcal{Y})$ `// a training data set`
      δ `// a predefined threshold`

Output: S_{best} `// a selected subset`

```
 1 begin
 2     for i ← 1 to N do
 3         calculate SU(Xᵢ, 𝒴) for Xᵢ;
 4         if SU(Xᵢ, C) > δ then
 5             append Xᵢ to S'ₗᵢₛₜ;
 6         end if
 7     end for
 8     order S'ₗᵢₛₜ in descending SU(Xᵢ, 𝒴) value;
 9     Xⱼ ← getFirstElement(S'ₗᵢₛₜ);
10     repeat
11         Xᵢ ← getNextElement(S'ₗᵢₛₜ, Xⱼ);
12         if Xᵢ ≠ NULL then
13             repeat
14                 if SU(Xᵢ, Xⱼ) ≥ SU(Xᵢ, 𝒴) then
15                     remove Xᵢ from S'ₗᵢₛₜ;
16                 end if
17                 Xᵢ ← getNextElement(S'ₗᵢₛₜ, Xᵢ);
18             until Xᵢ = NULL;
19         end if
20         Xⱼ ← getNextElement(S'ₗᵢₛₜ, Xⱼ);
21     until Xⱼ = NULL;
22     S_best = S'ₗᵢₛₜ;
23 end
```

As it can be seen, the algorithm starts by ordering the features according to their symmetrical uncertainty with respect to the class. In this step, a feature is considered relevant if it exceeds a predefined threshold. Let X_1 be the first feature from S'_{list}. Then the algorithm verifies if X_1 is a AMb of $X_i (i > 1)$. If it is, then X_i is removed from the set of relevant features. The above process is repeated until there are no features in S'_{list}.

2.2   Multivariate Approach

In order to assess the dependency among features from a subset, the concept of total correlation [12,15] provides an effective way to compute it. Given $X_1, \ldots, X_n$, denoted as $X_{1:n}$, the total correlation is defined as follows:

$$C(X_{1:n}) := \sum_{i=1}^{n} H(X_i) - H(X_{1:n}) \tag{9}$$

with $H(X_{1:n})$ the mulivariate joint entropy. It can be noted that for $n = 2$, the total correlation is equivalent to the bivariate mutual information.

In order to restrict the values of $C(X_{1:n})$ to the range $[0, 1]$, as in the case of SU, we have to normalize. The Normalized Total Correlation (NTC) can be defined as:

$$NTC(X_{1:n}) := \frac{C(X_{1:n}) - C_{min}}{C_{max} - C_{min}} \tag{10}$$

The maximum total correlation occurs when one of the variables determines all of the other variables and is given by Eq. 11, while the minimum is given by Eq. 12.

$$C_{max} := \sum_{i=1}^{n} H(X_i) - \max_{X_i} H(X_i) \tag{11}$$

$$C_{min} := \{0; \sum_{i=1}^{n} H(X_i) - \log_2 m\} \tag{12}$$

With m the sample size. If the sample is large enough, $C_{min} = 0$. However, the number of samples necessary increase exponentially with the number of features. In general samples are not so large and, therefore, $C_{min} \neq 0$. The lower values total correlation can obtain in these cases is given by $C(X_{1:n}) = \sum_{i=1}^{n} H(X_i) - \log_2 m$. However, This expression can be negative if m is large enough. Therefore, we have to select between 0 and the minimum possible value, Now we can use this measure to define the Approximate Multivariate Markov blanket (AMMb) as follows:

Definition 3 (Approximate Multivariate Markov blanket (AMMb)).
Given a feature X_i and a subset S_j ($X_i \notin S_j$), and given a class label $\mathcal{Y}$ then S_j forms an approximate Markov blanket for X_i iff $NTC(X_i, \mathcal{Y}) \leq NTC(X_i, S_j)$.

We can use the AMMb in the FCBF algorithm. The pseudocode of the resulting algorithm, denoted as FCBF$_{ntc}$, is presented in Algorithm 2 and differs, from the original strategy in the us of NTC instead of SU and in the following. Let X_1 be the first feature from S'_{list}. Then the algorithm verifies if X_1 is a AMMb

---

Algorithm 2. FCBF$_{ntc}$

    Input: $S(X_1, X_2, \ldots, X_N, \mathcal{Y})$ // a training data set
          δ // a predefined threshold
    Output: S_{best} // a selected subset

```
1  begin
2  |   for i ← 1 to N do
3  |   |   calculate NTC(Xᵢ, 𝒴) for Xᵢ;
4  |   |   if NTC(Xᵢ, C) > δ then
5  |   |   |   append Xᵢ to S'ₗᵢₛₜ;
6  |   |   end if
7  |   end for
8  |   order S'ₗᵢₛₜ in descending SU(Xᵢ, 𝒴) value;
9  |   Xⱼ ← getFirstElement(S'ₗᵢₛₜ);
10 |   S ← Xⱼ;
11 |   repeat
12 |   |   Xᵢ ← getNextElement(S'ₗᵢₛₜ, Xⱼ);
13 |   |   if Xᵢ ≠ NULL then
14 |   |   |   repeat
15 |   |   |   |   if NTC(Xᵢ, S) ≥ NTC(Xᵢ, 𝒴) then
16 |   |   |   |   |   remove Xᵢ from S'ₗᵢₛₜ;
17 |   |   |   |   end if
18 |   |   |   |   Xᵢ ← getNextElement(S'ₗᵢₛₜ, Xᵢ);
19 |   |   |   until Xᵢ = NULL;
20 |   |   end if
21 |   |   Xⱼ ← getNextElement(S'ₗᵢₛₜ, Xⱼ);
22 |   |   S ← Xⱼ;
23 |   until Xⱼ = NULL;
24 |   S_best = S'ₗᵢₛₜ;
25 end
```

of $X_i(i > 1)$. If it is, then X_i is removed from the set of relevant features. In the second iteration, let X_3 be the next feature from the S'_{list}. Then, the algorithm verifies if $\{X_1, X_3\}$ is a AMMb of $X_i(i > 3)$ and this process is repeated until there are no features in S'_{list}.

3   Data

This section describes the datasets used in this work for assessing the goodness of our proposal. First, we analyze the AMb approach using synthetic data. This kind of data provides a controlled environment scenario for analyzing potencial strengths and limitations of the proposal. In a second step, we tested the proposal on real datasets taken from the UCI repository [11]. The characteristics of the datasets are explained below.

3.1   Synthetic Datasets

We use the LED synthetic data, which consist of 7 boolean features and 10 concepts, the set of decimal digits. LED displays contain 7 light-emitting diodes and so all the 7 features are relevant. We add irrelevant features for testing if the proposal is able to find the relevant ones. We also add noise in order to further test our approach. Given a percentage of noise P_n a feature will have a a probability equal to P_n of being inverted. We generate several versions of this dataset as specified in Table 1.

Table 1. Summary of synthetic datasets.

dataset	#samples	#irr. features	noise (%)
LED	1000	$\{0, 50, 100\}$	$\{0, 10, 20\}$

3.2   UCI Datasets

Table 2 summarises the characteristics of the chosen datasets. The first two columns correspond to the name of the datasets as it appears in the UCI repository and the identifier (id) used in forthcoming tables. The following two columns show the total number of instances and the number of features. Finally, the last column presents the number of labels.

4   Experiments and Results

This section describes the experiments performed for testing our proposal. In particular, the objectives of the experimentation are:

Table 2. Characteristics of the datasets.

Dataset	id	#inst.	#feat.	#labels
Balance scale	bsc	625	4	3
Nursery	nur	12960	8	5
Pima diabetes	pdi	768	8	2
Page blocks	pbl	5473	10	5
Wine	win	178	13	3
Ionosphere	ion	351	34	2
Spambase	spa	4601	57	2
Sonar	son	208	60	2

- to evaluate the proposed multivariate AMb approach and compare it with the original proposal.
- to test the performance of $FCBF_{ntc}$ compared to state of the art algorithms from the feature selection problem.

As already stated, in the first experiment, we use synthetic datasets and analyze the number of relevant features identified, as well as the total number of features selected. Since we want to compare the proposed measure with the orginal one, we compare the FCBF$_{ntc}$ with the FCBF. In the second set of experiments, we considered real world datasets. Classification error, the number of features selected and the robustness of the solutions found are used for assessing the performances of the different strategies tested. 10 fold cross-validation is used in order to assess model quality. In this case we compare the proposal with FCBF, Best First (BF) and Sequential Forward Selection (SFS).

Robustness or stability [6,9,10] of feature subset selection strategies measures the sensitivity to variations of a feature selection algorithm. We quantify the robustness with the Jaccard index [14], which is defined as the size of the intersection divided by the size of the union of the sets. Let A and B be subsets of features such that $A, B \subseteq \mathcal{X}$. The Jaccard index for such subsets $\mathcal{I}_J(A, B)$ is defined as:

$$\mathcal{I}_J(A, B) = \frac{|A \cap B|}{|A \cup B|}. \tag{13}$$

Given a set of solutions $\mathcal{S} = \{S_1, \ldots, S_m\}$, the approach for estimating the stability, $\Sigma(S)$, among this set of solutions consists of averaging the pairwise $\mathcal{I}_J(\cdot, \cdot)$ (Σ) similarities

$$\Sigma(\mathcal{S}) = \frac{2}{m(m-1)} \sum_{i=1}^{m-1} \sum_{j=i+1}^{m} \mathcal{I}_J(S_i, S_j).$$

Higher values correspond to more stable subsets.

For computing the classification error, we use the Naive Bayes classifier due to its popularity and good results achieved. We compare our proposal against the Sequential Forward Selection (SFS) and the Best First (BF) due to their well performance in general. All experiments have been developed using Weka [4], and the source code is available upon request.

Finally, we applied statistical tests to support the conclusions. Following the guidelines proposed by Demšar [3], we apply the Wilcoxon signed-ranks test, which is a non-parametric alternative to the paired t-test.

4.1 Synthetic Datasets

Table 3 shows the results obtained by $FCBF_{ntc}$ and FCBF on synthetic datasets. The first column refers to the number of features. Then, the percentage of noise followed by the number of features selected by each algorithm. As we can see, both algorithms find the 7 relevant features except for FCBF that fails on the first dataset. However, FCBF adds irrelevant features when increasing the complexity of the dataset, both the dimensionality and the noise.

Table 3. Summary of the results achieved by $FCBF_{ntc}$ and FCBF on synthetic datasets.

#feats.	noise (%)	$FCBF_{ntc}$	FCBF
7	0	7	6
	10	7	7
	20	7	7
50	0	7	22
	10	7	23
	20	7	24
100	0	7	30
	10	7	31
	20	7	32

4.2 UCI Datasets

Table 4 presents the accuracy achieved by each feature selection algorithm. The first column refers to the id of the dataset. Then, for each algorithm, the mean accuracy achieved on each dataset is reported, together with its respective standard deviation.

In general, all algorithms show similar results except on the nur, spa and son datasets. On nur, $FCBF_{ntc}$ and FCBF outperform BF and SFS. On spa, BF and SFS achieve better result while on son, FCBF is the best algorithm. However, on average, all algorithms achieve very close values. Moreover, differences are not statistical significant.

The size of the solutions found is presented in Table 5. As it can be noticed, the $FCBF_{ntc}$ is the algorithm the achieves, on average, the higher reduction.

Table 4. Mean accuracy values with their respective standard deviation obtained by NB classifier after applying algorithms $FCBF_{ntc}$, FCBF, BF and SFS.

id	Accuracy			
	$FCBF_{ntc}$	FCBF	BF	SFS
bsc	90.56 ± 1.75	90.56 ± 1.75	90.56 ± 1.75	90.56 ± 1.75
nur	89.90 ± 0.73	90.31 ± 0.50	70.97 ± 1.02	70.97 ± 1.02
pdi	76.17 ± 4.54	77.21 ± 4.18	76.04 ± 4.64	76.04 ± 4.64
hpbl	94.13 ± 0.87	93.20 ± 1.26	94.52 ± 0.52	94.52 ± 0.52
win	97.19 ± 3.96	97.75 ± 3.92	96.67 ± 4.68	96.67 ± 4.68
io	88.61 ± 6.85	89.17 ± 5.00	89.17 ± 6.29	89.17 ± 6.29
spa	79.09 ± 1.58	77.00 ± 1.06	86.70 ± 1.22	86.70 ± 1.22
son	65.76 ± 14.78	70.62 ± 7.54	67.24 ± 8.66	67.24 ± 8.66
mean	85.18	85.73	83.98	83.98
P-val		0.553	0.673	0.673

Only the differences between $FCBF_{ntc}$ and FCBF were found significant with a confidence level of $\alpha = 0.95$.

Finally, the robustness is shown in Table 6. As with the accuracy, all algorithms show similar results. Although on average BF and SFS are more stable, these differences are not statistically significant.

Table 5. Dimensionality reduction achieved, with their respective standard deviation, achieved by algorithms $FCBF_{ntc}$, FCBF, BF and SFS.

id	#features			
	$FCBF_{ntc}$	FCBF	BF	SFS
bsc	4.0 ± 0.00	4.0 ± 0.00	4.0 ± 0.00	4.0 ± 0.00
nur	7.0 ± 0.00	8.0 ± 0.00	1.0 ± 0.00	1.0 ± 0.00
pdi	3.0 ± 0.00	3.8 ± 0.42	3.2 ± 0.42	3.2 ± 0.42
pbl	4.0 ± 0.00	3.7 ± 0.48	6.0 ± 0.00	6.0 ± 0.00
win	4.3 ± 0.67	9.6 ± 0.52	8.2 ± 0.63	7.8 ± 0.92
ion	4.1 ± 0.57	5.3 ± 0.67	12.6 ± 2.27	12.6 ± 2.27
spa	5.0 ± 0.00	15.2 ± 0.92	10.0 ± 0.00	10.0 ± 0.00
son	5.0 ± 0.00	9.6 ± 0.7	17.7 ± 1.42	17.7 ± 1.42
mean	4.55	7.4	7.84	7.79
P-val		0.035	0.151	0.151

Table 6. Robustness achieved by the algorithms $FCBF_{ntc}$, FCBF, BF and SFS.

id	Accuracy			
	$FCBF_{ntc}$	FCBF	BF	SFS
bsc	1.00	1.00	1.00	1.00
nur	1.00	1.00	1.00	1.00
pdi	1.00	0.91	0.91	0.91
pbl	0.92	0.60	1.00	1.00
win	0.79	0.93	0.89	0.82
ion	0.66	0.60	0.58	0.58
spa	1.00	0.91	1.00	1.00
son	0.42	0.57	0.81	0.81
mean	0.85	0.82	0.90	0.89
P-val		0.834	0.590	1.00

5   Conclusions and Future Works

In this work we address the feature selection problem by extending the concept of approximate Markov blanket in order to consider the interaction among subsets of features. We have extended the symmetrical uncertainty measure to the multivariate case by using the total correlation measure.

Results show that the multivariate measure overcomes the limitation of the bivariate one detecting interactions not observable by the bivariate case. As a consecuence, $FCBF_{ntc}$ can find smaller subsets of features with similar predictive power to the bivariate case. Moreover, the robustness of the solution is also similar.

When compared to other popular strategies, our proposal is also competitive as it achieves a similar accuracy and robustness while reducing, on average, the size of the solutions.

As future work, we will study the performance on high dimensional datasets from several domains and study the theoretical properties of the multivariate SU.

Acknowledgment. This work has been partially supported by the project TIN2015-64776-C3-2-R. Miguel García-Torres acknowledges the financial support of CONACyT-Paraguay (14-VIN-009). Christian E. Schaerer acknowledges PRONII-CONACyT-Paraguay. Part of the computer time was provided by the Centro Informático Científico de Andalucía (CIC).

References

1. Bell, D., Wang, H.: A formalism for relevance and its application in feature subset selection. Mach. Learn. **41**(2), 175–195 (2000)
2. Caruana, R., Freitag, D.: How useful is relevance?. In: Working Notes of the AAAI Fall Symposium on Relevance, pp. 25–29 (1994)

3. Demšar, J.: Statistical comparisons of classifiers over multiple data sets. J. Mach. Learn. Res. **7**, 1–30 (2006)
4. Hall, M.A., Frank, E., Holmes, G., Pfahringer, B., Reutemann, P., Witten, I.H.: The WEKA data mining software: An update. SIGKDD Explor. **11**(1), 10–18 (2009)
5. John, G.H., Kohavi, R., Pfleger, K.: Irrelevant features and the subset selection problem. In: Proceedings of the Eleventh International Conference on Machine Learning, pp. 121–1129. Morgan Kaufmann (1994)
6. Kalousis, A., Prados, J., Hilario, M.: Stability of feature selection algorithms: A study on high-dimensional spaces. Knowl. Inf. Syst. **12**(1), 95–116 (2007)
7. Kohavi, R., John, G.H.: Wrappers for feature subset selection. Artif. Intell. **97**(1–2), 273–324 (1997)
8. Koller, D., Sahami, M.: Toward optimal feature selection. In: Proceedings of the Thirteenth International Conference on Machine Learning, pp. 284–292 (1996)
9. Křížek, P., Kittler, J., Hlaváč, V.: Improving stability of feature selection methods. In: Kropatsch, W.G., Kampel, M., Hanbury, A. (eds.) CAIP 2007. LNCS, vol. 4673, pp. 929–936. Springer, Heidelberg (2007)
10. Kuncheva, L.I.: A stability index for feature selection. In: Proceedings of the 25th IASTED International Multi-Conference, pp. 390–395 (2007)
11. Lichman, M.: UCI Machine Learning Repository. Kluwer Academic, Dordrecht (2013)
12. McGill, W.J.: Multivariate information transmission. Trans. IRE Prof. Group Inf. Theor. **4**, 93–111 (1954)
13. Quinlan, J.R.: C4.5: Programs for Machine Learning. Morgan Kaufmann Publishers Inc., San Francisco (1993)
14. Saeys, Y., Abeel, T., Van de Peer, Y.: Robust feature selection using ensemble feature selection techniques. In: Daelemans, W., Goethals, B., Morik, K. (eds.) ECML PKDD 2008, Part II. LNCS (LNAI), vol. 5212, pp. 313–325. Springer, Heidelberg (2008)
15. Watanabe, S.: Information theoretical analysis of multivariate correlation. IBM J. Res. Develop. **4**(1), 66–82 (1960)
16. Yu, L., Liu, H.: Efficient feature selection via analysis of relevance and redundancy. J. Mach. Learn. Res. **5**, 1205–1224 (2004)

Student Performance Prediction Applying Missing Data Imputation in Electrical Engineering Studies Degree

Concepción Crespo-Turrado[1], José Luis Casteleiro-Roca[2(✉)],
Fernando Sánchez-Lasheras[3], José Antonio López-Vázquez[2],
Francisco Javier de Cos Juez[3], José Luis Calvo-Rolle[2],
and Emilio Corchado[4]

[1] Maintenance Department, University of Oviedo,
San Francisco 3, 33007 Oviedo, Spain
[2] Departamento de Ingeniería Industrial,
University of A Coruña, 15405 A Coruña, Spain
jose.luis.casteleiro@udc.es
[3] Department of Construction and Manufacturing Engineering,
University of Oviedo, Campus de Viesques, 33204 Gijón, Spain
[4] Departamento de Informática y Automática, University of Salamanca,
Plaza de la Merced s/n, 37008 Salamanca, Salamanca, Spain

Abstract. Nowadays the student performance and its evaluation is a challenge in general terms. Frequently, the students' scores of a specific curriculum have several fails due to different reasons. In this context, the lack of data of any of student scores adversely affects any future analysis to be done for achieving conclusions. When this occurs, a data imputation process must be performed in order to substitute the data that is missing for estimated values. This paper presents a comparison between two data imputation methods developed by the authors in previous researches, the Adaptive Assignation Algorithm (AAA) based on Multivariate Adaptive Regression Splines (MARS) and other technique called Multivariate Imputation by Chained Equations (MICE). The results obtained demonstrate that the proposed methods allow good results, specially the AAA algorithm.

Keywords: Student performance · Data imputation · MARS · MICE · AAA

1 Introduction

According with the guidance of quality assurance systems under the European Higher Education Area (EHEA), the studies tracking is regulated under a legal point of view, and of course is obligatory for official university degrees [1]. Under this point of view, the internal quality systems of the educational institutions, with the aim of on-going improvement, try to enhance their quality ratios or indicators in terms of academic results and performance [2]. This fact causes that the faculties or higher education schools need tools to support or assists on this task [3, 4].

© Springer International Publishing Switzerland 2016
F. Martínez-Álvarez et al. (Eds.): HAIS 2016, LNAI 9648, pp. 126–135, 2016.
DOI: 10.1007/978-3-319-32034-2_11

As a previous work for achieving a tool for making decisions, usually, it is necessary a way to obtain the required knowledge. Traditionally, in past research works, the common method is to obtain a model based on a dataset of the historical, well through traditional techniques or through other ones more advanced [5–8].

The above method could be a problem in general terms, given the need to have previous cases with a similar performance [9–13]. Also, it is necessary remark that the case under study could change. If it is the case, the model must be adaptive for the novel cases with different casuistic and performance [14–17]. In this sense, the imputation methods based on evolutionary methods could be a good solution to accomplish the present described problem.

This paper evaluates two imputation methods, which allows the system to fill in the missing data of any of the students' scores that are used in this research. One of the algorithms, the AAA (Adaptive Assignation Algorithm) [18], is based on Multivariate adaptive regression splines and the other one is the MICE (Multivariate Imputation by Chained Equations) [19]. The first one has a good performance in general terms, when the percentage of missing data for a case is reduced; when the sample is not in that way, the second method is more appropriate. The right combination of the both algorithms is a good solution that requires to stablish the border application of both.

This paper is structured in the following way. After the present section, the case of study is described, it consist on the students' scores dataset of the Electrical Engineering Studies Degree of the University of A Coruña. Then, the techniques for missing data imputation are shown. The results section shows the achieved outcomes with the imputation over the dataset for three different cases over the case of study. After that, the conclusions and future works are presented.

2   Case of Study

The students' scores in the Electrical Engineering Studies Degree of the University of A Coruña compose the dataset used in this research since course 2001/2002 until 2008/2009. The dataset includes the scores for each subject in the degree; nine subjects in the first year, another nine in the second year, seven in the last year, and the final project.

The data also includes the scores and the way to access to the University studies; in Spain, there are two different ways, from secondary school or from vocational education and training. Moreover, the scores for the subjects in the degree include not only the mark; the times used to pass each subject is also include.

The dataset under study has all the data. It is an important fact to test the performance of the used algorithms on this study. It will be possible to emulate several different percentages of missing values, and compare the both methods with the aim to stablish the right frontier of the both methods application. Then, with the combination, it will be obtained a hybrid model to increase the applicability of the method in a wide range of possibilities.

3   The Used Data Imputation Techniques

In this section the data imputation techniques employed on the present research are described.

3.1   The MICE Algorithm

The MICE algorithm developed by van Buuren and Groothuis-Oudshoorn [20] is a Markov Chain Monte Carlo Method where the state space is the collection of all imputed values. Like any other Markov Chain, in order to converge, the MICE algorithm needs to satisfy the three following properties [21–23]:

- Irreducible: The chain must be able to reach all parts of the state space.
- Aperiodic: The chain should not oscillate between different states.
- Recurrence: Any Markov chain can be considered as recurrent if the probability that the Markov chain starting from i will return to i is equal to one.

In practice, the convergence of the MICE algorithm is achieved after a relatively low number of iterations, usually somewhere between 5 and 20 [23]. According to the experience of the algorithm creator, in general, five iterations are enough, but some special circumstances would require a greater number of iterations. In the case of the present research, and due to the performance of the results obtained when compared with the other methods applied, five iterations were considered to be enough. This number of iterations is much lower than in other applications of the Markov Chain Monte Carlo methods, which often require thousands of iterations. In spite of these, and from a researcher point of view and experience, it must be also remarked that in the most common of the applications each iteration of the MICE algorithm would take several minutes or even a few hours. Furthermore, the duration of each iteration is mainly linked with the number of variables involved in the calculus and not with the number of cases. It must be taken into consideration that imputed data can have a considerable amount of random noise, depending on the strength of the relations between the variables. So in those cases in which there are low correlations among variables or they are completely independent, the algorithm convergence will be faster. Finally, high rates of missing data (20 % or more) would slow down the convergence process work. The MICE algorithm [23] for the imputation of multivariate missing data consist on the following steps:

1. Specify an imputation model $P(Y_j^{mis}|Y_j^{obs}, Y_{-j}, R)$ for variable Y_j with $j = 1, \ldots, p$
   The MICE algorithm obtains the posterior distribution of R by sampling interactive from the above represented conditional formula. The parameters R are specific to the respective conditional densities and are not necessarily the product of a factorization of the true joint distribution.
2. For each j, fill in starting imputation Y_j^0 by random draws from Y_j^{obs}

3. peat for $t = 1, \ldots, T$ (iterations)
4. Repeat for $j = 1, \ldots, p$ (variables)
5. Define $Y^t_{-j} = (Y^t_1, \ldots, Y^t_{j-1}, Y^{t-1}_{j+1}, \ldots, Y^{t-1}_p)$ as the currently complete data except Y_j
6. Draw $\emptyset^t_j \sim P\left(\emptyset^t_j | Y^{obs}_j, Y^t_{-j}, R\right)$
7. Draw imputations $Y^t_j \sim P\left(Y^{mis}_j | Y^{obs}_j, Y^t_{-j}, R, \emptyset^t_j\right)$
8. End repeat j
9. End repeat t

In the algorithm referred to, Y represents a $n \times p$ matrix of partially-observed sample data, R is a $n \times p$ matrix, 0–1 response indicators of Y, and $\emptyset$ represents the parameters space. Please note that in MICE imputation [24], initial guesses for all missing elements are provided for the $n \times p$ matrix of partially observed sample. For each variable with missing elements, the data are divided into two subsets, one of them containing all the missing data. The subset with all available data is regressed on all other variables. Then, the missing subset is predicted from the regression and the missing values are replaced with those obtained from the regression. This procedure is repeated for all variables with missing elements. After this, all the missing elements are imputed according to the algorithm explained above, the regression and predictions are repeated until the stop criterion is reached. In this case, until a certain number of consecutive iterates fall within the specified tolerance for each of the imputed values.

3.2   The AAA Algorithm

In order to explain the AAA, let's assume that we have a dataset formed by n different variables $v_1, v_2, \ldots, v_n$. In order to calculate the missing values of the i-th column, all the rows with no missing value in the said column are employed. Then, a certain number of MARS models are calculated. It is possible to find rows with very different amounts of missing data from 0 (no missing data) to n (all values are missing). Those columns with all values missing will be removed and will be neither used for the model calculation nor imputed. Therefore any amount of missing data from 0 to $n - 2$ is feasible (all variables but one with missing values).

In other words, if the dataset is formed by variables $v_1, v_2, \ldots, v_n$ and we want to estimate the missing values in column v_i, then the maximum number of different MARS models that would be computed for this variable (and in general for each column) is as follows: $\sum_{k=1}^{n-1} \binom{n-1}{k}$. For the case of the data under study in this research, with 10 different variables, a maximum of 5,110 distinct MARS models would be trained (511 for each variable).

After the calculation of all the available models, the missing data of each row will be calculated using those models that employ all the available non-missing variables of the row. In those cases in which no model was calculated, the missing data will be replaced by the median of the column. Please note in that the case of large data sets with a not-too-high percentage of missing data, these will be an unfrequent case. As a general rule for the algorithm, it has been decided that when certain value can be estimated using more than one MARS model, it must be estimated using the MARS model with the largest number of input variables; the value would be estimated by any of those models chosen at random. Finally, in those exceptional cases in which no model is available for estimation, the median value of the variable will be used for the imputation.

3.3   Models Validation

Leave-one-out cross-validation has been used to analyze the spatial error of interpolated data [25, 26]. This procedure involves using eight of the nine stations in the model to obtain the estimated value in the ninth station (this one is left out) in order to calculate Mean Square Error RMSE and Mean Absolute Error (MAE) for this station. The process is repeated nine times, once for each station.

The performance of the three methods has been evaluated using common statistics: Root RMSE, MAE:

$$RMSE = \sum\nolimits_{i=1}^{n} \sqrt{\frac{1}{n}(\widehat{G_i} - G_i)^2} \tag{1}$$

$$MAE = \frac{1}{n}\sum\nolimits_{i=1}^{n} \left|\widehat{G_i} - G_i\right| \tag{2}$$

$$RMSE(\%) = \frac{RMSE}{\frac{1}{n}\sum_{i=1}^{n} G_i} \times 100 \tag{3}$$

$$MAE(\%) = \frac{MAE}{\frac{1}{n}\sum_{i=1}^{n} G_i} \times 100 \tag{4}$$

where G_i and $\widehat{G_i}$ are the measurements and the model-estimated, and n is the number of data points of the validation set. The RMSE weights large estimation errors more strongly than small errors and it is considered a very important model validation metric. Also, MAE is a useful complement of the measured-modeled scatter plot near the 1-to-1 line [24].

4   Results

To calculate the performance of each algorithm, several test where made with different quantity of missing data. First of all, it is necessary to remark that, for the results show in the tables, only ten columns of the total dataset have been taking into account. Each column represents a different subject, and the selection was made randomly. In all tests, the percentage of missing data is always the same, 10 %, but the real missing data was varied from 1 to more than three, depending on the test.

Table 1 shows the performance of each algorithm with only 1 value missing in each case. It is possible to appreciate that the AAA algorithm is clearly better than MICE.

Table 1. Results for algorithm with 1 missing value

	MAE		MAD		RMSE	
	MICE	AAA	MICE	AAA	MICE	AAA
Column 1	0,15013	3,33e-15	0,07413	1,32e-15	0,25495	3,41e-15
Column 2	1,00e-03	1,11e-15	1,20e-03	0	0,00325	1,17e-15
Column 3	2,10e-03	8,44e-15	1,01e-03	1,25e-14	0,00247	8,45e-15
Column 4	0,07502	7,77e-15	0,07412	1,98e-15	0,11180	7,93e-15
Column 5	0,07503	5,11e-15	1,53e-03	0	0,15019	5,12e-15
Column 6	1,01734	5,11e-15	1,40805	1,32e-15	1,20623	5,24e-15
Column 7	0,19235	6,66e-16	2,36e-03	0	0,21015	1,33e-15
Column 8	0,02492	1,78e-15	0,02313	1,32e-15	0,04502	1,99e-15
Column 9	1,25013	1,55e-15	1,48260	0	1,36931	1,60e-15
Column 10	0,75024	2,89e-15	0,88956	0	0,90135	2,91e-15

In Table 2, the performance was calculated for 2 missing values. In this case, as in the previous one, the AAA algorithm is clearly better than MICE, but the different between each algorithm performance is reduced.

Table 2. Results for algorithm with 2 of missing values

	MAE		MAD		RMSE	
	MICE	AAA	MICE	AAA	MICE	AAA
Column 1	0,22265	5,08e-05	0,11597	5,82e-05	0,35759	4,90e-06
Column 2	0,09623	8,26e-05	0,10724	4,36e-05	0,03246	4,08e-05
Column 3	0,01146	9,28e-05	0,03063	3,00e-06	0,02834	4,16e-05
Column 4	0,11066	6,47e-05	0,08836	5,62e-05	0,16341	6,84e-05
Column 5	0,12991	3,09e-05	0,04132	2,92e-05	0,22379	9,68e-05
Column 6	1,07473	7,28e-06	1,43598	3,69e-05	1,23973	5,79e-05
Column 7	0,26962	4,01e-05	0,09282	5,15e-05	0,22093	8,40e-05
Column 8	0,10302	6,47e-05	0,07025	3,14e-05	0,05451	7,37e-05
Column 9	1,34970	1,13e-05	1,49259	2,32e-05	1,46712	4,40e-05
Column 10	0,80736	6,71e-05	0,96982	2,71e-06	0,94504	9,29e-05

The results present in Table 3, shows that when the missing values increase until 3, the MICE algorithm has better performance than the AAA.

With the aim to obtain the best results, a hybrid of the two algorithms was accomplished. The results of this hybrid system are shown in Table 4. In this table, the percentage of missing values is fixed to 10 %, but the number of missing values is random. When the missing values are less than 3 the algorithm selected is the AAA, and the MICE is the chosen one in the other cases.

Table 3. Results for algorithm with 3 of missing values

	MAE		MAD		RMSE	
	MICE	AAA	MICE	AAA	MICE	AAA
Column 1	0,29825	1,29788	0,21251	0,97760	0,37785	0,33879
Column 2	0,10030	0,32404	0,23003	0,68342	0,08148	0,88620
Column 3	0,23256	0,76501	0,14919	1,28895	0,06039	1,19963
Column 4	0,22723	1,01881	0,21624	0,30309	0,32788	1,18293
Column 5	0,18359	0,66619	0,13611	0,46380	0,29628	0,84689
Column 6	1,14205	0,93627	1,61320	1,10473	1,36929	0,91176
Column 7	0,37556	0,78123	0,10937	0,68277	0,32463	0,72429
Column 8	0,14983	1,18887	0,14077	1,05084	0,06936	0,42409
Column 9	1,44081	1,01170	1,56163	1,21070	1,49719	0,94814
Column 10	0,89382	0,94070	1,01722	0,32494	1,09256	1,19549

Table 4. Results for algorithm with random missing values and hybrid combination

	MAE		MAD		RMSE	
	MICE	AAA	MICE	AAA	MICE	AAA
Column 1	0,23592	4,66e-03	0,12653	4,87e-03	0,32118	8,18e-03
Column 2	0,04535	3,35e-03	0,10256	4,34e-03	0,11206	9,72e-03
Column 3	0,06909	8,09e-03	0,04011	1,03e-03	0,10750	1,72e-03
Column 4	0,18674	5,70e-03	0,12873	1,47e-03	0,13867	6,75e-03
Column 5	0,13655	6,68e-05	0,10169	5,25e-03	0,22239	7,44e-03
Column 6	1,11443	4,64e-03	1,41752	4,09e-03	1,30626	3,11e-03
Column 7	0,23217	6,50e-03	0,10877	8,66e-03	0,23569	7,44e-03
Column 8	0,09843	5,59e-03	0,12228	3,51e-03	0,14228	4,42e-03
Column 9	1,33824	6,13e-03	1,58086	7,90e-03	1,39444	6,70e-03
Column 10	0,85448	7,54e-04	0,94990	6,71e-03	0,91529	5,02e-03

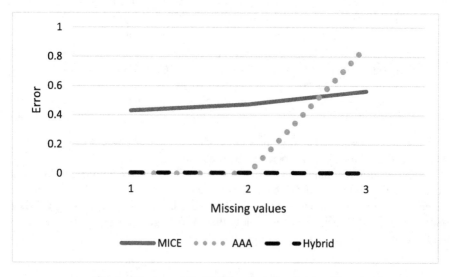

Fig. 1. Plotting of the RMSE values for the algorithms

Figure 1 shows the evolution of the RMSE for the two algorithms and the hybrid combination. The hybrid algorithm is not the best one for every case, but has the values for the RMSE constant independently on the number of missing values. The blue continued line represents the MICE algorithm; the red dotted line means the AAA algorithm, and the black dashed line is the combined algorithm results.

5 Conclusions

Very good results have been obtained in general terms with the data imputation techniques employed on this study.

It is possible to predict the scores of the students for the three cases contemplated, assuming the data do not exist, and comparing the estimate results with the real dataset. The average of RMSE for MICE was 0.50759 varying from 2.47e-3 to 1.54849; for AAA, the average of RMSE was 0.29130 with a minimum of 3.11e-31 and a maximum of 1.29216. The hybrid combination of these two algorithms achieved 4.92e-3 as average of RMSE, varying from 4.26e-5 to 9.72e-3.

These techniques could be used to predict lacks data and then, accomplish studies about students' performance taken into account all the cases.

In future research the use of support vector machines (SVM) [26, 27] and hybrid methods [28–30] will be explored by the authors in order to find a new algorithm with even higher performance.

Acknowledgments. Authors appreciate support from the Spanish Economics and Competitiveness Ministry, through grant AYA2014-57648-P and the Government of the Principality of Asturias (Consejería de Economía y Empleo), through grant FC-15-GRUPIN14-017.

References

1. http://www.ehea.info/
2. Francisco, H.G.: Ferreira and jérémie gignoux. the measurement of educational inequality: achievement and opportunity. World Bank Econ. Rev. **28**(2), 210–246 (2014). first published online February 20, 2013 doi:10.1093/wber/lht004
3. Grissom, J.A., Kalogrides, D., Loeb, S.: Using student test scores to measure principal performance. Educ. Eval. Policy Anal. **37**, 3–28 (2015). first published on March 10, 2014 doi:10.3102/0162373714523831
4. López-Vázquez, J.A., Orosa, J.A., Calvo-Rolle, J.L., Cos Juez, F.J., Castelerio-Roca, J.L., Costa, A.M.A: New way to improve subject selection in engineering degree studies. In: International Joint Conference: CISIS 2015 and ICEUTE 2015 (2015) doi:10.1007/978-3-319-19713-5_47
5. Kokkinos, C.M., Kargiotidis, A., Markos, A.: The relationship between learning and study strategies and big five personality traits among junior university student teachers. Learn. Individ. Differ. **43**, 39–47 (2015). ISSN 1041-6080, doi: 10.1016/j.lindif.2015.08.031
6. Freeman, S., Eddy, S.L., McDonough, M., Smith, M.K., Okoroafor, N., Jordt, H., Wenderoth, M.P.: Active learning increases student performance in science, engineering, and mathematics. Proc. Nat. Acad. Sci. **111**(23), 8410–8415 (2014)

7. Cook, W.D., Tone, K., Zhu, J.: Data envelopment analysis: Prior to choosing a model. Omega **44**, 1–4 (2014). ISSN 0305-0483, http://dx.doi.org/10.1016/j.omega.2013.09.004

8. Anderman, E.M., Gimbert, B., O'Connell, A.A., Riegel, L.: Approaches to academic growth assessment. Br. J. Educ. Psychol. **85**(2), 138–153 (2015)

9. Calvo-Rolle, J.L., Machón-Gonzalez, I., López-Garcia, H.: Neuro-robust controller for non-linear systems. Dyna **86**(3), 308–317 (2011). doi:10.6036/3949

10. Ghanghermeh, A., Roshan, G., Orosa, J.A., Calvo-Rolle, J.L., Costa, Á.M.: New climatic indicators for improving urban sprawl: a case study of Tehran City. Entropy **15**(3), 999–1013 (2013)

11. Alaiz Moretón, H., Calvo Rolle, J.L., García, I., Alonso Alvarez, A.: Formalization and practical implementation of a conceptual model for PID controller tuning. Asian J. Control **13**(6), 773–784 (2011)

12. Casteleiro-Roca, J.L., Calvo-Rolle, J.L., Meizoso-López, M.C., Piñón-Pazos, A.J., Rodríguez-Gómez, B.A.: Bio-inspired model of ground temperature behavior on the horizontal geothermal exchanger of an installation based on a heat pump. Neurocomputting **150**, 90–98 (2015)

13. Casteleiro-Roca, J.L., Quintián, H., Calvo-Rolle, J.L., Corchado, E., Meizoso-López, M.C., Piñón-Pazos, A.: An intelligent fault detection system for a heat pump installation based on a geothermal heat exchanger. J. Appl. Logic (2015)

14. Osborn, J., CosJuez, F.J., Guzman, D., Butterley, T., Myers, R., Guesalaga, A.: Using artificial neural networks for open-loop tomography. Opt. Express **20**(3), 2420–2434 (2012)

15. Guzmán, D., Cos Juez, F.J., Myers, R., Guesalaga, A., Sánchez-Lasheras, F.: Modeling a MEMS deformable mirror using non-parametric estimation techniques. Opt. Express **18**(20), 21356–21369 (2010)

16. Cos Juez, F.J., Sánchez-Lasheras, F., García Nieto, P.J., Suárez Suárez, M.A.: A new data mining methodology applied to the modelling of the influence of diet and lifestyle on the value of bone mineral density in post-menopausal women. Int. J. Comput. Math. **86**(10–11), 1878–1887 (2009)

17. García Nieto, P.J., Alonso Fernández, J.R., Sánchez Lasheras, F., Cos Juez, F.J., Díaz Muñiz, C.: A new improved study of cyanotoxins presence from experimental cyanobacteria concentrations in the Trasona reservoir (Northern Spain) using the MARS technique. Sci. Total Environ. **430**, 88–92 (2012)

18. Crespo Turrado, C., Sánchez Lasheras, F., Calvo-Rolle, J.L., Piñón-Pazos, A.J., de Cos Juez, F.J.: A new missing data imputation algorithm applied to electrical data loggers. Sensors **15**, 31069–31082 (2015). doi:10.3390/s151229842

19. Turrado, C., López, M., Lasheras, F., Gómez, B., Rollé, J., Juez, F.: Missing data imputation of solar radiation data under different atmospheric conditions. Sensors 14 (2014). doi:10.3390/s141120382

20. Van Buuren, S., Groothuis-Oudshoorn, K.: Mice: multivariate imputation by chained equations in R. J. Stat. Softw. **45**, 3 (2011)

21. Tierny, L.: Introduction to general state-space Markov chain theory. In: Gilks, W.R., Richardson, S., Spiegelhalter, D.J. (eds.) Markov Chain Monte Carlo in Practice, pp. 59–71. Chapman & Hall, London (1996)

22. Van Buuren, S.: Flexible Imputation of Missing Data. Chapman & Hall/CRC, London, UK (2012)

23. Liu, Y., Brown, S.D.: Comparison of five iterative imputation methods for multivariate classification. Chemom. Intell. Lab. **120**, 106–115 (2013)

24. Perez, R., Lorenz, E., Pelland, S., Beauharnois, M., van Knowe, G., Hemker, K., Heinemannb, D., Remunde, J., Müllere, S.C., Traunmüllerf, W., et al.: Comparison of numerical weather prediction solar irradiance forecasts in the US. Can. Eur. Sol. Energy **94**, 305–326 (2013)

25. Gutierrez-Corea, F.V., Manso-Callejo, M.A., Moreno-Regidor, M.P., Velasco-Gómez, J.: Spatial estimation of sub-hour global horizontal irradiance based on official observations and remote sensors. Sensors **14**, 6758–6787 (2014)

26. Tiengrod, P., Wongseree, W.: A comparison of spatial interpolation methods for surface temperature in Thailand. In: Proceedings of the International Computer Science and Engineering Conference (ICSEC), Nakorn Pathom, Thailand, 4–6 September 2013, pp. 174–178

27. Liu, Y., Brown, S.D.: Comparison of five iterative imputation methods for multivariate classification. Chemom. Intell. Lab. Syst. 120 (2013) doi:10.1016/j.chemolab.2012.11.010

28. García Nieto, P.J., Alonso Fernández, J.R., de Cos Juez, F.J., Sánchez Lasheras, F., Díaz Muñiz, C.: Hybrid modelling based on support vector regression with genetic algorithms in forecasting the cyanotoxins presence in the Trasona reservoir (Northern Spain). Environ. Res. 122 (2013) doi:10.1016/j.envres.2013.01.001

29. Quintian, H., Calvo-Rolle, J.L., Corchado, E.: A hybrid regression system based on local models for solar energy prediction. Informatica. 25 (2014) doi:10.15388/Informatica. 2014.14

30. Manuel Vilar-Martinez, X., Montero-Sousa, J.A., Calvo-Rolle, J.L., Casteleiro-Roca, J.L.: Expert system development to assist on the verification of "TACAN" system performance. Dyna. 89 (2014) doi:10.6036/5756

Accuracy Increase on Evolving Product Unit Neural Networks via Feature Subset Selection

Antonio J. Tallón-Ballesteros[1,2]([✉]), José C. Riquelme[2], and Roberto Ruiz[1]

[1] Area of Computer Science, Pablo de Olavide University, Seville, Spain
ajtalbal@upo.es
[2] Department of Languages and Computer Systems,
University of Seville, Seville, Spain

Abstract. A framework that combines feature selection with evolutionary artificial neural networks is presented. This paper copes with neural networks that are applied in classification tasks. In machine learning area, feature selection is one of the most common techniques for preprocessing the data. A set of filters have been taken into consideration to assess the proposal. The experimentation has been conducted on nine data sets from the UCI repository that report test error rates about fifteen percent or above with reference classifiers such as C4.5 or 1-NN. The new proposal significantly improves the baseline framework, both approaches based on evolutionary product unit neural networks. Also several classifiers have been tried in order to illustrate the performance of the different methods considered.

1 Introduction

Many techniques addressing the classification problem [1] have been presented by the machine learning community. Depending on the nature of the algorithm we can distinguish, among others, neural networks, rule-based classifiers and decision trees. Neural networks models play an important role in pattern recognition [13]. The possible inputs to an Artificial Neural Network (ANN) could be extremely large in the context of many practical problems. There may be some redundancy among different inputs. A huge number of inputs to an ANN increase its size and thus require more training data and longer training times in order to achieve reasonable generalization ability. Pre-processing is often needed to reduce the number of inputs to an ANN.

This paper aims at improving the accuracy and getting simpler neural models with a lower number of inputs and, if possible, containing a lower number of hidden neurons. The kind of the neural networks that are in the scope of the current work are feed-forward neural networks composed by product units in the hidden layer. Basically, the training of the models is carried out by an evolutionary programming algorithm [4]. More concretely we utilise a framework following a master-slave approach, where the master distributes a configuration to slave processes. A preliminary study of this base approach is described in [16].

© Springer International Publishing Switzerland 2016
F. Martínez-Álvarez et al. (Eds.): HAIS 2016, LNAI 9648, pp. 136–148, 2016.
DOI: 10.1007/978-3-319-32034-2_12

Now, the novel ingredient is a preprocessing phase prior to the training of the classification models.

The remainder of this paper is organised as follows: Sect. 2 describes some concepts about the training of Product Unit Neural Networks (PUNNs), the experimental design distribution and feature selection; Sect. 3 presents proposal; Sect. 4 details the conducted experimentation; then Sect. 5 shows and analyzes the results obtained; finally, Sect. 6 states the concluding remarks.

2   Methodology

2.1   Product Unit Neural Networks and Training Procedure

Among the different types of neural network architectures, the most popular are feed-forward ones. Within this kind, single hidden-layer networks are very powerful due to their universal approximation property. Multiplicative ANNs [17] contain nodes that multiply their inputs instead of adding them. This class of networks comprises such types as sigma-pi networks and product unit neural networks. The latter type was introduced by R. Durbin and D. Rumelhart [5] and is the study object of the current paper. The training of the neural networks is performed by means of an evolutionary programming algorithm to simultaneously learn the architecture and weights of the PUNN classification model. The neural network topology is a three-layer architecture, with k (number of features of the problem at hand) nodes in the input layer, m ones and a bias one in the hidden layer and a number of nodes equals to the number of classes minus one in the output layer. The m value is determined by the training algorithm. The transfer function of each node in the hidden and output layers is the identity function. We have considered a standard soft-max activation function, associated with the g network model with J classes, given by:

$$g_j(\mathbf{x}) = \frac{exp\, f_j(\mathbf{x})}{\sum_{j=1}^{J} exp\, f_j(\mathbf{x})} \quad j = 1, ..., J \tag{1}$$

where $f_j(\mathbf{x})$ is the output of node j for pattern $\mathbf{x}$ and $g_j(\mathbf{x})$ is the probability that this pattern belongs to class j. Given a training set $D = (x_i, yi)\ i = 1, ..., N$, a function of cross-entropy error is used to evaluate a network g with the instances of a problem, which is reflected in the following expression:

$$l(g) = -\frac{1}{N} \sum_{i=1}^{N} \sum_{j=1}^{J} (y_i^j ln(g_j(\mathbf{x}_i))) \tag{2}$$

and substituting g_j defined in (2),

$$l(g) = -\frac{1}{N} \sum_{i=1}^{N} \left(-\sum_{j=1}^{J} y_i^j f_j(\mathbf{x_i}) + ln(\sum_{j=1}^{J} exp\, f_j(\mathbf{x}_i)) \right) \tag{3}$$

where y_i^j is the target value for class j with pattern $\mathbf{x_i}$ ($y_i^j = 1$ if $\mathbf{x_i} \in$ class j and $y_i^j = 0$ otherwise), $f_j(\mathbf{x_i})$ is the output value of the neural network for the output neuron j with pattern $\mathbf{x_i}$. Observe that soft-max transformation produces probabilities that sum to one and therefore the outputs can be interpreted as the conditional probability of class membership. Thus, the number of nodes in the output layer is equal to the number of classes minus one in the problem.

Since the EA objective is to minimize the chosen error function, a fitness function is used in the form $A(g) = (1 + l(g))^{-1}$.

The main issues about the evolutionary training algorithm are briefly explained next. The search begins with a random initial population and, for each iteration, the population is modified using a population-update algorithm founded on parametric and structural mutations. The algorithm loops are repeated until the maximum number of generations, in each case, is reached or until the best individual or the population mean fitness does not improve during $gen - without - improving$ (20 in this paper) generations. The population is subjected to the operations of replication and mutation. More details and common parameter values of the algorithm are found in [16]. Crossover is not used due to its potential disadvantages in evolving artificial networks. With these properties the algorithm falls into the class of evolutionary programming.

2.2   Experimental Design Distribution

The starting framework of the current work is named Experimental Design Distribution (EDD) and follows a master-slave programming model. The master process prepares a base configuration that is distributed to all the slave processes that update the received configuration. Depending on the identity of the slave the task to be performed is different in the sense that may act on a concrete parameter doing a specific operation with a single value of the base configuration. Next, each process of every type runs the training algorithm described in the previous subsection using the proper (base/updated) configuration. The advantage of this framework is that a single configuration file and the number of slaves to be spawned is required. EDD is able to distribute two or three parameters over a maximum of eight computing nodes, that is, each process is mapped to one processor that is used in a exclusive way. We may have one master and seven slave processes. This is the first approach published in [16]. There we came to the empirical conclusion that is very useful to distribute three parameters. From the eight configurations of that proposal, the configurations that do not reduce the number of generations get better results. This fact motivates us to only consider hereinafter the first four configurations of the approach delivering three parameters among the processing system. In other words, it is just the same that asserting that the maximum number of neurons in the hidden layer and the parameter value associated with the parametrical mutation are distributed among four computation nodes.

2.3   Feature Selection

Feature selection may be defined as the problem of picking up a subset of features that are necessary and sufficient to describe the target concept [9]. A taxonomy of the feature selection algorithms may be based on the attribute evaluation measure: depending on the type (filter or wrapper technique) or on the way that features are evaluated (individual or subset evaluation). The filter model relies on general characteristics of the data (such as consistency, correlation and distance) to assess and select feature subsets without involving any data mining algorithm. The wrapper model requires a predetermined mining algorithm and uses its performance as evaluation criterion. This paper pays attention to feature subset selection implemented as filters. In this context, it is a fact that two kinds of features are generally perceived as being unnecessary: features that are irrelevant to the target concept, and features that are redundant given other features. BIRS (Best Incremental Ranked Subset [15]) method was proposed in a previous work to obtain relevant features and to remove redundancy. These features selected are considered as input variables to the network models that we get in this paper via EDD framework. Since BIRS belongs to a hybrid category, the selection process does not follow the typical paths and is divided into two phases: in the first one, features are evaluated individually, providing a ranking based on a criterion; in phase two, a feature subset evaluator is applied to a certain number of features in the previous ranking according to a search strategy. BIRS can use any evaluator in the two stages. In the current contribution, BIRS uses as a subset evaluator CFS (Correlation-based Feature Selection [6]) and CNS (CoNSistency based measure [10] -that are established on correlation and consistency concepts- at the second phase, and SOAP (Selection Of Attributes by Projection [14]) measure and the own subset evaluator at the first phase as a ranking evaluator. Thus, in the experiments, spBI_CNS indicates that SOAP is utilised as an individual measure in the first part of BIRS, and CNS is employed as a subset evaluator in the second part. In the same way, cfBI_CFS denotes that CFS evaluator will be used in both part of the BIRS algorithm.

3   Proposal Description

The current paper introduces *Experimental Design Distribution with Feature Selection* (EDDFS) framework, a combination of some FS methods, one by one independently, with EDD. First of all, some feature selectors are applied in an independent way to the training set of all data sets in order to obtain a list of attributes, for each of them, that it is considered for training and test phases. In this way, two subsets (training and test subset) are generated, where only most relevant features are included. It is important to remark that the feature selection is performed only with training data; the test subset has exactly the same features as the reduced training set. These subsets are taken as input to the evolutionary algorithm. EDDFS methodology operates with four feature selectors. As a result of the FS stage, a list of relevant features is obtained with each of the FS methods for each data set. The EDDFS properties are the

Table 1. Configurations of the EDD (baseline) and EDDFS frameworks

Framework								
	EDD				EDDFS			
♯$Configuration$	1	2	3	4	$1'$	$2'$	$3'$	$4'$
♯$Neurons$ (**neu**)	neu	$neu+1$	neu	$neu+1$	neu'	$neu'+1$	neu'	$neu'+1$
♯$Gener.$ (**gen**)	gen	gen	gen	gen	gen'	gen'	gen'	gen'
α_2	1	1	1.5	1.5	1	1	1.5	1.5

following: (a) PUNNs have been utilised, with a number of neurons in the input layer equal to the number of variables in the problem; a hidden layer with a number of nodes that depends on the data set to be classified and the number of selected features; and the number of nodes in the output layer equal to the number of classes minus one because a soft-max type probabilistic approach has been used; (b) four experiments have been performed for each problem, where two different values have been used for -associated with the residual of the updating expression of the output-layer weights- and the number of neurons in the hidden layer; (c) it employs similar terminology to aforementioned EDD; (d) four different configurations (1', 2', 3' and 4') are applied to subsets obtained with each of the selectors, for each data set. The parameters of each configuration are neu, gen and α_2. The first two ones take specific values depending on the data set and the last one depends on the configuration number (1', ...). Table 1 shows the main aspects of both EDD and EDDFS configurations.

4   Experimentation

Table 2 summarizes the data sets employed. All of them have been downloaded from the *University of California at Irivine* (UCI) repository [2]. Since we are using neural networks, all nominal variables have been converted to binary ones; due to this, sometimes the number of inputs is greater than the number of features. Also, the missing values have been replaced in the case of nominal variables by the mode or, when concerning continuous variables, by the mean, taking into account the full data set. These data sets have in common that present error rates in test phase about 15 % or above with reference classifiers such as C4.5 or 1-NN without feature selection. The number of samples in the training and test sets ensues from the splitting of the data sets following a experimental design via a cross validation technique called $hold-out$ that consists of dividing the data into two sets: a training and a test set. In our case, the sizes of the training and test sets are three and one quarters of the number of patterns in the problem, respectively; these percentages are similar to those used in [11]. More exactly, we have utilised a stratified holdout where the two sets are stratified [7] so that the class distribution of the samples in each set is approximately the same as in the original data set.

Table 2. Summary of the data sets and specific parameter values for EDD and EDDFS frameworks

Data set	Size	Train.	Test	Feat.	Inp.	Cl.	neu; gen	neu'; gen'
Breast	286	215	71	9	15	2	9; 500	7; 500
Heart	270	202	68	13	13	2	6; 500	4; 25
Hepatitis	155	117	38	19	19	2	3; 100	3; 100
Parkinsons	195	146	49	23	22	2	6; 500	3; 500
Pima	768	576	192	8	8	2	3; 120	3; 120
Promoter	106	80	26	58	114	2	11; 500	5; 300
Waveform	5000	3750	1250	40	40	3	3; 500	3; 500
Winequality-red	1599	1196	403	11	11	6	6; 300	4; 300
Yeast	1484	1112	372	8	8	10	11; 500	11; 500

Regards to EDD methodology, the concrete values of *neu* and *gen* parameters depend on the data set and are shown in the eighth last columns of Table 2. The decision about the number of neurons in the hidden-layer is a very difficult task in the scope of neural networks; we have done a preliminary study splitting the training set in two stratified sets with three and one quarters on the patterns and exploring the range [2–12] for the number of hidden neurons. Concerning the number of generations, we have defined three kinds of values: small (100–120), medium (300) and large (500). In EDDFS, again there are two parameters: *neu* and *gen*, whose values, neu' and gen', are defined for each data set. The assignment of values in EDD is not trivial, but now in EDDFS this decision is more difficult because there are four FS methods and the values are common for all of them. Kwak and Choi [8] have also considered this idea. The problem of finding the best architectures in neural networks that employ input feature selection remains unsolved. In most of cases the number of neurons is defined by us with a lower value than model EDD. There is no heuristics to guide this process, so we have used values at a guess. Regards the number of generations, the values are the same than in previous methodology except in the case of Promoter and Heart data sets. In the former, the dimensionality reduction is very important and the generation number has been change to medium value. In the latter the algorithms converges soon and a very small value (25) is utilised.

Table 3 depicts the methods used in the experimentation regarding the data preparation stage by means feature selection. There are four ones with and one without feature selection that belong respectively to EDDFS (the current proposal) and EDD frameworks. Last column defines an abbreviated name for each of them that is employed in next sections.

As previously mentioned, four FS methods have been applied to each data set. Table 4 illustrates, for each data set, the number of inputs of the original train set (see column labelled $F0$) and those that have been obtained with the different feature selectors (see columns labelled F1-4) along with the reduction

Table 3. List of filters based on feature subset selection employed in the empirical study

Feature selector name	Search method	Subset evaluator	Framework	Abbreviation
–	*None*	*None*	*EDD*	*F*0
spBI_CFS	*spBI*	*CFS*	*EDDFS*	*F*1
cfBI_CFS	*cfBI*	*CFS*	*EDDFS*	*F*2
spBI_CNS	*spBI*	*CNS*	*EDDFS*	*F*3
cnBI_CNS	*cnBI*	*CNS*	*EDDFS*	*F*4

percentage in the inputs of each selector compared to the original data set. Last row shows the average of the number of inputs or reduction percentage of the test bed for each experimented method on this paper. The reduction percentage of the number of inputs is defined as:

$$Reduction\_of\_Inputs(\%) = \left(1 - \frac{Inputs(Fi)}{Inputs(F0)}\right) 100 \quad i = 1, ..., 4 \qquad (4)$$

where i is the FS method index and $Inputs(j)$ represents the number of inputs of a given data set with method j. In all cases, FS methods successfully decreased the data dimensionality by selecting, in mean, much less than the half of the original features. Precisely, the number of selected features fluctuates between a quarter and a third of the original features. F2 method achieves a reduction percentage, on average, of 63.34 % (from 27.78 to 6.56 features in average), which is the highest overall average value obtained. Individually, Promoter data set has the highest reduction rate, above a 92 % in all cases.

Table 4. Number and reduction (%) of inputs with EDD (baseline) and EDDFS frameworks

Data set	Inputs					Reduction (%)			
	*F*0	*F*1	*F*2	*F*3	*F*4	*F*1	*F*2	*F*3	*F*4
Breast	15	4	4	2	2	73.33	73.33	86.67	86.67
Heart	13	7	7	8	9	46.15	46.15	38.46	30.77
Hepatitis	19	10	10	11	5	47.37	47.37	42.11	73.68
Parkinsons	22	5	5	7	6	77.27	77.27	68.18	72.73
Pima	8	3	3	4	5	62.50	62.50	50.00	37.50
Promoter	114	7	7	8	7	93.86	93.86	92.98	93.86
Waveform	40	14	14	15	15	65.00	65.00	62.5	62.50
Winequality − red	11	5	5	8	8	54.55	54.55	27.27	27.27
Yeast	8	5	4	7	7	37.50	50.00	12.50	12.50
Average	27.78	6.67	6.56	7.78	7.11	61.95	63.34	53.41	55.28

We follow the guidelines pointed out by J. Demšar [3] to perform nonparametric statistical tests. Iman-Davenport and Bonferroni-Dunn (Dunn, 1961) tests have been performed. The critical difference (CD) for Bonferroni-Dunn test can be computed from critical values, k and N. The considered significance levels have been 0.05 for Iman-Davenport test, and 0.05 and 0.10 for the post-hoc method.

5   Results

This section depicts the results obtained, measured in accuracy in the test set or in the test subset depending on that feature selection has been considered or not. First of all, we present the results obtained with EDD and EDDFS. After that, a statistical analysis compares EDD versus EDDFS to determine whether there are significant differences between applying or not feature selection with PUNN. Next, a second experiment compares, for each feature selector, the best mean values obtained with the current proposal to other classifiers using the same reduced data sets. Hence, in regard to EDD, the results have been extracted from next subsection for F1-4 methods.

5.1   Results Applying EDD and EDDFS

The results obtained by applying the EDD framework [16] are presented, along with those obtained with EDDFS. In the case of EDD, there were 8 configurations, denoted in the following way: 1, 2, ... 8. As already mentioned, this paper only deals with the first four configurations. In EDDFS, the four existing configurations are 1', ..., 4'. Table 5 shows the mean and standard deviation (SD) of the test accuracies for each data set for a total of 30 runs. From the analysis of the data, it can be concluded, from a purely descriptive point of view, that the EDDFS framework obtains best results for all data sets. Always, the SD reduction with EDDFS is clear and it expresses more homogeneous results compared to EDD.

Statistical Analysis. In this subsubsection we compare EDD and EDDFS methodologies by means of nonparametric statistical tests. To determine whether there are significant differences we apply an Iman-Davenport test. It compares the average ranks of the algorithms, where a low rank value indicates a good algorithm performance and a high value a bad algorithm performance. The average ranks of all methods, without (F0) and with FS (F1-4) are 4.78, 2.33, 2.56, 3.06 and 2.28, respectively. According to Iman-Davenport test results, since the statistic $F_F = 6.10$ is higher than the critical value at $(F(4, 32) = 2.67)$ the null-hypothesis is rejected. Therefore, we apply a post-hoc Bonferroni-Dunn test that compares a number of methods with a control method, by determining whether the average ranks differ by at least the CD. In our case, we make a comparison of the methods that employ FS (F1-4) versus the control method (F0) that does not use FS. CDs obtained by Bonferroni-Dunn test are 1.86 (at $\alpha = 0.05$)

Table 5. Results obtained in the test-bed by means of EDD and EDDFS frameworks

Data set	Filter	Mean ± SD			
		Config.			
		1/1′	2/2′	3/3′	4/4′
Breast	F0	63.85 ± 3.81	63.00 ± 3.24	64.27 ± 3.89	63.43 ± 3.80
	F1	70.84 ± 1.92	70.93 ± 1.59	70.18 ± 1.77	70.00 ± 1.92
	F2	70.84 ± 1.92	70.93 ± 1.59	70.18 ± 1.77	70.00 ± 1.92
	F3	69.20 ± 0.48	69.10 ± 0.35	69.06 ± 0.25	69.06 ± 0.25
	F4	69.20 ± 0.48	69.10 ± 0.35	69.06 ± 0.25	69.06 ± 0.25
Heart	F0	75.93 ± 2.40	75.83 ± 3.27	76.23 ± 2.48	76.03 ± 3.50
	F1	76.23 ± 1.86	76.47 ± 2.12	75.93 ± 2.33	77.50 ± 2.01
	F2	76.23 ± 1.86	76.47 ± 2.12	75.93 ± 2.33	77.50 ± 2.01
	F3	76.08 ± 2.50	75.98 ± 2.30	76.47 ± 2.01	75.59 ± 2.37
	F4	77.40 ± 2.10	76.76 ± 2.09	77.89 ± 2.49	77.99 ± 1.79
Hepatitis	F0	84.47 ± 4.49	85.52 ± 4.67	84.47 ± 4.55	84.29 ± 5.33
	F1	88.77 ± 2.49	88.77 ± 2.93	88.95 ± 2.80	89.91 ± 2.59
	F2	88.77 ± 2.49	88.77 ± 2.93	88.95 ± 2.80	89.91 ± 2.59
	F3	89.04 ± 2.40	89.30 ± 2.49	89.56 ± 2.13	89.47 ± 2.85
	F4	86.67 ± 1.53	86.67 ± 1.82	86.40 ± 1.40	86.32 ± 1.45
Parkinsons	F0	79.66 ± 5.01	78.16 ± 4.77	78.98 ± 4.05	79.32 ± 4.76
	F1	79.66 ± 2.37	79.32 ± 2.32	79.93 ± 2.15	79.05 ± 2.83
	F2	79.66 ± 2.37	79.32 ± 2.32	79.93 ± 2.15	79.05 ± 2.83
	F3	80.27 ± 4.23	81.84 ± 4.20	80.61 ± 3.07	80.14 ± 3.90
	F4	78.03 ± 1.16	80.07 ± 2.82	78.78 ± 1.98	79.66 ± 3.24
Pima	F0	77.33 ± 2.36	78.61 ± 1.88	76.96 ± 1.67	77.69 ± 1.79
	F1	79.54 ± 0.90	79.49 ± 0.79	79.60 ± 0.87	79.89 ± 0.92
	F2	79.54 ± 0.90	79.49 ± 0.79	79.60 ± 0.87	79.89 ± 0.92
	F3	75.48 ± 1.42	75.19 ± 1.26	75.00 ± 1.17	75.31 ± 1.51
	F4	78.42 ± 1.09	78.76 ± 1.13	78.73 ± 1.06	78.71 ± 1.47
Promoter	F0	59.74 ± 9.30	58.21 ± 9.67	60.51 ± 10.00	55.51 ± 10.03
	F1	84.48 ± 3.97	84.62 ± 3.78	83.20 ± 3.97	82.94 ± 4.12
	F2	84.48 ± 3.97	84.62 ± 3.78	83.20 ± 3.97	82.94 ± 4.12
	F3	67.43 ± 5.77	67.05 ± 5.11	66.15 ± 5.56	67.94 ± 5.74
	F4	75.89 ± 4.39	75.51 ± 4.45	76.41 ± 3.74	76.53 ± 4.55
Waveform	F0	81.43 ± 2.10	82.78 ± 0.64	82.05 ± 1.64	84.32 ± 1.73
	F1	84.97 ± 1.13	86.54 ± 0.48	84.92 ± 0.98	86.30 ± 0.95
	F2	84.97 ± 1.13	86.54 ± 0.48	84.92 ± 0.98	86.30 ± 0.95
	F3	85.39 ± 1.41	85.78 ± 0.74	85.20 ± 1.14	86.37 ± 0.84
	F4	84.87 ± 0.93	86.75 ± 0.57	85.55 ± 1.21	85.66 ± 0.80

(Continued)

Table 5. *(Continued)*

Data set	Filter	Mean $\pm$ SD			
Winequality – red	F0	61.03 ± 1.30	60.80 ± 1.25	61.16 ± 1.20	60.98 ± 1.42
	F1	61.67 ± 1.10	61.49 ± 0.99	61.21 ± 1.11	61.15 ± 1.30
	F2	61.67 ± 1.10	61.49 ± 0.99	61.21 ± 1.11	61.15 ± 1.30
	F3	61.70 ± 1.06	61.54 ± 1.10	61.75 ± 1.01	61.66 ± 1.05
	F4	61.70 ± 1.06	61.54 ± 1.10	61.75 ± 1.01	61.66 ± 1.05
Yeast	F0	59.18 ± 1.17	59.62 ± 1.27	58.50 ± 1.74	59.18 ± 1.83
	F1	59.82 ± 1.22	59.53 ± 1.36	58.95 ± 1.14	59.72 ± 1.46
	F2	54.86 ± 1.39	54.37 ± 1.16	54.16 ± 1.56	54.84 ± 1.35
	F3	60.10 ± 1.41	60.36 ± 1.16	59.93 ± 1.85	60.20 ± 1.46
	F4	60.10 ± 1.41	60.36 ± 1.16	59.93 ± 1.85	60.20 ± 1.46
Average	F0	71.40	71.39	71.46	71.20
	F1	76.22	76.35	75.87	76.27
	F2	75.67	75.78	75.34	75.73
	F3	73.85	74.02	73.75	73.97
	F4	74.70	75.06	74.94	75.09

and 1.67 (at $\alpha = 0.10$). The ranking difference with F0 are 2.45 with F1, 2.22 with F2, 1.72 with F3 and 2.50 with F4. Thus, there are significant differences between EDD applying each of the FS methods and without FS. The statistical tests points out that PUNN performance improves significantly pre-processing the data set with any of the FS methods employed in this paper. Summarising, EDDFS improves significantly EDD. However, F4 is better from the point of view of ranking difference, sharing the statistical significance level with F1 and F2.

5.2   Results Obtained with State-of-the-art Classifiers

Now, a comparison is performed between EDDFS and other machine learning algorithms. These methods are C4.5 [12], k-nearest neighbours (k-NN), -where k is 1-, SVM and PART. Since, C4.5, 1-NN, SVM and PART are implemented in Weka tool [18], we have used the same cross-validation, thus the same instances in each of the partitions, that in the first experiment. Regarding the parameters, the algorithms have been run with Weka default values. We have reported in Table 6 the results without and with FS for each data set and algorithm. From a purely descriptive analysis of the results, we can assert the following. Taking into account the data set without any FS the SVM and EDD algorithm achieves the best result in four out of nine data sets; C4.5 classifiers get once the highest accuracies. In average, SVM has the better accuracy (74.95 %), followed by EDD (72.21 %) and the remaining algorithms range from 67.28 % to 69.32 %. Applying FS, it can be concluded that the EDD method (EDDFS, the current

Table 6. Results obtained in nine data sets for several classifiers with and without feature subset selection

Data set	Filter	C4.5	1-NN	SVM	PART	EDD
Breast	$F0$	70.42	64.79	64.79	69.01	64.27
	$F1$	69.01	70.42	66.20	71.83	70.93
	$F2$	69.01	70.42	66.20	71.83	70.93
	$F3$	69.01	70.42	64.79	69.01	69.20
	$F4$	69.01	70.42	64.79	69.01	69.20
Heart	$F0$	70.59	73.53	76.47	73.53	76.23
	$F1$	73.53	73.53	76.47	77.94	77.50
	$F2$	73.53	73.53	76.47	77.94	77.50
	$F3$	73.53	75.00	76.47	75.00	76.47
	$F4$	72.06	75.00	76.47	75.00	77.99
Hepatitis	$F0$	84.21	86.84	89.47	81.58	85.52
	$F1$	84.21	89.47	86.84	84.21	89.91
	$F2$	84.21	89.47	86.84	84.21	89.91
	$F3$	89.47	92.11	89.47	86.84	89.56
	$F4$	89.47	84.21	89.47	84.21	86.67
Parkinsons	$F0$	71.43	77.55	75.51	75.51	79.66
	$F1$	75.51	79.59	75.51	77.55	79.93
	$F2$	75.51	79.59	75.51	77.55	79.93
	$F3$	75.51	81.63	75.51	75.51	81.84
	$F4$	79.59	79.59	75.51	81.63	80.07
Pima	$F0$	74.48	73.96	78.13	74.48	78.61
	$F1$	76.04	74.48	77.60	76.04	79.89
	$F2$	76.04	74.48	77.60	76.04	79.89
	$F3$	69.79	71.88	73.96	72.92	75.48
	$F4$	74.48	67.19	78.65	74.48	78.76
Promoter	$F0$	69.23	65.38	88.46	53.85	60.51
	$F1$	73.08	57.69	84.62	80.77	84.62
	$F2$	73.08	57.69	84.62	80.77	84.62
	$F3$	76.92	61.54	76.92	80.77	67.94
	$F4$	80.77	57.69	84.62	76.92	76.53
Waveform	$F0$	74.8	68.96	86.24	76.88	84.32
	$F1$	74.40	75.36	86.88	77.04	86.54
	$F2$	74.40	75.36	86.88	77.04	86.54
	$F3$	74.88	74.88	87.12	79.92	86.37
	$F4$	74.40	76.64	87.12	79.68	86.75

(Continued)

Table 6. *(Continued)*

Data set	Filter	C4.5	1-NN	SVM	PART	EDD
Winequality − red	F0	53.85	49.88	59.55	51.36	61.16
	F1	50.87	48.88	59.80	52.11	61.67
	F2	50.87	48.88	59.80	52.11	61.67
	F3	50.12	49.63	58.81	52.85	61.75
	F4	50.12	49.63	58.81	52.85	61.75
Yeast	F0	54.84	48.39	55.91	56.72	59.62
	F1	53.49	48.92	54.03	54.84	59.82
	F2	54.30	45.97	53.76	51.08	54.86
	F3	54.03	49.46	54.84	54.30	60.36
	F4	54.03	49.46	54.84	54.30	60.36
Average	F0	69.32	67.70	74.95	68.10	72.21
	F1	70.02	68.71	74.22	72.48	76.76
	F2	70.11	68.38	74.19	72.06	76.21
	F3	70.36	69.62	73.10	71.90	74.33
	F4	71.55	67.76	74.48	72.01	75.34

contribution) obtains the best result for five out of nine data sets; SVM yield the highest performance for two data sets and finally 1-NN and PART report the best accuracy once. Furthermore, the EDD reports the highest mean accuracy (76.76 %) followed by the SVM method (74.48 %). Both statements confirm the best behaviour of the product units. EDDFS with F1 is competitive with SVM. According to the results, the application of a preprocessing for SVM is not needed because the behaviour is better than with the reduced data sets; nevertheless, the performance of EDDFS overcomes SVM.

6 Conclusions

This paper presented a framework called EDDFS that combines FS with EDD in the context of product unit neural networks trained with an evolutionary programming approach. The models obtained with the proposal have the advantages that are more accurate and more simple, bearing in mind the number of inputs and/or the number of nodes in the hidden-layer. An empirical study on nine UCI classification problems, that present test error rates about a 15 percent or above with C4.5 or 1-NN classifiers, has been performed to compare EDDFS and EDD methodologies. Nonparametric statistical tests have been applied and the main conclusions achieved are as follows. The FS methods help to improve significantly the accuracy of the models with product units in all cases, although with three out of the four ones the performance is higher in terms of level significance. In regard to the comparison with other classifiers, EDDFS is better than SVM.

Acknowledgments. This work has been partially subsidized by TIN2011-28956-C02-02 and TIN2014-55894-C2-R projects of the Spanish Inter-Ministerial Commission of Science and Technology (MICYT), FEDER funds and the P11-TIC-7528 project of the "Junta de Andalucía" (Spain).

References

1. Aggarwal, C.C.: An introduction to data classification. In: Data Classification: Algorithms and Applications, p. 1 (2014)
2. Bache, K., Lichman, M.: UCI machine learning repository online (2015)
3. Demšar, J.: Statistical comparisons of classifiers over multiple data sets. J. Mach. Learn. Res. **7**, 1–30 (2006)
4. Downing, K.L.: Intelligence Emerging: Adaptivity and Search in Evolving Neural Systems. MIT Press, Cambridge (2015)
5. Durbin, R., Rumelhart, D.: Products units: a computationally powerful and biologically plausible extension to backpropagation networks. Neural Comput. **1**(1), 133–142 (1989)
6. Hall, M.A.: Correlation-based feature selection for discrete and numeric class machine learning. In: Proceedings of the Seventeenth International Conference on Machine Learning (ICML), pp. 359–366. Morgan Kaufmann, San Francisco (2000)
7. Kohavi, R.: A study of cross-validation and bootstrap for accuracy estimation and model selection. In: Proceedings of the 14th International Joint Conference on Artificial Intelligence (IJCAI), vol. 14, pp. 1137–1145 (1995)
8. Kwak, N., Choi, C.-H.: Input feature selection for classification problems. IEEE Trans. Neural Netw. **13**(1), 143–159 (2002)
9. Liu, H., Motoda, H.: Feature Selection for Knowledge Discovery and Data Mining, vol. 454. Springer Science & Business Media, New York (2012)
10. Liu, H., Setiono, R.: A probabilistic approach to feature selection - a filter solution. In: Proceedings of the thirteenth International Conference on Machine Learning (ICML), pp. 319–327, Italy. Morgan Kaufmann (1996)
11. Prechelt, L.: Proben1: A set of neural network benchmark problems and benchmarking rules (1994)
12. Quinlan, J.R.: C4.5: Programming for machine learning. Morgan Kauffmann, San Francisco (1993)
13. Rojas, R.: Neural Networks: A Systematic Introduction. Springer Science & Business Media, New York (2013)
14. Ruiz, R., Riquelme, J.C., Aguilar-Ruiz, J.S.: Projection-based measure for efficient feature selection. J. Intell. Fuzzy Syst. **12**(3–4), 175–183 (2002)
15. Ruiz, R., Riquelme, J.C., Aguilar-Ruiz, J.S.: Incremental wrapper-based gene selection from microarray expression data for cancer classification. Pattern Recogn. **39**(12), 2383–2392 (2006)
16. Tallón-Ballesteros, A.J., Gutiérrez-Peña, P.A., Hervás-Martínez, C.: Distribution of the search of evolutionary product unit neural networks for classification. arXiv preprint (2012). arxiv:1205.3336
17. Wang, J.: On the trainability, stability, representability, and realizability of artificial neural networks. Ph.D. thesis, Case Western Reserve University (1991)
18. Witten, I.H., Frank, E.: Data Mining: Practical Machine Learning Tools and Techniques. Data Management Systems. Morgan Kaufmann, San Francisco (2005)

Time Series

Rainfall Prediction: A Deep Learning Approach

Emilcy Hernández[1]([✉]), Victor Sanchez-Anguix[2], Vicente Julian[3],
Javier Palanca[3], and Néstor Duque[4]

[1] Departamento de Ingeniería de la Organización,
Universidad Nacional de Colombia,
Carrera 80 No 65-223 - Núcleo Robledo, Medellín, Colombia
ejhernandezle@unal.edu.co

[2] School of Computing, Electronics and Maths, Coventry University,
Gulson Road, Coventry CV1 2JH, UK
ac0872@coventry.ac.uk

[3] Departamento de Sistemas Informaticos y Computacion,
Universitat Politècnica de València, Cami de Vera s/n, 46022 Valencia, Spain
{vinglada,jpalanca}@dsic.upv.es

[4] Departamento de Informática y Computación,
Universidad Nacional de Colombia,
Campus La Nubia, Bloque Q, Piso 2, Manizales, Colombia
ndduqueme@unal.edu.co

Abstract. Previous work has shown that the prediction of meteorological conditions through methods based on artificial intelligence can get satisfactory results. Forecasts of meteorological time series can help decision-making processes carried out by organizations responsible of disaster prevention. We introduce an architecture based on Deep Learning for the prediction of the accumulated daily precipitation for the next day. More specifically, it includes an autoencoder for reducing and capturing non-linear relationships between attributes, and a multilayer perceptron for the prediction task. This architecture is compared with other previous proposals and it demonstrates an improvement on the ability to predict the accumulated daily precipitation for the next day.

Keywords: Artificial neural networks · Deep learning · Meteorological data · Rainfall prediction

1 Introduction

Rainfall prediction remains a serious concern and has attracted the attention of governments, industries, risk management entities, as well as the scientific community. Rainfall is a climatic factor that affects many human activities like agricultural production, construction, power generation, forestry and tourism, among others [1]. To this extent, rainfall prediction is essential since this variable is the one with the highest correlation with adverse natural events such as landslides, flooding, mass movements and avalanches. These incidents have

© Springer International Publishing Switzerland 2016
F. Martínez-Álvarez et al. (Eds.): HAIS 2016, LNAI 9648, pp. 151–162, 2016.
DOI: 10.1007/978-3-319-32034-2_13

affected society for years [2]. Therefore, having an appropriate approach for rainfall prediction makes it possible to take preventive and mitigation measures for these natural phenomena [3].

Also these predictions facilitate the supervision of agriculture activities, construction, tourism, transport, and health, among others. For agencies responsible for disaster prevention, providing accurate meteorological predictions can help decision-making in the face of possible occurrence of natural events.

For achieving these predictions there are a number of methods, ranging from naive methods, to those that use more complex techniques such as artificial intelligence (AI), artificial neural networks (ANNs) being one of the most valuable and attractive methods for forecasting tasks. In prediction, ANNs, as opposed to traditional methods in meteorology, are based on self-adaptive mechanisms that learn from examples and capture functional relationships between data, even if the relationships are unknown or difficult to describe [4].

Over the last few years, Deep Learning has been used as a successful mechanism in ANN for solving complex problems [5]. Deep Learning is a general term used to refer to a series of multilayer architectures that are trained using unsupervised algorithms. The main improvement is learning a compact, valid, and non-linear representation of data via unsupervised methods, with the hope that the new data representation contributes to the prediction task at hand. This approach has been successfully applied to fields like computer vision, image recognition, natural language processing, and bioinformatics [6]. Deep learning has shown promise for modeling time-series data through techniques like Restricted Boltzmann Machine (RBM), Conditional RBM, Autoencoder, Recurrent neural network, Convolution and pooling, Hidden Markov Model [7].

In this experimental study we use data gathered from a meteorological station located in a central area of Manizales, Colombia. The data gathered comprises more than a decade of measurements taken in real time and stored by Instituto de Estudios Ambientales (IDEA) of Universad Nacional de Colombia, also located in the same city. In order to perform forecasts, a deep architecture combining the use of an autoencoder and a multilayer perceptron is used. For testing the validity of the proposed model, we optimized the parameters of the deep architecture and tested the resulting network via a series of error measurement criteria. The results show that the proposed architecture outperforms the state of the art in the task of predicting the accumulated daily precipitation for the next day.

The structure of the paper is as follows: Sect. 2 describes previous approaches for the prediction of meteorological variables, mainly precipitation; Sect. 3 contains a description our proposed architecture, the techniques used for forecasting, and details of the dataset employed as case of study; meanwhile Sect. 4 shows the experiments realized and the results obtained. Finally, in Sect. 5 the conclusions and future work are presented.

2   Related Work

With the influence of weather in social and economic activities, prediction of atmospheric phenomena like rainfall would contribute to the prevention of adverse events. In the last few years, several approaches have been proposed in order to deal with this goal. There is extensive research carried out in the area of rainfall prediction, and particularly, one can notice the efficacy of neural networks for the problem.

Sawale & Gupta [8] present an algorithm based on an ANN that predicts atmospheric conditions from a dataset that includes the variable temperature, humidity and wind speed. The authors employed a hybrid architecture composed by a Back Propagation Network (BPN) and a Hopfield Network (HN). The output from the BPN is fed into the HN, which is in charge of making the actual predictions. The approach proposed is able to determine the non-linear relationship that exists between the historical data of parameters: temperature, wind speed,humidity, etc., and from this make a prediction of what the weather. In the paper does not define the time horizon to which the forecasts are made.

Luk et al. [9] present a model which aims to identify the spatio-temporal data necessary for achieving more accurate and short-term (5 min 30 min) rainfall prediction for an urban catchment in Sydney, Australia. An ANN is used to predict rainfall based on historical rainfall patterns from a series of measurements carried out in a basin study. To achieve this, the authors compared the accuracy of the predictions made by ANN configured with different variables of delay and number of inputs. The study found that the network that used a lower lag obtained better performance.

Beltrn-Castro et al. [10] adopt a decomposition and ensemble principle for daily rainfall forecasting. The decomposition technique employed is the Ensemble Empirical Mode Decomposition (EEMD), wich divides the original data into a set of simple components. Moreover, a Feed Forward Neural Network (FNN) is used as a forecasting tool for model each component. The model was tested in a case study with rainfall data registered in a meteorological station from Manizales city, Colombia. In this case study only the accumulated precipitation variable from past days was used as an input for predictions of daily rainfall of next day.

Abhishek et al. [11] proposed the use of ANNs for predicting the monthly average rainfall in an area of India characterized by monsoon type climate. The presented case study used data of eight-month per year. In these months, there is certainty that rainfall events will be present. The authors use the average humidity and average wind speed as explanatory variables. The experiments were carried out with three types of different networks: Feed Forward Back Propagation, Layer Recurrent, and Cascaded Feed Forward Back Propagation. Then, the results obtained with each network are compared, finding that the type of network that obtained the best results was Feed Forward Back Propagation.

Liu et al. [12] propose an alternative over the previous model. They explore the use of genetic algorithms as a feature selection algorithm, an then Nave Bayes as the predictive algorithm. The problem is decomposed into two prediction problems: rainfall event (i.e., a binary prediction problem), and a categorization of rainfall in case that rainfall is present (i.e., light, moderate and strong rainfall). The adoption of genetic algorithms for the selection of inputs, shows that it is possible to reduce the complexity of the dataset obtaining similar or slightly better performance.

Liu et al. (2014) proposed a model based on Deep Learning (DL). In their research they apply Deep Neural Network (DNN) to process massive data involving datasets of almost 30 years (1-1-1983 to 31-12-2012) of environmental records provided by the Hong Kong Observatory (HKO). The data is used to predict the weather change in the next 24 hours, given four variables: temperature, dew point, Mean Sea Level Pressures (MSLP) and wind speed. The results obtained for authors show that the DNN provide a good feature space for weather datasets and a potential tool for the feature fusion of time series problems. However they do not predict with their model more difcult weather data, such as rainfall dataset [13].

Finally, Grover et al. (2015) presented a Model for Weather Forecasting which makes predictions by considering the joint influence of climatic essential variables. For the case of study, they took data of winds, temperature, pressure and dew point from 2009 to 2015 observed in 60 points in the United States. The proposal has a novel hybrid model with discriminative and generative components for spatio-temporal inferences about the variables mentioned above. The proposed architecture combines a bottom-up predictor for each individual variable with a top-down deep belief network that models the joint statistical relationships. Another key component in the framework is a data-driven kernel, which is given on a similarity function learned automatically from the data. The kernel is used to assign long-range dependencies through the space and to ensure that inferences respecting the natural laws. The model is called "Deep Hybrid Model" and the results obtained are compared with other model proposed in [14] and with the model used by the National Oceanic and Atmospheric Administration (NOAA) of the United States, showing a better performance than these [15]. Forecasts are made at 6, 12 and 24 hours; however, the rainfall is not predicted.

Summarizing the literature review concludes that the ANN are one of the intelligent systems that has been used more for studies of weather prediction. In general, neural networks are an appropriate mechanism when undertaking systems and phenomena with nonlinear dynamics, as in the case of meteorological phenomena. Likewise, the Deep Learning is seen as a new promising strategy for forecasting meteorological variables.

3   Data Preparation

The problem solved at this paper is that of predicting the accumulated rainfall precipitation for the next day, by using data gathered in the previous days. More specifically, we employed data from a meteorological station located in a central area of Manizales. The station makes transmissions every five minutes, which are grouped into a daily time series covering from 2002 to 2013.

The dataset used for model validation contains a total of forty-seven explanatory characteristics, including temperature, relative humidity, barometric pressure, sun brightness, speed and direction of wind, and other derivatives of the

Table 1. Details of dataset

Input column	Description	Observation
1-3	Rainfall in the last 3 days ago	
4	Rainfall average 5 days ago	Measurement unit: mm
5	Difference between the temperature at 4:00 and 24:00	
6-8	Temperature in the last 3 days ago	
9	Temperature average 5 days ago	Measurement unit: C
10	Difference between the temperature at 4:00 and 24:00	
11-13	Barometric pressure in the last 3 days ago	
14	Barometric pressure average 5 days ago	Measurement unit: hPa
15	Difference between the barometric pressure at 4:00 and 24:00	
16-18	Relative humidity in the last 3 days ago	Measurement unit: %
19	Relative humidity average 5 days ago	
20-22	Wind speed in the last 3 days ago	Measurement unit: m/s
23-25	Sun brightness in the last 3 days ago	Measurement unit: W/m2
26	Sun brightness average 5 days ago	
27	Dew point temperature	Measurement unit: C
28-39	Month value of the input records	12 components are used, i.e., February: 010000000000 May: 000010000010
40-47	Prevaling wind direction	North: 10000000 Northeast: 01000000 East: 00100000 Southeast: 00010000 South: 00001000 Southwest: 00000100 West: 00000010 Northwest: 00000001

main variables. The reader can observe a description of all of these variables at Table 1.

The data is taken from an environmental datawarehouse administered by IDEA. The data stored in the datawarehouse has been preprocessed. More specifically it has undergone an ETL (Extract, Transform and Load) [16] process in order to achieve data integrity and standardization [17].

The dataset is divided into training, validation and testing with a percentage of 70, 15 and 15 percent respectively. Therefore, from the total of 4216 samples conforming the dataset, 2952 were randomly selected as training. From the rest, 632 samples were selected for validation, and the remaining 632 samples were kept for testing.

Once the data has been extracted and divided into training, test, and validation, we normalized variables to a $[0, 1]$ interval in order to avoid effects of scale in our deep learning architecture. The normalization method employed for the dataset can be observed in the Eq. (1), where a_i represents a value to normalize for the i-th variable, min_{a_i} is the minimum valor registered for this variable in the training set and max_{a_i} is the maximum valor registered for this variable in the training set.

$$V_i = \frac{a_i - min_{a_i}}{max_{a_i} - min_{a_i}} \tag{1}$$

4　Proposed Architecture

In this section, we describe the general architecture of our proposed model. As mentioned throughout the paper, we employ a deep learning architecture to predict the accumulated rainfall for the next day. The architecture is composed of two networks: an autoencoder network and a multilayer perceptron network. The autoencoder network is responsible to feature selection and as mentioned in [7], the autoencoder is a deep learning technique promise for the feature treatment in time series. A multilayer perceptron network is responsible for classification, prediction task. Next we will detail each network.

The first element in our architecture is the autoencoder. An autoencoder is an unsupervised network that aims to extract non-linear features for a data input. Being more specific, an autoencoder is composed by three layers: the input layer, a hidden layer using the sigmoid activation function, and the output layer. Differently to classic neural networks, autoencoders are trained so that the output layer attempts to be as similar as possible to the input layer. This way, the hidden layer results in a non-linear compact representation of the input layer, achieved thanks to the sigmoid activation function. The rationale behind this transformation is that data will be more compact (i.e., less prone to overfitting) and hopefully some interesting non-linear relationships that improve the explanation of the output variable have been discovered. In our architecture, the type of autoencoder that we employed is a denoising autoencoder [18] provided by Theano [19], a Python GPU-based library for mathematical optimization.

The hidden layer of the autoencoder, the non-linear compact representation of the original input, is directly connected to a Multilayer perceptron. This network is the one responsible for making predictions in our problem, by taking the new problem representation as an input. The MLP consists of one hidden layer and uses the sigmoid activation function. Figure 1 presents our architecture, it shows in detail the input and output layers and the way in which the autoencoder connects to the MLP network.

Figure 2 presents a general overview of all the system. Data is extracted for the data storage by means of a query, and then the information is normalized in order to be used by the autoencoder. The autoencoder builds the compact non-linear representation of the data and then it is fed to the MLP, which is responsible for making the predictions. In Table 2 are presented in detail the values tested in each parameter.

5　Experiments

In order to evaluate the performance of the proposed criteria we use the Mean Square Error (MSE) and the Root Mean Square Error (RMSE) as measurement errors. Let $\hat{Y}_i$ be a vector of n predictions and Y_i be the vector of observed values corresponding to the expected output of the function which generates the prediction, then MSE and RMSE can be calculated according to the Eq. (2).

$$MSE = \frac{1}{n} \sum_{i=1}^{n} (Y_i - \hat{Y}_i)^2$$

$$RMSE = \sqrt{MSE}$$

(2)

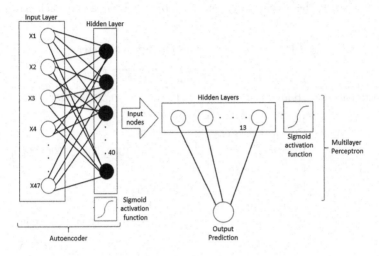

Fig. 1. Architecture: autoencoder and MLP.

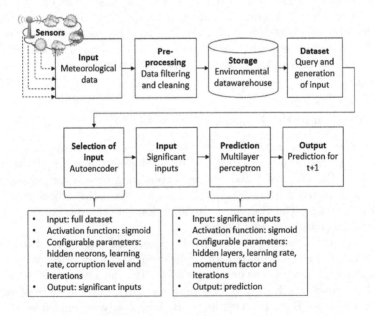

Fig. 2. Flow of the proposed method.

5.1 Optimizing the Proposed Network Architecture

Multiple network architectures were implemented with different configurations for the autoencoder and the MLP. The trainings and tests were carried out in parallel on a cluster consisting of 72 nodes. Initially, several combinations of value parameters were tested in order to look for the best possible architecture configuration. More specifically, we carried out a grid search for the following set of parameters, the Table 2 presents the approved values for each parameter.

Table 2. Approved values for each parameter

	Parameter	Values
Autoencoder	Hidden neurons	[11, 13, 19, 23, 29, 35, 40, 45]
	Learning rate	[0.1, 0.3, 0.9]
	Corruption level	[0.1, 0.3, 0.9]
	Iterations	[33, 100, 300, 1000, 3000, 5000, 9000]
MLP	Hidden layers	[10, 13, 19]
	Learning rate	[0.1, 0.3, 0.9]
	Momentum factor	[0.1, 0.3, 0.9]
	Iterations	[33, 100, 300, 1000, 3000, 5000, 9000]

Once carried out the tests, we found that the best configuration for the autoencoder was the following: 40 hidden neurons, 0.9 of learning rate, 0.1 for corruption level, and 5000 iterations of training. In the case of the MLP configuration, the best result was adjusted with the following combination of values: 13 hidden layers, 0.3 of learning rate, 0.9 of momentum factor and 1000 iterations of training.

5.2 Evaluation of the Proposed Network

Once optimized, the results of our network were compared with a wide range of methods: a naive approach consisting on predicting the accumulated rainfall of $t - 1$ for t (Naive 1), a naive approach consisting on always predicting the average accumulated rainfall (Naive 2), an optimized MLP whose parameters were optimized with the training and validation set, the method proposed in [11], and the method proposed in [10].

The two latter models [10,11] have been selected mainly for two reasons: they provide enough information for replication, and they attempt to predict the rainfall for the next day as our proposal. In [11], the authors test three types of neural networks: Back Propagation network (BP), Layer Recurrent network (LR), and Cascaded Back-Propagation (CBP). Similarly, we optimized the three types of networks proposed by [11] via a grid search on prospective parameters. In [10], the authors use Ensemble Empirical Mode Decomposition (EEMD) and

Feed-forward Neural Networks (FNN) to predict accumulated rainfall on the next day. Similarly to the authors, we configured the their network to take the last two days of data as input, and we set the EEMD to split the signal into nine different components which is fed into nine different FNN that form a prediction via summation of each prediction.

The results for this experiment can be observed in Table 3. The experiment shows the average MSE and RMSE for the best network configuration of each implemented method. The average is calculated by training each network 30 times and evaluating the MSE and RMSE against the test set. This allows us to capture statistical differences between the different networks. Error measures were calculated on the desnormalized data, that is, in the original unit of measurement.

Table 3. Results obtained by the different approaches

Method	MSE	RMSE
Autoencoder and MLP	40.11	6.33
MLP	42.34	6.51
Naive 1	132.82	11.52
Naive 2	88.43	9.40
Abhishek et al. (BP) [11]	93.51	9.67
Abhishek et al. (LR) [11]	81.72	9.04
Abhishek et al. (CBP) [11]	81.36	9.02
Beltran et al. [10]	98.73	9.94

It can be appreciated in the table above that our proposed method (Autoencoder and MLP) achieves a lower MSE and RMSE on average, with the single MLP being the next best algorithm. In order to assess whether both methods were statistically different, we carried out two one-tailed t-test ($\alpha = 0.01$) with the results obtained from both methods (one for the MSE and another for the RMSE). The null hypothesis for the test is that the average for both methods is equal, whereas the alternative hypothesis is that the difference between the average obtained by our method (Autoencoder and MLP) and the single MLP is less than zero. The first t-test was run with data from the MSE, and it obtained a p-value of $2.2E - 16$ supporting the alternative hypothesis and then assessing that our proposal was able to obtain a statistically lower average on the MSE than the single MLP. The second t-test was run for the RMSE and it obtained again a p-value of $2.2E - 16$ and, thus, concluding that our proposed method obtains lower RMSE than the single MLP. Hence, in both cases it is shown that our proposal is the best one for the case study.

We decided to explore further the results obtained by our proposal. For that matter, we compared the predictions obtained by our architecture with the real values for those data instances. Figure 3 shows the prediction with the proposed

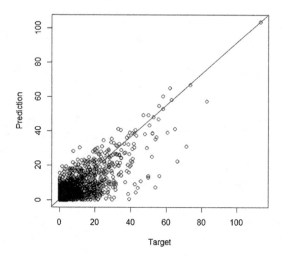

Fig. 3. Target versus prediction.

architecture versus the target data in the original unit of measurement. The horizontal axis represents the real value, whereas the vertical axis represents the prediction obtained by our algorithm. A perfect prediction would be place in a straight line with slope equal to one and intercept equal to zero. As it is possible to observe, data points tend to follow a straight line around the aforementioned straight line. This specially true for days with heavy rain, which are the focus of our study. For days with light rainfall (less than 20mm[1]), which are less interesting for our study as we aim to predict risk scenarios, the predictions tend to be less accurate and deviate from the target value. This indicates that there is room for improvement in the proposed architecture, and one of our goals in the future is improving the predictions for such cases.

6   Conclusions and Future Work

This paper has presented a deep learning approach based on the use of autoencoders and neural networks to predict the accumulated precipitation for the next day. The approach forecasts the daily accumulated rainfall in a specific meteorological station located in a central area of Manizales city (Colombia). The proposed architecture has been compared with other state of the art methods. The results suggest that our proposed architecture outperform other approaches in terms of the MSE and the RMSE.

As future work, we plan to improve our architecture for light rain scenarios. It should be highlighted that the focus of our study was precisely the opposite, heavy rain scenarios, as they are the scenarios that may lead to negative consequences (e.g., landslides). Additionally, we also plan to test other types of

---

[1] This threshold was obtained by talking with domain experts.

deep learning architecture like deep belief networks based on Restricted Boltzmann Machines [20] or multiple stacked denoising autoencoders. Moreover, we also consider the inclusion of new input features. More specifically, we plan to include data points of neighbor stations (considering neighborhood as stations with geographical proximity and similar altitude).

Acknowledgements. This work is partially supported by the MINECO/FEDER TIN2012-36586-C03-01 of the Spanish government.

The authors thank the Instituto de Estudios Ambientales - IDEA, of Universidad Nacional de Colombia - Sede Manizales for their help in obtaining the data and guidance regarding the operation of environmental monitoring networks and hydrometeorological stations.

References

1. World Health Organization: Climate Change and Human Health: Risks and Responses. World Health Organization, January 2003
2. Alcntara-Ayala, I.: Geomorphology, natural hazards, vulnerability and prevention of natural disasters in developing countries. Geomorphology **47**(24), 107–124 (2002)
3. Nicholls, N.: Atmospheric and climatic hazards: Improved monitoring and prediction for disaster mitigation. Natural Hazards **23**(2–3), 137–155 (2001)
4. Zhang, G., Eddy Patuwo, B., Hu, M.Y.: Forecasting with artificial neural networks: The state of the art. Int. J. Forecast. **14**(1), 35–62 (1998)
5. Bengio, Y.: Learning deep architectures for AI. Found. Trends Mach. Learn. **2**(1), 1–127 (2009)
6. Arel, I., Rose, D.C., Karnowski, T.P.: Deep machine learning - A new frontier in artificial intelligence research. IEEE Comput. Intell. Mag. **5**(4), 13–18 (2010)
7. Lngkvist, M., Karlsson, L., Loutfi, A.: A review of unsupervised feature learning and deep learning for time-series modeling. Pattern Recogn. Lett. **42**, 11–24 (2014)
8. Sawale, G.J., Gupta, S.R.: Use of artificial neural network in data mining for weather forecasting. Int. J. Comput. Sci. Appl. **6**(2), 383–387 (2013)
9. Luk, K.C., Ball, J.E., Sharma, A.: A study of optimal model lag and spatial inputs to artificial neural network for rainfall forecasting. J. Hydrol. **227**(14), 56–65 (2000)
10. Beltrán-Castro, J., Valencia-Aguirre, J., Orozco-Alzate, M., Castellanos-Domínguez, G., Travieso-González, C.M.: Rainfall forecasting based on ensemble empirical mode decomposition and neural networks. In: Joya, G., Gabestany, J., Rojas, I. (eds.) IWANN 2013, Part I. LNCS, vol. 7902, pp. 471–480. Springer, Heidelberg (2013)
11. Abhishek, K., Kumar, A., Ranjan, R., Kumar, S.: A rainfall prediction model using artificial neural network. In: 2012 IEEE Control and System Graduate Research Colloquium (ICSGRC), pp. 82–87, July 2012
12. Liu, J.N.K., Li, B.N.L., Dillon, T.S.: An improved naive Bayesian classifier technique coupled with a novel input solution method [rainfall prediction]. IEEE Trans. Syst. Man Cybern. Part C: Appl. Rev. **2**, 249–256 (2001)
13. James, N.K., Liu, Y.H., You, J.J., Chan, P.W.: Deep Neural Network Based Feature Representation for Weather Forecasting, 261–267 (2014)

14. Kapoor, A., Horvitz, Z., Laube, S., Horvitz, E.: Airplanes aloft as a sensor network for wind forecasting. In: Proceedings of the 13th International Symposium on Information Processing in Sensor Networks, IPSN 2014, pp. 25–34. Piscataway, NJ, USA, IEEE Press (2014)
15. Grover, A., Kapoor, A., Horvitz, E.: A Deep Hybrid Model for Weather Forecasting, pp. 379–386. Sydney (2015)
16. Vassiliadis, P.: A survey of extracttransformload technology. Int. J. Data Warehouse Min. **5**(3), 1–27 (2009)
17. Duque-Mndez, N.D., Orozco-Alzate, M., Vlez, J.J.: Hydro-meteorological data analysis using OLAP techniques. DYNA **81**(185), 160 (2014)
18. Vincent, P., Larochelle, H., Bengio, Y., Manzagol, P.-A.: Extracting and composing robust features with denoising autoencoders. In: Proceedings of the 25th International Conference on Machine Learning, ICML 2008, pp. 1096–1103. ACM, New York, NY, USA (2008)
19. LISA lab. Deep Learning Tutorials DeepLearning 0.1 documentation
20. Larochelle, H., Bengio, Y.: Classification using discriminative restricted boltzmann machines. In: Proceedings of the 25th International Conference on Machine Learning, ICML 2008, pp. 536–543. ACM, New York, NY, USA (2008)

Time Series Representation by a Novel Hybrid Segmentation Algorithm

Antonio Manuel Durán-Rosal[1(✉)], Pedro Antonio Gutiérrez-Peña[1],
Francisco José Martínez-Estudillo[2], and César Hervás-Martínez[1]

[1] Department of Computer Science and Numerical Analysis, University of Córdoba,
Rabanales Campus, Albert Einstein Building, 14071 Córdoba, Spain
{i92duroa,pagutierrez,chervas}@uco.es
[2] Department of Quantitative Methods, Loyola Andalucía University,
Escritor Castilla Aguayo 4, 14004 Córdoba, Spain
fjmestud@uloyola.es

Abstract. Time series representation can be approached by segmentation genetic algorithms (GAs) with the purpose of automatically finding segments approximating the time series with the lowest possible error. Although this is an interesting data mining field, obtaining the optimal segmentation of time series in different scopes is a very challenging task. In this way, very accurate algorithms are needed. On the other hand, it is well-known that GAs are relatively poor when finding the precise optimum solution in the region where they converge. Thus, this paper presents a hybrid GA algorithm including a local search method, aimed to improve the quality of the final solution. The local search algorithm is based on two well-known algorithms: Bottom-Up and Top-Down. A real-world time series in the Spanish Stock Market field (IBEX35) and a synthetic database (Donoho-Johnstone) used in other researches were used to test the proposed methodology.

Keywords: Time series segmentation · Hybrid algorithms · Time series representation · Spanish stock market index · Synthetic database

1 Introduction

Recently, the ubiquity of temporal data has initiated significant research and development efforts in the field of data mining. In this sense, time series can be easily obtained from financial and scientific applications, being one of the main sources of temporal datasets. Data mining in time series databases involves several tasks. One important task is the segmentation of time series, which consists

This work has been subsidized by the project TIN2014-54583-C2-1-R of the Spanish Ministerial Commission of Science and Technology (MICYT), FEDER funds and the P11-TIC-7508 project of the Junta de Andalucía (Spain). Antonio M. Durán-Rosal's research has been subsidized by the FPU Predoctoral Program (Spanish Ministry of Education and Science), grant reference FPU14/03039.

© Springer International Publishing Switzerland 2016
F. Martínez-Álvarez et al. (Eds.): HAIS 2016, LNAI 9648, pp. 163–173, 2016.
DOI: 10.1007/978-3-319-32034-2_14

in cutting the time series in some specific points, trying to achieve different objectives. The two main objectives in time series segmentation are now described.

One the one hand, discovering useful patterns in the time series is an appealing objective [1]. Das *et al.* [2] used a fixed-length window to segment the time series and represent it using the resulting simple patterns. Related with this, the characterization of strange events or special patterns in a time series (which are known as "tipping points") [3] can be used to discover common patterns which occur before these events and to extract conclusions about their nature. Finally, finding segments is also a way to discover temporal patterns or anomalies [4].

On the other hand, simplifying the time series by a segmentation algorithm is an option to alleviate the difficulty of processing, analysing or mining time series databases, given their continuous nature. Previous approaches [5,6] suggest dividing the time series using previously identified change points and substituting the segments with suitable approximations. We focus on a simplification based on piecewise linear approximation (PLA), which is able to reduce the number of points in the time series with a minimum reduction of information [7].

Genetic algorithms (GAs) are able to perform a global multi-point search, converging to high quality areas. For this reason, they are considered robust heuristics. However, they are not good at finding the precise optimum solution in these areas [8]. To solve this problem, during the last years, local optimization has been incorporated to GAs to refine their results. The idea is to combine genetic algorithms, as global explorers, with these local search (LS) procedures, which are good at finding local optima (local exploiters), resulting in what is usually known as hybrid algorithms.

There are several ways in which a LS procedure can be combined with an EAs. The way the combination is done is extremely important in terms of accuracy and computational efficiency, and the best balance of local exploitation and global exploration has to be obtained. Some of the strategies previously used include the multistart approach, the Lamarckian learning, the Baldwinian learning, the partial Lamarckianism and the process of random linkage [9–11].

In this paper, we propose a hybrid genetic algorithm for segmenting time-series and reducing their dimensionality using the PLA. The methodology combines a GA (global explorer) and a new LS procedure based on the well-known Bottom-Up and Top-Down methods [7]. The LS process consists in removing a number of cut points by the Bottom-Up methodology and, then, add the same number of points using the Top-Down procedure.

The LS is applied to the best solution obtained by the GA in the last generation, to find the precise local optimum around the final solution thanks to the high quality area returned by the GA. The results of the algorithm have been obtained with and without the LS process, and compared to the original Bottom-Up and Top-Down procedures. To test the performance of the proposed hybrid method, it is applied to a hard real-world time series in the Stock Market field (IBEX 35) and to the synthetic database Donoho-Jonhstone.

The rest of the paper is organized as follows. Section 2 includes the characteristics of the proposed algorithm, while Sect. 3 presents the description of the time series, the experiments performed and the discussion about the results. Finally, Sect. 4 establishes the conclusions.

2   Hybrid Segmentation Algorithm

2.1   Summary of the Algorithm

Given a time series $Y = \{y_n\}_{n=1}^{N}$, our objective is to divide the values of y_n into m consecutive subsets or segments, where the error of the approximation of these m segments should be as less as possible. Note that the search space is wide, its size being $\binom{N}{m}$.

The time indexes $(n = 1, \dots, N)$ are divided into segments: $s_1 = \{y_1, \dots, y_{t_1}\}$, $s_2 = \{y_{t_1}, \dots, y_{t_2}\}, \dots, s_m = \{y_{t_{m-1}}, \dots, y_N\}$, where the ts are the different cut points subscripted in ascending order $(t_1 < t_2 < \dots < t_{m-1})$. The cut points are the only points which belong to two segments (the segment before and the segment after). The values of the cut points, $t_i, i = 1, \dots, m - 1$, have to be determined by the algorithm. In this work, we have approximated each segment using a linear interpolation between the initial and final cut points of the segment. The main steps of the algorithm are summarized in Fig. 1.

2.2   Genetic Algorithm

The characteristics of the GA are defined as follows.

Chromosome Representation. Each individual chromosome (c) consists of an array of binary values, where the length of the chromosome is the time series length, N. Each position c_{t_i} stores whether the time index t_i of the time series represents a cut point for the evaluated solution. In this way, $\sum_{i=1}^{N} c_{t_i} = m$.

Initial Population. The population of the GA is a set P of binary vectors of length N, where m positions are $1s$ (the cut points, which are randomly chosen with a uniform distribution) and the rest are $0s$.

Fitness Evaluation. The goal of this kind of segmentation procedure is to reduce the error between the complete time series and its approximation. The fitness function could be defined as minimizing the difference between each real value of the time series and the corresponding approximation. The error of the i-th point in the chromosome c is defined as $e_i(c) = y_i - \bar{y}_i$, where y_i is the real value, and $\bar{y}_i(c)$ is the approximation of the chromosome c. We have considered two different fitness functions, which lead to very different results:

- The first function is the Root Mean Squared Error (RMSE), and it is calculated as follows:

$$RMSE(c) = \sqrt{MSE_c} = \sqrt{\frac{1}{m} \sum_{s=1}^{m} MSE_{c,s}}$$
$$= \sqrt{\frac{1}{m} \sum_{s=1}^{m} \frac{1}{t_s - t_{s-1} + 1} \sum_{i=t_{s-1}}^{t_s} e_i^2(c)}$$

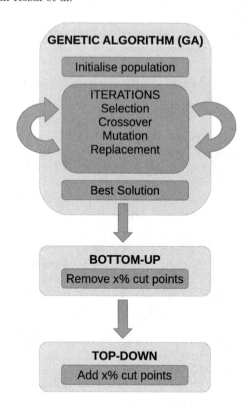

Fig. 1. Main steps for the proposed hybrid algorithm

where $MSE_s(c)$ is the Mean Squared Error (MSE) of each segment s, and MSE_c is the average value of the $MSE_{c,s}$ for all segments.

– The second function (called RMSEp, the error being averaged at a point-level), is obtained as follows:

$$RMSEp(c) = \sqrt{\frac{1}{N}SSE(c)} = \sqrt{\frac{1}{N}\sum_{i=1}^{N}e_i^2(c)}$$

where, as can be seen, the Sum of Square Errors ($SSE(c)$) is used, which does not average the errors of the points for each segment.

As both metrics have to be minimised, the fitness function is defined as $f = \frac{1}{1+RMSE}$ and $f = \frac{1}{1+RMSEp}$, respectively, which are bounded in the interval $[0,1]$.

Selection and Replacement Processes. All the individuals are considered for reproduction and generation of offspring. However, a replacement process is applied to the joint offspring and parent populations by roulette wheel selection. The selection process promotes diversity, but the replacement process is promoting selective pressure.

Mutation and Crossover Operators. Two kinds of operators are included in the algorithm to reduce the dependency with respect to the initial population and escape from local optima:

- Mutation operator: the probability p_m of performing any mutation is decided by the user. The kind of mutation applied to the individual is randomly selected from the following two operators: cyclic rotation to the left or to the right, where the number of positions in the chromosome are randomly chosen in the interval $[1, N - 1]$
- Crossover operator: For each parent individual (c^1), the crossover operator is applied with a given probability p_c. The operator randomly selects the other parent (c^2) and a time index (t_j). Then, those positions $t_i \geq t_j$ where $c^1_{t_i} = 1 \wedge c^2_{t_i} = 0$ are interchanged and also those where $c^1_{t_i} = 1 \wedge c^2_{t_i} = 0$. However, in order to maintain the same number of cutting points in the offspring, the maximum number of interchanges allowed is the minimum of the number of positions where the conditions are fulfilled.

2.3 Local Search

When the genetic algorithm is finished, the best solution in the last generation, is improved by with two well-known segmentation algorithms: **Bottom-Up** and **Top-Down**. On the one hand, in each iteration, Bottom-Up consists in merging the two adjacent segments with the lowest cost of merging (lowest error after merging). On the other hand, Top-Down is the natural complement to the Bottom-Up algorithm, recursively partitioning the time series until some stopping criteria (related with the error) is met. The proposed local search method removes a percentage of cut points using the Bottom-up strategy and then adds the same number of cut point with the Top-Down technique.

To use these algorithms, we have modified the implementation proposed in [7], in such a way that, for both, the stopping criteria is the number of segments to merge or cut, respectively. Note that the implementation of Top-Down presented in [7] is recursive method, so we have transformed it into an iterative method to know how many points have been added up to a given iteration.

3 Experimental Results and Discussion

The experiments performed and the results obtained are analysed in this section.

3.1 Time Series Analysed

In this paper, we evaluate the performance of the algorithm in two time series from different areas, to test its adaptability in various problems. The series considered are the following ones:

- The first time series is the IBEX35. It is one of the official indexes of the Madrid Stock Market, which is composed of the most liquid values listed in the Computer Assisted Trading System. In our study, we have considered the daily closing prices of this index from 4th January 1992 to 26th September 2014, presenting thus a total of 5730 observations[1]. The complete time series can be seen in Fig. 2(a).
- The second time series is extracted from a benchmark repository used by the neural net and machine learning community [12–14]. The datasets in this repository tend to have many inputs, either no noise of lots of noise, and little to moderate nonlinearity. The Donoho-Jonhstone benchmarks consist of four functions (called Blocks, Bumps, Heavisine, and Doppler) to which random noise can be added to produce an infinitive number of data sets. In our experiments, we used the function Blocks with medium noise, with a total of 2048 observations[2]. The complete time series is included in Fig. 3(a).

As we can check, the time series have different length and comes from different sources.

3.2 Experimental Setting

The experimental design for the time series under study is presented in this subsection.

Both fitness fuctions (RMSE and RMSEp) were considered in different experiments. The GA was configured with the following parameter values, obtained by a *trial and error* procedure. The number of individuals of the population is fixed to $P = 100$. The crossover probability is taken as $p_c = 0.8$ and the mutation probability as $p_c = 0.2$. The maximum number of generations is configured as $g = 200$. The number of points of the aproximation was established at $m = 2.5N\%$, where N is the length of the time series. The percentage of cut points to perform the LS procedure after the GA is set to 40 %. Given the stochastic nature of GAs, the algorithm was run 30 times with different seeds, and we obtained the mean and the standard deviation of these results. When applying only LS procedures, one single result is recorded are these are deterministic methods.

3.3 Discussion

Tables 1, 2 and 3 include, respectively, the results obtained using RMSE as fitness function (for GAs) or cutting/merging criterion (for LS procedures), those obtained using RMSEp and the correlation coefficient (r^2) of the approximated time series with respect to the original one. For this last table, in the case of GAs, the best fitness solution of the 30 ones has been selected.

First of all, we compare the performance of the GA without LS (GTSS) to the performance obtained when hybridizing it with the LS procedure (HTTS).

---

[1] The corresponding values can be downloaded at https://es.finance.yahoo.com/.

[2] The time series can be downloaded at https://sites.google.com/site/icdmmdl/.

Table 1. Results (Mean±StandardDeviation for the GAs or one single result for the LS methods) of the different algorithms using RMSE as the fitness function (for the GAs) or as the cutting/merging criterion (for the LS methods).

Algorithm	IBEX	Donoho-Johnstone
GTSS	*188.604 ± 11.933*	1.716 ± 0.226
HTSS	**160.185 ± 8.045**	*1.531 ± 0.193*
BOTTOM-UP	211.799	2.127
TOP-DOWN	206.729	**1.144**

Table 2. Results (Mean±StandardDeviation for the GAs or one single result for the LS methods) of the different algorithms using RMSEp as the fitness function (for the GAs) or as the cut/merge criterion (for the LS methods).

Algorithm	IBEX	Donoho-Johnstone
GTSS	280.905 ± 9.551	2.927 ± 0.080
HTSS	**204.195 ± 3.641**	**2.581 ± 0.054**
BOTTOM-UP	*210.321*	*2.639*
TOP-DOWN	269.801	3.466

Table 3. Correlation coefficient comparing the similarity of the approximated time series with the original one.

Fitness	IBEX		Donoho-Johnstone	
	RMSE - r^2	RMSEp - r^2	RMSE - r^2	RMSEp - r^2
HTSS	0.9932	**0.9982**	0.5560	**0.9407**
BOTTOM-UP	0.9973	*0.9980*	0.9275	*0.9351*
TOP-DOWN	0.8230	0.9967	0.1053	0.8810

On the one hand, results in Table 1 show that, when considering RMSE as fitness function, we reduce to a great extent the RMSE if the LS procedure is applied after the GA. Furthermore, the dispersion of the results (standard deviation) is also lower, what indicates that the algorithm tends to provide similar solutions in terms of fitness. On the other hand, Table 2 shows that the same can be observed when using the RMSEp function. The improvement is even greater in this case, because it reduces the RMSEp in 76 points for the IBEX time series and 0.4 for Dohono-Johnstone. The dispersion is still relatively low.

Comparing the GAs with respect to the LS algorithms, the following observations can be made. Table 1 shows that the best approximation is obtained by the HTSS method in the case of IBEX and using the RMSE fitness function. Furthermore, GTSS obtains better RMSE than LS algorithms. In Donoho-Jonhstone time series, the best approximation in terms of RMSE is Top-Down. However, we should take into account that the RMSE function can be deceiving for this

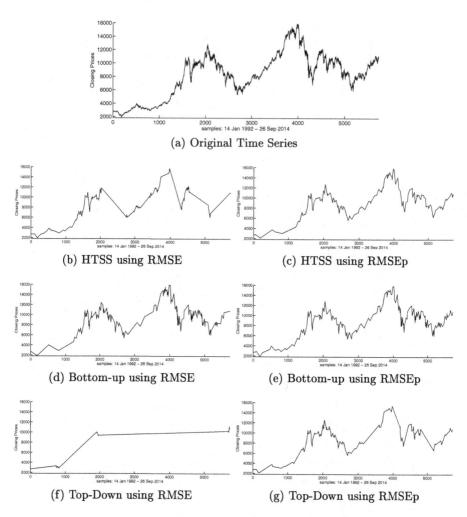

Fig. 2. Original IBEX time series and approximations by the different methods compared.

purpose because it tries to minimize the MSE of the different segments, independently of their length. In this way, Top-Down minimises the error for a part of the time series with a lot of very short segments, the RMSE counteracting the error of the long segments with those errors of the short ones. This problem can be observed in the columns of the RMSE fitness function of Table 3, where the approximation of IBEX with Top-Down is the worst in terms of r^2 using RMSE and RMSEp, and the approximation of Donoho-Jonhstone is also bad using HTSS and TOP-DOWN. We can observe graphically this problem in Fig. 3(b), (f) and Fig. 2(f). For this reason, RMSE function is not suitable for representing the global error of the time series approximation, and we recommend using RMSEp.

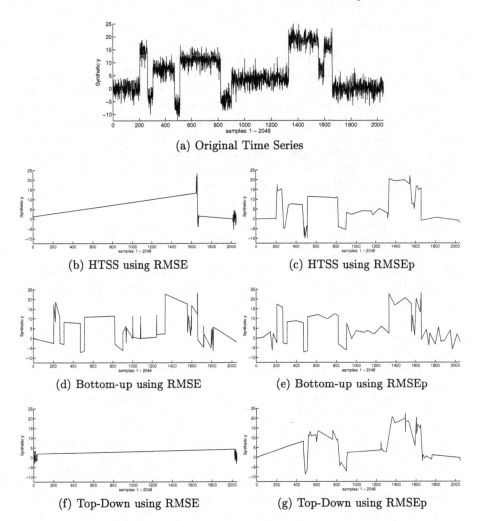

Fig. 3. Original Donoho-Jonhstone time series and approximations by the different methods compared.

Results with RMSEp are more confident, because the best methods in Table 2 are HTSS and Bottom-Up, both methods showing a good graphical behaviour in Figs. 2 and 3 and a good correlation coefficient in Table 3. It is important to mention that, using this metric, we reduce the problem of the RMSE for Top-Down, and we totally avoid it for the case of HTSS.

Finally, as said before, the best approximation in terms of r^2 are obtained with the HTSS algorithm. Although Bottom-Up obtains similar results in r^2, HTSS is better in error terms, so it is the recommended algorithm for future tasks.

4   Conclusions

This paper presents a novel hybrid time series segmentation method to simplify time series using PLAs, combining a GA with a LS. The LS sequentially applies Bottom-Up and Top-Down methods. We have tested the method in two time-series: the Spanish Stock market IBEX35 index and the synthetic Donoho-Johnstone database, showing that the results are better with the hybrid method than with LS algorithms. Experiments also reveals that the RMSE metric does not lead to a good global approximation of the time series. In this sense, the RMSEp is a better option, where the error is averaged at a point level.

We plan to extend this work in several directions:

- To use more time series for validating the conclusions.
- To test the proposed method in other tasks, as classification or clustering, comparing the results in these tasks using the original time series and the approximated versions.
- To approximate the time series applying linear regression instead of linear interpolation, or even using polynomials with degree greater than one, not necessarily linear.

References

1. Chung, F.L., Fu, T.C., Ng, V., Luk, R.W.: An evolutionary approach to pattern-based time series segmentation. IEEE Trans. Evol. Comput. **8**(5), 471–489 (2004)
2. Das, G., Lin, K., Mannila, H., Renganathan, G., Smyth, P.: Rule discovery from time series, pp. 16–22. AAAI Press (1998)
3. Nikolaou, A., Gutiérrez, P., Durán, A., Dicaire, I., Fernández-Navarro, F., Hervás-Martínez, C.: Detection of early warning signals in paleoclimate data using agenetic time series segmentation algorithm. Clim. Dyn. **44**(7), 1919–1933 (2014)
4. Fuchs, E., Gruber, T., Nitschke, J., Sick, B.: On-line motif detection in time series with swiftmotif. Pattern Recogn. **42**(11), 3015–3031 (2009)
5. Oliver, J., Forbes, C.: Bayesian approaches to segmenting a simple time series. Technical Report 14/97, Monash University, Department of Econometrics and Business Statistics (1997)
6. Oliver, J.J., Baxter, R.A., Wallace, C.S.: Minimum message length segmentation. In: Wu, X., Kotagiri, R., Korb, K. (eds.) PAKDD 1998. LNCS, vol. 1394, pp. 222–233. Springer, Heidelberg (1998)
7. Keogh, E.J., Chu, S., Hart, D., Pazzani, M.: Segmenting Time Series: A Survey and Novel Approach. In: Last, M., Kandel, A., Bunke, H. (eds.) Data Mining in Time Series Databases. Series in Machine Perception and Artificial Intelligence, vol. 57, pp. 1–22. World Scientific Publishing Company (2004)
8. Houck, C.R., Joines, J.A., Kay, M.G., Wilson, J.R.: Empirical investigation of the benefits of partial lamarckianism. Evol. Comput. **5**(1), 31–60 (1997)
9. Kolen, A., Pesch, E.: Genetic local search in combinatorial optimization. Discrete Appl. Math. **48**(3), 273–284 (1994)
10. Joines, J.A., Kay, M.G.: Utilizing hybrid genetic algorithms. In: Sarker, R., Mohammadian, M., Yao, X. (eds.) Evolutionary Optimization. International Series in Operations Research & Management Science, vol. 48, pp. 199–228. Springer, US (2002)

11. van Ulder, N.L.J., Aarts, E.H.L., Bandelt, H.J., Laarhoven, P.J.M., Pesch, E.: Genetic local search algorithms for the travelling salesman problem. In: Schwefel, H.-P., Mánner, R. (eds.) PPSN I. LNCS, vol. 496, pp. 109–116. Springer, Heidelberg (1991)

12. Donoho, D.L., Johnstone, J.M.: Ideal spatial adaptation by wavelet shrinkage. Biometrika $81(3)$, 425–455 (1994)

13. Donoho, D.L., Johnstone, I.M., Kerkyacharian, G., Picard, D.: Wavelet shrinkage: asymptopia? J. Royal Stat. Soc. Ser. B (Methodol.) $57(2)$, 301–369 (1995)

14. Donoho, D.L., Johnstone, I.M.: Adapting to unknown smoothness via wavelet shrinkage. J. Am. Stat. Assoc. 90, 1200–1224 (1995)

A Nearest Neighbours-Based Algorithm for Big Time Series Data Forecasting

Ricardo L. Talavera-Llames[1], Rubén Pérez-Chacón[1],
María Martínez-Ballesteros[2], Alicia Troncoso[1],
and Francisco Martínez-Álvarez[1(✉)]

[1] Division of Computer Science, Universidad Pablo de Olavide, 41013 Seville, Spain
{rltallla,ali,fmaralv}@upo.es, rpercha@alu.upo.es
[2] Department of Computer Science, University of Seville, Seville, Spain
mariamartinez@us.es

Abstract. A forecasting algorithm for big data time series is presented in this work. A nearest neighbours-based strategy is adopted as the main core of the algorithm. A detailed explanation on how to adapt and implement the algorithm to handle big data is provided. Although some parts remain iterative, and consequently requires an enhanced implementation, execution times are considered as satisfactory. The performance of the proposed approach has been tested on real-world data related to electricity consumption from a public Spanish university, by using a Spark cluster.

Keywords: Big data · Nearest neighbours · Time series · Forecasting

1 Introduction

Recent technological advances have led to a rapid and huge data storage. In fact, 90 % of existing data in the world have been generated in the last decade. In this context, the improvement of the current data mining techniques is necessary to process, manage and discover knowledge from this big volume of information. The modern term big data [10] is used to refer to this evolution. Sensor networks, typically associated with smart cities, are one of the main sources of big data generation and can be found in diverse areas such as energy, traffic or the environment.

The popular MapReduce paradigm [4] has been recently proposed by Google for big data parallel processing. This paradigm has been widely used by Apache Hadoop [15], which is an open source software implemented in Java and based on a distributed storage system called Hadoop Distributed File System (HDFS). However, the limitations of the MapReduce paradigm to develop iterative algorithms have promoted that other proposals emerge, such as Apache Spark [6]. Apache Spark is also an open source software project that allows the multipass computations, provides high-level operators, uses diverse languages (Java, Python, R) in addition to its own language called Scala, and finally, offers the machine learning library MLlib [5].

© Springer International Publishing Switzerland 2016
F. Martínez-Álvarez et al. (Eds.): HAIS 2016, LNAI 9648, pp. 174–185, 2016.
DOI: 10.1007/978-3-319-32034-2_15

In this work, an efficient forecasting algorithm for big data is introduced. The proposed method is based on the well-known nearest neighbours techniques [3] in machine learning. This choice is due to the good results reported when applied to datasets of small or moderate size. The algorithm has been developed in the framework Apache Spark under the Scala programming language. The algorithm has been tested on real–world big datasets, namely energy consumption, collected from a sensor network located in several buildings of a public university.

The rest of the paper is structured as follows. Section 2 describes a review of the existing literature related to the nearest neighbours algorithms for time series forecasting and to the different approaches of the nearest neighbours for big data published in recent years. In Sect. 3 the proposed method based on nearest neighbours to forecast big data time series is presented. Section 4 presents the experimental results corresponding to the prediction of the energy consumption coming from a sensor network of building facilities. Section 5 closes the paper giving some final conclusions.

2   Related Work

Predicting the future has fascinated human beings since its early existence. Accurate predictions are essential in economical activities as remarkable forecasting errors in certain areas may incur large economic losses. Therefore, many of these efforts can be noticed in everyday events such as energy management, natural disasters, telecommunications, pollution, and so forth.

The methods for time series forecasting can be roughly classified as follows: classical Box and Jenkins-based methods such as ARMA, ARIMA, ARCH or GARCH [1] and data mining techniques (the reader is referred to [9] for a taxonomy of these techniques applied to energy time series forecasting). Namely, data mining techniques based on the k nearest neighbours (kNN) have been successfully applied, providing competitive results [7,8,14]. However, these methods cannot be applied when big time series have to be predicted due to the high computational cost of the kNN.

Consequently, several MapReduce-based approaches to address the kNN algorithm in big data scenarios have been recently proposed. The authors in [17] study parallel kNN joins in a MapReduce programming model that involves both the join and the NN search to produce the k nearest neighbours of each point in a new dataset from an original dataset. In particular, both exact (H-BRJ) and approximate (H-zkNNJ) algorithms are proposed to perform efficient parallel kNN joins on big data. In [11], an algorithm is proposed to address the problem of the fast nearest neighbour approximate search of binary features in high dimensional spaces using the message passing interface (MPI) specification. A MapReduce-based framework focused on several instance reduction methods is proposed in [13] to reduce the computational cost and storage requirements of the kNN classification algorithm.

In the context of this work, the kNN query is usually required in a wide range of sensor network applications. In fact, authors in [16] propose a MapReduce-based algorithm to generalize the spatio-textual kNN join in large-scale data.

This algorithm aims at searching text-similar and k-nearest sensors to a query set containing more than one query point.

Furthermore, other distributed architectures such as GPU have been used to address parallel versions of the kNN algorithm [2], also allowing a fast and scalable meta-feature generation for highly dimensional and sparse datasets.

Alternatively, the MLlib does not include any Spark implementation of the kNN algorithm, in spite of providing several traditional algorithms such as k-means, decision tree, among others. Thus, several parallel implementations of the kNN algorithm have been proposed in the literature. For instance, the work presented in [12] provides a Spark implementation in Java of the kNN and the SVM-Pegasos algorithms to compare the scalability of this parallelization technology with the MPI/OpenMP on a Beowulf cluster architecture. This kNN Spark implementation maps the Euclidean distance from each training sample to a test sample.

3   Methodology

This section describes the methodology proposed in order to forecast big data time series. In particular, Sect. 3.1 introduces the methodology itself and in Sect. 3.2 how it is implemented to be used in Spark.

3.1   Time Series Forecasting Based on Nearest Neighbours

This section describes the technique applied to time series forecasting based on the kNN algorithm.

Given the electricity consumption recorded in the past, up to c_i, the problem consists in predicting the h consecutive measures for electricity consumption (note that h is the prediction horizon).

Let $C_i \in \mathbb{R}^h$ be a vector composed of the h values to be predicted:

$$C_i = [c_{i+1}, c_{i+2}, \ldots, c_{i+h}] \tag{1}$$

Then, the associated vector $CC_i \in \mathbb{R}^w$ is defined by gathering the consumption contained in a window composed of w consecutive samples, from values of the vector C_i backwards, as follows:

$$CC_i = [c_{i-w+1}, c_{i-w+2}, \ldots, c_{i-1}, c_i] \tag{2}$$

For any couple of vectors, CC_i and CC_j, a distance can be defined as:

$$\text{dist}(i, j) = \|CC_i - CC_j\| \tag{3}$$

where $\|\cdot\|$ represents a suitable vector norm (the Euclidean norm has been used in this work).

The weighted nearest neighbours (WNN) method first identifies the k nearest neighbours of vector CC_i, where k is a number to be determined and *neighbourhood* in this context is measured according to (3) as afore mentioned. This leads to the neighbour set, NS:

$$NS = \left\{ \text{set of } k \text{ indexes, } q_1, \ldots, q_k, \text{ such that } CC_{q_j} \text{ closest to vector } CC_i \right\} \tag{4}$$

in which q_1 and q_k refer to the first and k-th neighbours respectively, in order of distance.

According to the WNN methodology, the h electricity consumptions are predicted by linearly combining the consumptions of the k vectors succeeding those in NS, that is,

$$C_i = \frac{1}{\sum_{j=1}^{k} \alpha_j} \cdot \sum_{j=1}^{k} \alpha_j C_{q_j} \tag{5}$$

where the weighting factors α_j are obtained from,

$$\alpha_j = \frac{1}{(\text{dist}(CC_{q_j}, CC_i))^2} \tag{6}$$

Obviously, α_j when $j = k$ (furthest neighbour) is lesser than α_j when $j = 1$ (nearest neighbour). Note also that, although the w consumptions contained in CC_i are used to determine the nearest neighbours, only the h consumptions of the vectors C_{q_j} are relevant in determining C_i.

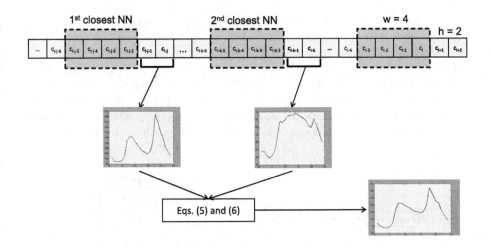

Fig. 1. Illustration of the WNN approach.

In order to find candidate neighbours, q_j, a window of w samples is simply slid along the entire dataset.

Figure 1 illustrates the basic idea behind the WNN algorithm, with $k = 2$ and $w = 4$. Values c_{i+1} and c_{i+2} ($h = 2$) are the target prediction. As $w = 4$, values $[c_{i-3}, c_{i-2}, c_{i-1}, c_i]$ are chosen as window. Later, minimal distances calculated according to Eq. (3) are searched for in the historical data. Sequences of values $s_1 = [c_{i-j-5}, ..., c_{i-j-2}]$ and $s_2 = [c_{i-k-5}, ..., c_{i-k-2}]$ are identified as the two nearest neighbours. In particular, s_2 is closer to w than s_1, and would therefore be denoted as q_2 and q_1, respectively. Finally, the forecast is performed by considering the h next samples to s_1 and s_2, according to Eqs. (5) and (6).

3.2   Algorithm Implementation for Apache Spark

The algorithm described in Sect. 3.1 has been implemented for Apache Spark, making the most of the RDD variables of Spark, in order to use it in a distributed way. This strategy makes the analysis of the datasets more efficient and faster. Therefore, every RDD created is split in blocks of the same size across the nodes that integrate the cluster, as it is shown in Fig. 2.

For a proper execution of the algorithm, several variables have to be defined from the beginning. These are:

1. The initial time series to be analysed.
2. The size of the window w whose values are taken as a pattern to look for the nearest neighbours.
3. The number of values h that needs to be predicted.
4. The number of nearest neighbours k that are going to be selected.

Since overwriting RDD variables cannot be done in Spark, a new RDD is created in each step of the algorithm. Hence, every time this section refers to a new transaction it means that a new RDD is being created.

Firstly, the data is loaded in Spark, split into different fields and finally just the energy consumption is selected, as shown in Fig. 3(a). An extra field with a numeric index is also added in this transaction. So the initial dataset in Spark is a RDD with just two fields, identification number with the position of the value of the time series, and the consumption itself (see Fig. 3(b)). Remark that, as

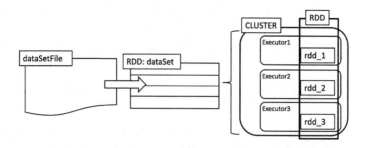

Fig. 2. Creation of a RDD variable in Spark and how it is managed in a cluster.

before mentioned, this data is split automatically across the nodes of the cluster. In a second transaction, the previous dataset is separated in two subsets, test set (TES) and training set (TRS), as Fig. 3(c) shows. TRS will be used to train the algorithm, whereas TES will be used to predict results and to check the accuracy of the prediction, comparing each predicted value to the actual one.

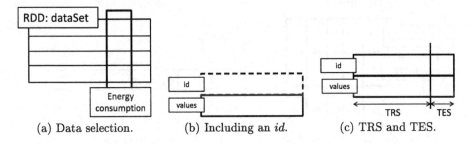

(a) Data selection.   (b) Including an *id*.   (c) TRS and TES.

Fig. 3. Data preprocessing.

The next transaction only uses TRS for training purposes. Therefore, the w previous values to the h values to be predicted are selected as the pattern in this iteration, as depicted in Fig. 4(a). Now, the main goal is to store every possible subset of w values that can be formed of which their h future values are known. To achieve this, the windows w has to be shifted h values from the end of the time series, and from there, the w subsequent values are selected. Next iteration will repeat the same process as is illustrated in Fig. 4(b). For the following transaction, the TRS is divided in subsets of h values, as shown in Fig. 4(c). Thanks to map transformations that Spark provides to its RDD, this is done in one instruction all over the RDD located in the cluster. The key in this transaction is to group values just in one action without doing several iterations like it would have been done in other languages (Java 8's Stream is, perhaps, the sole exception). In this case, the RDD from the previous transaction is grouped by the rule id/h. As a result, the new RDD will contain a numeric id of the subsets following by their corresponding h values. This can be seen in Fig. 4(d), where $idGrouping$ is the numeric id of each subset and h_i represents each subset of h values of the time series. In particular,

$$h_i = [c_{i \cdot h+1}, c_{i \cdot h+2}, ..., c_{(i+1) \cdot h}] \tag{7}$$

For instance, in the figure, h_0 is formed by the h values whose index id divided by h is 0, that is, $[c_1, c_2, ..., c_h]$.

As the formation of each subset of w values depends on the h_i previous subsets, a new RDD will be created with these subsets focusing on the RDD from the transaction before. So in this transaction, a dataset is also formed with the subsets of w values as well as the numeric id that matches with the RDD that contains the subsets h_i. This is represented in Fig. 5(a), where $idGrouping$

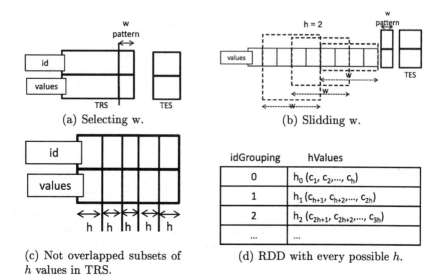

(a) Selecting w.

(b) Slidding w.

(c) Not overlapped subsets of
h values in TRS.

(d) RDD with every possible h.

Fig. 4. kNN in Spark, phase 1.

is the numeric id of the subset and w_i represents each subset of w previous values to the h values of the subset h_i.

$$w_i = [c_{i \cdot h - (w-1)}, ..., c_{i \cdot h - 1}, c_{i \cdot h}] \tag{8}$$

Due to the size of the windows w is usually greater than h, it can be observed that w_i cannot be defined when it does not exist w consecutive values previous to the values of h_i. For the same reason, it would be necessary not to look at just the values of the subset h_{i-1}, but in the w/h subsets before to build the subset w_i. This can be seen in Fig. 5(b), where the values for the w_2, for instance, are going to be formed by the values of the w/h previous h_i, in this case, h_0 and h_1.

In the next transformation, both RDDs need to be joined. Again, and thanks to the fact that both datasets share the same numeric id, Spark allows to do so by a simple action, obtaining a new RDD with the grouping id, the w values of the time series and the h values that follows it. This transaction can be seen in Fig. 5(c).

At this time the pattern w is compared to each w_i, obtaining the new field distance, which is calculated by the Euclidean distance and added to the previous RDD with just one action over Spark. Thus, the new dataset will contain the numeric id $idGrouping$, the w_i, the h_i and the distance d_i between the w pattern and w_i. This is shown in Fig. 6(a).

The next step of the algorithm sorts the previous RDD according to the distance, which Spark does rapidly just indicating the field for which the whole RDD is going to be sorted.

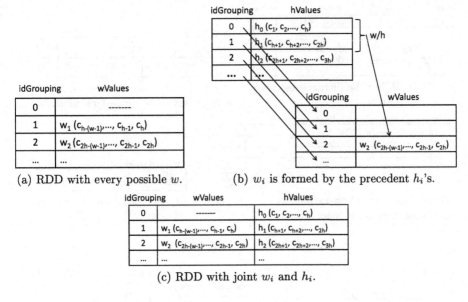

(a) RDD with every possible w.   (b) w_i is formed by the precedent h_i's.

(c) RDD with joint w_i and h_i.

Fig. 5. kNN in Spark, phase 2.

After that, just the k nearest neighbours will be chosen. This is explained in Fig. 6(b), where k is the number of nearest neighbours to be selected.

The next transaction will calculate the prediction, applying the formulas (5) and (6). In Spark, before the value is predicted, it is necessary to do intermediate calculations. First, each value of each h_i is divided by the square distance. This is done in Spark with a new map transformation, adding a new field with the values of $h_i/(d_i)^2$. And finally, each of these fields needs to be summed, which in Spark is done with a reduce action over the field obtaining a number. This is illustrated in detail in Fig. 6(c), where the new columns z_j represents the division of the j-th value of each h_i between its square distance $(d_i)^2$, *sum* represents the sum of each column and *reduce$_j$* is the name of the variable that gather that number. So first column z_1 will be the division of each $c_{i \cdot h+1}$ of each h_i between the distance $(d_i)^2$, then it will be summed and saved in the variable *reduce$_1$*. Then, it is just necessary to divide each sum of each field with the sum of the inverse of the square distance (reduceDist variable), obtaining the h values predicted as shown in Fig. 6(d).

Once all the predictions for the h values are made, the process begins again to obtain the following h forecasts, but this time updating the TRS, as shown in Fig. 7(a), where TRS *old* represents the initial TRS; and TRS *new* the new one including the previous TRS and the h real values previously predicted. The algorithm will then stop when the total predictions have the same size as the TES. This can be seen in Fig. 7(b). The final step lies in comparing the prediction with the real values in TES applying the formula of the mean relative error, defined in Eq. (9), as shown in Fig. 7(c).

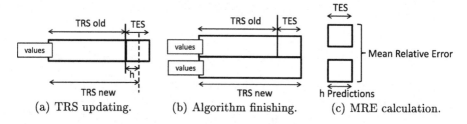

idGrouping	wValues	hValues	distance
0	------	h_0 (c_1, c_2,..., c_h)	---
1	w_1 ($c_{h-(w-1)}$,..., c_{h-1}, c_h)	h_1 (c_{h+1}, c_{h+2},..., c_{2h})	d_1
2	w_2 ($c_{2h-(w-1)}$,..., c_{2h-1}, c_{2h})	h_2 (c_{2h+1}, c_{2h+2},..., c_{3h})	d_2
3	w_3 ($c_{3h-(w-1)}$,..., c_{3h-1}, c_{3h})	h_3 (c_{3h+1}, c_{3h+2},..., c_{4h})	d_3
...	...	...	...

(a) RDD adding the distance between w_i and w pattern.

idGrouping	wValues	hValues	distance
3	w_3 ($c_{3h-(w-1)}$,..., c_{3h-1}, c_{3h})	h_3 (c_{3h+1}, c_{3h+2},..., c_{4h})	d_3
1	w_1 ($c_{h-(w-1)}$,..., c_{h-1}, c_h)	h_1 (c_{h+1}, c_{h+2},..., c_{2h})	d_1
2	w_2 ($c_{2h-(w-1)}$,..., c_{2h-1}, c_{2h})	h_2 (c_{2h+1}, c_{2h+2},..., c_{3h})	d_2
...	...	...	...

(b) Sorting by smaller distance and selecting just the k nearest neighbours.

idGrouping	wValues	hValues	distance	z_1	z_2
3	w_3 ($c_{3h-(w-1)}$,..., c_{3h-1}, c_{3h})	h_3 (c_{3h+1}, c_{3h+2},..., c_{4h})	d3		
1	w_1 ($c_{h-(w-1)}$,..., c_{h-1}, c_h)	h_1 (c_{h+1}, c_{h+2},..., c_{2h})	d_1		
...	...	...	...		
...	...	...	...		

$\fbox{sum}$ $\fbox{sum}$ $\fbox{sum}$
reduce$_1$ reduce$_2$

(c) RDD adding suboperations as columns before doing reduce sums actions.

Prediction of h values

reduce$_1$ reduceDist	reduce$_2$ reduceDist	...	reduce$_h$ reduceDist

(d) Computation of the prediction.

Fig. 6. kNN in Spark, phase 3.

(a) TRS updating.   (b) Algorithm finishing.   (c) MRE calculation.

Fig. 7. kNN in Spark, phase 4.

4   Results

This section presents the results obtained from the application of the proposed methodology to electricity consumption big data time series. Hence, Sect. 4.1 describes the used datasets. The experimental setup carried out is detailed in Sect. 4.2. Finally, the results are discussed in Sect. 4.3.

4.1   Datasets Description

The datasets used are related to the electrical energy consumption in two buildings located at a public university for years 2011, 2012 and 2013. The consumption is measured every fifteen minutes during this period. This makes a total of 35040 instances for years 2011 and 2013, and 35136 for the year 2012. TES consists of the the last three months of 2013 for both datasets.

Note that there were several missing values ($< 3\%$). In particular, some values are equal to 0. However, subsequent time stamps store the accumulated consumption for such instances. Therefore, the cleaning process consisted in searching for such 0 values and assuming that consumption had been constant during these periods of time. That is, the stored value after zeros is divided by the number of consecutive registered zeros and assigned to each one.

4.2 Design of Experiments

The proposed algorithm requires several variables to be executed. Since this is a preliminary study, an exhaustive analysis of best values has not been carried out and the following considerations have been taken into account:

1. The size of the window (w) has been set to 96, which represents all the values for a whole day.
2. As for the forecast horizon (h), it was firstly set to $h = 48$ (12 h) and secondly to $h = 96$ (24 h).
3. The number of nearest neighbours (k) varies from one to five.

The algorithm has been executed using each dataset described in Sect. 4.1 varying the aforementioned parameter settings (w, h and k). In short, each dataset has been executed 10 times.

To evaluate the runtime costs of the algorithm, each complete experimentation for each dataset has been executed using two processors, summing 20 executions in total.

The experimentation has been launched on a cluster, which consists of 2 Intel Xeon E7-4820 processors at 2 GHz, 18 MB cache, 8 cores per processor and 64 GB of main memory working under Linux Ubuntu. The cluster works with Apache Spark 1.4.1 and Hadoop 2.3.

Finally, in order to assess the performance of the algorithm, the well-known mean relative error (MRE) measure has been selected. Its formula is:

$$MRE = \frac{1}{N} \sum_{i=1}^{N} \frac{|v_{pred} - v_{actual}|}{v_{actual}} \tag{9}$$

where v_{pred} stands for the predicted values and v_{acutal} for the actual consumption values.

4.3 Electricity Consumption Big Data Time Series Forecasting

This section shows the results of applying the methodology proposed in Sect. 3.1 to the datasets described in Sect. 4.1 over the cluster described in Sect. 4.2. The algorithm has been tested on the last three months in the year 2013, for both buildings, resulting in 8832 forecasted instances.

Table 1 summarizes the results obtained for the first building. Analogously, Table 2 shows the results obtained for the second building. Note that the column *Duration* collects execution times in minutes. The values for the rightmost columns show the MRE associated with each k.

It can be noticed that to facilitate future comparative analysis, only two processors have been used. Additionally, horizons of prediction has been set to

Table 1. Electricity consumption forecasting for the first building.

w	h	Duration	$k = 1$	$k = 2$	$k = 3$	$k = 4$	$k = 5$
96	48	143.99	0.3184	0.2902	0.3025	0.3132	0.3090
96	96	53.00	0.4653	0.4243	0.4530	0.4773	0.4708

Table 2. Electricity consumption forecasting for the second building.

w	h	Duration	$k = 1$	$k = 2$	$k = 3$	$k = 4$	$k = 5$
96	48	143.79	0.3052	0.2749	0.2870	0.2912	0.3030
96	96	53.13	0.4807	0.4159	0.4407	0.4452	0.4686

48 (12 h) and 96 samples (24 h), thus representing usual short-term forecasting horizons in electricity consumptions.

It can be seen in both tables that the execution time varies along with the size of the h, up to 66 %. This is because the higher the value of h is, the lesser number of distances has to be computed. It can also be noticed that small values of k do not make significant difference to the accuracy of the predictions. In fact it just changes from one k to another by 5 %. Farthest studies need to be carried out to select the optimal k.

It must be admitted that the execution time is expected to be improved in future versions. This is partly due to the fact that the calculation of every w_i is the only part of the algorithm which is not made in a parallelized way, but in an iterative way. Since previous h_i must be checked to compute w_i, in some cases, two subsets w_i and w_j may have values from the same h_i. This means that for every w_i, all the previous h_i's need to be individually checked, and just the ones after it are discarded. In short, a formula that creates every w_i from the original time series following a MapReduce schema have not been found so far. Obviously, future research will address this issue.

5   Conclusions

An algorithm to forecast big data time series has been proposed. In particular, the algorithm is based on the weighted nearest neighbours paradigm. This work describes how to design it in Spark. It also provides results for real-world time series, e.g. electricity consumption for several buildings at a public university. The implementation has been launched on a 2-processor cluster generating satisfactory results in terms of both MRE and execution time. Future work is directed in integrating the code in the Spark MLlib as well as in reducing its computational cost.

Acknowledgments. The authors would like to thank the Spanish Ministry of Economy and Competitiveness, Junta de Andalucía, Fundación Pública Andaluza Centro de Estudios Andaluces and Universidad Pablo de Olavide for the support under projects TIN2014-55894-C2-R, P12-TIC-1728, PRY153/14 and APPB813097, respectively.

References

1. Box, G., Jenkins, G.: Time Series Analysis: Forecasting and Control. John Wiley and Sons, Hoboken (2008)
2. Canuto, S., Gonçalves, M., Santos, W., Rosa, T., Martins, W.: An efficient and scalable metafeature-based document classification approach based on massively parallel computing. In: Proceedings of the International ACM SIGIR Conference on Research and Development in Information Retrieval, pp. 333–342 (2015)
3. Cover, T.M., Hart, P.E.: Nearest neighbor pattern classification. IEEE Trans. Inf. Theor. **13**(1), 21–27 (1967)
4. Dean, J., Ghemawat, S.: Mapreduce: simplified data processing on large clusters. Commun. ACM **51**(1), 107–113 (2008)
5. Machine Learning Library (MLlib) for Spark (2015). http://spark.apache.org/docs/latest/mllib-guide.html
6. Hamstra, M., Karau, H., Zaharia, M., Knwinski, A., Wendell, P.: Learning Spark: Lightning-Fast Big Analytics. O' Really Media, Sebastopol (2015)
7. Martínez-Álvarez, F., Troncoso, A., Riquelme, J.C., Aguilar, J.S.: Discovery of motifs to forecast outlier occurrence in time series. Pattern Recogn. Lett. **32**, 1652–1665 (2011)
8. Martínez-Álvarez, F., Troncoso, A., Riquelme, J.C., Aguilar, J.S.: Energy time series forecasting based on pattern sequence similarity. IEEE Trans. Knowl. Data Eng. **23**, 1230–1243 (2011)
9. Martínez-Álvarez, F., Troncoso, A., Asencio-Cortés, G., Riquelme, J.: A survey on data mining techniques applied to electricity-related time series forecasting. Energies **8**(11), 12361 (2015)
10. Minelli, M., Chambers, M., Dhiraj, A.: Big Data, Big Analytics: Emerging Business Intelligence and Analytics Trends for Today's Businesses. John Wiley and Sons, Hoboken (2013)
11. Muja, M., Lowe, D.G.: Scalable nearest neighbor algorithms for high dimensional data. IEEE Trans. Pattern Anal. Mach. Intell. **36**(11), 2227–2240 (2014)
12. Reyes-Ortiz, J.L., Oneto, L., Anguita, D.: Big data analytics in the cloud: spark on hadoop vs MPI/OpenMP on beowulf. Procedia Comput. Sci. **53**, 121–130 (2015)
13. Triguero, I., Peralta, D., Bacardit, J., García, S., Herrera, F.: MRPR: a mapreduce solution for prototype reduction in big data classification. Neurocomputing **150**, 331–345 (2015)
14. Troncoso, A., Riquelme, J.C., Riquelme, J.M., Martínez, J.L., Gómez, A.: Electricity market price forecasting based on weighted nearest neighbours techniques. IEEE Trans. Power Syst. **22**(3), 1294–1301 (2007)
15. White, T.: Hadoop, The Definitive Guide. O' Really Media, Sebastopol (2012)
16. Yang, M., Zheng, L., Lu, Y., Guo, M., Li, J.: Cloud-assisted spatio-textual k nearest neighbor joins in sensor networks. In: Proceedings of the Industrial Networks and Intelligent Systems, pp. 12–17 (2015)
17. Zhang, C., Li, F., Jestes, J.: Efficient parallel kNN joins for large data in mapreduce. In: Proceedings of the International Conference on Extending Database Technology, pp. 38–49 (2012)

Active Learning Classifier for Streaming Data

Michał Woźniak[1]([✉]), Bogusław Cyganek[2,3], Andrzej Kasprzak[1],
Paweł Ksieniewicz[1], and Krzysztof Walkowiak[1]

[1] Department of Systems and Computer Networks,
Faculty of Electronics, Wrocław University of Technology,
Wybrzeże Wyspiańskiego 27, 50-370 Wrocław, Poland
{michal.wozniak,andrzej.kasprzak,pawel.ksieniewicz,
krzysztof.walkowiak}@pwr.edu.pl
[2] ENGINE Center, Wrocław University of Technology,
Wybrzeże Wyspiańskiego 27, 50-370 Wrocław, Poland
cyganek@agh.edu.pl
[3] AGH University of Science and Technology, Al. Mickiewicza 30,
30-059 Krakow, Poland

Abstract. This work reports the research on active learning approach applied to the data stream classification. The chosen characteristics of the proposed frameworks were evaluated on the basis of the wide range of computer experiments carried out on the three benchmark data streams. Obtained results confirmed the usability of proposed method to the data stream classification with the presence of incremental concept drift.

Keywords: Pattern classification · Data stream classification · Active learning

1 Introduction and Related Works

Designing the appropriate models for data stream classification is nowadays focus of intense research, because canonical classifiers usually do not take into consideration that the statistical dependencies between the observations of incoming objects and their classifications may change during. Such phenomena is called *concept drift* [13] and we may meet it in many practical issues, as spam filtering, intrusion detection/prevention, or recognition of client behaviour to enumerate only a few. There are several taxonomies of concept drift. The first one is considering its rapidity, then we can distinguish sudden concept drift and smooth one. We can also distinguish two types of such an event, according to its influence on the probabilistic characteristics of the classification task [6]:

- virtual concept drift means that changes do not impact the decision boundaries (some say the *posterior* probabilities do not change, but it is disputable), but affect the probability density functions [12].
- real concept drift means that changes affect the *posterior* probabilities and may impact unconditional probability density function [13].

© Springer International Publishing Switzerland 2016
F. Martínez-Álvarez et al. (Eds.): HAIS 2016, LNAI 9648, pp. 186–197, 2016.
DOI: 10.1007/978-3-319-32034-2_16

From the classification point of view, the real concept drift is important because it can strongly affect the shape of the decision boundary. The virtual drift does not affect the decision rule, especially taking into consideration the Bayes decision theory [5]. Additionally, during the designing a data stream classifier we should take also into consideration the limitation of the resources as memory and computational power, as well that we are not able have access all labels of learning examples. In this work we will mostly focus on the problem related to cost of labelling. The most of the classifier devoted to data stream or drifted data streams use supervised learning algorithms, which could produce a classifier on the basis of labelled examples. Unfortunately, from the practical point of view it is hard to be granted that labels are always available, e.g.,

- Medical diagnosis - human expert should always verifies the diagnosis, i.e., we have to ensure the continuous access to the human expert.
- Credit application (the true label is available ca. 2 years after the decision);
- Spam filtering - user should confirm the decision if incoming mail is legitimate or not.

In this approach we should take into consideration the cost of data labelling, which is usually passed over. Let us notice that labels are usually assigned by human experts and therefore they can not label all new examples if they come too fast. Therefore methods of classifier design which could produce the recognition system on the basis of a partially labelled set of examples (especially if learner could point out the interesting example to be labelled) [7].

Changes are discovered by monitoring the unlabelled input data and discover novelties related to outlier detection, or by monitoring classification accuracy [9]. Constant update of a classifier is accomplished by using incremental learning methods that allow adding new training data during the exploitation of a classifier or by dataset windowing.

Therefore, developing methods which are able to effectively deal with this phenomena has become an increasing issue in the intense researches. In general, the following approaches can be considered to deal with the above problem.

- Rebuilding a classification model if new data becomes available. It is very expensive and impossible from a practical point of view, and especially for which the concept drift occurs rapidly.
- Detecting concept changes in new data, and if these changes are *sufficiently* significant then rebuilding the classifier.
- Adopting an incremental learning algorithm for the classification model.

Our work will focus on a hybrid aproach which is combination of online learning approach and sliding windows method with forgetting. The online learning relates to the family of algorithms that continuously update the classifier parameters, while processing the incoming data.Online learners have to meet some basic requirements [4]:

- Each learning example must be processed only once in the course of training.
- The system should consume only limited memory and processing time, irrespective of the execution time and amount of data processed.

– The training process can be paused at any time, and its accuracy should not be lower than that of a classifier trained on batch data collected up to the given time.

We should also mention algorithms that incorporate the forgetting mechanism. This approach is based on the assumption that the recently arrived data are the most relevant, because they contain characteristics of the current context. However, their relevance diminishes with the passage of time. Therefore, narrowing the range of data to those that were most recently read may help form a dataset that embodies the actual context. There are three possible strategies here:

– selecting the instances by means of a sliding window that cuts off older instances [13];
– weighting the data according to their relevance; and
– applying boosting-based algorithms that focus on misclassified instances [3].

When dealing with the sliding window the main question is how to adjust the window size. On the one hand, a shorter window allows focusing on the emerging context, though data may not be representative for a longer lasting context. On the other hand, a wider window may result in mixing the instances representing different contexts [10].

Therefore, certain advanced algorithms adjust the window size dynamically depending on the detected state (e.g., FLORA2 [13] and ADWIN2 [1]). In more sophisticated algorithms, multiple windows may even be used [11].

2   Active Learning Classifier for Data Stream

Let us propose the classifier learning framework which employs the active learning paradigm. This framework works as the block classifier, because it collects the data in the form of chunk, but for each chunk the online learner is used. The decision about the object labelling depends on two parameters:

– threshold - which is responsible for choosing the "interesting" examples, i.e., if support function related with the decision is lower than a given threshold the the object seems to be interesting and algorithm is asking for its label.
– The label will be assigned (i.e., algorithm will pay for it) only in the case if its budget related to a given chunk will allows to pay for it. For each chunk only limited percentage of the objects could be labelled (depends on parameter budget).

Because the data stream is collected in the form of chunk, but each of them is processing incrementally, therefore before its analysis the order of the collected objects is randomizing. The idea of the algorithm is presented in Algorithm 1.

Algorithm 1. Active learning classifier for data stream

Require: input data stream,
    n - data chunk size,
    incremental training procedure(),
    classifier(),
    budget - max. percent of labeled example in a chunk,
    treshold
1: $i \leftarrow 0$
2: initialize classifier
3: **repeat**
4:     collect new data chunk $DS_i = \{x_i^1, x_i^2, ..., x_i^n\}$
5:     set random order of collected examples in DS_i
6:     **for** $j = 0$ **to** n **do**
7:        support $\leftarrow max$ (support function value returned by the classifier for x_i^j)
8:        **if** *support* $<$ *treshold* **then**
9:           **if** *budget* > 0 **then**
10:             ask for the label of the jth example
11:             classifier $\leftarrow$ incremental training procedure(x_j)
12:             *budget* $\leftarrow$ *budget* $- 1$
13:           **end if**
14:        **end if**
15:     **end for**
16:     $i \leftarrow i + 1$
17: **until** end of the input data stream

---

3   Experiments

3.1   Goals

The goal of the experiment is to check dependencies between algorithm's parameters (chunk size, threshold and budged for labelling) and the accuracy and stability of the classifier. The experiments were carried out for the 3 artificially generated data streams available in MOA (WaveformGeneratorDrift, RandomTreeGenerator, LEDGeneratorDrift) and 3 online learners as minimal distance classifier (k-NN), Naïve Bayes and Perceptron.

Software Environment. All experiments were carried out in the programing language Java using MOA (Massive Online Analysis) experimental software environment[1]. MOA [2] is a very popular framework for data stream analysis. It includes tools for evaluation and a collection of machine learning algorithms. The MOA project is related to WEKA software [8] developed by the same team from University of Waikato, New Zealand.

---

[1] http://moa.cms.waikato.ac.nz/.

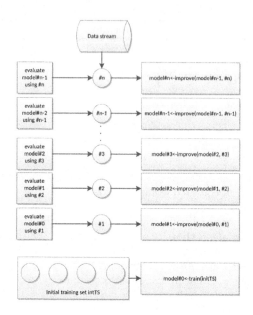

Fig. 1. Idea of test and train evaluation.

Table 1. Result of the experiments for k-NN classifier and LEDGeneratorDrift stream.

ch-s	tresh.	bud.	acc.	sd	ch-s	tresh.	bud.	acc.	sd
10	0.25	0.125	38.74	6.36	100	0.5	0.5	59.94	2.57
10	0.25	0.25	38.28	4.92	100	0.5	0.75	58.43	2.34
10	0.25	0.5	42.73	4.65	100	0.75	0.125	62.93	4.60
10	0.25	0.75	32.78	2.96	100	0.75	0.25	63.75	3.32
10	0.5	0.125	52.63	9.78	100	0.75	0.5	64.11	2.88
10	0.5	0.25	54.42	8.02	100	0.75	0.75	64.02	2.44
10	0.5	0.5	58.51	6.45	1000	0.25	0.125	38.43	2.27
10	0.5	0.75	58.93	6.57	1000	0.25	0.25	35.31	2.37
10	0.75	0.125	57.65	11.95	1000	0.25	0.5	41.77	2.09
10	0.75	0.25	60.01	9.29	1000	0.25	0.75	35.25	2.33
10	0.75	0.5	61.81	7.71	1000	0.5	0.125	56.65	1.92
10	0.75	0.75	62.26	7.20	1000	0.5	0.25	56.63	1.66
100	0.25	0.125	35.49	2.93	1000	0.5	0.5	60.94	1.75
100	0.25	0.25	38.5	2.99	1000	0.5	0.75	60.99	1.45
100	0.25	0.5	33.83	2.84	1000	0.75	0.125	64.82	1.38
100	0.25	0.75	32.71	3.43	1000	0.75	0.25	64.37	1.35
100	0.5	0.125	55.74	3.52	1000	0.75	0.5	63.87	1.58
100	0.5	0.25	55.45	2.79	1000	0.75	0.75	64.18	1.40

Table 2. Result of the experiments for k-NN classifier and RandomTreeGenerator stream.

ch-s	tresh.	bud.	acc.	sd	ch-s	tresh.	bud.	acc.	sd
10	0.25	0.125	58.54	3.36	100	0.5	0.5	57.93	3.17
10	0.25	0.25	58.54	3.36	100	0.5	0.75	60.75	3.15
10	0.25	0.5	41.45	3.44	100	0.75	0.125	75.44	2.49
10	0.25	0.75	58.54	3.36	100	0.75	0.25	75.63	2.59
10	0.5	0.125	58.54	3.36	100	0.75	0.5	76.04	2.26
10	0.5	0.25	59.31	3.26	100	0.75	0.75	75.72	2.32
10	0.5	0.5	60.94	3.00	1000	0.25	0.125	57.69	3.12
10	0.5	0.75	58.54	3.36	1000	0.25	0.25	42.31	3.12
10	0.75	0.125	73.40	4.78	1000	0.25	0.5	57.69	3.12
10	0.75	0.25	74.76	4.03	1000	0.25	0.75	57.69	3.12
10	0.75	0.5	74.79	3.97	1000	0.5	0.125	59.28	2.57
10	0.75	0.75	75.10	3.84	1000	0.5	0.25	64.16	2.38
100	0.25	0.125	57.93	3.17	1000	0.5	0.5	61.11	2.47
100	0.25	0.25	57.60	3.14	1000	0.5	0.75	57.69	3.12
100	0.25	0.5	57.93	3.17	1000	0.75	0.125	76.06	1.76
100	0.25	0.75	42.07	3.17	1000	0.75	0.25	75.96	1.64
100	0.5	0.125	57.93	3.17	1000	0.75	0.5	76.28	1.33
100	0.5	0.25	57.93	3.17	1000	0.75	0.75	75.79	1.86

Error Evaluation. The new model is trained on a given data chunk, but the error is estimated on the basis on the next (unseen) portion of data. Such a method is called "test and train" or "block evaluation method" [2] and its idea is depicted in Fig. 1.

3.2   Results

The results of the experiments are presented in Tables 1, 2, 3, 4, 5, 6, 7, 8 and 9. The abbreviations used in the column description: ch-s - chunk size, tresh.- treshold, bud. - budget, acc.-accuracy, sd - standard deviation.

3.3   Discussion

We realize that the scope of the experiments we carried out is limited and derived remarks are limited to the tested methods and three data stream generators only. In this case formulating general conclusions is very risky, but the preliminary results are quite promising, therefore we would like to continue the work on active learning methods applied to online learning in the future. Let's focus on some interesting observations:

Table 3. Result of the experiments for k-NN classifier and WaveformGeneratorDrift stream.

ch-s	tresh.	bud.	acc.	sd	ch-s	tresh.	bud.	acc.	sd
10	0.25	0.125	48.44	4.79	100	0.5	0.5	65.01	2.94
10	0.25	0.25	33.23	3.17	100	0.5	0.75	71.12	2.65
10	0.25	0.5	33.22	3.18	100	0.75	0.125	79.50	2.34
10	0.25	0.75	65.71	3.26	100	0.75	0.25	81.87	2.23
10	0.5	0.125	65.16	5.25	100	0.75	0.5	80.49	2.04
10	0.5	0.25	74.95	5.26	100	0.75	0.75	81.02	2.43
10	0.5	0.5	75.54	3.80	1000	0.25	0.125	57.70	2.76
10	0.5	0.75	69.54	3.27	1000	0.25	0.25	33.25	3.12
10	0.75	0.125	77.24	8.55	1000	0.25	0.5	74.18	2.46
10	0.75	0.25	77.85	6.83	1000	0.25	0.75	33.43	2.96
10	0.75	0.5	80.33	3.48	1000	0.5	0.125	72.09	2.35
10	0.75	0.75	80.96	3.56	1000	0.5	0.25	75.98	2.12
100	0.25	0.125	50.40	3.23	1000	0.5	0.5	73.13	2.24
100	0.25	0.25	61.23	3.17	1000	0.5	0.75	74.95	2.16
100	0.25	0.5	33.40	2.94	1000	0.75	0.125	80.57	1.79
100	0.25	0.75	33.40	2.94	1000	0.75	0.25	80.39	2.06
100	0.5	0.125	61.28	3.19	1000	0.75	0.5	81.48	1.56
100	0.5	0.25	72.38	2.91	1000	0.75	0.75	81.51	1.50

Table 4. Result of the experiments for Naive Bayes classifier and LEDGeneratorDrift stream.

ch-s	tresh.	bud.	acc.	sd	ch-s	tresh.	bud.	acc.	sd
10	0.25	0.125	35.65	4.05	100	0.5	0.5	62.13	3.16
10	0.25	0.25	42.38	4.05	100	0.5	0.75	66.70	3.08
10	0.25	0.5	35.14	5.18	100	0.75	0.125	73.61	3.75
10	0.25	0.75	36.79	3.08	100	0.75	0.25	73.81	3.39
10	0.5	0.125	58.04	10.34	100	0.75	0.5	73.65	2.94
10	0.5	0.25	61.97	8.14	100	0.75	0.75	74.05	2.87
10	0.5	0.5	62.46	5.37	1000	0.25	0.125	48.26	3.26
10	0.5	0.75	65.84	4.60	1000	0.25	0.25	50.70	3.32
10	0.75	0.125	68.87	12.05	1000	0.25	0.5	38.87	3.02
10	0.75	0.25	70.65	10.10	1000	0.25	0.75	45.90	3.14
10	0.75	0.5	72.20	6.70	1000	0.5	0.125	61.81	3.11

(Continued)

Table 4. (*Continued*)

ch-s	tresh.	bud.	acc.	sd	ch-s	tresh.	bud.	acc.	sd
10	0.75	0.75	72.28	7.03	1000	0.5	0.25	61.45	2.97
100	0.25	0.125	39.83	3.40	1000	0.5	0.5	68.35	3.14
100	0.25	0.25	42.64	11.25	1000	0.5	0.75	67.34	3.05
100	0.25	0.5	38.99	3.20	1000	0.75	0.125	73.85	2.85
100	0.25	0.75	32.5	2.97	1000	0.75	0.25	74.04	2.76
100	0.5	0.125	61.04	3.55	1000	0.75	0.5	73.95	2.83
100	0.5	0.25	67.01	3.26	1000	0.75	0.75	73.89	2.78

Table 5. Result of the experiments for k-NN classifier and RandomTreeGenerator stream.

ch-s	tresh.	bud.	acc.	sd	ch-s	tresh.	bud.	acc.	sd
10	0.25	0.125	41.47	3.36	100	0.5	0.5	57.93	3.17
10	0.25	0.25	56.72	3.15	100	0.5	0.75	61.36	6.07
10	0.25	0.5	58.49	3.28	100	0.75	0.125	73.57	3.00
10	0.25	0.75	41.47	3.36	100	0.75	0.25	73.68	2.92
10	0.5	0.125	58.36	3.21	100	0.75	0.5	73.54	2.92
10	0.5	0.25	58.48	3.32	100	0.75	0.75	73.58	2.96
10	0.5	0.5	60.60	3.07	1000	0.25	0.125	42.31	3.12
10	0.5	0.75	57.85	4.01	1000	0.25	0.25	42.31	3.13
10	0.75	0.125	72.63	3.84	1000	0.25	0.5	42.31	3.12
10	0.75	0.25	72.59	4.29	1000	0.25	0.75	57.69	3.12
10	0.75	0.5	72.83	3.67	1000	0.5	0.125	65.79	3.07
10	0.75	0.75	73.08	3.30	1000	0.5	0.25	59.30	3.14
100	0.25	0.125	42.07	3.17	1000	0.5	0.5	60.10	4.30
100	0.25	0.25	42.07	3.17	1000	0.5	0.75	57.48	3.20
100	0.25	0.5	57.93	3.17	1000	0.75	0.125	73.67	2.88
100	0.25	0.75	42.7	3.17	1000	0.75	0.25	73.64	2.79
100	0.5	0.125	58.25	3.24	1000	0.75	0.5	73.58	2.755818
100	0.5	0.25	57.31	3.17	1000	0.75	0.75	73.54	2.877642

- The experiments confirmed that proposed approach can adapt to changing concept returning a quite stable classifier, especially for a quite big data chunk.
- It's a strong dependency between threshold and the classifier accuracy. For the quite big data chunk (100 and 1000) the high threshold (0.75) guarantees the stable classifier. Usually, for the mentioned above treshold value the stability and accuracy do not depend on the budget.

Table 6. Result of the experiments for Naive Bayes classifier and WaveformGenera-torDrift stream.

ch-s	tresh.	bud.	acc.	sd	ch-s	tresh.	bud.	acc.	sd
10	0.25	0.125	33.49	3.04	100	0.5	0.5	72.45	2.82
10	0.25	0.25	42.90	3.13	100	0.5	0.75	74.00	2.84
10	0.25	0.5	43.53	2.93	100	0.75	0.125	80.29	2.70
10	0.25	0.75	33.49	3.044	100	0.75	0.25	80.04	2.67
10	0.5	0.125	70.78	5.19	100	0.75	0.5	81.30	2.56
10	0.5	0.25	70.28	4.29	100	0.75	0.75	81.54	2.57
10	0.5	0.5	66.31	2.95	1000	0.25	0.125	60.06	3.09
10	0.5	0.75	70.60	2.78	1000	0.25	0.25	58.47	3.18
10	0.75	0.125	79.48	6.44	1000	0.25	0.5	33.25	3.12
10	0.75	0.25	78.72	5.93	1000	0.25	0.75	33.25	3.12
10	0.75	0.5	80.83	3.08	1000	0.5	0.125	74.38	2.56
10	0.75	0.75	80.70	3.11	1000	0.5	0.25	69.73	2.869869
100	0.25	0.125	63.30	3.15	1000	0.5	0.5	61.24	2.96
100	0.25	0.25	75.04	2.87	1000	0.5	0.75	71.30	2.68
100	0.25	0.5	33.70	3.09	1000	0.75	0.125	80.25	2.34
100	0.25	0.75	46.13	3.23	1000	0.75	0.25	80.39	2.45
100	0.5	0.125	58.61	3.06	1000	0.75	0.5	80.89	2.28
100	0.5	0.25	62.32	3.29	1000	0.75	0.75	81.00	2.31

Table 7. Result of the experiments for Perceptron classifier and LEDGeneratorDrift stream.

ch-s	tresh.	bud.	acc.	sd	ch-s	tresh.	bud.	acc.	sd
10	0.25	0.125	36.57	7.36	100	0.5	0.5	58.35	3.95
10	0.25	0.25	38.14	5.92	100	0.5	0.75	66.00	3.46
10	0.25	0.5	44.07	5.70	100	0.75	0.125	71.18	7.61
10	0.25	0.75	39.44	4.48	100	0.75	0.25	72.19	5.70
10	0.5	0.125	51.30	11.62	100	0.75	0.5	72.84	4.53
10	0.5	0.25	54.56	10.44	100	0.75	0.75	73.27	4.10
10	0.5	0.5	61.42	10.45	1000	0.25	0.125	32.30	2.99
10	0.5	0.75	56.57	7.44	1000	0.25	0.25	33.46	3.61
10	0.75	0.125	62.14	15.26	1000	0.25	0.5	47.59	3.31
10	0.75	0.25	64.75	13.22	1000	0.25	0.75	32.83	3.19
10	0.75	0.5	67.84	11.61	1000	0.5	0.125	59.29	3.84

(*Continued*)

Table 7. (*Continued*)

ch-s	tresh.	bud.	acc.	sd	ch-s	tresh.	bud.	acc.	sd
10	0.75	0.75	68.38	11.06	1000	0.5	0.25	60.032	3.21
100	0.25	0.125	39.28	3.32	1000	0.5	0.5	64.45	3.23
100	0.25	0.25	37.73	3.12	1000	0.5	0.75	66.09	3.02
100	0.25	0.5	39.75	3.11	1000	0.75	0.125	73.51	3.02
100	0.25	0.75	42.17	3.19	1000	0.75	0.25	73.66	2.77
100	0.5	0.125	60.75	5.40	1000	0.75	0.5	73.66	2.62
100	0.5	0.25	60.23	4.24	1000	0.75	0.75	73.67	2.58

Table 8. Result of the experiments for Perceptron classifier and RandomTreeGenerator stream.

ch-s	tresh.	bud.	acc.	sd	ch-s	tresh.	bud.	acc.	sd
10	0.25	0.125	58.54	3.36	100	0.5	0.5	57.93	3.17
10	0.25	0.25	41.47	3.36	100	0.5	0.75	57.90	3.18
10	0.25	0.5	41.47	3.36	100	0.75	0.125	61.38	4.38
10	0.25	0.75	41.47	3.36	100	0.75	0.25	63.28	3.97
10	0.5	0.125	58.54	3.36	100	0.75	0.5	64.45	3.30
10	0.5	0.25	58.54	3.36	100	0.75	0.75	64.10	3.45
10	0.5	0.5	57.85	3.40	1000	0.25	0.125	57.69	3.12
10	0.5	0.75	58.54	3.36	1000	0.25	0.25	42.31	3.13
10	0.75	0.125	60.53	3.94	1000	0.25	0.5	42.31	3.12
10	0.75	0.25	62.08	4.72	1000	0.25	0.75	57.69	3.12
10	0.75	0.5	63.30	3.66	1000	0.5	0.125	57.54	3.11
10	0.75	0.75	63.52	3.76	1000	0.5	0.25	57.74	3.11
100	0.25	0.125	42.07	3.17	1000	0.5	0.5	58.10	3.06
100	0.25	0.25	57.93	3.17	1000	0.5	0.75	58.15	3.13
100	0.25	0.5	57.93	3.17	1000	0.75	0.125	59.17	3.78
100	0.25	0.75	42.07	3.17	1000	0.75	0.25	64.35	3.26
100	0.5	0.125	57.93	3.17	1000	0.75	0.5	64.66	3.03
100	0.5	0.25	57.64	3.178	1000	0.75	0.75	64.85	2.94

- For small chunk size the budget plays an important role. Its increasing causes that the model achieves better quality.
- It is obvious, but confirmed by the experiments that the accuracy and stability depend on chunk size, but for the biggest chunk size (1000) we observed the quality and stability detoration, what is probably causes by the fact that the chunks cover more than one model.

Table 9. Result of the experiments for Perceptron classifier and WaveformGenerator-Drift stream.

ch-s	tresh.	bud.	acc.	sd	ch-s	tresh.	bud.	acc.	sd
10	0.25	0.125	50.30	3.24	100	0.5	0.5	59.44	3.10
10	0.25	0.25	51.01	3.19	100	0.5	0.75	70.3	2.96
10	0.25	0.5	33.49	3.044	100	0.75	0.125	74.87	8.53
10	0.25	0.75	33.02	2.98	100	0.75	0.25	78.27	7.93
10	0.5	0.125	62.78	3.32	100	0.75	0.5	80.94	4.52
10	0.5	0.25	75.98	8.22	100	0.75	0.75	80.54	4.08
10	0.5	0.5	67.77	8.61	1000	0.25	0.125	33.39	2.82
10	0.5	0.75	53.10	5.31	1000	0.25	0.25	33.10	3.04
10	0.75	0.125	66.65	10.46	1000	0.25	0.5	33.10	3.04
10	0.75	0.25	69.94	12.26	1000	0.25	0.75	33.34	3.00
10	0.75	0.5	72.17	11.19	1000	0.5	0.125	62.25	3.22
10	0.75	0.75	76.28	7.41	1000	0.5	0.25	69.90	3.05
100	0.25	0.125	62.64	3.10	1000	0.5	0.5	60.36	3.22
100	0.25	0.25	33.40	2.94	1000	0.5	0.75	58.41	3.84
100	0.25	0.5	33.31	2.95	1000	0.75	0.125	81.15	3.15
100	0.25	0.75	61.79	3.16	1000	0.75	0.25	82.01	2.62
100	0.5	0.125	62.74	3.22	1000	0.75	0.5	80.64	3.69
100	0.5	0.25	61.89	5.07	1000	0.75	0.75	77.73	6.99

4   Conclusions

We realize that the scope of the experiments we carried out is limited. In this case formulating general conclusions is very risky, but the preliminary results are quite promising, therefore we would like to continue the work on active learning approach in the future.

In the near future we are going to:

- Carrying out experiments on the wider number of datasets, especially for the streams with and without concept drift.
- Applying the proposed approach to the classifier ensemble.
- Evaluating the proposed algorithm behavior for more type of concept drift and maybe employ concept drift detector to establish the chunk size dynamically.

Acknowledgement. This work was supported by the Polish National Science Centre under the grant no. DEC-2013/09/B/ST6/02264. This work was supported by EC under FP7, Coordination and Support Action, Grant Agreement Number 316097, ENGINE European Research Centre of Network Intelligence for Innovation Enhancement (http://engine.pwr.wroc.pl/). All computer experiments were carried out using computer equipment sponsored by ENGINE project.

References

1. Bifet, A., Gavalda R.: Learning from time-changing data with adaptive windowing. In: Proceedings of the Seventh SIAM International Conference on Data Mining. SIAM, Minneapolis, Minnesota, USA, 26–28 April 2007
2. Bifet, A., Holmes, G., Kirkby, R., Pfahringer, B.: Moa: massive online analysis. J. Mach. Learn. Res. **11**, 1601–1604 (2010)
3. Bifet, A., Holmes, G., Pfahringer, B., Kirkby, R., Gavaldà, R.: New ensemble methods for evolving data streams. In: Proceedings of the 15th ACM SIGKDD International Conference on Knowledge Discovery and Data Mining, KDD 2009, pp. 139–148. ACM, New York (2009)
4. Domingos, P., Hulten, G.: A general framework for mining massive data streams. J. Comput. Graph. Stat. **12**, 945–949 (2003)
5. Duda, R.O., Hart, P.E., Stork, D.G.: Pattern Classification, 2nd edn. Wiley, New York (2001)
6. Gama, J., Zliobaite, I., Bifet, A., Pechenizkiy, M., Bouchachia, A.: A survey on concept drift adaptation. ACM Comput. Surv. (2013, in press)
7. Greiner, R., Grove, A.J., Roth, D.: Learning cost-sensitive active classifiers. Artif. Intell. **139**(2), 137–174 (2002)
8. Hall, M., Frank, E., Holmes, G., Pfahringer, B., Reutemann, P., Witten, I.H.: The weka data mining software: an update. SIGKDD Explor. Newsl. **11**(1), 10–18 (2009)
9. Kuncheva, L.I.: Combining Pattern Classifiers: Methods and Algorithms. Wiley, New York (2004)
10. Kurlej, B., Wozniak, M.: Impact of window size in active learning of evolving data streams. In: Proceedings of the 45th International Conference on Modelling and Simulation of Systems, MOSIS 2011, pp. 56–62 (2011)
11. Lazarescu, M.M., Venkatesh, S., Bui, H.H.: Using multiple windows to track concept drift. Intell. Data Anal. **8**(1), 29–59 (2004)
12. Widmer, G., Kubat, M.: Effective learning in dynamic environments by explicit context tracking. In: Brazdil, P.B. (ed.) ECML 1993. LNCS, vol. 667, pp. 227–243. Springer, Heidelberg (1993)
13. Widmer, G., Kubat, M.: Learning in the presence of concept drift and hidden contexts. Mach. Learn. **23**(1), 69–101 (1996)

Bio-inspired Models and Evolutionary Computation

Application of Genetic Algorithms and Heuristic Techniques for the Identification and Classification of the Information Used by a Recipe Recommender

Cristian Peñaranda[✉], Soledad Valero, Vicente Julian, and Javier Palanca

Departamento de Sistemas Informáticos y Computación (DSIC),
Universitat Politècnica de València, Camino de Vera s/n, 46020 Valencia, Spain
cpenaranda@dsic.upv.es

Abstract. Most of existing applications for locating and retrieving information are currently oriented towards offering personalized recommendations using well-known recommender techniques as content-based or collaborative filtering. Nevertheless, automatic information retrieval approaches still lack of an efficient analysis, integration and adaptation of the retrieved information. This can be observed mainly when information comes from different sources. In this way, the application of intelligent techniques can offer an interesting approach for solving this kind of complex processes. This paper employs an evolutive approach in order to improve the retrieval process of correct nutritional information of ingredients in an on-line recommender system of cooking recipes. The proposed algorithm has been tested over real data. Moreover, some heuristics have been included in order to improve the obtained results.

Keywords: Genetic algorithms · Heuristics · NoSQL

1 Introduction

Today, Internet is the most important vehicle and storage for information. As Internet evolves and grows, the act of locating and consulting relevant information available over the net becomes more and more complicated. In most cases, current toolkits for locating and retrieving information are oriented towards offering personalized recommendations using traditional recommender systems. These systems base their recommendations on quantitative measures of similarity between the user's preferences and the current items to recommend (i.e. content-based recommenders [14]), between the user's profile and the profile of other users with similar preferences (i.e. collaborative filtering recommenders [15]) and on combinations of both (i.e. hybrid recommenders [3]). For a correct performance of these recommenders, it is necessary an automatic and efficient analysis of the information prior to their use in the recommendation process. However, it is still needed an improvement and optimization of the degree of

© Springer International Publishing Switzerland 2016
F. Martínez-Álvarez et al. (Eds.): HAIS 2016, LNAI 9648, pp. 201–212, 2016.
DOI: 10.1007/978-3-319-32034-2_17

automatization in these search and retrieval processes. The application of intelligent techniques in this kind of complex processes can offer an interesting approach for solving that problems in an efficient and flexible way.

One example of this problem is the case of Receteame.com[1] which is an on-line recommender of cooking recipes in spanish. Specifically, Receteame.com is a website that uses a persuasive social recommender system to offer new recipes customized for each user. In order to do this, the system retrieves recipes from the Internet, automatically calculates their nutritional information and dietary restrictions and uses this information to make recommendations. These automatic retrieval processes suffer the previously commented problem.

Concretely, the automatic calculation of nutritional information and dietary restrictions needs the integration and adaptation of information from different sources and without a uniform format. For the moment, the website automatically accesses to the United States Department of Agriculture (USDA)[2] database that contains nutritional information of a large number of ingredients in English.

The main problem using this database is finding the correct nutritional information of a particular ingredient. Therefore, only the 36 % of cases the database return the desired ingredient in the first position of the result set. One possible explanation for this behaviour is that USDA describes its ingredients using features, but these features do not follow a fixed structure. For example, Fig. 1 shows the description of three ingredients in USDA. The first is "apple" and it contains the keyword at the beginning of the description. On the other hand, we have the ingredient "cooked bacon" where its keyword is in the second position (the first position corresponds to the category). Finally in the "meatless bacon" case, the word bacon appears in the first position. These examples state that an ontology is not followed to describe ingredients in this database, so a fixed structure to describe ingredients is not used.

```
1  Apples  , raw      , with skin
2  Pork    , bacon    , cooked
3  Bacon   , meatless
```

Fig. 1. Example of the structure of different ingredients.

In order to improve the quality of the result sets, we decided to dump the USDA database to a new MongoDB database and use the text search feature of MongoDB[3]. This feature of MongoDB allowed us to give more priority to some fields over others, in order to improve the search by means of reducing the impact of the lack of an ontology to describe ingredients. This text search feature also searches the stem words to improve results. Thus, using this feature

---

[1] Available in http://receteame.com/.

[2] Database available in http://ndb.nal.usda.gov/ndb/foods.

[3] NoSQL database which uses a JSON document structure type, available in https://www.mongodb.org/.

we wanted to organize the structure of the ingredient description in the database. First, we divided the ingredient descriptions into feature fields (using commas of the description as split separators), so each ingredient description had up to eleven feature fields. Finally, we created weighted indexes for these feature fields. These weights allowed MongoDB to give more priority to some feature fields over others, in order to improve the searching.

However, as it was previously mentioned, due to the lack of an ontology for describing the ingredients, it was not possible to fix a priori the best value for each weight and it was necessary to search the best combination of possible values for them. But the dimension of the combinatorial space of this search was so high to tackle it with traditional search algorithms. In this way, we decided to apply a genetic algorithm to determine the set of weighted indexes which improve the result sets offered by MongoDB when an ingredient is searched in the USDA database. The use of evolutionary algorithms as a way to evolve an ontology can be considered a novel application and has been succesfully employed in recent works like [10, 11]. Moreover, we decided to develop and apply heuristics to the obtained result sets in order to improve, as much as possible, the rate of times in which the desired ingredient description is finally returned.

Therefore, in this paper a genetic algorithm and the heuristics we have developed are presented. Also, we show the results of applying them to searching of ingredient descriptions. The rest of the paper is organized as follows. Section 2 is dedicated to explain the GA and results of applying it. Section 3 describes the developed heuristics, showing also the final performance achieved using them. Finally, conclusions and future works are presented.

2 Specification of the Proposed Genetic Algorithm

Genetic algorithms (GAs) are general purpose search algorithms that use principles inspired by natural genetic populations to evolve solutions to problems [7, 9]. These algorithms have had a great measure of success in search and optimization problems. The reason for a great part of their success is their ability to exploit the information accumulated about an initially unknown search space in order to bias subsequent searches into useful subspaces. This is their key feature, particularly in large, complex, and poorly understood search spaces, where classical search tools (enumerative, heuristic, etc.) are inappropriate. GAs offer a valid approach to problems that requires efficient and effective search techniques.

In our case, the developed GA seeks the best combination of values of the weighted indexes of each feature field in which an ingredient description was organized in order to use the text searching tool of MongoDB. The GA starts with a random initial population, that is, a set of possible solutions (starting generation), which evolves using selection, crossover and mutation genetic operators, producing new generations of possible sets of weights. These operators are explained below.

2.1   Codification

Each ingredient had up to eleven feature fields, so we decided to use individuals with eleven genes where each gene adopts real values [9,13]. These values correspond to the weight of the index of each feature of an ingredient description, that is, the priority of this feature. Therefore, in our case, the codification of a possible solution or individual is $I_0 = (c_1, c_2, ..., c_{11})$, where $c_i \in [V_{min}, V_{max}]$, $\forall_{1 \leq i \leq 11}$, being c_i the value of the weight of the feature field i, and V_{min} and V_{max} the minimum and maximum value attainable by genes. The MongoDB database set $V_{min} = 1$ and $V_{max} = 99999$. In order to reduce the search space, we reduced V_{max} to 9901, and applied intervals of 100 units. Figure 2 shows an example of the codification used.

c1	c2	c3	c4	c5	c6	c7	c8	c9	c10	c11
1	6501	101	6401	201	101	201	4801	9901	801	1001

Fig. 2. Coding example of an individual where each gene corresponds to the importance of each feature field which describe an ingredient in the database MongoDB.

2.2   Starting Generation

The first step of our GA is to obtain a random starting generation, with a population size of 1000 individuals. Thus, each new individual is computed as follows: $I_0 = (c_1, c_2, ..., c_{11})$, where each gene $c_i = random[1, 9901]$, $\forall_{1 \leq i \leq 11}$, being c_i the value of the weight (importance) of the feature field i. Also, two or more genes can have the same value. Furthermore, as it was mentioned in Sect. 2.1, each gene value gets a result at intervals of 100 units.

2.3   GA Operators

From the starting generation, our approach obtains new generations applying two operators: crossover and mutation. The crossover operator gets new possible solutions from other selected as parents, whereas mutation tries to keep the diversity in the following generations.

Crossover Operator. We have used the tournament selection method in order to choose the individuals which will act as parents in the crossover operator [2,4,6]. This method selects an individual with the best fitness from a pool of randomly selected individuals in the population. In our case, the pool size was of 100 individual. Each individual is selected as parent only one time.

The crossover operator used in this GA is BLX-alpha [5], where two individuals (parents) are selected to create new individuals. Therefore, $h_i \in [c_{min} - \alpha I, c_{max} + \alpha I]$, where h_i is the value of the gene of the new individual, c_{min} and

c_{max} are the minimum and maximum values of the genes i of the parents, and $I = c_{max} - c_{min}$.

Every couple of individuals are crossed using a different α values at the same time, in a similar way to applied in [8]. Specifically, we use α values of 0.2, 0.4 and 0.6, getting 2, 4 and 2 new individuals respectively. Finally, only the two individuals with better fitness are selected as offspring.

Mutation Operator. This operator was applied over the population with a probability of 5 %. Concretely, we used the non uniform mutation proposed by [12], which focuses on a more localized search the higher the current generation is. Moreover, when an individual is selected to be mutated, the number of genes to be finally mutated also are randomly selected.

2.4   Fitness Function

When looking for ingredient descriptions in the database, we expect that the desired ingredient was found in the first position of the result set. Thus, to evaluate each weight set (individual), we seek N ingredients in the database. Then, we store the position in which the expected description is found in the returned result set. When the ingredient is not found, we assign the position 101 as a punishment. Finally, we compute the Eq. 1 to obtain the fitness value of each individual. The maximum attainable value for this function is 1, and our GA tries to maximize it.

$$ fitness = \frac{N}{\sum_{i=1}^{N} position_i} \tag{1} $$

2.5   Getting the New Generation

In each generation the GA operators produce new individuals, which are added to the current one, increasing the population size. In order to prevent performance problems, each new generation is obtained by means of reducing the population of the current one, in order to achieve a stable population size from one generation to the following one. Thus, we have used the stochastic universal sampling [1] as a method to reduce the population. This is a proportional selection method where individuals with good fitness are more likely to be chosen. Moreover, we also use an elitist strategy where the best individual is always chosen to survive.

2.6   Results

Our GA has a stable population of 1000 individuals. Moreover, it gets 100 generations as maximum. Also, if the maximum fitness value found is not improved in 5 generations, it stops. Our GA has a random behavior, so we run the GA 10 different times with the same starting data, in order to get statistically significant results.

In Fig. 3, we can observe the evolution of the GA in with respect to the average values of ten tests performed in each generation. This value represents an average fitness of individuals of the ten tests that pertain to the same generation. Besides, we can observe the mean square error in each generation. The GA tries to maximize the fitness value achieved, where the best fitness value correspond with a set of weights capable of find the desired ingredient descriptions in the first position of the result set returned by the database. From the first to the sixth generation, we see a fast evolution of average fitness value (0.07). But from the sixth to the twentieth generation, we can observe how this improvement grows more slowly (0.03).

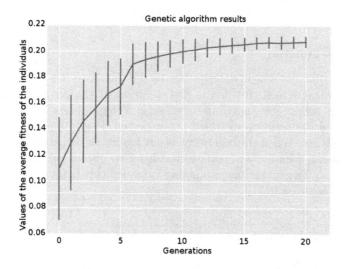

Fig. 3. Evolution of the GA execution with 20 generations.

Moreover, in Fig. 4 we can observe two different results in the same figure. The first result represents the initial success rate without applying the GA. The second result represents the success rate applying the GA in each generation. We calculate the success rate comparing the first ingredient of the database with the expected ingredient. Then, the success rate is the percentage of expected ingredients in the first position of the database. We can see the evolution of the success rate obtained by the GA, which obtains a 55 % success rate. This is an acceptable improvement, compared with the initial success rate of 36 %.

After performing several tests, we found the weighted indexes that obtain the best success rate. In Fig. 5 we can see this weighted indexes obtained with the GA proposed. With this weighted indexes, we obtained a 55 % success rate which supposes an increase of 36 % compared to the initial situation. This is an interesting improvement regarding the initial situation. However, we are still far from a 100 % success rate. So, in next section we are going to introduce new heuristics that improve even more this success rate.

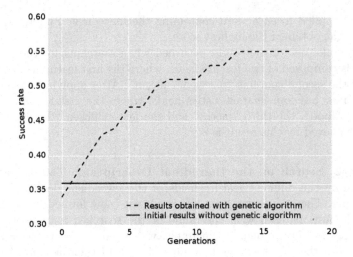

Fig. 4. Comparison between the initial success rate without applying the GA and the success rate applying the algorithm.

c1	c2	c3	c4	c5	c6	c7	c8	c9	c10	c11
9401	5801	4701	4801	3401	2801	6801	5101	1101	5001	901

Fig. 5. End configuration of feature fields.

3   Heuristics

After obtaining the best set of weights with the GA that obtained a 55 % success rate, we searched each ingredient in the database to further improve the success rate. We observed that 98 % of ingredients were in the top ten returned by database. Therefore, we decided to implement different heuristics that help us to improve the results obtained from the database. These heuristics choose a result from the top ten returned by the database in each searching process, trying to get the correct description of the ingredient. Following, the developed heuristics are explained in detail.

Heuristic 1: Feature Fields Division. We have split the ingredient description into eleven feature fields in the database. This heuristic divides the fields of features by each word and creates new feature fields, eliminating *stop words*. These new features fields contain one word. Then, we search the ingredient in these new feature fields. If the ingredient appears in the first positions of the result, we consider it is more likely to be the chosen result. Thus, we apply a score depending on the position in which the ingredient appears. If the ingredient appears in the first position, the result would have a score of 100, and this score is decremented by fives while the position of this ingredient increases. This heuristic is applied to each word containing the ingredient. Finally, we choose the result that obtained the highest score.

For example, one of the results returned when searching for the ingredient "chicken" is composed of two feature fields, where the first feature contains "fast food" and the second contains "pieces of chicken". After applying this heuristic, the result now has four characteristics fields, where the first feature is "fast", the second "food", the third "pieces" and the last "chicken". In this example, the score achieved by this result is 85.

Heuristic 2: Search on the Ingredient Description. This heuristic proposes to unify the different feature fields of the ingredient description into a unique string. Then, it selects from the result set (now formed by strings) the item which best matches with the name of the searched ingredient, that is, the sentence used in the query. Concretely, we search this sentence in the new descriptions in the result set, and we give to each of them a score depending on how the sentence matches with the description. We have measured that each description of the result set has up 131 characters. If the sentence matches, we give him a score of 150. This value is decremented one by one when the ingredient is found at a greater distance. If the ingredient is not found, the score is equal to zero. In the Algorithm 1, we can see how this heuristic behaves.

Algorithm 1. Heuristic 2

Require:
    search: Name of the searched ingredient;
    resultList: Result set obtained by database;
Ensure:
    bestResult: Result with the best score;

1 bestResult = " "; bestScore = 0;
2 **for** $i = 0 \rightarrow resultList.Size - 1$ **do**
3   resultList[i].convertToString();
4   score = resultList[i].index(search);
        ▷ If *search* are in the first position obtain 150, else decremented one by one when is found at a greater distance and 0 if not in *resultList*[i]
5   **if** $(score > bestScore)$ **then**
6   bestScore = score; bestResult = resultList[i];

Heuristic 3: Removing Non Predominant Groups. We decided to remove those results that belong to the minority group within the top ten results. Each ingredient belongs to a group, but in the top ten results we have different groups. In this heuristic, we suppose that the ingredient belongs to the predominant group. This is, the group which appears more times in the top ten results.

Heuristic 4: Oriented Search Feature Ingredient. Statistically, most of the ingredients have the word "raw" or "whole" in his description, so we decided to give more priority to those results that contain these words. First, we divide the feature fields of the ingredient description by each word and create new feature fields, eliminating *stop words*. Second, we search the words "raw" and "whole" in these new feature fields. We suppose that if these words appear in the first positions of the result, it is more likely to be the desired result. If some of these words appears in the first position, the result would get a score of 100, and this value is decremented by five while the position of these words increases. We choose from the result set the result which has the higher score. We can pre-calculate the value of this heuristic before executing the search.

Heuristic 5: Combined Heuristic. After analyzing the results of previous heuristics, we applied all heuristics that had obtained a higher success rate of 50 %. Therefore, this new heuristic offers a final score which combines the scores given by the heuristics 1, 2 and 4.

First of all, we normalized the score received by each result from each heuristics by means of dividing it by the maximum score allowed by that heuristic. Next, the maximum scores of each heuristic is explained:

- *Features fields division.* Scores depend on the position where the ingredient is. These scores may have up to one hundred per each word in the ingredient description($100 * n$ being n the number of words in the ingredient).
- *Search on the ingredient description.* In this heuristic we can obtain a maximum score of 150. This maximum score corresponds to the ingredient description that is exactly matching at the beginning of the result.
- *Oriented search feature ingredient.* This heuristic works just like the division of the feature fields. We search for two words ("raw" and "whole"). Thus, the maximum score is 200.

After the normalization of the scores given by the heuristics, we conducted a study to estimate the value of weights associated with each heuristic. These values apply priorities to heuristics. We gave each heuristic different weights, where these weights have values between zero and one with steps of 0.2.

In Eq. 2 we can see how the different scores are combined to offer a new value after applying this combined heuristic. Note that the equation is applied to each result i from the result set, where *words* is the number of words in the ingredient name we are seeking, where *heuristic1*, *heuristic2* and *heuristic4* refer to the score obtained after apply the corresponding heuristic to the result i, and where W, U and V are the value of the weights that will get to perform the permutation tests.

$$Value_i = W * heuristic1(i)/(100 * words)$$
$$+ U * heuristic2(i)/150 \qquad (2)$$
$$+ V * heuristic4(i)/200$$

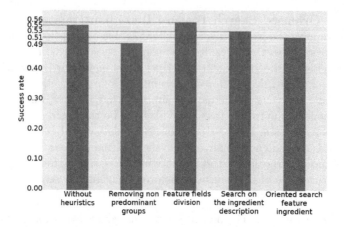

Fig. 6. Comparative between different heuristics

H1	H2	H4	Success rate (%)
0.2	0.0	0.0	56
0.4	0.0	0.0	56
0.6	0.0	0.0	56
0.8	0.0	0.0	56
1.0	0.0	0.0	56
0.0	0.0	0.0	55
0.2	0.4	0.2	54
0.2	0.8	0.4	54
0.4	1.0	0.2	54

Fig. 7. Hit percentage of expected result when searching for the ingredients. "$H1$" corresponds to the weight of the heuristic 1. "$H2$" corresponds to the weight of the heuristic 2. "$H4$" corresponds to the weight of the heuristic 4.

After applying the designed heuristics, we see in Fig. 6 the hit rate of each heuristic. In the heuristic 3, which removes non predominant groups, we obtained a hit rate of 49 %. This heuristic is worse than the hit rate we obtained when applying the GA. Moreover, the heuristic 1 that made features fields division has achieved a rate of 56 %. This heuristic improved the hit rate obtained by the GA. Finally, with the heuristic 2 which made a search on the ingredient description and the heuristic 4 which made a oriented search feature ingredient, we get a hit rate of 53 % and 51 % respectively.

Finally, with the heuristic 5 we have performed a test with different permutations of weights of all heuristics that had obtained a higher success rate of 50 %. We can see different permutations of weights used in the heuristic 5 and the success rate obtained in Fig. 7. We see that the values obtained in combined heuristic are not promising. The maximum hit rate obtained is 56 %. This hit rate is the same as applying only the heuristic 1 which obtained a 56 % hits. Therefore, we reject this heuristic.

4 Conclusions

In cooking recipes, we can find different ways to name the same ingredient. In this paper, we use the database of worldwide reference USDA trying to automatize the process to obtain nutritional information of ingredients. To do this, we dumped the USDA database to a MongoDB database, and divided to classify the ingredient description in eleven feature fields to improve the search results with weighted indexes.

We proposed a GA that will help us find the correct result. This GA finds the best weighted indexes associated with each of the feature fields of ingredients. Without using the GA, we had a success rate of 36 %. After applying the GA, we obtained a success rate of 55 %, which is 53 % better than the initial success rate. The next step was explore the use of different heuristics that could help us to improve the results obtained.

Therefore, we decided to implement five heuristics. These heuristics choose a result from the top ten returned in the search of the database using the best combination of weights obtained by the GA. After that, we observed that heuristic 1 obtains the best success rate. This heuristic divides the fields of features by each word and creates new feature fields, eliminating *stopwords*. We search the full ingredient description in these new feature fields. If the ingredient appears in the first positions of the result is more likely to be the result chosen. We obtained a 56 % success rate employing this heuristic 1, which is better than the initial success rate of 36 %.

As future work, we will create subsets of ingredients, considering its food group: beverage, spice, dairy, etc. Then, we will obtain, using the GA, the most appropriate weights of each feature of ingredient descriptions in that group. Also, we will apply the described heuristics to the results obtained using the subsets, in order to improve them. Another prospect could be the development of new heuristics that exploit the way in which the ingredients are stored in the database.

References

1. Baker, J.E.: Reducing bias and inefficiency in the selection algorithm. In: Proceedings of the Second International Conference on Genetic Algorithms and Their Application, pp. 14–21. L. Erlbaum Associates Inc., Hillsdale (1987)
2. Brindle, A.: Genetic algorithms for function optimization. Ph.D. thesis, University of Alberta, Department of Computer Science, Edmonton (1981)
3. Burke, R.: Hybrid recommender systems: survey and experiments. User Model. User-Adap. Inter. **12**(4), 331–370 (2002)
4. Chakraborty, M., Chakraborty, U.K.: An analysis of linear ranking and binary tournament selection in genetic algorithms. In: Proceedings of the International Conference on Information, Communications and Signal Processing ICICS 1997, pp. 407–411. IEEE, Singapore, 9–12 September 1997

5. Eshelman, L.J., David Schaffer, J.: Real-coded genetic algorithms and interval-schemata. In: Darrel Whitley, L. (ed.) Foundations of Genetic Algorithms 2, pp. 187–202. Morgan Kaufmann Publishers, San Mateo (1993)
6. Goldberg, D.E., Deb, K.: A comparative analisys of selection schemes used in genetic algorithms, pp. 69–93. Morgan Kaufmann, San Mateo (1991)
7. Goldberg, D.E.: Genetic Algorithms in Search, Optimization, and Machine Learning. Addison-Wesley, Reading (1989)
8. Herrera, F., Lozano, E., Pé, E., Sánchez, A.M., Villar, P.: Multiple crossover per couple with selection of the two best offspring: an experimental study with the blx-α crossover operator for real-coded genetic algorithms. In: Garijo, F.J., Riquelme, J.-C., Toro, M. (eds.) IBERAMIA 2002. LNCS (LNAI), vol. 2527. Springer, Heidelberg (2002)
9. Herrera, F., Lozano, M., Verdegay, J.L.: Tackling real-coded genetic algorithms. operators and tools for behavioural analysis. Artif. Intell. Rev. **12**, 265–319 (1998)
10. Matei, O., Contras, D.: Advanced genetic operators in the context of evolutionary ontology. In: 2015 IEEE Congress on Evolutionary Computation (CEC), pp. 9–14, May 2015
11. Matei, O., Contras, D., Pop, P.: Applying evolutionary computation for evolving ontologies. In: 2014 IEEE Congress on Evolutionary Computation (CEC), pp. 1520–1527, July 2014
12. Michalewicz, Z.: Genetic Algorithms+Data Structures=Evolution Programs. Springer, New York (1992)
13. Ortiz, D., Hervas, C., Muñoz, J.: Genetic algorithm with crossover based on confidence interval as an alternative to traditional nonlinear regression methods. In: 9th European Symposium On Artificial Neural Networks. ESANN 2001, pp. 193–198, Bruges, Belgium (2001)
14. Pazzani, M.J., Billsus, D.: Content-based recommendation systems. In: Brusilovsky, P., Kobsa, A., Nejdl, W. (eds.) Adaptive Web 2007. LNCS, vol. 4321, pp. 325–341. Springer, Heidelberg (2007)
15. Schafer, J.B., Frankowski, D., Herlocker, J., Sen, S.: Collaborative filtering recommender systems. In: Brusilovsky, P., Kobsa, A., Nejdl, W. (eds.) Adaptive Web 2007. LNCS, vol. 4321, pp. 291–324. Springer, Heidelberg (2007)

A New Visualization Tool in Many-Objective Optimization Problems

Roozbeh Haghnazar Koochaksaraei[1(✉)], Rasul Enayatifar[1],
and Frederico Gadelha Guimarães[2]

[1] Graduate Program in Electrical Engineering, Federal University of Minas Gerais,
Av. Antônio Carlos 6627, Belo Horizonte, MG 31270-901, Brazil
roozbeh.haghnazar@gmail.com
[2] Department of Electrical Engineering,
Universidade Federal de Minas Gerais, Belo Horizonte, Brazil
fredericoguimaraes@ufmg.br

Abstract. During the past decade, development in the field of
multi-objective optimization (MOO) and multi-criteria decision-making
(MCDM) has led to the so-called many-objective optimization problems
(many-MOO), which involve from half a dozen to a few dozens of simultaneous objectives. Many algorithms have been proposed in order to
approach the scalability issues involved when trying to solve many-MOO
problems. One of these issues is related to the visualization of solutions
and relations between them in high dimensional objective space. In this
paper we introduce a new visualization tool in order to better illustrate the behavior and relations between objectives in order to assist
understanding of the problem by the decision-maker. The understanding
provided by the proposed tool can be used to redesign the optimization problem and possibly reduce the number of objectives or transform
some of them into constraints, leading to an iterative and also interactive
design and optimize cycle.

1 Introduction

Real-world problems inherently involve conflicting objectives, making multi-
objective optimization (MOO) a major field of research. Traditionally, conflicting
objectives can be modelled in an optimization problem as individual objectives,
aggregated objectives or individuals constraint functions. When there are few
objectives involved, evolutionary algorithms have become successful methods for
searching approximations of the Pareto-optimal set of solutions, which represent
the trade-offs involved in the problem [1,2].

During the last decade, the poor scalability of the available state-of-the-
art methods for multiobjective optimization (MOO) has drawn the attention of
researchers in the field, leading to new developments and algorithms not only
for MOO but also for multi-criteria decision-making (MCDM). The research
focused on problems with more than four objectives is collectively known as
many-objective optimization or simply many-MOO [3]. The performance of current optimization algorithms in this class of problems is not satisfactory yet

© Springer International Publishing Switzerland 2016
F. Martínez-Álvarez et al. (Eds.): HAIS 2016, LNAI 9648, pp. 213–224, 2016.
DOI: 10.1007/978-3-319-32034-2_18

despite all the progress in the field. Moreover, there is still some debate about the practical necessity of optimizing problems with many objectives. Some scientists argue that many-MOO problems are in fact ill-designed or not well stated. Despite this criticism, one can actually find many papers with practical applications involving many-MOO. In a recent survey [4], the authors point out some challenges for many-MOO, namely: (i) loss of pressure in dominance guided evolutionary search algorithms; (ii) poor efficiency of genetic operators to generate better offspring, (iii) scalability of the Pareto, (iv) visualization of solutions in a high dimensional objective (or criteria) space.

When the number of possible alternative solutions grow, which is easily the case in many-MOO, the number of relations and information hidden in the data increase, causing difficulties to analyze them. Presenting huge amount of data and information has been a serious challenge in recent years. Traditional tools such as tables and graphs cannot accommodate the amount of data in a way that enable users to explore adequately their relations and characteristics. For this reasons, researchers in data visualization field have been trying to devise tools to address this problem.

Different types of analyses are needed to improve the process of solving many-MOO. One of the analysis that will be the goal of this paper is capturing the conflict and harmony between objectives that should be considered simultaneously. This visualization can be helpful to gain knowledge about the characteristics of the optimization problem in hand. This understanding can enable the designer to modify the previous formulation by for instance deciding to aggregate (or eliminate altogether) objectives that are not in conflict. Therefore it is important to realize the relations between objectives when approaching many-MOO problems, before actually performing any decision [3,5,6]. One important and significant usage of the proposed method is in the removal of redundant objectives [3,5–10].

Brockhoff and Zitzler [7,8] presented a method to reduce objectives geared towards direct integration into the evolutionary search. This algorithm depends on the dominance structure. Saxena et al. [10] applied Principal Component Analysis (PCA) of objective values to find the relations between objectives. The PCA has been designed to handle non-linear relations among the objectives by embedding the method inside of the NSGA-II. There are some more studies conducted on the new techniques based on PCA and unfolding maximum variance for non-linear reduction through developing independent solutions among the non-dominant ones.

In this paper, we introduce a new visualization tool in order to better illustrate the behavior and relations between objectives in order to assist understanding of the problem by the decision-maker/optimizer. The understanding provided by the proposed tool can be used to redesign the optimization problem and possibly reduce the number of objectives or transform some of them into constraints, leading to an iterative and also interactive design and optimize cycle. Therefore, the proposed visualization tool integrates data visualization with MOO, for analyzing data collected from many-MOO to assist problem understanding and problem-solving. The paper is organized in order to present the visualization tool developed to show the relations among objectives simultaneously, those relations are called Many-Objective Dependencies (MOD), which represent the harmonies and conflicts between objectives in the problem. That is inspired by the chord diagram, and the designer has tried to improve its features based on the needs and the goals. Also, later it can be seen that the tool has this potential to provide useful information to show different states of relations between objectives in several regions of one or more objectives and boundary details. Although this tool is used to show the relation among objectives in the objective space, it has strong potential to be applied to the design space as well.

2   Related Work

The three important and famous tools which are used in current studies [3,9,11], are parallel coordinate graph, radar graph and scatter graph. The first two tools can be very powerful. This section will review and compare them.

Figure 1 illustrates a scatter plot, which shows the dispersion of solutions in the objective space according to values of the objective functions. However, this kind of scatter plots cannot show the relations among objectives. Although for two or three dimensional objective space, this tool can present accurate information [12], since the scatter plot gives the true representation of the Pareto front. As it can be seen in Fig. 1, 2D scatter plots can be more useful to present the overview of the Pareto front and it can present the density and dispersion of solutions among the objectives.

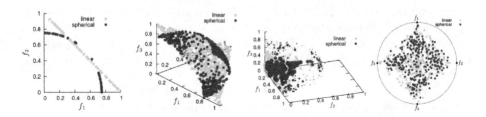

Fig. 1. Scatter graph can show the density of solutions in the space

The next popular tool is the parallel coordinate graph. This graph has some parallel columns representing each normalized objective. Each solution is represented as a line connecting the values of the objective functions for that solution, see Fig. 2. Multiple solutions are represented as multiple lines with different colors. Crossing lines between adjacent objectives in the graph represent a conflict, since one solution is decreasing for one objective while the other is increasing. Parallel lines and no crossing lines between adjacent objectives represent harmony between these objectives for those solutions.

The first graph in Fig. 2 illustrates a problem with 12 objectives. The solutions were generated artificially. It is clear to see that objectives 1 and 2 are

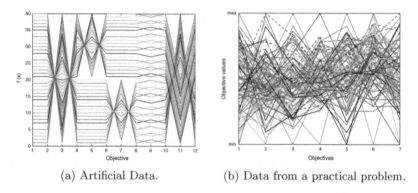

(a) Artificial Data.   (b) Data from a practical problem.

Fig. 2. Parallel Coordinate graph can show the values of solutions on each objective (Color figure online).

in perfect harmony, while objectives 2 and 3 are in conflict, since higher values in objective 2 lead to lower values in objective 3. More complex relations between the objectives can be seen between objectives 4 and 5, in which there is conflict for higher values of these objectives but harmony for lower values; and between objectives 6 and 7, in which there is the opposite. Considering minimization problems, conflict for lower values are more relevant to the designer than conflict for higher values.

However, in practical scenarios using real data, the situation can be more messy, as illustrated in the second graph of Fig. 2, becoming hard to draw conclusions. Some useful conclusions can still be drawn from this analysis, specially if the solutions are grouped with same colours using some similarity measure. One important limitation of this method is that it only shows the relations between adjacent objectives in the graph. If the designer reorders the objectives, it is possible to visualize different relations but this leads to a combinatorial problem.

The Radar Graph [3,12] is an extension of the parallel coordinate graph when the first and the last objectives are made adjacent too. Therefore it is possible to visualize the relation between the first and the last objectives in the radar graph, which is not possible in the parallel coordinate graph. Figure 3 depicts the radar graph for the two previous examples.

Section 3 will present the proposed tool, which was designed to overcome some of the problems discussed here.

3   Proposed Tool

There are some variables in design language that help designers to devise a good tool based on their needs [12]. These variables are position, size & length, shape, value, and color. Each one of those variables have their own characteristics and power to serve a purpose. Position is the strongest variable and shape is great to recognize many classes and color can be useful for qualitative data. The order of

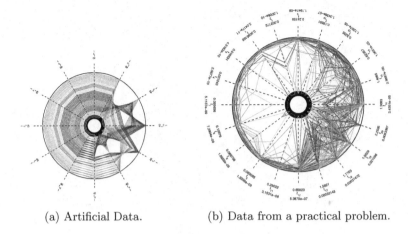

(a) Artificial Data.   (b) Data from a practical problem.

Fig. 3. Radar graph.

effective impact can be, position & length, area & angle, ratio scale and finally we can say that 3D and Gradient are the least effective and can be the last option.

This research has aimed at creating an innovative tool that provides users with enough information about the relations between objectives, which helps them to understand the problem, then being able to reduce the number of objectives. In the proposed tool, we adopt the visual information-seeking mantra, also known as *Shneiderman Mantra*, as the design concept [14–16]. The Shneiderman Mantra summarizes visual design guidelines and provides a framework for designing information visualization tools. According to this concept, the first step of visualizing data should be the overview and after that zooming and filtering can help the user to have detailed information. To show the details, linking and highlighting help users to see on demand the accurate information that is useful for them.

3.1   Overview Step

Figure 4 shows the overview of data to the user according to the mentioned points. The range of each objective is represented along an arc, forming a circle. Solutions in the objective space, in this case a three-dimensional one, are represented by individual lines connecting the corresponding values of the objectives for that solution. There are two kinds of overview in this frame. The first kind of view shows the links individually connecting one value of an objective to another value of a different objective for the same solution. For example in Fig. 4, there are two links in the end point of the *Obj0* that connect to the first points of *Obj1*, *Obj2*, showing that there is conflict between these objectives. In Fig. 4, we used 50 solutions to the DTLZ-2 problem with three objectives, taken from the DTLZ benchmark functions.

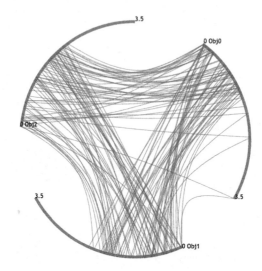

Fig. 4. Relation of three objectives in DTLZ-2 using 50 solutions.

Another kind of general information which has been extracted from this overview is the overall pattern of conflict or harmony between objectives. Looking more closely, the links from the lower bound of the objectives are denser, since this is a minimization problem. The slightly denser pattern of links from the lower bound of *Obj0* to the lower band of *Obj1* and the another dense pattern from the lower bound of *Obj1* to the middle bound of *Obj2* show some line crossings, that demonstrates some moderate conflict between these objectives. Totally, as it was shown, you can extract the nature or essence of the problem or objective space through the chaos or discipline of links or the density of them, which can make a visual pattern.

3.2   Detail Step

It is clear that the user needs more information than what the overview presents. Since having enough information is necessary to make the best decision, visualization tools should be able to produce and present enough and appropriate information for the end user based on the problem, needs and goals. According to *Shneiderman Mantra*, after presenting the overview, the tool should provide more details. Also, *linking & highlighting* can be a good way for giving and presenting more details to the end users [12]. On the other hand, all links are available in the tool and highlighting can improve the presentation condition when there is too many of them.

Figure 5 presents the tool in situations with 3 and 12 objectives, where many solutions have been produced on them. This amount of data makes a mess of links with different patterns, the end user is simply not able to have clear information in detail. That is why the designer should provide hovering for links in order

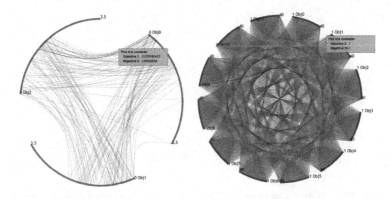

Fig. 5. Highlighting a specific link to get the detail information

to giving information about a specific solution, which contains the value of the solution in the objectives through the highlighting technique [12,13].

For instance, in the left picture you can see the link of a solution between *Obj0* and *Obj1*, which has the value of 0.07 in the first objective and 1.39 on the third objective. Therefore, the user can understand and realize that this highlighted link shows a little conflict between first and third objectives, because it has connected the lower bound of first objective to the middle range of third one. On the right, it is presented the tool with 12 objectives, showing the link between *Obj1* and *Obj9* that has the value 1 for both of them. It shows a high harmony for this solution between these two objectives.

It is recognizable that this level of details is not enough to realize the harmony and conflict of information. For this reason, we tried to provide complementary way to have a total and details view in one window. As mentioned before, the main goal of this visualization tool is illustrating the relations among objectives to realize and find harmonies and conflicts between them. Based on the main goal, a strategy is needed which can help to have a flexible comparison among the different boundaries and intervals of objectives. Hence, we need to have information about the amount of harmony in intervals of an objective with other ones. Having relations information and view in an specific range of the objectives is useful for the analysis.

To support the above requisite, the designer has provided and designed the *frame focus* facility to have a flexible analysis. This feature is depicted in Fig. 6, which presents the relationship among objectives for the special interval of one objective. For instance, in a three-objective space the lower bound of *Obj1* has been selected and there are some links that connect this interval to the other objectives. As it is shown, this bound has links to the lower, middle and upper bounds of *Obj0* and also has connections to the lower and middle bounds of *Obj2*. These visual information shows the appropriate conflict between second objective and two others in lower bound. In addition, the same analysis for the 12-objective space demonstrates a more regular link pattern.

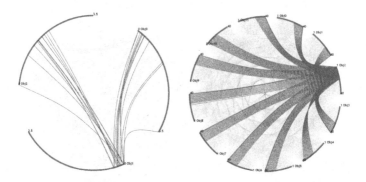

Fig. 6. Specify an interval to find relationships between objectives

All of the extracted information is helpful in different comparison purposes. As it is shown in Fig. 7, there is a comparison between different boundaries of *Obj1* with the other objectives in 3-objective space, which is useful in order to find the trade-off behavior in the objective space. For example, the selected region in the lower boundary of second objective has connections to all the regions of the first objective and first half of the third objective. Meanwhile, the middle boundary of second objective has connections to the lower half part of the first and lower and middle part of the third objectives. Therefore, the user can realize the different trade-offs in different regions of *Obj1* in this space. This comparison and analysis about the behavior of several intervals of an objective can be helpful when there is not full harmony or full conflict between objectives.

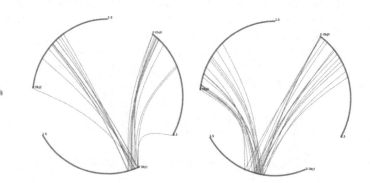

Fig. 7. Comparing the objectives in different regions

A feature that can distinct a powerful visualization tool is its ability to accommodate for a wide range of analyses. For example, the several forms of comparing the links and connection between objectives. The user should be able to extract different information from various viewpoints of the objective space and possible solutions. The designer has tried to design and implement a useful tool to present the necessary information.

Another way to perform a useful comparison between different intervals of objectives is using multi-color links in separated frames in one view as shown in Fig. 8. This figure shows the behavior of different regions of objectives in terms of their relationships with the others. This feature enables the user to assess trade-offs of the problem in different regions of objectives at the same time.

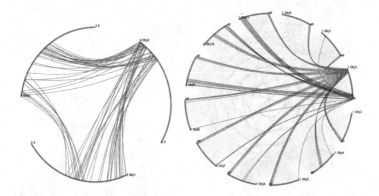

Fig. 8. Comparing the objective trade-offs in different regions in different goals (Color figure online)

4   Experimental Results

In this section we compare the proposed method with the radar graph and parallel coordinate using the same data. As it can be seen in Fig. 9 there are three different tools which were applied to the same dataset. In Fig. 9a the adjacent objectives were changed to show the harmony as much as possible. To this end, the designer tried to replace the axis which has different values in one objective with the axis which has the same values, placing them as neighbors. In this way, the user can see the harmony as well. In this case, it has been illustrated that Radar graph is more useful than the others, and after that parallel coordinator is in the second place. The proposed tool has a messy overview, specially with the increasing number of objectives at overview level. Nonetheless, all three tools suffer from the increase in number of solutions and objectives.

In the next step, the ability of tools for showing the details for a solution is assessed. In this level the tools should be able to show the information of each solution, or the user should be able to specify whatever she/he wants among all solutions.

In the current tools color has been selected as an attribute to separately consider items from the others. However, in this work, the designer believes that color is not a suitable attribute. Instead of just color, it was opted for highlighting as a technique and action in addition to color as an attribute to specify items.

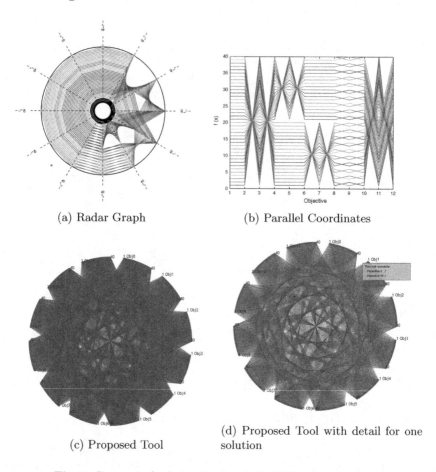

(a) Radar Graph

(b) Parallel Coordinates

(c) Proposed Tool

(d) Proposed Tool with detail for one solution

Fig. 9. Comparison of visualization tools (Color figure online)

When the number of items is too large, using color as an attribute can confuse the users. So instead of that highlighting can be more helpful.

As it is clear in Fig. 9d, the proposed tool can use highlighting and changing color as an action in addition to attributes to show and present items considered by the user.

Next area of comparison is the flexibility to realize relations. It means that the user should be able to see the relations between objectives in several ways. At first, it is assumed that the user needs to check out the relation between objectives with the other objectives simultaneously. Figure 10 shows the abilities of the proposed method for comparing different intervals.

In the proposed tool, it is possible to see the ability to draw a frame in the considered region and check the relations of that region of that objective with the others in the same time. The user can also check and compare different regions in one or more objectives simultaneously as shown in Fig. 10d.

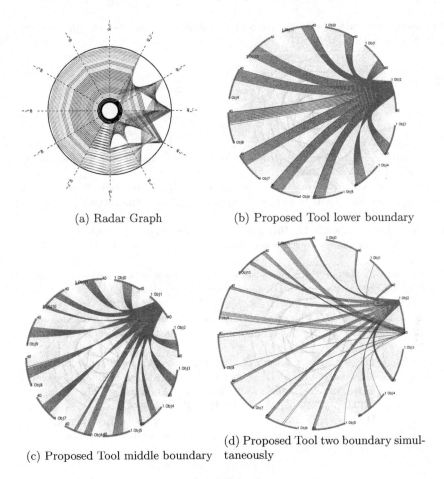

(a) Radar Graph

(b) Proposed Tool lower boundary

(c) Proposed Tool middle boundary

(d) Proposed Tool two boundary simultaneously

Fig. 10. Specified boundaries

5   Conclusion

In this paper the authors have tried to address the deficiency of current visualization tools, by integrating data visualization tools with MOO, for analyzing data obtained as the result of a many-MOO algorithm. This paper has introduced a new visualization tool in order to better illustrate the behavior and relations between objectives to assist understanding of the problem by the decision-maker/optimizer. The understanding provided by the proposed tool can be used to redesign the optimization problem and possibly reduce the number of objectives or transform some of them into constraints. The experiments have illustrated the advantages and potential of the proposed method for many-MOO visualization.

Acknowledgements. This work has been supported by the Brazilian agencies CAPES, CNPq and FAPEMIG.

References

1. Deb, K.: Multi-Objective Optimization Using Evolutionary Algorithms. Wiley, New York (2001)
2. Coello, C.A.C., Lamont, G.B., Veldhuizen, D.A.V.: Evolutionary Algorithms for Solving Multi-Objective Problems (Genetic and Evolutionary Computation). Springer, New York (2006)
3. de Freitas, A.R., Fleming, P.J., Guimarães, F.G.: Aggregation Trees for visualization and dimension reduction in many-objective optimization. Inf. Sci. **298**, 288–314 (2015)
4. von Lücken, C., Barán, B., Brizuela, C.: A survey on multi-objective evolutionary algorithms for many-objective problems. Comput. Optim. Appl. **58**(3), 707–756 (2014)
5. Giuliani, M., Galelli, S., Soncini-Sessa, R.: A dimensionality reduction approach for many-objective Markov Decision Processes: application to a water reservoir operation problem. Environ. Model. Softw. **57**, 101–114 (2014)
6. Čuček, L., Klemeš, J.J., Kravanja, Z.: Objective dimensionality reduction method within multi-objective optimisation considering total footprints. J. Cleaner Prod. **71**, 75–86 (2014)
7. Brockhoff, D., Zitzler, E.: Are all objectives necessary? on dimensionality reduction in evolutionary multiobjective optimization. In: Runarsson, T.P., Beyer, H.-G., Burke, E.K., Merelo-Guervós, J.J., Whitley, L.D., Yao, X. (eds.) PPSN 2006. LNCS, vol. 4193, pp. 533–542. Springer, Heidelberg (2006)
8. Brockhoff, D., Zitzler, E.: Dimensionality reduction in multiobjective optimization with (partial) dominance structure preservation: generalized minimum objective subset problems. TIK Report 247 (2006)
9. Freitas, A.R., Fleming, P.J., Guimaraes, F.G.: A non-parametric harmony-based objective reduction method for many-objective optimization. In: International Conference on Systems, Man, and Cybernetics (SMC), pp. 651–656 (2013)
10. Saxena, D.K., Deb, K.: Non-linear dimensionality reduction procedures for certain large-dimensional multi-objective optimization problems: employing correntropy and a novel maximum variance unfolding. In: Obayashi, S., Deb, K., Poloni, C., Hiroyasu, T., Murata, T. (eds.) EMO 2007. LNCS, vol. 4403, pp. 772–787. Springer, Heidelberg (2007)
11. Tusar, T., Filipic, B.: Visualization of pareto front approximations in evolutionary multiobjective optimization: a critical review and the prosection method. IEEE Trans. Evol. Comput. **19**(2), 225–245 (2015)
12. Ward, M.O., Grinstein, G., Keim, D.: Interactive Data Visualization: Foundations, Techniques, and Applications. CRC Press, Natick (2010)
13. Fry, B.: Visualizing Data: Exploring and Explaining Data with the Processing Environment. O'Reilly Media Inc., Sebastopol (2007)
14. http://www.infovis-wiki.net/index.php/Visual_Information-Seeking_Mantra
15. http://www.codingthearchitecture.com/2015/01/08/shneidermans_mantra.html
16. http://faculty.washington.edu/jtenenbg/courses/360/f04/sessions/schneidermanGoldenRules.html

A Novel Adaptive Genetic Algorithm for Mobility Management in Cellular Networks

Zakaria Abd El Moiz Dahi[1(✉)], Chaker Mezioud[1], and Enrique Alba[2]

[1] Department of Fundamental Computer Science and Its Application,
Constantine 2 University, Constantine, Algeria
{zakaria.dahi,chaker.mezioud}@univ-constantine2.dz
[2] Dep. de Lenguajes y Ciencias de la Computación, Málaga University,
Málaga, Spain
eat@lcc.uma.es

Abstract. Metaheuristics are promising tools to use when addressing optimisation problems. On the other hand, most of them are hand-tuned through a long and exhaustive process. In fact, this task requires advanced knowledge about the algorithm used and the problem treated. This constraint restricts their use only to pure abstract scientific research and by expert users. In such a context, their further application by non-experts in real-life fields will be impossible. A promising solution to this issue is the inclusion of adaptation within the search process of these algorithms. On the basis of this idea, this paper demonstrates that simple adaptation strategies can lead to more flexible algorithms for real-world fields, also more efficient when compared to the hand-tuned ones and finally more usable by non-expert users. Seven variants of the Genetic Algorithm (GA) based on different adaptation strategies are proposed. As benchmark problem, an NP-complete real-world optimisation problem in advanced cellular networks, the mobility management task. It is used to assess the efficiency of the proposed variants. The latter were compared against the state-of-the-art algorithm: the Differential Evolution algorithm (DE), and showed promising results.

Keywords: Evolutionary computation · Adaptation · Cellular networks

1 Introduction

Due to the limitations of the exhaustive-based search methods, metaheuristics appear as a promising tool to use when tackling optimisation problems. The Genetic Algorithm (GA) is one of the first-proposed Evolutionary Algorithms (EAs) [10], and also one of the most studied ones.

The main motivation behind the use of metaheuristics is ultimately solving real-world problems, which often requires a problem-specific algorithm design. The complex customisation of algorithms to a specific problem either needs a specialist or limits the field of application to scientific research. Indeed, most

© Springer International Publishing Switzerland 2016
F. Martínez-Álvarez et al. (Eds.): HAIS 2016, LNAI 9648, pp. 225–237, 2016.
DOI: 10.1007/978-3-319-32034-2_19

of the scientific works propose powerful algorithms without further consideration for their industrial application. Furthermore, there is a growing demand for
optimisation software usable by non-specialists within an industrial development
environment. A promising way to do this is to supply the industry with intelligent algorithms containing a mechanism that modifies the parameters without
external control [1]. Many schemes of adaptation exist in the literature, but all
can be regrouped in three categories [1]: deterministic, adaptive and self-adaptive
algorithms. In this paper we are intrested in the first class.

Customer tracking and mobility management are key factors in communication networks in general and especially in cellular networks (2G, EDGE, GPRS,
3G, 3G$^+$, LTE, 4G). In fact, any dysfunction of this task may alter the service quality of the network itself causing call drops and other issues. Regarding
the actual high standards of the mobile phone industry, these kinds of failure
are unacceptable for the telephony operators and the users as well. Thus, the
mobility management is one of the most challenging optimisation issues in cellular networks. It has been formulated as a binary optimisation problem and was
proven to be NP-complete [8].

This paper *investigates/proves* whether simple strategies of adaptation can
lead to more flexible, efficient and usable algorithms. Seven deterministically-
adaptive variants of the genetic algorithm are proposed based on several adaptation strategies with different complexities and behaviour. The performances
of the proposed variants is assessed by solving the mobility management problem. The state-of-the-art algorithm Differential Evolution (DE) is taken as an
efficient competitor.

The remainder of the paper is structured as follows. In Sect. 2, basic concepts
related to the GA, adaptation within EAs and finally the mobility management
problem are presented. In Sect. 3, the proposed variants of the genetic algorithm
are introduced. Section 4 is dedicated to the experimental results and their discussion. Finally, we conclude the paper in Sect. 5.

2   Basic Concepts

In this section, we introduce basic concepts of the genetic algorithm, adaptation
within evolutionary algorithms and finally the mobility management task.

2.1   The Genetic Algorithm

The genetic algorithm was first proposed by Holland [10]. It was born from the
attempt to mimic the natural process of reproduction and evolution. Thus, the
idea of the GA is to evolve a set of individuals toward a fitter state by applying
a series of selection, variation, evaluation and replacement phases.

The GA starts by *initializing* a population of N individuals $\overrightarrow{X}$ of size L,
where each individual $\overrightarrow{X}_{i=1...N} = \{X_{(i,1)}, X_{(i,2)}, ..., X_{(i,L)}\}$. The latter are
evaluated using the fitness function of the problem being addressed. Then, the
best individual $\overrightarrow{X_*}$ is extracted.

After, at each iteration of the algorithm, firstly we *select* M individual parents $\overrightarrow{P}$ according to a given strategy. Secondly, the selected parents $\overrightarrow{P}_{i=1...M}$ are perturbed using *variation* operators such as the mutation and crossover in order to produce $(N - M)$ new offspring $\overrightarrow{O}$. The crossover consists of exchanging parts of the individual parents at some chosen points. The amount of information exchanged and the number of crossover operations performed are ruled by both the type of crossover used and the crossover probability $P_c \in [0,1]$. After, the mutation operator randomly mutates the values of genes in each produced offspring $\overrightarrow{O}_{i=1...(N-M)}$. The number of mutation operations is determined by a mutation probability $P_m \in [0,1]$. Thirdly, the produced offspring are *evaluated* using the objective function of the problem being tackled.

Finally, having the old population of parents and the newly-produced offspring, a replacement phase is performed in order to determine what will be the composition of the population for the next iteration. However, the GA mechanics are left as a black box due to the existence of several types of selection, crossover, mutation and replacement.

2.2   Adaptation Within Evolutionary Algorithms

Adaptation within EAs reflects the attempt to mimic processes of natural evolution. State-of-the-art EA implementations often require a deep algorithmic knowledge from the user in order to choose appropriate parameters values for solving a specific optimisation problem. Even for an expert, the parameters configuration for an optimal performance is hard to find. The idea of automatic adaptation is to evolve these parameters values according to a given scheme. A classification of these schemes can be made according on how they are performed. Many classifications exist, but we opt for the taxonomy proposed in [1].

Parameter Tuning: Is the scheme used whenever the parameters have constant values throughout the run of the EA (i.e. there is no adaptation). Consequently, an external agent or a manual mechanism is needed to tune the desired parameters and to choose the most appropriate values.

Dynamic: It appears whenever there is some mechanism that modifies a parameter without any external control. The class of EA that uses this scheme can be further subdivided into other specific subschemes.

- **Deterministic:** This scheme takes place if the value of a parameter is tuned constantly by some deterministic rule. This rule modifies the strategy parameter deterministically without using any feedback from the EA. This scheme is the one we are intrested in our work.
- **Adaptive:** This scheme takes place if there is some form of *feedback* got from the EA that is used to set the direction *or/and* magnitude of the change to the strategy parameters.
- **Self-adaptive:** In this scheme the parameters are encoded with the variables and can evolve as well as the solution itself.

2.3   Studied Adaptation Strategies

Many parameters could be adapted such as P_c, the selection pressure, the population size, ... etc. But in our work the one that will undergo the adaptation is the mutation probability P_m. This is very simple but it could be very powerful at the same time. Adaptation in general is about three issues: When to adapt (i.e. period)? In which direction (i.e. increase or decrease)? How much (i.e. the amplitude of change)? Our scientific methodology consists of using strategies that deal with these issues in different manners and with an increasing level of complexity and with different directions of evolution in order to represent a wide range of mathematical adaptation behaviour. We firstly opt for the use of a canonical *monotone adaptation*: *linearly-decreasing* and *linearly-increasing*. Then, we use a more complex adaptation strategy (i.e. non-monotone) called *oscillatory*. In this perspective, we opt for the *sinusoidal wave* with a *decreasing* and *increasing amplitude* [6]. Finally, we use several specialized state-of-the-art strategies whose the efficiency is well-established. Thus, we opt for the ones studied in [4,7,9].

This is done in order to answer some questions such as: does adaptation allow producing better algorithms than the hand-tuned ones? Does designing more efficient algorithms imply using more complex adaptation schemes? Ultimately, is the adaptation a real solution for conceiving better algorithms?

It is worth to mention that within the next sections the variable N corresponds to the size of the population, L refers to the length of the individual, *Maxit* refers to the maximum number of iterations and finally t represents the actual iteration.

The Linear Adaptation Strategy: This strategy is based on adding (i.e. when increasing) or subtracting (i.e. when decreasing) at each iteration "t" of the algorithm a constant "*step*" from the previous P_m value at iteration $(t-1)$. The step size used is computed using Formula (1).

$$Step = \frac{UB - LB}{Maxit} \tag{1}$$

$$P_m(t+1) = P_m(t) \pm Step \tag{2}$$

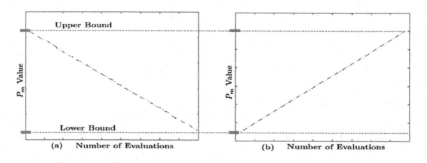

Fig. 1. Linear adaptation strategies: (a) decreasing and (b) increasing

Variables UB and LB are the upper and lower bounds of the interval where the P_m value is supposed to evolve. Figure 1(a) and (b) show the resulting evolution of P_m value when using the linearly-decreasing and linearly-increasing adaptation strategies, respectively.

The Oscillatory Adaptation Strategy: This strategy is based on the formula defining a *sinusoidal wave* with a *decreasing* or an *increasing amplitude*. Formula (3) defines the sinusoidal wave with an increasing amplitude, whereas Formula (4) highlights the new terms that differentiate the sinusoidal wave with an increasing from the one with a decreasing amplitude.

$$P_m(t) = P_{m_0} * \left(sin(2\pi * freq * t) * \frac{t}{Maxit} + 1 \right) \tag{3}$$

$$\frac{Maxit - t}{Maxit} \tag{4}$$

The variable *"freq"* is a parameter that controls the frequency of the wave and P_{m_0} is the value from where the evolution starts. Figure 2(a) and (b) show the resulting evolution of the P_m value when using the oscillatory-decreasing and oscillatory-increasing adaptation strategies, respectively.

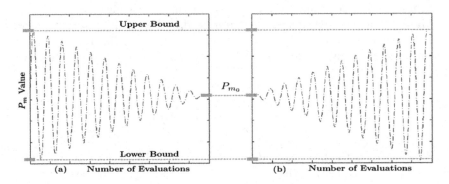

Fig. 2. Oscillatory adaptation strategies: decreasing and increasing amplitude

State-of-the-art Adaptation Strategies. These strategies were proposed in [4,7,9]. In the following, each one of them is introduced.

- **Bäck Strategy:** It was proposed by Bäck et al. [4]. It is defined by Formula (5).

$$P_m(t) = \left(2 + \frac{L - 2}{Maxit - 1} * t \right)^{-1} \tag{5}$$

- **Forgaty Strategy:** It was proposed by Fogarty [7]. It is defined by Formula (6).

$$P_m(t) = \frac{1}{240} + 0.11375 2^t \tag{6}$$

- **Hesser Strategy:** It was proposed by Hesser and Männer in [9]. It is defined by Formula (7), where C_1, C_2 and C_3 are constants.

$$P_m(t) = \sqrt{\frac{C_1}{C_2} \frac{exp(-C_3 t/2)}{N\sqrt{L}}} \tag{7}$$

2.4   Mobility Management in Cellular Networks

In order to assess the efficiency of our proposed approaches, we could go for an academic problem as much of the literature does. But instead, we wanted to improve the interest of our study by considering a real-problem such as mobility management.

Tracking mobile users is a key factor and a sensitive issue in cellular phone networks (2G, EDGE, GPRS, 3G, $3G^+$, LTE, 4G) [11] and other wired or wireless networks (vehicular, sensor, etc.). The optimisation of this task implies the optimisation of two sub-tasks which are: the paging and the location-update. Two main schemes of mobility management exist; the paging scheme and the location area-update-based scheme. The latter includes two main types; dynamic and static. The reporting cell scheme is one of the most practical static-location-update-based schemes [11]. In this last one, one seek to find the optimal network configuration that determines the reporting and non-reporting cells.

The reporting cell scheme was first proposed by Hac and Zhou in [8]. They assessed that it is NP-complete. Then, it has been modelled in [12] as a binary optimisation problem, where the objective function to optimize is defined by Formula (8).

$$Minimize: L_c = \beta * \sum_{i \in RC} N_{Lu}(i) + \sum_{i=0}^{Tc} N_P(i) * V(i) \tag{8}$$

Here $N_{Lu}(i)$ is the location-update cost associated to the ith cell and RC is the set of reporting cells in the network. $N_p(i)$ is the paging cost associated to the ith cell and Tc is the number of cells in the network. $V(i)$ is the vinicity factor associated to the ith cell. The vinicity factor depends on the type of the cell itself. If it is a reporting cell, the vinicity factor can be calculated as the number of non-reporting cells from where one can reach the reporting cell. If the cell is a non-reporting cell, the vinicity factor can be calculated as the maximum vinicity factor of the reporting cells from where one can reach the non-reporting cell. The parameter β is a ratio to balance the objective function. In fact, the cost of location-update is considered to be 10 times much higher than the cost of paging. Thus, usually in the literature β is set to 10. Figure 3 illustrates a potential solution of the reporting cell problem for a network with eight cells, where the 1st, 4th and the 8th cells are reporting cells, while the 2nd 3rd, 5th, 6th and the 7th are non-reporting cells.

1	0	0	1	0	0	0	1
1st	2nd	3rd	4th	5th	6th	7th	8th

Fig. 3. Solution instance for the mobility management problem

3   The Proposed Approach

In this paper, seven deterministically-adaptive variants of the genetic algorithm are proposed. The proposed variants are enhanced generational elitist genetic algorithms. In this section, a detailed description of the main operators and phases of the proposed approaches is given. Please note that the term L used in the next sections refers to the length of the chromosome. In the case of the mobility management problem, L corresponds to the size of the network.

3.1   Initialisation

At this step, a first population of N chromosomes is generated randomly by assigning to each gene of each chromosome either the value 1 or 0. A random number "$rand$" is generated from a standard uniform distribution. If $rand \geqslant 0.5$ then the gene will have the value 1, otherwise it will have the value 0.

3.2   Selection

In this step, $(N/2)$ couples are formed from the N chromosomes existing in the population. A binary tournament selection is used to select the parents and create the couples that will constitutes the mating pool that will undergo the reproduction phase. To create a couple, the best of two randomly-chosen parents is mated with a second individual selected from two other randomly-chosen parents. The process is repeated $(N/2)$ times.

3.3   Reproduction

In this step, the $(N/2)$ couples of parents will undergo a series of genetic operators (i.e. crossover and mutation) to produce N new offspring.

Crossover: A two-point crossover is performed. This mechanism is ruled by a probability of crossover $P_c \in [0,1]$. In our case P_c is set to 1. For each couple of parents, a random number "$rand$" is generated from a standard uniform distribution. If $rand \leqslant P_c$, the crossover is performed on the current couple, otherwise the parents are copied and considered as new offspring.

When applying the two-point crossover, two splitting-points are chosen randomly from the interval $[1, L]$. Then, the parents are swapped at these points. The zones delimited by the head, the first switch point, the second switch point and the tail of the two parents are exchanged.

Mutation: After the crossover operator, mutation is applied on the produced offspring. This operator is ruled by a mutation probability $P_m \in [0,1]$. But in our case it is set to $(1/L)$. The mutation consists in a bit-flip. For each gene of each one of the produced offspring, a random number "*rand*" is generated from a standard uniform distribution. If $rand \leqslant P_m$, the mutation is performed on the current gene. The gene is then flipped to the other state, otherwise it is kept as it is. In this work the value of P_m is driven using different adaptation strategies explained in Sect. 2.3.

3.4   Evaluation and Replacement

In this step, the produced offspring are evaluated using Formula (8). A generational elitist strategy (μ,λ) is used to extract the N best individuals (i.e. from the union of both produced offspring λ at generation (t) and the parents μ at generation $(t-1)$) that will constitute the new population of individuals at generation $(t+1)$. The latter will undergo the next generation of genetical operators. Detailed pseudo-code of the proposed approaches is available in the hyperlink[1].

On the basis of the strategy of adaptation used for the mutation probability P_m, we propose in this work seven new adaptive variants of the genetic algorithm. The first two proposed variants are based on a linear adaptation. The LD-GA (for Linearly-Decreasing adaptation strategy based Genetic Algorithm) that uses a linearly-decreasing strategy. The second variant called LI-GA (for Linearly-Increasing adaptation strategy based Genetic Algorithm) that is based on a linear increasing strategy.

The two next variants are based on the oscillatory adaptation. The OD-GA (for Oscillatory-Decreasing adaptation strategy based Genetic Algorithm) which is based on a sinusoidal strategy with a decreasing amplitude. The OI-GA (for Oscillatory-Increasing adaptation strategy based Genetic Algorithm) that is based on a sinusoidal strategy with an increasing amplitude.

The three last adaptation strategies are the state-of-the-art ones. Firstly, the B-GA (for Bäck adaptation strategy based Genetic Algorithm) which is based on the strategy proposed by Bäck et al. [4]. Secondly, the F-GA (for Forgaty adaptation strategy based Genetic Algorithm) which is based on the strategy proposed by Forgaty in [7]. Finally, the H-GA (for Hesser adaptation strategy based Genetic Algorithm) which is based on the strategy proposed by Hesser et al. [9].

4   Experimental Results and Analysis

All our tests are carried out using an Intel I3 core with 2 GB Ram and a Linux OS. The implementation is done using Matlab 7.12.0 (R2011a). Experiments are run using a cluster of 16 physical machines. Parallel processing of fitness evaluations is performed. The latter are equally split over 4 cores.

---

[1] Appendix: http://tinyurl.com/Appendix-Hyperlink.

The scalability of the proposed variants is assessed using different-sized instances of the reporting cell problem. Twelve instances of 4×4, 6×6, 8×8 and 10×10 cells are used. The instances were generated on the basis of realistic patterns. The instances are provided by the University of Malaga, Spain. They have been previously used in [2,3,5] and are available in[2].

On the basis of state-of-the-art works that already studied the GA behaviour and parameters [1], for the LI-GA, LD-GA, OI-GA and OD-GA, the Lower Bound (LB) is set to ($1/L$), where L is the chromosome length (in our case the size of the network). The Upper Bound (UB) is set to 0.3. For the OI-GA and OD-GA, the frequency *freq* is set to 0.7 and P_{m_0} is set to the middle of the interval $[(1/L), 0.3]$ after a parameter tuning experiment. Finally, for the variant H-GA, the constant C_1, C_2 and C_3 are set to 0.4, 0.6 and 0.9, respectively.

The proposed variants are compared to one of the state-of-the-art metaheuristic used to solve the mobility management task in cellular networks, which is the Differential Evolution algorithm (DE) [2,3].

For consistency and fair comparison with the DE, we use the same experimental parameters used in [2,3]. Thus, experiments are performed until reaching the termination criterion of 175000 fitness evaluations (including the evaluation of the initial population). We use 175 individuals, 1000 iterations and all the algorithms are repeated for 30 runs. Several results are reported such as: the *best*, the *worst* fitness, the *mean* and *standard deviation* of the fitnesses over 30 executions. We also report *#hits*; which represents how many times the proposed variants were able to reach the results obtained by the differential evolution algorithm. The variable *#evals*; represents the mean of the number of fitness evaluations needed to the proposed variants to obtain the same best results as the ones obtained by the differential evolution algorithm. The variable *Time* is the average time needed to the proposed approach to reach the same results reached by the differential evolution and it is expressed in seconds.

It is worth to mention that metrics *#hits*, *#evals* and *Time* are recorded every time the proposed variants achieve the same/better results obtained by the DE. The comparison is based on the best solution reported through 30 executions. Statistical analysis tests are also performed such as the one-sample Kolmogorov-Smirnov test, the Brown-Forsythe test, the Kruskal-Wallis one-way analysis of variance test and a multiple comparison test is used to determine which is the best "self* plan". All tests are performed using a level significance equal to 5 %. Detailed-numerical results of the above-mentioned tests are available in the hyperlink[3].

4.1   Numerical Results

Table 1 shows the numerical results obtained when using the proposed variants of the genetic algorithm to tackle networks of size 4×4, 6×6, 8×8 and 10×10 cells, respectively. It is worth to mention that the symbol "-" is used whenever the proposed variants achieve results worst than the ones obtained by the DE.

---

[2] Benchmark Instances: http://oplink.lcc.uma.es/problems/mmp.html.

[3] Appendix: http://tinyurl.com/Appendix-Hyperlink.

4.2   Discussion and Interpretation

On the basis of the metric *"Mean"* of Table 1, one can note that all the variants except the B-GA achieve the same results for networks 1, 2 and 3 of size 4×4 cells. Considering now networks of size 6×6 cells, the OI-GA variant is the best one, whereas for network 2, the OI-GA, OD-GA and F-GA are the best ones. For network 3, the OI-GA and OD-GA are the best variants. For networks of size 8×8 cells, the F-GA is the best one, while for networks 2 and 3, the OI-GA is the best one. Finally, for networks of size 10×10 cells, the OI-GA is assessed to be the best variant for networks 1, 2 and 3. Also, on the basis of the metric *"Mean"* of Table 1, the B-GA is assessed to be the worst variant in all networks, whereas the OI-GA is assessed to be the best one for all networks.

When considering the metric *"#evals"* of the best variants found in each one of the problem instances, one can observe that F-GA is the best variant when tackling network 1 of size 4×4 cells, whereas for network 2 it is the LD-GA the best one and finally for network 3, the LI-GA is assessed to be the best one. Let us consider now networks of size 6×6 cells, the H-GA is assessed to be the best variant for networks 1, 2 and 3. When tackling networks of size 8×8 cells, the OD-GA is found to be the best variant for networks 2 and 3. Finally, when tackling instance 3 of size 10×10 cells, the F-GA is found to be the best variant.

Taking again the same metric, the worst variant assessed for networks 1 and 3 of size 4×4 cells is the OD-GA, while for network 2 it is H-GA. When tackling networks of size 6×6 cells, OI-GA is assessed to be the worst variant. Finally, the LD-GA is found to be the worst variant for network 2 of size 8×8 cells, whereas for network 3 it is OI-GA the worst one.

Considering now the metric *"#hits"* of Table 1, all the variants except the B-GA achieve the same results for networks of size 4×4 cells. Let us take now networks of size 6×6 cells, the OI-GA is assessed to be the best variant for network 1, while for network 2 it is OI-GA, OD-GA and F-GA the best ones. For network 3, both OI-GA and OD-GA are the best variants. When tackling networks of size 8×8 cells, the OI-GA is found to be the best variant for networks 2 and 3. Finally, for network 3 of size 10×10 cells, the F-GA is found to be the best variant. Also, on the basis of the metric *"#hits"* of Table 1, the B-GA is found to be the worst variant in all problem instances, whereas the OI-GA is assessed to be the best one.

With regards to results of Table 1, the proposed variants are able to achieve results as good as those obtained by the differential evolution algorithm in 8 out of 12 instances. On the other hand, the proposed variants were outperformed by the DE in 3 out of 12 networks: network 1 of size 8×8 cells and networks 1 and 2 of size 10×10 cells. Finally, the proposed variant F-GA was able to outperform the differential evolution algorithm in network 3 of size 10×10 cells. This fact is even more interesting since we are proposing adaptive variants of a simple algorithm that is able to outperform a more complex and specialized one.

Statistical results of the Kruskal-Wallis and also the Post-Hoc tests[4] support the numerical results obtained in Table 1. The null-hypothesis is rejected for each

---

[4] Appendix: http://tinyurl.com/Appendix-Hyperlink.

Table 1. Numerical results when tackling networks 1, 2 and 3 of sizes 4×4, 6×6, 8×8 and 10×10 cells

4×4 and 6×6 Cells

Network	Size	Algorithm	Best	Worst	Mean	STD	#hits	#evals	Time (Second)
Network 1	4×4	LI-GA	98535	98535	98535.00	0.00	30\30	4515	486.07
		LD-GA	98535	98535	98535.00	0.00	30\30	1313	909.80
		OI-GA	98535	98535	98535.00	0.00	30\30	2013	1104.26
		OD-GA	98535	98535	98535.00	0.00	30\30	5448	2933.02
		B-GA	99008	101717	100122.07	869.69	0\30	–	–
		F-GA	98535	98535	98535.00	0.00	30\30	1196	618.65
		H-GA	98535	98535	98535.00	0.00	30\30	1266	416.66
Network 2	4×4	LI-GA	97156	97156	97156.00	0.00	30\30	4732	491.92
		LD-GA	97156	97156	97156.00	0.00	30\30	1234	835.43
		OI-GA	97156	97156	97156.00	0.00	30\30	2536	1165.96
		OD-GA	97156	97156	97156.00	0.00	30\30	4521	2770.21
		B-GA	98061	99762	98061.54	129.90	0\30	–	–
		F-GA	97156	97156	97156.00	0.00	30\30	2536	592.81
		H-GA	97156	97156	97156.00	0.00	30\30	5448	412.95
Network 3	4×4	LI-GA	95038	95038	95038.00	0.00	30\30	529	476.20
		LD-GA	95038	95038	95038.00	0.00	30\30	1324	5446.30
		OI-GA	95038	95038	95038.00	0.00	30\30	1692	1117.42
		OD-GA	95038	95038	95038.00	0.00	30\30	5297	3063.61
		B-GA	100796	103794	103119.33	678.91	0\30	–	–
		F-GA	95038	95038	95038.00	0.00	30\30	1225	693.67
		H-GA	95038	95038	95038.00	0.00	30\30	1155	481.34
Network 1	6×6	LI-GA	177290	192226	187856.87	3133.63	0\30	23742	8004.08
		LD-GA	173701	180077	175406.64	1715.60	06\30	67206	10114.83
		OI-GA	173701	173701	173701.00	0.00	30\30	28804	7222.07
		OD-GA	173701	175241	173841.06	432.06	27\30	–	–
		B-GA	197796	211585	205028.40	3630.18	0\30	–	–
		F-GA	173701	175241	174265.67	754.80	18\30	19172	2133.06
		H-GA	173701	178764	174941.97	1310.49	8\30	7919	1590.97
Network 2	6×6	LI-GA	184679	200720	194312.83	3157.27	0\30	7126	6598.24
		LD-GA	182331	189980	182934.23	1936.13	25\30	43488	10573.60
		OI-GA	182331	182331	182331.00	0.00	30\30	10745	6953.95
		OD-GA	182331	182331	182331.00	0.00	30\30	–	–
		B-GA	203729	215583	212149.37	2998.38	0\30	–	–
		F-GA	182331	182331	182331.00	0.00	30\30	4585	2164.86
		H-GA	182331	190630	183335.23	2341.88	26\30	4193	1486.46
Network 3	6×6	LI-GA	179570	186464	184053.27	1859.13	0\30	19128	6247.19
		LD-GA	174519	177218	175375.30	905.78	10\30	61752	10230.03
		OI-GA	174519	174519	174519.00	0.00	30\30	17885	6670.68
		OD-GA	174519	174519	174519.00	0.00	30\30	–	–
		B-GA	186290	202684	192601.27	3891.20	0\30	–	–
		F-GA	174519	175504	174551.83	179.84	29\30	12298	2098.87
		H-GA	174519	179550	175197.40	1153.46	14\30	5025	1249.48

8×8 and 10×10 Cells

Network	Size	Algorithm	Best	Worst	Mean	STD	#hits	#evals	Time (Second)
Network 1	8×8	LI-GA	33319	345066	340587.27	3065.09	0\30	–	–
		LD-GA	309347	320774	316210.59	2914.01	0\30	–	–
		OI-GA	311171	312925	312308.38	501.70	0\30	–	–
		OD-GA	311061	315876	312997.38	927.59	0\30	–	–
		B-GA	351634	376767	365901.77	5354.80	0\30	–	–
		F-GA	309293	314369	312103.50	873.99	0\30	–	–
		H-GA	310826	321769	315714.87	2627.36	0\30	–	–
Network 2	8×8	LI-GA	322459	333588	328461.37	2279.05	0\30	–	–
		LD-GA	287149	306890	300030.00	4535.41	1\30	160300	16031.62
		OI-GA	287149	299771	287236.41	478.71	29\30	147809	24764.68
		OD-GA	287149	298792	291023.59	4115.78	8\30	48541	22417.85
		B-GA	335937	354756	344118.37	3539.03	0\30	–	–
		F-GA	287149	301687	292361.30	4885.99	10\30	50698	4326.33
		H-GA	289135	307033	297015.17	4478.10	0\30	–	–
Network 3	8×8	LI-GA	295479	307558	301704.63	3115.72	0\30	–	–
		LD-GA	264204	284236	273250.03	4356.34	1\30	151550	15355.78
		OI-GA	264204	265324	264533.16	360.97	7\30	158350	24002.78
		OD-GA	264204	270809	266238.28	1619.11	2\30	68950	21267.24
		B-GA	305227	330492	318052.43	5247.21	0\30	–	–
		F-GA	264204	273613	265607.77	2312.06	9\30	95317	4241.02
		H-GA	267906	285729	274041.03	3951.37	0\30	–	–
Network 1	10×10	LI-GA	439956	455604	448217.37	3701.25	0\30	–	–
		LD-GA	387378	423108	411205.72	7719.00	0\30	–	–
		OI-GA	387104	394176	390531.47	1944.25	0\30	–	–
		OD-GA	393400	407044	399798.00	3554.94	0\30	–	–
		B-GA	467234	518118	495418.03	12786.56	0\30	–	–
		F-GA	387533	399335	391764.13	3091.07	0\30	–	–
		H-GA	402363	423246	411628.53	5663.68	0\30	–	–
Network 2	10×10	LI-GA	394878	411262	404379.97	4268.57	0\30	–	–
		LD-GA	360036	383744	373484.13	4317.90	0\30	–	–
		OI-GA	359623	370021	362320.88	2057.44	0\30	–	–
		OD-GA	364176	375084	369959.41	2532.46	0\30	–	–
		B-GA	431470	464161	448291.17	8962.47	0\30	–	–
		F-GA	359296	369765	363737.67	2959.43	0\30	–	–
		H-GA	366198	379584	373051.00	3648.64	0\30	–	–
Network 3	10×10	LI-GA	408509	415977	412496.37	2001.49	0\30	–	–
		LD-GA	375973	392676	386675.09	3797.95	0\30	–	–
		OI-GA	372938	382155	376900.28	2386.55	0\30	–	–
		OD-GA	377392	391608	384021.88	2957.58	0\30	–	–
		B-GA	426019	468344	448430.43	10362.73	0\30	–	–
		F-GA	371203	384354	378158.27	3063.30	1\30	144025	13823.44
		H-GA	381591	391108	386459.57	2430.45	0\30	–	–

one of the instances which confirms that a difference exists in the distribution of the proposed variants. Also, statistical ranking of the Post-Hoc confirm the promising efficiency of the proposed variants.

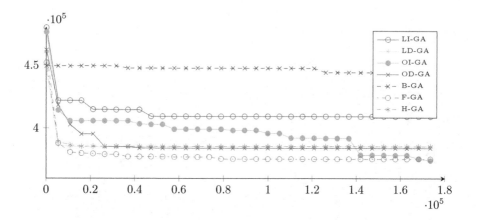

Fig. 4. Fitness evolution for network 3 of size 10×10 cells

Figure 4 shows the fitness evolution when using the deterministically-adaptive variants of the genetic algorithm for tackling network 3 of size 10×10 cells. One can see that the F-GA has the quickest converegnce rate and B-GA has the slowest one, while the remaining variants OI-GA, OD-GA, LI-GA, LD-GA and H-GA have a moderate convergence rate when comparing with the F-GA and B-GA. However, no clear link can be seen between the type of adaptation strategy (i.e. linear and oscillatory) or the direction of evolution (i.e. increasing and decreasing) and the produced convergence rate.

5   Conclusions

In this paper, a deterministically-adaptive genetic algorithm based on seven adaptation strategies was presented. The proposed variants were assessed for solving the mobility management problem in advanced cellular networks. The state-of-the-art algorithm differential evolution was taken as a comparison basis.

The experiments showed that the proposed approach based on the sinusoidal adaptation is the best one. They also showed that the use of adaptation within EAs can lead to more efficient algorithms when comparing to the hand-tuned ones. They demonstrated also that designing more efficient adaptive algorithms does not imply using more complex adaptation schemes. As perspective, we intend to study more complex and unexplored strategies of adaptation in order to solve efficiently the mobility management in advanced cellular networks.

Acknowledgments. Prof. Alba acknowledges partial support from Spanish-plus-FEDER project TIN2014-57341-R

References

1. Alba, E., Dorronsoro, B.: The exploration/exploitation tradeoff in dynamic cellular genetic algorithms. IEEE Trans. Evol. Comput. **9**(2), 126–142 (2005)
2. Almeida-Luz, S., Vega-Rodríguez, M., Gomez-Pulido, J., Sanchez-Perez, J.: Applying differential evolution to the reporting cells problem. In: Proceedings of the International Multiconference on Computer Science and Information Technology (IMCSIT), pp. 65–71. IEEE (2008)
3. Almeida-Luz, S., Vega-Rodríguez, M., Gómez-Púlido, J., Sánchez-Pérez, J.: Differential evolution for solving the mobile location management. Appl. Soft Comput. **11**(1), 410–427 (2011)
4. Bäck, T., Schütz, M.: Intelligent mutation rate control in canonical genetic algorithms. In: Michalewicz, M., Raś, Z.W. (eds.) ISMIS 1996. LNCS, vol. 1079, pp. 158–167. Springer, Heidelberg (1996)
5. Berrocal-Plaza, V., Vega-Rodríguez, M.A., Sánchez-Pérez, J.M.: A strength pareto approach to solve the reporting cells planning problem. In: Murgante, B., et al. (eds.) ICCSA 2014, Part VI. LNCS, vol. 8584, pp. 212–223. Springer, Heidelberg (2014)
6. Dahi, Z., Chaker, M., Draa, A.: Deterministically-adaptive genetic algorithm to solve binary communication problems: application on the error correcting code problem. In: Proceedings of the International Conference on Intelligent Information Processing, Security and Advanced Communication (IPAC 2015), pp. 79:1–79:5 (2015)
7. Fogarty, T.: Varying the probability of mutation in the genetic algorithm. In: Proceedings of the 3rd International Conference on Genetic Algorithms, pp. 104–109. Morgan Kaufmann Publishers Inc. (1989)
8. Hac, A., Zhou, X.: Locating strategies for personal communication networks: a novel tracking strategy. IEEE J. Sel. Areas Commun. **15**(8), 1425–1436 (1997)
9. Hesser, J., M"anner, R.: Towards an optimal mutation probability for genetic algorithms. In: Schwefel, H.-P., Männer, R. (eds.) PPSN 1990. LNCS, vol. 496, pp. 23–32. Springer, Heidelberg (1991)
10. Holland, J.: Genetic algorithms and adaptation. Adapt. Control of Ill-Defined Syst. **16**, 317–333 (1984)
11. Razavi, S.: Tracking area planning in cellular networks. Ph.D. thesis, Department of Science and Technology Linkoping University Norrkoping Sweden (2011)
12. Subrata, R., Zomaya, A.: Artificial life techniques for reporting cell planning in mobile computing. In: Proceedings of the Workshop on Biologically Inspired Solutions to Parallel Processing Problems (BioSP3) (2002)

Bio-Inspired Algorithms and Preferences for Multi-objective Problems

Daniel Cinalli[1]([✉]), Luis Martí[1], Nayat Sanchez-Pi[2],
and Ana Cristina Bicharra Garcia[1]

[1] Universidade Federal Fluminense, Rio de Janeiro, Brazil
{dcinalli,lmarti,bicharra}@ic.uff.br
[2] Universidade do Estado do Rio de Janeiro, Rio de Janeiro, Brazil
nayat@ime.uerj.br

Abstract. Multi-objective optimization evolutionary algorithms have been applied to solve many real-life decision problems. Most of them require the management of trade-offs between multiple objectives. Reference point approaches highlight a preferred set of solutions in relevant areas of Pareto frontier and support the decision makers to take more confidence evaluation. This paper extends some well-known algorithms to work with collective preferences and interactive techniques. In order to analyse the results driven by the online reference points, two new performance indicators are introduced and tested against some synthetic problem.

Keywords: Collective intelligence · Preferences · Reference points · Evolutionary multi-objective optimization algorithms

1 Introduction

Multi-objective optimization problems (MOPs) simultaneously optimize a set of objective functions. Formally posed, a MOP can be defined as min $F(x) = \{f_1(x), \dots, f_k(x)\}$, where $x = \langle x_1, \dots, x_n \rangle \in \Omega$ is an n-dimensional vector of decision variables. The solution of a MOP is a (possibly infinite) Pareto-optimal set $P_S = \{x \in \Omega | \nexists y \in \Omega : y \prec x\}$ that contains all the elements of Ω that not Pareto-dominated ($\prec$) by any other element [2]. Elements of P_S represent different trade-offs between the objective functions values. The projection of P_S through $F()$ is known as the Pareto-optimal front, P_F.

The application of evolutionary algorithms to MOPs has prompted the creation of multi-objective optimization evolutionary algorithms (MOEAs) [2]. They approximate the P_S as a discrete set of points.

Having a solution to a MOP, a decision maker (DM) must identify which of those solutions are the ones that satisfy her/his preferences and would be realized in practice. This task can be rather complex and requires in-depth knowledge of the problem being solved, something that is impossible in many practical situations.

© Springer International Publishing Switzerland 2016
F. Martínez-Álvarez et al. (Eds.): HAIS 2016, LNAI 9648, pp. 238–249, 2016.
DOI: 10.1007/978-3-319-32034-2_20

Reference points and interactive techniques can be used to mitigate these inconveniences and support the DM in reaching a proper specification. These approaches also allow the optimization algorithm to focus on areas of interest and thus reaching satisfactory solutions at a lower computational cost.

In practice, however, optimization problems pose difficulties in defining *a priori* reference points or preferences. In this regard, collective intelligence reference points obtained by the interaction and aggregation of multiple opinions can be used to produce an accurate representation of preferences and, hence, reference points. This approach can also eliminate the unilateral choice bias that can be introduced by a single DM. Collective environments can improve MOEAs with cognitive and subjective evaluation to find better solutions in more relevant regions of P_F.

This work incorporates online interactive collective preferences and interactive behaviour into three existing MOEAs: NSGA-II [6], SPEA2 [12] and SMS-EMOA [1] and, therefore, introduces a collective intelligence version of them. Similarly, while working in this task it became evident the lack of adequate performance indicators that take into account preferences. Therefore, as part of the paper are also introduced two new performance indicators that are used to evaluate the quality of the P_F approximation driven by the online collective preferences.

The paper proceeds with Sect. 2 that covers some required formal foundations regarding reference points and collective intelligence. Section 3 introduces the novel interactive MOEAs. Subsequently, Sect. 4 presents the new performance indicators that are to be used later on. After that, Sect. 5 analyzes the performance of the algorithms when faced with benchmark problem. Finally, conclusive remarks and future work directions are put forward.

2   Foundations

Preferences are user-defined parameters and denote values or subjective impressions regarding the trade-offs points. It transforms qualitative feelings into quantitative values to bias the search during the optimization phase and restrict the objective space. In this sense, a reliable preference vector improves the trade-off answers obtained.

The reference point approach concentrates the search of Pareto non-dominated solutions near a selected point. It is based on the achievement scalarizing function that uses a reference point to capture the desired values of the objective functions. Let z^0 be a reference point for an n-objective optimization problem of minimizing $F(x) = \{f_1(x), ..., f_k(x)\}$, the reference point scalarizing function can be stated as follows:

$$\sigma\left(z, z^0, \lambda, \rho\right) = \max_{i=1,...,k}\left\{\lambda_i(z_i - z_i^0)\right\} + \rho\sum_{i=1}^{k}\lambda_i\left(z_i - z_i^0\right), \tag{1}$$

where $z \in \mathcal{Z}$ is one objective vector, $z^0 = \langle z_1^0, ..., z_k^0 \rangle$ is a reference point vector, σ is a mapping from $\mathbb{R}^k$ onto $\mathbb{R}$, $\lambda = \langle \lambda_1, ..., \lambda_k \rangle$ is a scaling coefficients vector, and ρ is an arbitrary small positive number. Therefore, the achievement problem can be rebuilt as: min $\sigma\left(z, z^0, \lambda, \rho\right)$.

A subset X of $\mathbb{R}^n$ is convex if for any two pair of solutions $x^1, x^2 \in X$ and $\alpha \in [0, 1]$, the following condition is true: $\alpha x^1 + (1 - \alpha)x^2 \in X$. The intersection of all the convex sets containing a given subset X of $\mathbb{R}^n$ is called the convex hull of X. The convex hull of a set of points is the smallest convex set that contains the points.

The *convex hull of individual minima* (CHIM) is the set of points in $\mathbb{R}^k$ that are convex combinations of $F_i^* - F^*$:

$$\mathcal{H} = \left\{ \Phi\beta : \beta \in \mathbb{R}^k, \sum_{i=1}^{k} \beta_i = 1, \beta_i \geq 0 \right\} \tag{2}$$

where x_i^* is the global minimizers of $f_i(x)$, $\forall i \in \{1, \ldots, k\}$. Let $F_i^* = F(x_i^*), \forall i \in \{1, \ldots, k\}$; and Φ is a pay-off matrix $k \times k$ whose the ith column is $F_i^* - F^*$.

Since the beginning of 2000, the development of social network technologies and interactive online systems has promoted a broader understanding of the "intelligence" concept. A new phenomenon appeared based not only on the cognition of one individual, but also placed on a network of relationships with other people and the external world. The field known as collective intelligence (COIN) [9] is defined as the self-organized group intelligence arisen from participatory and collaboration actions of many individuals. Shared tasks or issues are handled by singular contributions in such a manner that their aggregation process creates better results and solves more problems than each particular contribution separately.

Inside collective environment, contributions come from different people. Clustering algorithms distinguish the users with similar preferences to perform a cooperative evolution or decision making choice. A mixture model is a probabilistic model to reveal distributions of observations in the overall population. Given a data set $Y = \{y_1, \ldots, y_N\}$ where y_i is a d-dimensional vector measurement with the points created from density $p(y)$, a finite mixture model is defined as:

$$p\left(y|\Theta\right) = \sum_{k=1}^{K} \alpha_k p_k\left(y|z_k, \theta_k\right) \tag{3}$$

Let $K \geq 1$ be the number of components, $p_k\left(y|z_k, \theta_k\right)$ be the mixture components where each k is a density or distribution over $p(y)$ and parameters θ_k, $z = \langle z_1, \ldots, z_k \rangle$ be a K-ary random variable defining the identity of the mixture component that produced y and $\alpha_k = p_k\left(z_k\right)$ are the mixture weights representing the probability that y was generated by component k. Hence, the parameters for a mixture model is $\Theta = \{\alpha_1, \ldots, \alpha_K, \theta_1, \ldots, \theta_K\}$, $1 \leq k \leq K$.

The Central Limit Theorem [8], explains why many applications that are influenced by a large number of random factors have a probability density function that approximates a Gaussian distribution. Let Y be a sequence of random variables that are identically and independently distributed, with mean μ and variance σ^2. The distribution of the normalised sum $S_n = \frac{1}{\sqrt{n}}(\boldsymbol{y}_1 + \ldots + \boldsymbol{y}_N)$ approaches the Gaussian distribution, $G(\mu, \sigma^2)$, as $n \to \infty$.

In a Gaussian mixture model, each of the K components is a Gaussian density with parameters $\theta = \{\boldsymbol{\mu_k}, \Sigma_k\}$, $\boldsymbol{y} \in \mathbb{R}^d$ and function as:

$$p_k\left(\boldsymbol{y}|\theta_k\right) = \frac{1}{(2\pi)^{d/2}\,|\Sigma_k|^{1/2}}e^{-\frac{1}{2}(\boldsymbol{y}-\boldsymbol{\mu_k})^t\,\Sigma_k^{-1}(\boldsymbol{y}-\boldsymbol{\mu_k})} \tag{4}$$

3 Interactive Algorithms

Interactive genetic algorithms (IGA) were successfully applied to get feedbacks of transitional results during the evolution process. IGA incorporates external evaluation to support problems whose optimization objectives are complex to be defined by *a-priori* exact functions. It employs users' subjectivities as fitness values to drive the search engine.

As the purpose of this study is the enhancement of MOEAs through the use of the collective preferences, interactive genetic algorithms are an appropriate technique to support this goal. The new algorithms are extensions of the classical MOEAs: NSGA-II, SPEA2 and SMS-EMOA. The main changes on the original methods are the incorporation of COIN into the selection procedure; the transformation of the continuous evolutionary process into an interactive one; and the adoption of reference points to drive the search towards relevant regions in Pareto-optimal front.

3.1 CI-NSGA-II

One of the new algorithms is a variation of NSGA-II [6]. The NSGA-II is a non-domination based genetic algorithm for multi-objective optimization. It adopts two main concepts: a density information for diversity and a fast non-dominated sorting in the population. The crowding distance uses the size of the largest cuboid enclosing two neighboring solutions to estimate the density of points in the front. The non-dominated sorting places each individual into a specific front such that the first front τ_1 is a non-dominant set, the second front τ_2 is dominated only by the individuals in τ_1 and so on. Each solution inside the front τ_n receives a rank equal to its non-domination level n.

The selection operator uses the rank (i_{rank}) and crowding distance (i_{dist}) in a binary tournament. The partial order $\prec_c$ between two individuals i and j, for example, prefers the minor domination rank if they are from different fronts or otherwise, the one with higher values of crowding distance.

$$i \prec_c j := i_{rank} < j_{rank} \vee (i_{rank} = j_{rank} \wedge i_{dist} > j_{dist}) \tag{5}$$

In Algorithm 1, the new CI-NSGA-II converts the original NSGA-II into an interactive process. The subroutine *CollectiveContributions()* suspends the evolution progress and submits some individuals from population to the users' evaluation. In this research, the individuals received can be analyzed in two different ways: (a) a pairwise comparison allows the selection of the best candidate between two or more individuals; (b) a dynamic game scenario stimulates the participant creativity to improve or produce new individuals. Both approaches discover online reference points.

Algorithm 1. The Collective Intelligence NSGA-II.

```
1:  generation ← numgeneration
2:  block ← subsetgeneration               ▷ iteration interval
3:  while i < generation do
4:      while block do
5:          offspring ← Tournament(pop)
6:          offspring ← Crossover(offspring)
7:          offspring ← Mutation(offspring)
8:          pop ← COIN Selection(offspring)
9:          i + +
10:     end while
11:     contributions ← CollectiveContributions(front)
12:     pop ← contributions
13:     Θ ← ExpectationMaximization(contributions)
14:     pop ← ReferencePoint Distance(pop, Θ)
15: end while
```

Inside collective environment, the contributions come from different people. Assuming the Central Limit Theorem [8], the inputs have a distribution that is approximately Gaussian. Therefore, after each collective interaction, the subroutine *ExpectationMaximization()* gets the users' collaboration as a Gaussian Mixture model to emulate the evaluation landscape of all participants' preferences.

The expectation maximization approach creates online reference points (Θ) for search optimization. Whether the user's collaboration is a simple vote on the best individual presented to him (pairwise comparison) or a complete re-edited individual, the clustering algorithm distinguishes the users with similar preferences to perform a cooperative evolution and a decision making choice through the collective reference points.

The procedure *ReferencePointDistance()* calculates the minimum distance from each point in the population to the nearest collective reference points in Θ. This way, the point near the reference point is favoured and stored in the new population. CI-NSGA-II develops a partial order similar to the NSGA-II procedure, but replaces the crowding distance operator by the distance to collective reference points (i_{ref}).

$$i \prec_c j := i_{rank} < j_{rank} \vee (i_{rank} = j_{rank} \wedge i_{ref} < j_{ref}) \tag{6}$$

CI-NSGA-II prioritizes the points close to the online collective reference point. The algorithm consumes preference information to explore satisfactory solutions for DMs.

3.2   CI-SMS-EMOA

The SMS-EMOA [1] is a steady-state algorithm that applies the non-dominated sorting as a ranking criterion and the hypervolume measure (S) as a selection operator.

After the non-domination ranking, the next step is to update the last front population, P_{worst}. It replaces the member with the minimum contribution to P_{worst} hypervolume by a new individual that increases the hypervolume covered by the population.

The new algorithm CI-SMS-EMOA converts the original SMS-EMOA into an interactive process. The *CollectiveContributions()* and *ExpectationMaximization()* subroutines have the same purpose and work as the CI-NSGA-II.

The selection operation, performed by the *COIN Selection()* procedure, prefers individuals with minor domination rank (i_{rank}). If they belong to the same front, the one with the maximum contribution to the hypervolume of the set and the closest reference point distance (i_{ref}) is selected.

A procedure *Hype-RefPoint Distance()* gets the hypervolume contribution (S) and calculates the minimum distance from each solution in the population to the nearest collective reference points in Θ. This way, the point with high hypervolume value and short reference point distance is favoured and stored in the new population.

3.3   CI-SPEA2

The strength pareto evolutionary algorithm 2 (SPEA2) [12] developed a fitness assignment strategy based on the number of individuals that one solution dominates and it is dominated by. SPEA2 implements elitism by keeping an external population (archive) of size N. The archive preserves the best solutions since the beginning of the evolution.

The strength $ST(i)$ for each individual i is the number of population members it dominates: $ST(i) = |\{j : j \in P_t \oplus \bar{P}_t \wedge i \prec j\}|$; where $\oplus$ is the multiset union, P_t and $\bar{P}_t$ are the population and archive population at generation t, respectively. The fitness $F(i)$ for a individual i is given by the strength of its dominators: $F(i) = \sum ST(j)$; where $j \in P_t \vee \bar{P}_t$, $j \prec i$. High values of $F(i)$ means the individual i is dominated by many others and $F(i) = 0$ corresponds to a non-dominated individual.

SPEA2 uses a nearest density estimation technique, adapted from the kNN method, to distinguish individuals having the same fitness values. This density function is a function of the distance to the k-th nearest data point and it is added to the fitness function F.

In the new algorithm CI-SPEA2, subroutine *COIN Selection()* computes the strength of all individuals and the non-dominated members are copied to the archive $\bar{P}_t$. The k-th nearest data point used to calculate the original density function in SPEA2 was substituted by the collective reference points Θ. If the archive $|\bar{P}_t| \leq N$, the algorithm chooses the nearest individuals to the collective reference point until the archive size is reached. Otherwise, if $|\bar{P}_t| > N$, it removes the more distant ones proportionally to the number of individuals in each reference point cluster. This way, the archive keeps the same distribution of points around its reference points.

4   Performance Indicators

Several performance indicators are used to evaluate the outcome sets of MOEAs. They measure the quality of the Pareto front approximation and allow comparison between different algorithms. There exist a variety of approaches that analyse the distribution of points in objective function space and the accuracy in terms of convergence.

The Pareto-optimal front coverage indicator, $D_{S \to P_F}$, is a proximity indicator that defines the distance between an achieved approximation set S and their closest counterpart in the current Pareto-optimal front:

$$D_{S \to P_F}(S) = \frac{1}{|S|} \sum_{x \in S} \min_{x' \in P_S} \{d(x, x')\}, \tag{7}$$

where d is the Euclidean distance between two points. Small values of $D_{S \to P_F}$ indicate proximity to the P_F.

However, some others indicators like: coverage of two sets, diversity and the hypervolume could not be employed in this study. Because their values depend on the spread of solutions in the whole Pareto front and, on contrary, the proposed algorithms aim to obtain subsets of solutions close to the collective reference points. There is a lack of performance indicators that focus only on the proportion of occupied area in P_F. For that reason, the following subsection presents two new ones.

4.1   Referential Cluster Variance Indicator

Instead of a good spread of solutions along P_F, the method proposed in this work wants to obtain subsets of solutions close to the collective reference point. In this context, a small cluster variance means the individuals from the sample $Y = \{y_1, \ldots, y_N\}$ of size N are clustered closely around the population mean (μ) or the reference point (z^0). A low dispersion for a group of preferred points in P_F denotes a better efficiency of the approach tested. The referential cluster variance indicator κ is represented as follows:

$$\kappa = \frac{1}{N} \sum_{i=1}^{N} (y_i - \mu)^2 \tag{8}$$

In cases with more than one collective reference point (z^j), the points are clustered based on the closest distance to one of the reference points: $C_j = \{a \in \mathbb{R}^k : \|a - z^j\| \le \|a - z^i\|, \forall i\}$. Cluster C_j consists of all points for which z^j is the closest. The referential cluster variance is calculated to each cluster separately.

4.2   Hull Volume Indicator

Convex hull is a well-known geometric object widely used in various fields such as: shape analysis, pattern recognition, geographical information systems, image processing, etc. It has been also applied in the multi-objective optimization scenario.

The Normal Boundary Intersection method (NBI) [4] projects elements of the CHIM towards the boundary $\partial \mathcal{Z}$ of the objective space $\mathcal{Z}$ through a normal vector N. The intersection point between $\partial \mathcal{Z}$ and N the normal pointing is a Pareto optimal point, if the P_F surface is convex. Martínez and Coello [10] introduced an archiving strategy based on the CHIM to find evenly distributed points along the P_F. Their convex hull multi-objective evolutionary algorithm (CH-MOEA) uses an archiving mechanism that stores non-dominated solutions which are orthogonal to each point of CHIM ($h \in \mathcal{H}$). Likewise, Shan-Fan et al. [11] presented a MOEA where the non-dominated solutions are picked out from dominated solutions by the quick convex hulls algorithm.

The idea of convex hull can be borrowed and applied as a performance indicator to measure the quality of the non-dominated points around the collective reference points. Connecting the closest final points to each reference point will produce a facet representation of the P_F. The volume of the convex hull can be used as a scalar indicator for the distribution of points in P_F. Small values of the hull volume (Ψ) indicate concentrate points.

Non-convex problems can use alpha shapes to determine a concave hull of theirs points in P_F. The alpha shape is a subgraph of the Delaunay triangulation. The value of alpha (α) controls the geometric design of the shape. For large α values the shape approaches to the boundary of the convex hull. On the other hand, as α decreases the shape shows more cavities.

5   Experimental Results

This section presents some results of CI-NSGA-II, CI-SPEA2 and CI-SMS-EMOA. The scalable multi-objective test problems from the ZDT, DTLZ and WFG problem sets [2] have a known optimal front and can be used to benchmark the outcome of the algorithms. Their features cover different classes of MOPs: convex P_F, non-contiguous convex parts, non-convex, multi-modal, etc. For those reasons, the test problems subject the new algorithms to distinct optimization difficulties and compare their results.

The experiment emulates the collectivity by developing some virtual DMs (robots). Each robot has a predefined point in the objective space which will be used to direct robots' votes in a pairwise comparison between two individuals from Pareto front. Therefore, the robot votes on a solution according to the closest distance between its predefined point and each of the two candidates. Figure 1 illustrates candidates $c1$ and $c2$ with their respectively distances to the predefined point, $d1$ and $d2$. As $d1 < d2$, the robot would vote on $c1$. The robots create the collective reference points with a better reasoning strategy than simply random choice. It is important to notice that the collective reference point is built on the similarity of answers (votes) after the Gaussian Mixture model and cannot be confused with the robots' predefined points.

Very few MOEAs consider more than one user for reference point selection or evolutionary interaction. They neglect a collective scenario where many users

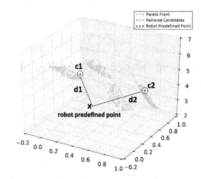

Fig. 1. The robot's predefined point will choose candidate c1 because the distance $d1 < d2$.

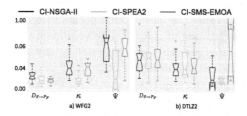

Fig. 2. Indicators for WFG2 and DTLZ2 tests.

could actively interact and take part of the decision process throughout the optimization. Furthermore, the new algorithms choose the reference points interactively. The references are not defined *a-priori*, like the R-NSGA-II from Deb [7], nor indicated by the DM as the middle point in the Light Beam approach [5]. Rather, all the references are discovered online with the support of a genuine collective intelligence of many users.

In this experiment, the robots abstract the collectivity within a controlled environment. So the algorithms can be tested, compared and better understood in their working principles. The quantity of online reference points is directly related to the number of k clusters in the Gaussian Mixture model.

The front coverage ($D_{S \rightarrow P_F}$), the referential cluster variance (κ) and the hull volume (Ψ) indicators were used to measure the quality of the algorithms. In addition to the Gaussian Mixture model, the K-means algorithm was implemented to bring a different clustering technique into the analysis of the algorithms. But the performance of Gaussian Mixture for these benchmarking cases was consistently better.

After 30 independent executions per algorithm on each test problem, the box plots were used to represent and support a valid judgment of the quality of the solutions and how different algorithms compare with each other. Figure 2 shows the distribution of the performance indicators for WFG2 and DTLZ2 problems in the form of box plots.

Table 1. Results of the Conover-Inman statistical hypothesis tests based on the mean values. Green cells (+) denote cases where the algorithm in the row statistically was better than the one in the column. Cells marked in red (−) are cases where the method in the column yielded statistically better results when compared to the method in the row.

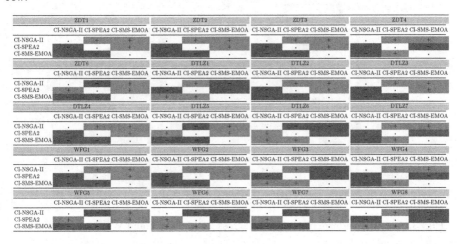

Although box plots allow a visual comparison of the results, it is necessary to go beyond reporting the descriptive statistics of the performance indicators and apply a statistical hypothesis test. The Conover-Inman procedure [3] is a non-parametric method for testing equality of population medians. It can be implemented in a pairwise manner to determine if the results of one algorithm were significantly better than those of the other. A significance level, α, of 0.05 was used for all tests. Table 1 contains the results of the statistical analysis for all the test problems based on the mean values.

The process of discovering the best algorithm is rather difficult as it implies cross-examining and comparing the results of their performance indicators. Figure 3 present a more integrative representation by grouping their indicators. A higher value of average performance ranking implies that the algorithm consistently achieved lower values of the indicators being assessed. In this case, lower values mean better convergence to P_F and higher concentration around the collective reference points. For a given set of algorithms $A_1, \ldots, A_K$, a set of P test problem instances $\Phi_1, \ldots, \Phi_P$, the function δ is defined as:

$$\delta\left(A_i, A_j, \Phi_p\right) = \begin{cases} 1 & \text{if } A_i \gg A_j \text{ solving } \Phi_p \\ 0 & \text{otherwise} \end{cases} \tag{9}$$

where the relation $A_i \gg A_j$ defines if A_i is better than A_j when solving the problem instance Φ_p in terms of the performance indicators: $D_{S \to P_F}$, κ and Ψ. Relying on δ, the performance index $P_p(A_i)$ of a given algorithm A_i when solving Φ_p is then computed as: $P_p(A_i) = \sum_{j=1, j \neq i}^{K} \delta\left(A_i, A_j, \Phi_p\right)$.

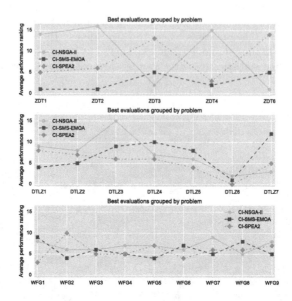

Fig. 3. Average performance ranking across ZDT, DTLZ and WFG test problems.

The CI-NSGA-II with Gaussian Mixture model consistently outperformed the others algorithms in most cases. Concerning the convergence indicator, CI-NSGA-II was ranked best in 16 of 21 test functions, except for ZDT1, ZDTL6, DTLZ1, WFG6 and WFG8. The CI-SPEA2 and CI-SMS-EMOA have a similar performance on WFG tests. It is worth noticing that ZDT4 experiment demonstrated a premature convergence around the online reference points. A better control of the extent of obtained solutions must be investigated to avoid this behaviour.

In summary, the interactive MOEAs and their collective reference points proved to be well matched for the range of ZDT, DTLZ and WFG test problems.

6   Final Remarks

In this work we have introduced new algorithms to improve the successive stages of evolution via dynamic group preferences. The interactive algorithms can apprehend people's heterogeneity and common sense to guide the search through relevant regions of Pareto-optimal front.

The new approaches have been tested successfully in benchmarking problems. Two different performance indicators were presented with the intention to measure the proportion of occupied area in P_F.

Currently, we have been exploring different features of the evolutionary process, such as: the usage of COIN as a local search for new individuals and opening the population for users' update to augment its quality. Replacing the robots by human collaborators, this research has a simulated environment[1] that

---

[1] http://playcanv.as/p/1ARj738G.

represents the facility location problem. In this context, individuals from the evolutionary algorithm population are distributed to the participants who have to fix and change the position arrangement or the resource distribution in the scenario. This simulated environment promotes the collaboration and supports rational improvements in the quality of the population. The algorithms (CI-NSGA-II, CI-SMS-EMOA, CI-SPEA2) introduced and compared here are used to iteratively refine the search parameters with collective preferences.

In the near future, we plan to work on creative solutions unfolded by the participants and possibly explore non-explicit objectives hidden in more complex scenario. Furthermore, we intent to apply directional information from the collective reference points during the evolution process. This way, the technique can extract the intelligence of the crowds and, at the same time, minimize the interruptions of the algorithm.

Acknowledgments. This work was partially funded by CNPq BJT Project 407851/2012-7, FAPERJ APQ1 Project 211.500/2015, FAPERJ APQ1 Project 211.451/2015.

References

1. Beume, N., Naujoks, B., Emmerich, M.: SMS-EMOA: Multiobjective selection based on dominated hypervolume. Eur. J. Oper. Res. **181**(3), 1653–1669 (2007)
2. Coello, C.C., Lamont, G.B., Van Veldhuizen, D.A.: Evolutionary Algorithms for Solving Multi-Objective Problems. Springer, New York (2007)
3. Conover, W.: Practical Nonparametric Statistics. Wiley, New York (1999)
4. Das, I., Dennis, J.E.: Normal-boundary intersection: a new method for generating the pareto surface in nonlinear multicriteria optimization problems. SIAM J. Optim. **8**(3), 631–657 (1998)
5. Deb, K., Kumar, A.: Light beam search based multi-objective optimization using evolutionary algorithms. In: IEEE Congress on Evolutionary Computation, 2007, CEC 2007, pp. 2125–2132. IEEE (2007)
6. Deb, K., Pratap, A., Agarwal, S., Meyarivan, T.: A fast and elitist multiobjective genetic algorithm: NSGA-II. IEEE Trans. Evol. Comput. **6**(2), 182–197 (2002)
7. Deb, K., Sundar, J., Udaya Bhaskara Rao, N., Chaudhuri, S.: Reference point based multi-objective optimization using evolutionary algorithms. Int. J. Comput. Intell. Res. **2**(3), 273–286 (2006)
8. Grinstead, C.M., Snell, J.L.: Introduction to Probability. American Mathematical Soc., Providence (2012)
9. Malone, T.W., Laubacher, R., Dellarocas, C.: Harnessing crowds: mapping the genome of collective intelligence (2009)
10. Martınez, S.Z., Coello, C.A.C.: An archiving strategy based on the convex hull of individual minima for MOEAs (2010)
11. Shan-Fan, J., Xiong, S.W., Zhuo-Wang, J.: The multi-objective differential evolution algorithm based on quick convex hull algorithms. In: Fifth International Conference on Natural Computation, 2009, ICNC 2009, vol. 4, pp. 469–473. IEEE (2009)
12. Zitzler, E., Laumanns, M., Thiele, L.: SPEA2: Improving the strength pareto evolutionary algorithm (2001)

Assessment of Multi-Objective Optimization Algorithms for Parametric Identification of a Li-Ion Battery Model

Yuviny Echevarría[1](✉), Luciano Sánchez[1], and Cecilio Blanco[2]

[1] Department of Computer Science, University of Oviedo, Gijón, Spain
yuviny@gmail.com, luciano@uniovi.es
[2] Department of Electrical Engineering, University of Oviedo, Gijón, Spain
cecilio@uniovi.es

Abstract. The identification of intelligent models of Li-Ion batteries is a major issue in Electrical Vehicular Technology. On the one hand, the fitness of such models depends on the recursive evaluation of a set of nonlinear differential equations over a representative path in the state space, which is a time consuming task. On the other hand, battery models are intrinsically unstable, and small differences in the initial state or the system, as well as imprecisions in the parameter values, may trigger large differences in the output. Hence, learning battery models from data is a complex multi-modal problem and the parameters of these models must be determined with a high accuracy. In addition to this, producing a dynamical model of a battery is a multi-criteria problem, because the predictive capabilities of the model must be estimated in both the voltage and the temperature domains. In this paper, a selection of state-of-the-art Multi-Objective Optimization Algorithms (SPEA2, NSGA-II, OMOPSO, NSGA-III and MOEA/D) are assessed with regard to their suitability for identifying a model of a Li-Ion battery. The dominance relations that occur between the Pareto fronts are discussed in terms of binary additive ϵ-quality indicators. It is concluded that each of the standard implementations of these algorithms has different issues with this particular problem, MOEA/D and NSGA-III being the best overall alternatives.

Keywords: Multi-Objective Optimization Algorithms · Li-Ion battery model · Parametric identification

1 Introduction

Battery Management Systems (BMS) are electronic subsystems governing the charge and discharge processes of batteries in Electric Vehicles (EVs). BMSs include hardware and software layers to perform a continuous monitoring of current, voltage and temperature of the battery and implement battery models for the estimation of different latent variables. Among these hidden variables,

© Springer International Publishing Switzerland 2016
F. Martínez-Álvarez et al. (Eds.): HAIS 2016, LNAI 9648, pp. 250–260, 2016.
DOI: 10.1007/978-3-319-32034-2_21

the State of Charge (SoC) is directly related to the EV range and thus the SoC is one of the most important readings in the drivers' dashboard.

The development of accurate battery models is a difficult task, because batteries are complex and instable electrochemical systems [1]. One of the most extended battery model groups are the so-called electrical Equivalent Circuit Models (ECMs). Commonly, ECMs estimate one output of the system from inputs [2–4]. The most frequently used ECMs for voltage estimation were recently reviewed by Hu [5]. Also, in [6] an offspring methodology of ECMs was proposed for determining the internal characteristics of dynamical systems by means of semi-physical models. These last models used current, battery and ambient temperatures as inputs, and were able to predict battery voltage and temperature, and at the same time some state variables, such as the SoC and the Open Circuit Voltage (OCV). This last methodology will be used in this work.

The parametric identification of a multi-output dynamical system is often intended to minimize the Mean Squared Error (MSE) between the observed output variables and the model. The MSE of a multi-output model is defined as the sum of the MSEs of all output variables. This definition has clear benefits, as the fitness of a model is a scalar value that can be optimized by standard methods. However, such an assessment of the error of a model strongly depends on the chosen physical units. For instance, a single model will be assigned two different errors if voltage and temperature are measured in millivolts and degrees Fahrenheit, or in volts and degrees Celsius. Because of this, in this work it is proposed that the battery model is regarded as a multi-criteria problem, and MSEs of voltage and temperature are not combined into a scalar value. It is remarked that this methodology has not been used in the past in the field of battery modeling, but there is prior art in other engineering areas. For instance, Efstratiadis made a review of ten year of study in the calibration of dynamical hydrological modeling with multi-criteria approaches [7].

In the particular case of semi-physical battery modeling, empirical observations suggest us that the fitness landscape of this problem contains many local minima, reaffirming the complexity of the parameter identification. Also, the accuracy of the model with respect to the MSE demands a high accuracy in order to obtain a well-fitted output curve (at least four significant figures for each parameter, according to our own experimentation). Lastly, the objective function of this problem identification has a high computational cost, thus algorithms that require a low number of evaluations are preferred.

The main idea in this paper is therefore to assess some state-of-the-art multi-criteria optimization algorithms and determine whether they are suitable for performing multi-criteria parametric identification of semi-physical battery models. Five Multi-Objetive Optimization Algorithms were chosen for this study: SPEA2 [8], NSGA-II [9], OMOPSO [10], NSGA-III [11] and MOEA/D [12]. It is remarked that a comparison between multi-criteria algorithms has certain technical difficulties on its own, as the assessment of the Pareto Fronts (PF) from different Multi-Objective Optimization Algorithms (MOOAs) is by itself a current research topic [13,14]. This study is based on Zitzler's binary additive ϵ-indicator to assess the different dominance relations between PFs [15].

The structure of the present paper is as follows: in Sect. 2, the battery model is outlined for the convenience of the reader. Section 3 contains a brief review of the MOOAs that are related to the problem at hand. Section 4 contains experimental tests and discuss the obtained results. The paper concludes in Sect. 5.

2 Semi-physical Model for Li-Ion Battery

The most popular ECM for Li-Ion Battery is a simple first-order RC model [16, 17]. The disadvantages of this RC model, that are shared by nearly all ECMs for batteries, are two: (i) the voltage of the battery cannot be estimated when no current is circulating through the circuit (ii) this kind of model ignores temperature effects. The semi-physical model studied in this work can be depicted as an equivalent circuit comprising non-linear impedances described by means of Fuzzy Rule-Based Systems (FRBSs). In this respect, intelligent models of elements akin to a resistance and a capacitor are defined by mean of fuzzy rules, and the dynamics of the whole model is defined by a set of differential equations where the FRBSs are non-linear embedded blocks (see Fig. 1).

The inputs of the model are: (i) the current i_B applied to the battery, positive or negative in charge or discharge process respectively; (ii) the ambient temperature T_A. On the other hand, the outputs are the battery voltage v_B and the battery temperature T_B.

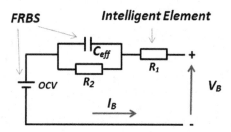

Fig. 1. First-Order ECM for the semi-physical battery model.

The stored charge in the battery Q is time-dependent and represented by the charge of the capacitor; $Q = C_{\text{eff}} \cdot v_{C_{\text{eff}}}$. The effective capacity C_{eff} depends of the charge Q, the current i_B and the temperature of the battery T_B. The limited speed of the electrochemical process is modeled by a dependence between charge and capacity which is governed by an exponential decay with a time constant τ. In the limit (or in the presence of very small charge/discharge currents) this can be simplified to

$$v_B = i_B R_1 + \text{OCV}(Q) + \eta(Q, T_B, i_B) \tag{1}$$

R_1 is the series resistance in the RC equivalent circuit, OCV is an FRBS that depends on Q, η represents the over-potential in the charge/discharge process and the time evolution of the system is described by the following nonlinear differential equation:

$$\dot{\eta} = -\tau(i_B) \cdot (\eta - f(Q, T_B, i_B) \cdot i_B) \tag{2}$$

The forcing function is the product

$$f(Q, T_B, i_B) \cdot i_B = \begin{cases} f^+(Q, T_B) \cdot i_B & \text{when charging} \\ f^-(Q, T_B) \cdot i_B & \text{when discharging} \end{cases} \tag{3}$$

where f^+ and f^- are FRBS that depend on the charge and the battery temperature. The heat balance (that has also been simplified to facilitate a better understanding of the model) is defined by the next dynamical equation:

$$\dot{T}_B = (\alpha(Q) + \beta T_B) \cdot i_B^2 + \gamma \cdot (T_B - T_A) \tag{4}$$

where α is another FRBS that depend of Q. Moreover, β and γ are constants, related with heating and cooling rates. The term $\alpha(Q) + \beta T_B) \cdot i_B^2$ models the internal heating when charging/discharging the battery.

The differential equations are integrated by means of the implicit Euler's method (backward Euler's method), which is adequate for a slow system like this. The obtained discretized equations are:

$$v_B(t) = i_B(t)R_1 + \text{OCV}(Q) + \eta(t) \tag{5}$$

$$\eta(t + \Delta t) = \frac{\eta(t) + \Delta t \cdot \tau(i_B) \cdot i_B \cdot f(Q, T_B, i_B)}{1 + \tau(i_B)\Delta t} \tag{6}$$

$$T_B(t + \Delta t) = \frac{T_B(t) + \Delta t \cdot (\alpha(Q)i_B^2(t + \Delta t) - \gamma T_B(t + \Delta t))}{1 - \Delta t \cdot (\beta i_B^2(t + \Delta t) - \gamma)} \tag{7}$$

The parametric identification of the discrete model defined by Eqs. 5, 6 and 7 consists therefore in finding the following unknown parameters

1. The constant R_1, γ, β;
2. The constants resulting from $\tau(i_B) = \begin{cases} \tau_+ & \text{when } i_B > 0 \\ \tau_0 & \text{when } i_B = 0 \\ \tau_- & \text{when } i_B < 0 \end{cases}$
3. The consequents defining OCV;
4. The consequents defining f^+, f^- for $i_B > 0$ and $i_B < 0$;
5. The consequents defining α;
6. The initial states Q_0, T_{B0} and V_{B0};
7. The antecedent for FRBS related with the voltage output;
8. Finally, the antecedent for FRBS related with temperature.

The fuzzy rules in the model are zeroth-order Takagi–Sugeno–Kang type in which the antecedents are AND combinations of statements. For example, the following rule is part of the knowledge base of the forcing function $f^-(Q, T_B)$:

If Q is LOW and T_B is HRT, then $f^-(Q, T_B) = 5.3$

where Q and T_B are described by eight linguistic terms with triangular fuzzy sets joined to left and right trapezoidal for the extremes. The linguistic variable (Q) charge are: "VERY LOW (VL) CHARGE", "LOW (L) CHARGE", "QUASI LOW (QL) CHARGE", "MEDIUM LOW (ML) CHARGE", "MEDIUM HIGH (MH) CHARGE", "QUASI HIGH (QH) CHARGE", "HIGH (H) CHARGE", and "VERY HIGH (VH) CHARGE". The linguistic terms for the variable T_B is based on the rise of temperature (RT): ("VLRT", "LRT", "QLRT", "MLRT", "MHRT", "QHRT", "HRT", "VHRT"). Moreover, the current i_B use three terms: "POSITIVE", "ZERO" and "NEGATIVE". All fuzzy memberships in this model are part of strong fuzzy partitions as was explained in [18,19].

3   Multi-Objective Approach for Semi-physical Models

The use of MOOAs to solve multi-objective optimization problems has been studied by many authors in applications with very large search spaces, uncertainty and noise where traditional deterministic optimization algorithms are impossible. The problem of multi-objective parameter identification for dynamical models is complex in all application areas, as explained in Sect. 1.

In the present study, some of the most representative algorithms for multi-objective optimization have been selected. The list is by no means complete, but includes some of the most popular approaches in multi-criteria system identification. On the one hand, Zitzler's Strength Pareto Evolutionary Algorithm (SPEA2) [8] and Deb's Nondominated Sorting Genetic Algorithm (NSGA-II) [9]. The main idea under NSGA-II was to alleviate the computational complexity, proposing a non-elitism approach and eliminating the need of the sharing parameter in precedent techniques. A third version of this last algorithm has been recently published (NSGA-III) [11]. In the same spirit, a multi-objective evolutionary algorithm based on decomposition (MOEA/D) that was proposed in [12], is also included in this study. MOEA/D is based on conventional aggregation approaches in which the multi-criteria problem is decomposed into a number of scalar objective optimization problems. Lastly, the same authors of NSGA-III and MOEA/D jointly proposed a new algorithm named MOEA/DD [20]. The new approach exploits the merits of the concepts of dominance and decomposition to obtain a balance between convergence and diversity. MOEA/DD is suitable for problems with a high number of objectives and therefore it is not suitable for the model proposed in this paper, however it might suit future developments with a higher number of criteria, related with the internal electrochemical characteristics of the battery. On the other hand, the swarm intelligence approach OMOPSO [10] is an improving of Particle Swarm Optimization for Multi-Objective Problems based on Pareto dominance and using the crowding factor for the selection of leaders. There are many recent applications of PSO in battery modeling [21,22], thus it was decided to include OMOPSO in the comparative.

The multi-criteria problem for the semi-physical battery model studied in this work (Sect. 2) can be formulated as follows. Given $\vec{x_\theta}$, that is the vector of unknown parameters of the model, and the feasible set X (X comprises the upper and lower bounds of the parameters along with the semantic restrictions of the fuzzy rules), the problem that must be solved is

$$\min F(\vec{x_\theta}) = \left(E_v(\vec{x_\theta}), E_T(\vec{x_\theta})\right) \quad \vec{x_\theta} \in X \tag{8}$$

where the functions E_v and E_T are

$$E_v = \sum_{i=1}^{N} \left\{V_B(t_0 + i\Delta t) - V_B^{\text{TRUE}}(t_0 + i\Delta t)\right\}^2 \tag{9}$$

$$E_T = \sum_{i=1}^{N} \left\{T_B(t_0 + i\Delta t) - T_B^{\text{TRUE}}(t_0 + i\Delta t)\right\}^2 \tag{10}$$

The constrains of the problem are:

1. $R_1 > 0$;
2. $\tau_+ > 0$, $\tau_- > 0$ and $\tau_0 > 0$;
3. Each set of numbers defining OCV are monotonically increasing with Q;
4. Each set of numbers defining the model FRBS are also comonotonical with respect to its corresponding input variable.

4   Experimental Results

In the first part of this section, the experimental setup that was chosen for acquiring the battery data is described. In a second part, the methodology that was used to compare the different Pareto Fronts is explained. The numerical results are presented and discussed in the third subsection.

4.1   Experimental Setup and Electronic Instrumentation

All battery data was collected in the Battery Test Laboratory at the University of Oviedo, Spain. The equipment comprises a SBT 10050 battery test system from PEC with an ICP 750 climate chamber from Memmert. Different charging and discharging protocols were performed for sampling current, voltage and temperature. The tested cell was a pouch from European Batteries, whose rated capacity C is 42 Ah, with a weight of 1010 g. The performance characteristics sheet provided by the manufacturer indicates that the average operating voltage is 3.2 V, the charge and discharge cut-off voltages are 3.65 V and 2.5 V respectively.

The dataset for this study consists in a 0.1 Hz sampling at different discharge currents C/3, C/2 and C rates (14 A, 21A and 42A) in several charge-discharge cycles[1]. The standard charging method provided by the manufacturer was used in all cases and the temperature inside the chamber was fixed to 23 degrees Celsius. The Fig. 2 shows a standard charge, resting period and discharge cycle at C rate.

---

[1] Data publicly available at http://www.unioviedo.es/batterylab/.

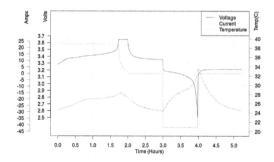

Fig. 2. Voltage, current and battery temperature with standard charge and discharge at C rate.

4.2 Statistical Experimental Design

For each of the dataset (DS-C/3, DS-C/2 and DS-C), all algorithms (SPEA2, NSGA-II, OMOPSO, NSGA-III and MOEA/D) were launched ten times. The Pareto front was built by combining all non-dominated models that were found by each algorithm at these ten iterations.

All evolutionary algorithms used the same population size, mutation and crossover probabilities (0.1 and 0.9 respectively), selected from empirical observation. Specific crossover and bounded mutation operators were designed that preserved the restrictions described in the preceding section. It is remarked that the original semi-physical model in [19] made use of a multi-objetive Simulated Annealing hybridized with a local search, that cannot be applied to multicriteria problems. The experiment programming core is based on Java framework for multi-objective optimization, jMetal version 5 [23].

Different operators exist that can be used for examining the different dominance relations between Pareto fronts in the experiments. Following [15], unary quality indicators were not the best choice, because they oversimplify the comparisons and the binary additive ϵ-indicator measure was selected to assess the different techniques instead. This metric is defined as follows [24]:

$$I_{\varepsilon+}(A, B) = \inf \left\{ \varepsilon \in \mathbb{R} \mid \forall b \in B \, \exists a \in A : a \succeq_{\varepsilon+} b \right\} \tag{11}$$

where $A, B \in X$, ϵ express the minimum factor that we can add to each objective value in $b \in B$ and the resulting objective is still weakly dominated by $a \in A$. When $I_{\epsilon+}(A, B) < 0$, A strictly dominates B ($A \succ\succ B$). If $I_{\epsilon+}(A, B) = 0$ and $I_{\epsilon+}(B, A) = 0$, then A and B represent the same PF. Otherwise, if $I_{\epsilon+}(A, B) \leq 0$ and $I_{\epsilon+}(B, A) > 0$ then A is better than B ($A \triangleright B$). If both epsilon are greater than zero A and B are incomparable ($A \parallel B$).

4.3 Numerical Results and Discussion

An example of the obtained results is depicted in the Fig. 3. The outcomes of each studied MOOAs are shown in Fig. 3a. The input dataset (DS-C) is representative of a standard battery charge, resting period and discharge at constant current of 42 A. On the other hand, Fig. 3b shows a zoom plot at the resulting PF of NSGA-III with dataset DS-C/3 as input. It is remarked that NSGA-III did improve NSGA-II in certain problems (see Fig. 3a for the particular case of the dataset DS-C). Notwithstanding this, the differences were not significant for many cases. Notice also that, in the resulting PF from MOEA/D all solutions are concentrated in the same area of the PF (Fig. 3a), while SPEA2 was able to explore a larger area.

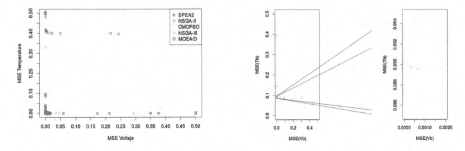

Fig. 3. Outcomes of the studied algorithms (a) PFs of all algorithms with dataset DS-C as input (b) Zoom plot of NSGA-III solutions for dataset DS-C/3.

A parameter set of the models found by MOEA/D for the dataset DS-C were included in Fig. 4. Notice the differences in the voltage and temperature curves of the model in term of Volts and degrees Celsius respectively.

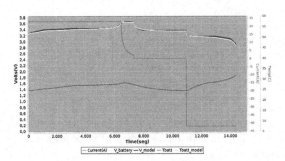

Fig. 4. Semi-physical model output from a dominant solution of MOEA/D with DS-C.

Another criticism that can be made about the studied algorithms is that none of the PFs dominate the model found by the ad-hoc hybrid algorithm proposed in [19]. This result clearly signals that a specific hybrid multi-objective algorithm might be possible that improves state-of-the-art of MOOAs for this particular application. The accuracy of the ad-hoc hybrid algorithm is depicted in Fig. 5

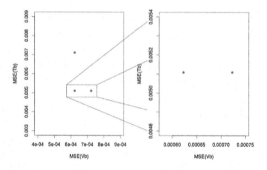

Fig. 5. PF accuracy of the ad-hoc hybrid algorithm proposed in [19] with dataset DS-C/3 as input.

Table 1. Binary Additive Epsilon Indicator relations between the studied algorithms.

		A = SPEA2		A = NSGA-II		A = OMOPSO		A = NSGA-III		A = MOEA/D		A = AD-HOC	
		$I_{\epsilon+}(A,B)$	relation	$I_{\epsilon+}(A,B)$	relation	$I_{\epsilon+}(A,B)$	relation	$I_{\epsilon+}(A,B)$	relation	$I_{\epsilon+}(A,B)$	relation	$I_{\epsilon+}(A,B)$	relation
	B = SPEA2	0	=	0.0042		3.38E-5		0.0046		0.0032		-1.75e-5	
	B = NSGA-II	-5.62E-4	▷	0	=	-5.31E-4		0.0020		0.0016		-5.82e-4	
DS-C	B = OMOPSO	0.0052	‖	0.0087	◁	0	=	0.0091		0.0058		-5.13e-5	
	B = NSGA-III	1.62E-6	‖	0.0015	‖	3.53E-5	‖	0	=	0.0031		-1.60e-5	
	B = MOEA/D	0.0025	‖	0.0068	‖	-0.0010	▷	0.0070	‖	0	=	-1.10e-3	
	B = AD-HOC	**0.0796**	◁	**0.0823**	◁	**0.0750**	◁	**0.0841**	◁	**0.0770**	◁	**0**	=
	B = SPEA2	0	=	0.0070		0.0070		0.0170		0.0063		-4.30e-5	
	B = NSGA-II	-4.44E-4	▷	0	=	0.0041		0.0132		0.0010		-4.88e-4	
DS-C/2	B = OMOPSO	2.25E-4	‖	0.0032	‖	0		0.0104		0.0023		-1.88e-5	
	B = NSGA-III	-3.84E-4	‖	0.0010	‖	-4.08E-4	=	0		0.0011		-4.27e-4	
	B = MOEA/D	-9.43E-4	▷	0.0035	‖	0.0039	‖	0.0130	‖	0	=	-9.87e-4	
	B = AD-HOC	**0.0542**	◁	**0.0612**	◁	**0.0612**	◁	**0.0703**	◁	**0.0592**	◁	**0**	=
	B = SPEA2	0	=	0.0433		8.69E-4		5.21E-4		0.0070		-1.23E-4	
	B = NSGA-II	-5.26E-4	▷	0	=	-1.82E-4		-4.12E-4		0.0016		-1.97E-4	
DS-C/3	B = OMOPSO	1.89E-4	‖	0.0425	◁	0	=	3.001E-4		0.0063		-4.66E-4	
	B = NSGA-III	4.69E-6	‖	0.0430	◁	7.54E-4	‖	0	=	0.0067		-1.18E-4	
	B = MOEA/D	-0.0013	▷	0.0382	‖	-9.67E-4	▷	-0.0013	▷	0	=	-1.43E-3	
	B = AD-HOC	**0.3486**	◁	**0.0862**	◁	**0.3494**	◁	**0.3487**	◁	**0.3534**	◁	**0**	=

for the particular case of dataset DS-C/3. All in all, the solutions of the studied MOOAs are reasonable from a practical point of view and serve as a baseline for future developments.

Finally, in Table 1 the dominance relationships of the five assessed algorithms are shown for the different datasets, along with the ad-hoc hybrid algorithm. The lower triangular matrix for each dataset dimension shows the relationships based on the indicators $I_{\epsilon+}(A,B)$ and $I_{\epsilon+}(B,A)$. Observe that neither NSGA-II nor OMOPSO had an exceedingly good performance. If ad-hoc algorithm is excluded the incomparability between PFs is the most frequent result, showing that the performance of all studied algorithms is roughly the same. The performance of SPEA2 is acceptable (and a good sampling of the PF was found by this algorithm, as mentioned) but the computational cost is higher than that of other algorithms with similar performance. MOED/D was among the best algorithms for the parametric identification, however, all of the models found with this technique were localized in the same region of the PF.

5 Conclusion

An empirical study has been presented where different multicriteria optimization algorithms have been applied to a specific problem of parametric identification of a semi-physical battery model. This is a particularly complex problem where domain specific knowledge can be used to alleviate the computational burden, and as such ad-hoc methods were proposed that found a very accurate solution. In this paper it has been shown that none of the out-of-the box algorithms were able to find a Pareto front containing solutions that dominate the model found by the ad-hoc method. This means that specific multicriteria algorithms are possible that can improve state-of-the-art MOOAs at this specific problem, and the results presented here may serve as a baseline for these future developments.

Acknowledgements. This work funded by the Eureka SD project (agreement number 2013-2591), that is supported by the Erasmus Mundus programme of the European Union. In addition, was supported by the Spanish Ministry of Science and Innovation (MICINN) and the Regional Ministry of the Principality of Asturias under Grants TIN2014-56967-R, DPI2013-46541-R and FC-15-GRUPIN14-073.

References

1. Waag, W., Fleischer, C., Sauer, D.U.: Critical review of the methods for monitoring of lithium-ion batteries in electric and hybrid vehicles. J. Power Sources **258**, 321–339 (2014)
2. Zhang, C., Li, K., Pei, L., Zhu, C.: An integrated approach for real-time model-based state-of-charge estimation of lithium-ion batteries. J. Power Sources **283**, 24–36 (2015)
3. Feng, T., Yang, L., Zhao, X., Zhang, H., Qiang, J.: Online identification of lithium-ion battery parameters based on an improved equivalent-circuit model and its implementation on battery state-of-power prediction. J. Power Sources **281**, 192–203 (2015)
4. Xu, J., Cao, B., Chen, Z., Zou, Z.: An online state of charge estimation method with reduced prior battery testing information. Int. J. Electr. Power Energ. Syst. **63**, 178–184 (2014)
5. Hu, X., Li, S., Peng, H.: A comparative study of equivalent circuit models for Li-ion batteries. J. Power Sources **198**, 359–367 (2012)
6. Sánchez, L., Couso, I., González, M.: A design methodology for semi-physical fuzzy models applied to the dynamic characterization of LiFePO4 batteries. Appl. Soft Comput. **14**, 269–288 (2014)
7. Efstratiadis, A., Koutsoyiannis, D.: One decade of multi-objective calibration approaches in hydrological modelling: a review. Hydrol. Sci. J. **55**(1), 58–78 (2010)

260 Y. Echevarría et al.

8. Zitzler, E., Laumanns, M., Thiele, L.: SPEA2: improving the strength pareto evolutionary algorithm, pp. 95–100 (2001)
9. Deb, K., Pratap, A., Agarwal, S., Meyarivan, T.: A fast and elitist multiobjective genetic algorithm: NSGA-II. IEEE Trans. Evol. Comput. **6**(2), 182–197 (2002)
10. Sierra, M.R., Coello, C.A.C.: Improving PSO-based multi-objective optimization using crowding, mutation and ϵ-dominance. In: Coello Coello, C.A., Hernández Aguirre, A., Zitzler, E. (eds.) EMO 2005. LNCS, vol. 3410, pp. 505–519. Springer, Heidelberg (2005)
11. Deb, K., Jain, H.: An evolutionary many-objective optimization algorithm using reference-point-based nondominated sorting approach, Part I: solving problems with box constraints. IEEE Trans. Evol. Comput. **18**(4), 577–601 (2014)
12. Zhang, Q., Li, H.: MOEA/D: a multiobjective evolutionary algorithm based on decomposition. IEEE Trans. Evol. Comput. **11**(6), 712–731 (2007)
13. Deb, K.: Multi-objective optimization. In: Burke, E.K., Kendall, G. (eds.) Search Methodologies, pp. 403–449. Springer, New York (2014)
14. Tutum, C.C., Deb, K.: A multimodal approach for evolutionary multi-objective optimization (MEMO): proof-of-principle results. In: Gaspar-Cunha, A., Henggeler Antunes, C., Coello, C.C. (eds.) EMO 2015. LNCS, vol. 9018, pp. 3–18. Springer, Heidelberg (2015)
15. Zitzler, E., Laumanns, M., Thiele, L., Fonseca, C.M., da Fonseca, V.G.: Why quality assessment of multiobjective optimizers is difficult. In: Proceedings of the Genetic and Evolutionary Computation Conference, GECCO 2002, pp. 666–674. Morgan Kaufmann Publishers Inc., July 2002
16. Cuma, M.U., Koroglu, T.: A comprehensive review on estimation strategies used in hybrid and battery electric vehicles. Renew. Sustain. Energ. Rev. **42**, 517–531 (2015)
17. Linden, D.: Linden's Handbook of Batteries, 4th edn. McGraw-Hill Education, New York (2011)
18. Blanco, C., Sanchez, L., Gonzalez, M., Anton, J.C., Garcia, V., Viera, J.C.: An equivalent circuit model with variable effective capacity for LiFePO4 batteries. IEEE Trans. Veh. Technol. **63**(8), 3592–3599 (2014)
19. Sanchez, L., Blanco, C., Anton, J.C., Garcia, V., Gonzalez, M., Viera, J.C.: A variable effective capacity model for LiFePO4 traction batteries using computational intelligence techniques. IEEE Trans. Ind. Electron. **62**(1), 555–563 (2015)
20. Li, K., Deb, K., Zhang, Q., Kwong, S.: An evolutionary many-objective optimization algorithm based on dominance and decomposition. IEEE Trans. Evol. Comput. **19**(5), 694–716 (2015)
21. Xian, W., Long, B., Li, M., Wang, H.: Prognostics of lithium-ion batteries based on the verhulst model, particle swarm optimization and particle filter. IEEE Trans. Instrum. Meas. **63**(1), 2–17 (2014)
22. Hu, C., Jain, G., Zhang, P., Schmidt, C., Gomadam, P., Gorka, T.: Data-driven method based on particle swarm optimization and k-nearest neighbor regression for estimating capacity of lithium-ion battery. Appl. Energy **129**, 49–55 (2014)
23. Nebro, A.J., Durillo, J.J., Vergne, M.: Redesigning the jMetal multi-objective optimization framework. In: Proceedings of the Companion Publication of the 2015 on Genetic and Evolutionary Computation Conference - GECCO Companion 2015, pp. 1093–1100. ACM Press, New York, July 2015
24. Zitzler, E., Thiele, L., Laumanns, M., Fonseca, C., da Fonseca, V.: Performance assessment of multiobjective optimizers: an analysis and review. IEEE Trans. Evol. Comput. **7**(2), 117–132 (2003)

Comparing ACO Approaches in Epilepsy Seizures

Paula Vergara[1], José R. Villar[1(✉)], Enrique de la Cal[1], Manuel Menéndez[2],
and Javier Sedano[3]

[1] Computer Science Department, University of Oviedo, Oviedo, Spain
{U032599,villarjose,delacal}@uniovi.es
[2] Morphology and Cellular Biology Department, University of Oviedo, Oviedo, Spain
menendezgmanuel@uniovi.es
[3] Instituto Tecnológico de Castilla y León, Burgos, Spain
javier.sedano@itcl.es

Abstract. Epilepsy is a neurological illness causing disturbances in the nervous system. In recent studies, a wearable device has been developed and a Hybrid Artificial Intelligent System has been proposed for enhancing the anamnesis in the case of new patients or patients with severe convulsions. Among the different Artificial Intelligent techniques that have been proposed during the last years for Epilepsy Convulsions Identification (ECI), Ant Colony Optimization (ACO) has been found as one of the most efficient alternatives in order to learn Fuzzy Rule Based Classifiers (FRBC) to tackle with this problem.

This study proposes the comparative of two different ACO based learning strategies: the Pittsburg FRBC learning by means of Ant Colony Systems (ACS) and the Michigan FRBC learning using the Ant-Miner+ algorithm. Different alternatives for both strategies are also analyzed.

The obtained results show the Pittsburg ACS learning as a very promising solution for mio-clonic ECI. The Ant-Miner+ based Michigan strategy doesn't perform well for this research, which is mainly due to the reduced number of features considered in the experimentation.

1 Introduction

Epilepsy is a core neurological disorder that has an intense impact in the everyday life of people living with the disease. Monitoring patients living with epilepsy is always challenging, as seizures usually affect consciousness. This monitoring relies on the patient and relatives for registering the episode information, which is not always feasible. Developing a wearable device for epilepsy monitoring would therefore eventually complete the anamnesis, enhancing medical diagnosis and treatment settings.

The development of low-cost wearable devices focused the research on developing models for the assistance in the anamnesis, mainly centered on Epilepsy Convulsion Identification (ECI). The majority of the approaches are based on the video surveillance combined with, i.e., electrocardiograms [1,2]. The use of

© Springer International Publishing Switzerland 2016
F. Martínez-Álvarez et al. (Eds.): HAIS 2016, LNAI 9648, pp. 261–272, 2016.
DOI: 10.1007/978-3-319-32034-2_22

3D accelerometer (3DACC) has also been reported in the literature for the study of certain types of epilepsy convulsions, specially those that have a clear impact on the motor system [3]. Most of the 3DACC based solutions make use of thresholds for discriminating among the possible patient's states [4] or including extra information from other types of sensors [1].

Although the performance of these methods is really high, the fact that all of them work on constrained areas -like laboratories or specific rooms- and the restriction on the activities the patient can be carrying on just before a convulsion are far too serious, restraining the generalization of these approaches. On the other hand, several products, like [5–8], have been introduced in the press. However, the products are not in the market, and, the most important, the approaches are not always suited to the normal life: several of them makes use of several sensors located in different positions of the body, while others propose the use of a wearable clothes that are really uncomfortable or even impossible to use in normal life. For sure, these solutions are focused on patients suffering plenty of convulsions per week.

Recently, two different approaches have been proposed for ECI, the first one based on Genetic Fuzzy Finite State Machines (GFFSM) [9] and the second based on Fuzzy Rule Based Classifiers (FRBC) learned by means of Ant Colony Optimization (ACO) [10].

Briefly, GFFSMs are Fuzzy Finite State Machines, where the states are the problem classes, the transitions are Fuzzy Rules, and the input variables are partitioned with a priory defined granularity [11,12]. In [9], a realistic experimentation was performed with several healthy participants simulating ECIs through following a well defined protocol designed by the medical staff. This realistic data and the 5×2 cross validation scheme applied on the participants -shuffling the participants to became part of the training and testing data sets for each fold instead of shuffling the time series- allowed not only the learning the GFFSM models but also the validation and robustness test of the obtained models: this was possible as long as the training and the validation data sets included data from a similar number of participants. It was shown that shuffling the participants generated more general models than using Leave-One-Out on the participants or when using typical cross validation schemes where the time series are shuffled independently of the participant.

This study focuses on learning generalized Fuzzy Rule Based Classifier FRBC models in order to identify ECIs using Ant Colony Optimization (ACO). The learning proposal of [10] is expanded with the two main approaches of learning FRBCs (Pittburgs and Michigan) using the same cross-validation scheme. The Pittsburg and Michigan approaches were inspired in the representation suggested in [13] using Ant Colony System (ACS) and in [14] with Ant-Miner+, respectively. Furthermore, different variations in the partitioning and in the Fuzzy Rule base dimensionality are analyzed. Finally, the Ant-Miner+ is also applied to learn Rule Based Classifiers (RBC) in order to compare the performance of the different methods.

The organization of this paper is as follows. In the next section, an overview of the complete approach is detailed. Afterwards, an exhaustive experimentation for comparing the different approaches is presented, including the discussion on the results. Finally, the conclusions remarks are drawn.

2   FRBC Learning Metaheuristics for ECI

The different options that have been analyzed for the identification of epilepsy convulsions are presented in Fig. 2. In a previous work, the GFFSM learning solution presented in [11] was adapted for the ECI problem [9,12]; we would refer the interested readers to the mentioned references for further description of this solution. The main advantage of these GFFSM models lies on the steady state of the classifier's output, generating a non-fluctuation class proposal. Nevertheless, its learning complexity and the time spent in training these models highly penalize this model learning approach.

An alternative to the GFFSM is the FRBC learning without any type state machine. In case the partitioning of the Fuzzy variables is given, learning FRBC can be seen as the optimization of a combinatorial problem; in this type of problems, ACO has been reported as a very successful technique.

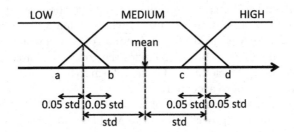

Fig. 1. Calculation of the partition relevant points -a, b, c and d- based on the mean and std values of the variable for the class EPILEPSY.

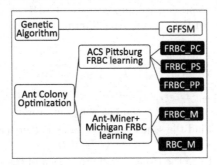

Fig. 2. A scheme of the learning approach and the variations considered in this study. Refer to the text for a description.

There is a wide variety of methods for the generation of fuzzy partitions, from the uniform partitioning to more sophisticated and elaborated methods based on examples, i.e., clustering among others. In this study, the partitioning of the Fuzzy variables is determined by computing the statistics of the different variables for the samples belonging to the class Epilepsy [10]. This partitioning is referred from now on as the statistical partitioning scheme Fig. 1, and makes use of three linguistic labels -LOW., MID, HIGH- per variable. Uniformly distributed fuzzy trapezoidal membership functions were assigned to each label.

Figure 2 shows the taxonomy of strategies tackled in this paper. On the one hand, a Pittsburg FRBC learning strategy by means of Ant Colony Systems (ACS) as proposed in [13] is presented with different flavors: learning a complete rule based (FRBC_PC), learning a subset of rules -thus reducing the cardinality of the rule set- (FRBC_PS), and a pruning stage (FRBC_PP) in order to chose the best set of rules from those proposed in the FRBC_PC model.

On the other hand, Ant-Miner+ is proposed to learn FRBC models in a Michigan fashion. Therefore, the original Ant-Miner+ algorithm -which was developed for learning RBCs- is extended to learn the Fuzzy Rules (FR). As a result, the Ant-Miner+ proposal in this study generates FRBC_M or RBC_M according to the parameters and the given partitioning. Consequently, different models can be learned using the Ant-Miner+ adaptation proposed in this research.

From now on, and as stated in previous research [9], three variables have been chosen as the most representative from the whole domain of features, namely, the Signal Magnitude Area (SMA), the Amount of Movement (AoM) and the Time Between Peaks (TBP). Table 1 includes the equations for computing these features from the body acceleration. Peaks differing the mean in at least 0.9 of the standard deviation were accepted.

The next subsections deal with all of these aspects: Subsect. 2.1 includes the details of the Pittsburg approach, while the Michigan approach is explained in Subsect. 2.2.

Table 1. The input variables used in this study. A sliding window of size w=32 samples with a shift of 16 samples, at a sampling rate of 16 Hz. $b_{c,i}$ stands for the body acceleration extracted from the 3DACC data filtering the gravity.

Transformation	Calculation
$SMA_t(\vec{s})$	$\frac{1}{w}\sum_{i=1}^{w}(|b_{x,t-i}| + |b_{y,t-i}| + |b_{z,t-i}|)$
$AoM_t(\vec{s})$	$\sum_{i=1}^{i=w}\sum_{c\in\{x,y,z\}}|max(b_{c,t-i}) - min(b_{c,t-i})|$
$TBP_t(\vec{s})$	Computed with the following algorithm:
	1. Find the sequences with value higher than mean+K*std within the window ($K = 0.9$)
	2. Keep the rising points from each of these sequences
	3. Measure the mean time between them

2.1   Pittsburg Learning of Generalized FRBC Models

Following the proposal for learning FRBC detailed in [13], the best set of non-null support fuzzy rules according to the current partition was obtained in a Pittsburg fashion by means of ACO. Accordingly, any FR_r has the format depicted: "IF X_1 is $A_{1,r} \wedge X_2$ is $A_{2,r} \wedge \cdots \wedge X_N$ is $A_{N,r}$ THEN Y is S_r", where there are N input variables, $A_{i,r}$ is corresponding label used in rule FR_r for the i variable, Y is the output class and S_r is class assigned to rule FR_r. The single winner inference is the Fuzzy Reasoning method. The combination of antecedents as the nodes in the input layer and the available classes as destination nodes in the output layer [10].

The Ant Colony System (ACS) algorithm used is proposed in [15]. In this algorithm, each ant represents a combination of non-null support fuzzy rules. However, some slight adaptations were proposed in [13].

The pheromone update is calculated accordingly with the ACS, computing the fitness of the individual as the inverse of the Mean Absolute classification Error (see Eq. 1), where N is the number of available samples for training (or testing), and x_n and y_n refer to the input vector and model's output, respectively.

$$MAE = \frac{1}{N} \sum_{n=1}^{N} |y_n - FRBC(x_n)| \tag{1}$$

ACO based FRBC learning as stated in [13] learns Pittsburg models including the complete set of available rules. When the number of features is reduced this solution might be valid, but the complexity increases as the cardinality of the input domain does. Therefore, some filtering is introduced in order to evaluate if simpler models perform better. One simple method is to limit the number of rules in the classifier, forcing the models to include only a predefined number of rules.

Additionally, two simple pruning methods are introduced: the up-bottom (UB) and the bottom-up (BU) pruning. The UB starts once the final Pittsburg model has been learned and, in subsequent iterations, evaluates the model without a rule, eliminating those rules for which the model performs better without them. The process stops when no increase in the performance is obtained. Conversely, the BU pruning starts from an empty model, and in repeated iterations adds the rule that introduces the best performance in the model. In both cases, a limit in the number of the filtered rules is fixed a priory.

In the following, a FRBC learned with the original Pittsburg approach presented in [13] is referred as FRBC_PC (PC stands for Pittsburg fashion, Complete fuzzy rule base), while those FRBCs learned using a reduced set of rule in a Pittsburg style are referred as FRBC_PS (PS stands for Pittsburg fashion, fuzzy rule base Subset). The models obtained from the FRBC_PC models after pruning are referred as FRBC_PP_UB or FRBC_PP_BU, respectively, where PP stands for using Pittsburg modeling and Pruning afterwards.

2.2   Ant-Miner+ for Learning FRBCs with Michigan Style

According to [14, 16–19], ACO allows to learn classification rules and, particularly, FR as described in Subsect. 2.1. To do so, the approach moves from the ACS algorithm to the Ant-Miner+ [14, 20]. However, some modifications are needed in the heuristic function for computing the path costs.

The construction of the graphs starts by choosing the rule class. To do so, the available samples are analyzed and the minority class is selected. Afterwards, the inner nodes are generated. An inner node represents the antecedent of the rule, thus it includes a label from each of the input variables. Only the nodes with support in the current data set are included. The process is illustrated in Fig. 3. It is worth noticing that in this approach we do not extend the graph with all the variables; instead, we condense the variable label combination in a single node. As long as, on the one hand, the rules are not allow to include more than a single label from a variable and, on the other hand, Ant-Miner+ includes a label from each variable in any rule, this simplification does not affect the performance of the algorithm but reduces the computation cost.

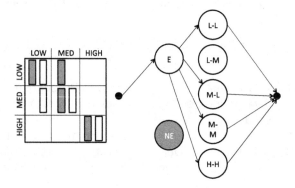

Fig. 3. The construction of a graph. The table in the left part is calculated, according to the current data set. The minority class is chosen as the starting point, and labeled as node E. Only the nodes that have support for class E are considered. Therefore, the node Low-Med has no edge, thus it does not belong to the graph -it is included only for the explanation-.

The early stopping condition is accomplished using the train-validation-test approach detailed in [14], but with a light variation. The validation data set will be chosen among those selected for testing, and the participant will be held for validation purposes until the rule extraction process ends. For the next rule extraction, a new random participant will be chosen. However, the validation participant will be also kept within the test data.

In Ant-Miner+, the samples included in the data set varies, extracting from the learning process those samples that have been explained by the previously chosen rules. However, in the context of this study, the concept of an explained sample needs further details. Similarly to [21], in this study a very simple approach is used.

Let the rule FR_r be defined by the pair $< ant_r, S_r >$, with ant_r being the combination of labels from each variable that represents the antecedent part of the rule and S_r being the class the rule proposes. A sample $< \vec{X}, Y >$ is totally explained by a rule FR_r when $w_r(\vec{X}) \geq \alpha_{exp} \wedge Y == S_r$, with $\alpha_{exp} > 0.5$. Additionally, a sample is not explained when by a rule FR_r when $(Y \neq S_r) \vee (w_r(\vec{X}) < 0.5)$. Otherwise, the sample is partially explained.

Let us call $E_{F_r}^{\alpha_{exp}}$ the set of samples from the data set for which $w_r(\vec{X}) \geq \alpha_{exp}$. Then, the heuristic to determine the cost of each path is computed as Eq. 2, where r refers to a valid antecedent combination. The pheromone evaporation and update are accomplished using the coverage criteria from the Ant-Miner+ (see Eq. 3), with $\rho \in [0.8, 0.99]$. Finally, Q_{best}^+ is computed as stated in Eq. 4. Due to the simplification of the graph construction explained before, the first term in Eq. 4 corresponds with the $\eta_{S_r ant_r}$ for the best ant found so far.

$$\eta_{S_r ant_r} = \frac{|< \vec{X}, Y > \in E_{F_r}^{\alpha_{exp}} \wedge Y == S_r|}{\sum_{S_r} |< \vec{X}, Y > \in E_{F_r}^{\alpha_{exp}}|} \tag{2}$$

$$\tau_{S_r,r}(t+1) = \rho \times \tau_{S_r,r}(t) + \frac{Q_{best}^+}{10} \tag{3}$$

$$Q^+ = \frac{|< \vec{X}, Y > \in E_{F_r}^{\alpha_{exp}} \wedge Y == S_r|}{\sum_{S_r} |< \vec{X}, Y > \in E_{F_r}^{\alpha_{exp}}|} + \frac{|< \vec{X}, Y > \in E_{F_r}^{\alpha_{exp}} \wedge Y == S_r|}{|< \vec{X}, Y >|} \tag{4}$$

The pruning is a simple procedure that removes a variable at a time, evaluating the new pruned rule and keeping the best combination found so far. This removing of a variable is repeated until there is no improvement on the performance of the current rule.

The Ant-Miner+ was originally proposed for learning rule based classifiers with categorical attributes. Therefore, we also learn this type of models just by changing the type of partition from Fuzzy to Interval. For the case of Fuzzy learning, the partition scheme is based on those explained in the previous Sect. 2. For the case of categorical attributes, the partitioning scheme is adapted by creating intervals at the membership function cross-points, as shown in Fig. 4. From now on, we will refer to the FRBC and RBC learned in Michigan style as FRBC_M and RBC_M respectively.

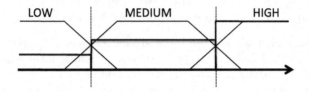

Fig. 4. Adapting the Fuzzy partition to a categorical input domain. The cross-points lead to the definition of the categories.

3   Experimentation and Results

The experimentation compares the different FRBC learning approaches; Subsect. 3.2 has been devoted for this topic. The data set gathering, preprocessing, the cross validation issues and the parameters are explained in the next subsection.

3.1   Materials and Methods

In a previous study [9,10], a realistic experimentation concerning 6 participants carrying out 10 trial runs of 4 activities (epilepsy convulsion simulation, running, sawing and walking) is described. Each participant wore a 3DACC bracelet, the sampling frequency has been set to 16 Hz. The obtained data set is used in this study for evaluating this approach.

The cross validation (cv) method is 5×2 cv based on shuffling the participants, as it was the best suite in the former research. This means that help of the population is keep for training, the other half for testing. The training data set includes the time series (TS) from the activities epilepsy convulsion simulation, running and sawing; however, only the 60 % of these TS has been used in training. The remaining 40 %, together with the walking activity TS, have been used in combination with the all the TS from the testing participants. This arrangement allows to evaluate how the models behave with unseen TS from the training participant, but also to evaluate the generalization capabilities of the different techniques.

In this study, whenever the FRBS is learned using the Pittsburg approach the following set of parameters holds: 300 iterations, the number of ants per iteration is the total number of rules with positive support (22 rules), $\rho = 0.6$, $\psi = 0.6$, $\beta = 2$, $q_0 = 0.2$. When a reduced set of rules is fixed, then it is specify with a suffix. For instance, "_Xr" refers to limit to X the number of rules of the FBRBC. For the Michigan experimentation the parameters are fixed as follows. 300 iterations, the number of ants for iterations is ten, $\rho = 0.85$, $\psi = 0.85$, $\alpha = 1$, $\beta = 2$, $[\tau_{max} \tau_{min}] = [1 \ 0]$, $\alpha_{exp} = 0, 6$. This experimentation was performed by FRBC_M and RBC_M. In all the cases, the parameters were set based on the literature.

3.2   Evaluating the Effect of the Partitioning in the ACO Pittsburg Learning and Ant-Miner+ Michigan Approach

This comparison includes all the methods outlined in the previous section, together with the GFFSM. The aim is to determine which of the learning strategies and techniques performs better in the context of ECI. The best FRBC_PC model found for each fold of the cross validation was pruned using bottom-up and up-bottom schemes, generating the FRBC_PP_BU and FRBC_PP_UB models respectively. Furthermore, the FRBC_PS models with the limits of 5 and 10 rules were trained with 5×2 cv. The Michigan methods, FRBC_M and RBC_M, were the same models as shown in previous section.

Two analysis have been carried out. On the one hand, the classification capabilities of each technique are evaluated based on the MAE (see Eq. 1). For this purpose, Table 2 and Fig. 5 show the numerical results obtained with all the methods.

On the other hand, the generalization capabilities of the methods are analyzed. To do so, the evolution of the outcomes from each method for all the available TS belonging to the testing participants have been plotted. That is, the best model found for each fold using a learning technique is evaluated for each of the TS belonging to the participants in the corresponding testing fold.

Plotting all of these outcomes for a technique and participant generates figures like the depicted in Fig. 6. In this figure, the outcomes of the best GFFSM (left part) and FRBC_PC (right part) models found for the first fold are shown. Each subplot includes the desire output and the model output. Using these figures allows to evaluate at a single glance whether the models generalization performance: the higher the number of false alarms the worse the generalization capabilities. Also, the steadies the output is the better.

Table 2. MAE Results for the best individual found in each fold evaluated with the test data set.

Fold	GFFSM	FRBC_PC	FRBC_PS 5 rules	FRBC_PS 10 rules	FRBC _PP_BU 10 rules	FRBC_PP_UB 10 rules	FRBC_M	RBC_M
1	0.0377	0.0281	0.1202	0.1135	0.0308	0.0281	0.4986	0.4986
2	0.0386	0.1144	0.1184	0.1089	0.0669	0.0686	0.1243	0.4986
3	0.0403	0.0292	0.1181	0.1053	0.0339	0.0363	0.1243	0.4927
4	0.0414	0.0172	0.1163	0.1102	0.0308	0.0285	0.4927	0.4993
5	0.0395	0.1000	0.1206	0.1514	0.0674	0.1050	0.4927	0.1207
6	0.0364	0.0253	0.1211	0.1104	0.0308	0.0290	0.4986	0.4986
7	0.0393	0.0274	0.1176	0.0728	0.0324	0.0340	0.4927	0.4993
8	0.0369	0.0185	0.1158	0.1113	0.0308	0.0286	0.4927	0.1207
9	0.0386	0.0305	0.1187	0.1067	0.0308	0.0281	0.4986	0.4986
10	0.0381	0.0978	0.1189	0.1087	0.0655	0.0999	0.1243	0.4993
mean	0.0387	0.0488	0.1186	0.1099	0.0420	0.0486	0.3839	0.4226
median	0.0386	0.0287	0.1185	0.1095	0.0316	0.0315	0.4927	0.4986
std	0.0015	0.0386	0.0017	0.0178	0.0161	0.0293	0.1700	0.1510

Very interesting findings are extracted from the classification results in Table 2. Firstly, restricting the Ant-Miner+ to a predefined partition scheme is not worthy as long as the performance is rather poor. Secondly, the same happens to learning models with a restricted number of rules, like for the FRPC_PS; this is rather strange as we expected a similar behavior as for the FRBC_PP_xx methods. Thirdly, the performance of the GFFSM models are pretty good and robust, with very similar behavior independently of the fold. Furthermore, the FRBC_PC models perform better in the majority of the folds but in three of them, for which the error measurement is really high. This result points to the suitability of the ACO approach, but introducing a tuning stage for improving the robustness of the method. Perhaps, introducing a final stage for tuning the partition scheme could lead to a better performance of the technique. Finally, it

Fig. 5. Boxplot of the test MAE results for the best model found in each fold for the different models: from left to right, GFFSM, FRBC_PC, FRBC_PS_5r, FRBC_PS_10r, FRBC_PP_BU_10r, FRBC_PP_UB_10r, FRBC_M and RBC_M.

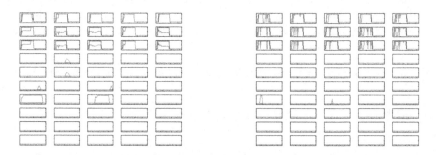

Fig. 6. Evolution of the output of the GFFSM (on the left figure) and FRBC_PC (on the right figure) model with different Test Time Series for participant 1.

is very interesting that for those FRBC_PC models with pretty bad performance, the corresponding FRBC_PP_UB and FRBC_PP_BU enhance the final results. Graphically, these facts can be observed in Fig. 5.

Let us focus now on the generalization capabilities of the models based on their deployment with unseen participants from the testing data set. That is, we are going to analyze how the model's outputs are when faced against TS from participants that were included in the test data set.

Figure 6 include the evolution for the GFFSM and FRBC_PC, correspondingly. In all of them, the first three rows include epilepsy episodes, while the remaining rows are -from up to bottom- for sawing (2 rows), running (2 rows) and walking (3 rows). All of these latter rows do not include epilepsy episodes.

From Fig. 6 it can be seen that the output of the GFFSM model is much more steady than those belonging to the FRBC_PC models. However, there are several TS classified as epilepsy episodes that are not, that is, they are false positives. Furthermore, for the three first rows, the output of the GFFSM introduces uncertainties in the class prediction -those values not higher than 0.5, for instance-. These results suggest that using typical classification error measurements enhance the results but do not avoid such false alarms; that is, provided there are not too many, the classification error measurement will have a low value. Perhaps this problem can be tackle by introducing event based error measurements. These measurements must consider discrepancies in the shape factor between the model's output and the expected output.

4   Conclusions and Future Work

Two different strategies, based in ACO, are analyzed. The first one, a Pittsburg scheme by means of Ant Colony Systems (ACS) is presented with different flavors: learning a complete rule based, learning a subset of rules, and a pruning stage in order to chose the best set of rules. Ant-Miner+ is proposed as second strategy to learn FRBC models in a Michigan fashion. Therefore, the original Ant-Miner+ approach for learning RBCs is extended to learn the FR.

The best results are obtained for the GFFSM in terms of robustness; however, the FRBC_PC combined with the pruning stage whenever the performance is enhanced also generates valid solutions. The remaining techniques seems to be dependent on the initial partition scheme, mainly for the case of Ant-Miner+.

ON the other hand, the generalization capabilities of the FRBC_PC seems to be better than those of the GFFSM. The fluctuation for the epilepsy episodes suggests that introducing a final filtering stage sounds interesting. For instance, this filtering could be a voting scheme on a sliding window with a configurable size; with this simple extra stage the output of the models would be more robust and steady.

Acknowledgments. This research has been funded by the Spanish Ministry of Science and Innovation, under projects MICIN-12-TIN2011-24302 and MINECO-15-TIN2014-56967-R, and Junta de Castilla y León projects BIO/BU09/14 and SACYL 2013 GRS/822/A/13.

References

1. de Vel, A.V., Cuppens, K., Bonroy, B., Milosevic, M., Huffel, S.V., Vanrumste, B., Lagae, L., Ceulemans, B.: Long-term home monitoring of hypermotor seizures by patient-worn accelerometers. Epilepsy Behav. **26**(1), 118–125 (2013)
2. Ramgopal, S., Thome-Souza, S., Jackson, M., Kadish, N.E., Fernández, I.S., Klehm, J., Bosl, W., Reinsberger, C., Schachter, S., Loddenkemper, T.: Seizure detection, seizure prediction, and closed-loop warning systems in epilepsy. Epilepsy Behav. **37**, 291–307 (2014)
3. Cogan, D., Pouyan, M., Nourani, M., Harvey, J.: A wrist-worn biosensor system for assessment of neurological status. In: 36th Annual International Conference of the IEEE Engineering in Medicine and Biology Society, pp. 5748–5751 (2014)
4. Nijsen, T., Cluitmans, P., Arends, J., Griep, P.: Detection of subtle nocturnal motor activity from 3-d accelerometry recordings in epilepsy patients. IEEE Trans. Biomed. Eng. **54**(11), 2073–2081 (2007)
5. Bioserenity: Neuronaute (2015). https://www.bioserenity.com/. Accessed 1 October 2015

6. Scientist, N.: Nokia app powers portable brain scanner (2011). https://www. newscientist.com/article/smartphone-brain-scanner/. Accessed 1 October 2015
7. Pandher, P., Bhullar, K.: Smartphone applications for seizure management. Health Inform. J. **18**, 1–12 (2014)
8. Ranganathan, L.N., Chinnadurai, S.A., Samivel, B., Kesavamurthy, B., Mehndirata, M.M.: Application of mobile phones in epilepsy care. Int. J. Epilepsy **2**, 28–37 (2014)
9. Villar, J.R., Menéndez, M., Sedano, J., de la Cal, E., González, V.: Analyzing accelerometer data for epilepsy episode recognition. In: 10th International Conference on Soft Computing Models in Industrial and Environmental Applications, Advances in Intelligent Systems and Computing, vol. 368, pp. 39–48. Springer (2015)
10. Vergara, P., Villar, J.R., Cal, E., Menéndez, M., Sedano, J.: Fuzzy rule learning with ACO in epilepsy crisis identification. In: In Evaluation for the 2015 11th International Conference on Innovations in Information Technology (IIT 2015), Dubai, UAE, November 2015
11. Alvarez-Alvarez, A., Triviño, G., Cordón, O.: Human gait modeling using a genetic fuzzy finite state machine. IEEE Trans. Fuzzy Syst. **20**(2), 205–223 (2012)
12. Villar, J.R., González, S., Sedano, J., Chira, C., Trejo-Gabriel-Galan, J.M.: Improving human activity recognition and its application in early stroke diagnosis. Int. J. Neural Syst. **25**(4) (2015). doi:10.1142/S0129065714500361
13. Casillas, J., Cordón, O., Herrera, F.: Learning Fuzzy Rules Using Ant Colony Optimization Algorithms, pp. 13–21. University of Granada, Granada (2000)
14. Martens, D., Backer, M.D., Haesen, R., Vanthienen, J., Snoeck, M., Baesens, B.: Classification with ant colony optimization. IEEE Trans. Evol. Comput. **11**, 651–665 (2007)
15. Dorigo, M., Gambardella, L.: Ant colony system: a cooperative learning approach to the traveling salesman problem. IEEE Trans. Evol. Comput. **1**(1), 53–66 (1997)
16. Parpinelli, R., Lopes, H., Freitas, A.: Data mining with an ant colony optimization algorithm. IEEE Trans. Evol. Comput. **6**(4), 321–332 (2002)
17. Otero, F.E.B., Freitas, A.A., Johnson, C.G.: cAnt-Miner: an ant colony classification algorithm to cope with continuous attributes. In: Dorigo, M., Birattari, M., Blum, C., Clerc, M., Stützle, T., Winfield, A.F.T. (eds.) ANTS 2008. LNCS, vol. 5217, pp. 48–59. Springer, Heidelberg (2008)
18. Salama, K.M., Otero, F.E.B.: Using a unified measure function for heuristics, discretization, and rule quality evaluation in ant-miner. In: Proceedings of the 2013 IEEE Congress on Evolutionary Computation, IEEE, pp. 900–907 (2013)
19. Villar, J.R., Menéndez, M., Sedano, J., de la Cal, E., González, V.: Learning fuzzy rules through ant optimization, lasso and dirichlet mixtures. In: Proceedings of the IEEE International Conference on Fuzzy Systems (FUZZ-IEEE), IEEE 2014, pp. 2558–2565 (2014)
20. Martens, D., Baesens, B., Fawcett, T.: Editorial survey: swarm intelligence for data mining. Mach. Learn. **82**, 1–42 (2011)
21. Sánchez, L., Otero, J.: Boosting fuzzy rules in classification problems under single-winner inference. Int. J. Intell. Syst. **22**, 1021–1034 (2007)

Estimating the Maximum Power Delivered by Concentrating Photovoltaics Technology Through Atmospheric Conditions Using a Differential Evolution Approach

Cristobal J. Carmona[1]([⊠]), F. Pulgar[2], Antonio Jesús Rivera-Rivas[2],
Maria Jose del Jesus[2], and J. Aguilera[3]

[1] Department of Civil Engineering, University of Burgos, 09006 Burgos, Spain
cjcarmona@ubu.es
[2] Department of Computer Science, University of Jaén, 23071 Jaén, Spain
{fpulgar,arivera,mjjesus}@ujaen.es
[3] Department of Electronics and Automatization Engineering,
University of Jaén, 23071 Jaén, Spain
aguilera@ujaen.es

Abstract. The Concentrating Photovoltaic technology is focused on the generation of electricity reducing the associated costs. The main characteristics is to concentrate the sunlight in solar cells by means of optical device such as plastic or glass material. This technology could contribute with several benefits to our environmental. This paper presents a new study of the Concentrating Photovoltaic technology with the analysis of the solar spectrum considering the impact of the direct normal irradiance spectral distribution. In this way, a estimation of regression coefficients for the spectral matching ratio multivariable regression and the average photon energy multivarible regression are obtained through a differential evolution approach. The accurate calculation of the model parameters reveals relations among the atmospheric conditions very useful for the experts.

Keywords: Regression solar · Data mining · Differential evolution · Concentrating Photovoltaic technology

1 Introduction

The main aim of Concentrating Photovoltaic (CPV) technology is to generate electricity with a lower associated cost. Regarding this purpose, the sunlight is concentrated in the solar cell by means of an optical device, deriving in an increase of the cell efficiency and a resulting reduction of the required cell area to generate the same power. These optical devices are commonly made of plastic or glass material, which are significantly cheaper than the solar cells. CPV modules are, in most of the cases, based on Multijunction (MJ) solar cells, which moreover tend to be composed of a serial layout of high efficiency semiconductor

© Springer International Publishing Switzerland 2016
F. Martínez-Álvarez et al. (Eds.): HAIS 2016, LNAI 9648, pp. 273–282, 2016.
DOI: 10.1007/978-3-319-32034-2_23

materials [13]. This technology has numerous benefits like higher energy density, higher efficiency, needs of lower surface and lower semiconductor material requirements [5]. Nevertheless, some technical and economic barriers must be removed to reduce the electricity production costs using this technology and to make it really competitive.

Because the bankability of a CPV Plant is an important topic to pave the way toward a sustained growth of this technology and this bankability is based on energy yield prediction under real atmospheric conditions, an accurate estimate of the maximum power (P_M) of the CPV modules is crucial [9,14]. The accurate calculation of this P_M would allow to estimate the electric production of a CPV power plant and the analysis of its costs and profitability, with the consequent benefits for the commercial development of this CPV technology. The calculation of the P_M delivered by a CPV module under specific environmental parameters is not a trivial issue. A generalized problem which concerns to the lack of an international standard method for outdoor power rating of CPV modules, is perceived by investors as a worrying item. The American Society for Testing and Materials (ASTM) E2527-06 is, until now, the unique standard which allows calculating the maximum power delivered by a CPV module under specific atmospheric conditions. However, this standard does not consider the spectral distribution as one of these input environmental conditions. As it has been previously studied by several researchers the spectral distribution of the direct normal irradiance has an important effect on the electrical behaviour of CPV modules. Due to the latter, its inclusion in the modelling has a paramount relevance. In this work, two different variables have been used to include this spectral influence: the Spectral Machine Radio (SMR) and the Average Photon Energy (APE).

This work proposes the use of two different equations for SMR and APE. The first equation must be implemented when the DNI spectral distribution has a higher red-content than the standard one; otherwise, the second equation will be used when the incident direct spectrum has a higher blue-content than the standard. This estimation model is, at the same time and with the objective of increasing its accuracy, divided into two different spectrum intervals. The optimisation of these equations is analysed through different proposals such as differential evolution (DE), support vector machine (SVM), artificial neural networks, etc. Results obtained in the experimental study show a good behaviour of the DE algorithm in order to model through multiple linear equations the P_M, as a function of the following atmospheric conditions: DNI, T_A, W_S, and DNI spectral distribution through two alternative indexes: SMR and APE. The regression coefficients with the best fir to the equations are obtained through the algorithm with the lowest error in the prediction of the P_M.

The contribution is organized as follows: Sect. 2 describes the main properties of CPV technology analysing the influential atmospheric conditions in order to measure the electric performance of the CPV modules, and the use of two indexes to define the influence of DNI spectral distribution on the CPV modules' electrical performance. Section 3 outlines the experimental framework and shows the results obtained, and finally, some concluding remarks are outlined.

2   CPV Technology

The main aim of the CPV technology is to contribute to the generation of electricity with a lower cost, by using the least possible amount of material. Most of CPV modules available in the market use high efficient MJ solar cells, with an optical device to focus the solar radiation in the MJ solar cell surface. The required optical device must include a primary optics, that is in charge of collecting and concentrating the *DNI*, and a secondary optics to uniformly distribute the sunlight from the primary optic, along the whole surface of the solar cell [11]. Due to the latter, only the direct component of the global radiation is used, in other words, the diffuse component is not exploited. The assembly of various solar cells, with their respective complementary elements, constitutes a CPV module. Finally, it is necessary to use a tracking system to hold the CPV module and to orient it towards the Sun, in such way that the component solar cells are, at every moment, perpendicularly disposed to the solar ray [16].

2.1   Study of Influential Atmospheric Conditions on the Electric Performance of CPV Modules

The *DNI* is considered as the main atmospheric parameter which influences the outdoor electric performance of a CPV module. The relation between *DNI* and P_M is almost linear, so its effect is predominant.

Using the *DNI* as the integration value along the whole wavelength range for a specific photovoltaic (PV) device is a common practice. Nevertheless, we can consider the *DNI* value for each wavelength value, obtaining the *solar spectrum distribution*. As has been widely demonstrated, the *DNI*, as well as its spectral distribution, have an important influence on the electric performance of MJ solar cells. It is well known that the MJ solar cells temperature affect to their electric performance. In this sense, the temperature has an almost negligible positive effect on the short circuit current delivered by the MJ solar cell, and a negative predominant effect on both the open circuit voltage and P_M [10,12,19,23]. The same behaviour is observed when analyzing the impact of the temperature on the electric performance of CPV modules equipped with MJ solar cells [21]. However, the own disposition of the MJ solar cells inside the CPV module makes it very difficult to measure their temperature. In this work, T_A is considered as influential factor, given a direct relation between cell temperature and T_A [1,2].

The consideration of the W_S as one of the influential factors whose contribution must be added in the equation proposed by the ASTM E-2527-09 standard. In this way, W_S can perform a positive refrigerating effect on the electric performance of a CPV system, cooling the MJ solar cells which compose the module down, and obtaining therefore a better behaviour [4]. However, high W_S values can also exert a negative effect of misalignment on the tracker [15], displacing the MJ solar cells from their optimum arrangement in the solar beam direct trajectory.

A review of the main models for estimating the P_M of CPV modules has been recently published [22]. However, it must be taken into account that, when talking about standard power rating methods, the ASTM E2527-09 methodology is the unique model in CPV field.

2.2 The Use of *SMR* and *APE* Indexes to Characterise the *DNI* Spectral Distribution

The influence of the solar spectrum distribution on the electric performance of CPV modules can be considered from two different indexes: *SMR* and *APE*. On the one hand, *SMR* is defined as a index which expresses the ratio between the effective *DNI* received by two different junctions (top and middle) of the MJ solar cells which compose the CPV module [6]. When the incident solar spectrum differs from the AM 1.5D standard, the effective *DNI* collected by each of these junctions could be different, so the photocurrent generated by the whole MJ solar cell is limited by the junction generating a lower photocurrent at each moment. The *SMR* index is calculated as follows:

$$SMR\,(AM1.5D)^{TOP-junction}_{MIDDLE-junction} = \frac{DNI_{TOP-junction}}{DNI_{MIDDLE-junction}} \qquad (1)$$

where $DNI_{TOP-juntion}$ and $DNI_{MIDDLE-junction}$ represent the effective *DNI* collected by the top and middle junction, respectively. Attending to the last equation, there are three different possibilities:

- $SMR < 1$, the incident spectral distribution is red-richer than the standard one, which means that the middle junction collected an effective *DNI* higher than the one collected by the top junction, being this last the limiting junction.
- $SMR > 1$, the incident spectral distribution is blue-richer than the standard one, which means that the top junction collected an effective *DNI* higher than the one collected by the middle junction, being this last the limiting junction.
- $SMR = 1$, top and middle junctions collected the same effective *DNI*, which means that the incident spectrum coincides with the AM1.5D standard one.

The *SMR* influence on the normalized Short Circuit Current (ISC_N) -and therefore on the P_M- generated by a CPV module were normalized in terms of *DNI*, to avoid its predominant effect. As can be appreciated, under *SMR* values lower than 1, this factor has a positive influence on the electric performance of the CPV module. In other words, increasing values of *SMR* makes the module to produce a higher ISC_N. Otherwise, when *SMR* values are close to 1 (which means spectral distributions close to the AM1.5D standard one), the module is working in an optimum way. Under *SMR* values higher than 1, this parameter has a negative influence, making the module to deliver a lower value of ISC_N.

On the other hand, *APE* index is defined as a unique value which characterises the shape of the *DNI* spectral distribution between a determined wavelength range [17]. As increasing the value of the *APE* index, the incident spectrum is expected to have a higher blue content. The *APE* index can be obtained by calculating the following equation:

$$\frac{\int_a^b E_\lambda(\lambda)d\lambda}{\int_a^b \phi_\lambda(\lambda)d\lambda} \qquad (2)$$

where:

- E_λ ($W\,(m^2 \cdot nm)$): Spectral irradiance.
- ϕ ($1/(m^2 \cdot nm \cdot s)$): Spectral photon flux density (ratio between the spectral irradiance E_λ and the energy of the photon of wavelength *lambda*).
- a and b are considered as the integration limits and depend on the spectro-radiometer specifications.

The APE index has been introduced as a remarkable parameter to describe, in an easy way, the impact of the solar spectrum change in different PV solar technologies [20].

There is an intrinsic relation between APE and SMR which is almost linear, except when the solar spectral distribution has high red-content, in which APE values are lower than expected. In this way, it is possible to obtain a first degree polynomial expression to define this relation, without entailing a big error:

$$f(x) = p_1 x + p_2 \tag{3}$$

Coefficients (with 95 % of confidence bounds):

- $p_1 = 0.34\,(0.3385, 0.3414)$
- $p_2 = 1.487\,(1.485, 1.488)$

Goodness of fit (values given by $Matlab_{TM}$ curve fitting toolbox):

- $R - square$: 0.9601
- $RMSE$: 0.00644

From the last obtained equation, it is possible to calculate the APE value which corresponds to the AM1.5D standard spectral distribution, or in other words, the APE value which corresponds to $SMR = 1$. As can be observed, the maximum of the function was found for SMR values closer to the unit, under which the CPV module should work on its optimum manner. Because of that, $SMR = 1$, that according to the linear relation between SMR and APE corresponds to $APE = 1.83$, is going to be considered as the turning point to the definition of the model proposed in this paper, dividing it into two different spectral intervals. This turning point corresponds to the AM 1.5D standard spectral distribution.

3   Experimental Study

The data were obtained from one model of CPV modules, whose main characteristics are solar cells type $Multijunction - GaInP/Ga(In)As/Ge$ with 25 solar cells and a concentration factor of 550. The measures were acquired at the rooftop of the Higher Polytechnical School of Jaén during the period between March 2013 and November 2013, forming a whole dataset composed of 8780 samples in the case of the module $M1$. The atmospheric measures were registered every 5 min using the outdoor devices specified in Table 1 and described below:

Table 1. Measurement of atmospheric conditions by outdoor devices.

Atmospheric condition	Units	Outdoor device	Measures range
DNI	(W/m^2)	Pyheliometer	[140–1024]
Spectrum APE	(eV)	Spectro − radiometer	[1.59–1.87]
Spectrum SMR	(−)	Spectro − heliometer	[0.40–1.13]
T_A	(°C)	Spectro − heliometer	[11.39–41.82]
W_S	(m/s)	Anemometer	[0.04–20.50]

- A Kipp & Zonnen[TM] CHP 1 pyrheliometer to the measurement of the direct normal irradiance (DNI).
- An EKO[TM] MS700 spectro-radiometer with a collimator tube to the measurement of the direct normal spectral Irradiance distribution with a wavelength range of 350–1050 nm. From the measurement of the spectrum distribution the APE value is calculated.
- A Triband spectro-heliometer composed by three component cells, with the same structure of the MJ solar cells which compose the analysed CPV modules. In this way it is possible to independently measure the effective irradiance collected by each junction, and so calculate the SMR index.
- A meteorological Station formed by a Young[TM] 41382VC relative humidity & temperature probe to register the T_A and a Young[TM] 05305VM anemometer to measure the W_S.

The analysis of the data is performed in two stages. Firstly, an experimental study with different algorithms is performed in order to measure the mean squared error (MSE) of the P_M for the module, i.e. the MSE between real P_M values and P_M values predicted. Next, the regression coefficients obtained for the approach with the best results and more interpretable are presented. Algorithms included in the experimental study are outlined below:

- The DE algorithm is a stochastic algorithm for optimising and searching based on the natural evolution process and it was defined by Storn and Price [24] as a versatile function optimiser where mutation is emphasised. DE uses a mutation operator to promote the diversity in the population where a scaled difference between an original individual and several randomly selected individuals from the same population is performed. Subsequently to the result a recombination operator is applied in order to lead the search for an optimal solution.
- A multiple linear regression (MLR) method based on [8] where the most popular estimation method for the coefficients, least squares, pick them to minimize the residual sum of squares.
- Wang and Mendel (WM) [25] is a method for generating fuzzy rules by supervised learning. This fuzzy classical approach divides the input and fuzzy spaces of the given numerical data into fuzzy regions and generates a linguistic fuzzy rule for each fuzzy region (if it is possible) from the given data. The fuzzy rule

based system uses the t-norm product and centroid defuzzification formula to determine the output

- Classification and regression trees ($CART$) [3] is a kind of decision tree that can produce either classification or regression trees, depending on the given output variable. This decision tree is composed of: Rules for splitting data at a tree node based on the values of the input variables; Stopping rules for stablishing when a branch is terminal; an output value for the dependent variable in each terminal node.
- The SVM model uses the sequential minimal optimization training algorithm and treats a given problem in terms of solving a quadratic optimization problem. The $NUSVR$ [7], also called $vSVM$, for regression problems is an extension of the traditional SVM and it aims to build a loss function.
- $MLPConjGrad$ [18] uses the conjugate gradient algorithm to adjust weight values of a multilayer perceptron. Compared to gradient descent, the conjugate gradient algorithm takes a more direct path to the optimal set of weight values. Usually, the conjugate gradient is significantly faster and more robust than the gradient descent. The conjugate gradient also does not require the user to specify learning rate and momentum parameters.

It is important to separate with respect to the interpretability of the algorithms in order to analyse the possibility to know the regression coefficients in the P_M equations. In this way, we could divide algorithms in two groups: Interpretable (DE, MLR, WM and $CART$) and non-interpretable ($NUSVR$ and $MLPConjGrad$). Finally, it is important to remark that the experimentation process is performed through a separation between training and test dataset. In this case, we use 80 % (training) of the whole dataset to calculate the regression coefficients that best fit the equations which compose the proposed model. Otherwise, 20 % (test) of the whole dataset was used to validate the predictive capacity of the proposed model.

Table 2. MSE test results obtained to the CPV module under study

Index	Interpretable models				Non interpretable	
	DE	MLR	WM	CART	NUSVR	MLPConjGrad
$SMR < 1$	**8.35**	9.31	16.83	8.36	8.80	**5.34**
$SMR \geq 1$	**7.47**	7.58	32.92	8.25	7.99	**7.23**
$APE < 1.83$	**8.41**	9.45	20.08	8.59	11.27	**6.24**
$APE \geq 1.83$	**6.79**	6.90	37.37	8.21	7.24	**6.55**

The MSE are shown in Table 2. The algorithm with the best results is the $MLPConjGrad$. However, it is impossible to analyse the regression coefficients with this algorithm because they are considered "black box" and it is very difficult to show relations, coefficients, impact and so on between the variables. In this way, the following algorithm with best results is the DE. This approach is interpretable and these results show the capacity to solve the proposed multiple linear regression model with MSE values within the interval [6.79–8.41]. In Table 3, the regression coefficients obtained by the DE algorithm for the analysed CPV module are presented.

Table 3. Regression coefficients obtained by DE methodology for the CPV modules

Index	a_1	a_2	a_3	a_4	a_5
$SMR < 1$	0.076423	−1.63E-05	−1.11E-04	3.00E-04	0.062229
$SMR \geq 1$	0.150911	−9.48E-06	−3.63E-04	3.38E-04	−0.012287
$APE < 1.83$	−0.178408	−1.66E-05	−1.53E-04	3.01E-04	0.174229
$APE \geq 1.83$	0.219101	−8.79E-06	−3.75E-04	3.06E-04	−0.044181

According to the regression coefficients calculated by the DE-proposal for the module, it can be remarked:

– Almost linear relation between DNI and P_M delivered by CPV modules. This can be appreciated due to the low values of a_2 coefficients compared to a_1 ones.
– Very slight negative influence of T_A on the P_M delivered by CPV modules. This influence is given by a_3 regression coefficients.
– Very slight positive influence of W_S on the P_M delivered by CPV modules. This influence is given by a_4 regression coefficients.
– As it was predicted, a positive influence of the DNI spectral distribution on the P_M of the CPV modules for values of $SMR < 1$ or $APE < 1.83$ is observed: when increasing the value of SMR or APE, the P_M is increased. This influence is given by a_5 regression coefficients for the first spectral interval.
– Negative influence of the DNI spectral distribution on the P_M of the CPV modules for values of $SMR \geq 1$ or $APE \geq 1.83$. In this way, when increasing the value of SMR or APE, the P_M is decreased. This effect is perceptible through the analysis of a_5 regression coefficients for the second spectral interval.

The multivariable regression model presented in this paper is very important as it allows obtaining the regression coefficient which quantify the influence of different atmospheric conditions on the P_M delivered by a CPV module. This functionally can not be achieved by an ANN model.

4   Conclusions

The multivariable regression model proposed in this work is based on the ASTM E-2527-09. This standard defines a methodology to calculate the P_M delivered by CPV modules or systems, through the resolution of a multiple linear equation based on the following input atmospheric conditions: DNI, T_A and W_S.

To calculate this P_M value, the regression coefficients which compose the multiple linear equation must be previously calculated. Nevertheless, the methodology proposed by the ASTM E-2527-09 has a big drawback, as it does not consider the influence of the solar spectrum distribution. In this work, the standard methodology has been modified in order to make it more accurate. This modification consists on adding an additional term which quantifies the influence of the DNI spectral distribution on the P_M delivered by CPV modules. The proposed model allows to consider this additional term through the use of two alternative indexes: SMR and APE. In this way, the applicability of the model is increased as it can be implemented from the measurement acquired through a triband spectro-heliometer (SMR) or a spectro-radiometer(APE).

The P_M values obtained by the model (through the regression coefficients calculated by means of DE) under determined atmospheric conditions, were compared with the corresponding real P_M values for one analysed CPV modules. As a result, it is concluded that the proposed model obtained good MSE values within of a considerable range of powerful lower than 3 %. Specifically, In PV field, errors between [0–2]% are classified as a very good predictions, in the interval between [2–3.5]% as good, and within the range [3.5–5]% they are considered as satisfying.

Acknowledgments. This work was supported by the Spanish Science and Innovation Department under project ENE2009-08302, by the Department of Science and Innovation of the Regional Government of Andalucia under project P09-TEP-5045, and by Spanish Ministry of Economy and Competitiveness under project TIN2015-68454-R (FEDER Founds).

References

1. Almonacid, F., Pérez-Higueras, P., Fernández, E., Rodrigo, P.: Relation between the cell temperature of a hcpv module and atmospheric parameters. Solar Energy Mater. Solar Cells **105**, 322–327 (2012)
2. Antón, I., Martínez, M., Rubio, F., Núñez, R., Herrero, R., Domínguez, C., Victoria, M., Askins, S., Sala, G.: Power rating of cpv systems based on spectrally corrected dni, vol. 1477, pp. 331–335 (2012)
3. Breiman, L., Friedman, J.H., Olshen, R.A., Stone, C.J.: Classification and Regression Trees. Chapman & Hall, New York (1984)
4. Castro, M., Domínguez, C., Núez, R., Antón, I., Sala, G., Araki, K.: Detailed effects of wind on the field performance of a 50 kw cpv demonstration plant. In: AIP Conference Proceedings, vol. 1556, pp. 256–260 (2013)
5. Chan, N., Brindley, H., Ekins-Daukes, N.: Impact of individual atmospheric parameters on cpv system power, energy yield and cost of energy. Prog. Photovoltaics **22**, 1080–1095 (2014)
6. C. Domínguez, I. Askins, S. Antón, and G. Sala. Indoor characterization of cpv modules using helios 3198 solar simulator. In: 24th European Photovoltaic Solar Energy Conference and Exhibition, pp. 165–169 (2009)
7. Fan, R., Chen, P., Lin, C.: Working set selection using the second order information for training svm. J. Mach. Learn. Res. **6**, 1889–1918 (2005)

8. Flury, B., Riedwyl, H.: Multiple linear regression. In: Multivariate Statistics, pp. 54–74 (1988)
9. Gupta, R.: CPV: expansion and bankability required. Renew. Energy focus 14(4), 12–13 (2013)
10. Helmers, H., Schachtner, M., Bett, A.: Influence of temperature and irradiance on triple-junction solar subcells. Solar Energy Mater. Solar Cells 116, 144–152 (2013)
11. Herrero, R., Victoria, M., Domínguez, C., Askins, S., Antón, I., Sala, G.: Concentration photovoltaic optical system irradiance distribution measurements and its effect on multi-junction solar cells. Prog. Photovoltaics Res. Appl. 20(4), 423–430 (2012)
12. Kinsey, G., Hebert, P., Barbour, K., Krut, D., Cotal, H., Sherif, R.: Concentrator multijunction solar cell characteristics under variable intensity and temperature. Prog. Photovoltaics Res. Appl. 16(6), 503–508 (2008)
13. Law, D., King, R., Yoon, H., Archer, M., Boca, A., Fetzer, C., Mesropian, S., Isshiki, T., Haddad, M., Edmondson, K., Bhusari, D., Yen, J., Sherif, R., Atwater, H., Karam, N.: Future technology pathways of terrestrial iii-v multijunction solar cells for concentrator photovoltaic systems. Solar Energy Mater. Solar Cells 94(8), 1314–1318 (2010)
14. Leloux, J., Lorenzo, E., Garca-Domingo, B., Gueymard, J.A.C.: A bankable method of assessing the performance of a cpv plant. Appl. Energy 118(C), 1–11 (2014)
15. Lin, C.-K., Fang, J.-Y.: Analysis of structural deformation and concentrator misalignment in a roll-tilt solar tracker. In: AIP Conference Proceedings, vol. 1556, pp. 210–213 (2013)
16. Luque, A., Sala, G., Luque-Heredia, I.: Photovoltaic concentration at the onset of its commercial deployment. Prog. Photovoltaics Res. Appl. 14(5), 413–428 (2006)
17. Minemoto, T., Nakada, Y., Takahashi, H., Takakura, H.: Uniqueness verification of solar spectrum index of average photon energy for evaluating outdoor performance of photovoltaic modules. Solar Energy 83(8), 1294–1299 (2009)
18. Moller, M.F.: A scaled conjugate gradient algorithm for fast supervised learning. Neural Netw. 6(4), 525–533 (1993)
19. Nishioka, K., Takamoto, T., Agui, T., Kaneiwa, M., Uraoka, Y., Fuyuki, T.: Annual output estimation of concentrator photovoltaic systems using high-efficiency ingap/ingaas/ge triple-junction solar cells based on experimental solar cell's characteristics and field-test meteorological data. Solar Energy Mater. Solar Cells 90(1), 57–67 (2006)
20. Nofuentes, G., García-Domingo, B., Muoz, J., Chenlo, F.: Analysis of the dependence of the spectral factor of some pv technologies on the solar spectrum distribution. Appl. Energy 113, 302–309 (2014)
21. Peharz, G., Ferrer Rodríguez, J., Siefer, G., Bett, A.: Investigations on the temperature dependence of cpv modules equipped with triple-junction solar cells. Prog. Photovoltaics Res. Appl. 19(1), 54–60 (2011)
22. Rodrigo, P., Fernández, E., Almonacid, F., Pérez-Higueras, P.: Models for the electrical characterization of high concentration photovoltaic cells and modules: a review. Renew. Sustain. Energy Rev. 26, 752–760 (2013)
23. Siefer, G., Bett, A.: Analysis of temperature coefficients for III-V multi-junction concentrator cells. Prog. Photovoltaics Res. Appl. 22(5), 515–524 (2014)
24. Storn, R., Price, K.: Differential evolution: a simple and efficient adaptive scheme forglobal optimization over continuous spaces.Technical report TR-95-012 (1995)
25. Wang, L.X., Mendel, J.M.: Generating fuzzy rules by learning from examples. IEEE Trans. Syst. Man Cybern. 22(6), 1414–1427 (1992)

A Hybrid Bio-inspired ELECTRE Approach for Decision Making in Purchasing Agricultural Equipment

Dragan Simić[1](✉), Jovana Gajić[2], Vladimir Ilin[1], Vasa Svirčević[3], and Svetlana Simić[4]

[1] Faculty of Technical Sciences, University of Novi Sad, Trg Dositeja
Obradovića 6, 21000 Novi Sad, Serbia
dsimic@eunet.rs, v.ilin@uns.ac.rs
[2] Faculty of Economics, University of Novi Sad,
Segedinski put 9–11, 24000 Subotica, Serbia
j.gajic@yahoo.com
[3] Lames Ltd., Jarački put bb., 22000 Sremska Mitrovica, Serbia
vasasv@hotmail.com
[4] Faculty of Medicine, University of Novi Sad,
Hajduk Veljkova 1–9, 21000 Novi Sad, Serbia
drdragansimic@gmail.com

Abstract. Agricultural management is an interdisciplinary approach. This paper discusses decision making in purchasing agricultural equipment. Methodological hybrid bio-inspired and ELECTRE I method is proposed here and it is shown how such a model can be used for complete ranking model. The proposed hybrid bio-inspired ELECTRE I method is implemented on real-world data set. The experimental results in our research could be well compared with PROMETHEE II method presented in our previously study.

Keywords: Agricultural equipment · Genetic algorithm · ELECTRE · Ranking

1 Introduction

Nowadays, the planet's population is increasing dramatically, and agriculture became commercial, and precision agriculture and sustainable agriculture are a part of it. Agricultural management is an interdisciplinary approach. Determination of optimum land use type for an area involves examination of data originating from various domains, and sources such as soil science, social science, meteorology, management science are included in decision making when it comes to purchasing agricultural equipment. During the last decades a multitude of methods has been developed which are able to solve complex decision problems which require the consideration of multiple objectives or criteria and are used in many various real-world problems [1].

This research for ranking alternatives for decision making in purchasing agricultural equipment is based on our previous research [2]. Two different methods there are used: ELimination Et Choix Traduisant la REalitá (ELECTRE) and Preference Ranking Organization METHods for Enrichment Evaluations (PROMETHEE). In that

© Springer International Publishing Switzerland 2016
F. Martínez-Álvarez et al. (Eds.): HAIS 2016, LNAI 9648, pp. 283–295, 2016.
DOI: 10.1007/978-3-319-32034-2_24

previous research ELECTRE I method is used and then the experimental results are compared with the results obtained by PROMETHEE II ranking method.

The rest of the paper is organized in the following way: Section 2 provides some approaches about agricultural decision making and related work. Section 3 proposes methodology of hybrid genetic algorithm (GA) and ELECTRE I method. Choosing and decision making when it comes to agricultural equipment as well as real-world data set, are shown in Sect. 4. An application of this hybrid model's experimental results, complete ranking, and comparison with experimental results obtained by PROMETHEE II method are presented in Sect. 5. And finally, Sect. 6 gives concluding remarks.

2   Agricultural Decision Making and Related Work

The decision making environment in agriculture is complex. Three possible approaches to the theoretical study of agriculture are recognized: the first assumes that the physical environment controls agricultural decision making; the second can be called economic determinism; and the third recognizes a further set of influences on agriculture which is not based on economic or physical-environmental factors [3].

Decision making and strategy selection to agricultural development of Zanjan province in Iran is discussed in [4]. There is an analysis of usage of agricultural mechanization by *SWOT-AHP* method. Application of Data Envelopment Analysis as a multi-criteria decision making methodology is tested for Sri Ram Sagar Project, Andhra Pradesh, India to select the suitable irrigation planning alternative, and it is shown in [5].

An approach and a practical example of ranking the agricultural producers who applied to the Provincial Fund for Agricultural Development of Vojvodina Province (Serbia) for loans for purchasing irrigation equipment is presented in [6]. The system is based on AHP group decision making and consistency ratio and total Euclidean distance is used to "weight" involved decision makers.

3   A Hybrid Bio-Inspired ELECTRE Model

The origins of ELECTRE methods go back to 1965 at the European consultancy company SEMA, as ELECTRE I (electre one) and it was first introduced in [7].

3.1   Multiple Criteria Decision Making ELECTRE I Model

We assume that A_1, A_2,..., A_m are m possible alternatives for optimum purchase of agricultural equipment in multi-criteria decision making, C_1, C_2,..., C_n are criteria used to describe the alternative characters, after the assignment, defined as x_{ij} for the degree of alternative A_i with respect to criteria C_j. Let W_n be the weight for importance of C_n, which is determined by decision maker experience. The computation flow process of ELECTRE I method is the following.

Step 1. Normalization of matrix and weighted matrix.

Considering concepts on the interval numbers of decision matrix, the normalized matrix of $R_{ij} = [r_{ij}]$ is calculated by:

$$r_{ij} = \frac{x_{ij}}{\sqrt{\sum_{i=1}^{m} x_{ij}^2}} \tag{1}$$

The weighted matrix depends on normalized matrix assigned to it, and is given by:

$$V_{ij} = R \times W = \begin{bmatrix} r_{11} \cdot w_1 & r_{12} \cdot w_2 & \cdots & r_{1n} \cdot w_n \\ r_{21} \cdot w_1 & r_{22} \cdot w_2 & \cdots & r_{2n} \cdot w_n \\ \cdots & \cdots & \cdots & \cdots \\ r_{m1} \cdot w_1 & r_{m2} \cdot w_2 & \cdots & r_{mn} \cdot w_n \end{bmatrix} \tag{2}$$

Where $0 \leq w_1, w_2, \ldots, w_n \leq 1$. The weights of attributes are expressed by these constants. Besides, the correlation coefficients of normalized interval numbers are between 0 and 1.

Step 2. Ascertainment of concordance and discordance interval sets.

Considering that reliability design scheme decision is a multi-attribute decision with preference information, the decision rules are reasoned by the concordance and discordance interval sets, and then the attribute sets are obtained through these decision rules. Let $A = \{a, b, c, \cdots\}$ denote a finite set of alternatives, in the following formulation we divide the attribute sets into two different sets of concordance interval set (C_{ab}) and discordance interval set (D_{ab}). The concordance interval set is applied to describe the dominance query if the following condition is satisfied:

$$C_{ab} = \{j \mid x_{aj} \geq x_{bj}\} \tag{3}$$

On complementation of C_{ab}, we obtain the discordance interval set (D_{ab}) using (4):

$$D_{ab} = \{j \mid x_{aj} < x_{bj}\} \tag{4}$$

Step 3. Calculation of the concordance interval matrix.

According to the deciders' preference for alternatives, the concordance interval index (C_{ab}) between A_a and A_a is obtained using (5):

$$C_{ab} = \sum_{j \in C_{ab}} w_j \tag{5}$$

The concordance index indicates the preference of the assertion "A outranks B". The concordance interval matrix can be formulated in the following way:

$$C = \begin{bmatrix} - & c(1,2) & \cdots & c(1,m) \\ c(2,1) & - & \cdots & c(2,m) \\ \vdots & \vdots & \ddots & \vdots \\ c(m,1) & c(m,2) & \cdots & - \end{bmatrix} \tag{6}$$

Step 4. Calculation of the discordance interval matrix.

First, it is the discordance index of $d(a, b)$, which can be viewed as the preference of discontent in decision of scheme a rather than scheme b. It is defined:

$$d(a,b) = \frac{\max_{j \in D_{ab}} |v_{aj} - v_{bj}|}{\max_{j \in J, m, n \in I} |v_{mj} - v_{nj}|} \tag{7}$$

Here scheme m, n is used to calculate the weighted normalized value among all scheme target attributes. Then, using discordance interval index sets, we can obtain discordance interval matrix as:

$$D = \begin{bmatrix} - & d(1,2) & \cdots & d(1,m) \\ d(2,1) & - & \cdots & d(2,m) \\ \vdots & \vdots & \ddots & \vdots \\ d(m,1) & d(m,2) & \cdots & - \end{bmatrix} \tag{8}$$

Step 5. Determine the concordance index matrix.

The concordance index matrix for satisfaction measurement problem can be written in the following way:

$$\bar{c} = \sum_{a=1}^{m} \sum_{b}^{b} c(a,b) / m(m-1) \tag{9}$$

Here $\bar{c}$ is the critical value, which can be determined by average dominance index. Thus, a Boolean matrix (E) is given by:

$$\begin{cases} e(ab) = 1 & if \quad c(ab) \geq \bar{c} \\ e(ab) = 0 & if \quad c(ab) < \bar{c} \end{cases} \tag{10}$$

Step 6. Determine the discordance index matrix.

The preference of dissatisfaction is can be measured by discordance index:

$$\bar{d} = \frac{\sum_{a=1}^{m} \sum_{b}^{b} d(ab)}{m(m-1)} \tag{11}$$

And, the discordance index matrix (F) is given by:

$$\begin{cases} f(ab) = 1 & \text{if} \quad d(ab) \geq \overline{d} \\ f(ab) = 0 & \text{if} \quad d(ab) < \overline{d} \end{cases} \tag{12}$$

Step 7. Calculate *decision matrix* (aggregate dominance matrix) and compare alternatives according *veto* threshold values on attributes.

To take into account the imperfect character of the evaluation of actions, ELECTRE methods make use of discrimination (indifference and preference) thresholds. This leads to a pseudo-criterion model on each criterion. Indifference and preference thresholds, as *veto* threshold values on attributes [8], express the power attributed to a given criterion to be against the assertion "*a* outranks *b*" ("*a is at least as good as b*"), when the difference of the evaluation between $f(a, b)$ and $e(a, b)$ is greater than this thresholds. These thresholds can be constant along a scale or it can also vary. The final comparison and decision are done on aggregate dominance matrix.

3.2   Application of Bio-Inspired Ranking Method

One of the methods of comparison which has been widely used in this connection is that of ranking. The ranking method suffers from a serious drawback when the quality considered is not known with certainty to be representable by a linear variable. The method of offering judgment for two objects at time is known as the method of paired comparisons [9]. It is interesting to mention a research paper [10] from 1972, where a family of models for paired-comparison data that generalize the Bradley-Terry-Luce (BTL) model are proposed.

ELECTRE I is an outranking method, and it is therefore purpose ranking model for estimating choice parameters from paired-comparison data. The implemented ranking model is based on two research papers [11, 12].

Unlike previously mentioned research, in this research, a different approach to optimization *fitness* function is implemented. The *fitness* function is given by data represented by the *decision matrix* from (Step 7). To minimize *fitness* function, genetic algorithm is used. Ranking discovery framework and calculation for *fitness* function is presented in Fig. 1, where $N_{gen} = 30$ and $N_{top} = 10$ are user-specified parameters.

The GA is non-deterministic in that all mutations and breeding are made on a random basis and even individuals with poor fitness may have an opportunity to influence future generations. An individual's contributions to future generations depend on its fitness. The proposed method, makes any of general models (BTL) easy to specify and to estimate their parameters. The implemented GA function eliminates the time-consuming task of constructing the likelihood function by hand for every single model.

1. Generate an initial population
2. Perform the following sub-steps on training N_{gen} generations:
    2.1 Use each rank to score and rank the collection
    2.2 Calculate the fitness of each rank
    2.3 Record the top N_{top} ranks
    2.4 Create new population by:
        a) Reproduction
        b) Crossover
        c) Mutation
3. Apply the recorded ($N_{gen} \times N_{top}$) candidate ranks to select the best performance as the unique discovery output.

Fig. 1. Ranking discovery framework

4   Choosing and Decision Making for Agricultural Equipment

This research for decision making in purchasing agricultural equipment continues our existing study: Application of ELECTRE and PROMETHEE methods in agricultural decision making [2] from 2105. The implementation of multi-criteria-decision model ELECTRE I is continued and it is extended with bio-inspired ranking model, based on genetic algorithm.

4.1   Data Collection - Combine Harvester

During our previous research [2] detailed data were collected. The data set cover following data: combine harvester - with technical and economic characteristics presented in Table 1. In this example: farmer would like to purchase combine harvester class Tucano serial 300 or serial 400. On the first view both of them are suitable, but he needs to choose the best possible alternative.

Table 1. The criteria and technical and economic characteristics of a combine harvester

	Engine power (kW)	Number of straw-walkers	Delivery date	Manufacture year	Engine manufacturer	Price €	Volume of the harvest bunker
	max	*max*	*min*	*max*	*max*	*min*	*max*
Tucano 320	150	5	30	2015	Mercedes	120 000	6500
Tucano 340	205	6	30	2015	Mercedes	130 000	7500
Tucano 430	190	5	90	2015	Mercedes	140 000	8000
Tucano 440	205	6	45	2015	Mercedes	150 000	8500
Tucano 450	220	6	60	2015	Mercedes	160 000	9000

5 Experimental Results

The experimental results are presented in following subsections.

5.1 Experimental Results - Combine Harvester

Weights for importance of decision making criteria determined by decision maker experience: 0.2; 0.1; 0.1; 0.1; 0.1; 0.3; 0.1.

Table 2. Quantifications matrix

	C1	C2	C3	C4	C5	C6	C7
	max	max	min	max	max	min	max
A1	150	5	30	2015	10	120000	6500
A2	205	6	30	2015	10	130000	7500
A3	190	5	90	2015	10	140000	8000
A4	205	6	45	2015	10	150000	8500
A5	220	6	60	2015	10	160000	9000

Table 3. Normalized matrix

	C1	C2	C3	C4	C5	C6	C7
	max	max	min	max	max	min	max
A1	0.34317	0.39777	0.24077	0.44721	0.44721	0.38138	0.40914
A2	0.46900	0.47733	0.24077	0.44721	0.44721	0.41316	0.47209
A3	0.43469	0.39777	0.72231	0.44721	0.44721	0.44494	0.05035
A4	0.46900	0.47733	0.36115	0.44721	0.44721	0.47673	0.53503
A5	0.50332	0.47733	0.48154	0.44721	0.44721	0.50851	0.56650
Weights	0.2	0.1	0.1	0.1	0.1	0.3	0.1

Table 4. Weighted matrix depends on normalized matrix

	C1	C2	C3	C4	C5	C6	C7
	max	max	min	max	max	min	max
A1	0.068635	0.039778	0.024077	0.044721	0.044721	0.114416	0.040915
A2	0.093801	0.047733	0.024077	0.044721	0.044721	0.123950	0.047209
A3	0.086938	0.039778	0.072232	0.044721	0.044721	0.133485	0.005036
A4	0.093801	0.047733	0.036116	0.044721	0.044721	0.143019	0.053504
A5	0.100665	0.047733	0.048154	0.044721	0.044721	0.152554	0.056651

Table 5. Concordance and discordance index matrix

	C1	C2	C3	C4	C5	C6	C7	
	max	max	min	max	max	min	max	
A1 A1	1	1	1	1	1	1	1	1
A1 A2	0	0	1	1	1	1	0	0.6
A1 A3	0	1	1	1	1	1	1	0.8
A1 A4	0	0	1	1	1	1	0	0.6
A1 A5	0	0	1	1	1	1	0	0.6
A2 A1	1	1	1	1	1	0	1	0.7
A2 A2	1	1	1	1	1	1	1	1
A2 A3	1	1	1	1	1	1	1	1
A2 A4	1	1	1	1	1	1	0	0.9
A2 A5	0	1	1	1	1	1	0	0.7
A3 A1	1	1	0	1	1	0	0	0.5
A3 A2	0	0	0	1	1	0	0	0.2
A3 A3	1	1	1	1	1	1	1	1
A3 A4	0	0	0	1	1	1	0	0.5
A3 A5	0	0	0	1	1	1	0	0.5
A4 A1	1	1	0	1	1	0	1	0.6
A4 A2	1	1	0	1	1	0	1	0.6
A4 A3	1	1	1	1	1	0	1	0.7
A4 A4	1	1	1	1	1	1	1	1
A4 A5	0	1	1	1	1	1	0	0.7
A5 A1	1	1	0	1	1	0	1	0.6
A5 A2	1	1	0	1	1	0	1	0.6
A5 A3	1	1	1	1	1	0	1	0.7
A5 A4	1	1	0	1	1	0	1	0.6
A5 A5	1	1	1	1	1	1	1	1

Comparison of alternatives according *veto* threshold values on attributes is used in Table 6 to get outranking between alternatives. *Veto* threshold values on attributes are chosen on the basis of empirical experience and they are: 0.4 and 0.6.

The experimental result by ELECTRE I method are presented in Tables 1, 2, 3, 4, 5 and 6. The most important is decision matrix - *aggregate dominance matrix*, and comparisons (outranking) alternatives according to *veto* threshold values on attributes are presented in column *Dominance* in Table 6.

According to this outranking method, the optimal alternative for a farmer would be Tucan 450 (A5), which dominates all the variations. Both this method and PROMETHEE II method agree that the A3 is the worst possible alternative. In ELECTRE I method it does not dominate over any other alternative. After A5, a farmer should choose either combine harvester A2 or A4. These two alternatives provide the same results and are the best possible alternatives after the optimal one, that is, combine harvester A5 [2].

Table 6. Decision matrix - aggregate dominance matrix - and compare alternatives according veto threshold values on attributes

	C1	C2	C3	C4	C5	C6	C7			
	max	*max*	*min*	*max*	*max*	*min*	*max*	MAX	Comparison	Dominance
A1 A1	0	0	0	0	0	0	0	0	0	–
A1 A2	0,02516	0,00795	0	0	0	0,00953	0,00629	0,02516	0,48757	Dominance
A1 A3	0,01830	0	0,04815	0	0	0,01906	−0,03588	0,04815	0,93294	False
A1 A4	0,02516	0,00795	0,01203	0	0	0,02860	0,01258	0,02860	0,55417	Dominance
A1 A5	0,03203	0,00795	0,02407	0	0	0,03813	0,01573	0,03813	0,73890	False
A2 A1	−0,02517	−0,00796	0	0	0	−0,00953	−0,00629	0	0	Dominance
A2 A2	0	0	0	0	0	0	0	0	0	–
A2 A3	−0,00686	−0,00796	0,04815	0	0	0,00953	−0,04217	0,04815	0,93294	False
A2 A4	0	0	0,01203	0	0	0,01906	0,00629	0,01906	0,36945	Dominance
A2 A5	0,00686	0	0,02407	0	0	0,02860	0,00944	0,02860	0,55417	Dominance
A3 A1	−0,0183	0	−0,04815	0	0	−0,01907	0,03587	0,03587	0,69512	False
A3 A2	0,00686	0,00795	−0,04815	0	0	-0,00953	0,04217	0,04217	0,81707	False
A3 A3	0	0	0	0	0	0	0	0	0	–
A3 A4	0,00686	0,00795	−0,03612	0	0	0,00953	0,04846	0,04846	0,93902	False
A3 A5	0,01372	0,00795	−0,02408	0	0	0,01906	0,05161	0,05161	1	False
A4 A1	−0,02517	−0,00796	−0,01204	0	0	−0,0286	−0,01259	0	0	Dominance
A4 A2	0	0	−0,01204	0	0	−0,01907	−0,00629	0	0	Dominance
A4 A3	−0,00686	-0,00796	0,03611	0	0	−0,00953	−0,04847	0,03611	0,69971	False
A4 A4	0	0	0	0	0	0	0	0	0	–
A4 A5	0,00686	0	0,01203	0	0	0,00953	0,00314	0,01203	0,23323	Dominance
A5 A1	−0,03203	−0,00796	−0,02408	0	0	−0,03814	−0,01574	0	0	Dominance
A5 A2	−0,00686	0	−0,02408	0	0	−0,0286	−0,00944	0	0	Dominance
A5 A3	−0,01373	−0,00796	0,02407	0	0	−0,01907	−0,05162	0,02407	0,46647	Dominance
A5 A4	−0,00686	0	−0,01204	0	0	−0,00953	−0,00315	0	0	Dominance
A5 A5	0	0	0	0	0	0	0	0	0	–

Table 7. Ranking alternatives for estimating choice parameters from paired-comparison data in aggregate dominance matrix

	A1	A2	A3	A4	A5
C1	0.5293	0.0079	0.2658	0.1401	0
C2	0.3719	0.1443	0.2978	0	0.0763
C3	0.2963	0.2624	0	0.1863	0.2156
C4	0.2000	0.2000	0.2000	0.2000	0.2000
C5	0.2000	0.2000	0.2000	0.2000	0.2000
C6	0.2624	0.2963	0.2494	0.2156	0
C7	0.3183	0.0716	0.4927	0.0993	0
$\sum$	**2.1782**	**1.1825**	**1.7057**	**1.0413**	**0.6919**
Rank	V	III	IV	II	I

Ranking alternatives for estimating choice parameters from paired-comparison data in aggregate dominance matrix are presented in Table 7. The ranking alternatives are presented in row $\sum$. The minimal value presents the best solution, that is, the best alternative. The row $\sum$ also shows that the best alternative is A5 for estimation choice parameters are 0.6919. The second best alternative is A4, with estimation choice parameters 1.0413, and the third best alternative is A2, and the forth is A3. The lowest ranking alternative is A1 with maximum estimation choice parameters 2.1782.

5.2   Complete Ranking PROMETHEE II Method - Experimental Results

Software Visual PROMETHEE is used for complete ranking in PROMETHEE II method in our previous study is shown in Fig. 2 [2]. It is important to mention that, data set used here is the same as data set used in ELECTRE I method.

Fig. 2. Complete Ranking graph usage by PROMETHEE II

Figure 2 presents the graph which shows that the action that dominates the others is action number two A2. The second best alternative is A1, and the next alternative is A4, and then the A5, and at the very end as the least favorable alternative is A3. If we look at the graph above, in A2 only criterion number 7, which represents the criterion of bunkers' volume, does not correspond to this type of combine. Also, in alternative A4 we can see that only one criterion is not met, and this is the price. It also seems logical given that farmers prefer lower prices. The worst possible alternative is, by all means, the alternative A3. There are much more unmet then met criteria here.

5.3   Discussion on Experimental Results

Table 8 compared the experimental results obtained by implementation of three methods: (1) ELECTRE I; (2) Hybrid Bio-Inspired ELECTRE I; (3) PROMETHEE II. It also shows the average placement and final rank.

The experimental results obtained by the outranking ELECTRE I method and complete ranking hybrid bio-inspired ELECTRE I method can be compared. In both methods A5 is the best choice. Alternatives A4 and A2 are almost the same, and very close. And, finally, alternatives A1 and A3 are the worst decisions.

On the other side, the experimental results obtained by all three decision making methods can be compared. For that reason, the average placement of three methods is calculated and according to it, the *Final Rank - hypothetic* is determined. Looking at the average placement, it could be concluded that A2 and A5 are the best solution, since for both of them the *Final Rank* is one. Not so far on average placement is A4,

Table 8. Comparison of experimental results of implemented methods

Alternative	Method			Average placement	Final Rank
	ELECTRE I	GA + ELECTRE	PROMETHEE II		*hypothetic*
A1	4	5	2	3.66	4
A2	2	3	1	2	1
A3	5	4	5	4.66	5
A4	2	2	3	2.33	3
A5	1	1	4	2	1

it occupies the third place. The fourth place is A1 mostly because of good placement in PROMETHEE II method. Finally, A3 is definitely the worst solution when it comes to purchasing agricultural equipment – in this case, combine harvester.

Also, difference in placement of A1 in different experimental results could be discussed. Alternative one in ELECTRE I method occupies first two places, while PROMETHEE II method gave it very low fourth placement although it does not meet only one criterion – *price*, and has the highest weighted coefficient values.

5.4 Experimental Results - Purchasing Irrigation Equipment

Weights for importance of decision making criteria in purchasing irrigation equipment are determined by decision maker experience: 0.3; 0.3; 0.2; 0.2 (Table 9).

Table 9. Quantifications matrix

	C1	C2	C3	C4
	min	*min*	*max*	*max*
A1	1178	9750	10	30
A2	1252	18500	10	40
A3	1337	11500	7	35
A4	1094	10000	10	40
A5	1265	110000	12	113

Table 10. Ranking alternatives for estimating choice parameters in purchasing irrigation equipment

	A1	A2	A3	A4	A5
C1	0.2999	0.2348	0	0.2840	0.1969
C2	0.2649	0.2652	0.2433	0.2331	0
C3	0.2061	0.2351	0.3357	0.1714	0
C4	0.2649	0.2433	0.2331	0.2652	0
Σ	**1.0358**	**0.9784**	**0.8121**	**0.9537**	**0.1969**
Rank	V	IV	II	III	I

Ranking alternatives for estimating choice parameters from paired-comparison data usage by GA + ELECTRE I method in purchasing irrigation equipment are presented in Table 10. The row $\sum$ shows that the best alternative is A5 for estimation choice parameters are 0.1969. The lowest ranking alternative is A1 with maximum estimation choice parameters 1.0358.

Table 11. Comparison of experimental results of implemented methods

Alternative	Method			Average placement	Final Rank
	ELECTRE I	Hybrid Bio-Inspired ELECTRE	PROMETHEE II		*hypothetic*
A1	–	5	2	3.5	3
A2	–	4	3	3.5	3
A3	5	2	5	4	5
A4	–	3	1	2	1
A5	1	1	4	2	1

If the experimental results are compared, Table 11, it can be seen that there are significant discrepancies for different methods. Therefore, the system for decision making in purchasing agricultural equipment could be combined with some other methods for calculating relative importance of criteria such as AHP, MACBETH or MAUT, instead of assigning the weighted coefficient values for importance of criteria by decision maker experience.

6   Conclusion and Future Work

This paper presents the hybrid bio-inspired ELECTRE I method for ranking the most suitable purchasing agricultural equipment. In general it uses a bio-inspired approach, particularly genetic algorithm for ranking alternatives. ELECTRE I method is outranking method and this research extended it to complete ranking ELECTRE I method. This research continues our previous study.

The proposed hybrid GA + ELECTRE I method is described and implemented on real-world data set presented in our previously mentioned study. The first thing that can be concluded is that proposed hybrid method could be used as completely ranking method. Comparing the obtained experimental results with the experimental results obtained by PROMETHEE II method it could be noted that there is a discrepancy when it comes to certain alternatives.

Experimental results encourage further research. In future research, the hybrid system could be tested with some other methods for calculating relative importance of criteria, instead of assigning weighted coefficient values for importance of criteria by decision maker experience.

Acknowledgments. The authors acknowledge the support for research project TR 36030, funded by the Ministry of Science and Technological Development of Serbia.

References

1. Simić, D., Svirčević, V., Simić, S.: An approach of steel plates fault diagnosis in multiple classes decision making. In: Polycarpou, M., de Carvalho, A.C., Pan, J.-S., Woźniak, M., Quintian, H., Corchado, E. (eds.) HAIS 2014. LNCS, vol. 8480, pp. 86–97. Springer, Heidelberg (2014)
2. Gajić, J.: Primena ELECTRE i PROMETHEE metoda u donošenju odluka u poljoprivredi. (ELECTRE and PROMETHEE method application in agricultural decision making). Master thesis, University of Novi Sad, Faculty of Economics (2105)
3. Tarrant, J.R.: Agricultural Geography (Problems in modern geography). David & Charles, Newton Abbot (1974)
4. Nasab, M.N., Azizi, M.: Strategy for agricultural development in Zanjan city, Iran: Application of SWOT-AHP method. Annual meeting of the ISAHP (2014). http://www.isahp.org/uploads/p743933.pdf (accessed January 12, 2016)
5. Raju, K.S., Kumar, D.N.: Ranking irrigation planning alternatives using data envelopment analysis. Water Resour. Manage 20(4), 553–566 (2006)
6. Srdjević, Z., Blagojević, B., Srdjević, B.: AHP based group decision making in ranking loan applicants for purchasing irrigation equipment: a case study. Bul. J. Agr. Sci. 17(4), 531–543 (2011)
7. Benayoun, R., Roy, B., Sussman, N.: Manual de reference du programme electre. Note De Synthese et Formaton 25 (1966)
8. Sen, P., Yang, J.-B.: Multiple Criteria Decision Support in Engineering Design. Springer, Heidelberg (1998)
9. Kendall, M.G., Smith, B.B.: On the method of paired comparisons. Biometrika 31(3/4), 324–345 (1940)
10. Tversky, A.: Elimination by aspects: A theory of choice. Psychol. Rev. 79, 281–299 (1972)
11. Wickelmaier, F., Schmid, C.: A Matlab function to estimate choice model parameters from paired-comparison data. Behav. Res. Methods Instrum. Comput. 36(1), 29–40 (2004)
12. Svensson, C.-M., Coombes, S., Peirce, J.W.: Using evolutionary algorithms for fitting high-dimensional models to neuronal data. Neuroinformatics 10(2), 199–218 (2012)

Learning Algorithms

Evaluating the Difficulty of Instances of the Travelling Salesman Problem in the Nearby of the Optimal Solution Based on Random Walk Exploration

Miguel Cárdenas-Montes[(✉)]

Department of Fundamental Research, Centro de Investigaciones Energéticas
Medioambientales y Tecnológicas, Madrid, Spain
miguel.cardenas@ciemat.es

Abstract. Combinatorial optimization is one of the main research areas
in Evolutionary Computing and Operational Research, and the Travelling Salesman Problem one of their most popular problems. The never
ending quest of researchers for new and more difficult combinatorial
problems to stress their evolutionary algorithms leads to investigate how
to measure the difficulty of Travelling Salesman Problem instances. By
developing methodologies for separating ease from difficult instances,
researchers will be confident about the performance of their algorithms.
In this proof-of-concept, a methodology for evaluating the difficulty of
instances of the Travelling Salesman Problem in the nearby of the optimal
solution is proposed. This methodology is based on the use of Random
Walk to explore the closeness area of the optimal solution. Instances
with a more pronounced gradient towards the optimal solution might be
considered easier than instances exhibiting almost a null gradient. The
exploration of this gradient is done by starting from the optimal tour and
later modifying it with a Random Walk process. The aim is to propose
a methodology to evaluate the difficulty of instances of Travelling Salesman Problem, which can be applied to other combinatorial-problems
instances. As a consequence of this work, a methodology to evaluate the
difficulty of Travelling Salesman Problem instances is proposed and confronted to a wide set of instances, and finally a rank of their difficulty is
stated.

Keywords: Travelling Salesman Problem · Instance difficulty · Combinatorial optimization

1 Introduction

Together with other classical combinatorial problems, such as: N-Queen, Knapsack, and Partition Number Problem, Travelling Salesman Problem (TSP) is
one of the most popular problems in combinatorial optimization. The quest for
searching high-quality solutions to these problems has fostered the development

© Springer International Publishing Switzerland 2016
F. Martínez-Álvarez et al. (Eds.): HAIS 2016, LNAI 9648, pp. 299–310, 2016.
DOI: 10.1007/978-3-319-32034-2_25

of cutting-edge evolutionary algorithms (see Blum [1] for a review). The numerous variants of TSP [2,3] is the result of the search of more difficult variants of the problem for stressing more advanced heuristics and metaheuristics. However, in the investigation of the performance of the heuristics and metaheuristics proposed to solve this kind of problems, it lacks a great bulk of references to the intrinsic difficulty or the hardness of the instances of the TSP. TSP aims to find the minimal tour among N cities or points by passing only once by all cities and returning to the starting point, and it is considered as NP-hard [4], but it does not mean that all instances of the problem have the same difficulty.

The study of the TSP instances is mainly performed two type of instances: real instances consisting of the cities of a real region or country, and randomly generated cities.

Among the variants of the TSP, it should be underlined the Asymmetric Travelling Salesman Problem (ATSP), in which the travel cost from the city i to j is different to the reverse travel. ATSP is considered more challenge than symmetric TSP.

Usually benchmark instances of TSP and other combinatorial problems are used to report the strengths and weaknesses of combinatorial algorithms. To incorporate metrics to evaluate the difficulty of the instance might provide information about the better capability to find high-quality sub-optimal solutions among two or more algorithms.

In this work, a methodology based on Random Walk is proposed to evaluate the difficulty of the TSP instances in the nearby of the optimal solution. The outlook of the methodology is as follows: starting from the optimal solution, a set of steps are performed by using Random Walk. The Random Walk allows the fitness worsens from the optimal. How far the fitness worsens is an indicator of the slope towards the minimum (optimum).

The intuition of this process is that when the nearby of the minimum has a strong slope towards the optimal solution, it will be ease for the algorithm to find this optimal solution, and therefore, the instance can be considered as an instance of low difficulty. So that, by perturbing the optimal through Random Walk, the process will generate solutions with fitness much worse than the optimal one (Fig. 1(a)).

By making the reverse reasoning, when the fitness varies slowly from the optimal value —a small gradient is exhibited by the fitness towards the minimum—, then the instance can be labelled as one of high difficulty. So that, by starting from the optimal solution, the Random Walk process will only generate slightly-worsened solutions. This is graphically illustrated in Fig. 1(b).

The proposed methodology allows the use of diverse indicators as numerical value of the difficulty of the TSP instance. In the initial conception of this work, to untie the methodology for evaluating the difficulty and the metric to provide a numerical value of the difficulty was a requirement. Along the analysis of the results diverse metrics will be proposed and compared.

Following the previous intuition, the squared area in Fig. 1 is a potential indicator of the difficulty of the instance. A larger area (Fig. 1(a)) indicates that

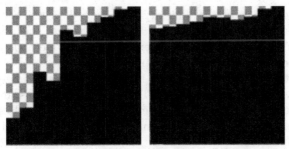

(a) Example of easy instance. (b) Example of difficult instance.

Fig. 1. The figures illustrate the intuition of the use of Random Walk for evaluating the difficulty of the TSP instance. In Fig. 1(a), the fitness quickly differentiates from the optimum value when mutating the optimal tour with Random Walk. In this case, there is a strong gradient towards the optimum value. However in Fig. 1(b), the fitness does not significantly vary from the optimum value. This figure shows a moderate slope of the fitness landscape toward the optimum value when mutating the optimal tour with Random Walk. For convenience, in the two figures the worse fitness after 10 steps is identical. Therefore, following this intuition the difficulty of the TSP instance is inversely related to the grey-squared area. This area is obtained by subtracting the total area of the rectangle with dimensions of number of steps times maximum fitness reached in Random Walk process to the sum of the fitness values in the Random Walk process.

the instance is easier to solver than a smaller area (Fig. 1(b)). The values of this area generated during the Random Walk process has to be treated as a random variable. In Sect. 4, this indicator and others are used to evaluate the hardness of diverse TSP instances.

Considering the core of the methodology, it can be applied to evaluate the difficulty of other instances of combinatorial problems. The only requirement is to have the optimal solution or a very high-quality solution of these instances, the later application of the Random Walk process to worsen the optimal solution and the evaluation of those worsened solutions. Besides, in order to apply the proposed methodology the behaviour of the fitness landscape should be smooth in the nearby of the optimal solution.

Unfortunately, the methodology to evaluate the difficulty of TSP instances has some limitations. They have to be recognised in order to avoid extrapolating it beyond its natural scope. The recognition of the limitations should foster further research to widen the applicability of the methodology. Furthermore, the very final aim is to extrapolate the methodology to be able to measure the difficulty of instances of other combinatorial problems, and for this purpose, it is worthy to recognize the restricted scope of this initial proof-of-concept.

Among the limitations of this proof-of-concept, it should be cited the requirement of knowing the optimal tour of the TSP instance. Alternatives methodologies for instances without known optimal tour will be addressed in the future.

Besides, the evaluation of the difficulty is restricted to the behaviour of the instance in the nearby of the optimal tour. Evaluating the difficulty of the instances in wider areas will required a extension of the methodology and probably the incorporation of more complex metrics.

The rest of the paper is organized as follows: Sect. 2 summarizes the Related Work and previous efforts done. The TSP and its instances are depicted at Sect. 3.1. Section 3.2 describes the experimental setup. The Results and the Analysis are discussed in Sect. 4. And finally, the Conclusions and Future Work are presented in Sect. 5.

2   Related Work

From the historical point of view, in [5] two algorithms for solving TSP are presented. This work uses as benchmark two TSP instances with 13 cities and 9 cities respectively. Comparing with the current problem sizes, these tiny problem sizes are revealing how the capacity to produce high-quality solutions has evolved, and therefore, the need of a set of hard TSP instances to fairly evaluate the ground-breaking heuristics and metaheuristics. For a more complete review of the problem, the reader is referred to [2,3] for more information.

In [6], the objective is to predict the relationships between the performance of algorithms and the critical features of instances. The paper provides a methodology to discern if the metadata is sufficient for predicting the behaviour of the instances, ease or hard. In this work, the experimental set-up is composed of instances of 100 cities randomly generated in a square area of 400 units. The TSP instances are evolved using a evolutionary algorithm, particularly a genetic algorithm: new instances are created by using uniform crossover and mutation. The criterion for classifying as easy or as hard the instances is based on the effort done by two Lin-Kernighan heuristic methods [7] to solve the TSP instance: chained Lin-Kernighan [8] and Lin-Kernighan with cluster compensation [9].

The existence of a transition phase in TSP is cited in [10]. This issue arises from the transformation of the TSP into a binary decision problem under the question, *can an algorithm find a solution with a tour length less that l?*. The transition phase ease-hard-ease in relation to the difficulty to find a new solution to a TSP instance with a shorter tour length is analysed. Authors place this transition phase at $\frac{l}{\sqrt{N \cdot A}} \approx 0.75$, where N is the number of particles or cities, A the area covered by the cities and l the tour length. In Sect. 4.3, the values of this parameter, also cited and used in [6], are confronted with the methodology proposed in the current work. The rank generated by the Random Walk approach is compared with the coordinate of the ease-hard-ease transition phase, $\frac{l}{\sqrt{N \cdot A}}$.

In [11] a major revision and extension of [6] is done by extending the methodology to the most popular combinational problems: assignment problem, knapsack problem, bin-packing problem, graph problem timetabling and constraint satisfaction.

3   Methodology

3.1   Travelling Salesman Problem and Instances

The TSP can be expressed as shown in Eqs. 1 and 2.

$$x_{ij} = \begin{cases} 1 & \text{the path goes from city } i \text{ to city } j \\ 0 & \text{otherwise} \end{cases} \tag{1}$$

where $x_{ij} = 1$ if city i is connected with city j, and $x_{ij} = 0$ otherwise.

For $i = 0, ..., n$, let u_i be an artificial variable, and finally take c_{ij} to be the distance from city i to city j. Then TSP can be written as shown in Eq. 2.

$$\min \sum_{i=0}^{n} \sum_{j\neq i, j=0}^{n} c_{ij} x_{ij}$$

$$0 \leq x_{ij} \leq 1 \qquad\qquad i, j = 0, \cdots, n$$

$$u_i \in \mathbf{Z} \qquad\qquad i = 0, \cdots, n$$

$$\sum_{i=0, i\neq j}^{n} x_{ij} = 1 \qquad\qquad j = 0, \cdots, n \tag{2}$$

$$\sum_{j=0, j\neq i}^{n} x_{ij} = 1 \qquad\qquad i = 0, \cdots, n$$

$$u_i - u_j + n x_{ij} \leq n - 1 \qquad 1 \leq i \neq j \leq n$$

The purpose of TSP is to find the shortest tour between a set of cities. In the symmetric version of TSP —variant used in this work—, the cost of joining two cities does not depend on the departure city, only on the pair of cities.

The TSP instances (Fig. 2) used as benchmarks in this work have been extracted from http://comopt.ifi.uni-heidelberg.de/software/TSPLIB95/. Among the instances published in this site, those with optimal solution have been selected. Besides, several instances were selected under the criterion of having 100 points. This allows a study of the difficulty of instances of equal size. Other instances were selected under the criterion of having a number of points slightly lower or larger than 100, to facilitate the mapping of the difficulty in function of the number of points. Instances varying more than two orders of magnitude in relation to the smallest one have been skipped. So that, efforts to evaluate the difficulty relative among instances which encompass from tens to hundreds of cities are done.

The list of TSP instances includes: ulysses22 (Fig. 2(a)), st70 (Fig. 2(b)), pr76 (Fig. 2(c)), kroA100 (Fig. 2(d)), kroD100 (Fig. 2(e)), rd100 (Fig. 2(f)), gr120 (Fig. 2(g)), and gr202 (Fig. 2(h)). The figure in the names indicates the number of cities conforming the TSP instance.

With this selection of TSP instances, it is expected to cover a wide range of cases, so that, different difficulty instances are evaluated.

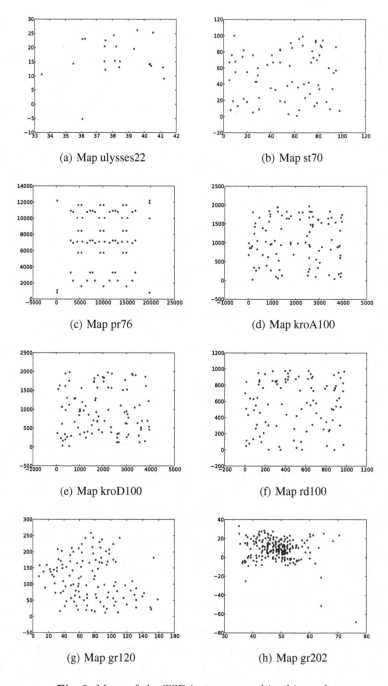

(a) Map ulysses22

(b) Map st70

(c) Map pr76

(d) Map kroA100

(e) Map kroD100

(f) Map rd100

(g) Map gr120

(h) Map gr202

Fig. 2. Maps of the TSP instances used in this work.

3.2   Experimental Setup

All the numerical experiments have been executed in a machine with two Intel Xeon X5570 processors at 2.93 GHz and 8 GB of RAM. Python 2.6.6 has been used for the prototype. As pseudorandom number generator, a subroutine based on Mersenne Twister [12] has been used.

4   Analysis

In this section the proposed methodology and the metrics are confronted to the TSP instances used in this work (Fig. 2). Furthermore, the methodology is compared with previous works about difficulty evaluation of TSP instances.

4.1   How Far from the Optimal Fitness?

The proposed methodology can be linked to diverse metrics. These metrics are the final indicator of the difficulty of the TSP instances. Once the Random Walk process has provided the fitness evolution after n steps, the values of the fitness function during this process allow implementing diverse metrics.

For example, the highest fitness value reached in the 25 steps of the Random Walk process (Fig. 3(a)), or the mean fitness of the 25 steps (Fig. 3(b)) might be used as indicator of how far from the optimal solution has evolved the fitness; and therefore, the slope towards the optimal fitness value. When comparing with the optimal fitness values, these metrics give an intuition of the difficulty of the instances.

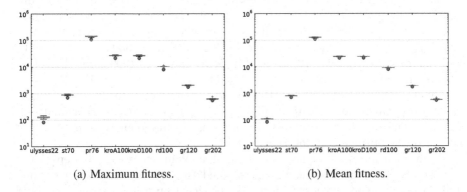

(a) Maximum fitness.   (b) Mean fitness.

Fig. 3. Maximum fitness reached and mean fitness after 25 Random Walk steps. Values produced by 10 executions. For each TSP instance, the point indicates the optimal fitness value.

It is expected that more difficult instances will produce fitness values less away from the optimal fitness values, whereas less difficult instances will produce

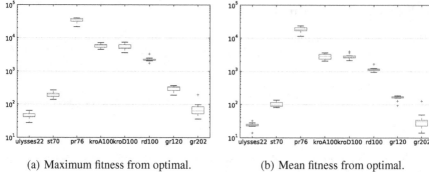

(a) Maximum fitness from optimal.   (b) Mean fitness from optimal.

Fig. 4. Difference from the optimal fitness to the maximum reached and mean fitness after 25 Random Walk steps. Values produced by 10 executions. Higher values indicates higher hardness.

fitness values farther from the optimal value. Difficult instances will slight evolve from the nearby of the optimal solutions, so that the difference between the optimal fitness value and the maximum or the mean fitness after 25 Random Walk steps should not be large. Oppositely, for ease instances the strong gradient towards the optimal fitness will produce, after the Random Walk process, fitness values will be very distant from optimal one. These values are shown in Fig. 4. In this figure, the y-coordinate represents how far from the optimal fitness the Random Walk process worsens the fitness.

It is important to verify how the behaviour exhibited in Fig. 4 varies for a larger number of steps in the Random Walk. By increasing the steps, areas beyond the nearby of the optimal solution are explored. These areas might differently behave that the nearby of the optimal solutions, e.g. stagnation fitness zones, variation of the slope of the fitness, or even local minimum areas. In Figs. 5 and 6, the maximum fitness for 100 steps (Fig. 5(a)) and 1000 steps (Fig. 6(a)), and the mean fitness after 100 steps (Fig. 5(b)) and after 1000 steps (Fig. 6(b)) are presented for comparison purposes with the case of 25 steps (Fig. 4).

By observing the difficulty relative among the instances for 25 steps (Fig. 4) and the equivalent for 100 steps (Fig. 5), it is perceived at equivalent pattern. Therefore, when using either 25 or 100 steps in the Random Walk process, the nearby of the optimal solution is explored.

Even for a much larger number of Random Walk steps —1000 steps— the hardness rank of the instances is maintained (Fig. 6). So that, when ranking TSP instances, computational efforts can be saved by using a reduced number of steps without impact on the hardness rank.

4.2   Area as Metric

As it was previously mentioned, the intuition about the difficulty of the TSP instance can be measured as the area not covered in the rectangle with dimensions of number of steps and maximum fitness reached in Random Walk process

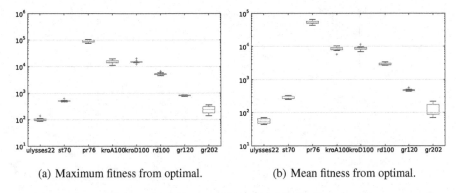

(a) Maximum fitness from optimal.   (b) Mean fitness from optimal.

Fig. 5. Difference from the optimal fitness to the maximum reached and mean fitness after 100 Random Walk steps. Values produced by 10 executions. Higher values indicates higher hardness.

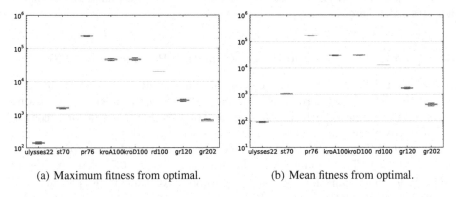

(a) Maximum fitness from optimal.   (b) Mean fitness from optimal.

Fig. 6. Difference from the optimal fitness to the maximum reached and mean fitness after 1000 Random Walk steps. Values produced by 10 executions. Higher values indicates higher hardness.

(see Fig. 1). For the TSP instances used in this work, the values of this metric —10 executions— is presented in Fig. 7 for the case of 25 Random Walk steps.

For this metric, the hardness rank is consistent in the difficulty relative among the TSP instances predicted with the Random Walk methodology by using the metric of the area (Fig. 7) and the other metrics (Fig. 4). It is remarkable that in comparison with the previous metrics, the area not covered shown a larger variance than the other metrics.

From the metrics in this section, it can be stated that hardness of the TSP instances seem not directly related with the number of cities. TSP instance with two-hundred cities, e.g. gr202, seems less difficult than others with one-hundred cities, e.g. gr120.

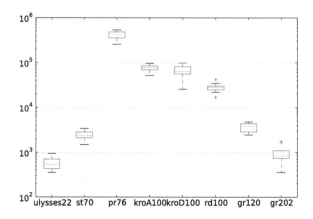

Fig. 7. Mean value and standard deviation of the area not covered as it is shown in Fig. 1. Values obtained for 25 Random Walk steps and 10 executions. Higher values indicates higher hardness.

4.3   Comparison with the Phase Transition Parameter for TSP

In [10], for Euclidean TSP instances in the plane indicates the existence of a phase transition —ease-hard-ease— for the TSP decision problem when seeking a answer to the question if a tour with length less than l exists for a certain instance. Given the parameters, A the area where the cities are spread out and N the number of cities, the decision problem becomes more difficult for instances with $\frac{l}{\sqrt{N \cdot A}} \approx 0.75$. Therefore, the closeness of $\frac{l}{\sqrt{N \cdot A}}$ to 0.75 can provide an auxiliary hardness rank for comparison purposes. At Table 1 this parameter is calculated for the TSP instances of this work.

Comparing the hardness ranks in Figs. 4 and 7 and the values of the critical parameter $\frac{l}{\sqrt{N \cdot A}}$ (Table 1), except for the instance pr76, the difficulty relative among the TSP instances predicted with the Random Walk methodology coincides with the closeness of the hard phase in the transition ease-hard-ease. This coincidence reinforces the confidence in the hardness rank produced with the Random Walk methodology.

From the critical parameter $\frac{l}{\sqrt{N \cdot A}}$ and the results of the metrics presented in this work, two alternatives hardness ranks can be presented. Firstly, from the parameter $\frac{l}{\sqrt{N \cdot A}}$ the scale of increasing hardness is as follows: kroA100 > kroD100 > gr120 > rd100 > pr76 > gr202 > st70 > ulysses22; whereas from the previous metrics, e.g. the area not covered (Sect. 4.2) the scale is as follows: pr76 > kroA100 > kroD100 > rd100 > gr120 > st70 > gr202 > ulysses22. Although a great coincidence is produced for certain TSP instances, the discrepancies and their origin deserve further research. For example, it should be analysed the role of the regular pattern in the harness differences for pr76 instance.

Table 1. Values of the transition phase parameter $\frac{l}{\sqrt{N \cdot A}}$ in [10] for the TSP instances used in this work. Transition phase ease-hard-ease occurs at $\frac{l}{\sqrt{N \cdot A}} \approx 0.75$, so that instances with closer values of this parameter to 0.75 are considered as harder instances.

	Critical parameter: $\frac{l}{\sqrt{N \cdot A}}$	$\left|\frac{l}{\sqrt{N \cdot A}} - 0.75\right|$
ulysses22	1.121	0.371
st70	0.862	0.112
pr76	0.829	0.079
kroA100	0.769	0.019
kroD100	0.770	0.020
rd100	0.813	0.063
gr120	0.810	0.060
gr202	1.859	1.109

5   Conclusions and Future Work

In this paper, a methodology for evaluating the difficulty of TSP instances has been proposed and evaluated. The evaluation of the difficulty of the TSP instances is relevant in order to separate difficult instances from ease ones and, therefore, to intensively stress the evolutionary algorithms created to solve them. The methodology proposed in this work is based on the use of Random Walk to evaluate the gradient of the fitness landscape in the nearby of the optimal solution.

The methodology has been confronted to a wide set of TSP instances. As a consequence of the application of the methodology to the TSP instances, they can be ranked by their difficulty. Furthermore, the comparison of this difficulty rank of TSP instances is in agreement with previously published ranks. This reinforces the confidence in the use of the proposed methodology to evaluated the difficulty of TSP instances in the nearby of the optimal solution.

As future work, the study of other instances of the TSP problems is proposed, so that a larger difficulty rank be produced. The study will include the analysis of other variants of TSP. As it has been mentioned, the proposed methodology is restricted to a particular scenario, the nearby of the optimal solution. Furthermore, some limitations have been also mentioned along the work. Therefore, to widen the scope of the applicability of the methodology is a major issue for future work. Besides, the effect of the distribution of the cities in the area once corrected of the area extension where they are placed and its influence in the hardness of the instance is also proposed as future work. Finally, the acquisition of the capacity to evaluated the harness of instances opens new possibilities for hardening instances.

Acknowledgement. The research leading to these results has received funding by the Spanish Ministry of Economy and Competitiveness (MINECO) for funding support through the grant FPA2013-47804-C2-1-R, and "Unidad de Excelencia María de Maeztu": CIEMAT - FÍSICA DE PARTÍCULAS through the grant MDM-2015-0509.

References

1. Blum, C.: Hybrid metaheuristics in combinatorial optimization: a tutorial. In: Dediu, A.-H., Martín-Vide, C., Truthe, B. (eds.) TPNC 2012. LNCS, vol. 7505, pp. 1–10. Springer, Heidelberg (2012)
2. Gutin, G., Punnen, A.P. (eds.): The Traveling Salesman Problem and Its Variations. Combinatorial Optimization. Kluwer Academic, Dordrecht (2002)
3. Applegate, D.L., Bixby, R.E., Chvatal, V., Cook, W.J.: The Traveling Salesman Problem: A Computational Study. Princeton Series in Applied Mathematics. Princeton University Press, Princeton (2007)
4. Garey, M.R., Johnson, D.S.: Computers and Intractability: A Guide to the Theory of NP-Completeness. W. H. Freeman, San Francisco (1979)
5. Lin, S.: Computer solutions of the traveling salesman problem. Bell Syst. Tech. J. **44**(10), 2245–2269 (1965)
6. Smith-Miles, K., van Hemert, J., Lim, X.Y.: Understanding TSP difficulty by learning from evolved instances. In: Blum, C., Battiti, R. (eds.) LION 4. LNCS, vol. 6073, pp. 266–280. Springer, Heidelberg (2010)
7. Lin, S., Kernighan, B.W.: An effective heuristic algorithm for the travelling-salesman problem. Oper. Res. **21**, 498–516 (1973)
8. Applegate, D., Cook, W.J., Rohe, A.: Chained lin-kernighan for large traveling salesman problems. INFORMS J. Comput. **15**(1), 82–92 (2003)
9. Johnson, D.S., McGeoch, L.A.: Experimental Analysis of Heuristics for the STSP. Wiley, New York (2001)
10. Gent, I.P., Walsh, T.: The TSP phase transition. Artif. Intell. **88**(1–2), 349–358 (1996)
11. Smith-Miles, K., Lopes, L.: Measuring instance difficulty for combinatorial optimization problems. Comput. OR **39**(5), 875–889 (2012)
12. Matsumoto, M., Nishimura, T.: Mersenne twister: a 623-dimensionally equidistributed uniform pseudorandom number generator. ACM Trans. Model. Comput. Simul. **8**(1), 3–30 (1999)

A Nearest Hyperrectangle Monotonic Learning Method

Javier García[1], José-Ramón Cano[2], and Salvador García[3(✉)]

[1] Department of Computer Science, University of Jaén, 23071 Jaén, Spain
jgf00002@red.ujaen.es
[2] Department of Computer Science, University of Jaén, EPS of Linares,
Calle Alfonso X El Sabio S/N, 23700 Linares, Jaén, Spain
jrcano@ujaen.es
[3] Department of Computer Science and Artificial Intelligence,
University of Granada, 18071 Granada, Spain
salvagl@decsai.ugr.es

Abstract. We can find real prediction learning problems whose class attribute is represented by ordinal values that should increase with some of the explaining attributes. They are known as classification problems with monotonicity constraints. In this contribution, our goal is to formalize the nearest hyperrectangle learning approach to manage monotonicity constraints. The idea behind it is to retain objects in $\mathbb{R}^n$, which can be either single points or hyperrectangles or rules into a combined model. The approach is checked with experimental analysis involving wide range of monotonic data sets. The results reported, verified by nonparametric statistical tests, show that our approach is very competitive with well-known techniques for monotonic classification.

Keywords: Monotonic classification · Instance-based learning · Rule induction · Nested generalized examples

1 Introduction

The monotonicity constraint in classification is very common in practice and many data mining algorithms have been adapted to be able to handle such constraints in one form or another. They are problems whose examples are described by attributes with ordered values and monotonicity constraints are present: a higher value of an attribute of an example, fixing other attributes' values, should not decrease its class assignment. On way to deal with monotonicity is imposing constraints for learning only monotone classification functions. Proposals of this type are: classification trees and rule induction [5,11,13], neural networks [8], and instance-based learning [4].

Exemplar-based learning considers a set of methods widely used in machine learning and data mining [10]. The most famous algorithm belonging to this family is the k-Nearest Neighbor (k-NN). A similar scheme is based on the Nested Generalized Exemplar (NGE) theory [14]. In NGE theory, generalizations

© Springer International Publishing Switzerland 2016
F. Martínez-Álvarez et al. (Eds.): HAIS 2016, LNAI 9648, pp. 311–322, 2016.
DOI: 10.1007/978-3-319-32034-2_26

take the form of hyperrectangles in $\mathbb{R}^n$ [15]. With respect to instance-based classification [1], these generalizations increase the understanding of the data stored and the achievement of a substantial compression of the data, reducing the storage requirements. Considering rule induction [9], the ability of modeling decision surfaces by hybridizations between distance-based methods (Voronoi diagrams) and parallel axis separators could improve the performance of the models in domains with clusters of exemplars or exemplars strung out along a curve.

In this contribution, we propose NGE learning to monotonic classification tasks, aiming at increasing accuracy for this type of problem by means of generating monotone generalized examples to perform the classification rule. We compare our approach with other monotonic example-based learning models, such as monotonic k-NN [7], OLM [4] and OSDL [12]. The reason behind this choice is based upon the fact that these three methods are the most known models for instance-based learning in monotonic classification. The results show an improvement in accuracy whereas the number of examples stored in the final subset is further reduced.

The contribution is organized as follows. In Sect. 2 we present some background concepts: the ordinal classification with monotonic constraints and NGE learning. Section 3 is devoted to describing our proposal of NGE and its adaptation to satisfy the monotonicity constraints. Section 4 describes the experimental framework and examines the results obtained in the empirical study, and presents a discussion and analysis. Finally, Sect. 5 concludes the contribution.

2 Background

We will define the monotonic classification problem in Subsect. 2.1. The NGE classification will be described in Subsect. 2.2.

2.1 Monotonic Classification

Ordinal classification problems are those in which the class is neither numeric nor nominal. Instead, the class values are ordered. For instance, a worker can be described as "excellent", "good" or "bad", and a bond can be evaluated as "AAA", "AA", "A", "A-", etc. A monotonic classifier is one that will not violate monotonicity constraints. Informally, the monotonic classification implies that the assigned class values are monotonically non-decreasing (in ordinal order) with the attribute values. More formally, let $\{\mathbf{x}_i, \text{class}(\mathbf{x}_i)\}$ denote a set of examples with attribute vector $\mathbf{x}_i = (\mathbf{x}_{i,1}, \ldots, \mathbf{x}_{i,n})$ and a class, class$(\mathbf{x}_i)$, being m the number of instances and n the number of attributes. Let $\mathbf{x}_i \succeq \mathbf{x}_h$ if $\forall_{j=1,\ldots,n}, \mathbf{x}_{i,j} \geq \mathbf{x}_{h,j}$.

A data set $\{\mathbf{x}_i, \text{class}(\mathbf{x}_i)\}$ is monotonic if and only if all the pairs of examples i, h are monotonic with respect to each other [5] (see Eq. 1).

$$\mathbf{x}_i \succeq \mathbf{x}_h \implies \text{class}(\mathbf{x}_i) \geq \text{class}(\mathbf{x}_h), \forall_{i,h} \tag{1}$$

2.2   NGE Learning

NGE is a learning paradigm based on class exemplars, where an induced hypothesis has the graphical shape of a set of hyperrectangles in $\mathbb{R}^n$. Exemplars of classes are either hyperrectangles or single instances [14]. The input of an NGE system is a set of training examples, each described as a vector of pairs *numeric_attribute/value* and an associated class. Attributes can either be numerical or categorical. Numerical attributes are usually normalized in the $[0,1]$ interval.

In NGE, an initial set of hyperrectangles in $\mathbb{R}^n$ formed by single points directly taken from the data is generalized into a smaller set of hyperrectangles regarding the elements that it contains. Choosing which hyperrectangle is generalized from a subset of points or other hyperrectangles and how it is generalized depends on the concrete NGE algorithm employed.

The matching process is one of the central features in NGE learning and it allows some customization, if desired. Generally speaking, this process computes the distance between a new example and an exemplar memory object (a generalized example). Let the example to be classified be termed as x_0 and the generalized example as G, regardless of whether G is formed by a single point or a hyperrectangle if it has some volume.

The model computes a match score between x_0 and G by measuring the Euclidean distance between two objects. The Euclidean distance is well-known when G is a single point. Otherwise, the distance is computed as follows (considering numerical attributes):

$$D_{x_0 G} = \sqrt{\sum_{j=1}^{n} \left(\frac{\mathrm{dif}_j}{\max_j - \min_j} \right)^2} \qquad (2)$$

$$\mathrm{dif}_j = \begin{cases} x_{0,j} - \max(G_j) & \text{when } x_{0,j} > \max(G_j), \\ \min(G_j) - x_{0,j} & \text{when } x_{0,j} < \min(G_j), \\ 0 & \text{otherwise} \end{cases} \qquad (3)$$

where m is the number of attributes of the data, $x_{0,j}$ is the value of the jth attribute of the example x_0, $\max(G_j)$ and $\min(G_j)$ are the maximum and minimum values of G for the jth attribute and $\max_j$ and $\min_j$ are the maximum and minimum values for jth attribute in training data, respectively.

The distance measure represents the length of a line dropped perpendicularly from the point x_0 to the nearest surface, edge or corner of G. Note that internal points in a hyperrectangle have a distance of 0 to that rectangle. In the case of overlapping rectangles, several strategies could be implemented, but it is usually accepted that a point falling in the overlapping area belongs to the smaller rectangle (the size of a hyperrectangle is defined in terms of volume). The volume is computed following the indications given in [15]. In nominal attributes, the distance is 0 when two attributes have the same categorical label, and 1 on the contrary.

3   Monotonic Nested Generalized Exemplar Learning: MoNGEL

The method proposed in this contribution, named Monotonic Nested Generalized Exemplar Learning (MoNGEL), is thoroughly explained in this section. This method builds a model obtaining a set of rules which do not violate the monotonicity restrictions from the set of training instances trying to preserve as much as possible the behavior of the algorithms based on instances. First, in Sect. 3.1 we explain some definitions required to understand the proposed model, and after, in Sect. 3.2 we describe the phases of the building of the model.

3.1   Definitions

We represent each instance with $\mathbf{x}_i = (\mathbf{x}_{i,1}; \mathbf{x}_{i,2}; \ldots; \mathbf{x}_{i,n}; \text{class}(\mathbf{x}_i))$, where $\mathbf{x}_{i,j}$ is the input value of the instance i in the jth attribute, n is the total number of input attributes and $\text{class}(\mathbf{x}_i)$ is the class or output value of the instance i. Let the rules be denoted by $R : (\prod_j A_j; C)$, where A_j is a condition belonging to the antecedent and C is the response. A formal definition is given next:

$$
R : A_1 \times A_2 \times \cdots \times A_n \Rightarrow C, \tag{4}
$$
$$
\text{with } A_j = \begin{cases} [j_{\min}, j_{\max}] & \text{if numerical,} \\ \{\alpha, \beta, \ldots\} & \text{if nominal,} \end{cases}
$$
$$
C = \text{a value of the class,}
$$

where $j_{\min}$ and $j_{\max}$ are the minimum and maximum boundaries for the condition j respectively, and $\alpha, \beta, \ldots$ are the possible categorical values belonging to the domain of the jth attribute, if it is nominal.

The rules should not break monotonicity in the sense we saw in Subsect. 2.1. Hence, we define a partial order relation in the set of disjoint rules (where R and R' are disjoint if $\exists j, A_j \cap A'_j = \emptyset$), deciding when a condition is higher than, lower than or equal to another:

$$
A_j \preceq A'_j \text{ if } j\text{th attribute is numeric and } j_{\max} \leq j'_{\min} \tag{5}
$$
$$
\text{or if } j\text{th attribute is nominal and } A_j \subseteq A'_j,
$$
$$
A_j \succeq A'_j \text{ if } j\text{th attribute is numeric and } j_{\max} \geq j'_{\min}
$$
$$
\text{or if } j\text{th attribute is nominal and } A'_j \subseteq A_j,
$$
$$
A_j = A'_j \text{ if } j\text{th attribute is numeric and } j_{\min} = j'_{\min} \text{ and } j_{\max} = j'_{\max}
$$
$$
\text{or if } j\text{th attribute is nominal and } A_j \equiv A'_j.
$$

Then let two rules R and R' be defined as:

$$
R \preceq R' \text{ if } A_j \preceq A'_j \ \forall j \text{ and } \exists l, 1 \leq l \leq n, A_l < A'_l, \tag{6}
$$
$$
R = R' \text{ if } A_j = A'_j \ \forall j,
$$
$$
R \succeq R' \text{ if } A_j \succeq A'_j \ \forall j \text{ and } \exists l, 1 \leq l \leq n, A_l > A'_l.
$$

Two rules are comparable if $R \preceq R'$ or $R \succeq R'$, and non-comparable in contrary case, since we cannot establish an order between them. Hence, a rule $R : (\prod_j A_j, C)$ will be anti-monotonic with respect to another $R' : (\prod_j A'_j, C')$ if:

$$R \preceq R' \text{ and } C > C' \text{ or} \qquad (7)$$
$$R \succeq R' \text{ and } C < C' \text{ or}$$
$$R = R' \text{ and } C \neq C'.$$

The distance between an instance $\mathbf{x}_i$ and a rule R is defined as follows:

$$D_{\mathbf{x}_i R} = \sqrt{\sum_{j=1}^{n} \left(\frac{\mathrm{dis}_j}{\mathrm{Range}} \right)^2}, \qquad (8)$$

where dis_j and Range are defined differently depending on the type of the jth attribute. If the jth attribute is numeric:

$$\mathrm{Range} = \max_j - \min_j, \qquad (9)$$

$$\mathrm{dis}_j = \begin{cases} \mathbf{x}_{i,j} - j_{\max} & \text{if } \mathbf{x}_{i,j} > j_{\max}, \\ j_{\min} - \mathbf{x}_{i,j} & \text{if } \mathbf{x}_{i,j} < j_{\min}, \\ 0 & \text{otherwise.} \end{cases}$$

If the jth attribute is nominal:

$$\mathrm{dis}_j = \begin{cases} 0 & \mathbf{x}_{i,j} \in A_j, \\ 1 & \text{otherwise,} \end{cases} \qquad (10)$$
$$\mathrm{Range} = \text{Number of possible values of the } j\text{th attribute.}$$

where $\mathbf{x}_{i,j}$ is the value of the jth attribute of the instance i, $j_{\max}$ and $j_{\min}$ are the maximum and minimum values of the rule R in the jth attribute and $\max_j$ and $\min_j$ are the maximum and minimum values of the jth attribute in the data set.

The distance between two rules R and R' is defined as:

$$D_{RR'} = \sqrt{\sum_{j=1}^{n} \left(\frac{\mathrm{dis}_j}{\mathrm{Range}} \right)^2}, \qquad (11)$$

where dis_j and Range are defined as:

$$\mathrm{dis}_j = \left| \frac{j_{\max} + j_{\min}}{2} - \frac{j'_{\max} + j'_{\min}}{2} \right|, \qquad (12)$$
$$\mathrm{Range} = \max_j - \min_j,$$

if the jth attribute is numeric and

$$\mathrm{dis}_j = 1 - \frac{\#(A_j \cap A'_j)}{\#(A_j \cup A'_j)}, \qquad (13)$$

if the jth attribute is nominal. The geometrical interpretation of the distances is given next. The measured distance between an instance and a rule is equivalent to the length of a line dropped perpendicularly from the instance to the nearest surface, edge or corner of the rule. Furthermore, the measured distance between two rules is the real distance between the average points of each condition by considering numeric attributes (Eq. 12) and the dissimilarity between each condition by considering nominal attributes (Eq. 13).

3.2   Model Building

Our algorithm follows the steps of the batch operating form of NGE studied in [15]. In summary, firstly all the instances are transformed to zero-dimensional rules, formed by a single point, and are gathered to obtain an initial set of rules. Secondly, for every rule, the comparable rule of the same class and with minimum distance is searched for within the set of rules. Each rule is then iteratively generalized (or expanded) to cover the nearest rule until a non-comparable rule or a rule with a different class value is found. Finally, an anti-monotonic test is conducted aiming at removing those rules which are anti-monotonic to each other, trying to remove the smallest number of rules.

In the initialization phase of the rules set, all instances are transformed to rules of dimension zero (the limits of the numerical ranges are equal and nominal sets consist of a single value). Then, the rules are sorted by their class value in descending order to discern the subset of rules for each class. Finally, the repeated rules are removed from the rules set with the goal of ignoring the repeated examples from the training set. We can see this process in more detail in Algorithm 1.

Algorithm 1. Initialization phase

S, Set of Rules.
$S = \emptyset$.
For each instance $\mathbf{x}_i$ of the training set
    $\mathbf{x}_i$ is transformed to a rule R_i of dimension 0.
    $S = S \bigcup R_i$.
Sort the rules in S by its class value in descending order, obtaining the subset S_C for each class.
Remove the repeated rules in all S_C.

In the next phase, known as the generalization phase, all the rules are checked to find that which is comparable, has the same class value and has the minimum distance. If it exists, it will be replaced by a generalized rule which covers both, provided that the new generalized rule does not overlap with any existing rule of the same class. This process is then repeated until there is no possibility of generalizing anymore. This phase is sensitive to the order of presentation of instances, hence the algorithm incorporates a randomization process on the order of presentation of instances for each class. The procedure is depicted in Algorithm 2.

The *Generalize* procedure receives the rules $R : (\prod_j A_j, C)$ and $R' : (\prod_j A'_j, C)$ as input, and computes an output rule $R'' : (\prod_j A''_j, C)$ given by:

$$R'' : A''_1 \times A''_2 \times \cdots \times A''_n \Rightarrow C, \qquad (14)$$
$$\text{with } A''_j = \begin{cases} [\min(j_{\min}, j'_{\min}), \max(j_{\max}, j'_{\max})] & \text{if numerical,} \\ A_j \bigcup A'_j & \text{if nominal.} \end{cases}$$

Algorithm 2. Generalization phase

Repeat
    For each class C
        Randomize the order of presentation of rules for class
        For each rule $R_i \in S_C$
            Find the nearest rule $R'_i \in S_C$ such that it is comparable with R_i.
            If R'_i exists
                $R''_i = Generalize(R_i, R'_i)$.
                If for all $R_j \in S_C$, R_j and R''_i are disjoints
                    Delete R'_i.
                Replace R_i by R''_i.
Until no generalization is done.

Finally, in the last phase called removal of anti-monotonic rules, we construct a monotonicity violation matrix $N = n_{ip}$ where $n_{ip} = 1$ if the rule i is anti-monotonic with the rule p and $n_{ip} = 0$ if the rule i is not anti-monotonic with the rule p. It is worth mentioning that not to be anti-monotonic is not equal to being monotonic, because two rules could also not be comparable. Afterwards, we calculate the number of violations of each of the rules and register this value in a list $V = v_i$. Once we have computed v_i for all rules, we find the maximum value of the list V, $v_{\max}$, and remove the rule R_i that corresponds to $v_{\max}$. In case of a tie, the rule covering fewer instances is removed. In the case of a next tie in terms of number of instances, a random chosen rule is then removed. Afterwards, both the matrix N and the vector V is updated and the process is repeated until no violations of monotonicity are registered; that is, until $v_i = 0$, $\forall i$. The detailed procedure is illustrated in Algorithm 3.

Algorithm 3. Elimination of anti-monotonic rules

Construct the monotonicity violation matrix N, and the list V.
While i exists such that $v_i > 0$
    Obtain the row having the greatest number of monotonicity violations in V.
    In case of a tie, locate that row representing the rule which covers the smallest number of instances: p. If there are more than one row, choose one randomly.
    Remove the row p and column p in N.
    Update the list V according to N.

Once the set of rules is built, the classification is performed by computing the distance of the instance with all the rules stored. The nearest rule makes the decision of class by using its output value C. In case of a tie, or when two or more rules have a distance of zero to the instance to classify, choose the rule with smaller volume (according to the initial motivation of NGE learning which attempts to learn generalizations with exceptions [14]), which is calculated with the following formula:

$$V(R) = \prod_j L_j, \tag{15}$$

where L_j is computed for each condition as

$$L_j = \begin{cases} j_{\max} - j_{\min} & \text{if numerical and } j_{\max} \neq j_{\min}, \\ 1 & \text{if numerical and } j_{\max} = j_{\min}, \\ \frac{\#(A_j)}{|A_j|} & \text{if nominal,} \end{cases} \tag{16}$$

where $\#(A_j)$ is the number of categorical elements covered by the rule in the jth attribute and $|A_j|$ is the number of possible values of the jth attribute (equal to Range used previously).

4   Experimental Framework, Results and Analysis

This section exhibits the methodology used in the experimental study that compares our proposal with other monotonic learning approaches: OLM, OSDL and k-NN. We will show the configuration of the experiment: monotonic data sets and parameters for the algorithms used.

In this study, the classifiers are run over 21 data sets from the KEEL-data set and UCI repositories[1] [2,3], 4 classical ordinal classification data sets from [6][2] and another 3 from regression problems which were transformed into classification problems by discretizing the class value in [7][3], maintaining the same order. In the former 20 standard classification data sets, the class attribute is transformed into an ordinal attribute, assigning each category a number in such way that the number of pairs of non monotonic examples is minimized. The choice of parameters has been done according to the standards and recommendations given by the authors in the original proposal papers.

As performance metrics, we consider Accuracy, Mean Absolute Error (MAE) and the number of rules that form the models built by the algorithms.

4.1   Results and Analysis

This section shows the results obtained in the experimental study as well as the analysis based on them. Tables 1 and 2 report the results measured by accuracy and MAE in test data and the number of rules for each approach considered in this contribution, except for the OSDL algorithm. The best case in each data set is stressed in bold. The last row in each table shows the average considering all data sets.

At a glance, observing Tables 1 and 2 we can make the following analyses:

– The MoNGEL proposal yields the best average result in accuracy over test data. It is slightly more accurate than k-NN and much more accurate than OLM and OSDL.

---

[1] Australian, Automobile, Bands, Cleveland, Dermatology, Glass, Heart, Hepatitis, Housevotes, Ionosphere, Iris, Mammographic, Newthyroid, Pima, Saheart, Segment, Sonar, Titanic, Vowel, Wine, Wisconsin.
[2] ERA, ESL, LEV, SWD.
[3] Auto-mpg, Bostonhousing, MachineCPU.

Table 1. Accuracy and MAE reported by all algorithms in all data sets

Datasets	Accuracy								MAE							
	OLM		OSDL		KNN		MoNGEL		OLM		OSDL		KNN		MoNGEL	
	Ave	Std	Ave	Std	Ave	Std	Ave	Std	Ave	Std	Ave	Std	Ave	Std	Ave	Std
Australian	0.7232	0.0620	**0.8319**	0.0646	0.7043	0.0464	0.6797	0.1557	0.2768	0.0620	**0.1681**	0.0646	0.2957	0.0464	0.3203	0.1557
Auto-mpg4classes	0.6812	0.0571	0.3854	0.0553	**0.6859**	0.0571	0.6119	0.0661	**0.3879**	0.0797	0.8291	0.0741	0.3962	0.0741	0.5414	0.0906
Automobile	0.2333	0.1327	0.3758	0.1168	0.6921	0.0698	**0.8308**	0.0881	2.1046	0.4104	0.8958	0.2259	0.4783	0.1356	**0.2508**	0.1242
Bands	0.3807	0.0159	0.6274	0.0459	0.6439	0.0380	**0.6764**	0.0578	0.6193	0.0159	0.3726	0.0459	0.3561	0.0380	**0.3236**	0.0578
Bostonhousing4classes	0.3003	0.0247	0.2569	0.0111	**0.5616**	0.0709	0.5019	0.0608	1.3045	0.0773	1.0099	0.0332	**0.6238**	0.1182	0.8261	0.0943
Cleveland	**0.5793**	0.0490	0.5421	0.0604	0.5595	0.0622	0.5353	0.0830	0.8311	0.1243	0.7848	0.1361	**0.6823**	0.1174	0.8159	0.1873
Dermatology	0.4499	0.0474	0.1593	0.0544	0.8073	0.0487	**0.8128**	0.0559	1.3821	0.1193	1.6421	0.1372	0.4665	0.1297	**0.3858**	0.1313
Era	**1.0000**	0.0000	**1.0000**	0.0000	**1.0000**	0.0000	**1.0000**	0.0000	**0.0000**	0.0000	**0.0000**	0.0000	**0.0000**	0.0000	**0.0000**	0.0000
Esl	0.9179	0.0228	0.9364	0.0324	**0.9384**	0.0402	0.9365	0.0322	0.0923	0.0284	**0.0656**	0.0341	0.0719	0.0492	0.0738	0.0411
Glass	0.3175	0.0243	0.3223	0.0222	**0.6732**	0.0877	0.6686	0.0805	1.7994	0.0461	1.8000	0.1764	**0.6409**	0.2160	0.6435	0.1382
Heart	0.6704	0.0767	0.6259	0.0672	0.7296	0.0952	**0.7667**	0.0938	0.3296	0.0767	0.3741	0.0672	0.2704	0.0952	**0.2333**	0.0938
Hepatitis	0.2375	0.0875	0.8000	0.0612	0.8000	0.1392	**0.8125**	0.1008	0.7625	0.0875	0.2000	0.0612	0.2000	0.1392	**0.1875**	0.1008
Housevotes	0.9047	0.0696	0.9096	0.0450	**0.9486**	0.0420	0.9005	0.0519	0.0953	0.0696	0.0904	0.0450	**0.0514**	0.0420	0.0995	0.0519
Ionosphere	0.6580	0.0346	0.7237	0.0921	0.7603	0.0784	**0.7917**	0.0760	0.3420	0.0346	0.2763	0.0921	0.2397	0.0784	**0.2083**	0.0760
Iris	0.9000	0.0447	0.3733	0.0442	**0.9867**	0.0267	0.9533	0.0521	0.1000	0.0447	0.9067	0.1200	**0.0133**	0.0267	0.0467	0.0521
Lev	**1.0000**	0.0000	**1.0000**	0.0000	**1.0000**	0.0000	**1.0000**	0.0000	**0.0000**	0.0000	**0.0000**	0.0000	**0.0000**	0.0000	**0.0000**	0.0000
Machinecpu4classes	0.6267	0.0877	0.6362	0.1031	**0.6893**	0.1222	0.6562	0.1263	0.5031	0.1279	0.4067	0.1226	**0.4062**	0.1698	0.5107	0.2137
Mammographic	**0.9892**	0.0114	0.9831	0.0154	0.9843	0.0143	0.9855	0.0072	**0.0108**	0.0114	0.0169	0.0154	0.0157	0.0143	**0.0145**	0.0072
Newthyroid	0.6223	0.0751	0.1818	0.0403	0.8002	0.0586	**0.8271**	0.0534	0.5504	0.1367	0.8413	0.0638	0.2879	0.0669	**0.2476**	0.0829
Pima	0.8151	0.0403	0.6224	0.0147	**0.8515**	0.0253	0.8321	0.0343	0.1849	0.0403	0.3776	0.0147	**0.1485**	0.0253	0.1679	0.0343
Saheart	0.6862	0.0322	0.6839	0.0862	0.6905	0.0637	**0.6950**	0.0548	0.3138	0.0322	0.3161	0.0862	0.3095	0.0637	**0.3050**	0.0548
Segment	0.3061	0.0176	0.1684	0.0060	0.9645	0.0102	**0.9710**	0.0061	2.4022	0.0576	2.8597	0.1965	0.0684	0.0164	**0.0515**	0.0096
Sonar	0.4662	0.0162	0.5724	0.0764	0.8267	0.0687	**0.8645**	0.0842	0.5338	0.0162	0.4276	0.0764	0.1733	0.0687	**0.1355**	0.0842
Swd	**1.0000**	0.0000	**1.0000**	0.0000	**1.0000**	0.0000	**1.0000**	0.0000	**0.0000**	0.0000	**0.0000**	0.0000	**0.0000**	0.0000	**0.0000**	0.0000
Titanic	**1.0000**	0.0000	**1.0000**	0.0000	**1.0000**	0.0000	0.9949	0.0068	**0.0000**	0.0000	**0.0000**	0.0000	**0.0000**	0.0000	**0.0000**	0.0000
Vowel	0.0909	0.0072	0.0859	0.0081	0.9788	0.0071	0.7301	0.1024	5.0000	0.0000	4.8273	0.2312	0.0444	0.0240	**0.0101**	0.0156
Wine	0.3484	0.0341	0.3314	0.0284	0.8088	0.0798	**0.9796**	0.0227	0.9660	0.0734	0.9667	0.0759	**0.2696**	0.1210	0.3369	0.1401
Wisconsin	0.8815	0.0412	0.9547	0.0188	0.9781	0.0198	0.9796	0.0227	0.1185	0.0412	0.0453	0.0188	0.0219	0.0198	**0.0204**	0.0227
Average	0.6352	0.0397	0.6104	0.0418	**0.8237**	0.0490	0.8220	0.0555	0.7504	0.0648	0.7322	0.0791	**0.2333**	0.0687	0.2413	0.0736

Table 2. Number of rules reported by all algorithms in all data sets

	Number of Rules					
	OLM		KNN		MoNGEL	
Datasets	Ave	Std	Ave	Std	Ave	Std
Australian	**2.1**	0.30	621	0.00	47.9	3.33
Auto-mpg4classes	**160**	5.92	352	0.00	243.9	3.27
Automobile	**113.3**	2.19	143	0.00	120.2	2.27
Bands	**323.6**	1.20	328	0.00	324.4	1.02
Bostonhousing4classes	**418**	3.71	455	0.00	433.7	1.95
Cleveland	**199**	2.83	267	0.00	230.8	1.78
Dermatology	**276.1**	3.08	322	0.00	289.5	2.01
Era	**33**	0.00	900	0.00	34	0.00
Esl	**49.9**	1.58	439	0.00	83	1.90
Glass	**190**	0.89	192	0.00	190	0.89
Heart	**159.7**	4.78	243	0.00	199.8	1.66
Hepatitis	**66.1**	0.83	72	0.00	67.8	0.60
Housevotes	**38.1**	3.88	208	0.00	146.5	2.58
Ionosphere	**265.7**	4.73	315	0.00	287.5	2.01
Iris	**18.6**	1.02	135	0.00	48.2	1.78
Lev	**33.4**	0.00	900	0.00	52.7	0.46
Machinecpu4classes	**93**	2.19	188	0.00	113.7	1.85
Mammographic	**21**	1.10	747	0.00	87.6	2.87
Newthyroid	**90.5**	2.38	193	0.00	122.3	2.00
Pima	**190.1**	7.78	691	0.00	472.8	4.38
Saheart	**226**	6.59	415	0.00	313.9	3.53
Segment	**1861.6**	4.29	2079	0.00	1868.5	3.96
Sonar	187.2	0.40	**187**	0.00	187.2	0.40
Swd	**62**	0.00	900	0.00	82.9	0.70
Titanic	**2**	0.00	1980	0.00	3	0.00
Vowel	**891**	0.00	**891**	0.00	**891**	0.00
Wine	**146.1**	2.17	160	0.00	151	1.10
Wisconsin	**72.4**	5.00	614	0.00	201.9	2.74
Average	**221.1**	2.5	533.8	0.00	260.6	1.8

- The k-NN proposal gets the best average result in MAE over test data. MoN-GEL obtains a very close result to k-NN, but it is clearly better than OLM and OSDL.
- The OLM proposal achieves the best average result in the number of rules over test data. However, MoNGEL is very close to OLM in this aspect and much better than k-NN and OSDL, which use the whole training set to classify.

Table 3. Wilcoxon test report

Algorithm	Accuracy	MAE	Number of rules
OLM	+(0.000)	+(0.000)	=(1)
OSDL	+(0.000)	+(0.001)	—
k-NN	=(1)	=(1)	+(0.000)

Table 4. Rankings obtained by the Friedman test

Algorithm	Accuracy	MAE	Number of rules
OLM	3.0357	3.1071	**1.0893**
OSDL	3.2321	3.0536	—
k-NN	**1.8393**	**1.875**	2.9286
MonGEL	1.8929	1.9643	1.9821

Table 3 collects the results of applying the Wilcoxon test to MoNGEL and the rest of the methods studied in this contribution. In each one of the cells, three symbols can appear: +, = or −. They represent either that MoNGEL outperforms (+), is similar to (=) or is worse (−) in performance than the rest of the methods. The value in brackets is the p-value obtained in the comparison. Other statistical studies can be performed by using non-parametric multiple comparison tests. These types of procedures study the set of results obtained by all the algorithms to compute a ranking that takes into account the multiple comparison. The smaller the ranking, the better the algorithm is. Rankings of the Friedman test are depicted in Table 4.

According to the statistical tests, MoNGEL is the best approach compared with the other techniques, except in the number of rules where OLM is the best. Also, our algorithm significantly outperforms OLM and OSDL in accuracy and MAE. No differences are reported when comparing it with k-NN.

5   Concluding Remarks

The goal of this contribution was to present a proposal of an algorithm for nested generalized exemplar learning for classification with monotonicity constraints named Monotonic Nested Generalized Exemplar Learning (MoNGEL). It creates an initial set of rules from the training data and then it performs a generalization process focused on maximizing the accuracy while minimizing the number of instances retained and conserving the anti-monotonic index. The results showed that MoNGEL allows us to obtain very precise models with few rules. We have compared it with well-known monotonic learning approaches and the effectiveness of our approach is very competitive.

As future work, we are interested in the application of NGE learning to large monotonic data sets by considering data with a large number of instances and attributes. We will adopt different schemes for optimizing the selection and/or positioning of hyperrectangles in $\mathbb{R}^n$, including real-coding evolutionary algorithms such as differential evolution algorithms.

Acknowledgments. This work was partially supported by the Spanish Ministry of Science and Technology under project TIN2014-57251-P and the Andalusian Research Plans P11-TIC-7765, P10-TIC-6858.

References

1. Aha, D.W. (ed.): Lazy Learning. Springer, Heidelberg (1997)
2. Alcala-Fdez, J., Fernández, A., Luengo, J., Derrac, J., García, S., Sánchez, L., Herrera, F.: KEEL data-mining software tool: data set repository, integration of algorithms and experimental analysis framework. J. Multiple-Valued Logic Soft Comput. **17**(2–3), 255–287 (2011)
3. Bache, K., Lichman, M.: UCI machine learning repository (2013). http://archive. ics.uci.edu/ml
4. Ben-David, A.: Automatic generation of symbolic multiattribute ordinal knowledge-based dsss: methodology and applications. Decis. Sci. **23**, 1357–1372 (1992)
5. Ben-David, A.: Monotonicity maintenance in information-theoretic machine learning algorithms. Mach. Learn. **19**(1), 29–43 (1995)
6. Ben-David, A., Sterling, L., Pao, Y.H.: Learning, classification of monotonic ordinal concepts. Comput. Intell. **5**, 45–49 (1989)
7. Duivesteijn, W., Feelders, A.: Nearest neighbour classification with monotonicity constraints. In: Daelemans, W., Goethals, B., Morik, K. (eds.) ECML PKDD 2008, Part I. LNCS (LNAI), vol. 5211, pp. 301–316. Springer, Heidelberg (2008)
8. Fernández-Navarro, F., Riccardi, A., Carloni, S.: Ordinal neural networks without iterative tuning. IEEE Trans. Neural Netw. Learn. Syst. **25**(11), 2075–2085 (2014)
9. Fürnkranz, J.: Separate-and-conquer rule learning. Artif. Intell. Rev. **13**, 3–54 (1999)
10. Han, J., Kamber, M.: Data Mining: Concepts and Techniques. Morgan Kaufmann Publishers Inc., Burlington (2011)
11. Hu, Q., Che, X., Zhang, L., Zhang, D., Guo, M., Yu, D.: Rank entropy-based decision trees for monotonic classification. IEEE Trans. Knowl. Data Eng. **24**(11), 2052–2064 (2012)
12. Lievens, S., Baets, B.D., Cao-Van, K.: A probabilistic framework for the design of instance-based supervised ranking algorithms in an ordinal setting. Ann. Oper. Res. **163**(1), 115–142 (2008)
13. Potharst, R., Feelders, A.J.: Classification trees for problems with monotonicity constraints. SIGKDD Explor. **4**(1), 1–10 (2002)
14. Salzberg, S.: A nearest hyperrectangle learning method. Mach. Learn. **6**(3), 251–276 (1991)
15. Wettschereck, D., Dietterich, T.G.: An experimental comparison of the nearest-neighbor and nearest-hyperrectangle algorithms. Mach. Learn. **19**(1), 5–27 (1995)

Knowledge Modeling by ELM in RL
for SRHT Problem

Jose Manuel Lopez-Guede$^{(\boxtimes)}$, Asier Garmendia, and Manuel Graña

Computational Intelligence Group,
Basque Country University (UPV/EHU), Leioa, Spain
jm.lopez@ehu.es

Abstract. Single Robot Hose Transport (SRHT) is a limit case of
Linked Multicomponent Robotic Systems (L-MCRS), when one robot
moves the tip of a hose to a desired position, while the other hose
extreme is attached to a source position. Reinforcement Learning (RL)
algorithms have been applied to learn autonomously the robot control
with success. However, RL algorithms produce large and intractable data
structures. This paper addresses the problem by learning an Extreme
Learning Machine (ELM) from the state-action value Q-table, obtaining
very relevant data reduction. In this paper we evaluate empirically a classification strategy to formulate ELM learning to provide approximations
to the Q-table, obtaining very promising results.

1 Introduction

Linked Multi-Component Robotic Systems (L-MCRS) [1] are composed of a collection of autonomous robots linked by a non-rigid uni-dimensional link introducing additional non-linearities. The final objective in this field is to design the
control of L-MCRS to achieve desired behaviors by autonomous learning.

Single Robot Hose Transport (SRHT) is a paradigmatic trasportation task
example of the transportation of a hose by one robot in its simplest form. The
task to be accomplished by the robot is to bring the tip of the hose to an arbitrarily designated destination point. We have worked on this paradigmatic task
[2–4] achieving that the robot learns autonomously how to solve the control task
by means of Reinforcement Learning (RL) [5] algorithms. These approaches are
derived from the Q-Learning [6] and TRQ-Learning [7] algorithms. The size of
the resulting structres of this learning process (Q-tables) grows exponentially
with several factors. For practical applications, a compact functional representation of Q-tables is desired.

This paper tackle this problem by learning approximations to the maps
encoded by those large size Q-tables using Extreme Learning Machines (ELM).
The data for training and testing consists in the Q-table entries, so the ELM is
desired to predict the actual action that would be selected by the optimal policy
according to the given Q-table.

The structure of the paper is as follows. Section 2 reviews the some methods
involved in the present work. Section 3 introduces the hose control problem and

© Springer International Publishing Switzerland 2016
F. Martínez-Álvarez et al. (Eds.): HAIS 2016, LNAI 9648, pp. 323–331, 2016.
DOI: 10.1007/978-3-319-32034-2_27

states the related problem of data structures size. Section 4 describes tested approacheto build an approximations to the Q-table by ELM learning. The experimental design is described in Sect. 5, while Sect. 6 discusses the results. Finally, Sect. 7 gives our conclusions.

2 Background

2.1 Reinforcement Learning

Reinforcement Learning [5] is a class of learning algorithms which assumes that the environment-agent system can be modeled as a discrete time stochastic process formalized as a Markov Decision Process (MDP) [8,9].

Markov Decision Process (MDP). A Markov Decision Process (MDP) is defined by the tuple $< S, A, T, R >$, where S is the state space, A the action repertoire, specifically A_s are the actions allowed in state $s \in S$, $T : S \times A_s \times S \to \mathbb{R}$ is the probabilistic state transition function, and $R : S \times A_s \to \mathbb{R}$ is the immediate reward function. A policy $\pi : S \to A_s$ is the probabilistic decision of the action $a \in A_s$ to be taken in state $s \in S$. Reinforcement Learning procedures looks for optimal action selection policies maximizing the total reward received by the agent.

Algorithm 1. TRQ-Learning algorithm

Input: empty structures $T(s,a)$, $R(s,a)$, $Q(s,a)$
Output:
-$T(s,a)$: containing the transitions of the system
-$R(s,a)$: containing the reward function of the system
-$Q(s,a)$: containing the optimal policy
Initialize $Q(s,a)$ with arbitrary random values
Initialize $T(s,a) = \emptyset$, $R(s,a) = 0$, $\forall s \in S$, $\forall a \in A$
Repeat (for each episode):
  Initialize s
  Repeat (for each step of episode):
    Choose a from s using policy derived from Q
    if $T(s,a) \neq \emptyset$
      $s' \leftarrow T(s,a)$
      $r \leftarrow R(s,a)$
    else
      Take action a, observe reward r and new state s'
      $T(s,a) \leftarrow s'$
      $R(s,a) \leftarrow r$
    $Q(s,a) \leftarrow Q(s,a) + \alpha \left[r + \gamma \max_a Q(s',a) - Q(s,a) \right]$
    $s \leftarrow s'$
  until s is terminal

Q-Learning. Q-Learning [10] is an unsupervised model free Reinforcement Learning algorithm that learns the optimal policy in environments specified by Finite MDP (S and A are finite sets). The main idea of the algorithm is to fill a look-up table $Q(s, a)$ of dimensions $|S| \times |A|$, which is initialized arbitrarily.

It has been proved [11] that, for a discrete FMDP environment, the Q-Learning algorithm converges with probability one to the optimal policy if α decrease complies with the stochastic gradient convergence conditions and if all actions are infinitely sampled in all states.

TRQ-Learning. TRQ-Learning [7] is an algorithm derived from Q-Learning which performs an ad-hoc model learning, i.e., besides learning the optimal policy to solve the proposed task, it also learns the response of the environment to the agent's actions. Its update rule is similar to the Q-Learning's rule, but it involves additional data structures $T(s, a)$ and $R(s, a)$ storing the learned transition and the reward functions, respectively, as specified in Algorithm 1. TRQ-Learning is faster than Q-Learning, and it is also more successful [7], because the agent learns the environment's response to its actions by means of its transition and reward functions.

2.2   Extreme Learning Machines

Extreme Learning Machines (ELMs) [12,13] are classified as Single-Hidden Layer Feedforward Networks (SLFNs). They can be trained without iterative tuning, which confers them several interesting characteristics compared to classical back-propagation algorithm: they are easy to use, they require minimal human intervention, they have a faster learning speed and a higher generalization performance, and they are suitable for several nonlinear activation functions.

3   Statement of the Problem

In previous sections we stated that we have solved the autonomous learning of the L-MCRS using the TRQ-Learning algorithm. We have used different state models and different spatial discretization steps in our RL processes, obtaining different Q-tables. Our instance of L-MCRS working space is a square of $4\,m^2$ and to build the state space representation, we have used two spatial discretization steps per axis: $0,5\,m$ and $0,2\,m$. Table 1 contains the specification of the state models, spatial discretization steps and size of state space, which is the number of rows in the learned Q-table. The agent's perception of states in model $X^{(a)}$ is less complex than in model $X^{(b)}$, and so on. The description of the individual components of the state variables of Table 1 are in Table 2.

However, a new problem arises once the agent has learned autonomously the Q-table encoding the state-action value function to solve the task, because it needs to store it for actual robot operation. The size of the Q-table depends mainly on the cardinality of the set S (denoted $|S|$), which in its turn depends on the state model that is not unique. More complex models give better results with

Table 1. Different state models used in the MDP specification

State model	Discretization	$|S|$
$X^{(a)} = \{\mathbf{p}_r, \mathbf{p}_g, i\}$	$0, 5\,m$	512
	$0, 2\,m$	20,000
$X^{(b)} = \{\mathbf{p}_r, \mathbf{p}_g, i, \mathbf{p}_1, \mathbf{p}_2\}$	$0, 5\,m$	131,072
$X^{(c)} = \{\mathbf{p}_r, \mathbf{p}_g, i, \mathbf{v}_r\}$	$0, 5\,m$	8,192
$X^{(d)} = \{\mathbf{p}_r, \mathbf{p}_g, i, c, \mathbf{v}_r\}$	$0, 5\,m$	16,384

Table 2. Description of the state variables (and their components) composing several state models

Variable	Comp.	Type	Description
$\mathbf{p}_r$	x_r	Discretized	x coordinate of the robot's position $\mathbf{p}_r$
	y_r	Discretized	y coordinate of the robot's position $\mathbf{p}_r$
$\mathbf{p}_g$	x_g	Discretized	x coordinate of the goal's position $\mathbf{p}_g$
	y_g	Discretized	y coordinate of the goal's position $\mathbf{p}_g$
i		Binary	set if the line $\overline{\mathbf{p}_r\mathbf{p}_g}$ intersects the linking element of the L-MCRS
c		Binary	set if the box with corners $\mathbf{p}_r$ and $\mathbf{p}_g$ intersects the linking element of the L-MCRS
$\mathbf{p}_1$	$\mathbf{p}_{1_x}$	Discretized	x coordinate position of a point of the hose
	$\mathbf{p}_{1_y}$	Discretized	y coordinate position of a point of the hose
$\mathbf{p}_2$	$\mathbf{p}_{2_x}$	Discretized	x coordinate position of a point of the hose
	$\mathbf{p}_{2_y}$	Discretized	y coordinate position of a point of the hose
$\mathbf{v}_r$	v_N	Binary	set to 1 if collision after performing the *North* action is predicted
	v_S	Binary	set to 1 if collision after performing the *South* action is predicted
	v_E	Binary	set to 1 if collision after performing the *East* action is predicted
	v_W	Binary	set to 1 if collision after performing the *West* action is predicted

large Q-tables. Besides the variables of the system state, the spatial discretization step used in those variables is very important because it has a great impact in $|S|$. We can assume that the learned Q-table is a tabular encoding of the state-action value function. To deal with the problem of large size of the Q-table we have considered to train an artificial neural network [14–16] fitting it to obtain a compact representation of the knowledge contained the Q-table.

4   Q-Table Learning by ELMs

The approximation of the Q-table by means of an ELM consists in using the Q-table entries as the data for training and testing of the ELM, therefore the obtained ELM is a functional approximation of the Q-table. Q-tables have as many rows as states reached during the RL training process (n states), and as many columns as actions that can be executed by the agent (m actions). In our application, n depends on the one state model that has been used (see Table 1 for a estimation of $n = |S|$ in each case), and the number of actions is always $m = 4$ ($A = \{North, South, East, West\}$, i.e., the available movements of the robot).

We have modeled the task of learning a Q-table as a classification task: given a particular state of the system, the ELM must learn the maximum value action in that state according to the information contained in the Q-table. Thus we have a multi-label classification problem, where the set S of states is partitioned in four classes and each class is a subsets of S containing all the states whose best action is the same.

5   Experimental Setup

We have used the four different state models that are in Table 1. For the first state model, two different discretization steps have been used ($0, 5\,m$ and $0, 2\,m$), while with the remaining state models only a discretization step of $0, 5\,m$ has been used. For each combination of state model and discretization step, we started from the original Q-table as generated by the learning process carried out with TRQ-Learning algorithm. Then we perform random selection of the 75 % of the table entries as the train set and the remaining 25 % as the test set. We also have considered normalizing the input attributes of the train and the test sets into the range $[-1, 1]$. So, we have two versions of each training and testing dataset: raw unnormalized and normalized datasets. Besides, for each one of these two versions we have generated several subversions by the addition of noise to each input attribute based on uniformly distributed pseudo-random numbers in the range $r \in [-1, 1]$ and weighted by a parameter $noisew \in [0, 100]$, as indicated in the Eq. (1):

$$attribute \leftarrow attribute.\{1 + [noisew \cdot (2r - 1)]\} \qquad (1)$$

We have used values of $noisew \in \{0, 1, 5, 10, 20\}$. This combination of parameters means that we have 10 different training and testing datasets for each combination of state model and discretization step.

Finally, regarding the ELM networks, they have a typical structure. The used activation function in the hidden nodes are sigmoidal, sine, hardlim, triangular basis function and radial basis function. We have used a number of values of hidden nodes, more specifically we have used logarithmically equally spaced integer values between 1 and 1000, giving 43 different values. For all the resulting combinations of number of nodes and activation function, we have executed 10 trials and we have measured individual and mean values.

6   Experimental Results

The accuracy results of this approximation are given in Tables 3 and 4, for different state models.

Table 3. Accuracy results for classification learning of the Q-tables obtained with the model state $X^{(a)}$

Step	Norm	Noise	Classification accuracy
0.5	No	0	0,61
"	"	1	0,57
"	"	5	0,60
"	"	10	0,60
"	"	20	0,57
"	Yes	0	0,60
"	"	1	0,60
"	"	5	0,53
"	"	10	0,59
"	"	20	0,53
0.2	No	0	0,72
"	"	1	0,71
"	"	5	0,70
"	"	10	0,70
"	"	20	0,70
"	Yes	0	0,71
"	"	1	0,72
"	"	5	0,70
"	"	10	0,71
"	v	20	0,70

The best accuracy is 72 %, however, there is a great advantage in using ELMs because the space saving is significant. In Table 5 we can see the space requirements to store the original Q-table for each combination of state model and discretization step, while Table 6 contains the space requirements to store the ELM that has been tested more in detail. For the case of $X^{(d)} = \{\mathbf{p}_r, \mathbf{p}_g, i, c, \mathbf{v}_r\}$ and *discretization step* $= 0, 5\,m$, the space saving is 99, 18 %, i.e., only the 0, 82 % of the original space is needed.

Table 4. Accuracy results for Classification learning of the Q-tables obtained with the model state $X^{(b)}$, $X^{(c)}$, $X^{(d)}$ and the discretization step of $0,50\,m$

State	Norm	Noise	Classification accuracy
$X^{(3)}$	No	0	0,65
"	"	1	0,66
"	"	5	0,65
"	"	10	0,64
"	"	20	0,65
"	Yes	0	0,64
"	"	1	0,66
"	"	5	0,66
"	"	10	0,64
"	"	20	0,61
$X^{(4)}$	No	0	0,67
"	"	1	0,67
"	"	5	0,70
"	"	10	0,68
"	"	20	0,65
"	Yes	0	0,66
"	"	1	0,68
"	"	5	0,66
"	"	10	0,65
"	"	20	0,66
$X^{(5)}$	No	0	0,69
"	"	1	0,69
"	"	5	0,65
"	"	10	0,69
"	"	20	0,68
"	Yes	0	0,66
"	"	1	0,68
"	"	5	0,66
"	"	10	0,66
"	"	20	0,65

Table 5. Different state models, their maximum success ratios and the Q-table required storage size measured in Kbytes.

State model	Discretization	Q size
$X^{(a)}$	$0,5\,m$	424
	$0,2\,m$	15.213
$X^{(b)}$	$0,5\,m$	7.575
$X^{(c)}$	$0,5\,m$	3.133
$X^{(d)}$	$0,5\,m$	4.777

Table 6. Space requirements of the best ELM learning the Q-table as a classification problem $\left(X^{(d)}\right)$.

	Matrix	*Size*	*KB*
$X^{(d)} = \{\mathbf{p}_r,\ \mathbf{p}_g,\ i,\ c,\ \mathbf{v}_r\}\,0,5\,m$	Bias hidden	282×1	2
	Input weight	282×10	22
	Output weight	282×4	9
	Total		39

7   Conclusions

In this paper we have addressed one practical problem when Linked Multi-Component Robotic Systems (L-MCRS) learn autonomously complex behaviors through Reinforcement Learning: the large size of the data structures needed to contain the learned Q-tables. We have given a short background on Markov Decision Processes, Reinforcement Learning (more specifically on Q-Learning and TRQ-Learning algorithms) and Extreme Learning Machines. We have explained the specific problem of autonomous learning in L-MCRS with RL algorithms: the large size of the data structures which contains the knowledge. To deal with this problem, we have proposed to compute their approximation using ELMs. Promising results were obtained because classification accuracy reached the 72 %, and the space savings to store the Q-table knowledge have reached more than the 99 %.

Acknowledgements. The research was supported by the Computational Intelligence Group, funded by the Basque Government with grant IT874-13.

References

1. Duro, R., Graña, M., de Lope, J.: On the potential contributions of hybrid intelligent approaches to multicomponen robotic system development. Inf. Sci. **180**(14), 2635–2648 (2010)

2. López-Guede, J.M., Graña, M., Zulueta, E.: On distributed cooperative control for the manipulation of a hose by a multirobot system. In: Corchado, E., Abraham, A., Pedrycz, W. (eds.) HAIS 2008. LNCS (LNAI), vol. 5271, pp. 673–679. Springer, Heidelberg (2008)

3. Fernandez-Gauna, B., Lopez-Guede, J., Zulueta, E., Graña, M.: Learning hose transport control with Q-Learning. Neural Netw. World **20**(7), 913–923 (2010)

4. Fernandez-Gauna, B., Lopez-Guede, J.M., Zulueta, E., Echegoyen, Z., Graña, M.: Basic results and experiments on robotic multi-agent system for hose deployment and transportation. Int. J. Artif. Intell. **6**(S11), 183–202 (2011)

5. Sutton, R., Barto, A.: Reinforcement Learning: An Introduction. MIT Press, Cambridge (1998)

6. Watkins, C., Dayan, P.: Q-Learning. Mach. Learn. **8**(3–4), 279–292 (1992)

7. Lopez-Guede, J.M., Fernandez-Gauna, B., Graña, M., Zulueta, E.: Improving the control of single robot hose transport. Cybern. Syst. **43**(4), 261–275 (2012)

8. Bellman, R.: A Markovian decision process. Indiana Univ. Math. J. **6**, 679–684 (1957)

9. Tijms, H.: Discrete Time Markov Decision Processes, pp. 233–277. Wiley, Hoboken (2004)

10. Watkins, C.: Learning from delayed rewards. In: Ph.D. dissertation, University of Cambridge, England (1989)

11. Watkins, C., Dayan, P.: Technical note: Q-Learning. Mach. Learn. **8**, 279–292 (1992)

12. Huang, D.H.W.G.-B., Lan, Y.: Extreme learning machines: a survey. Int. J. Mach. Learn. Cybern. **2**(2), 107–122 (2011)

13. Huang, G.-B., Zhu, Q.-Y., Siew, C.-K.: Extreme learning machine: theory and applications. Neurocomputing **70**(1–3), 489–501 (2006)

14. Widrow, B., Lehr, M.: 30 years of adaptive neural networks: perceptron, madaline, and backpropagation. Proc. IEEE **78**(9), 1415–1442 (1990)

15. Lopez-Guede, J.M., Graña, M., Zulueta, E., Barambones, O.: Economical implementation of control loops for multi-robot systems. In: Köppen, M., Kasabov, N., Coghill, G. (eds.) ICONIP 2008, Part I. LNCS, vol. 5506, pp. 1053–1059. Springer, Heidelberg (2009). Revised Selected Papers, Part I

16. Lopez-Guede, J.M., Fernandez-Gauna, B., Graña, M., Zulueta, E.: Multi-robot systems control implementation. In: Robot Learning, pp. 137–150. SCIYO (2010)

Can Metalearning Be Applied to Transfer on Heterogeneous Datasets?

Catarina Félix[1,2(✉)], Carlos Soares[1,3], and Alípio Jorge[2,4]

[1] INESC TEC, Porto, Portugal
cfo@inescporto.pt
[2] Faculdade de Ciências da Universidade do Porto, Porto, Portugal
amjorge@fc.up.pt
[3] Faculdade de Engenharia da Universidade do Porto, Porto, Portugal
csoares@fe.up.pt
[4] LIAAD-INESC TEC, Porto, Portugal

Abstract. Machine learning processes consist in collecting data, obtaining a model and applying it to a given task. Given a new task, the standard approach is to restart the learning process and obtain a new model. However, previous learning experience can be exploited to assist the new learning process. The two most studied approaches for this are metalearning and transfer learning. Metalearning can be used for selecting the predictive model to use on a new dataset. Transfer learning allows the reuse of knowledge from previous tasks. However, when multiple heterogeneous tasks are available as potential sources for transfer, the question is which one to use. One approach to address this problem is metalearning. In this paper we investigate the feasibility of this approach. We propose a method to transfer weights from a source trained neural network to initialize a network that models a potentially very different target dataset. Our experiments with 14 datasets indicate that this method enables faster convergence without significant difference in accuracy provided that the source task is adequately chosen. This means that there is potential for applying metalearning to support transfer between heterogeneous datasets.

1 Introduction

Machine learning processes consist of (1) collecting training data for the new task; (2) obtaining a model; (3) applying the model to new data. This is done even when the new task is related to previously solved tasks, for example, when there are relationships between variables or between the processes used to obtain the models.

There are two approaches to using previous learning experience in new tasks: metalearning and transfer learning. Both use information about a domain to learn efficiently and effectively in a new one. Metalearning typically focuses on the choice of a learning algorithm while transfer learning tries to reuse the models obtained from previous tasks. This suggests that transfer learning and metalearning may be used together.

© Springer International Publishing Switzerland 2016
F. Martínez-Álvarez et al. (Eds.): HAIS 2016, LNAI 9648, pp. 332–343, 2016.
DOI: 10.1007/978-3-319-32034-2_28

Our ultimate aim is to investigate if metalearning can be used to support transfer learning in tasks consisting of heterogeneous data, reducing computational cost without loss in predictive performance and, eventually, cutting down the time data scientists need to invest in the process.

The method for using metalearning to support transfer learning is illustrated id Fig. 1 and has three steps:

1. **Source selection step:** finding the best source problem for approaching our new target problem;
2. **Transfer step:** adapting the source model and use some of its components (or characteristics) in the target model;
3. **Learning step:** training the target model (adapted from the source model) on the target data.

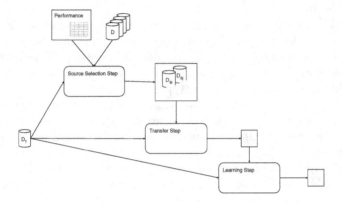

Fig. 1. Method for using metalearning

In this paper we propose a method for the transfer step. We show that if we find a good solution for the meta step, the transfer step can improve the learning speed, even with very simple methods. Future work is to develop a process for the meta step.

2   Metalearning and Transfer Learning

This section presents the basic concepts related with our work. First we describe metalearning, some of its methods and examples of use. After that, we present transfer learning, its motivation, operation mode and some techniques used. Finally, we describe some examples of the combination of metalearning and transfer learning.

2.1   Metalearning

Metalearning is typically used for algorithm recommendation: helping in the process of selecting a predictive algorithm to use on a new dataset. It also aims at taking advantage of the repetitive use of a given method over a set of similar tasks.

There are several applications of metalearning: combining base learners, namely using several learners together to create a composite model that better predicts the result; bias management, mostly used for data streams that require context adaptation due to the fact that the domain is not static; and transferring metaknowledge across tasks. But metalearning is mostly used for the algorithm recommendation, as described next.

Algorithm Recommendation. Choosing the best algorithm for processing a given dataset is a difficult process. Besides, algorithms normally have parameters that affect its efficiency and tuning them can be a difficult and slow task. This constitutes the motivation for the Algorithm Selection Problem [1], originally formulated by Rice [2].

This problem consists in determining the best algorithm to use for a certain dataset. The metalearning approach takes advantage of information previously obtained on several datasets and also on several algorithms. This knowledge is used to build a metamodel that, given a new dataset, predicts which is(are) the most suitable algorithm(s).

Earlier applications of metalearning addressed the most common tasks - classification [3], regression [4] and time series [5]. These approaches were then extended to selecting parameter settings for a single algorithm [6], the whole data mining process [7] and also to problems from domains other than machine learning, e.g.: different optimization problems [8,9]. More recently, they were also used to deal with new problems in data mining: data streams [10].

2.2 Transfer Learning

A definition of transfer learning is: given a source domain D_S and a learning task T_S, a target domain D_T and a learning task T_T, transfer learning aims to improve the process of learning of the target predictive function $f_T(.)$ in D_T using the knowledge in D_S and T_S, where $D_S \neq D_T$, or $T_S \neq T_T$ [11].

Transfer learning allows algorithms to adapt to new tasks based on the knowledge obtained in previous ones. The three main research issues in this topic are related to *what*, *how* and *when* to transfer.

What to Transfer? This question concerns the type of information transferred between problems: instance-transfer, where instances from the source domain are used together with the ones on the target domain, to use more training data for the target model, as in the TrAdaBoost [12] algorithm; feature-representation-transfer, where a set of feature representations is extracted from the source domain and is transferred to become a new feature representation of the target domain [13]; parameter-transfer that consists of transferring some of the parameters of the source to the target model, assuming that the models for related tasks share some parameters [14]; and relational-knowledge-transfer, that consists in trying to transfer the knowledge about data between the domains, as is the case of TAMAR [15], that maps a source Markov Logic Network to the target domain and revises only its incorrect portions.

How to Transfer? After knowing what to transfer, the focus is on *how to transfer?*, that is, on the development of learning algorithms to perform the transfer. Approaches to this question can be characterized in two dimensions: the type of algorithm and the type of data used. As for the algorithm the approaches were based, for example, in neural networks [16,17], naive bayes [18] or decision trees [19,20]. In what concerns the data some consider propositional data [16, 18,20,21], while others use more complex types, such as graphs [19].

When to Transfer? The last question is concerned with the situations in which the transfer should be performed. Ultimately, the objective is to avoid *negative transfer*, i.e. when, instead of improving the performance, the transfer can even harm the learning process in the target task. Some approaches have been proposed to identify when transfer learning will hurt the performance of the algorithm instead of improving it (e.g. [18]).

2.3   Metalearning and Transfer Learning

Some work has been performed in using metalearning together with transfer learning.

Metafeatures are used in [22] for calculating similarities between the datasets. The algorithms used for this task is the *k-nearest neighbors*. The best configurations for the selected source domain are then transferred for the target domain.

In [23], metalearning is used to find matrix transformations capable of producing good kernel matrices for the source tasks. These transformations can be used to compute the kernel matrix for new related tasks. Another example is [24], where metalearning is used to construct a new classification algorithm that will be applied to new problems.

The results are evaluated by performance measures as accuracy [24] and more precisely by the area under the ROC curve in [22,23].

The transferred objects found on the studied papers are SVM parameter settings in [22], the kernel matrices in [23] and the *parameter function* (responsible for mapping statistics to parameters in "bag-of-words" text classification problems) in [24].

3   Weight Transfer in Neural Networks

In this section we propose a method, with four variants, for transferring weights from a source neural network, specifically a Multilayer Perceptron, to a target one. As explained above, the aim is to reduce the computational time needed for the target network to converge.

We start by revisiting the concept of neural network and then describe the weight transfer method and also the mapping method used for the weight transfer.

3.1   Neural Networks

Neural networks have been used for problems in diverse areas, such as: pattern recognition, prediction, optimization, associative memory, and control [25].

The neural networks considered in this work are composed by three layers of neurons: input, hidden and output. Figure 2 shows an example of a neural network with this structure designed for a dataset with three input and one output variables.

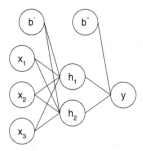

Fig. 2. Example of a neural network

The neurons in the input layer correspond to the independent variables of the dataset (x_1, x_2 and x_3) and there is an extra neuron for the bias (b'). The number of neurons in the hidden layer can vary and it is one of the parameters of the algorithm. In the example the neural network has two hidden neurons: h_1 and h_2. This layer also has an additional bias neuron (b''). The neuron on the output layer (y) corresponds to the dependent variable of the dataset.

There are connections between input and hidden layers and, also, between the latter and the output layer. The connections have associated weights, which are adjusted in each iteration of the network to better predict the output variable. A neural network is initialized with a set of weights and, after converging or reaching the (parametrized) maximum number of iterations, outputs the adjusted set of weights.

3.2   Weight Transfer Method

In our method, we transfer the weights from a (source) network to another (target) network according to Algorithm 1.

The input D_S corresponds to the source dataset that is composed by the independent variables $x_i : i \in \{1,\ldots,n\}$ and the dependent variable y_S. D_T is the target dataset and consists of $x_j : j \in \{1,\ldots,n\}$ as independent and y_T as

Input: D_S, D_T, N_S
Output: $N_{T \leftarrow S}$

1   Map $vars(D_S)$ into $vars(D_T)$
2   **foreach** $x_j \in vars(D_T)$ **do**
3      $w_{x_j, h_p} = w_{M^F_{x_j}, h_p}$
4   **end**
5   **foreach** *hidden node h of* N_T **do**
6      $w_{h_p, y_T} = w_{h_p, y_S}$
7   **end**
8   **foreach** *bias node b of* N_T **do**
9      $w_{b'_T, h_p} = w_{b'_S, h_p}$
10     $w_{b''_T, y_T} = w_{b''_S, y_S}$
11   **end**

Algorithm 1. Transfer algorithm

dependent variables. N_S is the neural network learned from the source dataset with a randomly generated initial set of weights.

The first step of the algorithm consists in mapping the variables from the source to the ones on the target datasets. The mapping process is explained in 3.3.

After this, for each mapping $M^F_{x_j} = x_i$, we transfer every weight originating in the neuron corresponding to x_i in N_S to the connections with origin in x_j in N_T (line 3 in the algorithm).

The weights of the connections with origin in hidden (h_p) and bias (b' and b'') neurons are directly transferred, since N_S and N_T have the same hidden layer configuration (lines 6, 9 and 10 in the algorithm, respectively).

3.3 Mapping Method

The mapping process is performed independently of the transfer step and uses the entire dataset. The mapping method is represented by the generic mapping

$$M^F_{x_j} = x_i$$

that assigns to each target variable the most adequate source variable.

This generic mapping can be instantiated with different specific mapping functions (F):

– Kullback-Leibler (KL) divergence

$$M^{KL}_{x_j} = argmin_i\{KL(x_j, x_i)\}, \forall i \in \{1 \ldots n\}, j \in \{1 \ldots m\}$$

– Pearson, Spearman and Kendall correlations

$$M^C_{x_j} = argmin_i\{|corr(x_j, y_T) - corr(x_i, y_S)|\}, \forall i \in \{1 \ldots n\}, j \in \{1 \ldots m\}$$

We also use random mapping and compare the improvement of the resulting neural networks with the ones obtained when using the mapping functions mentioned above.

4   Experiment

Now that we have described the weight transfer method, we will perform an exhaustive experiment using 14 datasets. Our hypothesis is that a neural network algorithm can converge faster on a target dataset if the initial weights are transferred from a source network trained on a well chosen source dataset.

For that purpose, we test the methods proposed here on all source/target combinations (the source is always different from the target) and pick, for each target, the best source.

We assess the results of our methods against the usual random weight initialization method. If the best source/target pairing shortens the convergence time when compared to the baseline, then we have evidence to support our hypothesis.

The experiment was performed using datasets retrieved from UCI [26] (Table 1). Most of the datasets are heterogeneous, i.e. generated from very different processes (i.e. they are represented by very different sets of variables). However, some of the problems used have more than one target variable, and, thus, originate more than one dataset.

This means that these datasets are related, as they share the same independent variables, with the same values.

4.1   Experiment Description

We performed the experiment using neural networks with ten neurons in the hidden layer. Our objective is to assess the potential improvement that the right transfer of weights brings to the learning time of a target neural network.

This improvement is calculated by comparing the time needed for the network to converge when using:

- randomly generated initial weights
- weights transferred from another neural network

The experiment is performed for every possible combination of source/target datasets.

It is organized into two steps as illustrated by the boxes in Fig. 3: the source learning step and the target learning step.

The source learning step (top of the figure) consists in learning a neural network with standard randomly generated initial weights (W_S) for each dataset (D_S) considered. After the learning process we store the error (MSE_S), duration of the process ($duration_S$) and the best set of weights found (W_S^L).

This is repeated twenty times to outwit the effect of using random values to initialize the network. Thus, we get twenty sets of weights for transfer. Although this is performed for all the datasets considered, to simplify, we only represent one dataset.

We call it source dataset (D_S) because the weights used for the transfer in the second part will be the ones learned here.

Table 1. Datasets used for the experiment

Problem	Derived dataset
Concrete compressive strength	ConcreteCompressiveStrength
Wine quality - red	WineQuality-red
Wine quality - white	WineQuality-white
Challenger USA space shuttle O-ring - erosion only	o-ring-erosion-only
Challenger USA space shuttle O-ring - erosion or blowby	o-ring-erosion-or-blowby
Concrete slump test	slumpTestSLUMP
	slumpTestFLOW
	slumpTestCompressiveStrength
Parkinsons telemonitoring	parkinsonsMotorUPDRS
	parkinsonsTotalUPDRS
Airfoil self-noise	airfoilSelfNoise
Energy efficiency	ENB2012-Y1
	ENB2012-Y2
Yacht hydrodynamics	yachtHydrodynamics

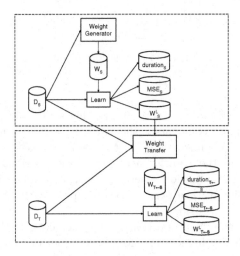

Fig. 3. Experiment workflow

The target learning step (bottom of the figure) consists of learning a neural network for the dataset considered (target dataset - D_T), by initializing it with weights transferred from one of the other datasets instead of randomly generated ones.

4.2 Results

In our experiment we measure the improvement achieved by transferring weights from another neural network – the source network –, considering the time needed for a neural network to converge (duration). We consider that an improvement has occurred when $duration_r > duration_t$, where $duration_r$ refers to the network with randomly generated initial weights and $duration_t$ refers to the network with initial weights transferred the source network.

The heat map on the left of Fig. 4 shows the percentage of improvements of the best transfer for each target dataset (y axis) when using each of the mapping methods (x axis).

A red (dark) square corresponds to having almost 100 % probability of improvement in the target dataset Y when using the mapping method X. The lighter the square, the closest this probability is to 0 %. Grey squares correspond to the cases where the transfer worsened the result instead of improving it. The histogram on the right shows the frequency with which the percentage of improvements occur, using the same color code. The mapping methods correspond to the ones shown in Table 2.

Table 2. Average percentage of improvements by mapping method

	Mapping measure	Average
1	Random	40.25 %
2	KL-divergence	56.43 %
3	Pearson correlation	57.86 %
4	Spearman correlation	65.00 %
5	Kendall correlation	58.57 %

As discussed earlier, our goal is to assess whether the right choice of source dataset could lead to improvements in the learning process of the target datasets. To investigate this, we analyze the best possible transfer observed for each dataset, instead of all the transferences, as in the previous paragraph. This approach simulates the situation where the source problem is optimally chosen. Table 2 shows the average percentage of improvement of the best transfer for each of the methods considered.

Here we can see that the proportion of improvements for the proposed mapping methods are clearly higher than for the random mapping. While random mapping of variables can improve the time of convergence of the network in around 40 % of the times, a similarity-based mapping can improve it in up to 65 % of the times, with the mapping functions considered. This suggests that we can benefit from the transfer of weights from a network previously trained on a different problem to a new network.

However, this benefit only occurs if the source problem is well chosen. One approach that can be used for that purpose is metalearning. Given a new target problem for which we want to train a network, a metalearning approach aims to select the most adequate source dataset based on characteristics of the datasets, usually referred to as metafeatures. The next step in our work is to investigate a metalearning approach for that purpose.

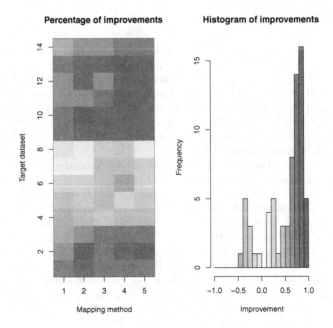

Fig. 4. Percentage of improvements for the best results

5   Conclusions and Future Work

In this paper we have proposed one specific method for transferring weights from a source network to another. This method has four variants based on different similarity measures between dataset variables: KL divergence and the Pearson, Spearman and Kendall correlation coefficients. In our experiments we have shown that transferring weights can accelerate the learning of the target network as long as the source network is well chosen. This suggests that we can benefit from a metalearning approach that is able to select a good source problem given a new one. In other words, it indicates that metalearning can be used to support transfer learning.

As future work, we wish to identify the appropriate problem characteristics (metafeatures) to be used for selecting the best variable (and dataset) to use as source in the transfer to a target network. The similarity between datasets will be used to determine the dataset whose network will be the best one to transfer the weights from. The similarity between variables will be used to determine the mapping to be used when transferring the weights between neural networks.

Acknowledgments. This project has received funding from the Electronic Component Systems for European Leadership Joint Undertaking under grant agreement No 662189. This Joint Undertaking receives support from the European Union's Horizon 2020 research and innovation programme and Spain, Finland, Denmark, Belgium, Netherlands, Portugal, Italy, Austria, United Kingdom, Hungary, Slovenia, Germany.

References

1. Brazdil, P., Giraud-Carrier, C.G., Soares, C., Vilalta, R.: Metalearning - Applications to Data Mining. Cognitive Technologies. Springer, Berlin (2009)
2. Rice, J.R.: The algorithm selection problem. Adv. Comput. **15**, 65–118 (1976)
3. Brazdil, P., Soares, C., da Costa, J.P.: Ranking learning algorithms: using IBL and meta-learning on accuracy and time results. Mach. Learn. **50**(3), 251–277 (2003)
4. Gama, J., Brazdil, P.: Characterization of classification algorithms. In: Pinto-Ferreira, C., Mamede, N.J. (eds.) EPIA 1995. LNCS (LNAI), vol. 990, pp. 189–200. Springer, Heidelberg (1995)
5. Prudêncio, R.B.C., Ludermir, T.B.: Meta-learning approaches to selecting time series models. Neurocomputing **61**, 121–137 (2004)
6. Gomes, T.A.F., Prudêncio, R.B.C., Soares, C., Rossi, A.L.D., Carvalho, A.C.P.L.F.: Combining meta-learning and search techniques to select parameters for support vector machines. Neurocomputing **75**(1), 3–13 (2012)
7. Serban, F., Vanschoren, J., Kietz, J.U., Bernstein, A.: A survey of intelligent assistants for data analysis. ACM Comput. Surv. **45**(3), 31:1–31:35 (2013)
8. Abreu, P., Soares, C., Valente, J.M.S.: Selection of heuristics for the job-shop scheduling problem based on the prediction of gaps in machines. In: Stützle, T. (ed.) LION 3. LNCS, vol. 5851, pp. 134–147. Springer, Heidelberg (2009)
9. Smith-Miles, K.: Cross-disciplinary perspectives on meta-learning for algorithm selection. ACM Comput. Surv. **41**(1), 6:1–6:25 (2009)
10. Gama, J., Kosina, P.: Learning about the learning process. In: Gama, J., Bradley, E., Hollmén, J. (eds.) IDA 2011. LNCS, vol. 7014, pp. 162–172. Springer, Heidelberg (2011)
11. Pan, S.J., Yang, Q.: A survey on transfer learning. IEEE Trans. Knowl. Data Eng. **22**(10), 1345–1359 (2010)
12. Dai, W., Yang, Q., Xue, G., Yu, Y.: Boosting for transfer learning. In: Proceedings of the Twenty-Fourth International Conference on Machine Learning (ICML 2007), pp. 193–200, Corvallis, Oregon, USA, 20–24 June 2007
13. Blitzer, J., McDonald, R., Pereira, F.: Domain adaptation with structural correspondence learning. In: Proceedings of the 2006 Conference on Empirical Methods in Natural Language Processing, pp. 120–128. Association for Computational Linguistics (2006)
14. Gao, J., Fan, W., Jiang, J., Han, J.: Knowledge transfer via multiple model local structure mapping. In: International Conference on Knowledge Discovery and Data Mining, Las Vegas, NV (2008)
15. Mihalkova, L., Huynh, T., Mooney, R.J.: Mapping and revising markov logic networks for transfer learning. In: Proceedings of the 22nd National Conference on Artificial Intelligence, pp. 608–614. AAAI (2007)
16. Pratt, L.Y., Pratt, L.Y., Hanson, S.J., Giles, C.L., Cowan, J.D.: Discriminability-based transfer between neural networks. In: Advances in Neural Information Processing Systems 5, pp. 204–211. Morgan Kaufmann (1993)
17. Silver, D.L., Poirier, R., Currie, D.: Inductive transfer with context-sensitive neural networks. Mach. Learn. **73**(3), 313–336 (2008)
18. Rosenstein, M.T., Marx, Z., Kaelbling, L.P., Dietterich, T.G.: To transfer or not to transfer. In: NIPS 2005 Workshop, Inductive Transfer: 10 Years Later (2005)
19. Ramon, J., Driessens, K., Croonenborghs, T.: Transfer learning in reinforcement learning problems through partial policy recycling. In: Kok, J.N., Koronacki, J., Lopez de Mantaras, R., Matwin, S., Mladenič, D., Skowron, A. (eds.) ECML 2007. LNCS (LNAI), vol. 4701, pp. 699–707. Springer, Heidelberg (2007)

20. Mahmud, M., Ray, S.: Transfer learning using kolmogorov complexity: basic theory and empirical evaluations. In: Advances in Neural Information Processing Systems, pp. 985–992 (2007)
21. Eaton, E., desJardins, M., Lane, T.: Modeling transfer relationships between learning tasks for improved inductive transfer. In: Daelemans, W., Goethals, B., Morik, K. (eds.) ECML PKDD 2008, Part I. LNCS (LNAI), vol. 5211, pp. 317–332. Springer, Heidelberg (2008)
22. Biondi, G., Prati, R.: Setting parameters for support vector machines using transfer learning. J. Intell. Robot. Syst. **80**(1), 295–311 (2015)
23. Aiolli, F.: Transfer learning by kernel meta-learning. In: ICML Unsupervised and Transfer Learning, pp. 81–95 (2012)
24. Do, C., Ng, A.Y.: Transfer learning for text classification. In: NIPS (2005)
25. Jain, A.K., Mao, J., Mohiuddin, K.: Artificial neural networks: a tutorial. Computer **3**, 31–44 (1996)
26. Bache, K., Lichman, M.: UCI machine learning repository (2013). http://archive.ics.uci.edu/ml

Smart Sketchpad: Using Machine Learning to Provide Contextually Relevant Examples to Artists

Michael Fischer[✉] and Monica Lam

Computer Science Department Stanford, Stanford University,
Stanford, CA 94305-9035, USA
{mfischer,lam}@cs.stanford.edu

Abstract. Sketching is a way for artists to generate ideas quickly, explore alternatives with less risk, and encourage discussions. How might computational tools amplify the abilities of artists? This paper introduces Smart Sketchpad, a digital sketchpad that uses machine learning to identify what is being sketched. The sketchpad then shows example images, color pallets, and subject information. The goal of Smart Sketchpad is to increase an artist's ability to get ideas down with higher fidelity by making it easier to reference and include existing example works. Our study compares traditional sketching on a phone to Smart Sketchpad. We found that introducing examples during the sketching process leads to higher satisfaction of the sketch by the artist and an external expert.

Keywords: Sketching · Machine learning · Content-aware software

1 Introduction

There is a marketing legend about an instant cake mix that only required the addition of water but sold poorly because home cooks felt guilty about not having to do much work. The marketers found there was an "emotional imperative to bake cakes from scratch". To fix the problem they released "ads at persuading bakers to view the plain cake layers as merely 'step number one'". "You can put your effort into glorifying your cake with frosting, dreaming up an exciting trim that puts your own label on it." [1] The art, they argued, began after the cake came out of the oven. The cake layers were elements of a larger goal, an overall cake creation with frosting, filling, and decorations that allowed for a higher level of creativity from the baker. Similarly, in this paper, we examine how a computer can assist with "step number one" of the sketching. The goal is to allow the user more time to add the creative details that make a sketch their own.

Typically, to create interesting and good-looking work, an artist must think about content, color, and composition, given the constraint of how much time or effort that they can spend working on the project [2]. We seek to address this problem by providing a sketch interface where the artist can make use of example content and color pallets that are targeted at what the artist is sketching. The system works as a search system. The input to the search system is a sketch that is labeled by a machine learning algorithm based on prior examples. The results of the search are:

© Springer International Publishing Switzerland 2016
F. Martínez-Álvarez et al. (Eds.): HAIS 2016, LNAI 9648, pp. 344–352, 2016.
DOI: 10.1007/978-3-319-32034-2_29

(1) Line drawn images from an online image search.
(2) Color pallets from a repository of user generated color pallets.
(3) A reference to an encyclopedia article on the subject being drawn.

By referring to the related images and colors, the user can get inspiration from an example design, use parts of the example design, or directly add the example design by dragging and dropping it onto their composition.

In this paper we describe the user interface, how it was constructed, and the results of our study. We found that users and an external expert rated drawings produced with the help of the smart interface higher than those produced with the control sketch interface (Fig. 1).

2   Related Work

2.1   Examples

Our future ideas and creations are based on our prior experiences [3, 4]. Recognizing exemplary content is easier (and perhaps a precursor) to creating exemplary content. To this end, research has looked into how to provide examples within a computer interface [5, 6] to improve outcomes in creativity and productivity. There is still debate though that looking at examples may limit forms of creative thinking [7].

2.2   Sketching

Sketching is a commonly accepted practice of design and is how some designers convey their work [8, 9]. Algorithms have been developed that can identify simple sketches of objects about as accurately as humans [10].

2.3   Color

Color theory is closely linked to the physiology of our visual system and perception. Color is known to be matched to context [11, 12]. This research was then extended into the data visualization field by introducing an algorithm for automatic selection of semantically-resonant colors to represent data [13].

3   System

3.1   User Flow

The artist starts with a blank canvas. The control canvas has a button to change the brush color, an undo button, an erase all button, and a button to save the images to the server. After every stroke, the image is sent to the server.

When the server is more than 80 % confident it has found a match, the interface goes into smart mode. In smart mode, the artist has the option to tap a button at the top of the screen to display example images. The example images can be dragged and resized on

Fig. 1. Users were asked to draw a cat that could be put on a birthday card to a friend. On the left are sketches that were drawn using the control interface. On the right are sketches that were drawn with the help of examples images and colors that were suggested by the Smart Sketchpad.

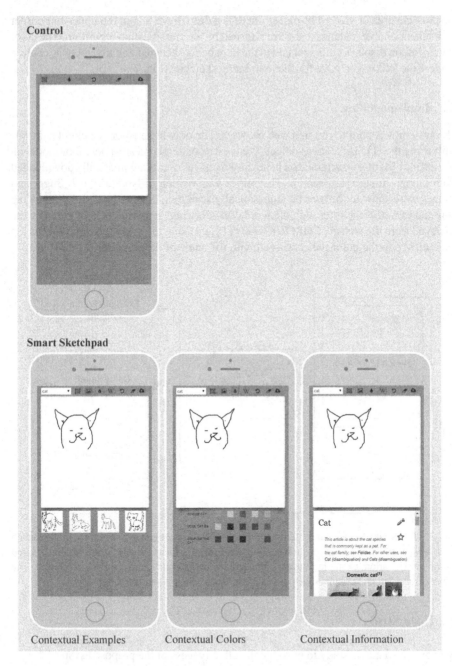

Fig. 2. The control sketchpad interface (top). The Smart Sketchpad (bottom). Smart Sketchpad provides contextual information about what is being sketched. Example images can be dragged onto the canvas (bottom-left). Color pallets related to the content being sketched are displayed (bottom-center). Contextual information about the subject is available from Wikipedia (bottom-right).

the drawing area or viewed in-place. There is a drop down box in the upper-left corner with other possible matches that were returned by the classification algorithm. The color palette button displays colors related to the item being sketched. Finally, there is a button to view the Wikipedia page for the item being sketched (Fig. 2).

3.2 Implementation

The system was built to run in a web browser. The drawing area on the client side was built using the HTML5 canvas object. We used a condensed nearest neighbor model on MetaMind [14] that was trained on hand drawn images of cats automatically downloaded from Google Image [15] search. The server was written in Node.JS [16]. Suggested images were show to the user by automatically searching Google Images using the tag returned from the classifier with the word "line drawing" appended. Color pallets were retrieved from the website COLOURlovers [17] by using their API to search for the top three most popular color pallets tagged with the name of the classifier (Fig. 3).

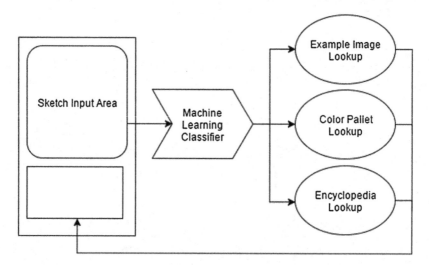

Fig. 3. The Smart Sketchpad system architecture. The user begins by sketching in the sketch input area. The sketch acts as a search query that the machine learning algorithm classifies. Based on the classification, example images, color pallets, and an encyclopedia entry are found. The information from the lookup is then displayed in the box below the sketch input area.

4   User Study

We conducted a user study to evaluate the effectiveness of the proposed system. Using the prompt:

```
You forgot to get a present for your friend's birthday
party. The party starts in 5 min. Your friend likes cats.
Draw a cat for their present.
```

4.1 Participants

Six university students participated in the study (Table 1). Three self-identified as "experienced" sketchers and three self-identified as "novice" sketchers.

Table 1. The profile of the participants. Half were novice user and half were experienced users. An external evaluator always chose the sketches from the Smart Sketchpad as being better.

#	User's Sketching Experience	User's Rating of Image (Control)	User's Rating of Image (Smart)	Expert's Choice of Image
1	Experienced	1	4	Smart
2	Novice	2	4	Smart
3	Experienced	3	5	Smart
4	Experienced	3	3	Smart
5	Novice	4	5	Smart
6	Novice	4	6	Smart

4.2 Apparatus

A Motorola G, 3rd generation mobile phone was used for the evaluation. An optional capacitive stylus was provided and all participants chose to use it.

4.3 Procedure

At the beginning of the test we let participants test the interface and to get familiar with the system for approximately 2 mins.

Using the prompt above, each participant created two sketches on a mobile phone. In both cases they were encouraged to make the sketch as best as they could and to notify the examiner when they were done.

One sketch was with the smart system disabled. The other sketch was with the smart system enabled. The conditions were counter-balanced to control for ordering effects.

Using within-subject testing may have accounted for some learning effects. We were aware of this and made the decision that doing between-subject testing would make evaluating our experimental condition difficult because of the high degree of variability in subject's artistic ability and style.

During the session we used a think aloud protocol to gather data about how the user thought about the design challenge. After completing the sketch the users answered a questionnaire about their experience. At the end, the user and examiner had an informal talk to find out more about questions not in the questionnaire or to examine a particular area in more depth.

We had an outside expert review the pairs of images produced. They were told to choose an image based on which they would be more excited to receive as a birthday gift from a friend. Within a pair, the control and smart sketchpad images were randomly ordered. The expert was not told about the context of the experiment.

5   Results

5.1   Quantitative Assessment

The result shows that in all but one case users were more satisfied with their result when using Smart Sketchpad. That user, who had advanced artistic skills, felt the same about both of their images.

In all cases, the expert chose sketches done using the Smart Sketchpad as the one they would prefer to receive.

Every user looked at the examples in the Smart Sketchpad condition. Four users used the example as a template.

Only two users picked the same image of the four that were offered. There was no clear definition of what a "best" cat template looked like between users.

All users said they sketch to capture an idea, two users said they also sketch for enjoyment.

All users completed the task in less than five minutes and none asked for more time. All users also said that they would like to use the system again. All users except for one experienced user were satisfied with the example images provided. Two experienced users asked for more color choices.

5.2   Qualitative Assessment

The results of our qualitative assessment show that users used the examples because they thought that they provided a better foundation than what they could do. Some sample comments:

> The reference gave me something I could work from. I didn't have to figure out how to draw a cat by myself.

> I liked that I could get a pre-drawn outline because it was way better than anything I could have done.

> When I saw the pre-drawn cat outlines I decided to just use that because it was better than anything I could have drawn, and I got lazy.

Users then took the opportunity to add to the existing image their own additions.

> I used the image itself and drew some lines on it for texture and color so that it would look nicer.

> I just put additions onto the photo of a cat that I liked best.

Two of the more experienced sketchers used the examples as counter examples or to correct misconceptions that they had.

> I drew something different from that in order to avoid drawing a stereotyped image.

> The reference images were useful in correcting some misconceptions I had about anatomy.

Using examples fit into the existing workflow of some of the users but having it built into the interface made it easier to access.

Typically I have a pretty strong idea, but I'll look around Pinterest or flip through drawing books to develop it more.

One user wanted the examples to be less concrete and allow for more creativity.

It feels like cheating to use an image of a cat for drawing in the drawing. Potentially would be better if I could use it to outline then remove the image.

The color pallet was popular with users. Having color pallets that other people had validated that went together was found to be helpful. Although some felt restricted and wanted more color options.

The colors weren't as complementary as the ones in the smart interface.

The colors generally went together better because I didn't have to chose them.

I wanted a color that wasn't in the color list and I didn't know what to do.

I think the colors kind of restricted me - I originally envisioned a blue cat but I had to make a normal, brownish-orange cat because that's the colors that were given to me.

Only one user looked at the Wikipedia page. Although three others mentioned that they would have looked at the page if they were sketching something that they were not familiar with or wanted to find information about other things that they could add to the sketch.

6   Discussion

The feedback that was received about the system was positive and users were interested in continuing to use the smart interface.

An area that we found interesting was that three of the four users that used a template in the smart condition also included other elements (grass, a ball, clouds, or a flower) to embellish their drawing. This was done without any prompt, whereas the people that did not use the template did not embellish their work with anything else. A possible explanation of this behavior could be that users who used the example images as a template had more time left to focus on the other areas of their sketch.

Based on this observation, we will follow up this work with a test to determine how the smart interface is used when composing a larger, more complex work that involves multiple sub-elements. We are interested to investigate how the usage of the tool changes as the drawing goes from a small sketch to a larger composition. We'd be looking to see if the usage of the tool increases as the complexity of the final image increases.

Based on user feedback, another area that we would like to further explore is to give the user the option of producing their own search query for the system with either text or speech instead of having to use an image. The original idea was to be able to match the type of image being drawn; a cat in a certain pose generates an example of a cat in that pose. However, we found that users typically start drawing with a concept in their mind as opposed to a specific image of a cat in their mind, although we expect this to vary across use cases.

Bringing examples into the sketching interface supported the natural workflow that some users already did on a desktop computer. One remarked how this system would be useful when they only had their phone available to them.

We can also improve the training set of the images that can be recognized with the machine learning algorithm by adding all images sketched using the system back into the training set. Perhaps the system could then be used as a semantic authoring system for sketches.

Overall, we found that contextual suggestions improve the output of users as rated by both themselves and by an outside expert.

References

1. Shapiro, L.: Something from the Oven: Reinventing Dinner in 1950's America. Viking, New York (2004)
2. Sketching: the Visual Thinking Power Tool. http://alistapart.com/article/sketching-the-visual-thinking-power-tool
3. Smith, S., Ward, T., Schumacher, J.: Constraining effects of examples in a creative generation task. Mem. Cogn. **21**(6), 837–845 (1993)
4. Gentner, D., Holyoak, K.J., Kokinov, B.N.: The Analogical Mind: Perspectives from Cognitive Science. MIT Press, Cambridge (2001)
5. Kumar, R., Talton, J., Ahmad, S., Klemmer, S.: Bricolage: example-based retargeting for web design. In: Proceedings of the SIGCHI Conference on Human Factors in Computing Systems (CHI 2011), pp. 2197–2206. ACM, New York (2011)
6. Lee, B., Srivastava, S., Kumar, R., Brafman, R., Klemmer, S.: Designing with interactive example galleries. In: Proceedings of the SIGCHI Conference on Human Factors in Computing Systems (CHI 2010), pp. 2257–2266. ACM, New York (2010)
7. Schank, R., Childers, P.: The Creative Attitude: Learning to Ask and Answer the Right Questions. Macmillan, New York (1988)
8. Design thinking. (2015, October 13). In Wikipedia, The Free Encyclopedia. Retrieved 17:54, October 14, 2015, from https://en.wikipedia.org/w/index.php?title=Design_thinking
9. Newman, M. W., Landay, J.A.: Sitemaps, storyboards, and specifications: a sketch of Web site design practice. In: Boyarski, D., Kellogg, W.A. (eds.) Proceedings of the 3rd Conference on Designing Interactive Systems: Processes, Practices, Methods, and Techniques (DIS 2000), pp. 263–274. ACM, New York (2000)
10. Eitz, M., Hays, J., Alexa, M.: How do humans sketch objects? ACM Trans. Graph. **31**(4), Article 44, 10 p., July 2012
11. van de Weijer, J., Schmid, C., Verbeek, J., Larlus, D.: Learning color names for real-world applications. Trans. Img. Proc. **18**(7), 1512–1523 (2009)
12. Schauerte, B.; Stiefelhagen, R.: Learning robust color name models from web images. In: 2012 21st International Conference on Pattern Recognition (ICPR), pp. 3598–3601, November 11–15, 2012
13. Lin, S., Fortuna, J., Kulkarni, C., Stone, M., Heer, J.: Selecting semantically-resonant colors for data visualization. In: Proceedings of the 15th Eurographics Conference on Visualization (EuroVis 2013), pp. 401–410. The Eurographs Association & John Wiley & Sons, Ltd., Chichester (2013)
14. MetaMind. https://www.metamind.io
15. Google Images. https://www.google.com/imghp
16. Node.JS.. http://nodejs.org/
17. COLOURlovers. http://www.colourlovers.com/

An Analysis of the Hardness of Novel TSP Iberian Instances

Gloria Cerasela Crişan[1], Camelia-M. Pintea[2(✉)], Petrică Pop[2], and Oliviu Matei[2]

[1] Vasile Alecsandri University of Bacău, 600115 Bacăsu, Romania
ceraselacrisan@ub.ro
[2] Technical University Cluj-Napoca, 430122 Baia Mare, Romania
dr.camelia.pintea@ieee.org, petrica.pop@cunbm.utcluj.ro,
oliviu.matei@holisun.com

Abstract. The scope of this paper is to introduce two novel TSP instances based on the freely available geographic coordinates of the main cities from Spain and Portugal. We analyze in the case of the described instances the hardness, the quality of the provided solutions and the corresponding running times, using the Lin-Kernighan heuristic algorithm with different starting solutions and Applegate et al's branch and cut algorithm.

Keywords: TSP · Heuristics · Geographic coordinates

1 Introduction

One of the oldest, most investigated and challenging problems in Operations Research is the Traveling Salesman Problem (TSP). Given a number of cities and the cost of the journey between any two cities, TSP aims to find a minimum cost closed tour with the property that each city is visited exactly once. Such a tour is called Hamiltonian.

Some variants of TSP have been approached more than 150 years ago by the mathematicians William Rowan Hamilton and Thomas Penyngton Kirkman. By the half of the last century, the problem received its current name and became one of the intensely studied academic problems as more and more applications were revealed. The most important result in TSP theoretical research was delivered in 1972 by Richard Karp, who showed that TSP is NP-hard [21]. This means that it is very probable that no polynomial-time algorithm exists for solving the worst TSP cases.

In the literature there have been considered several variants of the TSP modeling real-life applications: the prize collecting TSP [3], the fuzzy TSP [15,30], the uncertain and dynamic TSP [10], the bottleneck TSP [35], the multiple traveling salesman problem (mTSP) [4], the generalized traveling salesman problem (GTSP) [29], etc.

© Springer International Publishing Switzerland 2016
F. Martínez-Álvarez et al. (Eds.): HAIS 2016, LNAI 9648, pp. 353–364, 2016.
DOI: 10.1007/978-3-319-32034-2_30

TSP applications span on broad domains. Manufacturing industry can benefit from well designed drilling [20] or computer wiring patterns [22], efficient dispatching methods are crucial in transportation industry and logistics [7]. Optimal production sequence [26], mobile robot path planning optimization [6] and X-ray crystallography [5] are other important domains where TSP is applied. For a survey on the TSP, its history and current developments we refer to [1,8,14,32].

Nowadays the Internet provides many freely available data and tools for modeling and simulating complex real-life situations. One of these is the presence of the Global Positioning Systems (GPS) coordinates on dedicated websites. This system offers spatial data structures able to be integrated in custom-designed platforms and applications. In this paper we are using the GPS coordinates to define new Traveling Salesman Problem (TSP) instances for the Iberian Peninsula.

The rest of our paper is organized as follows: in Sect. 2 we provide an overview of the available TSP instances, solvers and algorithmic solutions. Section 3 describes the novel Iberian TSP instances and in Sect. 4 we present our computational experiments followed by an analysis of the obtained results. Finally, the last Section concludes the paper with some remarks and further suggestions.

2   Available TSP Instances, Solvers and Algorithmic Solutions

Probably the most known and used TSP instance collections are provided in [36,37]. TSPLIB [36] mainly contains geographic instances with up to 85,900 cities. The instances from [37] are grouped based on several characteristics: if the distance function is symmetric or not; if the distance function is Euclidean, Geographic or it has other explicit analytic form, or is specified as a matrix. An important feature of these TSP instances beside their size is the distribution of the data within the given space.

Recently, the attention of the research community focuses on real-world difficult instances, in an effort to bridge the academic research with industrial needs. Several TSP instances specified by geographic coordinates are studied in [17,33]. In 2014, the Romanian instance was introduced by Crişan and Pintea [11].

The GEOM distance introduced for the World TSP instance from [37] directly handles the geographic coordinates. It is designed to provide the distances in meters, while the old GEO norm uses integer kilometers. As there are large regions with high node density, we have chosen to work with the GEOM version, for its higher accuracy.

Currently, the best exact TSP solver is *Concorde*, written in ANSI C by David Applegate, Robert E. Bixby, Vasek Chvatal and William J. Cook, and freely available for academic use [25]. In 2006, Concorde solved *pla*85900, the largest instance currently known to be solved to optimality. Other online solvers are available at [19,28].

Solving large TSP instances requires massive computational resources. For example, *pla*85900 needed 136 years of CPU equivalent time with *Concorde*, making the solving process hard to replicate [2]. As real-world situations often accept close-to-optimum solutions, researchers designed and implemented many efficient heuristic approaches to TSP. We describe in the following the most known heuristic algorithms for solving the TSP.

Constructive heuristics quickly build from scratch a good-enough solution, using a strategy for adding until completion edges to the tour. Local search heuristics start from an initial tour and iterates some transformation for shortening it, until no improvement can be made. Often the current implementations are hybrid, including both approaches.

The TSP literature describes very efficient constructive heuristics. *Genetic Algorithms* keep a pool of tours and improve their quality using operators inspired by the Darwinian evolution: crossover and mutation, and maintaining the shorter tours in the pool [31]. Evolutionary algorithms are also used in other applications as for example classification [34] or for solving the Component selection problem [38]. *Ant Colony Optimization* is inspired by the way an ant colony manages to find the shortest path from food to nest. It uses a collection of agents that concurrently construct tours, by adding one edge at each step. For a specific agent staying in a specific city, the next city is chosen based on its closeness and on the intensity of the artificial pheromone on the corresponding edge. After the agents complete their tours, the pheromone is deposited on good tours, and the process is repeated [16].

The *Greedy* method starts by increasingly sorting the edges by their lengths in a list. It constructs the tour by selecting from the list only the edges that do not prematurely close circuits, and do not connect cities with degree 2. The *Borůvka* strategy is better for large instances, as it works in parallel. It was initially devised for solving the minimum spanning tree problem, but it can be used for TSP with a minor modification. It works with a set of tour components, and at each step it lowers the numbers of components, until just one remains, connecting all the nodes. At the beginning, each component consists of just one city. At each step, each component is connected with other one by an edge with lowest cost and the degrees of the adjacent cities less than 2 [27]. *Quick Borůvka* is a variant introduced in [1]. It uses a fixed order of the cities; at each step it connects the first city with a degree less than 2 with the nearest eligible city.

Local search heuristics for TSP use a strategy to repeatedly adjust an existing tour in order to lower its length. The well-known *Lin-Kernighan* heuristic is described in [23]. The *2-opt* move applied to a tour delivers the shortest tour obtained from the initial one by excluding two edges and adding other edges that reconstruct the tour. If the result has the same length with the initial tour, then other more complicate moves can be done. The *3-opt* move tries to lower the length of a tour by deleting three edges and reconnecting the tour in a shortest way. The general λ-*opt* move constructs a tour from an existing one by deleting λ edges and reconnecting the λ parts in the most efficient way.

The *Lin-Kernighan* solving method starts from a tour and applies *2-opt* moves until no improvement is made. It dynamically continues with ascending values of λ, deciding after each value if λ should be increased, or the algorithm stops [23].

In our experiments we used hybrid algorithms involving the *Lin-Kernighan* heuristic and the exact solution provided by *Concorde*. The hybrid models are based on the solutions given by *Borůvka*, Quick *Borůvka*, *Greedy* and *Random* algorithms.

3   The Proposed TSP Data Sets: The Spanish and Portuguese TSP Instances with GIS Features

In this section, we introduce the first, as far as we know, Spanish and Portuguese TSP instances based on geographic coordinates. We extracted the data from the online repository [18]. The distance between any two nodes is the orthodromic, great circle distance, which is the shortest distance between two points on the surface of a sphere. In this case, the distance is measured along the surface of the Earth as opposed to a straight line passing through the Earth's interior. We intended to model the Iberian Peninsula as a TSP instance in the most correct way, so we used the geodesic distance instead of the 2D Euclidean one.

The geographic coordinate for a specific point on the Earth surface is a pair of decimal values for latitude and longitude. The coordinates for the instances we used were transformed to comply with the GEOM norm. In 2014, the first TSP Romanian national instance *romania2950.tsp* was introduced in a similar way [11]. Specifying the nodes of a TSP instance through the geographic coordinates allows its approach with modern applications based on GIS services. For example, the dynamics of the phenomena manifested on large territories could be simulated using Geoinformatics systems and packages. Data collected by aerial devices could be integrated with data gathered by land sensors. Ecological, geographical, meteorological or environmental complex models could use such modern TSP instances, providing support for accurate predictions at large scale.

Current developments of Computational Geosciences provide many data collections freely available for academic use. For example, the list of the Spanish provinces sorted by the number of their localities is in [24]. Based on this list, Spain has 8111 human settlements. As we intended to be coherent in working with data for the whole Iberian Peninsula, we searched for collections at continental level. From the available data we chose [18], which offers world geographic coordinates for localities with more than 15,000 inhabitants. Thus we derived the Spanish and Portuguese TSP instances available for download at [12,13]. A cumulative instance, called Iberian, was also constructed.

4   Numerical Experiments

Our experiments investigate the behavior of the Lin-Kernighan heuristic method on real-life instances specified by geographic coordinates and with GEOM norm. Our first goal is to study the balance between the quality of the solutions and the time needed for obtaining them. We used the online version of Concorde, executing 15 tries for the Lin-Kernighan heuristic algorithm on Spanish, Portuguese and the cumulative, Iberian instance newly introduced. The results are presented in Table 1.

Table 1. The comparative results of the newly introduced TSP instances using the Concorde online tool.

Instances	# nodes	CPLEX		Lin-Kernighan	
		Length (m)	Time (s)	Length (m)	Time (s)
Spain	567	12988919	9.43	12991587.47	1.70
Portugal	113	5068330	0.62	5068330.00	0.22
Spain and Portugal	680	16059232	21.12	16073695.80	1.93

The investigated heuristic method perfectly works on the Portuguese instance in one-third of the time needed by the exact solver. On Spanish instance, it offers a solution which is 0.02 % close to the optimum in one fifth of the time needed to exactly solve it. The Iberian instance produces in less than one-tenth time fraction a result which is 0.09 % close to the optimum. We can conclude the first part of our investigation: the implicit settings of the online Lin-Kernighan solver provide extremely good results when considering both the solutions quality and the running time.

Our second goal is to study the influence of the hybridization of the Lin-Kernighan method with other constructive method. Concorde offers an offline solver with more settings than the online application. We used the offline version on an AMD E-450 CPU computer with 1.6 GB RAM. From the application menu, we were able to choose the Lin-Kernighan implementation starting from an initial solution constructed with: *Borůvka*, Greedy, Quick *Borůvka*, or Random method. For each initial method, we constructed fifteen tours and collected the results. Table 2 includes a statistical analysis: the average lengths, the standard deviations and the percentage errors.

Figures 1, 2, 3 4 and 5 illustrate the solutions of the considered algorithms for five consecutive runs. Visual representations of the Spanish solution are in the Figs. 1 and 2. The *Borůvka* method is more constant, as its five overlapped solutions do not generate large sub-tours. Quick *Borůvka* and Greedy methods introduce more diversity in the solutions, as their superposed representations have obvious sub-tours (for example, connecting the Canary islands with the mainland). The Portuguese instance was exactly solved in each case due to the small dimension of the dataset (Fig. 3).

Table 2. Average lengths and standard deviations for Lin-Kernighan with starting tour generated with four different methods.

Statistic analysis	Spain instance	Portugal instance	Spain and Portugal instance
Borůvka (B)			
Avg length (m)	12992659.07	5068330.0	16079282.27
Std. dev.	2360.25	0.0	23952.40
Percentage error (%)	0.029	0.0	0.125
Greedy (G)			
Avg length (m)	12992659.20	5068330.0	16079538.60
Std. dev.	2593.63	0.0	24640.16
Percentage error (%)	0.029	0.0	0.126
Quick Borůvka(Q)			
Avg length (m)	12992150.07	5068330.0	16077071.27
Std. dev.	2977.92	0.0	24810.00
Percentage error (%)	0.025	0.0	0.111
Random (R)			
Avg length (m)	12992942.47	5068330.0	16076542.80
Std. dev	2966.75	0.0	23489.09
Percentage error (%)	0.031	0.0	0.108

Clearly the solutions provided for the largest instance are similar. Figures 4 and 5 are dedicated to the Iberian instance: all the methods provide solutions that can be hardly discerned. Only very attentive exploration of the images reveals small differences, for example in the Seville province.

The quality of the solution delivered by the Lin-Kernighan method is measured by the percentage error (the difference between the average length of the solutions and the optimum length, divided by the optimum length). The average lengths were each time less than 0.13 % greater than the exact solution. When starting from a Quick *Borůvka* Spanish solution, the Lin-Kernighan method was the most effective; on the Iberian instance it delivers the second-best result.

From the stability point of view, solving the Spanish instance led to significant differences: *Borůvka* initial solution seems to introduce stability in the solution set. Conversely, Quick *Borůvka* initial solution introduces high diversity in the final results. But for larger instance (Spanish instance has 567 nodes and the Iberian instance has 680 nodes) the influence of the initial choice diminishes. Both the average length and the standard deviation are quite close and the power of the Lin-Kernighan method strongly manifests: it seems to be indifferent to the initial solution.

In order to statistically investigate the influence of the hybridization method, we used the non-parametric, independent samples Mann-Whitney U-test (Wilcoxon rank-sum test) [9] with two tails and the significance level 0.05. We paired in all the possible ways the numerical series formed by each type of initial solution and we investigate if the null hypothesis "the methods chosen for the initial solution have the same influence on the length of the final result" could be rejected.

We considered all the series (*Borůvka*, Greedy, Quick *Borůvka*, or Random) each formed by 30 numbers representing the lengths for each execution (15 tries for Spain and 15 for the Iberian instance). We excluded the 15 identical results for the Portuguese instance. In each case, the distribution was approximately normal; therefore, the Z-value was used. The results presented in Table 3 provide that the null hypothesis is not rejected for each tested pair.

Table 3. Statistic analysis: Mann-Whitney U-test with two tails and the significance level 0.05.

Pair of initial methods	*Borůvka*, Greedy	*Borůvka*, Quick *Borůvka*	*Borůvka*, Random	Greedy, Quick *Borůvka*	Greedy, Random	Quick *Borůvka*, Random
U	446.5	401.0	429.5	415.0	438.0	426.5
Z	0.0444	0.7170	0.2957	−0.5101	0.1700	−0.3400
p	0.9681	0.47152	0.76418	0.61006	0.86502	0.72786

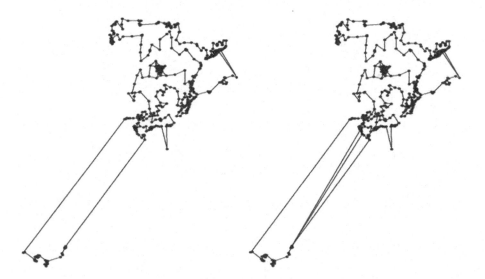

Fig. 1. Solutions for the Spain TSP instances [12] using as starting algorithm for Lin-Kernighan: *Borůvka* (left) and Quick *Borůvka* (right).

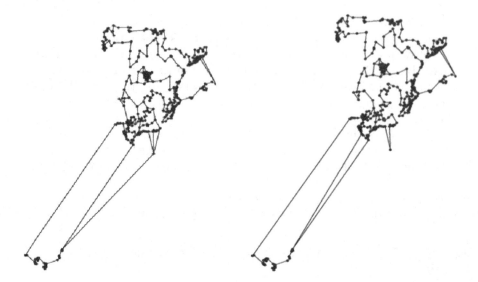

Fig. 2. Solutions for the Spain TSP instance [12] using as starting algorithm for Lin-Kernighan: greedy (left) and random techniques (right).

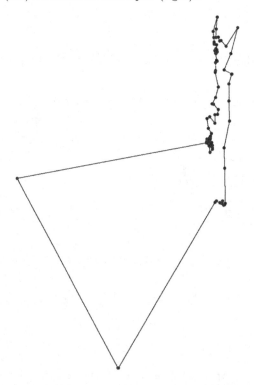

Fig. 3. The solution for the Portugal TSP instance [13].

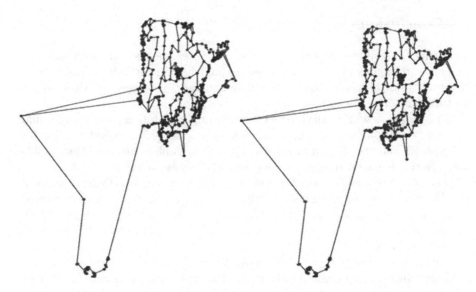

Fig. 4. Solutions for the Iberian region TSP instance [12, 13] using as starting algorithm for Lin-Kernighan: *Borůvka* (left) and Quick *Borůvka* (right).

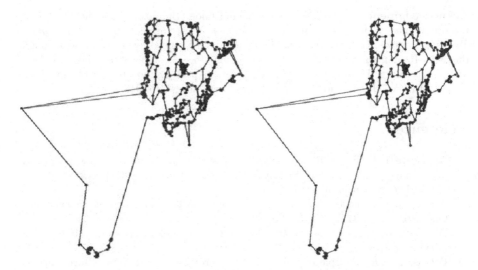

Fig. 5. Solutions for the Iberian region TSP instance [12, 13] using as starting algorithm for Lin-Kernighan: greedy (left) and random techniques (right).

Our second part of the investigation shows that for the real-world instances studied here, the Lin-Kernighan method is stable. In conclusion, our empiric study illustrates the efficiency and stability of the Lin-Kernighan implementation offered by Concorde.

5 Conclusions

This paper introduces two national TSP instances specified through the geographic coordinates of the main localities and having orthodromic distances. Several hybridizations for the Lin-Kernighan method were used and their results on these instances are compared.

This study shows that the online Concorde implementation provides optimum solutions on Portuguese instance, and rapidly produces a very good solution for the Spanish and the Iberian instances. The offline implementation shows stable and effective behavior on the instance with the highest number of nodes.

The statistic analysis we performed on the effect of the hybridization of the Lin-Kernighan implementation with four other heuristic methods showed minor differences in the quality of the results. The diversity decreases when the dimension of the TSP instance increases, making us to expect a very good stability on large instances.

Future work needs to be done in order to construct more real-life TSP instances and to empirically study the influence of their structure, clustering and/or spanning area on the quality, stability or effectiveness of other solving methods.

Acknowledgment. The study was conducted under the auspices of the IEEE-CIS Interdisciplinary Emergent Technologies task force and the project "Bacău and Lugano-Teaching Informatics for a Sustainable Society", co-financed by Switzerland through the Swiss-Romanian Cooperation Programme to reduce economic and social disparities within the enlarged European Union. This work is partly supported by the ProSEco project of EU's 7th FP, under the grant agreement no. NMP-2013 609143.

References

1. Applegate, D.L., Bixby, R.E., Chvátal, V., Cook, W.J.: Princeton Series in Applied Mathematics. The Traveling Salesman Problem: A Computational. Princeton University Press, Princeton (2007)
2. Applegate, D.L., et al.: Certification of an optimal TSP tour through 85,900 cities. Oper. Res. Lett. **37**(1), 11–15 (2009)
3. Balas, E.: The prize collecting traveling salesman problem. Networks **19**, 621–636 (1989)
4. Bektas, T.: The multiple traveling salesman problem: an overview of formulations and solution procedures. OMEGA: Int. J. Manage. Sci. **34**(3), 209–219 (2006)
5. Bland, R.G., Shallcross, D.F.: Large travelling salesman problems arising from experiments in X-ray crystallography: a preliminary report on computation. Oper. Res. Lett. **8**(3), 125–128 (1989)
6. Brassai, S.T., Iantovics, B., Enachescu, C.: Optimization of robotic mobile agent navigation. Stud. Inform. Control **21**(4), 403–412 (2012)
7. Clarke, G., Wright, J.: Scheduling of vehicles from a central depot to a number of delivery points. Oper. Res. **12**(4), 568–581 (1964)
8. Cook, W.J.: In Pursuit of the Traveling Salesman: Mathematics at the Limits of Computation. Princeton University Press, Princeton (2014)

9. Corder, G.W., Foreman, D.I.: Nonparametric Statistics: A Step-by-Step Approach. Wiley, New Jersey (2014)
10. Crişan, G.C., Nechita, E., Palade, V.: Ant-based system analysis on the traveling salesman problem under real-world settings. In: Hatzilygeroudis, I., Palade, V., Prentzas, J. (eds.) Combinations of Intelligent Methods and Applications, vol. 46, pp. 39–59. Springer, Heidelberg (2016)
11. Crişan, C., Pintea, C.-M.: Romania2950 dataset (2014). doi:10.13140/2.1.4706.8165
12. Crişan, C., Pintea, C.-M.: Spain TSP instance (2015). doi:10.13140/RG.2.1.2331.2727
13. Crişan, C., Pintea, C.-M.: Portugal TSP instance (2015). doi:10.13140/RG.2.1.4944.5209
14. Crişan, G.C.: Ant algorithms in artificial intelligence. Ph.D thesis, Al.I.Cuza Unversity of Iasi, Romania (2007)
15. Crişan, G.C., Nechita, E.: Solving fuzzy TSP with ant algorithms. Int. J. Comput. Commun. Control **3**, 228–231 (2008)
16. Dorigo, M., Gambardella, L.M.: Ant colonies for traveling salesman problem. BioSystems **43**, 73–81 (1997)
17. Eldrandaly, K.A., Abdallah, A.F.: A novel GIS-based decision-making framework for the school bus routing problem. Geo-spat. Inf. Sci. **15**(1), 51–59 (2012)
18. GeoNames download page. http://www.geonames.org/export/
19. Google Developers TSP Application. https://developers.google.com/optimization/routing/tsp?hl=en
20. Grötschel, M., Jünger, M., Reinelt, G.: Optimal control of plotting and drilling machines: a case study. Math. Methods Oper. Res. **35**(1), 61–84 (1991)
21. Karp, R.M.: Reducibility among combinatorial problems. In: Miller, R.E., Thatcher, J.W. (eds.) Complexity of Computer Computations, pp. 85–103. Plenum, New York (1972)
22. Lenstra, J.K., Kan, A.H.G.: Some simple applications of the traveling salesman problem. Oper. Res. **26**, 717–733 (1975)
23. Lin, S., Kernighan, B.W.: An effective heuristic algorithm for the traveling-salesman problem. Oper. Res. **21**(2), 498–516 (1973)
24. List of the Spanish provinces. http://en.classora.com
25. NEOS server for Concorde. http://neos.mcs.anl.gov/neos/solvers/co:concorde/TSP.html
26. Nahmias, S., Lennon, O.T.: Production and Operations Analysis, 7th edn. Waveland Press, Long Grove (2015)
27. Nešetřil, J., Milková, E., Nešetřilová, H.: Otakar Borůvka on minimum spanning tree problem: translation of both the 1926 papers, comments, history. Discrete Math. **233**(1–3), 3–36 (2001)
28. OptiMap solver. http://www.gebweb.net/optimap/
29. Pintea, C.-M.: A lnifying survey of agent-based approaches for equality-generalized traveling salesman problem. Informatica **26**(3), 509–522 (2015)
30. Pintea, C.-M., Ludwig, S.A., Crişan, G.-C.: Adaptability of a discrete PSO algorithm applied to the traveling salesman problem with fuzzy data. In: IEEE International Conference on Fuzzy Systems (FUZZ-IEEE), pp. 1–6 (2015)
31. Potvin, J.-Y.: Genetic algorithms for the traveling salesman problem. Ann. Oper. Res. **63**(3), 337–370 (1996)
32. Reinelt, G. (ed.): TSP. LNCS, vol. 840. Springer, Heidelberg (1994)
33. Rodríguez, A., Ruiz, R.: The effect of the asymmetry of road transportation networks on the traveling salesman problem. Comput. Oper. Res. **39**, 1566–1576 (2012)

34. Stoean, C., Stoean, R.: Support Vector Machines and Evolutionary Algorithms for Classification. Springer, Heidelberg (2014)
35. Shapiro, D.M.: Algorithms for the solution of the optimal cost and bottleneck traveling salesman problems. Sc.D. thesis, Washington University, St. Louis, MO (1966)
36. TSPLIB. http://www.iwr.uni-heidelberg.de/groups/comopt/software/tsplib95
37. TSP data. www.math.uwaterloo.ca/tsp/data/
38. Vescan, A., Grosan, C.: A hybrid evolutionary multiobjective approach for the component selection problem. In: Corchado, E., Abraham, A., Pedrycz, W. (eds.) HAIS 2008. LNCS (LNAI), vol. 5271, pp. 164–171. Springer, Heidelberg (2008)

A Data Structure to Speed-Up Machine Learning Algorithms on Massive Datasets

Francisco Padillo[1], J.M. Luna[1], Alberto Cano[2], and Sebastián Ventura[1(✉)]

[1] Department of Computer Science and Numerical Analysis, University of Cordoba,
Rabanales Campus, 14071 Cordoba, Spain
{i12paruf,jmluna,sventura}@uco.es
[2] Department of Computer Science, School of Engineering,
Virginia Commonwealth University, 401 W. Main St, East Hall,
E4251, Richmond, VA, USA
acano@vcu.edu

Abstract. Data processing in a fast and efficient way is an important functionality in machine learning, especially with the growing interest in data storage. This exponential increment in data size has hampered traditional techniques for data analysis and data processing, giving rise to a new set of methodologies under the term Big Data. Many efficient algorithms for machine learning have been proposed, facing up time and main memory requirements. Nevertheless, this process could still become hard when the number of features or records is extremely high. In this paper, the goal is not to propose new efficient algorithms but a new data structure that could be used by a variety of existing algorithms without modifying their original schemata. Moreover, the proposed data structure enables sparse datasets to be massively reduced, efficiently processing the data input into a new data structure output. The results demonstrate that the proposed data structure is highly promising, reducing the amount of storage and improving query performance.

Keywords: Machine learning · Data structure · Massive data

1 Introduction

Big Data is a buzzword used for managing huge amount of data generated from many sources such as social media, mobile devices, web log data, etc. Although, the origin of the term Big Data dates back to 1997 [1], nowadays it is a reality. The increasing amount of electronically available data have given rise to increasingly large datasets, which exceed the capacity of traditional machine learning algorithms with respect to memory consumption and performance in reasonable time. Hence, there is a necessity for speeding up machine learning and data mining processes [2]. The use of datasets in the order of terabytes is a usual thing, and the processing of such large datasets in a efficient way is of great interest in many fields, especially in machine learning where data are the cornerstone. Machine learning algorithms need to scan through the data for obtaining the

© Springer International Publishing Switzerland 2016
F. Martínez-Álvarez et al. (Eds.): HAIS 2016, LNAI 9648, pp. 365–376, 2016.
DOI: 10.1007/978-3-319-32034-2_31

statistic to solve or optimize model parameters. It calls for intensive computing to access the large-scale data frequently.

Thereby, the goal of this work is to describe a suitable data structure that enables to reduce the data size and provides a faster access to the stored information. The required memory storage reduction is achieved by sorting data in a special way using a shuffling strategy based on the Hamming distance (HD) [3]. An inverted index construction [4] and a compression step using a run length encoding (RLE) [5] are also employed. The resulting data reorganization allows fitting more data into main memory achieving faster data accesses.

The data structure is properly designed to be easily adapted to future parallelizations, although the experimental study is carried out in a sequential way. Thus, the results are not influenced by the parallelization but only by the data representation. The application of the proposed data structure to machine learning algorithms is highly promising, achieving excellent computational time and memory requirements. For example, its use in an algorithm that requires many data accesses reveals high efficiency, achieving reduction ratios above 90 % in almost all cases. Datasets primarily populated with zeros or sparse datasets are also considered in our proposal, achieving a reduction of elements in almost 50 %.

This paper is structured as follows. Section 2 provides a relevant Background. Sections 3 describes the proposed data structure. Section 4 describes the experiments and discusses the results. Finally, Sect. 5 outlines some concluding remarks achieved in this work.

2   Background

Nowadays, a large volume of data are being collected to achieve a better decision making process. Many different sources of data, such as social network interactions or servers constantly recording about what the online users are doing, are being collected and grouped provoking that data are totally heterogeneous. Our capability for data generation had never been so powerful and enormous since almost the invention of the information technology in the early 19th century. As a large volume of non-processed data are being collected, the process of extracting knowledge from massive datasets is more and more unfeasible [6]. But the worst of all of this, is that instead of having more information, people feel less proficient in decision making.

Although many different algorithms have been proposed on machine learning, almost of all them have something in common: many data accesses are required [7]. When few data are considered, traditional machine learning algorithms work without any issue, but it does not occur in the same way with massive datasets, especially, with algorithms such as k-nearest neighbor (KNN) [8] where the data size is the cornerstone.

KNN [8] computes the distances from the query point to all the n points in the data set and picks the closet point. Thus, if our data set has N instances, it will require to iterate over the whole dataset N times, as a rule of thumb this methodology is incapable of handling massive data set due to its data size.

Hence, there is an increasing interest in the reduction of computational and memory requirements, so speeding up the data accesses in tool-kits such as Weka [9] is a very alluring challenge.

3   Massive Data Structure

In this work, a novel and highly effective data representation to efficiently process multiple heterogeneous datasets is proposed. In this sense, it simplifies and reorganizes data items in order to reduce the data size and provide a faster access to the stored information, guaranteeing the validity, accuracy, usability and integrity of the original data.

Our proposal is based on the fact that the specific order of the records in a dataset is not as important as the their own feature values are. When these features are deeply analyzed, it is discovered that their values are not so different as they seem at first glance. Even when the feature under analysis represents a continuous domain, the number of distinct values is not so high.

Fig. 1. Workflow of the methodology used to create the new data structure

The proposed data structure is completely hidden and transparent for the end user. No knowledge about how the data are organized is required. Also, an easy and simple yet expressive API similar is proposed[1].

Figure 1 shows a overview of the methodology used to create the new data structure, whose steps are detailed in the following sections. Firstly, the shuffling strategy is carried out enabling data to be sorted by HD. Secondly, an index construction is performed to create an efficient data structure. Finally, a compression process is implemented, based on RLE.

3.1   Shuffling Strategy

As mentioned above, a major characteristic of any dataset in Big Data is its similarity among records. In fact, in Big Data is possible to find millions or even billions of instances, thus the probability is greater than in small datasets. Hence, the higher the number of records of a dataset, the more probable is that two records share similar feature values, or even being completely the same, thereby these records could be clustered in a same set of features. To achieve it, a shuffling strategy based on a similarity metric rather than a distance metric is proposed. In concrete, HD is used as a similarity metric, where similar records

---

[1] Information about the API is available in: http://www.uco.es/grupos/kdis/kdiswiki/SpeedingUpML.

Step 1

Input data	Sorted data	HD
b, 0.0, 0	c, 0.5, 0	2

Step 2

Input data	Sorted data	HD
a, 0.0, 1	b, 0.0, 0	3
	c, 0.5, 0	3

Step 3

Input data	Sorted data	HD
a, 0.5, 0	b, 0.0, 0	2
	c, 0.5, 0	2
	a, 0.0, 1	2

Step 4

Input data	Sorted data	HD
a, ?, 0	b, 0.0, 0	2
	c, 0.5, 0	2
	a, 0.0, 1	2
	a, 0.5, 0	1

Step 5

Input data	Sorted data	HD
a, 0.5, 1	b, 0.0, 0	2
	c, 0.5, 0	3
	a, 0.0, 1	1
	a, 0.5, 0	1
	a, ?, 0	2

Step 6

Input data	Sorted data	HD
	b, 0.0, 0	
	c, 0.5, 0	
	a, 0.0, 1	
	a, 0.5, 0	
	a, 0.5, 1	
	a, ?, 0	

Fig. 2. Shuffling strategy based on the HD between set of records. HD is used as a similarity metric, enabling the number of different values for each transaction to be calculated

are clustered in order to minimize the number of changes in the feature values from one record to another. On this way, data sharing the same values could be merged in a subsequent compression process.

HD is used as a form of determining the number of distinct values comprised in two records, because two records in a dataset tend to be similar when their features share the same values. Thus, the lower the HD value, the higher the probability that both instances are clustered in the same group. In order to clarify this point, consider an heterogeneous set of records which comprises three features or attributes defined into different domains: first attribute is defined in a discrete domain, comprising the values a, b or c; second and third attributes are defined in a continuous domain, comprising any real or integer value respectively. Additionally, a missing value with the symbol '?' has been added, to demonstrate that the proposal is also applicable to this type of values. In this regard, we introduce the shuffling strategy by considering a set of heterogeneous records that comprise three different kind of values: categorical, numeric, and missing.

As shown in Fig. 2, the proposed shuffling strategy begins with the first record, which is added to the new dataset. When a new record is considered, the approach calculates the HD from this record to each one of the N stored. The new record is stored close to the most similar existing record. In such a situation where two or more records are equally promising to be chosen, the last one is selected since no one could be considered to be better than another. Finally, it should be noted that this is a one pass process, so this reordering process can also be done on streaming data.

The idea behind this shuffling strategy is to group similar attributes that could be joined in a subsequent compression process. Thus, it is interesting to check the dataset as a set of features that could be grouped. Once the shuffling strategy is performed, the dataset could be considered as the transpose of the resulting sorted data, considering three lists of features for this sample dataset: $Attribute1 : \{b, c, a, a, a\}$, $Attribute2 : \{0.0, 0.5, 0.0, 0.5, 0.5, ?\}$, and $Attribute3 : \{0, 0, 1, 0, 1, 0\}$.

3.2   Index Construction

This part is considered as one of the most important procedure of the proposed methodology. Once the shuffling strategy is carried out and the data is sorted by the similarity between transactions, an efficient structure to organize and compress data is required. The goal of this procedure is to map the index of attribute values according to the transactions satisfied, which could be joined when consecutive transactions share the same value (RLE).

This process gets as input data *(sorted_data)* the set of transactions reshuffled according to the similarities between pairs of transactions. Later, it follows an inverted index methodology, assigning a key-value pair to each list of features or attributes, providing a new data structure where the attribute value have pointers to any transaction index satisfied by the attribute value.

In order to demonstrate the efficiency of the index construction, we have carried out the computational and space complexity analysis. Firstly, it should be noted that the computational complexity depends on the number of unique values considered in the whole set of attributes ($\mathcal{X}_{unique\_values}$) and the number of instances ($\mathcal{X}_{num\_instances}$). Thus, we determine that the computational complexity of this process is $\mathcal{O}(\mathcal{X}_{unique\_values} \times \mathcal{X}_{num\_instances})$. Secondly, the space complexity of this index construction process also depends on the number of unique values considered in the whole set of attributes ($\mathcal{X}_{unique\_values}$) and the number of instances or transactions ($\mathcal{X}_{num\_instances}$). Hence, we could state that the final space complexity for the index construction process is $\mathcal{O}(\mathcal{X}_{unique\_values} \times \mathcal{X}_{num\_instances})$.

Figure 3 illustrates the new data structure once the inverted index construction is applied to the sample dataset (lists of features) described above. It should be noted that each value is unique, so a discrete or categorical attribute is considered in the same way as a numerical one. The main difference lies in the number of unique values. Thus, each feature points out its values, and each value points out its indexes. For instance, as is shown in Fig. 3, the *Attribute1* feature describes three different values: *a*, *b*, and *c* where each of these values match a pointers to the indexes of the instances satisfied by the attribute value.

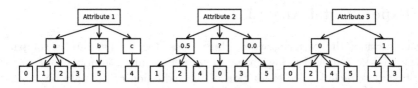

Fig. 3. Inverted index mapping takes the set of features and produces a set of intermediate key-value pairs comprising the feature values and the instances satisfied

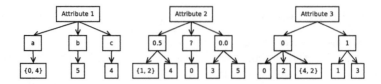

Fig. 4. Resulting data structure once the RLE is applied on the new data structure. Note that in pointers $\{x, k\}$, x denotes the start index and k is the total number of consecutive transactions containing the same feature value

3.3   Compression Process

Once the data structure is obtained, a compression procedure is performed. This is based on an idea similar to a RLE compression, where the data structure is simplified, enabling lower memory requirements and speeding up the data access. RLE is a form of data compression in which sequences of data having the same values occur in a consecutive way. Considering the aforementioned data structure (see Fig. 3), the consecutive indexes for each attribute could be grouped into a 2-tuple that defines a starting index and the total number of consecutive transactions containing the same feature value $\{index, displacement\}$. In this regard, the resulting data structure (see Fig. 4) is compressed thanks to the clustering of consecutive indexes.

Similarly to the analysis carried out for the index construction, the computational and the space complexity of the compression procedure have been analyzed. Firstly, the computational complexity only depends on the number of unique values considered in the whole set of attributes ($\mathcal{X}_{unique\_values}$) since a compression step is considered for each one of the unique values. Thus, the computational complexity of this process is $\mathcal{O}(\mathcal{X}_{unique\_values})$. Secondly, the space complexity of this compression process also depends on the number of unique values considered in the whole set of attributes ($\mathcal{X}_{unique\_values}$) and the number of instances or transactions ($\mathcal{X}_{num\_instances}$). Hence, the final space complexity for the compression process is $\mathcal{O}(\mathcal{X}_{unique\_values} \times \mathcal{X}_{num\_instances})$.

4   Experimental Analysis

In this section, the performance of the proposed data structure is compared to the well-known ARFF file format. Our benchmark comprises four tasks[2]. The first task includes the evaluation of the reduction of the data on the new representation. In the second task, the memory requirements required to save the data are analyzed. Then, the computational time to run a set of queries and to load the dataset is described. Finally, the proposed data structure is applied on a well-known machine learning algorithm that requires many data accesses like the KNN [8] algorithm. Table 1 shows the datasets information, the number of

---

[2] Due to space limitations, we have put a table with the results for each dataset at the website http://www.uco.es/grupos/kdis/kdiswiki/SpeedingUpML.

instances and attributes. Multiple datasets with different sizes are considered to evaluate the performance of the proposal, these have been categorized as dense and sparse datasets. It should be noted that an special format of ARFF highly optimized for sparse data (Sparse ARFF) has been considered.

Table 1 contains the dataset information, the reduction ratio in term of number of elements, file size, object file size, memory used, time to load dataset, time to load object and time for some queries. An explanation of all of this will be developed in further sections.

It should be noted that all the experiments were carried out without any kind of parallelization since the goal is to demonstrate that the proposed data structure is highly efficient by itself, in order to make a fair comparison with ARFF format. Also, the data structure is properly designed to be easily adapted to future parallelizations.

4.1   Data Reduction

In this first analysis, the behavior of the proposed methodology is studied in term of data size reduction. Our proposal has been compared to other famous compression algorithms such as, the universal compressor *Zip* [10] and the *Krimp* Algorithm [11], in order to know which level of compression could be achieved. Figure 5 shows a box-plot that quantifies the file size once different compressions have been applied to the original data. Although, the goal of this work is not to propose a new compression algorithm but an efficient data structure, it has been considered interesting to show how the proposed data structure behaves in terms of data compression. It gets over the *krimp* algorithm, and as expected our data structure does not get over about *Zip* compression, whose unique aim is to compress data. However, in our proposal the query can be executed directly on the compressed data without decompression unlike *Zip* compression.

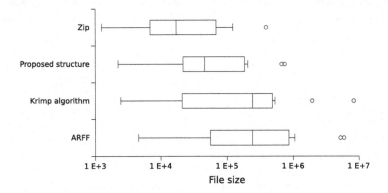

Fig. 5. A box-plot representing the file size of different massive datasets once different compression methods are applied with respect to original file size

As shown in Fig. 5, data are massively reduced in the new methodology since attribute values and instances are clustered. As forth-column in Table 1 shows, the reduction ratio (reduction of the size of our proposal with regards of ARFF) is even higher in sparse datasets, where data is represented by using less than 50 % of the elements required with the ARFF representation in the worst case scenario, whereas in the best a 6.27 % of the original number of elements are used.

Regarding the file size, the results illustrate a high reduction in many cases (see fifth-column in Table 1). For instance, using the *KDDCup99* dataset, the ARFF file size is 529.14 MBytes, whereas our proposal file size is 13.42 MBytes, so the data have been compressed in a 2.54 % of the original data size. This surprising reduction is obtained thanks to the data clustering since this dataset includes many repeated feature values that are easily grouped. Similarly, the data object for the dataset under analysis is extremely better than the one provided by ARFF, as the data object size illustrates (see sixth-column in Table 1). Our proposal object size is 17.35 MBytes, supposing only a 0.99 % of the original object size.

Nevertheless, this extremely high reduction is not always possible, and some datasets do not enable good ensembles of attribute values. For instance, datasets that comprises many different numerical values as *P53* dataset, which includes 5408 attributes comprising a continuous domain, having all instances unique numerical values. For this specific dataset, the reduction is not so high because there is no possible clustering of feature values, yet the data access is faster as it is shown in subsequent sections.

4.2   Memory Requirements

In this second study, the memory requirements to save the datasets in main memory are analyzed. Figure 6 shows a box-plot comparing the memory required to save them in main memory. The reduction ratio obtained in the memory use is very high, allowing of using big datasets on machines with small memory capacities.

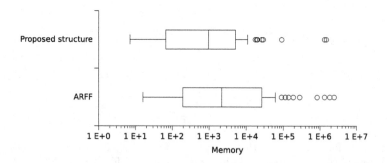

Fig. 6. A box-plot comparing the memory used for our proposal vs the original ARFF file

Analyzing the *KDDCup99* dataset (see seventh-column in Table 1), only 16 MBytes of memory are required by using the new data structure, meanwhile the ARFF structure needs close to 2 GBytes of memory. Thus, our proposal only needs a 1 % of its original memory size, these results open a new perspective in machine learning where huge data sizes could be analyzed that in the past were unfeasible.

The *P53* dataset is again the worst result obtained, the demanded memory has been reduced from 1.33 MBytes to 1.32 MBytes. As this dataset is primarily populated with different values, only a reduction ratio of 0.51 % has been achieved. Nevertheless, the reduction is highly promising in the rest of datasets.

4.3   Loading Time and Data Queries

In a third study, the loading time is analyzed, as the Fig. 7 shows, the new data representation enables the data to be loaded faster. This reduction is much more pronounced when dealing with data objects instead of plain text files (see eight and nineth-column on Table 1). In this regard, the reduction ratio is higher than 90 % of the original time in most of the datasets, demonstrating that ARFF datasets are much more time-consuming to be loaded. For example, although the memory used for the *P53* dataset could not be improved, the loading time has been reduced substantially, using only a 40 % of the original time. This reduction ratio in loading time is not so high for the sparse datasets since this type of data have already a very efficient and optimized representation, however a difference of Sparse ARFF the memory requirements have been reduced. Again, the loading time has been improved reducing on this way the computation time for machine learning algorithms, which need to read the whole dataset multiple times.

The time required to run a set of predefined queries is illustrated in the last column of Table 1. In order to do a fair comparison, the data queries were defined to comprise any kind of attributes of the datasets. Thus, for a dataset it is run as many queries as the number of attributes, so the time required from a dataset to another cannot be compared, but the comparison of queries runtime between ARFF and our proposal for a dataset is fair since they run the same query to the same attributes.

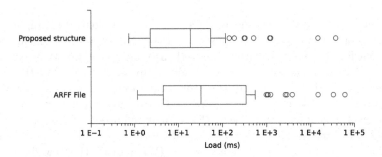

Fig. 7. A box-plot representing the loading time of different massive datasets

Table 1. Datasets information (number of instances and attributes) and reduction ratios obtained by the proposed data structure: number of elements, plain file size, object file size, memory size, plain file loading time, object file loading time and runtime queries.

Dataset	Instances	Atts	Reduct. elements	Reduct. File (KB)	Reduct. Obj (KB)	Reduct. Memo.	Reduct. LoadFile	Reduct. LoadObj	Reduct. Queries
				Dense datasets					
Iris	150	5	20.53%	60.00%	58.33%	56.25%	36.21%	35.82%	60.61%
Glass	214	10	17.57%	30.77%	36.00%	65.54%	13.56%	25.10%	76.92%
Bupa	345	7	17.60%	14.29%	46.67%	56.41%	12.68%	61.71%	82.80%
Diabetes	768	9	13.54%	36.36%	41.03%	51.04%	9.29%	75.68%	84.95%
Pima	768	9	13.73%	36.36%	41.03%	51.04%	10.48%	76.94%	84.72%
Vote	435	17	74.36%	72.22%	86.49%	82.42%	58.19%	61.02%	80.00%
Tic-tac-toe	958	10	58.48%	65.38%	83.81%	84.73%	40.21%	79.33%	89.83%
Australian	690	15	49.14%	34.62%	64.08%	66.39%	25.28%	63.45%	85.34%
Sonar	208	61	1.50%	2.33%	10.71%	14.17%	11.80%	44.64%	85.57%
Yeast	1,484	9	34.88%	36.84%	58.11%	62.30%	19.44%	68.80%	90.65%
Vowel	990	14	24.95%	7.87%	41.73%	46.39%	24.24%	75.04%	72.09%
Cmc	1,473	10	67.07%	58.06%	83.02%	85.05%	45.14%	80.57%	92.90%
Ankara	1,609	10	9.75%	9.46%	36.99%	46.19%	7.19%	78.87%	86.76%
WDBC	569	31	3.16%	4.17%	14.56%	20.45%	13.37%	67.89%	73.06%
German	1,000	21	47.20%	63.29%	70.56%	70.74%	45.17%	68.34%	91.62%
Soybean	683	36	83.05%	93.21%	90.00%	78.04%	81.96%	59.13%	88.99%
Page-blocks	5,472	11	21.49%	12.55%	32.70%	24.73%	8.87%	16.21%	70.56%
Nursery	12,690	8	72.99%	94.11%	91.49%	92.77%	85.22%	97.62%	87.37%
Chess	3,196	37	92.26%	90.87%	96.18%	95.58%	88.03%	88.36%	86.96%
HillValley	1,212	101	0.87%	1.00%	4.90%	7.57%	35.79%	61.59%	53.05%
Mushroom	5,644	23	90.36%	88.58%	95.51%	94.94%	85.21%	91.81%	86.25%
Twonorm	7,400	21	4.73%	1.39%	18.79%	27.32%	28.45%	91.84%	48.27%
Penbased	10,992	17	12.37%	10.63%	31.91%	39.53%	22.24%	90.29%	76.64%
Kr-vs-k	28,056	7	70.65%	74.42%	90.27%	92.12%	63.73%	98.39%	90.74%
Magic	19,020	11	9.01%	2.57%	31.63%	42.82%	16.07%	96.48%	42.79%
Satimage	6,435	37	2.61%	4.16%	16.07%	21.17%	8.33%	83.71%	78.18%
Letter	20,000	16	46.82%	44.54%	79.11%	81.25%	38.21%	95.34%	96.99%
Electricity	45,312	9	27.83%	19.64%	49.85%	58.46%	2.72%	95.02%	52.53%
Shuttle	58,000	10	77.10%	76.23%	87.52%	89.22%	71.63%	97.20%	94.03%
Adult	48,842	14	71.47%	85.90%	83.70%	37.30%	75.44%	97.14%	44.36%
Coil2000	9,822	86	84.84%	81.08%	92.42%	92.19%	81.21%	88.30%	92.75%
MovieLens	943	1,682	85.93%	82.44%	90.62%	87.01%	83.68%	28.26%	69.13%
Connect-4	67,557	43	90.46%	88.78%	95.58%	95.76%	88.84%	98.71%	83.42%
Fars	100,968	30	88.42%	98.36%	93.24%	92.77%	95.44%	98.08%	91.84%
Comedy	1,138,562	3	72.72%	88.68%	91.49%	87.82%	82.28%	94.20%	96.13%
Airlines	539,383	8	79.57%	82.94%	92.41%	93.26%	74.10%	95.06%	99.83%
Poker-lsn	829,201	11	80.77%	77.16%	92.77%	93.95%	70.63%	99.54%	96.97%
Poker	1,025,009	11	60.32%	54.10%	85.08%	87.52%	58.19%	99.23%	95.80%
Census	299,284	42	85.01%	95.46%	90.79%	91.05%	88.61%	94.76%	40.90%
KDDcup99-10	494,020	42	97.05%	96.21%	98.29%	97.95%	95.53%	93.00%	97.10%
Covtype	581,012	55	86.23%	71.03%	89.26%	89.74%	69.01%	97.59%	59.69%
Donation	5,749,132	12	83.08%	70.85%	87.10%	89.10%	0.36%	99.51%	40.76%
P53	31,420	5,409	0.25%	0.18%	0.47%	0.51%	38.09%	39.01%	51.05%
KDDcup99	4,898,431	42	98.00%	97.46%	99.01%	98.97%	96.28%	99.16%	98.11%
				Sparse datasets					
Internet-ads	3,279	1,559	78.82%	71.50%	78.91%	65.42%	61.12%	46.56%	90.09%
Dexter	600	20,000	49.65%	34.85%	43.50%	34.66%	14.85%	31.82%	8.67%
Reuters	15,564	47,237	49.29%	5.56%	17.69%	23.18%	10.75%	35.60%	81.94%
Imdb	120,919	1,002	48.06%	1.59%	21.08%	29.84%	6.24%	94.31%	99.85%
KDD09	100,000	15,002	66.60%	32.39%	36.58%	39.25%	25.28%	41.75%	74.32%
Url	2,396,130	3,231,962	93.73%	88.34%	89.36%	84.01%	87.16%	58.78%	78.03%

Results illustrate that, for dense datasets, the reduction rate is higher than 40 %, demonstrating that the proposed data structure is very promising to be used in machine learning algorithms, since their running time would be extremely reduced. This reduction is not so high in all the sparse datasets, but the results are still very good. For instance, the *Reuters* dataset, which comprises 47,237 attributes and 15,564 instances, requires 491 s to compute the data queries in our proposal format, whereas the ARFF format requires 2,722 seconds to run the same set of queries, an improvement of 81.94 %.

Unlike the memory requirements for the *P53* dataset, the new data structure enables a faster data access for this dataset. Thus, it demonstrates that,

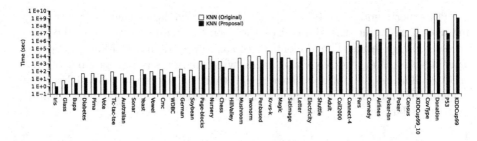

Fig. 8. Runtime in seconds when both the original and the proposed data structure are applied to the KNN algorithm using a varied set of massive datasets

even when the dataset cannot be massively reduced, the data access could be improved. The reduction ratio is higher than 40 % in all the dense datasets. As for the sparse datasets, the results depicted in Table 1 show a good behavior even when the new data structure is compared to sparse ARFF, which is highly optimized.

4.4 Performance on Machine Learning

Finally, we evaluate the performance of the proposal under the use of a well-known machine learning algorithm such as the k-nearest neighbor (KNN) algorithm [8], which requires many data accesses. By means of this study, we want to demonstrate that the proposed data structure not only enables the data size to be reduced but it also reduces the access time to data and therefore, it reduces the runtime in high time-consuming machine learning algorithms.

The Fig. 8 shows the performance using our proposal, which is extremely promising, highly reducing the execution time. For instance, the runtime on the *KDDCup99* dataset is reduced to about a third. The runtime on the *P53* has been improved in spite of this dataset obtained the worst results in almost all the previous studies. It is interesting to point out that the reduction in almost all of the datasets is noteworthy, allowing of reducing the runtime significantly.

Regarding the sparse datasets, the reduction ratio is still very good, demonstrating that the proposed data structure behaves very well when it is applied on a machine learning algorithm.

5   Concluding Remarks

In this paper, a novel data structure for machine learning was proposed. The new data structure provides a highly effective representation to efficiently process multiple heterogeneous datasets. This is an important functionality in machine learning, where the fast data access is a cornerstone. The motivation and idea behind our approach is to improve the performance of existing algorithms without any modification in their original schemata. Thus, it is a great advantage since the performance capabilities of many existing algorithms could be improved.

The experimental results reveal that the proposed data structure is extremely promising, reducing the data size, the memory requirements and the data accesses in high levels. The model has been also applied on a well-known machine learning algorithm, the KNN algorithm, which requires a high number of data accesses. The results obtained have shown that the use of the proposed schema is highly recommended in the field of machine learning, especially when dealing with large datasets.

Acknowledgments. This research was supported by the Spanish Ministry of Economy and Competitiveness, project TIN-2014-55252-P, and by FEDER funds.

References

1. Cox, M., Ellsworth, D.: Application-controlled demand paging for out-of-core visualization. In: Proceedings of the 8th Conference on Visualization 1997, VIS 1997, pp. 235-ff. IEEE Computer Society Press, Los Alamitos (1997)
2. Cano, A., Luna, J.M., Ventura, S.: High performance evaluation of evolutionary-mined association rules on gpus. J. Supercomput. **66**(3), 1438–1461 (2013)
3. Deza, M.M., Deza, E.: Encyclopedia of Distances. Springer, Berlin (2009)
4. Luk, R., Lam, W.: Efficient in-memory extensible inverted file. Inform. Syst. **32**(5), 733–754 (2007)
5. Abadi, D., Madden, S., Ferreira, M.: Integrating compression and execution in column-oriented database systems. In: Proceedings of the ACM SIGMOD International Conference on Management of Data, pp. 671–682. SIGMOD Conference, Chicago, Illinois, USA (2006)
6. Rajaraman, A., Ullman, J.D.: Mining of Massive Datasets. Cambridge University Press, New York (2011)
7. Wu, X., Zhu, X., Wu, G.Q., Ding, W.: Data mining with big data. IEEE Trans. Knowl. Data Eng. **26**(1), 97–107 (2014)
8. Cover, T., Hart, P.: Nearest neighbor pattern classification. IEEE Trans. Inf. Theory **13**(1), 21–27 (1967)
9. Hall, M., Frank, E., Holmes, G., Pfahringer, B., Reutemannr, P., Witten, I.H.: The WEKA data mining software: an update. SIGKDD Explor. **11**, 10–18 (2009)
10. Cover, T.M., Thomas, J.A.: Elements of Information Theory (Chap. 3), 2nd edn. Wiley-Interscience (2006)
11. Vreeken, J., Leeuwen, M., Siebes, A.: Krimp: mining itemsets that compress. Data Min. Knowl. Discovery **23**(1), 169–214 (2011)

A Sensory Control System for Adjusting Group Emotion Using Bayesian Networks and Reinforcement Learning

Jun-Ho Kim, Ki-Hoon Kim, and Sung-Bae Cho[✉]

Department of Computer Science, Yonsei University, Seoul, Korea
barabarada@sclab.yonsei.ac.kr, aruwad.open@gmail.com,
sbcho@yonsei.ac.kr

Abstract. The relationship between sensory stimuli and emotion has been actively investigated, but it is relatively undisclosed to determine appropriate stimuli for inducing the target emotion for a group of people in the same space like school, hospital, store, etc. In this paper, we propose a stimuli control system to adjust group emotion in a closed space, especially kindergarten. The proposed system predicts the next emotion of a group of people using modular tree-structured Bayesian networks, and controls the stimuli appropriate to the target emotion using utility table initialized by domain knowledge and adapted by reinforcement learning as the cases of stimuli and emotions are cumulated. To evaluate the proposed system, the real data were collected for five days from a kindergarten where the sensor and stimulus devices were installed. We obtained 84 % of prediction accuracy, and 56.2 % of stimuli control accuracy. Moreover, in the scenario tests on math and music classes, we could control the stimuli to fit the target emotion with 63.2 % and 76.3 % accuracies, respectively.

1 Introduction

The emotion can affect human's mind. Recently, the services to promote user's purchase and educational satisfaction by sensory stimuli have been actively investigated. For an example, emotion can affect to the effect of education, and some curricula are designed so that the students feel specific emotion. Table 1 shows the elements that can be measured and controlled in an educational institute, especially kindergarten. These elements are selected by teachers in the kindergarten. They affect children's emotion, but do not disturb the curricula of kindergarten. Conventional studies utilize many devices like electrode attached on subject's skin, but they disturb education and can affect to subject's emotion.

In this paper, we propose a group emotion control system in kindergarten class by controlling stimuli. Even though kindergarten is a target domain in this paper, the proposed method can be easily applied to any space that requires to control stimuli for inducing appropriate emotion. The proposed system is composed of the two parts of predicting emotion and determining stimuli as shown in Fig. 1. At the first part, the next emotion is predicted using modular tree-structured Bayesian networks. At the second part, the proper stimuli to change it to the target emotion are determined by utility table, which is initialized by domain knowledge and adapted by reinforcement learning.

© Springer International Publishing Switzerland 2016
F. Martínez-Álvarez et al. (Eds.): HAIS 2016, LNAI 9648, pp. 377–388, 2016.
DOI: 10.1007/978-3-319-32034-2_32

Table 1. The elements to be measured and controlled in kindergarten

Type	Stimulus	State
Visual	Lux	200 lx, 700 lx, 1000 lx
	Color temperature	1000 K, 3000 K, 7000 K
	Video	V_1, V_2, V_3, V_4 (Pre-defined videos)
Auditory	Sound	S_1, S_2, S_3, S_4 (Pre-defined sounds)
	Volume	20 db, 40 db, 60 db
Olfactory	Scent	lavender, lemon, jasmine, rose
Tactile	Temperature	18 °C, 23 °C, 25 °C, 28 °C
	Humidity	30 %, 40 %, 50 %, 70 %

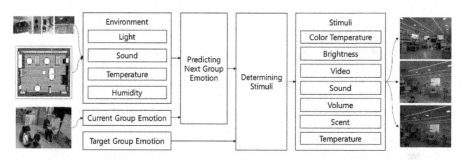

Fig. 1. A process of controlling stimuli for inducing emotion in the kindergarten

2   Related Works

Predicting emotion from data such as facial, vocal, and text has been the focus of a large number of studies over the past several decades. Table 2 shows the emotion recognition research which use raw-data.

Table 2. Studies to predict emotion

Authors	Input	Proposed method
Black and Yacoob [4]	Image	Rule-based
Eyharabide et al. [5]	Text	Ontology
Yacoub et al. [6]	Speech	k-Nearest neighbor, Support vector machine, Neural network, Decision tree
Lee et al. [7]	Speech	Decision tree
Utane and Nalbalwar [8]	Speech	Hidden Markov Model
Hayamizu et al. [9]	Facial image, Speech	Bayesian networks
Ivon, et al. [11]	Facial image, GSR, Accelerometer	Bayesian networks

Black extracted features from facial image and defined rules to classify emotion [4]. Eyharabide recognized emotion using ontology and applied it to e-learning service [5]. Yacoub compared four types of classification method using speech data [6]. Lee classified speech data for human and robot interaction [7]. The robot recognizes emotion and responds depending on the current states of emotion. Utane applied emotion recognition to natural conversation between human and computer [8]. Hayamizu designed Bayesian network to recognize group emotion considering the previous state of emotion [9]. Previous works focused on accurate recognition using personal data. However, in the emotional service, we cannot use personal data like speech or face. We have to predict emotion from information on specific environment that usually come from multimodal sensors. We proposed the Bayesian network to predict group emotion before, but it is not constructed as a complete system [10].

3 The Proposed System

In this paper, we deal with not the specific emotions such as happiness, sadness, anger, etc., but four groups of emotions based on Valance-Arousal (V-A) model proposed by Russell [2]. In this model, emotions can be mapped on a space of positive-negative degree and arousal-relax degree, leading to one of four emotions such as positive-arousal (P-A), positive-relax (P-R), negative-arousal (N-A), and negative-relax (N-R) as shown in Fig. 2.

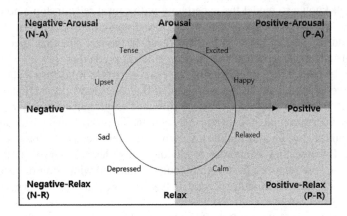

Fig. 2. Arousal-variance model for representing emotions

Based on this emotion model, the proposed system is as shown in Fig. 3. Bayesian networks predict the next emotion, and utility table finds proper stimuli for target emotion. The utility table is initialized by domain knowledge and adapted by reinforcement learning.

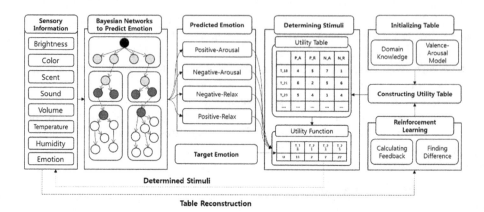

Fig. 3. The overall structure of the proposed system

3.1   Emotion Prediction by Bayesian Networks

To determine the proper stimuli, the emotion of a group of people has to be predicted from environment information. Bayesian networks are used to predict emotion because they are well-known to model the uncertainty with causal relationship among events. We can construct single Bayesian network from domain knowledge provided by the literature and teachers in kindergarten. However, in the real situation, there are quite many events and evidences that hinders from efficient prediction.

In order to reduce the complexity of Bayesian network, we devise a sophisticated method to model it with modular tree-structured Bayesian networks. At first, we design the modular Bayesian networks to adopt different environments easily by utilizing Markov boundary to find boundaries between modules [12]. After calculating the Markov boundary, we find the middle nodes that are overlapped more than two Markov boundaries. Because they are border of modules, modules are divided by the middle nodes, and they are removed from both modules connected with a pair of virtual nodes inserted in each module. Modules M_i and M_j can be represented as follows:

$$M_i = \left(B_i(TBN) - Md_{ij}\right) \cup V_{ij}$$
$$M_j = \left(B_j(TBN) - Md_{ij}\right) \cup V_{ji} \tag{1}$$
$$V_{ij} = V_{ji} = \left\{S_0, S_2, \ldots, S_n\right\}$$

Md_{ij} is a middle node between M_i and M_j, and V_{ij} means the virtual node that is in M_i and connects M_i and M_j. Virtual nodes have the same states and conditional probability table with the middle node. Virtual nodes in a pair have the same probability in each state. By this process, we can construct modular Bayesian networks.

Next, each module of Bayesian network is converted into a tree-structured Bayesian network. Maximum spanning tree algorithm is used to find connections that strongly affect to prediction performance. Figure 4 shows the conversion algorithm. The weight of edge means the influence when the edge is removed. Suppose the states of two nodes

```
Input: Single Bayesian Network (SBN)
Output: Tree-Structured Bayesian Network (TBN)

TBN = SBN;
Remove all nodes in TBN;
while (Nᵢ is node in SBN)
    Select node Nᵢ;
    Select edge set Eᵢ that includes every edge of Nᵢ;
while (Eᵢ is not empty)
    Select edge Eᵢⱼ that has maximum weight in Eᵢ;
    Make connection Nᵢ and Nⱼ in TBN;
    if (cycleExist(TBN))
        Delete connection between Nᵢ and Nⱼ;
        Delete Eᵢⱼ from Eᵢ;
    else
        Escape the loop;
```

Fig. 4. A conversion algorithm to tree-structured Bayesian network

be X and Y, and the state of output node be C. Then, we can represent the weight of each node I_p as follows:

$$I_p(X, Y) = \sum_{x \in X, y \in Y, c \in C} P(x, y, c) log \frac{p(x, y|c)}{p(x|c)p(y|c)}. \tag{2}$$

After calculating the weight of each edge, we can construct a maximum spanning tree from a module of Bayesian network. Edges are sorted in decreasing order, and is selected every edge that makes no cycle.

The final Bayesian networks constructed to predict emotions in the kindergarten classes have six modules and fifty-five nodes as shown in Fig. 5. The constructed modules are grouped to three parts: "Collecting stimuli data" part, "Combining stimulus" part, and "Predicting emotion" part. There are four modules for collecting stimuli data: touch, sight, hearing, and olfactory sensors. They collect stimuli data from each sense like sound type or volume. "Combining stimuli" module gathers their results, and combines data and the emotion classified from the stimuli. "Predicting emotion" module predicts emotion from the previous emotion, current emotion, and the result of "Combining stimuli" module.

3.2 Stimuli Control by Utility Table

Because emotion is given as probabilities, which represent the uncertainties of emotion, decision making problem can be modeled as POMDP. Q-value would be calculated as weighted sum of Q-values (denoted as EQ) with each probability, as shown in Eq. (3).

The final stimulus is selected as O_{j*}^{a} s.t. $EQ\left(O_{j*}^{a}\right) > EQ\left(O_{j}^{a}\right)$ for $\forall j$, where $j =$ value index of the ath stimulus given, and $k =$ index of emotion.

$$EQ(O_{j}^{a}) = \sum P(k) * Q(s, a) \qquad (3)$$

Because the effect of actions can be known after the action has been taken, we do not know whether unchosen actions are good or bad. The proposed system uses the domain knowledge to initialize the utility table, substituting exploration process manually. Since the data represent the effect to individual emotion, positive, negative, arousal and relax, the proposed system first maps these values onto the V-A plane. Figure 6 shows the mapping algorithm ($N_i\left(O_{j}^{a}\right) =$ number of descriptions with the jth value given and the ath stimulus to the ith emotion). In the first step, $N_i\left(O_{j}^{a}\right)$ values are counted for all i's.

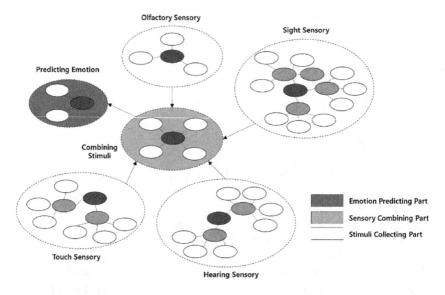

Fig. 5. Modular Bayesian networks to predict emotion in the kindergarten classes

Then, $P\left(O_{j}^{a}\right)$, mapped point, is calculated by their distance. Steps 3 and 4 in Fig. 6 approximate $P\left(O_{j}^{a}\right)$ to the nearest NWc point, with Euclidian distance. Since each NWc represents the membership value to each quadrant, utility values are calculated by a set of linear transition functions using NWc ($S =$ adjusting constant, $NWc = (Xc, Yc)$, $f_i =$ utility value for the ith quadrant).

Step 1: for $\forall\ 1\leqq i \leqq 4$, count the number of words describing O_j^a with given i, and set $N_i(O_j^a)$.

Step 2: calculate $P(O_j^a) = (P_x, P_y) = (N_1(O_j^a) - N_2(O_j^a), N_3(O_j^a) - N_4(O_j^a))$.

Step 3: for $\forall\ 1\leqq c \leqq 12$,
    calculate $d_c(P(O_j^a)) = \sqrt{(Px - Xc)^2 + (Py - Yc)^2}$

Step 4 : select NWc^* s.t. $d_{c^*}(P(O_j^a)) < d_c(P(O_j^a))$ for $\forall\ 1\leqq c \leqq 12$

Fig. 6. An algorithm to initialize utility table

$$
\begin{aligned}
f_1(X_c, Y_c) &= (X_c + Y_c) + S \\
f_2(X_c, Y_c) &= (X_c - Y_c) + S \\
f_3(X_c, Y_c) &= (-X_c + Y_c) + S \\
f_4(X_c, Y_c) &= (-X_c - Y_c) + S
\end{aligned} \tag{4}
$$

The proposed system uses the current emotion and selected stimuli for every period except the first period, and calculates reward $r_{t+1}(s_t, a_t)$ so to update utility table as follows.

$$
Q_{t+1}(s_t, a_t) \leftarrow (1 - \alpha)Q_t(s_t, a_t) + \alpha r_{t+1}(s_t, a_t) \tag{5}
$$

In this equation, α means the reflection rate of data that are gathered from the stimuli control system. If α is zero, the table will not be updated; if α is 1, the table will be reconstructed entirely.

4 Experimental Results

4.1 Data Description

The real data were collected from ten children at the kindergarten classes, where volume indicator, thermometer, hydroscope, illuminometer, and color sensor were installed, as shown in Fig. 7. Thermometer, humidity sensor, microphone, brightness sensor, and color sensor were installed at the wall. We can control temperature, light (for brightness and color temperature), video, sound, and scent. VIBRA system [13] was used to measure the emotion, and the teacher in the class was asked to provide the group emotion.

The data at the classes were collected for five days, and two classes in a day. Sensor data were sampled at every minute and each class was given in twenty minutes. In total, the dataset for all classes amounts to two-hundred instances of brightness, color temperature, humidity, volume, sound, video, scent, current emotion, and next emotion.

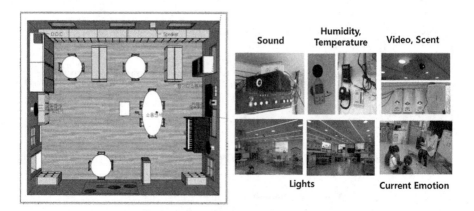

Fig. 7. The kindergarten class that data were collected

4.2   Experiments on Emotion Prediction

The accuracy of emotion prediction was compared with single and tree-structured Bayesian networks, and other classification methods: Decision Tree (DT), Multi-Layer Perception (MLP), K-Nearest Neighbor (KNN), and Support Vector Machine (SVM). Classification methods were evaluated by five-fold cross validation.

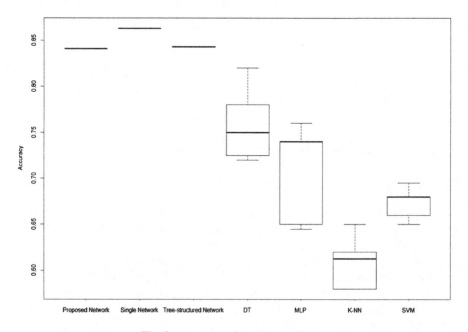

Fig. 8. Accuracy of emotion prediction

Figure 8 shows the accuracy of emotion prediction. The proposed method shows the accuracy of 84 %, which is little lower than single Bayesian network, but much higher than other classification methods. This means the proposed method has better perform-ance than other classification methods, and similar performance with single Bayesian network. When we need faster method with competitive accuracy, the proposed method might be better than single Bayesian network.

4.3   Experiments on Stimuli Control

Figure 9 shows the accuracies of a baseline system without reinforcement learning and the proposed system. 65-minutes data with unclean data excluded were used for the test and 10-fold cross validation was conducted. An accuracy of the baseline system is 39.66 % with standard deviation of 8.82 %, and 15.51 % increase of accuracy is obtained by applying reinforcement learning. Since the utility values of failed cases in the baseline system are not incremented, the specificity is calculated as 100 % for given data.

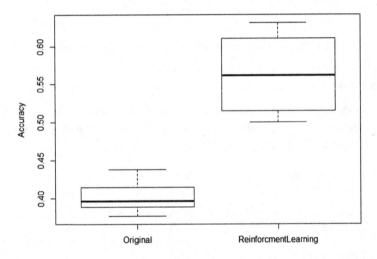

Fig. 9. Accuracy of stimuli control

Figure 10 shows the improvement of accuracy for each update of utility table. As the baseline system does not update, its accuracy is constant at initial accuracy (39.66 %). Improvements are mainly occurred in the 45~50-minutes and 60~65-minutes sections, primarily contributions of success of the second class' color temperature of 6,800 K to the correction of the third class' mis-controlled color temperature of 5,000 K. As shown in the result, enough time is needed to exploit the result of learning, as improvements are mainly occurred in the latter part.

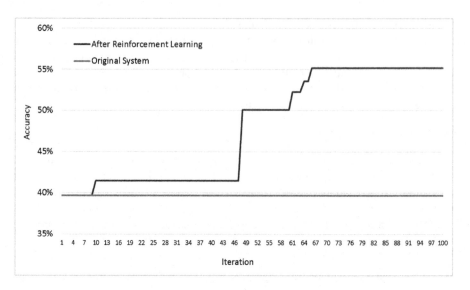

Fig. 10. Accuracy improvements with reinforcement learning

4.4 Scenario Test

To confirm the operational performance, we conducted experiments on a couple of scenarios that include math and music contents at the kindergarten (see Table 3). A scenario composed of three parts was performed in twenty minutes.

Table 3. Two scenarios of math and music classes at the kindergarten

Type		0~5 min	5~15 min	15~20 min
Math	Activity	Finding number	Calculating number	Presenting result
	Target emotion	P-A	P-R	P-A
Music	Activity	Listening	Singing together	Singing alternately
	Target emotion	P-A	P-A	P-R

Figure 11 shows the achievement for math and music scenarios. Achievement is calculated by comparing target and real emotions. If two emotions are the same, it is calculated as 100 %. If two emotions are the same at only one dimension (positive-negative or arousal-relax), it is calculated as 50 %. In the figure, the music scenario has higher achievement than the math scenario, possibly because music is more emotional than math.

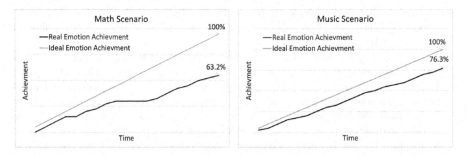

Fig. 11. Emotional achievements for the two scenarios

5   Concluding Remarks

In this paper, we have proposed a sensory stimuli control system to change group emotion at kindergarten classes. The proposed system consists of emotion prediction part and stimuli determination part. Modular tree-structured Bayesian networks are used to predict emotion from environment. They produce more than 80 % accuracy with less complexity, and the performance is much better than other classification methods. It shows better performance for classifying positive and arousal emotions than negative and relax emotions. Utility values are used to determine the stimuli from targeted and predicted emotions, and reinforcement learning is used to adapt the utility table from cumulated data. For the future works, we need to collect more data to verify the proposed system, especially for negative emotions, and apply the system to a variety of domains.

Acknowledgements.   This work was supported by the Industrial Strategic Technology Development Program, 10044828, Development of Augmenting Multisensory Technology for Enhancing Significant Effects on the Service Industry, funded by the Ministry of Trade, Industry and Energy (MI, Korea).

References

1. Brave, S., Nass, C.: The Human-Computer Interaction Handbook: Fundamentals, Evolving Technologies and Emerging Applications, pp. 81–96. CRC Press, Boca Raton (2003)
2. Mehrabian, A., Russell, J.: An Approach to Environmental Psychology. MIT Press, Cambridge (1974)
3. Donovan, R., Rossiter, J.: Store atmosphere: an environmental psychology approach. J. Retail. **58**(1), 34–57 (1982)
4. Black, M., Yacoob, Y.: Tracking and recognizing rigid and non-rigid facial motions using local parametric models of image motion. In: International Conference on Computer Vision, pp. 374–381 (1995)
5. Eyharabide, V., Amandi, A., Courgeon, M., Clavel, C., Zakaria, C., Martin, J.: An ontology for predicting students' emotions during a quiz. In: IEEE Workshop on Affective Computational Intelligence, pp. 1–8 (2011)

6. Yacoub, S., Simske, S., Lin, X., Burns, J.: Recognition of emotions in interactive voice response systems. In: 8th European Conference on Speech Communication and Technology, pp. 1–4 (2003)
7. Lee, C., Mover, E., Busso, C., Lee, S., Narayanan, S.: Emotion recognition using a hierarchical binary decision tree approach. Speech Commun. **53**, 1162–1171 (2011)
8. Utane, A., Nalbalwar, S.: Emotion recognition through speech using Gaussian mixture model and hidden Markov model. Int. J. Adv. Res. Comput. Sci. Software Eng. **3**, 742–746 (2013)
9. Hayamizu, T., Mutsuo, S., Miyawaki, K., Mori, H., Nishiguchi, S., Yamashita, N.: Group emotion estimation using Bayesian network based on facial expression and prosodic information. In: International Conference on Control System, Computing and Engineering, pp. 23–25 (2012)
10. Kim, J., Cho, S.-B.: Predicting group emotion in kindergarten classes by modular Bayesian networks. In: 7th International Conference on Soft Computing and Pattern Recognition, pp. 298–302 (2015)
11. Ivon, A., James, R., Beverly, W.: Using an intelligent tutor and math fluency training to improve math performance. Int. J. Artif. Intell. Educ. **21**(1–2), 135–152 (2011)
12. Yang, K., Cho, S.-B.: Modular dynamic Bayesian network based on Markov boundary for emotion prediction in multi-sensory environment. In: 10th International Conference on Natural Computation, pp. 1131–1136 (2014)
13. Park, J., Kim, J., Hwang, S.: The study on emotional classification algorithm using Vibraimage technology. In: ACED Asian Conference on Ergonomics and Design (2014)
14. Romero, C., Ventura, S., Pechenizkiy, M., Baker, RSJd: Handbook of Educational Data Mining, pp. 323–338. CRC Press, Boca Raton (2010)

Video and Image

Identification of Plant Textures in Agricultural Images by Principal Component Analysis

Martín Montalvo[1(✉)], María Guijarro[2], José Miguel Guerrero[1], and Ángela Ribeiro[3]

[1] Department of Software Engineering and Artificial Intelligence,
School of Computer Science, University Complutense of Madrid, Madrid, Spain
mmontalvo@ucm.es
[2] Department of Computer Architecture and Automatic,
School of Computer Science, University Complutense of Madrid, Madrid, Spain
mguijarro@ucm.es
[3] Centre for Automation and Robotics, (CSIC-UPM), Arganda del Rey, 28500 Madrid, Spain

Abstract. In precision agriculture the extraction of green parts is a very important task. One of the biggest issues, when it comes to computer vision, is image segmentation, which has motivated the research conducted in this work. Our goal is the segmentation of vegetative and soil parts in the images. For this proposal a novel method of segmentation is defined in which different vegetation indices are calculated and through the reduction of components by principal component analysis (PCA) we obtain an enhanced greyscale image. Finally, by Otsu thresholding, we binarize the grayscale image isolating the green parts from the other elements in the image.

Keywords: Segmentation image · Principal component analysis · Thresholding · Agricultural images · Precision agriculture

1 Introduction

Up to the present, due to the increasing use of artificial vision sensors in precision agriculture (PA), it is becoming increasingly important to study different techniques to obtain accurate information. These sensors are in autonomous vehicles and should provide autonomously responses [1].

Recently, important progress in agricultural field images processing has been achieved and automatic segmentation methods have been applied for soil and green parts identification in images oriented toward PA [2, 3].

As we are working with images in outdoor conditions, we have the problem of providing a good automatic segmentation. The main objective is to discern between soil and vegetation, in order to apply the appropriate treatment in the proper areas [4].

Along literature, we can find several strategies, which have been proposed for segmenting agricultural images, specifically oriented towards green segmentation.

Under this approach we can find techniques based in visible spectral indices, including the excess green index (ExG, [5, 6]), the excess red index (ExR, [7]), the colour index of vegetation extraction (CIVE, [8]), and the excess green minus excess red index

© Springer International Publishing Switzerland 2016
F. Martínez-Álvarez et al. (Eds.): HAIS 2016, LNAI 9648, pp. 391–401, 2016.
DOI: 10.1007/978-3-319-32034-2_33

(ExGR, [9]). In addition, the vegetative index (VEG) described in [10], which was designed to cope with the variability of natural daylight illumination. All these approaches are used in our research selecting the best information from each. It is important remark the need to fix a threshold for final segmentation.

Different combinations of these vegetative indices, in order to obtain an improved image, are described in several works. The most relevant in our study are listed. Meyer et al. [11] used the information belonging to ExR and ExG applying unsupervised approaches, including fuzzy clustering, for segmenting regions of interest. Zheng et al. [12, 13] defined the segmentation of green vegetation as a binary classification problem, using a supervised mean-shift algorithm and the color spaces used were RGB, LUV and HSI. Guijarro et al. [14] combines four spectral indices and applies a fuzzy clustering-based strategy for discriminating plants and soil and at a second stage crop and weeds. Guerrero et al. [15] applied support vector machines as learning strategy to discriminate between plants with high and low degrees of greenness.

Numerous papers were focused on the use of principal component analysis (PCA) in agricultural images. The main objective of this method [16] is to reduce the dimensionality of the data set using a change of coordinates. This technique has already been used previously in the field of agriculture for tasks such as in [17] where the technique is used to distinguish plants cranberry in satellite images, in [18] where it is used to check for changes in land for agriculture or [19] where the PCA analysis is used to differentiate leaves of strawberries through geometric descriptors.

Therefore, this paper designed a new combination of vegetative indices using the PCA, with which we obtain a new grey image stressing accurately the vegetative areas. Once we have the enhanced grey image, we used the Otsu thresholding [20] in order to obtain a binary image where the vegetative parts in the image are distinguished.

2   Materials and Methods

In this section, the set of images, which are used in the present study, and the proposed strategy used to identify green plants on the field are detailed.

2.1   Images

All images used for this study belongs to maize crops and were acquired with a SVS-4050CFLGEA industrial digital camera of SVS-VISTEK company. The images were obtained during the months of April and May 2013 and 2014 in a 1.7-ha experimental field of maize on La Poveda Research Station, Arganda del Rey, Madrid. All acquisitions were spaced in the time by several days, in this way it is possible to obtain some sets of images with different growth state and different environmental lightening conditions. Camera intrinsic and extrinsic parameters with witch images have been taken: pitch angle = 20°, roll angle = 0, yaw angle = 0°, height that camera was placed = 1.5 m and the focal length was 8 mm. Images were saved as 24-bit color images in Red, Green and Blue (RGB) color space in the BMP format and the resolutions is 2336 × 1756 pixels. The SVS camera is able to archive a frame rate of 16 with the previous resolution. The images were processed with the Image Processing Toolbox from Matlab 2015a. A representative image captured for this camera and used for this study is showed in Fig. 1(a).

Due to the big resolution images, each captured image was divided into smaller sub-images for getting easily the ground-truth of each image. The sub-images has a 400×400 pixel resolution except the sub-images of corners that have 335×400, 400×151 or 335×441 pixels resolution depending of corner. With this division there would be 30 sub-images per image, but from all these sub-images those which contain a part of a color panel must be discarded. This panel was used for other purposes unrelated to present investigation and can be viewed at the bottom of Fig. 1(a). If the sub-images containing the panel are not considered, there are 22 sub-images per image. These sub-images were used to test the methods of this study. A representative image and a sub-images are showed in Fig. 1(a) y (b) respectively.

a)   *b)*

Fig. 1. (*a*) Original image captured with SVS camera; (*b*) sub-image of image show in (*a*).

2.2   Principal Component Analysis

PCA is one of the most widespread techniques for taking high-dimensional data and reducing the number of variables under consideration to achieve a reduction of the problem complexity and represent it in a more tractable form.

PCA's method reduces the dimension of source data by projecting the data from a n-dimensional space to a m-dimensional subspace, where n > m. In statistical practice, the PCA method is used to find the linear combinations with large variance. In several problems the amount of variables under consideration is too large to handle. Since it is the variance in these studies that are of interest, to discard the linear combinations with small variances and study only those with large variances is a manner of reducing the number of variables to treat. Another perspective to analyze the method is a change to another coordinate system. Transforming the original vector variable to the vector variable of PCA is equivalent to a rotation of coordinate axes that has inherent statistical properties [21].

For this study, the aim is to reduce the dimensionality of the existing data in multiple grayscale images to a single grayscale image, equivalent to reduce an n-dimensional space to a one-dimensional space. For this specific use of case, the sequence of steps to apply PCA to our data set is detailed in part (c) Combination of basis indices by PCA, Sect. 2.3.

2.3 Plant Identification

The proposed strategy is based on PCA and consists of two automatic phases, segmentation and thresholding, which are described in next subsections in depth:

1. Segmentation phase. This phase consists in to quantify the greenness presents in the field of the image. A value is assigned to each pixel of the image and this value symbolizes the greenness of pixel. This phase is composed of three processes: normalization image, calculation of basis indices and combination of basis indices by PCA.
2. Thresholding phase. In this phase, the pixels that represent a part of the presented object in the scene are classified in two groups, green plants and others elements. This classification is based on the greenness values obtained in segmentation phase and the Otsu method.

A scheme of the proposed strategy is showed in Fig. 2.

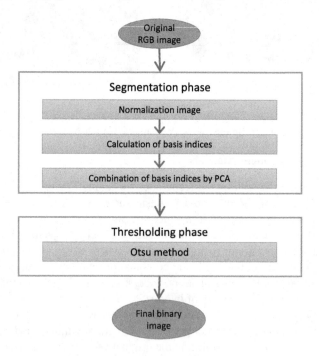

Fig. 2. Scheme of the proposed strategy

Segmentation Phase Based on PCA

This phase can be divided in three steps: (a) normalization image, (b) calculation of basis indices and (c) combination of basis indices by PCA.

(a) Normalization image

Once the image is captured by camera in the RGB color model, the first step is to obtain a grayscale image from the previous RGB image. This segmentation process is focused on the separation of green plants (crop and weeds) from the rest (soil, stones and others). Grayscale image represent the greenness in the field of the original image, in such way that in such way that the more value pixel has, the more probability pixel will be a plant.

Before to transform the original image in RGB color space to a grayscale image, two normalizations widely used in the literature [22, 23] are needed:

The first normalization is given by:

$$R_n = \frac{R}{R_{max}}, G_n = \frac{G}{G_{max}}, B_n = \frac{B}{B_{max}} \tag{1}$$

Where R, G and B are the pixel's values of channels Red, Green and Blue respectively and $R_{max}, G_{max}, B_{max}$ are the maximum values in the original images for the channels Red, Green and Blue o the maximum pixel value. After this first normalization the pixel's values are between 0 and 1, i.e. in the range [0,1].

The second normalization is performed to reach the sum of the three channels' values for a given pixel is equals to unity, as follows:

$$r = \frac{R_n}{R_n + G_n + B_n}, g = \frac{G_n}{R_n + G_n + B_n}, b = \frac{B_n}{R_n + G_n + B_n} r + g + b = 1 \tag{2}$$

Where R_n, G_n, B_n are the previous normalized RGB pixel's values ranging from 0 to 1.

(b) Calculation of basis indices

At this point, the pixels' values have been normalized and the next step is to compute the different vegetation indices. Each index uses information from the color image normalized in the previous step to obtain a grayscale image and combine them by PCA. The indices are calculated from the 3-channel normalized image according to the following rules:

$ExG = 2g - r - b$ [5] [6]	$ExGR = 3g - 2.4r - b$ [9]
$VEG = \frac{g}{r^a b^{1-a}}$ $a = 0.667$ [10]	$NDI = \frac{g-r}{g+r}$ [24]
$CIVE = 0.441r - 0.811g + 0.385b + 18.78745$ [8]	

Where r, g and b are the pixel's values of channels Red, Green and Blue after the normalization step respectively.

(c) Combination of basis indices by PCA

In the last step of the segmentation phase, a new index used to determine the existing greenery in the image must be created by combining the above indices, ExG, ExGR, CIVE, VEG and NDI. The weight that contributes each of these indices will be determined by PCA.

Given a set of t images to be processed, original RGB images, with a resolution of $u \times v$ pixels, a set V of $m = t \times u \times v$ vectors is defined, $V = \{v_1, v_2, \ldots, v_m\}$. There is the same number of vectors as the sum of the pixels of all images, therefore each vector represents a different pixel of each images.

Since each vector represents a pixel of the image, the vector will be composed of five features. These features will be the value of that pixel in each of the grayscale images provided by the vegetative indices, *ExG, ExGR, CIVE, VEG* and *NDI*. Therefore, for each pixel i and its values given by the five vegetative indices, we have the vector $v_i = \{ExG_i, ExGR_i, CIVE_i, VEG_i, NDI_i\}$.

The weights, which represent the participation of each index in the final image, are calculated as follow. All these vectors, v_i, are represented in matrix mode by X *(see expression 3)*, where the columns are the pixels' values of previous five indices.

$$X = \begin{pmatrix} v_1 \\ v_2 \\ \vdots \\ v_m \end{pmatrix} = \begin{pmatrix} ExG_1 & ExGR_1 & CIVE_1 & VEG_1 & NDI_1 \\ ExG_2 & ExGR_2 & CIVE_2 & VEG_2 & NDI_2 \\ \vdots & \vdots & \vdots & \vdots & \vdots \\ ExG_m & ExGR_m & CIVE_m & VEG_m & NDI_m \end{pmatrix}$$

$$= \left\{ \begin{array}{ccccc} \vdots & \vdots & \vdots & \vdots & \vdots \\ ExG & ExGR & CIVE & VEG & NDI \\ \vdots & \vdots & \vdots & \vdots & \vdots \end{array} \right\}$$

(3)

Data should be centered, that is, every variable should have mean zero, so apply:

$$\hat{X} = X - S \times R$$

where S is a column vector de m one's and R is a row vector of 5 elements defined as:

$$R = \left\{ \sum_{j=1}^{m} ExG_j, \sum_{j=1}^{m} ExGR_j, \sum_{j=1}^{m} CIVE_j, \sum_{j=1}^{m} VEG_j, \sum_{j=1}^{m} NDI_j, \right\}$$

(4)

Next step consists in calculate the covariance matrix of $\hat{X}$, and get the eigenvalues, D, and eigenvectors, W, of the covariance matrix C.

$$C = covariance(\hat{X})$$

(5)

$$D = \{\lambda_1, \lambda_2, \ldots, \lambda_n\}$$

(6)

$$W = \{w_1, w_2, \ldots, w_n\} \quad w_i = \{w_i^{ExG}, w_i^{ExGR}, w_i^{CIVE}, w_i^{VEG}, w_i^{NDI}\}$$

(7)

where λ_i is the corresponding eigenvalue of eigenvector w_i and w_i^n is the n-th component of w_i. The eigenvalues give the total variance described by each variable and the eigenvectors are the principal components of the original data.

Eigenvalues are ordered form largest to smallest, all eigenvalues must be positive. The principal component is determined by the largest eigenvalue, being his corresponding eigenvector. The projection method is achieved by multiplying the principal component associated with the greatest eigenvalue for the matrix with information of all grayscale images, X, managing to reduce the dimensionality of the data. If λ_t is the largest eigenvalue then w_t will be the principal component. Finally, the original data are summarized according to:

$$X^F = X \times w_t = \begin{pmatrix} ExG_1 & ExGR_1 & CIVE_1 & VEG_1 & NDI_1 \\ ExG_2 & ExGR_2 & CIVE_2 & VEG_2 & NDI_2 \\ \vdots & \vdots & \vdots & \vdots & \vdots \\ ExG_m & ExGR_m & CIVE_m & VEG_m & NDI_m \end{pmatrix} \times \begin{pmatrix} w_t^{ExG} \\ w_t^{ExGR} \\ w_t^{CIVE} \\ w_t^{VEG} \\ w_t^{NDI} \end{pmatrix} \tag{8}$$

According to Eq. (8), a grayscale image, X^F, is achieved from the original five grayscales images, X, being X^F the projection of X. Finally, in Fig. 3 the enhanced grey image is obtained by this new approach using the principal component.

Fig. 3. Grayscale image of Fig. 1(a) obtained by PCA

Thresholding Phase
The next and last objective is to determine which pixels belong to green plants and which pixels belong to other elements present in the grayscale image. In grayscale image obtained by PCA exists different levels of values to express the greenness of the image, see Fig. 3. The higher value of a pixel, the higher the greenness of that pixel and the probability of which pixel will be a green plant, so the problem become a thresholding problem. To achieve the goal, several methods of automatic thresholding were studied, and among them the method of Otsu [20] is selected. The Otsu's method maximizes the between-class variance and minimizes the within-class variance. The between-class variance refers to the difference between group of green plants and group of other

elements present in the scene. The within-class variance refers to the similarity of the pixels within each group (the group of green plants and the group of others elements).

After applying thresholding by the method of Otsu a threshold is obtained. The pixels whose value is greater than or equal to the threshold are considered as green plants and pixels which are less than this threshold are belonging to another group, as summarized in the following decision rule:

$$\begin{cases} if v(p) \geq t \rightarrow p \in GP \\ if v(p) < t \rightarrow p \in OT \end{cases} \tag{9}$$

where p is a pixel of the image, $v(p)$ is the value of pixel p in the grayscale image obtained by PCA, GP is the group of pixels considered as green plants and OT is the group of pixels considered as others elements in the scene.

Following the previous decision rule (9) a binary image where the pixels identified as green plants are labeled with white and the other black pixels with the color is obtained. In Fig. 4 is showed the Fig. 3 binarized by Otsu's method.

Fig. 4. Binarized image of Fig. 3 by Otsu's method

3 Results

The methods and algorithms explain in this paper were development in the software Matlab 2015a [25] using the Image Processing Toolbox. The used computer was a conventional laptop.

The performance of the proposed vegetation index, based on PCA (IPCA), is tested by comparison with the simple methods and also with another method based on a combining strategy of basic indices used in this work. The chosen vegetation index for the comparative is the index COM [14] The COM index combines some of the indices used in IPCA so it is a good candidate to compare. The used method to provide a quantitative value in the measure is based on a set of ground-truth images. Ground-truth images are made from original RGB images using the following steps:

- Pixels whose green component is greater than red and blue ones simultaneously at least in a 10 % are labeled as white (green plants).
- Pixels whose red or blue component is greater than others two at least in a 10 % are labeled as black (background).
- Pixels that still are not labeled are manually labeled according to the human expert criterion.

The above steps are not part of the algorithm, they are used to make the ground-truth image so we can evaluate the error rate.

For the experiment, 24 full size images have been used, being 22 sub-images per full size image, resulting 528 sub-images as described in Sect. 2.1. Of the total images, 350 sub-images have been randomly chosen for computing the weights by PCA. The others 178 images have been used for the comparative. The whole procedure of the proposed strategy take 250 ms on average.

After apply all steps of the proposed strategy to the set of 350 sub-images, the averaged values of weights obtained for the IPCA are finally the following: $w^{ExG} = 0.4319, w^{ExGR} = 0.4506, w^{CIVE} = -0.4353, w^{NDI} = 0.4777, w^{VEG} = 0.4390$

The metrics used for comparison is the average of the error rate, being the error rate equals to number of misclassified pixels by the total number of pixels (Table 1).

Table 1. Error rates for each of the vegetation indices

INDEX	ExG	ExGR	CIVE	NDI	VEG	COM	IPCA
% error	11,15	11,21	10,42	12,05	19,14	8,93	8,07

As we can see our new approach improves the simple indices by a significant percentage. Regarding the index COM, our contribution improves the error in a quantitative way more than qualitative. Figure 5 shows a zoom performed on the bottom of Fig. 1 and obtained by the COM and IPCA indices. As we can observe in this figure, the use of new IPCA index reduces the noise of the image more than the COM index.

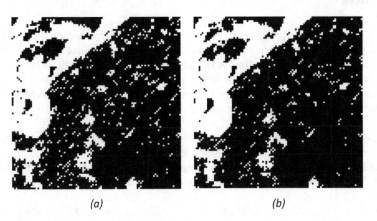

(a)   (b)

Fig. 5. Zoom of central bottom area of binary image by COM (a) and by PCA (b) of Fig. 4

4 Conclusions

In this work we propose a novel strategy for plant detection, which consist of two main phases. In the first one, the kernel of the contribution, a segmentation of an agricultural image is performed. This segmentation extracts the greenness of the image by combining several simple indices by the use of the principal component analysis obtaining a new index, called IPCA. This new index gives to each simple index a weight using the eigenvector associated with the largest eigenvalue. Once the new enhanced grey image is obtained, in the second phase, a thresholding is performed in order to binarize the image and detect the green plants.

This method has been compared with the simple indices and COM method, which has the same goal combining different simple indices. In view of the results, it can be concluded that IPCA shows a better behavior in detecting green plants than simple indices in a significant percentage of improvement. In the comparison with the COM index we can conclude that our results improve the percentage in a quantitative sense more than qualitative. To prove the qualitative improvement, we prepare the zoom of an image in order to observe the contribution in the noise reduction by our method, IPCA.

In precision agriculture, the detection of green plants in images is a very important task. In our opinion, the use of this new index, based on principal component analysis, provides a good combination of the information about the greenery from the simple indices. Thus, for each index, this method takes the most significant information improving the image segmentation, being a helpful contribution in this area.

Acknowledgments. The authors wish to acknowledge to the project AGL2014-52465-C4-3-R, supported by the Ministerio de Educación y Ciencia of Spain within the Plan Nacional de I + D + i, for its support and coordination work.

References

1. Davies, G., Casady, W., Massey, R.: Precision agriculture: an introduction [En línea] (1998). http://extension.missouri.edu/explorepdf/envqual/wq0450.pdf. Último acceso 25 11 2015
2. Ahmed, F., Al-Mamun, H.A., Bari, A.H., Hossain, E., Kwan, P.: Classification of crops and weeds from digital images: a support vector machine approach. Crop Prot. **40**, 98–104 (2012)
3. Montalvo, M., Guerrero, J.M., Romeo, J., Emmi, L., Guijarro, M., Pajares, M.: Automatic expert system for weeds/crops identification in images from maize fields. Expert Syst. Appl. **40**(1), 75–82 (2013)
4. Onyango, C.M., Marchant, J.A.: Segmentation of row crop plants from weeds using colour and morphology. Comput. Electron. Agric. **39**, 141–155 (2003)
5. Woebbecke, D.M., Meyer, G.E., Von Bargen, K., Mortensen, D.A.: Shape features for identifying young weeds using image analysis. Trans. Am. Soc. Agric. Biol. Eng. **38**(1), 271–281 (1995)
6. Ribeiro, A., Fernández-Quintanilla, C., Barroso, J., García-Alegre, M.C.: Development of an image analysis system for estimation of weed. In: Proceedings of 5th European Conference on Precision Agriculture (5ECPA), pp. 169–174 (2005)

7. Meyer, G., Metha, T., Kocher, M., Mortensen, D., Samal, A.: Textural imaging and discriminant analysis for distinguishing weeds for spot spraying. Trans. ASAE **41**(4), 1189–1197 (1998)
8. Kataoka, T., Kaneko, T., Okamoto, H., Hata, S.: Crop growth estimation system using machine vision. In: The 2003 IEEE/ASME International Conference on Advanced Intelligent Mechatronics, vol. 2, pp. 1079–1083 (2003)
9. Neto, J.C.: A Combined Statistical–Soft Computing Approach for Classification and Mapping Weed Species in Minimum Tillage Systems. University of Nebraska, Lincoln (2004)
10. Hague, T., Tillet, N., Wheeler, H.: Automated crop and weed monitoring in widely spaced cereals. Precis. Agric. **1**(1), 95–113 (2006)
11. Meyer, G.E., Camargo-Neto, J., Jones, D.D., Hindman, T.W.: Intensified fuzzy clusters for classifying plant, soil, and residue regions of interest from color images. Comput. Electron. Agric. **42**, 161–180 (2004)
12. Zheng, L., Shi, D., Zhang, J.: Segmentation of green vegetation of crop canopy images based on mean shift and Fisher linear discriminate. Pattern Recogn. Lett. (2010)
13. Zheng, L., Zhang, J., Wang, Q.: Mean-shift-based color segmentation of images containing green vegetation. Comput. Electron. Agric. **65**, 93–98 (2009)
14. Guijarro, M., Pajares, G., Riomoros, I., Herrera, P.J., Burgos-Artizzu, X.P., Ribeiro, A.: Automatic segmentation of relevant textures in agricultural images. Comput. Electron. Agric. **75**(1), 75–83 (2011)
15. Guerrero, J.M., Pajares, G., Montalvo, M., Romeo, J., Guijarro, M.: Support vector machines for crop/weeds identification in maize fields. Expert Syst. Appl. **39**(12), 1149–1155 (2012)
16. Sewell, M.: http://www.stats.org.uk [En línea]. http://www.stats.org.uk/pca. Último acceso 28 05 2015
17. Panda, S.S., Hoogenboom, G., Paz, J.: Distinguishing blueberry bushes from mixed vegetation land use using high resolution satellite imagery and geospatial techniques. Comput. Electron. Agric. **67**, 51–58 (2009)
18. Hanh, N.T.T., Dien, T.N.: Application of Principal Component Analysis Technique to Multispectral Image LANDSAT for Monitoring Change of Agricultural Land in the North Delta, Vietnam. Asian Association on Remote Sensing (2013)
19. Wang, J., Han, Y., Fu, Z., Li, D., Chen, J., Wang, S.: Edge geometric measurement based principal component analysis in strawberry leaf images. In: Li, D., Chen, Y. (eds.) Computer and Computing Technologies in Agriculture VI, Part I. IFIP AICT, vol. 392, pp. 58–68. Springer, Heidelberg (2013)
20. Otsu, N.: A threshold selection method from gray-level histogram. IEEE Trans. Syst. Man Cybern. **9**, 62–66 (1979)
21. Anderson, T.W.: An Introduction to Multivariate Statistical Analysis. Wiley-Interscience, Hoboboken (2003)
22. Gée, C., Bossu, J., Jones, G., Truchetet, F.: Crop/weed discrimination in perspective agronomic images. Comput. Electron. Agric. **60**, 49–59 (2008)
23. Montalvo, M., Pajares, G., Guerrero, J.M., Romeo, J., Guijarro, M., Ribeiro, A., Ruz, J.J., Cruz, J.J.: Automatic detection of crops rows in maize fields with high weeds pressure. Expert Syst. Appl. **39**, 11889–11897 (2012)
24. Pérez, A.J., López, F., Benllock, J.V., Christensen, S.: Colour and shape analysis techniques for weed detection in cereal fields. Comput. Electron. Agric. **25**, 197–212 (2000)
25. MathWorks. Accelerating the pace of engineering and science [En línea]. http://www.mathworks.com. Último acceso 1 10 2015

Automatic Image-Based Method for Quantitative Analysis of Photosynthetic Cell Cultures

Alzbeta Vlachynska[1(✉)], Jan Cerveny[2], Vratislav Cmiel[3],
and Tomas Turecek[1]

[1] Tomas Bata University in Zlin, Zlin, Czech Republic
{vlachynska,tturecek}@fai.utb.cz
[2] Global Change Research Institute CAS, Brno, Czech Republic
cerveny.j@czechglobe.cz
[3] Brno University of Technology, Brno, Czech Republic
cmiel@feec.vutbr.cz

Abstract. This work deals with an automatic quantitative analysis of photo-synthetic cell cultures. It uses images captured by a confocal fluorescent microscope for automatic determination the number of cells in sample containing complex 3D structure of cell clusters. Experiments were performed on the confocal microscope Leica TCS SP8 X. The cell nuclei were stained by SYBR® Green fluorescent DNA binding marker. In the first step we used combination of adaptive thresholding to found out areas where nuclei were located. Proposed segmentation steps allowed reduction of noise and artefacts. Z-axis position was obtained as a location of peak from intensity profile. Finally model of scene can be created by emplacement of spheres with adequate diameter to found 3D coordinates. Number of cells per volumetric unit were determined in structurally different culture samples of cell cultures *Chenopodium rubrum* (Cr) and *Solanum lycopersicum* (To). The results were verified by manual counting.

Keywords: Automated cell counting · Image segmentation · Plant cell · Suspension cultures · 3D reconstruction · Visualization

1 Introduction

Plant cell suspension cultures are considered as attractive model systems to address various aspects of defense response, ion transport, secondary metabolite production, gene regulation and signal transduction. Single cells or small clusters of cells are grown in strictly controlled environmental conditions. Low concentrations of substances and short incubation times are sufficient to elicit cellular reactions because there is no barrier (e.g. cuticula) and no thick cell layers have to be penetrated. Plant cells are safer and less expensive to cultivate than mammalian cells and are easier to scale up [1]. Plant cell suspension cultures also offer several advantages over whole plant, including shorter production cycles, easily controlled environments and the lack of biotic and abiotic contaminants [2].

© Springer International Publishing Switzerland 2016
F. Martínez-Álvarez et al. (Eds.): HAIS 2016, LNAI 9648, pp. 402–413, 2016.
DOI: 10.1007/978-3-319-32034-2_34

Cell suspension cultures of a number of plant species and tissues have been established, but only a limited number of species are photoautotrophic (PA) cultures, which grow in the absence of any reduced carbon source and solely utilize photosynthesis to provide energy and carbon for grow. Plant suspension cultures are considered as a source of valuable products such as sweeteners, pharmaceuticals, flavours and enzymes. Moreover, the industrial production of plant compounds from these cell cultures would save natural resources [2–4].

In order to characterize, understand and control such production platforms accurately, it is important to determine quantitative properties of biological systems to allow detailed and comparative evaluation of cells productivity. Plant cells often form clusters or multi-cell aggregates several millimetres in diameter [5]. Such clustering makes identification of individual cell's special properties difficult, e.g. individual cells-counting or morphological properties quantification (Fig. 1).

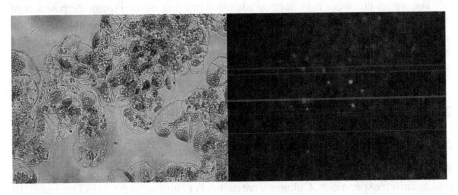

Fig. 1. Cell culture *Chenopodium rubnum*. Microscop iMIC system (FEIMunich GmbH, Germany) including objective with 40x ZOOM (UApochromat, NA 0,90). Left side – transmitted light, right side - SYBR® green fluorescence data (blue excitation 490 nm) (Color figure online).

Several cell counting protocols and instruments have been developed for homogeneous suspensions cell count determination of mammalian and bacterial cells, but these methods tend to be unsuitable for plant cell suspension cultures. The most of them were produced by applying methods to generate single cells and count them using a hemocytometer. Treatments that can produce single cells include the maceration of cell clusters with CrO_3, enzymatic digestion of the middle lamella, and protoplast generation, but they are expensive and time consuming and usually irreproducible. Many cells are lost during preparation, and the precise number of cells in culture cannot be determined [6, 7].

There are some efforts to establish counting system for plant cells without hemocytometry. Lamboursain and Jolicoeur (2005) described an approach in which the total fluorescence signal from stained nuclei was analysed in a microplate reader and the cell number was estimated by referring to standards with known cell numbers [8]. However, the accuracy of this method was influenced by the cell cycle, which determines the size of the nucleus and the degree of chromatin condensation.

Image-based cell counting algorithms is usually managed by analysis of fluorescence microscopy images. Havenith et al. (2014) used confocal microscope to acquire bigger area of sample in contract to standard fluorescence microscopy [9]. Because they scan and analyse only one image from one sample, they estimated a false negative detection, where dividing nuclei were close together or where cell clustering caused nuclei to overlap in the image. In such cases the software counted only one nucleus instead of two or more. There could be considerable amount of such nuclei in multi-cell aggregates, which will lead to significant error in the computation.

The problem could be solved by high resolution confocal microscopy approach, allowing large data acquisition and subsequent 3D reconstruction of observed scene. Unfortunately, conventional confocal microscope software designed for confocal data processing and analysis has considerable limitations. Cells cannot be separated from the background and detected individually. Automated calculation or sorting of individual objects according to different parameters is not possible.

The aim of this work is to develop advanced imaging method using the potential of 3D imaging by confocal fluorescence microscopy and computational techniques for the automatic determination of cell counts in a sample containing complex system of plant cells with corresponding intensity and spatial distribution, which would require only limited sample processing. The work summarizes results of the Master thesis [16].

2   Materials and Methods

2.1   Used Plant Cell Suspension Cultures

We used plant cell suspension cultures of *Chenopodium rubrum* and *Solanum lycopersicum* in our experiments. Cultures were routinely cultivated in 50 ml MS medium [10] in 100-ml glass Erlenmeyer flasks under sterile conditions at a temperature of 25 °C, supplied with 2 % of CO2 enriched air and continuously illuminated by modest warm white light (100 μmoll (photons) $m^{-2}s^{-1}$).

2.2   Fluorescence Staining

The 1 ml dense cell suspension (directly from flask) were centrifuged (3000x g, 5 min) and the supernatant was replaced with 1 ml 20 % fixation solution methanol/Acetic Acid (3:1). Mixture was re-suspended and incubated for 10 min at room temperature. 1 ml sample of fixed cells was washed with distilled water and transferred to a new tube. DNA within cells located in nuclei was stained with 10 μl SYBR® Green fluorescence marker (Invitrogen, Ltd., Paisley, UK) from 1/100 diluted stock solution in DMSO. Then the sample was incubated min 10 min at room temperature in darkness.

Since each cell has only one nucleus, it is possible to count the number of nuclei corresponding to the number of cells in structurally complex plant suspension culture clusters.

2.3 Data Acquisition

The data was acquired by Leica TCS SP8 X confocal microscope including HCPL APO CS objective with 10X magnification. The dye was excited by 490 nm laser. White Light Laser (WLL) was used for the excitation. The fluorescence response was detected by photomultiplier including tuneable spectral filter opened in effective emission range of 510–550 nm.

Spatial resolution of output images was selected as 512×512 pixels to allow faster z-axis screening. The size of the sample volume was adjusted individually according to the displayed scene. The z-axis scanning step was set to 2 μm. Such spacing generates enough Z-axis samples to ensure safe detection of each nuclei due to their expected size of approximately 5–15 μm. Size of nuclei for each type of plant cell suspension is typically well conserved and can be easily estimated from pre-screening images. The spacing and the spatial resolution were chosen at a low level to avoid photo bleaching or even cell death. The acquired data was then exported in a lossless TIFF image format for further processing (Fig. 2).

2.4 Algorithm for Nuclei Segmentation

The first necessary step before modelling the microscopic scene and subsequent analysis of cellular nuclei is segmentation of nuclei from fluoroscopic images. One of the most common method for solving the nuclei recognition problem is the region growing one – watershed algorithm. Many region growing algorithms result in over-segmented images, i.e. too many object regions are formed. The gradient-weighted distance transform with hybrid 3D watershed algorithm has been introduced by Line et al. (2003) [11]. The over segmentation was treated by model-based approach during the post processing. They achieved in average 97 % of correctly segmented nuclei in images of rat brain cells. Cloppet F., Boucher (2008) discuss segmentation of overlapping or aggregating nuclei from Hutchinson-Gilford Progeria Syndrome cells [12]. The automatic thresholding method and subsequent watershed algorithm with prior information optimization and gradient input image has been used, where the rate of well-segmented nuclei was 96 %.

Edge-based segmentation techniques, which try to connect local maxima of the gradient image, often run into problems when trying to produce closed curves. Zanella et al. (2010) introduced the segmentation algorithm based on edge detection on early zebrafish embryogenesis cells. They used generalized 3D Hough transform and Subjective Surfaces to find out closed curves [13].

Cell nuclei are usually convex and do not show narrow waists. The shape of the cell nuclei itself can therefore be used for a priori modelling, or as an object-specific feature, in the search for a suitable segmentation method discriminating between single nucleus and clusters of nuclei. Yang and Parvin (2002) presented a 3D blob segmentation method based on elliptic feature calculation, convex hull computations and size discrimination [14]. A careful choice of a scale parameter is essential, and the edges of the resulting objects will not necessary be aligned with the edges of the nuclei.

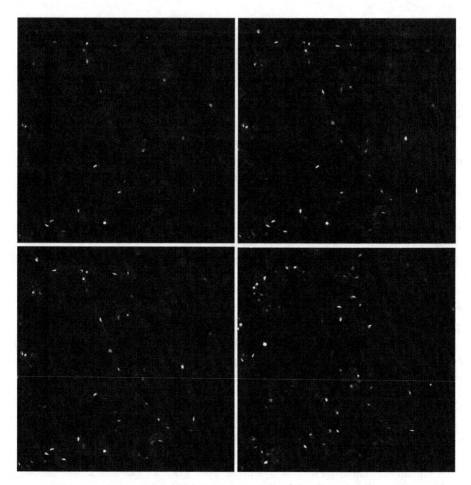

Fig. 2. Plant cell *Solanum lycopersicum* (To) – 1st, 5th, 10th, and 15th slice of sample. HCPL APO CS objective with 10X magnification

None of the above described methods will alone produce a satisfactory result on images of fluorescence-stained nuclei in tissue if (1) there are intensity variations within the nuclei, (2) the image background is variable and (3) the nuclei are clustered. Here we present a method in which we combined the intensity information, the shape of the nuclei and the position of nuclei in related slices for improved segmentation. Our approach is based on global and local thresholding, morphologic operations and determination of object properties. This approach ensures sufficient segmentation accuracy with low computational complexity that is important for high-throughput image processing of statistically significant cell population sample. Only green channel from confocal image data, representing DNA stain fluorescence signal, is taken into account in our algorithm. Simplified block scheme of discussed approach is outlined in Fig. 3.

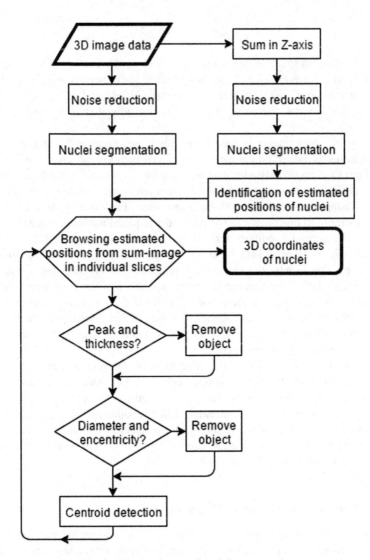

Fig. 3. Block scheme of nuclei segmentation

2.5   2D Nuclei Segmentation

The first step of our approach is segmentation of objects in each slice. Simultaneously is done the segmentation of estimated positions of nuclei in sum-image, which is created as normalized summation of whole 3D image data over Z-axis.

The segmentation optionally begins by reduction of the noise which can be caused by many artificial sources, notably the inhomogeneous distribution of fluorescent agent in cells, thermal noise of electrical instruments and photon noise. This task is performed by 2D convolution with Gaussian kernel with variance 6^2. Gaussian coefficients of convolution kernel can be computed as

$$g(x, y) = e^{-(x^2 + y^2)/2 \cdot 6^2} \tag{1}$$

where g is a Gaussian function on coordinates x and y [15]. The signal-to-noise ratio is improved by the above mentioned filtering which leads to better recognition of nuclei objects in background, but also some information is lost and computing time rise. Because of this reasons, the noise reduction is use only if it is necessary, on poor quality pictures.

The main of segmentation is done by thresholding. Because the brightness of the individual cores is rather different, we use a combination of simple and adaptive thresholding. One-pixel (indicating the presence of the nucleus) is only added to the resulting image if the corresponding pixel of the input image satisfies the condition of a simple and adaptive thresholding at the same time. First thresholding condition is determined simply as one threshold indicating the required minimum intensity of pixel brightness. The second condition, for adaptive thresholding, compare the brightness values of the processed pixel with the average brightness of the surrounding pixels. It is determined by two inputs: the size of the pixel neighbourhood, that is taken into account for calculating the average intensity, and the number indicating how many times must be the brightness of the processed pixel in the input image higher than the average brightness of its neighbourhood. The size of surrounding region is counted from excepted proportions of nuclei. This process leads to binary image where white areas are approximately detected nuclei.

The image is further modified after thresholding. Objects smaller than 10px are removed. Than we use morphological operation open with structure element disc.

Specific conditions for filtration, thresholding and morphological operation are set to each species of plant cell suspension. Slightly different settings are used for sum-image and individual slices. We use stricter parameters to individual slices than to sum-image, where we do not want to lose any object, which will possibly be a nucleus. Individual used setting is shown in Tables 2 and 4.

2.6   3D Segmentation and Scene Modelling

The main task is to detect and count nuclei in 3D reconstructed images. For this, segmented sum-image, segmented slice images, and approximate size and eccentricity of nucleus is needed. The basis of analysis is the sum-image, where segmented objects are counted and identified. All slices are scanned in area of each object found in sum-image. We assume, that objects can often overlap in sum-image, but they are divided by their z-coordinate and then located in different slice-images. Number of one-pixels in each slice-image, on the position of processed object, is mounted to the variable, which length corresponds to the number of slices. This variable can be treated as a one-dimensional signal.

One nucleus can occur in several successive slices due to small z-axis scanning step. We need to determine the centre of the nucleus. If the nucleus is spherical object, then its centre is located in the equatorial plane, namely those which has the most one-pixels. Ideally, the size of object gradually increases up to a maximum of equatorial plane and subsequently decrease in a similar manner. Rendering it such a signal we got concave function.

However, it is not so easy in reality. The area of each object varies due to noise and segmentation inaccuracy. There are many local maxima on the main peak. We choose the peak only, if the signal value between two adjusted signal peaks decrease below 20 % of the desired average nucleus size. This prevent multiple-detection of one nucleus.

The identified object is further tested. We analyse the size and the eccentricity. Only object, which satisfies both conditions is counted. The size of the object is compared with an expected size of nuclei. If the object is smaller than the defined range around this value (+−25 %), it is excluded from the computation. If it is bigger, we try to segment this object by watershed and then we test diameters of new object again.

The eccentricity of object is evaluated after testing the size. We compare major and minor axes length of the ellipse that has the same normalized second central moments as the object. The ratio of major and minor axes will be nearly one for a circle. The ratio is one of required input settings.

If the analysed object is finally accepted as nucleus type, its centre coordinates are determined. X-axis and Y-axis positions are derived from 2D binary image as the intersection of minor and major axis of the object. Z-axis position is obtained as a position of peak maxima from intensity profile. Finally model of scene can be created by emplacement of spheres with adequate diameter to find complete 3D coordinates. Now it is possible to prepare subsequent analyses like nuclei space distribution measurement, intensity-distribution measurement, size-distribution, etc. Final 3D reconstructed model is shown in Fig. 4.

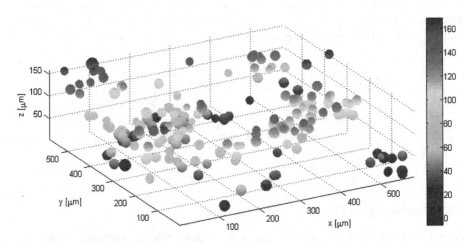

Fig. 4. Model of microscopic scene. Simulated nuclei distribution with depth colour coding (Color figure online).

3   Results

3.1   Validation of Segmentation Results

The proposed algorithm was verified on 2 data sets of *Chenopodium rubrum* plant suspension cells. In each set the number of nuclei was manually counted by biologist using the ImageJ-based image visualization program Fiji which allows to detect the positions of the nuclei in 3D space. The results of automatic and manual counts are compared in Table 1. The difference between the results did not exceed 5 % in either of evaluated samples.

Table 1. Validation of segmentation results

Experiment	Sample 1	Sample 2
Manual counted nuclei [-]	65	190
Automatically counted nuclei [-]	63	182
Incorrect counted nuclei [-]	2	8
Error [%]	3.1	4.2

3.2   Determination of the Number of Cells in 1 ml of Plant Cell Sample

The cell culture of *Chenopodium rubrum* (Cr) and *Solanum lycopersicum* (To) were used to determine the number of cells in 1 ml of the sample (cells concentration). Several independent measurements were done on each sample. Cells concentration should be permanent for each sample. Minor deviations are caused by random selection of scanning area. It is possible to achieve a result which describes the properties of the sample as a whole by repeated scanning of various locations on one sample. Counting results of plant culture *Chenopodium rubnum* are shown in Table 3 and results of plant culture *Solanum lycopersicum* are in Table 5.

Table 2. Segmentation settings - *Chenopodium rubum* (Cr)

	Sum-image	Slices
Min. brightness [%]	2	3
Size of neighbourhood [px]	30	30
Multiple	1	1
Morphological o.	Open	Open

3.3   Computational Complexity of Algorithm

On a 2.20GHZ CPU and 4 GB RAM memory computer, our algorithm needs from 20 s to 90 s to process set of images and calculate number of nuclei in the sample. Processing time depends mainly on the number of scanned slices (denote as n) and the number of examined objects in images (denote as m). The computational complexity is than simply determined by multiplication of these two factors (m*n).

Table 3. Counting results of plant culture *Chenopodium rubnum* (Cr)

Sample	Sample volume [μm^3]	Number of cells in image	Number of cells in 1 ml
Cr 1	775.0 × 775.0 × 34.62	222	1.068*10^7
Cr 2	775.0 × 775.0 × 121.20	741	1.018*10^7
Cr 3	775.0 × 775.0 × 88.62	553	1.039*10^7
Average	–	–	1.042*10^7
St. deviation	–	–	2.51*10^5 (2.41 %)

Table 4. Segmentation settings - *Solanum lycopersicum* (To)

	Sum-image	Slices
Min. brightness [%]	5	3
Size of neighbourhood [px]	30	30
Multiple	1	2
Morphological o.	Open	Open

Table 5. Counting results of plant culture *Solanum lycopersicum* (To)

Sample	Sample volume [μm^3]	Number of cells in image	Number of cells in 1 ml
To 1	911.76 × 911.76 × 84.59	172	2.446*10^6
To 2	911.76 × 911.76 × 104.74	203	2.331*10^6
To 3	775.0 × 775.0 × 88.62	319	2.190*10^6
Average	–	–	2.322*10^6
St. deviation	–	–	1.28*10^5 (5.52 %)

4   Conclusion

We developed a new method for counting plant cells based on a combination of nuclear staining, automated fluorescence microscopy and image analysis. The method benefits from a simple sample preparation technique that do not require sample homogenization or even single cell generation, or use of an external standard. The main problem that occurred during the segmentation process was the threshold parameter tuning. Any other parameters could be set automatically according to resolution of image data and prior knowledge about physiologically relevant size and shape of detected nuclei. Specific for photosynthetic plant cell cultures is also chlorophyll auto-fluorescence that makes analysis of images acquired using fluorescence imaging techniques more diffi-cult to apply.

The algorithm accuracy depends on manual tuning of parameters for different cell cultures. The current parametrization and user interface is designed for slightly more technically experienced user. Tuning of the method is most determined by quality of data acquisition. The biggest issue for discussed image analysis is caused by chlorophyll auto-fluorescence typical for photosynthetic organisms imaging. Simplification and automation of segmentation process is a part of future research in this topic.

We used this method for counting *Chenopodium* and tomato cells and demonstrated stability of results. The method is automated and, thus, large numbers of nuclei could be counted more rapidly and accurately than manual counting methods. Plant cells were counted in 3D volume, which allows us to model a microscopic scene. We assume applicability to other types of identified objects and organisms, such as lipid bodies or microalgae cultures and their products due to the versatility of the proposed algorithm.

Acknowledgment. This work was supported by the Internal Grant Agency at TBU in Zlín, project No. IGA/CebiaTech/2016/007 and by the Ministry of Education, Youth and Sports of CR within the National Sustainability Program I (NPU I), grant number LO1415 (J.C.).

References

1. Schillberg, S., Raven, N., Fischer, R., Twyman, R.M., Schiermeyer, A.: Molecular farming of pharmaceutical proteins using plant suspension cell and tissue cultures. Curr. Pharm. Des. **19**(31), 5531–5542 (2013)
2. Roitsch, T., Sinha, A.K.: Application of photoautotrophic suspension cultures in plant science. Photosynthetica **40**(4), 481–492 (2002)
3. Hampp, C., Richter, A., Osorio, S., Zellnig, G., Sinha, A.K., Jammer, A., et al.: Establishment of a photoautotrophic cell suspension culture of arabidopsis thaliana for photosynthetic, metabolic, and signaling studies. Mol. Plant **5**(2), 524–527 (2012)
4. Husemann, W., Barz, W.: Photoautotrophic growth and photosynthesis in cell suspension cultures of Chenopodium rubrum. Physiol Plantarum **40**(2), 77–81 (1977)
5. Naill, M.C., Roberts, S.C.: Preparation of single cells from aggregated Taxus suspension cultures for population analysis. Biotechnol. Bioeng. **86**(7), 817–826 (2004)
6. de Gunst, M.C.M., Harkes, P.A.A., Val, J., van Zwet, W.R., Libbenga, K.: Modeling the growth of a batch culture of plant-cells - a corpuscular approach. Enzyme Microb. Technol. **12**(1), 61–71 (1990)
7. Nicoloso, F.T., Val, J., Vanderkeur, M., Vaniren, F., Kijne, J.W.: Flow-cytometric cell counting and dna estimation for the study of plant-cell population-dynamics. Plant Cell, Tissue Organ Cult. **39**(3), 251–259 (1994)
8. Lamboursain, L., Jolicoeur, M.: Determination of cell concentration in a plant cell suspension using a fluorescence microplate reader. Plant Cell Rep. **23**(10–11), 665–672 (2005)
9. Havenith, H., Raven, N., Di Fiore, S., Fischer, R., Schillberg, S.: Image-based analysis of cell-specific productivity for plant cell suspension cultures. Plant Cell, Tissue Organ Cult. **117**(3), 393–399 (2014)
10. Murashige, T., Skoog, F.: A revised medium for rapid growth and bio assays with tobacco tissue cultures. Physiol. Plant. **15**, 473–497 (1962)
11. Lin, G., Adiga, U., Olson, K., Guzowski, J.F., Barnes, C.A., Roysam, B.: A hybrid 3D watershed algorithm incorporating gradient cues and object models for automatic segmentation of nuclei in confocal image stacks. Cytometry A **56**(1), 23–36 (2003)

12. Cloppet, F., Boucher, A.: Segmentation of overlapping/aggregating nuclei cells in biological images. In: 19th International Conference on Pattern Recognition, vols. 1–6, pp. 789–792 (2008)
13. Zanella, C., Campana, M., Rizzi, B., Melani, C., Sanguinetti, G., Bourgine, P., et al.: Cells segmentation from 3-D confocal images of early Zebrafish embryogenesis. IEEE Trans. Image Process. **19**(3), 770–781 (2010)
14. Yang, Q., Parvin, B.: CHEF: convex hull of elliptic features for 3D blob detection. In: Proceedings of the 16th International Conference on Pattern Recognition, vol 2, pp. 282–285 (2002)
15. Nixon, M.S., Aguado, A.S.: Feature Extraction and Image Processing. Newnes, Oxford (2002)
16. Vlachynska, A.: Photosynthetic cell suspension cultures quantitative image data processing. MSc thesis (Czech language), Brno University of Technology, Brno, May 2015

Fall Detection Using Body-Worn Accelerometer and Depth Maps Acquired by Active Camera

Michal Kepski[2] and Bogdan Kwolek[1(✉)]

[1] AGH University of Science and Technology, 30 Mickiewicza Av.,
30-059 Krakow, Poland
[2] University of Rzeszow, 16c Rejtana Av., 35-959 Rzeszów, Poland
http://home.agh.edu.pl/~bkw/contact.html

Abstract. In the presented system to person fall detection a body-worn accelerometer is used to indicate a potential fall and a ceiling-mounted depth sensor is utilized to authenticate fall alert. In order to expand the observation area the depth sensor has been mounted on a pan-tilt motorized head. If the person acceleration is above a preset threshold the system uses a lying pose detector as well as examines a dynamic feature to authenticate the fall. Thus, more costly fall authentication is not executed frame-by-frame, but instead we fetch from a circular buffer a sequence of depth maps acquired prior to the fall and then process them to confirm fall alert. We show that promising results in terms of sensitivity and specificity can be obtained on publicly available UR Fall Detection dataset.

Keywords: Smart home · Human behavior analysis · Fall detection

1 Introduction

The main goal of user-centered ubiquitous computing is to sense changes in human environments in order to provide effective personal assistance. It is expected that the use of ubiquitous computing and ambient intelligence can help to meet the societal challenges posed by aging of population [1]. Smart home technology [2] is considered as important part of the ubiquitous computing. One of the most critical factors limiting the realization of ambient intelligence in broader scale is limited number of cost-effective and energy-efficient devices for human activity monitoring and/or power saving modules for ubiquitous computing. One of the most promising areas of applications of the embedded vision is healthcare [3]. Particularly, embedded vision technology has strong potential to considerably change the healthcare at home, for example through mobile phone applications that monitor the user's state of health and report it to a medical center.

With the aim to enable prolonged independent living in a safe and homely environment, automatic fall detection is an important task [4]. Inertial sensors such as accelerometers and gyroscopes have proven to be very useful in the analysis of motion patterns [5]. Compared to vision sensors, wearable inertial sensors

© Springer International Publishing Switzerland 2016
F. Martínez-Álvarez et al. (Eds.): HAIS 2016, LNAI 9648, pp. 414–426, 2016.
DOI: 10.1007/978-3-319-32034-2_35

offer advantages in terms of size, weight, ease of use and, most importantly, power consumption and costs of use. They permit data collection outside of laboratory environments and are considered as one of the best sensors for ubiquitous health monitoring [3]. In context-aware systems various kinds of sensors are usually deployed in the environment in order to detect falls. The most common sensors are cameras, microphones, floor sensors and pressure sensors. One of their advantages is that the person undergoing monitoring does not need to wear any special device. A short time ago the Kinect's sensor has been proposed to be employed in fall detection [4,6,7]. As demonstrated in [6,7], the depth maps delivered by Kinect are sufficient to delineate the person from the background. Moreover, due to using speckle pattern of infrared laser light to estimate the dense depth maps, the object detection can be done any time. A recent survey [4] discusses several approaches to Kinect-based fall detection. However, the available algorithms do not achieve both high sensitivity and specificity. By combining video or depth maps and acceleration data, the detection of emergency situations [7,8] as well as activity recognition [9] can be improved greatly.

2   Embedded System for Fall Detection

The system detects fall events on the basis of depth maps acquired by a ceiling-mounted Kinect sensor as well as motion data, which is acquired by a body-worn accelerometer. To expand the observation area a pan-tilt head is used to rotate the Kinect and to follow a moving person. Initially, a nearest neighbor interpolation is executed to fill the holes in the depth map and to get the map with meaningful values for all pixels. The interpolation is based on the median filter with a 5×5 window. To improve the delineation of the person in the depth maps the algorithm extracts the floor and then removes their corresponding pixels from the depth map. Given the extracted person's blob in the last depth map, the algorithm uses it as seed region in the subsequent region growing, which is responsible for delineation of the person from the background depth map in the current frame. Afterwards, a Support Vector Machine (SVM) is utilized optionally to acknowledge the person presence within the depth blob. Then, the center of gravity of the blob is determined. Finally, given the person's centroid, the pan-tilt head rotates the Kinect to keep the target in the central part of the depth maps. Given the delineated person, lying pose and dynamic transition classifiers are executed to raise alarm in case of fall event. The features describing the dynamic transitions are calculated using depth maps, which are continuously stored in a circular buffer. Thanks to the use of the accelerometer, the cascade classifier responsible for fall detection is not executed frame-by-frame, but is triggered only if a person acceleration is above a preset threshold, see Fig. 1.

A system for fall detection should to be as cheap as possible in order to be affordable for the elderly. It should also be easy-to-install and consume least amount energy. Hence, our system consists of inexpensive sensing devices such as Kinect, an accelerometer worn on human body, a low-cost pan-tilt unit, and low-cost PandaBoard at which the algorithms are executed. The PandaBoard was

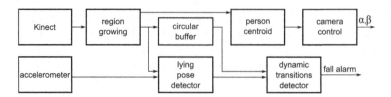

Fig. 1. Block diagram of the embedded system for fall detection using depth maps and body-worn accelerometer.

selected for the implementation of the application since it offers high performance at a low cost with only 3.5 W power consumption under full load. The data from the accelerometer are transmitted wirelessly to the processing unit. The Kinect sensor (Asus Xtion Pro Live) is connected to the board via USB. The microcontroller of the head is connected with the PandaBoard through I2C bus.

Figure 2 depicts sample images, which were captured by ceiling-mounted Kinect. As we can observe, thanks to the pan-tilt head the observation area is broaden. For the Kinect sensor mounted on the height of 2.6 m from the floor, the observation area is about $5.5\,m^2$. Owing to the use of the pan-tilt unit, the Kinect is able to examine a room of average size, say $15-20\,m^2$. The RGB images are not processed and they are used only for visualization purposes.

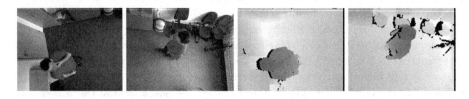

Fig. 2. Example top-view images captured by Kinect mounted on pan-tilt head, RGB images (top row), depth images (bottom row).

3   Person Delineation Using Active Pan-Tilt Depth Sensor

The pursuing a moving person is achieved by a series of saccades of the pan-tilt head to keep the detected object in central part of permanently acquired depth maps. The object position is expressed as the centroid of the delineated area. Below we detail the depth region growing that delineates the person undergoing tracking in maps acquired by an active camera. We also present an algorithm that supports locating the person's head in case of region chaining.

3.1   Delineation of Person Using Region Growing

The person is delineated from the background assuming that he/she occupies an integrated region in 3D space. Owing to extracting the floor in advance, we avoid incorporating of the neighboring pixels from the floor into the person region. The developed depth region growing starts with selecting a seed point in a current frame. Assuming that there is a common depth region between regions belonging to a person in two consecutive frames, such seed region is determined using the **and** operator between the previously delineated depth region belonging to person and the current depth map. Afterwards, the algorithm repeatedly seeks all neighboring pixels of the current region. The selected pixels are sorted according to their depth similarities and then they are stored in a list of candidate pixels. The depth similarity is the Euclidean distance between the depth values of a pixel from such a list and its closest pixel from the current region. It is employed in order to verify if a neighboring pixel around a region pixel is allowed to be merged with the region.

3.2   Finding Human in Depth Maps

Ordinary region growing algorithms suffer from the problem of region chaining (overspill), which occurs when two regions are grown into one region while they are actually separated from each other, see also Fig. 3a. In order to improve the delineation of the person in such situations as well as to improve the pursuing of the person by the active camera, we execute a person detector. The detector permits also automatic initialization of person tracking. The person detection is done by a SVM for linear classification that is built on Histogram of Oriented Depths (HOD) features [10]. The HOD descriptors locally encode the orientation of depth changes, see Fig. 3c. In our approach they are calculated in sub-windows, which are scaled according to their distances to the camera. The scaling is according to the distance between the camera and the closest pixels from the sub-window. Such sub-windows of fixed size are then subdivided into cells. The descriptors are calculated for each cell and then the oriented depth gradients are collected into 1D histograms.

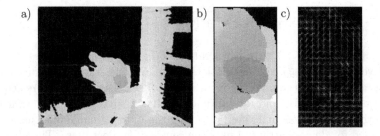

Fig. 3. Illustrative oversegmentation of the person blob (a), extracted head (b) and corresponding HOD (c).

4   Feature Extraction

At the beginning of this Section we show how we indicate falls on the basis of motion data. Afterwards, we discuss lying pose recognition in depth maps acquired by the overhead depth sensor. Finally, we present features describing dynamic transitions.

4.1   Fall Indicating Using Body-Worn Accelerometer

Compared to vision-based motion analysis systems, wearable sensors offer several advantages, particularly in terms of cost, ease of use and, most importantly, portability. They are the only sensors that are used in real fall detection systems as well as outside of laboratory. However, despite many advantages, the inertial sensors-based technology does not meet the seniors' needs, because some activities of daily living are erroneously reported as falls. Present smartphones serve not only as communication and computing devices, but they also come with a rich set of embedded sensors, such as accelerometer, gyroscope and digital compass. Therefore, increasing interest on using this technology for fall detection is observed and the number of relevant papers grows considerably. Being aware of shortcomings of current solutions we believe that such technology will be significantly enhanced and in combination with small devices like smart watches it will be very useful in fall detection. Thus, our system processes data from a wireless body-worn accelerometer.

A lot of different techniques for inertial sensors were proposed to achieve reliable fall detection [5]. Frequently, a single body-worn sensor (tri-axial accelerometer or gyroscope, or both embedded in an IMU) is used to indicate person fall. Tri-axial accelerometer is the most commonly used device. The accelerometer-based algorithms raise the alarm when the signal reaches a certain threshold value. In [11] an accelerometer-based algorithm, relying on change in body orientation has been proposed. It signals potential fall if the root sum vector of the three squared accelerometer outputs exceeds an assumed threshold.

In our algorithm a fall is indicated if the Total Sum Vector SV_{total} is greater than 2.5 g. The value of SV_{total} has been calculated in the following manner:

$$SV_{total}(t) = \sqrt{A_x^2(t) + A_y^2(t) + A_z^2(t)} \tag{1}$$

where $A_x(t)$, $A_y(t)$, $A_z(t)$ is the acceleration in the $x-$, $y-$, and $z-$axes at time t, respectively. The SV_{total} contains both the dynamic and static acceleration components, and thus it is equal to 1 g for standing. The sensor signals were acquired at a frequency of 256 Hz and resolution of 12 bits. A survey of the relevant literature reveals that for a single inertial device the most valuable information can be obtained for devices attached near the centre of subject mass. Therefore, the accelerometer was attached near the spine on the lower back using an elastic belt around the waist.

4.2   Lying Pose Recognition

The lying pose has been distinguished from ADLs using classifiers trained on features representing the extracted person in the depth maps. We selected 214 maps from UR Fall Detection (URFD) dataset[1] with normal activities like walking, sitting down on a chair, taking or putting an object from floor, bending right. Such representative images were then used to train a k-NN classifier and a linear SVM classifier responsible for checking whether a person is lying on the floor. Both classifiers have been trained on three features:

- H/H_{max} - a ratio of head-floor distance to the height of the person
- $area$ - a ratio expressing the person's area in the image to the area of the blob at assumed distance to the camera, representing a top-view of the person
- l/w - a ratio of major length to major width of a blob representing the person on the depth image.

4.3   Dynamic Transitions for Fall Detection

Person fall entails an abrupt and significant change of head-floor distance with accompanying change from a vertical orientation to horizontal one. The distance of the person's centroid to the floor also changes significantly and rapidly during the accidental fall period. In the images acquired from a ceiling-mounted camera the area ratio also changes considerably in the case of the fall. Thus, through analysis of the cues above mentioned we can determine whether a transition of the body is intentional or not.

In order to incorporate the information about the speed of the head towards the floor we utilize the following ratio:

$$h(t) = \frac{H(t)}{H(t - \Delta T)} \qquad (2)$$

where $H(t)$ is determined in the moment of the impact, and $H(t - \Delta T)$ is calculated ΔT before the fall. It quite reliably characterizes the dynamics of the fall using a ceiling-mounted Kinect. In the depth images from an overhead camera the peak value of $H(t)/H(t - \Delta T)$ is far below one. The ratio $H(t)/H(t - \Delta T)$ can also be determined by analysis of depth image pairs and searching for some local minima, which are below a threshold value. However, the use of accelerometer as indicator of the potential fall simplifies calculation of this ratio since the time t can be determined easily and with low computational cost. Figure 4 demonstrates sample plots of $H(t)/H(t - \Delta T)$ for accidental fall and intentional lying on the floor. As we can observe, for ΔT equal to 600 ms the Threshold that is set to 0.6 has been exceeded for the fall.

If the lying pose classifier has decided that person is lying on the floor, the threshold-based classifier is executed to examine if the dynamic transition of the head in the depth maps is smaller than 0.6. Thus, the final decision about the

---

[1] http://fenix.univ.rzeszow.pl/~mkepski/ds/uf.html.

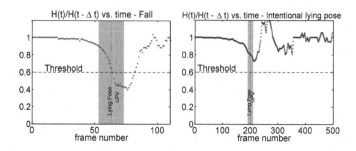

Fig. 4. $H(t)/H(t - \Delta T)$ vs. time for fall and intentional lying pose.

fall is taken by the chain of the classifiers. The discussed chain of the classifiers consists of accelerometer based classifier deciding about the potential fall, as well as lying pose and dynamic transition classifiers, which take decisions on the basis of the depth maps. The resulting fall detection classifier has lower false positive rate.

5 Real-Time Data Processing

The fall detection system runs under Linux operating system. The application executes five main concurrent processes that communicate via message queues. The message queues provide asynchronous communication between processes. The first process is accountable for acquiring motion data from the wearable device, the second one acquires depth maps from the Kinect, third process is responsible for preprocessing inertial and depth data, fourth one is accountable for person tracking and camera control, whereas the fifth process is responsible for data classification and triggering the fall alarm. The dual-core processor of the utilized PandaBoard allows parallel execution of acquisition and processing processes. The motion data are acquired with 256 Hz and transmitted wirelessly via Bluetooth to the processing device. The depth images are acquired using OpenNI (Open Natural Interaction) library with a frame rate up to 30 fps.

The region growing is executed in 37 ms, on average. This means that the person detection and tracking can be done with 25 Hz. The SVM-based classifier for distinguishing between falls and non-falls has been trained off-line on a PC. It has been trained using LIBSVM software [12]. The SVM model obtained in such a way has been used to implement the fall predictor, executed on the PandaBoard. The principle behind k-NN methods is to seek a predefined number of training samples closest in a distance to the classified example, and then to predict the label from these. This means that the k-NN algorithm does not learn anything from the training data and just utilizes the training data itself for the classification. As a result, there is no learning cost and all the cost is dedicated to determining the decision. A naive neighbor search implementation involves the brute-force computation of distances in D dimensions between the current example and all instances in the dataset. To handle computational burden of the brute-force neighbor search, the kd-tree data structure has been used to store the ADL and fall examples. Given such a data structure determined in advance during training, the nearest neighbor of an example in question can be determined with only $O(\log(N))$ distance computations.

6   Experimental Results

A system for fall detection should be inexpensive, ought to preserve user's privacy, work any time, and in particular it should exhibit both high sensitivity and specificity. The discussed system has been designed to fulfill the requirements mentioned above. A high detection accuracy has been achieved through scrupulous selection of the ingredients of the system as well as arrangement of scenarios for training and evaluation. In the subsequent subsections we present the dataset, evaluation results of the fall detector, and performance of person detector and tracker.

6.1   Fall Detection Dataset

The fall detector has been trained and evaluated on image sequences from URFD dataset. The dataset contains both depth images and acceleration data acquired by body-worn accelerometer [13]. The depth data were acquired by a ceiling-mounted Kinect Xbox 360 with 30 fps, whereas the motion data were acquired by x-IMU device with sampling rate of 256 Hz. The motion data contains the acceleration over time in the $x-$, $y-$, and $z-$axes together with the precalculated SV_{total} values. The x-IMU device was worn near the pelvis. All depth images are synchronized with motion data. Thirty simulated falls were recorded by two static Kinect devices. The first Kinect was situated in front of the scene and placed at the height of about 1 m, whereas the second ceiling-mounted Kinect was placed at the height of 2.6 m. The dataset recorded by the ceiling-mounted Kinect contains thirty image/acceleration sequences with 30 falls. The total number of the frames amounts to 3000. Two kinds of falls were simulated by five persons, namely from standing position and from sitting on the chair. The part of dataset, which was recorded by the frontal Kinect additionally contains 40 image/acceleration sequences with typical ADLs sitting down, crouching down, picking-up an object from the floor, and ten sequences with fall-like activities as quick lying on the floor and lying on the bed/couch.

6.2   Evaluation of the Fall Detector

The fall detection system can be configured to utilize both accelerometric and depth data or depth data only. When the accelerometer is involved at indicating that the person's movement is above some preset threshold, the impact can be detected more reliably in comparison to configuration using only depth data. The results are better since the depth map analysis is used to confirm the fall detection hypothesis indicated on the basis of examination of acceleration data from body-worn device. The use of the accelerometer as an indicator of the potential fall simplifies also the extracting of the dynamic features since the time of the impact can be determined easily, see also (2).

At the beginning we conducted experiments to determine acceleration thresholds for fall detection, using accelerometric measurements. Two voluntary subjects performed typical daily activities consisting in walking, taking or putting an object from floor, bending right or left to lift an object, sitting down on a chair, tying laces, crouching down and lying. Simulated falls (forward, backward, and lateral) were performed in an office towards a carpet with thickness of about 2 cm. The accelerometer was worn near the spine on the lower back using an elastic belt around the waist. For the carried out daily activities during half an hour experiment the acceleration values 2.5–3g were exceeded several times. Hence, large amounts of false alarms would be triggered if the fall detection was carried out only on the basis of the acceleration data. One of the conclusions from the discussed experiments is that the acceleration threshold set to 2.5 allows us to indicate all fall and fall-like activities as non-ADLs.

The algorithm for lying pose recognition has been evaluated on 875 representative images from UR Fall Detection Dataset of which 60 % were training examples. Since the discussed sequences were recorded using the static sensor, the person has been delineated through the differencing the current depth map from the depth reference map [7]. The depth reference maps were extracted in advance. A linear SVM and a k-NN with 5 neighbors classifiers have been trained on features discussed in Sect. 4.2 to discriminate between falls and ADLs. In Table 1 are shown results, which were obtained by the classifiers mentioned above. As we can notice, the results achieved by k-NN and SVM-based lying pose detectors are identical. They are promising in terms of both sensitivity and accuracy.

Table 1. Performance of lying pose detection on depth maps from URFD dataset [%].

			True		
			Fall	No Fall	
Estimated	SVM	Fall	244	9	Accuracy=97.52% Precision=96.44%
		No fall	4	268	
		Sens.= 98.39% Spec.= 96.75%			
	k-NN	Fall	244	10	Accuracy=97.33% Precision=96.06%
		No fall	4	267	
		Sens.= 98.39% Spec.= 96.39%			

Afterwards, we evaluated the usefulness of the dynamic feature. The experiments aimed at improving the distinguishing between the intentional lying on the floor from the accidental falling. At the beginning we investigated the classification accuracy with regard to decision criterions. Figure 5 depicts the receiver operating characteristic (ROC) curve for the dynamic feature, which illustrates the performance of a binary classifier for varying discrimination threshold. The best classification accuracy has been obtained for ΔT=500 ms and Threshold=0.525. Two students attending in the evaluations found that a cascade classifier consisting of lying pose detector and dynamic transition detector has almost null ratio of false alarms. They found that the main reason of the false alarms is imperfect detection of the moment of the body impact. The cascade classifier combined with the accelerometer demonstrated null false alarm. In particular, all falls were detected properly on the images from URFD dataset.

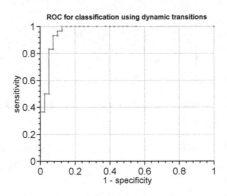

Fig. 5. Receiver operating characteristic (ROC) for dynamic feature.

6.3 Evaluation of Person Detector and Tracker

When a static ceiling-mounted camera is used, the person can be extracted reliably and with low computational burden through differencing the current depth map from the accommodated on-line depth reference map of the scene [7]. On the basis of such a depth reference map the person can be extracted in about 50 ms. However, as mentioned previously, the observation area of ceiling-mounted Kinect is quite small. Thanks to pan-tilt capabilities the monitoring area of the system can be extended considerably. On the other hand, more sophisticated and time consuming techniques are needed to delineate the person followed by an active camera.

Initially, the region growing has been evaluated in depth maps from URFD dataset. In all frames the person was extracted satisfactorily. Afterwards, the region growing has been evaluated on five sequences acquired by the active camera. In the discussed experiments with active camera, the aim was not only to extract in real-time the person, but also to keep he/she in the central part of the depth maps. Prior to the delineation of the subject using region growing, the camera was static for a while, and he/she was initially extracted through differencing the current depth map from the depth reference map of the scene. In all frames from the utilized sequences, including maps with intentional falls, all main body parts were extracted. Figure 6 depicts some results with delineated person, which were obtained on depth images acquired by the active camera. As we already mentioned, on the PandaBoard the average time of person delineation using region growing is from 35 ms to 40 ms depending on the blob size. Sample video illustrating person tracking with the pan-tilt depth camera can be found at the following url: http://fenix.univ.rzeszow.pl/~mkepski/demo/act.mp4.

Fig. 6. Region growing - based person delineation on depth maps.

The person detector has been evaluated on 254 positive samples and 638 negative samples of which 60 % were used for training. The images with delineated person were scaled according to distance of his/her head to the camera. They were also rotated to a canonical pose using the axis of the person's blob. Table 2 shows results that were obtained using the detector discussed in Sect. 3.2. As we can observe, the results are better if the silhouettes are rotated to the canonical pose. On the other hand, the difference is not significant, and this means that the algorithm is quite resistant to various head poses. This is because the gradients on the head in depth images seen from an overhead camera form elliptical like structures. The discussed results were obtained for HOD cell size equal to 8×8. On the PandaBoard a single person detection can be done in 41 ms.

Table 2. Performance of person detection [%]

	accuracy	precision	sensitiv.	specificity
rotat.	99.45	98.21	100.0	99.22
no rotat.	98.91	98.18	98.18	99.22

As we mentioned in Subsect. 3.2, in some circumstances, during person extraction on the basis of the region growing a person oversegmentation can take place. In such situations the person detector has been found to be useful since it helps to authenticate location of the person in such oversegmented depth maps. Let us consider a fall scenario, where a person is seating at the chair and is oversegmented as demonstrated on Fig. 3a. After the fall we have time t that is indicated by the threshold-based trigger. We then fetch a depth image from the circular buffer, which had been acquired 600 ms earlier. For simplicity, let us assume that this is image depicted on Fig. 3a. Given such a depth image, we execute HOG-SVM head detector to determine the location of the centroid of the head blob. After a while, i.e. max after a few seconds, we can determine $H(t)/H(t - \Delta T)$. Even if after the fall the person is still oversegmented, we can determine $H(t)$ easily because a lying person occupies areas below 40 cm from the ground. This way, we avoid to perform fall detection on features not belonging to person undergoing monitoring.

7 Conclusions

In this paper we presented an embedded system for fall detection using a ceiling-mounted depth sensor. In the proposed architecture a body-worn accelerometer is utilized to indicate an eventual fall, whereas the Kinect sensor is used to authenticate it. In order to expand the observation area the Kinect has been mounted on a pan-tilt head. We demonstrated that owing to thresholding of the motion data we can considerably reduce the computing overheads for processing the depth data. We then showed that a depth sensor can reliably distinguish between such filtered events and the falls. In consequence, the depth maps are not processed frame-by-frame, but instead a circular buffer is used to store the depth maps for processing them in the case of possible fall. The detection performance of the system has been evaluated on UR Fall Detection dataset. The presented embedded system works 365/7/24 days and hours, permits reliable and unobtrusive fall detection as well as preserves privacy of the user.

Acknowledgment. This work was supported by Polish National Science Center (NCN) under a research grant 2014/15/B/ST6/02808 and a grant 11.11.230.124.

References

1. Friedewald, M., Raabe, O.: Ubiquitous computing: an overview of technology impacts. Telemat. Inf. **28**(2), 55–65 (2011)
2. Wilson, C., Hargreaves, T., Hauxwell, R.: Smart homes and their users: a systematic analysis and key challenges. Pers. Ubiquitous Comp. **19**, 463–476 (2015)
3. Acampora, G., Cook, D., Rashidi, P., Vasilakos, A.: A survey on ambient intelligence in healthcare. Proc. IEEE **101**(12), 2470–2494 (2013)
4. Webster, D., Celik, O.: Systematic review of Kinect applications in elderly care and stroke rehabilitation. J. NeuroEngineering Rehabil. **11**, 1 (2014)
5. Bourke, A., O'Brien, J., Lyons, G.: Evaluation of a threshold-based tri-axial accelerometer fall detection algorithm. Gait Posture **26**(2), 194–199 (2007)
6. Rougier, C., Auvinet, E., Rousseau, J., Mignotte, M., Meunier, J.: Fall detection from depth map video sequences. In: Abdulrazak, B., Giroux, S., Bouchard, B., Pigot, H., Mokhtari, M. (eds.) ICOST 2011. LNCS, vol. 6719, pp. 121–128. Springer, Heidelberg (2011)
7. Kepski, M., Kwolek, B.: Fall detection on embedded platform using kinect and wireless accelerometer. In: Miesenberger, K., Karshmer, A., Penaz, P., Zagler, W. (eds.) ICCHP 2012, Part II. LNCS, vol. 7383, pp. 407–414. Springer, Heidelberg (2012)

8. Cuppens, K., Chen, C.W., Wong, K.B.Y., Van de Vel, A., Lagae, L., Ceulemans, B., Tuytelaars, T., Van Huffel, S., Vanrumste, B., Aghajan, H.: Integrating video and accelerometer signals for nocturnal epileptic seizure detection. In: Proceedings of the 14th ACM International Conference on Multimodal Interaction, pp. 161–164, New York, NY (2012)

9. Chen, C., Jafari, R., Kehtarnavaz, N.: Improving human action recognition using fusion of depth camera and inertial sensors. IEEE Trans. HMS **45**, 51–61 (2015)

10. Spinello, L., Arras, K.: People detection in RGB-D data. In: IEEE/RSJ International Conference on IROS, pp. 3838–3843, September 2011

11. Chen, J., Kwong, K., Chang, D., Luk, J., Bajcsy, R.: Wearable sensors for reliable fall detection. In: International Conference on Engineering in Medicine and Biology Society, pp. 3551–3554 (2005)

12. Chang, C.C., Lin, C.J.: LIBSVM: a library for support vector machines. ACM Trans. Intell. Syst. Technol. **2**(3), 1–27 (2011)

13. Kepski, M., Kwolek, B.: Fall detection using ceiling-mounted 3d depth camera. In: International Joint Conference on Computer Vision Theory and Applications (VISAPP), vol. 2, pp. 640–647

Classification of Melanoma Presence and Thickness Based on Computational Image Analysis

Javier Sánchez-Monedero[1]([⊠]), Aurora Sáez[2], María Pérez-Ortiz[1],
Pedro Antonio Gutiérrez[3], and Cesar Hervás-Martínez[3]

[1] Department of Quantitative Methods, Universidad Loyola Andalucía,
Escritor Castilla Aguayo, 4, 14004 Córdoba, Spain
{jsanchez,mariaperez}@uloyola.es
[2] Signal Theory and Communications Department, University of Seville,
41092 Seville, Spain
aurorasaez@us.es
[3] Department of Computer Science and Numerical Analysis, Campus de Rabanales,
Edificio Albert Einstein, University of Córdoba, 14071 Córdoba, Spain
{pagutierrez,chervas}@uco.es

Abstract. Melanoma is a type of cancer that occurs on the skin. Only in the US, 50,000–100,000 patients are yearly diagnosed with melanoma. Five year survival rate highly depends on early detection, varying between 99 % and 15 % depending on the melanoma stage. Melanoma is typically identified with a visual inspection and lately confirmed and classified by a biopsy. In this work, we propose a hybrid system combining features which describe melanoma images together with machine learning models that learn to distinguish melanoma lesions. Although previous works distinguish melanoma and non-melanoma images, those works focus only in the binary case. Opposed to this, we propose to consider finer classification levels within a five class learning problem. We evaluate the performance of several nominal and ordinal classifiers using four performance metrics to provide highlights of several aspects of classification performance, achieving promising results.

Keywords: Melanoma · Feature extraction · Dermoscopic image · Computer vision · Machine learning · Multi-class · Ordinal classification · Imbalanced classification

1 Introduction

Melanoma is a malignancy of melanocytes, which are the cells that produce the pigment melanin that colors the skin, hair and eyes. The most common type

This work was partly financed by a grant provided by the TIN2014-54583-C2-1-R project of the Spanish Ministry of Economy and Competitively (MINECO), by FEDER Funds and by the P11-TIC-7508 project of the Junta de Andalucía, Spain.

© Springer International Publishing Switzerland 2016
F. Martínez-Álvarez et al. (Eds.): HAIS 2016, LNAI 9648, pp. 427–438, 2016.
DOI: 10.1007/978-3-319-32034-2_36

of melanoma is called cutaneous melanoma and occurs on the skin. In the US, approximately 73,870 melanomas will be diagnosed by the end of 2015, with around 9,940 resulting in death [1]. In Europe, approximately 100,000 cases are yearly diagnosed with similar death ratio [2]. In medicine, it is well accepted that only early detection can reduce mortality, since the prognosis of patients with melanoma depends on the thickness of the tumor at the time of surgical treatment [3].

Melanoma must be detected at an early stage, this is, before the tumour has penetrated the epidermis (i.e., before the thickness is higher than $> 0.76\,\mathrm{mm}$). In that case, the five year survival rate is about 99 %, otherwise it drops to 15 % for patients with advanced disease [4].

Detection methods consist on a visual inspection with a dermatoscope performed by trained professionals, which demands a posterior biopsy based on visual findings. However, in the late years, tools to aid or to improve the prognosis are being developed [4], which are mainly based on dermoscopic images analysis. Although many lines are being investigated, images analysis based methods have the advantage of being easier and cheaper to combine with current detection methods.

Recently, computerized dermoscopy image analysis systems have been proposed to assist the diagnosis of pigmented lesions [5]. Most of the works in the literature focus on distinguishing melanomas from benign lesions [6,7]. Nevertheless, going further into a finer melanoma classification is a recent and necessary topic with scarce related works. Rubegni et al. [8] address the characterization of two types of melanoma based on their thickness. This work uses 49 features related to color, geometry and texture, extracted from a private database of 141 images obtained with a hardware system of the company.

In this paper, we develop a system to distinguish non-melanoma from melanoma cases, the latter being labeled using four categories related to the thickness of the tumor. Up to our best knowledge, it is the first time that the five class scenario is considered for this challenging problem. To do so, we evaluate the performance of a bank of multi-class learners to establish a performance baseline. The multi-class classifiers chosen are nominal (obviating the ordinal nature of the labels) and ordinal models (including order information in the classifiers).

The proposed system considers a step of feature extraction, in which features regarding both the distinction between melanoma/benign lesion and the depth of melanoma are taken into account. Features for distinguishing melanoma and non-melanoma are based on the ABCD method, a useful tool for the diagnosis of pigmented lesions. This method analyzes four clinical characteristics to identify a malignant melanoma: asymmetry (A), border irregularity (B), color variegation (C) and differential structures (D). Features to estimate the melanoma thickness are based on clinical findings that correlate certain characteristics present in dermoscopic images and tumor depth [9].

The contributions of the present work are the following. Firstly, we propose to jointly solve two different challenges: classify non-melanoma and melanoma cases, and provide a finer-grain classification based on tumor depth. Secondly, to support this goal, an extensive feature extraction step is considered to describe different types of lesions with 86 variables. Finally, we perform a selection of advanced machine learning methods including ordinal classification ones, which have been proved to be, in general, more suitable for these type of problems.

The rest of the paper is organized as follows. Section 2 presents the clinical problem and the image database, and Sect. 3 describes the set of features selected to describe the images. Section 4 briefly summarizes the machine learning methods used to build the prediction models. The experiments performed and results are depicted in Sect. 5. The paper finalizes outlining some conclusions and three possible future research lines.

2   Breslow's Depth and Database

Tumor thickness is directly correlated with greater access to lymph capillaries, which is a common method of cancer spread, then, related to prognosis. When the melanoma is confined to the epidermis, it is called 'in situ' melanoma, and it is curable by adequate removal surgery. However, as the cancerous cells grown into the deeper layer of the skin (the dermis), it is known as invasive melanoma, whose survival rate worsens with the depth of invasion.

The Breslow index is a method for prognosis of patients survival [9]. It measures the depth of the melanoma invasion by means of pathological examination after incisional or excisional biopsy of the suspected lesion [9]. It consists on a vertical measurement in millimeters from the top of the granular layer of the epidermis to its deepest part within the dermis. In addition, it represents the main parameter used to establish the surgical margins excision width [10,11], as well as to decide to perform a sentinel lymph node biopsy (SNB) [10], which is a surgical procedure to determine if cancer has spread into the lymphatic system. Accordingly, measuring melanoma thickness before surgical excision is crucial in order to assess the high or low risk of progression, and consequently to ensure adequate excision margins avoiding a second more radical operation and to perform SNB if needed.

Table 1. Stages of melanoma according to thicknes, number of patterns in each class and Imbalance Ratio (IR)

Stage	Location	Class	Number of patterns	Imbalance ratio
Non-melanoma	-	1	313	0.159
Stage 0	In situ	2	64	1.556
Stage I	<0.76 mm	3	102	0.902
Stage II	0.76 mm - 1.50 mm	4	54	1.881
Stage III	>1.50 mm	5	29	3.676
			Total patterns	Mean IR
			562	1.635

Table 1 includes different stages of thickness based on the Breslow index. In this work, we collect 556 images from the Interactive Atlas of Dermoscopy [12], which is a multimedia project for medical education with pigmented skin lesions images in which all lesions were biopsied and diagnosed histopathologically. The database images can be analysed using five classes: non-melanoma case and four stages of melanoma depth. The number of patterns belonging to each class is also included in Table 1, as well as the imbalance ratio.

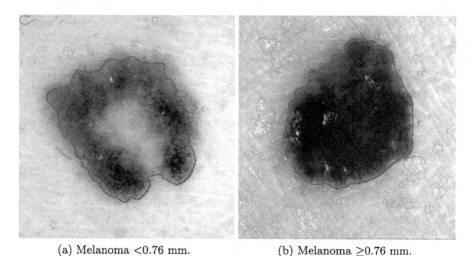

(a) Melanoma <0.76 mm.   (b) Melanoma ≥0.76 mm.

Fig. 1. Examples of segmented melanomas

All the images have the same resolution (768 × 512 pixels). The images were segmented using the automatic segmentation algorithm proposed in [13], in which an edge based level-set technique is applied together with a perceptually adapted color gradient [14]. Figure 1 presents examples of two segmented melanomas.

3   Feature Extraction

The feature extraction process proposed in this paper aims to mimic dermatologist assessment, by using discriminative characteristics defined in the clinical ABCD rule (in order to distinguish between benign lesions and melanomas) and features inspired by the findings derived from clinical studies regarding the correlation between certain characteristics seen in dermoscopic images and melanoma thickness. A total of 86 descriptors ($x_1 - x_{86}$) based on shape, color and texture are extracted.

Regarding the ABCD method, asymmetry (A) and border irregularity (B) are characterized by the shape features, color variegation (C) by the feature that represents the number of colors present in a lesion and differential structures (D) by texture features, especially, by those based on a Markov random field model, that allow to identify different dermoscopic structures, as was proposed in [13].

3.1   Shape Features

As it has been mentioned, shape features were extracted to satisfy the asymmetry (A) and irregularity border (B) criteria. We compute circularity index (computed as 4π multiplied by lesion area, divided by its squared perimeter) (x_1), perimeter normalized by the equivalent perimeter (perimeter of a circle with the same area as the lesion) (x_2), the variance of the distance of the border lesion points from the centroid location (x_3), eccentricity (a measure of elongation) (x_4) [7] and length of major axis of the lesion normalized with respect to the equivalent diameter (diameter of a circle with the same area as the lesion) (x_5). In order to evaluate the lesion asymmetry, first, the major axis orientation of the lesion was calculated, and secondly, it was rotated these degrees clockwise to align the principal axes with the image (x and y) axes. The lesion was then hypothetically folded about the x-axis, and the percentage of overlapping area with respect to the total area of the lesion was computed to obtain the horizontal asymmetry (x_6). The same procedure was performed for the y-axis to obtain vertical asymmetry (x_7). If the process is repeated taking into account the percentage of overlapping pixels assigned to the same color (see Sect. 3.2 for the color assignation), we compute the color horizontal asymmetry (x_8) and the color horizontal asymmetry (x_9).

3.2   Color Features

Color features play an important role in the estimation of depth of the melanoma. Different dermoscopic structures discriminative in the melanoma thickness estimation are associated with different colors. We extract features related to the six colors present in the pigmented lesions: black, dark brown, light brown, blue-gray, red and white [15]. These colors appear depending on the depth of the melanoma [16]: black melanin appears when it is located in the stratum corneum and upper epidermis; brown is associated with deeper location in the epidermis; gray and blue are related to location in the dermis; red is associated with dilation of blood vessels; and white with scaring and/or regression. To describe these colors, we propose to segment each lesion into their constituting colors by a similar approach to that proposed by Seidenari et al. [17]. We developed a color palette formed by 144 patches that present unequivocally one of the six possible colors. This palette was used to extract the color regions of the lesions from the patches according to a nearest neighbor approach. Each pixel of the image was assigned to the color patch that minimized its Euclidean distance in the CIE $L^*a^*b^*$ color space. From this color identification, we extracted six descriptors $(x_{10}-x_{15})$ that represent the percentage of the lesion area classified as these colors, one (x_{16}) that represents the number of colors that each lesion presents (color criterion of ABCD), and 24 additional statistical descriptors of the color (mean, standard deviation, kurtosis, and skewness of each color) $(x_{17}-x_{40})$.

3.3   Pigment Network Features

Pigment network is a dermoscopic structure, cited by many authors as one of the most discriminative features for melanoma thickness [10, 18–20], being inversely correlated with melanoma depth [12]. A pigment network is a regular grid of brownish lines over a diffuse light-brown background [12]. We detect this structure seeking the 'holes' of the network by applying a filtering and thresholding step by the Otsu's method [21]. Finally, we apply the two conditions relative to area size and color proposed in the work of Sadeghi et al. [22] in order to remove those wrongly detected areas. The features extracted from this detection are network density ratio (x_{41}), number of nodes (x_{42}) and number of links or edges (x_{43}).

3.4 Texture Features

Other dermoscopic structures have been found to have relation with the depth of melanoma such as vascular pattern [10,18], blue-gray veil [10,18], white scar-like areas [19], and dots or globules [20]. These are usually associated with texture features.

To try to capture properties of different structures, we extract three sets of texture features from three different approaches: 19 features from the gray level co-occurrence matrix (GLCM) [23] ($x_{44} - x_{62}$), 18 features based on a Markov random field (MRF) model [13] ($x_{63} - x_{80}$) and 6 features from local binary pattern (LBP) histograms ($x_{81} - x_{86}$).

4 Classification Methods

In this section, we summarize the machine learning methods used for the experiments. We have selected two families of methods: nominal and ordinal multi-class learners. The ordinal classifiers are methods designed to improve performance when the nature of the problem presents an order relationship between categories. These methods present the advantage of reducing the magnitude of the errors and exploiting the ordering information imbued in the labels. In addition, many ordinal classification methods are single-model methods, in contrast with their nominal counterparts. For instance, in the case of logistic regression the ordinal classification method model is a single-model one, whereas the nominal implementation is an ensemble of binary models. The methods selected are the following:

– Although it is a statistical method, Logistic Regression (LR) is included in many machine learning studies, since it provides a baseline for comparisons with other methods and it yields very good performance in some datasets. Here we use three variants of LR:
  • Multinomial Logistic Regression (MLR) is a model composed of several binary LR models. It uses the "one against all" scheme to extend the binary models to the multi-class case. In this work we use the `mnrfit` function of Matlab, which implements MLR.
  • SimpleLogistic algorithm fits a multinomial LR model using the LogitBoost algorithm, adding one simple LR model per class in each iteration to build the final logistic regression model [24].

- The Proportional Odds Model (POM) adapts the standard logistic regression to the ordinal case. For the POM model, the `mnrfit` function of Matlab software has been used.
- Logistic regression with artificial neural network hidden neurons is a methodology proposed in [25,26], which adds non-linear transformations of the input space to the LR model, this capturing non linear relationships the data. We use the proposal called "Logistic regression using Initial variables and Product Units" (LIPU), trained with the methodology presented in [27].
- Support Vector Machines (SVMs) are the most popular kernel methods:
  - SVM multi-classifier (SVC) with the "one against one" approach [28] is considered as a nominal method.
  - The SVM for ordinal regression with implicit constraints (SVORIM) [29] is a threshold method for ordinal regression and has shown very good performance in this context [30].
  - RED-SVM by [31] applies the reduction from cost-sensitive ordinal ranking to weighted binary classification (RED) framework to SVM.
- Kernel Discriminant Learning for Ordinal Regression (KDLOR) [32] extends the Kernel Discriminant Analysis (KDA) to ordinal classification using a rank constraint.

Experiments of SVC, SVORIM, RED-SVM, KDLOR, POM and MLR have been done with ORCA [30] software[1]. LIPU source code is available on a public website[2]. For SimpleLogistic experiments, we use the *SLogistic* method available at Weka [33].

5 Experiments

This section includes a description of the experiments performed and an analysis of the results.

5.1 Performance Evaluation

Selection of proper classification evaluation metrics strongly depends on the problem requirements. In our case, due to the relevance of the model precision in patients survival, we have selected several performance metrics to have multiple views of the model performance. In addition, Table 1 reveals the imbalanced nature in the classification problem, therefore demanding specific metrics which take all classes into account. We have selected metrics to evaluate global accuracy, the balance of the performance for all the classes and the ordinal magnitude of the errors. The four selected metrics are:

---

[1] https://github.com/ayrna/orca.
[2] http://www.uco.es/grupos/ayrna/en/partitions-and-datasets/#
paguitierrez2011ieeetnn.

– Accuracy (Acc) is the percentage of correctly classified patterns and represents the global performance of the classification task:

$$Acc = 100 \cdot \frac{1}{N} \sum_{i=1}^{N} [\![\hat{y}_i = y_i]\!],$$

where $[\![c]\!]$ is the indicator function, being equal to 1 if c is true, and to 0 otherwise. Acc values range is $[0, 100]$.

– Minimum Sensitivity (MS) is proposed to measure imbalanced multi-class model performance [34], and it is defined as the minimum per class Sensitivity (S_i): $MS = 100 \cdot \min \{S_i; \; i = 1, \dots, J\}$, where J is the number of classes, and S_i is the accuracy taking only patterns from class $\mathcal{C}_i$ into account.

– GM: The geometric mean of the sensitivities for each class is typically used to evaluate performance in imbalanced problems [35]:

$$GM = 100 \cdot \sqrt[J]{\prod_{j=1}^{J} S_j},$$

where J is the number of classes and S_j is the accuracy of the classifier for patterns of class j. GM varies from 0 to 100. The case of $GM = 0$ means that the classifier is not correctly labeling any pattern of one or more classes.

– Mean Absolute Error (MAE) is the average deviation in absolute value of the predicted class from the true class. It is an ordinal classification metric, and, for imbalanced datasets, this measure should be modified to consider the relative frequency of the classes, deriving in the *Average MAE* ($AMAE$) [36]:

$$AMAE = \frac{1}{J} \sum_{j=1}^{J} MAE_j = \frac{1}{J} \sum_{q=1}^{J} \frac{1}{n_q} \sum_{i=1}^{n_q} e(\mathbf{x}_i),$$

where $e(\mathbf{x}_i) = |\mathcal{O}(y_i) - \mathcal{O}(\hat{y}_i)|$ is the distance between the true and the predicted ranks, $\mathcal{O}(\mathcal{C}_q) = q$ is the position of the q-th label, n_q is the number of patterns of class $\mathcal{C}_q$, and $AMAE$ values range from 0 to $J - 1$.

Experiments are performed using a 10-fold cross-validation with features standardized using the mean and the standard deviation of the training fold. MLR, POM and Simple Logistic do not have hyper-parameters to be tuned. Parameters associated to LIPU are adjusted to those values presented in [27], with the exception of the minimum and maximum number of hidden product unit nodes, which are 1 and 5, respectively, the population size, which is set to 500 individuals, and the maximum number of generations adjusted to 150. For the rest of methods, to adjust the hyper-parameters, a nested cross-validation is applied to the training data of each fold, with a grid search validating the parameter values (value ranges are those recommended in [30]). The criteria for selecting the parameters is $AMAE$, because preliminary experiments using other metrics, such as Acc, led to models ignoring at least one of the classes ($MS = 0.00\%$ and $GM = 0.00\%$).

Table 2. Experimental results considering four classification performance metrics.

Method/Metric	AMAE	Acc	GM	MS
Nominal classifiers				
MLR	0.887	63.17	38.48	*28.13*
SLogistic	0.799	*68.15*	*40.03*	16.67
LIPU	**0.773**	**68.51**	39.12	14.81
SVC	0.924	65.30	34.85	20.69
Ordinal classifiers				
POM	0.837	63.52	36.78	20.69
KDLOR	*0.791*	57.65	**42.26**	*28.13*
REDSVM	0.859	61.57	36.74	23.44
SVORIM	0.820	59.96	39.46	**29.63**

To compare performance, the metrics are calculated on a matrix which is the sum of all generalization confusion matrices from the 10 folds. This provides a more robust evaluation point of view for MS and GM when having classes with few patterns.

5.2 Results

Table 2 shows the experimental results according to the performance evaluation described in Sect. 5.1. The first conclusion is that the problem is a challenging classification task, for which it is difficult to correctly classify all the classes. The best performance considering Acc is obtained by LIPU and SLogistic, while, methods with better performance in the minority classes (KDLOR and SVORIM for GM and MS) obtain it at the cost of global Acc. Considering the performance for the four metrics, KDLOR, LIPU and SLogistic are probably the ones with a better balance. Moreover, the POM results are also interesting, presenting a good average performance in the four metrics. The advantage of POM is that it is a linear probabilistic model that can be interpreted to further analyze the influence of features in the discrimination of each class. Finally, apart from LIPU, which is an evolutionary algorithm, classical ordinal methods perform acceptably in this application, presenting generally a better ordering of the classes compared to their nominal counterparts. In terms of family of methods, we can conclude that logistic regression and its variants (MLR, SLogistic, LIPU and POM) present good performance even though being linear classifiers. This can be explained due to the high number of features available and low number of patterns, which ease to find linear boundaries to differentiate the five classes. In general, ensemble methods (MLR and SVC) have suitable performance for all the classes (measured in GM AND MS metrics). These methods build several binary models with the purpose of classify each class separately, thus minimizing the effect of the imbalance. Finally, as expected all the ordinal regression methods have an overall best performance in ordinal metrics.

Table 3. Generalization confusion matrices for LIPU, KDLOR and SLogistic models.

	LIPU					KDLOR					SLogistic				
	C_1	C_2	C_3	C_4	C_5	C_1	C_2	C_3	C_4	C_5	C_1	C_2	C_3	C_4	C_5
C_1	296	3	10	2	2	235	59	14	4	1	295	2	10	4	2
C_2	12	25	23	2	2	14	18	20	12	0	14	24	22	3	1
C_3	22	16	45	14	5	9	27	34	26	6	25	16	43	13	5
C_4	6	6	27	8	7	5	8	8	25	8	6	3	29	9	7
C_5	1	1	7	9	11	2	1	5	9	12	2	1	9	5	12

To better analyze the results, Table 3 shows generalization confusion matrices corresponding to LIPU, KDLOR and SLogistic models. As shown, the improvement in *Acc* is done at the expense of losing performance for some classes. In the case of LIPU and SLogistic, the models tends to classify all the patterns in class three (C_3).

6   Conclusions

In this paper, we present a hybrid system based on computational image analysis and machine learning to develop a tool for automatic detection of melanoma presence and severity. We extract image features related to shape, color, pigment network and texture to describe benign and several malign stage cases.

The performance results are promising, thus indicating that the type of features extracted describe the lesions properly. The use of several performance metrics reveals the necessity of improving classification accuracy for all the classes, but specifically for minority classes, which corresponds, in addition, to the worst prognosis survival expectation.

As future work, several lines can be explored. Firstly, most of the features we have included are aimed at discriminating thickness of melanomas, but more specific features to distinguish non-melanoma from melanoma patterns can be included. Adding more features of these type would probably improve class separability between the first class and the rest of classes. Secondly, more patterns should be included in the database, specially those corresponding to the minority classes. In this direction, oversampling techniques may be explored. Finally, due to the different performance obtained for the different models, this encourages the use of ensemble models to tackle this classification problem.

References

1. Institute, N.C.:Seer stat fact sheets: melanoma of the skin (2015). http://seer. cancer.gov/statfacts/html/melan.html. Accessed 15 December 2015
2. For Research on Cancer. World Health Organization, I.A.:Cancer factsheet. Malignant melanoma of skin (2015). http://eco.iarc.fr/eucan/Cancer.aspx?Cancer=20. Accessed 15 Dec 2015

3. Pizzichetta, M., Argenziano, G., Talamini, R., Piccolo, D., Gatti, A., Trevisan, G., Sasso, G., Veronesi, A., Carbone, A., Peter Soyer, H.: Dermoscopic criteria for melanoma in situ are similar to those for early invasive melanoma. Cancer **91**, 992–997 (2001)
4. Herman, C.: Emerging technologies for the detection of melanoma: achieving better outcomes. Clin. Cosmet. Invest. Dermatol. **5**, 195–212 (2012)
5. Maglogiannis, I., Doukas, C.N.: Overview of advanced computer vision systems for skin lesions characterization. IEEE Trans. Inf.Technol. Biomed. **13**, 721–733 (2009)
6. Garnavi, R., Aldeen, M., Bailey, J.: Computer-aided diagnosis of melanoma using border- and wavelet-based texture analysis. IEEE Trans. Inf. Technol. Biomed. **16**, 1239–1252 (2012)
7. Celebi, M., Kingravi, H., Uddin, B., Iyatomi, H., Aslandogan, Y., Stoecker, W., Moss, R.: A methodological approach to the classification of dermoscopy images. Comput. Med. Imaging Graph. **31**, 362–373 (2007)
8. Rubegni, P., Cevenini, G., Sbano, P., Burroni, M., Zalaudek, I., Risulo, M., Dell'Eva, G., Nami, N., Martino, A., Fimiani, M.: Evaluation of cutaneous melanoma thickness by digital dermoscopy analysis: a retrospective study. Melanoma Res. **20**, 212–217 (2010)
9. Amouroux, M., Blondel, W.: Non-invasive determination of Breslow index. In: Cao, M.Y. (ed.) Current Management of Malignant Melanoma, pp. 29–44. InTech (2011)
10. Stante, M., De Giorgi, V., Cappugi, P., Giannotti, B., Carli, P.: Non-invasive analysis of melanoma thickness by means of dermoscopy: a retrospective study. Melanoma Res. **11**, 147–152 (2001)
11. Lens, M.B., Nathan, P., Bataille, V.: Excision margins for primary cutaneous melanoma: updated pooled analysis of randomized controlled trials. Arch. Surg. **142**, 885–891 (2007)
12. Argenziano, G., Soyer, H., et al.: Interactive Atlas of Dermoscopy. EDRA-Medical Publishing and New Media, Milan (2000)
13. Sáez, A., Serrano, C., Acha, B.: Model-based classification methods of global patterns in dermoscopic images. IEEE Trans. Med. Imaging **33**, 1137–1147 (2014)
14. Sáez, A., Mendoza, C.S., Acha, B., Serrano, C.: Development and evaluation of perceptually adapted colour gradients. IET Image Proc. **7**, 355–363 (2013)
15. Soyer, H., Argenziano, G., Hofmann-Wellenhof, R., Johr, R.: Color Atlas of Melanocytic Lesions of the Skin. Springer, Heidelberg (2010)
16. Weismann, K., Lorentzen, H.F.: Dermoscopic color perspective. Arch. Dermatol. **142**, 1250 (2006)
17. Seidenari, S., Pellacani, G., Grana, C.: Computer description of colours in dermoscopic melanocytic lesion images reproducing clinical assessment. Br. J. Dermatol. **149**, 523–529 (2003)
18. Argenziano, G., Fabbrocini, G., Carli, P., De Giorgi, V., Delfino, M.: Clinical and dermatoscopic criteria for the preoperative evaluation of cutaneous melanoma thickness. J. Am. Acad. Dermatol. **40**, 61–68 (1999)
19. Lorentzen, H., Weismann, K., Grønhøj Larsen, F.: Dermatoscopic prediction of melanoma thickness using latent trait analysis and likelihood ratios. Acta Derm. Venereol. **81**, 38–41 (2001)
20. da Silva, V., Ikino, J., Sens, M., Nunes, D., Di Giunta, G.: Dermoscopic features of thin melanomas: a comparative study of melanoma in situ and invasive melanomas smaller than or equal to 1mm [características dermatoscópicas de melanomas finos: Estudo comparativo entre melanomas in situ e melanomas invasivos menores ou iguais a 1mm]. Anais Brasileiros de Dermatologia **88**, 712–717 (2013)

21. Otsu, N.: Threshold selection method from gray-level histograms. IEEE Trans. Syst. Man Cybern. **SMC–9**, 62–66 (1979). (cited By 10522)
22. Sadeghi, M., Razmara, M., Lee, T., Atkins, M.: A novel method for detection of pigment network in dermoscopic images using graphs. Comput. Med. Imaging Graph. **35**, 137–143 (2011)
23. Haralick, R., Shanmugam, K., Dinstein, I.: Textural features for image classification. IEEE Trans. Syst. Man Cybern. **SMC3**, 610–621 (1973)
24. Landwehr, N., Hall, M., Frank, E.: Logistic model trees. Mach. Learn. **59**, 161–205 (2005)
25. Hervás-Martínez, C., Martínez-Estudillo, F.J., Carbonero-Ruz, M.: Multilogistic regression by means of evolutionary product-unit neural networks. Neural Netw. **21**, 951–961 (2008)
26. Hervás-Martínez, C., Martínez-Estudillo, F.: Logistic regression using covariates obtained by product-unit neural network models. Pattern Recogn. **40**, 52–64 (2007)
27. Gutiérrez, P.A., Hervás-Martínez, C., Martínez-Estudillo, F.J.: Logistic regression by means of evolutionary radial basis function neural networks. IEEE Trans. Neural Networks **22**, 246–263 (2011)
28. Chang, C.C., Lin, C.J.: LIBSVM: a library for support vector machines. ACM Trans. Intell. Syst. Technol. **2**, 27:1–27:27 (2011)
29. Chu, W., Keerthi, S.S.: Support vector ordinal regression. Neural Comput. **19**, 792–815 (2007)
30. Gutiérrez, P., Pérez-Ortiz, M., Sánchez-Monedero, J., Fernandez-Navarro, F., Hervás-Martínez, C.: Ordinal regression methods: survey and experimental study. IEEE Trans. Knowl. Data Eng. **28**, 127–146 (2016)
31. Lin, H.T., Li, L.: Reduction from cost-sensitive ordinal ranking to weighted binary classification. Neural Comput. **24**, 1329–1367 (2012)
32. Sun, B.Y., Li, J., Wu, D.D., Zhang, X.M., Li, W.B.: Kernel discriminant learning for ordinal regression. IEEE Trans. Knowl. Data Eng. **22**, 906–910 (2010)
33. Hall, M., Frank, E., Holmes, G., Pfahringer, B., Reutemann, P., Witten, I.H.: The WEKA data mining software: an update. Spec. Interest Group Knowl. Discov. Data Min. Explorer Newsl. **11**, 10–18 (2009)
34. Fernández-Caballero, J.C., Martínez-Estudillo, F.J., Hervás-Martínez, C., Gutiérrez, P.A.: Sensitivity versus accuracy in multiclass problems using memetic pareto evolutionary neural networks. IEEE Trans. Neural Networks **21**, 750–770 (2010)
35. Kubat, M., Matwin, S.: Addressing the curse of imbalanced training sets: one-sided selection. In: Proceedings of the 14th International Conference on Machine Learning, pp. 179–186. Morgan Kaufmann (1997)
36. Baccianella, S., Esuli, A., Sebastiani, F.: Evaluation measures for ordinal regression. In: Proceedings of the Ninth International Conference on Intelligent Systems Design and Applications (ISDA 2009), pp. 283–287. IEEE Computer Society, San Mateo, CA (2009)

Classification and Cluster Analysis

Solution to Data Imbalance Problem in Application Layer Anomaly Detection Systems

Rafał Kozik[(✉)] and Michał Choraś

Institute of Telecommunications and Computer Science,
UTP University of Science and Technology in Bydgoszcz, Bydgoszcz, Poland
{rafal.kozik,michal.choras}@utp.edu.pl

Abstract. Currently, we can observe the increasing number of successful cyber attacks which use vulnerable web pages which allow the hacker
(or cracker) to breach the network security (e.g. to deliver a malicious
content). This trend is caused by the web applications complexity and
diversity, which make it difficult to provide the effective and efficient
cyber security countermeasures. Moreover, there are lots of different
obfuscation techniques that allow the attacker to overcome signature-
based attacks detections mechanisms. Therefore, in this paper we propose
a machine-learning web-layer anomaly detection system that adapts our
algorithm for packet segmentation and an ensemble of REPTree classifiers. In our experiments we prove that this approach can substantially increase the effectiveness of cyber attacks detection. Moreover, we
present the solution to counter the data imbalance problem in cyber
security.

Keywords: Data imbalance · Anomaly detection · Ensemble of classifiers · Application layer attacks · Web application security

1 Introduction

The motivation of our work and results presented in this paper come from the
current view and analysis of the cyber crime landscape. As always in the history of the world, when a technology is created end evolves, it can be used for
good and criminal purposes. The same happened with the quick evolution of the
communication networks and web applications which are now often the source
or the target of so called cyber crime. Currently, two common trends in cyber
attacks are:

– The growing number and importance of attacks in the application layer. Such
  situation is also reflected in attacks ranking e.g. by OWASP [1] where SQLIA
  (SQL Injection Attack) and XSS (Cross Site Scripting) are top-ranked. Some
  recent examples of critical systems vulnerable to attacks in the application
  layer are attack on flight management system in Poland.

© Springer International Publishing Switzerland 2016
F. Martínez-Álvarez et al. (Eds.): HAIS 2016, LNAI 9648, pp. 441–450, 2016.
DOI: 10.1007/978-3-319-32034-2_37

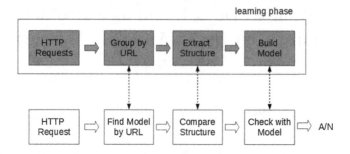

Fig. 1. The proposed algorithm overview. It adapts batch processing approach to machine learning. First, the model is established on learning data, afterwards new data samples are compared with the model in order to detect a cyber attack. The method returns binary result (A/N), where A indicates *anomaly* and N *normal*.

- The growing number of behavioural attacks (e.g. phishing bank accounts and worms STUXNET [2], Black.Energy [3], Havex [4]).

Our work is focused on countering and detecting cyber attacks in the application layer. We specifically focus on SQLIA and XSS attacks which are currently top-ranked. Moreover, in this paper we present the solution to another common problem in cyber security research and community. Typically, while analysing network traffic, the problem of data imbalance occurs. In fact, there are much more un-attacked normal data traces or logs than those containing cyber attacks. Therefore, typically in most databases and reported research results the traces containing attacks are under-represented. Such problem is rarely addressed and not yet apparent, and there are not many works addressing this challenge.

Our paper is structured as follows: in Sect. 2 our innovative approach is presented. In Sect. 3, we address the challenge of data imbalance and present the classification based on the ensemble of hybrid classifiers. The experimental set-up, the benchmark data and the results are presented in Sect. 4. Conclusions are given thereafter.

2   Proposed Approach

The high-level idea of our method is presented in Fig. 1. It adapts the machine learning supervised algorithms in order to build the model representing normal and anomalous content of the request sent from client to server. In this paper we analyse HTTP (Hypertext Transfer Protocol) requests. During the learning phase we apply classical batch processing, where the learner receives the whole learning dataset and returns the model (classifier) as the result.

During the learning phase, the algorithm groups the HTTP requests by the URL (Uniform Resource Locator) addresses which have a textual form. For the correctly formatted HTTP request, the first line contains the HTTP method name and an URL address of the resource the request is sent to. The URL addresses can be parametrised with so called query string (e.g. $?param1 = value\&param2 = value$). However, these parameters can contain malicious code, therefore; we collect this data for further analysis. We also collect request content that appears after the HTTP header. Such approach is quite common for majority of signature-based application attacks detection techniques.

It must be noticed, that we build the model (shown in Fig. 1) for each unique URL address. This allows us to divide the dataset into smaller subsets and to convey the learning phase on each part simultaneously. Obviously, this reduces the problem complexity and decreases the computation time.

Commonly, signature-based tools (e.g. PHP-IDS, Apache ModSecurity) use pre-defined patters to find potentially dangerous character sequences (e.g. SQL injection trials). However, the tools mentioned above make some prior assumption about the HTTP request structures. For instance, PHP-IDS assumes "application/x-www-form-urlencoded" type of encoding. However, there are many ways to serialise user data sent from the HTML form to the web server such as SOAP or GWT-RCP. It may also happen that a web application will use its own serialisation algorithm (possibly combined with other methods). In such cases, the challenge of analysing user data becomes even more difficult.

Therefore, in our approach we apply analysis technique that allows us to identify the structure of the HTTP request from historical data. The collected raw data extracted from HTTP requests is analysed to identify common sequences of characters (we call them tokens) and their positions in the consecutive HTTP calls. Obviously, there will be sequences that are unique and will not be repeated in other sequences. Therefore, we capture that sequences to measure the distribution of characters. As a result the request made by client to a specific resource identified by URL address will be described by common tokens and histograms of characters.

The tokens extraction is not a trivial task, because single token can appear at different positions in consecutive HTTP requests. Moreover the distance between tokens may also vary. Additionally, it may happen that one token is a sub-token of another, or tokens can appear in different order.

The challenge is to find the longest common substring that occurs in at least k of m analysed sequences. However, it is shown in [6] that this problem can be transformed to color-set-size (CSS) problem and solved in $O(n)$ time. For CSS problem we define general rooted tree (also called GST – Generalized Suffix Tree) with n leaves where each leaf is associated with a color c, such that $c \in C$, where $C = 1, ..., m$ (m is associated with number of analysed sequences). The color size for vertex v is the number of unique (different) leaf colors in the sub-tree rooted at v. More implementation details and proof of the algorithm complexity is shown in [6].

Once the set of tokens common for all the analysed sequences is identified, further processing is needed. First of all, to build HTTP request model, we need to identify the right subset of tokens and their order.

To address tokens alignment problem, we may formulate it as discrete knapsack problem: "given a set of items, each with a mass and a value, determine which item to include in a collection so that the total weight is less than or equal to a given limit and the total value is as large as possible". In our case single token represents item. We assign the value to each token (in current implementation we favour longer tokens over shorter) and mass – position of token in a sequence. The limit in our case is determined by analysed sequences.

More formally, given n tokens of value v_i, we want to solve the optimisation problem described by Eq. 1.

$$
\begin{aligned}
\underset{x}{\text{maximise}} \quad & C(x) = \sum_{i=0}^{n} v_i x_i \\
\text{subject to} \quad & \sum_{i=0}^{n} w_i x_i \le W, \; x_i \in \{0, 1\}.
\end{aligned}
\tag{1}
$$

To solve this optimisation problem we adapted genetic algorithms with classical binary chromosome encoding schema and one point crossover. The chromosome in our algorithm represents candidate solution and is a string of bits (1 indicates that given token is taken to build the structure of request, while 0 is used to reject given token).

Once the tokens are identified, we describe the sequences between tokens using their statistical properties.

3   Data Classification

For the data classification problem we adapted classifiers hybridisation method. Our main goal was to address the problem of data imbalance (usually we have only a few examples of attacks while having large volume of data representing normal traffic samples) and to increase the effectiveness of attack detection by adapting an ensemble of one-class classifiers. As it is explained in [9] there is no single pattern recognition algorithm that is suitable for all problems. In fact, each classifier has its own domain of competence. Therefore, the approaches exploiting the strength of the individual classifiers have been proposed over the last decade. The reason why the researchers are focusing on an ensemble of classifiers is the fact that combined classifiers [8]:

- can improve the overall effectiveness of recognition,
- can be easier deployed in distributed systems,
- allow overcoming the initialization problem of many machine-learning methods (e.g. k-means, tree learner, GMM).

3.1   Addressing Data Imbalance

In our research we consider the two-class recognition problem (normal and anomalous HTTP requests). Therefore, we can propose a simple and a straight-forward way to address the data imbalance, by assigning an appropriate weight to majority and minority classes. More precisely, we want to assign the minority class a higher importance, since we want to detect as may attacks as possible, but still having a reasonably low ratio of false positives. Therefore, if the learning method minimises the number of errors, it will produce classifier that bias toward the majority class is reduced.

In our approach we used a cost matrix represented by Eq. 2, where

$$M = \begin{bmatrix} 0 & m_P \\ m_N & 0 \end{bmatrix} \tag{2}$$

the m_P indicates the penalty for classifying a normal request as anomalous (see Eq. 3), m_N indicates the penalty for misclassifying an anomalous request as a normal one,

$$m_P = 1 - \frac{\bar{P}}{\bar{P} + \bar{N}} \tag{3}$$

$\bar{P}$ indicates the cardinality of a set containing only normal requests, and $\bar{N}$ the cardinality of set containing an anomalous requests, respectively.

$$m_N = 1 - \frac{\bar{N}}{\bar{P} + \bar{N}} \tag{4}$$

3.2 Building Hybrid Classifiers

Another manner in which we want to improve anomaly detection efficiency is the application of ensemble of hybrid classifiers. One of the issues when producing an ensemble of classifiers is the diversity problem. Although, the formal definition does not exist, it can be intuitively perceived as the correlation and the similarity of classifiers results. For instance, if the outputs produced by a pool of classifiers are similar, the classifier will have a poor diversity, and thus we may not expect a performance improvement.

According to [8], there are the following methods that allow improving us diversity, namely:

- to use a different partition of data to train the classifiers,
- to exploit a local specialisation of given classifiers.
- to use a different sub-set of feature.

In order to address the diversity problem we applied the boosting techniques. In our approach we selected REPTree classifiers that comprise the ensemble. The REPTree (Reduced Error Pruning Tree) [10] is a machine learning technique that uses pruned decision tree. REP Tree algorithm generates multiple regression trees in each iteration. Afterwards, it chooses the best one. It uses regression tree adapting variance and information gain (by measuring the entropy). The algorithm prunes the tree using a back fitting method.

The reason why we selected above-mentioned classifier is twofold. First of all, REPTree classifier is often used with bagging and boosting techniques [11] and secondly it is also efficient and simplistic (so it can be applied to real-time applications like cyber attacks and anomalies detection) [10].

4   Experiments

4.1   Dataset Used During Experiments

Apart from proposing any intrusion and anomaly detection techniques, cyber security researchers usually have to overcome the problem of the lack of data for testing. In contrary to other pattern recognition domains, there are not many relevant datasets available. Some researchers still use databases like DARPA or KDD'99, but those are very old and outdated (and papers using such data are usually rejected). Some researchers create their own datasets, which are usually useless since those are not shared and do not contain large amount of realistic data. On the other hand, the real (even anonimized) commercial network data containing cyber attacks is not shared and available.

To solve such problems, in this paper we use known benchmark dataset for web application cyber attacks and anomalies detection CSIC'10 [7] (quite recent one in comparison to other known datasets). However, it is already 5 years old and does not contain some of the recent web application anomalies. Therefore, we decided to enhance it with additional data coming from the monitoring of requests to real web application (Fig. 2).

During the experiment we measured the effectiveness of our method using publicly available CSIC'10 dataset that was extended by additional traffic samples. We intended to incorporate into the original dataset the traffic volume that will contain wider variety of HTTP requests, which were generated by more up-to-date web applications. The original dataset currently contains mainly requests that are complied with "application/x-www-form-urlencoded" encoding standard. However, the modern web applications are currently using also different

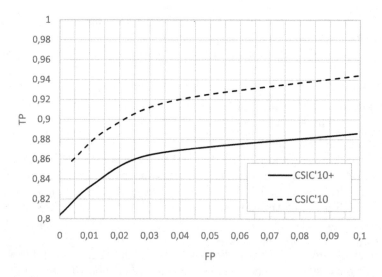

Fig. 2. Receiver Operating Characteristic curves showing the accuracy of ICD-based method for original and extended CSIC'10 dataset.

types of request content, e.g. "application/json", "text/x-gwt-rpc", or any other proprietary types.

We increased the original CSIC'10 dataset by 3.6 %. We added 2.08 % of normal samples (around 1500 requests) and 7.9 % of new attacks (around 2000 of anomalous requests). To gather these samples we set up a GWT-based web application that provides feature-rich GIS (Geographic Information System). In this application we identified several malicious code injection vulnerabilities. We used these vulnerabilities to convey cyber attacks.

4.2 Obtained Results

In our experiments we investigated hybridisation technique, which combines REP Tree classifier whit AdaBoost approach. We have compared our approach with different detection mechanisms to show that our technique indeed allows as to improve detection rates and to lower the number of false positives. The results are presented in Table 1.

Because we use character distribution as a feature vector, we used the method proposed in [5] as a baseline for results evaluation. In [5] authors used χ^2-test (Eq. 5) to measure the fitness of the tested sample with so called ICD. The ICD (Idealised Character Distribution) is an averaged character distribution of requests that are considered normal. In the (Eq. 5) E_i is $i - th$ bin for ICD and O_i is the $i - th$ bin for the observed distribution.

$$\chi^2 = \sum_{i=0}^{n} \frac{(O_i - E_i)^2}{E_i} \tag{5}$$

The method proposed in [5] assumes that all HTTP requests are encoded using "application/x-www-form-urlencoded" encoding type.

Table 1. Comparison of different approaches for anomaly-based cyber attacks detection.

Method	DR	FP	Precision	F-measure
OurMethod + AdaBoost	0,915	0,007	0,98	0,915
BodyParse + AdaBoost	0,915	0,01	0,98	0,917
OurMethod + Chi	0,911	0,007	0,981	0,911
BodyParse + Chi	0,834	0,011	0,965	0,834

In our experiments we have measured different performance characteristics in order to compare adapted in our work classifiers ensembles. For evaluation we adapted classical 10-fold cross validation.

The reported results measurements are:

– *TP Rate* - True Positive Rate (also Detection Rate) indicating the percentage of detected HTTP requests labelled as anomalous.

– *FP Rate* - False Positive Rate indicating the percentage normal HTTP requests labelled (incorrectly) as anomalous.
– *Precision* - number of True Positives divided by the sum of False Positives and True Positives.
– *F-Measure* - calculated according to the following equation:

$$F - Measure = 2 \cdot \frac{Precision * Recall}{Precision + Recall} \tag{6}$$

In this equation *Recall* is equivalent to *TP Rate*.

In all cases we used 10 iterations to establish the ensemble of classifiers (10-fold cross-validation test). In all the experiments we used a paired t-test to judge the results at 0.5 statistical significance level.

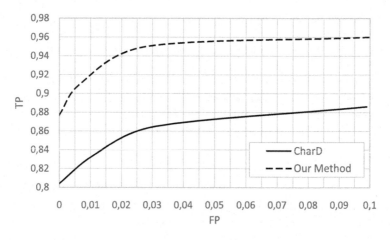

Fig. 3. Receiver Operating Characteristic curves showing the accuracy of the proposed segmentation method with respect to classical HTTP standard-based approach (CharD - Character Distribution). Both methods use histograms of characters.

Firstly, we have adapted classical HTTP body parameters request segmentation combined with χ^2 metrics of character distribution (in table indicated as BodyParse + Chi). This method assumes that HTTP request is fully compliant with RFC 2616 (Hypertext Transfer Protocol). It means that data sent from web browser to http server is encoded as a sequence of key-values separated by ampersand (e.g. key1 = val1&key2 = val2). It can be noticed that such method obtains fairly-satisfactory results achieving more than 80 % of attacks detection ration while having 1.1 % of false positives.

In contrary, our method (in table indicated as OurMethod + AdaBoost) combined with cost sensitive boosting method for ensemble of classifiers building, allows us to improve the results significantly. As it is shown in Table 1 this approach achieves more than 91 % of attacks detection of ration while having 0.7 % of false positives. Both of these characteristics are statistically better. Moreover, in the Fig. 3 we show the Receiver Operating Characteristic curve for our method compared with the character distribution method combined with χ^2 metric (in figure indicated as CharD).

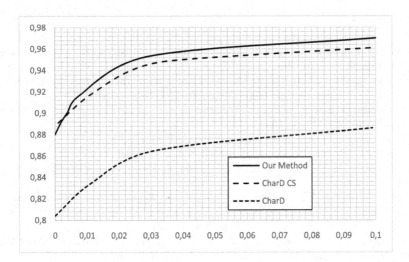

Fig. 4. Receiver Operating Characteristic curves showing the accuracy of the proposed segmentation method.

In Fig. 4 we have presented ROC curves for our method compared with other approaches. It can be noticed that our method is superior to body param-based segmentation technique. However, the difference is not so significant when we compare body param segmentation technique enhanced with AdaBoost cost-sensitive method. Moreover, our packet segmentation method (in figure indicated as CharD CS) combined with χ^2 statistics (instead of AdaBoosting) allowed us to achieve almost identical results. It means that, combining our method with AdaBoosting does not improve results significantly in this case.

5   Conclusions and Further Work

In this paper we have investigated different approaches for anomaly-based cyber attacks detection in application layer. Particularly, we have proposed the request segmentation technique enhanced with ensemble-based classification approach. In our case and for chosen dataset, the cost-sensitive ensemble AdaBoosting hybridisation techniques improve significantly the classical body param segmentation technique. Moreover, we proposed the solution for data imbalance in network cyber security domain the problem which is apparent but often forgotten by researchers.

Conducted experiments show that this approach allows us to satisfactory high attack detection rates while having low rates of false positives. One of the advantages of proposed technique is fact that the structure extraction step, applied before the classification, allows us to divide dataset into smaller parts, and thus to decrease the time required for learning the classifier.

References

1. OWASP Top 10 2013. OWASP project homepage. https://www.owasp.org/index. php/Top_10_2013-Top_10
2. Stuxnet malware. http://www.kaspersky.com/about/news/virus/2014/Stuxnet-Patient-Zero-First-Victims-of-the-Infamous-Worm-Revealed
3. Black Energy botnet. http://www.kaspersky.com/about/news/virus/2010/Most_wanted_the_Black_Energy_bot
4. https://ics-cert.us-cert.gov/alerts/ICS-ALERT-14-176-02A
5. Kruegel, C., Vigna, G.: Anomaly detection of web-based attacks. In: Proceedings of the 10th ACM Conference on Computer and Communications Security, pp. 251–261 (2003)
6. Chi, L., Hui, K.: Color set size problem with applications to string matching. In: Apostolico, A., Galil, Z., Manber, U., Crochemore, M. (eds.) CPM 1992. LNCS, vol. 644, pp. 230–243. Springer, Heidelberg (1992)
7. Torrano-Gimnez, C., Prez-Villegas, A., Alvarez, G.: The HTTP dataset CSIC 2010. http://users.aber.ac.uk/pds7/csic_dataset/csic2010http.html
8. Wozniak, M.: Hybrid Classifiers: Methods of Data, Knowledge, and Classifier Combination. Studies in Computational Intelligence. Springer, Heidelberg (2013)
9. Wolpert, D.H.: The supervised learning no-free-lunch theorems, In: Proceedings of 6th Online World Conference on Soft Computing in Industrial Applications, pp. 25–42 (2001)
10. Frank, E.: Data Mining: Practical Machine Learning Tools and Techniques. Morgan Kaufmann Series in Data Management Systems, 2nd edn. Morgan Kaufmann, San Francisco (2005)
11. Quinlan, J.: Simplifying decision trees. I. J. Man Mach. Stud. **27**(3), 221–234 (1987)
12. Jayanthi, S.K., Sasikala, S.: REPTree classifier for identifying link spam in web search engines. IJSC **3**(2), 498–505 (2013)

Ordinal Evolutionary Artificial Neural Networks for Solving an Imbalanced Liver Transplantation Problem

Manuel Dorado-Moreno[1]([✉]), María Pérez-Ortiz[2,3],
María Dolores Ayllón-Terán[3], Pedro Antonio Gutiérrez[1],
and Cesar Hervás-Martínez[1]

[1] Department of Computer Science and Numerical Analysis, University of Córdoba,
Rabanales Campus, Albert Einstein Building, 14071 Córdoba, Spain
{i92domom,pagutierrez,chervas}@uco.es
[2] Department of Mathematics and Engineering,
Universidad Loyola Andalucía, Córdoba, Spain
i82perom@uco.es
[3] Liver Transplantation Unit, Reina Sofía Hospital, Córdoba, Spain
lolesat83@hotmail.com

Abstract. Ordinal regression considers classification problems where there exists a natural ordering among the categories. In this learning setting, thresholds models are one of the most used and successful techniques. On the other hand, liver transplantation is a widely-used treatment for patients with a terminal liver disease. This paper considers the survival time of the recipient to perform an appropriate donor-recipient matching, which is a highly imbalanced classification problem. An artificial neural network model applied to ordinal classification is used, combining evolutionary and gradient-descent algorithms to optimize its parameters, together with an ordinal over-sampling technique. The evolutionary algorithm applies a modified fitness function able to deal with the ordinal imbalanced nature of the dataset. The results show that the proposed model leads to competitive performance for this problem.

Keywords: Ordinal regression · Artificial neural networks · Imbalanced classification · Liver transplantation · Donor-recipient matching

1 Introduction

Liver transplantation is an accepted treatment for patients who present end-stage liver disease. However, transplantation is restricted by the lack of suitable

This work has been subsidized by the TIN2014-54583-C2-1-R project of the Spanish Ministerial Commission of Science and Technology (MICYT), FEDER funds and the P2011-TIC-7508 project of the "Junta de Andalucía" (Spain). The authors M. Dorado-Moreno, M. Pérez-Ortíz and M.D. Ayllón-Terán have contributed equally to the preparation of this paper.

© Springer International Publishing Switzerland 2016
F. Martínez-Álvarez et al. (Eds.): HAIS 2016, LNAI 9648, pp. 451–462, 2016.
DOI: 10.1007/978-3-319-32034-2_38

liver donors and this imbalance results in significant waiting list deaths. Besides clinical judgement on whether, when and how to transplant, clinical scores such as the Model for End-stage Liver Disease score (MELD) may aid clinical decision. MELD is based on the "sickest-first" principle, where the only aspect considered is information concerning the recipient. However, these scores rely on conventional statistical methodologies that carry inherent limitations [1], possibly leading to suboptimal performance. The development of machine learning (ML) algorithms accounting for a multiplicity of factors led to the generation of robust and accurate prediction models. In this way, new trends in biomedicine have considered ML techniques [2–5]. There has been recent research using conventional statistical methods in donor-recipient problems [6,7] and also using some ML techniques [8–10]. Several methods have been developed and applied to find a better system to prioritize recipients on the waiting list [11–13]. In this sense, this paper presents a new model for computing donor-recipient best compatibility via evolutionary artificial neural networks.

The classification of patterns into naturally ordered labels is referred to as ordinal regression or ordinal classification. This learning paradigm, although still mostly unexplored, is spreading rapidly and receiving a lot of attention from the pattern recognition and machine learning communities [14], given its applicability to real world problems. Thresholds models [14–16] are one of the most common methodologies for ordinal classification. These methodologies try to estimate two elements:

- A function $g(\mathbf{x})$ to predict the nature of the latent variable.
- A vector of thresholds $\boldsymbol{\beta}_0 = \left(\beta_0^1, \beta_0^2, \ldots, \beta_0^{J-1}\right) \in \mathbb{R}^{J-1}$ (where J is the number of classes in the problem) to represent the intervals in the range of $g(\mathbf{x})$, where $\beta_0^1 \leq \beta_0^2 \leq \ldots \leq \beta_0^{J-1}$.

For example, if the categories of an ordinal regression problem associated to the size of a tumor are {*very small, small, medium, big, very big*}, a threshold model would try to uncover the latent variable, and the thresholds would divide this latent variable into the considered categories.

There has been a great deal of work on probabilistic linear regression models for ordinal response variables [16,17]. These models are known as Cumulative Link Models (CLMs) and they are based on the idea of modelling the cumulative probability of each pattern to belong to a class lower than or equal to the class which is being considered. The proportional odds model (POM) [16] is the first model in this category, being a probabilistic model which leads to linear decision boundaries, given that the latent function $g(\cdot)$ is a linear model. This probabilistic model resembles the threshold model structure, although the linearity of $g(\cdot)$ can limit its applicability for real datasets. POM is commonly used in medicine, and several articles consider it when dealing with ordinal data, e.g. endometriosis [18], medical scoring systems [19] or imsomnia problems [20].

On the other hand, the classification paradigm when one or several categories present a much lower prior probability is known as imbalanced classification [21,22], and it generally poses a serious hindrance for the learning process of

ML algorithms. Different perspectives have been considered for this topic: sampling data approaches (over-sampling groups of interesting and rare examples or under-sampling majority classes) and algorithmic ones (e.g. cost-sensitive learning).

Concerning previous studies, cost-sensitive learning has been proved to lead to over-fitting [23], thus data approaches are usually preferred. In the same vein, some studies suggest that over-sampling is more useful and powerful than under-sampling for highly imbalanced and complex datasets [22], given the potential loss of meaningful information.

Recently, a new over-sampling methodology has been proposed for ordinal problems [24], where the data is over-sampled considering the order among the categories. This technique is used in this paper to deal with the imbalanced nature of the liver transplantation problem considered. The classification model considered is an evolutionary artificial neural network, which is optimized using an evolutionary algorithm with a modified fitness function, adding specifically designed costs to deal with the characteristics of the dataset. The results obtained combining the over-sampling technique with the imbalanced fitness function are better than those of the original methodologies and competitive with respect to state-of-the-art methods.

The rest of the paper is organised as follows: Sect. 2 presents the methodology proposed, while Sect. 3 presents and discusses the experimental results. The last section summarises the main contributions of the paper.

2   Methodology

This section describes the classification algorithm proposed and the over-sampling techniques used to deal with the imbalanced nature of the data.

The goal in ordinal classification is to assign an input vector $\mathbf{x}$ to one of J discrete classes $\mathcal{C}_j, j \in \{1, \ldots, J\}$, where there exists a given ordering among the labels $\mathcal{C}_1 \prec \mathcal{C}_2 \prec \cdots \prec \mathcal{C}_J$, $\prec$ denoting this order information. Hence, the objective is to find a prediction rule, $C : \mathcal{X} \to \mathcal{Y}$, by using an i.i.d. training sample $X = \{\mathbf{x}_i, y_i\}_{i=1}^{N}$, where N is the number of training patterns, $\mathbf{x}_i \in \mathcal{X}$, $y_i \in \mathcal{Y}$, $\mathcal{X} \subset \mathbb{R}^k$ is the k-dimensional input space, and $\mathcal{Y} = \{\mathcal{C}_1, \mathcal{C}_2, \ldots, \mathcal{C}_J\}$ is the label space.

2.1   Proposed Ordinal Classifier

An adaptation of the POM to artificial neural networks is used in this work. This adaptation is based on two elements: the first one is a second hidden linear layer with only one node whose inputs are the non-linear transformations of the first hidden layer. The task of this node is to project the values into a line, to impose an order. Apart from this one-node linear layer, an output layer is included with one bias for each class, whose objective is to set the optimum thresholds to classify the patterns in the class they belong to.

The structure of our model is presented in Fig. 1 which has two main parts. The part at the bottom is formed by sigmoidal unit (SU) neurons,

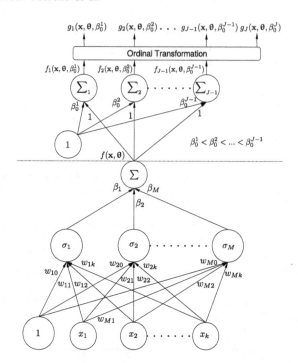

Fig. 1. Neural Network model for ordinal classification

where $\mathbf{x} = (x_1, \ldots, x_k)$, is the vector of input variables, and k is the number of variables in the database. $\mathbf{W} = \{\mathbf{w}_1 \ldots \mathbf{w}_M\}$ is the matrix of weights of the connections from the input nodes to the hidden layer SU nodes (for each neuron, $\mathbf{w}_j = \{w_{j0}, w_{j1}, \ldots w_{jk}\}$, w_{j0} being the bias of the neuron), and σ is the sigmoidal function.

The upper part of the figure shows a single node in the second hidden layer of the model, which is the one that performs the linear transformation of the POM model. Its result, $f(\mathbf{x}, \boldsymbol{\theta})$, where $\boldsymbol{\theta} = \{\mathbf{W}, \beta_1, \ldots, \beta_M\}$, is connected, together with a second bias, to the output layer, where J is the number of classes, and $\beta_0^0, \ldots, \beta_0^{J-1}$ are the thresholds for the different classes. These $J - 1$ thresholds are able to separate the J classes, but they have to fulfill the order constraint shown in the figure. Finally, the output layer obtains the outputs of the model, $f_j(\mathbf{x}, \boldsymbol{\theta}, \beta_0^j)$, for $j \in \{1, \ldots, J-1\}$. These outputs are transformed into a probability $(g_j(\mathbf{x}, \boldsymbol{\theta}, \beta_0^j))$, using the POM model structure. $g_j(\mathbf{x}, \boldsymbol{\theta}, \beta_0^j)$ is the probability that each pattern has to belong to the different classes, and the class with the greatest probability is the one selected by the neural network.

2.2   Training Algorithm and Proposed Fitness Function

In this section, the hybrid algorithm to estimate the architecture and parameters of the model is presented. The objective of the algorithm is to design a hybrid neural network with optimal structure and weights for each ordinal classification problem. The details about the algorithm can be found in [25], where an evolutionary programming (EP) method is combined with a local search function. In this paper, we modify the fitness function of the EP method to deal with the problem of imbalanced classification. The fitness function is a mean squared error with ordinal costs, which is given by the following expression:

$$l(\boldsymbol{\theta}, \boldsymbol{\beta}_0) = -\frac{1}{N} \sum_{i=1}^{N} \sum_{j=1}^{J} IM(\mathcal{C}_j) \cdot c(y_i, j) \cdot \left(g_j(\mathbf{x}, \boldsymbol{\theta}, \beta_0^j) - y_i^{(j)} \right)^2, \qquad (1)$$

where several symbols must be clarified. $\mathbf{y}_i = (y_i^{(0)}, y_i^{(1)}, \ldots, y_i^{(J)})$ is a 1-of-J encoding vector of the label from pattern $\mathbf{x}_i$ (i.e. $y_i^{(j)} = 1$ if the pattern $\mathbf{x}_i$ belongs to class j, and 0 otherwise), y_i is the corresponding index (i.e. $y_i = \arg_j(y_i^{(j)} = 1)$), $\boldsymbol{\beta}_0 = (\beta_0^1, \ldots, \beta_0^{J-1})$ and $\boldsymbol{\theta}$ are the vector of biases and the vector of parameters of the ranking function, respectively, and $c(y_i, j)$ is an ordinal cost function in the following form:

$$c(y_i, j) = \begin{cases} (J/2)(J-1), & \text{if } y_i = j \\ |y_i - j|, & \text{if } y_i \neq j \end{cases}. \qquad (2)$$

This cost function gives higher importance to the errors of the classifier as the number of classes between predicted and true ranks increases. The value $(J/2)(J-1)$ corresponds to the maximum sum of the costs for a class (i.e. the sum of the costs for the extreme classes). $IM(\mathcal{C}_j)$ is the main proposal of this paper, a modification of the fitness function in order to deal with the imbalanced nature of the problem, returning a higher cost when missclassifying a pattern which belongs to a minority class. $IM(\mathcal{C}_j)$ is given by the following expression:

$$IM(\mathcal{C}_j) = \frac{1 - \frac{N_j}{N}}{\sum_{j=1}^{J} 1 - \frac{N_j}{N}} = \frac{N - N_j}{N(J-1)}, \qquad j = 1, \ldots, J, \qquad (3)$$

where N_j corresponds to the number of patterns of class j. This corresponds to the normalized imbalance ratio of the class.

2.3   Ordinal Over-Sampling

Three over-sampling techniques are used to preprocess the dataset. Their main idea is to generate new synthetic patterns in a space where there exists an ordering relation among the classes. These methods are based on a graph perspective, to easily include the ordering information in the synthetic pattern generation process.

Roughly speaking, the over-sampling techniques considered make use of different graph operations to create a representative data-driven manifold that exploits the order of the classes [24]. The strategies tested in this paper are:

1. Ordinal Graph-based Over-sampling via Neighbourhood information using a probability function for the Intra-class edges (OGO-NI). In this case, the

manifold structure is constructed based on a simple neighbourhood analysis, and new synthetic patterns are created using a probabilistic approach.
2. Ordinal Graph-based Over-sampling via Shortest Paths using a probability function for the intra-class edges (OGO-SP). The manifold is constructed using the previous mentioned neighbourhood analysis, but it is refined computing the shortest paths in the graph.
3. Ordinal Graph-based Over-sampling via Interior Shortest Paths (OGO-ISP). The technique for constructing the graph is the same than in OGO-SP but in this case the probabilistic approach for constructing new patterns is also used.

Specific details about these methods can be consulted in [24].

3   Experiments

In this section, a description of the multi-state liver transplantation dataset is given, followed by the methods compared, the measures evaluated and the results obtained.

3.1   Dataset Description

First of all, a multi-centred retrospective analysis of 7 Spanish Liver Transplant units was made. Recipient and donor characteristics were reported at the time of transplant. Patients undergoing partial, split or living-donor liver transplantation and patients undergoing combined or multivisceral transplants were excluded from the study. Liver Transplantation units were homogeneously distributed throughout Spain. The dataset constructed has 634 patterns (donor-recipient pairs) corresponding to the years 2007 and 2008.

In addition, the dataset was completed with information about donor-recipient pairs from the King's College Hospital (London), to perform a supra-national study of donor-recipient allocation in liver transplantation. To obtain a similar number of patterns, only reported pairs of recipients over eighteen years of age between January 2002 and December 2010 were included. Thus, a dataset containing 858 English donor-recipient pairs were collected. In order to merge the datasets, several variables were selected, 16 recipient variables, 17 donor variables and 5 surgically related variables. Furthermore, all patients were followed from the date of transplant until death, graft loss or completion of the first year after the liver transplant. The resulting dataset was comprised of 1406 patterns.

To solve the donor-recipient matching problem, the dependent variable is the class label which is equal to 1 when representing graft loss up to the first 15 days after the transplant, equal to 2 if the loss occurs between 15 days and 3 months, equal to 3 when the loss is after 3 months and before a year, and, finally, the last class corresponds to the patterns which do not present graft loss after the first year and is represented by label 4. Further details about the dataset and the variables selected can be seen in [11].

3.2   Evaluated Methodologies

To tackle the donor-recipient problem, the methodology described in Sect. 2 has been referred to as IMbalanced Ordinal neural NETwork (IM-ORNET). The experiments were designed to compare several methodologies with the proposal:

- Ordinal neural NETwork (ORNET). The algorithm presented in [25], where the fitness function is the one presented in Sect. 2 without considering the cost $IM(\mathcal{C}_j)$.
- Support Vector Classifier using the one-versus-one approach (SVC) [26].
- Proportional Odds Model (POM) [16].
- Extreme Learning Machine for Ordinal Regression (ELMOR) [27].
- Error Correcting output codes cascade model with Support Vector Machines (ECSVM) [11].
- Kernel Discriminant Leaning for Ordinal Regression (KDLOR) [15].
- REDuction scheme for ordinal regression using Support Vector Machines (REDSVM) [28].

3.3   Evaluation Metrics

Several measures can be considered for evaluating ordinal classifiers. The most common ones in machine learning are the Mean Absolute Error (MAE) and the Mean Zero-one Error (MZE) [14], being $MZE = 1 - Acc$, where Acc is the accuracy or correct classification rate. However, these measures may not be the best option, for example, when measuring performance in the presence of class imbalances [29], and/or when the costs of different errors vary markedly. In this way, three different metrics are used in this paper.

The correct classification rate or accuracy (Acc) is defined by:

$$Acc = \frac{1}{N} \sum_{i=1}^{N} (I(y_i^* = y_i)), \tag{4}$$

where $I(\cdot)$ is the zero-one loss function, y_i is the desired output for pattern $\mathbf{x}i$, y_i^* is the prediction of the model and N is the total number of patterns in the dataset. Acc values vary from 0 to 1 and it represents global performance in the classification task. It does not take the category order into account and it is not recommended for imbalanced datasets.

The geometric mean of the sensitivities of each class (GMS) is an average of the percentage of the correct classification per class:

$$GMS = \sqrt[J]{\prod_{j=1}^{J} S_j}, \tag{5}$$

where $S_j = \frac{1}{N_j} \sum_{i=1}^{N_j} (I(y_i^* = y_i))$ is the sensitivity of the j-th class, i.e. the ratio of patterns correctly predicted as belonging to the j-th class.

The average mean absolute error ($AMAE$) [29] is the mean of MAE classification errors throughout the classes, where MAE is the average absolute deviation of the predicted class from the true class (in number of categories on the ordinal scale). It is able to mitigate the effect of imbalanced class distributions. Let MAE_j be the MAE for a given j-th class:

$$MAE_j = \frac{1}{N_j} \sum_{i=1}^{N_j} |\mathcal{O}(y_i) - \mathcal{O}(y_i^*)|, \ 1 \leq j \leq J, \tag{6}$$

where $\mathcal{O}(\mathcal{C}_j) = j$, $1 \leq j \leq J$, i.e. $\mathcal{O}(y_j)$ is the order of class label y_j. Then, the $AMAE$ measure can be defined in the following way:

$$AMAE = \frac{1}{J} \sum_{j=1}^{J} MAE_j. \tag{7}$$

MAE values range from 0 to $J - 1$, as do those of $AMAE$.

3.4   Experimental Setting

For evaluation of the results, a stratified 10-fold technique was used to divide the data, and the results were taken as the mean and standard deviation of the measures for the test sets over the 10 obtained models.

The parameters for all methods except ORNET and IM-ORNET were chosen using a 5-fold nested cross-validation. The final parameter combination was the one which obtained, in mean, the best average performance for the validation sets, where the metric used was the GMS. The kernel selected for all the kernel methods (SVC, ECSVM, KDLOR and REDSVM) was the Gaussian one, $K(\mathbf{x}, \mathbf{y}) = \exp\left(-\frac{\|\mathbf{x}-\mathbf{y}\|^2}{\sigma^2}\right)$ where σ is the kernel width. For every tested kernel method, the kernel width was selected within these values $\{10^{-3}, 10^{-2}, \ldots, 10^3\}$, as was the cost parameter associated to the SVM methods. For the ELMOR methodology, the sigmoidal units were used, and the number of hidden neurons was selected within the values $H \in \{5, 10, 20, 30, 40, 50, 60, 70, 80, 90, 100\}$.

For the ORNET and IM-ORNET methodologies, the hidden layer was composed by sigmoidal basis functions, the minimum number of hidden neurons was 20 and the maximum was set to 30. In order to set these parameters, a preliminary experiment was done with one partition of the dataset. A 5-fold cross-validation (using only the training split) was performed and repeated with the following minimum numbers of hidden nodes $\{5, 10, 15 \ldots, 30\}$. The maximum number of hidden neurons was always set to 10 units more to give the evolutionary algorithm enough freedom to search for the optimum classifier. The population size and the number of generations was set to 500.

Several works in the literature have considered the over-sampling of classes that present an imbalanced ratio (IR) higher than 1.5 [30,31]. In this work we consider the same threshold for deciding to apply over-sampling to a certain class and for computing the number of necessary synthetic patterns. In this case,

Table 1. Means and standard deviations $(Mean \pm SD)$ of Acc, GMS and $AMAE$ for the test sets

Method	Dataset	Acc	GMS	$AMAE$
Nominal methods				
SVC	Original	81.45 ± 5.56	0.00 ± 0.00	1.492 ± 0.033
SVC	OGO-NI	76.81 ± 2.10	0.00 ± 0.00	1.468 ± 0.054
SVC	OGO-SP	76.46 ± 1.74	0.00 ± 0.00	1.447 ± 0.078
SVC	OGO-ISP	76.32 ± 2.94	0.00 ± 0.00	1.449 ± 0.056
Ordinal methods				
ORNET	Original	71.84 ± 3.15	0.00 ± 0.00	1.393 ± 0.078
ORNET	OGO-NI	66.24 ± 3.05	5.03 ± 10.74	1.396 ± 0.116
ORNET	OGO-SP	66.74 ± 3.21	4.4 ± 9.27	1.431 ± 0.089
ORNET	OGO-ISP	68.23 ± 4.96	2.62 ± 8.28	1.393 ± 0.078
IM-ORNET	Original	84.85 ± 0.91	0.00 ± 0.00	1.501 ± 0.002
IM-ORNET	OGO-NI	69.08 ± 3.54	*5.29 ± 11.17*	1.367 ± 0.072
IM-ORNET	OGO-SP	71.13 ± 2.99	**7.47 ± 12.08**	1.354 ± 0.113
IM-ORNET	OGO-ISP	66.95 ± 6.09	2.66 ± 8.41	1.421 ± 0.092
POM	Original	*84.85 ± 0.91*	0.00 ± 0.00	1.501 ± 0.002
POM	OGO-NI	64.86 ± 3.20	0.00 ± 0.00	1.299 ± 0.083
POM	OGO-SP	65.64 ± 4.44	0.00 ± 0.00	1.304 ± 0.084
POM	OGO-ISP	62.10 ± 11.17	0.00 ± 0.00	1.301 ± 0.096
ELMOR	Original	**85.21 ± 0.27**	0.00 ± 0.00	1.500 ± 0.000
ELMOR	OGO-NI	62.09 ± 3.94	0.00 ± 0.00	1.336 ± 0.063
ELMOR	OGO-SP	64.58 ± 2.87	2.13 ± 6.72	1.294 ± 0.101
ELMOR	OGO-ISP	61.39 ± 8.81	0.00 ± 0.00	1.322 ± 0.087
ECSVM	Original	66.28 ± 4.08	2.28 ± 7.20	1.333 ± 0.109
ECSVM	OGO-NI	83.00 ± 1.67	0.00 ± 0.00	1.493 ± 0.057
ECSVM	OGO-SP	83.00 ± 2.16	0.00 ± 0.00	1.503 ± 0.044
ECSVM	OGO-ISP	83.00 ± 1.25	0.00 ± 0.00	1.503 ± 0.041
KDLOR	Original	50.50 ± 3.96	5.22 ± 11.05	1.355 ± 0.159
KDLOR	OGO-NI	54.56 ± 4.31	2.79 ± 8.81	**1.206 ± 0.064**
KDLOR	OGO-SP	54.70 ± 4.85	0.00 ± 0.00	*1.240 ± 0.078*
KDLOR	OGO-ISP	54.27 ± 5.33	3.05 ± 9.63	1.224 ± 0.085
REDSVM	Original	83.35 ± 5.95	0.00 ± 0.00	1.481 ± 0.061
REDSVM	OGO-NI	66.00 ± 3.64	0.00 ± 0.00	1.295 ± 0.047
REDSVM	OGO-SP	64.65 ± 3.09	0.00 ± 0.00	1.336 ± 0.027
REDSVM	OGO-ISP	64.23 ± 3.42	0.00 ± 0.00	1.320 ± 0.056

The best result is in **bold** face and the second best result is in *italics*.

we over-sample the first three classes of the dataset, which present a pattern distribution of {69, 75, 64}, as opposed to the majority class which is composed of 1198.

3.5   Results

Table 1 shows the results obtained for the different algorithms considered with the four versions of the dataset (the original one and three versions obtained by applying the three over-sampling methods presented in Sect. 2.3). Observing the results in Table 1, different methods can be emphasized depending on the evaluation metric considered. In this dataset, it is important to obtain a trade-off between all the metrics included, aiming then at an accurate model that also respects the classification and order of minority classes. Note that a $GMS = 0\%$ means that at least one class is always misclassified. If we only focus on Acc, the best model is obtained by ELMOR using the original dataset, but this result, examining GMS and $AMAE$ scores, shows that nearly all the patterns are classified in the predominant class, obtaining what is known as a trivial classifier. Note that most classifiers are in this case trivial ones, showing the difficulty of the considered application.

The best $AMAE$ model is obtained by KDLOR using the OGO-NI technique. The corresponding GMS score is 2.79% in average (which is, at least, higher than 0%), and its $AMAE$ shows that this classifier tends to respect the order of the label space (i.e., generally, it will not missclassify a pattern belonging to class 0 in class 3, for example). The results of the nominal methodology (SVC) shows a bad $AMAE$ score, because these methodologies do not consider the order of the classes. Finally, combining IM-ORNET with the OGO-SP over-sampling technique, the best GMS score is obtained. In other words, it is the combination which better classifies all the classes in mean. Acc and $AMAE$ scores are also competitive.

Finally, it can be concluded that the application of the different over-sampling techniques tends to improve GMS results, especially when used in conjunction with the neural network methodologies proposed in this paper (ORNET and IM-ORNET), and that the results obtained in this paper by IM-ORNET improves those obtained for the same problem in previous studies [11] by the ECSVM methodology.

4   Conclusions

This paper proposes a new fitness function for an evolutionary artificial neural network in imbalanced problems, together with the application of an ordinal over-sampling technique to palliate the skewness of the distribution of the patterns belonging to each class. The proposal (IM-ORNET) is evaluated in a extremely imbalanced liver transplantation problem and it improves the results with respect to previous works [11], obtaining a good balance in performance for all the metrics considered. The application of the ordinal over-sampling techniques is able to improve the results for minority classes, without harming the ordinal structure of the dataset.

Some future researching lines include extending the database to include more European hospitals and applying the model in a real environment to check its performance when compared to the use of the MELD score. Another possible future research line is to dynamically adjust the weights introduced for each class ($IM(\mathcal{C}_j)$) depending on the average performance of the population for each of the classes, instead of using static weights.

References

1. Breiman, L.: Statistical modeling: The two cultures. Stat. Sci. **16**(3), 199–231 (2001)
2. Kotsiantis, S.B., Zaharakis, I.D., Pintelas, P.E.: Machine learning: a review of classification and combining techniques. Artif. Intell. Rev. **26**(3), 159–190 (2006)
3. Yardimci, A.: Soft computing in medicine. Appl. Soft Comput. **9**(3), 1029–1043 (2009)
4. Li, W., Coats, M., Zhang, J., McKenna, S.J.: Discriminating dysplasia: Optical tomographic texture analysis of colorectal polyps. Med. Image Anal. **26**, 57–69 (2015)
5. Jimenez, F., Sanchez, G., Juarez, J.M.: Multi-objective evolutionary algorithms for fuzzy classification in survival prediction. Artif. Intell. Med. **60**, 197–219 (2014)
6. Gooleyand, T.A., Chienand, J.W., Pergamand, S.A., Hingoraniand, S., Sorrorand, M.L., Boeckhand, M., Martinand, P.J., Sandmaierand, B.M., Marrand, K.A., Appelbaumand, F.R., Storband, R., McDonaldand, G.B.: Reduced mortality after allogeneic hematopoietic-cell transplantation. N. Engl. J. Med. **363**(22), 2091–2101 (2010)
7. Mazzaferro, V., Llovet, J.M., Miceli, R., et al.: Predicting survival after liver transplantation in patients with hepatocellular carcinoma beyond the milan criteria: a retrospective, exploratory analysis. Lancet Oncol. **10**, 30–43 (2009)
8. Delen, D., Oztekin, A., Kong, Z.: A machine learning-based approach to prognostic analysis of thoracic transplantations. Artif. Intell. Med. **49**, 33–42 (2010)
9. Shouval, R., Bondi, O., Mishan, H., Shimoni, A., Unger, R., Nagler, A.: Application of machine learning algorithms for clinical predictive modeling: a data-mining approach in SCT. Bone Marrow Transplant. **49**, 332–337 (2014)
10. Shouval, R., Labopin, M., Bondi, O., Mishan-Shamay, H., et al.: Prediction of allogeneic hematopoietic stem-cell transplantation mortality 100 days after transplantation using a machine learning algorithm: A european group for blood and marrow transplantation acute leukemia working party retrospective data mining study. J. Clin. Oncol. **33**(28), 3144–3151 (2015)
11. Pérez-Ortiz, M., Cruz-Ramírez, M., Ayllón-Terán, M., Heaton, N., Ciria, R., Hervás-Martínez, C.: An organ allocation system for liver transplantation based on ordinal regression. Appl. Soft Comput. **14**, 88–98 (2014)
12. Cruz-Ramírez, M., Hervás-Martínez, C., Gutiérrez, P.A., Pérez-Ortiz, M., Briceño, J., de la Mata, M.: Memetic Pareto differential evolutionary neural network used to solve an unbalanced liver transplantation problem. Soft. Comput. **17**, 275–284 (2012)
13. Pérez-Ortiz, M., Gutiérrez, P.A., Hervás-Martínez, C., Briceño, J., de la Mata, M.: An ensemble approach for ordinal threshold models applied to liver transplantation. In: Proceedings of the the 2012 International Joint Conference on Neural Networks (IJCNN), pp. 2795–2802 (2012)

14. Gutiérrez, P.A., Pérez-Ortiz, M., Sánchez-Monedero, J., Fernandez-Navarro, F., Hervás-Martínez, C.: Ordinal regression methods: survey and experimental study. IEEE Trans. Knowl. Data Eng. **28**, 127–146 (2015)
15. Sun, B.Y., Li, J., Wu, D.D., Zhang, X.M., Li, W.B.: Kernel discriminant learning for ordinal regression. IEEE Trans. Knowl. Data Eng. **22**, 906–910 (2010)
16. McCullagh, P.: Regression models for ordinal data. J. Roy. Stat. Soc. B (Methodol.) **42**(2), 109–142 (1980)
17. Agresti, A.: Analysis of Ordinal Categorical Data. Wiley series in probability and mathematical statistics. Applied probability and statistics. Wiley, Chichester (1984)
18. Chapron, C., Fauconnier, A., Dubuisson, J.B., Barakat, H., Vieira, M., Breart, G.: Deep infilltrating endometriosis: relation between severity of dysmenorrhoea and extent of disease. Hum. Reprod. **18**(4), 760–766 (2003)
19. Feldmann, U., Steudel, I.: Methods of ordinal classification applied to medical scoring systems. Stat. Med. **19**, 575–586 (2000)
20. LeBlanc, M., Beaulieu-Bonneau, S., Merette, C., Savard, J., Ivers, H., Morin, C.M.: Psychological and health-related quality of life factors associated with insomnia in a population-based sample. J. Psychosom. Res. **63**, 157–166 (2007)
21. He, H., Garcia, E.A.: Learning from imbalanced data. IEEE Trans. Knowl. Data Eng. **21**(9), 1263–1284 (2009)
22. Japkowicz, N., Stephen, S.: The class imbalance problem: a systematic study. Intell. Data Anal. **6**(5), 429–449 (2002)
23. Galar, M., Fernández, A., Barrenechea, E., Bustince, H., Herrera, F.: A review on ensembles for the class imbalance problem: bagging-, boosting-, and hybrid-based approaches. IEEE Trans. Syst. Man Cybern. Part C: Appl. Rev. **42**(4), 463–484 (2012)
24. Pérez-Ortiz, M., Gutiérrez, P., Hervás-Martínez, C., Yao, X.: Graph-based approaches for over-sampling in the context of ordinal regression. IEEE Trans. Knowl. Data Eng. **27**(5), 1233–1245 (2015)
25. Dorado-Moreno, M., Gutiérrez, P.A., Hervás-Martínez, C.: Ordinal classification using hybrid artificial neural networks with projection and kernel basis functions. In: Corchado, E., Snášel, V., Abraham, A., Woźniak, M., Graña, M., Cho, S.-B. (eds.) HAIS 2012, Part II. LNCS, vol. 7209, pp. 319–330. Springer, Heidelberg (2012)
26. Hsu, C.W., Lin, C.J.: A comparison of methods for multi-class support vector machines. IEEE Trans. Neural Netw. **13**(2), 415–425 (2002)
27. Deng, W.Y., Zheng, Q.H., Lian, S., Chen, L., Wang, X.: Ordinal extreme learning machine. Neurocomputing **74**(1–3), 447–456 (2010)
28. Lin, H.T., Li, L.: Reduction from cost-sensitive ordinal ranking to weighted binary classification. Neural Comput. **24**(5), 1329–1367 (2012)
29. Baccianella, S., Esuli, A., Sebastiani, F.: Evaluation measures for ordinal regression. In: Proccedings of the Ninth International Conference on Intelligent Systems Design and Applications, ISDA 2009, pp. 283–287 (2009)
30. Fernández, A., García, S., del Jesus, M.J., Herrera, F.: A study of the behaviour of linguistic fuzzy rule based classification systems in the framework of imbalanced data-sets. Fuzzy Sets Syst. **159**(18), 2378–2398 (2008)
31. Fernández-Navarro, F., Hervás-Martínez, C., Antonio Gutiérrez, P.: A dynamic over-sampling procedure based on sensitivity for multi-class problems. Pattern Recogn. **44**(8), 1821–1833 (2011)

A Fuzzy-Based Approach for the Multilevel Component Selection Problem

Andreea Vescan[✉] and Camelia Şerban

Computer Science Department, Babes-Bolyai University,
1, M. Kogalniceanu, Cluj-Napoca, Romania
{avescan,camelia}@cs.ubbcluj.ro

Abstract. Component-based Software Engineering uses components to construct systems, being a means to increase productivity by promoting software reuse. This work deals with the Component Selection Problem in a multilevel system structure. A fuzzy-based approach is used to construct the required system starting from the set of requirements, using both functional and non-functional requirements. For each selection step, the fuzzy clustering approach groups similar components in order to select the best candidate component that provide the needed required interfaces. To evaluate our approach, we discuss a case study for building a Reservation System. We compare the fuzzy-based approach with an evolutionary-based approach using a metric that assess the overall architecture of the obtained systems, from the coupling and cohesion perspective.

Keywords: Component selection · Metrics · Fuzzy analysis · Architecture assessment

1 Introduction

Component-Based Software Engineering (CBSE) is concerned with designing, selecting and composing components [5]. As the popularity of this approach and hence number of commercially available software components grows, selecting a set of components to satisfy a set of requirements while minimizing a set of various objectives (as cost, number of used components) is becoming more difficult. The problems of identification and selection the right software components out of a range of choices to satisfy a set of requirements have received considerable attention in the field of CBSE during the last two decades [2,7].

In this paper, we address the Component Selection Problem (CSP) [14]. Informally, our problem is to select a set of components from a components repository which can satisfy a given set of requirements while minimizing/maximizing various criteria. Components are themselves compositions of components. This give rise to the idea of composition levels, where a component on level i may be decomposed (using more components) at level $i+1$ or compositions at level $i+1$ serves as component at level i. The multilevel approach was proposed in [13].

© Springer International Publishing Switzerland 2016
F. Martínez-Álvarez et al. (Eds.): HAIS 2016, LNAI 9648, pp. 463–474, 2016.
DOI: 10.1007/978-3-319-32034-2_39

The motivation to propose this approach is two fold. Firstly, this paper presents a systematic approach to describe component-based systems having a *multilevel structure*. This offers a means to abstract details not needed in a certain level. Secondly, the proposed approach takes also into consideration *non-functional requirements*: functionality metric and cost of a component, i.e. cost of the solution. The final obtained system is assessed by measuring coupling and cohesion that are internal attributes influencing reusability and maintenability external quality attributes.

The paper is organized as follows: Sect. 2 presents a short introduction on components and metrics, i.e. the used component model and the metrics used for selection. Section 3 presents the proposed approach, formulating the problem, presenting the metrics used for selection criteria and the fuzzy-based algorithm to construct the final system. Section 4 presents a case study. We have compared the obtained solution by our algorithm with the solution obtained by an evolutionary algorithm. Finally, Sect. 5 summarizes the contributions of this work and outlines directions for further research.

2   Background: Component Model and Metrics

To provide a discussion context for configuration we first describe the assumptions about components and their compositions. The metrics used in our fuzzy-based selection algorithm are also described in this section.

2.1   Component Model

A component is an independent software package that provides functionality via well defined interfaces. Assembling components [5] is called composition. Composition involves putting components together and connecting provided functionality to required functionality.

A graphical representation of our view of components is given in Fig. 1. See details about component specification elements in [13].

There are two type of components: *simple component* (specified by inports, outports and a function) and *compound component* - is a group of connected components in which the output of a component is used as input by another component from the assembly. In Fig. 1 we have designed the compound component by fill in the box. See [4,13] for more details.

2.2   Metrics for Selection Criteria and Architecture Evaluation

Selecting the best component alternative among components that sometimes provide similar functionalities needs to appeal to knowledge on quality attributes such as, for example, maintainability, reusability and extensibility. Therefore evaluation of these components is of utmost importance and software metrics are a means to quantify those attributes considered important for the system that will be built.

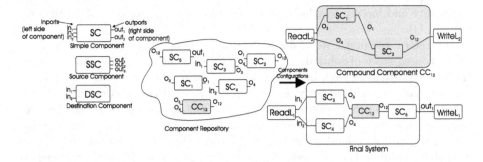

Fig. 1. Components graphical representation and components assembly construction reasoning.

Component Related Metrics. As it has already been mentioned above, we need to evaluate the available set of components in order select the best candidate. This evaluation is based on some criteria (quality attributes) that are important for the final system. These attributes are quantified using the metrics stated in the following:

- The *cost (C)* of a component metric is defined as the overall cost of acquisition and adaptation of that component.
- The *Functionality* metric (F) is defined as the ratio between the number of required services of the system that are provided by the component and the number of required services of the system.

The influence of these metrics values over the quality attributes previously mentioned has been discussed in [12].

Architecture Related Metrics. In our research, the system is built using a multilevel approach (see paper [13] for details). In such an hierarchical system, every compound component is decomposed into a subsystem that will be part of the next higher level. The first level solution defines the modules of the system. In this approach, a module can be viewed as a set of one or more components whose composition forms a subsystem of the final system. Each module has to provide a set of functionalities which define the module's interface [1].

Taking into account the interactions between components, the proposed decomposition approach brings us additional information that can be used to assess coupling and cohesion. It is well known that these internal attributes have a great impact [6] on external quality attributes like reusability, understandability and modularity which are of great importance for a component-based system [1,9,10]. A quantitative approach to measure and assess the solutions of software modularity based on the criteria of minimal coupling and maximal cohesion was proposed in [1]. Coupling measures the interactions among software modules while cohesion measured interactions among the software components which are within a software module. A good software system should possess software modules with high cohesion and low coupling. A highly cohesive module exhibits high reusability and loosely coupled systems enable easy maintenance of a software system [11].

Therefore, the first level of decomposition solution minimizes coupling, as a direct consequence of minimizing the number of components for solution, and the decomposition of each composed component at the next levels maximizes the modules cohesion, identifying the interactions between components of the same module. To define coupling and cohesion metrics for software modules, we take into account the interactions between components. Therefore, coupling for a software module refers to the external interactions of components regarding with that module, whereas cohesion refers to internal interactions of components for that module. In this research, we use the Intramodular Coupling Density metric (ICD) proposed by Abreu and Goulao [1]. They proposed a quantitative approach for measuring coupling and cohesion at the module level. The ICD metric was also used by [8], adapted for component-based system approach.

The definition of **ICD metric** [8], used in our approach is given as follows:

$$ICD_j = \frac{(CI_{IN})_j + 1}{(CI_{IN})_j + (CI_{OUT})_j} \tag{1}$$

ICD_j is the intra-modular coupling density for the jth module; $(CI_{IN})_j$ is the number of component interactions within the jth module; and $(CI_{OUT})_j$ is the number of component interactions between the jth module and other modules.

As a remark, in order to satisfy the principle of "maximize cohesion within modules while minimizing the coupling between them", the value of ICD metric has to be as near as possible to the value 1.

3   Proposed Algorithm Description

3.1   Component Selection Problem Formulation

An informal specification of our aim is described next. It is needed to construct a final system specified by input data (that is given) and output data (what is required to compute). We can see the final system as a compound component and thus the input data becomes the required interfaces of the component and the output data becomes the provided interfaces and in this context we have the required interfaces as provided data and we need to configure the internal structure of the final compound component by offering the provided interfaces. In Fig. 2 all the above discussion is graphically represented.

A formal definition of the problem (seen as a compound component) [14] is as follows. Consider SR the set of final system requirements (the provided functionalities of the final compound component) as $SR = \{r_1, r_2, ..., r_n\}$ and SC the set of components (repository) available for selection as $SC = \{c_1, c_2, ..., c_m\}$. Each component c_i can satisfy a subset of the requirements from SR (the provided functionalities) denoted $SP_{c_i} = \{p_{i_1}, p_{i_2}, ..., p_{i_k}\}$ and has a set of requirements denoted $SR_{c_i} = \{r_{i_1}, r_{i_2}, ..., r_{i_h}\}$. The goal is to find a set of components Sol in such a way that every requirement r_j $(j = \overline{1, n})$ from the set SR can be

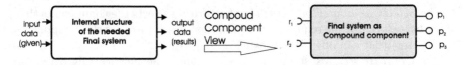

Fig. 2. Graphically representation of the problem formulation.

assigned a component c_i from *Sol* where r_j is in SP_{c_i} $(i = \overline{1, m})$, while minimizing/maximizing various criteria.

3.2   Metrics for Component Classification

In the following, each component c_i from SC is described by a 2-dimensional vector, $c_i = (F, C)$. Next, our goal is to group similar components regarding the defined attributes. To obtain this, we use a clustering approach [17]. The objects to be clustered are components from our repository and the characteristics of these objects are the corresponding metrics values. The next problem is the selection of one component out of a set of possibilities. After obtaining the final system we use ICD metric to measure the "degree" of reusability and maintenance of it.

3.3   Algorithm Description

In this section we propose a new algorithm for the Component Selection Problem defined in Sect. 3.1. Our algorithm is based on selected metrics and fuzzy clustering approach described before. The objects to be clustered are components, each component being identified by a vector of metrics values. Our focus is to group similar objects in order to select the best candidate. The fuzzy clustering algorithm (Fuzzy n-means algorithm) used to determine the fuzzy partition of the set of components is described in [3]. Taking these into account, we next give the proposed algorithm: SR-set of requirements and SC-set of components and their metrics values represent input, and Sol- obtained solution represents output.

```
program MF-CS (SR, SC, Sol)
  begin
      while (SR is not empty)
          CC := SelectCandidateComponents(SR,SC);
          ComputeMetrics(CC, SR);
          FuzzyPartitionDet(CC, A, B);
          c := SelectBestComponent(CC, A, B);
          AddToSol(Sol,c);
          UpdateSR(SR, c, CC);
  end.
```

The *SelectCandidateComponents* subalgorithm selects the components that satisfy at least one of the requirements from the SR, i.e. provides the components (the CC set) that can offer functionalities from SR.

The *ComputeMetrics* subalgorithms computes the metrics values for the Functionality and Cost quality criteria.

The *FuzzyPartitionDet(CC, A, B)* subalgorithm computes a fuzzy partition of the set CC. The fuzzy sets obtained after the first splitting are A, B, i.e. the candidate components set is partitioned in two sets, A, i.e. B considering Functionality and Cost metrics values.

The *SelectBestComponent* subalgorithm is described next. From the set of possible candidates we have to select one of them. There are two different cases that may appear: all these components belong to the same cluster, or some of them are in the first cluster and the others in the second one. For the first case, we select the component with the maximum membership degree for that class. Regarding the second case we proceed in the following way: the best candidate from each cluster is identified, and then some criteria (first Functionality, then Cost) are considered to choose one of them. For this reason, the component set is split in two clusters. In future research we will apply a divisive hierarchical algorithm and the initial partition will be further split.

The *AddToSol* algorithm adds the selected component to the final solution.

The *UpdateSR* algorithm updates the set of SR by the dependencies appeared by selecting component c and removes the requirements that were provided by selecting component c.

4   Case Study

In order to validate our approach we have used the following case study for building a *Reservation System* is developed. The system allows booking several types of items (hotel, car, ... etc.), by different types of customers, having thus different types of offers. Four modules that define the business logic of this system are identified: *Offer Module* (provides transactions on making a reservation and getting a notification), *LoyaltyPrg Module* (responsible for the loyalty program for old clients), *ReservationType Module* (managing different types of booking offers) and *Customer Module* (provides information about customers). Two of the four modules mentioned above, *LoyaltyPrg Module* and *Offer Module*, are described at level 1 as compound components which are further decomposed at next levels whereas, the modules *ReservationType* and *Customer Module* are simple components and remain unchanged over modules decomposition. The components and the structure of (one) solution may be found at [16].

4.1   Component Selection Problem Formulation

Having specified two input data (customerData, calendarData) and two output data (doneReservation, requestConfirmation) needed to be computed, and having a set of 126 available components, the goal is to find a subset of the given components such that all the requirements are satisfied considering the functionality and cost criteria previously specified. The set of requirements $SR = \{r_3, r_4\}$ (view as provided interfaces $\{p_3, p_4\}$, see the discussion in Sect. 3.1) and the set of components $SC = \{c_0, c_1, c_2, c_3, c_4, c_5, c_6, ..., c_{126}\}$ are given. The final system has as input data (transformed in required interfaces) the set $\{r_1, r_2\}$.

Remark. The component repository may be found at [16]. There are many components that may provide the same functionality with different requirements interfaces. The components from the repository system have been numbered for better management and utilization of the algorithm.

4.2 Solution Obtained by the Proposed Algorithm

In the first step of the algorithm the set of requirements needed to be satisfied is: $\{r_3, r_4\}$. Considering the remark on Sect. 3.1, these requirements are "transformed" in provided interfaces, thus we "search" components that contain these provided interfaces.

Remark. The criteria that help us decide which of the two components should be chosen to be part of the final solution are based on two metrics values that quantify: functionality and cost. When the functionality criterion has the same value for both components, the cost criterion is considered. If all the criteria are equal one of the components is randomly selected.

Construction of Level 1. Applying the [3] algorithm we obtained the results in Table 1. The components that offer these requirements are split in the following clusters (representative components for a cluster are written in bold): A contains $\{c_{12}, c_{16}, c_3\}$ with the most representative being c_{12} and the cluster B contains $\{c_{25}, c_{18}, c_4, c_{24}, c_{10}, c_{13}\}$ with the most representative being c_{25}. To decide which of c_{12} and c_{25} components should be chosen, we consider the metrics-based criteria selection mention above. In this case, the c_{12} component is chosen due to the functionality criterion.

Table 1. The final partition (representative components for a cluster are written in bold) for the set of 9 components (level 1)

Class	c_{12}	c_{16}	c_3	c_4	c_{25}	c_{10}	c_{13}	c_{18}	c_{24}
A	**0.99**	**0.99**	**0.99**	0.09	0.02	0.03	0.16	0.23	0.50
B	0.01	0.01	0.01	**0.91**	**0.98**	**0.97**	**0.84**	**0.77**	**0.50**

The new set of remaining requirements is $\{r_5, r_7, r_8, r_{11}\}$, i.e. the provided interfaces $\{p_5, p_7, p_8, p_{11}\}$. The components that offer these requirements are again grouped in two clusters. Based on the same rules, between the c_6 and c_2 components, the component c_2 (that provides $\{p_7, p_8\}$ was chosen. A new partition is created for the remained set of provided interfaces, and between c_6 and

c_{21} components, the first one is selected (that provides $\{p_5\}$). From components $\{c_{21}, c_{15}, c_{22}\}$ that have the same Functionality metric value and the same Cost, one is chosen randomly, i.e. c_{21}.

The obtained solution (constructing first level) contains the components: $\{cc_{12}, cc_2, c_6, c_{21}\}$ and has the cost 153. Components c_2 and c_{12} are compound components.

Construction of Level 2. Until now we have constructed the first level of the system. The solution from the first level contains two compound components, thus we need to apply the same algorithm for each compound component.

The requirements needed to be satisfy for component C_2 are: $\{r_7, r_8\}$. The components that offer these requirements are split in the following clusters: A contains $\{c_{27}, c_{54}, c_{35}, c_{53}, c_{29}, c_{49}, c_{38}, c_{44}, c_{55}\}$ with the most representative being c_{27} and the cluster B contains $\{c_{43}, c_{31}, c_{37}\}$ with the most representative being c_{43}. In Table 2 the degrees are presented (representative components for a cluster are written in bold). To decide which of c_{27} and c_{43} components should be chosen, we consider the metrics-based criteria selection mention above. In this case, the c_{27} component is chosen due to the cost criterion.

Table 2. The final partition (representative components for a cluster are written in bold) for the set of 12 components (level 2)

Class	c_{38}	c_{29}	c_{49}	c_{37}	c_{43}	c_{44}	c_{27}	c_{54}	c_{35}	c_{31}	c_{53}	c_{55}
A	**0.98**	**0.98**	**0.98**	0.10	0.01	**0.90**	**0.99**	**0.99**	**0.99**	0.03	**0.99**	**0.79**
B	0.02	0.02	0.02	**0.90**	**0.99**	0.10	0.01	0.01	0.01	**0.97**	0.01	0.21

After choosing the c_{27} component, the only requirement needs to be satisfied is r_7. All the components that offer this functionality are again grouped in one cluster, thus the chosen component is c_{38}.

The new set of remaining requirements is $\{r_{37}, r_{34}\}$, i.e. the provided interfaces $\{p_{37}, p_{34}\}$. The components that offer these requirements are again grouped in two clusters. Based on the same rules, between the c_{33} and c_{26} components, the component c_{26} was chosen. After choosing the c_{26} component, the only requirement needs to be satisfied is r_{37}. All the components that offer this functionality are grouped in the same cluster, thus the chosen component is c_{33}.

The new set of remaining requirements is $\{r_6, r_{35}\}$, i.e. the provided interfaces $\{p_6, p_{35}\}$. The provided interface p_6 is provided by the final system, i.e. is satisfied. For the p_{35} the components have the same Functionality and Cost, thus one is chosen randomly, i.e. c_{50}.

The new set of remaining requirements is $\{r_{10}, r_{36}\}$, i.e. the provided interfaces $\{p_{10}, p_{36}\}$. The provided interface p_{10} is provided by the final system, i.e. is satisfied. For the p_{36} the components have the same Functionality and Cost, thus one is chosen randomly, i.e. c_{50} that also was previously selected.

The obtained solution (constructing component c_2) contains the components: $\{c_{27}, c_{38}, c_{26}, c_{33}, c_{50}\}$ and has the cost 52.

The requirements needed to be satisfy for component C_{12} are: $\{r_3, r_4\}$. The components that offer these requirements are split in the following clusters: A contains $\{c_{59},\ c_{70},\ c_{74}\}$ with the most representative being c_{59} and the cluster B contains $\{c_{57},\ c_{60},\ c_{69},\ c_{75}\}$ with the most representative being c_{57}. To decide which of c_{59} and c_{57} components should be chosen, we consider the metrics-based criteria selection mention above. In this case, the c_{57} component is chosen due to the functionality criterion.

The new set of remaining requirements is $\{r_5,\ r_{54}\}$, i.e. the provided interfaces $\{p_5,\ p_{54}\}$. The provided interface p_5 is provided by the final system, i.e. is satisfied. For the p_{54} the components have the same Functionality and Cost, thus one is chosen randomly, i.e. c_{68} that also was previously selected.

The new set of remaining requirements is $\{r_{11},\ r_{55}\}$, i.e. the provided interfaces $\{p_{11},\ p_{55}\}$. The provided interface p_{11} is provided by the final system, i.e. is satisfied. For the p_{55} the components have the same Functionality and Cost, thus one is chosen randomly, i.e. c_{63} that also was previously selected.

The obtained solution (constructing component c_{12}) contains the components: $\{c_{57}, c_{68}, c_{63}\}$ and has the cost 56. Components c_{26}, c_{33} and c_{57} are compound components.

Construction of Level 3. Until now we have constructed the second level of the system. The solution from the second level contains two compound components, thus we need to apply the same algorithm for each compound component.

The requirement needed to be satisfy for component C_{26} is: $\{r_{34}\}$. The components that offer this requirement are split in the following clusters: A contains $\{c_{81}\}$ with the most representative being c_{81} and the cluster B contains $\{c_{77},\ c_{80},\ c_{84},\ c_{78}\}$ with the most representative being c_{77}. To decide which of c_{81} and c_{77} components should be chosen, we consider the metrics-based criteria selection mention above. In this case, the c_{77} component is chosen due to the cost criterion.

The new set of requirements is $\{r_{65}\}$, i.e. the provided interfaces $\{p_{65}\}$. The components have the same Functionality and Cost, thus one is chosen randomly, i.e. c_{83}.

The obtained solution (constructing component c_{26}) contains the components: $\{c_{77}, c_{83}\}$ and has the cost 15. There no other compound components.

The requirement needed to be satisfy for component C_{33} is: $\{r_{37}\}$. The components that offer this requirement are split in the following clusters: A contains $\{c_{88},\ c_{97},\ c_{90}\}$ with the most representative being c_{88} and the cluster B contains $\{c_{89},\ c_{95}\}$ with the most representative being c_{89}. To decide which of c_{88} and c_{89} components should be chosen, we consider the metrics-based criteria selection mention above. In this case, the c_{89} component is chosen due to the cost criterion.

The new set of requirements is $\{r_{72},\ r_{73},\ r_{74}\}$, i.e. the provided interfaces $\{p_{72},\ p_{73},\ p_{74}\}$. The components that offer these requirements are split in the following clusters: A contains $\{c_{101}\}$ and the cluster B contains $\{c_{94}\}$. To decide which of c_{101} and c_{94} components should be chosen, we consider the metrics-based criteria selection mention above. In this case, the c_{101} component is chosen due to the functionality criterion. The remained set of requirements are provided by the component c_{94}.

The obtained solution (constructing component c_{33}) contains the components: $\{c_{89}, c_{101}, c_{94}\}$ and has the cost 26. There no other compound components.

The requirements needed to be satisfy for component C_{57} are: $\{r_3,\ r_4\}$. The components that offer this requirement are split in the following clusters: A contains $\{c_{104},\ c_{115},\ c_{107},\ c_{109}\}$ with the most representative being c_{104} and the cluster B contains $\{c_{123},\ c_{108},\ c_{113},\ c_{126}\}$ with the most representative being c_{123}. To decide which of c_{104} and c_{123} components should be chosen, we consider the metrics-based criteria selection mention above. In this case, the c_{104} component is chosen due to the functionality criterion.

The new set of requirements is $\{r_{78},\ r_{79}\}$, i.e. the provided interfaces $\{p_{78},\ p_{79}\}$. The components that offer these requirements are split in the following clusters: A contains $\{c_{114},\ c_{118},\ c_{111}\}$ and the cluster B contains $\{c_{110}, c_{105}, c_{116}\}$. To decide which of c_{114} and c_{110} components should be chosen, we consider the metrics-based criteria selection mention above. In this case, the c_{110} component is chosen due to the cost criterion.

The new set of requirements is $\{r_{79}\}$, i.e. the provided interfaces $\{p_{79}\}$. The components have the same Functionality and Cost, thus one is chosen randomly, i.e. c_{114}.

The obtained solution (constructing component c_{57}) contains the components: $\{c_{104}, c_{110}, c_{114}\}$ and has the cost 33. There no other compound components.

4.3   Comparison: Evolutionary Algorithm Vs. Fuzzy-Based Selection

The problem of selecting components from a set of available components was also discussed in several papers using various approaches. We compare our approach with an evolutionary-based approach.

An approach for the same selection problem that uses principles of evolutionary computation and multiobjective optimization was proposed in [15]. The problem is formulated as a multiple objective optimization problem having two objectives: the total cost of the components used and the number of components used. Both objectives are to be minimized.

In order to compare our approach with those mention before, we describe in Table 3 the obtained solution for the evolutionary algorithm and in Table 4 the solution obtained for the fuzzy-based approach.

Result Analysis: The solutions obtained with the evolutionary algorithm (EA) approach and with the fuzzy-based approach are compared from the cost and ICD (internal metric value that influence the external quality attributes reusability and maintainability) perspectives: EA approach obtained the solution with cost 153 and ICD=0.5313 and the Fuzzy-based approach the solution with cost 159 and ICD=0.5376.

Thus, we select a solution based on one criteria (that is important to us, either [reusability&maintainability] or cost) on the expense of the other criteria. There is a trade-off between cost and [reusability&maintainability].

Table 3. ICD metric values for best solution with cost = 153 using evolutionary algorithm.

CI_{IN}	m_1	m_2	m_3	m_4
L_1	0	0	0	0
L_2	0	4	0	2
L_3	0	7	0	7
CI_{OUT}	2	5	3	4
ICD_m	0.5000	0.6667	0.3333	0.6250
ICD	0.5313			

Table 4. ICD metric values for the obtained solution with cost = 159 using the fuzzy-based selection algorithm.

CI_{IN}	m_1	m_2	m_3	m_4
L_1	0	0	0	0
L_2	0	4	0	2
L_3	0	8	0	7
CI_{OUT}	2	5	3	4
ICD_m	0.5000	0.6923	0.3333	0.6250
ICD	0.5376			

5 Conclusions and Future Work

A new algorithm based on metrics and fuzzy clustering analysis that addresses the problem of component selection in the multilevel system structure was proposed in this paper. We use both functional and non-functional criteria when selecting the best candidate component for each selection step.

We evaluate our approach using a case study. We have compared our fuzzy-based approach with an evolutionary based approach: we have obtained better solutions from different perspective: considering either cost or reusability and maintainability quality attributes.

We will focus our future work on three main fronts: to apply this approach for more case studies; to apply other fuzzy clustering algorithms in order to obtain the needed classification, and to select more relevant metrics.

References

1. e Abreu, F.B., Goulao, M.: Coupling and cohesion as modularization drivers: are we being over-persuaded? In: Conference on Software Maintenance and Reengineering, pp. 47–57 (2001)
2. Becker, C., Rauber, A.: Improving component selection and monitoring with controlled experimentation and automated measurements. Inf. Softw. Technol. **52**(6), 641–655 (2010)
3. Bezdek, J.: Pattern Recognition with Fuzzy Objective Function Algorithms. Plenum Press, New York (1981)
4. Cox, P., Song, B.: A formal model for component-based software. In: Symposium on Visual/Multimedia Approaches to Programming and Software Engineering, pp. 304–311 (2001)
5. Crnkovic, I.: Building Reliable Component-Based Software Systems. Artech House Inc., Norwood (2002)
6. Fenton, N.E.: Software Metrics: A Rigorous Approach. Chapman and Hall, London (1991)
7. Iribarne, L., Troya, J., Vallecillo, A.: Selecting software components with multiple interfaces. In: The EUROMICRO Conference Component-Based Software Engineering, pp. 26–32 (2002)

8. Kwong, C., Mu, L., Tang, J., Luo, X.: Optimization of software components selection for component-based software system development. Comput. Ind. Eng. **58**(1), 618–624 (2010)

9. Bertrand, M.: Software Engineering. Addison-Wesley, Longman Publishing Co., Inc., Boston (2001)

10. Parsa, S., Bushehrian, O.: A framework to investigate and evaluate genetic clustering algorithms for automatic modularization of software systems. In: International Conference on Computational Science, pp. 699–702 (2004)

11. Seker, R., van der Merwe, A.J., Kotze, P., Tanik, M.M., Paul, R.: Assessment of coupling and cohesion for component based software by using Shannon languages. J. Integr. Des. Process Sci. **8**, 33–43 (2004)

12. Vescan, A.: A metrics-based evolutionary approach for the component selection problem. In: The International Conference on Computer Modelling and Simulation, pp. 83–88 (2009)

13. Vescan, A., Grosan, C.: Evolutionary multiobjective approach for multilevel component composition. Studia Univ. Babes-Bolyai, Informatica **LV**(4), 18–32 (2010)

14. Vescan, A., Grosan, C., Yang, S.: A hybrid evolutionary multiobjective approach for the dynamic component selection problem. In: The International Conference on Hybrid Intelligent Systems, pp. 714–721 (2011)

15. Vescan, A., Serban, C.: Multilevel component selection optimisation and metrics-based architecture evaluation. Soft Comput. J. 0, 1–1 (2015, submitted)

16. Vescan, A., Serban, C.: Details on case study for the multilevel componentselection optimisation approach (2016). http://www.cs.ubbcluj.ro/~avescan/?q=node/95

17. Zadeh, L.: Fuzzy sets. Inf. Control **8**, 338–353 (1965)

A Clustering-Based Method for Team Formation in Learning Environments

Marta Guijarro-Mata-García[1](✉), Maria Guijarro[1], and Rubén Fuentes-Fernández[2]

[1] Department of Computer Architecture and Automatic, School of Computer Science, University Complutense of Madrid, c/Profesor José García Santesmases 9, 28040 Madrid, Spain
mguijarro@ucm.es
[2] Group of Agent-Based, Social, and Interdisciplinary Applications (GRASIA), School of Computer Science, University Complutense of Madrid, c/Profesor José García Santesmases 9, 28040 Madrid, Spain
ruben@fdi.ucm.es

Abstract. Teamwork is acquiring a growing relevance in learning environments. In many cases, it is a useful and meaningful way to organize the learning activities and improve their outcomes. Moreover, related skills are needed for the professional life of students. This situation makes necessary the availability of support techniques to manage the different aspects of teamwork in educational settings. A key aspect is the organization of teams. Literature offers alternatives to assess students and make up teams, but they are focused on particular and isolated aspects. This work proposes a novel methodology to develop tailored student assessments from the integration of multiple pre-existent evaluation techniques. These new techniques evaluate features belonging to student's profiles, and use the results to create groups that improve their learning experience. The process is based on clustering techniques and has three-stage. In the first one, lecturers identify features they consider relevant in their context (e.g. leadership, ability to communicate, or spatial skills) and test to asses them. Then, the training stage identifies the combinations of feature values from those tests that characterize high-performance teams, i.e. teams where group learning results are over the average in its context. Finally, the classification stage uses those values to determine which students should belong to which teams, trying to replicate the distribution of student's profiles in the best teams, and thus their results. The paper reports the experiments performed so far to evaluate the method in a computer engineering school.

Keywords: Teamwork · Group learning · Collaborative learning · Student's profile · Team formation · Classification · Clustering

1 Introduction

Teamwork has a growing presence at all levels in education [7]. This interest is fuelled by two main reasons. First, there is evidence that group-based learning enhances the educational experience and outcome in many cases. In particular, it helps students to develop teamwork skills, and also others like autonomy and adaptability [4]. This kind

© Springer International Publishing Switzerland 2016
F. Martínez-Álvarez et al. (Eds.): HAIS 2016, LNAI 9648, pp. 475–486, 2016.
DOI: 10.1007/978-3-319-32034-2_40

of competencies is highly demanded in our rapidly changing societies. Second, this approach can also help to deal with constraints on resources like time and budget.

Literature [4, 7, 10, 13] offers theories, techniques, and tools to manage the different aspects of teamwork in diverse educational settings. Despite its wide range, this support usually presents some limitations when applied in real settings. It largely relies on the skills and experience of lecturers to apply them. Methods are frequently described through only some principles or general ideas [4]. Even when they are reported with a high level of detail (see examples in [6]), it is difficult that they consider all the situations that can appear in the actual classroom. Moreover, there is usually a lack of automated support, so lecturers' workload can be increased. When this support is available (see for instance the tools for team formation in [2]), this is tied to specific aspects of techniques, so lecturers cannot use or combine it in a flexible way.

To address these issues and facilitate taking advantage of the already available methods, our work proposes the use of general classification techniques to create assessment techniques tailored to specific aspects of the teamwork of students. In particular, this paper applies this approach to team formation for learning activities.

There are multiple techniques to constitute students' teams [6], such as randomly, student-selected, the jigsaw, or according to learning styles. Their applicability can depend on the setting. For instance, the jigsaw method is only useful in collaborative learning settings, as it makes that every student in a group prepares a topic to teach that new expertise to the rest of the group.

Our work adopts a different perspective and approaches team formation from the experience in previous courses. The hypothesis is that, in a given context, there are combinations of features that characterize students in high-performance teams. A high-performance team is here one that gets learning results over the average, according to the goals of the course. When these combinations of features have been identified in previous courses using techniques for assessment and classification, lecturers can look for the same combinations when making up new teams. This approach generalizes, for instance, team formation based on learning profiles. In it, profiles indicate the students' features to consider, and the target distribution of profiles in teams is the team formation criteria.

This process can be implemented in a customizable assistant tool to semi-automate it. The tool allows lecturers selecting the tests to consider, introducing the historical data from previous courses, obtaining the students' input for their assessment, and creating the teams from it. The key issue is the classification of teams from student's features. For this purpose, the system applies clustering techniques.

The approach has been evaluated in the context of engineering studies in higher education. The results show the suitability of the method to make up the teams, and its flexibility to deal with variations in the distribution of the students' profiles. Nevertheless, conclusive results on whether the approach actually improves the learning results of students still need further experimentation.

The rest of the paper is organized as follows. Section 2 introduces the methodology for team formation, and Sect. 3 shows its application in the aforementioned case study. The results of our approach are compared with related work in Sect. 4. Finally, Sect. 5 discusses some conclusions and future lines of work.

2 Methodology

The proposed method is intended for group formation in environments where students need to carry out teamwork. It is general in the sense that it does not depend on any specific pedagogical approach (e.g. group learning, collaborative learning, or competition), can consider different student's feature (e.g. learning profile, teamwork competencies, or level of expertise), and different assessment methods. The method works in three stages: identification of features to evaluate, method training, and classification.

Lecturers start identifying features that they consider relevant in their learning context. These include individual skills they want to improve and also those they consider relevant for teamwork. For instance, lecturers can want to work on communicative and critical thinking skills, and for it, they consider that teams should avoid mixing people too dominant with others who are much more less, as the first ones would dominate any initiative.

In this first stage, lecturers also need to find assessment resources that allow them to evaluate the previous features. Our approach does not require a unique resource for this. On the contrary, it can use multiple resources to evaluate the same or different features. For instance, the case study in this paper applies two tests, [1] to assess the learning style of students and [5] for the style of collaborative learning in Learning Management Systems (LMSs). As [5] is built over the theoretical basis of [1], the experiment also illustrates how the approach allows us to determine whether tests are complementary or redundant.

The chosen tests determine the actual features to consider in the classification. Each test T_i classifies students using a vector of features $F_{i,j}$. In this way, when a student k is assessed using test T_i, s/he is characterized as a vector of values $x_{k,i,j}$. These features and data are the input for the clustering algorithm.

The second stage performs the training of the method. It includes the training of the clustering algorithm to identify students' profiles, the composition of the first groups looking for different combinations of students' profiles, and the observation of the results of these teams.

It starts evaluating a first set of students with the selected tests. Each student is characterized as a vector x of size f with the values for the F features, which are the different features in the union of the sets $F_{i,j}$ after removing duplicates. These values correspond to the students' answers to the T_i tests. X is the set of the x vectors for all students. The algorithm, trained with the data in X, identifies clusters in students' profiles, that is, similar combinations of values for the F features.

In the second part of this stage, lecturers assign students to groups. They look to get groups that represent different distributions of clusters.

At the end of the second stage, lecturers gather the evaluations of these initial groups. This information indicates which combinations of students' clusters in groups are getting the best results, and thus characterize the desirable high-performance teams.

The final third stage of our approach uses the trained algorithm to make up the new teams. Lecturers assess new students using the previous process, but this time they constitute teams following the recommended combinations of clusters.

Next subsections give the details of the clustering algorithm used in our approach. It describes both the training and classification stages.

2.1 Clustering Algorithm

Our clustering algorithm works in two stages. Firstly, it performs a training process with a set of input (i.e. the *patterns* in classification literature, characterized as the previously mentioned x vectors) that corresponds to the initial group of students. This stage determines the number of clusters and its characterization in terms of students' features. Secondly, the algorithm is applied for classification over new data. It indicates for each new input the class (i.e. *cluster*) it belongs to. Our scheme applies here a fuzzy classifier, as literature reports this kind of classifier has a good performance with similar data [14]. Figure 1 shows both processes.

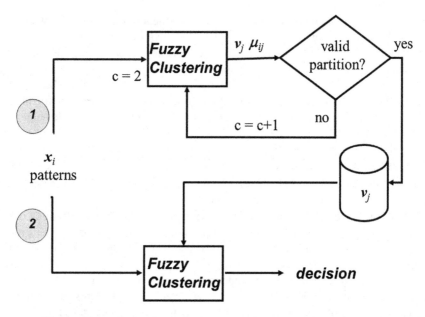

Fig. 1. Clustering algorithm with training (1) and classification (2) stages.

The Training Process. During the training phase, the algorithm considers the set X of n training patterns, i.e. $X = \{x_1, x_2, \dots, x_n\}, x_i \in R^f$. Note that the clustering algorithm requires that the domain of the features in F is $\mathbb{R}$, so conversions may be needed.

Each sample is to be assigned to a given class, where the number of possible classes is c. Each class is identified as w_j, where $j = 1 \dots c$. The problem is to assign each pattern sample to a class and compute the cluster prototypes. For such purpose, our work chooses the well-tested Fuzzy Clustering Framework (FCF), which has been customized and tailored to work in an unsupervised way [8]. The original FCF computes for each x_i at the iteration k its membership grade and updates the cluster centers according to Eq. (1).

$$\mu_{ij}(k) = \frac{1}{\sum_{r=1}^{C} (d_{ij}(k)/d_{ir}(k))^{\frac{2}{m-1}}}$$

$$v_j(k+1) = \frac{\sum_{i=1}^{n} \mu_{ij}^m(k) x_i}{\sum_{i=1}^{n} \mu_{ij}^m(k)} \tag{1}$$

Where d is the squared Euclidean distance, m is called the exponent weight, the vector v contains the cluster centers, and the vector μ is formed by the membership grades. The stopping criterion of the iteration process is achieved when $\left\| \mu_{ij}(k+1) - \mu_{ij}(k) \right\| < \varepsilon \, \forall ij$ or a number N of iterations is reached. The number of classes is initially set to 2. After the fuzzy clustering process, a partition of the input training patterns is obtained, where each cluster j has associated its center v_j. Also, for each sample i, its corresponding membership grades (μ_{ij}, of belonging to each cluster j) are computed. The cluster centers are stored to be considered later.

The next step is the cluster validation. This is carried out by computing the *Partition Coefficient* (PC) for the available classes as follows:

$$PC(U;c) = \frac{1}{n} \sum_{i=1}^{n} \sum_{j=1}^{c} \left(\mu_{ij} \right)^2 \tag{2}$$

The maximum value of *PC* for different values of c determines the best partition, i.e. the best number of classes for the set of training samples available. Values of *PC* near 1 indicate that the partition is acceptable, as the *PC* is upper bounded by 1.

The Classification Process. During the classification process, the new sets X of n patterns are classified in the clusters obtained in the training phase. With such purpose, the method recovers the v_j cluster centers stored during the training process. During this phase, given a pattern x_i, it is classified as belonging to the cluster j if $\mu_{ij} > \mu_{ik} \forall k \neq j$, where the membership grades are computed according to (1).

3   Case Study

The method described in this paper has been preliminarily tested in the context of the engineering studies of the Computer Science School of the University Complutense in Madrid (Spain) during course 2012–2013. The chosen group corresponded to the Language Processors (LP) subject, which had 80 students initially enrolled that academic year.

The LP course was organized around classroom sessions and group projects. Lecturers used classroom sessions to introduce the relevant theory and discuss exercises and individual assignments. Students also developed a compiler in their projects, grouped in teams of 10–12 students. These projects were intended to apply the subject knowledge and improve teamwork skills. In all the works, lecturers and students made an extensive use of software tools to support their tasks, being the main one the university LMS.

In this context, lecturers were interested in improving the way to constitute the teams. Two important aspects of the student profiles were their learning styles (particularly regarding autonomy, flexibility, and abstraction, and application capabilities), and their skills to make use software tools for collaborative learning.

Next subsections discuss the different aspects of the experiment. Section 3.1 presents the tests applied to evaluate students, Sect. 3.2 its execution, and Sect. 3.3 the discussion on the observed results.

3.1 Assessment Tests

Researchers chose for the experiment the two tests [1, 5] previously mentioned (see Sect. 2) and the features they consider. Both of them have available online tools that were used with students to obtain their assessment.

The first test [1] classifies students according to their general learning style. It considers four not mutually exclusive categories: *active, reflexive, theoretical,* and *pragmatic.* For each category, a student can get a mark from 0 to 20. A questionnaire with 80 questions, approximately 20 questions for each category, is used to obtain those scores.

The scores in [1] are not absolute, but relative values. They must be compared with the results of the group (in our context the classroom mates) the students belong to. For instance, a given student can obtain a score of 13 for the *reflexive* category, but that can only be interpreted as the student is a kind of reflexive student when compared to the average of her/his classmates.

The second test [5] is focused on how students use software tools, in particular LMSs, when they are involved in collaborative learning experiences. It is inspired by the work in [1] and follows a similar approach. This test identifies four categories: *participating, researching, structuring and planning,* and *concrete and producing.* In this case, the test includes 40 yes/no questions, and students can obtain a score from 0 to 10 for each category. As previously, the scores are relative.

At that point of the experiment, researchers could not find in literature information on whether the categories proposed in both works [1, 5] were or not overlapping. As work in [5] states that it is based on [1], it could be possible that its categories were partly redundant after considering those from [1]. This was an additional question to solve with the classification of students in clusters.

3.2 Experiment

The proposed clustering method works in three stages. The first two (i.e. identification of features and tests, and training) were performed at the beginning of the academic year, and the third one (i.e. classification) at the beginning of the second semester.

The method uses patterns characterized by a feature vector x. As mentioned above, the features considered in the vector depend on the information from the tests performed to each student. This information is obtained in the first stage. In the case of tests from works [1, 5], each one is focused on different aspects of students and learning. Both identify four categories to which students can belong to different extents. Thus, the set F of features extracted from tests initially corresponds to the eight categories present in them. The x vectors that characterize students in the course are 8-dimensional, where its components are the percentages of each profile in both tests.

The second stage started passing the tests to students. The result is the set X of vectors that characterize students according to the features in F. The result of applying the clustering algorithm (see Sect. 2.1) is shown in Table 1.

Table 1. Clusters for the set of feature vectors X.

Cluster	Values of features (as %)							
	Active	Reflexive	Theoretical	Pragmatic	Participating	Researching	Structuring & planning	Concrete & producing
1	39.14	11.93	14.33	34.57	40.19	11.35	13.59	34.84
2	8.66	38.55	41.90	10.86	25.05	55.23	10.36	9.34
3	15.26	54.91	11.48	18.33	11.50	14.15	25.60	48.73

There are three clusters 1–3. Cluster 1 contains high values for features *active, pragmatic, participating*, and *concrete and producing*; cluster 2 is dominated by the *theoretical* and *researching* features; and cluster 3 has high values for features *reflexive* and *concrete and producing*. As the table shows, there is no correspondence between categories from both tests, so their profiles are not the same. Thus, the experiment continued with all the eight categories.

In order to evaluate the methodology, researchers split students in two groups, the control A and experimental B ones. Each group had half of the class, thus 40 students. The project assignment had two deliveries, one in February and another in June. In the A group, students chose their teammates in the first semester, as it is usually done within the course. In the B group, researchers split students in four teams with different percentages of students of the different clusters. This looked for the best performing combinations. Team B1 included an even distribution of all clusters (33 % of students of each one), and in teams B2, B3, and B4, clusters 1, 2, and 3 respectively dominated, i.e. they had a higher percentage of students in that group than the other two clusters.

These eight teams worked together for the first semester, until the February assignment. This was evaluated both at the individual and group levels through a project report and individual interviews. The students and researchers also discussed the main issues that appeared in the teamwork.

Table 2 shows the team marks from the project reports. Ratings are given considering 0 as the lowest score and 10 being the highest score.

Teams B2 and B3 obtained the higher marks regarding the developed product, but also from the point of view of the teamwork. Their collaboration to build the solution was better than in other cases, and they were able to manage effectively their conflicts. On the

Table 2. Team marks for the February asignment.

Group	Assignment marks - February
A1	8,75
A2	6
A3	7,5
A4	4
B1	6,5
B2	9
B3	9,5
B4	Not presented

contrary, team B1 experienced communication and misunderstanding problems, and B4 was unable to meet the deadline. In the A group, A1 was the best performing team, with a high mark for the compiler and a good management of teamwork. Teams A2, A3, and A4 were average in the class, both in terms of their marks and their collaboration.

In the second semester, researchers rebuilt teams. This time, all of them were constituted following the recommendations on cluster combinations obtained in the first semester. The best teams regarding their marks and teamwork were B2 and B3. Researchers kept them to ensure their proper progress, and were able to make up four more teams following their cluster distribution. In this way, teams C1–C3 followed the B2 distribution, being C1 the former B2, and C4–C6 followed the B3 distribution, being C4 the former B3. For the remaining teams, it was not possible to follow the recommended distribution. However, it was possible to make up teams C7 and C8 following the distribution of B1, the following best performing team in the B group of the first semester. In order to improve their performance, these groups had additional support from lecturers regarding their organization of the teamwork and communication in the team.

Table 3. Team marks for the June asignment.

Group	Assignment marks - June
C1 (former B2)	9
C2	8,75
C3	6,5
C4 (former B3)	9,5
C5	3,5
C6	8
C7	Not presented
C8	7,5

Table 3 shows the marks for the project in the second semester. Teams C1, C2, C4, and C6 got high marks, and also evaluated as good their collaborative work. Note that C1 and C4 teams are B2 and B3 from the first semester, and returned to get good scores. They are groups that have worked together along the course, so their collaborative work was reinforced getting good results. Team C8 also got good marks, improving the performance of several of their members regarding the first semester. They were also able to improve their teamwork by using additional support tools for teamwork (mainly Trello[1]). Team C3 passed the assignment, but with lower marks. Teams C5 and C7 did not succeed with the June assignment. The first one delivered the project, but it did not meet the minimum requirements, and the second team did not deliver any result before the deadline.

3.3 Discussion

The results obtained from the currently limited experimentation are not conclusive. Regarding the assignment marks, there was only a slight improvement in the second semester as shown in Table 4. The best performing teams were the same all over the year. In both semesters, one of the groups failed the assignment and other was unable to meet the deadline.

Table 4. Comparison of project marks by teams between semesters.

Mark interval	Groups	
	1st semester	2nd semester
≥ 9	B2, B3	C1 (former B2), C4 (former B3)
[8, 9)	A1	C2, C6
[7, 8)	A3	C8
[6, 7)	A2, B1	C3
[5, 6)	–	–
<5	A4	C5
Not presented	B4	C7

These results were better for teamwork. Students had a better impression of their performance in this aspect and the management of teams in the second semester. In fact, some groups, particularly C8, took initiatives on their own to amend this aspect. In any case, this could be due to the experience they gained on teamwork in the first semester: for the second one they had a better idea on how to work and what they needed to fix.

Regarding the experiment design, some issues need to be fixed. First, figures are low to be significant. The researchers are currently gathering information on additional courses. Second, the analysis of cluster combinations needs to be extended to consider other variants in group composition. Third, teams have to remain the same all over the academic year to obtain a better evaluation of teamwork that shows whether there is an improvement with the method.

---

[1] https://trello.com/.

4   Related Work

Literature presents multiple works in team formation [4, 7, 10, 13]. Simple techniques do not carry out any preliminary analysis of potential team members. Examples of them are random formation, student-chosen, or the jigsaw method already mentioned in the introduction. However, in most cases, there is an assessment of some members' features to use them in team formation. In the case of learning teams, these features are usually linked to learning styles and teamwork skills.

Works that use learning styles consider that some combinations of these styles in teams make possible improving the skills of their different members. Through the interaction with students with better learning skills, students with worse habits can evaluate their own skills, find other models, and apply them in practice. An example of this kind of work is [12] based on the Vermunt's learning styles. In it, meaning-directed and reproduction-directed styles are considered as good models for the undirected style. An additional observed result in some of these works is that certain combinations of learning styles also improve interactions in teams.

When teamwork skills are at the forefront, works mainly consider two groups of features. Some focus on general good features for teamwork [3], such as communicative, flexible, or thinking in team goals. The criterion for team formation is to choose people suitable to work with others. The other approach looks for combining people that are able to play complementary roles in teams. For instance, the 6HTFS method [9] tries to put in teams different roles, such as brainstormers or devil's advocates.

In some cases, the previous techniques have related support tools that help in the assessment. For instance, the work in [12] has related tools to recommend team formation from students' tests.

A common limitation of all the proposed methods is that they are tied to the features and tests described in the original work. They do not support adaptation to include new features that allow them adapting to different settings. For instance, when working with profiles in teams with the 6HTFS method [9] or learning styles in [12], there are no guides to include the assessment of critical thinking as shown in [11]. In this case, this hinders the capability of lecturers to integrate those researches to make different kinds of team for less standard or more challenging assignments. In this sense, our work is a first attempt in this novel line of work.

5   Conclusions

This work aims to provide a general method to integrate multiple techniques for the creation of groups in courses where collaborative work is important. This allows lecturers addressing in their classrooms combinations of team members' features that original works do not consider. The proposed method makes up teams by learning about the combinations of students' skills that appear in high-performance teams.

The method is a three-stage process based on clustering techniques. In the first one, lecturers study the features of their students and the needs of the course subject, and select the tests to asses them. Then, the training stage identifies the clusters of students' features, makes up teams with different combinations of those clusters, evaluates them, and sorts the combinations according to their performance. Finally, the third stage creates new teams trying to maximize the presence of the best combinations of clusters.

The method was tested in an experiment performed in the context of the engineering studies of the Computer Science School in a Spanish university. The experiment integrated two sets of students' features, one about learning styles and other on the use of virtual environments for collaborative learning. The results support the suitability of the approach to integrate different techniques for assessing students and grouping their profiles. However, results were not conclusive regarding team formation from the students' profiles, with only a slight improvement when applying the technique.

The work performed so far shows several lines of future work. Further experimentation needs to be performed with additional courses and students, and over the span of multiple academic years. This is required to complete the assessment of the method. The method also has to be described more formally to facilitate its application by lecturers without previous knowledge of clustering techniques.

Acknowledgements. This work has been done in the context of the project "Desarrollo Colaborativo de Soluciones AAL (ColoSAAL)", supported by the Spanish Ministry for Economy and Competitiviness, with grant TIN2014-57028-R. Also, we acknowledge support from the "Programa de Creación y Consolidación de Grupos de Investigación UCM-BSCH" for group GR3/14, and the project "Modelo de asistente semi-automático para procesos de aprendizaje presenciales" (372) of the program "Proyectos de Innovación y Mejora de la Calidad Docente - 2015" (Projects for Innovation and Improvement of Education Quality) of the University Complutense of Madrid.

References

1. Alonso, C.M., Gallego, D.J., Honey, P.: Learning Styles – What They Are – How to Assess Them – How to Improve Our Own Learning Style (original in Spanish "Los estilos de aprendizaje - Qué son - Cómo diagnosticarlos - Cómo mejorar el propio estilo de aprendizaje"). Editorial Mensajero (1994)
2. Ardaiz-Villanueva, O., Nicuesa-Chacón, X., Brene-Artazcoz, O., Sanz-de-Acedo-Lizarraga, M.L., Sanz-de-Acedo-Baquedano, M.T.: Evaluation of computer tools for idea generation and team formation in project-based learning. Comput. Educ. **56**(3), 700–711 (2011)
3. Baker, D.P., Salas, E.: Principles for measuring teamwork skills. Hum. Factors J. Hum. Factors Ergon. Soc. **34**(4), 469–475 (1992)
4. Barkley, E.F., Cross, K.P., Major, C.H.: Collaborative Learning Techniques – A Handbook for College Faculty. Wiley, San Francisco (2014)
5. Barros, D.M.V.: Collaborative learning styles for E-learning (original in Portuguese "Estilo de aprendizagem colaborativo para o e-learning"). Linhas **12**(2), 31–43 (2011)
6. Deibel, K.: Team formation methods for increasing interaction during in-class group work. ACM SIGCSE Bull. **37**(3), 291–295 (2005)
7. Gregory, R., Thorley, L.: Using Group-Based Learning in Higher Education. Routledge, London (2013)
8. Guijarro, M., Pajares, G., Abreu, R.: A new unsupervised hybrid classifier for natural textures in images. In: Corchado, E., Corchado, J.M., Abraham, A. (eds.) Innovations in Hybrid Intelligent Systems. AISC, vol. 44, pp. 280–287. Springer, Heidelberg (2007)

9. Jensen, D., Feland, J., Bowe, M., Self, B.: A 6-hats based team formation strategy – development and comparison with an MBTI based approach. In: Proceedings of the ASEE Annual Conference (2000)

10. Michaelsen, L.K., Sweet, M., Parmelee, D.X.: Team-based learning – small group learning's next big step. In: New Directions for Teaching and Learning, vol. 103, no. 116. Wiley, Hoboken (2011)

11. Newman, D.R., Webb, B., Cochrane, C.: A content analysis method to measure critical thinking in face-to-face and computer supported group learning. Interpers. Comput. Technol. 3(2), 56–77 (1995)

12. Sancho-Thomas, P., Fuentes-Fernández, R., Fernández-Manjón, B.: Learning teamwork skills in university programming courses. Comput. Educ. 53(2), 517–531 (2009)

13. Slavin, R.E.: Cooperative Learning – Theory, Research, and Practice. Allyn and Bacon, Boston (1990)

14. Zimmermann, H.-J.: Fuzzy Set Theory — and its Applications. Springer, Dordrecht (1991)

R Ultimate Multilabel Dataset Repository

Francisco Charte[1(✉)], David Charte[1], Antonio Rivera[2], María José del Jesus[2], and Francisco Herrera[1]

[1] Department of Computer Science and Artificial Intelligence, University of Granada, Granada, Spain
{fcharte,herrera}@ugr.es, fdavidcl@correo.ugr.es
[2] Department of Computer Science, University of Jaén, Jaén, Spain
{arivera,mjjesus}@ujaen.es
http://sci2s.ugr.es, http://simidat.ujaen.es

Abstract. Multilabeled data is everywhere on the Internet. From news on digital media and entries published in blogs, to videos hosted in Youtube, every object is usually tagged with a set of labels. This way they can be categorized into several non-exclusive groups. However, publicly available multilabel datasets (MLDs) are not so common. There is a handful of websites providing a few of them, using disparate file formats. Finding proper MLDs, converting them into the correct format and locating the appropriate bibliographic data to cite them are some of the difficulties usually confronted by researchers and practitioners.

In this paper RUMDR (*R Ultimate Multilabel Dataset Repository*), a new multilabel dataset repository aimed to fuse all public MLDs, is introduced, along with mldr.datasets, an R package which eases the process of retrieving MLDs and their bibliographic information, exporting them to the desired file formats and partitioning them.

Keywords: Multilabel · Datasets · R · Software

1 Introduction

Multilabel classification (MLC) is a sort of machine learning technique characterized by the fact that each data sample is associated to a group of labels or tags. MLC is useful in many different fields, including protein classification [1], image labeling [2], tag suggestion [3], and text categorization [4]. Several dozens of multilabel datasets (MLDs) have been produced from these areas in late years, and some of them are publicly available in web repositories.

The research in MLC algorithms [5,6], as well as in preprocessing methods [7,8] has been extraordinary, with hundreds of proposals already published. These development efforts rely on the availability of MLDs in order to test their behavior and performance. In the initial stages, a decade ago, MLDs were not publicly available, so most authors produced them by themselves. Some of those MLDs are now sparsely hosted in several web repositories and disparate file formats, a situation that does not ease the work in new developments.

© Springer International Publishing Switzerland 2016
F. Martínez-Álvarez et al. (Eds.): HAIS 2016, LNAI 9648, pp. 487–499, 2016.
DOI: 10.1007/978-3-319-32034-2_41

In addition to the data itself, in the adequate format to work with it, the corresponding bibliographic information to properly give attribution to who produced the MLD is also needed. Sometimes finding this piece of data can be very time consuming. Also, to conduct empirical experiments the MLDs usually have to be partitioned, obtaining training and test folds. Therefore, new research attempts have to fulfill the process of locating the MLDs along with the bibliographic data, converting them to the desired format and partitioning them. Additional steps would be obtaining basic characterization metrics from these MLDs, determining how many labels they have, how frequent each label is, their complexity, etc.

Aiming to ease most of the steps in the described process, two new proposals are made on this paper:

- **RUMDR:** The *R Ultimate Multilabel Dataset Repository* is a GitHub[1] Repository that collects the MLDs publicly available and provides them under an unified file format.
- **mldr.datasets**: It is an R package that automates the use of RUMDR, providing functions to download the MLDs, recover their bibliographic information, export them to several file formats and partition them, among other tasks.

This paper is structured as follows. In Sect. 2 the previous works aimed to provide multilabel datasets repositories are enumerated and their main characteristics are shown. Section 3 describes the content of RUMDR, our ultimate multilabel dataset repository, and how it has been structured. How to use the mldr.datasets package to download MLDs, obtain information about them, partitioning and exporting them is the goal of Sect. 4. Lastly, some conclusions are provided in Sect. 5.

2   Related Work

Many early multilabel works produced original MLDs, and some authors published them in their own web page or other publicly accessible web sites, allowing third parties to use them. For instance, the datasets created by the authors of [3] are available at http://figshare.com/articles/Multilabel_datasets_from_Stack_Exchange_forums/1385315. Many of these MLDs were compiled, mainly by developers of MLC tools, giving rise to public repositories such as the following:

- **LibSVM:** This is a well-known library for Support Vector Machines (SVM) [9], and their authors maintain a repository with all kind of datasets, including binary, multiclass and multilabel[2] ones. The file format is similar to CSV (*Comma-Separated Values*), but with a sparse representation and locating the labels at the beginning of each row.

---

[1] http://GitHub.com.

[2] https://www.csie.ntu.edu.tw/~cjlin/libsvmtools/datasets/multilabel.html.

- **MEKA:** It is a multilabel software tool designed by Read [10] and founded on WEKA. Its associated repository[3] provides over 20 MLDs. The file format is ARFF, but with a special header that indicates how many attributes are labels. Those are always located at the beginning.
- **Mulan:** This is probably the leading multilabel software [11], including reference implementation for many of the published MLC algorithms. The Mulan repository[4] is also the largest one, with more than 25 MLDs available at this moment. The base file format is ARFF, but the labels can be any position since their names are supplied in a separate XML file.
- **KEEL:** It is a general purpose data mining software tool [12], similar to WEKA, and it also has an associated dataset repository[5] which includes some MLDs. The file format is also ARFF-based, but with specific header fields that indicate which attributes are labels.

As can be seen, the goal of each one of these repositories is to provide the MLDs in the correct file format for the tool they are interested in. To use the MLDs which are exclusively available in one of the repositories, for instance some of the Mulan datasets, with another tools, such as LibSVM, MEKA or KEEL, a previous conversion step is mandatory.

3   The R Ultimate Multilabel Dataset Repository

Although some specific multilabel software programs, such as Mulan, are actively used to work in new multilabel developments, none of them stand out for their ease of use as exploratory data analysis tools, or for their ability to be interactively used to develop algorithm prototypes. On the contrary, these are tasks in which the use of R [13] is prominent. Its large collection of packages makes data analysis and visualization easier, as well as the creation of proofs of concept for new methods.

Regarding the processing of multilabeled data, the main exploratory analysis tasks can be accomplished by means of the mldr package [14]. It only includes three typical MLDs (genbase, emotions and birds), but it is able to load any other MLD in Mulan and MEKA formats. We have used the functionality in mldr, along with some custom R code, to build RUMDR. This new repository holds all the publicly available MLDs, taken from the previously mentioned repositories and translated to a common format.

In this section the file format of RUMDR MLDs and the structure of the repository are detailed. Furthermore, the list of MLDs initially provided by RUMDR is also enumerated.

---

[3] http://sourceforge.net/projects/meka/files/Datasets/.

[4] http://mulan.sourceforge.net/datasets-mlc.html.

[5] http://sci2s.ugr.es/keel/multilabel.php.

3.1 RUMDR Structure and File Format

RUMDR is a multilabel dataset repository hosted at https://github.com/ fcharte/mldr.datasets. It is a public GitHub repository which also hosts the source code of the mldr.datasets package described in Sect. 4. The repository has two folders containing MLDs:

- **data:** It holds 10 small and medium sized MLDs, such as birds, emotions, genbase, medical and slashdot. They are among the most used in the literature.
- **additional-data:** It holds 52 additional MLDs. Some of them are subsets of bigger datasets, such as rcv1sub1 to rcv1sub5 which are five subsets of the well-known RCV1 text corpus from Reuters.

The purpose of grouping the MLDs into two different sets is to ease the functionality of the mldr.datasets package, as will be further explained. All the files stored into these two folders have the same file format. They are standard .rda[6] R files, thus can be loaded into the current workspace by simply typing load('filename.rda') at the R console. This would get into memory an R object with the same name but without the .rda extension.

Once the object is in memory, it can be queried to access the data it contains through the syntax object$dataset. In addition, information about the labels, labelsets and other metrics can be obtained by querying object$labels, object$labelsets and object$measures, respectively.

3.2 Datasets in RUMDR

At launch time RUMDR holds more than forty distinct MLDs, including several subsets of large datasets and also some pre-partitioned datasets. They sum 62 individual .rda files in total. 41 of them originate from the text field, 15 more from the image field, 3 from the sound/music field, 2 from the protein/genetics area, and the last one from the video field. The name of each one, the number of individual objects, where they come from and the folder where they are stored within the repository are shown in Table 1.

Most cases consist in only one MLD, but there are some special situations. These must be detailed to be able to use them:

- **corel16k:** These MLDs, there are 10 in total with names from corel16k001 to corel16k010, are subsets of the Corel image database [29]. Each one holds almost 14 000 instances and the same set of input features, but there are slight differences in the sets of labels.
- **EUR-Lex:** There are six files in this set, named eurlexdc_tra, eurlexdc_test, eurlexev_tra, eurlexev_test, eurlexsm_tra and eurlexsm_test. They correspond to the train and test partitions of the directory codes (dc), EUROVOC descriptors (ev), and subject matters (sm) of the EUR-Lex dataset [19]. Each object consist in a list of 10 folds.

---

[6] This is a compressed file format of the representation of R objects in memory.

Table 1. MLDs initially included in RUMDR

Field	Name	# MLDs	Reference	Folder
Text	20ng	1	[15]	data
	bibtex	1	[16]	additional-data
	bookmarks	1	[16]	additional-data
	delicious	1	[17]	additional-data
	enron	1	[18]	additional-data
	EUR-Lex	6	[19]	additional-data
	imdb	1	[20]	additional-data
	langlog	1	[21]	data
	medical	1	[22]	data
	ohsumed	1	[23]	additiona-data
	rcv1v2	5	[4]	additional-data
	reuters	1	[21]	additional-data
	slashdot	1	[20]	data
	stackexchange	6	[3]	data & additional-data
	tmc2007	2	[24]	additional-data
	yahoo	11	[25]	additional-data
Sound/music	birds	1	[26]	data
	cal500	1	[27]	data
	emotions	1	[28]	data
Image	corel16k	10	[29]	additional-data
	corel5k	1	[30]	additional-data
	flags	1	[31]	data
	nus-wide	2	[2]	additional-data
	scene	1	[32]	additional-data
Video	mediamill	1	[33]	additional-data
Protein/genetics	genbase	1	[34]	data
	yeast	1	[1]	additional-data

- **nus-wide:** The original NUS-WIDE dataset [2] used a set of 500 input features to represent each image. An alternative version, with 128 input features, is also available. The former is accessible as nuswide_BoW, while the latter is named nuswide_VLAD.
- **rcv1v2** and **reuters:** The Reuters corpus, best known as RCV1-v2 (*Reuters Corpus Volume 1 version 2*) [4], is a large text corpus generated from news published by Reuters. The .rda files rcv1sub1 to rcv1sub5 consist in five MLDs which are subsets of RCV1-v2, containing 6 000 instances each one of them while preserving all the input features. The reuters MLD [21] is a reduced version with only 500 input features.

- **stackexchange:** It is a collection of six MLDs generated from text collected in a selection of Stack Exchange forums [3]. The individual files are stackex_chess, stackex_chemistry, stackex_coffee, stackex_cooking, stackex_cs and stackex_philosophy.
- **yahoo:** As the previous case, this also consists of a collection of MLDs. They were produced from text extracted from the web, specifically from the Yahoo! web directory. There are a total of 11 MLDs, named yahoo_arts, yahoo_business, yahoo_computers, yahoo_education, yahoo_entertainment, yahoo_health, yahoo_recreation, yahoo_reference, yahoo_science, yahoo_social and yahoo_society.

4   The mldr.datasets Package

Although RUMDR is valuable by itself, as an unified multilabel repository from where almost all available MLDs can be download in a common file format, we aimed to increase its usefulness by pairing it with a specific software package. This is an R package named mldr.datasets, and it is already available on CRAN (*The Comprehensive R Archive Network*). Therefore, it can be installed from the R command line by simply typing `install.packages('mldr.datasets')`, then loaded into memory with `library(mldr.datasets)`.

Once loaded, the ten MLDs hosted in the data folder of RUMDR will be immediately available as they are embedded into the package. This means that queries such as `emotions$measures`, `genbase$labels` or `flags$labelsets` can be entered to get general information about emotions, label information from genbase and data related to the labelsets in flags. The list of the remainder datasets, those that can be downloaded at any time, is retrieved with the `mldrs()` function. This returns a table as the shown in Fig. 1.

To load any of the additional MLDs, those that are not embedded into the package, there are two alternatives. The first one is calling the function that shares the same name that the desired MLD, for instance `bibtex()`, `corel5k()` or `scene()`. The second way consists in using the function `check_n_load.mldr()`, providing as argument the name of the MLD. Assuming that a new MLD called **newmld** existed at RUMDR, entering `check_n_load.mldr('newmld')` in the R command line would download and install it in our system. Either way, regardless of the function used, firstly whether the needed MLD is locally available will be checked. If so, it is simply loaded into memory. Otherwise, the corresponding file is downloaded from RUMDR, copied to the local installation of mldr.datasets, and then loaded.

The MLDs in memory are R objects with class `mldr`, and the mldr.datasets package includes several functions to deal with this type of objects, easing the process of obtaining bibliographic information, partitioning them and exporting them. They are explained below.

	X	Name	Description	Instances	Attributes	Labels
1	1	bibtex	Dataset with BibTeX entries	7395	1836	159
2	2	bookmarks	Dataset with data from web bookmarks and their ca>	87856	2100	208
3	3	corel16k001	Datasets with data from the Corel image collectio>	13766	500	153
4	4	corel16k002	Datasets with data from the Corel image collectio>	13761	500	164
5	5	corel16k003	Datasets with data from the Corel image collectio>	13760	500	154
6	6	corel16k004	Datasets with data from the Corel image collectio>	13837	500	162
7	7	corel16k005	Datasets with data from the Corel image collectio>	13847	500	160
8	8	corel16k006	Datasets with data from the Corel image collectio>	13859	500	162
9	9	corel16k007	Datasets with data from the Corel image collectio>	13915	500	174
10	10	corel16k008	Datasets with data from the Corel image collectio>	13864	500	168
11	11	corel16k009	Datasets with data from the Corel image collectio>	13884	500	173
12	12	corel16k010	Datasets with data from the Corel image collectio>	13618	500	144
13	13	corel5k	Dataset with data from the Corel image collection	5000	499	374
14	14	delicious	Dataset generated from the del.icio.\ site bookm>	16105	500	983
15	15	enron	Dataset with email messages and the folders where>	1702	1001	53
16	16	eurlexdc_test	List with 10 folds of the test data from the EUR>	1935	5000	412
17	17	eurlexdc_tra	List with 10 folds of the train data from the EU>	17413	5000	412
18	18	eurlexev_test	List with 10 folds of the test data from the EUR>	1935	5000	3993
19	19	eurlexev_tra	List with 10 folds of the train data from the EU>	17413	5000	3993

Fig. 1. List of additional mldrs.

4.1 Obtaining BibTeX Entries

All MLDs hosted in RUMDR hold bibliographic information, specifically BibTeX
entries that can be used while writing new works with LaTeX. The entry associated to an MLD can be retrieved by means of the generic function toBibtex(),
delivering the mldr object as parameter. The raw entry can be copied to the
clipboard or displayed in the R console, as shown in Fig. 2.

```
Console D:/FCharte/Estudios/mldr/mldr/
>
> toBibtex(emotions)
[1] "@incollection{,\n  title = \"Multi-Label Classification of Emotions in Music\",\n  a
uthor = \"Wieczorkowska, A. and Synak, P. and Ra'{s}, Z.\",\n  booktitle = \"Intelligent
Information Processing and Web Mining\",\n  year = \"2006\",\n  volume = \"35\",\n  chapt
er = \"30\",\n  pages = \"307--315\"\n}"
>
> cat(toBibtex(genbase))
@inproceedings{,
    title = "Protein Classification with Multiple Algorithms",
    author = "Diplaris, S. and Tsoumakas, G. and Mitkas, P. and Vlahavas, I.",
    booktitle = "Proc. 10th Panhellenic Conference on Informatics, Volos, Greece, PCI05",
    year = "2005",
    pages = "448--456"
}
>
```

Fig. 2. Obtaining bibliographic information from MLDs.

The BibTeX entries of all MLDs in RUMDR are also available in the
README[7] file stored in the additional-data folder of the repository.

---

[7] https://github.com/fcharte/mldr.datasets/blob/master/additional-data/
README.md.

4.2   Theoretical Complexity Score

All mldr objects have a member called **measures** containing disparate characterization metrics, such as the number of instances, attributes and labels, imbalance
levels, etc. mldr.datasets adds a data item to this member, named **tcs**, with the
value of a metric introduced in [35], TCS (*Theoretical Complexity Score*). It
is computed as shown in (1), f being the number of input features and k the
number of labels of the dataset D.

$$TCS(D) = \log(f \times k \times |unique\ labelsets|) \tag{1}$$

The goal of this new metric is to give a glimpse of how hard would be for
a classifier to learn from each MLD. Theoretically, the bigger the input and
output spaces are, the more complex the generated model will be, making it more
difficult to properly adjust. The number of different combinations of labelsets is
also a factor to be considered while working in the multilabel field.

Relying on the precalculated TCS values of the MLDs, it is easy to sort them
according to their theoretical complexity, as shown in Fig. 3. This information
can be useful to chose the MLDs to be used in a new experimentation.

```
Console D:/FCharte/Estudios/mldr/mldr/
>
> as.matrix(sort(sapply(data(package = "mldr.datasets")$result[,3], function(mld) get(mld
)$measures$tcs)))
                    [,1]
flags           8.879333
emotions        9.364262
scene          10.183389
birds          13.395470
genbase        13.839914
ng20           13.916803
slashdot       15.124688
cal500         15.597163
medical        15.628586
langlog        16.946263
stackex_chess  18.779425
>
```

Fig. 3. Embedded MLDs in mldr.datasets sorted according to their TCS value.

4.3   Partitioning MLDs

With few exceptions, such as the MLDs generated from the EUR-Lex datasets,
all files available in RUMDR contain full datasets. Prior to their usage in any
experiment they have to be partitioned, obtaining training and test partitions
with subsets of the instances they contain. The mldr.datasets package provides
two functions to accomplish this task:

- **random.kfolds()**: Randomly samples the instances in the dataset until the
  desired number of folds is produced.

- `stratified.kfolds()`: It was introduced in [35]. First groups the instances into strata attending to the frequency of the labels appearing in them, then each strata is randomly sampled to divide it into the number of desired folds. This way the distribution of rare samples among the folds results more balanced.

Both functions take as input the same parameters, the MLD to be partitioned, the number of folds and the seed for the random generator. The last two arguments have default values, 5 for the number of folds and 10 as seed. The obtained result is a list with as many items as folds the user asked for. Each item consists of a `train` and a `test` element, both mldr objects that can be used in the same way as the full MLD. The example shown in Fig. 4 demonstrates the use of both functions.

```
Console D:/FCharte/Estudios/mldr/mldr/

>
> emotions.folds <- random.kfolds(emotions)
> summary(emotions.folds[[1]]$train)
  num.attributes num.instances num.inputs num.labels num.labelsets num.single.labelsets
1             78           474         72          6            25                      2
  max.frequency cardinality   density   meanIR    scumble scumble.cv      tcs
1            65    1.848101 0.3080169 1.488775 0.01166691   1.359773 9.287301
>
> emotions.folds <- stratified.kfolds(emotions, k = 10)
> summary(emotions.folds[[4]]$test)
  num.attributes num.instances num.inputs num.labels num.labelsets num.single.labelsets
1             78            60         72          6            14                      2
  max.frequency cardinality   density   meanIR    scumble scumble.cv      tcs
1             9    1.883333 0.3138889 1.555556 0.01600574   1.029966 8.707483
>
>
```

Fig. 4. Partitioning the emotions MLD randomly and stratifiedly

4.4 Exporting MLDs to Other File Formats

Even though R is an environment from which the MLDs can be explored, analyzed and given as input to different preprocessing and learning algorithms, it could be interesting to use them with other software tools, such as the aforementioned Mulan, MEKA, etc. This is a task that the mldr.datasets package considerably simplifies through the `write.mldr()` function. It is able to export any MLD to Mulan, MEKA, KEEL, LibSVM and CSV formats, using dense or sparse representation in the first three cases.

An invocation to `write.mldr()` needs at least one parameter, but it can take three additional ones. The names and goal of each parameter are the following:

- `mld`: It can be an mldr object or the result returned by the `random.kfolds()` and `stratified.kfolds()` functions. In the latter case write operation is performed for each training and test partition.

- `format`: This parameter can be a string or a vector of strings, stating the formats the MLD have to be exported to. The valid values are 'MULAN', 'MEKA', 'KEEL', 'LIBSVM' and 'CSV'. By default c('MULAN', 'MEKA') is used. That means that the MLD will be written in these two formats.
- `sparse`: It is applicable only with Mulan, MEKA and KEEL file formats, all of them based on the WEKA ARFF format. By default it gets the `FALSE` value, thus dense representation of features is used. Assigning it the `TRUE` value a disperse representation will be used.
- `basename`: One call to `write.mldr()` can create several files. The Mulan format produces one .arff and one .xml file. The CSV format generates two, one with the data and another one with the labels. In addition, if a partitioned datasets is given as input two files, one for test and one for training, will be written for each partition. With this parameter the base name for all these files is established. By default, mldr.datasets looks for a `name` member in the mldr object. If it is present, it is used as basename; otherwise the value 'unnamed_mldr' is used.

A single call as the shown below will partition the given MLD into 10 subsets and write it in the five file formats supported by the package, generating 120 files in total:

```
write.mldr(stratified.kfolds(emotions, k = 10),
    format = c('MULAN', 'MEKA', 'KEEL', 'LIBSVM', 'CSV'),
    basename = 'emotions')
```

5   Conclusions

The process of analyzing, researching and putting into practice new multilabel solutions demands the availability of enough datasets, in the proper format and with the corresponding bibliographic information. Additional data about its structure and complexity are also quite useful. The automation of these MLDs manipulation tasks is the goal of RUMDR and the associated mldr.datasets R package.

RUMDR is a new repository in which almost all publicly available multilabel datasets have been collected, being stored in a common file format. The mldr.datasets package is a software tool that eases the loading of these MLDs from R, as well as the retrieval of metrics and bibliographic information and the partitioning and exporting to several file formats.

The main goal behind the development of RUMDR and mldr.datasets has been to make easier the work of researchers and practitioners interested in multilabeled data. The repository will be maintained by incorporating new MLDs that may be published in the future.

Acknowledgments. This work was partially supported by the Spanish Ministry of Science and Technology under projects TIN2014-57251-P and TIN2012-33856, and the Andalusian regional projects P10-TIC-06858 and P11-TIC-7765.

References

1. Elisseeff, A., Weston, J.: A kernel method for multi-labelled classification. In: Advances in Neural Information Processing Systems 14, vol. 14, pp. 681–687. MIT Press (2001)
2. Chua, T.-S., Tang, J., Hong, R., Li, H., Luo, Z., Zheng, Y.: NUS-WIDE: a real-world web image database from National University of Singapore. In: Proceedings of the ACM International Conference on Image and Video Retrieval, p. 48. ACM (2009)
3. Charte, F., Rivera, A.J., del Jesus, M.J., Herrera, F.: QUINTA: a questiontagging assistant to improve the answering ratio in electronic forums. In: EUROCON 2015 - International Conference on Computer as a Tool (EUROCON), pp. 1–6. IEEE (2015). doi:10.1109/EUROCON.2015.7313677
4. Lewis, D.D., Yang, Y., Rose, T.G., Li, F.: RCV1: a new benchmark collection for text categorization research. J. Mach. Learn. Res. 5, 361–397 (2004)
5. Gibaja, E., Ventura, S.: Multi-label learning: a review of the state of the art and ongoing research. Wiley Interdisc. Rev. Data Min. Knowl. Discov. 4(6), 411–444 (2014). doi:10.1002/widm.1139
6. Zhang, M., Zhou, Z.: A review on multi-label learning algorithms. IEEE Trans. Knowl. Data Eng. 26(8), 1819–1837 (2014). doi:10.1109/TKDE.2013.39
7. Charte, F., Rivera, A.J., del Jesus, M.J., Herrera, F.: Addressing imbalance in multilabel classification: measures and random resampling algorithms. Neurocomputing 163, 3–16 (2015). doi:10.1016/j.neucom.2014.08.091
8. Charte, F., Rivera, A.J., del Jesus, M.J., Herrera, F.: MLSMOTE: approaching imbalanced multilabel learning through synthetic instance generation. Know. Based Syst. 89, 385–397 (2015). doi:10.1016/j.knosys.2015.07.019
9. Chang, C.-C., Lin, C.-J.: Libsvm: a library for support vector machines. ACM Trans. Intell. Syst. Technol. 2(3), 27:1–27:27 (2011). doi:10.1145/1961189.1961199
10. Read, J., Reutemann, P.: MEKA multi-label dataset repository. http://meka.sourceforge.net/#datasets
11. Tsoumakas, G., Xioufis, E.S., Vilcek, J., Vlahavas, I.: MULAN: a Java library for multi-label learning. J. Mach. Learn. Res. 12, 2411–2414 (2011)
12. Alcala-Fdez, J., Fernández, A., Luengo, J., Derrac, J., García, S., Sánchez, L., Herrera, F.: Keel data-mining software tool: data set repository and integration of algorithms and experimental analysis framework. J. Multiple-Valued Logic Soft Comput. 17(2–3), 255–287 (2011)
13. R Core Team, R: A Language and Environmentfor Statistical Computing, R Foundation for Statistical Computing, Vienna, Austria (2014). http://www.R-project.org/
14. Charte, F., Charte, D.: Working with multilabel datasets in R: the mldr package. R J. 7(2), 149–162 (2015)
15. Lang, K.: Newsweeder: Learning to filter netnews. In: Proceedings of the 12th International Conference on Machine Learning, pp. 331–339 (1995)
16. Katakis, I., Tsoumakas, G., Vlahavas, I.: Multilabel text classifcation for automatedtag suggestion. In: Proceedings of the ECML PKDD 2008 Discovery Challenge, Antwerp, Belgium, pp. 75–83 (2008)
17. Tsoumakas, G., Katakis, I., Vlahavas, I.: Effective and effcient multilabel classiffcationin domains with large number of labels. In: Proceedings of the ECML/PKDD Workshop on Mining Multidimensional Data, MMD 2008, Antwerp, Belgium, pp. 30–44 (2008)

18. Klimt, B., Yang, Y.: The enron corpus: a new dataset for email classification research. In: Boulicaut, J.-F., Esposito, F., Giannotti, F., Pedreschi, D. (eds.) ECML 2004. LNCS (LNAI), vol. 3201, pp. 217–226. Springer, Heidelberg (2004). doi:10.1007/978-3-540-30115-8_22

19. Loza Mencía, E., Fürnkranz, J.: Efficient pairwise multilabel classification for large-scale problems in the legal domain. In: Daelemans, W., Goethals, B., Morik, K. (eds.) ECML PKDD 2008, Part II. LNCS (LNAI), vol. 5212, pp. 50–65. Springer, Heidelberg (2008)

20. Read, J., Pfahringer, B., Holmes, G., Frank, E.: Classifier chains for multi-label classification. Mach. Learn. **85**, 333–359 (2011). doi:10.1007/s10994-011-5256-5

21. Read, J.: Scalable multi-label classification. Ph.D. thesis, University of Waikato (2010)

22. Crammer, K., Dredze, M., Ganchev, K., Talukdar, P.P., Carroll, S.: Automatic code assignment to medical text. In: Proceeding of the Workshop on Biological, Translational, and Clinical Language Processing, BioNLP 2007, Prague, Czech Republic, pp. 129–136 (2007)

23. Joachims, T.: Text categorization with suport vector machines: learning with many relevant features. In: Nédellec, C., Rouveirol, C. (eds.) ECML 1998. LNCS, vol. 1398, pp. 137–142. Springer, Heidelberg (1998)

24. Srivastava, A.N., Zane-Ulman, B.: Discovering recurring anomalies in text reports regarding complex space systems. In: IEEE Aerospace Conference, pp. 3853–3862 (2005). doi:10.1109/AERO.2005.1559692

25. Ueda, N., Saito, K.: Parametric mixture models for multi-labeled text. In: Advances in Neural Information Processing Systems, pp. 721–728 (2002)

26. Briggs, F., Lakshminarayanan, B., Neal, L., Fern, X.Z., Raich, R., Hadley, S.J.K., Hadley, A.S., Betts, M.G.: Acoustic classification of multiple simultaneous bird species: a multi-instance multi-label approach. J. Acoust. Soc. Am. **131**(6), 4640–4650 (2012)

27. Turnbull, D., Barrington, L., Torres, D., Lanckriet, G.: Semantic annotation and retrieval of music and sound effects. IEEE Audio Speech Lang. Process. **16**(2), 467–476 (2008). doi:10.1109/TASL.2007.913750

28. Wieczorkowska, A., Synak, P., Raś, Z.: Multi-label classification of emotions in music. In: Klopotek, M.A., Wierzchori, S.T., Trojanowski, K. (eds.) Intelligent Information Processing and Web Mining. ASC, pp. 307–315. Springer, Heidelberg (2006). doi:10.1007/3-540-33521-8_30

29. Barnard, K., Duygulu, P., Forsyth, D., de Freitas, N., Blei, D.M., Jordan, M.I.: Matching words and pictures. J. Mach. Learn. Res. **3**, 1107–1135 (2003)

30. Duygulu, P., Barnard, K., de Freitas, J.F.G., Forsyth, D.: Object recognition as machine translation: learning a lexicon for a fixed image vocabulary. In: Heyden, A., Sparr, G., Nielsen, M., Johansen, P. (eds.) ECCV 2002, Part IV. LNCS, vol. 2353, pp. 97–112. Springer, Heidelberg (2002). doi:10.1007/3-540-47979-1_7

31. Gonçalves, E.C., Plastino, A., Freitas, A.A.: A genetic algorithm for optimizing the label ordering in multi-label classifier chains. In: Proceedings of the 25th IEEE International Conference on Tools with Artificial Intelligence (ICTAI 2013), pp. 469–476 (2013)

32. Boutell, M., Luo, J., Shen, X., Brown, C.: Learning multi-label scene classification. Pattern Recogn. **37**(9), 1757–1771 (2004). doi:10.1016/j.patcog.2004.03.009

33. Snoek, C.G.M., Worring, M., van Gemert, J.C., Geusebroek, J.M., Smeulders, A.W.M.: The challenge problem for automated detection of 101 semantic concepts in multimedia. In: Proceedings of the 14th Annual ACM International Conference on Multimedia, MULTIMEDIA 2006, Santa Barbara, CA, USA, pp. 421–430 (2006). doi:10.1145/1180639.1180727

34. Diplaris, S., Tsoumakas, G., Mitkas, P.A., Vlahavas, I.P.: Protein classification with multiple algorithms. In: Bozanis, P., Houstis, E.N. (eds.) PCI 2005. LNCS, vol. 3746, pp. 448–456. Springer, Heidelberg (2005). doi:10.1007/11573036_42

35. Charte, F., Rivera, A., del Jesus, M.J., Herrera, F.: On the impact of dataset complexity and sampling strategy in multilabel classifiers performance. In: Martínez-Álvarez, F., Troncoso, A., Quintián, H., Corchado, E. (eds.) HAIS 2016. LNCS (LNAI), vol. 9648, pp. 500–511. Springer, Switzerland (2016)

On the Impact of Dataset Complexity and Sampling Strategy in Multilabel Classifiers Performance

Francisco Charte[1]([⊠]), Antonio Rivera[2], María José del Jesus[2], and Francisco Herrera[1]

[1] Department of Computer Science and Artificial Intelligence, University of Granada, Granada, Spain
{fcharte,herrera}@ugr.es
[2] Department of Computer Science, University of Jaén, Jaén, Spain
{arivera,mjjesus}@ujaen.es
http://sci2s.ugr.es, http://simidat.ujaen.es

Abstract. Multilabel classification (MLC) is an increasingly widespread data mining technique. Its goal is to categorize patterns in several non-exclusive groups, and it is applied in fields such as news categorization, image labeling and music classification. Comparatively speaking, MLC is a more complex task than multiclass and binary classification, since the classifier must learn the presence of various outputs at once from the same set of predictive variables. The own nature of the data the classifier has to deal with implies a certain complexity degree. How to measure this complexness level strictly from the data characteristics would be an interesting objective. At the same time, the strategy used to partition the data also influences the sample patterns the algorithm has at its disposal to train the classifier. In MLC random sampling is commonly used to accomplish this task.

This paper introduces TCS (*Theoretical Complexity Score*), a new characterization metric aimed to assess the intrinsic complexity of a multilabel dataset, as well as a novel stratified sampling method specifically designed to fit the traits of multilabeled data. A detailed description of both proposals is provided, along with empirical results of their suitability for their respective duties.

Keywords: Multilabel classification · Complexity · Metrics · Partitioning

1 Introduction

Unlike multiclass and binary classification, where the classifier has to predict only one output, multilabel classification (MLC) must learn the associations between the patterns' features and several outputs at once. Each output indicates if a certain label is relevant to the data sample or not, thus the algorithms have to work with a set of binary predictions. Nowadays MLC is being applied to

© Springer International Publishing Switzerland 2016
F. Martínez-Álvarez et al. (Eds.): HAIS 2016, LNAI 9648, pp. 500–511, 2016.
DOI: 10.1007/978-3-319-32034-2_42

automate tag suggestion [1], categorize text documents [2], label incoming images [3], etc. A introduction to MLC and a recent review on MLC techniques and related topics can be found in [4,5], respectively.

Most of the aforementioned tasks involve working with large multilabel datasets (MLDs) having disparate numbers of input features, instances, labels, combinations of labels, etc. Undoubtedly some of these traits, such as the number of instances, determine at some extent the time necessary to train a classifier. Beyond this fact, it would be desirable to know in advance the difficulties a certain MLD can present and how its complexity can affect the classifier performance.

A second circumstance which potentially affects MLC algorithms performance is the way MLDs have been partitioned. There are MLDs containing only a few samples, sometimes only one, as representatives of rare labels. Random sampling, which is the mainstream strategy used in the multilabel field, can throw these few samples all on either the training or the test partition. Both cases will probably decrease the performance of the classifier.

The main aim of this paper is to study how the complexity of MLDs and the sampling strategy impacts classification results. For doing so, two proposals are introduced:

- A new characterization metric, called TCS (*Theoretical Complexity Score*), will allow to know the complexity of an MLD in advance, prior to use it to train a classifier. It is computed from the basic MLD traits.
- A novel stratified sampling method for partitioning datasets, aiming to improve label distribution among training and test partitions, thus providing the classifier a fairer representation of each label. It is built upon an stratification strategy, grouping instances containing labels with similar frequencies.

This paper is structured as follows. Section 2 explains how different complexity factors influence classification results and introduces the TCS metric. In Sect. 3 the problems of random sampling are described, and a new stratified sampling method is presented. The suitability of these two proposals is experimentally tested in Sect. 4. Lastly, in Sect. 5 some conclusions are drawn.

2   Assessing a Multilabel Dataset Complexity

Data complexity [6] is an intensively studied aspect in different fields, including classification. How to measure it and its influence in specific problems, such as imbalanced [7] learning and noise filtering [8], have been already faced in traditional classification. Regarding MLC, some studies related to imbalance [9] measurement and other complexity facts, such as the concurrence among frequent and infrequent labels [10], have been also published.

The interest here is to determine an intrinsic and easily interpretable complexity metric for MLDs. In this context, complexity has to be understood as the set of traits of the MLD that will make the learned model both more ineffective and inefficient.

2.1   Factors Influencing the Complexity of MLDs

In order to design such a metric firstly the main traits of any MLD and its implications in learning a MLC model have to be analyzed. The considered factors are the following:

- **Number of data instances:** The number of rows in an MLD determine the amount of available patterns to train and then test any model. While it is true that a larger quantity of data samples also implies more time devoted to training, having more instances does not necessarily means that the resulting model will be more complex. In fact, training a classifier with enough representative patterns is usually associated to a better performance.
- **Number of input features:** In machine learning the curse of dimensionality [11] is a very well-known problem. As the number of input features growths, so does the dimensions of the space where the patterns are located. Working in a high-dimensional space makes more difficult tasks such as measuring distances among patterns and finding analytical solutions. Most MLDs have a large number of features, thus it is a factor to be taken into account.
- **Number of labels:** In traditional classification the algorithms only have one output to learn, whether it is binary or multiclass. By contrast, MLDs have hundreds or thousands of labels. The larger is the number of labels the more complex would be the model to generate. There are many MLC methods based on binarization techniques [12–15], and the number of labels has a direct impact in both the time used to train each binary classifier and the complexity of the overall algorithm. This, no doubt, is another factor to consider.
- **Number of labelsets:** The labels in an MLD appear producing different combinations, usually known as labelsets. The number of distinct labelsets is another aspect to bear in mind, since there are many MLC methods [16–19] based on training multiclass classifiers using the labelsets as class identifiers. Some of them produce simpler subsets of labels through pruning, random combinations and clustering approaches. In general, the larger is the amount of different combinations the more complex will be the final solution.

2.2   Theoretical Complexity Score

Building on the premises just enumerated, the proposed TCS metric is computed as indicated in (1). Let f be the number of input features, k the number of labels and ls the number of distinct labelsets. The logarithm of the product of these three factors will provide a theoretical complexity score, based only on the basic traits of the MLD[1] and easier to interpret than the raw product.

$$TCS(D) = \log(f \times k \times ls) \tag{1}$$

---

[1] In practice there would be other factors also influencing the classifiers performance, such as data sparseness, imbalance levels, concurrence among rare and frequent labels, etc.

The main goals in defining this metric, in addition to assess the complexity of an MLD, were ease of computation and interpretation, providing a straightforward measurement.

If there were an extremely simple MLD, having only one input attribute, two labels (on the contrary it would not be multilabel), and four different labelsets (the number of combinations two labels can produce), its TCS value would be $\log(1 \times 2 \times 4) \approx 2$. Table 1 shows the number of attributes, labels, labelsets and TCS for twenty MLDs commonly used on the literature, ordered according to their TCS value. As can be seen emotions and scene, two of the most popular MLDs, are the simplest ones. The two MLDs from genetics/proteins field, genbase and yeast, are more complex. Multimedia datasets, such as mediamill and corel5k, are located at the middle of the table. Some of the MLDs coming from text media, such as delicious, bookmarks, EURLex, etc., appear as the most complex ones.

Table 1. MLDs ordered according to their theoretical complexity score

Dataset	TCS	Attributes	Labels	Labelsets
emotions	9.364	72	6	27
scene	10.183	294	6	15
yeast	12.562	103	14	198
genbase	13.840	1 186	27	32
cal500	15.597	68	174	502
medical	15.629	1 449	45	94
enron	17.503	1 001	53	753
reuters	17.548	500	103	811
mediamill	18.191	120	101	6 555
corel16k001	19.722	500	153	4 803
corel5k	20.200	499	374	3 175
stackex-cs	20.532	635	274	4 749
bibtex	20.541	1 836	159	2 856
tmc2007	21.093	49 060	22	1 341
eurlex-sm	21.646	5 000	201	2 504
eurlex-dc	21.925	5 000	412	1 615
rcv1subset1	22.313	47 236	101	1 028
delicious	22.773	500	983	15 806
bookmarks	22.848	2 150	208	18 716
eurlex-ev	26.519	5 000	3 993	16 467

3   Sampling Multilabel Datasets

Almost all studies and proposals in the multilabel field imply some classification experimentation. Hold out, 2×5 and 10 folds cross validation are among the most common schemes, always with the same strategy to chose the patterns included in train and test partitions, random sampling. Despite the fact that some other sampling strategies [20] have been described for some time, the random approach is still the most used option.

Random sampling does a good work in selecting training and test patterns when most labels have enough representation in the MLD. However, sometimes it could be a risky strategy. That some labels have only one or two patterns representing them in the MLD is quite usual. Random sampling can place all of them either in the training or the test partition. To avoid this problem a stratified sampling approach can be used.

3.1   Stratified Sampling of MLDs

Stratified sampling is a usual technique in cross validation [21] for traditional classification. Since only one class is assigned to each instance, it is possible to compute the distribution of each class in the whole dataset and then draw the equivalent proportion of samples for training and testing. On the contrary, samples in an MLD are associated to several labels at once. If one instance is chosen for the train partition because it holds a certain label, it must be taken into account that some other labels are also included in the operation since they jointly appear with the selected one.

In [20] a stratified iterative method for sampling MLDs is proposed. It goes label by label through the MLDs, choosing individual samples and updating a set of counters. Due to its iterative nature it is a slow method when compared with random sampling, specially with MLDs having thousands of labels. Nonetheless, the authors stated that it was able to improve the classifier performance while dealing with some MLDs.

3.2   Stratified Random Sampling Method

The method outlined in Algorithm 1 is a new proposal to partition MLDs. It follows a stratified random sampling approach, but unlike the one in [20] it is not iterative by label.

In line 3 a weight is computed for each instance in the MLD. It is obtained as the product of the relative frequencies of active labels in the data sample. If one or more rare labels appear in it, the score will be very low. On the contrary, the occurrence of one or more common labels will produce a higher value. The number of active labels also influences this score. The larger is the set of labels in the instance the lower will be the score. The goal is to group instances with a similar label distribution relying in a simple procedure.

Once the instances have been ordered according to their weight (line 5), they are divided into as many strata as folds have been requested. Each training

---

Algorithm 1. Partitioning method based on stratified random sampling

---

1: **function** STRATIFIED.KFOLDS(MLD D, Integer $nfolds$)
2:    **for each** *instance i* **in** D **do**
3:        $D_{i_w} \leftarrow \prod freq(l \in D_i)$ ▷ Weight for each instance
4:    **end for**
5:    $D \leftarrow$ SortBy(D_w)   ▷ Sort instances according to their weight
6:    ▷ Group samples with similar weight in separate strata
7:    **for** $i = 1$ **to** $nfolds$ **do**
8:        $strata_i \leftarrow D_{|D|/nfolds*(i-1)} - D_{|D|/nfolds*i}$
9:    **end for**
10:   **for** $i = 1$ **to** $nfolds$ **do**   ▷ Generate nfolds folds
11:       **for** $j = 1$ **to** $nfolds$ **do**   ▷ Taking part of the samples in each stratum
12:           $trainfold_i \Leftarrow$ drawRandomly($strata_j, |D|/nfolds \times (nfolds - 1)$)
13:           $testfold_i \Leftarrow strata_j - trainfold_j$ ▷ Remainder samples in stratum
14:       **end for**
15:   **end for**
16:   **return** ($trainfold, testfold$)
17: **end function**

---

partition gets a portion of each stratum proportional to the number of samples in D and the number of folds. The remainder samples in the stratum are given to the test partition. The samples in each stratum are randomly picked.

4   Experimentation

Aiming to validate the usefulness of the two proposals made in the previous sections, five MLDs with diverse TCS values have been selected from Table 1. Those are emotions, yeast, enron, stackex-cs and delicious. All of them can be downloaded from the R Ultimate Multilabel Dataset Repository [22], and they can be partitioned randomly or using the stratified strategy described in Sect. 3 by means of the mldr.datasets[2] R package.

The datasets were partitioned using 10 fcv, once randomly and once with stratified random sampling. These partitions were given as input to tree multilabel classifiers, one based on binarization (BR [12]), one based on label combinations (LP [16]), and one on lazy learning adapted to multilabel data (ML-kNN [23]). From the results produced by the classifiers three general performance metrics, Accuracy (2), Precision (3) and Recall (4) have been computed to analyze the meaningfulness of the TCS metric. Another two more specific metrics, MacroPrecision and MacroRecall, have been obtained to compare the two sampling strategies. The macro-averaging strategy (5) allows the calculation of any standard performance metric label by label, then averaging to obtain the final measure. In these equations n is the number of instances in the MLD, Y_i the real labelset associated to i-th instance, Z_i the predicted one, k the number of

---

[2] https://cran.r-project.org/web/packages/mldr.datasets/index.html.

labels in $\mathcal{L}$, and TP, FP, TN and FN stand for *True Positives*, *False Positives*, *True Negatives* and *False Negatives*, respectively.

$$Accuracy = \frac{1}{n} \sum_{i=1}^{n} \frac{|Y_i \cap Z_i|}{|Y_i \cup Z_i|} \tag{2}$$

$$Precision = \frac{1}{n} \sum_{i=1}^{n} \frac{|Y_i \cap Z_i|}{|Z_i|} \tag{3}$$

$$Recall = \frac{1}{n} \sum_{i=1}^{n} \frac{|Y_i \cap Z_i|}{|Y_i|} \tag{4}$$

$$MacroMet = \frac{1}{k} \sum_{l \in \mathcal{L}} EvalMet(TP_l, FP_l, TN_l, FN_l) \tag{5}$$

4.1   Influence of Complexity in Classifier Performance

To analyze how the intrinsic complexity of each MLD influences the classifiers performance, Figs. 1, 2 and 3 shows for each classifier the Accuracy, Precision and Recall values along with TCS. The x-axis corresponds to the five MLDs ordered according to their complexity.

From these plots observation that higher TCS values are correlated to worse performances can be easily deduced. For the LP algorithm the three evaluation metrics show a similar behavior, whereas for BR and ML-kNN Precision seems to be less affected than Recall and Accuracy. To formally analyze this relationship, a Pearson correlation test was applied over the TCS and performance values for

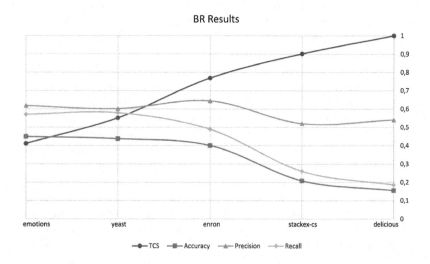

Fig. 1. Performance measures with respect to TCS values for the BR algorithm.

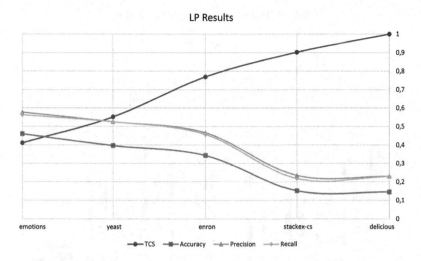

Fig. 2. Performance measures with respect to TCS values for the LP algorithm.

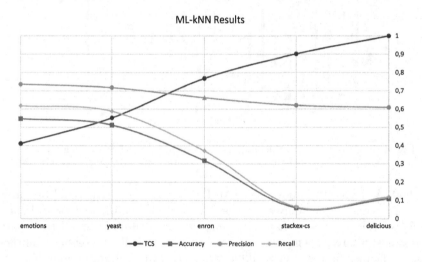

Fig. 3. Performance measures with respect to TCS values for the ML-kNN algorithm.

each metric and algorithm. The obtained results are the shown in Table 2. As can be seen, with the exception of Precision and BR, all the results are above 0.9 in absolute value, meaning that a strong correlation exists. The negative values imply an inverse relation, thus the higher is TCS the worse would be the result.

4.2 Influence of Sampling Strategy in Classifier Performance

Once the partitions for each MLD using the two sampling strategies are generated, it would be useful to know how potentially problematic cases affect each

Table 2. Pearson correlation test results

Algorithm	Accuracy	Precision	Recall
BR	$-0,91$	$-0,67$	$-0,93$
LP	$-0,95$	$-0,94$	$-0,93$
ML-kNN	$-0,96$	$-0,99$	$-0,95$

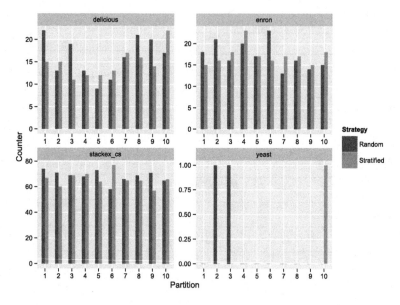

Fig. 4. Occurrences of problematic cases depending on the sampling strategy.

method. As mentioned above, some MLDs contain labels that could be considered as rare, since they only appear once or twice in the whole dataset. Using a 10 fcv scheme, it is easy that these singular cases fall down in the train partition almost always, leaving the test set with poor or null representation of these labels. The own sampling method guarantees that at least once they will appear in the test partition.

The plots in Fig. 4 show the amount of labels with one or none occurrences in the test set produced by each strategy. Here "Random" refers to the classical random approach and "Stratified" to the proposed stratified random sampling. The emotions MLD does not have any case, thus his plot would be empty. Looking at delicious, for instance, it can be verified that for folds 1, 3, 8 and 9 the random sampling clearly produces more problematic cases than the stratified approach. Only for fold 10 the result is definitely worse for the stratified strategy. With stackex-cs the differences appear to be smaller due to the y-axis scale. In more than half of the folds the stratified strategy worked better than the random one. The yeast MLD is not affected by the described problem as much as the other ones. There are two folds in which the random approach produced one

Table 3. Performance measures for each MLD, algorithm and sampling strategy

Dataset	Algorithm	Macro Precision		Macro Recall	
		Random	Stratified	Random	Stratified
delicious	BR	0.4882	**0.4919**	0.0696	**0.0705**
	LP	0.1113	**0.1114**	**0.1101**	0.1095
	ML-kNN	**0.6385**	0.6134	**0.0433**	0.0420
emotions	BR	0.5961	**0.5997**	0.5578	**0.5832**
	LP	**0.5761**	0.5573	0.5565	**0.5631**
	ML-kNN	**0.7439**	0.7122	**0.6051**	0.5837
enron	BR	0.4556	**0.4780**	**0.1684**	0.1667
	LP	**0.1855**	0.1696	**0.1657**	0.1536
	ML-kNN	0.5942	**0.6266**	0.0880	**0.0899**
stackex-cs	BR	**0.4026**	0.3864	**0.1160**	0.1156
	LP	**0.0964**	0.0937	**0.0911**	0.0847
	ML-kNN	**0.6242**	0.5876	**0.0200**	0.0184
yeast	BR	0.4425	**0.4576**	0.3817	**0.3971**
	LP	0.3764	**0.3784**	0.3762	**0.3814**
	ML-kNN	0.6783	**0.6803**	0.3503	**0.3515**

problematic case, against only one for the proposed stratified method. Lastly, enron has the most mixed situation, with large and small differences in both ways.

The results produced by the classifiers were, in general, better for the stratified strategy in those partitions where it produced less problematic cases. The same was applicable for the random approach. Since the results obtained from cross validation are always average values, these differences tend to compensate among them. These final evaluation measures are the shown in Table 3. Best values are highlighted in bold.

Overall there is a tie between the two strategies. Although there are MLDs working better with the stratified one, such as yeast, and others with the random alternative, such as stackex-cs, the remainder MLDs reflect a mixed behavior. Even though there are some noticeable differences between the results produced by the two strategies, most of them are in the order of a few thousandths.

5 Conclusions

The performance of a multilabel classifier is influenced by a plethora of circumstances, starting with the own model goodness, the learning process and the traits (imbalance, missing values, outliers, label concurrence, etc.) of the data used to train it. We hypothesized that two key aspects could be the inherent complexity of the data and the strategy used to partition the MLDs, and described two useful tools to face them.

With the proposed TCS metric the theoretical complexity of any MLD can be quickly and easily computed. As has been demonstrated with experimental results, a clear correlation between the TCS level and the performance of the tested MLC algorithms can be established. Therefore, this metric could be used to know in advance if an MLD would obtain better or worse classification results than others depending on their TCS values.

Regarding the sampling strategies to partition the datasets, the most used approach in MLC is the random way. It can produce some problems with certain MLDs, as has been explained, that could be solved with an stratified strategy. Such a method has been proposed, and its behavior has been compared with the standard random sampling. Although it clearly improved the balanced presence of rare labels among folds in some cases, the classifiers performance did not show fair overall differences. A further more extensive analysis, including additional MLDs, algorithms and sampling strategies, will be needed to determine which could be the best way for MLD partitioning.

Acknowledgments. This work was partially supported by the Spanish Ministry of Science and Technology under projects TIN2014-57251-P and TIN2012-33856, and the Andalusian regional projects P10-TIC-06858 and P11-TIC-7765.

References

1. Charte, F., Rivera, A.J., del Jesus, M.J., Herrera, F.: QUINTA: a question tagging assistant to improve the answering ratio in electronic forums. In: EUROCON 2015 - International Conference on Computer as a Tool (EUROCON), pp. 1–6. IEEE (2015). doi:10.1109/EUROCON.2015.7313677

2. Klimt, B., Yang, Y.: The enron corpus: a new dataset for email classification research. In: Boulicaut, J.-F., Esposito, F., Giannotti, F., Pedreschi, D. (eds.) ECML 2004. LNCS (LNAI), vol. 3201, pp. 217–226. Springer, Heidelberg (2004). doi:10.1007/978-3-540-30115-8_22

3. Duygulu, P., Barnard, K., de Freitas, J.F.G., Forsyth, D.: Object recognition as machine translation: learning a lexicon for a fixed image vocabulary. In: Heyden, A., Sparr, G., Nielsen, M., Johansen, P. (eds.) ECCV 2002, Part IV. LNCS, vol. 2353, pp. 97–112. Springer, Heidelberg (2002). doi:10.1007/3-540-47979-1_7

4. Gibaja, E., Ventura, S.: A tutorial on multilabel learning. ACM Comput. Surv. **47**(3), 1–38 (2015). doi:10.1145/2716262

5. Gibaja, E., Ventura, S.: Multi-label learning: a review of the state of the art and ongoing research. Wiley Interdisc. Rev. Data Min. Knowl. Discovery **4**(6), 411–444 (2014). doi:10.1002/widm.1139

6. Ho, T.K., Basu, M.: Complexity measures of supervised classification problems. IEEE Trans. Pattern Anal. Mach. Intell. **24**(3), 289–300 (2002)

7. Luengo, J., Fernández, A., García, S., Herrera, F.: Addressing data complexity for imbalanced data sets: analysis of smote-based oversampling and evolutionary undersampling. Soft. Comput. **15**(10), 1909–1936 (2011). doi:10.1007/s00500-010-0625-8

8. Sáez, J.A., Luengo, J., Herrera, F.: Predicting noise filtering efficacy with data complexity measures for nearest neighbor classification. Pattern Recogn. **46**(1), 355–364 (2013). doi:10.1016/j.patcog.2012.07.009

9. Charte, F., Rivera, A.J., del Jesus, M.J., Herrera, F.: Addressing imbalance in multilabel classification: measures and random resampling algorithms. Neurocomputing **163**, 3–16 (2015). doi:10.1016/j.neucom.2014.08.091
10. Charte, F., Rivera, A., del Jesus, M.J., Herrera, F.: Concurrence among imbalanced labels and its influence on multilabel resampling algorithms. In: Polycarpou, M., Carvalho, A.C.P.L.F., Pan, J.-S., Woźniak, M., Quintian, H., Corchado, E. (eds.) HAIS 2014. LNCS, vol. 8480, pp. 110–121. Springer, Heidelberg (2014). doi:10.1007/978-3-319-07617-1_10
11. Bellman, R.: Dynamic programming and lagrange multipliers. Proc. Natl. Acad. Sci. U.S.A. **42**(10), 767 (1956)
12. Godbole, S., Sarawagi, S.: Discriminative methods for multi-labeled classification. Adv. Knowl. Discovery Data Min. **3056**, 22–30 (2004). doi:10.1007/978-3-540-24775-3_5
13. Hüllermeier, E., Fürnkranz, J., Cheng, W., Brinker, K.: Label ranking by learning pairwise preferences. Artif. Intell. **172**(16), 1897–1916 (2008). doi:10.1016/j.artint.2008.08.002
14. Fürnkranz, J., Hüllermeier, E., Loza Mencía, E., Brinker, K.: Multilabel classification via calibrated label ranking. Mach. Learn. **73**, 133–153 (2008). doi:10.1007/s10994-008-5064-8
15. Read, J., Pfahringer, B., Holmes, G., Frank, E.: Classifier chains for multi-label classification. Mach. Learn. **85**, 333–359 (2011). doi:10.1007/s10994-011-5256-5
16. Boutell, M., Luo, J., Shen, X., Brown, C.: Learning multi-label scene classification. Pattern Recogn. **37**(9), 1757–1771 (2004). doi:10.1016/j.patcog.2004.03.009
17. Tsoumakas, G., Katakis, I., Vlahavas, I.: Effective and efficient multilabel classification in domains with large number of labels. In: Proceedings of the ECML/PKDD Workshop on Mining Multidimensional Data, Antwerp, Belgium, MMD 2008, pp. 30–44 (2008)
18. Read, J.: A pruned problem transformation method for multi-label classification. In: Proceedings of the 2008 New Zealand Computer Science Research Student Conference (NZCSRS 2008), pp. 143–150 (2008)
19. Tsoumakas, G., Vlahavas, I.P.: Random k-labelsets: an ensemble method for multilabel classification. In: Kok, J.N., Koronacki, J., Lopez de Mantaras, R., Matwin, S., Mladenič, D., Skowron, A. (eds.) ECML 2007. LNCS (LNAI), vol. 4701, pp. 406–417. Springer, Heidelberg (2007). doi:10.1007/978-3-540-74958-5_38
20. Sechidis, K., Tsoumakas, G., Vlahavas, I.: On the stratification of multi-label data. In: Gunopulos, D., Hofmann, T., Malerba, D., Vazirgiannis, M. (eds.) ECML PKDD 2011, Part III. LNCS, vol. 6913, pp. 145–158. Springer, Heidelberg (2011). doi:10.1007/978-3-642-23808-6_10
21. Refaeilzadeh, P., Tang, L., Liu, H.: Cross-validation. In: Liu, L., Özsu, M.T. (eds.) Encyclopedia of Database Systems, pp. 532–538. Springer, New York (2009). doi:10.1007/978-0-387-39940-9_565
22. Charte, F., Charte, D., Rivera, A., del Jesus, M.J., Herrera, F.: R ultimate multilabel dataset repository. In: Martínez-Álvarez, F., Troncoso, A., Quintián, H., Corchado, E. (eds.) HAIS 2016. LNCS (LNAI), vol. 9648, pp. 487–499 Springer, Switzerland (2016)
23. Zhang, M., Zhou, Z.: ML-KNN: a lazy learning approach to multi-label learning. Pattern Recogn. **40**(7), 2038–2048 (2007). doi:10.1016/j.patcog.2006.12.019

Managing Monotonicity in Classification by a Pruned AdaBoost

Sergio González[(✉)], Francisco Herrera, and Salvador García

Department of Computer Science and Artificial Intelligence, University of Granada,
18071 Granada, Spain
{sergiogvz,herrera,salvagl}@decsai.ugr.es

Abstract. In classification problems with ordinal monotonic constraints, the class variable should raise in accordance with a subset of explanatory variables. Models generated by standard classifiers do not guarantee to fulfill these monotonicity constraints. Therefore, some algorithms have been designed to deal with these problems. In the particular case of the decision trees, the growing and pruning mechanisms have been modified in order to produce monotonic trees. Recently, also ensembles have been adapted toward this problem, providing a good trade-off between accuracy and monotonicity degree. In this paper we study the behaviour of these decision tree mechanisms built on an AdaBoost scheme. We combine these techniques with a simple ensemble pruning method based on the degree of monotonicity. After an exhaustive experimental analysis, we deduce that the AdaBoost achieves a better predictive performance than standard algorithms, while holding also the monotonicity restriction.

Keywords: Monotonic classification · Decision tree induction · AdaBoost · Ensemble pruning

1 Introduction

The classification of examples in ordered categories has drawn the interest of the data mining practitioners over the last years. This popular problem has been named with several terms, such as ordinal classification or ordinal regression. However all these share a common singularity in the data: the class or output attribute is ordinal. Monotonic classification [1], also known as classification with monotonicity constraints, is an ordinal classification problem with clear monotonic restrictions: a greater value of an attribute in an example, maintaining other values fixed, should not decrease its class assignment [2].

Rule induction [3], decision trees [4] and hyperrectangles learning algorithms [5] are some of the most promising methods to deal with monotonic classification, thanks to their capacity to build legible models which are preferred on real monotonic applications. Furthermore, these techniques have been successfully integrated into ensemble-type classifiers, empowering the accomplished

© Springer International Publishing Switzerland 2016
F. Martínez-Álvarez et al. (Eds.): HAIS 2016, LNAI 9648, pp. 512–523, 2016.
DOI: 10.1007/978-3-319-32034-2_43

performance [6]. In [7], a bootstrapping-type ensemble based on decision trees is proposed for ordinal classification. The proposal fuses, by the intersection, the different space partitions built by the decision trees trained with the different samples bags. Afterwards, a relabelling of these regions is performed in order to maintain the consistency of the ordinal constraints. This consistency avoids the presence of big disparities in the output decision, when small changes in input data are found. Even though this restriction could be useful, it does not take in consideration the monotonic constraints. Recently, ensembles turn to be promising classifiers in the monotonic classification problem, such as Monotonic Random Forest [8] which is built on the monotonic decision trees mechanisms. However, a classifier selection based on the degree of monotonicity was needed to enhance its monotonicity, and this technique is known as ensemble pruning [9]. Boosting-based ensembles have been also proposed related to decision rules. In particular, the proposals in [10,11] follows a greedy procedure for monotone rules induction, similar to a boosting technique. AdaBoost [12] is probably the most popular boosting-based ensemble of general purpose.

The general purpose of this paper is to motivate the use of the AdaBoost algorithm in classification with monotonic constraints and to offer a good trade-off between accurate predictive performance and the construction of monotonic models. The monotonicity ordering-based pruning mechanism based on the non-monotonicity index will support the second goal.

This contribution is organized as follows. In Sect. 2 we introduce the ordinal classification with monotonic constraints. Section 3 is devoted to describe our proposal of AdaBoost and its adaptation to satisfy the monotonicity constraints. Section 4 illustrates the experimental framework and examines the results obtained in the empirical study, presenting a discussion and analysis. Finally, Sect. 5 concludes the contribution.

2   Monotonic Classification

Ordinal classification problems are those whose class values are ordered, but neither they are nominal nor numeric. Despite of having an ordinal scale, the class lacks a precise notion of distance between its values, in contrast to a numeric scale. For example, products, such as phones or vehicles, can be described as "high-", "mid-" or "low-range", and employees can be evaluated as "excellent", "good" or "bad". Theses types of evaluation or categorization are very common in our daily life, thus ordinal classification problems are such important topics.

To consider a classifier as monotonic, it should not violate the monotonicity constraints. Informally, the monotonic classification signifies that the predicted class values are monotonically non-decreasing (in ordinal order) with the feature values. More formally, let $\{\mathbf{x}_i, \text{class}(\mathbf{x}_i)\}$ denote a set of instances with feature vector $\mathbf{x}_i = (\mathbf{x}_{i,1}, \ldots, \mathbf{x}_{i,m})$ and a class, $\text{class}(\mathbf{x}_i)$, being n the number of examples and m the number of features. Let $\mathbf{x}_i \succeq \mathbf{x}_h$ if $\forall_{j=1,\ldots,m}, \mathbf{x}_{i,j} \geq \mathbf{x}_{h,j}$. A data set $\{\mathbf{x}_i, \text{class}(\mathbf{x}_i)\}$ can be considered monotonic if and only if all the pairs of instances i, h are monotonic with respect to each other [13].

Some monotonic ordinal classifiers need monotonic data sets to successfully built, nonetheless others have been designed with the capacity of construct monotonic models by learning from non-monotonic data sets as well.

3   Monotonic AdaBoost

In this section, we describe our proposal to deal with the monotonic classification. AdaBoost is a well-known boosting ensemble which obtains highly accurate predictive models. We have designed some modifications that generates partially monotonic models, while maintaining this level of accuracy. Like other ensembles, AdaBoost can take, as its core classifier, nearly every unique classifier preferring weak learners, however we decide to use decision trees, due to its relevance in monotonic classification. It worth to point out that the AdaBoost version implemented and shown in Algorithm 1 is the one described in [14].

AdaBoost or Adaptive Boosting was formulated by Freund and Schapire as a way to adapts the boosting scheme to the mistakes made in previous iterations. With this purpose, the algorithm incorporates two different techniques during different phases: during the training of the classifiers of the ensemble and in the combination of the predictive results.

The first adaptation is achieved by giving a weight to each sample according to its previous classification, in order to reinforce, during the training of the weak learners, the importance of those samples which have not been correctly classified yet. The ensemble starts with a weights distribution where all samples have the same relevance, as shown in the Line 2 of the Algorithm 1. After each training phase, the error rate of the previous weak classifier ϵ_i is computed, in our version, as the sum of the weights of the misclassified samples, represented in the Line 6. This rate is used to reduce the weights of the correctly classified samples as exhibited in Line 17. Thanks to this reduction, the next classifier is tweaked in favor of the misclassified samples.

In addition, AdaBoost also includes weights for each trained classifier during the combination of the predictions. The weight given to a certain classifier α_i is inversely proportional to its error rate ϵ_i, as manifested in Line 14. At last, the final output is computed by the majority voting of the weighted decision of each learner.

The modifications done for this contribution are more directed to the decision trees built by the AdaBoost and their diversity, than to its boosting scheme. The splitting procedure of the tree has been changed to ensure that the monotonicity constraints are managed. Also the diversity of the ensemble have been enhanced thanks to the introduction of a new random factor related to the degree of monotonicity. Finally, the aggregation of the results are guided by the ensemble pruning method, prioritizing the most monotonic models.

As previously mentioned, our proposal uses decision trees with a modified splitting method. This procedure was first introduced by Ben-David in the MID algorithm [13]. This decision tree classifier selects the best feature to expand a node attending to the *total-ambiguity*-score as a criterion. This measurement is

---

Algorithm 1. Monotonic AdaBoost algorithm.

1: **function** MONADABOOST(D - dataset, $nTrees$ - number of random trees built, R_{limit} - importance factor for monotonic constrains, T - Threshold used in the pruning procedure, S - the predicted version of D, w weights for each examples)

2:     **initialize:** $S = \{\}$, $Trees[1..nTrees]$, $NMIs[1..nTrees]$, $w_i = 1/N$

3:     **for** i in $[1,nTrees]$ **do**

4:         $rand = Random(1, R_{limit})$

5:         $C_i = Build\_Tree(D, w, rand)$

6:         $\epsilon_i = \sum_{x_j \in D : C_i(x_j) \neq y_j} w_j$

7:         **if** $\epsilon_i > 0.5$ **then**

8:             $\alpha_i = 0$

9:             $w_j = 1/N$

10:         **else if** $\epsilon_i = 0$ **then**

11:             $\alpha_i = 10$

12:             $w_j = 1/N$

13:         **else**

14:             $\alpha_i = \frac{1}{2} ln \frac{1-\epsilon_i}{\epsilon_i}$

15:             **for** x_j in D **do**

16:                 **if** $C_i(x_j) = y_j$ **then**

17:                     $w_j = w_j/2(1 - \epsilon_i)$

18:                 **end if**

19:             **end for**

20:             $Normalize(w)$

21:         **end if**

22:     **end for**

23:     $Trees = Sort(Trees, NMIs, \alpha_m)$

24:     **for** i in $[1, \lceil nTrees * T \rceil]$ **do**

25:         $\widehat{Trees} \leftarrow Trees[i]$

26:     **end for**

27:     **for** d in D **do**

28:         $S \leftarrow Predict\_Majority\_Voting(\widehat{Trees}, d, \alpha_m)$

29:     **end for**

30:     **return** S

31: **end function**

---

computed as the aggregation of the E-score of the ID3 algorithm and the *order-ambiguity*-score weighted by the parameter R (Eq. 1). The *order-ambiguity*-score is defined as shown in Eq. 2, based on the Non Monotonic Index (NMI). This index measures the rate of number of violations of monotonicity constraints, as non-monotonic branch pairs, divided by the total number of instances in a data set.

$$Total\text{-}ambiguity\text{-}score = E\text{-}score + R * A \qquad (1)$$

In the particular case of our contribution, the MID-C4.5 have been chosen to build every weighted tree of the ensemble. The MID-C4.5 uses the information gain of the standard C4.5 decision tree as first term of the *total-ambiguity*-score, instead of the entropy of the ID3. Thanks to this change, we accomplish the initial objective of being able to manage monotonicity with the well-known ensemble.

$$A = \begin{cases} 0 & \text{if } NMI = 0 \\ -(\log_2 NMI)^{-1} & \text{otherwise} \end{cases} \qquad (2)$$

The parameter R, introduced together with the MID algorithm, represents the significance of the monotonicity in splitting process guided by the computed value of the *total-ambiguity-score*, that is, the factor which weight the contribution of the *order-ambiguity-score*. As greater as R is set, more important are the monotonicity constraints considered. We include this factor as a manner to further diversify and randomise the different trees grown in the AdaBoost and at the same time, we induce the tree ramification procedure to be dictated by the monotonicity considerations. In order to achieve this, each tree is grown from the start with a distinct factor R, chosen as a random value from 1 to R_{limit}, being put as a parameter as it is shown in Algorithm 1.

Finally, we incorporate a ensemble pruning based on a simple threshold mechanism to the final aggregation of the different results during the prediction process of the class of each instance. Rather than combining every grown decision trees, in order to guess the class value through the majority vote of the predictions, we select, within a given threshold, the most monotonic trees measured by their Non-Monotonic-Indices, ending Lines 23–28 of the Algorithm 1. Having this aim, our Monotonic AdaBoost sorts the different learnt trees by their NMIs in increasing order (Line 23) and the pruning method chooses the first n trees, being n the product of the total number of grown trees and the threshold T within the interval (0,1], as exhibited in Line 24. After analysing the results shown on the next section, we have noticed that there is a certain range from where to choose the proper value for T having acceptable results. The value chosen should be within [0.3, 0.7]. This permits us to adjust the value according to the monotonicity and accuracy necessities of a given problem. For getting a balanced result, we recommend to set it at 0.50.

4   Experimental Framework, Results and Analysis

In this section, we describe the experimental framework used to compare and analyse the performance of the AdaBoost algorithm for monotonic classification.

4.1   Experimental Methodology

The experimental methodology is presented next by explaining some basic elements:

- Data Sets: In this experiment, 50 monotonic data sets are used. Most of them are standard data sets commonly found in the classification scope and selected from KEEL repository [15] which have been relabelled following the method applied in the experimental framework of [16]. This relabelling process

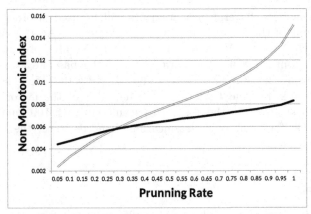

(a) Average NMI of the RF and AdaBoost depending on the pruning rate.

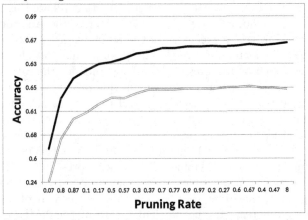

(b) Average accuracy of the RF and AdaBoost depending on the pruning rate.

Fig. 1. Effect of the pruning rate in the ensembles. AdaBoost is represented by the thick black line and RF, by hollow grey line.

applied first transforms the labels to ordinal values. Afterwards, it relabels all instances which violates the monotonicity constraints, performing the fewer changes possible. This procedure changes the class distributions and complexities of the data sets but maintains the number of examples and attributes. Four classical monotonic data sets have been also added: *ERA*, *ESL*, *LEV*, *SWD*.

– Compared algorithms: Our proposal will be compared with three decision trees: MID-C4.5 [13], MID-CART [4] and MID-RankTree [17]; and other ensemble based on Random Forests that have been also adapted to deal with monotonicity constraints: MID-RF [8].

- Evaluation metrics: Several measurements will be used in order to evaluate the behaviour of the algorithms compared: Accuracy (Acc); Mean Absolute Error (MAE) [18]; Non Monotonic Index (NMI); Number of Leaves (NL).
- Parameters configuration: The parameters of the baseline algorithms were extracted from the standard ones in KEEL software [15]. The maximum depth for RankTree and CART is 90. The value of the factor R for MID is 1. AdaBoost also uses the standard parameters with 100 number of trees built, however for monotonic classifications it needs to set the $R_{limit} = 100$ and Threshold= 0.5.

4.2   Results

This section is devoted to explain the results collected from the runs of the different classifiers using the setting described in the previous subsection.

Firstly, it is worth to present the experiment that allowed us to select the best value for the monotonicity pruning parameter of the AdaBoost proposal. The trees grown during the execution of the ensemble are sorted by their Non Monotonic Index in increasing order. The pruning method chooses the trees using a threshold coming from 0.05 to 1. This stands for the ratio of trees that will conform the final classifier. In this way, if this ratio is set to 1, all the trees will be considered to form the ensemble and if its value is 0.2, only 20 % of the most monotonic trees will be used during the aggregation of the results.

This exact study has been applied to both compared ensembles, MID-AdaBoost and MID-RF. Figure 1 exhibits the influence of this pruning ratio previously explained in the two ensembles. The values represented for both graphics are associated with the mean values of accuracy and NMI of the 50 data sets.

Observing Fig. 1, we can easily notice that the behaviour of these two classifiers is slightly different. In the particular case of the NMI (Fig. 1a), there exists, for the RF, a clear turning point around the rate value of 0.5 where the curve starts to grow with a steep slope. In contrast, for the AdaBoost, the NMI increases gradually and approximately constant and with moderate slope. Therefore, from the threshold value 0.3, all the values observed in the AdaBoost are lower than the RF ones, enlarging their differences as the pruning rate gets bigger. Just when the pruning parameter overtakes the value 0.9 for the AdaBoost algorithm, it equals its NMI value with the optimal value obtained by the RF with the recommended 0.5 threshold.

On the other hand, the general performance in terms of accuracy is similar, with the exception of the much better results obtained by the AdaBoost. As shown in the Fig. 1b, both have a great rise in the very beginning, starting their over-fitting around the value 0.6.

Due to these two previously exemplified facts, we deduce that there is a certain interval from where to select the proper value for this pruning threshold, maintaining highly acceptable results. We believe that the value of this parameter should be chosen from the interval [0.3, 0.7]. This allows us to calibrate the parameter according to the monotonicity and accuracy necessities.

Table 1. Accuracy and MAE results reported.

	Accuracy					Mean absolute error				
	MID AdaBoost	MID RF	MID C4.5	MID CART	MID RankTree	MID AdaBoost	MID RF	MID C4.5	MID CART	MID RankTree
Appendicitis	0.8888	0.8667	0.8964	0.8864	**0.9064**	0.1112	0.1333	0.1036	0.1136	**0.0936**
Australian	0.7986	0.8261	0.8029	0.8319	**0.8362**	0.2014	0.1739	0.1971	0.1681	**0.1638**
Auto-mpg	**0.6664**	0.6529	0.6247	0.4489	0.6223	**0.4195**	0.4630	0.4851	1.0335	0.5001
Automobile	**0.8792**	0.8039	0.8250	0.7304	0.7429	**0.2063**	0.3069	0.2688	0.4696	0.4263
Balance	**0.9878**	0.9830	0.9777	0.9777	0.9856	**0.0149**	0.0186	0.0239	0.0271	0.0176
Bostonhousing	0.6405	**0.6483**	0.5674	0.4982	0.5237	**0.4917**	0.4958	0.6102	0.7504	0.6856
Breast	**0.7634**	0.7597	0.7337	0.6933	0.7440	0.2366	0.2403	0.2663	0.3067	0.2560
Bupa	**0.8133**	0.7981	0.7508	0.7534	0.7879	**0.1867**	0.2019	0.2492	0.2466	0.2121
Car	0.9350	0.8731	**0.9433**	0.8183	0.9386	0.0747	0.1609	**0.0666**	0.2396	0.0735
Cleveland	0.5607	**0.5644**	0.4909	0.5284	0.5253	**0.6757**	0.6893	0.8332	0.8014	0.8586
Contraceptive	**0.8581**	0.8185	0.7991	0.5601	0.7719	**0.1781**	0.2351	0.2552	0.6449	0.2844
Crx	**0.8301**	0.8290	0.7903	0.7933	0.7839	**0.1699**	0.1710	0.2097	0.2067	0.2161
Dermatology	**0.8698**	0.8633	0.8437	0.8408	0.7512	0.2867	**0.2810**	0.3325	0.3465	0.5339
Ecoli	**0.6533**	0.6441	0.6074	0.5750	0.5779	**0.9725**	1.0802	1.0549	1.5201	1.1250
ERA	1.0000	1.0000	1.0000	1.0000	1.0000	0.0000	0.0000	0.0000	0.0000	0.0000
ESL	**0.9433**	0.9043	0.9159	0.6162	0.9344	**0.0689**	0.1107	0.1026	0.5788	0.0738
Flare	**0.9493**	0.9025	0.9165	0.6380	0.9456	**0.0644**	0.1256	0.1191	0.6479	0.0826
Glass	0.7462	**0.7464**	0.6773	0.6258	0.6883	0.5362	**0.4934**	0.6929	0.7747	0.6747
Haberman	**0.9594**	0.9291	0.9177	0.9312	0.9537	**0.0406**	0.0709	0.0823	0.0688	0.0463
Hayes-Roth	**0.9792**	0.9042	0.9438	0.7688	0.8500	**0.0208**	0.1104	0.0563	0.2500	0.1688
Heart	0.8185	**0.8235**	0.7926	0.7593	0.8111	0.1815	**0.1765**	0.2074	0.2407	0.1889
Hepatitis	**0.9000**	0.8917	0.7750	0.8375	**0.9000**	**0.1000**	0.1083	0.2250	0.1625	**0.1000**
Housevotes	**0.9828**	0.9528	0.9741	0.8750	0.9266	**0.0172**	0.0472	0.0259	0.1250	0.0734
Ionosphere	**0.8879**	0.8832	0.8348	0.7863	0.7810	**0.1121**	0.1168	0.1652	0.2137	0.2190
Iris	0.9733	0.9711	0.9667	0.9733	**0.9867**	0.0267	0.0289	0.0333	0.0267	**0.0133**
Led7digit	**0.9727**	0.8600	0.9520	0.7880	0.9660	0.0780	0.3800	0.1140	0.6780	**0.0700**
LEV	1.0000	0.9993	1.0000	0.6990	1.0000	0.0000	0.0007	0.0000	0.4450	0.0000
Lymphography	0.7816	**0.7819**	0.7705	0.6767	0.6900	0.2317	**0.2314**	0.2567	0.3633	0.3714
Machinecpu	**0.6634**	0.6520	0.5638	0.4398	0.6369	**0.4386**	0.4741	0.6086	0.7564	0.4726
Mammographic	0.9880	0.9763	0.9831	0.9735	**0.9904**	0.0120	0.0237	0.0169	0.0265	**0.0096**
Monk-2	0.9776	**0.9807**	0.9746	0.9792	0.9769	0.0224	**0.0193**	0.0254	0.0208	0.0232
Movement_libras	**0.6981**	0.6796	0.5194	0.5583	0.5333	1.0815	1.1602	2.0306	1.7861	1.8528
Newthyroid	0.8469	**0.8621**	0.8279	0.8511	0.8329	0.2012	**0.1905**	0.2186	0.1909	0.2139
Pima	0.8607	**0.8702**	0.8242	0.7837	0.8007	0.1393	**0.1298**	0.1758	0.2163	0.1993
Post-operative	**0.7958**	0.6968	0.6333	0.4403	0.7403	**0.2412**	0.3773	0.4806	0.7292	0.3153
Saheart	0.7289	**0.7302**	0.6627	0.6645	0.6624	0.2711	**0.2698**	0.3373	0.3355	0.3376
Segment	**0.9831**	0.9759	0.9649	0.9632	0.9602	**0.0336**	0.0447	0.0610	0.0671	0.0723
Sonar	**0.8089**	0.8042	0.7681	0.7250	0.7648	**0.1911**	0.1958	0.2319	0.2750	0.2352
Spectfheart	**0.8040**	0.8028	0.7379	0.7412	0.7339	**0.1960**	0.1972	0.2621	0.2588	0.2661
SWD	1.0000	0.9993	1.0000	0.3820	1.0000	0.0000	0.0007	0.0000	1.0240	0.0000
tae	**0.9053**	0.8278	0.8483	0.5904	0.8417	**0.1125**	0.1921	0.1650	0.5283	0.1913
Titanic	1.0000	1.0000	1.0000	1.0000	1.0000	0.0000	0.0000	0.0000	0.0000	0.0000
Vehicle	**0.7515**	0.7409	0.6904	0.6384	0.6644	0.4827	0.4929	0.5661	0.6475	0.6334
Vowel	**0.9714**	0.9525	0.7758	0.2182	0.7778	**0.0710**	0.1010	0.6242	2.9313	0.5232
Wdbc	**0.7247**	0.7183	0.6768	0.6749	0.6713	**0.2753**	0.2817	0.3232	0.3251	0.3287
Windsorhousing	**0.9151**	0.8932	0.8939	0.8738	0.8664	**0.0849**	0.1068	0.1061	0.1262	0.1336
Wine	0.7598	**0.7926**	0.6794	0.7297	0.7578	0.3395	**0.2882**	0.4219	0.3719	0.3154
Wisconsin	0.9722	**0.9747**	0.9591	0.9693	0.9591	0.0278	**0.0253**	0.0409	0.0307	0.0409
Yeast	**0.4106**	0.4095	0.3659	0.2811	0.3639	**1.5920**	1.7143	1.8605	3.1107	1.8111
Zoo	**0.8352**	0.7427	0.8127	0.4564	0.8127	**0.3912**	0.7000	0.4727	1.8073	0.4336
Average	**0.8488**	0.8313	0.8051	0.7169	0.8056	**0.2382**	0.2727	0.3213	0.5403	0.3188

Table 2. Number of leaves and NMI results reported.

	Number of leaves					Non monotonic index				
	MID AdaBoost	MID RF	MID C4.5	MID CART	MID RankTree	MID AdaBoost	MID RF	MID C4.5	MID CART	MID RankTree
Appendicitis	8.1	**5.2**	7.0	11.2	10.6	0.0194	0.0352	0.0353	0.1592	**0.1499**
Australian	18.9	9.7	**8.2**	90.0	90.1	0.0023	0.0120	0.0131	**0.0008**	0.0034
Auto-mpg	61.5	**43.3**	65.6	90.0	130.0	**0.0003**	0.0006	**0.0003**	**0.0003**	0.2300
Automobile	38.9	62.0	56.9	80.6	**35.8**	**0.0003**	**0.0003**	0.0006	0.3764	0.4684
Balance	13.0	**6.7**	9.6	90.0	17.1	**0.0090**	0.0211	0.0106	0.0220	0.1946
Bostonhousing	73.8	**55.2**	83.0	135.9	156.4	**0.0002**	0.0004	**0.0002**	0.3375	0.3595
Breast	117.6	95.3	118.6	90.0	**71.7**	0.0001	0.0001	0.0001	**0.0000**	0.2498
Bupa	33.3	**16.9**	23.3	77.2	57.5	**0.0011**	0.0050	0.0025	0.1501	0.2218
Car	258.0	128.3	125.4	**91.4**	180.0	**0.0000**	**0.0000**	0.0001	0.0378	0.2624
Cleveland	48.9	**36.1**	61.1	104.5	107.0	0.0005	0.0009	**0.0003**	0.2528	0.2428
Contraceptive	188.0	112.3	163.0	**94.6**	382.4	**0.0000**	**0.0000**	**0.0000**	0.0280	0.2517
Crx	**90.4**	122.9	154.5	92.2	103.2	0.0001	**0.0000**	0.0001	0.0335	0.2762
Dermatology	40.3	**25.9**	26.1	109.9	71.8	**0.0008**	0.0014	0.0013	0.2647	0.3781
Ecoli	59.6	**33.7**	50.7	115.4	116.3	**0.0004**	0.0012	0.0005	0.2507	0.2853
ERA	28.2	31.0	28.5	**27.4**	36.0	0.0025	**0.0021**	0.0026	0.2153	0.2633
ESL	55.7	**36.7**	39.9	112.1	85.4	**0.0005**	0.0009	0.0006	0.3047	0.1189
Flare	241.4	**87.0**	146.8	91.4	100.4	**0.0000**	0.0002	0.0001	0.0623	0.3625
Glass	29.2	**21.7**	27.8	49.7	54.0	**0.0015**	0.0026	0.0016	0.3378	0.4485
Haberman	20.5	**13.2**	17.4	39.2	30.0	**0.0039**	0.0082	0.0057	0.1518	0.2181
Hayes-Roth	16.1	**12.9**	15.4	94.9	38.8	**0.0059**	0.0074	0.0076	0.0571	0.3026
Heart	25.7	**20.2**	30.8	55.9	44.3	0.0015	0.0025	**0.0012**	0.1677	0.2009
Hepatitis	6.1	**5.1**	7.9	9.9	10.7	**0.0137**	0.0261	0.0187	0.1761	0.2527
Housevotes	10.8	12.8	**6.8**	82.6	18.7	0.0124	**0.0073**	0.0184	0.0766	0.3653
Ionosphere	20.8	**16.0**	19.9	91.5	39.8	**0.0025**	0.0042	0.0040	0.0498	0.2236
Iris	5.4	5.1	**4.6**	8.1	7.7	**0.0384**	0.0487	0.1114	0.2539	0.2552
Led7digit	41.3	**19.1**	34.6	90.1	50.5	**0.0011**	0.0040	0.0016	0.0233	0.2547
LEV	39.1	46.4	**36.4**	101.1	47.3	0.0013	**0.0009**	0.0016	0.1472	0.2545
Lymphography	35.0	31.2	**30.5**	91.2	39.3	**0.0008**	0.0013	0.0015	0.0453	0.4516
Machinecpu	35.6	**25.8**	35.7	93.6	79.9	0.0009	0.0017	**0.0008**	0.0488	0.2028
Mammographic	13.6	13.1	**11.8**	92.2	18.4	**0.0069**	0.0072	0.0085	0.1064	0.1985
Monk-2	13.5	**5.4**	12.6	91.8	20.8	**0.0073**	0.0184	0.0093	0.0369	0.1589
Movement_libras	60.5	**47.2**	66.1	104.2	128.4	0.0004	0.0005	**0.0003**	0.2691	0.3227
Newthyroid	21.8	**11.9**	12.6	39.2	29.0	**0.0032**	0.0098	0.0086	0.2520	0.2378
Pima	59.6	**32.4**	44.7	108.5	98.7	**0.0004**	0.0014	0.0007	0.1469	0.2052
Post-operative	23.0	**18.6**	27.9	91.0	33.0	0.0020	0.0040	**0.0018**	0.0352	0.3957
Saheart	44.2	**26.5**	47.7	82.1	94.5	0.0006	0.0020	**0.0006**	0.1845	0.2179
Segment	62.9	56.4	**47.8**	77.9	84.2	0.0004	**0.0004**	0.0006	0.3421	0.4048
Sonar	13.4	**13.0**	15.7	21.5	21.3	**0.0056**	0.0063	0.0063	0.1842	0.2222
Spectfheart	19.0	**14.3**	22.3	37.8	32.0	**0.0024**	0.0047	0.0032	0.1830	0.3067
SWD	58.0	69.3	**53.5**	90.0	62.3	0.0006	0.0004	0.0007	**0.0000**	0.2728
Tae	21.1	**15.0**	16.3	93.4	36.9	**0.0031**	0.0061	0.0041	0.0424	0.2397
Titanic	**3.0**	4.0	4.0	4.0	4.0	0.1667	**0.1163**	0.1667	0.1667	0.1667
Vehicle	96.4	**71.3**	99.8	147.6	178.8	0.0001	0.0002	**0.0001**	0.3101	0.2928
Vowel	100.6	102.5	102.5	**94.9**	198.0	0.0001	**0.0001**	0.0001	0.0590	0.3976
Wdbc	47.2	**31.5**	53.1	84.1	86.6	0.0005	0.0013	**0.0005**	0.2172	0.2267
Windsorhousing	42.2	**24.6**	35.0	62.6	79.5	**0.0007**	0.0015	**0.0007**	0.1852	0.1837
Wine	18.9	**13.8**	18.8	30.6	34.8	0.0033	0.0062	**0.0040**	0.2524	0.3337
Wisconsin	17.1	**12.4**	16.8	57.0	27.0	**0.0048**	0.0075	0.0050	0.0766	0.1854
Yeast	318.1	231.6	349.3	**129.8**	802.5	**0.0000**	**0.0000**	**0.0000**	0.2918	0.3101
Zoo	22.8	**13.5**	16.6	90.0	25.2	**0.0031**	0.0090	0.0049	0.0200	0.5680
Average	54.7	**39.3**	50.2	78.8	86.1	**0.0067**	0.0080	0.0094	0.1479	0.2719

Table 3. Summary table for statistical inference outcome: Ranks and APVs

	Acc		MAE		NL		NMI	
	Ranks	APVs	Ranks	APVs	Ranks	APVs	Ranks	APVs
MID-AdaBoost	**1.600**	—	**1.620**	—	2.660	0.001	**1.500**	—
MID-RF	2.480	0.005	2.540	0.003	**1.640**	—	2.560	0.000
MID-C4.5	3.41	0.000	3.390	0.000	2.42	0.013	2.240	0.019
MID-CART	4.22	0.000	4.210	0.000	4.11	0.000	3.890	0.000
MID-RankTree	3.29	0.000	3.240	0.000	4.17	0.000	4.810	0.000

For balanced result, we recommend to set it at 0.50. Under our suggested settings of pruning and random choice of R parameter, we compare the AdaBoost algorithm with the other contestant classifiers. Table 1 exhibits the performance results measured as accuracy and MAE, whereas Table 2 offers the complexity of the trees as number of leaves and the NMIs. These results have been obtained from the algorithms executions over monotonic data sets, in terms of average values of the three runs of 10-fcv.

To further check the results, we incorporate a statistical analysis based on non parametric tests. The results gathered from the execution of the Friedman test and the Holm post-hoc procedure are depicted in Table 3. Additionally, the Adjusted P-Value (APV) [19] computed by the Holm procedure is given for the algorithms whose ranking is not the best in each group.

4.3 Analysis

From this study, we may stress the following conclusions:

- In terms of accuracy, the goodness of the Monotonic AdaBoost with ensemble pruning based on NMI thresholding is absolutely clear. In the Fig. 1b, we have seen how all average results of our proposal are over the RF results, probably the second best algorith. In Tables 1 and 3, we can notice that the AdaBoost outperforms the other 4 classifiers by a significant difference.
- The right part of the Table 1 shows a similar result in term of MAE, having even a greater difference with the next algorithm, MID-RF. This accomplishment can be predictable, when such a overwhelming superiority in terms of accuracy was obtained.
- In contrast, Monotonic AdaBoost is the third worst algorithm in term of complexity of the model as shown in Tables 2 and 3. The AdaBoost scheme permits to obtain great predictive performance in spite of more complex models, even selecting the most monotonic and simple trees built, thanks to the pruning procedure.
- Following the tendency of the two first measurements, Tables 2 and 3 reflect better monotonic results in terms of NMI for MID-AdaBoost. Our proposal obtained the minimum value of NMI for the majority of data sets.

5   Concluding Remarks

The aim of this paper is to present and to study the AdaBoost proposal for the ordinal monotonic classification problem. To fulfil with the correct adaptation to this problem, we incorporate as core classifier of the ensemble a MID-based decision tree that allows it to start managing the monotonicity constraints. In order to further diversify the trees built in the ensemble and, at the same time, to enhance the monotonicity of the final model, the monotonicity importance factor of the splitting procedure of the trees is selected randomly within a certain given range. After growing of all the decision trees, an ensemble pruning method based on the monotonicity degree of each model picks the subset of the most monotonic decision trees to be considered for the aggregation of the final predictions. After an intensive experimental analysis, we conclude that AdaBoost is a very promising algorithm to deal with this problem, obtaining very accurate predictive models while maintaining the monotonicity constraints.

Acknowledgments. This work was partially supported by the Spanish Ministry of Science and Technology under project TIN2014-57251-P and the Andalusian Research Plans P11-TIC-7765, P10-TIC-6858.

References

1. Ben-David, A., Sterling, L., Pao, Y.H.: Learning, classification of monotonic ordinal concepts. Comput. Intell. **5**, 45–49 (1989)
2. Kotłowski, W., Słowiński, R.: On nonparametric ordinal classification with monotonicity constraints. IEEE Trans. Knowl. Data Eng. **25**, 2576–2589 (2013)
3. Furnkranz, J., Gamberger, D., Lavrac, N.: Foundations of Rule Learning. Springer, Berlin (2012)
4. Rokach, L., Maimon, O.: Data Mining with Decision Trees: Theory and Applications, 2nd edn. World Scientific, River Edge (2014)
5. Garca, J., Fardoun, H., Alghazzawi, D., Cano, J.R., Garca, S.:Mongel: monotonic nested generalized exemplar learning. Pattern Anal. Appl. 1–12 (2015)
6. Wozniak, M., Graña, M., Corchado, E.: A survey of multiple classifier systems as hybrid systems. Inf. Fusion **16**, 3–17 (2014)
7. Sousa, R., Cardoso, J.: Ensemble of decision trees with global constraints for ordinal classification. In: 2011 11th International Conference on Intelligent Systems Design and Applications (ISDA), pp. 1164–1169 (2011)
8. González, S., Herrera, F., García, S.: Monotonic random forest with an ensemble pruning mechanism based on the degree of monotonicity. New Gener. Comput. **33**, 367–388 (2015)
9. Martínez-Muñoz, G., Hernández-Lobato, D., Suárez, A.: An analysis of ensemble pruning techniques based on ordered aggregation. IEEE Trans. Pattern Anal. Mach. Intell. **31**, 245–259 (2009)
10. Dembczyński, K., Kotłowski, W., Słowiński, R.: Ensemble of decision rules for ordinal classification with monotonicity constraints. In: Wang, G., Li, T., Grzymala-Busse, J.W., Miao, D., Skowron, A., Yao, Y. (eds.) RSKT 2008. LNCS (LNAI), vol. 5009, pp. 260–267. Springer, Heidelberg (2008)

11. Dembczyński, K., Kotłowski, W., Słowiński, R.: Learning rule ensembles for ordinal classification with monotonicity constraints. Fundamenta Informaticae **94**, 163–178 (2009)
12. Freund, Y., Schapire, R.E.: A decision-theoretic generalization of on-line learning and an application to boosting. J. Comput. Syst. Sci. **55**, 119–139 (1997)
13. Ben-David, A.: Monotonicity maintenance in information-theoretic machine learning algorithms. Mach. Learn. **19**, 29–43 (1995)
14. Webb, G.: Multiboosting: a technique for combining boosting and wagging. Mach. Learn. **40**, 159–196 (2000)
15. Alcala-Fdez, J., Fernández, A., Luengo, J., Derrac, J., García, S., Sánchez, L., Herrera, F.: KEEL data-mining software tool: data set repository, integration of algorithms and experimental analysis framework. J. Multiple-Valued Logic Soft Comput. **17**, 255–287 (2011)
16. Duivesteijn, W., Feelders, A.: Nearest neighbour classification with monotonicity constraints. In: Daelemans, W., Goethals, B., Morik, K. (eds.) ECML PKDD 2008, Part I. LNCS (LNAI), vol. 5211, pp. 301–316. Springer, Heidelberg (2008)
17. Xia, F., Zhang, W., Li, F., Yang, Y.: Ranking with decision tree. Knowl. Inf. Syst. **17**, 381–395 (2008)
18. Japkowicz, N., Shah, M. (eds.): Evaluating Learning Algorithms: A Classification Perspective. Cambridge University Press, Cambridge (2011)
19. García, S., Fernández, A., Luengo, J., Herrera, F.: Advanced nonparametric tests for multiple comparisons in the design of experiments in computational intelligence and data mining: Experimental analysis of power. Inf. Sci. **180**, 2044–2064 (2010)

Model Selection for Financial Distress Prediction by Aggregating TOPSIS and PROMETHEE Rankings

Vicente García[1], Ana I. Marqués[2], L. Cleofas-Sánchez[3],
and José Salvador Sánchez[3(✉)]

[1] División Multidisciplinaria de Ciudad Universitaria, Universidad Autónoma
de Ciudad Juárez, 32310 Ciudad Juárez, Chihuahua, Mexico
[2] Department of Business Administration and Marketing, Universitat Jaume I,
Castelló de la Plana, Spain
[3] Institute of New Imaging Technologies, Department of Computer Languages
and Systems, Universitat Jaume I, 12071 Castelló de la Plana, Spain
sanchez@uji.es

Abstract. Many models have been explored for financial distress prediction, but no consistent conclusions have been drawn on which method shows the best behavior when different performance evaluation measures are employed. Accordingly, this paper proposes the integration of the ranking scores given by two popular multiple-criteria decision-making tools as an important step to help decision makers in selecting the model(s) properly. Selection of the most appropriate prediction method is here shaped as a multiple-criteria decision-making problem that involves a number of performance measures (criteria) and a set of techniques (alternatives). An empirical study is carried out to assess the performance of ten algorithms over six real-life bankruptcy and credit risk databases. The results reveal that the use of a unique performance measure often leads to contradictory conclusions, while the multiple-criteria decision-making techniques may yield a more reliable analysis. Besides, these allow the decision makers to weight the relevance of the individual performance metrics as a function of each particular problem.

Keywords: Model selection · Multi-criteria decision-making · Financial distress · TOPSIS · PROMETHEE

1 Introduction

The lingering international financial crisis and the recommendations issued by the Basel Committee on Banking Supervision have led to increasing attention of financial institutions on credit and operational risk assessment, converting this into a critical task because of the heavy losses associated with wrong decisions. One major risk for financial institutions comes from the difficulty to distinguish the creditworthy applicants from those who will probably default on repayments.

© Springer International Publishing Switzerland 2016
F. Martínez-Álvarez et al. (Eds.): HAIS 2016, LNAI 9648, pp. 524–535, 2016.
DOI: 10.1007/978-3-319-32034-2_44

The most traditional approaches to bankruptcy and credit risk management have been based upon subjective judgments made by human financial experts, using past experiences and some standard guiding principles, but the considerable increase in business demands and database sizes have brought about the development of more formal and accurate methods to efficiently assess the financial risk. The adoption of statistical and operations research models (e.g., logistic regression, discriminant analysis, or linear and quadratic programming) represented a first step in that direction [18,23,30]. However, some assumptions of the statistical procedures, such as the multivariate normality for explanatory variables, are frequently violated in practice, thus making them theoretically invalid for finite samples [10]. During the last decade, efforts have focused on the deployment of data mining techniques such as artificial neural networks [3,5,14], support vector machines [4,20,28] and classifier ensembles [19,29,31,32], to design and implement solutions for financial risk prediction. In contrast with statistical models, data mining methods do not assume any specific prior knowledge, but automatically extract information from the examples available.

From a practical point of view, financial distress prediction can be defined as a binary classification problem where a new observation must be categorized into one of the two predefined classes based on a number of input variables. These collect a variety of information that describes socio-demographic characteristics and economic conditions of the applicants, and then the model has to produce the output in terms of their creditworthiness. In its most usual form, financial distress prediction aims at assigning customers to either good (those who are liable to reimburse the financial obligation) or bad (those debtors with high probability of defaulting on repayments). Assuming a set of m past observations $S = \{(x_1, y_1), \ldots, (x_m, y_m)\}$, where each sample x_i is characterized by D explanatory variables, $x_{i1}, x_{i2}, \ldots x_{iD}$, and y_i denotes the class (good/bad, defaulter/non-defaulter, positive/negative), then a model F has to predict the value y for a new case $\mathbf{x}$, that is, $F(\mathbf{x}) = y$.

Many comparative studies of a variety of financial risk prediction models have been conducted, but their conclusions may vary depending on the performance measure evaluated. For example, Desai et al. [7] concluded that customized neural networks perform better than linear models when measuring the percentage of bad applicants correctly classified, whereas logistic regression yields better results in terms of percentage of good and bad applicants correctly classified. Yobas et al. [33] found that linear discriminant analysis outperforms neural networks, genetic algorithms and decision trees in the proportion of samples correctly classified. Baesens et al. [4] showed that the support vector machines achieve the highest accuracy rate, while the neural networks perform the best in terms of the area under the ROC curve. Bensic et al. [5] suggested that the predictive accuracy of probabilistic neural networks is superior to that of logistic regression, CART decision trees, radial basis function, multi-layer perceptron and learning vector quantization. Antonakis and Sfakianakis [2] evaluated the performance of k-nearest neighbors decision rule, multi-layer perceptron, decision trees, logistic regression, linear discriminant analysis and naïve Bayes, showing that the k-nearest neighbors rule achieved the highest accuracy and the neural network was the best method in terms of the Gini coefficient. Wang et al. [32] found that stacking and bagging using a decision tree as base classifier achieve the best performance in terms of accuracy, type-I error and type-II error.

Disagreement of these and many other related studies suggests that there exists no prediction algorithm that could be superior for any performance measure. However, model selection constitutes an issue of particular interest in financial risk management, which indicates the need of more powerful methods to evaluate the prediction performance of a set of classifiers. Bearing the limitations of individual performance measures in mind, the purpose of this paper is to introduce an aggregated multiple-criteria decision-making (MCDM) method for a more comprehensive assessment of financial distress prediction models. To this end, the TOPSIS and PROMETHEE algorithms are employed to rank a collection of classifiers based on a set of metrics and then their ranking scores are combined to provide a single scalar, demonstrating that the use of this technique allows for stronger conclusions regarding the performance of prediction models.

2   Multiple-Criteria Decision-Making

Assessing the performance of prediction models means to take more than one criterion of interest into account, usually weighting this against the gains of other complementary criteria. Under this consideration, model selection can be viewed as an example of MCDM problems. Generally speaking, MCDM constitutes a branch of operations research that comprises several analytical tools to judge the pros and cons of a finite set of alternatives (or choices) based on a finite set of criteria (or attributes), with the aim of making a reliable decision [15,27].

Within the context of financial risk prediction, the MCDM methods should allow decision makers to choose the model that achieves a closely optimal trade-off of the assessment criteria of interest. A general MCDM problem can be expressed in the form of a $(M \times N)$ decision matrix as that given in Table 1, where M is the number of alternatives (prediction models) and N denotes the number of decision criteria (performance measures).

Popular examples of the many MCDM methods proposed in the literature are TOPSIS and PROMETHEE, which provide interesting advantages over other techniques [24]: (i) a solution that represents the rationale of human choice;

Table 1. Decision matrix for an MCDM problem (z_{ij} indicates the value of alternative A_i when evaluated in terms of criterion C_j)

	C_1	C_1	$\cdots$	C_N
A_1	z_{11}	z_{12}	$\cdots$	z_{1N}
A_2	z_{21}	z_{22}	$\cdots$	z_{2N}
$\vdots$	$\vdots$	$\vdots$	$\ddots$	$\vdots$
A_M	z_{M1}	z_{M2}	$\cdots$	z_{MN}

(ii) a scalar value that accounts for both the best and worst alternatives; and (iii) a simple computation procedure that can be easily implemented into a spreadsheet.

2.1 TOPSIS

The basic principle behind TOPSIS is to find the best alternative by simultaneously minimizing the distance to the positive ideal solution and maximizing the distance to the negative ideal solution [11]. The positive ideal solution is formed as a composite of the best performance values exhibited by any alternative for each criterion, whereas the negative ideal solution is the composite of the worst performance values.

Assuming a problem with M alternatives and N criteria defined as in Table 1, the stepwise procedure of TOPSIS can be implemented as follows:

Algorithm 1. TOPSIS

1: Calculate the normalized decision matrix, where the normalized value n_{ij} of the original score z_{ij} is calculated as
$$n_{ij} = \frac{z_{ij}}{\sqrt{\sum_{i=1}^{M} z_{ij}^2}} \quad i = 1, \ldots, M \quad j = 1, \ldots, N$$

2: Calculate the weighted normalized values $v_{ij} = w_j z_{ij}$, where w_j is the weight of the criterion C_j and $\sum_{j=1}^{N} w_j = 1$

3: Determine the positive ideal A^+ and negative ideal A^- solutions
$$A^+ = \{v_1^+, \ldots, v_N^+\} = \{(\max_j v_{ij} | i \in I), (\min_j v_{ij} | i \in J)\}$$
$$A^- = \{v_1^-, \ldots, v_N^-\} = \{(\min_j v_{ij} | i \in I), (\max_j v_{ij} | i \in J)\}$$
where I and J are associated with benefit and cost criteria, respectively

4: Calculate the separation of each alternative from the positive ideal solution and that from the negative ideal solution using the N-dimensional Euclidean distance
$$d_j^+ = \sqrt{\sum_{j=1}^{N} (v_{ij} - v_j^+)^2} \text{ and } d_j^- = \sqrt{\sum_{j=1}^{N} (v_{ij} - v_j^-)^2} \quad i = 1, \ldots, M$$

5: Calculate the relative closeness to the ideal solution. The relative closeness of the alternative A_i with respect to A^+ is defined as $R_i^+ = \frac{d_i^-}{d_i^+ + d_i^-}$ $\quad i = 1, \ldots, M$

6: Rank alternatives according to the descending order of the index R_i^+

Note that the TOPSIS model provides a complete ranking of alternatives according to their global utilities and it does not require criterion preferences to be independent [11].

2.2 PROMETHEE

The objective of the PROMETHEE method [6] is to rank alternatives based on their values over different criteria. As an outranking technique, it quantifies a

---

Algorithm 2. PROMETHEE

1: For each pair (A_i, A_j) of a finite set of alternatives $A = \{A_1, A_2, \ldots, A_M\}$, calculate aggregated preference indices as follows:

$$\pi(A_i, A_j) = \sum_{k=1}^{N} P_k(A_i, A_j)w_k \quad \text{and} \quad \pi(A_j, A_i) = \sum_{k=1}^{N} P_k(A_j, A_i)w_k$$

where w_k is the normalized weight of the criterion C_k. $\pi(A_i, A_j)$ indicates how A_i is preferred to A_j and $\pi(A_j, A_i)$ indicates how A_j is preferred to A_i. $P_k(A_i, A_j)$ and $P_k(A_j, A_i)$ are the preference functions for alternatives A_i and A_j, respectively

2: Define the positive and the negative preference flows as

$$\phi^+(A_i) = \tfrac{1}{M-1} \sum_{a \in A} \pi(A_i, a) \quad \text{and} \quad \phi^-(A_i) = \tfrac{1}{M-1} \sum_{a \in A} \pi(a, A_i)$$

3: Compute the net preference flow for each alternative as $\phi(A_i) = \phi^+(A_i) - \phi^-(A_i)$

---

ranking through the pairwise comparisons (differences) between the criterion values describing the alternatives. It makes use of the concept of preference flow: the positive preference flow indicates how an alternative is outranking all the other alternatives, whereas the negative preference flow indicates how an alternative is outranked by the remaining alternatives. The procedure of PROMETHEE can be expressed in a series of steps as follows:

When $\phi(A_i) > 0$, A_i is more outranking all the alternatives on all evaluation criteria. Conversely, when $\phi(A_i) < 0$, A_i is more outranked. The alternative A_i with the maximum net preference flow $\phi(A_i)$ is deemed as the best.

3   Experimental Methodology

This study evaluates the performance of a set of financial distress prediction models by means of TOPSIS and PROMETHEE, with the aim of demonstrating that the MCDM tools are superior to a unique metric for making better decisions about which prediction technique is the most appropriate for a particular financial problem. The TOPSIS and PROMETHEE models have been conducted through the Sanna software [12], while the classifiers here tested have been implemented using the WEKA toolkit [8] with the default parameter values: Bayesian network (BNet), multi-layer perceptron (MLP), radial basis function (RBF), support vector machine (SVM), naïve Bayes classifier (NBC), logistic regression (logR), nearest neighbor rule (1NN), RIPPER propositional rule learner, and C4.5 and CART decision trees.

3.1   Data Sets

Experiments have been carried out on six real-life financial data sets. The Australian and German databases have been taken from the UCI Machine Learning Database Repository (http://archive.ics.uci.edu/ml/). The Australian data set consists of 690 instances of MasterCard applicants, 307 of which have been identified as creditworthy and 383 as non-creditworthy applicants; each example has 14 explanatory variables (6 numerical and 8 categorical). The German credit data set refers to a credit screening application in a German bank, containing observations on 24 numerical attributes for 1000 past applicants: 700 examples of creditworthy applicants and 300 cases whose credit should not be granted. The Iranian data set comes from a modification to a corporate client database of a small private bank in Iran [22]. It consists of 950 examples labeled as good customers and 50 as bad customers, each one described by 27 input attributes. The Polish data set contains bankruptcy information of 120 companies recorded over a two-year period [21], with 112 bankruptcy accounts and 128 good status accounts. The Thomas database, which comes with the book by Thomas et al. [26], collects 12 input variables to describe the data of 1125 applicants for a credit product. Finally, the UCSD data set corresponds to a subset with samples randomly chosen from the database used in the 2007 Data Mining Contest organized by the University of California San Diego and Fair Isaac Corporation. This is a completely balanced data set with 2500 examples from each class and 38 variables.

3.2 Experimental Set-Up

As data are rather limited, the performance of the prediction models has been assessed with 5-fold cross-validation because this is quite reliable. Each original database has been divided into five blocks, using four subset for training and the remaining one for testing purposes. Ten repetitions have been run for each trial. Thus the results from classifying the test samples have been averaged across the 50 runs and then evaluated with some standard performance measures and analyzed with TOPSIS and PROMETHEE.

Typical performance evaluation scores in the field of financial distress include accuracy, Gini coefficient, Kolmogorov-Smirnov statistic, root mean squared error, area under the ROC curve, geometric mean of accuracies, or type-I and type-II errors [1,9,26], among others. For a two-class problem, as is the case of the databases here experimented, most of these metrics can be easily derived from a (2×2) confusion matrix where each entry contains the number of correct (true positive, true negative) or incorrect (false positive, false negative) predictions.

Many financial systems often use the accuracy to evaluate the performance of the prediction models, thus representing the proportion of the correctly predicted cases on a particular data set. However, empirical and theoretical evidences show that this measure is strongly biased with respect to data imbalance and proportions of correct and incorrect predictions. Because financial data are commonly imbalanced, the area under the ROC curve (AUC) has been suggested as an appropriate evaluator without regard to class distribution or misclassification costs [4,16]. The AUC for a binary problem can be roughly defined as the arithmetic average of the mean predictions for each class [25]:

$$AUC = \frac{sensitivity + specificity}{2} \tag{1}$$

where the sensitivity (or true positive rate, TPrate) measures the percentage of good applicants that have been predicted correctly, and the specificity (or true negative rate, TNrate) is the percentage of bad applicants predicted as bad.

Another measure often used in skewed domains is the geometric mean of accuracies, which intends to maximize the predictive accuracy on each class while keeping them balanced (the difference between TPrate and TNrate is small). It punishes those models that produce large disparities in accuracy between classes. It is worth noting that the geometric mean of accuracies closely relates with the distance to perfect classification in the ROC space.

$$Gmean = \sqrt{sensitivity \cdot specificity} \tag{2}$$

The root mean squared error (RMSE) is another common performance measure used in general prediction problems. Let $p_1, p_2, \ldots, p_m$ and $a_1, a_2, \ldots, a_m$ be the predicted and actual outputs on the test samples, respectively. The RMSE allows to quantify the difference between the predictions and the true labels, measuring the deviation of the classification model from the target value [13].

$$RMSE = \sqrt{\frac{1}{m} \sum_{i=1}^{m} (p_i - a_i)^2} \tag{3}$$

4   Results

Figure 1 plots the average results of five performance measures achieved with each prediction model. The values of RMSE has not been included because the meaning of this metric is opposite to that of the others, that is, lower values of RMSE indicate a better performing model.

Table 2 shows the results of six performance evaluation measures (accuracy, RMSE, TPrate, TNrate, AUC, and Gmean) averaged over the six experimental data sets. For each measure, the best performing model has been highlighted in bold. When analyzing the behavior by means of the predictive accuracy, logR, SVM, RIPPER and CART were the classifiers with the highest average rates. With the RMSE measure, logistic regression and CART appeared to be the best classifiers. Assessment of performance by means of the true positive rate suggested that logR, the RBF neural network and the CART decision tree were the best performing algorithm. The naïve Bayes classifier yielded the highest true negative rate. By using AUC, the best model corresponded to logistic regression, whereas the 1NN decision rule outperformed the remaining classifiers in terms of the geometric mean of accuracies.

From Fig. 1 and Table 2, it seems obvious that there is no classification algorithm that achieves the best results across all measures and therefore, one might draw different conclusions about the best performing model depending on the performance evaluation measure used. For example, the TNrate indicates that the naïve Bayes classifier is the most suitable method, the AUC proposes the

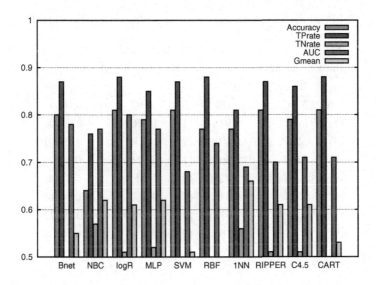

Fig. 1. Average values of five performance measures over different prediction models

Table 2. Performance results averaged over the six experimental databases

	Accuracy	RMSE	TPrate	TNrate	AUC	Gmean
BNet	0.80	0.39	0.87	0.48	0.78	0.55
NBC	0.64	0.54	0.76	**0.57**	0.77	0.62
logR	**0.81**	**0.37**	**0.88**	0.51	**0.80**	0.61
MLP	0.79	0.40	0.85	0.52	0.77	0.62
SVM	**0.81**	0.43	0.87	0.50	0.68	0.51
RBF	0.77	0.39	**0.88**	0.42	0.74	0.49
1NN	0.77	0.47	0.81	0.56	0.69	**0.66**
RIPPER	**0.81**	0.38	0.87	0.51	0.70	0.61
C4.5	0.79	0.40	0.86	0.51	0.71	0.61
CART	**0.81**	**0.37**	**0.88**	0.48	0.71	0.53
Weight	0.04762	0.23810	0.09524	0.14286	0.19048	0.28571

logistic regression model as the best algorithm, and the geometric mean of accuracies suggests that the 1NN rule is the most accurate technique. These contradictory outcomes describe a realistic situation in which two analysts might make radically different decisions depending on how they have evaluated the performance of a given financial risk prediction system. These are good examples of practical situations where we believe that MCDM methods should be taken into consideration in order to make more reliable, consistent decisions.

The problems associated with the use of individual performance evaluation measures led to experiment with the two MCDM techniques chosen for the

Table 3. Preference ranking with TOPSIS and PROMETHEE

TOPSIS			PROMETHEE		
Rank	Alternative	Score	Rank	Alternative	Score
(4)	BNet	0.78659	(4)	BNet	0.06349
(10)	NBC	0.20299	(5)	NBC	0.00529
(1)	logR	0.91444	(1)	logR	0.61905
(3)	MLP	0.80115	(2)	MLP	0.29101
(8)	SVM	0.59485	(10)	SVM	−0.57672
(7)	RBF	0.72369	(9)	RBF	−0.31746
(9)	1NN	0.44631	(7)	1NN	−0.04762
(2)	RIPPER	0.87712	(3)	RIPPER	0.19577
(6)	C4.5	0.76144	(8)	C4.5	−0.18519
(5)	CART	0.78476	(6)	CART	−0.04762

present study. Although assigning weights to alternatives is nontrivial, here the weight of each performance measure used in TOPSIS and PROMETHEE methods were set according to its relative relevance for the financial risk prediction task. For example, AUC and Gmean are significant metrics in this practical domain because they select optimal models independently of the class distribution and the cost associated to each class [13]. On the other hand, the misclassification cost associated with false positives is generally much higher than the misclassification cost associated with false negatives [17]. The weights were then normalized in the interval $[0, 1]$ such that the sum of all weights was equal to 1 (see the last row in Table 2).

Table 3 summarizes the ranking of prediction models given by TOPSIS and PROMETHEE, respectively. The results are straightforward: the higher the ranking, the better the classifier. From the analysis with these two MCDM tools, the logistic regression model seemed to be the best performing algorithm, whereas the RIPPER rule learner and the MLP neural network were among the top-three ranked classifiers. These results indicate that TOPSIS and PROMETHEE, which gave similar rankings, can be useful to make accurate decisions in financial risk prediction problems.

Paradoxically, despite the claims of many authors, the SVM appeared to be one of the worst alternatives for financial distress prediction when TOPSIS and PROMETHEE were used for model selection. Such disagreement may be due to the use of inappropriate performance evaluation measures, while the MCDM tools are able to correct their misleading results.

Even though the ranks given by TOPSIS and PROMETHEE were quite similar, we further defined an aggregated ranking score as the mean of the values of the two methods for each prediction model (or alternative) i. This aggregated score allows to combine the rankings of TOPSIS and PROMETHEE in an easy, fair manner as follows:

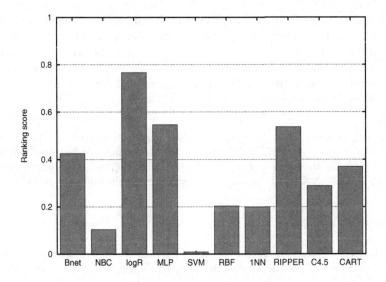

Fig. 2. Aggregated ranking scores

$$Aggregated\_Score_i = \frac{score_i(t) + score_i(p)}{2} \tag{4}$$

where $score_i(t)$ and $score_i(p)$ are the scores given by TOPSIS and PROMETHEE, respectively.

By plotting the aggregated score, Fig. 2 provides a better representation of the decisions made, showing the superiority of the logistic regression model over the other methods and the poor performance of SVM.

5   Concluding Remarks

This paper advocates the application of MCDM methods to evaluate the performance of financial risk prediction models. It has empirically been demonstrated that the use of single performance evaluation measures may lead to unreliable conclusions regarding the best performing algorithm, thus making difficult the selection of the most accurate model for a particular financial problem.

Two popular MCDM techniques, TOPSIS and PROMETHEE, have been tested in the experiments over six real-life financial data sets, using ten prediction models (alternatives) and six performance evaluation measures (criteria). The assessment of classifiers through single performance measures has given contradictory results, in the sense that different metrics have proposed different algorithms as the best alternative. This suggests that financial risk prediction is a real-world problem where MCDM tools should be applied to consistently evaluate a set of models and select the most appropriate one for each particular problem. Both TOPSIS and PROMETHEE have indicated that logistic regression, RIPPER and MLP are the best prediction models when the performance is evaluated with a composite of measures.

Besides, an aggregated score defined as a linear combination of the ranking values given by TOPSIS and PROMETHEE has also been introduced. The most interesting advantages of this new score are: (i) it transforms the individual rankings of two MCDM methods into a single scalar which allows to make more consistent decisions; (ii) its graphical representation allows to clearly understand the decisions made by an analyst.

Acknowledgement. This work has partially been supported by the Spanish Ministry of Economy [TIN2013-46522-P], the Generalitat Valenciana [PROME-TEOII/2014/062], the Mexican PRODEP [DSA/103.5/15/7004] and the Mexican Science and Technology Council through the Postdoctoral Fellowship Program [232167].

References

1. Abdou, H., Pointon, J.: Credit scoring, statistical techniques and evaluation criteria: a review of the literature. Intell. Syst. Account. Finance Manage. **18**(2–3), 59–88 (2011)
2. Antonakis, A., Sfakianakis, M.E.: Assessing naïve Bayes as a method for screening credit applicants. J. Appl. Stat. **36**(5), 537–545 (2009)
3. Atiya, A.: Bankruptcy prediction for credit risk using neural networks: a survey and new results. IEEE Trans. Neural Netw. **12**(4), 929–935 (2001)
4. Baesens, B., Gestel, T.V., Viaene, S., Stepanova, M., Suykens, J., Vanthienen, J.: Benchmarking state-of-the-art classification algorithms for credit scoring. J. Oper. Res. Soc. **54**(6), 627–635 (2003)
5. Bensic, M., Sarlija, N., Zekic-Susac, M.: Modelling small-business credit scoring by using logistic regression, neural networks and decision trees. Intell. Syst. Account. Finance Manage. **13**(3), 133–150 (2005)
6. Brans, J.P., Vincke, P.: A preference ranking organisation method: the PROMETHEE method for multiple criteria decision-making. Manage. Sci. **31**(6), 647–656 (1985)
7. Desai, V., Crook, J., Overstreet, G.: A comparison of neural networks and linear scoring models in the credit union environment. Eur. J. Oper. Res. **95**(1), 24–37 (1996)
8. Hall, M., Frank, E., Holmes, G., Pfahringer, B., Reutemann, P., Witten, I.: The WEKA data mining software: an update. SIGKDD Explor. Newslett. **11**(1), 10–18 (2009)
9. Hand, D.: Good practice in retail credit scorecard assessment. J. Oper. Res. Soc. **56**(9), 1109–1117 (2005)
10. Huang, Z., Chen, H., Hsu, C.J., Chen, W.H., Wu, S.: Credit rating analysis with support vector machines and neural networks: a market comparative study. Decis. Support Syst. **37**(4), 543–558 (2004)
11. Hwang, C.L., Yoon, K.: Multiple Attribute Decision Making - Methods and Applications. Springer, New York (1981)
12. Jablonsky, J.: Software support for multiple criteria decision making problems. Manage. Inf. Syst. **4**(2), 29–34 (2009)
13. Japkowicz, N., Shah, M.: Evaluating Learning Algorithms: a Classifier Perspective. Cambridge University Press, New York (2011)

14. du Jardin, P.: Predicting bankruptcy using neural networks and other classification methods: the influence of variable selection techniques on model accuracy. Neurocomputing **73**(10–12), 2047–2060 (2010)
15. Köksalan, M., Wallenius, J., Zionts, S.: Multiple Criteria Decision Making: From Early History to the 21st Century. World Scientific, Singapore (2011)
16. Lee, J.S., Zhu, D.: When costs are unequal and unknown: a subtree graftingapproach for unbalanced data classification. Decis. Sci. **42**(4), 803–829 (2011)
17. Lee, T.S., Chen, I.F.: A two-stage hybrid credit scoring model using artificial neural networks and multivariate adaptive regression splines. Expert Syst. Appl. **28**(4), 743–752 (2005)
18. Lee, T.S., Chiu, C.C., Chou, Y.C., Lu, C.J.: Mining the customer credit using classification and regression tree and multivariate adaptive regression splines. Comput. Stat. Data Anal. **50**(4), 1113–1130 (2006)
19. Marqués, A., García, V., Sánchez, J.: Two-level classifier ensembles for credit risk assessment. Expert Syst. Appl. **39**(12), 10916–10922 (2012)
20. Min, J., Lee, Y.C.: Bankruptcy prediction using support vector machine with optimal choice of kernel function parameters. Expert Syst. Appl. **28**(4), 603–614 (2005)
21. Pietruszkiewicz, W.: Dynamical systems and nonlinear Kalman filtering applied in classification. In: Proceedings of the 7th IEEE International Conference on Cybernetic Intelligent Systems, London, UK, pp. 263–268 (2008)
22. Sabzevari, H., Soleymani, M., Noorbakhsh, E.: A comparison between statistical and data mining methods for credit scoring in case of limited available data. In: Proceedings of the 3rd CRC Credit Scoring Conference, Edinburgh, UK (2007)
23. Shi, Y., Peng, Y., Kou, G., Chen, Z.: Classifying credit card accounts for business intelligence and decision making: a multiple-criteria quadratic programming approach. Int. J. Inf. Technol. Decis. Making **4**(4), 581–599 (2005)
24. Shih, H.S., Shyur, H.J., Lee, E.: An extension of TOPSIS for group decision making. Math. Comput. Model. **45**(7–8), 801–813 (2007)
25. Sokolova, M., Lapalme, G.: A systematic analysis of performance measures for classification tasks. Inf. Process. Manage. **45**(4), 427–437 (2009)
26. Thomas, L., Edelman, D., Crook, J.: Credit Scoring and Its Applications. SIAM, Philadelphia (2002)
27. Triantaphyllou, E.: Multi-criteria decision making methods. Multi-Criteria Decision Making Methods: a Comparative Study. Applied Optimization, pp. 5–21. Springer, Berlin (2000)
28. Trustorff, J.H., Konrad, P., Leker, J.: Credit risk prediction using support vector machines. Rev. Quant. Finance Account. **36**(4), 565–581 (2011)
29. Tsai, C.F., Wu, J.W.: Using neural network ensembles for bankruptcy prediction and credit scoring. Expert Syst. Appl. **34**(4), 2639–2649 (2008)
30. Tseng, F., Lin, L.: A quadratic interval logit model for forecasting bankruptcy. Omega **13**(1), 85–91 (2005)
31. Twala, B.: Combining classifiers for credit risk prediction. J. Syst. Sci. Syst. Eng. **18**(3), 292–311 (2009)
32. Wang, G., Hao, J., Ma, J., Jiang, H.: A comparative assessment of ensemble learning for credit scoring. Expert Syst. Appl. **38**(1), 223–230 (2011)
33. Yobas, M., Crook, J., Ross, P.: Credit scoring using neural and evolutionary techniques. IMA J. Math. Appl. Bus. Ind. **11**(4), 111–125 (2000)

Combining k-Nearest Neighbor and Centroid Neighbor Classifier for Fast and Robust Classification

Wiesław Chmielnicki[✉]

Faculty of Physics, Astronomy and Applied Computer Science,
Jagiellonian University, Kraków, Poland
wieslaw.chmielnicki@uj.edu.pl
http://www.fais.uj.edu.pl

Abstract. The k-NN classifier is one of the most known and widely used nonparametric classifiers. The k-NN rule is optimal in the asymptotic case which means that its classification error aims for Bayes error if the number of the training samples approaches infinity. A lot of alternative extensions of the traditional k-NN have been developed to improve the classification accuracy. However, it is also well-known fact that when the number of the samples grows it can become very inefficient because we have to compute all the distances from the testing sample to every sample from the training data set. In this paper, a simple method which addresses this issue is proposed. Combining k-NN classifier with the centroid neighbor classifier improves the speed of the algorithm without changing the results of the original k-NN. In fact usage confusion matrices and excluding outliers makes the resulting algorithm much faster and robust.

Keywords: k-NN classifier · Confusion matrix · Statistical classifiers · Supervised classification · Multiclass classifiers

1 Introduction

The k-Nearest Neighbor (k-NN) is very simple yet very efficient nonparametric classifier. It has been widely used in many applications because of its simplicity, effectiveness and intuitiveness. The k-NN classifies the unknown sample according to the k closest samples from the training data set i.e. the label of the most frequent class among those neighbors will be assigned to this sample. The k-NN method is theoretically and empirically described in [10].

The traditional k-NN classifier has two main drawbacks. First, we have to find out the k nearest neighboring samples, so all the distances between unknown sample x and the training samples must be calculated. If the training set contains a very large number of the samples and the feature vector describing the sample is high dimensional this can stand a problem, especially for the real time

© Springer International Publishing Switzerland 2016
F. Martínez-Álvarez et al. (Eds.): HAIS 2016, LNAI 9648, pp. 536–548, 2016.
DOI: 10.1007/978-3-319-32034-2_45

applications. Second, all the training samples are treated equally, so even several outliers can significantly worsen the result. Especially 1-NN classifier is very sensitive even for a single outlier [14].

Recently, many extensions of the traditional k-NN have been developed. Most of them focused on the improving the classification accuracy, for example in [1,19,22]. There are some weighted voting schemes used [11,12] or in other solutions some different algorithms are used to employ the labels of k nearest neighbors to weight classifiers applied for the classification [23]. There are also some approaches using centroids of the classes, for example in [13].

The real world problem which we have to solve was to classify the gestures made by hand with the mobile device (using the data from accelerometer). Our first choice was a Support Vector Machine (SVM) classifier [26]. The hybrid discriminative/generative approach (SVM-RDA classifier) described in [3,5] had been used.

The usage of SVM-RDA classifier was successful but the speed of the algorithm has not been satisfactory. Additionally, one more requirement had to be fulfilled i.e. algorithm should efficiently add new samples to the training data set. However, the learning phase of the SVM algorithm is computationally demanding it also requires calculating of the two parameters C and γ which should be chosen, for example using grid-search procedure [2].

All these requirements caused that the decision to use the k-NN algorithm has been made. Adding the new sample, even the sample representing the new class is quite straightforward in this approach. We just have to add the sample to the training data set. However, the growing number of the samples provokes the new problem with the speed of the algorithm on mobile devices.

So, in this approach the focus is on the speed of the k-NN algorithm instead of the classification accuracy. Using the distance from the centroids of the classes we can limit the number of the samples from the training data set that have to be considered during the classification phase. This approach and the usage of the confusion matrices improves the speed of the program without impact on the classification error. Additionally introducing a method which eliminates outliers achieves more robust and stable algorithm.

The rest of this paper is organized as follows: Sect. 2 describes the k-NN and centroids neighbor classifiers, Sect. 3 introduces proposed method, Sect. 4 is dedicated to the experiments conducted to test the solution, Sect. 5 shows the experimental results and finally in Sect. 6 conclusions are discussed.

2   The k-NN and Centroid Neighbor Classifiers

In this section both classifiers are presented. The description does not go into the details because both classifiers are very simple and widely known. Instead, the focus is on the strong aspects of the presented algorithms. Additionally their drawbacks are pointed out and there are suggestions how to ease them.

2.1   The k-NN Classifier

The k-nearest neighbors rule is one of the oldest and simplest methods for pattern classification. The k-NN rule classifies each sample in the three steps. First, we calculate the distance between the sample x and all the others samples x_i from the training data set. Second step is to get k closest samples from the set and finally we assign the label to the sample x according to majority voting scheme i.e. we say that x belong to c_i class when most of the k samples belongs to this class.

So, if we denote the set $S(x) = \{(x_i, y_i)\}_{i=1}^{k}$ which has been created from the samples of the training data set according to the distance $d(x, x_i)$. Often the Euclidean or Manhattan distance is used:

$$d(x, x_i) = \sqrt{\sum_{j=1}^{m}(x_j, x_{ij})^2} \quad or \quad d(x, x_i) = \sqrt{\sum_{j=1}^{m}|x_j, x_{ij}|} \tag{1}$$

where the m is the number of features and x_j is the j-th value of the feature of the vector x and x_{ij} is the j-th value of the feature of the vector x_i.

The class label is determined by the majority voting scheme which means calculating the following formula:

$$y = \arg\max_{c_j} \sum_{(x_i, y_i) \in S} \delta(c_j, y_i) \tag{2}$$

where $\delta(c_j, y_i)$ have the value one if $c_j = y_i$ and zero otherwise.

We see that if $k > 1$ and the number of the classes $K \geq 2$ then the number of the samples belonging to two different classes might be equal i.e. $\sum \delta(c_j, y_i)$ can be equal for c_j, c_k, $j \neq k$. In these cases we can just choose the arbitrary label or we can use 1-NN rule to settle the draw.

Of course the performance of the method depends crucially on the distance metric used to identify nearest neighbors. Usually the metric is adapted to the particular problem. There are many papers showing that k-NN classification rule can be significantly improved by learning a distance metric from labeled examples [6,20,27]. However even usage of the simple Euclidean or Manhattan distance provides very good results in many applications.

The asymptotic classification error of k-NN tends to the optimal Bayes error rate as $k \to \infty$ while $k/N \to 0$ when N grows to infinity, and the error is bounded by approximately twice the Bayes error if $k = 1$ [7]. This asymptotic classification performance and the simplicity of implementation makes k-NN a powerful classification approach. However, with one objection: We should have a very large training data set. Additionally, this theoretical behavior usually cannot be obtained because k-NN is very sensitive to the outliers and the noise (especially when the value of k is small). These two drawbacks are addressed in the presented approach.

2.2   The Centroid Neighbor Classifier

This classifier is based on the assumption that the distances between the samples belonging to the same class should be minimal. There are several methods based on this assumption. For example, the Fisher linear discriminant analysis [10] which project the original space into a new space in which distance between classes is enlarged while distance within class is narrowed.

The centroid neighbor classifier calculates the centers (also called centroids) of each class and then assigns the unknown sample to the class which centroid is the closest. So, the classification rule is:

$$y = \arg\max_i = dist(x, \mu_i) \tag{3}$$

where μ_i are the centroids of the classes for $i = 1, \ldots, K$ calculated using the samples from the training data set as follows:

$$\mu_i = \frac{1}{N_i} \sum_{j=1}^{N_i} x_j \tag{4}$$

where N_i is the number of the samples representing i-th class and x_j are the samples belonging to this class.

We see from the above formula that this classifier is much faster. Its computational complexity is $O(1)$ comparing to $O(n)$ for k-NN. We calculate only the distances between the sample x and all centroids. This classifier is much more robust to the outliers especially when we have a large number of the samples representing each class because the individual outliers have almost no impact on the centroid.

However, this method often suffers from the inductive bias or model misfit [16,24]. It also achieves very bad results on problems presented in Fig. 1. The problem on the left is called "Japanese flag" data set [28]. We see that it is impossible to correctly classify these data sets using centroid rule (for "Japanese flag" the centroids are almost the same) but k-NN rule will get quite good

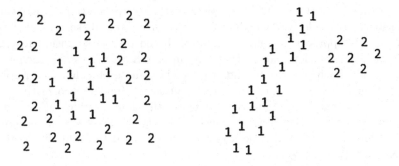

Fig. 1. The data sets for which the centroid classifier fails

results. These examples do not mean that k-NN is always better than the centroid neighbor classifier. Some authors claims [18] that the centroid classifier often outperforms the k-NN algorithm on the real data sets.

3   The Proposed Approach

The problem with k-NN classifier is that we would like to have as many samples in the training data set as possible because it improves the recognition ratio but on the other hand when the number of the samples in the training data set grows we have to calculate a lot of distances. The calculation of the distance is computationally expensive especially when the feature vector is high dimensional.

Let us consider the problem depicted in the Fig. 2. We see that instead of calculating all distances we can calculate the distances between the samples from three neighboring classes only: {1, 2, 7}. The problem is that we don't know which samples we should include in our calculation procedure.

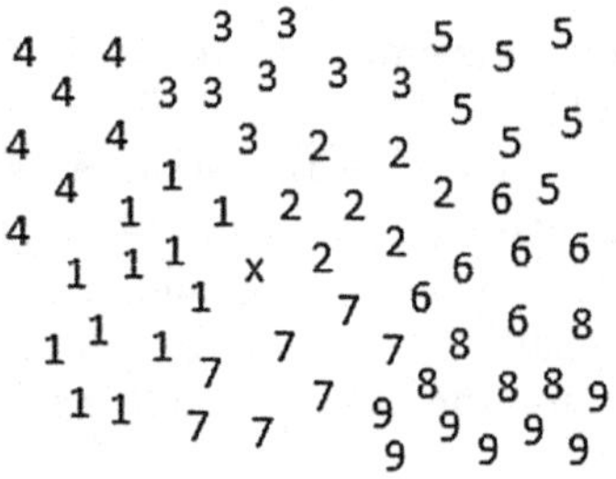

Fig. 2. The sample "x" among the samples from the training data set

The simple solution is to use the centroids of the classes and calculate the distances to all samples representing the classes with the nearest centroids. However the problem is how many centroids we should consider or what value of the distance should be the limit. The answer to these two questions is not simple and probably it would be dependent from the current database.

So in this approach a different solution based on the confusion matrix is proposed. The confusion matrix is a square matrix KxK where K is the number of the classes. Each row corresponds to one class and each column corresponds to one of the classes to which the sample is classified (maybe incorrectly). Each cell (i, j) of the matrix contains the number of the samples which belong to i-th class but has been classified as j-th class. The original k-NN algorithm running on the training data set with k-crossvalidation is used to build the confusion matrix.

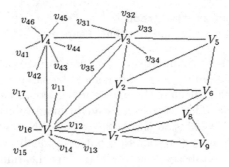

Fig. 3. The example of the confusion graph

The next step is to build the confusion graph which will be used by our algorithm. The graph has two kinds of vertices: $\{V_i\}_{i=1}^K$ for all centroids and $\{v_{ij}\}_{j=1}^{N_i}$ for each sample from the training data set. The vertices V_i and V_j are connected by the edge if and only if the value in the cell (i,j) of the confusion matrix is greater than zero. The vertex v_{ij} is connected to the vertex V_j if and only if it belongs to the class which centroid is represented by V_j. All edges are labeled with the distances between samples or centroids.

The example of the confusion graph is presented on the Fig. 3. For the clarity of the picture the $\{v_{ij}\}$ vertices (representing samples) are placed for V_4, V_1 and V_3 vertices only. We can see that if the unknown sample x will be closest to the centroid represented by V_4 vertex then we will calculate only the distances between all v_{ij} vertices which are connected by the edges with V_4, V_3 and V_1 respectively i.e. $\{v_{4j}\}_{j=1}^{N_4}$, $\{v_{3j}\}_{j=1}^{N_3}$ and $\{v_{1j}\}_{j=1}^{N_1}$.

As it has been stated earlier there is also a problem with the outliers. If we use the original k-NN method there is no way to eliminate them. However, when we combine it with the centroid neighbor we have the centroid of each class. So we can calculate the standard deviation of each class using the formula below:

$$\sigma_i = \sqrt{\frac{1}{N_i}\sum_{j=1}^{N_i}(x_j - \mu_j)^2} \tag{5}$$

where the μ_j are the centroids of the classes calculated using formula (4).

We can throw away all the samples that are more distant from the centroid of his own class than 2σ and in this way get rid of all outliers. We assume that the samples in the training data set are distributed normally, so 95 % of the samples should be within this 2σ distance. This procedure means that we remove the edges between centroid V_i and the samples v_{ij} which lies outside 2σ boundary.

So finally we build the confusion graph using the following steps:

```
(1) Calculate all centroids for all classes
(2) Create the confusion matrix using original k-NN algorithm
(3) Create the confusion graph on the basis of the matrix
```

(4) Label all edges of the graph
(5) Remove the edges for the distant samples

This approach has two main advantages: first, using centroids and the confusion matrix we eliminate a large number of the samples. So at the testing phase we do not have to calculate these distances. Second, we eliminate outlying samples using 2σ rule. These two rules lead to more robust and much faster algorithm. Let's call it Confusion Graph k-NN (CG k-NN). It works pretty well for our problem with gesture recognition but additionally we tested it against three other different databases from UCI Machine Learning Repository [25]. These experiments and the results are described in the next two sections.

If we carefully examine the algorithm we see that we can improve its speed in yet another way. The k-NN algorithm using confusion graph consists of the following steps (to simplify the description let's assume that $k = 1$):

```
(1) dmin = MAX_DISTANCE;
(2) vmin = -1;
(3) V = getClosestVertex(x, confGraph);
(4) for all v connected to V
(5)     dmin, vmin = min(dmin, dist(x, v));
(6) for all Vi connected to V
(7)     for all v connected to Vi
(8)         dmin, vmin = min(dmin, dist(x, v));
(9) Assign the label of vmin~to the x
```

Let us look at the Fig. 4. We would like to classify the unknown sample x. Now, we are looking at the samples connected to the V_i centroid and the current minimum distance is equal to d_{min}. The next step of the algorithm would be to calculate the distance between the sample x and v_3. However, we know the value of the distance d_i between x and the centroid and the value of the distance d_{3i} between the sample v_3 and the centroid.

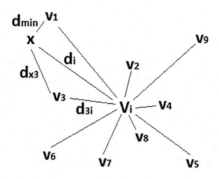

Fig. 4. The example of the confusion graph

On the other hand we know that d is the distance function what means that it has to meet the triangle inequality i.e. $d_i \leq d_{3i} + d_{x3}$. So, it comes from this inequality that $d_{x3} \geq d_i - d_{3i}$ and therefore if $d_{min} < d_i - d_{3i}$ we don't have to calculate d_{x3} distance. In this way we can skip a lot of distance calculations which are expensive replacing them by just one subtraction.

We can gain even more when we are looking for other centroid vertices. Let us look closer at the Fig. 5. We know the distance d_{xi} between unknown sample x and the centroid V_i (it is computed in the step 3 of the algorithm). Let's recall that we excluded all samples from the training data set that are more distant than $2\sigma_i$ from the vertex V_i. It is obvious that the closest sample connected with V_i centroid cannot be closer than $d_{xi} - 2\sigma_i$, so if d_{min} is less than this value then there is no sense to calculate any distance between vertices v_i connected to the V_i centroid.

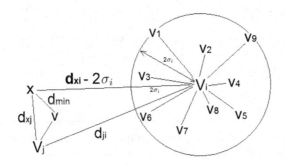

Fig. 5. The example of the confusion graph

The modified algorithm is much faster than CG k-NN presented above. What is more important, excluding these vertices from the calculation has no effect on the final result. Additionally this approach can be also extended for different values of k although it is less effective. In this case the value of d_{min} store the value of the maximum value of the distance from k nearest neighbor distances. This algorithm with additional procedure minimizing the number of distance calculations we call Fast CG k-NN (FCG k-NN).

4   The Experiment

The proposed algorithm works well for the problem with gesture recognition on mobile devices but it has been also tested on several different databases from UCI Machine Learning Repository [25]. Three databases with different characteristics have been selected. The number of the classes is between 10 and 100, the number of features varies from 126 to 1500 and the number of samples from 698 to 700000. The detailed specification can be found in the Table 1.

Table 1. The databases used in the experiments

Database name	Number of		
	Classes	Samples	Features
Gestures	16	4800	1500
Proteins	27	698	126
Leafs	100	1600	192
Digits	10	700000	192

Table 2. The results using 1-NN classifier

Database name	Method	
	1-NN [%]	CG 1-NN [%]
Gestures	81.1–85.5–92.7	83.2–86.1–92.6
Proteins	44.3–46.4–50.6	45.2–46.9–50.8
Leafs	85.5–88.1–91.9	86.1–88.5–92.3
Digits	92.7–94.3–97.8	92.9–94.4–97.8

The feature vector used for the Gestures database are the time-series from accelerometer normalized to the same number of values for all readings. The feature vector for Proteins problem is described in [8,9] and for Leafs database in [21]. The digits database is in fact Modified NIST database [15,17]. The feature vector extracted from this database is described in [4].

For each database the confusion matrix using 7-NN algorithm has been created using the k-crossvalidation procedure ($k = 7$) on the training data set. Finally all samples outside 2σ limit has been excluded. The last step was to calculate the recognition ratio for CG 1-NN and FCG 1-NN algorithm. This also has been done using k-crossvalidation procedure (with $k = 7$). However, another different partitions has been used i.e. different from these that has been used for calculating confusion matrices. Then the same procedure has been repeated for 3-NN, 5-NN and 7-NN classifiers.

The presented algorithm should be faster and more robust than the original k-NN algorithm. So the number of the distances required to obtain the result has been computed and additionally the time for all algorithm runs has been compared.

Although the original problem has been implemented on the mobile phone and under android operating system the experiments has been conducted on the desktop computer.

5   The Results

The Table 2 shows the results obtained from the experiments. There are three results in each column which present minimum - average - maximum classification ratio for 1-NN and CG 1-NN algorithm. The results from FCG 1-NN algorithm are not present because there is no difference between CG and FCG according to the classification ratio.

We see that the proposed method achieves slightly better recognition ratios than the original k-NN algorithm. We also see that the results are more stable. The difference between maximum and minimum results is lower. However, the improvement according to the classifications ratios has not been expected.

The Table 3 shows the same comparison between 1-NN, 3-NN, 5-NN and 7-NN classifiers. The average value of the classification ratio is presented. We see that the results are comparable. We can even notice the slight increase of the recognition ratio but it is possible that it is not statistically significant.

The number of the calculated distances and the time needed to classify all the samples is presented in the Table 4. In the columns we have the average number of the distances between the samples we have to compute to classify one unknown sample and the time we need to classify all the samples. The time is relative to 1-NN classifier i.e. for 1-NN classifier it is always 100 %.

And finally in the Table 5 the results for the k-NN classifiers with different k values are presented. We see the increase of the speed of the algorithm according to original k-NN. We can also notice that usage of CG modification increases the speed of the algorithm from 2.82–12.39 and FCG from 2.93–15.43. Of course the gain is better for the problems with a large number of the classes.

Table 3. The results using k-NN classifier (for k = 1, 3, 5 and 7)

Database name	Method							
	1-NN	CG 1-NN	3-NN	CG 3-NN	5-NN	CG 5-NN	7-NN	CG 7-NN
Gestures	85.5 %	86.1 %	85.9 %	86.3 %	86.1 %	86.4 %	86.1 %	86.4 %
Proteins	46.4 %	46.9 %	44.2 %	44.9 %	43.1 %	43.7 %	42.0 %	42.5 %
Leafs	88.1 %	88.5 %	87.2 %	87.9 %	86.5 %	87.1 %	85.0 %	85.3 %
Digits	94.3 %	94.4 %	95.5 %	95.5 %	95.9 %	95.9 %	96.2 %	96.2 %

Table 4. The number of distances calculated by 1-NN, CG 1-NN and FCG 1-NN classifiers

Database name	Method		
	1-NN	CG 1-NN	FCG 1-NN
Gestures	4114 (100 %)	964 (22.6 %)	632(16.8 %)
Proteins	598 (100 %)	224 (35.2 %)	187 (32.6 %)
Leafs	1371 (100 %)	117 (8.1 %)	82 (6.5 %)
Digits	$6 * 10^5$ (100 %)	$2.3 * 10^5$ (37.2 %)	$1.1 * 10^5$ (19.3 %)

Table 5. The increase of the speed for CG k-NN and FCG k-NN algorithms

Database name	Method							
	1-NN		3-NN		5-NN		7-NN	
	CG	FCG	CG	FCG	CG	FCG	CG	FCG
Gestures	4.42	5.95	4.45	5.54	4.41	5.31	4.39	5.17
Proteins	2.84	3.07	2.84	3.02	2.83	2.99	2.82	2.93
Leafs	12.39	15.43	12.35	15.12	12.36	14.97	12.36	14.84
Digits	2.69	5.18	2.67	5.01	2.68	4.97	2.69	4.93

6   Conclusions

The proposed solution accelerates the algorithm of the gesture recognition about 6 times and the recognition ratios remain at the same level as those achieved using the original k-NN approach. Similar results have been obtained for the three other UCI databases with different characteristics producing much faster algorithms.

The proposed solution solved the problem with the gesture recognition on mobile devices and also proved to be efficient for three other problems from UCI Machine Learning Repository. As we can see from the Table 3 the results are nearly the same for different values of the k.

There are two drawbacks of the proposed method. First there is additional overhead connected to calculating centroids and standard deviations of the classes. However, this is done on the training phase of the algorithm and in most of the classification tasks the time of the training phase is not important. Second problem appears when we would like to retrain the algorithm using additional samples. This operation is straightforward for the original k-NN, we just add the samples to the training data set. In this approach it is not possible because the confusion graph should be updated.

Reconstructing the confusion graph when we add single sample will be completely inefficient, so we can just add the new v_i vertex to the graph or we can postpone the addition and run the procedure of updating confusion graph when the number of extra samples exceeds some preset value.

There are still some open questions that could be addressed. We can look for the algorithm which can remove some edges between the centroids in the way that will not affect the classification ratio achieved by the algorithm. The number of these edges is crucial according to the efficiency of the solution. We can also look for some additional criteria which allow us to remove some edges between samples and centroids. It would be especially effective when we have a lot of the samples representing each class.

References

1. Altincay, H.: Improving the k-nearest neighbour rule: using geometrical neighbour-hoods and manifold-based metrics. Expert Syst. Wiley Online Libr. **28**(4), 391–406 (2011)
2. Chang, C.C., Lin, C.J.: LIBSVM: a library for support vector machines (2001). Software available at http://www.csie.ntu.edu.tw/~cjlin/libsvm
3. Chmielnicki, W., Stąpor, K.: Protein fold recognition with combined SVM-RDA classifier. In: Graña Romay, M., Corchado, E., Garcia Sebastian, M.T. (eds.) HAIS 2010, Part I. LNCS (LNAI), vol. 6076, pp. 162–169. Springer, Heidelberg (2010)
4. Chmielnicki, W., Stapor, K.: Investigation of normalization techniques and their impact on a recognition rate in handwritten numeral recognition. Schedae Informaticae **19**, 53–77 (2010)
5. Chmielnicki, W., Stapor, K.: A hybrid discriminative/generative approach to protein fold recognition. Neurocomputing **75**(1), 194–198 (2012)
6. Domeniconi, C., Gunopulos, D., Peng, J.: Large margin nearest neighbor classifiers. IEEE Trans. Neural Netw. **16**(4), 899–909 (2005)
7. Devijver, P.A., Kittler, J.: Pattern Recognition: A Statistical Approach. Prentice Hall, Englewood Cliffs (1982)
8. Ding, C.H., Dubchak, I.: Multi-class protein fold recognition using support vector machines and neural networks. Bioinformatics **17**, 349–358 (2001)
9. Dubchak, I., Muchnik, I., Kim, S.H.: Protein folding class predictor for SCOP: approach based on global descriptors. In: Proceedings ISMB (1997)
10. Duda, R.O., Hart, P.E., Stork, D.G.: Pattern Classification, 2nd edn. Wiley, New York (2000)
11. Dudani, S.: The distance-weighted k-nearest neighbor rule. IEEE Trans. Syst. Man Cybern. **6**(4), 325–327 (1976)
12. Gou, J., Xiong, T., Kuang, Y.: A novel weighted voting for k-nearest neighbor rule. J. Comput. **6**(5), 833–840 (2011)
13. Gou, J., Du, L., Xiong, T.: Weighted k-nearest centroid neighbor classification. J. Comput. Inf. Syst. **8**(2), 851–860 (2012)
14. Jiang, Y., Zhou, Z.-H.: Editing training data for kNN classifiers with neural network ensemble. In: Yin, F.-L., Wang, J., Guo, C. (eds.) ISNN 2004. LNCS, vol. 3173, pp. 356–361. Springer, Heidelberg (2004)
15. LeCun, Y., et al.: Comparison of learning algorithms for handwritten digit recognition. In: Fogelman-Soulie, F., Gallinari, P. (eds.) Proceedings of the International Conference on Artificial Neural Networks, France, Nanterre, pp. 53–60 (1995)
16. Liu, Y., Yang, Y., Carbonell, J.: Boosting to correct inductive bias in text classification. In: 11th ACM International Conference on Information and Knowledge Management, pp. 348–355 (2002)
17. The MNIST database of handwritten digits (2015). http://yann.lecun.com/exdb/mnist/
18. Petitjean, F., Forestier, G., Webb, G., Nicholson, A., Chen, Y., Keogh, E.: Faster and more accurate classification of time series by exploiting a novel dynamic time warping averaging algorithm. Knowl. Inf. Syst. 1–26 (2015). doi:10.1007/s10115-015-0878-8
19. Sanchez, J.S., Marques, A.: An LVQ-based adaptive algorithm for learning from very small codebooks. Neurocomputing **69**(7–9), 922–927 (2006)
20. Shalev-Shwartz, S., Singer, Y., Ng, A.: Online and batch learning of pseudo-metrics. In: Proceedings of the 21st International Conference on Machine Learning, Banff, Canada (2004)

21. Silva, P.F.B., Marçal, A.R.S., Almeida da Silva, R.: Evaluation of features for leaf discrimination. In: Kamel, M., Campilho, A. (eds.) ICIAR 2013. LNCS, vol. 7950, pp. 197–204. Springer, Heidelberg (2013)

22. Sun, S., Huang, R.: An adaptive k-nearest neighbor algorithm. In: Proceedings of the 7th International Conference on Fuzzy Systems and Knowledge Discovery, pp. 91–94 (2010)

23. Sun, S.: Local within-class accuracies for weighting individual outputs in multiple classifier systems. Pattern Recogn. Lett. **31**(2), 119–124 (2010)

24. Tan, S.: An improved centroid classifier for text categorization. Expert Syst. Appl. **35**(1), 279–285 (2008)

25. UCI Machine Learning Repository (2015). http://archive.ics.uci.edu/ml/datasets.html

26. Vapnik, V.: The Nature of Statistical Learning Theory. Springer, New York (1995)

27. Weinberger, K., Saul, L.: Distance metric learning for large margin nearest neighbor classification. J. Mach. Learn. Res. **10**, 207–244 (2009)

28. Xi, X., Ueno, K., Keogh, E., Lee, D.: Converting nonparametric distance-based classification to anytime algorithms. Pattern Anal. Appl. **11**(3–4), 321–336 (2008)

A First Study on the Use of Boosting for Class Noise Reparation

Pablo Morales Álvarez$^{(\boxtimes)}$, Julián Luengo, and Francisco Herrera

Department of Computer Science and Artificial Intelligence, CITIC-UGR,
University of Granada, 18071 Granada, Spain
pablomorales@correo.ugr.es, {julianlm,herrera}@decsai.ugr.es

Abstract. Class noise refers to the incorrect labeling of examples in classification, and is known to negatively affect the performance of classifiers. In this contribution, we propose a boosting-based hybrid algorithm that combines data removal and data reparation to deal with noisy instances. A experimental procedure to compare its performance against no-preprocessing is developed and analyzed, laying the foundations for future works.

Keywords: Data reparation · Data filtering · Class noise · Boosting · Classification

1 Introduction

The main goal of Data Mining (DM) consists of extracting useful and valuable knowledge out of large amounts of raw data [6,15]. Evidently, the relevance and interest of this knowledge is strongly influenced by the quality of the used data, and this turns preprocessing into one of the most crucial and time-consuming steps in the DM process [14,22]. In this stage, a very common problem is the presence of *noise* in the dataset, i.e. corrupted data items not following the general distribution of the dataset, which can lead to excessively complex models with deteriorated performance [31]. We focus our interest on classification task, where two types of noise are distinguished: *class noise*, when it affects to the class label of the instances, and *attribute noise*, when it affects to the rest of attributes. The former is known to be the most disruptive one [24,30]. Consequently, many recent works, including this contribution, are devoted to overcome it or at least to minimize its effects (see [10] for a comprehensive and updated survey).

Among the approaches followed to address this problem, data reparation is one of most delicate, since incorrect relabeling may dramatically harm the borders between classes, leading to deteriorated accuracy for later classifiers [8,20]. This supposes a significant lack of literature and methods on the subject, which usually prevents researchers and practitioners from taking advantage of reparation benefits.

In this contribution, we propose using the well-known boosting mechanism [11,12] to introduce a hybrid algorithm that combines data removal and data

© Springer International Publishing Switzerland 2016
F. Martínez-Álvarez et al. (Eds.): HAIS 2016, LNAI 9648, pp. 549–559, 2016.
DOI: 10.1007/978-3-319-32034-2_46

reparation. The reason for the choice of boosting is twofold: its sensitivity to noise allows for detecting noisy instances through the values of their weights, and the reliability of the ensemble of classifiers built along the different iterations allows for evaluating the most likely class for the noisy instances and somehow quantify its confidence.

We will develop a experimental study to compare our proposal against "no preprocessing", considering 13 datasets and noise levels from 0 % to 35 % by increments of 5 %. To leave out exernal effects on the noise treatment, we will avoid using robust classifiers in the evaluation, taking 1-NN instead. Finally, we will include a Wilcoxon signed-rank test to assess the statistical evidence of enhancement.

The layout of the contribution is as follows: in Sect. 2 we set the context for our proposal, including previous related works (Sect. 2.1), and some relevant notes on boosting (Sect. 2.2). In Sect. 3, our novel hybrid algorithm is detailed and analyzed. Section 4 addresses the empirical evaluation, setting the experimental framework in Sect. 4.1 and explaining the results in Sect. 4.2. Some conclusions, comments, and future directions are included in Sect. 5.

2 Background and Related Work

In this section we set the context for our proposal. Specifically, Sect. 2.1 briefly reviews the main techniques for class noise preprocessing, focusing on reparation. Section 2.2 includes some appropriate comments on the use of boosting.

2.1 Tackling Class Noise Preprocessing

In the literature, there are two main ways to deal with class noise [30]: *algorithm level approaches* [7,23], which attempt to create robust classification algorithms that are little influenced by the presence of noise, and *data level approaches* [5,13], which try to develop strategies to cleanse the dataset as a previous step to the fit of the classifier. We will follow the second approach, since it allows to carry out the preprocessing just once and apply any classifier therafter, whereas the first treatment is specific for each classification algorithm.

In the chosen approach, the most classical procedure consists of detecting polluted instances and *removing* them from the dataset. Such algorithms are commonly called *filters*, and the detection step can be accomplished by means of different paradigms, such as ensemble-based techniques (e.g. Ensemble Filter (EF), see [5]), iterative procedures (e.g. Iterative Partitioning Filter (IPF), see [17]), or metric-based mechanisms (e.g. Saturation Filter (SF), see [13]).

However, there exist also other interesting ideas, like additionally allowing for data *reparation* (or *relabeling*) rather than only *removal* [3,18,21,25,33]. In fact, data is usually difficult to obtain, and getting rid of instances inexorably leads to loss of information, so it could be avoided when the real class can be guessed with a considerable level of confidence. This damage for the learning process is even worse in specific frameworks such as imbalanced classification [28].

The discussion between data filtering, data reparation, and their possible synergy is a dynamic and challenging research area: several studies warn about the dangers of incorrectly relabeling instances [8,20], whereas many others claim the problems derived from removing too many instances from the dataset [18,27]. Hence, most proposals in the subject try to develop an appropriate trade-off to address the problem.

Among these algorithms that integrate data reparation, we can find different approaches: techniques based on votes from an ensemble of classifiers [3], methods based on noise measurements and thresholds [25], nearest neighbors-related techniques [2,18], approaches based on neighborhood graphs [19,21], and other particular mechanisms like in [32,33], where neural networks and decision trees are used respectively under a similar idea. As we will comment in Sect. 3, our algorithm somehow combines the two first approaches by means of *boosting*.

2.2 Elements of Boosting

Boosting [12] is a well-known ensemble mechanism to enhance the performance of a single classifier (called the *weak classifier*, although it is not necessarily a simple one) along several iterations. Briefly, it trains that same classifier in different rounds, focusing each time in those instances misclassified in the previous step. Once the ensemble is completed, it combines the predictions of all those weak classifiers, weighted by their training accuracy, to classify previously unobserved instances.

One of the greatest exponent of this technique is AdaBoost (Adaptive Boosting) algorithm [11], which distinguishes between binary classification task (AdaBoost.M1 algorithm) and general classification (AdaBoost.M2 algorithm, which includes the notion of "pseudo-loss"). Since the former is the most popular and easy-to-handle version, in this first study we will focus on binary classification, postponing the general framework with AdaBoost.M2 for future studies (see Sect. 5).

The described procedure of boosting makes it prone to overfit noisy instances [9], with weak classifiers persistently misclassifying them and thus getting high values for their weights. Interestingly, this can be used as an indicator to detect corrupted items. For instance, in [16] the authors present a classifier called ORBoost (Outlier Removal Boosting), a noise-robust adaptation of AdaBoost which removes in each iteration those instances whose weight exceeds an appropriate threshold. Likewise, in [29] the values of certain evaluation metrics associated to the boosting process, called *edge* and *margin*, are used to detect noisy instances.

Our proposal elaborates over these ideas, and integrates the possibility of reparation based on the predictions from the underlying ensemble of classifiers.

3   Noise Reparation Using AdaBoost

Before going into specific details, let us summarize the key ideas which define our cleansing algorithm:

1. We apply the scheme of AdaBoost.M1, with its particular weights update [11,12]. Recall we are dealing with binary classification in this first approach.
2. In each iteration, we detect as "potentially noisy" those instances whose weight is over a certain threshold.
3. Those instances are either removed, relabeled or kept unchanged depending on the predictions from the underlying ensemble of weak classifiers built until that round.

Notice that points 3 and 2 above correspond to the two first approaches explained in last paragraph of Sect. 2.1 as typical ways to address the problem of noise data reparation: on the one hand, techniques based on ensembles, and on the other hand those relying on noise measurements and thresholds.

Now, let us enumerate the specific parameters and elements that allow for tuning our proposal. Their default values for the experimentation will be provided in Sect. 4.1:

- T: number of iterations for the AdaBoost mechanism.
- $weakCL$: the weak classifier used in each round.
- $NoiseTH$: threshold for considering an instance as potentially noisy (recall point 2 above).
- $RepTH, KeepTH$: respectively, thresholds for repairing or keeping those potentially noisy items (recall point 3 above).

The process is sketched in Algorithm 1. It starts with an uniform distribution of weights, i.e. $\omega_1(i) = 1/m$ for all $i = 1, \ldots, m$, where m denotes the initial number of instances in the dataset. For each iteration $t = 1, \ldots, T$, the well-known process of AdaBoost.M1 is applied, obtaining a weak classifier h_t with an associated confidence $\beta_t \in (0, +\infty)$, and updating the weights to $\{\omega_{t+1}(i)\}_i$ (the range of i will progressively decrease as removal occurs). Then, we select those instances $i_1, \ldots, i_k$ whose weight exceeds the threshold $noiseTH$. In order to analyze them, we consider the corresponding predictions of the weak classifiers $h_1, \ldots, h_t$ built until that iteration, weighted by their confidence values $\beta_1, \ldots, \beta_t$. Normalizing, we have k pairs of values $(c_{11}, c_{12}), \ldots, (c_{k1}, c_{k2})$ in the interval $[0, 1]$, describing the confidence of each "suspicious" instance belonging to each one of the two classes. Now, for each $j = 1, \ldots, k$, we take the class c with highest confidence between c_{j1} and c_{j2}:

- If c is the actual class of the instance in that step, it is kept unchanged if the confidence is greater than $KeepTH$, and removed otherwise.
- If c is not the actual class of the instance in that step, it is relabeled if the confidence is greater than $RepTH$, and removed otherwise..

Before going into next iteration, the weights of relabeled instances are initialized to $1/m_t$, with m_t the number of instances in the dataset after iteration t, the weights of those analyzed but kept instances are given back its previous value (before exceeding the threshold), and the rest of weights are not modified. After proper normalization, the process gets into next round.

Algorithm 1. AdaBoost-based approach for filtering and repairing.

Input: Dataset D with m initial instances, and tuning parameters T, *weakCL*, *NoiseTH, RepTH, KeepTH*.

Initialize: Weights $\omega_1(i) = 1/m$ for all $i = 1, \ldots, m$.

for $t = 1, \ldots, T$ **do**

    Apply AdaBoost.M1 to obtain weak classifier h_t with confidence β_t.

    Update weights to ω_{t+1} following AdaBoost.M1 scheme.

    Select "potentially noisy instances": $i_1, \ldots, i_k$ such that $\omega_{t+1}(i_j) > NoiseTH$.

    for $j = 1, \ldots, k$ **do**

        Compute c_{j1} and c_{j2} confidences for i_j belonging to class 1 and 2 respectively, based on predictions from $h_1, \ldots, h_t$ weighted by $\beta_1, \ldots, \beta_t$.

        Put $c = \max(c_{j1}, c_{j2})$ and $\gamma \in \{1, 2\}$ the correspondent class.

        if class(i_j)$= \gamma$ **then**

            if $c > KeepTH$ **then**

                Keep instance i_j in D unchanged.

            else

                Remove instance i_j from D.

            end if

        end if

        if class(i_j)$\neq \gamma$ **then**

            if $c > RepTH$ **then**

                Relabel instance i_j in D with class γ.

            else

                Remove instance i_j from D.

            end if

        end if

    end for

    Weights for relabeled items are initialized to $1/m_t$, with m_t current size of D.

    Weights for analyzed but kept items are set back to ω_t.

    Weights are re-normalized.

end for

return D

---

4 Experiments

In this section we develop a experimental study to compare our preprocessing proposal against no preprocessing. Specific framework and parameters are fixed in Sect. 4.1, whereas results are shown and analyzed in Sect. 4.2.

4.1   Experimental Framework

In order to assess the performance of our proposal, we consider 13 datasets for binary classification from KEEL dataset repository[1] [1]. Table 1 summarizes the main features of these datasets.

Table 1. Datasets used in the experimental study. #EX denotes the number of examples or instances, and #AT the number of attributes (apart from the class).

Dataset	banana	german	heart	ionosphere	magic	monk	phoneme
#EX	5300	1000	270	351	19020	432	5404
#AT	2	20	13	33	10	6	5
Dataset	pima	ring	sonar	spambase	twonorm	wdbc	
#EX	768	7400	208	4597	7400	569	
#AT	8	20	60	57	20	30	

A stratified 5-folds cross validation scheme is used to test the accuracy of 1-NN classifier without preprocessing and after applying our preprocessing algorithm. Noise levels from 0 % to 35 %, by increments of 5 %, are introduced in the training sets following a *uniform class noise scheme* [26]: the corresponding percentage of examples are corrupted randomly replacing their class labels by other ones from the set of classes. Thus, using this scheme, both classes may be affected by the noise.

In total, two runs of the same scheme (for preprocessing and no preprocessing), with eight noise levels, five train-test pairs, and thirteen datasets, adds up to $2 \times 8 \times 5 \times 13 = 1040$ experiments.

Finally, before going into the results, let us specify the default values for our algorithm's tuning parameters:

1. $T = 50$ iterations.
2. CART decision tree [4] is taken as weak classifier, which is a classical choice for boosting.
3. The noise threshold *NoiseTH* is set to depend on the size of the dataset, concretely $NoiseTH = 10/m$, where m is the initial number of instances.
4. Both *RepTH* and *KeepTH* are chosen so that "repairing" or "keeping" holds when the highest confidence is double the next one. In two-class classification, this implies $RepTH = KeepTH = 2/3$.

4.2   Analysis of Results

Complete results of the experiments are shown in Table 2. Since there are five train-test pairs for each dataset and noise level, the precision displayed is the mean value of test accuracy.

---

[1] http://keel.es/datasets.php.

Table 2. Classification accuracy for 1-NN with no preprocessing (NP) and with preprocessing (P). Results are given for each dataset and noise level considered, highlighting in each case in bold the best option between NP and P (in case of ties, both options are bolded). Since we are just displaying three decimal places, there are pairs of precision values which seem to be equal but actually differ (see for instance the dataset "sonar" at 20 % noise level).

	0 %		5 %		10 %		15 %	
	NP	P	NP	P	NP	P	NP	P
banana	0.872	**0.900**	0.855	**0.894**	0.833	**0.869**	0.817	**0.817**
german	0.683	**0.735**	0.668	**0.715**	0.659	**0.690**	0.654	**0.679**
heart	0.744	**0.807**	0.730	**0.804**	0.722	**0.796**	0.711	**0.770**
ionosphere	0.855	**0.858**	**0.843**	0.840	0.803	**0.846**	0.786	**0.832**
magic	0.816	**0.842**	0.800	**0.803**	0.784	**0.785**	**0.767**	**0.767**
monk	0.734	**0.752**	0.724	**0.738**	0.724	**0.761**	0.704	**0.771**
phoneme	**0.899**	0.863	0.880	**0.886**	0.863	**0.867**	**0.842**	**0.842**
pima	0.692	**0.763**	0.671	**0.745**	0.672	**0.751**	0.656	**0.691**
ring	0.748	**0.760**	0.733	**0.748**	0.729	**0.749**	0.710	**0.752**
sonar	**0.846**	0.836	0.832	**0.856**	0.827	**0.841**	0.822	**0.827**
spambase	**0.909**	0.906	0.889	**0.908**	0.871	**0.908**	0.849	**0.904**
twonorm	0.949	**0.966**	0.928	**0.965**	0.909	**0.967**	0.879	**0.965**
wdbc	0.946	**0.949**	0.919	**0.951**	0.896	**0.956**	0.888	**0.958**
	20 %		25 %		30 %		35 %	
	NP	P	NP	P	NP	P	NP	P
banana	**0.798**	**0.798**	**0.765**	**0.765**	**0.763**	**0.763**	**0.743**	**0.743**
german	0.657	**0.670**	0.626	**0.634**	0.616	**0.618**	0.630	**0.638**
heart	0.641	**0.722**	0.674	**0.733**	0.681	**0.726**	0.689	**0.719**
ionosphere	0.775	**0.838**	0.761	**0.852**	0.761	**0.843**	0.758	**0.852**
magic	**0.751**	**0.751**	**0.741**	**0.741**	**0.721**	**0.721**	**0.704**	**0.704**
monk	0.699	**0.769**	0.697	**0.722**	0.657	**0.674**	0.641	**0.669**
phoneme	**0.817**	**0.817**	**0.804**	**0.804**	**0.773**	**0.773**	**0.761**	**0.761**
pima	0.643	**0.664**	0.664	**0.681**	0.650	**0.663**	**0.609**	0.606
ring	0.698	**0.733**	**0.687**	**0.687**	**0.672**	**0.672**	**0.670**	**0.670**
sonar	**0.769**	**0.769**	0.779	**0.803**	0.692	**0.712**	0.803	**0.812**
spambase	0.831	**0.833**	**0.811**	**0.811**	**0.788**	**0.788**	**0.782**	**0.782**
twonorm	0.859	**0.965**	0.831	**0.835**	**0.817**	**0.817**	**0.787**	**0.787**
wdbc	0.828	**0.953**	0.822	**0.946**	0.840	**0.944**	0.812	**0.954**

Table 3. Explicit comparison between preprocessing and no preprocessing for classification accuracy with 1-NN. A symbol '+' denotes the proposed algorithm outperforms the no preprocessing. Symbols '=' and '−' indicate equality or deterioration respectively.

	0	5	10	15	20	25	30	35
banana	+	+	+	=	=	=	=	=
german	+	+	+	+	+	+	+	+
heart	+	+	+	+	+	+	+	+
ionosphere	+	−	+	+	+	+	+	+
magic	+	+	+	=	=	=	=	=
monk	+	+	+	+	+	+	+	+
phoneme	−	+	+	=	=	=	=	=
pima	+	+	+	+	+	+	+	−
ring	+	+	+	+	+	+	=	=
sonar	−	+	+	+	+	+	+	+
spambase	−	+	+	+	+	=	=	=
twonorm	+	+	+	+	+	+	+	=
wdbc	+	+	+	+	+	+	+	+
+	10	12	13	10	10	9	8	6
= +	10	12	13	13	13	13	13	12

Table 3 summarizes the direct comparison between preprocessing and no-preprocessing in a more illustrative and clear fashion. Briefly, we can conclude that our method allows for accurate preprocessing while noise does not remove too much information and patterns from the dataset, when it passes to exhibit an appropriately conservative behavior. Indeed, penultimate row reveals that our algorithm (strictly) improves accuracy at low noise levels (even at 0 % level, when no artificial noise is introduced), and that this enhancement progressively decreases as noise grows. Moreover, last row shows that our algorithm avoids incorrect reparation or unsure filtering for those higher noise levels, where precision does not deteriorate with respect to no-preprocessing.

In fact, this behavior is a natural consequence of the internal mechanism of our algorithm: as noise level grows, the precision of the weak classifier used in the boosting scheme decreases, leading to high error rates ϵ_t at each iteration. When these values get close to random guessing (i.e. $\epsilon_t \approx 0.5$), the AdaBoost weights updating scheme becomes trivial, leading to a very similar weight distribution for next round. Hence, the boosting process gets stalled, and the proposed preprocessing has no effect. This will be further discussed in Sect. 5.

To check the statistical evidence of enhancement, Table 4 shows the results of a Wilcoxon signed-rank test for each noise level, with the alternative hypothesis that our method improves the precision accuracy. Low p-values let us refuse

Table 4. Results from Wilcoxon signed-rank test applied to compare our preprocessing proposal with no preprocessing, obtained for each noise level. R^+ and R^- denote, respectively, the sum of ranks for preprocessing and no preprocessing.

	0 %	5 %	10 %	15 %	20 %	25 %	30 %	35 %
R^+	75	90	91	55	55	45	36	27
R^-	16	1	0	0	0	0	0	1
p-value	0.0199	0.0002	0.0001	0.003	0.003	0.0046	0.0071	0.0173

the null hypothesis at all noise levels, even at very low significance levels for moderate amounts of noise.

5 Conclusions and Future Work

In this first study on the use of boosting for class noise reparation, we motivate and suggest a novel cleansing algorithm, which is then shown to outperform no preprocessing in a experimental study. Results displayed in Tables 2, 3 and 4 are promising and lay the foundations for deeper works. These extensions may address several interesting aspects:

- General classification problem, with more than two classes. In principle, the same algorithm based on AdaBoost.M1 can be applied with minor modifications in the tuning parameters. However, AdaBoost.M2 is a specific adaptation developed by the same authors for general classification [11,12], and could lead to better performance of the preprocessing mechanism too.
- Dealing with high noise levels. We explained in last Sect. 4.2 how our algorithm gets stalled in presence of considerable noise levels, producing no effect. This can be regarded as a safe mechanism to avoid filtering or repairing when there is not much certainty about it. However, a bit more flexible behaviors could be explored so that, at these noise levels, preprocessing also improves, at least slightly, the lack of it.
- Experimental studies can be extended at least in two directions: a wider range of classifiers (including robust ones) could be used to assess the performance of our preprocessing approach, and direct comparison against most popular cleansing algorithms might be tackled.

All these extensions can motivate, or even require, a deep and challenging comparison between the two approaches we are dealing with: data filtering and data reparation.

Acknowledgments. This work was supported by the National Research Project TIN2014-57251-P and Andalusian Research Plans P10-TIC-6858 and P11-TIC-7765. P.M. Álvarez also holds ICARO contract 135849 from University of Granada.

References

1. Alcalá, J., Fernández, A., Luengo, J., Derrac, J., García, S., Sánchez, L., Herrera, F.: Keel data-mining software tool: Data set repository, integration of algorithms and experimental analysis framework. J. Multiple-Valued Logic Soft Comput. **17**(2–3), 255–287 (2010)
2. Barandela, R., Gasca, E.: Decontamination of training samples for supervised pattern recognition methods. In: Amin, A., Pudil, P., Ferri, F., Iñesta, J.M. (eds.) SPR 2000 and SSPR 2000. LNCS, vol. 1876, pp. 621–630. Springer, Heidelberg (2000)
3. Barandela, R., Valdovinos, R.M., Sánchez, J.S.: New applications of ensembles of classifiers. Pattern Anal. Appl. **6**(3), 245–256 (2003)
4. Breiman, L., Friedman, J., Stone, C.J., Olshen, R.A.: Classification and Regression Trees. CRC Press, Boca Raton (1984)
5. Brodley, C.E., Friedl, M.A.: Identifying mislabeled training data. J. Artif. Intell. Res. **11**, 131–167 (1999)
6. Cherkassky, V., Mulier, F.M.: Learning from Data: Concepts, Theory, and Methods. John Wiley & Sons, New York (2007)
7. Cohen, W.W.: Fast effective rule induction. In: Proceedings of the Twelfth International Conference on Machine Learning, pp. 115–123, July 1995
8. Cuendet, S., Hakkani-Tür, D., Shriberg, E.: Automatic labeling inconsistencies detection and correction for sentence unit segmentation in conversational speech. In: Popescu-Belis, A., Renals, S., Bourlard, H. (eds.) MLMI 2007. LNCS, vol. 4892, pp. 144–155. Springer, Heidelberg (2008)
9. Dietterich, T.G.: An experimental comparison of three methods for constructing ensembles of decision trees: Bagging, boosting, and randomization. Mach. learn. **40**(2), 139–157 (2000)
10. Frénay, B., Verleysen, M.: Classification in the presence of label noise: A survey. IEEE Trans. Neural Netw. Learn. Syst. **25**(5), 845–869 (2014)
11. Freund, Y., Schapire, R.E.: A decision-theoretic generalization of on-line learning and an application to boosting. J. Comput. Syst. Sci. **55**(1), 119–139 (1997)
12. Freund, Y., Schapire, R.E.: Boosting: Foundations and algorithms. MIT press, Cambridge (2012)
13. Gamberger, D., Lavrac, N., Groselj, C.: Experiments with noise filtering in a medical domain. In: ICML, pp. 143–151, June 1999
14. García, S., Luengo, J., Herrera, F.: Data Preprocessing in Data Mining. Springer, New York (2015)
15. Hastie, T., Tibshirani, R., Friedman, J., Franklin, J.: The elements of statistical learning: Data mining, inference and prediction. Math. Intel. **27**(2), 83–85 (2005)
16. Karmaker, A., Kwek, S.: A boosting approach to remove class label noise. In: Fifth International Conference on Hybrid Intelligent Systems, 2005, HIS 2005. p. 6. IEEE, November 2005
17. Khoshgoftaar, T.M., Rebours, P.: Improving software quality prediction by noise filtering techniques. J. Comput. Sci. Technol. **22**(3), 387–396 (2007)
18. Koplowitz, J., Brown, T.A.: On the relation of performance to editing in nearest neighbor rules. Pattern Recogn. **13**(3), 251–255 (1981)
19. Lallich, S., Muhlenbach, F., Zighed, D.A.: Improving classification by removing or relabeling mislabeled instances. In: Hacid, M.-S., Raś, Z.W., Zighed, D.A., Kodratoff, Y. (eds.) ISMIS 2002. LNCS (LNAI), vol. 2366, pp. 5–15. Springer, Heidelberg (2002)

20. Miranda, A.L.B., Garcia, L.P.F., Carvalho, A.C.P.L.F., Lorena, A.C.: Use of classification algorithms in noise detection and elimination. In: Corchado, E., Wu, X., Oja, E., Herrero, A., Baruque, B. (eds.) HAIS 2009. LNCS, vol. 5572, pp. 417–424. Springer, Heidelberg (2009)
21. Muhlenbach, F., Lallich, S., Zighed, D.A.: Identifying and handling mislabelled instances. J. Intell. Inf. Syst. **22**(1), 89–109 (2004)
22. Pyle, D.: Data Preparation for Data Mining, vol. 1. Morgan Kaufmann, San Francisco (1999)
23. Quinlan, J.R.: C4.5: Programs for Machine Learning. Elsevier, Amsterdam (2014)
24. Sáez, J.A., Galar, M., Luengo, J., Herrera, F.: Analyzing the presence of noise in multi-class problems: Alleviating its influence with the one-vs-one decomposition. Knowl. Inf. Syst. **38**(1), 179–206 (2014)
25. Sun, J.W., Zhao, F.Y., Wang, C.J., Chen, S.F.: Identifying and correcting mislabeled training instances. In: Future Generation Communication and Networking (FGCN 2007), vol. 1, pp. 244–250. IEEE, December 2007
26. Teng, C.M.: Correcting noisy data. In: ICML, pp. 239–248, June 1999
27. Teng, C.M.: Dealing with data corruption in remote sensing. In: Famili, A.F., Kok, J.N., Peña, J.M., Siebes, A., Feelders, A. (eds.) IDA 2005. LNCS, vol. 3646, pp. 452–463. Springer, Heidelberg (2005)
28. Van Hulse, J., Khoshgoftaar, T.: Knowledge discovery from imbalanced and noisy data. Data Knowl. Eng. **68**(12), 1513–1542 (2009)
29. Wheway, V.: Using boosting to detect noisy data. In: Kowalczyk, R., Loke, S.W., Reed, N.E., Graham, G. (eds.) PRICAI-WS 2000. LNCS (LNAI), vol. 2112, pp. 123–130. Springer, Heidelberg (2001)
30. Wu, X., Zhu, X.: Class noise vs. attribute noise: A quantitative study. Artif. Intell. Rev. **22**(3), 177–210 (2004)
31. Wu, X., Zhu, X.: Mining with noise knowledge: Error-aware data mining. IEEE Trans. Syst. Man Cybern. Part A: Syst. Hum. **38**(4), 917–932 (2008)
32. Zeng, X., Martinez, T.R.: An algorithm for correcting mislabeled data. Intel. Data Anal. **5**(6), 491–502 (2001)
33. Zeng, X., Martinez, T.R.: Using decision trees and soft labeling to filter mislabeled data. J. Intell. Syst. **17**(4), 331–354 (2008)

Ensemble of HOSVD Generated Tensor Subspace Classifiers with Optimal Tensor Flattening Directions

Bogusław Cyganek[1,2(✉)], Michał Woźniak[2], and Dariusz Jankowski[2]

[1] AGH University of Science and Technology, Al. Mickiewicza 30, 30-059 Kraków, Poland
cyganek@agh.edu.pl
[2] Wroclaw University of Technology, Wybrzeże Wyspiańskiego 27, 50-370 Wrocław, Poland
Michal.Wozniak@pwr.wroc.pl, dariusz.jankowski@pwr.edu.pl

Abstract. The paper presents a modified method of building ensembles of tensor classifiers for direct multidimensional pattern recognition in tensor subspaces. The novelty of the proposed solution is a method of lowering tensor subspace dimensions by rotation of the training pattern to their optimal directions. These are obtained computing and analyzing phase histograms of the structural tensor computed from the training images. The proposed improvement allows for a significant increase of the classification accuracy which favorably compares to the best methods cited in literature.

Keywords: Pattern classification · Ensemble of classifiers · Tensor · Higher-Order Singular Value Decomposition

1 Introduction

The new approach to pattern classification involves direct account for the multidimensionality of the input patterns. Classification methods which have their roots in 1D vector spaces are extended to direct processing of N-D patterns without prior vectorization, where $N > 1$ stands for dimensionality of the input patters. Examples of such patterns are ubiquitous, such as monochrome, color and hyperspectral images, video streams, sensor data, market selling data, to name a few. Direct processing and more accurate classification of such patterns started to be possible after a number of seminal achievements in their representation with tensors, as well as development of a number of tensor decomposition algorithms [1, 12, 15, 16, 25].

In this paper we extend the works on tensor based pattern classification in the subspaces spanned by the Higher-Order Singular Value Decomposition (HOSVD) of the prototype pattern tensors. The original HOSVD method was proposed by Savas and Eldén [23]. Then, the method was extended to the ensemble of HOSVD by Cyganek [3–5], as well as to higher dimensions in the paper by Cyganek and Woźniak [7]. The main modification, presented in this paper, consists of lowering the HOSVD subspace dimensions based on computation of the dominating signal directions in the input patterns. This allows their rotations which has an effect of increasing information concentration along the columns or rows of the matrices obtained from flattening of the prototype tensors.

© Springer International Publishing Switzerland 2016
F. Martínez-Álvarez et al. (Eds.): HAIS 2016, LNAI 9648, pp. 560–571, 2016.
DOI: 10.1007/978-3-319-32034-2_47

This method, originally proposed by Letexier *et al.* to the Wiener filtering of digital signals, was never applied to higher-order classification methods, however [18]. In this paper we show that it allows significant increase of the classification accuracy of the HOSVD based tensor classifiers, as well. Moreover, we also propose an original and efficient method for computation of the dominating orientations in the image patterns. For this purpose, the structural tensor (ST) is employed – the ST phase values, computed in the image areas of high magnitude of the stick component, are used to select a dominating orientation. This is then used to rotate all the input patterns.

The rest of the paper is organized as follows. Section 2.1 presents theory on HOSVD based tensor classifiers. Section 2.2 deals with construction of the ensemble of the HOSVD classifiers. In Sect. 2.3 details of selecting the optimal flattening directions for pattern tensors are presented. Experimental results are included in Sect. 3. The paper ends with conclusions in Sect. 4.

2 Pattern Classification in the HOSVD Induced Tensor Subspaces

For multi-dimensional data, such as images, video, sell values, etc. It was shown that tensor based classifiers have an advantage over classifiers operating with vectorized versions of the input patterns. In a tensor approach each degree of freedom is represented by a separate index of a tensor [1]. Details of tensor processing can be found in literature, e.g. in [5, 12].

2.1 The HOSVD Tensor Classifier with Optimal Tensor Flattening Directions

In this method training patterns are contained in a prototype tensor [2, 5, 7]. This tensor is then HOSVD decomposed to construct orthogonal tensor subspaces of some dimensions [1, 15, 12]. The interesting observation is that the bases are spanned by orthogonal tensors, rather than simple vectors as, for instance, in the classical PCA approach.

The HOSVD method allows any P-dimensional tensor $\mathcal{T} \in \mathfrak{R}^{N_1 \times N_2 \times \ldots N_m \times \ldots N_n \times \ldots N_P}$ to be equivalently represented as follows [15, 16]

$$\mathcal{T} = \mathcal{Z} \times_1 \mathbf{S}_1 \times_2 \mathbf{S}_2 \ldots \times_P \mathbf{S}_P, \tag{1}$$

where $\times_k$ denotes a k-mode product of a tensor and a matrix, $\mathbf{S}_k$ are $N_k \times N_k$ unitary mode matrices, $\mathcal{Z} \in \mathfrak{R}^{N_1 \times N_2 \times \ldots N_m \times \ldots N_n \times \ldots N_P}$ is a core tensor fulfills a number of properties [15, 16]. For 3D tensors, used in this paper, the above formula can be equivalently represented as follows

$$\mathcal{T} = \left(\mathcal{Z} \times_1 \mathbf{S}_1 \times_2 \mathbf{S}_2 \right) \times_3 \mathbf{S}_3. \tag{2}$$

It can be shown that the factor in parenthesis in formula (2) and for each value of the third dimension, constitute orthogonal tensors, i.e. the ones which when multiplied give 0. Thus, (2) can be rewritten as

$$\mathcal{T} = \sum_{h=1}^{N_3} \mathcal{T}_h \times_3 \mathbf{s}_3^h. \tag{3}$$

where $\mathbf{s}_3^h$ are columns of the unitary matrix $\mathbf{S}_3$. Because each $\mathcal{T}_h$ is of dimension 2, then $\times_3$ stands for the outer product of a 2D tensor and 1D vectors $\mathbf{s}_3^h$. Computation of $\mathcal{T}_h$ can be done after simple rearrangement of the equation

$$\mathcal{T} \times_3 \mathbf{S}_3^T = \left(\mathcal{Z} \times_1 \mathbf{S}_1 \times_2 \mathbf{S}_2 \right). \tag{4}$$

Finally, $\mathbf{S}_3$ can be computed after the SVD decomposition of the 3rd mode flattened matrix $\mathbf{T}_{(3)}$ of the tensor $\mathcal{T}$, i.e.

$$\mathbf{T}_{(3)} = \mathbf{S}_3 \mathbf{V}_3 \mathbf{D}_3^T. \tag{5}$$

The orthogonal property of $\mathcal{T}_h$ in (3) can be used for building orthogonal tensor subspaces which can be used for pattern recognition. One set of tensor bases is used to represent only one class training patterns. For multi-class problems, a set of $\hat{\mathcal{T}}_h^i$ is built (hat means tensor normalization). In the recognition stage, given a test pattern $\mathbf{X}$, its projections into each of the spaces spanned by the set of the bases $\hat{\mathcal{T}}_h^i$ in is computed. An output class c is the one which minimizes the following expression [5, 23]

$$c = \arg\min_i \left\{ \sum_{h=1}^{N^i \leq N_3^i} \left\langle \hat{\mathcal{T}}_h^i, \mathbf{X} \right\rangle^2 \right\}. \tag{6}$$

However, an important aspect of the above computations is the choice of the number of important components N^i used in the summation in (6).

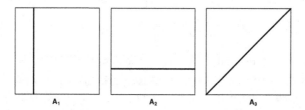

Fig. 1. The idea of subspace dimensions for three matrices with zero elements except the shown lines. The rank of the matrices A_1 and A_2 is 1, whereas A_3 can be a full rank matrix.

These depend on a content of the input patterns. More specifically, as shown in the paper by Letexier *et al.* in the context of Wiener filtering of signals, when signal gradients are more aligned with the horizontal or vertical directions of the storing them matrices, then the resulting number of important components in the SVD decomposition gets minimized [18, 21]. Figure 1 illustrates this idea with three matrices of zero elements except the shown black lines. The rank of the matrices $\mathbf{A}_1$ and $\mathbf{A}_2$ is 1, whereas $\mathbf{A}_3$ can be a full rank matrix. To translate this idea to our framework, when constructing pattern tensor $\mathcal{T}$ we propose first to compute the dominating orientation of all the patterns, and then to rotate them in accordance with this orientation. This way processed patterns create the orientation aligned pattern tensors $\mathcal{T}$. This can be explained by analysis of the formula (4). Although to compute the base tensors $\mathcal{T}_h$ we don't need to directly compute $\mathbf{S}_1$ and $\mathbf{S}_2$, since only one decomposition (5) needs to be processed. However, when patterns in $\mathcal{T}$ are horizontally and vertically aligned, the important number of components will be minimized. Certainly, a possibility of computing a single dominating orientation depends on content of the input patterns (images in our case). For some datasets this cannot be even possible. However, as shown in experiments, such prior rotation of patterns can significantly increase accuracy of classification.

2.2 Construction of the Ensemble of HOSVD Based Classifiers

Figure 2 shows architecture of the ensemble of the HOSVD classifiers. All training and testing data are preprocessed with the Image Euclidean Transformation, as described in [4]. Then, each HOSVD is trained with only a partition of the training dataset obtained in the bagging process and rotated to their principal orientations, as already discussed.

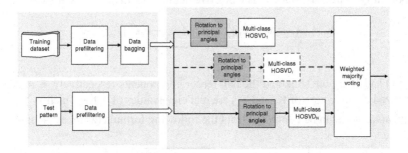

Fig. 2. Data flow in the proposed construction of the HOSVD ensemble of classifiers

The outputs of the multi-class HOSVD classifiers are governed by the majority voting algorithm which shows advantage over a simple majority voting scheme [27].

2.3 Selecting Optimal Tensor Flattening Directions for Image Patterns

Computation of the dominating orientation of the input patterns – a key technique to the system presented in this paper – is proposed to be done with the structural tensor. Such a method was devised by Cyganek to classification of the road signs [2]. In this section we briefly outline this method. Further details can be found in the book [5].

For color or monochrome 2D images, ST relies on computation of the averaged products of local signal gradients. As shown, this allows reliable discrimination of basic signal changes in each local neighborhood of pixels. This way, straight line, but also corners, can be easily computed.

For 2D images, ST is a 2 × 2 matrix **K** with the following components

$$K_{ij}(\rho, \xi) = G_\rho(R_i^{(\xi)} R_j^{(\xi)}), \tag{7}$$

where $R_i^{(\xi)}$ is a ξ-tap discrete differentiating operator, $G\rho$ is a Gaussian smoothing kernel with scale ρ. In our framework, $R_i^{(\xi)}$ is a 5 × 5 derivative filter and $G\rho$ is a 5 × 5 Gaussian smoothing mask. The tensor **K** is positive definite, so its eigenvector looks like follows

$$\mathbf{e} = \begin{bmatrix} K_{11} - K_{22} & 2K_{12} \end{bmatrix}^T, \tag{8}$$

where $ATAN_2$ denotes the arcus-tangent function of a quotient of its two arguments, which is also defined when its second argument approaches zero (result is $\pm \pi/2$ based on a sign of the first argument). In the next step, phase φ of a local structure represented by **e** is computed as follows

$$\varphi(\mathbf{e}) = ATAN_2\big(2K_{12},\ K_{11} - K_{22} \big), \tag{9}$$

Values of the phase φ are put into the phase histograms (in our experiments with 180 bins). However, the values of φ are computed exclusively in the areas of strong stick component **Q** of the ST. Since **K** is a positive definite it can be represented as follows:

$$\mathbf{K} = \big(\lambda_1 - \lambda_2\big) \underbrace{\bar{\mathbf{e}}_1 \bar{\mathbf{e}}_1^T}_{Q} + \lambda_2 \underbrace{\big(\bar{\mathbf{e}}_1 \bar{\mathbf{e}}_1^T + \bar{\mathbf{e}}_2 \bar{\mathbf{e}}_2^T\big)}_{B}, \tag{10}$$

where **Q** and **B** are the stick and the ball tensor components respectively, $\bar{\mathbf{e}}_1$ and $\bar{\mathbf{e}}_2$ are normalized eigenvectors of **K**, and $\lambda_{1,2}$ are real eigenvalues of **T** for which $\lambda_1 \geq \lambda_2 \geq 0$. Eigenvalues of **K** can be computed from the following formula (λ_1 takes '+'):

$$\lambda_{1,2} = \frac{1}{2}\left[\big(K_{11} + K_{22}\big) \pm \sqrt{\big(K_{11} - K_{22}\big)^2 + 4K_{12}^2}\right]. \tag{11}$$

It is easy to observe that areas corresponding only to the stick component pose high value of λ_1 with small λ_2 at the same time. Therefore the criteria for areas for computation of the important orientations need to fulfil the following condition

$$\frac{\lambda_2}{\lambda_1} \leq \kappa, \tag{12}$$

where κ is a threshold value, which in the experiments was less than 0.2. Inserting (11) into (12) yields

$$p \geq \frac{1 - \kappa}{1 + \kappa}, \tag{13}$$

where

$$p = \frac{\sqrt{\left(K_{11} - K_{22}\right) + 4K_{12}^2}}{K_{11} + K_{22}}, \text{ for } K_{11} + K_{22} \neq 0. \tag{14}$$

Detailed algorithm for computation of the phase histograms in image areas with high stick-like structures is described in [2].

3   Experimental Results

The presented ensemble of HOSVD classifiers were tested on the handwritten digits database USPS [10, 28]. It is a common test-set for comparison of different versions of this type of tensor based classifiers, such as in the paper by Savas and Eldén [23], as well as by Cyganek [3, 4]. The dataset, which examples are shown in Fig. 3, includes selected and preprocessed 16×16 gray level scans of the handwritten digits from the envelopes of the U.S. Postal Service. Table 1 presents the numbers of training and testing patterns for each digit in the dataset. There is a total number of 7291 training and 2007 testing patterns, respectively. The patterns are relatively difficult for machine classification since the reported human error is 2.5 %. For this purpose it was also used for comparison of other classifiers [17, 23].

Fig. 3.   Views of some training (left) and testing (right) patterns from the USPS database [10, 17].

The system was implemented in C ++ in the Microsoft Visual 2013 framework and with help of the tensor library described in [5]. All experiments were conducted on the laptop machine endowed with the Intel® Core™ i7-4800MQ CPU @2.7 GHz, memory 32 GB RAM, OS 64-bit Windows 7.

Table 1.   Numbers of training and testing digits in the USPS database.

Pattern	"0"	"1"	"2"	"3"	"4"	"5"	"6"	"7"	"8"	"9"
#Train	1194	1005	731	658	652	556	664	645	542	644
#Test	359	264	198	166	200	160	170	147	166	177

As already mentioned, the main novelty proposed in this paper is rotation to the principal direction of the patterns before fed to the HOSVD classifiers. Thanks to this, a number of important components of each of the HOSVD classifiers gets reduced which results in higher accuracy compared to the not pre-processed data. The principal directions are found for each set of training patterns for a given class. For visual patterns, as the ones used in the presented experiments, for this purpose we propose an analysis of the

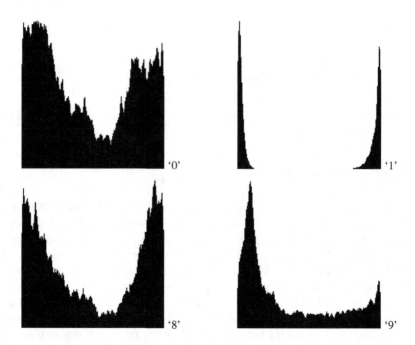

Fig. 4. Common histograms of the dominating phase orientations for the training patterns of the digits '0', '1', '8', and '9'. Each histogram contains 180 bins and is normalized. Image orientations are taken from the image areas characteristic of high magnitude of the stick component of the structural tensor.

phase histograms obtained from the stick components of the structural tensor. There is only one principal component computed for all the patterns of a given class (i.e. a digit in this case). Figure 4 depicts a number of such common phase histograms for digits "0", "1", "8", and "9", respectively. It can be easily noticed that for some patterns, a dominating direction is not uniquely determined. Nevertheless, in our approach we choose an angle which corresponds to the highest bin in a histogram.

Figure 5 shows rotated input patterns for some examples of digits '0' and '4' from the training dataset. As visible, rotations horizontally align a dominating orientation of the patterns. Thanks to this, a much lower number of important components conveys important information on the training set. Average accuracies of recognition of each

Fig. 5. View of the rotated input patterns for some examples of digits '0' and '4'. Rotation is done to horizontally align a dominating orientation of the patterns.

digit from the handwritten USPS dataset, as well as the average accuracy are contained in Table 2. Bagging data denotes a number of training data randomly chosen for each bag during the training, whereas #Ensem denotes a number of HOSVD classifiers in each ensemble, which we choose to be 1, 5, and 11 in this test. It is visible that for the ensembles of (members/bagging size) 11/64, 11/192, 5/256, the best accuracies of 0.988, 0.986, and 0.987 are obtained (i.e. an average error rate of 1.3 %). This shows up to be the best results when compared to the competitive results presented in literature (see Table 3).

Table 2. Average accuracies of recognition of each digit from the handwritten USPS dataset, as well as the average accuracy. Bagging data denotes a number of training data randomly chosen for each bag during the training. #Ensem. denotes number of HOSVD classifiers in each ensemble (1, 5, and 11).

Bagging data	64			192			256		
#Ensem Digit	1	5	11	1	5	11	1	5	11
"0"	0.994	0.994	0.991	0.988	0.991	0.994	0.991	0.991	0.991
"1"	0.988	0.988	0.988	0.988	0.988	0.988	0.988	0.988	0.988
"2"	0.954	0.989	0.989	0.964	0.979	0.994	0.979	0.994	0.984
"3"	0.963	0.93	0.993	0.891	0.981	0.969	0.987	0.993	0.963
"4"	0.95	0.955	0.975	0.93	0.955	0.965	0.98	0.955	0.975
"5"	0.987	0.981	0.987	0.956	0.968	0.993	0.962	0.987	0.981
"6"	1	1	1	0.982	1	1	1	1	1
"7"	0.972	0.965	0.979	0.972	0.972	0.979	0.965	0.979	0.986
"8"	0.975	0.993	1	0.963	0.987	0.993	0.975	0.987	0.987
"9"	1	0.988	0.983	0.977	0.988	0.983	0.983	0.994	0.988
Av.Accuracy	0.979	0.979	**0.988**	0.961	0.981	**0.986**	0.981	**0.987**	0.984

Table 3. Comparison of the mean accuracy values of different classification methods for the USPS dataset reported in the literature.

Author(s)	Method Description	Av. accuracy
Savas and Eldén [23]	Single HOSVD multi-classifiers, noise added	0.95
Maji & Malik [19, 20]	PHOG, SVM (rbf, $\gamma = 0.1$)	0.973
Decoste & Schölkopf B [8]	Raw pixels, VSV (poly, d = 3)	0.968
Cyganek [4]	Ensemble of HOSVD, IMED	0.945
Cyganek et al. [6]	Chordal tensor kernel, raw pixels	0.949
This paper	Ensemble of HOSVD, IMED, patterns rotated to dominating directions	**0.987**

Let us notice that the best accuracy can be obtained with different combination of the number of ensembles and the amount of data randomly drawn by the bagging procedure. Also, accuracy increases to some point with increase of the bagging set. However, in all the cases shown in Table 2 a single classifier gives inferior results compared to an ensemble.

The results shown in Table 3 are cited based on the accuracies reported by other authors in respect to the best classification of the USPS dataset.

Finally, Figs. 6 and 7 show plots of the ensemble averaged accuracy value for the best arrangement presented in Table 2. Namely, two times accuracy of the ensemble was measured in respect to an ensemble of 5 member and different bagging sets, as well as different size ensembles and fixed bagging set to 256 patterns, respectively. We notice, that in respect to these two parameters there is an optimum, as shown in Fig. 7. However, this can change from run to run, since a random aspect is due to the bagging process. Also, we can observe that for a larger number of members in an ensemble, the accuracy drops.

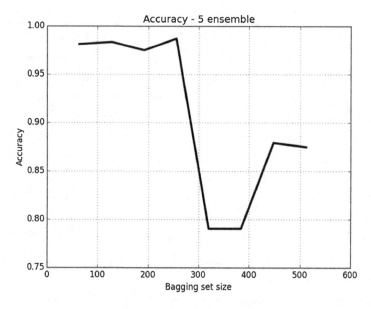

Fig. 6. Ensemble accuracy for an ensemble of 5 members and different bagging sets.

This can be due to a loss of diversity in the case of classifiers with repeated data sets coming from the bagging process.

As already mentioned, the output of the ensemble was estimated based on the majority voting scheme.

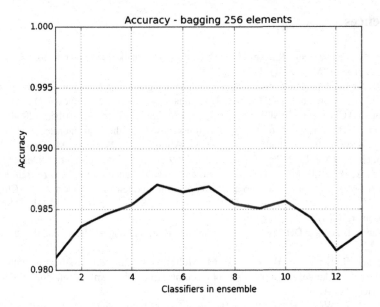

Fig. 7. Accuracy for a fixed bagging of 256 data and 1-13 classifiers in an ensemble.

4   Conclusions

In this paper an extended version of our previous work on image classification with the ensemble of the HOSVD tensor based classifiers is presented [3, 4]. The main modification presented in this paper is rotation of the input patterns for each class in directions of their dominating orientations. These, in turn, are obtained by computation and analysis of the phase histograms of the structural tensor, which correspond to edges in the images. However, application of the structural tensor allows computation of these orientations in the image areas characteristic of strong stick component of this tensor. This allows reliable differentiation between strong signal changes due to true edges from signals associated with noise and other non-linear structures. Rotation of the input patterns allows significant reduction of dimensions of the subspaces obtained from flattened versions of the prototype pattern tensor. In effect, much higher accuracies of the final classification ensemble are obtained which compare favorably to the results presented in literature. Last but not least, the method allows real-time response due to simple decision formula. Further work will focus upon speeding-up the training process, as well as on verification of the method with other types of signals and data.

Acknowledgement. This work was supported by the Polish National Science Centre under the grant no. DEC-2013/09/B/ST6/02264. This work was supported by EC under FP7, Coordination and Support Action, Grant Agreement Number 316097, ENGINE – European Research Centre of Network Intelligence for Innovation Enhancement (http://engine.pwr.wroc.pl/). All computer experiments were carried out using computer equipment sponsored by ENGINE project.

References

1. Cichocki, A., Zdunek, R., Amari, S.: Nonnegative matrix and tensor factorization. IEEE Signal Process. Mag. **25**(1), 142–145 (2008)
2. Cyganek, B.: A real-time vision system for traffic signs recognition invariant to translation, rotation and scale. In: Blanc-Talon, J., Bourennane, S., Philips, W., Popescu, D., Scheunders, P. (eds.) ACIVS 2008. LNCS, vol. 5259, pp. 278–289. Springer, Heidelberg (2008)
3. Cyganek, B.: Ensemble of tensor classifiers based on the higher-order singular value decomposition. In: Corchado, E., Snášel, V., Abraham, A., Woźniak, M., Graña, M., Cho, S.-B. (eds.) HAIS 2012, Part II. LNCS, vol. 7209, pp. 578–589. Springer, Heidelberg (2012)
4. Cyganek, B.: Embedding of the extended euclidean distance into pattern recognition with higher-order singular value decomposition of prototype tensors. In: Cortesi, A., Chaki, N., Saeed, K., Wierzchoń, S. (eds.) CISIM 2012. LNCS, vol. 7564, pp. 180–190. Springer, Heidelberg (2012)
5. Cyganek, B., Object Detection and Recognition in Digital Images: Theory and Practice, Wiley (2013)
6. Cyganek, B., Krawczyk, B., Woźniak, M.: Multidimensional data classification with chordal distance based kernel and support vector machines. Eng. Appl. Artif. Intell. **46**, 10–22 (2015). Elsevier, Part A
7. Cyganek, B., Woźniak, M.: An improved vehicle logo recognition using a classifier ensemble based on pattern tensor representation and decomposition. New Gener. Comput. **33**(4), 389–408 (2015). Springer
8. Decoste, D., Schölkopf, B.: Training invariant support vector machines. Mach. Learn. **46**(1–3), 161–190 (2002)
9. Grandvalet, Y.: Bagging equalizes influence. Mach. Learn. **55**, 251–270 (2004)
10. Hull, J.: A database for handwritten text recognition research. IEEE Trans. Pattern Anal. Mach. Intell. **16**(5), 550–554 (1994)
11. Kittler, J., Hatef, M., Duing, R.P.W., Matas, J.: On Combining Classifiers. IEEE PAMI **20**(3), 226–239 (1998)
12. Kolda, T.G., Bader, B.W.: Tensor decompositions and applications. SIAM Rev. **51**(3), 455–500 (2008)
13. Krawczyk, B.: One-class classifier ensemble pruning and weighting with firefly algorithm. Neurocomputing **150**, 490–500 (2015)
14. Kuncheva, L.I.: Combining Pattern Classifiers, Methods and Algorithms. Wiley Interscience, Chichester (2005)
15. Lathauwer, de L.: Signal processing based on multilinear algebra. Ph.D dissertation, Katholieke Universiteit Leuven (1997)
16. de Lathauwer, L., de Moor, B., Vandewalle, J.: A multilinear singular value decomposition. SIAM J. Matrix Anal. Appl. **21**(4), 1253–1278 (2000)
17. LeCun, Y., Bottou, L., Bengio, Y., Haffner, P.: Gradient-based learning applied to document recognition. Proc. IEEE Speech Image Process. **86**(11), 2278–2324 (1998)
18. Letexier, D., Bourennane, S., Blanc-Talon, J.: Main flattening directions and Quadtree decomposition for multiway Wiener filtering. Signal, Image Video Process. **1**(3), 253–265 (2007)
19. Maji, S., Malik, J.: Fast and Accurate Digit Classification. Technical report no. UCB/EECS-2009-159, University of California at Berkeley (2009)
20. Maji, S., Berg, A.C., Malik, J.: Efficient classification for additive kernel SVMs. IEEE Trans. Pattern Anal. Mach. Intell. **35**(1), 66–77 (2013)

21. Marot, J., Fossati, C., Bourennane, S.: About advances in tensor data denoising methods. EURASIP J. Adv. Signal Process. **2008**(1), 1–12 (2008)
22. Polikar, R.: Ensemble Based Systems in Decision Making. IEEE Circuits and Systems Magazine **6**(3), 21–45 (2006)
23. Savas, B., Eldén, L.: Handwritten digit classification using higher order singular value decomposition. Pattern Recogn. **40**, 993–1003 (2007)
24. Theodoridis, S., Koutroumbas, K.: Pattern Recognition, 4th edn. Academic Press, London (2009)
25. Vasilescu, M.O., Terzopoulos, D.: Multilinear analysis of image ensembles: tensorfaces. In: Heyden, A., Sparr, G., Nielsen, M., Johansen, P. (eds.) ECCV 2002, Part I. LNCS, vol. 2350, pp. 447–460. Springer, Heidelberg (2002)
26. Woźniak, M.: A hybrid decision tree training method using data streams. Knowl. Inf. Syst. **29**(2), 335–347 (2011)
27. Woźniak, M., Grana, M., Corchado, E.: A survey of multiple classifier systems as hybrid systems. Inf. Fusion **16**(1), 3–17 (2014)
28. www-stat.stanford.edu/~tibs/ElemStatLearn/

Applications

Evaluation of Decision Trees Algorithms for Position Reconstruction in Argon Dark Matter Experiment

Miguel Cárdenas-Montes[✉], Bárbara Montes, Roberto Santorelli,
and Luciano Romero, on behalf of Argon Dark Matter Collaboration

Department of Fundamental Research,
Centro de Investigaciones Energéticas Medioambientales y Tecnológicas,
Madrid, Spain
{miguel.cardenas,barbara.montes,roberto.santorelli,
luciano.romero}@ciemat.es

Abstract. Nowadays, Dark Matter search constitutes one of the most challenging scientific activity. During the last decades several detectors have been developed to evidence the signal of interactions between Dark Matter and ordinary matter. The Argon Dark Matter detector, placed in the Canfranc Underground Laboratory in Spain is the first ton-scale liquid-Ar experiment in operation for Dark Matter direct detection. In parallel to the development of other engineering issues, computational methods are being applied to maximize the exploitation of generated data. In this work, two algorithms based on decision trees —Generalized Boosted Regression Models and Random Forests— are employed to reconstruct the position of the interaction in Argon Dark Matter detector. These two algorithms are confronted to a Montecarlo data set reproducing the physical behaviour of Argon Dark Matter detector. In this work, an in-depth study of the position reconstruction of the interaction is performed for both algorithms, including a study of the distribution of errors.

Keywords: Decision tree · Random forests · Regression · R · Argon dark matter experiment · Dark matter search · Position reconstruction

1 Introduction

It is accepted today in the scientific community that roughly 85 % of the matter in the Universe is in some form of non-baryonic matter that neither emits nor absorbs electromagnetic radiation. That Dark Matter component could explain many astrophysical and cosmological phenomena, ranging from internal motions of galaxies to the large scale inhomogeneities in the cosmic microwave background radiation and the dynamics of colliding galaxy clusters that could be, otherwise, not accounted only considering the visible matter.

One possible hypothesis regarding the Dark Matter nature is motivated by the elementary particle physics, in forms of undiscovered elementary particles

© Springer International Publishing Switzerland 2016
F. Martínez-Álvarez et al. (Eds.): HAIS 2016, LNAI 9648, pp. 575–587, 2016.
DOI: 10.1007/978-3-319-32034-2_48

foreseen by the supersymmetric extension of the Standard Model. The leading candidate is a cold thermal Weakly Interacting Massive Particles (WIMP) relic from the Big Bang which interact only weakly with the ordinary matter and that could be nowadays part of a massive halo that pervades our galaxy.

Typically there are three classes of WIMP searches: direct detection in shielded underground detectors; indirect detection with satellites, balloons, and ground-based telescopes looking for signals of Dark Matter annihilation; and detection at particle colliders where Dark Matter particles may be directly produced in high-energy collisions.

The detection of the elastic collisions —with energy in the order of tens of keV (kiloelectronvolt)— produced by the Dark Matter with the nuclei of the ordinary matter is the most used way to directly detect WIMPs. A great variety of different detector experiment, located in underground laboratories, have been used during the recent years to identify those extremely rare signals by achieving a sufficiently low energy threshold as well as low enough background. One of the most promising technologies is based on noble liquids time projection chambers (TPC), which can provide important and additional background suppressions through the measurement of the interaction multiplicity and the 3D reconstruction of its position. In fact it is expected that the WIMP-nucleus scatterings are uniformly distributed inside the detector and only one scattering is produced per time. At the same time the background, typically given by the external radiation or by the natural radioactivity, tends to be located near the border of the active volume and can produce two or more scatterings at the same time.

The Argon Dark Matter experiment (ArDM) can be classified as direct detection experiment. In direct detection experiments, the detection of WIMPs from the galactic halo is made via elastic scattering off ordinary target nuclei. ArDM is an one-ton scale liquid-Ar detector installed in the Canfranc Underground Laboratory in Spain.

In the past, the position reconstruction in experiments such as ArDM, XENON10, and XENON100 has been based on the use the Artificial Neural Networks (NN). By using the input signals from the detectors composing the experiment, the NN algorithm is able to reconstruct the position where the interaction has taken place. In this work, we explore the use of two algorithms based on decision trees —Generalized Boosted Regression Models [1,2] and Random Forests [3]— to reconstruct the position of the interaction in the ArDM experiment. Due to the current status of the experiment, the evaluation is performed with Montecarlo data.

In Ensemble Methods [4,5], several models are combined in order to improve the performance of the algorithm prediction. Frequently, the Ensemble Methods outperform the individual base models which compose them, at the same time that they overcome the problem of the overfitting. These individual models have to be somehow different among them. This can be achieved by building them in a relatively different manner. Two examples of this are Bagging [6] and Boosting, whose the most relevant representative is AdaBoost algorithm.

In Bagging, each individual member is trained with a bootstrap sample of the training data, which in turn generates slightly different models. Random Forest incorporates Bagging and Random Subspaces [7]. At each node, a subset of variables is selected for the decision about the division. The final prediction of the ensemble is the average of the predictions of its individual members.

In Boosting, each training sample has a weight, initially equal for all of them. After the construction and prediction of the first model of the ensemble, the weights are modified, giving more importance to those samples which are misclassified. In the next iteration, the previously misclassified samples hold a stronger consideration for the model, so that it should improve their prediction. By repeating the process, the ensemble will consist of a set of individual models with an increasing capacity to correctly predict the training samples. As previously, the final prediction of the ensemble is the average of the predictions of its individual members.

Concerning the Montecarlo data set, it is composed of one-million events isotropically distributed inside the volume of the detector [8]. The simulation framework GEometry ANd Tracking (GEANT4) was used to simulate the detector geometry and physics processes taking place in the detector. This data set is used for the training and the test sets in this work.

The rest of the paper is organized as follows: Sect. 2 summarizes the Related Work and previous efforts done. In Sect. 3.1, the most relevant details about the ArDM experiment are presented. The decision tree algorithms used in this work are reviewed in Sects. 3.2 and 3.3. The Results and the Analysis are displayed in Sect. 4. Finally, the Conclusions are presented in Sect. 5.

2   Related Work

Regarding the previous efforts done in position reconstruction in Dark Matter detection experiments, in [9], a neural network (NN) is used for reconstructing the events position in the xy-plane of the detector of XENON10 Dark Matter experiment, but not for z-coordinate. The event z-coordinate is inferred from direct signals in the detector and it is not based on regression algorithms. For xy-plane event reconstruction, a feed-forward NN composed of 2 hidden layers with an hyperbolic tangent as activation function is applied. This NN is trained with $4 \cdot 10^4$ simulated events. Each input event is a vector with the signals of photomultipliers normalized by the sum of their signals. A comparison has been carried out between NN and χ^2 minimization, leading to a better performance for the NN.

The XENON100 Dark Matter experiment [10] is the follow-up of XENON10, with a larger active volume, 62 kg of liquid xenon, faced to the 14 kg of XENON10, being both installed at the Gran Sasso Underground Laboratory in Italy. In [10], NN and Support Vector Machine for xy-plane event reconstruction are employed. Most of the considerations of the previous version of the experiment are applicable to XENON100. Among the differences, the main one is the new structure of the NN composed of a single hidden layer with 30 neurons.

Concerning the scientific literature about the ArDM experiment, in-depth description about the design, the construction, the operation of the facility as well as the initial physics results can be found in [11–14].

Similarly to XENON experiments, in ArDM experiment NN has been used for position reconstruction [8] in the ArDM experiment. In this case, diverse NNs have been created and tested by using JavaNNS [15]. The 3D position reconstruction has been performed for the Montecarlo data set as well as for data emerging from ArDM filled with gas Ar and later with liquid Ar, although the later ones are still in an early stage. In both studies the configuration was: a NN composed of 24 input neurons[1], 24 neurons in a single hidden layer with hyperbolic tangent as activation function and 1 neuron for the coordinate output. With this configuration, three NN were created corresponding to x-, y- or z-coordinate. This configuration with 1 neuron for the coordinate output was used when filling with liquid argon, and 3 neurons when filling with gas argon.

In the current work, we investigate the use of two implementations based on decision trees to position reconstruction in ArDM experiment. To the authors' knowledge, no similar works in this line have been proposed.

3 Methodology

3.1 The ArDM Experiment

The Argon Dark Matter (ArDM) experiment consists of a ton-scale double-phase liquid-gas argon time projection chamber installed in the Canfranc Underground Laboratory (LSC) in Spain (Fig. 1). The experiment is designed for measuring the elastic scattering of WIMPs from argon nuclei. The nuclei recoil could be measurable by observing free electrons from ionization and photons from scintillation. Experiments based on noble liquids are currently leading the field of direct Dark Matter detection. These experiments have progressively increased the target mass of detectors until the current size in the one-ton scale.

Briefly, the experimental set-up (Fig. 2) consists of a cylindrical dewar with 80 cm diameter and 100 cm as vertical direction. The vessel is filled of ultra-clean liquid argon with a weight of 850 kg. At the top —immersed in gas argon— and at the bottom —in liquid argon— of the device two arrays of 12 photomultipliers. The signal received by the 24 photomultipliers is the input array for the position reconstruction algorithms. When processing the signal of the photomultipliers, the expected output is the position (x, y, z) of the interaction in the detector. Since, few Dark Matter events are expected to be observed, background events are reduced by appropriate shielding of the detector and also by selecting highly radiopure materials for its components. Due to the quasi-cylindrical symmetry, the results presented in the current work focus on x- and z-coordinates; while, for the sake of the conciseness, skipping the reconstruction of y-coordinate.

---

[1] The use of 24 neurons in the input and hidden layers is due to the fact that the ArDM experiment holds 24 photomultipliers. See Sect. 3.1 for further details.

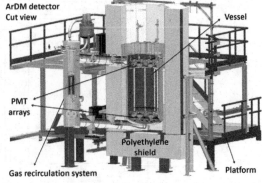

(a) ArDM Detector in Hall
A of LSC.

(b) Schema of ArDM Experiment

Fig. 1. Image of the ArDM Experiment installed in Hall A of LSC (Fig. 1(a)) and schema of the installation (Fig. 1(b)). The facility was constructed and initially operated at CERN. In early 2012 the transfer to its final place in the LSC was initiated with the installation of the vessel and the majority of the cryogenic parts.

More details of ArDM experiment can be found in the scientific literature [8,11–13]. In these publications, physics and engineering issues are in-depth described.

3.2 Generalized Boosted Regression Models

Generalized Boosted Regression Models (GBM) is an implementation of AdaBoost algorithm [1] and Friedman's gradient boosting machine [2]. Similarly to other boosting methods, gradient boosting combines diverse weak learners to construct a single strong learner. The Friedman's gradient boosting algorithm is rawly as follows: the output-value is used as a first guess for predicting all observations. The residuals for the model are computed (loss function). At each step of gradient boosting, the model is widened by adding a new weak learner, in such a way that the overall learner predicts better. In order to avoid overfitting, the number of gradient boosting iterations can be used as regularization parameter. Other regularization mechanism is the shrinkage. It is done by reducing or shrinking the impact of each additional tree. The intuition is that it is better to improve a model by taking many small steps than a smaller number of large steps.

In this work the R package *GBM* [16] is used with the following configuration: Gaussian distribution (squared error), shrinkage parameter 0.05, 3 as maximum depth of variable interactions, the fraction of the training set observations randomly selected to propose the next tree in the expansion and the train fraction are 0.5, and minimum number of observations in the trees terminal nodes equal to 20. The training data set encompasses $4 \cdot 10^4$ instances, whereas the validation one encompasses $5 \cdot 10^4$ instances.

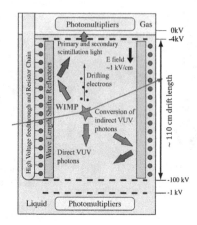

Fig. 2. Schematic description of light production and detection in the ArDM Experiment.

3.3   Random Forests

Random Forests (RF) [3] is a decision trees algorithm which incorporates ensemble learning. Random Forests is composed of many independent classification trees. Each tree is grown to the largest extent possible (no pruning). Random Forests incorporates Bagging for creating each tree —each tree corresponds to a individual model in the ensemble—. Each tree is trained with a slightly different training set. In RF, these training sets are bootstrap sets.

In addition to use a different bootstrap sample for each tree —bagging— RF proposes an additional layer of randomness. A random selection of features is executed to split each node, random subspace method [7]. In each node split, the best ones among a subset of predictors are randomly selected among the overall predictors. Thanks to this construction, Random Forests minimizes the overfitting risk, and at the same time is specially recommended when dealing with large high-dimensional data sets.

In order to perform a classification or a regression action for a new instance, this instance is predicted by each tree composing the Random Forest. In case of classification, the class of the new object is assigned by the majority of votes. If the case corresponds to a regression, the average value of each tree is calculated and assigned to the new instance.

In detail the algorithm works as follows: one tier of the data with replacement is randomly selected (*out of bag data*, OOB) while the rest of the data is the *learning sample*, LS. The LS is used to fit a tree without pruning. In each split only a randomly sub-set of predictors, approximately one tier, is used.

Due to the construction mechanism, Random Forests encompasses some relevant features, among others: high accuracy, estimation of the importance of variables, handling of unbalanced data set, or proximity measure.

In this work the R package *randomForest* [17] is used with a configuration of a total of 200 trees and the vote not normalized. The training data set encompasses $4 \cdot 10^4$ instances, whereas the validation one encompasses $5 \cdot 10^4$ instances.

4   Results and Dicussion

In this section the two algorithms proposed for position reconstruction are confronted to the Montecarlo data set. The analysis focusses on how well the position is reconstructed through the histogram of errors —difference between the predicted and the real value of the coordinate— and the distribution of the errors with the value of the coordinate. Due to the quasi-cylindrical symmetry of device, the analysis is done for x- and z-coordinates.

4.1   Application of Generalized Boosted Regression Models for Position Reconstruction

In Fig. 3, the histograms of errors in the position reconstruction of samples in validation set for x- and z-coordinates are presented. The figures correspond to the difference between the value of the x-coordinate predicted with GBM and the real x-coordinate (Fig. 3(a)), and the equivalent of the z-coordinate (Fig. 3(b)). These two coordinates have been chosen because of detector geometry they behave differently, whereas x- and y-coordinates behave similarly.

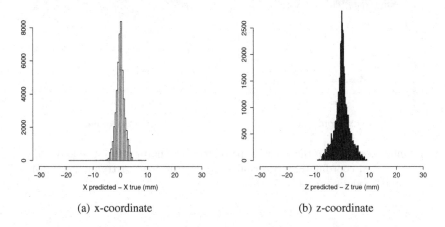

(a) x-coordinate   (b) z-coordinate

Fig. 3. Histogram of errors between the values of predicted coordinate with GBM and real coordinate. GBM configuration: 200 trees, a training set of $4 \cdot 10^4$ instances and a validation set of $5 \cdot 10^4$ instances. Histogram is composed of 100 bins.

By using GBM, the reconstruction of x- and z-coordinates are done in excellent agreement with real data. For all the instance, z-coordinate reconstruction is performed within an error margin of ±10 mm, whereas for x-coordinate the difference has a wider range, from -18 to $+10$ mm. Taking into account that the dewar size in x-coordinate is 800 mm and in z-coordinate 1200 mm, it is appreciated the excellent agreement between the real coordinates and their predictions. The mean squared error for the reconstruction of the x-coordinate of validation set is 2.5 mm, whereas for the z-coordinate is 6.7 mm.

The errors of x-coordinate can be characterized by a mean value and standard deviation of: 0.03 ± 1.64, whereas for the z-coordinate these values are -0.06 ± 2.61. These results will be used later for comparison purposes between the performance of GBM and RF. Furthermore, for the 95 % of errors their absolute value is lower than 3.0 mm for x-coordinate, and 5.6 mm for z-coordinate.

It is also relevant to observe if the largest differences between real and predicted coordinates are produced in a specific coordinate or otherwise if the differences are randomly distributed across the range of the coordinate. In Fig. 4, the difference between predicted values and real values versus real values is shown. For both coordinates a certain pattern in the distribution of the differences is observed. This distribution of the differences is not random, and this fact might be consequences in the reconstruction of experimental data.

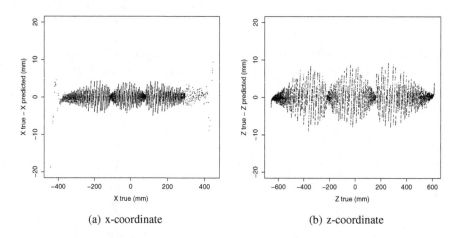

(a) x-coordinate   (b) z-coordinate

Fig. 4. Difference between the values of predicted coordinate with GBM and real coordinate versus real coordinate. GBM configuration: 200 trees, a training set of $4 \cdot 10^4$ instances and a validation set of $5 \cdot 10^4$ instances.

4.2   Application of Random Forest for Position Reconstruction

Similarly to the previous studies, the histograms for the differences between the values predicted of x-coordinate and z-coordinate and the real x-coordinate and z-coordinate in validation data set when using Random Forest for position reconstruction are presented in Fig. 5. These histograms should provide an intuition about how well these coordinates are reconstructed, how large the differences between real an reconstructed coordinate can be, and how much the differences are concentrated or scattered around zero.

By comparing the histograms of errors for RF (Fig. 5) and GBM (Fig. 3), it is observed how RF produces some few cases with larger reconstruction errors than GBM. They reach up to -150 mm for z-coordinate, being in all cases larger than ± 50 mm. However, RF is able to concentrate more instances reconstructed with very low error. The central bins of RF histograms hold more than $2 \cdot 10^4$ counts, whereas the equivalent bins of GBM hold around $8 \cdot 10^3$ counts for x-coordinate and $2.5 \cdot 10^3$ counts for z-coordinate.

The mean value and standard deviation of the errors for x-coordinate is -0.015 ± 2.29, whereas for z-coordinate is -0.06 ± 3.79. Comparing with the equivalent results for GBM, RF produces very similar mean error values, but incrementing their variance. The mean squared error for the reconstruction of the x-coordinate of validation set is 5.1 mm, whereas for the z-coordinate is 19.8 mm. In both cases, the mean squared errors are slightly larger for RF than for GBM, but still they are acceptable for the position reconstruction in the experiment. Finally, for the 95 % of errors their absolute value is lower than 2.7 mm for x-coordinate, and 5.7 mm for z-coordinate. These figures are similar to their equivalent of GBM.

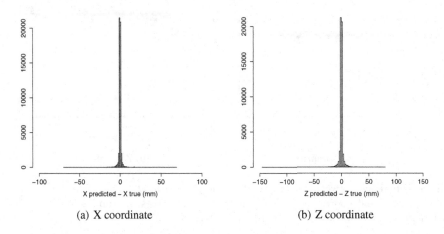

(a) X coordinate   (b) Z coordinate

Fig. 5. Histogram of differences between the values of predicted coordinate with RF and real coordinate. RF configuration: 200 trees, a training set of $4 \cdot 10^4$ instances and a validation set of $5 \cdot 10^4$ instances. Histogram is composed of 100 bins.

Regarding the errors distribution versus the involved coordinate, RF does not show any pattern (Fig. 6). Except for the values placed at the extremes of the device, errors are randomly distributed along the x-coordinate (Fig. 6(a)) and z-coordinate (Fig. 6(b)).

Larger errors in the position reconstruction for the limits of the device than for other internal positions appear for both algorithms. This is an algorithmic effect. The algorithms can not reconstruct positions beyond the extreme positions in the training data set. This is verified by reducing the size of the training data set and observing how the intensity of the errors at the limits of the coordinates increases. For the sake of conciseness, these results are skipped. Independently of algorithm used in the reconstruction, the two peaks at the extremes of the coordinates arising from the lack of the events are observed (Figs. 4(a), 6(a)). Not only the intensity of the peaks increases with the reduction of the training set size, a displacement of the peaks towards values closer to zero appears.

Comparing RF and GBM, the absence of pattern in the errors in RF is noticed against the use of GBM. The error pattern in GBM appears independently of the configuration employed[2]. The configuration shown in Sect. 3.2 is a trade-off between the lowest errors in the position reconstruction and a moderate processing time. In any case, both algorithms maintain the errors in the reconstruction in very low values, which qualify for the position reconstruction in ArDM Experiment.

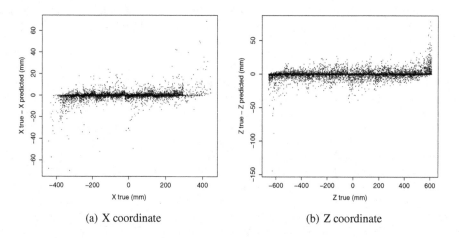

(a) X coordinate   (b) Z coordinate

Fig. 6. Difference between the values of predicted coordinate with RF and real coordinate versus real coordinate. RF configuration: 200 trees, a training set of $4 \cdot 10^4$ instances and a validation set of $5 \cdot 10^4$ instances.

Finally, in Fig. 7 the position reconstruction of Montecarlo data set, x-coordinate versus z-coordinate, is presented. The aim is to gain intuition about the reconstruction for the whole device and to observe the presence of patterns or voids in certain areas of the device.

A second issue is to investigate if the pattern generated by GBM algorithm is translated to this bi-dimensional reconstruction. Visually it is difficult to ascertain if the position reconstruction with GBM (Fig. 7(a)) shows some patterns

---

[2] In the case of GBM the origin of the patter in the errors is more controversial. Effectively it is associated to the use of this type of decision tree for this dataset. Further research is necessary to explain the origin of pattern shown in Fig. 4

in opposition to the reconstruction with RF (Fig. 7(b)) which seems completely random. This issue is relevant for position reconstructing in experimental data sets, and therefore, it deserves further research in future work.

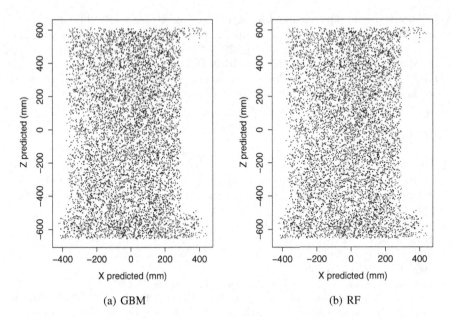

(a) GBM   (b) RF

Fig. 7. Representation of predicted x-coordinate versus z-coordinate with GBM (Fig. 7(a)) and RF (Fig. 7(b)).

5   Conclusions

In this paper, two algorithms: Random Forests and Generalized Boosted Regression Models have been tested for position reconstruction of simulated data in ArDM experiment. For both algorithms, the distribution of errors between the real and the reconstructed coordinates has been analysed in frequency and in relation to the real position. Due to the quasi-symmetric of the device, the work has focussed on x- and z-coordinates. For both coordinates, a high accuracy is achieved, although Random Forests produces a higher variance in the error values than Generalized Boosted Regression Models.

Regarding the performance of GBM, independently of the coordinate, a certain pattern in the position reconstruction is observed. In further studies — specially those including real data, the consequences of this pattern in the position reconstruction have to be elucidated. When using RF for position reconstruction, this pattern is not observed.

As future work, the evaluation of other variants of decision trees algorithms and other algorithms with position prediction capacity such as neural networks is proposed. Besides, the accuracy exhibited by Random Forests and Generalized Boosted Regression Models with simulated date has to be confirmed with experimental data.

Acknowledgment. The research leading to these results has received funding by the Spanish Ministry of Economy and Competitiveness (MINECO) for funding support through the grants FPA2012-30811, FPA2013-47804-C2-1-R, and "Unidad de Excelencia María de Maeztu": CIEMAT - FÍSICA DE PARTÍCULAS through the grant MDM-2015-0509. The authors acknowledge the kind support of the whole ArDM collaboration by making available the Monte Carlo simulation.

References

1. Freund, Y., Schapire, R.E.: A decision-theoretic generalization of on-line learning and an application to boosting. J. Comput. Syst. Sci. **55**(1), 119–139 (1997)
2. Friedman, J.H.: Greedy function approximation: a gradient boosting machine. Ann. Stat. **29**, 1189–1232 (2000)
3. Breiman, L.: Random forests. Mach. Learn. **45**(1), 5–32 (2001)
4. Kuncheva, L.I.: Ensemble methods. In: Combining Pattern Classifiers: Methods and Algorithms, 2nd edn, pp. 186–229. John Wiley & Sons, Inc. (2014). doi:10.1002/9781118914564.ch6
5. Pardo, C., Rodríguez, J.J., Díez-Pastor, J.F., García-Osorio, C.: Random oracles for regression ensembles. In: Okun, O., Valentini, G., Re, M. (eds.) Ensembles in Machine Learning Applications. SCI, vol. 373, pp. 181–199. Springer, Heidelberg (2011)
6. Breiman, L.: Bagging predictors. Mach. Learn. **24**(2), 123–140 (1996)
7. Ho, T.K.: The random subspace method for constructing decision forests. IEEE Trans. Pattern Anal. Mach. Intell. **20**(8), 832–844 (1998)
8. Montes Nuñez, B.R.: Data Analysis of the Argon Dark Matter Experiment and Background Studies. Ph.D. thesis, Facultad de Ciencias Físicas, Universidad Complutense de Madrid. (2015)
9. Aprile, E., Angle, J., Arneodo, F., Baudis, L., Bernstein, A., Bolozdynya, A., Brusov, P., Coelho, L., Dahl, C., DeViveiros, L., Ferella, A., Fernandes, L., Fiorucci, S., Gaitskell, R., Giboni, K., Gomez, R., Hasty, R., Kastens, L., Kwong, J., Lopes, J., Madden, N., Manalaysay, A., Manzur, A., McKinsey, D., Monzani, M., Ni, K., Oberlack, U., Orboeck, J., Orlandi, D., Plante, G., Santorelli, R., dos Santos, J., Shagin, P., Shutt, T., Sorensen, P., Schulte, S., Tatananni, E., Winant, C., Yamashita, M.: Design and performance of the XENON10 dark matter experiment. Astropart. Phys. **34**(9), 679–698 (2011)
10. Aprile, E., Arisaka, K., Arneodo, F., Askin, A., Baudis, L., Behrens, A., Brown, E., Cardoso, J., Choi, B., Cline, D., Fattori, S., Ferella, A., Giboni, K., Kish, A., Lam, C., Lang, R., Lim, K., Lopes, J., Undagoitia, T.M., Mei, Y., Fernandez, A.M., Ni, K., Oberlack, U., Orrigo, S., Pantic, E., Plante, G., Ribeiro, A., Santorelli, R., dos Santos, J., Schumann, M., Shagin, P., Teymourian, A., Tziaferi, E., Wang, H., Yamashita, M.: The XENON100 dark matter experiment. Astropart. Phys. **35**(9), 573–590 (2012)
11. Regenfus, C.: The ArDM collaboration: the argon dark matter experiment ArDM. J. Phys.: Conf. Ser. **203**(1), 012024 (2010)

12. Marchionni, A., Amsler, C., Badertscher, A., Boccone, V., Bueno, A., Carmona-Benitez, M.C., Coleman, J., Creus, W., Curioni, A., Daniel, M., Dawe, E.J., Degunda, U., Gendotti, A., Epprecht, L., Horikawa, S., Kaufmann, L., Knecht, L., Laffranchi, M., Lazzaro, C., Lightfoot, P.K., Lussi, D., Lozano, J., Mavrokoridis, K., Melgarejo, A., Mijakowski, P., Natterer, G., Navas-Concha, S., Otyugova, P., de Prado, M., Przewlocki, P., Regenfus, C., Resnati, F., Robinson, M., Rochet, J., Romero, L., Rondio, E., Rubbia, A., Scotto-Lavina, L., Spooner, N.J.C., Strauss, T., Touramanis, C., Ulbricht, J., Viant, T.: ArDM: a ton-scale LAr detector for direct dark matter searches. J. Phys.: Conf. Ser. **308**(1), 012006 (2011)
13. Badertscher, A., et al.: Status of the ArDM Experiment: first results from gaseous argon operation in deep underground environment (2013)
14. Boccone, V.: The ArDM collaboration: the ArDM project: a liquid argon TPC for dark matter detection. J. Phys.: Conf. Ser. **160**(1), 012032 (2009)
15. Zell, A.: Java Neural Network Simulator (JavaNNS) (2013). http://www.ra.cs.uni-tuebingen.de/software/JavaNNS/
16. Ridgeway, G.: Generalized boosted models: a guide to the GBM package (2005)
17. Liaw, A., Wiener, M.: Classification and regression by randomForest. R News **2**(3), 18–22 (2002)

A Preliminary Study of the Suitability of Deep Learning to Improve LiDAR-Derived Biomass Estimation

Jorge García-Gutiérrez[1]([✉]), Eduardo González-Ferreiro[2,3],
Daniel Mateos-García[1], and José C. Riquelme-Santos[1]

[1] Department of Computer Languages and Systems,
University of Seville, Seville, Spain
{jorgarcia,mateosg,riquelme}@us.es
[2] Sustainable Forest Management Unit, Department of Agroforestry Engineering,
University of Santiago de Compostela, Santiago de Compostela, Spain
edu.g.ferreiro@gmail.com
[3] Department of Forest Ecosystems and Society,
Oregon State University, Corvallis, OR, USA

Abstract. Light Detection and Ranging (LiDAR) is a remote sensor able to extract three-dimensional information about forest structure. Biophysical models have taken advantage of the use of LiDAR-derived information to improve their accuracy. Multiple Linear Regression (MLR) is the most common method in the literature regarding biomass estimation to define the relation between the set of field measurements and the statistics extracted from a LiDAR flight. Unfortunately, there exist open issues regarding the generalization of models from one area to another due to the lack of knowledge about noise distribution, relationship between statistical features and risk of overfitting. Autoencoders (a type of deep neural network) has been applied to improve the results of machine learning techniques in recent times by undoing possible data corruption process and improving feature selection. This paper presents a preliminary comparison between the use of MLR with and without preprocessing by autoencoders on real LiDAR data from two areas in the province of Lugo (Galizia, Spain). The results show that autoencoders statistically increased the quality of MLR estimations by around 15–30%.

Keywords: Deep learning · LiDAR · Regression · Remote sensing · Soft computing

1 Introduction

Light Detection and Ranging (LiDAR) is a remote laser-based technology able to measure the distance from the source to an object or surface in addition to x-y position. LiDAR sensors have transformed the work previously done with

© Springer International Publishing Switzerland 2016
F. Martínez-Álvarez et al. (Eds.): HAIS 2016, LNAI 9648, pp. 588–596, 2016.
DOI: 10.1007/978-3-319-32034-2_49

expensive or not always-feasible fieldwork. One of the most important disciplines where LiDAR has become an important tool is forestry, specially for estimating forest biomass [1]. Biomass estimation is a key process in forestry management and also, is closely related to climate change since forests are important carbon deposits on Earth [2].

Regarding LiDAR and biomass estimation, researchers have focused on deriving variables related to the LiDAR's ability to extract vertical information and then, worked on establishing relations with field measurements [3]. Multiple linear regression (MLR) has usually been the selected technique to find those relations [4]. The main advantage of using MLR has been the simplicity and clarity of the resulting model, although other techniques have already proven to be more suitable for regression [5].

Regardless the technique selected, main concerns about LiDAR-derived models are related to their suitability to be applied from one area to another (overfitting) [6]. Scale-dependence is well-known in the literature [7] which makes researchers try to work at regional levels [8] in order to facilitate the carbon stocks calculation but with lower accuracy in the models. Regardless the selected scale, models have also problems related to noise in the LiDAR signal [9] which makes researchers avoid intensity (an important component in LiDAR data related to reflectance of the objects) because of the difficulties to well calibrate and sensitivity to multiple returns (which are often found in forested areas) [10]. All these problems are translated to the classical framework where MLR is applied to develop biomass estimation models. In this context, there is a need to explore new ways to reduce noise in LiDAR data whilst at the same time, clarify the relation between LiDAR-derived statistical features.

In recent times, deep learning has emerged as an important tool in machine learning. Deep learning is defined as a branch of machine learning that exploit layers of non-linear information (in the fashion of neural networks), supervised or unsupervised feature extraction and transformation, and for pattern analysis and classification [11]. Autoencoders are a special type of deep neural network, whose output vectors are a (a presumably better) representation of the original input. They are often used for learning an effective or encoding representation of the original data as input vectors in the hidden layers. Vincent et al. [12,13] showed that the use of autoencoders to denoise training data could lead to an improvement of the performance of classification/regression tasks.

Our aim in this work is to compare the results of the classical MLR for biomass estimation with and without a preprocessing based on the use of autoencoders. Experiments carried out in two different areas of the province of Lugo (Galizia, Spain) are statistically validated and discussed.

The rest of the paper is organized as follows. Section 2 provides a description of the LiDAR data used in this work and the methodology followed to carry out the experimentation in Sect. 2. The results achieved, their statistical validation and the main findings are shown in Sect. 3. Finally, Sect. 4 is devoted to summarize the conclusions and to discuss future lines of work.

2   Materials and Method

2.1   Experimental Datasets

Aerial LiDAR data used for this study was flown in two forest areas in the northwest of the Iberian Peninsula (Fig. 1, more details about both areas can be found in Gonzalez-Ferreiro et al. [14]).

Field data from the two study sites were collected to obtain the dependent variables. 39 and 54 instances (one per training plot in a study site) were located and measured on site A and B, respectively. From every study site, two different datasets were generated. One with the maximum resolution provided for the flight and another with a lower level of 0.5 pulses $\times$ m^{-1}.

Biomass fractions of each tree were estimated according to the field measurements (heights and diameters) and the equations for Eucalyptus globulus (site A) and Pinus radiata (site B) reported by [15]. For every plot, biomass fractions were used to calculate the following stand variables in per hectarea basis: stand

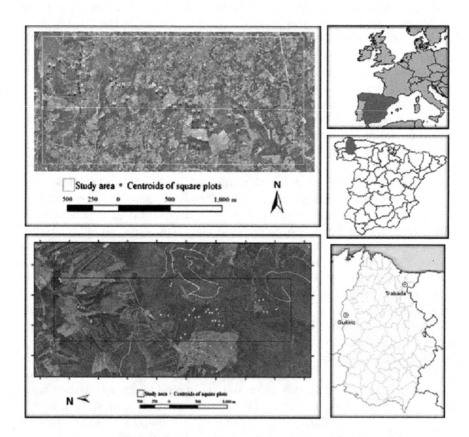

Fig. 1. Study sites located in NW of Spain. Bottom: study site of Trabada (site A). Top: study site of Guitiriz (site B).

crown biomass (W_{cr}), stand stem biomass (W_{st}) and stand aboveground biomass (W_{abg}) for both sites A and B. Additionally, stand basal area (G), dominant height (H_d), mean height (H_m) and stand volume (V) were computed for site B.

FUSION software [16] also provided the variables related to the height and return intensity distributions within the limits of the field plots. Table 1 shows the complete set of metrics and the corresponding abbreviations used in this paper.

From field data and the statistics obtained from LiDAR we built the experimental datasets. Each dataset was compose of the 48 independent variables (*coverFP* and *returns* in Table 1 plus the rest calculated for LiDAR intensity and heights distributions) extracted from LiDAR data and a dependent variable

Table 1. Statistics extracted from the LiDAR flights' heights and intensities used as independent variables for the regression.

Description	Abbreviation
Percentage of first returns over 2 m	coverFP
Number of returns above 2 m	returns
Minimum	min
Maximum	max
Mean	mean
Mode	mode
Standard deviation	SD
Variance	V
Interquartile distance	ID
Skewness	Skw
Kurtosis	Kurt
Average absolute deviation	AAD
25th percentile	P25
50th percentile	P50
75th percentile	P75
5th percentile	P05
10th percentile	P10
20th percentile	P20
30th percentile	P30
40th percentile	P40
60th percentile	P60
70th percentile	P70
80th percentile	P80
90th percentile	P90
95th percentile	P95

(fieldwork-derived forest variable). This procedure gave a total of 20 datasets (obtained for the ten biophysical variables and the two different resolutions of LiDAR-derived feature extraction).

2.2 Autoencoders

We used a traditional autoencoder model [17] to improve MLR performance. An autoencoder is a type of neural network which tries to learn an identity function defining a code/decode transformation. Thus, it firstly takes an input vector x and maps it to a hidden representation y through a deterministic mapping $y = f(x) = s(Wx + b)$, parametrized by W, b. W is a weight matrix and b is a bias vector. The resulting latent representation y is then mapped back to a *reconstructed* vector z in input space $z = g(y) = s(W'y + b')$. Every instance $x(i)$ is thus mapped to a corresponding $y(i)$ and a reconstruction $z(i)$ (see Fig. 2). The parameters of both transformations are calculated to minimize an error function between input and output usually based on the traditional squared error function.

In this work, the selected implementation of the autoencoder was obtained from Weka [18] source repository. The autoencoder was implemented as an unsupervised filter with two optional extra steps (normalization and standardization). We worked with just one hidden layer (since single-hidden-layer neural networks are universal approximators [19]) and the number of units in the hidden layer was set up to the number of features plus one (non-linear autoencoders with more hidden units than inputs have experimentally yielded useful representations [20]).

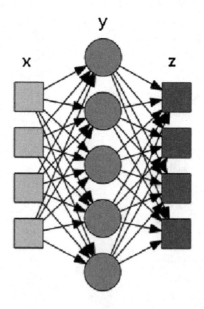

Fig. 2. Autoencoder structure.

2.3 Experimental Framework

In this work, we tested MLR with and without autoencoder preprocessing, applied to the 20 datasets with the 48 independent variables.

Coefficient of correlation (R) was selected to establish the comparison as was done in recent bibliography [21] although we also included root mean square error $(RMSE)$ in the results section for information purpose. The coefficients were obtained in a process of 5-fold cross-validation on each dataset repeated five times. The mean value of the five repetitions was recorded for each technique and dataset in order to obtain robust results (independent from the random selection of folds).

Feature selection based on the well-known M5' filter from Weka was applied to avoid the Hughes phenomenon [22] in all the cases. Optionally, normalization and standardization were applied. Thus, experiments were repeated for every dataset and each compared technique (simple MLR and MLR with autoencoder) with no extra filtering, normalization, and standardization. Then, we selected the best R obtained by each technique and every dataset regardless the optimal filtering setup.

Finally, a T-student or Wilcoxon test (depending on whether or not parametric conditions are met) was applied to statistically validate the results [23].

3 Results

The results obtained by each option can be found in Table 2. If R is used as the reference measure of quality, we can observe that in 14 out of 20 cases, the use of an autoencoder improved the results obtained by MLR. If $RMSE$ is the quality measure, the results are even better (18 out of 20).

After the generation of the quality results for the models, a statistical analysis was applied by using the open-source platform StatService [24] to check the significance in the differences in terms of R. T-student test is usually used for pairwise comparison of results if parametric conditions (homoscedasticity, independence, normality) are met [25]. However, Shapiro-Wilk test rejected the normality hypothesis of the results with a p-value under 0.026 for an $\alpha = 0.05$, and therefore, a non-parametric test such as Wilcoxon's was selected.

Wilcoxon test firstly obtains the average ranks taking into account the position of the compared results with respect to each other. Thus, a value of 1 for a rank would mean a model was the best for a test case, while a rank of 2 would mean it was the worst. Later, the test statistically validates the differences in the mean ranks. In our case, MLR without autoencoding obtained a mean ranking of 1.7 and with the use of an autoencoder reached a mean ranking of 1.1. Taking into account that the Wilcoxon statistic was 164.5 with 1 and 18 degrees of freedom and its corresponding p-value was 0.024, so we could state that the use of an autoencoder significantly improved MLR performance under an $\alpha = 0.05$.

Regarding the results obtained, we can observe that when an autoencoder is applied the improvement of $RMSE$ is around 15 % in average whilst it is 30 %

Table 2. Results obtained by MLR with (column 'Auto') and without (column 'Simple') autoencoding. The best in bold.

Site	Resolution	Biophysical variable	R		RMSE	
			Simple	Auto	Simple	Auto
Trabada	0.5	W_{cr}	0.41	**0.64**	7663.42	**5570.10**
		W_{st}	0.4	**0.74**	50424.57	**36029.75**
		W_{abg}	0.44	**0.69**	61899.45	**47395.80**
	4	W_{cr}	0.36	**0.69**	6200.81	**4553.23**
		W_{st}	0.30	**0.81**	51109.90	**31582.79**
		W_{abg}	0.27	**0.77**	56869.20	**36324.06**
Guitiriz	0.5	W_{cr}	**0.65**	0.55	10236.60	**9675.70**
		W_{st}	0.61	**0.72**	65573.57	**46515.49**
		W_{abg}	0.61	**0.69**	62827.15	**59505.88**
		G	0.50	**0.52**	12.58	**11.63**
		H_d	0.71	**0.79**	2.93	**2.84**
		H_m	0.76	**0.78**	2.48	**2.41**
		V	**0.68**	0.67	133.71	**125.00**
	8	W_{cr}	**0.76**	0.53	**9127.03**	9709.39
		W_{st}	**0.71**	0.69	58881.87	**45201.21**
		W_{abg}	0.69	**0.72**	63302.99	**54142.08**
		G	0.60	**0.64**	11.07	**10.63**
		H_d	0.76	**0.81**	3.44	**2.79**
		H_m	**0.78**	0.71	2.51	**2.18**
		V	**0.74**	0.70	**112.57**	121.22

if we compare averaged R. Similar results have reported [12] that demonstrated that the use of autoencoders bring benefits for other machine learning techniques such as Support Vector Machines. Our results show that parametric techniques can also be boosted by this type of preprocessing.

Among the possible reasons for such a good performance of autoencoders, we should outline that LiDAR-derived data is generated in several steps which may involve noise generation. Vincent et al. [13] showed how to develop denoising autoencoders which focus in noise reduction. Although the one applied in this work cannot be seen as a complete denoising autoencoder, the benefit could still be present due to the own nature of autoencoders which establish a mechanism to code/decode data avoiding spurious influence.

Also, notice that LiDAR-derived statistical features are usually limited and hand-crafted. These features might not have to completely describe the complexity in a forest area. In that case, relations between statistics could be explored by an autoencoder in order to find a better data representation by features combination. Taking into account that autoencoders take almost-negligible training time for small datasets (a common situation in forestry due to fieldwork high costs), their use is strongly advised.

Finally but not less important, autoencoders could have also decreased the risk of overfitting introducing some degree of distortion in training data although this possibility needs a deeper study to be confirmed.

4   Conclusions

This paper presented a preliminary study of the use of autoencoders to improve LiDAR-derived biomass estimation by MLR. The experimentation was carried out on real data from two areas in the province of Lugo (Galizia, Spain). The results showed that autoencoders statistically improved the use of classical MLR for biomass estimation. Nevertheless, results confirmed that autoencoders are a valuable tool to preprocess LiDAR-derived features by getting noise reduction and feature discovering.

Future work should address gaps not covered in this work. Thus, we must complete the framework with a deeper comparison with other types of autoencoders (denoising encoders, sparse encoders, etc.) and regression techniques (regression trees, Gaussian processes, etc.). We should also study the influence of the number of hidden units. Finally, we must assess autoencoders to avoid overfitting and thus overcome the problems to apply models from one area to another.

References

1. Wulder, M.A., Bater, C.W., Coops, N.C., Hilker, T., White, J.C.: The role of LiDAR in sustainable forest management. Forest. Chron. **84**(6), 807–826 (2008)
2. Hansen, E.H., Gobakken, T., Solberg, S., Kangas, A., Ene, L., Mauya, E., Nsset, E.: Relative efficiency of ALS and InSAR for biomass estimation in a tanzanian rainforest. Remote Sens. **7**(8), 9865 (2015)
3. Gonzlez-Ferreiro, E., Miranda, D., Barreiro-Fernandez, L., Bujan, S., Garcia-Gutierrez, J., Dieguez-Aranda, U.: Modelling stand biomass fractions in galician eucalyptus globulus plantations by use of different LiDAR pulse densities. For. Syst. **22**(3), 510–525 (2013)
4. Muss, J.D., Mladenoff, D.J., Townsend, P.A.: A pseudo-waveform technique to assess forest structure using discrete LiDAR data. Remote Sens. Environ. **115**(3), 824–835 (2011)
5. Garcia-Gutierrez, J., Martinez-Alvarez, F., Troncoso, A., Riquelme, J.: A comparison of machine learning regression techniques for LiDAR-derived estimation of forest variables. Neurocomputing **167**, 24–31 (2015)
6. Bouvier, M., Durrieu, S., Fournier, R.A., Renaud, J.P.: Generalizing predictive models of forest inventory attributes using an area-based approach with airborne LiDAR data. Remote Sens. Environ. **156**, 322–334 (2015)
7. Zhao, K., Popescu, S., Nelson, R.: LiDAR remote sensing of forest biomass: A scale-invariant estimation approach using airborne lasers. Remote Sens. Environ. **113**(1), 182–196 (2009)

8. Hayashi, M., Saigusa, N., Yamagata, Y., Hirano, T.: Regional forest biomass estimation using ICESat/GLAS spaceborne LiDAR over borneo. Carbon Manage. **6**(1–2), 19–33 (2015)
9. Cao, N., Zhu, C., Kai, Y., Yan, P.: A method of background noise reduction in LiDAR data. Appl. Phys. B **113**(1), 115–123 (2013)
10. Hofle, B., Pfeifer, N.: Correction of laser scanning intensity data: Data and model-driven approaches. ISPRS J. Photogrammetry Remote Sens. **63**, 1415–1433 (2007)
11. Deng, L., Yu, D.: Deep learning: Methods and applications. Found. Trends Signal Process. **7**, 3–4 (2014)
12. Vincent, P., Larochelle, H., Bengio, Y., Manzagol, P.: Extracting and composing robust features with denoising autoencoders. In: Proceedings of the Twenty-fifth International Conference on Machine Learning (ICML 2008), pp. 1096–1103. ACM (2008)
13. Vincent, P., Larochelle, H., Lajoie, I., Bengio, Y., Manzagol, P.A.: Stacked denoising autoencoders: Learning useful representations in a deep network with a local denoising criterion. J. Mach. Learn. Res. **11**, 3371–3408 (2010)
14. Gonzalez-Ferreiro, E., Dieguez-Aranda, U., Miranda, D.: Estimation of stand variables in pinus radiata d. don plantations using different LiDAR pulse densities. Forestry **85**(2), 281–292 (2012)
15. Diéguez-Aranda, U., Rojo-Alboreca, A., Castedo-Dorado, F., González, J.A., Barrio-Anta, M., Crecente-Campo, F., González-González, J., Pérez-Cruzado, C., Rodríguez-Soalleiro, R., López-Sánchez, C., Balboa-Murias, M., Gorgoso-Varela, J.J., Sánchez-Rodríguez, F.: Herramientas selvícolas para la gestión forestal sostenible en Galicia, vol. 259. Consellería do Medio Rural, Xunta de Galicia (2009)
16. McGaughey, R.: FUSION/LDV: software for LIDAR data analysis and visualization. In: US Department of Agriculture, Forest Service, Pacific Northwest Research Station, Seattle (2009)
17. Bengio, Y.: Learning deep architectures for AI. Found. Trends Mach. Learn. **2**(1), 1–127 (2009)
18. Hall, M., Frank, E., Holmes, G., Pfahringer, B., Reutemann, P., Witten, I.H.: The WEKA data mining software: An update. SIGKDD Explor. **11**(1), 10–18 (2009)
19. Hassoun, M.: Fundamentals of Artificial Neural Networks. MIT Press, Cambridge (1995)
20. Bengio, Y., Lamblin, P., Popovici, D., Larochelle, H.: Greedy layer-wise training of deep networks. In: Schölkopf, B., Platt, J., Hoffman, T., (eds.) Advances in Neural Information Processing Systems, vol. 19, pp. 153–160. MIT Press (2007)
21. Zhao, K., Popescu, S., Meng, X., Pang, Y., Agca, M.: Characterizing forest canopy structure with LiDAR composite metrics and machine learning. Remote Sens. Environ. **115**(8), 1978–1996 (2011)
22. Hughes, G.F.: On the mean accuracy of statistical pattern recognizers. IEEE Trans. Inf. Theory **14**, 55–63 (1968)
23. Fay, M., Proschan, M.: Wilcoxon-mann-whitney or t-test? On assumptions for hypothesis tests and multiple interpretations of decision rules. Stat. Surv. **4**, 1–39 (2010)
24. Parejo, J.A., García, J., Ruiz-Cortés, A., Riquelme, J.C.: Statservice: Herramienta de análisis estadístico como soporte para la investigación con metaheurísticas. In: Actas del VIII Congreso Expañol sobre Metaheurísticas, Algoritmos Evolutivos y Bio-inspirados (2012)
25. Demsar, J.: Statistical comparisons of classifiers over multiple data sets. J. Mach. Learn. Res. **7**, 1–30 (2006)

Fisher Score-Based Feature Selection for Ordinal Classification: A Social Survey on Subjective Well-Being

María Pérez-Ortiz[1][(✉)], Mercedes Torres-Jiménez[1], Pedro Antonio Gutiérrez[2], Javier Sánchez-Monedero[1], and César Hervás-Martínez[2]

[1] Department of Quantitative Methods, Universidad Loyola Andalucía, Córdoba, Spain
{i82perom,jsanchezm}@uco.es, mtorres@uloyola.es
[2] Department of Computer Science and Numerical Analysis, University of Córdoba, Córdoba, Spain
{pagutierrez,chervas}@uco.es

Abstract. This paper approaches the problem of feature selection in the context of ordinal classification problems. To do so, an ordinal version of the Fisher score is proposed. We test this new strategy considering data from an European social survey concerning subjective well-being, in order to understand and identify the most important variables for a person's happiness, which is represented using ordered categories. The input variables have been chosen according to previous research, and these have been categorised in the following groups: demographics, daily activities, social well-being, health and habits, community well-being and personality/opinion. The proposed strategy shows promising results and performs significantly better than its nominal counterpart, therefore validating the need of developing specific ordinal feature selection methods. Furthermore, the results of this paper can shed some light on the human psyche by analysing the most and less frequently selected variables.

1 Introduction

The nature of well-being is a topic that has exercised the minds of moral philosophers for centuries [1]. Recently, research on happiness has gained importance, not only in the psychology area, but also in other fields like economics [2]. A number of nations have begun to develop measures of subjective well-being [3] to complement traditional measures of national well-being, such as the Gross Domestic Product. Well-being research is usually clustered into two camps [1], focusing either on subjective well-being or psychological well-being. On the one hand, subjective well-being is understood as having an emotional component of the balance between positive and negative affect and a cognitive component of

This work has been subsidised by the TIN2014-54583-C2-1-R project of the Spanish Ministerial Commission of Science and Technology (MICYT), FEDER funds and the P11-TIC-7508 project of the "Junta de Andalucía" (Spain).

© Springer International Publishing Switzerland 2016
F. Martínez-Álvarez et al. (Eds.): HAIS 2016, LNAI 9648, pp. 597–608, 2016.
DOI: 10.1007/978-3-319-32034-2_50

judgements about life satisfaction. On the other hand, psychological well-being has been defined as "engagement with existential challenges of life" [4]. Given the diversity of perspectives on the definition of subjective and psychological well-being, it is not surprising that different measurements have been considered in each case. In empirical research, a number of studies suggests that subjective and psychological well-being are two related, but distinct, constructs [4].

Nowadays, machine learning represents one of the most actively researched technical fields, mainly because of its applicability to very different domains. Given the lack of empirical agreement on the structure of well-being and the use of non-validated measures in previous studies, the current study examines these issues using machine learning techniques and data from the European Social Survey (ESS)[1]. The ESS includes a large sample of European inhabitants and validated well-being measures. It is an academically driven cross-national survey and has been conducted every two years across Europe. The survey measures the attitudes, beliefs and behaviour patterns of diverse populations in more than thirty nations, involving strict random probability sampling, a minimum target response rate of 70 % and rigorous translation protocols. The interviews include questions on a variety of core topics: social trust, political interest and participation, socio-political orientations, social exclusion, national, ethnic and religious allegiances, health and social determinants, immigration, human values, demographics and socioeconomics.

This paper presents a new strategy to perform feature selection in ordinal classification [5]. Ordinal classification comprises those classification problems where the variable to predict follows a natural order (e.g. in Likert scales, as the case considered here). More specifically, we develop a novel feature selection methodology based on the well-known Fisher score [6]. The proposed technique promotes features that maintain the order among the classes and is used in this paper to analyse which are the factors influencing subjective well-being to a larger extent.

The remainder of the paper is structured as follows: Sect. 2 presents the data considered; Sect. 3 presents some previous notions and the proposed strategy for feature selection; Sect. 4 analyses and presents the results obtained; and finally, Sect. 5 outlines some conclusions and final remarks.

2   Social Survey on Subjective Well-Being

The survey data conducted in 2014 from 15 European Union countries have been selected according to the availability of information (all persons aged 15 and over, resident within private households, regardless of their nationality, citizenship, language or legal status, in the following participating countries: Austria, Belgium, Czech Republic, Denmark, Estonia, Finland, France, Germany, Ireland, Netherlands, Slovenia, Sweden and Switzerland). Different variables have been selected to predict the level of well-being of European citizens, considering the

---

[1] http://www.europeansocialsurvey.org/.

components that influences happiness according to previous research [7]. These variables have been classified into six different groups:

- Demographics: different factors including country, age, gender, education, familiar composition, financial matters, etc.
- Daily activities: this group considers different variables that indicate how people spend their time (e.g. number of working hours, main activity, employment contract, number of hours watching TV, etc.).
- Social well-being: these variables are related to the social environment of the person (e.g. how often they take part in social activities, the number of people they are living with, how many people they can discuss personal matters with, etc.).
- Health and habits: including how often they practice sports, how often they eat vegetables, subjective general health, how often they drink alcohol, smoking behaviour, quality of sleep, and others.
- Community well-being: related to the sense of engagement they have with the area they live. It includes politic and environmental aspects (e.g. whether they feel close to their country, how interested they are in politics, how satisfied they are with economy/health services/education/government in their country, placement on left-right scale, etc.).
- Personality/opinion: how religious they are, whether it is important to be rich/free/humble/adventurous, whether they would allow immigrants from poorer countries to settle in their country, whether most people can be trusted or not, etc.

The study comprise a set of 56 different variables: a large number of them (38) represent Likert scales (i.e. ordinal) and are codified using a numeric scale, 7 are numeric, 6 of them are binary, and finally, there are 5 nominal variables, which are transformed to binary ones, resulting then in a total set of 91 variables. The total number of cases is $28,137$, excluding those with responses "don't know", "no answer" or "refusal" in the dependent variable, which is how happy they are in a Likert scale (from 0 to 10). Three different datasets are considered, using different number of levels for the subjective well-being: all the 11 possible answers (referred to as SW-11c), 5 classes (SW-5c, where $C_1 = \{0, 1, 2\}$, $C_2 = \{3, 4\}$, $C_3 = \{5, 6\}$, $C_4 = \{7, 8\}$ and $C_5 = \{9, 10\}$) and 3 classes (SW-3c, where $C_1 = \{0, 1, 2, 3\}$, $C_2 = \{4, 5, 6, 7\}$ and $C_3 = \{8, 9, 10\}$).

Values such as "don't know", "no answer" or "refusal" in the independent variables have been considered as missing values and have been imputed using the Event Covering algorithm, as suggested in [8] for approximate models such as neural networks, support vector machines and other statistical methods.

3 Methodology

This section describes some previous notions (the paradigm of ordinal classification and the Fisher score) and proposes an ordinal feature selection method.

3.1   Previous Notions

Ordinal Classification and Ordinal Feature Selection. The classification of patterns into naturally ordered labels is referred to as ordinal regression or ordinal classification. This learning paradigm, although still mostly unexplored, is spreading rapidly and receiving a lot of attention from the pattern recognition and machine learning communities [5,9], given its applicability to real world problems. This paradigm shares properties of classification and regression. In contrast to multinomial classification, there exists some ordering among the elements of $\mathcal{Y}$ (the labelling space) and both standard classifiers and the zero-one loss function do not capture and reflect this ordering. Concerning regression, $\mathcal{Y}$ is a non-metric space, so the distances between categories are not known.

As an explanatory example, consider the case of financial trading where an agent predicts not only whether to buy an asset, but also the investment. The different situations could be categorised as {"no investment", "little investment", "big investment", "huge investment"}. A natural order among the classes exists in this case, and a necessity of penalising differently the misclassification errors (it should not be considered equal misclassifying a "no investment" instance with a "huge investment" one than misclassifying it with "little investment").

The goal in ordinal classification is to assign an input vector $\mathbf{x}$ to one of K discrete classes $\mathcal{C}_k, k \in \{1, \ldots, K\}$, where there exists a given ordering between the labels, $\mathcal{C}_1 \prec \mathcal{C}_2 \prec \cdots \prec \mathcal{C}_K$, $\prec$ denoting this order information. Hence, the objective is to find a prediction rule $C : \mathcal{X} \to \mathcal{Y}$ by using an i.i.d. training sample $X = \{\mathbf{x}_i, y_i\}_{i=1}^N$, where N is the number of training patterns, $\mathbf{x}_i \in \mathcal{X}$, $y_i \in \mathcal{Y}$, $\mathcal{X} \subset \mathbb{R}^d$ is the d-dimensional input space and $\mathcal{Y} = \{\mathcal{C}_1, \mathcal{C}_2, \ldots, \mathcal{C}_K\}$ is the label space. For convenience, denote by $\mathbf{X}_i$ to the set of patterns belonging to $\mathcal{C}_i$.

Despite the novelty of ordinal classification, there is some research concerning new prediction strategies for these problems. However, there are aspects of ordinal classification that are receiving less attention. This is the case of feature selection methods in ordinal classification, where the number of approaches is still low [10,11]. Like some of the strategies in the feature selection literature, these techniques rely on a discretisation of the input space. In this paper, we devise a new strategy for ordinal feature selection that is free of this requirement.

Fisher Score for Feature Selection. The problem of supervised feature selection is now described. Given a dataset $\{\mathbf{x}_i, y_i\}_{i=1}^N$, we aim to find a feature subset of size m (where $m < d$) that contains the most informative features.

The Fisher score for feature selection [6] was proposed as an heuristic strategy for computing an independent score for each feature using the well-known notion of the Fisher ratio. Let μ_k^i and σ_k^i be the mean and standard deviation of the k-th class and i-th feature (and μ^i and σ^i the mean and standard deviation of the whole dataset for the i-th feature). The Fisher score for the i-th feature $(\mathbf{x}^i)$ can be computed as:

$$F(\mathbf{x}^i) = \frac{\sum_{k=1}^K N_k (\mu_k^i - \mu^i)^2}{\sum_{k=1}^K N_k (\sigma_k^i)^2}, \tag{1}$$

where N_k is the number of patterns of class $\mathcal{C}_k$. Since this score is computed independently, the features selected may represent a suboptimal set. Furthermore, this heuristic may fail to select redundant features or those with a high aggregated discriminative power. This technique is named as Nominal Feature Selection (NFS) in the experimental results.

3.2 Proposed Feature Selection Strategy

In this paper, we reformulate the nominal Fisher score F to deal with ordinal data (named it as F_O). In this regard, we include a weighting term that introduces a higher cost for distant classes. This cost will force the feature selection method to focus more on those features that help to discriminate classes that are far in the ordinal scale (in order to avoid the above-mentioned misclassification errors). The formulation proposed is the maximise the following score:

$$F_O(\mathbf{x}^i) = \frac{\sum_{k=1}^{K} \sum_{j=1}^{K} |k - j| (\mu_k^i - \mu_j^i)^2}{(K - 1) \sum_{k=1}^{K} (\sigma_k^i)^2}, \tag{2}$$

where $|k - j|$ is the cost of misclassifying a pattern from class $\mathcal{C}_k$ in class $\mathcal{C}_j$.

Apart from the fact that more distant classes in the ordinal scale should present a higher distance between them, there is another ordinal requirement which can be introduced in the feature selection stage. As said before, the labelling space is non-metric, therefore we can not introduce a distance relation among the different classes. However, from the ordinal classification definition it can be stated that $d(\mathcal{C}_k, \mathcal{C}_j) < d(\mathcal{C}_k, \mathcal{C}_h), \forall \{k, j, h, | k \neq j \neq h \wedge (k < j < h \vee k > j > h)\}$. These ordinal requirements can be introduced by the score:

$$O_R(\mathbf{x}^i) = \frac{\sum_{k=1}^{K-2} \sum_{j=k+1}^{K-1} \sum_{h=j+1}^{K} [\![((\mu_k^i - \mu_h^i)^2 - (\mu_k^i - \mu_j^i)^2) > 0]\!]}{\sum_{j=2}^{K-1} (K - j)}, \tag{3}$$

being $[\![\cdot]\!]$ a Boolean test which is 1 if the inner condition is true, and 0 otherwise. This O_R score measures the number of ordinal requirements fulfilled for a specific feature i. To include both terms in the feature selection process, we compute a weighted mean of both scores in the following manner:

$$F_{OR}(\mathbf{x}^i) = \alpha \cdot F_O(\mathbf{x}^i) + (1 - \alpha) O_R(\mathbf{x}^i), \tag{4}$$

where $\alpha \in (0, 1)$.

Up to now, we have defined the distance between the classes $\mathcal{C}_z$ and $\mathcal{C}_j$ as $d_s^i(\mathcal{C}_z, \mathcal{C}_j) = (\mu_z^i - \mu_j^i)^2$ (note that this formulation presents problems with non-linear, multimodal or non-normal data). Alternative metrics have been proposed for measuring the distance between classes [12]. In this way, we consider other notions of distance between sets of points, such as the mean distance:

$$d_m^i(\mathcal{C}_z, \mathcal{C}_j) = \frac{1}{N_z \cdot N_j} \sum_{\mathbf{x}_h^i \in \mathcal{C}_z} \sum_{\mathbf{x}_v^i \in \mathcal{C}_j} (x_h^i - x_v^i)^2, \tag{5}$$

where the idea is to compute the mean distance between each pair of patterns of different classes. Another alternative is the sum of minimum distances:

$$d_{\mathrm{md}}^i(\mathcal{C}_z, \mathcal{C}_j) = \frac{1}{2} \left(\sum_{\mathbf{x}_h^i \in \mathcal{C}_z} \Delta_{\mathrm{m}}(\mathbf{x}_h^i, \mathcal{C}_j) + \sum_{\mathbf{x}_v^i \in \mathcal{C}_j} \Delta_{\mathrm{m}}(\mathbf{x}_v^i, \mathcal{C}_z) \right), \qquad (6)$$

where $\Delta_{\mathrm{m}}(\mathbf{x}_h^i, \mathcal{C}_j) = \min_{\mathbf{x}_v^i \in \mathcal{C}_j} d(\mathbf{x}_h^i, \mathbf{x}_v^i)$ and d represents the Euclidean distance. Finally, the Hausdorff distance is defined as:

$$d_{\mathrm{h}}^i(\mathcal{C}_z, \mathcal{C}_j) = \max\{ \max_{\mathbf{x}_h^i \in \mathcal{C}_z} \Delta_{\mathrm{m}}(\mathbf{x}_h^i, \mathcal{C}_j), \max_{\mathbf{x}_v^i \in \mathcal{C}_j} \Delta_{\mathrm{m}}(\mathbf{x}_v^i, \mathcal{C}_z) \}. \qquad (7)$$

In the experiments of this paper, we will test these three alternative approaches for computing inter-class distances.

4   Experimental Results

Regarding the experimental setup, a stratified holdout technique was applied to randomly divide the datasets 30 times, using 5 % of the patterns for training (approximately 1400 patterns) and the remaining 95 % for testing. The partitions were the same for all methods and one model was obtained and evaluated (in the test set) for each split. Finally, the results are computed as the mean and standard deviation of the measures over the 30 test sets. The classification method chosen is the reformulation of Kernel Discriminant Analysis for Ordinal Regression (KDLOR), because of its relation to the Fisher score [13].

4.1   Methodologies Tested

Different methods are compared:

- No feature selection. These results are obtained with the KDLOR classification method using the whole set of features.
- Nominal Feature Selection (NFS). In this case, we use the nominal version of the Fisher score.
- Ordinal Feature Selection (OFS) with d_{s} as distance metric.
- Ordinal Feature Selection using the mean distance (OFSMean). In this case, d_{m} is used as distance metric.
- Ordinal Feature Selection using the min distance (OFSMin). In this case, d_{md} is used as distance metric.
- Ordinal Feature Selection using the Hausdorff distance (OFSHausdorff). In this case, d_{h} is used as distance metric.

The value α for all the ordinal feature selection methods is fixed to $\alpha = 0.5$. For all feature selection methods, features are ranked according to the corresponding score, and then a percentage of the best features is retained (where the percentages tested are $10\%, 20\%, \ldots, 90\%$). Concerning the parameters selected for the classification method, a Gaussian kernel is used for KDLOR, $K(\mathbf{x}, \mathbf{y}) = \exp\left(-\frac{\|\mathbf{x}-\mathbf{y}\|^2}{\sigma^2} \right)$, where σ is the kernel width which has been cross-validated using a 5-fold nested procedure over the training set and the range $\{10^{-3}, \ldots, 10^3\}$.

4.2   Evaluation Metrics

Several measures can be considered for evaluating ordinal classifiers, such as the Mean Absolute Error (MAE) or the accuracy or Acc [5]. In this work, two metrics have been used:

- Acc is the ratio of correctly classified patterns:

$$Acc = \frac{1}{N} \sum_{i=1}^{N} [\![y_i^* = y_i]\!],$$

where y_i is the desired output for pattern i and y_i^* is the prediction.
- Acc and MAE may not be the best option when measuring performance in the presence of class imbalances [14]. The average mean absolute error ($AMAE$) is the mean of MAE classification errors throughout the classes, where MAE is the average absolute deviation of the predicted class from the true class. Let MAE_k be the MAE for a given k-th class:

$$MAE_k = \frac{1}{N_k} \sum_{i=1}^{N_k} |\mathcal{O}(y_i) - \mathcal{O}(y_i^*)|, \ 1 \leq k \leq K,$$

where $\mathcal{O}(\mathcal{C}_k) = k$, $1 \leq k \leq K$, i.e. $\mathcal{O}(y_i)$ is the order of class label y_i. Then, the $AMAE$ measure can be defined in the following way:

$$AMAE = \frac{1}{K} \sum_{k=1}^{K} MAE_k,$$

MAE values range from 0 to $K - 1$, as do those of $AMAE$. This metric has been chosen given the imbalanced nature of the problem considered.

4.3   Results

The results obtained for all the methods can be seen in Table 1 for Acc and Table 2 for $AMAE$, from which several conclusions can be drawn. Note that the results without feature selection are also included in the Tables for the three datasets. Firstly, the performance of the base algorithm (i.e. with no feature selection) can be improved in some cases (e.g. in SW-5c), and there are reduction levels where the reduced datasets perform relatively similar to the base ones (e.g. with 30 % of features), which is interesting for model interpretability purposes and to reduce computational time. Secondly, the results are in general promising (considering the difficulty of the problem). Finally, the proposed technique performs better than the nominal counterpart (specially when the Hausdorff distance is used).

To quantify whether a statistical difference exists among the algorithms compared, a procedure is employed to compare multiple classifiers in multiple datasets [15]. Tables 1 and 2 also shows the result of applying the non-parametric

Table 1. *Acc* mean and standard deviation (Mean ± SD) obtained by all the methodologies compared as a function of the percentage of features selected.

	NFS	OFS	OFSMean	OFSMin	OFSHausdorff
Perc. of features	SW-3c, result without FS: 68.99 ± 0.53				
10 %	46.31 ± 2.55	49.02 ± 3.75	*49.41 ± 2.29*	45.11 ± 4.67	**55.52 ± 4.55**
20 %	**56.83 ± 4.45**	*56.76 ± 6.28*	53.14 ± 1.41	49.59 ± 2.46	49.99 ± 2.58
30 %	60.25 ± 0.21	*60.35 ± 0.09*	52.36 ± 1.32	60.14 ± 0.57	**65.26 ± 0.67**
40 %	*60.34 ± 0.27*	60.33 ± 0.18	56.69 ± 1.31	62.14 ± 0.83	**65.01 ± 0.80**
50 %	60.40 ± 0.07	*60.41 ± 0.05*	60.32 ± 0.12	64.21 ± 0.71	**64.22 ± 0.65**
60 %	59.93 ± 1.00	60.05 ± 0.82	59.53 ± 1.01	*66.48 ± 0.66*	**66.49 ± 0.63**
70 %	60.36 ± 0.51	60.77 ± 0.74	61.74 ± 0.69	**67.37 ± 0.62**	*67.36 ± 0.68*
80 %	62.91 ± 0.52	63.46 ± 0.68	64.27 ± 0.69	**68.39 ± 0.51**	*68.28 ± 0.48*
90 %	66.09 ± 0.52	66.18 ± 0.51	66.98 ± 0.64	*68.87 ± 0.50*	**68.89 ± 0.54**
Perc. of features	SW-5c, result without FS: 50.22 ± 0.49				
10 %	*30.38 ± 3.49*	**32.41 ± 4.24**	26.62 ± 9.84	22.10 ± 3.26	22.73 ± 3.16
20 %	38.15 ± 10.35	**44.75 ± 7.18**	29.63 ± 3.69	*42.32 ± 3.73*	42.28 ± 3.73
30 %	*48.67 ± 0.25*	48.40 ± 2.24	38.17 ± 1.67	**48.84 ± 0.06**	**48.84 ± 0.06**
40 %	48.82 ± 0.07	*48.84 ± 0.04*	42.84 ± 0.83	**48.86 ± 0.02**	**48.86 ± 0.02**
50 %	*48.84 ± 0.01*	**48.85 ± 0.01**	47.65 ± 0.50	48.69 ± 0.42	48.67 ± 0.43
60 %	48.85 ± 0.00	48.85 ± 0.00	48.85 ± 0.01	*49.72 ± 0.59*	**50.74 ± 0.66**
70 %	48.82 ± 0.18	48.84 ± 0.05	48.78 ± 0.18	*50.80 ± 0.41*	**51.10 ± 0.40**
80 %	48.88 ± 0.22	49.05 ± 0.35	49.51 ± 0.34	*50.88 ± 0.31*	**51.48 ± 0.22**
90 %	49.88 ± 0.33	49.94 ± 0.30	50.21 ± 0.27	*50.42 ± 0.23*	**51.08 ± 0.20**
Perc. of features	SW-11c, result without FS: 30.09 ± 0.34				
10 %	10.85 ± 3.72	**15.82 ± 3.27**	6.70 ± 4.80	14.35 ± 2.34	*14.60 ± 2.56*
20 %	17.97 ± 6.07	*24.58 ± 6.61*	13.06 ± 2.86	22.52 ± 3.10	**27.88 ± 4.08**
30 %	*30.49 ± 0.30*	29.80 ± 3.12	19.30 ± 1.07	**30.71 ± 0.08**	30.33 ± 1.14
40 %	*30.59 ± 0.41*	**30.60 ± 0.49**	21.83 ± 1.46	29.07 ± 2.37	27.78 ± 0.47
50 %	*30.51 ± 0.28*	**30.61 ± 0.20**	30.01 ± 1.35	27.54 ± 0.86	29.38 ± 0.41
60 %	**30.73 ± 0.03**	**30.73 ± 0.04**	*30.35 ± 1.32*	28.77 ± 0.57	30.18 ± 0.36
70 %	*29.47 ± 1.99*	28.51 ± 2.01	27.39 ± 1.26	29.41 ± 0.47	**30.37 ± 0.31**
80 %	27.66 ± 0.37	28.13 ± 0.48	28.53 ± 0.51	*29.79 ± 0.34*	**30.20 ± 0.35**
90 %	29.01 ± 0.28	29.21 ± 0.27	29.44 ± 0.40	*29.98 ± 0.35*	**30.11 ± 0.31**
Average	43.777	44.639	41.233	*44.977*	**45.838**
Ranking	3.519	2.778	3.981	*2.759*	**1.963**
Friedman's test	Confidence interval $C_0 = (0, F_{(\alpha=0.05)} = 2.459)$. F-val.$_{Acc}$: 8.278 $\notin C_0$.				

The best performing method is in **bold** face and the second one in *italics*.

statistical Friedman's test (for a significance level of $\alpha = 0.05$) to the mean *Acc* and *AMAE* rankings. The test rejected the null-hypothesis that all of the algorithms perform similarly in mean ranking for both metrics.

On the basis of this rejection and following the guidelines in [15], we consider the best performing method as control method for the following test. We compare this method to the rest according to their rankings. It has been noted that the

Table 2. *AMAE* mean and standard deviation (Mean ± SD) obtained by all the methodologies compared as a function of the percentage of features selected.

	NFS	OFS	OFSMean	OFSMin	OFSHausdorff
Perc. of features	SW-3c, result without FS: 0.581 ± 0.010				
10 %	0.877 ± 0.037	0.891 ± 0.039	0.870 ± 0.036	*0.825 ± 0.049*	**0.780 ± 0.054**
20 %	0.947 ± 0.057	0.955 ± 0.084	**0.756 ± 0.020**	*0.757 ± 0.035*	0.758 ± 0.052
30 %	0.996 ± 0.006	0.999 ± 0.002	*0.731 ± 0.019*	0.917 ± 0.105	**0.606 ± 0.108**
40 %	0.997 ± 0.009	0.997 ± 0.007	0.913 ± 0.046	*0.647 ± 0.014*	**0.606 ± 0.014**
50 %	0.997 ± 0.003	0.999 ± 0.002	0.997 ± 0.006	*0.631 ± 0.009*	**0.630 ± 0.009**
60 %	0.952 ± 0.098	0.950 ± 0.102	*0.806 ± 0.140*	**0.610 ± 0.007**	0.610 ± 0.008
70 %	0.777 ± 0.114	0.730 ± 0.075	*0.677 ± 0.020*	**0.600 ± 0.007**	0.600 ± 0.008
80 %	0.678 ± 0.016	0.668 ± 0.016	0.645 ± 0.017	**0.588 ± 0.009**	*0.589 ± 0.009*
90 %	0.630 ± 0.014	0.629 ± 0.015	*0.609 ± 0.014*	**0.581 ± 0.008**	**0.581 ± 0.008**
Perc. of features	SW-5c, result without FS: 1.294 ± 0.052				
10 %	*1.619 ± 0.098*	**1.590 ± 0.107**	1.668 ± 0.192	1.678 ± 0.116	1.668 ± 0.097
20 %	1.490 ± 0.199	1.460 ± 0.168	1.486 ± 0.085	*1.349 ± 0.080*	**1.347 ± 0.079**
30 %	*1.401 ± 0.001*	1.413 ± 0.070	1.404 ± 0.023	**1.399 ± 0.001**	**1.399 ± 0.001**
40 %	**1.400 ± 0.001**	**1.400 ± 0.000**	*1.410 ± 0.014*	**1.400 ± 0.000**	**1.400 ± 0.000**
50 %	1.400 ± 0.000	1.400 ± 0.000	1.401 ± 0.005	*1.356 ± 0.100*	**1.339 ± 0.112**
60 %	1.400 ± 0.000	1.400 ± 0.000	1.400 ± 0.000	*1.160 ± 0.049*	**1.137 ± 0.066**
70 %	1.396 ± 0.022	1.396 ± 0.023	1.370 ± 0.062	*1.192 ± 0.021*	**1.145 ± 0.023**
80 %	1.358 ± 0.050	1.336 ± 0.054	1.280 ± 0.045	*1.249 ± 0.017*	**1.181 ± 0.017**
90 %	1.304 ± 0.028	1.297 ± 0.022	*1.284 ± 0.016*	1.294 ± 0.010	**1.232 ± 0.010**
Perc. of features	SW-11c, result without FS: 2.884 ± 0.015				
10 %	3.986 ± 0.353	**3.774 ± 0.255**	4.530 ± 0.634	*3.381 ± 0.229*	3.384 ± 0.200
20 %	3.670 ± 0.425	3.549 ± 0.146	3.696 ± 0.333	**3.143 ± 0.145**	*3.404 ± 0.215*
30 %	3.535 ± 0.011	3.514 ± 0.111	**3.298 ± 0.150**	3.546 ± 0.001	*3.494 ± 0.143*
40 %	3.535 ± 0.025	3.537 ± 0.030	*3.246 ± 0.087*	3.264 ± 0.403	**2.656 ± 0.049**
50 %	3.528 ± 0.018	3.534 ± 0.017	3.520 ± 0.076	*2.767 ± 0.157*	**2.685 ± 0.040**
60 %	3.543 ± 0.003	3.542 ± 0.004	3.497 ± 0.167	*2.765 ± 0.047*	**2.739 ± 0.030**
70 %	3.386 ± 0.248	3.222 ± 0.289	2.943 ± 0.212	*2.802 ± 0.035*	**2.799 ± 0.025**
80 %	2.976 ±'0.024	2.929 ± 0.036	2.861 ± 0.046	**2.843 ± 0.021**	*2.848 ± 0.020*
90 %	2.913 ± 0.022	2.905 ± 0.023	2.875 ± 0.028	*2.870 ± 0.018*	**2.867 ± 0.016**
Average	1.914	1.889	1.858	*1.712*	**1.647**
Ranking	4.185	3.852	3.093	*2.370*	**1.500**
Friedman's test	Confidence interval $C_0 = (0, F_{(\alpha=0.05)} = 2.459)$. F-val.$_{AMAE}$: 23.859 $\notin C_0$.				

The best performing method is in **bold** face and the second one in *italics*.

approach of comparing all classifiers to each other in a post-hoc test is not as sensitive as the approach of comparing all classifiers to a given classifier (a control method). One approach to this latter type of comparison is the Holm's test. The test statistics for comparing the i-th and j-th method using this procedure is: $z = \dfrac{R_i - R_j}{\sqrt{\frac{J(J+1)}{6T}}}$, where J is the number of algorithms, T is the number of datasets and R_i is the mean ranking of the i-th method. The z value is used to find the corresponding probability from the table of the normal distribution, which is then compared with an appropriate level of significance α. Holm's test adjusts the value for α in order to compensate for multiple comparisons. This is done

Table 3. Results of the Holm procedure using OFSHausdorff as control method: corrected α values, compared method and p-values, ordered by comparisons (i).

Control alg.: OFSHausdorff		Acc	
i	$\alpha_{0.05}^{*}$	Method	p_i
1	0.01250	OFSMean	0.00000_{++}
2	0.01667	NFS	0.00003_{++}
3	0.02500	OFS	0.05830
4	0.05000	OFSMin	0.06425
Control alg.: OFSHausdorff		$AMAE$	
i	$\alpha_{0.05}^{*}$	Method	p_i
1	0.01250	NFS	0.00000_{++}
2	0.01667	OFS	0.00000_{++}
3	0.02500	OFSMean	0.00002_{++}
4	0.05000	OFSMin	0.04312_{++}

Win ($++$) with statistical significant difference for $\alpha = 0.05$

in a step-up procedure that sequentially tests the hypotheses ordered by their significance. We will denote the ordered p-values by $p_1, p_2, \ldots, p_q$ so that $p_1 \leq p_2 \leq \ldots \leq p_q$. Holm's test compares each p_i with $\alpha_{\text{Holm}}^{*} = \alpha/(J - i)$, starting from the most significant p value. If p_1 is below $\alpha/(J - 1)$, the corresponding hypothesis is rejected, and we allow to compare p_2 with $\alpha/(J - 2)$. If the second hypothesis is rejected, the test proceeds with the third, and so on.

Table 3 shows the result of the Holm's test when comparing the best performing technique (i.e. OFSHausdorff) to the rest of algorithms. It can be seen that this method outperforms the rest of techniques for $AMAE$ and specifically OFSMean and NFS for Acc, when $\alpha = 0.05$. This result validates the Hausdorff distance in this context and shows that the ordinal nature of the data should be considered when performing feature selection. The results not only improve when considering ordinal measures (i.e. $AMAE$) but also nominal ones (such as Acc), meaning that the method can benefit from the order constraint introduced.

4.4 Discussion

As stated before, the authors consider that a percentage of 30 % features represents a good option, since it allows to have a relatively accurate model with an increased interpretability (70 % of the variables are removed). In this section, we examine the variables (associated to this 30 %) that are of largest importance to the characterisation of happiness, considering the version of the dataset with 3 classes and the OFSHausdorff method. Note that the feature selection method does not consider aggregated sets of features, and therefore is not able to discover redundant variables of interactions between them. Since we considered 30 different train data partitions, we have 30 different results. The following variables 'have been selected at least in 15 models: variables related to the country (meaning that there could be other factors of vital importance to the characterisation of well-being, such as the state of economy of the country, the weather, etc.), gender, variables related to love relationships (single, legally married, living with partner, etc.), general level of health, whether the person is daily hampered by illness or if he/she belongs to a minority ethnic, the number of times the person felt depressed previous week, the quality of the sleep, whether the person gives importance to be rich and to have expensive belongings, religiosity and whether the person would allow entry of immigrants from poorer countries.

Several conclusions can be drawn from these results. Firstly, the environment in which a person lives significantly influences their well-being and so do other demographic variables (e.g. familiar composition, gender or belonging to a minority ethnic). Secondly, both physical and mental health have an impact on subjective well-being. Finally, the group of variables related to personality and opinions also play a vital role in the classification of happiness.

The variables selected when considering 70 % of features were also examined in order to study variables that were selected by very few models. Note from Table 1 that 70 % represents also an interesting threshold, as it is the point from which the performance usually starts to degrade. In this case, the range of variables present in at least in 15 models includes additional variables concerning: social well-being (feeling of loneliness and inability to get going, number of people to discuss personal matters with, involvement in social activities and conflicts at home when growing up), health and habits (diet/sport/alcohol/smoking behaviour, inability to get medical consultation or treatment), daily activity (specifically the main activity, the number of hours watching TV per week and whether the person improved their knowledge/skills in the last year), other demographic factors (such as the domicile, the type of contract or the familiar composition), community well-being (interest in politics, closeness to country, satisfaction with health and education in country) and, finally, personality (whether it is important to be modest and to seek for adventures, whether the person thinks that other people try to take advantage of them and the feeling of safety walking alone in local area at night). Conversely, there is a set of variables that have been selected in very few models (in this case we consider variables selected in less than 10 models). These variables are the following: age, weight, number of hours working, people responsible for at job, financial difficulties when growing up, years of education, number of people living with, satisfaction with government and economy (as opposed to health and education that were selected as relevant), whether politicians care what people think and the number of hours helping others (family, friends or neighbours).

5   Conclusions

This paper presents a feature selection strategy for classification problems where the dependent variable follows a natural order. We construct a dataset for predicting subjective well-being across different European countries that includes 56 variables of different components of happiness. The results show that there are some factors, such as the environment where the person lives, the physical and mental health and the personality, that are of great influence to subjective well-being. Moreover, the performance of the proposed method is competitive against its nominal counterpart, which demonstrates the necessity of developing more specific techniques for domains such as the ordinal classification one.

References

1. Linley, P.A., Maltby, J., Wood, A.M., Osborne, G., Hurling, R.: Measuring happiness: the higher order factor structure of subjective and psychological well-being measures. Pers. Individ. Differ. **47**, 878–884 (2009)
2. Diener, E.: Subjective well-being: the science of happiness and a proposal for a national index. Am. Psychol. **55**, 34–43 (2000)
3. Self, A., Thomas, J., Randall, C.: Measuring national well-being: Life in the uk (2012). Accessed 8 December 2015
4. Keyes, C.L., Shmotkin, D., Ryff, C.D.: Optimizing well-being: the empirical encounter of two traditions. J. Pers. Soc. Psychol. **82**, 1007 (2002)
5. Gutiérrez, P.A., Pérez-Ortiz, M., Sánchez-Monedero, J., Fernández-Navarro, F., Hervás-Martínez, C.: Ordinal regression methods: survey and experimental study. IEEE Trans. Knowl. Data Eng. **28**, 127–146 (2016)
6. Gu, Q., Li, Z., Han, J.: Generalized fisher score for feature selection. CoRR abs/1202.3725 (2012)
7. Bixter, M.T.: Happiness, political orientation, and religiosity. Personality Individ. Differ. **72**, 7–11 (2015)
8. Luengo, J., García, S., Herrera, F.: On the choice of the best imputation methods for missing values considering three groups of classification methods. Knowl. Inf. Syst. **32**, 77–108 (2012)
9. Pérez-Ortiz, M., Gutiérrez, P.A., Hervás-Martínez, C.: Projection-based ensemble learning for ordinal regression. IEEE Trans. Cybern. **44**, 681–694 (2014)
10. Baccianella, S., Esuli, A., Sebastiani, F.: Feature selection for ordinal text classification. Neural Comput. **26**, 557–591 (2014)
11. Mukras, R., Wiratunga, N., Lothian, R., Chakraborti, S., Harper, D.: Information gain feature selection for ordinal text classification using probability redistribution. In: The IJCAI 2007 Workshop on Text Mining and Link Analysis, Hyderabad, IN (2007)
12. Eiter, T., Mannila, H.: Distance measures for point sets and their computation. Acta Inform. **34**, 103–133 (1997)
13. Sun, B.Y., Li, J., Wu, D.D., Zhang, X.M., Li, W.B.: Kernel discriminant learning for ordinal regression. IEEE Trans. Knowl. Data Eng. **22**, 906–910 (2010)
14. Baccianella, S., Esuli, A., Sebastiani, F.: Evaluation measures for ordinal regression. In: Proceedings of the Ninth International Conference on Intelligent Systems Design and Applications (ISDA 2009), Pisa, Italy (2009)
15. Demsar, J.: Statistical comparisons of classifiers over multiple data sets. J. Mach. Learn. Res. **7**, 1–30 (2006)

A Soft Computing Approach to Optimize the Clarification Process in Wastewater Treatment

Marina Corral Bobadilla[1(✉)], Roberto Fernandez Martinez[2],
Ruben Lostado Lorza[1], Fatima Somovilla Gomez[1],
and Eliseo P. Vergara Gonzalez[1]

[1] Mechanical Engineering Department, University of La Rioja, Logroño, Spain
marina.corral@unirioja.es
[2] Department of Electrical Engineering, University of the Basque Country
UPV/EHU, Bilbao, Spain

Abstract. The coagulation process allows for the removal of colloidal particles suspended in wastewater. Estimating the amount of coagulant required to effectively remove these colloidal particles is usually determined experimentally by the jar test. The configuration of this test is often performed in an iterative manner which has the disadvantage of requiring a significant period of experimentation and an excessive amount of coagulant consumption. This study proposes a methodology to determine the optimum natural coagulant dose while at the same time eliminating the maximum amount of colloidal particles suspended in the wastewater. An estimation of the amount of colloidal particles removed from the wastewater is determined by the turbidity in a standardized jar test, which is applied to the wastewater at the wastewater treatment plant in Logroño (Spain). The methodology proposed is based on the combined use of soft computing techniques and evolutionary techniques based on Genetic Algorithms (GA). Firstly, a group of regression models based on neural networks techniques was performed to predict the final turbidity of a wastewater sample taking into consideration a configuration of jar test inputs. The jar test inputs are: initial turbidity, natural coagulant dosage, temperature, mix speed and mix time. Finally, the best combination of jar test inputs to obtain the optimum natural coagulant dose, while also eliminating the maximum amount of colloidal particles, was achieved by applying evolutionary optimization techniques to the most accurate regression models obtained beforehand.

Keywords: Soft computing techniques · Optimization · Coagulation process · Wastewater treatment

1 Introduction

Water is vital for all aspects of life. Wastewater management directly impacts the biological diversity of aquatic ecosystems, as it disrupts the fundamental integrity of our life support systems. Wastewater management is considered an integrated part of the ecosystem that covers across all areas including fresh and marine water. Due to the

© Springer International Publishing Switzerland 2016
F. Martínez-Álvarez et al. (Eds.): HAIS 2016, LNAI 9648, pp. 609–620, 2016.
DOI: 10.1007/978-3-319-32034-2_51

fact that fresh water travels through the entire hydrological system (from mountain tops to the seas), the entire range of activities capture, divert, extract, treat and reuse water to sustain our communities and economies throughout the watershed. Most human activities do not normally return water to its the watershed from which it was previously extracted. A staggering 80 %–90 % of all wastewater generated in developing countries is discharged directly into the surface water watershed. Wastewater contains harmful dissolved or suspended matter. Unregulated discharge of wastewater harms biological diversity, natural resilience and the planet's capacity to provide fundamental ecosystem services, which in turn impacts both rural and urban populations and affects a range of sectors from healthcare to industry, agriculture, fisheries and tourism [1]. The processes of coagulation-flocculation followed by sedimentation and filtration are employed around the globe in wastewater treatment processes before discharging treated water to the river. Solid-liquid separation through coagulation process is considered an important process in wastewater primary treatment [2]. The coagulation process is effective, straightforward to operate, and widely employed to treat industrial effluent or wastewater. The selection process and the coagulant dose added to wastewater is an extremely important task. In this regard, many researchers have conducted studies on inorganic coagulant (aluminum and ferric sulphates and chlorides), synthetic organic polymers (polyacrylamide derivatives and polyethylene amine) [3–5]. In recent years, the use of natural organic coagulant has gradually grown mainly because of its effectiveness in removing colloidal particles, as well as its low cost compared to other synthetic and inorganic coagulants [6]. And furthermore, organic coagulants do not contain metals in their chemical composition and do not absorb alkalinity from the environment, since they does not undergo hydrolysis in solution. With all these characteristics, this coagulant consistently presents an effective performance. Many factors, including the type of coagulant, coagulant dosage, effluent pH, mix speed, mix time and temperature can influence the coagulation process [7]. Therefore, optimizing these factors or inputs is crucial to increasing coagulation treatment efficiency. Normally, the wastewater adjustment process at treatment plants is performed by varying only one of these factors considered in the process, while the other factors remain constant. However, this approach consumes large amounts of time and coagulant due to the large number of experiments that are necessary [8]. The estimation of the amount of coagulant required to effectively remove these colloidal particles is usually determined experimentally by the jar test (See Fig. 1). Thus, the use of models based on soft computing and machine learning methods has proven to be useful for solving engineering and optimization problems [9–11]. In the field of wastewater treatment and purification, some researchers have used regression models based on data mining techniques to model and optimize some of the most influential factors in the coagulation-flocculation process. Thus, for example, in [12], water quality was modeled considering turbidity and the final color of the wastewater using Artificial Neural Networks (ANN). In addition, the optimal chemical dose of flocculants needed to maximize wastewater depuration of wastewater was obtained. Others researchers [13] have employed Multiple Linear Regression (MLR) and ANN to model residual aluminum and turbidity in treated water. In said study, a large number of factors or inputs were considered (twenty-three features), such as: pH, hardness, color, conductivity, silicates, turbidity, etc. More recently, two types of Support Vector

Machine (SVM) using two different kernel functions (radial basis function and polynomial function) and K-Nearest Neighbors (KNN) were analyzed in order to predict coagulant dosage in water treatment plants considering a given value of turbidity of several wastewater samples [14]. In this case, the input parameters considered were pH, temperature and dosage. In the present study, several regression models based on neural networks techniques were initially proposed to predict the optimum natural dosage of coagulant obtained from acacia in order to determine the final turbidity of a wastewater sample considering the following jar test inputs: initial turbidity, natural coagulant dosage, temperature, mix speed and mix time. Finally, the most accurate combination of jar test inputs to obtain the optimum natural coagulant dose, while also eliminating the maximum amount of colloidal particles, was achieved by applying evolutionary optimization techniques based on Genetic Algorithms (GA).

Fig. 1. Jar test in wastewater treatment plant using Acacia coagulant

2   Methodology

2.1   Design of Experiments and Design Matrix

The statistical Design of Experiments (DoE) is a structured and systematized method of experimentation in which all factors are varied simultaneously over a set of experimental runs in order to determine the relationship between the factors affecting the output response of the process. DoE [15] is used in experimental tasks to minimize the number of experiments and to obtain an adequately amount of detail to support a hypothesis. In general, the hypothesis is that a number of controllable variables (inputs or design factors) and uncontrollable variables (noise factors) determine the number of responses (outputs) with a continuous and differentiable function. Several methods have been proposed to develop DoE, but all of them involve the construction of a design matrix (inputs) and measuring the outputs or responses of the experiments [16]. In this study, the input parameters used for the experiments are time (t), speed (S), temperature (T), initial turbidity (iniTurb), and coagulant dosage (cuaDose); and the output is the final turbidity of the treated water (finalTurb). The design (Table 1) was performed using Central Composite Design (CCD) [17], which is a fractional three-level design that reduces the number of experiments in comparison with a full three-level design. Reducing the number of experiments in this case is important due to the difficultly involved in preparing each experiment's initial samples.

Table 1. Input parameters and levels

Input	Notation	Magnitude	Levels		
			-1	0	1
Time	t	Sec	30	90	120
Speed	S	Rpm	50	75	100
Temperature	T	°C	10	15	20
Initial turbidity	iniTurb	NTU	40	90	140
Coagulant dosage	cuaDose	Ml	1	3	6

According to the input parameters and levels included in Table 1 and using the R statistical analysis tool [18], 42 experiments were generated with their corresponding inputs (Table 2).

Table 2. Design matrix and samples obtained following the CCD DoE

Inputs				Output		
Sample	t	S	T	iniTurb	cuaDose	finalTurb
1	30	50	20	140	6.0	38.9
2	120	100	20	140	6.0	2.8
...	...	...	...	...	...	...
41	75	75	20	90	3.5	10.63
42	75	75	15	90	6.0	9.72

The output (final turbidity) was measured by a turbidimeterTN-100 once the laboratory tests were done.

2.2 Neural Networks

There are numerous regression techniques inherently based on a nonlinear nature. One of the most intensively studied and applied techniques are neural networks [19, 20]. Neural networks are powerful nonlinear regression techniques inspired by brain biological neural networks. They usually present a system of interconnected neurons with numeric weights and biases that can predict the value of an output. Many approaches have studied how a neural network can create an output regression from several inputs. In the present study only four of the most significant techniques based on neural networks, both classical and advanced, were performed. Bayesian regularized neural networks (BFNN): this function uses bayesian regularization for feed-forward neural networks, where the weight and bias values are optimized according to Levenberg-Marquardt optimization [21, 22] to improve their generalization qualities. During this optimization, an initial selection of weight is performed by the Nguyen and Widrow algorithm [23], and the error is minimized by the Gauss-Newton algorithm [22]. Extreme learning machine (ELM): this learning algorithm is based on a feedforward neural network with a single layer of hidden nodes where the weights that connect inputs to hidden neurons are randomly chosen, and the output weights are analytically determined, providing a satisfactory generalization performance and a minimal computational cost [24–26]. Averaged Neural Network (AFNN): this learning algorithm uses the classical feed-forward neural network defined by Ripley [20], but given to this technique's random initializations (random initial values in their learning procedures), the same neural network model is fit using different random number seeds and the outputs from each network are averaged [27]. Quantile regression neural network (QRNN): this function fits a censored quantile regression neural network model for the tau-quantile by minimizing a cost function based on the Huber norm approximation to the tilted absolute value and ramp functions. Furthermore, in this case, bootstrap aggregation is applied, calculating an average of an ensemble of bagged models that tend to alleviate overfitting [28–30].

2.3 Model Selection Criteria

The neural networks models were trained using 50 times repeated 10-fold cross-validation, as their calculation times are not very high and allowed the entire training dataset obtained from the DoE to be used, including 42 entries, to create the models. This method involves dividing the initial database into 10 subsets, building the model with 9 subsets and calculating the error with the other partial sample of the dataset. This procedure is repeated 50 times obtaining other errors. And finally, the error is calculated as the arithmetic mean of all the errors occurring during the process [31–33]. Once the different algorithms had been trained while some of the most significant parameters were tuned, a selection was conducted of those parameters with the greatest predictive performance. The coefficients indicative of the error used to evaluate the accuracy of the predictions were the Root Mean Square Error (RMSE) and its standard deviation. Once the most accurate models were selected, they were tested with new samples. 10 new experiments were performed in the laboratory to test the actual degree of generalization of the selected models.

2.4 Optimization Based on Genetic Algorithms

And finally, using GA, the optimization of the process was performed according to several objective functions. The regression models with the greatest generalization capacity were employed to perform a search of the best combinations of inputs in order to achieve the aforementioned objectives: determine the optimum natural coagulant dose and eliminate the maximum amount of colloidal particles. This search for the best combination of inputs was performed by applying evolutionary optimization techniques based on GA. The use of evolutionary techniques based on genetic algorithms to optimize industrial processes [34, 35] based on the results obtained from real experimental data has been confirmed by the literature.

3 Results

3.1 Analysis of Uncertainty

An analysis of variance, ANOVA, was performed to assess the uncertainty in the experimental measurements based on the proposed DoE. The final turbidity of the treated water was analyzed against the input variables. The p-values obtained exhibit low values for two of the variables, especially over time, which indicates that the observed relationships are statistically significant. Thus, when the p-value is lower than 0.1, it is considered — with a low level of uncertainty — that the null hypothesis, being that the model has no predictive capability, can be confidently rejected. For example, in this case, time and cuaDose both satisfy this condition, and speed is close to satisfying this condition as well (Table 3).

Table 3. Results obtained from the analysis of variance of final turbidity. Significant codes according to p-value: '***' 0.001, '**' 0.01, '*' 0.05,'.' 0.1.

	Deg. of freedom	Sums of squares	Mean squares	F ratios	p-value	
Time	1	0.50116	0.50116	15.3874	0.0009142	***
Speed	1	0.09548	0.09548	2.9314	0.1031440	
Temp	1	0.00000	0.00000	0.0000	0.9968026	
iniTurb	1	0.04162	0.04162	1.2777	0.2723867	
cuaDose	1	0.20548	0.20548	6.3090	0.0212072	*
Residuals	19	0.61882	0.03257			

3.2 Neural Networks

The creation of regression models to predict the final turbidity of treated water incorporated classical and advanced machine learning techniques based on neural networks. In addition, in order to be able to compare linear and nonlinear techniques, linear regression (LR) was performed as well. In this case, the method was conducted in the following way: firstly, 42 experiments were performed according to the proposed DoE. The dataset obtained from the experiments was normalized between 0 and 1. Thereafter, these 42 instances were used to train the models using 50 times repeated cross-validation. During this training, and to have the possibility of comparing the accuracy of the models, the RMSE and its standard deviation were obtained. At the same time, during this training, a tuning of the most important parameters of each algorithm was performed to improve the prediction capability. For example, Fig. 2 shows the RMSE of the variable 'final turbidity' during the training of a feedforward

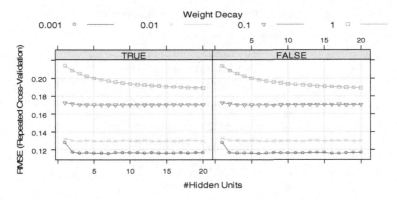

Fig. 2. Results obtained from training period (50 times repeated cross-validation) using AFNN to predict the final turbidity of the water. Values of the most accurate configuration: weight decay = 0.001, hidden neurons = 2, and bagging method applied.

neural network when parameters like the number of neurons and weight decay vary in two situations: when bagging is applied or when not.

And furthermore, in order to be able to test the models with new and previously unused data during the training, 10 new experiments were performed and tested. These new instances were chosen randomly so as to reveal the entire space of possibilities of the problem from the previous DoE, and thereby avoid overtraining the models. The results obtained are listed in Table 4.

Table 4. Results obtained during training and testing stage for the output variable (the most accurate and selected variables are in bold)

Model	Training (cross validation)		Testing
	RMSE (%)	RMSE SD (%)	RMSE (%)
BFNN	**10.04**	**5.56**	**22.22**
ELM	15.21	6.94	25.73
AFNN	11.58	6.77	22.95
QRNN	14.04	7.37	24.93
LR	15.26	7.04	25.17

From this comparison it is concluded that the most accurate model is the BFNN. The list of obtained weights and biases for this model (a neural network with a hidden layer with two neurons) are shown in Table 5. Also, α (equal to $\frac{1}{2\sigma_\theta^2}$, where σ_θ^2 is a dispersion parameter for weights and biases) obtained is equal to 0.561, β (equal to $\frac{1}{2\sigma_e^2}$, where σ_e^2 is a dispersion parameter for the error of the function) is equal to 24.325, and the values of E_W (sum of squares of network parameters: weights and biases) and E_D (error sum of squares) are respectively 11.426 and 0.599.

Table 5. Parameters of the selected model

Neuron	1	2
ω_k	0.7520925	−0.27187975
b_k	−2.4240337	−0.02826183
$\beta_1^{[k]}$	−0.9208434	0.84650768
$\beta_2^{[k]}$	−0.2406589	0.27899223
$\beta_3^{[k]}$	0.3959223	0.11409175
$\beta_4^{[k]}$	1.2513062	0.80114163
$\beta_5^{[k]}$	−0.7394062	0.53470159

3.3   Optimization Based on Genetic Algorithms

The optimization process to find the best combination of inputs was conducted as follows: firstly, a number of 1000 individuals or combinations of inputs (time, speed, temp, iniTurb, cuaDose) from the initial generation was randomly generated. Subsequently, and based on these individuals, the final turbidity was obtained applying the BFNN selected. Two objective functions were analyzed in this case: the objective function F_1 implemented to minimize the final turbidity (Eq. 1), and the objective function F_2, implemented to minimize the final turbidity; but at the same time the coagulant dosage was applied (Eq. 2) where both variables were applied with a weight w_1 and w_2.

$$F_1 = \min(\mathit{finalTurb}) \tag{1}$$

$$F_2 = \min(w_1 \cdot \mathit{finalTurb} + w_2 \cdot \mathit{coaDose}) \tag{2}$$

The next generations (first generation and subsequent generations) were generated using selection, crossover and mutation. The new generation was comprised as follows:

- 25 % comprised the best individuals from the previous generation.
- 60 % comprised individuals obtained by crossover.
- The remaining 15 % was obtained by random mutation.

The minimization of objective functions was performed according to four values of initial turbidity: 50, 75, 100, and 125 NTU. Tables 6 and 7 show the values of the inputs obtained by using GA and which meet the objective functions. In addition, Fig. 3 shows the evolution of the fitness function along the first new GA generations, in this case using the fitness function F_1, when the input iniTurb is equal to 150 NTU.

And finally, to appreciate the real effectiveness of the process, the values obtained in the optimization process were experimentally probed. Tables 8 and 9 show the real values, for all the cases, obtained from experiments performed in the laboratory.

Table 6. Value of the studied variables that meets the objective function F_1 for an initial turbidity of 50, 75, 100 and 125 NTU.

	iniTurb (NTU)			
	50	75	100	125
Time	119.8	119.79	117.9	117.78
Speed	88.89	88.83	96.2	85.18
Temp	17.79	17.97	19.62	18.01
iniTurb	50	75	100	125
cuaDose	4.98	4.98	4.97	4.64
finalTurb	5.68	2.86	1.13	1.13

Table 7. Value of the studied variables that meets the objective function F_2 for an initial turbidity of 50, 75, 100 and 125 NTU.

	iniTurb (NTU)			
	50	75	100	125
Time	101.79	117.98	118.17	118.01
Speed	89.89	88.81	89.88	88.99
Temp	19.76	19.76	17.98	12.46
iniTurb	50.00	75.00	100.00	125.00
cuaDose	1.00	1.00	1.00	1.00
finalTurb	23.40	12.46	8.45	6.43

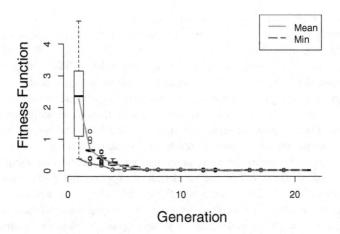

Fig. 3. Evolution of the fitness function along the new GA generations (just first 20 generations. Red line: mean of the error of each population. Blue line: minimum error of each population) (Color figure online).

Table 8. Value of the studied variables obtained from the experiments for an initial turbidity of 50, 75, 100 and 125 NTU when the objective function was F_1.

	iniTurb (NTU)			
	50	75	100	125
Time	120.00	120.00	118.00	118.00
Speed	89.00	88.00	96.00	85.00
Temp	17.80	18.20	19.40	18.00
iniTurb	55.00	72.90	98.00	126.00
cuaDose	5.00	5.00	4.95	4.65
finalTurb	2.56	3.03	1.58	2.40

Table 9. Value of the studied variables obtained from the experiments for an initial turbidity of 50, 75, 100 and 125 NTU when the objective function was F_2.

	iniTurb (NTU)			
	50	75	100	125
Time	100.00	118.00	118.00	120.00
Speed	90.00	89.00	89.00	89.00
Temp	19.70	20.10	18.40	13.00
iniTurb	45.00	76.00	100.00	132.00
cuaDose	1.00	1.00	1.00	1.00
finalTurb	12.17	22.10	12.10	25.40

4   Conclusions

Determining the amount of coagulant necessary to clarify a wastewater sample represents a complicated task, which is usually conducted in an approximate manner by way of a jar test. This study details a methodology to optimize the coagulant dose required in order to eliminate as much of the suspended solids from a wastewater sample as possible. Initially, and based on a CCD design of experiments, a series of jar tests was performed in order to obtain the final turbidity of a wastewater sample with the following inputs: initial turbidity, natural coagulant dosage, temperature, mix speed and mix time. Then, a group of regression models based on neural networks techniques were performed to predict the final turbidity of a wastewater sample taking into consideration a configuration of the aforementioned jar test inputs. The adequacy of the model was verified effectively by the validation of experimental data. In this case, the Bayesian regularized neural networks was the model with the strongest generalization ability in terms of predicting the final turbidity considering the aforementioned inputs were considered. The best combinations of jar test inputs to obtain the optimum natural coagulant dose while also eliminating the maximum amount of colloidal particles was determined by applying evolutionary optimization techniques to the BFNN model. Two objective functions were analyzed in this case: the objective function F_1 implemented to minimize the final turbidity, and the objective function F_2, implemented to minimize the final turbidity, but at the same time the coagulant dosage was also applied. The results obtained for the cases studied herein demonstrate that the coagulant dose required for the first case studied is approximately 5 ml (4.65 ml–5 ml), while the coagulant dosage required for the second case is 1 ml.

Acknowledgements. The authors wish to thank Servyeco Group for providing partial support for this study and to the University of the Basque Country for its support through the project US15/18 OMETESA.

References

1. Corcoran, E., Nellemann, C., Baker, E., Bos, R., Osborn, D., Savelli, H.: Sick water? the central role of wastewater management in sustainable development. A Rapid Response Assessment. In: United Nations Environment Programme, UN-HABITAT, GRID-Arendal (2010)
2. Lee, K.E., Morad, N., Teng, T.T., Poh, B.T.: Development, characterization and the application of hybrid materials in coagulation/flocculation of wastewater: a review. Chem. Eng. J. **203**, 370–386 (2012)
3. Boisvert, J.P., To, T.C., Berrak, A., Jolicoeur, C.: Phosphate adsorption in flocculation processes of aluminium sulphate and poly-aluminium-silicate-sulphate. Water Res. **31**(8), 1939–1946 (1997)
4. Gao, B.Y., Yue, Q.Y., Wang, B.J., Chu, Y.B.: Poly-aluminum-silicate-chloride (PASiC)—a new type of composite inorganic polymer coagulant. Colloids Surf., A **229**(1), 121–127 (2003)
5. Sinha, S., Yoon, Y., Amy, G., Yoon, J.: Determining the effectiveness of conventional and alternative coagulants through effective characterization schemes. Chemosphere **57**(9), 1115–1122 (2004)
6. Ahmad, A.L., Yasin, N.M., Derek, C.J.C., Lim, J.K.: Optimization of microalgae coagulation process using chitosan. Chem. Eng. J. **173**(3), 879–882 (2011)
7. Wang, Y., Chen, K., Mo, L., Li, J., Xu, J.: Optimization of coagulation-flocculation process for papermaking-reconstituted tobacco slice wastewater treatment using response surface methodology. J. Ind. Eng. Chem. **20**, 391–396 (2014)
8. Wu, T.Y., Mohammad, A.W., Jahim, J.M., Anuar, N.: Optimized reused and bioconversion from retentate of pre-filtered palm oil mill effluent (POME) into microbial protease by Aspergillus terreus using response surface methodology. J. Chem. Technol. Biotechnol. **84**, 1390–1396 (2009)
9. Calvo-Rolle, J.L., Corchado, E.: A bio-inspired knowledge system for improving combined cycle plant control tuning. Neurocomputing **126**, 95–105 (2014)
10. Sedano, J., Curiel, L., Corchado, E., de la Cal, E., Villar, J.: A soft computing method for detecting lifetime building thermal insulation failures. Integr. Comput. Aided Eng. **17**(2), 103–115 (2010)
11. Lostado, R., Fernández, R., Mac Donald, B.J., Villanueva, P.M.: Combining soft computing techniques and the finite element method to design and optimize complex welded products. Integr. Comput. Aided Eng. **22**(2), 153–170 (2015)
12. Baxter, C.W., Zhang, Q., Stanley, S.J., Shariff, R., Tupas, R.R., Stark, H.L.: Drinking water quality and treatment: the use of artificial neural networks. Can. J. Civ. Eng. **28**(S1), 26–35 (2001)
13. Juntunen, P., Liukkonen, M., Pelo, M., Lehtola, M.J., Hiltunen, Y.: Modelling of water quality: an application to a water treatment process. Appl. Comput. Intell. Soft Comput. **2012**, 4 (2012)

14. Zhang, K., Achari, G., Li, H., Zargar, A., Sadiq, R.: Machine learning approaches to predict coagulant dosage in water treatment plants. Int. J. Syst. Assur. Eng. Manage. 4(2), 205–214 (2013)
15. Fisher, R.A.: The design of experiments. Oliver and Boyd, Edinburgh (1935)
16. Box, G.E., Behnken, D.W.: Some new three level designs for the study of quantitative variables. Technometrics 2(4), 455–475 (1960)
17. Montgomery, D.C.: Design and Analysis of Experiments. Wiley, New York (2008)
18. Team, R.C.: A language and environment for statistical computing. R foundation for Statistical Computing (2005)
19. Bishop, C.: Neural Networks for Pattern Recognition. Oxford University Press, Oxford (1995)
20. Ripley, B.: Pattern Recognition and Neural Networks. Cambridge University Press, Cambridge (1996)
21. MacKay, D.J.C.: Bayesian interpolation. Neural Comput. 4(3), 415–447 (1992)
22. Foresee, F.D., Hagan, M.T.: Auss-Newton approximation to Bayesian regularization. In: Proceedings of the 1997 International Joint Conference on Neural Networks. (1997)
23. Nguyen, D., Widrow, B.: Improving the learning speed of 2-layer neural networks by choosing initial values of the adaptive weights. Proc. IJCNN 3, 21–26 (1990)
24. Huang, G.B., Zhu, Q.Y., Siew, C.K.: Extreme learning machine: theory and applications. Neurocomputing 70, 489–501 (2006)
25. Huang, G.B., Ding, X., Zhou, H.: Optimization method based extreme learning machine for classification. Neurocomputing 74, 155–163 (2010)
26. Ding, S., Zhao, H., Zhang, Y., Xu, X., Nie, R.: Extreme learning machine: algorithm, theory and applications. Artif. Intell. Rev. 44(1), 103–115 (2015)
27. Funahashi, K.: On the approximate realization of continuous mappings by neural networks. Neural Netw. 2, 183–192 (1989)
28. Taylor, J.W.: A quantile regression neural network approach to estimating the conditional density of multiperiod returns. J. Forecast. 19(4), 299–311 (2000)
29. Guitton, A., Symes, W.W.: Robust inversion of seismic data using the Huber norm. Geophysics 68, 1310–1319 (2003)
30. Cannon, A.J.: Quantile regression neural networks: implementation in R and application to precipitation downscaling. Comput. Geosci. 37, 1277–1284 (2011)
31. Fernandez, R., Okariz, A., Ibarretxe, J., Iturrondobeitia, M., Guraya, T.: Use of decision tree models based on evolutionary algorithms for the morphological classification of reinforcing nano-particle aggregates. Comput. Mater. Sci. 92, 102–113 (2014)
32. Fernandez, R., Martinez de Pisón, F.J., Pernía, A.V., Lostado, R.: Predictive modelling in grape berry weight during maturation process: comparison of data mining, statistical and artificial intelligence techniques. Span. J. Agric. Res. 9(4), 1156–1167 (2011)
33. Illera, M., Lostado, R., Fernandez, R., Mac Donald, B.J.: Characterization of electrolytic tinplate materials via combined finite element and regression models. J. Strain Anal. Eng. Des. 49(6), 467–480 (2014)
34. Martinez de Pison, F.J., Lostado, R., Pernía, A., Lostado, R.: Optimising tension level-ling process by means of genetic algorithms and finite element method. Ironmaking Steelmaking 38, 45–52 (2011)
35. Lostado, R., Martínez de Pisón, F.J., Fernández, R., Fernández, J.: Using genetic algorithms to optimize the material behaviour model in finite element models of processes with cyclic loads. J. Strain Anal. Eng. Des. 46(2), 143–159 (2011)

A Proposed Methodology for Setting the Finite Element Models Based on Healthy Human Intervertebral Lumbar Discs

Fatima Somovilla Gomez[1][(✉)], Ruben Lostado Lorza[1],
Roberto Fernandez Martinez[2], Marina Corral Bobadilla[1],
and Ruben Escribano Garcia[3]

[1] Department of Mechanical Engineering, University of La Rioja,
Logroño, Spain
fatima.somovilla@unirioja.es
[2] Department of Electrical Engineering, University of the Basque Country
UPV/EHU, Bilbao, Spain
[3] Built Environment and Engineering, Leeds Beckett University, Leeds, UK

Abstract. The human intervertebral lumbar disc is a fibrocartilage structure that is located between the vertebrae of the spine. This structure consists of a nucleus pulposus, the annulus fibrosus and the cartilage endplate. The disc may be subjected to a complex combination of loads. The study of its mechanical properties and movement are used to evaluate the medical devices and implants. Some researchers have used the Finite Element Method (FEM) to model the disc and to study its biomechanics. Estimating the parameters to correctly define these models has the drawback that any small differences between the actual material and the simulation model based on FEM can be amplified enormously in the presence of nonlinearities. This paper sets out a fully automated method to determine the most appropriate material parameters to define the behavior of the human intervertebral lumbar disc models based on FEM. The methodology that is proposed is based on experimental data and the combined use of data mining techniques, Genetic Algorithms (GA) and the FEM. Firstly, based on standard tests (compression, axial rotation, shear, flexion, extension and lateral bending), three-dimensional parameterized Finite Element (FE) models were generated. Then, considering the parameters that define the proposed parameterized FE models, a Design of Experiment (DoE) was completed. For each of the standard tests, a regression technique based on Support Vector Machines (SVM) with different kernels was applied to model the stiffness and bulges of the intervertebral lumbar disc when the parameters of the FE models are changed. Finally, the best combination of parameters was achieved by applying evolutionary optimization techniques that are based on GA to the best, previously obtained regression models.

Keywords: Finite elements method · Support Vector Machines · Optimization · Genetic Algorithms · Biomechanics · Human intervertebral lumbar disc

© Springer International Publishing Switzerland 2016
F. Martínez-Álvarez et al. (Eds.): HAIS 2016, LNAI 9648, pp. 621–633, 2016.
DOI: 10.1007/978-3-319-32034-2_52

1 Introduction

The human intervertebral disc (IVD) is a fibrocartilage structure that is located between the vertebrae of the spine. It consists of a nucleus pulposus, the annulus fibrosus and the cartilage endplates. Its complex structure allows significant mobility between two adjacent vertebrae while transmitting considerable compressive loads from one vertebra to another. The healthy intervertebral disc provides mobility and spine flexibility during body movement, shock absorption and prevention of excessive wear of the facet joints during daily spine loading. It is very common to study the disc's mechanical properties and movement for the purpose of evaluating medical devices and implants, which are submitted to several standard tests (compression, flexion, extension, shear, lateral bending and axial rotation). In reality, the disks are subject to a complex combination of loads, such as those that are experienced during the movements of lifting, walking, sitting up and leaning. Some researchers have used the Finite Element Method (FEM) to model the intervertebral discs and to study its biomechanics. The finite element models (FE models) are usually validated by experimental studies that are based on dead people (cadavers). To ensure realistic results in modelling the intervertebral discs using the FEM, it is essential to have realistic FE models that are as close to experimental data as possible. Some researchers set the parameters that define the behavior of the FE models from tables or theoretical calculations. However, estimating the parameters in this way has the drawback that any small differences between the actual material model and the simulated FE model can be amplified enormously in the presence of material nonlinearities, large displacements and mechanical contacts. This means that determining the right parameters to define the FE model is a lengthy and complicated task, although essential if the results of the simulation are too closely resemble reality. There have been many FE studies of the biomechanics of the human intervertebral disk. One of the first FE studies of the intervertebral discs was developed in [1]. In this early work, an axisymmetry linear FE model with orthotropic formulation for the annulus fibrosus was considered, and the effects of material properties and geometry on the stress-distribution and intradiscal pressures were obtained. In a similar fashion, in [2] was developed an axisymmetry non-linear FE model, but the behavior of the nucleus was considered to be incompressible. Many of the FE models mentioned, and those that were proposed subsequently, were validated by experimental studies with a minimization of the error between the experimental data and the response obtained from the FE analysis (deformations, forces, rigidities, etc.) [3]. A large number of FE studies proposed methodologies to adjust the deformations [1], the reaction forces [2] and the intradiscal pressure [4] of the FE models proposed, but they were developed basically by the trial-error method. However, an optimization algorithm was developed in [5] to determine the relationship among the components of the annulus fibrosus, collagen fibers and ground substance of a FE model using the material properties of the different tissues that were extracted from the literature. For each bending moment, the stiffness of fibers was varied to approximate the Young's modulus of the ground substance in order to fulfil the required range of motion obtained from in vitro results with an accuracy of 99 %. In more recent work [6] a method that was based on differential evolution was proposed to calibrate the FE model of a functional spinal unit that was consisted of ligaments, facet joints, vertebral arch and nucleus pulposus. The loading conditions in the study were pure moments in flexion, extension, lateral bending and axial rotation. The current paper proposes a method to automate the process for adjusting the parameters that define a FE model of an intervertebral disc. It does so by combining FE models and Data Mining techniques when submitting the disc to a combination of standard tests (compression, torque, shear, flexion bending, extension bending and lateral bending loads). Using the parameters that define the FE models and the results that are obtained when they are submitted to the standard tests, a regression technique that is based on Vector Support Machines (SMV) was used with different kernel were obtained for modeling the stiffness and the bulges of the disc. Also, ordinary linear regression (LR) was applied to compare this linear technique with the previous nonlinear technique and to show the effect on the non-linearity. The regression models proposed were trained from the data obtained based on the DoE, using repeated cross-validation [7, 8]. Subsequently, these proposed models were tested with additional data that was chosen randomly from the entire space of possibilities. Once the best regression model for predicting stiffness and bulges had been selected, the parameters that define the FE models for an intervertebral when it is submitted to a combination of standard tests were obtained. This was done by applying evolutionary optimization techniques that are based on Genetic Algorithms (GA).

2   FE Model for Modeling the Intervertebral Disc

The fibrocartilage structure of the intervertebral disc (cartilage endplates, nucleus pulposus and annulus fibrosus) is usually considered to be incompressible like the elastomers. This is due to its soft tissue and high water content condition (See Fig. 1a). The cartilage endplate is a thin structure that surrounds all the nucleus pulposus and about one third of the annulus fibrosus. It is a hyaline cartilage that has a composition similar to that of a particular cartilage, but with less water. The nucleus pulposus helps to distribute pressure evenly across the disc. This prevents the development of stress concentrations that could damage the underlying vertebrae or their end plates. The nucleus of the disc acts as a shock absorber, absorbing the impact of the body's activities and keeping the two vertebrae separated. The annulus fibrosus is a ring structure that surrounds the nucleus pulposus. It is located between adjacent vertebrae. It consists of a complex network of collagen fibers that are embedded in a ground substance and arranged in a series of circumferential laminas that serves to resist the nucleus pressure in radial and tangential directions [9]. The annulus consists of concentric layers of fibrosus tissue. The fibers are surrounded by annulus ground substance. Over the years, several researchers have modeled with the FEM the intervertebral disc in a similar way. However, the relationship between the parameters that defines the annulus fibrosus, collagen fibers, ground substance and cartilage endplates of the FE models when the disc is submitted to standard tests has differed in each of the studies. In [10, 11] was considered the endplates cartilage with an isotropic formulation when the elastic modulus E and Poisson ratio μ where, respectively, 20 MPa and 0.3. Similarly the values of the endplates cartilage were considered in

[12, 13] to have E = 24 MPa and μ = 0.4, whereas in [7], values of E = 23.8 MPa and μ = 0.8 were used. In addition, in [14] the nucleus pulposus was considered to be incompressible. It used the Mooney-Rivlin model with the parameters of C_{10} = 0.12 and C_0 = 0.09 and μ = 0.4999. Similarly, in [15] the parameters were considered to be C_{10} = 0.0343 MPa and C_0 = 0.1369 MPa (E = 1.0 MPa and μ = 0.49). The literature provides a Young's modulus for the annulus ground substance that ranges from 2 MPa to 8 MPa. However the most commonly used value is 4.2 MPa. The Poisson ratio has the same value of 0.45, which suggest an almost incompressible material [16]. In [17, 18] the values of Young's modulus were taken as 4.2 and 10 MPa respectively. In regard to Poisson's ratio, the values ranged from 0.45 to 0.35. Some studies have chosen linear properties of the fibers, which provide an average Young's modulus of approximately 550 to 360 MPa and a Poisson ratio of 0.3 [19]. The FE model that is proposed in this paper considered the endplates cartilage with an isotropic formulation. In this case, the elastic modulus E and Poisson's ratio μ was assumed to range from 23 MPa to 55 MPa and 0.3 to 0.4 respectively. The nucleus pulposus was considered to be an incompressible and hyper-elastic Mooney-Rivlin model. The empirical constants of the material that is related to its rigidity C_{10} and C_0 ranged from 0.11 to 0.14 and from 0.02 to 0.04, respectively. The annulus fibrosus was assumed to be a matrix of four homogenous ground substance that were reinforced by collagen fibers (Fig. 1b). The fibers were organized in five different radial layers and oriented an angle of ±30° relative to the horizontal direction (Fig. 1c). The fibers were simulated by three-dimensional unidirectional line FE elements, and the homogenous ground substance was simulated as solid, eight-node, isoparametric FE elements. The groups of fibers 1&2, 3&4, 5&6, 7&8 and 9&10 considered a range for their Elastic Modulus E, and were considered from 550 to 360 MPa. Finally, the homogenous ground substance was considered to have an elastic modulus E and a Poisson's ratio μ in a range of 4.0 MPa to 4.2 MPa and 0.25 to 0.45 respectively. Table 1 summarizes the ranges of eleven different parameters that have been considered in this paper to model the different tissues that compose the intervertebral disc.

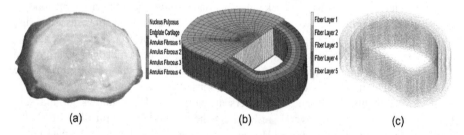

Fig. 1. (a) Human intervertebral lumbar disc obtained from a cadaver (b) Detailed view of the composite structure that is formed by the nucleus cartilage endplates, nucleus pulposus and annulus fibrosus (c) Detail of the orientation corresponding to the different five fiber layers (Color figure online).

Table 1. Range of the material parameters proposed for defining the behavior of the human intervertebral lumbar disc models based on FEM

Tissue	FE parameters		Tissue	FE parameters	
	Min.	Max.		Min.	Max
Nucleus Pulposus			**Annulus Fibrosus**		
C_{10}	0.11	0.14	Fiber 1&2	515.0	550.0
C_0	0.02	0.04	Fiber 3&4	503.0	515.0
Endplate			Fiber 5&6	455.0	503.0
E	23.0	55.0	Fiber 7&8	408.0	455.0
M	0.3	0.4	Fiber 9&10	360.0	408.0
–	–	–	E Annulus Fibrosus	4.0	4.2
–	–	–	μ Annulus Fibrosus	0.25	0.45

3 Setting the Proposed Finite Element Model

The material parameters for defining the behavior of the parameterized human disc FE model were adjusted after considering the following standard tests: compression, axial rotation, shear, flexion, extension and lateral bending. Table 2 shows the nine different stiffnesses and bulges obtained from the standard tests that were used to adjust the eleven parameters that define the behavior of FE model of the intervertebral disc.

Table 2. Different stiffnesses and bulges obtained from the standard tests that are used to adjust the parameters that define the behavior of the FE model of the intervertebral.

Test	Load used	Stiffness	Test	Load used	Stiffness
Compression	500 N	810 N/mm[20]	**Flexion**	5 N.m	1.18 Nm/°[19]
Axial Rotation	10 N.m	2.1 Nm/°[22]	**Extension**	4 N.m	1.53 Nm/°[24]
Shear	450 N	300 N/mm[23]	**Lateral Bending**	10.6 N.m	2.0 Nm/° [25]

Test	Bulge	Load used	Displacement
Compression	Anterior	500 N	0.5 mm[21]
Compression	Posterior	500 N	0.75 mm[21]
Compression	Lateral	500 N	0.35 mm[21]

4 Support Vector Machines

There are numerous regression techniques that are based inherently on a nonlinear nature. One of the most intensively studied and applied technique is SVM because of its performance as a universal approximation [26–28]. This technique is based on a kernel-based algorithm that has sparse solutions. Its predictions for new inputs depend on the kernel function evaluated at a subset of instances during a training stage. The goal of this technique is to find a function that minimizes the final error in Eq. 1.

$$y(x) = w^T \cdot \phi(x) + b \tag{1}$$

Where $y(x)$ is the predicted value, w is the vector with the parameters that define the model, b indicates the value of the bias and $\phi(x)$ is the function that fixes the feature-space transformation.

In this method, the error function used in simple linear regression (Eq. 2) is replaced by an ε-insensitive error function (Eq. 3) that assigns zero to values when the target and the predicted value difference are less than ε and keeps the value of the error function otherwise. In order to minimize Eq. 4, a cost (C) is assigned to the difference from the target:

$$\frac{1}{2} \sum_{n=1}^{N} [y_n - t_n]^2 + \frac{\lambda}{2} w^2 \tag{2}$$

$$E_\epsilon(y(x) - t) = \begin{cases} 0, & if\, |y(x) - t| < \epsilon \\ |y(x) - t| - \epsilon, & otherwise \end{cases} \tag{3}$$

$$C \sum_{n=1}^{N} E_\epsilon(y(x_n) - t_n) + \frac{1}{2} \|w^2\| \tag{4}$$

where $y(x)$ is the value predicted by Eq. 1, t is the searched target function, ϵ defines the margin where the function does not penalize and C define the cost of the penalization.

The process is optimized. Finally, the initial function (Eq. 1) becomes the more complex function (Eq. 5).

$$y(x) = \sum_{n=1}^{N} (\alpha_i - \alpha_i^*) x_i \cdot x + b \tag{5}$$

where α is a solution of the optimization problem that is obtained by Lagrangian theory.

Also, the function transforms the data to a higher dimensional feature space to improve the accuracy of the nonlinear problem. In this way, the final function becomes like Eq. 6.

$$y(x) = \sum_{n=1}^{N} (\alpha_i - \alpha_i^*) k(x_i, x) + b \tag{6}$$

Also, three kernels functions are used in this case: linear (Eq. 7), polynomial (Eq. 8) and Gaussian Radial Basis Function (RBF) (Eq. 9).

$$k(x_i, x) = x_i^T x \tag{7}$$

$$k(x_i, x) = \langle x_i \cdot x^d \rangle \tag{8}$$

$$k(x_i, x) = e^{-\frac{\|x_i - x^2\|}{2\sigma^2}} \tag{9}$$

R statistical software environment v2.15.3 was used to program the proposed methodologies, to develop the regression models and to perform the optimization based on GA [29, 30].

5 Results

5.1 Finite Element Results

Table 3 shows some of the 128 combinations of the material parameters (C_{10}, Fiber 12, AnnulusE, ...) that are generated using a two-level fractional factorial design [31] when the ranges shows in Table 1 are considered. In addition, this table shows the stiffnesses and bulges obtained from the parameterized FE models considered the material parameters when they are simulated to the standard tests (compression, axial rotation, shear, flexion, extension and lateral bending).

Table 3. Results obtained from the simulation of FE models when a combination of 128 material parameters are considered.

Run	C_{10}	Fiber12	AnnulusE	...	FlexRig	FlexLRig	TorsRig
1	0.11	515	4	...	1.635	1.998	3.593
2	0.14	515	4.2	...	1.762	1.581	3.264
3	0.11	515	4.2	...	1.646	1.320	3.150
...	...	...	...	...	...	...	
126	0.14	550	4	...	1.350	1.160	3.255
127	0.11	550	4	...	1.395	1.321	3.333
128	0.14	550	4.2	...	2.310	3.210	3.740

All these data formed the training dataset, and were used to generate the regression models. The following subsections show the process for generating and optimizing these models.

5.2 Modeling the Mechanical Behavior of the FE Model with a Regression Models Based on SVM

The process to obtain regression models that predict the stiffness and bulges of the intervertebral lumbar disc was based on the use of machine learning techniques that are based on SVM. In this case, the method was the following: Firstly, 128 experiments were performed according to the proposed DoE, in this case a two-level fractional factorial design. The dataset obtained from the experiments were normalized between 0 and 1. Thereafter, these 128 instances were used to train the models using 50 times repeated cross-validation. During this training, and to be able to compare the accuracy of the models, the Root Mean Squared Error (RMSE) (Eq. 10) and its standard deviation were obtained. At the same time, during the training, the most important parameters of each algorithm were tuned to improve the prediction capability. For example, Fig. 2 shows the RMSE of the variable 'TorsRig' while a SVM was being trained with a RBF kernel when parameters, such as the cost and sigma, were varying.

$$RMSE = \sqrt{\frac{1}{m} \cdot \sum_{k=1}^{m} \left(Y_{k\,REAL} - Y_{k\,PRE} \right)^2} \qquad (10)$$

In this case, $Y_{k\,REAL}$ and $Y_{k\,PRE}$ are, respectively, the values obtained from FE models and regression models that are based on SVM techniques, and m is the number of instances of the dataset.

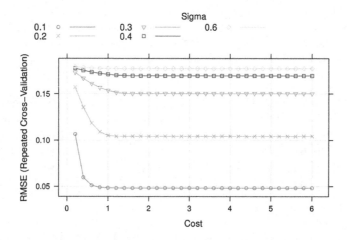

Fig. 2. Results obtained from the training period (50 times repeated cross-validation) using SVM with a RBF kernel to predict the 'TorsRig' feature. Values of the most accurate configuration: cost = 1.8 and sigma = 0.1 (Color figure online).

Since the models could be tested with data that was not used during the training stage, 30 new random simulations from the entire space of possibilities were conducted to test the models. These new instances were chosen randomly in an effort to uncover new possibilities of the problem from the previous DoE, and thereby avoid overtraining on the models. The results obtained from the training and the testing stages are shown in Table 4. Using these results, the most accurate models were selected, taking into consideration the training and testing results, but giving a greater weight to the testing results. This table shows the results of SVM with the three kernels applied and the results of the linear regression. In all cases, the nonlinear technique provided more accurate predictions than the linear technique.

5.3 Optimization Based on Genetic Algorithms

The regression models with the best generalization capacity (the ones mark in bold letters in Table 4) were used to set the parameters in the human intervertebral disc. This process was based on evolutionary optimization techniques that are based on GA. It was conducted as follows: Firstly, a number of 1000 individuals based on a combination of the studied features (C_{10}, C_0, Fiber12, Fiber34, Fiber56, Fiber78, Fiber910, AnnulusE, AnnulusU, CartilE, and CartilU) were randomly generated formed the initial generation. Later and based on these individuals, the values of output features (CompBulgeA, CompBulgeL, CompBulgeP, CompRig, ShearRig, ExteRig, FlexRig, FlexLRig, TorsRig) were obtained applying the selected regression models.

Table 4. Results obtained during the training and testing stage for the output variables (in bold letters the most accurate and selected ones)

Model	Training (Rep. Cross validation)		Testing	Training (Rep. Cross validation)		Testing
	RMSE (%)	RMSE SD (%)	RMSE (%)	RMSE (%)	RMSE SD (%)	RMSE (%)
	CompBulgeA			**CompBulgeL**		
SVM-Linear Kernel	**4.06**	**0.49**	**5.43**	**9.61**	**1.15**	**11.94**
SVM-Polynomial Kernel	3.13	0.50	5.58	3.55	0.49	12.54
SVM-RBF Kernel	7.30	0.66	12.48	8.74	0.82	17.78
LR	3.97	0.42	5.72	8.49	0.67	13.42
	CompBulgeP			**CompRig**		
SVM-Linear Kernel	**3.37**	**0.60**	**7.57**	**5.82**	**0.38**	**5.33**
SVM-Polynomial Kernel	3.11	0.67	7.61	3.36	0.22	5.41
SVM-RBF Kernel	6.58	0.65	11.66	8.65	0.60	15.46
LR	3.30	0.57	7.88	5.64	0.30	6.00
	ShearRig			**ExteRig**		
SVM-Linear Kernel	**2.38**	**0.42**	**7.64**	23.29	8.44	2.45
SVM-Polynomial Kernel	2.38	0.42	7.64	**22.71**	**4.87**	**1.50**
SVM-RBF Kernel	6.30	0.61	13.08	22.60	6.52	7.56
LR	2.37	0.41	7.80	23.55	4.97	10.99
	FlexRig			**FlexLRig**		
SVM-Linear Kernel	**7.23**	**0.86**	**6.97**	11.64	0.72	11.74
SVM-Polynomial Kernel	3.35	0.51	6.99	**3.22**	**0.14**	**11.70**
SVM-RBF Kernel	8.17	0.64	14.67	9.56	0.78	17.16
LR	7.02	0.64	7.88	9.67	0.48	11.80
	TorsRig					
SVM-Linear Kernel	**2.85**	**0.54**	**12.75**			
SVM-Polynomial	2.85	0.54	12.75			
SVM-RBF Kernel	4.83	0.78	14.25			
LR	2.88	0.56	12.77			

Then fitness values of the objective function F (Eq. 11) were calculated by minimizing the error between the values that were obtained from the selected regression models and the values that were obtained experimentally (See Table 2).

$$F = \min \left(\begin{array}{c} w_1 \cdot \Delta CompBulgeA + w_2 \cdot \Delta CompBulgeL + w_3 \cdot \Delta CompBulgeP + w_4 \cdot \Delta CompRig \\ + w_5 \Delta ShearRig + w_6 \Delta ExteRig + w_7 \Delta FlexRig + w_8 \Delta FlexLRig + w_9 \Delta TorsRig \end{array} \right)$$

$$(11)$$

where each of the Δ values in Eq. 11 was obtained in the same way, from the difference between the predicted values and the corresponding experimental data. For example, the value of $\Delta CompBulgeA$ was calculated according to Eq. 12.

$$\Delta CompBulgeA = \left| \frac{CompBulgeA - 0.5}{0.5} \right|$$

$$(12)$$

Also, all Δ values were associated with their corresponding weights (w_1 to w_9). In this case, all variables were considered at the same level of significance in the optimization. Therefore, their corresponding weights were fixed at 1. Then, the next generations (first generation and subsequent generations) were created using selection, crossing and mutation. The new generation was made up as follows:

- 25 % were the best individuals from the previous generation.
- 60 % were individuals obtained by crossover.
- The remaining 15 % were obtained by random mutation.

The minimization of the objective function F generated the values that are shown in Table 5. These values indicated the values closest to the real behavior of a healthy human intervertebral lumbar disc. With these values, a new FE model was simulated. It obtained a Mean Absolute Percentage Error (MAPE) equal to 6.17 %. This indicates that the methodology to optimize the lumbar disc is effective.

Table 5. Results obtained during training and testing stage for the output variables (in bold letters the most accurate and selected one)

Material Parameters		Output Variables from SVM		Output Variables from FEM	
C_{10}	C_0	Comp_bulgeA	CompbulgeL	Comp_bulgeA	CompbulgeL
0.133	0.035	0.342	0.127	0.352	0.140
Fiber12	**Fiber34**	**Comp_bulgeP**	**Comp_rigi**	**Comp_bulgeP**	**Comp_rigi**
515.352	503.390	0.761	1271.224	0.767	1237.623
Fiber56	**Fiber78**	**Cort_rigi**	**Exte_rigi**	**Cort_rigi**	**Exte_rigi**
455.511	408.071	272.381	2.695	271.122	2.052
Fiber910	**AnnulusE**	**Flex_rigi**	**FleL_rigi**	**Flex_rigi**	**FleL_rigi**
360.151	4.005	1.725	1.490	1.672	1.414
AnnulusU	**CartilE**	**Tors_rigi**	–	**Tors_rigi**	–
0.449	23.003	3.024	–	3.031	–
CartilU	–	–	–	–	–
0.373	–	–	–	–	–

6 Conclusions

To ensure realistic results in modelling biological tissues using the FEM, it is essential to have realistic FE models that are as close as possible to experimental data. This paper sets out a fully automated method based on experimental data and the combined use of data mining techniques, Genetic Algorithms (GA) and the FEM to determine the most appropriate material parameters of the human intervertebral lumbar disc models based on FEM. Firstly, based on standard tests, three-dimensional parameterized FE models were generated. For each of the standard tests, regression techniques based on SVM with different kernels were applied to model the stiffness and the bulges. Finally, the best combination of parameters was achieved by applying GA to the best regression models. The adequacy of the SVM models was verified by validation with FEM. The results demonstrate that the MAPE obtained between the models based on SVM and FEM was 6.17 %.

Acknowledgements. The authors wish to thanks the University of the Basque Country UPV/EHU for its support through Project US15/18 OMETESA.

References

1. Belytschko, T., Kulak, R.F., Schultz, A.B., Galante, J.O.: Finite element stress analysis of an intervertebral disc. J. Biomech. **7**, 276–285 (1974)
2. Kulak, R.F., Belytschko, T.B., Schultz, A.B., Galante, J.O.: Nonlinear behavior of the human intervertebral disc under axial load. J. Biomech. **9**(6), 377–386 (1976)
3. Panjabi, M.M., Brand, R.A., White, A.A.: Mechanical properties of the human thoracic spine. J. Bone Joint Surg. Am. **58**(5), 642–652 (1976)
4. Yang, K.H., King, A.I.: Mechanism of facet load transmission as a hypothesis for low-back pain. Spine **9**(6), 557–565 (1984)
5. Schmidt, H., Heuer, F., Simon, U., Kettler, A., Rohlmann, A., Claes, L., Wilke, H.J.: Application of a new calibration method for a three-dimensional finite element model of a human lumbar annulus fibrosus. Clin. Biomech. **21**(4), 337–344 (2006)
6. Ezquerro, F., Vacas, F.G., Postigo, S., Prado, M., Simón, A.: Calibration of the finite element model of a lumbar functional spinal unit using an optimization technique based on differential evolution. Med. Eng. Phys. **33**(1), 89–95 (2011)
7. Fernandez, R., Okariz, A., Ibarretxe, J., Iturrondobeitia, M., Guraya, T.: Use of decision tree models based on evolutionary algorithms for the morphological classification of reinforcing nano-particle aggregates. Comput. Mater. Sci. **92**, 102–113 (2014)
8. Fernandez, R., Martinez de Pisón, F.J., Pernía, A.V., Lostado, R.: Predictive modelling in grape berry weight during maturation process: Comparison of data mining, statistical and artificial intelligence techniques. Span. J. Agric. Res. **9**(4), 1156–1167 (2011)
9. González, R.A., Lacroix, D.: Biomechanical Study of Intervertebral Disc Degeneration. Polytechnic University of Catalonia, Barcelona (2012)
10. Lu, Y.M., Hutton, W.C., Gharpuray, V.M.: Do bending, twisting and diurnal fluid change in the disc affect the pro-pensity to prolapse? A viscoelastic finite element model. Spine **21**, 2570–2579 (1996)

11. Martinez, J.B., Oloyede, V.O.A., Broom, N.D.: Biomechanics of load-bearing of the intervertebral disc: an experimental and finite element model. Med. Eng. Phys. **19**(2), 145–156 (1997)

12. Kim, H.J., Chun, H.J., Kang, K.T., Lee, H.M., Chang, B.S., Lee, C.K., Yeom, J.S.: Finite element analysis for comparison of Spinous process Osteotomies technique with conventional Laminectomy as lumbar decompression procedure. Yonsei Med. J. **56**(1), 146–153 (2015)

13. Dicko, A.H., Tong-Yette, N., Gilles, B., Faure, F., Palombi, O.: Construction and validation of a hybrid lumbar spine model for the fast evaluation of intradiscal pressure and mobility. Int. J. Med. Health Biomed. Bioeng. Pharm. Eng. WASET **9**(2), 134–145 (2015)

14. Smit, T.H., Odgaard, A., Schneider, E.: Structure and function of vertebral trabecular bone. Spine **22**(24), 2823–2833 (1997)

15. Ibarz, E., Herrera, A., Más, Y., Rodríguez-Vela, J., Cegoñino, J., Puértolas, S., Gracia, L.: Development and kinematic verification of a finite element model for the lumbar spine: application to disc degeneration. Biomed. Res., Int (2012)

16. Baroud, G., Nemes, J., Heini, P., Steffen, T.: Load shift of the intervertebral disc after a vertebroplasty: a finite-element study. Eur. Spine J. **12**(4), 421–426 (2003)

17. Denozière, G., Ku, D.N.: Biomechanical comparison between fusion of two vertebrae and implantation of an artificial intervertebral disc. J. Biomech. **39**(4), 766–775 (2006)

18. Dietrich, M., Kedzior, K., Zagrajek, T.: A biomechanical model of the human spinal system. Proc. Inst. Mech. Eng. Part H-J. Eng. Med. **205**(1), 19–26 (1991)

19. Pitzen, T., Geisler, F.H., Matthis, D., Müller-Storz, H., Pederson, K., Steudel, W.I.: The influence of cancellous bone density on load sharing in human lumbar spine: a comparison between an intact and a surgically altered motion segment. Eur. Spine J. **10**(1), 23–29 (2001)

20. Rostedt, M., Ekström, L., Broman, H., Hansson, T.: Axial stiffness of human lumbar motion segments, force dependence. J. Biomech. **31**(6), 503–509 (1998)

21. Shirazi-Adl, S.A., Shrivastava, S.C., Ahmed, A.M.: Stress analysis of the lumbar disc-body unit in compression. A three-dimensional nonlinear finite element study. Spine **9**(2), 120–134 (1984)

22. Gardner-Morse, M.G., Stokes, I.A.: Structural behavior of human lumbar spinal motion segments. J. Biomech. **37**(2), 205–212 (2004)

23. Liu, Y.K., Ray, G.A.U.T.A.M., Hirsch, C.: The resistance of the lumbar spine to direct shear. Orthop. Clin. North Am. **6**(1), 33 (1975)

24. Guan, Y., Yoganandan, N., Zhang, J., Pintar, F.A., Cusick, J.F., Wolfla, C.E., Maiman, D.J.: Validation of a clinical finite element model of the human lumbosacral spine. Med. Biol. Eng. Comput. **44**(8), 633–641 (2006)

25. Schultz, A.B., Warwick, D.N., Berkson, M.H., Nachemson, A.L.: Mechanical properties of human lumbar spine motion segments—Part I: responses in flexion, extension, lateral bending, and torsion. J. Biomech. Eng. **101**(1), 46–52 (1979)

26. Vapnik, V., Golowich, S.E., Smola, A.: Support vector method for function approximation, regression estimation, and signal processing. In: Mozer, M., Jordan, M., Petsche, T. (eds.) Advances in Neural Information Processing Systems, pp. 281–287. MIT Press, Cambridge (1997)

27. Clarke, S.M., Griebsch, J.H., Simpson, T.W.: Analysis of support vector regression for approximation of complex engineering analyses. J. Mech. Des. Trans. ASME **127**(6), 1077–1087 (2005)

28. Bishop, C.M.: Pattern Recognition and Machine Learning. Springer, New York (2006)

29. R Core Team: R: a language and environment for statistical computing. R Foundation for Statistical Computing, Vienna, Austria (2013). http://www.R-project.org/
30. Kuhn, M., Contributions from Wing, J., Weston, S., Williams, A., Keefer, C., Engelhardt, A., Cooper, T., Mayer, Z., Kenkel, B.., The R Core Team, Benesty, M., Lescarbeau, R., Ziem, A., Scrucca, L.: Caret: classification and Regression Training. R package version 6.0-41 (2015)
31. Montgomery, D.C.: Design and Analysis of Experiments. Wiley, New Jersey (2008)

Passivity Based Control of Cyber Physical Systems Under Zero-Dynamics Attack

Fawad Hassan[1(✉)], Naeem Iqbal[1], Francisco Martínez-Álvarez[2],
and Khawaja M. Asim[1]

[1] Pakistan Institute of Engineering and Applied Sciences, Islamabad, Pakistan
[2] Division of Computer Science, Universidad Pablo de Olavide, 41013 Seville, Spain
fawad871@gmail.com

Abstract. Introduction of computer networks in communication and control of the industrial setups has given rise to the new concept of Cyber Physical System. These control systems are vulnerable to the stealthy cyber-attacks as they are connected to communication networks. Cyber Attacks can cause malfunctioning of plants i.e. abnormal operational behavior, instability, etc. So it is of prime importance to control the unit under cyber-attack in order to protect the whole setup from damage. Passivity is a system property that enables the system designer to devise an energy based control of general dynamic systems. In this paper passive architecture of Cyber Physical Systems is discussed. To prevent the excitation of unstable zeros of system in stealthy attacks like zero-dynamics attack, back-stepping technique is employed to make zero-dynamics of closed loop the system stable. This technique is also used to develop a control law that will prevent the system from reaching unstable region if it is under zero-dynamics attack.

Keywords: Cyber Physical System · Security · Back-steeping · Sensor network

1 Introduction

The sharing of computational and storage cloud has given rise to the concept of Cyber Physical Systems (CPS) [4] in recent years. A CPS is the collection of a number of distributed physical systems which are interconnected with computational networks for control purposes. The composition of computational resources, sensory equipment, actuators and communication equipment gives the broader view of modern real world CPS. Modern power grids, water resources, robotics and distributed process control systems etc. are the examples of CPS. As controllers and the process systems are spatially distributed so the involvement of computer networks is inevitable, that makes these systems vulnerable to the false control data injected by some hacker.

These cyber intrusions are a serious threat to the stability of CPS. Since a CPS contains different control systems and process systems, the overall stability

© Springer International Publishing Switzerland 2016
F. Martínez-Álvarez et al. (Eds.): HAIS 2016, LNAI 9648, pp. 634–646, 2016.
DOI: 10.1007/978-3-319-32034-2_53

of this system is not easy to ensure. Even if the individual sub part is stable and its performance is ensured, when it is deployed in network, their performance and stability are no longer guaranteed. So the conventional ways to ensure the stability cannot be employed.

The involvement of communication networks in control systems makes them vulnerable to the *cyber − attacks* [9]. A cyber-attack is an act from some hacker (a person or an organization) to target the computer control and communication systems to manipulate communicated data. In networked control systems there are several types of cyber-attacks, such as deception and denial of service attack, dynamic false data injection attack, replay attack or covert attack.

The purpose of attack can be explained as its effects on the system. Constraints are related to the ability of the system to detect the attack. Sensitive systems have well defined operating point constraints. So the notion of stable region is introduced to characterize the safety constraints. In order to make the control system attack resilient, control systems are made passive [6]. If the system is passive then its zero-dynamics are stable, so in case of attack (zero-dynamics attack) system won't go in the unstable region even if its zero-dynamics are excited.

For this purpose, a technique called *Back-Stepping* is proposed to be used in this work to make the zero-dynamics of system stable. Additionally, after introducing a thorough concept of passivity based-control CPS, a control law is developed to make the system passive. Later, its performance is tested on simulated datasets, showing that stabilization and passivation can be reached with the proposed technique.

The rest of the paper is structured as follows. Section 2 thoroughly discusses the term passivity in this context. Section 3 introduces the wave variable transform. Later in Sect. 4, the main components of control systems are described. The issue of zero-dynamics attack is introduced in Sect. 5. The proposed *Back-Stepping* approach is presented in Sect. 6. Finally, relevant conclusions derived from this work are found in Sect. 7.

2   Passivity

A system that uses the energy supplied to it without generating its own energy can be characterized as a passive system. So far, there are no techniques that can control the whole CPS as in general control of plant where a single or multiple controllers can control the plant. Now the property that has been used in designing of nonlinear control system is that of *passivity* or, more generally, *dissipativity* [2].

2.1   Background

There are different definitions for passive systems in mathematical terms [1]. But one thing in which all definitions agree is that the output energy of a system must be restrained so that the system does not generate more energy than it had initially absorbed.

Strictly input passive and strictly output passive systems having finite gain are said to be stable. Passive systems in terms of all observable states are Lyapunov-stable [10]. It is uniqueness of passive systems that, when they are connected in parallel configuration or in negative feedback configuration, the resulting connected system also remains passive. If the feedback loop is closed with any positive definite matrix, then discrete time passive plant can be considered as strictly output passive. It is to be noted that when delays are incorporated in the feedback configuration the network may loose its passiveness.

2.2   Basic Concept

Passive theory has been driven from the circuit analysis theory where the circuits with the passive elements are stable and dissipative [1]. Passivity generalizes the notion of energy by utilizing the energy storage function and energy supply function [7]. We consider general nonlinear function:

$$\dot{x} = f(x, u)$$
$$y = h(x, u) \tag{1}$$

where $x \in X \subset \Re^n$, $u \in U \subset \Re^n$, $y \in Y \subset \Re^n$ denotes the system state, input of the system and output of the system, respectively. Without loss of generality, it can be considered that $f(0,0) = 0$ and $h(0,0) = 0$. Also it is assumed that f is Lipschitz with respect to variable x. Now a dissipative system dissipates energy without generating its own energy. Energy supply rate $w(\cdot, \cdot)$ represents the energy being provided to the system, where $w : U \times Y$. The energy stored is internally can be represented as the energy storage function with the $V : X \rightarrow \Re^+$.

Definition 1. The system (1) is considered to be dissipative, if a non-negative energy storage function $V(x)$ exists such that the stored energy of the system is always restrained above by the input energy of the system over a finite interval of time $T \in [0, \infty)$. For the energy supply function $w(u, y)$

$$\int_0^\infty w(u, y)dt \geq V(x(T)) - V(x(0)) \tag{2}$$

This is a general definition of dissipativity. In practice, it is very difficult to exactly determine the energy supply rate for a system.

2.3   Interconnection of Systems

There are different topologies for the interconnection of systems. Two of them are very basic and important [1]: general feedback interconnection of systems (see Fig. 1) and the parallel interconnection of systems (see Fig. 2).

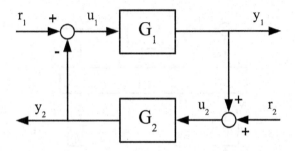

Fig. 1. Feedback interconnection of two systems

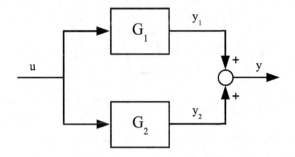

Fig. 2. parallel interconnection of two systems

3   Wave Variables

Wave variable transform was first introduced in [3] in order to solve the issue of delay free loop and also to guarantee the realizability of wave digital filter. Wave variables transformation is a bilinear transformation in which a minimum phase continuous time stable system is transformed to the discrete time minimum phase system and by this way the transformation preserves the passivity of the interconnected system.

The networks having a passive plant and a controller are generally connected with the help of power variables. The power variables are represented with an effort and flow variable pair product of which is power. These power variables are affected by communication delays, so the communication channel is no longer passive and this loss passivity can lead to instability. Wave variables filter allows the transmission of effort and flow variables over the network while it remains passive even when they are affected by arbitrary constant time delays and data loss.

If additional data is transmitted along with continuous wave variables, we can keep the channel passive while it is subjected to the variable time delays. Consider the networked control system as shown in Fig. 3.

System G_1 is the mapping $e_1 \rightarrow y_1$ and system G_2 is the mapping of $e_2 \rightarrow y_2$. One of the two system is passive and the other is the controller that is designed in such a way that it also remains passive. By considering the delays in the

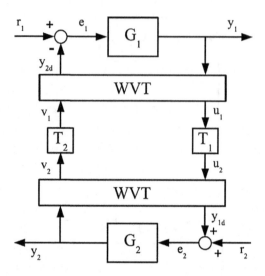

Fig. 3. Usage of wave variable transformation in networked scheme

system to be constant, It is possible that delay T_1 and delay T_2 are different. Now the signals can be shown as

$$u_2(t) = u_1(t - T_1)$$
$$v_1(t) = v_2(t - T_2) \tag{3}$$

The wave variable transformation (WVT) is the input-output coordinate transformation is shown below.

$$\begin{bmatrix} u_1 \\ v_1 \end{bmatrix} = \frac{1}{\sqrt{2b}} \begin{bmatrix} bI & I \\ bI & -I \end{bmatrix} \begin{bmatrix} y_1 \\ y_{2d} \end{bmatrix} \tag{4}$$

$$\begin{bmatrix} u_2 \\ v_2 \end{bmatrix} = \frac{1}{\sqrt{2b}} \begin{bmatrix} bI & I \\ bI & -I \end{bmatrix} \begin{bmatrix} y_{1d} \\ y_2 \end{bmatrix} \tag{5}$$

where b is the design parameter. The energy being supplied the network is the square of two waves u_2 and v_2 and output energy of the network is the square of u_2 and v_1. So the net energy increase is given as below.

$$V_N = \frac{1}{2} \int_{t_o}^t (u_1^T u_1 + v_2^T v_2 - u_2^T u_2 - v_1^T v_1) \, d\tau \tag{6}$$

When delays are constant then this expression can be shown as the net energy flowing into the network is positive.

$$V_N = \frac{1}{2} \int_{t_o}^t (u_1^T u_1 \, d\tau + \frac{1}{2} \int_{t-T_2}^t v_2^T v_2 \, d\tau \geq 0. \tag{7}$$

Even in more general cases, the quantity V_N is always non negative so that the network does not generate energy. According to the definition of energy stored in the network (6), it can be observed that the energy of G_1 side bounds the energy on the G_2 side of the network.

$$\frac{1}{2} \int_{t_o}^{t} (u_1^T u_1 - v_1^T v_1) \, d\tau \geq \int_{t_o}^{t} (v_2^T v_2 - u_2^T u_2) \, d\tau \tag{8}$$

$$\Rightarrow \int_{t_o}^{T} y_1^T y_{2d} \, d\tau \geq \int_{t_o}^{T} y_2^T y_{1d} \, d\tau \tag{9}$$

This is the fact is used to show the stability of interconnected system.

Theorem 6. Two nonlinear output strictly passive systems connected over a delayed network via the wave variable transformation shown in Fig. 3, the interconnected system will be l_2 stable, if the network delays are constant.

4   System Model

A control system connected to the network has the following main components [9]: physical plant, communication network, feedback controller, anomaly detector. This section reviews each of these components.

4.1   Plant Model

The physical plant model is treated in the discrete-time state-space model

$$x_{k+1} = Ax_k + B\tilde{u}_k + Gw_k + Ff_k, \quad y_k = Cx_k + v_k \tag{10}$$

where $x_k \in \Re^n$ is the state variable, $\tilde{u}_k \in \Re^q$ is the control action applied to the process, $y_k \in \Re^p$ is the measurement from the sensors at the sampling instant $k \in Z$ and $f_k \in \Re^d$ is the unknown signal showing the effects of anomalies that is generally denoted as fault signal in the control literature. w_k and v_k represent the process and measurement noise respectively. It is assumed that their sources are bounded by δ_w and δ_v i.e. $\bar{w} = ||Ew_k|| \leq \delta_w$ and $\bar{v} = ||Ev_k|| \leq \delta_v$. The plant operation is controlled by a communication channel (network). By using this network sensor measurements and actuator data is communicated, which at the plant side correspond to y_k and $\tilde{u}_k$, respectively.

For the controller side we represent the sensor data and actuator data by $\tilde{y}_k \in R^p$ and $u_k \in R^q$, respectively. The communication channel (network) can be unreliable so the data communication in between the plant and the controller may be changed due to noise or inaccuracies which results in unreliability in the communicated data at the plant side and also at the controller end. In this paper we do not consider the usual communication network effects (packet losses and delays). In order to avoid all these problems in communication, the network should be reliable and it should not affect the data communicated over it. The given physical plant model in (10) and while assuming the ideal control network, the control system connected to the network is said to have the nominal behavior if $f_k = 0$, $\tilde{u}_k = u_k$ and $\tilde{y}_k = y_k$. The violation of any of these conditions may cause abnormal behavior and poor performance of the system.

4.2   Feedback Controller

The feedback controller for the plant if given as below.

$$z_{k+1} = A_c Z_k + B_c \bar{y}_k, u_k = C_c z_k + D_c \bar{y}_k \tag{11}$$

where the states of the controller, $z_k \in \Re^m$, can also incorporate the process state error and tracking error estimates. For the plant and network model, the controller is required to be designed in such a way that minimum satisfactory performance is achieved under normal behavior.

4.3   Anomaly Detector

The purpose of the anomaly detector is to detect the variations in performance from nominal behavior of system. Anomaly detector is required to be with controller of the plant so it has access to $\tilde{y}_k$ and u_k. The structure of anomaly detector is observer based fault detection filter as shown below.

$$\hat{x}_{k|k} = A\hat{x}_{k-1|k-1} + Bu_{k-1} + K(\tilde{y}_k - \tilde{y}_{k|k-1}), \ r_k = V(\tilde{y}_k - \tilde{y}_{k|k}) \tag{12}$$

4.4   System Under Attack

We have model of closed loop network control system under attack as following:

$$\eta_{k+1} = A\eta_k + Ba_k + G \begin{bmatrix} w_k \\ v_k \end{bmatrix}, \tilde{y}_k = C\eta_k + Da_k + H \begin{bmatrix} w_k \\ v_k \end{bmatrix} \tag{13}$$

where system matrices are

$$A = \begin{bmatrix} A + BD_eC & BC_e \\ B_eC & A_e \end{bmatrix}, G = \begin{bmatrix} G & BD_e \\ 0 & B_e \end{bmatrix}, C = \begin{bmatrix} C & 0 \end{bmatrix}, H = \begin{bmatrix} 0 & I \end{bmatrix}$$

the system components under attack are now specified for the attack vector a_k, it also incorporates the fault signal f_k. Let us consider the plant and controller states to be augmented as $\eta_k = [x_k^T \ z_k^T]^T$.

Definition 8. For the time instant k, system is said to be protected if $x_k \ \varepsilon \ S_z$, where S_z is a non-empty closed and compact set.

Assumption. The system is in safe state if $x_{ko} \ \varepsilon \ S_z$ at the beginning of the attack. The effects of an attack performed on the control system can be assessed by observing whether the states of the system are in the safe set S_z during and after the attack. The attack is supposed to be successful if the states are driven out of the safe set.

As per attack constraints are concerned, these attacks are stealthy which means they cannot be detected at the output of the system. Also we consider the attack component comprises of only physical attack on the system and data deception attacks in the network and so we have the attack vector $a_k = [f_k^T \ b_k^{uT} \ b_{k+1}^{uT} \ b_k^{uT}]^T$ and attack signal $A_{ko}^{kf} = \{ a_{ko}, \ a_{k1}, \dots, a_{kf} \}$ then the stealthy attack is defined as follows.

Definition 9. The Attack signal A_{ko}^{kf} is stealthy if $||r_k|| < \delta_r + \delta_a, \forall\, k \geq k_o$.

This definition is dependent on the initial state of the system at k_o and also the noise terms w_k and v_k.

5   Zero-Dynamics Attack

Definition (9) is about the type of attack that are stealthy that means it cannot be detected at the output of the system [8]. So if $r_k^a = 0, k = k_o, ..., k_f$. The concept of stealthy attack is to design the policy of attack and attack signal A_{ko}^{kf} such that the residual signal r_k from the system controller system model and does not change the value due to the attack.

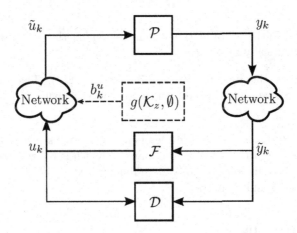

Fig. 4. Schematic of zero-dynamics attack

Attack Policy: So the attack strategy refers to the input signal a_k that makes the outputs of the control system under attack $\tilde{y}_k^a$ zero and its it illustrated in Fig. 4. Now the solution to the problem is provided by the sequence

$$a_k = gv^k \tag{14}$$

is specified by the input zero direction g and zeros of the system are v. For simple solution we consider a single instant when actuator data is compromised. In this situation zero-dynamics attack policy utilizes the information of the transmission zero-dynamics of the plant. Now the plant states due to the attack on the actuator data are given below.

$$x_{k+1}^a = Ax_k^a + Ba_k, \; y_k^a = Cx_k^a \tag{15}$$

with $a_k = b_k^u$. The discrete time system (15) with full column rank matrix B, the transmission zeros of the system can be calculated as the values $v \in C$ that the cause the matrix $P(v)$ to lose rank, where

$$P(v) = \begin{bmatrix} vI - A & -B \\ C & 0 \end{bmatrix} \qquad (16)$$

these values are non-minimum phase or minimum phase zeros depending on whether they are on left hand side or right hand side of frequency domain respectively. In discrete time system a zero is stable if the value of $|v|$ is less than 1 and unstable otherwise. The input zero direction is calculated as the solution of the following equation.

$$\begin{bmatrix} vI - A & -B \\ C & 0 \end{bmatrix} \begin{bmatrix} x_o \\ g \end{bmatrix} = \begin{bmatrix} 0 \\ 0 \end{bmatrix} \qquad (17)$$

where x_o is the initial state of the system for which the input sequence (14) results in an identically zero output, $\tilde{y}_k^a = 0 \ \forall k$.

Lemma 1. x_o is the initial state and it satisfies (17). The zero-dynamics attack generate state trajectories which are in the span of (x_o) i.e. $x_k^a \in span(x_o) \forall \ k \geq 0$.

System Knowledge: To calculate the open loop attack strategy it is required to have the exact information of zero-dynamics, which is represented as k_z. The calculation of transmission zeros of system requires exact knowledge of the plant dynamics i.e. A, B and C matrices.

6   Back-Stepping

A technique that is simple and known for the stabilization of feedback control systems is *back-stepping*. It is recursive Laypunov based technique which was introduced in early 1990s [5]. The concept of back-stepping is to develop a control function while considering state variables as virtual control and then designing controls for these virtual control variables. This technique can complete the objectives of stabilization and tracking. Consider a system such as

$$\dot{x} = f(x, u) \qquad (18)$$

Let the origin $x = 0$ is the equilibrium point for the system $\dot{x} = f(x, u)$ with $u = 0$. Assume that the state feedback law of the form $u = \phi(x)$. Now the new feedback system is given as

$$\dot{x} = f(x, \phi(x)) \qquad (19)$$

As the origin of an unforced system (19) is stable, then a positive definite energy function V can be devised for which $\dot{V}$ is negative definite in the neighborhood of origin.

6.1   General Case of Back-Stepping:

Here for the concept of back-stepping a general system of the following form is considered.

$$\dot{x} = f(x) + g(x)y$$
$$\dot{y} = u \tag{20}$$

where $x \ \varepsilon \ R^n$, $y \ \varepsilon \ R^n$, and $[x, y]^T \ R^{n+1}$ are the states of the system. u is the control input to the function $f, g \ : \ D \ \rightarrow \ R^n$ are supposed to be smooth. Here the following assumptions are made:

1. The function $f(.) \ : R^n \rightarrow \ R^n$ satisfies $f(0) = 0$. Thus the origin become the equilibrium point of the subsystem $\dot{x} = f(x)$.
2. Consider the subsystem (20) assume that state variable y as the independent input to this subsystem and the control law of the form

$$y = \phi(x) \ , \phi(0) = 0$$

the lypunov function $V_1 : D \rightarrow R^+$ such that

$$\dot{V}_1(x) = \frac{\partial V_1}{\partial x}[f(x) + g(x).\phi(x)] \leq -V_a(x) \leq 0 \quad \forall \ x\varepsilon \ D$$

where $V_a(.) \ : \ D \rightarrow R^+$ is positive semidefinite function in D.

By these assumptions the system (21) has a subsystem for which a stabilizing law already exists which is augmented with integrator subsystem.

6.2   Illustrative Example

Consider a third order system, such as:

$$\dot{x}_1 = x_2 + x_1^2$$
$$\dot{x}_2 = x_3 + x_2^2$$
$$\dot{x}_3 = u_2 \tag{21}$$
$$\dot{y} = -y + u_1$$

here in this system x_1, x_2 and x_3 are the states of the system and the control input is u. The purpose is to design the state feedback controller that makes the origin asymptotically stable.

From the first equation of (21) let $z_1 = x_1$ and so $\dot{z}_1 = \dot{x}_1$.

$$\dot{z}_1 = x_2 + x_1^2 \tag{22}$$

Let x_2 is virtual control for the above equation. The error dynamics of virtual control α_1 can be given as

$$z_2 = x_2 - \alpha_1 \tag{23}$$

This gives $\dot{z}_1 = z_2 + \alpha_1 + x_1^2$. For this a control is designed that stabilizes the above error dynamics. Laypunov function is given as

$$V_1 = \frac{1}{2}z_1^2 \tag{24}$$

Which gives $\dot{V}_1 = z_1(\alpha_1 + x_1^2) + z_1 z_2$. $z_2 = 0$. Choose $\alpha_1 = -x_1^2 - c_1 z_1$ so

$$\dot{V}_1 = -c_1 z_1^2 \tag{25}$$

where c_1 is design parameter and it is always positive i.e. $c_1 > 0$.

For the next step derivative of error dynamics (23).

$$\dot{z}_2 = x_3 + x_2^2 - \dot{\alpha}_1 \tag{26}$$

Here $\dot{\alpha}_1 = -(c_1 + 2x_1)(x_2 + x_1^2)$. for this step x_3 is virtual control i.e.

$$z_3 = x_3 - \alpha_2 \tag{27}$$

By using the value of x_3 from (27) $\dot{z}_2$ becomes

$$\dot{z}_2 = z_3 + \alpha_2 + x_2^2 + (c_1 + 2x_1)(x_2 + x_1^2) \tag{28}$$

Now Lyapunov function for this state is augmented with (24) i.e.

$$V_2 = V_1 + \frac{1}{2}z_2^2 \tag{29}$$

After calculations and putting $\alpha_2 = -z_1 - x_2^2$ and $z_3 = 0$, $\dot{V}_2$ becomes

$$\dot{V}_2 = -c_1 z_1^2 - c_2 z_2^2 \tag{30}$$

where c_2 is design parameter and it is always positive i.e. $c_2 > 0$.

From error dynamics (27) $\dot{z}_3 = \dot{x}_3 - \dot{\alpha}_2$, and with $\dot{\alpha}_2 = \frac{\partial \alpha_2}{\partial x_1}(x_2 + x_1^2) - \frac{\partial \alpha_2}{\partial x_2}(x_3 + x_2^2)$. Lyapunov function for the next state is given as

$$V_3 = V_2 + \frac{1}{2}z_3^2 \tag{31}$$

$\dot{V}_3$ is given as

$$\dot{V}_3 = -c_1 z_1^2 - c_2 z_2^2 - c_3 z_3^2 + z_3(u_2 + z_2 + c_3 z_3 + \frac{\partial \alpha_2}{\partial x_1}(x_2 + x_1^2) + \frac{\partial \alpha_2}{\partial x_2}(x_3 + x_2^2) \tag{32}$$

where c_3 is design parameter and $c_3 \geq 0$.

$$u_2 = -z_2 - c_3 z_3 + \frac{\partial \alpha_2}{\partial x_1}(x_2 + x_1^2) + \frac{\partial \alpha_2}{\partial x_2}(x_3 + x_2^2) \tag{33}$$

Then $\dot{V}_3 = \sum_{i=1}^{3} z_i \dot{z}_i = \sum_{i=1}^{3} -c_i z_i^2 < -\sigma||z||$ where σ is class K function. With the control law (33), zero-dynamics closed loop system is asymptotically stable. From $\dot{V}_3 = < -\sigma||z|| \le 0$, this it is obvious that $V_3(t) \le V_3(0)$ and thus z_1, z_2, z_3 are all bounded

$$\dot{z}_1 = -c_1 z_1^2 + z_2$$
$$\dot{z}_2 = -c_2 z_2^2 - z_1 + z_3 \qquad (34)$$
$$\dot{z}_3 = -c_3 z_3^2 - z_2$$

From (34) we can say that z_3 is stable which makes z_2 and hence z_1 stable. Define $\beta = -\dot{V}_3$ then $\int_0^t \beta(\tau)d\tau = v_3(0) - V_3(t)$. As $V_3(0)$ is bounded, and $V_3(t)$ is non-increasing and bounded, so $\lim_{t \to \infty} \int_0^t \beta(\tau)d\tau < \infty$. Also $\dot{\beta}$ is bounded, $\lim_{t \to \infty} \beta = 0$ holds due to Barbalat's lemma. So $z_1 \to 0$, $z_2 \to 0$ and $z_3 \to 0$, as $t \to \infty$,. By definition of virtual control variables $x_1, x_2, x_3, x_2^*, x_3^*$ the system states x_1, x_2, x_3 will converge to zero. So input u_2 can stabilize the system (21). Now in order to make the whole system passive and stable let $V_3=W$, then lyapunov function for the whole system is

$$V = W + \frac{1}{2}y^2 \qquad (35)$$

Then $\dot{V} = \dot{W} + y\dot{y}$, where $\dot{y} = -y + u_1$.

$$\dot{V} = \dot{W} + y\dot{y} \qquad (36)$$

from (32) value of $W=V_3$ is used. so

$$\dot{V} = -\frac{\partial W}{\partial z}\dot{z}|_{y=0} - y^2 + yu_1 \qquad (37)$$

$\dot{V} = -\frac{\partial W}{\partial z}\dot{z}|_{y=0} - y^2 + yu_1 \le -y^2 + yu_1$ this shows that system is strictly output passive. if we choose $u_1 = -\gamma y$, $\gamma > 0$ then $\dot{V} \le 0$ and $y(t) \to 0$ as $t \to \infty$. From La Salle's theorem and positive limit set all states x_1, x_2 and x_3, approach to zero. Hence system is zero state observable. So with suggested control law (33), system (21) is said to be asymptotically stable.

7   Conclusions

A thorough concept of Passivity based control of Cyber Physical Systems is presented. In order to make these system resilient to cyber-attack i.e. zero-dynamics attack, the stabilization of zero-dynamics of system and over all passivation of system is necessary. For this purpose $Back - stepping$ is used to stabilize a theoretical two input single output nonlinear system. For this system a control law is derived to make zero-dynamics closed loop system asymptotically stable.

Then another control law is developed using the same technique that makes the whole system passive. Hence the overall objective of stabilization of zero-dynamics and passivation of system is achieved.

Acknowledgements. The authors would like to thank Spanish Ministry of Economy and Competitiveness and Junta de Andalucía for the support under projects TIN2014-55894-C2-R and P12-TIC-1728, respectively.

References

1. Antsaklis, P.J., Goodwine, B., Gupta, V., McCourt, M.J., Wang, Y., Wu, P., Xia, M., Yu, H., Zhu, F.: Control of cyberphysical systems using passivity and dissipativity based methods. Eur. J. Control **19**(5), 379–388 (2013)
2. Bao, J., Lee, P.L.: Process Control - The Passive Systems Approach. Springer, London (2007)
3. Fettweis, A.: Wave digital filters: practice and theory. Proc. IEEE **74**(2), 270–327 (1986)
4. Khaitan, S.K., McCalley, J.D.: Design techniques and applications of cyberphysical systems: a survey. IEEE Syst. J. **9**(2), 350–365 (2014)
5. Kokotovic, K.V.: The joy of feedback: nonlinear and adaptive. IEEE Control Syst. Mag. **12**(2), 7–17 (1992)
6. Michalek, M.M., Kielczewski, M.: The concept of passive control assistance for docking maneuvers with n-trailer vehicles. IEEE/ASME Trans. Mechatron. **20**(5), 2075–2084 (2015)
7. Ortega, R., Mareels, I.: Energy-balancing passivity-based control. In: Proceedings of the IEEE American Control Conference, pp. 1265–1270 (2000)
8. Pasqualetti, F., Dorfler, F., Bullo, F.: Attack detection and identification in cyberphysical systems. IEEE Trans. Autom. Control **58**(11), 2715–2729 (2013)
9. Teixeira, A., Shames, I., Sandberg, H., Johansson, K.H.: A secure control framework for resource-limited adversaries. Automatica **51**, 135–148 (2015)
10. Zhao, J., Hill, D.J.: Dissipativity theory for switched systems. IEEE Trans. Autom. Control **53**(4), 941–953 (2008)

The Multivariate Entropy Triangle and Applications

Francisco José Valverde-Albacete$^{(\boxtimes)}$ and Carmen Peláez-Moreno

Departamento de Teoría de la Señal y de las Comunicaciones,
Universidad Carlos III de Madrid, 28911 Leganés, Spain
fva@tsc.uc3m.es

Abstract. We extend a framework for the analysis of classifiers to encompass also the analysis of data sets. Specifically, we generalize a balance equation and a visualization device, the Entropy Triangle, for multivariate distributions, not only bivariate ones. With such tools we analyze a handful of UCI machine learning task to start addressing the question of how information gets transformed through machine learning classification tasks.

1 Introduction and Motivation

As early as [1], there emerged an interest in better understanding how the transmission of information in the *multivariate setting*—that is, among multiple variables—compares to the *bivariate setting* used by Shannon for variables X and Y—input and output, respectively—in his seminal paper for the analysis of reliable communication systems [2].

Furthermore, the last 60 years of engineering practice have revealed that this setting is far broader than initially envisaged, and many problems, both theoretical and applied, can be characterized as "relating to the transmission of information", that is, in information-theoretical terms. For the scope of this paper we concentrate in the Machine Learning applications for the multivariate setting [3,4]:

For that purpose, let $\overline{X} = \{X_i \mid 1 \leq i \leq n\}$ be a set of discrete random variables with joint multivariate distribution $P_{\overline{X}} = P_{X_1 \ldots X_n}$, and their corresponding marginals $P_{X_i}(x_i) = \sum_{j \neq i} P_{\overline{X}}(\overline{x})$ where $\overline{x} = x_1 \ldots x_n$ is a tuple of n elements.

Typically, the $\overline{X}$ represent a set of features realized as a set of (vector of) observations, and this is all of the information characterizing an unsupervised learning task. On supervised tasks we may select one of the variables to represent a *class index* Y in this (categorical or discrete) setting. When the support of Y has more than two values $|\text{supp}(Y)| \geq 2$ we call this setting *multiclass classification*; if $|\text{supp}(Y)| = 2$, we call it *(binary) classification*. For this paper we will suppose that the classification variable Y is actually adjoined to variable vector $\overline{X}$ (see Sect. 3.3).

F.J. Valverde-Albacete—CPM & FVA have been partially supported by the Spanish Government-MinECo projects TEC2014-53390-P and TEC2014-61729-EXP.

© Springer International Publishing Switzerland 2016
F. Martínez-Álvarez et al. (Eds.): HAIS 2016, LNAI 9648, pp. 647–658, 2016.
DOI: 10.1007/978-3-319-32034-2_54

1.1   The Entropy Balance and the Entropy Triangle

For the original, simpler case of one input variable and one output variable, a new equation on the entropies around a bivariate joint distribution was introduced in [5] and later refined in [6]. It was named the *balance equation* and it leads to a visualization graph which is a ternary diagram, or *de Finetti diagram*, of entropies, also called the *entropy triangle (ET)*. Both tools have been used to evaluate multiclass classifiers in [7] using their joint distribution of results implicit in the confusion matrix over the classified as evaluated on the train and test data [3,4].

Both tools are based on an often overlooked decomposition of the joint entropy of two random variables [5]. Figure 1 depicts this decomposition showing the three crucial regions:

- The *divergence with respect to uniformity*, $\Delta H_{P_X \cdot P_Y}$, between the joint distribution where P_X and P_Y are independent and the uniform distributions with the same cardinality of events as P_X and P_Y.

$$\Delta H_{P_X \cdot P_Y} = H_{U_X \cdot U_Y} - H_{P_X \cdot P_Y}.$$

- The *mutual information*, $MI_{P_{XY}}$, quantifies the force of the stochastic binding between P_X and P_Y.

$$MI_{P_{XY}} = H_{P_X \cdot P_Y} - H_{P_{XY}}$$

- The *variation of information*, $VI_{P_{XY}}$, embodies the residual entropy, not used in binding the variables.

$$VI_{P_{XY}} = H_{P_{X|Y}} + H_{P_{Y|X}}$$

Each of these quantities provide intuitions into the behavior of P_X, P_Y and P_{XY} used to advantage in applications (cfr. Sect. 1.3), and we would like to reproduce them in a multivariate setting for applications like feature filtering [8] or multi-label classification [9].

Note that all of these quantities are positive. In fact from the previous decomposition the following *balance equation* is evident,

$$H_{U_X \cdot U_Y} = \Delta H_{P_X \cdot P_Y} + 2 * MI_{P_{XY}} + VI_{P_{XY}} \tag{1}$$
$$0 \le \Delta H_{P_X \cdot P_Y}, MI_{P_{XY}}, VI_{P_{XY}} \le H_{U_X \cdot U_Y}$$

where the bounds are easily obtained from distributional considerations [5].

1.2   From the Balance Equation to the Entropy Triangle

If we normalize (1) by the overall entropy $H_{U_X \cdot U_Y}$ we obtain

$$1 = \Delta' H_{P_X \cdot P_Y} + 2 * MI'_{P_{XY}} + VI'_{P_{XY}} \tag{2}$$
$$0 \le \Delta' H_{P_X \cdot P_Y}, MI'_{P_{XY}}, VI'_{P_{XY}} \le 1$$

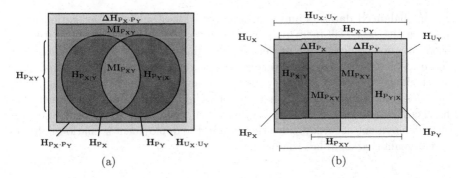

Fig. 1. Extended entropy diagrams related to a bivariate distribution, from [5]. The bounding rectangle is the joint entropy of two uniform (hence independent) distributions U_X and U_Y of the same cardinality as input probability distribution P_X and output P_Y, resp. The expected mutual information $MI_{P_{XY}}$ appears *twice* in (a) and this makes the diagram split for each variable symmetrically in (b).

Equation (2) is the 2-simplex in normalized $\Delta H'_{P_X \cdot P_Y} \times 2MI'_{P_{XY}} \times VI'_{P_{XY}}$ space. Each joint distribution P_{XY} can be characterized by its *joint entropy fractions*, $F(P_{XY}) = [\Delta H'_{P_{XY}}, 2 \times MI'_{P_{XY}}, VI'_{P_{XY}}]$. Its projection onto the plane with director vector $(1,1,1)$ is its *de Finetti (entropy) diagram*, represented in Fig. 2, so *every binary distribution shows as a point in the triangle*.

The de Finetti entropy diagram shows as an equilateral triangle, hence the alternative name *entropy triangle*, each of whose sides and vertices represents classifier performance-related *qualities*:

- The lower side is the geometric locus of distributions with independent marginals: if $P_{XY} = P_X \cdot P_Y$ then $F(P_{XY}) = [\cdot, 0, \cdot]$.
- The left side is the geometric locus of distributions with uniform marginals. If $P_X = U_X$ and $P_Y = U_Y$ then $F(P_{XY}) = [0, \cdot, \cdot]$.
- Finally, the right-hand side is the locus of distributions with identical marginals: if $P_X = P_Y$—that is, $H_{P_X} = H_{P_Y} = MI_{P_{XY}}$—then $F(P_{XY}) = [\cdot, \cdot, 0]$.

1.3 Application: Evaluating Classifiers

The evaluation of classifiers is fairly simple using the schematic in Fig. 2.

1. Classifiers on the bottom side of the triangle *transmit no mutual information* from input to output: they have not profited by being exposed to the data.
2. Classifiers on the right hand side have diagonal confusion matrices, hence *perfect (standard) accuracy*.
3. Classifiers on the left hand side operate on perfectly balanced data distributions, hence they are *solving the most difficult multiclass problem* (from the point of view of an uninformed decision).

Of course, combinations of these conditions provide specific kinds of classifiers. Those at the apex or close to it are obtaining the highest accuracy possible on very balanced datasets and transmitting a lot of mutual information hence they are the *best classifiers* possible. Those at or close to the left vertex are essentially not doing any job on very difficult data: they are *the worst classifiers*. Those at or close to the right vertex are not doing any job on very easy data for which they claim to have very high accuracy: they are *specialized (majority) classifiers* and our intuition is that they are the kind of classifiers that generate the accuracy paradox, whereby classifiers with higher test set accuracy provide lower deployment accuracy, since the data in the deployment scenario might not be as imbalanced as in lab conditions

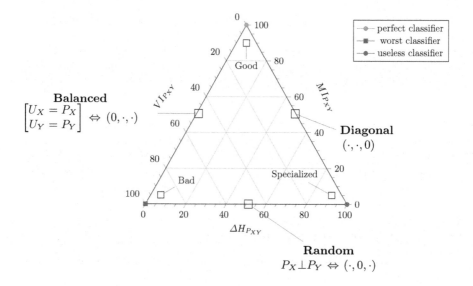

Fig. 2. Schematic Entropy Triangle showing interpretable zones and extreme cases of classifiers. The annotations on the center of each side are meant to hold for that whole side.

In just this guise, the ET has already been successfully used in the evaluation of Speech Recognition systems [5,10], sentiment analysis [7], and other classification tasks.

1.4   Motivation

We would like to use the balance equation and entropy triangle to investigate learning and performance limitations in the case of supervised and unsupervised tasks—that is, directly on the observation data—and not on the results of classification—that is, on the confusion matrices of classifiers.

For that purpose we would like to be able to access similar results *on the multivariate data (or data plus label data)*. But, instead of manipulating the total entropy around a joint distribution in the style of [11,12], we would like to consider a similar decomposition to that of the bivariate entropy triangle enumerated above.

For that purpose, we first review the theory and methods behind the balance equation and the entropy triangle, we then present the analogues for multivariate distributions, our main results, and a brief sketch of an application, to end with a discussion of solved and pending issues.

2   Methods

2.1   The Split Balance Equation and Entropy Triangle

In [5] it is reasoned how (1) may be split into two equations. Briefly, since both U_X and U_Y on the one hand and P_X and P_Y are independent as marginals of U_{XY} and Q_{XY}, respectively, we may write:

$$\Delta H_{P_X P_Y} = (H_{U_X} - H_{P_X}) + (H_{U_Y} - H_{P_Y}) = \Delta H_{P_X} + \Delta H_{P_Y} \qquad (3)$$

where

$$\Delta H_{P_X} = H_{U_X} - H_{P_X} \qquad\qquad \Delta H_{P_Y} = H_{U_Y} - H_{P_Y} \qquad (4)$$

This and the occurrence of twice the expected mutual information in Eq. (1) suggests a different information diagram, depicted in Fig. 1(b). Both variables X and Y now appear somehow decoupled—in the sense that the areas representing them are disjoint—yet there is a strong coupling in that the expected mutual information appears in both H_{P_X} and H_{P_Y}.

$$H_{U_X} = \Delta H_{P_X} + MI_{P_{XY}} + H_{P_{X|Y}} \qquad H_{U_Y} = \Delta H_{P_Y} + MI_{P_{XY}} + H_{P_{Y|X}}. \qquad (5)$$

The *split entropy triangle* focuses on these quantities *for each component variable or marginal distribution in the joint distribution*. They describe the *marginal fractions* of entropy when the normalization is done with H_{U_X} and H_{U_Y} respectively

$$F_X(P_{XY}) = [\Delta H'_{P_X}, MI'_{P_{XY}}, VI'_X = H'_{P_{X|Y}}] \qquad (6)$$
$$F_Y(P_{XY}) = [\Delta H'_{P_Y}, MI'_{P_{XY}}, VI'_Y = H'_{P_{Y|X}}]$$

hence we may consider the de Finetti marginal entropy diagrams for both F_X and F_Y to visualize the entropy changes from input to output.

3   Results

In this section we generalize the results presented in Sect. 2 to the multivariate setting. For that purpose, given a multivariate distribution $P_{\overline{X}}$, let $\Pi_{\overline{X}} = \prod_{i=1}^n P_{X_i}$ be the (jointly) independent distribution with similar marginals to $P_{\overline{X}}$ and $U_{\overline{X}} = \prod_{i=1}^n U_{X_i}$ be the uniform distribution with identical support.

3.1   The Multivariate Entropy Triangle

The Multivariate Balance Equation. For the purpose of highlighting the divergence with the uniform, we introduce:

$$\Delta H_{\Pi_{\overline{X}}} = H_{U_{\overline{X}}} - H_{\Pi_{\overline{X}}} \tag{7}$$

From a philosophical standpoint, we must also consider the fact that every random variable has a residual entropy which might not be explained away by the information provided by the other variables. $H_{P_{X_i | X_i^c}}$ where $X_i^c = \overline{X} \setminus \{X_i\}$.

We call *multivariate variation of information or multivariate residual entropy*, as a generalization of the same quantity in the bivariate case, the sum of these quantities across the set of random variables:

$$VI_{P_{\overline{X}}} = \sum_{i=1}^{n} H_{P_{X_i | X_i^c}} . \tag{8}$$

Both the divergence from uniformity and the variation of information have readily available interpretations as areas in the generalization of Fig. 1 that is represented in Fig. 3, as the yellow and red areas, respectively.

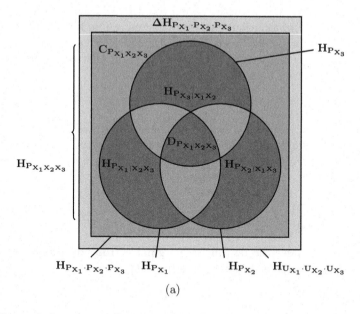

(a)

Fig. 3. Extended entropy diagram of a trivariate distribution. The bounding rectangle is the joint entropy of uniform (hence independent) distributions U_{X_i} of the same cardinality as distribution P_{X_i}. The green area is the sum of the multiinformation (total correlation) $C_{P_{\overline{X}}}$ and the dual total correlation $D_{P_{\overline{X}}}$. Th case illustrated is $n = 3$ since higher orders are difficult to visualize in this guise (Color figure online).

The differences with the bivariate case concentrate in the green areas of Fig. 3, instantiated for $n = 3$. The outer area represents the *total correlation* [13] or *multiinformation* [14]

$$C_{P_{\overline{X}}} = H_{\Pi_{\overline{X}}} - H_{P_{\overline{X}}} \tag{9}$$

while the inner area represents the *dual total correlation* [12, 15]

$$D_{P_{\overline{X}}} = H_{P_{\overline{X}}} - VI_{P_{\overline{X}}} \tag{10}$$

Each of these measures capture a different part of the stochastic binding between the diverse combinations of the variables in $\overline{X}$, as a correlate of the fact that they are represented by different areas.

For the multivariate case we propose to use the addition of both quantities as a third coordinate measuring this total amount of stochastic binding or correlation, and call it the *bound information of* $\overline{X}$,

$$M_{P_{\overline{X}}} = C_{P_{\overline{X}}} + D_{P_{\overline{X}}}. \tag{11}$$

Notice that in the bivariate case we have $C_{P_{XY}} = D_{P_{XY}} = MI_{P_{XY}}$ whence the total bound information was twice this quantity in (1), $M_{P_{XY}} = 2 \cdot MI_{P_{XY}}$.

In the new variables it is easy to write that

Theorem 1 (Multivariate Balance Equation). *Let* $P_{\overline{X}}$ *be an arbitrary discrete distribution over the set of random variables* $\overline{X}$. *Then, with the definitions above, the following balance equation holds*

$$H_{U_{\overline{X}}} = \Delta H_{\Pi_{\overline{X}}} + M_{P_{\overline{X}}} + VI_{P_{\overline{X}}} \tag{12}$$

Proof. A simple matter of adding together (7), (8) and (11) and cancelling terms. □

The Multivariate Entropy Triangle (MET). Similarly to the procedure (2), we may normalize the multivariate balance equation by $H_{U_{\overline{X}}}$ to obtain

$$1 = \Delta H'_{\Pi_{\overline{X}}} + M'_{P_{\overline{X}}} + VI'_{P_{\overline{X}}} \tag{13}$$
$$0 \leq \Delta H'_{\Pi_{\overline{X}}}, M'_{P_{\overline{X}}}, VI'_{P_{\overline{X}}} \leq 1$$

This also admits a representation in terms of a de Finetti diagram on the joint entropy fractions $F(P_{\overline{X}}) = [\Delta H'_{P_{\overline{X}}}, M'_{P_{\overline{X}}}, VI'_{P_{\overline{X}}}]$. with similar meaning as before:

- The lower side is the geometric locus of distributions with independent marginals: if $P_{\overline{X}} = \Pi_{\overline{X}} = \Pi_{i=1}^{n} P_{X_i}$ then $F(P_{\overline{X}}) = [\cdot, 0, \cdot]$.
- The left side is the geometric locus of distributions with uniform marginals. If $P_{X_i} = U_{X_i}, 1 \leq i \leq n$ then $F(P_{\overline{X}}) = [0, \cdot, \cdot]$.
- The right-hand side is the locus of distributions with identical marginals: if $P_{X_i} = P_{X_j}, i \neq j$ then $F(P_{\overline{X}}) = [\cdot, \cdot, 0]$.

3.2 The Multisplit Entropy Triangle

The Multisplit Balance Equation. Notice that since uniform distributions are independent, from (7) we may write:

$$\Delta H_{P_{\overline{X}}} = \sum_{i=1}^{n} H_{U_{X_i}} - \sum_{i=1}^{n} H_{P_{X_i}} = \sum_{i=1}^{n} H_{U_{X_i}} - H_{P_{X_i}} = \sum_{i=1}^{n} \Delta H_{P_{X_i}} \qquad (14)$$

where $\Delta H_{P_{X_i}} = H_{U_{X_i}} - H_{P_{X_i}}$ defines the divergence of each of the component random variables.

As in the case of $\Delta H_{P_{\overline{X}}}$ and $VI_{P_{\overline{X}}}$, $M_{P_{\overline{X}}}$ may be written in terms of the component entropies:

$$M_{P_{\overline{X}}} = (H_{\Pi_{\overline{X}}} - H_{P\overline{X}}) + (H_{P\overline{X}} - VI_{P_{\overline{X}}}) = H_{\Pi_{\overline{X}}} - VI_{P_{\overline{X}}}$$

$$= \sum_{i=1}^{n} H_{P_{X_i}} - \sum_{i=1}^{n} H_{P_{X_i \mid X_i^c}} = \sum_{i=1}^{n} (H_{P_{X_i}} - H_{P_{X_i \mid X_i^c}}) \qquad (15)$$

and let us call $M_{P_{X_i}} = H_{P_{X_i}} - H_{P_{X_i \mid X_i^c}}$, the *bound information (of X_i)*, the amount of entropy of P_{X_i} that is bound through dependences to the marginal distributions of different orders of $P_{X_i^c}$. This suggests that the decomposition of entropies hold individually. Indeed:

Theorem 2 (Multisplit Balance Equation). *Let $P_{\overline{X}}$ be an arbitrary discrete distribution over the set of random variables $\overline{X} = \{X_i\}_{i=1}^{n}$. Then, with the definitions above, the balance equation holds for each variable individually:*

$$H_{U_{X_i}} = \Delta H_{P_{X_i}} + M_{P_{X_i}} + H_{P_{X_i \mid X_i^c}}, \quad 1 \le i \le n \qquad (16)$$

Proof. We notice that:

$$H_{U_{X_i}} = (H_{U_{X_i}} - H_{P_{X_i}}) + (H_{P_{X_i}} - H_{P_{X_i \mid X_i^c}}) + H_{P_{X_i \mid X_i^c}}$$

and then we identify the terms with the names defined above.   □

Under this new point of view, the aggregate balance equation (12) is just the addition of the individual (16) over all random variables.

The Multivariate Split Triangle. It is clear that the normalization carried out for (2) and (15) can also be carried for the split balance equations (16), but in this case we use each of the individual $H_{U_{X_i}}$ to obtain:

$$1 = \Delta H'_{P_{X_i}} + M'_{P_{X_i}} + H'_{P_{X_i \mid X_i^c}}, \quad 1 \le i \le n \qquad (17)$$

$$0 \le \Delta H'_{P_{X_i}}, M'_{P_{X_i}}, H'_{P_{X_i \mid X_i^c}} \le 1$$

Then for each multivariate $\overline{X} = \{X_i\}_{i=1}^{n}$ we may write the coordinates in a de Finetti diagram as $F(P_{X_i}) = [\Delta H'_{P_{X_i}}, M'_{P_{X_i}}, VI'_{P_{X_i}}]$, with similar meaning as before. Notice, that despite the fact that these coordinates all refer to potentially different entropy levels, since the normalizing $H_{U_{X_i}}$ may be greatly different, in the normalized form they can all be represented in the same entropy triangle. Examples of the multisplit entropy triangle can be found in Fig. 5.

3.3 Application: Characterizing the Information Content of Datasets

We know tackle the problem of characterizing the information content of machine learning datasets. For that purpose, we used the R environment [16] and databases from the vcd [17] and mlbench [18] packages, some of which belong to the UCI repository [19]. The visualizations are done using our own R package[1]—under heavy development, at present—with the help of the ggtern package for drawing ternary diagrams [20].

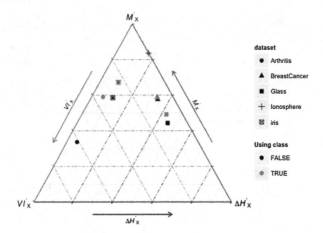

Fig. 4. Aggregated Multivariate Source Entropy Triangle for some datasets, considering their class label (black) and without it (red). Note how some databases' bound information $M_{P_{\overline{X}}}$ does not change (Ionosphere, BreastCancer), while others' may change wildly (Arthritis) (Color figure online).

To better assess the theory, instead of selecting unsupervised (clustering) data, we selected supervised multi-class classification data for the Arthritis,

Table 1. Some datasets considered in this study

	Dataset	Features	Class name	Num. Classes
1	Ionosphere	35	Class	2
2	iris	5	Species	3
3	Glass	10	Type	7
4	Arthritis	5	Improved	3
5	BreastCancer	11	Class	2

---

[1] https://github.com/FJValverde/entropies.git.

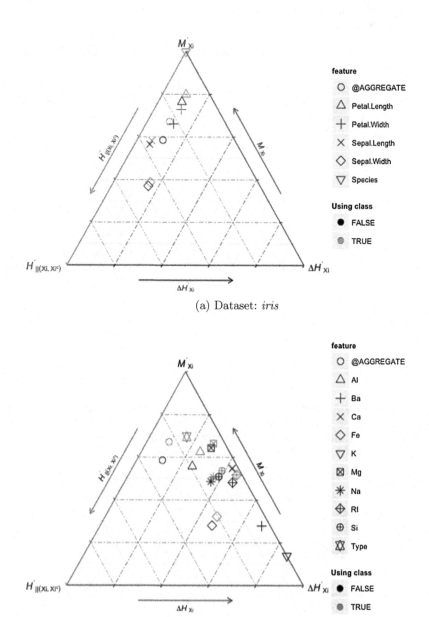

(a) Dataset: *iris*

(b) Dataset: *Glass*

Fig. 5. Multivariate Source Entropy Triangles for the iris **and** Glass **data with and without the class label,** *Species* **and** *Type*, **respectively.** The aggregate entropies as in the previous Figure are under label *AGGREGATE*

iris, Ionosphere, Glass and BreastCancer databases since they are wide-spread and practitioners already have their own intuition as to whether our inferences are likely or not. Table 1 lists their main characteristics.

Our main interest here is how does the inclusion of the classification label transform the entropies in the set. Figure 4 shows the plot of the balance of entropies for the five datasets under study, and we can see clearly that the shifting of the aggregate entropy balance when the class labels are added is a peculiarity of each dataset: some change wildly, like Arthritis, while other barely change, like Ionosphere. The rest are within those two extremes.

We interpret this to mean that for Ionosphere the information needed to characterize the label can already be found in the features, whereas in Arthritis this is not the case by far. To support this claim we look at how the individual features' balance change by the inclusion of the class label.

Figure 5 shows the multisplit ET for databases iris and Glass, that are among those that change their balance point somewhat. Whereas in iris the balance point of each feature rises slightly, betraying an increase in total bound information that is therefore translated to the aggregate balance, in Glass the increment is due to the increase in total bound information of only some of the features. Indeed, for Ionosphere (not shown), no feature increases its bound information.

4   Discussion and Further Work

We believe we have found an informative and promising representation for the entropic content of databases that deserves better exploration in further work. A brief analysis has shown that it is possible to detect which features contribute the most to the total bound information in a classification dataset, which is one of the "substances" whose transmission it to be maximized in classification tasks.

The combination of this representation with that already introduced will allow us to explore in future work how information is transmitted from the data in the datasets to the intelligence represented by classifiers in machine learning tasks, including multiclass and multilabel classification.

References

1. McGill, W.J.: Multivariate information transmission. Psychometrika **19**(2), 97–116 (1954)
2. Shannon, C.E.: A mathematical theory of Communication. Bell Syst. Techn. J. **XXVII**(3), 379–423 (1948)
3. Murphy, K.P.: Machine Learning. A Probabilistic Perspective. MIT Press, Cambridge (2012)
4. Theodoridis, S., Koutroumbas, K.: Pattern Recognition. Academic Press, Orlando (2006)

5. Valverde-Albacete, F.J., Peláez-Moreno, C.: Two information-theoretic tools to assess the performance of multi-class classifiers. Pattern Recogn. Lett. **31**(12), 1665–1671 (2010)
6. Valverde-Albacete, F.J., Peláez-Moreno, C.: 100% classification accuracy considered harmful: the normalized information transfer factor explains the accuracy paradox. PLOS ONE **9**(1), e84217 (2014)
7. Valverde-Albacete, F.J., Carrillo-de-Albornoz, J., Peláez-Moreno, C.: A proposal for new evaluation metrics and result visualization technique for sentiment analysis tasks. In: Forner, P., Müller, H., Paredes, R., Rosso, P., Stein, B. (eds.) CLEF 2013. LNCS, vol. 8138, pp. 41–52. Springer, Heidelberg (2013)
8. Brown, G., Pocock, A., Zhao, M.J., Luján, M.: Conditional likelihood maximisation: a unifying framework for information theoretic feature selection. J. Mach. Learn. Res. **13**(1), 27–66 (2012)
9. Gibaja, E., Ventura, S.: A tutorial on multilabel learning. ACM Comput. Surv. (CSUR) **47**(3), 1–38 (2015)
10. Mejía-Navarrete, D., Gallardo-Antolín, A., Peláez-Moreno, C., Valverde-Albacete, F.J.: Feature extraction assessment for an acoustic-event classification task using the entropy triangle. In: Interspeech 2010: 12th Annual Conference of the International Speech Communication Association (2011)
11. Han, T.S.: Linear dependence structure of the entropy space. Inf. Control **29**, 337–368 (1975)
12. Han, T.S.: Nonnegative entropy measures of multivariate symmetric correlations. Inf. Control **36**(2), 133–156 (1978)
13. Watanabe, S.: Information theoretical analysis of multivariate correlation. IBM Corp. J. Res. Dev. **4**(1), 66–82 (1960)
14. Studený, M., Vejnarová, J.: The multiinformation function as a tool for measuring stochastic dependence. In: Jordan, M.I. (ed.) Learning in Graphical Models. NATO ASI Series, vol. 89, pp. 261–297. Springer, Netherlands (1998)
15. Abdallah, S.A., Plumbley, M.D.: A measure of statistical complexity based on predictive information with application to finite spin systems. Phys. Lett. A **376**(4), 275–281 (2012)
16. R Core Team: R A Language and Environment for Statistical Computing. R Foundation for Statistical Computing, Vienna, Austria (2015)
17. Meyer, D., Zeileis, A., Hornik, K.: VCD: Visualizing Categorical Data. R package version 1.4-1 (2015)
18. Leisch, F., Dimitriadou, E.: mlbench: Machine Learning Benchmark Problems. R package version 2.1-1 (2010)
19. Lichman, M.: UCI Machine Learning Repository. University of California, Irvine (2013)
20. Hamilton, N.: ggtern: An Extension to ggplot2, for the Creation of Ternary Diagrams. R package version 1.0.6.1 (2015)

Motivational Engine with Sub-goal Identification in Neuroevolution Based Cognitive Robotics

Rodrigo Salgado, Abraham Prieto, Pilar Caamaño, Francisco Bellas, and Richard J. Duro[✉]

Integrated Group for Engineering Research, Universidade da Coruña, Ferrol, Spain
{rodrigo.salgado,abprieto,pcsobrino,francisco.bellas, richard}@udc.es
http://www.gii.udc.es

Abstract. A first approach towards a new motivational system for an autonomous robot that can learn chains of sub-goals leading to a final reward is proposed in this paper. The motivational system provides the motivation that guides the robot operation according to its knowledge of its sensorial space so that rewards are maximized during its lifetime. In order to do this, a motivational engine progressively and interactively creates an internal model of expected future reward (value function) for areas of the robot's state space, through a neuroevolutionary process, over samples obtained in the sensorial (state space) traces followed by the robot whenever it obtained a reward. To improve this modelling process, a strategy is proposed to decompose the global value function leading to the reward or goal into several more local ones, thus discovering sub-goals that simplify the whole learning process and that can be reused in the future. The motivational engine is tested in a simulated experiment with very promising results.

Keywords: Neuroevolution · Cognitive systems · Motivation · Autonomous robots

1 Introduction

This paper deals with motivations in the framework of cognitive architectures. The basic function of a motivational system is to allow an agent to choose between courses of action as a function of how appropriate the state space points they lead to are in order to improve the chances of achieving a goal (obtain a reward). Specifically, a motivational system must provide the agent with relative evaluations of state space points in terms of their usefulness to achieve a goal. Note that a goal in this paper is taken as a point in the state space of the agent where a reward (utility) is obtained. This way, the agent can choose the most appropriate action or behavior, out of those accessible to it from its current situation (point in state space), by evaluating the suitability of the point it will end up in. Goals have led to the concept of Extrinsic Motivations in the literature [1], mostly from a psychological viewpoint.

Computationally, what the agent requires is an internal function that compiles its experience related to how good the different areas of its state space were in terms of

© Springer International Publishing Switzerland 2016
F. Martínez-Álvarez et al. (Eds.): HAIS 2016, LNAI 9648, pp. 659–670, 2016.
DOI: 10.1007/978-3-319-32034-2_55

leading it to a goal. That is, a function that assigns a probability of achieving utility starting from that area and that leads the agent more naturally towards the goal along paths in its state space of monotonically increasing probability of expected utility. This is what is called a value function (*VF*). It is an internal representation created by the agent where it associates each point of its state space (ideally continuous) to this smoothed representation of the probability it has of reaching a goal from that particular point modulated by the expected utility value of the goal point. The ideal or optimal value function for a robot in a given environment or succession of environments is the one that allows the robot to achieve the largest accumulated reward during its lifetime. This function does not necessarily have to reflect the real utility provided by the environment, it just needs to be useful to achieve the maximum possible utility in a consistent manner. In this paper we address the problem of how to progressively construct this optimal value function through interaction with the environment and of how to restructure it to make it more accessible in complex situations.

We assume that the agent starts with no knowledge of its environment, it has no idea of what points in state space provide utility or how to reach them. Thus, initially the system needs to explore in order to find points that provide utility (goals) before it can start developing VFs that lead to those points. Examples of motivational approaches for exploration found in the literature are those guided by curiosity [2, 3], interestingness [4], exploration bonus [5]; among others. Many authors have resorted to these types of exploration drivers, which have traditionally been called Intrinsic Motivations [6]. The whole purpose of the study of motivational architectures is to achieve the right balance between intrinsic and extrinsic motivations and provide ways to construct representations of the value functions that are useful to the agent.

Due to the large and continuous state spaces that need to be addressed and the different tasks, constraints and dynamic environments a life-long learning robot must be able to handle, monolithic value functions for goals really make no sense. More versatile representations with partial reusable value functions corresponding to sub-goals that can be chained together to achieve a goal seem like a much more interesting approach. We define a sub-goal as a point in the agent´s state space that, even though it does not have to be directly linked to a reward (it may produce no reward at all), the agent deems that it is useful as a starting or intermediate point in order to reach one or several different goals. Thus, sub-goals are a construct of the agent to which it assigns value because its experience tells it that they facilitate achieving goals.

The identification of sub-goals and of how to combine them to achieve a goal are open research issues. Most authors address the identification problem through the analysis of the state space, discovering so-called bottleneck points or regions the agent frequently visits when a goal is successfully achieved [7]. Different approaches have been proposed for the identification of bottleneck points. In some, such as diverse density [7], Q-cut dynamics [8], betweenness centrality [9] or clustering [10], the authors analyze the graphs identifying the transitional states more frequently visited by the agents, but mostly over discrete valued state spaces. It is only recently that continuous domains are starting to be addressed. Examples of this are [11, 12].

In this paper we consider an initial integrated approximation to this complete problem in terms of how to adaptively combine intrinsic and extrinsic motivations into an integrated motivational architecture that allows an artificial agent to find goals and decompose them into sub-goals that can be chained to facilitate achieving the final goal. This approximation is based on a neuroevolutionarily learnt value function where the equilibrium between intrinsic and extrinsic motivations as well as its decomposition into sub-value functions is autonomously achieved.

2 Motivational Engine

The problem faced here can be formulated as follows: there is a robot in an unknown environment with an operational goal that must be achieved. There exists a *utility function* (U) that provides a scalar value, a reward, for some perceptual states $\tau_i(t)$. A *perceptual state* ($\tau(t)$) is a vector made up of the sensorial information the robot acquires from its environment in a given instant of time and it is a point in state space. We assume that the robot operates in a continuous dynamic environment, so the perceptual states are not discrete. Additionally, things can change producing a certain degree of dynamicity in the domain the robot has to deal with.

The objective of the motivational engine is to provide an estimated evaluation for any possible state according to a set of autonomously created motivations that guide its operation. Specifically, the motivational engine evaluates each possible future state τ ($t + 1$) based on three main motivational components: blind intrinsic motivation (I_b), extrinsic motivation (E) and competence based intrinsic motivation (I_{cb}).

Blind intrinsic motivation (I_b). This first component of the motivational system guides the robot behaviour towards the discovery of unvisited states in the perceptual space and operates as an explorative process. Its implementation is based on the concept of *novelty*, which is a distance measurement between perceptual states. To compute it, a trajectory buffer must be created that stores all the perceptual states the robot has experienced in the last M instants of time. Formally, the *novelty* of the k-th candidate state $\tau_{c,k}$ proposed by the action chooser is:

$$I_b = Nov_k = \frac{1}{M} \sum_{i=1}^{M} dist(\tau_{c,k} - \tau_i)^n \quad with\ k = 1\ to\ N$$

where n is a coefficient that regulates the balance between the relevance of distant and near states, τ_i is the i-th state on the trajectory buffer and N is the number of candidates considered.

Extrinsic motivation (E). The extrinsic motivation (E) guides the robot behavior towards maximizing the *utility function U*, this is, towards achieving the goal. In general, the perceptual states where the robot is able to sense utility are limited and scarce. Consequently, the robot must create an internal representation of the utility function to associate an *expected utility* to any possible perceptual state. Such internal representation is typically called a *value function (VF)* and models the previously mentioned association:

$$E = eu(t) = VF(\tau(t))$$

Thus, the extrinsic motivation (E) completely relies on the adequacy of the value function to represent the expected utility. Consequently, how this function is learnt is a key aspect of the motivational system.

In this work, *VF* learning is carried out through a neuroevolutionary approach, which is based on the learning scheme used in the Multilevel Darwinist Brain cognitive architecture [13]. This approach has the following features:

- It is an online procedure that evolves a population of ANNs that represent the *VF*.
- Each ANN is evaluated according to its prediction error over the perceptual traces that are stored in a *trace memory*, which is created as follows:
  - The perceptual states obtained during the robot operation are stored in a limited size FIFO buffer. When the robot reaches the goal state, the states remaining in the buffer are assigned a decreasing expected utility (following the classical scheme of eligibility traces used in Reinforcement Learning).
  - This list of perceptual states with an assigned utility make up a *trace* and the different traces are stored in a trace memory.
  - The trace memory has a configurable fixed capacity. When it is full, the oldest trace value is replaced by the new one.
- The population of ANNs is evolved in order to improve its predictions over the trace memory, but only for a small number of iterations to prevent its convergence towards that instance of the trace memory.
- Every time the trace memory is updated, evolution restarts from the same population.
- When the evolution finishes, the ANN with the highest fitness represents the *VF*.

As more traces are obtained by the robot, that is, as it reaches the goal more times, the *VF* becomes more accurate and, thus, the extrinsic motivation given by the *VF* is more reliable for guiding the robot operation.

Given the process and the problem, it is clear that the reliability of the expected utility provided by the value function is not constant, neither in time nor in (state) space. In the first stages of learning, there are only a small number of traces that can be used to learn the value function, so reliability remains low. Also, in regions that are far away from those where the goal was found, the *VF* is not reliable either. In order to allow the robot to make appropriate decisions, the reliability of the VF in its different regions must be taken in to account. To provide these reliability values, we combine into a certainty value the effects of two sources of uncertainty:

1. *Density certainty coefficient (C_d):* the set of traces is used to produce a sampling density model based on the distances between the samples in the traces and the candidate state. Poorly sampled areas will be associated to a lower reliability and those with higher sampling density to a higher reliability of the estimated *VF* value. This coefficient can be obtained using the following equation:

$$C_d = f(d^{-k}) = \begin{cases} 1 & \text{if } d^{-k} < d_{sat} \\ 1 - \dfrac{d^{-k} - d_{sat}}{d_{act} - d_{sat}} & \text{else} \end{cases}$$

with d^{-k} being the distance to the k-st closest sampled position stored in memory. Function f is defined by two parameters:

a. *Saturation distance (d_{sat}):* maximum distance to consider that the *VF* is completely reliable:

$$d_{sat} = \max\left(1, k * \sqrt[N]{\frac{\prod_{d=1 toN} Range_d}{N_{trace}}}\right)$$

where N is the number of sensors of the robot and N_{trace} the number of points in the trace memory, and $Range_d = \max(\tau_d) - \min(\tau_d)$, that is, the difference between the maximum and minimum value of each component of the perceptual state. Therefore, this parameter is dynamic and produces an approximation to an average distance between samples.

b. *Activation distance (d_{act}):* maximum distance to consider that the *VF* is valid.

$$d_{act} = 2 * d_{sat}$$

2. *Success certainty coefficient (C_s):* a second criterion to evaluate the reliability of the *VF* is the number of times (N_s) it guided the robot towards achieving the goal. This new coefficient is defined as:

$$Cs_i = \min\left(1, \left(\frac{N_s}{maxN_s}\right)^{\gamma}\right)$$

where γ is a reliability parameter that establishes the growth rate of this coefficient to control the relevance of the VF as a function of goal achievements. *maxN$_s$* defines the number of achievements required to set the success certainty to one.

Thus, a *global certainty coefficient (C_i)* associated to any state can be computed by combining these components:

$$C_i(\tau) = Cd_i(\tau) \cdot Cs_i(\tau)$$

The combination of the expected utility and the certainty of a state produce the resulting extrinsic evaluation of a state, which is what will finally guide the robot:

$$E_i(\tau) = C_i(\tau) \cdot eu(t)$$

Competence based intrinsic motivation (Icb$_i$). The last component of the motivational system is in charge guiding the robot to improve the *VF* model by improving the sampling of the traces used to learn it. That is, we assume that the initial traces are sub-optimal and scarce and therefore not representative enough to produce an adequate value function. This motivation seeks to expand the sampled area by seeking samples close to the boundaries of the certainty region of the value functions. To do it, we use the *saturation* and *activation* distances defined above to define the following equation for the competence based intrinsic motivation (I_{cb}):

$$Icb_i = g\left(d^{-k}\right) = \begin{cases} e^{-((x-d_{act})*\frac{2.5}{d_{sat}})^2} & if\ x < d_{act} \\ e^{-((x-d_{act})*\frac{2.5}{2*d_{sat}})^2} & otherwise \end{cases}$$

3 Sub-goal Identification

In order to reduce complexity, not to depend on trace length, and allow for knowledge reuse, it would be useful to be able to identify sub-goals that could be chained as needed in order to reach the final goals. In this line, we have developed a *sub-goal identification mechanism* with the aim of autonomously discovering sub-goals and, consequently, of dividing the whole problem into smaller ones.

The identification of sub-goals is carried out by the motivational engine based on the combination of a set of criteria that propose and evaluate certain regions of the state space to be considered as new sub-goals of the problem. Currently, the criteria we are using are the following:

1. **Density:** it selects regions of state space where there is a notorious increase in the density of points belonging to traces that leading to a goal (or sub-goal).
2. **Topology:** it may include regions with high connectivity towards neighboring regions of the space, bottlenecks, etc.
3. **Distance:** generally speaking, the adequacy of a sub-goal for restructuring the *VF* increases with the distance in the state space between this sub-goal and the rest of the sub-goals

This mechanism operates continuously from the beginning of each run and, when the combination of criteria allows it, selects a given region of the perceptual space as a sub-goal. Associated to these sub-goals, new value functions VF_i are also built to restructure the global value function.

Figure 1 displays a representation of a possible configuration of the perceptual space, with a global goal (blue circle) and two sub-goals (green and red circles) with their corresponding certainty regions. This setup implies that a given candidate state can be in the influence region of different value functions and a procedure must be enabled to combine them.

Generally, the extrinsic motivational value is provided as the highest expected utility value:

$$E_g = \max_i(E_i * C_i)$$

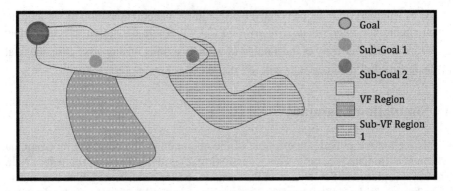

Fig. 1. Representation of different goals, sub-goals and their certainty regions (Color figure online)

Regarding the competence based intrinsic motivation (I_{cb}), the influence of each *VF* has been considered by inversely weighing the success certainty of their current *VF* to produce a global competence based intrinsic motivation value:

$$I_{cbg} = \left[1 - \prod_i Cs_i\right] * \frac{\sum_i\left[(1 - Cs_i) * I_{cbi}\right]}{\sum_i (1 - Cs_i)}$$

Being i, the index of the i-th value function.

Finally, for each candidate, n, the extrinsic E_{g_n} and intrinsic I_{cbg_n} values are combined into a final evaluation Ev_n for the nth candidate using the following expression:

$$Ev_n = \begin{cases} \dfrac{(1+C_{sgn})\cdot\in_{g_n}+(1-C_{sgn})\cdot I_{cbg_n}}{2} & \in_{g_n} > 0 \\ \dfrac{(1+C_{sgn})\cdot(\in_{g_n}+1)+(1-C_{sgn})\cdot I_{cbg_n}}{2} - 1 & else \end{cases}$$

$$\in_{gn} = \frac{\Delta E_{gn}}{max\Delta E_{gn}}$$

$$\Delta E_{gn} = E_{gn} - E_{g0}$$

$$max\Delta E_g = \frac{1}{N_t}$$

$\Delta \in_{gn}$ represents the increment in the extrinsic motivation for the nth candidate regarding the current extrinsic value (E_{g0}). $max\Delta E_g$ represents the maximum increment from one position to the next one. Since the traces are created associating a linearly decreasing expected utility, this increment is equal to the maximum expected utility divided by the size of the trace.

As as summary, it must be pointed out that in the general operation of the motivational engine, the *blind intrinsic motivation (I_b)* will guide the action selection while $E_c = I_{cb} = 0$ independently of the number of value functions. In any other case, the final evaluation of the candidate state will use the previous expression for Ev_n.

4   Simulation Example

In this section we provide an example of the operation of the complete motivational system in a simulated scenario. This scenario (Fig. 2) is divided into two parts by a wall. The robot is placed in the left part of the scenario, where it can sense a blue box and an green button. In the right side of the scenario there is a red ball (not seen by the robot as there is a wall in between). The robot is able to move on this environment and to reach the different objects. Hitting the button makes the wall open (it disappears) allowing the robot to see the ball. Whenever the robot reaches the ball, it automatically picks it up. Also, when the robot reaches the box carrying the ball, the ball is dropped in the box and the robot receives a reward. This event triggers a reset of the scenario and the robot is again placed in a random location on the left part of the arena.

With regards to the robot itself, it is provided with three sensors: distance to the green button (g), distance to the red ball (r) and distance to the blue box (b). When the robot cannot see the ball, the sensor returns the maximum distance it can measure. As for the actions (a), the robot can change its orientation by an angle between $-90°$ and $90°$, and then move fixed distance in that direction in a straight line. The robot state each iteration is given by $\tau(t) = (g,r,b)$.

This configuration implies that the robot has to learn a complex and ordered behavior. In order to achieve a reward it will first have to reach the button, then go and pick the ball, so that it can finally go to the box, drop it, and receive the reward. Initially the robot has no idea of where the reward is or of how to reach it. It will thus have to discover the reward and associate it to a point in its states space. After this it will have to learn to get to it from anywhere in the environment.

General configuration	
Iterations	20000
Candidate	32
Trace length	{10, 25, 50}
Size of memory traces	3 x trace length
Max number of sub-goals	{0, 1, 8}
Blind Intrinsic Motivation	
n	5
M	200
Extrinsic Motivation	
k	1
maxNS	20
gamma	1

Fig. 2. Simulated scenario (right) and parameters (left) used in the experiment (Color figure online)

In order to test the approach in this setup, the simulation was set up with the parameters shown on the left of Fig. 2, which were fixed for all the runs except for the size of the VF trace and the maximum number of sub-goals (and sub-VF) which were varied to test their influence on the results.

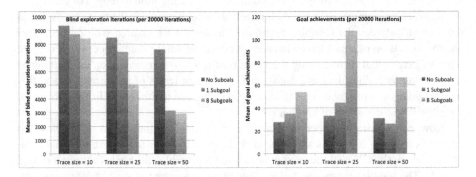

Fig. 3. Averaged results of 5 executions with different configurations of trace sizes and maximum number of allowed sub-goals (Color figure online)

Just to provide an indication of the influence of these variable parameters on the performance of the system we ran a series of tests where the global performance was measured using the number of goals achieved (for a fixed number of time steps) and the number of time steps that the blind intrinsic motivation was active (N_{bi}). The latter provides an indication of the coverage of the state space by the extrinsic motivation model. Figure 3 represents the averaged results of 5 executions with different trace

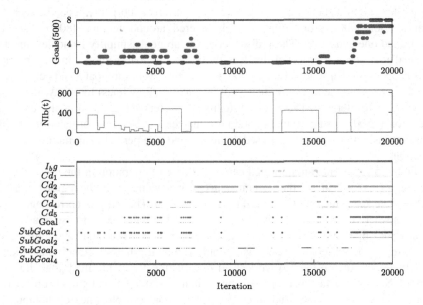

Fig. 4. Single execution with a trace size of 25 and 8 possible sub-goals (Color figure online)

lengths and maximum number of allowed sub-goals. The left graph shows the number of iterations that the robot was using blind exploration, and there is a clear inverse relationship between the trace size and N_{bi}, as well as between the number of sub-goals and N_{bi}. The right graph shows that introducing more sub-goals improves the performance of the system as it allows for the compensation of the limited length of the traces. In this problem, a value of 25 points for the trace length provides the best results due to the tradeoff between the complexity required to learn a VF created with longer traces and the limitation of small traces in order to cover the whole state space. What is more relevant here is that restructuring the value function into a combination or chaining of several simpler value functions (sub-goals) is clear in terms of performance, and this without going into its advantages in lifelong learning due to the reusability of sub-goals, which will be the subject of another paper.

Now, considering the operation of the motivational engine, Fig. 4 shows how the system is learning sub-goals and how to chain them in order to achieve the final goal. The trace length is 25 and the system is allowed 8 possible sub-goals (although it only used 5). The top plot represents the number of goals reached in the last 500 iterations. The central plot displays the average time the robot is using blind intrinsic exploration between two goal achievements ($N_{bi}(t)$). The bottom plot gives an idea of what is going on in terms of active VF and the achievement of goals and sub-goals. The certainty of each VF is depicted only when it is equal to one and the blind intrinsic component is also represented using a black line, which, as explained before, is activated when the robot is away from any certainty region. The colors corresponding to each element are indicated in the left of the graph.

The robot starts from a situation where it knows very little, as shown by the fact that it is not certain about anything (Cd values are not present), and explores intensively (strong black line). Sometimes it reaches the goal through exploration and this provides trace information that can be used later to try to discover sub-goals. It can be seen that near iteration 3000 the first sub-goal is discovered, around iteration 4800 it discovers the second one and so on. These discoveries of sub-goals simplify its achievement of the final goal, which is reflected clearly in the number of goals achieved in the top graph. This happens until around iteration 6000 where it discovers sub-goal 3 and gets trapped wandering around the area of influence of this goal (yellow lines) for many time steps. However, after iteration 15000 the system starts to recover again to finally converge (iteration 17500) to an extremely good performance and coverage of the scenario (the blind intrinsic motivation is not used anymore) and to a perfect chaining of the value functions.

Figure 5 represents an amplified capture of an early iteration in the process and a final one. There we can see the certainty and extrinsic values of all the regions along the path in state space the robot followed towards the goal. The left plot corresponds to an iteration where the robot is starting to learn. Thus, it initially needs to use blind exploration (black line) until it reaches an area where there is some certainty about the VF (in this case that of sub-goal 1, which is the only sub-goal it has adequately identified at that time and which it uses to work itself towards the VF of the final goal shown in purple). Notice also the always increasing evaluation of the VF that guides it first to the first sub-goal (green line) and after that to the goal (purple line) even though it tangentially goes through the second sub-goal. The right plot depicts the ideal behavior of the system at the end of a run. In this case, the whole of the state space is covered by VFs corresponding to the different sub-goals and, consequently, there are no iterations that require blind exploration. The robot can follow the increasing value of the VFs until it reaches the final goal. Thus, we can see the chained combination of VFs and sub-goals.

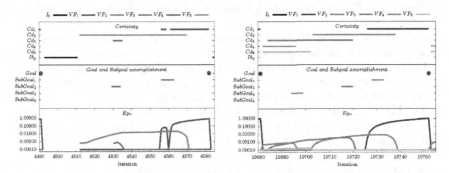

Fig. 5. Motivational engine operation in an early (left) and final (right) iteration (Color figure online)

5 Conclusions

A complete motivational system that involves the combination of intrinsic and extrinsic motivations as well as the automatic discovery and chaining of sub-goals is presented here. The system is based on a neuroevolutionary approach for learning the appropriate value functions that provide the agent with the information that allows it to choose the actions that will better lead it to its goal. This approach has shown very good results in problems where a complex combination of actions must be carried out in order to achieve the goal as shown in an example involving several steps and conditions for the goal to be achievable. We are now working on the application of this motivational engine within a Darwinist cognitive system for robots with the objective of making the robots capable of lifelong autonomous learning.

Acknowledgements. This work was partially funded by the EU's H2020 research and innovation programme under grant agreement No 640891 (DREAM project) and by the Xunta de Galicia and European Regional Development Funds under grants GRC 2013-050 and redTEIC network (R2014/037).

References

1. Ryan, R.M., Deci, E.L.: Intrinsic and extrinsic motivations: classic definitions and new directions. Contemp. Educ. Psychol. **25**, 54–67 (2000)
2. Scott, P.D., Markovitch, S.: Learning novel domains through curiosity and conjecture. In: Proceedings IJCAI 1989, pp. 669–674 (1989)

3. Shmidhuber, J.: Adaptive confidence and adaptive curiosity. Technical Report. Institut fur Informatik, Technische Universität Munchen (1991)
4. Lenat, D.B.: AM: an artificial intelligence approach to discovery in mathematics as heuristic search, Doctoral Dissertation No. STAN-CS-76-570, Department of Computer Science, Stanford University (1976)
5. Sutton, R.S.: Reinforcement learning architectures for animals. In: From Animals to Animats: Proceedings of the First International Conference on Simulation of Adaptive Behavior, pp. 288–296 (1991)
6. Oudeyer, P.Y., Kaplan, F.: What is intrinsic motivation? a typology of computational approaches. Front. Neurorobot. **1**(A.6), 1–14 (2007)
7. McGovern, A., Barto, A.: Automatic discovery of subgoals in reinforcement learning using diverse density. Technical report of the faculty publication series, Computer Science Department, University of Massachusetts, Amherst (2001)
8. Menache, I., Mannor, S., Shimkin, N.: Q-cut - dynamic discovery of sub-goals in reinforcement learning. In: Elomaa, T., Mannila, H., Toivonen, H. (eds.) ECML 2002. LNCS (LNAI), vol. 2430, pp. 295–306. Springer, Heidelberg (2002)
9. Simsek, O., Barto, A.: Betweenness centrality as a basis for forming skills. Technical report, Department of Computer Science, University of Massachusetts (2007)
10. Mannor, S., Menache, I., Hoze, A., Klein, U.: Dynamic abstraction in reinforcement learning via clustering. In: Proceedings of the Twenty-First International Conference on Machine Learning, pp. 560–567. ACM (2004)
11. Konidaris, G., Barto, A.: Sensorimotor abstraction selection for efficient, autonomous robot skill acquisition. In: 7th IEEE International Conference on Development and Learning, ICDL 2008, pp. 151–156, (2008)
12. Salge, C., Glackin, C., Polani, D.: Approximation of empowerment in the continuous domain. Adv. Complex Syst. **16**(1–2), 1250079 (2013)
13. Bellas, F., Duro, R.J., Faina, A., Souto, D.: Multilevel Darwinist Brain (MDB): artificial evolution in a cognitive architecture for real robots. IEEE Trans. Auton. Ment. Dev. **2**(4), 340–354 (2010)

Bioinformatics

TRIQ: A Comprehensive Evaluation Measure for Triclustering Algorithms

David Gutiérrez-Avilés and Cristina Rubio-Escudero[(✉)]

Department of Computer Science, University of Seville, Seville, Spain
davgutavi@gmail.com, crubioescudero@us.es

Abstract. Triclustering has shown to be a valuable tool for the analysis of microarray data since its appearance as an improvement of classical clustering and biclustering techniques. Triclustering relaxes the constraints for grouping and allows genes to be evaluated under a subset of experimental conditions and a subset of time points simultaneously. The authors previously presented a genetic algorithm, $TriGen$, that finds triclusters of gene expression dasta. They also defined three different fitness functions for $TriGen$: MSR_{3D}, LSL and MSL. In order to asses the results obtained by application of $TriGen$, a validity measure needs to be defined. Therefore, we present $TRIQ$, a validity measure which combines information from three different sources: (1) correlation among genes, conditions and times, (2) graphic validation of the patterns extracted and (3) functional annotations for the genes extracted.

Keywords: Triclustering · Validity measure · Genetic algorithms · Microarrays

1 Introduction

Data Mining has developed a vast amount of computational tools for the analysis of bioinformatics data and allows us to find new knowledge which is hidden for the human's eyesight. One of the most useful and studied approaches is the behavior pattern search in gene expression data from microarray experiments. These genes, that exhibit high correlation among their expression levels, could be involved in similar regulatory processes as relationship exists between correlation and functionality.

We focus on one behavior pattern searching technique, clustering, which analyzes the microarray dimensional space grouping genes and taking into account all experimental conditions. There are different approaches, having classic clustering techniques, which group genes based on all conditions [19], biclustering, which emerges as an evolution of clustering since it groups genes under some particular experimental conditions, and finally we have triclustering, that goes one step further by grouping genes under particular conditions and under particular time points [11], thus being capable of managing 3D data. Triclustering is therefore suitable for microarray experiment where time points are considered,

© Springer International Publishing Switzerland 2016
F. Martínez-Álvarez et al. (Eds.): HAIS 2016, LNAI 9648, pp. 673–684, 2016.
DOI: 10.1007/978-3-319-32034-2_56

which has great interest since it allows for a deep analysis of biological processes where temporary development is important.

Both biclustering and triclustering attack NP-hard problems, and thus algorithms based on heuristics are well suited for them. In [11] we presented the TriGen algorithm, a triclustering-genetic algorithm based on an evolutionary heuristic which finds patterns of similarity for genes on a three dimensional space, thus taking into account the gene,conditions and time factors.

Definition of fitness functions for the genetic algorithm is an essential task. In biclustering, a classic measure is the Mean Squared Residue (MSR) [6]. We have defined a three dimensions adaptation of this measure, MSR_{3D} [9]. Furthermore, we have defined two other fitness functions improving the behavior of MSR_{3D}. Both are based on the similarity among the slopes of the angles. The first one, Least Squared Lines (LSL) [12], measures the quality of a tricluster based on the similarity among the slopes of the angles formed by the least squares lines from each of the profiles formed by the genes, conditions and times of the tricluster. The second one, Multi Slope Measure (MSL) [10], measures the quality of a tricluster based on the similarity among the angles of the slopes formed by each profile formed by the genes, conditions and times of the tricluster.

The results obtained by the three proposed fitness functions have been validated in three different ways. First, by analyzing the correlation among the genes, conditions and times in each tricluster using two different correlation measures: Pearson [4] and Spearman [13]. Second, by a graphic validation of the patterns extracted based on the graphic representation, and third we have provided functional annotations for the genes extracted from the Gene Ontology project (GO) [1]. These three validation measures have been chosen since they are the standard ones for this topic as can be seen in [14,15,17,22,23].

However, we consider that providing a single evaluation measure capable of combining the information from the three mentioned sources of validation will be a great improvement. Therefore, in this work we propose $TRIQ$, a validation measure which combines the three previously proposed validation mechanisms (correlation, graphic validation and functional annotation of the genes).

2   Related Works

This section is to provide a general overview of triclustering published in literature. We particularly focus on the validation methods applied to assess the quality of the triclusters obtained.

In 2005, Zhao and Zaki [23] introduced the triCluster algorithm to extract patterns in 3D gene expression data. They presented a measure to assess triclusters's quality based on the symmetry property. They validated their triclusters based on their graphical representation and Gene Ontology (GO) results.

g-triCluster, an extended and generalized version of Zhao and Zaki's proposal, was published one year later [15]. The authors claimed that the symmetry property is not suitable for all patterns present in biological data and propose the Spearman rank correlation [20] as a more appropriate tricluster evaluation measure. The also showed validation results based on GO.

An evolutionary computation proposal was made in [16]. The fitness function defined is a multi-objective measure which tries to optimize three conflicting objectives: clusters size, homogeneity and gene-dimension variance of the 3D cluster. The tricluster quality validation was based on GO.

LagMiner was introduced in [22] to find time-lagged 3D clusters, what allows to find regulatory relationships among genes. It is based on a novel 3D cluster model called S^2D^3 Cluster. They evaluated their triclusters on homogeneity, regulation, minimum gene number, sample subspace size and time periods length. Their validation was based on graphical representation and GO results.

Hu *et al.* presented an approach focusing on the concept of Low-Variance 3-Cluster [14], which obeys the constraint of a low-variance distribution of cell values. This proposal uses a different functional enrichment tool called CLEAN [8], which uses GO as one of their components.

The work in [17] was focused on finding Temporal Dependency Association Rules, which relate patterns of behavior among genes. The rules obtained are to represent regulated relations among genes. They also validated their triclusters based on their graphical representation and GO results.

Summarizing, we see that the standard for validation of triclusters quality is based on their graphical representation and GO functional annotations.

3   Methodology

This section describes a novel methodology to evaluate the performance of triclustering algorithms on gene expression data. The goal is to introduce a single measure that globally assesses the quality of the triclusters generated by any triclustering algorithm. The new measure is called TRIcluster Quality ($TRIQ$).

This index takes into account three key aspects to assess the quality of triclusters obtained from gene expression data:

1. The level of biological notoriety of the clustered genes.
2. The graphic quality of the patterns that forms the tricluster.
3. The level of correlation of the tricluster's values.

Biological notoriety and graphical quality are standards in literature for tricluster quality assessment as seen in Sect. 2. Correlation has been included since it provides statistical information on the relation of dependence among the components of the triclusters (gene, condition and time) [4,13].

These three aspects are reflected within the framework $TRIQ$ in its four terms of the general equation: Biological Quality ($BIOQ$) or biological quality of triclusters, Graphical Quality (GRQ) or graphical quality of triclusters, Pearson Quality (PEQ) or value for the Pearson correlation of triclusters and Spearman Quality (SPQ) or values for the Spearman correlation.

The influence of each term is reflected in Eq. 1, where $TRIQ$ is defined as the weighted sum of each of the four aforementioned terms. Therefore, four associated weights must be defined: the weight for ($BIOQ$), denoted as W_{bio};

the weight for (GRQ), denoted as W_{gr}; the weight for (PEQ), denoted as W_{pe}; and the weight for (SPQ), denoted as W_{sp}.

$$TRIQ(TRI) = \frac{1}{W_{bio} + W_{gr} + W_{pe} + W_{sp}} *$$
$$[W_{bio} * BIOQ(TRI) + W_{gr} * GRQ(TRI)+ \qquad (1)$$
$$W_{pe} * PEQ(TRI) + W_{sp} * SPQ(TRI)]$$

3.1 BIOQ

The Gene Ontology Project (GO) [1] is a major bioinformatics initiative with the aim of standardizing the representation of gene and gene product attributes across species and databases. The biological quality of a tricluster is calculated based on the GO analysis that identifies, for a set of genes in a tricluster, the terms listed in each of the three available ontologies: biological processes, cellular components and molecular functions.

The GO analysis used in the calculation of $BIOQ$ is done with the software Ontologizer [3]. This analysis, besides identifying the annotated terms, performs the statistical analysis for the over-representation of those terms, also providing their p-value. However, it is also important to take into account how deep in the ontology the terms are annotated, with the deeper terms being more specific than the superficial ones [18]. In order to represent that information in the $BIOQ$ measure, the biological quality of a tricluster TRI is defined in Eq. 2 as the normalization of the biological significance, SIG_{bio}, of the set of genes TRI_G:

$$BIOQ(TRI) = \frac{SIG_{bio}(TRI_G)}{S_{l_{|LV|}}} \qquad (2)$$

where $S_{l_{|LV|}}$ denotes the value of maximum possible score for the total existing levels set LV, as established in Table 1.

The scoring system, in which the index is based, must be designed prior to the definition of SIG_{bio}. An interval for a given level $Inter_l$ is defined by a weight value w_l for the level, and by the lower and upper bounds (inf_l and sup_l, respectively), being an open-closed p-values interval (Eq. 3a). The set of existing LV consists of all levels with Inf_l smaller or equal to a minimum p-value, th. For each interval of each level $Inter_l$, the weight value w_l is the value of the previous level plus the level difference factor d (Eq. 3c.); Inf_l is defined as the division between the pitch factor interval s and the base interval b raised to the power of l factor (Eq. 3d), and sup_l is set to the division between s and b raised to the power of l minus 1 (Eq. 3e).

$$inter_l = \langle w_l, (inf_l, sup_l] \rangle \tag{3a}$$

$$LV = \forall\, l \in \mathbb{N} : inf_l \leq th \tag{3b}$$

$$w_l = [(l-1)*d] + 1 \tag{3c}$$

$$inf_l = \frac{s}{b^l} \tag{3d}$$

$$sup_l = \frac{s}{b^{(l-1)}} \tag{3e}$$

All biological significance intervals for the configuration detailed in Eq. 4 are shown in Table 1. For each row, weight (w_l) and range ($inter_l$) for each level (L) sorted in ascending order are shown. Each interval provides a set of p-values where their significance is directly related to the corresponding level, that is, a p-value is better the higher the level to which it belongs is (a p-value is better the closer to zero it is).

$$th = 1.0 \times 10^{-40}$$
$$d = 10.0$$
$$b = 10.0 \tag{4}$$
$$s = 1.0$$
$$LV = \{1, \ldots, 41\}$$

The biological significance for all genes in TRI_G is defined as the sum of the score for each level in the GO analysis (Eq. 5c), by taking into account all levels of l and predefined intervals $inter_l$.

S_l score for each level is defined as the multiplication of the concentration level (C_l) by the weight w_l and the level l, plus a function of maximum bonus dependent with the maximum level l_{max} found for all analyzed genes TRI_G (Eq. 5c). C_l is defined as the number of terms located on this level Te_l divided by the total of terms, Te, from the GO analysis results (Eq. 5c).

The bonus feature f_{bonus} is defined as the sum of the peak reached by TRI_G plus the bonus factor V_{bonus} (Eq. 5d).

$$SIG_{bio}(TRI_G) = \sum_{l \in LV} S_l \tag{5a}$$

$$S_l = [C_l * w_l * l] + f_{bonus}(l_{max}) \tag{5b}$$

$$C_l = \frac{Te_l}{Te} \tag{5c}$$

$$f_{bonus}(l_{max}) = l_{max} + V_{bonus} \tag{5d}$$

Table 1. Biological significance.

Level (l)	Weight (w_l)	Interval ($inter_l$)
41	401	(0.0E-00,1.0E-40]
40	391	(1.0E-40,1.0E-39]
39	381	(1.0E-39,1.0E-38]
38	371	(1.0E-38,1.0E-37]
37	361	(1.0E-37,1.0E-36]
36	351	(1.0E-36,1.0E-35]
35	341	(1.0E-35,1.0E-34]
34	331	(1.0E-34,1.0E-33]
33	321	(1.0E-33,1.0E-32]
32	311	(1.0E-32,1.0E-31]
31	301	(1.0E-31,1.0E-30]
30	291	(1.0E-30,1.0E-29]
29	281	(1.0E-29,1.0E-28]
28	271	(1.0E-28,1.0E-27]
27	261	(1.0E-27,1.0E-26]
26	251	(1.0E-26,1.0E-25]
25	241	(1.0E-25,1.0E-24]
24	231	(1.0E-24,1.0E-23]
23	221	(1.0E-23,1.0E-22]
22	211	(1.0E-22,1.0E-21]
21	201	(1.0E-21,1.0E-20]
20	191	(1.0E-20,1.0E-19]
19	181	(1.0E-19,1.0E-18]
18	171	(1.0E-18,1.0E-17]
17	161	(1.0E-17,1.0E-16]
16	151	(1.0E-16,1.0E-15]
15	141	(1.0E-15,1.0E-14]
14	131	(1.0E-14,1.0E-13]
13	121	(1.0E-13,1.0E-12]
12	111	(1.0E-12,1.0E-11]
11	101	(1.0E-11,1.0E-10]
10	91	(1.0E-10,1.0E-09]
9	81	(1.0E-09,1.0E-08]
8	71	(1.0E-08,1.0E-07]
7	61	(1.0E-07,1.0E-06]
6	51	(1.0E-06,1.0E-05]
5	41	(1.0E-05,1.0E-04]
4	31	(1.0E-04,1.0E-03]
3	21	(1.0E-03,1.0E-02]
2	11	(1.0E-02,1.0E-01]
1	1	(1.0E-01,1.0E-00]

3.2 GRQ

The graphic quality of a tricluster is a quantitative representation of a qualitative measure: how homogeneous the members of the tricluster are. This is widely used in literature for tricluster visual validation by means of graphically representing the triclusters on their three components: genes, conditions and time points [17,22,23].

We have quantified this information using the MSL measure [10], since it provides a numerical value of the similarity among the angles of the slopes formed by each profile for genes, conditions and times (see Fig. 1).

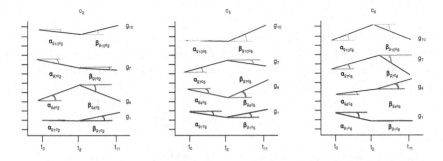

Fig. 1. Representation of how the MSL measure is calculated.

We define GRQ in Eq. 6 as one minus the normalization of MSL. Thus, a tricluster is graphically better the smaller the value of MSL is [10].

$$GRQ(TRI) = 1 - \frac{MSL(TRI)}{2\pi} \qquad (6)$$

3.3 PEQ and SPQ

Pearson [4] and Spearman [13] correlations have been chosen since they are the standard correlations measures and they are widely used in literature [15].

Random variables for a tricluster TRI are defined to calculate PEQ and SPQ, based on its subset of genes (Eq. 7a), conditions (Eq. 7b) and time stamps (Eq. 7c). Thus, every tricluster will have a set of random variables $vars$ composed of the combination of each gene and each experimental condition (Eq. 7d). Each of these variables will have a expression level for each time stamp (Eq. 7e).

For example, for a tricluster consisting of four genes g_1, g_4, g_8, g_{10}, two conditions c_3, c_7 and three time points t_1, t_3, t_5, random variables for eight possible combinations will be considered, each having three values (one per time stamp): $V_{g_1 c_3}, V_{g_1 c_7}, V_{g_4 c_3}, V_{g_4 c_7}, V_{g_8 c_3}, V_{g_8, c_7}, V_{g_{10} c_3}$ and $V_{g_1 c_7}$.

$$TRI_G = < g_0, g_1, \ldots, g_{|G|} > \tag{7a}$$

$$TRI_C = < c_0, c_1, \ldots, c_{|C|} > \tag{7b}$$

$$TRI_T = < t_0, t_1, \ldots, t_{|T|} > \tag{7c}$$

$$\forall g_i \in TRI_G, c_j \in TRI_C \; vars = \{V_{g_0 c_0}, V_{g_1 c_1}, \ldots, V_{g_{|G|} c_{|C|}}\} \tag{7d}$$

$$V_{g_i c_j} = < el_{g_i c_j t_0}, el_{g_i c_j t_1}, \ldots, el_{g_i c_j t_{|T|}} > \forall g_i \in TRI_G, c_j \in TRI_C, t_k \in TRI_T \tag{7e}$$

Given the set of variables $vars$, PEQ is defined as the sum of the absolute value of the Pearson correlation coefficient for each combination of each pair of variables in the set $vars$ divided by the number of such combinations (Eq. 8).

$$PEQ(TRI) = \frac{\sum_{V_{g_i c_j}, V_{g_k c_l} \in vars} |PE(V_{g_i c_j}, V_{g_k c_l})|}{\left[\frac{(|G||C|)^2 - |G||C|}{2}\right]} \tag{8}$$

Similarly, SPQ is defined as the sum of the absolute value of the Spearman correlation coefficient for each combination of each pair of variables in the set $vars$ divided by the number of such combinations (Eq. 9).

$$SPQ(TRI) = \frac{\sum_{V_{g_i c_j}, V_{g_k c_l} \in vars} |SP(V_{g_i c_j}, V_{g_k c_l})|}{\left[\frac{(|G||C|)^2 - |G||C|}{2}\right]} \tag{9}$$

4   Results

In this section we show the results obtained by application of $TRIQ$ to the tricluster solutions obtained using the three fitness function MSR_{3D}, LSL and MSL embedded in the $TriGen$ algorithm. Three different datasets have been used: the yeast cell cycle (*Saccharomyces Cerevisiae*) [21], in particular the *elutriation* experiment, an experiment with mice (*Mus Musculus*) called $GDS4510$ [7] and data from an experiments with humans (*Homo Sapiens*) called $GDS4472$ [5]. The last two datasets have been retrieved from Gene Expression Omnibus [2], a repository of high throughput gene expression data. All experiments examine the behavior of genes under conditions at certain times.

We show, for each of the datasets, the average values obtained upon execution of TriGen with each of the fitness functions (MSR, LSL and MSL) for $TRIQ$ in the triclusters obtained, as well as the individual values obtained for each of the measures involved in $TRIQ$: $BIOQ$, GRQ, PEQ and SPQ.

The weights for calculation of $TRIQ$ (see Eq. 1) have been set to the values shown in Eq. 10. Triclusters with greater biological and graphical quality are preferred, since Pearson and Spearman correlations are not typically critical, even if the information contained on them is greatly valuable.

$$W_{bio} = 0.5$$
$$W_{gr} = 0.4$$
$$W_{pe} = 0.05 \tag{10}$$
$$W_{sp} = 0.05$$

The value for the bonus parameter for the $BIOQ$ measure V_{bonus} is set to the value shown in Eq. 11:

$$V_{bonus} = 0$$
$$S_{l_{|LV|}} = [C_{l_{|LV|}} * w_{l_{|LV|}} * l_{|LV|}] + [l_{|LV|} * V_{bonus}] \tag{11}$$
$$= [1 * 401 * 41] + [41 + 0] = 16482$$

4.1 Yeast Cell Cycle Dataset

We have applied the TriGen algorithm to the yeast (*Saccharomyces Cerevisiae*) cell cycle problem [21]. The yeast cell cycle analysis project's goal is to identify all genes whose mRNA levels are regulated by the cell cycle. The resources used are public and available in http://genome-www.stanford.edu/cellcycle/. Here we can find information relative to gene expression values obtained from different experiments using microarrays. In particular, we have created a dataset $Delu_{3D}$ from the elutriation experiment with 7744 genes, 13 experimental conditions and 14 time points. Experimental conditions correspond to different statistical measures of the Cy3 and Cy5 channels while time points represent different moments of taking measures from 0 to 390 min.

Table 2. $TRIQ$ results for the Yeast Cell Cycle experiment.

Fitness function	$TRIQ$	$BIOQ$	GRQ	PEQ	SPQ
MSR_3D	0,2905	0,0001	0,5790	0,5901	0,5870
LSL	0,4530	0,0001	0,9181	0,8655	0,8479
MSL	0,4947	0,0001	0,9995	0,9400	0,9571

We see that MSL obtains the best values for $TRIQ$ in this experiment, as well as for GRQ, PEQ, and SPQ. LSL has the second better set of results, while the values for $BIOQ$ are very similar for the three fitness functions (Table 2).

4.2 Mouse GDS4510 Dataset

This dataset was obtained from GEO [2] with accession code GDS4510 and title *rd1 model of retinal degeneration: time course* [7]. In this experiment the degeneration of retinal cells in different individuals of home mouse (*Mus musculus*) is analyzed over 4 days just after birth, specifically on days 2, 4, 6 and 8. Our input dataset $DGDS4510_{3D}$ is composed of 22690 genes, 8 experimental conditions (one for each individual involved in the biological experiment) and 4 time points.

Table 3. $TRIQ$ results for the Mouse GDS4510 experiment.

Fitness function	$TRIQ$	$BIOQ$	GRQ	PEQ	SPQ
MSR_3D	0,3601	0,0003	0,7412	0,6400	0,6289
LSL	0,4117	0,0006	0,8486	0,7094	0,7298
MSL	0,4693	0,0013	0,9767	0,7807	0,7780

We see that, again, MSL obtains the best values for $TRIQ$, as well as for all separate measures involved. LSL has the second position (Table 3).

4.3   Human GDS4472 Dataset

This dataset has been obtained from GEO [2] under code GDS4472 titled *Transcription factor oncogene OTX2 silencing effect on D425 medulloblastoma cell line: time course* [5]. In this experiment we analyze the effect of doxycycline on medulloblastoma cancerous cells at six times after induction: 0, 8, 16, 24, 48 and 96 h. Our input dataset $DGSD4472_{3D}$ is composed by 54675 genes, 4 conditions (one for each individual involved) and 6 time points (one per hour).

Table 4. $TRIQ$ results for the Human GDS4472 experiment.

Fitness function	$TRIQ$	$BIOQ$	GRQ	PEQ	SPQ
MSR_3D	0,3128	0,0001	0,6215	0,6334	0,6490
LSL	0,4111	0,0050	0,8326	0,7779	0,7344
MSL	0,4422	0,0048	0,8983	0,7905	0,8182

We see how, for this dasatet also, MSL obtains the best values for $TRIQ$, as well as for GRQ, PEQ, and SPQ. MSL and LSL have very similar values for $BIOQ$, both improving MSR. LSL has the second better set of results (Table 4).

In a previous publication [10] we stated that MSL was the fitness function capable of extracting best tricluster solutions in terms of the three validation measures considered: correlation, graphic validation and functional annotations. We see how $TRIQ$ has successfully represented the three validation measures yielding the same validation results as in [10].

5   Conclusions

In this work we have presented a tricluster validation measure, $TRIQ$ capable to combine information from three different sources: correlation among the genes, conditions and times, graphic validation of the patterns extracted and functional annotations for the genes extracted.

We have applied $TRIQ$ to the triclusters obtained with three fitness functions previously defined by the authors: MSR_{3D}, LSL and MSL. The datasets used are the yeast cell cycle (*Saccharomyces Cerevisiae*), in particular the *elutriation* experiment, an experiment with mice (*Mus Musculus*) called $GDS4510$ and data from an experiments with humans (*Homo Sapiens*) called $GDS4472$.

We have shown that $TRIQ$ has successfully represented the three validation measures yielding the same validation results as in [10] where each of the components of $TRIQ$ ($BIOQ$, GRQ, PEQ, and SPQ) where applied separately.

Acknowledgments. The authors thank financial support by the Spanish Ministry of Science and Technology, projects TIN2011-28956-C02-02 and TIN2014-55894-C2-1-R and Junta de Andalucía's project P12-TIC-7528.

References

1. Ashburner, M., Ball, C.A., Blake, J.A., Botstein, D., Butler, H., Cherry, J.M., Davis, A.P., Dolinski, K., Dwight, S.S., Eppig, J.T., Harris, M.A., Hill, D.P., Issel-Tarver, L., Kasarskis, A., Lewis, S., Matese, J.C., Richardson, J.E., Ringwald, M., Rubin, G.M., Sherlock, G.: Gene ontology: tool for the unification of biology. Nat. Genet. **25**(1), 25–29 (2000)
2. Barrett, T., Wilhite, S.E., Ledoux, P., Evangelista, C., Kim, I.F., Tomashevsky, M., Marshall, K.A., Phillippy, K.H., Sherman, P.M., Holko, M., Yefanov, A., Lee, H., Zhang, N., Robertson, C.L., Serova, N., Davis, S., Soboleva, A.: NCBI GEO: archive for functional genomics data sets-update. Nucleic Acids Res. **41**, D991–D995 (2013)
3. Bauer, S., Grossmann, S., Vingron, M., Robinson, P.N.: Ontologizer 2.0–a multifunctional tool for GO term enrichment analysis and data exploration. Bioinformatics **24**(14), 1650–1651 (2008)
4. Benesty, J., Chen, J., Huang, Y., Cohen, I.: Pearson correlation coefficient. In: Noise Reduction in Speech Processing, pp. 1–4 (2009)
5. Bunt, J., Hasselt, N.E., Zwijnenburg, D.A., Hamdi, M., Koster, J., Versteeg, R., Kool, M.: OTX2 directly activates cell cycle genes and inhibits differentiation in medulloblastoma cells. Int. J. Cancer **131**(2), E21–E32 (2012)
6. Cheng, Y., Church, G.M.: Biclustering of expression data. In: Proceedings of the International Conference on Intelligent Systems for Molecular Biology, pp. 93–103 (2000)
7. Dickison, V.M., Richmond, A.M., Abu-Irqeba, A., Martak, J.G., Hoge, S.C.E., Brooks, M.J., Othman, M.I., Khanna, R., Mears, A.J., Chowdhury, A.Y., Swaroop, A., Ogilvie, J.M.: A role for prenylated rab acceptor 1 in vertebrate photoreceptor development. BMC Neurosci. **13**(1), ID152 (2012)
8. Freudenberg, J.M., Joshi, V.K., Hu, Z., Medvedovic, M.: Clean: clustering enrichment analysis. BMC Bioinformatics **10**(1), 234 (2009)

9. Gutiérrez-Avilés, D., Rubio-Escudero, C.: Mining 3D patterns from gene expression temporal data: a new tricluster evaluation measure. Sci. World J. 1–16, 2014 (2014)

10. Gutiérrez-Avilés, D., Rubio-Escudero, C.: MSL: a measure to evaluate three-dimensional patterns in gene expression data. Evol. Bioinform. 11, 121–135 (2015)

11. Gutiérrez-Avilés, D., Rubio-Escudero, C., Martínez-Álvarez, F., Riquelme, J.C.: TriGen: a genetic algorithm to mine triclusters in temporal gene expression data. Neurocomputing 132, 42–53 (2014)

12. Gutiérrez-Avilés, D., Rubio-escudero, C.: L.S.L: a new measure to evaluate triclusters. In: IEEE International Conference on Bioinformatics and Biomedicine, pp. 30–37 (2014)

13. Hauke, J., Kossowski, T.: Comparison of values of Pearson's and Spearman's correlation coefficients on the same sets of data. Quaestiones Geographicae 30(2), 87–93 (2011)

14. Hu, Z., Bhatnagar, R.: Algorithm for discovering low-variance 3-clusters from real-valued datasets. In: IEEE International Conference on Data Mining, pp. 236–245 (2010)

15. Jiang, H., Zhou, S., Guan, J., Zheng, Y.: gTRICLUSTER: a more general and effective 3D clustering algorithm for gene-sample-time microarray data. In: Li, J., Yang, Q., Tan, A.-H. (eds.) BioDM 2006. LNCS (LNBI), vol. 3916, pp. 48–59. Springer, Heidelberg (2006)

16. Liu, J., Li, Z., Hu, X., Chen, Y.: Multi-objective evolutionary algorithm for mining 3D clusters in gene-sample-time microarray data. In: 2008 IEEE International Conference on Granular Computing, No. 60573057, pp. 442–447. IEEE, August 2008

17. Liu, Y.-C., Lee, C.-H., Chen, W.-C., Shin, J.W., Hsu, H.-H., Tseng, V.S.: A novel method for mining temporally dependent association rules in three-dimensional microarray datasets. In: 2010 International Computer Symposium (ICS), pp. 759–764. IEEE (2010)

18. Romero-Zaliz, R.C., Rubio-Escudero, C., Cobb, J.P., Herrera, F., Cordón, O., Zwir, I.: A multiobjective evolutionary conceptual clustering methodology for gene annotation within structural databases: a case of study on the gene ontology database. IEEE Trans. Evol. Comput. 12(6), 679–701 (2008)

19. Rubio-Escudero, C., Martínez-Álvarez, F., Romero-Zaliz, R.C., Zwir, I.: Classification of gene expression profiles: comparison of k-means and expectation maximization algorithms. In: Proceedings of IEEE International Conference on Hybrid Intelligent Systems, pp. 831–836 (2008)

20. Spearman, C.: Correlation calculated from faulty data. Br. J. Psychol. 1904–1920 3(3), 271–295 (1910)

21. Spellman, P.T., Sherlock, G., Zhang, M.Q., Iyer, V.R., Anders, K., Eisen, M.B., Brown, P.O., Botstein, D., Futcher, B.: Comprehensive identification of cell cycle-regulated genes of the yeast saccharomyces cerevisiae by microarray hybridization. Mol. Biol. Cell 9(12), 3273–3297 (1998)

22. Xu, X., Lu, Y., Tan, K.L., Tung, A.K.H.: Finding time-lagged 3D clusters. In: Proceedings of the IEEE International Conference on Data Engineering, pp. 445–456 (2009)

23. Zhao, L., Zaki, M.J.: triCluster: an effective algorithm for mining coherent clusters in 3D microarray data. In: Proceedings of the ACM SIGMOD International Conference on Management of Data, pp. 694–705 (2005)

Biclustering of Gene Expression Data Based on *SimUI* Semantic Similarity Measure

Juan A. Nepomuceno[1]([✉]), Alicia Troncoso[2],
Isabel A. Nepomuceno-Chamorro[1], and Jesús S. Aguilar–Ruiz[2]

[1] Departamento de Lenguajes y Sistemas Informáticos,
Universidad de Sevilla, Seville, Spain
janepo@us.es
[2] Área de Informática, Universidad Pablo de Olavide, Seville, Spain

Abstract. Biclustering is an unsupervised machine learning technique that simultaneously clusters genes and conditions in gene expression data. Gene Ontology (GO) is usually used in this context to validate the biological relevance of the results. However, although the integration of biological information from different sources is one of the research directions in Bioinformatics, GO is not used in biclustering as an input data. A scatter search-based algorithm that integrates GO information during the biclustering search process is presented in this paper. SimUI is a GO semantic similarity measure that defines a distance between two genes. The algorithm optimizes a fitness function that uses SimUI to integrate the biological information stored in GO. Experimental results analyze the effect of integration of the biological information through this measure. A SimUI fitness function configuration is experimentally studied in a scatter search-based biclustering algorithm.

Keywords: Biclustering of gene expression data · Gene pairwise GO measures · Scatter search metaheuristic

1 Introduction

Biclustering is an unsupervised machine learning technique that searches local patterns. Although it was previously known with names as subspace clustering or coclustering, most of the biclustering algorithms have been presented in the context of gene expression data due to the nature of these data. Gene expression data report the information of how thousand of genes are expressed along dozens of samples or experimental conditions. These kinds of datasets motivate the interest of grouping genes only in a subset of samples and not in all of them. Therefore, biclustering simultaneously clusters genes (features) and conditions (instances). Due to the NP-hard nature of the algorithmic problem, most of the algorithms use different heuristic strategies [1]. It must be highlighted a family of algorithms based on evolutionary computation and metaheuristics [2,3].

Gene Ontology (GO) is a dictionary where each gene is annotated with a specific set of biological terms. These terms are classified in three domains: Biological Process (BP), Molecular Functions (MF) and Cellular Components (CC).

© Springer International Publishing Switzerland 2016
F. Martínez-Álvarez et al. (Eds.): HAIS 2016, LNAI 9648, pp. 685–693, 2016.
DOI: 10.1007/978-3-319-32034-2_57

The ontology has a tree structure. High levels in the tree structure have more general information and low levels have more specific information. Functional annotation files relate genes with their set of biological terms. Therefore, each gene is related with a set of GO terms. These kinds of files are usually used in biclustering in validation tasks to study the biological relevance of the results. The standard benchmark of comparison among biclustering algorithms is based on the use of functional annotation files [4]. However, although the integration of biological information is one of the research directions in Bioinformatics, this information is only used in validation but not as part of the search mechanism. Some new clustering [5] and biclustering [6] algorithms recently use GO annotation files to improve their searches processes in the context of gene expression data. These new search criteria use the information in gene expression matrices and in gene annotation files extracted from GO.

A concept of a distance among GO terms can be defined using a GO based-similarity measure. These measures evaluate the specificity of a GO term according the structure of the GO graph [7]. GO based-similarity measures can basically be classified in two groups: graph-based measures if they use the frequency of a term in the GO graph or (IC)-based measures if they use the depth in the GO graph. Otherwise, each gene in the gene annotation file is related with a set of terms. Therefore, a distance between two genes can be defined through a GO based-similarity measure.

SimUI measure is a graph-based GO similarity measure that evaluates the distance between two genes [8]. The idea of SimUI is counting the terms in the GO graph for each gene. This measure can be used to infer the biological relevance of a set of genes in a gene annotation file. The idea of this paper is to use the SimUI measure to introduce a biological bias during the search process in the biclustering algorithm. Therefore, the GO information is used as part of the search process to find the best results from a biological point of view. The proposed algorithm is a scatter search based-algorithm that sequentially finds each bicluster. The scatter search is a population based-metaheuristic where the evolutionary process is addressed by the evolution of a small set of solutions. This set of solutions is built according an equilibrium between an intensification and a diversity criterion. The proposed algorithm is based on the algorithm presented in [6]. Basically, a fitness function that evaluates the quality of each bicluster is optimized through a scatter search procedure. This merit function firstly evaluates the patterns in the bicluster using the gene expression matrix. Secondly, the biological relevance of the genes in the bicluster is also measured with SimUI that works with a gene annotation file.

The rest of the paper is organized as follows. The proposed algorithm is presented in Sect. 2. Firstly, the scatter search procedure is explained in Subsect. 2.1. Secondly, the SimUI based-fitness function is presented in Subsect. 2.2. Section 3 presents the experimental results to show that the performance of the algorithm is improved using SimUI. Finally, conclusions and future works are presented in Sect. 4.

2   Algorithm

The input data of the algorithm are basically a gene expression data matrix and a gene functional annotation file. Each row in the gene expression data matrix is the expression profile of a gene. Each column is a sample generated according a specific experimental condition. Gene functional annotation files provide biological information that is used to provide a biological bias during the bicluster search process. These files relate each gene with a set of biological terms as for example GO terms.

The proposed algorithm is a scatter search-based algorithm that optimizes a fitness function. This fitness function firstly uses the gene expression matrix information to define biclusters and secondly the functional annotation files to integrate the biological information. The search process is based on a scatter search metaheuristic procedure that is repeated to obtain each bicluster. It is important to note that the search procedure and the fitness function definition are independent.

2.1   Scatter Search Based-Procedure

Scatter search is a population based-metaheuristic where the evolution of a small and representative set of solutions is used to optimize a merit function. Each solution codifies a bicluster and at the end of the evolutionary process the best one represents the result. Each resultant bicluster is found using a scatter search procedure. Hence, the proposed algorithm repeats this procedure the number of times equal to the number of bicluster to discover. This procedure uses the same ideas that the algorithm presented in [9].

Solutions/biclusters are codified as two binary strings where the bits indicate their corresponding condition or gene in the gene expression matrix. The key idea in the scatter search process is the combination of intensification and diversification using a small set of solutions called the *reference set*. The intensification of solutions accelerates the search and the diversification avoids local minimum.

Figure 1 shows the scatter search scheme. The input basically is the gene expression matrix and the gene annotation file. Firstly, an *initial population* is built. The *diversification generation method* generates solutions as scatter as possible in order to contemplate different places in the search space. This method is based on the diversification method presented in [9], where a randomly seed solution is used to generate a set of diverse solutions. If x is a seed binary string, a new string x' is generated for each value of an integer $h = 1, 2, 3, \ldots, h_{max}$ as follows:

$$x'_{1+kh} = 1 - x_{1+kh} \quad \textbf{for} \quad k = 0, 1, 2, 3, \ldots, \lfloor n/h \rfloor \tag{1}$$

where $x = (x_1, \ldots, x_n)$, n is the number of bits, k takes values from 0 to the largest integer satisfying $k \leq n/h$, with the maximum value for h is $h_{max} = n/5$. All the remaining bits of x' are equal to those of x. Secondly, the *improvement method* changes each solution by other better solution from fitness function point

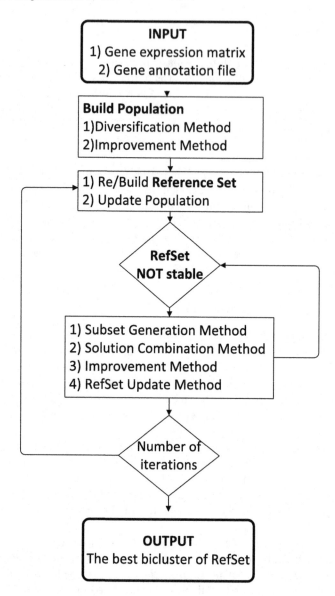

Fig. 1. Scatter search procedure to find a bicluster

of view. This method is a local search that intensifies the search process. Every improved solution is stored in the initial population.

The reference set is built according an intensification and a diversification criterion. Firstly, the half of the solutions in the reference set are most representative solutions from the initial population according to fitness function point of view. Secondly, the other half of solutions are the most scattered solutions respects the solutions previously considered. After that, the initial population is updated by removing these solutions in the reference set.

The reference set evolves until it is stable. Every new solution generated cannot improve from fitness point of view any solution previously stored in the reference set. Namely, every new solution is worse than the existent solutions in this set. New solutions are generated through the subset generation, solution combination and improvement method. The *subset generation method* builds new binary strings with uniform crossover operator usually used in genetics algorithms. The *solution combination method* builds new solutions combining with these strings. Each new solution is improved with the improvement method as it has previously commented. The *reference set update method* chooses the best solutions from the new generated solutions and the solutions in the reference set. This stability process of the reference set is repeated a number of times and the reference set is rebuilt. Finally, the best solution in the last reference set codifies the output bicluster. This procedure is repeated as many times as biclusters to discover. Note that the proposed algorithm obtains each bicluster through an independent scatter search procedure, which is a heuristic with a random nature. Therefore, the biclusters obtained are independent each other. The number of biclusters is an input parameter depending of the user needs or preferences.

2.2 *SimUI*-Based Fitness Function

A merit function is defined in order to characterize biclusters. The optimization of this function provides the resultant biclusters. Three different criteria are considered: the volume, the average correlation of the bicluster and finally, the *SimUI* measure of the set of genes. Given a bicluster composed by N genes and Q conditions, the fitness function is defined as follows:

$$f(B) = M_1 \cdot \frac{1}{N \cdot Q} + M_2 \cdot f_{corr}(B) + M_3 \cdot f_{SimUI}(B) \tag{2}$$

where the first term measures the volume, the second term measures the patterns in the gene expression matrix and the third one measures the information in GO of the set of genes according SimUI measure.

The average correlation is based on the correlation by pairs of genes. It has been previously used [9] and it is defined as:

$$f_{corr}(B) = 1 - \frac{1}{\binom{N}{2}} \sum_{i=1}^{N-1} \sum_{j=i+1}^{N} |\rho_{ij}| \tag{3}$$

where ρ_{ij} is the pearson correlation coefficient between the genes g_i and g_j. Note that this correlation is calculated using the rows and the columns in the submatrix generated with the bicluster information in the gene expression matrix. The best value for the correlation is equal to 1, and the goal is to minimize the fitness function, therefore f_{corr} is modified to have the best value in 0. The absolute value is considered to capture positive and negative correlations.

The third term in the fitness function measures the functional similarities among genes using SimUI GO measure. The gene annotation file is used to introduce the biological information in GO. This term is defined as follows:

$$f_{SimUI}(B) = 1 - \frac{1}{\binom{N}{2}} \sum_{i=1}^{N-1} \sum_{j=i+1}^{N} SimUI(g_i, g_j) \tag{4}$$

where $SimUI(g_i, g_j)$ is the SimUI measure for the genes g_i and g_j. Note that the best situation is a value equal to 1. For example, the measure of a gen with itself that is the maximum similarity. Hence, this term is also modified to find the optimum value in 0.

It is important to note that the first and the second term use the gene expression matrix and besides, the third term uses the gene functional annotation file. The parameters in Eq. (2) M_1, M_2 and M_3 control the importance of each term.

The **SimUI measure** is a gene pairwise GO measure based on counting in the graph of GO [7]. A distance between two genes is established according their functional similarity in GO. The gene annotation file is built such that each gene is related with a collection of GO terms. These terms include direct annotations of the genes and their ancestral terms up to the root node. Given two genes g_1 and g_2, the $SimUI$ measure is defined as follows:

$$SimUI(g_1, g_2) = \frac{COUNT_{t \in GO(g_1) \cap GO(g_2)}}{COUNT_{t \in GO(g_1) \cup GO(g_2)}} \tag{5}$$

where $COUNT$ is a function to count the number of GO terms. It must be noted that if there is not any annotation for g_1 and g_2, the measure is chosen equal to zero in order to represent a bad situation during the optimization process.

3   Experimental Results

The goal of the experiments is to study the influence of the SimUI measure as a mechanism to integrate biological information. The performance of the proposed algorithm is evaluated with and without any biological information integration. Note that if the third term (Eq. 2) is null there is not any biological information. In this case, the information captured by the gene annotation file is not used.

Table 1 presents the gene expression matrix size, the number of annotated genes in the matrix and a short description of the gene annotation file. The number of terms is the total number of GO terms in the gene annotation file. The average terms per gene is the average number of GO terms associated for each gene. A yeast dataset with accession number GDS1116 *GEO* repository has been used in these experiments. After being processed using *Babelomic* web tool, GDS116 gene expression matrix is composed by 882 genes and 131 conditions. The gene functional annotation file is a gene association file with the extension

Table 1. Functional annotations from GO for GDS1116 yeast dataset: input and validation data.

Dataset	Size	GO Functional annotation source	Number of genes	Number of terms	Avg. terms per gene
GDS1116	(882 × 131)	INPUT	798	1790	7.3
		BP domains	632	245	10.6
		MF domains	634	135	5.5
		CC domains	703	44	3.1

.goa_yeast downloaded from the additional information in the reference [8]. An extra file with the GO structure has been downloaded too. This file has the extension *.obo*.

The comparison criterion usually used in biclustering is the gene enrichment in the resultant biclusters [4]. A bicluster is said to be enriched if at least one enriched GO term is associated to it. The idea is that a group of genes is associated with any biological function in GO in this bicluster. Therefore it is biologically relevant. A ranking of algorithms can be defined depending on the percentage of enriched biclusters in their results. A gene annotation file is necessary to calculate the enrichment of biclusters but the same gene annotation file used as input could introduce a bias in the validation. Therefore, three gene annotation files have been generated for validation tasks different from the file used as input. The information of these files is also shown in Table 1. Three files for each GO domain have been generated using *Babelomic* web tool: for Biological Process (BP), Molecular Function (MF) and Cellular Component (CC).

The parameters configuration in the fitness function (Eq. 2) has been studied. The third term indicates SimUI term and it indicates if it is used to take the biological information from gene annotation file. Three parameter configurations are studied: (211), (212) and (221). Firstly, the fitness function configuration (211) gives the same importance to the average correlation (Eq. 3) that to the SimUI measure (Eq. 4). Secondly, the configuration (212) gives more importance to the SimUI over the average correlation. Finally, the average correlation is more relevant for the (221) configuration. If the parameter M_3 is equal to 0 there is only two possible configurations (210) and (220). It is important to note that the three terms in the fitness function vary between 0 to 1. Every configuration has the parameter M_1 equal to 2 due to the previous experience that shows that the volume must equal or more relevant that the average correlation in order to avoid trivial biclusters. It must be noted that several values varying from 1 to 2 for M_2 and M_3 were considered in previous studies [6] but the results did not show meaningful differences. (Namely, 1.0, 1.3, 1.5, 1.8 and 2).

Figure 2 shows a comparison among different fitness function configurations: (211), (212) and (221) for SimUI and (210) and (220) in the case that there is not any biological integration. The black bar, the grey and the white represent the BP, MF and CC GO domains respectively. They represents the percentage

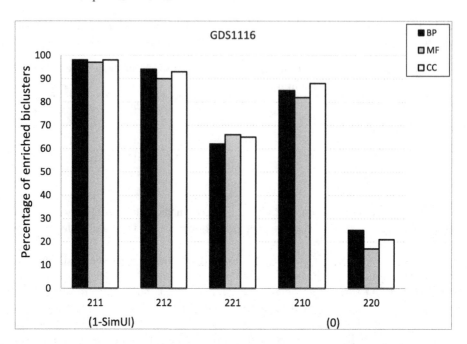

Fig. 2. Results with (1-SimUI) and without (0) biological information integration.

of enriched biclusters for each run of the algorithm. All runs have obtained 100 biclusters in order to have a high number of results to handle the random nature of the algorithm.

It can be observed in Fig. 2 that the best results are obtained when M_2 is equal to 1. In the case that SimUI is used, (211) and (221) has more percentage of enriched biclusters than (221). If there is not any biological integration, (210) obtains better results than (220). The configuration (211) obtains the best results and nearly the 100 % of biclusters are enriched. This case considers the average correlation (Eq. 3) and the SimUI measure (Eq. 4) with the same relevance in the fitness function (Eq. 2). The results for the three different domains BP, MF and CC present almost the same situation. These three domains has been considered in order to avoid any kind of bias in the validation. It is important to note that gene annotation file used as input is different from the files used to build Fig. 2.

The most relevant information that can be observed in Fig. 2 is that the integration of biological information using SimUI measure improves the results of the algorithm when there is not any kind of integration. (211) and (212) obtains better results than (210) and it also occurs with (221) respect (220).

4   Conclusions

A scatter search based-biclustering algorithm that integrates GO information has been presented in this paper. Each reported bicluster is the result of the optimization process of a fitness function. This fitness function evaluates the quality of each bicluster and SimUI similarity measure is used as a term to integrate the information stored in GO. The input data of the algorithm are the gene expression data and a gene annotation file. Thus, a biological bias is introduced in the search process to address the results to biologically relevant biclusters.

Experimental results have shown the effect of integration of the biological information through SimUI measure. Different parameters configurations have been studied and it can be concluded that SimUI based-fitness function helps to improve the algorithm performance. Future works will be focused on some improvements in the search procedure and the study of other gene pairwise GO measures.

Acknowledgements. We would like to thank Spanish Ministry of Science and Innovation, Junta de Andalucía and University Pablo de Olavide for the financial support under projects TIN2011-28956-C02-02, TIN2014-55894-C2-R, P12-TIC-1728 and APPB813097, respectively.

References

1. Eren, K., Deveci, M., Kucuktunc, O., Catalyurek, U.V.: A comparative analysis of biclustering algorithms for gene expression data. Briefings Bioinform. **14**(3), 279–292 (2013)
2. Divina, F., Aguilar-Ruiz, J.: A multi-objective approach to discover biclusters in microarray data. In: Proceedings of the 9th Annual Conference on Genetic and Evolutionary Computation, pp. 385–392. ACM, New York (2007)
3. Flores, J.L., Inza, I., Larrañaga, P., Calvo, B.: A new measure for gene expression biclustering based on non-parametric correlation. Comput. Methods Programs Biomed. **112**(3), 367–397 (2013)
4. Prelic, A., Bleuler, S., Zimmermann, P., Wille, A., Buhlmann, P., Gruissem, W., Hennig, L., Thiele, L., Zitzler, E.: A systematic comparison and evaluation of biclustering methods for gene expression data. Bioinformatics **22**(9), 1122–1129 (2006)
5. Verbanck, M., Le, S., Pages, J.: A new unsupervised gene clustering algorithm based on the integration of biological knowledge into expression data. BMC Bioinform. **14**(1), 42 (2013)
6. Nepomuceno, J.A., Troncoso, A., Nepomuceno-Chamorro, I.A., Aguilar-Ruiz, J.: Integrating biological knowledge based on functional annotations for biclustering of gene expression data. Comput. Methods Programs Biomed. **119**(3), 163–180 (2015)
7. Pesquita, C., Faria, D., Bastos, H., Ferreira, A., Falcao, A., Couto, F.: Metrics for go based protein semantic similarity: a systematic evaluation. BMC Bioinform. **9**(Suppl 5), S4 (2008)
8. Caniza, H., Romero, A.E., Heron, S., Yang, H., Devoto, A., Frasca, M., Mesiti, M., Valentini, G., Paccanaro, A.: Gossto: a stand-alone application and a web tool for calculating semantic similarities on the gene ontology. Bioinformatics **30**(15), 2235–2236 (2014)
9. Nepomuceno, J.A., Troncoso, A., Aguilar-Ruiz, J.: Biclustering of gene expression data by correlation-based scatter search. BioData Min. **4**(1), 3 (2011)

Discovery of Genes Implied in Cancer by Genetic Algorithms and Association Rules

Alejandro Sánchez Medina[1], Alberto Gil Pichardo[1],
Jose Manuel García-Heredia[2], and María Martínez-Ballesteros[3(✉)]

[1] University of Sevilla, Seville, Spain
`alesanmed@alum.us.es`, `albgilpic@alum.us.es`
[2] Department of Vegetal Biochemistry and Molecular Biology,
University of Seville, Seville, Spain
`jmgheredia@us.es`
[3] Department of Computer Science, University of Seville, Seville, Spain
`mariamartinez@us.es`

Abstract. This work proposes a methodology to identify genes highly related with cancer. In particular, a multi-objective evolutionary algorithm named CANGAR is applied to obtain quantitative association rules. This kind of rules are used to identify dependencies between genes and their expression levels. Hierarchical cluster analysis, fold-change and review of the literature have been considered to validate the relevance of the results obtained. The results show that the reported genes are consistent with prior knowledge and able to characterize cancer colon patients.

Keywords: Data mining · Association rules · Gene expression · Cancer

1 Introduction

The word cancer refers to a set of different complex diseases, characterized by an uncontrolled and pathogenic growth of cells as a tumor, driving to death without medical treatment. Due to the increase of life expectancy, cancer can be considered as the 21st century's disease. In fact, around one third of the total population will develop cancer during their lifetime [1]. This high percentage shows the importance of the development of adequate techniques for diagnosis and treatment of the different cancers.

The origin of cancer is mainly genetic, due to the accumulation of mutations in cells during lifetime. This enables them to become independent of the extracellular matrix, losing adherent properties and allowing them to metastasize to other tissues. During the period 1989–2008, around 15 % of all deaths due to malignant tumours were caused by colorectal cancer [2].

Data Mining has been used in cancer context for the diagnosis and prognosis of breast cancer [3]. This technique can help to detect it earlier reducing the mortality risk in patients. Indeed, data mining has been used in breast cancer

© Springer International Publishing Switzerland 2016
F. Martínez-Álvarez et al. (Eds.): HAIS 2016, LNAI 9648, pp. 694–705, 2016.
DOI: 10.1007/978-3-319-32034-2_58

to predict the survival rate of patients [4]. This allows that patients with lower survival rate may change their habits in order to increase it. Association Rules (hereafter AR) mining is a popular methodology in the field of Data Mining to discover significant and apparently hidden relations among attributes in a subspace of the dataset instances. In fact, the work presented in [5] proposes the application of fuzzy AR to find potential associations among prognostic factors in breast cancer. The well-known Apriori algorithm was applied to mine the AR between clinical factors and good survival outcomes in operation in [6].

The expression microarray technology [7] is composed of chips that show us the expression of a large number of genes of the patient, being impossible to perform a particular and individual study and statistical analysis. The goal of bioinformatics is to find genes involved in cancer progression. This is achieved by using normal and cancerous tissue samples.

In this work we propose a study to identify gene expression patterns in colon cancer microarray data using Quantitative Association rules (hereafter QAR). In particular, we have applied a multi-objective genetic algorithm, henceforth called CANGAR, to discover QAR with the aim to find genes probably associated with cancer according to their expression levels. The resulting genes of CANGAR may be studied in order to find out if they are implied or related in any way with a specific type of cancer.

The rest of the paper is structured as follows. Section 2 summarizes the main concepts of AR and quality measures in addition to the fold-change measures used to select the genes to be analyzed. Section 3 thoroughly describes the CANGAR approach to identify genes highly related to colon cancer patients. Section 4 presents and discuss the results obtained in the analysis proposed. Finally, Sect. 5 summarizes the conclusions drawn from the analysis performed.

2 Preliminaries

This section provides a brief description of QARs and quality measures, in addition to the fold-change measure commonly used in microarray analysis.

2.1 Quantitative Association Rules and Quality Measures

AR are implications like $X \Rightarrow Y$ where $X \bigcap Y = \emptyset$. But there are a subtype of AR that allows also to set an interval of membership for the attributes, those are called QAR [8]. For example, a QAR could be numerically expressed as:

$$GeneA \in [1,2] \ and \ GeneB \in [3,4] \Rightarrow GeneC \in [2,3]$$

The left-side and the right-side of an AR are known as antecedent and consequent, respectively. In this example, $GeneA$ and $GeneB$ belong to the antecedent and $GeneC$ belongs to the consequent.

Several probability-based measures exist to evaluate the generality and reliability of AR (and QAR) [9]. The most frequently measures used are support and confidence [10]. Table 1 summarizes the description and the mathematical definition of measures used in this work [11]. Note that the classical algorithms need to obtain some frequent item-sets before generating AR that satisfy minimum support and confidence thresholds. This is undoubtedly the most costly task in seeking AR. One of the most important algorithms for generating frequent item-sets, is the Apriori algorithm [12], which is based on the fact that if a set is frequent, all of it subsets will be frequent too, and the same in the other way.

The CANGAR algorithm does not require the generation of frequent itemset, since the intervals of QAR are evolved through the evolutionary process of CANGAR until those rules with best measures are obtained. Note that n(AB) is the number of occurrences of the rule $A \Rightarrow B$ in the dataset and $|D|$ is the total number of instances in the dataset.

Table 1. QAR quality measures

Measure	Equation
$Sup(A \Rightarrow B)$	$\frac{n(AB)}{|D|}$
$Conf(A \Rightarrow B)$	$\frac{Sup(A \Rightarrow B)}{Sup(A)}$
$Lift(A \Rightarrow B)$	$\frac{Sup(A \Rightarrow B)}{Sup(A)Sup(B)}$
$Conviction(A \Rightarrow B)$	$\frac{1 - Sup(B)}{1 - Conf(A \Rightarrow B)}$
$Gain(A \Rightarrow B)$	$Conf(A \Rightarrow B) - Sup(B)$
$Certainty\,factor(A \Rightarrow B)$	• If $Conf(A \Rightarrow B) \geq Sup(B)$: $\frac{Gain(A \Rightarrow B)}{1 - Sup(B)}$ • If $Conf(A \Rightarrow B) < Sup(B)$: $\frac{Gain(A \Rightarrow B)}{Sup(B)}$
$Leverage(A \Rightarrow B)$	$Sup(A \Rightarrow B) - Sup(A)Sup(B)$
$Accuracy(A \Rightarrow B)$	$Sup(A \Rightarrow B) + Sup(A \Rightarrow B)$
$Coverage(A \Rightarrow B)$	$\frac{Sup(A \Rightarrow B)}{Sup(B)}$
$Netconf(A \Rightarrow B)$	$\frac{Sup(A \Rightarrow B) - Sup(A)Sup(B)}{Sup(A)(1 - Sup(A))}$
$Yule's\,Q(A \Rightarrow B)$	$\frac{x - y}{x + y}$ s.t $x = Sup(A \Rightarrow B)(1 - Sup(B))$ $-Sup(A) + Sup(A \Rightarrow B)$ $y = (Sup(A) - Sup(A \Rightarrow B))(Sup(B)$ $-Sup(A \Rightarrow B))$

2.2   Differentially Expressed Genes in Microarray Data

In order to know if the change of expression of a specific gene is significant, cancer samples must be compared with normal samples using a parameter called fold change (FC). In that way, at least two different microarrays experiments must be performed. For the dataset used in this work, normal (control) samples come from the same patient, but from healthy tissue close to tumoral tissue. Expression of up to 20000 genes is determined by the mRNA level of each gene and measured by fluorescence differences. These differences must be translate from fluorescence intensity to real values, using some housekeeping genes (genes that are supposed to have a constant expression) to normalize the expression.

Higher mRNA expression are connected with a higher hybridization and, consequently, to a higher fluorescence that show higher expression values. In order to estimate the FC we have applied the following function:

$$FC = log_2(average(C)) - log_2(average(N)) \tag{1}$$

Where C is the expression gene set in cancer samples and N refers to the expression gene set in control samples.

Depending on FC value, we have two different gene behaviors in cancer:

– If FC>0, a gene is up-regulated, showing a higher expression in cancer cells
– If FC<0, a gene is down-regulated, showing a lower expression in cancer cells.

FC values can be analyzed using statistic inference or descriptive statistics. The first simply selects the genes with highest FC and with statistical significance. Descriptive statistics groups genes with similar expression patterns, allowing selecting a parameter to group genes with same behavior. Both due to the experiment and cancer biology, the previous analysis can be inappropriate to extract rules for this disease. In that way, small changes in gene expression of a specific gene can produce a great impact in cancer evolution. This makes necessary to use different parameters to define the role of genes in cancer. As consequence, we have designed a parametrized genetic algorithm to discover QAR able to deal with the expression levels of the genes.

3   Description of CANGAR Algorithm

This section describes the CANGAR algorithm used to mine QAR from microarray data of colon cancer patients. CANGAR is a multi-objective algorithm based on the well-known NSGA-II [13] that discovers QAR in continuous datasets. CANGAR provides rules with adaptive intervals, whereas the classical algorithms, such Apriori, requires a previous discretization of data. The search of the most suitable intervals is addressed by an evolutionary process in which the intervals are evolved to discover high quality QAR according to the objectives optimized.

The main features of CANGAR algorithm are presented in the following sections. Section 3.1 shows the pseudocode of CANGAR algorithm based on the NSGA-II algorithm. Section 3.2 describes the codification of the individuals of the population to represent a QAR. Section 3.3 details the genetic operators used to deal with the aforementioned individual representation.

3.1   Algorithm Pseudocode

In this section the pseudocode of CANGAR algorithm to obtain QAR is presented in Algorithm 1. Although the evolutionary scheme is based on the NSGA-II algorithm, the inherit scheme has been modified and new features have been added. For instance, an external population (P_E) is considered to include all the non-dominated solutions found. Furthermore, the population is restarted when the percentage of evolved individuals is lesser than a minimum threshold (Et).

The pseudocode is divided in four procedures. The main procedure is *Algorithm* (lines 7 – 17). This procedure performs a number of executions (num_{ex}), in which a set of Re rules are obtained to compose the final set of best rules (Bc) found by the algorithm. *Evolve* procedure (lines 18 – 31) represents the evolving process of the population. This procedure obtains the external population (P_E) when the generations limit (Gl) is reached. In each generation, the new population obtained is sorted and ranked according to the level of non-domination. Then, the external population (P_E) is updated with the non-dominated solutions that compose the first Pareto Front (P_{r0}).

Procedure *Next-generation* (lines 32 – 47) is devoted to build the next generation of the population. To fulfil this goal, the offspring population (D) is obtained by genetics operators. After that, these individuals and the current population (P_g) are merged into a new population (T). This new population (T) is sorted and ranked to obtain different fronts according to the level of non-domination of the individuals (F). The next generation (P_{g+1}) is composed of the N best individuals selected from F. Finally, the procedure *Update-external-population* (lines 48 – 51) updated the external population (P_E) taking into account the non-dominated solutions after performing the union between R and P_E.

3.2   Individual Representation

As the implemented algorithm seeks to do data mining with QAR, the chromosomes must represent those rules. To achieve that, the chromosomes include the following properties:

- **Antecedent**: Set of genes representing the rule antecedents.
- **Consequent**: Depending on the desired rules to be reported, two type of consequents have been considered.
  Type 1 Set of genes representing the rule consequent.
  Type 2 Fixed class. This can be used to fix, for example, if the patient has cancer or not. When the consequent is a gene or a set of them, this property is not used.
  In this work, consequent type 1 can be used to find relationships among genes and consequent type 2 can be used to find which genes are related with a type of patient.

In the context of this work, the genes, referring to the indivisible part of the chromosome, correspond to real genes. Due to the algorithm seeks to find genes implied in cancer, the chromosome genes would be real ones. Each gene has the following properties:

Algorithm 1. CANGAR pseudocode

1: **Input 1:** Number of executions (num_ex)
2: **Input 2:** Population size (N)
3: **Input 3:** Generations Limit (Gl)
4: **Input 4:** Rules per execution (Re)
5: **Input 5:** Evolve threshold (Et)
6: **Output:** Best rules found

7: **procedure** ALGORITHM(num_ex, N, Gl, Re, Et)
8:      $Bc \leftarrow \emptyset$
9:      **while** Executions $\leq$ num_ex **do**
10:         $P_0 \leftarrow$ initial-population(N)
11:         $Fp \leftarrow \emptyset$
12:         $Fp \leftarrow evolve(P_0, Gl, Et)$
13:         $I \leftarrow$ sort-by-distance($individuals(Fp)$)
14:         $Bc \leftarrow Bc \cup I[1 : Re]$
15:      **end while**
16:      **return** Bc
17: **end procedure**

18: **procedure** EVOLVE(P_g, Gl, Et)
19:      $P_E \leftarrow \emptyset$
20:      **while not** Gl **do**
21:         $P_g \leftarrow$ next-generation(P_g, Et)
22:         $Pr = (Pr_0, Pr_1, ...) \leftarrow$ non-dominated-sort(P_g)
23:         $P_E \leftarrow$ update-external-population(Pr_0)
24:         **if** percentage-evolved(P_g) $< Et$ **then**
25:            $P_g \leftarrow$ initial-population(N)
26:         **end if**
27:      **end while**
28:      $P_E \leftarrow$ filter(P_E)
29:      $P_E \leftarrow$ rankings(P_E)
30:      **return** P_E
31: **end procedure**

32: **procedure** NEXT-GENERATION(P_g, Et)
33:      $D \leftarrow descendants(P_g)$
34:      $T \leftarrow D \cup P_g$
35:      $F = (F_0, F_1, ...) \leftarrow$ non-dominated-sort(T)
36:      $i \leftarrow 0$
37:      $P_{g+1} \leftarrow \emptyset$
38:      **while** $|P_{g+1}| + |F_i| < N$ **do**
39:         $P_{g+1} \leftarrow P_{g+1} \cup F_i$
40:         $i \leftarrow i + 1$
41:      **end while**
42:      **if** $|P_{g+1}| < N$ **then**
43:         $F_i \leftarrow$ sort-by-distance(F_i)
44:         $P_{g+1} \leftarrow P_{g+1} \cup F_i[1 : |P_{g+1} - N|]$
45:      **end if**
46:      **return** P_{g+1}
47: **end procedure**

```
48: procedure UPDATE-EXTERNAL-POPULATION(R)
49:     P_E ← P_E ∪ R
50:     filter-dominated(P_E)
51: end procedure
```

- **Attribute**: Index referring to the column of this gene in the original dataset. This index is used for not to have to deal with strings, and get the gene name only once, at the end.
- **Lower Limit**: Real number showing the lower limit of the expression interval of the gene.
- **Upper Limit**: Real number showing the upper limit of the expression interval of the gene.

The lower and upper limits turns the AR into QAR, because they do not only link a gene with a state (normal or cancer) or other genes but also they link genes and their expression interval, with a state or with other genes and their expression interval.

3.3   Genetic Operators

Genetic operators are devoted to evolve the population for, starting with parents, generate better children. There are selection mechanisms to filter those individuals who are not good enough and apply the operators only to the best ones. In this work, two genetic operators, the mutation and crossover operator, have been defined to deal with the aforementioned individual representation.

Mutation Operator. Three mutation policies have been implemented.

- Generalisation of rules. The first one is for generalise rules. The policy remove a gene from the antecedent or consequent as long as the condition for minimum number of antecedents or consequents is satisfied.
- Specialisation of rules. The second one is a policy to specialise rules. It works the same way as the generalise policy, but adding a gene to the antecedent or consequent.
- Interval bounds. The last one do not add nor remove any gene from the rule, but takes one (in either the antecedent or the consequent) and mutates it's interval. This is made by taking a random point inside the current interval and generating a new one around this point.

Crossover Operator. The chosen crossover operator is based on taking a gene of each parent and give it to one child alternatively. To do that, the limit is taken as the number of genes of the biggest parent. Then, the genes are iterated one by one. In the first iteration, the gene of the first parent is given to the first child and the gene of the second parent is given to the second child. In the next one, the gene of the first parent is given to the second child and the gene of the second parent is given to the first child. The same process is done in every iteration.

If a gene can not be given to the corresponding child in one of those iterations (because that child already has that gene, for example) this iteration would be marked as invalid. Thus, the assignment regulation will not be reversed in the next iteration. Note that the interval bounds of the individuals are taken from the inherited gene of the parents in the crossover operator.

4   Experimentation

This section presents and analyzes the results obtained by CANGAR to discover relationships among set of genes related with patient that suffer colon cancer according to their expression levels. The cancer colon dataset used in the experimentation is presented in Sect. 4.1. Then, the parametrization of the algorithm is also described in Sect. 4.2. The results obtained in the experimental study are provided in Sect. 4.3.

4.1   Cancer Dataset

This work has used a public microarray gene expression dataset of patients with colon cancer referred as GSE21510 in the National Center for Biotechnology Information repository (NCBI) [14], using Robust Multi-Array Average (RMA) algorithm to standardize microarray data. The dataset is composed of 148 patients and 54675 genes expression profiles per patient. In order to check if the behavior of the database is the expected, we analyzed several known genes connected with colon cancer such as KLF4 [15] and BMI1 [16]. Once validated, we used this dataset applying the CANGAR algorithm to obtain QARs with genes highly related with cancer patients.

4.2   Parameter Settings

The CANGAR algorithm has several parameters to satisfy the user needs that are described as follows. The rule size can be controlled by the maximum number of attributes in the antecedents and the consequents. In this work, the minimum and maximum number of attributes in antecedents and consequents have been 1 and 4, respectively. The consequent can be a fixed class (typically *normal* or *cancer*) or a set of genes (type 1 and 2, respectively). Consequent type 1 have been used in this work. The rules obtained by CANGAR can be also filtered by setting minimum thresholds for several quality measures. For instance, a minimum support threshold of 0.1 and a minimum confidence threshold of 0.8 have been considered.

Other parameters are the maximum population size (100), the number of generations (100), the mutation rate (0.15) according to the three mutation policies (0.5 for the generalizing mutation, 0.1 for the specializing mutation and 0.4 for the interval bounds mutation) and the crossover rate (0.6). There is an option to avoid the algorithm stagnating using a threshold to set the minimum share of the population that have to evolve. In this case, a minimum percentage of individuals to evolve of 0.1 has been used. The objectives to be optimized by CANGAR regarding other previous studies [17] are Leverage, Netconf and Certainty Factor. Finally, the algorithm has be executed 5 times and the number of rules selected per execution has been 10.

4.3   Results

Several experiments have been performed using the aforementioned dataset and parameter settings to obtain a potential set of genes related with colon cancer. The CANGAR algorithm has been applied to obtain a set of QAR being fixed patient type (healthy or cancer) as consequent part. We are highly interested in those rules in which the patients type refers to patients suffering from colon cancer disease. Then, we have selected the top 100 of the most frequent genes that appear more than 20 % in the rules obtained by CANGAR. The selected genes have been validated by hierarchical cluster analysis, statistical and biological significance validation techniques and literature mining.

Hierarchical Cluster Analysis. A hierarchical cluster analysis has been conducted to cluster patients and genes with similar behaviour. This method is applied to assess the capability of the genes obtained by CANGAR to classify between healthy and cancer patients according to the changes in the expression levels (down-regulated or up-regulated). Alternatively, this hierarchical cluster analysis can be used to validate the changes of the expression levels detected by the intervals of the rules obtained by CANGAR.

Figure 1 displays the heatmap of control and cancer patients according to the top genes under study after applying the hierarchical cluster analysis. Note that data have been scaled and centered. The results are plotted as dendrograms. Spearman correlation and Pearson correlation have been used to cluster the columns (patients) and rows (genes), respectively. The resulting tree has been cut at specific height (1.5) with its corresponding clusters highlighted in the heatmap color bar.

In general, four groups can be observed according to the patient type and gene expression levels. Control and cancer patients are separated in different groups as can be observed in the X-axis of the heatmap (from left to right, respectively). The down-regulated genes and up-regulated genes for cancer patients are concentrated at the top-right and bottom-right parts of the heatmap, respectively. The more differences exist between the groups of genes and patients, the higher is its importance in cancer.

Biological Relevance. Using CANGAR algorithm we have found more than 90 altered genes in colon cancer samples. These genes have been classified in different groups regarding its main function in cancer [18] as can be observed in Table 2. The aforementioned functions are described as follows:

– **Cellular Proliferation/Death:** This is the main function involved in tumor transformation, thus these genes have been deeply studied in cancer. Here we

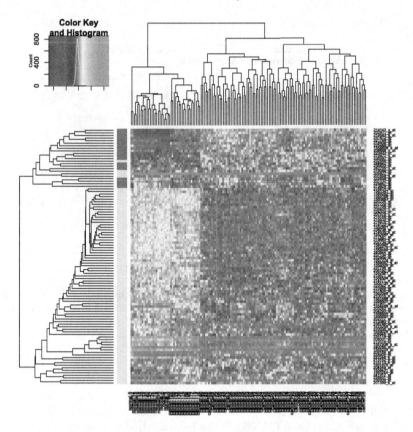

Fig. 1. Hierarchical cluster analysis of top genes.

find genes that take action in the cell cycle, like APC (Anaphase Promoter Complex) which is essential for mitosis.

- **Metastasis:** Invasion is one of the main characteristics of cancer cells, becoming independent from its environment and entering in blood circulation to reach other tissues. Here we can find genes related with cytoskeleton or matrix stabilization, like ACTN1 or ITIH2.
- **Angiogenesis:** cancer cells require high levels of glucose and oxygen, making necessary the develop of new blood vessels. Two genes (MED28 and TNFSF15) involved in angiogenesis have been identified using CANGAR algorithm.
- **Gene Expression Regulators:** cancer progression is characterized by important changes in gene expression, due to alterations in ribosome synthesis (RPL13A) or histone modification (PRDM9, HIST1H3H). In that way, we found downregulation of histone HIST1H3H, involved in heterochromatization, a process that turn-off gene transcription.
- **Other Component:** Many genes of the list are unknown or poorly characterized. In this way, the lack of information about the role in cancer of many of the found genes converts them in potential targets for new research.

Table 2. Functional classification of the genes found by CANGAR

Metastasis	Cellular Proliferation/ Death	Angiogenesis	Regulation of genetic expression	Other components
CCDC87	WWOX	MED28	MBNL1	CLIP 1
ACTN1	MAPK6	TNFSF15	PRDM9	ITSN2
ITIH2	MPP3		HNRNPLL	ARNT
PRP14	GFRA4		IKZF1	CLN8
MMP14	GPR137		RPL13A	CHST1
PPP1R9A	WNT5A		MIEF1	SLC30A9
GPM6	RXRA		RBP1	SLCO1B1
MYCN	APC		TCF3	ANKRD43
CEP350	STK38		HIST1H3H	ANKRD46
	CDC34		EIF3CL	RNF10
	R653		DNAZC13	PAM
	TNK1		HELQ	ACTR1A
	TRRAIP		SPOCD1	
	USP40		MIEF1	
	JAG1		PWRN2	
			HIST2H2AA3	
			RPL13A	

*Up-regulated genes with FC higher than 1.5 have been highlighted in light grey
*Down-regulated genes with FC lower than 1.5 has been highlighted in dark grey

5   Conclusions

In this work, we have presented the discovery of quantitative association rules in gene expression microarrays of cancer. In particular, the multi-objective evolutionary algorithm named CANGAR has been applied to discover hidden relations among genes according to their expression levels. Then, we identified the most frequent genes appearing in the rules in order to provide a subset of genes with potencial prognosis role in cancer. To validate the results, a hierarchical cluster analysis has been applied using the reported set of genes to validate the capability of characterization between control and cancer patients of them. Furthermore, the genes have been classified according their main function. As a future work, we intend to improve the validation of the results, to test the implication of the reported set of genes in different types of cancer and apply the CANGAR algorithm in other microarray datasets.

Acknowledgments. The financial support from the Spanish Ministry of Science and Technology, projects TIN2011-28956-C02-02 and TIN2014-55894-C2-1-R, and from the Junta de Andalucia, P11-TIC-7528 and P12-TIC-1728, is acknowledged.

References

1. Ellis, L., Woods, L.M., Estve, J., Eloranta, S., Coleman, M.P., Rachet, B.: Cancer incidence, survival and mortality: explaining the concepts. Int. J. Cancer **135**(8), 1774–1782 (2014)

2. López-Abente, G., Aragonés, N., Pérez-Gómez, B., Pollán, M., García-Pérez, J., Ramis, R., Fernández-Navarro, P.: Time trends in municipal distribution patterns of cancer mortality in spain. BMC Cancer **14**(1), 1–15 (2014)

3. Kharya, S.: Using data mining techniques for diagnosis and prognosis of cancer disease. CoRR abs/1205.1923 (2012)

4. Sarvestani, A., Safavi, A., Parandeh, N., Salehi, M.: Predicting breast cancer survivability using data mining techniques. In: 2nd International Conference on Software Technology and Engineering (ICSTE) 2010, vol. 2, pp. 227–231 (2010)

5. Lopez, F., Cuadros, M., Cano, C., Concha, A., Blanco, A.: Biomedical application of fuzzy association rules for identifying breast cancer biomarkers. Med. Biol. Eng. Comput. **50**(9), 981–990 (2012)

6. Tang, J.Y., Chuang, L.Y., Hsi, E., Lin, Y.D., Yang, C.H., Chang, H.W.: Identifying the association rules between clinicopathologic factors and higher survival performance in operation-centric oral cancer patients using the apriori algorithm. Biomed. Res. Int. **2013**, 7 (2013)

7. Slonim, D.K., Yanai, I.: Getting started in gene expression microarray analysis. PLoS Comput. Biol. **5**(10), e1000543 (2009)

8. Martínez-Ballesteros, M., Troncoso, A., Martínez-Álvarez, F., Riquelme, J.C.: Improving a multi-objective evolutionary algorithm to discover quantitative association rules. Knowl. Inf. Syst. 1–29 (2015)

9. Geng, L., Hamilton, H.: Interestingness measures for data mining: a survey. ACM Comput. Surv. **38**(3), 1–42 (2006)

10. Martínez-Ballesteros, M., Martínez-Álvarez, F., Troncoso, A., Riquelme, J.C.: Quantitative association rules applied to climatological time series forecasting. In: Corchado, Emilio, Yin, Hujun (eds.) IDEAL 2009. LNCS, vol. 5788, pp. 284–291. Springer, Heidelberg (2009)

11. Martínez-Ballesteros, M., Troncoso, A., Martínez-Álvarez, F., Riquelme, J.: Obtaining optimal quality measures for quantitative association rules. Neurocomputing **176**, 36–47 (2016)

12. Agrawal, R., Imieliński, T., Swami, A.: Mining association rules between sets of items in large databases. SIGMOD Rec. **22**(2), 207–216 (1993)

13. Deb, K., Pratap, A., Agarwal, S., Meyarivan, T.: A fast and elitist multiobjective genetic algorithm: NSGA-II. IEEE Trans. Evol. Comput. **6**(2), 182–197 (2002)

14. Tsukamoto, S., Ishikawa, T., Iida, S., Ishiguro, M., Mogushi, K., Mizushima, H., Uetake, H., Tanaka, H., Sugihara, K.: Clinical significance of osteoprotegerin expression in human colorectal cancer. Clin. Cancer Res. **17**(8), 2444–2450 (2011)

15. Hu, R., Zuo, Y., Zuo, L., Liu, C., Zhang, S., Wu, Q., Zhou, Q., Gui, S., Wei, W., Wang, Y.: Klf4 expression correlates with the degree of differentiation in colorectal cancer. Gut Liver **5**(2), 154 (2011)

16. Kreso, A., van Galen, P., Pedley, N.M., Lima-Fernandes, E., Frelin, C., Davis, T., Cao, L., Baiazitov, R., Du, W., Sydorenko, N., Moon, Y.C., Gibson, L., Wang, Y., Leung, C., Iscove, N.N., Arrowsmith, C.H., Szentgyorgyi, E., Gallinger, S., Dick, J.E., O'Brien, C.A.: Self-renewal as a therapeutic target in human colorectal cancer. Nat. Med. **20**(1), 29–36 (2014)

17. Martínez-Ballesteros, M., Martínez-Álvarez, F., Lora, A.T., Riquelme, J.C.: Selecting the best measures to discover quantitative association rules. Neurocomputing **126**, 3–14 (2014)

18. Hanahan, D., Weinberg, R.A.: Hallmarks of cancer: the next generation. Cell **144**(5), 646–674 (2015)

Extending Probabilistic Encoding for Discovering Biclusters in Gene Expression Data

Francisco Javier Gil-Cumbreras, Raúl Giráldez$^{(\boxtimes)}$, and Jesús S. Aguilar-Ruiz

School of Engineering, Pablo de Olavide University, Seville, Spain
{fjgilcum,giraldez,aguilar}@upo.es

Abstract. In this work, we have extended the experimental analysis about an encoding approach for evolutionary-based algorithms proposed in [1], called *probabilistic encoding*. The potential of this encoding for complex problems is huge, as candidate solutions represent regions, instead of points, of the search space. We have tested in the context of gene expression biclustering problem, in a selection of a well-known expression matrix datasets. The results obtained for the experimental analysis reveals a satisfactory performance in comparison with other evolutionary-based algorithms, and a high exploration power in very large search spaces.

1 Introduction

In the context of gene expression data analysis, microarray techniques allow to simultaneously measure the expression level of thousands of genes under different experimental conditions. The obtained data is usually organized in expression matrices, where each element stands for the expression level of a given gene under a specific experimental condition. Analysis of microarrays has become a critical aspect in biomedical research and is used with various aims, e.g., pattern recognition of genes [2] and prognosis and discovering of subtypes of diseases [3].

The application of biclustering techniques has been widely used in recent years in order to extract information from gene expression data [4]. Biclustering is a variant of clustering, in which the search is performed simultaneously on the rows and columns of the matrix. Thus, in the context of microarray analysis, it is possible to group genes that show similar behavior under subsets of conditions. These two-dimensional clusters are called biclusters.

Different techniques have been successfully applied in order to extract biclusters from microarrays. Among these, Evolutionary Algorithms (EAs) have obtained encouraging results [5–7].

The design of a suitable representation of the search space (encoding) is one of the most influential factors in the quality of the solutions found by an EA. Although there is no universal encoding scheme that is suitable for every optimization problem, there exist several standard encoding schemes studied in the literature, which have been successfully applied to many different problems. One of the simplest and most established schemes is the well-known binary

© Springer International Publishing Switzerland 2016
F. Martínez-Álvarez et al. (Eds.): HAIS 2016, LNAI 9648, pp. 706–717, 2016.
DOI: 10.1007/978-3-319-32034-2_59

encoding, where each candidate solution in the search space is represented with a bit string. The use of binary encoding is suitable for problems whose solutions can be naturally modeled using a set of boolean decision variables (BDV). However, when the problem to be solved is characterized by a level of uncertainty, a binary encoding might not be the best choice, since it will not allow to representation of the implicit uncertainty of the problem. Biclustering is a problem characterized by its level of uncertainty which is due to various reasons, such as the presence of missing values and noise in the expression matrix.

This aspect motivated some researchers [1] to design a new encoding schema, called *probabilistic encoding*, which extends the traditional binary encoding. This encoding allows to represent the uncertainty that could be present on specific values of some BDV in the solutions of optimization problems.

In this work, we try to delve deeper into the experimental analysis aspects of this encoding, in order to test the effectiveness of *probabilistic encoding* on finding biclusters in a selection of a well-known expression matrix datasets. Also, we show that the method proposed in [1] converges to a set of solutions.

This paper is organized as follows. Section 2 introduces the application of biclustering to microarray data. In Sect. 3, the probabilistic encoding is reviewed, while the algorithm and the fitness evaluation strategy is addressed and discussed out in Sect. 4. Section 5 presents and discusses the experimental results obtained. Finally, in Sect. 6, the main conclusions are summarized.

2   Biclustering on Expression Data

DNA microarray data are usually organized in an expression matrix (EM), where each element EM_{ij} represents the expression level of the ith gene under the jth experimental condition. Biclustering is capable of finding subgroups of genes that are intimately related across subgroups of conditions. In other words, by simultaneously clustering the rows and columns of the EM, it is possible to identify a sub-matrix of EM, defined by subsets of genes and conditions (bicluster) that are associated with specific biological functions. Later, biological analysis and experimentation could then confirm the significance of the found biclusters.

Nevertheless, the size of the expression matrix in real datasets typically makes the problem intractable to solve using exact methods, and requires the use of techniques based on search heuristics and therefore, the use of a measure establishing the quality of bicluster. In the literature, there are many references to different evaluation measures that quantify the quality of biclusters. One of most popular bicluster quality measures is the mean squared residue (henceforth MSR) [8], which measures the numerical coherence among the genes in a bicluster.

The lower the MSR, the better the numerical coherence among the genes is and, therefore, the better the quality of a bicluster. Thus, when the genes of a bicluster show exactly the same behaviour, with the only difference that they started with different initial values, then the MSR is equal to 0 [2]. Nevertheless, a MSR equals to 0 does not always identify a good bicluster. For instance, biclusters with genes that present a flat behaviour across all the experimental conditions (constant genes), will also have MSR equal to 0. The same holds for a trivial bicluster containing only one gene or condition. Obviously, such biclusters are not interesting and, therefore, should be avoided. For this reason, other measures may be used in combination with the MSR, such as mean row variance (henceforth MRV) [8] and volume (bicluster size). This is the case of IEPR[1] (*Identification and Exploitation of Promising Regions*) [1], wich aims to find biclusters with low MSR, high volume and relatively high MRV.

Thus, we can identify three objectives to be optimized and these objectives are usually in conflict with each other. MSR and MRV can be conflicting, as a perfect bicluster can be totally flat. MSR and volume are also typically conflicting, as when a bicluster has a non-zero MSR, it is always possible to remove a gene or a condition to lower the MSR [8]. For this reason, the problem of finding biclusters can be straightforwardly seen as a multi-objective problem [6]. Moreover, by addressing this problem as a multi-objective problem, it is not necessary to combine all the objectives into a single cost function, but a multi-objective EA might then be able to identify a set of incomparable (in the sense of Pareto) biclusters, typically sharing a single core set of highly coherent and with high variance genes and conditions, but representing different kinds of compromises among objectives.

Biclustering can be also described as a multi-modal problem [9]. In some multi-objective problems, the goal is to find a good sampling of the Pareto front of the problem, that is, extracting all the best different kinds of compromises between the different objectives. In biclustering, we are more interested in finding several different biclusters, identifying different underlying biological relations, even if these different biclusters exhibit similar kinds of compromise between objectives. Different biclusters will obviously involve different sets of genes and conditions, although those can have some genes and conditions in common [9]. In other words, different biclusters can overlap in the EM, so that some approaches develop effective methods for handling it [10].

3   Probabilistic Encoding

This section describes the main idea behind probabilistic encoding. In a classical evolutionary encoding, each gene of the chromosome represents a specific value. For example, in binary encoding, each gene can assume either value 1 or 0. It follows then that each gene establishes if the related feature is contained or not in the phenotype. This kind of representation is well suited for a variety of optimization problems, where a solution represents a single point in the search space. In other words, a solution is modeled as a particular evaluation of a single set of BDV. A solution is determined by selecting a set of traits as belonging to the solution (value 1), while the rest of the traits do not belong to the solution (value 0). BDV optimization problems are considered as the context to apply the standard binary encoding as representation.

---

[1] In [1], IEPR was named as MOBPEOC (*Multi-Objective Biclustering with Probabilistic Encoding and Overlapping Control*).

However, there are problems that are characterized by the presence of some level of uncertainty [11]. This usually means that the objective function has limited capacity to evaluate the quality of the solutions and, therefore, the algorithm may not be able to distinguish between the actual quality of solutions. In such a case, binary encoding becomes no longer a suitable option to represent such uncertain solutions. In uncertain BDV problems, it would then be desirable for an EA to be able to specify the presence of the traits in the solutions with a given level of uncertainty, in order to reflect the uncertainty contained in the problem. This motivated the proposal of *probabilistic encoding*.

The basic idea behind this encoding is that replaces the bits of binary encoding with probabilities, in such a way that each element of the genotype specifies the probability of the presence of its associated trait in the solution. Therefore, an individual of the population will not represent a single point in the search space, but rather a region of the search space. Instead of a binary individual, we have probabilistic individual that can represent many different candidate solutions.

This feature allows an EA adopting probabilistic encoding, to locate a promising region of the search space, which can contain the optimal solution, when the exact position of the optimal solution is uncertain. The population will evolve towards probabilistic individuals which share a set of traits, in such a way that the traits with higher probabilities will belong to a promising regions. They will be part of the optimal solution. The traits with lower probabilities will remain outside the promising region. In short, their probabilities converge respectively to 1 and 0. On the other hand, each individual has a set of traits whose probabilities denote a range of uncertainty. This set of remaining traits may form part of the solution or not and they define the size of promising region, since the traits with higher probabilities always form part of optimal solution. If there are T traits in the uncertainty range, the size of the promising region is 2^T, i.e., a potentially large region of solutions.

In any case, a mechanism is needed to determine the level of certainty that is assumed when incorporating each trait to a solution, based on the probability associated with the trait. This mechanism should have a minimum and maximum probability thresholds to determine what traits are present in a solution and which are not. In addition, the mechanism should deal with the traits that have an intermediate uncertainty among those thresholds. For this reason, it will be necessary to have two parameters, P_m and P_M, which determine the level of certainty that is supported when extracting the solutions contained in the regions represented by the probabilistic individuals. Therefore, the features v_i with probability of presence $P(v_i) >= P_M$, will be present in the solution and features v_i with probability of presence $P(v_i) <= P_m$, will not be present in the solution. For traits v_i whose probability is $P_m <= P(v_i) <= P_M$, a mechanism should be applied to determine whether or not to included v_i. These two parameters, P_m and P_M, are critical in the performance of the probabilistic encoding, and somehow define the levels of uncertainty that can be handled. If these two parameters were fixed with a value of 0.5, intermediate uncertainty margin would disappear and probabilistic encoding would degrade in such a way that probabilistic individual would represent a region that would contain a unique solution. If these thresholds are placed in very extreme points, extracting specific solutions contained in the regions defined by the probabilistic individuals is complicated and the process becomes substantially random. Therefore, this mechanism should be implemented in a EA that adopts probabilistic encoding and parameters, P_m and P_M, should be configured with values that allow dealing with the level of uncertainty of the problem to be solved.

Since a probabilistic individual can represent a potentially large region of solutions, the EA using probabilistic encoding can explore a larger area of the search space at each generation.

At the end of the evolutionary process, the EA would have located a promising region, i.e., a region that probably contains the optimal solution. It will be necessary to extract a specific solution to the problem from that region, which will be the best solution possible.

Other elements of the EA are affected when we use probabilistic encoding, like genetic operators and fitness evaluation strategy. The adjustments of these components were described in [1].

4   The Algorithm

In this section we will briefly review the features of the algorithm IEPR presented in [1]. The algorithm consists of two phases: Identification and Exploitation of Promising Regions.

For the first phase (Identification), we use a Multi-Objective Evolutionary Algorithm (MOEA) that adopts probabilistic encoding, in order to identify promising regions. Thus, an individual will consists of $N + M$ probabilities, where N and M are the number of genes and conditions of the microarray, respectively. This means that a probability is associated to each possible gene and condition. The population is initialized in such a way that a proportion of randomly selected genes and conditions receive a high probability value, while the remaining ones receive a low probability value, using two parameters for genes and conditions. These parameters allow to control the size of the regions created.

Genetic operators were adapted in IEPR in order to adopt probabilistic encoding. The algorithm makes use of three crossover operators and two mutations operators: uniform crossover, gene mean crossover, condition mean crossover, gene mutation and condition mutation. In gene mean crossover, the probabilities relative to the genes are computed as the average of the probabilities of the parents, while for probabilities relative to the conditions uniform crossover is used. Condition mean crossover works in a similar way, but computes the averages of the probabilities relative to the conditions. Gene and condition mutations replace a randomly picked gene/condition probability value by a randomly generated number in $[0, 1]$. The MOEA uses the niched Pareto selection mechanism proposed in [12] (Niched Pareto Genetic Algorithm, NPGA). As in

NPGA, IEPR adopts two phase selection mechanism. In particular, the selection scheme adopted is a tournament selection of size two. During the first step, the quality of the two selected individuals is evaluated using the domination relations in the current generation. If the first step of the tournament leads to a tie, continuously updated sharing is used to compute the niche count of both individuals in the provisional next generation. The individual that presents the lowest niche count is then selected. Unlike in [12], sharing distance is computed directly in the search space. This is due to that objective is not maintain diversity along the Pareto optimal front, but find different biclusters in a single run.

The MOEA optimizes three objectives that we already pointed out in Sect. 2. These are MSR, MRV and volume. Since with probabilistic encoding an individual represents a region of the search space, the evaluation of these measures should be conducted by a sampling process in this region, extracting a number of biclusters contained in it and calculating the average of such measures of each bicluster. Since a region can contain a potentially large number of biclusters, fitness evaluation strategy is a problem of high computational complexity for IEPR. In other words, extracting an excessive number of biclusters can penalize excessively the computation time. Whereas if we do not draw a sufficient number of biclusters in the region, the evaluation of the three objectives can be extremely inaccurate. Therefore we need to find a balance between these two situations, by calculating the three measures with a margin of error, and keeping the computational burden at reasonable level. In any case, it is necessary to perform an analysis of this sampling process, under the umbrella of statistical sampling, because that will allow us to define the number of samples needed to achieve a satisfactory level of confidence, according to the problem and the available data.

For the second phase (Exploitation), a local search procedure, namely simulated annealing (SA) [13], is used in order to discover interesting biclusters within the previously identified regions. Such regions are exploited in order to extract biclusters with low MSR from them. Each region is explored separately. The procedure starts with the bicluster containing all the genes and conditions with probability higher than 0.5. The local search then tries to improve the MSR by adding or removing one gene or condition at a time, according to the simulated annealing scheme. If the probability associated to a gene/condition is higher than the lower threshold Pm, then the gene/condition will always be included in the bicluster. In the same way, if the probability associated to a gene/condition is lower than the higher threshold PM, then the gene/condition will not be included in the bicluster.

5   Experiments and Results

As aforementioned, one of main aims of this work is to deepen on the experimental analysis about an encoding approach for evolutionary-based algorithms proposed in [1]. Thus, we have tested IEPR on eight well-known gene expression datasets. The list of the datasets, along with their features, is given in Table 1.

Table 1. Datasets used in the experimentation [14].

Dataset	Name	#Genes	#Conditions
Yeast	Yeast *Saccharomyces cerevisiae* cell cycle	2884	17
Human	Human B–cells	4026	96
Colon	Colon Cancer	2000	62
Malaria	Malaria *Plasmodium parasites* life cycle	3719	16
Embryonal	Embryonal tumors of the central nervous syst.	7129	60
Leukemia	Leukemia	7129	72
RatCNS	Rat Central Nervous System	112	9
Steminal	Steminal Cells	26127	30

Table 2. Parameters.

EA		SA	
Parameter	Value	Parameter	Value
Generations	1000	P_M	0.95
Population size	600	P_m	0.15
Min-max % gens (initialization)	0.05–4	Initial temp. Rows	2.0
Min-max % conditions (initialization)	90–100	Initial temp. Columns	30
P_M (Max. Prob. threshold)	0.7	Final temp. rows	0.0375
P_m (Min. Prob. threshold)	0.3	Final temp. columns	0.562
NI (% new individuals to reinitialization)	5	Temp. decrease ratio	0.90
Size of regions sample set	50		
Size of comparison set	510		
Niching Radius	0.85		
Scaling Factor	1		
Crossover probability	0.85		
Mutation probability	0.10		

These datasets are the same as were used in [14]. In this section, we have studied the convergence of IEPR and we have validated the size of sample set we used to assess measures of probabilistic individuals. Finally, from these experiments, we have extracted biclusters whose features will be analyze in this section.

Table 2 reports the parameter setting used for IEPR. These parameters were determined after several preliminary runs.

First, we have calculated the measures of a probabilistic population using sample sizes from 1 to 50. In Fig. 1, around 50 samples, we can see as the averages move in a limited range of values, which indicates its stabilization.

Other important issue is to verify that the MOEA of the first phase converges. We have performed an analysis of the three measures of the best 30

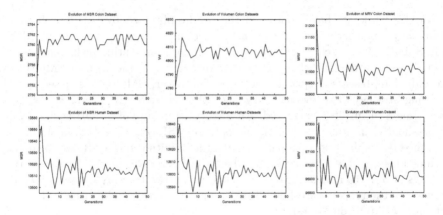

Fig. 1. Evolution of Measures with increasing of size of sample set.

individuals during 1000 generations. In Fig. 2, we can see results for human and colon datasets. In the case of colon dataset, volume is the one with more convergent behavior, stabilizing at around 14000, while MRV rises at first, and stabilizes at a range of 100, which is acceptable because it is an average of 30 individuals. This fluctuation is due to these measures are trying to reach the compromise between them. We can conclude that the same happens with MSR. MSR initially moves in very large ranges, while gradually reduces the level of variation. Regarding human dataset, MSR and MRV initially increase their values, but during the last hundreds of generations the fluctuations are bounded around 12600. Volume suffers a greater range of fluctuation, while trying to adopt a compromise with the other two values. Given these results, we can conclude that MOEA implementing the first phase has a convergent behavior.

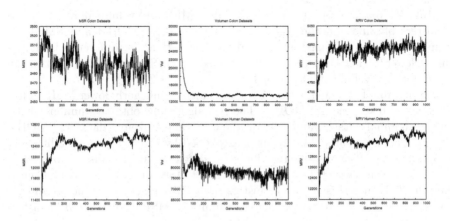

Fig. 2. Convergence of measures.

In this work, we have compared the results obtained by IEPR with those obtained by another MOEA for biclustering of microarray data, namely SMOB [14]. SMOB adopts a classical binary encoding for representing biclusters, where a bit is associated to each gene and condition. So in the case of SMOB, an individual represents a specific bicluster. Moreover, SMOB uses a sequential covering strategy. The evolutionary algorithm is executed several times, and each time a bicluster is extracted. An important feature of SMOB is the use of a thresholds δ in order to limit the acceptable MSR of a bicluster, as in [8].

Since IEPR does not use any threshold for limiting the MSR, we have also included results obtained by SMOB where the δ is relaxed. So we have used two settings of SMOB, namely SMOB-δ that uses a strict threshold, and SMOB-Δ, which uses the relaxed threshold. Table 3 reports the thresholds used by the two settings of SMOB on each dataset.

Table 3. Values of δ used in the settings of SMOB-δ and SMOB-Δ.

Dataset	δ in SMOB-δ	δ in SMOB-Δ
Yeast	300	3400
Human	1200	23000
Colon	500	3300
Malaria	600	19000
Embryonal	1800	10000
Leukemia	1800	23130700
RatCNS	5	11
Steminal	10	130

Tables 4, 5 and 6 report the average MSR, MRV and volume of one-hundred biclusters obtained on the eight datasets by IEPR, SMOB-δ and SMOB-Δ. A minus/plus symbol next to a result indicates that the difference is significantly lower/higher than the result obtained by IEPR, according to a two-tail t-test with a level of confidence of 1 %.

From Table 4, we can see that IEPR obtained significantly lower MSR on five datasets with respect to SMOB-δ. The two algorithms obtained similar results on the steminal dataset, and only on the colon and leukemia datasets SMOB-δ obtained better results. This result is explained by the fact that the threshold adopted by SMOB-δ on these two datasets limited the MSR of discovered biclusters to 500 in the case of the colon dataset and to 1800 in the case of the leukemia dataset. This means that any biclusters with MSR higher that the specified δ are discarded by SMOB. IEPR does not limit the MSR of discovered biclusters in any way.

We believe that this is an important advantage of IEPR, since using a wrong value of δ may prevent the algorithm from finding interesting biclusters.

Table 4. Average MSR obtained on each dataset.

Dataset	MSR		
	IEPR	SMOB-δ	SMOB-Δ
Yeast	$107.0_{\pm 12.2}$	$272.0_{\pm 25.0}$ +	$1062.1_{\pm 274.8}$ +
Human	$295.0_{\pm 218.7}$	$1103.6_{\pm 86.7}$ +	$10742.6_{\pm 2321.3}$ +
Colon	$916.3_{\pm 125.0}$	$455.3_{\pm 45.5}$ −	$2107.2_{\pm 306.3}$ +
Malaria	$311.5_{\pm 267.3}$	$449.7_{\pm 174.5}$ +	$12095.5_{\pm 2298.1}$ +
Embryonal	$9.1_{\pm 0.5}$	$398.2_{\pm 344.2}$ +	$803.0_{\pm 1243.1}$ +
Leukemia	$23538.4_{\pm 9498.6}$	$1533.2_{\pm 169.2}$ −	$4929089.4_{\pm 2938946.0}$ +
CnsRat	$0.6_{\pm 0.2}$	$1.6_{\pm 1.3}$ +	$2.2_{\pm 2.0}$ +
Steminal	$4.1_{\pm 0.5}$	$4.1_{\pm 2.1}$	$13.1_{\pm 12.9}$ +

We can also notice that if the threshold is relaxed, the average MSR of the biclusters discovered by SMOB is significantly higher that those obtained by IEPR on all the datasets.

Table 5. Average MRV obtained on each dataset.

Dataset	MRV		
	IEPR	SMOB-δ	SMOB-Δ
Yeast	$527.6_{\pm 99.2}$	$408.6_{\pm 77.2}$ −	$1245.2_{\pm 294.0}$ +
Human	$982.6_{\pm 354.1}$	$1412.1_{\pm 168.6}$ +	$11412.7_{\pm 2476.3}$ +
Colon	$3707.4_{\pm 345.6}$	$2836.8_{\pm 1026.7}$ −	$4876.2_{\pm 548.4}$ +
Malaria	$4454.6_{\pm 4562.0}$	$2667.4_{\pm 3765.7}$ −	$16707.7_{\pm 2914.7}$ +
Embryonal	$9.9_{\pm 0.5}$	$428.8_{\pm 366.0}$ +	$849.4_{\pm 1304.1}$ +
Leukemia	$23959.9_{\pm 9640.9}$	$2391.4_{\pm 660.1}$ −	$5269867.7_{\pm 3099017.9}$ +
CnsRat	$0.7_{\pm 0.3}$	$2.1_{\pm 1.6}$ +	$2.7_{\pm 2.3}$ +
Steminal	$4.1_{\pm 0.5}$	$4.5_{\pm 2.3}$	$13.8_{\pm 13.3}$ +

Regarding MRV, we can notice from Table 5, that on four datasets, namely yeast, colon, malaria and leukemia, IEPR obtained better results than SMOB-δ. On the other hand, on the human, embryonal and CnsRat, SMOB-δ obtained significantly better results. However, if we analyze these three cases, we can notice that the average MSR obtained by SMOB-δ on these three datasets was significantly higher than that obtained by IEPR. In general, to higher values of MSR corresponds higher values of MRV [8], since MSR and MRV are objectives that are typically in conflict with each other. We can also notice that the average MSR obtained by IEPR on the yeast and on the malaria dataset is lower than that obtained by SMOB-δ on the same datasets. If the threshold used by SMOB is relaxed, then the average MRV is significantly higher that the average MRV obtained by IEPR on all the datasets. However this results is again justified by the fact that in all the cases the MSR obtained by SMOB-Δ is significantly higher.

Finally, in Table 6, it is shown that IEPR always obtained biclusters characterized by a significant higher volume than the biclusters found by SMOB-δ.

Table 6. Average Volume obtained on each dataset.

Dataset	Volume		
	IEPR	SMOB-δ	SMOB-Δ
Yeast	$759.0_{\pm 166.4}$	$226.1_{\pm 77.3}$ −	$461.5_{\pm 95.0}$ −
Human	$363.8_{\pm 668.0}$	$362.2_{\pm 106.8}$ −	$1128.3_{\pm 260.4}$ +
Colon	$4790.4_{\pm 1519.8}$	$197.6_{\pm 85.1}$ −	$1172.5_{\pm 334.5}$ −
Malaria	$452.2_{\pm 674.8}$	$54.7_{\pm 31.5}$ −	$462.0_{\pm 108.2}$ +
Embryonal	$230266.7_{\pm 14973.8}$	$1456.2_{\pm 577.3}$ −	$1423.6_{\pm 519.3}$ −
Leukemia	$139609.4_{\pm 32628.0}$	$441.7_{\pm 141.2}$ −	$1132.2_{\pm 220.4}$ −
CnsRat	$353.2_{\pm 65.9}$	$128.5_{\pm 81.0}$ −	$128.6_{\pm 69.0}$ −
Steminal	$291095.0_{\pm 57256.9}$	$1312.5_{\pm 371.8}$ −	$1286.7_{\pm 399.4}$ −

This result is even more relevant if we consider that in five cases, the average MSR obtained by IEPR is significantly lower than the average MSR obtained by SMOB-δ. We know that the volume is in general in conflict with the MSR. However IEPR was capable of finding biclusters that present both low MSR and high volume. Even when δ is relaxed, SMOB is capable of discovering biclusters presenting higher volume only in two cases. As for the MRV, we must point out that also for the volume, the average MSR obtained by SMOB-Δ was higher than the one obtained by IEPR in all the cases. This observation explains why SMOB-Δ could find in two cases biclusters with higher volumes.

By considering the three objectives together, we can conclude that the results obtained by IEPR on the eight datasets are very satisfactory. In fact, in general, the biclusters discovered by IEPR are characterized by a lower MSR, a higher MRV and volume than those discovered by SMOB-δ. If the threshold is relaxed, we can then perform a fairer comparison of the two algorithms, since IEPR does not use any threshold to limit the MSR of the biclusters. In this case IEPR presents superior performances with respect to SMOB. In fact, SMOB-Δ obtains better results only as far as the MRV is concerned. However, the other two objectives are significantly worse than those obtained by IEPR.

6   Conclusions

In this paper we have reviewed the probabilistic encoding and the method proposed in [1]. We have discussed about the mechanism that deals with uncertainty and how the lower and higher thresholds of uncertainty can affect to effectiveness of this mechanism. Moreover, we have discussed about the fitness evaluation strategy and the number of biclusters we have to extract from a region defined by a probabilistic individual to obtain a balance between reliable measurements and acceptable computational burden.

In our experiments, we have used 50 samples from probabilistic individual to calculate the measures and we have confirmed the reliability of the results. Moreover, we also have proved the convergence of the MOEA used in the first phase of method.

Finally, the results obtained by our proposal were compared to those obtained by two variants of SMOB, a MOEA that uses a classical binary representation. The experimental analysis on eight gene expression datasets shows that IEPR provides excellent results in comparison with the other techniques, especially at exploring the search space when several objectives are under study. In addition, the probabilistic encoding reveals a high potential of use for solving complex problems with evolutionary techniques.

Acknowledgements. This research has been supported by the Spanish Ministry of Economy and Competitiveness under grants TIN2011-28956 and TIN2014-55894-C2-R.

References

1. Marcozzi, M., Divina, F., Aguilar-Ruiz, J.S., Vanhoof, W.: A novel probabilistic encoding for EAs applied to biclustering of microarray data. In: Proceedings of the 13th Annual Conference on Genetic and Evolutionary Computation, GECCO 2011, pp. 339–346. ACM, New York (2011)
2. Aguilar-Ruiz, J.S.: Shifting and scaling patterns from gene expression data. Bioinformatics **21**, 3840–3845 (2005)
3. Berrar, D.P., Dubitzky, W., Granzow, M.: A Practical Approach to Microarray Data Analysis. Springer Publishing Company, Incorporated, US (2003)
4. Madeira, S.C., Oliveira, A.L.: Biclustering algorithms for biological data analysis: a survey. IEEE Trans. Comput. Biol. Bioinform. **1**, 24–25 (2004)
5. Divina, F., Aguilar-Ruiz, J.S.: Biclustering of expression data with evolutionary computation. IEEE Trans. Knowl. Data Eng. **18**(5), 590–602 (2006)
6. Mitra, S., Banka, H.: Multi-objective evolutionary biclustering of gene expression data. Pattern Recogn. **39**(12), 2464–2477 (2006)
7. Pontes, B., Giráldez, R., Aguilar-Ruiz, J.: Configurable pattern-based evolutionary biclustering of gene expression data. Algorithms Mol. Biol. **8**(1), 1–22 (2013)
8. Cheng, Y., Church, G.M.: Biclustering of expression data. In: Proceedings of the Eighth International Conference on Intelligent Systems for Molecular Biology, pp. 93–103. AAAI Press (2000)
9. Yang, J., Wang, H., Wang, W., Yu, P.: Enhanced biclustering on expression data. In: Proceedings of the 3rd IEEE Symposium on BioInformatics and BioEngineering, BIBE 2003, p. 321. IEEE Computer Society, Washington, DC, USA (2003)
10. Pontes, B., Divina, F., Giráldez, R., Aguilar-Ruiz, J.S.: Improved biclustering on expression data through overlapping control. Int. J. Intell. Comput. Cybern. **3**(2), 293–309 (2010)
11. Cruz, C., González, J.R., Pelta, D.A.: Optimization in dynamic environments: a survey on problems, methods and measures. Soft Comput. **15**(7), 1427–1448 (2011)
12. Horn, J., Nafpliotis, N., Goldberg, D.E.: A niched pareto genetic algorithm for multiobjective optimization. In: Proceedings of the First IEEE Conference on Evolutionary Computation, 1994. IEEE World Congress on Computational Intelligence, vol. 1, pp. 82–87. IEEE (1994)
13. Kirkpatrick, S., Gelatt Jr., C.D., Vecchi, M.P.: Optimization by simulated annealing. Science **220**(4598), 671–680 (1983)
14. Divina, F., Pontes, B., Giraldez, R., Aguilar-Ruiz, J.S.: An effective measure for assessing the quality of biclusters. Comput. Biol. Med. **42**(2), 245–256 (2012)

Hybrid Intelligent Systems for Data Mining and Applications

A Hybrid Approach to Closeness in the Framework of Order of Magnitude Qualitative Reasoning

Alfredo Burrieza[1], Emilio Muñoz-Velasco[2(✉)], and Manuel Ojeda-Aciego[2]

[1] Dept. Filosofía, Universidad de Málaga, Málaga, Spain
burrieza@uma.es
[2] Dept. Matemática Aplicada, Universidad de Málaga, Málaga, Spain
{emilio,aciego}@ctima.uma.es

Abstract. Qualitative reasoning deals with information expressed in terms of qualitative classes and relations among them, such as comparability, negligibility or closeness. In this paper, we focus on the notion of closeness using a hybrid approach which is based on logic, order-of-magnitude reasoning, and on the so-called *proximity structures*; these structures will be used to decide the elements that are close to each other. Some of the intuitions of this approach are explained on the basis of examples. Moreover, we show some capabilities of the logic with respect to expressivity in order to denote particular positions of the proximity intervals.

1 Introduction

Qualitative Reasoning (QR) deals with information expressed in terms of qualitative classes and relations among them, such as comparability, negligibility or closeness. This theory has proven to be useful for solving problems about systems in absence of exact data. QR has found many applications in Artificial Intelligence [3–6,8–11]; even some logic-based approaches to QR can be seen in [2,12].

In this paper, we introduce an approach to the notions of closeness and negligibility which can be seen as hybrid in many ways: on the one hand, it considers jointly multi-modal logics and order-of-magnitude qualitative reasoning, in the line of [7]; on the other hand, it considers both the absolute and the relative approaches to order-of-magnitude, in which the former is a purely qualitative approach based on abstractions of quantitative values, whereas the latter is based on relations between quantitative values.

The qualitative approach we will consider here is more general than that given in [13] since we consider a qualitative class INF of *infinitesimals*, as it allows to somehow consider non-measurable quantities. Note that these infinitesimals will be interpreted as numbers indistinguishable from 0 in the sense that their difference cannot be measured, not in the sense of hyperreal numbers.

Partially supported by the Spanish research project TIN2012-39353-C04-01.

F. Martínez-Álvarez et al. (Eds.): HAIS 2016, LNAI 9648, pp. 721–729, 2016.
DOI: 10.1007/978-3-319-32034-2_60

The underlying idea of our notion of closeness, to be introduced later, is that two (quantitative) values are said to be *close* whenever they belong to a given area or *proximity interval*. This approach is purely crisp and does not use fuzzy set-related ideas as in [1], where a fuzzy set-based approach for handling relative orders of magnitude was introduced. The reason why closeness will be based on membership to a certain element of a given set of proximity intervals, instead of making distance-based assumptions, is that our goal is to define an abstract framework for dealing with natural or artificial barriers, for instance, two people are situated in both banks of a river, although they could be very close geometrically, it might be a long walk if they would like actually to meet; another example, now based on artificial barriers, can be seen with respect to full age, for instance, Alice is born on March 29 and Bob is born on March 30 in the same year (hence their ages are very close); for legal purposes, Alice reaches full age one day before Bob, hence it might happen that Alice would be allowed to participate on presidential elections on March 29 but Bob is not because he has not reached full age yet.

In this paper, we introduce a multimodal logic for order of magnitude reasoning which manages the notions of closeness and negligibility. The main contributions are a new definition of closeness (given in terms of the so-called proximity structures) and its treatment in a multimodal logic context.

The rest of the paper is organized as follows: Section 2 is devoted to the introduction of the framework, the qualitative classes and the notions of closeness and negligibility. The multimodal logic in introduced in Sect. 3, whereas soundness, completeness, decidability, and complexity are studied in Sect. 4. Finally, some conclusions and lines of future work are drawn in Sect. 5.

2 On the Notions of Closeness and Neglibility

We will consider a strictly ordered set of real numbers $(\mathbb{S}, <)$ divided into the following qualitative classes:

$$NL = (-\infty, -\gamma) \qquad\qquad PS = (+\alpha, +\beta]$$
$$NM = [-\gamma, -\beta) \qquad INF = [-\alpha, +\alpha] \qquad PM = (+\beta, +\gamma]$$
$$NS = [-\beta, -\alpha) \qquad\qquad PL = (+\gamma, +\infty)$$

Note that all the intervals are considered relative to $\mathbb{S}$.

The labels correspond to "negative large" (NL), "negative medium"(NM), "negative small" (NS), "infinitesimals" (INF), "positive small" (PS), "positive medium" (PM) and "positive large" (PL). It is worth to note that this classification is slightly more general than the standard one [13], since the qualitative class containing the element 0, i.e. INF, needs not be a singleton; this allows for considering values very close to zero as null values in practice, which is more in line with a qualitative approach where accurate measurements are not always possible.

Let us now introduce the notion of closeness. As stated in the introduction, the intuitive idea underlying our notion of closeness is that, in real life problems,

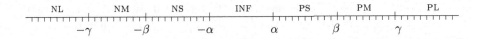

Fig. 1. Proximity intervals.

there are situations in which we consciously choose not to distinguish between *certain* pairs of elements (for instance, two cars priced 19 000 € and 18 000 € might be both acceptable, but perhaps 20 000 € is considered too expensive for our budget). Somehow, there exist some areas of indistinguishability so that x is said to be close to y if and only if both x and y belong to the same area (although, in the example, 18 000 and 20 000 are equidistant to 19 000, the psychological perception[1] is that 20 000 might be too expensive and, therefore, it is not considered close to 19 000).

We will consider each qualitative class to be divided into disjoint intervals called *proximity intervals*, as shown in Fig. 1. The qualitative class INF is itself one proximity interval.

Definition 1. *Let* $(\mathbb{S}, <)$ *be a strictly linear ordering divided into the qualitative classes defined above.*

- *An* r-proximity structure *is a finite set* $\mathcal{I}(\mathbb{S}) = \{I_1, I_2, \ldots, I_r\}$ *of* proximity intervals *in* $\mathbb{S}$, *such that:*
  1. *For all* $I_i, I_j \in \mathcal{I}(\mathbb{S})$, *if* $i \neq j$, *then* $I_i \cap I_j = \varnothing$.
  2. $I_1 \cup I_2 \cup \cdots \cup I_r = \mathbb{S}$.
  3. *For all* $x, y \in \mathbb{S}$ *and* $I_i \in \mathcal{I}(\mathbb{S})$, *if* $x, y \in I_i$, *then* x, y *belong to the same qualitative class.*
  4. INF $\in \mathcal{I}(\mathbb{S})$.
- *Given a proximity structure* $\mathcal{I}(\mathbb{S})$, *the binary relation of closeness* $\mathfrak{c}$ *is defined, for all* $x, y \in \mathbb{S}$, *as follows:* $x \,\mathfrak{c}\, y$ *if and only if there exists* $I_i \in \mathcal{I}(\mathbb{S})$ *such that* $x, y \in I_i$.

Notice that, as a consequence of item 3 above, each proximity interval is included in some qualitative class; this feature will be used later.

It is also worth to notice that, by definition, the number of proximity intervals is finite, regardless of the cardinality of the set $\mathbb{S}$. This choice is justified by the nature of the measuring devices that after reaching a certain limit, they do not distinguish among nearly equal amounts; for instance, consider the limits to represent numbers in a pocket calculator, thermometer, speedometer, etc.

As a result of considering just finitely many proximity intervals, it can be the case that two elements exist whose magnitudes are not comparable but, according to this approach, turn out to be comparable. In everyday life, we often face similar situations where excessively large quantities are no longer considered to have an appreciable difference. For instance, if the limit of users

---

[1] This is a well-known effect in marketing.

simultaneously connected to a server is, say, 1 000 000 users, it is clear that the response would be the same than if 10 000 000 users are connected to the server. In this case, although these quantities may not be comparable in absolute terms, they turn out to be comparable from the point of view of the response of the server. Nevertheless, if for some reason, we need these quantities to be not comparable, we have just to change the choice of the qualitative classes in our approach.

From now on, we will denote by $\mathcal{Q} = \{\text{NL, NM, NS, INF, PS, PM, PL}\}$ the set of qualitative classes, and by QC to any element of $\mathcal{Q}$.

The following proposition is an immediate consequence of the previous definition.

Proposition 1. *The relation* c *defined above has the following properties:*

1. c *is an equivalence relation on* $\mathbb{S}$.
2. *For all* $x, y, z \in \mathbb{S}$, *the following holds:*
   (a) *If* $x, y \in \text{INF}$, *then* x c y.
   (b) *For every* $QC \in \mathcal{Q}$, *if* $x \in QC$ *and* x c y, *then* $y \in QC$.

The informal notion of negligibility we will use in this paper is the following: x is said to be *negligible* with respect to y if and only if either (i) x is infinitesimal and y is not, or (ii) x is small (but not infinitesimal) and y is *sufficiently large*. Formally:

Definition 2. *Let* $(\mathbb{S}, <)$ *be a strictly linear divided into the qualitative classes defined above. The binary relation of negligibility* n *is defined on* $\mathbb{S}$ *as* x n y *if and only if one of the following situations holds:*

(i) $x \in \text{INF}$ *and* $y \notin \text{INF}$,
(ii) $x \in \text{NS} \cup \text{PS}$ *and* $y \in \text{NL} \cup \text{PL}$.

The following straightforward result states some interesting properties about the interaction between the relations of closeness and negligibility.

Proposition 2. *For all* $x, y, z \in \mathbb{S}$ *we have:*

(i) *If* x c y *and* y n z, *then* x n z.
(ii) *If* x n y *and* y c z, *then* x n z.

In order to further explain the underlying behavior of the definitions of closeness and negligibility, we include the following example.

Example 1. It does not rain very often in a city like Málaga (Spain), but there is a real danger of floods due to torrential rain. For this reason, there is a reservoir very close to the city in order to control the water flooding from the mountains. We represent the quantity of water in the reservoir by positive qualitative classes PS, PM, PL, and consider the proximity intervals, with a length that can be considered as non-significative with respect to the total quantity of water of the reservoir, for instance 1 000 litres. Using the previous definitions, we can express many interesting situations. For instance, assume that PS is the level of water in the reservoir considered OK (that is, safe), with PM a warning message must be shown, and PL is a dangerous situation that forces to open the floodgates. If the quantity of water x is OK, that is $x \in$ PS and some rain is expected, such as the quantity of water will increase to y, several results are possible out of which we detail the following: (a) if $x \mathrel{c} y$, then $y \in$ PS, meaning that if a small rain is expected, then the situation will remain OK and there is no need to open the floodgates; (b) if $x \mathrel{n} y$, then $y \in$ PL, which means that if a big rain is expected, the floodgates must be opened and some water has to be released.

The properties given in Proposition 2 can be used in this context. If a small rain is coming ($x \mathrel{c} y$) an after that a big rain is expected ($y \mathrel{n} z$), then the floodgates must be opened ($x \mathrel{n} z$), by using property (i). Similarly, property (ii) in Proposition 2 can be used whenever a big rain is coming ($x \mathrel{n} y$) followed by a small rain ($y \mathrel{c} z$), so the floodgates must be opened also ($x \mathrel{n} z$).

We now introduce the our logic that will allow to reason, for instance, in situations as the shown in the previous example.

3   Syntax and Semantics of $\mathcal{L}(MQ)^{\mathcal{P}}$

In this section, we will use as special modal connectives $\overrightarrow{\square}$ and $\overleftarrow{\square}$ to deal with the usual ordering $<$, so $\overrightarrow{\square}A$ and $\overleftarrow{\square}A$ have the informal readings: *A is true for all numbers greater than the current one* and *A is true for all number less than the current one*, respectively. Two other modal operators will be used, $\boxdot$ for closeness, where the informal reading of $\boxdot A$ is: *A is true for all number close to the current one*, and $\boxed{n}$ for negligibility, where $\boxed{n}A$ means *A is true for all number with respect to the current one is negligible*.

The alphabet of the language $\mathcal{L}(MQ)^{\mathcal{P}}$ is defined by using a stock of atoms or propositional variables, $\mathcal{V}$, the classical connectives $\neg, \wedge, \vee$ and $\rightarrow$; the constants for milestones $\alpha^-, \alpha^+, \beta^-, \beta^+, \gamma^-, \gamma^+$; a finite set $\mathcal{C}$ of constants for proximity intervals, $\mathcal{C} = \{c_1, \ldots, c_r\}$ [2]; the unary modal connectives $\overrightarrow{\square}, \overleftarrow{\square}, \boxed{n}, \boxdot$, and the parentheses '(' and ')'. We define the formulas of $\mathcal{L}(MQ)^{\mathcal{P}}$ as follows:

$$A = p \mid \xi \mid c_i \mid \neg A \mid (A \wedge A) \mid (A \vee A) \mid (A \rightarrow A) \mid \overrightarrow{\square}A \mid \overleftarrow{\square}A \mid \boxed{n}A \mid \boxdot A$$

where $p \in \mathcal{V}$, $\xi \in \{\alpha^+, \alpha^-, \beta^+, \beta^-, \gamma^+, \gamma^-\}$ and $c_i \in \mathcal{C}$. In order to refer to any constant for positive milestones as α^+ we will use ξ^+ and for negative ones as β^- we will use ξ^-.

The *mirror image* of a formula A is the result of replacing in A each occurrence of $\overrightarrow{\square}, \overleftarrow{\square}, \alpha^+, \beta^+$ and γ^+ respectively by $\overleftarrow{\square}, \overrightarrow{\square}, \alpha^-, \beta^-$ and γ^- and reciprocally.

We will use the symbols $\overrightarrow{\lozenge}, \overleftarrow{\lozenge}, \lozenge\!\!\!\!\diamond, \lozenge\!\!\!\!\diamond$ as abbreviations, respectively, of $\neg\overrightarrow{\square}\neg$, $\neg\overleftarrow{\square}\neg$, $\neg\boxdot\neg$ and $\neg\boxed{n}\neg$. Moreover, we will introduce nl, $\ldots$, pl as abbreviations

---

[2] There are at least as many elements in $\mathcal{C}$ as qualitative classes.

for qualitative classes, for instance, ps for $(\overleftarrow{\lozenge}\alpha^+ \wedge \overrightarrow{\lozenge}\beta^+) \vee \beta^+$. By means of qc we denote any element of the set $\{\mathsf{nl}, \mathsf{nm}, \mathsf{ns}, \mathsf{inf}, \mathsf{ps}, \mathsf{pm}, \mathsf{pl}\}$.

The cardinality r of the set $\mathcal{C}$ of constants for proximity intervals will play an important role since it, somehow, encodes the granularity of the underlying logic. This implies that, actually, *we are introducing a family of logics which depend parametrically on r.*

Definition 3. *A multimodal qualitative frame for $\mathcal{L}(MQ)^{\mathcal{P}}$ (a frame, for short) is a tuple $\Sigma = (\mathbb{S}, \mathcal{D}, <, \mathcal{I}(\mathbb{S}), \mathcal{P})$, where:*

1. $(\mathbb{S}, <)$ *is a strict linearly ordered set.*
2. $\mathcal{D} = \{+\alpha, -\alpha, +\beta, -\beta, +\gamma, -\gamma\}$ *is a set of designated points in $\mathbb{S}$ (called mile-stones).*
3. $\mathcal{I}(\mathbb{S})$ *is an r-proximity structure.*
4. $\mathcal{P}$ *is a bijection (called proximity function), $\mathcal{P}\colon \mathcal{C} \longrightarrow \mathcal{I}(\mathbb{S})$, that assigns to each proximity constant c a proximity interval.*

Notice that item 4 above means that every proximity interval corresponds to one and only one proximity constant.

Definition 4. *Let Σ be a frame for $\mathcal{L}(MQ)^{\mathcal{P}}$, a multimodal qualitative model on Σ (a MQ-model, for short) is an ordered pair $\mathcal{M} = (\Sigma, h)$, where h is a meaning function (or, interpretation) $h\colon \mathcal{V} \longrightarrow 2^{\mathbb{S}}$. Any interpretation can be uniquely extended to the set of all formulas in $\mathcal{L}(MQ)^{\mathcal{P}}$ (also denoted by h) by means of the usual conditions for the classical Boolean connectives and the following conditions:*

$$h(\overrightarrow{\square}A) = \{x \in \mathbb{S} \mid y \in h(A) \text{ for all } y \text{ such that } x < y\}$$
$$h(\overleftarrow{\square}A) = \{x \in \mathbb{S} \mid y \in h(A) \text{ for all } y \text{ such that } y < x\}$$
$$h(\boxdot A) = \{x \in \mathbb{S} \mid y \in h(A) \text{ for all } y \text{ such that } x \,\mathfrak{c}\, y\}$$
$$h(\boxminus A) = \{x \in \mathbb{S} \mid y \in h(A) \text{ for all } y \text{ such that } x \,\mathfrak{n}\, y\}$$
$$h(\alpha^+) = \{+\alpha\} \qquad h(\beta^+) = \{+\beta\} \qquad h(\gamma^+) = \{+\gamma\}$$
$$h(\alpha^-) = \{-\alpha\} \qquad h(\beta^-) = \{-\beta\} \qquad h(\gamma^-) = \{-\gamma\}$$
$$h(c_i) = \{x \in \mathbb{S} \mid x \in \mathcal{P}(c_i)\}$$

The definitions of *truth*, *satisfiability* and *validity* are the usual ones.

Example 2. The aim of this example is to specify in $\mathcal{L}(MQ)^{\mathcal{P}}$ the behavior of a device to automatically control the speed of a car. Assume the system has, ideally, to maintain the speed close to some speed limit v. For practical purposes, any value in an interval $[v - \varepsilon, v + \varepsilon]$ for small ε is admissible. The extreme points of this interval can then be considered as the milestones $-\alpha$ and $+\alpha$ of our frames; on the other hand, we will consider different levels of velocity in a qualitative approach ranging from *very slow* to *very fast*. We will introduce consequently the atoms $\mathsf{v}_{-3}, \mathsf{v}_{-2}, \mathsf{v}_{-1}, \mathsf{v}_0, \mathsf{v}_1, \mathsf{v}_2, \mathsf{v}_3$ associated to them (which are interpreted, respectively, as the qualitative classes NL, NM, NS, INF, PS, PM, PL and, moreover, v_0 represents the interval $[v - \varepsilon, v + \varepsilon]$).

We will introduce also the atoms `accelerate`, `maintain`, `release` and `brake` to describe actions of the system with their intuitive meaning.

Now we represent how the system works:

1. Whenever the speed is below the intended limit, then the engine is accelerated, whereas when the speed is within the admissible limits, the speed is maintained. Thus, we have the two formulas below

$$(v_{-3} \lor v_{-2} \lor v_{-1}) \to \texttt{accelerate} \qquad v_0 \to \texttt{maintain}$$

2. It can happen that the speed increases more than the limit allowed due to external factors, for instance when the road has negative slope, this way some rules are required to maintain the speed. Usually, when the car reaches the speed limit, the driver does not brake immediately but releases the accelerator instead, so that the air friction helps to recover an admissible speed. We accomplish this action precisely in the proximity interval immediately after v_0, which we will call, say, c. As a result, we have the two formulas

$$c \to (\overleftarrow{\Diamond} \alpha^+ \wedge \overleftarrow{\Box}(\overleftarrow{\Diamond} \alpha^+ \to c)) \qquad c \to \texttt{release}$$

3. When we are beyond the limit imposed by the interval c, then the system has to *actively* brake:

$$(\neg c \wedge \overleftarrow{\Diamond} c) \to \texttt{brake}$$

According to the intended meaning of the previous formulas, the atoms `accelerate`, `keep`, `release` and `brake` are true, respectively, at

$$\text{NL} \cup \text{NM} \cup \text{NS} \qquad \text{INF} \qquad I_c \qquad (\text{PS} \setminus I_c) \cup \text{PM} \cup \text{PL}$$

where I_c is the proximity interval represented by c. Note that the length of this interval depends on the granularity of the system; indeed, given the axiom **m1**, I_c should be included in the class PS.

Some consequences of the behavior of the system (specifically, valid formulas in the model) are the following:

`brake` $\to \overrightarrow{\Box}$`brake`
(If the system brakes at a specific speed, then it brakes at higher speeds)
`release` $\to \boxed{c}(v_1 \wedge \neg$`brake`$)$
(If the throttle is released at certain speed, then any small variation implies that the speed is still slightly fast and the system does not brake)
`release` $\to \boxed{n}(v_{-3} \to$ `accelerate`$)$
(If the throttle is released at certain speed and, by any circumstances, the speed decreases excessively, then it has to accelerate again)
`accelerate` $\to \boxed{c}\neg$`brake`
(If the system accelerates, it will not brake immediately)
$v_0 \to \overrightarrow{\Box}(v_2 \to \overleftarrow{\Diamond}$`release`$)$
(The throttle is released before reaching a fast speed)

4   On the Expressivity of $\mathcal{L}(MQ)^\mathcal{P}$ wrt Proximity Intervals

In this section, we consider the question whether it is possible to express the positions, with respect to the underlying ordering, of the proximity intervals within a qualitative class by means of formulas of $\mathcal{L}(MQ)^\mathcal{P}$. Specifically, is there a formula of $\mathcal{L}(MQ)^\mathcal{P}$ which is true, for instance, just in the n-th proximity interval of PS in any model? In what follows we will focus just on the values which are greater than $+\alpha$.

The following formula

$$\bigvee_{i=1}^{r} (c_i \wedge \overleftarrow{\Box}(\overleftarrow{\Diamond}\alpha^+ \to c_i) \wedge \overleftarrow{\Diamond}\alpha^+) \tag{1}$$

expresses the first proximity interval after $+\alpha$, in the sense that it is true just in the points belonging to that interval.

Formally, assume a model $\mathcal{M} = (\mathbb{S}, \mathcal{D}, <, \mathcal{I}(\mathbb{S}), \mathcal{P}, h)$ and let K be the first proximity interval after $+\alpha$ in $\mathcal{M}$. We will prove that the formula above is true in a point x (with respect to the model $\mathcal{M}$) if and only if $x \in K$.

Assume that c_k, for some $k \in \{1, \ldots, r\}$, is assigned by the function $\mathcal{P}$ to the interval K, that is, $\mathcal{P}(c_k) = K$.

1. Given $x \in K$ we have that $x \in h(c_k)$. Moreover, since $+\alpha < x$ and $+\alpha \in h(\alpha^+)$, then $\overleftarrow{\Diamond}\alpha^+ \in h(x)$. For all y smaller than x, we trivially have $y \in h(\overleftarrow{\Diamond}\alpha^+ \to c_k)$, then $x \in h(\overleftarrow{\Box}(\overleftarrow{\Diamond}\alpha^+ \to c_k))$. Thus, we have

$$x \in h(c_k \wedge \overleftarrow{\Box}(\overleftarrow{\Diamond}\alpha^+ \to c_k) \wedge \overleftarrow{\Diamond}\alpha^+)$$

   and, hence, the formula (1) is true in x.

2. Conversely, assume $x \notin K$. By definition of the proximity structure, we have that x belongs to some proximity interval $J \neq K$, and assume that $\mathcal{P}(c_j) = J$. In these conditions, the only disjunct of formula (1) that could be true in x would be the following

$$c_j \wedge \overleftarrow{\Box}(\overleftarrow{\Diamond}\alpha^+ \to c_j) \wedge \overleftarrow{\Diamond}\alpha^+$$

   Now, there are two possibilities:
   - If x is to the left of K, then clearly $x \notin h(\overleftarrow{\Diamond}\alpha^+)$
   - If x is to the right of K, then $x \notin h(\overleftarrow{\Box}(\overleftarrow{\Diamond}\alpha^+ \to c_j))$, because $\overleftarrow{\Diamond}\alpha^+ \to c_j$ is not true in the points of K.

   either of which proves that formula (1) is not true in x.

In the same manner, we can express the last proximity interval of the qualitative class PS, that is, the interval containing the milestone $+\beta$ can be defined as follows:

$$\bigvee_{i=1}^{r} (c_i \wedge \overrightarrow{\Box}((\beta^+ \vee \overrightarrow{\Diamond}\beta^+) \to c_i) \wedge \overrightarrow{\Diamond}(\beta^+ \vee \overrightarrow{\Diamond}\beta^+))$$

5 Conclusions and Future Work

Logics for order of magnitude reasoning are important to deal with situations where numerical values are either imprecise or unavailable. Negligibility and closeness are two important relations in the area of qualitative reasoning and, in this paper, we have presented a multimodal logic for order of magnitude reasoning which considers negligibility and a new approach to closeness, based on *proximity intervals*.

The notion of proximity interval turns out to be a useful tool to decide whether two elements are close to each other; in the formal language, proximity intervals are referred to by means of *proximity constants*. We have shown some capabilities of the logic with respect to expressivity in order to denote particular positions of the proximity intervals.

As future work, we have a twofold plan: on the one hand, to study completeness and the decidability of the logic, considering a tableau system for deciding the satisfiability of the formulas of our logic; other hand, we would like to study and develop other logics based on different notions of closeness and negligibility.

References

1. Ali, A., Dubois, D., Prade, H.: Qualitative reasoning based on fuzzy relative orders of magnitude. IEEE Trans. Fuzzy Syst. **11**(1), 9–23 (2003)
2. Bennett, B., Cohn, A., Wolter, F., Zakharyaschev, M.: Multi-dimensional modal logic as a framework for spatio-temporal reasoning. Appl. Intell. **17**(3), 239–251 (2002)
3. Burrieza, A., Muñoz-Velasco, E., Ojeda-Aciego, M.: A PDL approach for qualitative velocity. Int. J. Uncertainty Fuzziness Knowl. Based Syst. **19**(1), 11–26 (2011)
4. Chan, C.S., Coghill, G.M., Liu, H.: Recent advances in fuzzy qualitative reasoning. Int. J. Uncertainty Fuzziness Knowl. Based Syst. **19**(3), 417–422 (2011)
5. Chavez, G., Zerkle, D., Key, B., Shevitz, D.: Relating confidence to measured information uncertainty in qualitative reasoning. In: 2011 Annual Meeting of the North American Fuzzy Information Processing Society (NAFIPS), pp. 1–6. IEEE (2011)
6. Falcó, E., García-Lapresta, J.L., Llorenç, R.: Allowing agents to be imprecise: a proposal using multiple linguistic terms. Inf. Sci. **258**, 249–265 (2014). 2
7. Golińska-Pilarek, J., Muñoz-Velasco, E.: A hybrid qualitative approach for relative movements. Logic J. IGPL **23**(3), 410–420 (2015)
8. Liu, H., Brown, D.J., Coghill, G.M.: Fuzzy qualitative robot kinematics. IEEE Trans. Fuzzy Syst. **16**(3), 808–822 (2008)
9. Mossakowski, T., Moratz, R.: Qualitative reasoning about relative direction of oriented points. Artif. Intell. **180**, 34–45 (2012)
10. Muñoz-Velasco, E., Burrieza, A., Ojeda-Aciego, M.: A logic framework for reasoning with movement based on fuzzy qualitative representation. Fuzzy Sets Syst. **242**, 114–131 (2014)
11. Prats, F., Roselló, L., Sánchez, M., Agell, N.: Using *L*-fuzzy sets to introduce information theory into qualitative reasoning. Fuzzy Sets Syst. **236**, 73–90 (2014)
12. Shults, B., Kuipers, B.J.: Proving properties of continuous systems: qualitative simulation and temporal logic. Artif. Intell. **92**(1), 91–129 (1997)
13. Travé-Massuyès, L., Prats, F., Sánchez, M., Agell, N.: Relative and absolute order-of-magnitude models unified. Annal. Math. Artif. Intell. **45**, 323–341 (2005)

Hybrid Algorithm for Floor Detection Using GSM Signals in Indoor Localisation Task

Marcin Luckner[⊠] and Rafał Górak

Faculty of Mathematics and Information Science, Warsaw University of Technology,
ul. Koszykowa 75, 00–662 Warszawa, Poland
{mluckner,R.Gorak}@mini.pw.edu.pl

Abstract. One of challenging problems of indoor localisation based on GSM fingerprints is the detection of the current floor. We propose an off–line algorithm that labels fingerprints with the number of current floor. The algorithm uses one pass through the given route to learn the GSM fingerprints. After that the height on the testing passes of the same route can be estimated with high accuracy even for measures registered with various velocities and a month after the learning process. The two phase algorithm detects the points of a potential floor change. Next, the regression function normalises height of the change and calculates its direction. The obtained results are up to 40 % better than the results obtained by the pure regression.

1 Introduction

Indoor localisation based on cellular networks signal strengths is a specific approach to an indoor localisation because it does not need any additional infrastructure inside a building nor any specific localisation equipment except a common mobile phone.

Several works presented localisation system based on Global System for Mobile Communications (GSM) [1–3,10]. To sum up their results, it can be said that a horizontal localisation of a mobile phone can be done with relatively small error of a few meters. However, detection of the current floor is still a challenge.

The paper [12] presented a cellular network fingerprinting-based system, which determines the current floor on which a user with a mobile phone is located. The tests were done in 9 to 16-storey buildings. The system classified the floor correctly in up to 73 % of cases and nearly 100 % of measures were localised with an error less or equal to three floors. However, such results are not (rewarding) satisfying for lower buildings.

In this paper we solve the floor detection problem for the predefined route. After one passing through the monitoring route with a registration of GSM fingerprints we can, with high accuracy, label floors on the tracks that lead through a similar route. The system works for the tracks travelled with various velocities and registered a month after the learning trace.

© Springer International Publishing Switzerland 2016
F. Martínez-Álvarez et al. (Eds.): HAIS 2016, LNAI 9648, pp. 730–741, 2016.
DOI: 10.1007/978-3-319-32034-2_61

The system uses a hybrid solution that connects detection of the points that can be used to change a floor with regression of the height that allows us to estimate the direction and the height of the change.

The system works off–line. Therefore, it cannot be used in real–time applications, but it is useful to monitor the behaviour of paroling units both human and robots.

The remaining part of the paper is organised as follows: Sect. 2 describes the detection algorithm, Sect. 3 shows the application of the system to detect a floor for six tracks. The work is concluded in Sect. 4.

2   Floor Detection Algorithm

The task which is solved by the floor detection algorithm is to estimate a height of a tracked object during its pass through the building. The estimation is done for the sequence of vectors of GSM signals (fingerprints). Each vector was measured in the point defined by three coordinates: x, y, and z. However, in this paper only the z coordinate is taken into consideration.

The proposed algorithm consists of two phases. The first phase detects moments when the z coordinate can change its value. The second estimates the direction and magnitude of the height change . Both phases – presented in Fig. 1 – are described in detail below.

For initiation, the algorithm needs one record of the learning track. The learning track is an ordered set of mappings of fingerprints into a height. The preprocessing compares the z coordinate between two following points. If the height difference is bigger than 0.1 meters then the both points are labelled as a floor changing points (*Change*). In other case the points are labelled as stable floor points (*Stable*). It should be stressed that the learning track is the only knowledge about a building infrastructure including automatically collected information about the possibility of a floor change.

The points labelled as *Change* or *Stable* create the learning set for a classification method. The classification method is used to detect whether the given point should be labelled as *Change* on the base of observed signals. We tested the following classification methods: the RUSBoost algorithm [9] that is dedicated to discriminate imbalance classes; the One–Class SVM algorithm [8] that creates a classifier for one class; the SVM algorithm [11] that is a very popular binary classifier. They can be replaced by any other classification algorithm.

Figure 1a shows detection results for the learning track. The *Stable* points are marked with red circles and the *Change* points with blue stars.

The learning trace is used once again to train a regression function to estimate the height on the track on the base of the fingerprints. We used the bagging algorithm [7] for that task, but the algorithm can be replaced by another regression method.

After the classification method and the regression function are trained on the learning track it is possible to apply the floor estimation algorithm to other tracks that are passing through the same or similar set of points. If the beginning

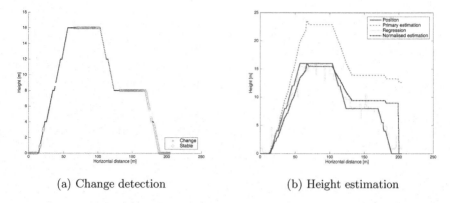

(a) Change detection   (b) Height estimation

Fig. 1. The two parts of the floor detection algorithm: the classification of the points of a floor change, the estimation and normalisation – using regression – of the height (Color figure online)

of the track is on the same level as the end, no additional information is necessary in the future estimation procedure.

On tracks the *Change* points are detected by the classification method. The change of the height can be estimated by an assumption that each *Change* point means a change of the height by d.

There are two issues in this step. The first one is the detection of the direction of the local change. The second one is the estimation of an absolute value of d for the whole track.

To solve the first issue the base height is set as zero. When the algorithm faces the sequence of *Change* points the regression of the height is calculated for all points of the sequence. If most of them are localised above the base level then the sequence is ascending. In the other case, the sequence is descending. Next the base level is changed by $\pm d \times n$ and the procedure is repeated for the next sequence of *Change* points.

The change of the height for the base height f and the sequence of n points can be calculated as

$$\delta f = n \times d \times \mathrm{sgn}\left(\sum_1^n \mathrm{sgn}(f - \hat{f}_i)\right), \tag{1}$$

where f_i is value of the regression function for the ith point and sgn is the signum function.

The second issue is solved by the following approach. First, the d is fixed as 16 cm, which is a common size of the step on the staircase. Next, the created estimation is normalised. The normalisation is done on the base of the regression function that estimates the height on the whole track.

The normalisation is done separately for the ascending and the descending part of the track. First, the last point of the descending sequence is localised and its position is labelled as h. For all points from 1 to h the normalised height $\bar{f}_i$ is calculated as

$$\bar{f}_i = \frac{max\hat{f}(f_i - \min_i(f_i))}{\max_i(f_i) - \min_i(f_i)} \text{ for } i = 1, \ldots, h, \tag{2}$$

where $\hat{f}$ is the regression function and f is the height estimated using formula (1).

The second part of points is normalised using the following formula

$$\bar{f}_i = \frac{\bar{f}_h(f_i - f_h)}{f_h - \min_i(f_i)} + \bar{f}_h \text{ for } i = h + 1, \ldots, n \tag{3}$$

Figure 1b shows the previous estimation f, the regression $\hat{f}$, and the normalised estimation $\bar{f}$ for the learning track 41944.

Finally, the obtained height function $\bar{f}$ is converted into discrete values to detect a current floor. For that, the continuous value $\bar{f}$ is divided by 4 and rounded to the nearest integer.

3 Results

The analysis will be conducted on data collected in the publicly accessible areas of a six floor academic building (including the ground floor). The building has an irregular shape. Its outer dimensions are around 50 by 70 m and its height is 24 m.

Data sets consist of vectors of the signal strengths from $\mathbb{R}^7$ labelled by the height of the point z. The elements of the data sets are commonly called fingerprints.

The fingerprinting approach for indoor localisation is to build a model based on a data set of training fingerprints. The fingerprints are vectors of signal strengths labelled with a localisation. In our case the localisation is defined by a height of the measuring point. Using a classification model one can now label a new vector of signal strengths (fingerprint) with an estimated height. More information on the building and the collected data can be found in [4,5].

The algorithm was tested on a scenario. The scenario is a real path that includes changes of the floor. Each scenario was recorded several times as multiple tracks. The first track was used as the learning set. The rest were used as the testing set. All tracks were registered by a mobile phone held in a hand.

The data was collected in several independent series – tracks. The scenario contains 7 tracks with GSM signals. The first track 41935 was used as the learning set. The rest of traces created the testing set. What is important is that two tracks 49055 and 49057 were recorded nearly a month after the recording of the learning track. Therefore, the results for these tracks will show us how well the presented method works after a long time.

The data was collected using the Android application created for the localisation system [6].

3.1   Floor Change Detection

All classifiers and all types of signals were evaluated separately. Evaluation for each track contains True Positive, False Positive, True Negative, and False Negative numbers. Additionally, True Positive Rate, False Positive Rate, Accuracy, and F1–measure were calculated.

Table 1 presents the results obtained for the learning track 41944 and tor the testing tracks. In the test GSM signal were used. As a classifier an SVM classifier was used.

Table 1. Height change detection using SVM

Track	TP	FP	TN	FN	TPR	FPR	ACC	F1
41944	155	50	597	60	0.72	0.08	0.87	0.74
41935	118	24	505	357	0.25	0.05	0.62	0.38
41942	235	29	538	135	0.64	0.05	0.82	0.74
41945	122	36	318	84	0.59	0.10	0.79	0.67
45268	205	9	639	146	0.58	0.01	0.84	0.73
49055	193	19	365	108	0.64	0.05	0.81	0.75
49057	174	10	262	144	0.55	0.04	0.74	0.69

Table 2 presents the results obtained for the learning track 41944 and tor the testing tracks. In the test GSM signals were used. As a classifier an RUSBoost classifier was used.

Table 2. Height change detection using RUSBoost

Track	TP	FP	TN	FN	TPR	FPR	ACC	F1
41944	187	18	573	84	0.69	0.03	0.88	0.79
41935	127	15	478	384	0.25	0.03	0.60	0.39
41942	242	22	501	172	0.58	0.04	0.79	0.71
41945	143	15	265	137	0.51	0.05	0.73	0.65
45268	190	24	604	181	0.51	0.04	0.79	0.65
49055	151	61	347	126	0.55	0.15	0.73	0.62
49057	81	103	292	114	0.42	0.26	0.63	0.43

Table 3 presents the results obtained for the learning track 41944 and tor the testing tracks. In the test GSM signals were used. As a classifier an One–Class SVM classifier was used.

We observe that the One–Class SVM cannot solve the detection problem. Most of the observations were classified to the same class. The results obtained

Table 3. Height change detection using One–Class SVM

Track	TP	FP	TN	FN	TPR	FPR	ACC	F1
41944	57	148	282	375	0.13	0.34	0.39	0.18
41935	71	71	529	333	0.18	0.12	0.60	0.26
41942	65	199	395	278	0.19	0.34	0.49	0.21
41945	45	113	219	183	0.20	0.34	0.47	0.23
45268	50	164	339	446	0.10	0.33	0.39	0.14
49055	35	177	388	85	0.29	0.31	0.62	0.21
49057	50	134	268	138	0.27	0.33	0.54	0.27

by the RUSBoost algorithm and the SVM method are similar, but generally the SVM method is better. Therefore, the SVM was selected as a floor change detection for the future works.

Figure 2 shows the results obtained by the SVM method for all testing classes. We see differences between tracks that may be a result of different speed during measures, which is suggested by different distances between measured points. However, the long segments of *Stable* points were mostly well detected.

3.2 Height Estimation

The height is a base for the future floor detection. To evaluate the results of this step of the algorithm, the obtained height estimation was compared with the results of the regression function. The metrics used to compare the methods are median, mean, and 80th percentile of the estimation and regression errors.

Table 4 compares the results of the height estimation based on the defection of height changes done by the SVM.

Table 4. Height estimation for scenario Main staircase using GSM signals and SVM

Track	Regression mean	Estimation mean	Regression median	Estimation median	Regression 80 percentile	Estimation 80 percentile
41944	0.44	1.49	0.16	1.41	0.76	1.42
41935	2.66	1.10	1.84	0.91	4.83	1.83
41942	2.34	3.10	1.62	3.37	4.63	4.41
41945	2.16	1.23	1.14	0.56	3.94	2.14
45268	2.38	0.82	1.56	0.56	4.45	1.10
49055	3.42	1.06	2.31	0.76	6.69	1.62
49057	3.47	1.47	2.83	0.91	6.08	2.20

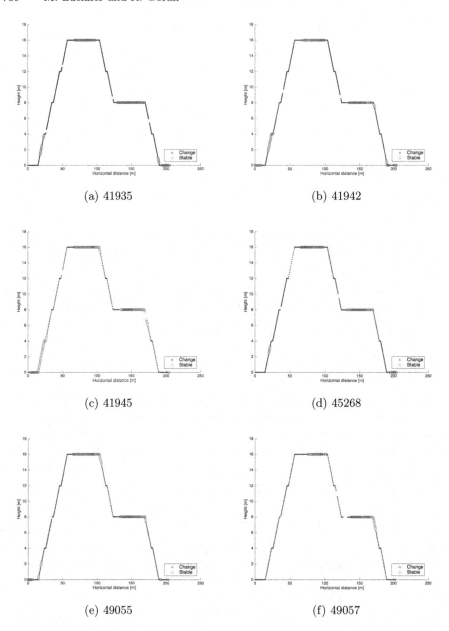

(a) 41935   (b) 41942

(c) 41945   (d) 45268

(e) 49055   (f) 49057

Fig. 2. Detection of points of floor change for the testing tracks

For us the most important is the threshold of 4 meters that is a floor height. If the height estimation is lower than this value we can assume that the floor will be correctly detected.

The regression error exceeds the limit of 4 meters for the 80th percentile of the measures. In case of the estimation in all cases – except track 41942 – the errors are much smaller. That allows us to assume that the floor detection accuracy can be greater than 80 % for these tracks.

Figure 3 shows the results obtained by the SVM method for all testing classes. The results obtained by regression are much more chaotic than the estimation results. Moreover, the estimated curve better reflects the original plot.

3.3   Floor Detection

The result of the algorithm is the number of the detected floor. The original number was calculated as an integer value of the z coordinate divided by the height of the floor. The same transformation was calculated for the regression function $\hat{f}$ and the estimated height $\bar{f}$.

Table 5 compares the results of the floor detection based on the detection of height changes done by the SVM. The two measures are compared. The first measure is the percent of correctly localised measuring points. The second measure is the longest distance with the correctly recognised floors.

Table 5. Floor detection using SVM

Track	Regression %	Estimation %	Regression [m]	Estimation [m]
41944	92.46	84.57	31.04	47.72
41935	49.30	81.27	22.41	50.89
41942	53.90	41.09	21.17	41.02
41945	60.89	75.54	50.87	50.87
45268	51.45	87.59	18.83	63.09
49055	42.77	82.92	17.17	50.27
49057	33.56	71.69	17.54	48.49

For all traces – except 41942 – the percent of points correctly localised on the floor is greater than 70 %. Figure 4 shows the estimation and the real position of the measure points. Analysing the worst results we can tell that the error for track 41942 is an effect of misclassification of the second floor. The second worst result – for track 49057 – is an effect of too narrow detection of the 4th floor.

Looking back on Fig. 3 we see how the final results are reflected in the previous estimations. In track 41942, the estimation goes too low and in track 49057 the regression does not reach the maximum of the real position plot.

It should be stressed that for both tracks that were measured a month after the learning track, the floor detection results are acceptable and better than the results obtained by the regression, taking into consideration both the percent of the correctly localised points and the longest correct distance.

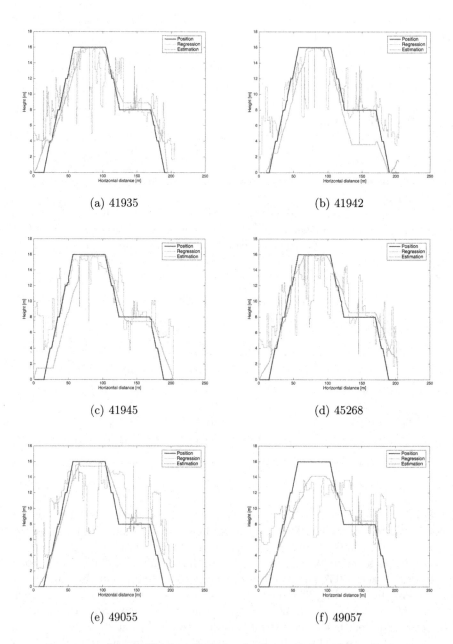

Fig. 3. Height estimation for the testing tracks

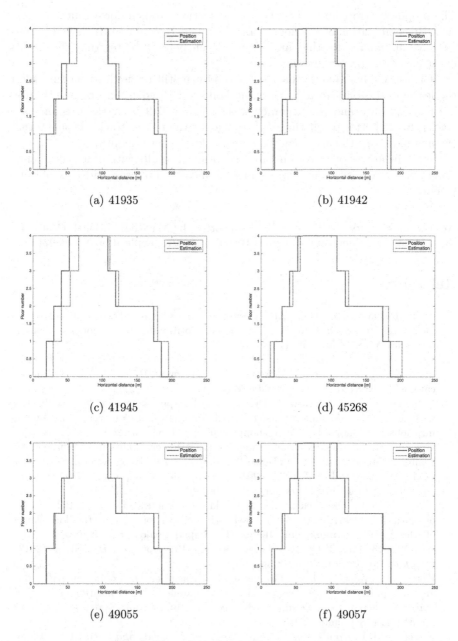

(a) 41935

(b) 41942

(c) 41945

(d) 45268

(e) 49055

(f) 49057

Fig. 4. Floor detection for the testing tracks

4   Conclusions

The proposed algorithm solves the floor detection problem for a route observation. By combination of the floor change points detection and the height regression, we obtain results that are several dozen percent better that the results obtained by the pure regression.

It is especially valuable that the method can still be used a long time after the learning session. We tested our method on data collected one month after the training data and the accuracy was 71.7 and 82.9 % for the two analysed tracks that is better result that the average for the rest of tracks. It shows that the method keeps the accuracy on the same level after a month.

In the future we want to compare the obtained results with other floor detection methods such as using pressure measurement and to use a wider set of route scenarios.

Acknowledgments. The research is supported by the the National Centre for Research and Development, grant No PBS2/B3/24/2014, application No 208921.

References

1. Ahriz, I., Oussar, Y., Denby, B., Dreyfus, G.: Carrier relevance study for indoor localization using GSM. In: 7th Workshop on Positioning Navigation and Communication (WPNC), pp. 168–173, March 2010
2. Brida, P., Cepel, P., Duha, J.: The accuracy of rss based positioning in GSM networks. In: International Conference on Microwaves, Radar Wireless Communications, MIKON 2006, pp. 541–544, May 2006
3. Denby, B., Oussar, Y., Ahriz, I., Dreyfus, G.: High-performance indoor localization with full-band GSM fingerprints. In: IEEE International Conference on Communications Workshops, ICC Workshopps 2009, pp. 1–5, June 2009
4. Grzenda, M.: On the prediction of floor identification credibility in RSS-based positioning techniques. In: Ali, M., Bosse, T., Hindriks, K.V., Hoogendoorn, M., Jonker, C.M., Treur, J. (eds.) IEA/AIE 2013. LNCS, vol. 7906, pp. 610–619. Springer, Heidelberg (2013). http://dx.doi.org/10.1007/978-3-642-38577-3_63
5. Karwowski, J., Okulewicz, M., Legierski, J.: Application of particle swarm optimization algorithm to neural network training process in the localization of the mobile terminal. In: Iliadis, L., Papadopoulos, H., Jayne, C. (eds.) EANN 2013, Part I. CCIS, vol. 383, pp. 122–131. Springer, Heidelberg (2013). http://dx.doi.org/10.1007/978-3-642-41013-0_13
6. Korbel, P., Wawrzyniak, P., Grabowski, S., Krasinska, D.: LocFusion API - programming interface for accurate multi-source mobile terminal positioning. In: Federated Conference on Computer Science and Information Systems (FedCSIS), pp. 819–823, September 2013
7. Kuncheva, L.I.: Combining Pattern Classifiers: Methods and Algorithms. Wiley-Interscience, Hoboken (2004)
8. Schölkopf, B., Platt, J.C., Shawe-Taylor, J.C., Smola, A.J., Williamson, R.C.: Estimating the support of a high-dimensional distribution. Neural Comput. **13**(7), 1443–1471 (2001). http://dx.doi.org/10.1162/089976601750264965

9. Seiffert, C., Khoshgoftaar, T., Van Hulse, J., Napolitano, A.: Rusboost: a hybrid approach to alleviating class imbalance. IEEE Trans. Syst. Man Cybern. Part B Cybern. **40**(1), 185–197 (2010)
10. Tian, Y., Denby, B., Ahriz, I., Roussel, P., Dreyfus, G.: Hybrid indoor localization using GSM fingerprints, embedded sensors and a particle filter. In: 11th International Symposium on Wireless Communications Systems (ISWCS), pp. 542–547, August 2014
11. Vapnik, V.: The Nature of Statistical Learning Theory. Information Science and Statistics. Springer, New York (1995)
12. Varshavsky, A., LaMarca, A., Hightower, J., de Lara, E.: The skyloc floor localization system. In: Fifth Annual IEEE International Conference on Pervasive Computing and Communications, PerCom 2007, pp. 125–134, March 2007

Hybrid Optimization Method Applied to Adaptive Splitting and Selection Algorithm

Pedro Lopez-Garcia[1]([✉]), Michał Woźniak[2], Enrique Onieva[1],
and Asier Perallos[1]

[1] Deusto Institute of Technology (DeustoTech), University of Deusto,
48007 Bilbao, Spain
{p.lopez,enrique.onieva,perallos}@deusto.es
[2] Department of Systems and Computer Networks,
Wrocław University of Technology,
Wybrzeże Wyspiańskiego 27, 50-370 Wrocław, Poland
michal.wozniak@pwr.edu.pl

Abstract. The paper presents an approach to train combined classifiers based on feature space splitting and selection of the best classifier ensemble to each subspace of feature space. The learning method uses a hybrid algorithm that combines a Genetic Algorithm and Cross Entropy Method. The proposed approach was evaluated on the basis of the comprehensive computer experiments run on balanced and imbalanced datasets, and compared with Cluster and Selection algorithm, improving the results obtained by this technique.

Keywords: Genetic algorithms · Cross entropy · Classification · Machine learning · Classifier ensemble · Hybrid optimization

1 Introduction

Classifier ensembles have been known for years and their usefulness has been confirmed in many practical tasks [19]. While designing such a system, selecting a valuable set of individuals plays a key role. It is obvious that such a set should group mutually complementary models [11]. Brown et al. [3] noticed that diversity of classifier set may be ensure by using implicitly or explicitly diversity maintaining algorithms. According to [13] the diversity of an individual classifiers may be ensured by one of the following approaches:

- Training each individual classifier to recognize a subset of classes only and then choose a combination rule that recovers the whole class set, as one-against-one or one-against-all strategies dedicated to binary and one-class classifiers or more sophisticated ECOC (*Error-Correcting Output Codes*) [5].
- Training individuals using different classifier models.
- Differentiating elementary classifier inputs [1], i.e.:
  1. using vertical or horizontal partitioning to train individuals on the basis on each partitions, i.e., using selected attributes or subsets of original data set;
  2. taking into consideration a local specialization of individual classifiers.

© Springer International Publishing Switzerland 2016
F. Martínez-Álvarez et al. (Eds.): HAIS 2016, LNAI 9648, pp. 742–750, 2016.
DOI: 10.1007/978-3-319-32034-2_62

In this work we will focus on the last strategy, because it allows to exploit local competencies of individuals [17], especially we would like to concentrate on the horizontal partitioning and selecting the most appriopriate classifier for each of the partition. Basically, we can found two main approaches related to the mentioned concept:

– Static classifier selection, where the relationship between the feature subspace and the assigned classifier is fixed. One of the first approach - clustering and selection (CS), was proposed by Kuncheva [12]. The extension of this concept - the adaptive splitting and selection algorithm (AdaSS), was published by Jackowski and Wozniak [9] (AdaSS).
– The dynamic classifier selection, in which the competencies of the individual classifiers are calculated during the classification operation [6].

This work deals with the static classifier selection and proposes a hybrid algorithm that combines a Genetic Algorithm (GA) and a Cross Entropy (CE) method as a method of classifier training. The main advantage of the proposed algorithm is the use of the exploration ability of a GA with the exploitation ability of a CE in order to make a feature-space partitioning and assigning classifier ensemble to each partition into one process. The main contribution of this work is that instead of evolutionary approach we propose to use original hybrid optimization method used as the training algorithm addresses the aforementioned problems.

The outline of this work is as follows. First, the propose the classification model and how the proposed method works is shown, then we present the results of the computer experiments. The last part concludes the work and formulates recommendations for further study.

2   Classifier Model

Firstly, let's present the classification model based on the feature space partitioning, which can exploit the local competencies of given classifiers. It assumes that the feature space $\mathcal{X}$ is partitioned into a set of H clusters

$$\mathcal{X} = \bigcup_{h=1}^{H} \hat{\mathcal{X}}_h, \quad \forall k,l \in \{1,...,H\}, \quad k \neq l, \quad \hat{\mathcal{X}}_k \cap \hat{\mathcal{X}}_l = \varnothing \tag{1}$$

where $\hat{\mathcal{X}}_h$ denotes the h-th constituent (cluster). The decision rule of such a combined classifier Ψ is given by the following decision rule

$$\Psi(x) = i \text{ if } \bar{\Psi}_h(x) = i \text{ and } x \in \hat{\mathcal{X}}_h. \tag{2}$$

where $\bar{\Psi}_h$ is a classifier assigned to the h-th cluster (called area classifier). It could be a classifier based on a single model or classifier ensemble as well. Meanwhile, we have to notice that the number of clusters H, which is an arbitrarily chosen parameter, plays a crucial role for the combined classifier accuracy.

On the one hand, a larger number of clusters makes a wider exploration of the local competencies of the area classifiers possible. On the other hand, it could lead the classifier overfitting. In this work, the parameter H is set to an unique value due to the aim of the work is to prove the performance of the proposed algorithm in this kind of problems.

3   GACE: Genetic Algorithm with Cross Entropy

While GA has proved its quality in many articles as searching algorithm [15,16], CE helps to focus the search in the best solution area [4,18]. The proposed algorithm is developed with the aim of taking advantage of the synergy between the exploration ability of a GA and the exploitation ability of a CE. The algorithm works as follow. An initial population (POP) is created randomly with a given number of individuals POP_{size}.

In each generation, POP_t is divided in two sub-populations, GA_{pop} and CE_{pop}, with GA_{size} and CE_{size} number of individuals respectively. These sub-populations are created in two different ways. In case of GA_{pop}, the individuals are chosen using the selection operator of a GA. On the other hand, the individuals chosen to form CE_{pop} are the CE_{size} best individuals in the population POP_t. Once these sub-populations are created, both works in a different way. Crossover and mutation operators are applied to GA_{pop}, while in CE_{pop} a Cross Entropy method is used. The new individuals created in both sub-populations are joined and they replace completely the previous population. Then, $POP_{size} = GA_{size} + CE_{size}$.

Algorithm 1 shows the pseudocode of the algorithm.

3.1   Use of the Proposal in Ensembles

In a formal way, one individual in the population is formed by two different parts: centroids of the areas (C), and the weights used to choose the ensembles response (W).

Centroids C is an array that contains c_h centroids, where h is the area where the centroid is used. In the case of the weights, W contains w_h matrices. Each matrix has a size of $k \times m$ values, where k is the number of classifiers used, and m the number of the classes in the dataset. Each value of a w_h matrix is the weight that classifier k has to determinate the class m while the fitness function is applied in area h. For example, $w_{2,3}$ is the weight for the classifier 2 to determinate the third class.

Then, each one of the possible solutions are represents as shown in Eq. 3:

$$Ind(C, W) = \begin{cases} C = (c_1, c_2, \dots c_n) \\ W = (w_1, w_2, \dots w_n) \end{cases} \tag{3}$$

Data: $POP_{size}, p_{ga}, p_c, p_m, L_r, p_{up}, T_{max}$
Result: *Best individual found*
1 $GA_{size} \leftarrow \| POP_{size} \cdot p_{ga} \|$
2 $CE_{size} \leftarrow POP_{size} - GA_{size}$
3 $n_{up} \leftarrow \| CE_{size} \cdot p_{up} \|$
4 $t \leftarrow 0$
5 $POP_0, \leftarrow$ Initialize(POP_{size})
6 $\overline{M} \leftarrow$ Initialize Means vector
7 $S \leftarrow$ Initialize Standard Deviation vector
8 Evaluate POP_0
9 **while** $t < T_{max}$ **do**
10     $GA_{pop} \leftarrow$ SelectionOperator(POP_t, GA_{size})
11     $CE_{pop} \leftarrow$ SelectBestSamples(POP_t, CE_{size})
12     $Offspring_{GA} \leftarrow$ Crossover(GA_{pop}, p_c)
13     $Offspring_{GA} \leftarrow$ Mutation($Offspring_{GA}, p_m$)
14     $Offspring_{CE} \leftarrow$ Generate($CE_{pop}, CE_{size}, \overline{M}, S$)
15     $\overline{M} \leftarrow UpdateMeans(L_r, \overline{M}, Offspring_{CE}, n_{up})$
16     $S \leftarrow UpdateDeviation(L_r, S, Offspring_{CE}, n_{up})$
17     $POP_{t+1} \leftarrow Offspring_{GA} \bigcup Offspring_{CE}$
18   Evaluate POP_{t+1}
19   Add the best individual found to POP_{t+1} if it is not in the population
20     $t \leftarrow t + 1$
21 **end**

Algorithm 1: Pseudocode of the workflow followed by the proposed method GACE

The algorithm is used to achieve the following goals:

1. Adjust the position and shape of the different centroids c_h in the feature space.
2. Tuning the weights of the classifiers w_h in the different areas and classes.

As it was explained in previous sections, the proposed algorithm creates an initial population. In this case, each value in c_h is initialized with a random number in the interval $[min, max]$, where min is the minimum value of variable $i - th$ can take, and max is the maximum value. In the case of weights, each value in matrix w_h is initialized randomly in the interval $[0, 1]$. While each c_h has a size equal to the number of variables in the feature space, each w_h has a size of k classifiers per m classes.

3.2 Operators of the Sub-populations

Different operators are used in each sub-population. For GA part, Tournament selection [7] is adopted as selection operator. The operator chooses two random individuals and compares them. The individual with the best fitness is selected. Using that method, GA_{size} individuals are chosen. As crossover operator, BLX-α [8] is used. This operator takes two parents and create new offspring generating random values inside an interval. Finally, Gaussian mutation [2] is taken as mutation operator. Every element of the individual $A = \{a_1, \cdots, a_i\}$ is updated according to a Normal Distribution with means a_i and standard deviation which depends on the length $R_{max} - R_{min}$, where R_{max} and R_{min} are the upper and lower bounds of the individual.

In the case of CE part, the algorithm maintains two different individuals called $\overline{M}$ and S, which keeps the means and the standard deviation respectively of the different part of the individuals in the population. These individuals have the same structure as a individual of the population, i.e., they have two different parts, one for centroids and another one for weights. Each part is used for created new individuals using CE method and they are updated in each generation.

In next section, details about the different parameters used in the experimentation are showed.

4   Experimentation

The principal objective of this work was to prove the ability of the proposed hybrid algorithm working with ensembles. The main goals of this research are listed below:

- To prove if the use of GACE to tune the different parts of an individual in a population can outperform the result of a single best classifier in a pool,
- To show if the use of different base classifier models in combination with GACE can offer good results in classification tasks,
- To know if the proposed algorithm works in a proper way as learning algorithm in ensemble problems.
- To compare GACE with Clustering and Selection (CS), in order to test if a more sophisticated training process can offer better results.
- To check if the proposal works in a proper way with balanced datasets and imbalanced ones.

4.1   Datasets

With the purpose of prove the quality of the proposal in different kind of datasets, six balanced and six imbalanced datasets are chosen from KEEL repository[1]. Then, a total of twelve datasets are used in this experimentation. Table 1 shows the name, size, and number of features and classes of the datasets. Besides, for imbalanced datasets, the Imbalance Ratio (IR) is shown.

4.2   Parameter Settings

As base classifiers, three different kind of models have been chosen:

- Minimal distance classifier, applied the 3-nearest neighbors (3-NN) algorithm.

---

[1] http://sci2s.ugr.es/keel/datasets.php.

Table 1. Details of each dataset used in the experimentation

No.	Name	Objects	Features	Classes	IR
1	Ecoli	336	7	8	-
2	Glass	214	9	7	-
3	Hepatitis	155	19	2	-
4	Iris	150	4	3	-
5	Vehicle	846	18	4	-
6	Yeast	1484	8	10	-
7	Ecoli1	336	7	8	1.86
8	Glass1	214	9	7	1.82
9	Pima	768	8	2	1.87
10	Iris0	150	4	3	2
11	Vehicle1	846	18	4	2.9
12	Yeast1	1484	8	10	2.46

- Neural Network (NN), trained with back-propagation algorithm. The number of neurons depend on the dataset used: input layer is equal to the number of features, output layer is equal to the number of classes, and neurons on hidden layer is equal to the half of the sum of neurons in input and output layers.
- Support Vector Machine (SVM) classifier, using the sequential minimal optimization procedure with a polynomial kernel as training method.

For each classifier type, a pool of three models is used in this experimentation. This pool is homogeneous, i.e. each classifier has the same type. In order to not have identical models at our disposal, each classifier is training with a part of the training dataset. Each of these parts are different and contain the same distribution of examples as the training dataset.

About the parameters of the algorithm used in the experimentation, POP_{size} has been set to 50, with a $GA_{size} = 40$. This value is taken that way because of the results obtained with it in other classification works, where a population with a higher GA_{size} gets lower errors [14]. Crossover probability p_c was set to 0.85 while mutation probability p_m was set to 0.1. As it was mentioned in previous section, the value of learning rate (L_r) was set to a value in the interval $[0.7, 0.9]$. In this case, $L_r = 0.7$. The number of samples used to update the value of means and deviation n_{up} is 0.4 of total CE_{size}. The number of areas H has been defined as $H = 3$ for this work, and the number of classifiers in each pool k was defined as 3. There are two stop conditions. One of them, reach a maximum number of generations T_{max} set to 200. The other one is, if the best solution does not change in 20 generations, the execution is finished. To sum up, all the parameters used in the experimentation are defined in Table 2.

Table 2. Values of the parameters used in the experimentation

Parameter	Symbol	Values
Population size	POP_{size}	50
GA pop. size	GA_{size}	40
CE pop. size	CE_{size}	10
Crossover probability	p_c	0.85
Mutation probability	p_m	0.1
Learning rate	l_r	0.7
No. update	n_{up}	0.4
No. of areas	H	3
No. of classifiers	k	3
No. of iterations	T_{max}	200

The experimentation was carried out in Matlab r2013, using PRTools Toolbox[2].

4.3   Results and Comparative

The proposal is compared against Cluster and Selection (CS) algorithm [12]. This technique divides the feature space into a number of given clusters using, in this case, K-means algorithm [10]. Then, CS selects the best classifier from the pool for each cluster according to its local accuracy. CS uses the same pool of classifiers as the proposal. Then, the results must be compared between the same classifiers.

As it was mentioned in the previous section, balanced and imbalanced datasets have been used to prove the quality of the developed algorithm. 5-Cross validation is used. Table 3 shows the error obtained in each one of the balanced datasets while, in Table 4, the results obtained in the imbalanced datasets are shown. The bold values are the best error obtained in each dataset and pool.

In balanced datasets, the three techniques used as classifiers obtain similar errors in all the datasets. $GACE_{SVM}$ obtains 3 out of 6 best values, where the biggest difference against the rest of the techniques is obtained in Iris dataset. The other 3 best values are obtained by $GACE_{KNN}$. The proposal obtains better results in all the datasets when it is compared with CS. The best errors using CS in balanced datasets are obtained when the individual classifiers are SVMs.

Although the errors are higher in imbalanced datasets than in balanced datasets, they are still low. As can be seen, $GACE_{SVM}$ obtains one of the best errors in 4 out of 6 datasets. $GACE_{KNN}$ obtain 2 out of 6 best values in Ecoli1 and Yeast1. In this case, CS best errors are obtained again when the classifiers in the pool are SVM.

---

[2] http://prtools.org/prtools/prtools-overview/.

Table 3. Errors obtained in balanced datasets

	Ecoli	Glass	Hepatitis	Iris	Vehicle	Yeast
$GACE_{KNN}$	**0.012**	0.006	**0.009**	0.020	0.010	**0.0006**
CS_{KNN}	0.084	0.073	0.043	0.24	0.037	0.070
$GACE_{NN}$	0.02	0.014	**0.009**	0.049	0.012	0.0002
CS_{NN}	0.083	0.071	0.046	0.238	0.047	0.076
$GACE_{SVM}$	0.018	**0.002**	0.010	**0.009**	**0.005**	0.001
CS_{SVM}	0.050	0.08	0.025	0.235	0.013	0.031

Table 4. Errors obtained in imbalanced datasets

	Ecoli1	Glass1	Pima	Iris0	Vehicle1	Yeast1
$GACE_{KNN}$	**0.016**	0.037	0.062	0.047	0.017	**0.031**
CS_{KNN}	0.077	0.076	0.067	0.102	0.091	0.088
$GACE_{NN}$	0.032	0.043	0.068	0.055	0.019	0.045
CS_{NN}	0.079	0.076	0.069	0.103	0.093	0.091
$GACE_{SVM}$	0.031	**0.036**	**0.021**	**0.034**	**0.016**	0.043
CS_{SVM}	0.041	0.054	0.047	0.084	0.072	0.066

5   Conclusions

In this work, a hybrid algorithm that combines a Genetic Algorithm with a Cross Entropy method has been applied as a learning method for ensembles classification. The algorithm has been used in balanced and imbalanced datasets due to prove its performance in different kind of datasets. The results obtained show the good performance of this algorithm in that kind of problems. In future works, a comparative with more literature techniques will be made. Besides, a heterogeneous pool of classifiers can be used instead of a homogeneous one. The number of datasets will be increased in future experimentations.

Acknowledgment. Pedro Lopez-Garcia, Enrique Onieva and Asier Perallos' work was supported by TIMON Project (Enhanced real time services for an optimized multimodal mobility relying on cooperative networks and open data). This project has received funding from the European Unions Horizon 2020 research and innovation programme under grant agreement No. 636220. Also, Michal Wozniak's work was supported by the Polish National Science Centre under the grant no. DEC-2013/09/B/ST6/02264 and by EC under FP7, Coordination and Support Action, Grant Agreement Number 316097, ENGINE - European Research Centre of Network Intelligence for Innovation Enhancement (http://engine.pwr.wroc.pl/). All computer experiments were carried out using computer equipment sponsored by ENGINE project.

References

1. Akhand, M.A.H., Murase, K.: Ensembles of neural networks based on the alteration of input feature values. Int. J. Neural Syst. **22**(1), 77–87 (2012)
2. Bäck, T., Schwefel, H.: An overview of evolutionary algorithms for parameter optimization. Evol. Comput. **1**(1), 1–23 (1993)
3. Brown, G., Wyatt, J.L., Harris, R., Yao, X.: Diversity creation methods: a survey and categorisation. Inf. Fusion **6**(1), 5–20 (2005)
4. Caballero, R., Hernndez-Daz, A.G., Laguna, M., Molina, J.: Cross entropy for multiobjective combinatorial optimization problems with linear relaxations. Eur. J. Oper. Res. **243**(2), 362–368 (2015)
5. Dietterich, T.G., Bakiri, G.: Solving multiclass learning problems via error-correcting output codes. J. Artif. Intell. Res. **2**, 263–286 (1995)
6. Giacinto, G., Roli, F.: Dynamic classifier selection based on multiple classifier behaviour. Pattern Recogn. **34**(9), 1879–1881 (2001)
7. Goldberg, D.E., Deb, K.: A comparative analysis of selection schemes used in genetic algorithms. Found. Genet. Algorithms **1**, 69–93 (1991)
8. Herrera, F., Lozano, M., Verdegay, J.L.: Tackling real-coded genetic algorithms: Operators and tools for behavioural analysis. Artif. Intell. Rev. **12**(4), 265–319 (1998)
9. Jackowski, K., Wozniak, M.: Algorithm of designing compound recognition system on the basis of combining classifiers with simultaneous splitting feature space into competence areas. Pattern Anal. Appl. **12**(4), 415–425 (2009)
10. Kanungo, T., Mount, D.M., Netanyahu, N.S., Piatko, C.D., Silverman, R., Wu, A.Y.: An efficient k-means clustering algorithm: analysis and implementation. IEEE Trans. Pattern Anal. Mach. Intell. **24**(7), 881–892 (2002)
11. Krogh, A., Vedelsby, J.: Neural network ensembles, cross validation, and active learning. Adv. Neural Inf. Process. Syst. **7**, 231–238 (1995)
12. L.I. Kuncheva. Clustering-and-selection model for classifier combination. In: Fourth International Conference on Knowledge-Based Intelligent Engineering Systems and Allied Technologies, Proceedings. vol. 1, pp. 185–188 (2000)
13. Kuncheva, L.I.: Combining Pattern Classifiers: Methods and Algorithms. Wiley-Interscience, Piscataway (2004)
14. Lopez-Garcia, P., Onieva, E., Osaba, E., Masegosa, A.D., Perallos, A.: A hybrid method for short-term traffic congestion forecasting using genetic algorithms and cross entropy. IEEE Trans. Intell. Transp. Syst. **17**(2), 557–569 (2016)
15. Onieva, E., Naranjo, J.E., Milanés, V., Alonso, J., García, R., Pérez, J.: Automatic lateral control for unmanned vehicles via genetic algorithms. Appl. Soft Comput. **11**(1), 1303–1309 (2011)
16. Osaba, E., Diaz, F., Onieva, E.: Golden ball: a novel meta-heuristic to solve combinatorial optimization problems based on soccer concepts. Appl. Intell. **41**(1), 145–166 (2014)
17. Rastrigin, L.A., Erenstein, R.H.: Method of Collective Recognition. Energoizdat, Moscow (1981)
18. Rubinstein, R.: The cross-entropy method for combinatorial and continuous optimization. Methodol. Comput. Appl. Probab. **1**(2), 127–190 (1999)
19. Wozniak, M., Graña, M., Corchado, E.: A survey of multiple classifier systems as hybrid systems. Inf. Fusion **16**, 3–17 (2014). Special Issue on Information Fusion in Hybrid Intelligent Fusion Systems

Hybrid Intelligent Model for Fault Detection of a Lithium Iron Phosphate Power Cell Used in Electric Vehicles

Héctor Quintián[1], José-Luis Casteleiro-Roca[2], Francisco Javier Perez-Castelo[2], José Luis Calvo-Rolle[2(✉)], and Emilio Corchado[1]

[1] Departamento de Informática y Automática, University of Salamanca, Plaza de la Merced s/n, 37008 Salamanca, Salamanca, Spain
hector.quintian@usal.es
[2] Departamento de Ingeniería Industrial, University of A Coruña, Avda. 19 de febrero s/n, 15495 Ferrol, A Coruña, Spain
jlcalvo@cdf.udc.es

Abstract. Currently, the electrical mobility and the intermittent power generation facilities problem are two of the main purposes of batteries. Batteries, in general terms, have a complex behavior. Due to the usual electrochemical nature of batteries, several tests are made to check their performance, and it is very useful to know a priori how they are working in each case. By checking the battery temperatures for a specific voltage and current value, this work describes a hybrid intelligent model aimed at making fault detection of a LFP (Lithium Iron Phosphate - LiFePO4) power cell type, used in Electric Vehicles. A large set of operating points is obtained from a real system to create the dataset for the operation range of the power cell. Clusters of the different behavior zones have been obtained to accomplish the solution. Some simple regression methods have been applied for each cluster. Polynomial Regression, Artificial Neural Networks and Support Vector Regression were the combined techniques to develop the hybrid intelligent model proposed. The novel hybrid model allows to be achieved good results in all the operating range, detecting all the faults tested.

Keywords: Power cell · Fault detection · Battery · Clustering · Artificial neural networks · Polynomial regression · LS-SVR

1 Introduction

Electric energy storage is one of the current solutions due to several reasons [1]. Examples of these motives are: the variation of energy production at renewable energy installations like wind farms, the necessity of finding a substitute for fossil fuels or to supply energy to portable devices [2]. An important consideration is that, electric vehicles and portable devices, in general terms, require higher autonomy and less weight [3]. The electric vehicles development case has the main problem of energy storage. However its use is unavoidable, despite reasons

© Springer International Publishing Switzerland 2016
F. Martínez-Álvarez et al. (Eds.): HAIS 2016, LNAI 9648, pp. 751–762, 2016.
DOI: 10.1007/978-3-319-32034-2_63

like preservation of the environment and, the fact that electric powertrains are more efficient than internal combustion engines [4].

One of the best candidates to accomplish the above mentioned problem in electric vehicles are batteries. Because of this fact, nowadays, there are some studies with the purpose of improving them. Among the different battery technologies, this paper is focused on Lithium Iron Phosphate - LiFePO4 (LFP) power cell type. Due to the importance of these kind of batteries, modeling them is very important, particularly their fault detection [5,6].

Fault detection is very important in all fields, and of course in engineering. There are a lot of works whose aim is this target. In [7–9] intelligent systems were developed to detect faults in a heat pump installation. [10] accomplish fault detection and isolation of automotive air conditioning systems using first principle models. Fault detection and isolation of bearings in a drive reducer of a hot steel rolling mill is described in [11].

The classic regression models are based on Multiple Regression Analysis (MRA) methods [12]. MRA-based methods are useful due to their applications in different subjects [13–15]; the first cite shows a model for cost prediction in the early state of projects, the second one proposes a method to evaluate suppliers performance. The main problem of these methods is their limitations in certain cases. For instance in [12,16–20] the common trouble is its non linearity and the different ways followed to solve them with approaches based on MRA techniques. Regression techniques based on Soft Computing could avoid some of the problems mentioned above. Several works have been developed with this goal. In [21] the prediction state of a model predictive control system is carried out by meta-classifiers. By combining multi regression analysis and artificial neural networks an optimizing overbreak prediction is made in [22]. In [23] failure detection and prediction in wind turbines is achieved by using intelligent techniques.

Despite the new methods to solve regression problems, there are cases where it is not possible to achieve a good performance of the model, for instances due to the high non-linearity of the system. Clustering could be a complementary solution as a previous step to apply regression to the dataset [24]. K-Means clustering algorithms are often employed with this purpose [25,26]. With this method, the dataset is divided into subsets (clusters), depending on the features of the input data. Then, regression is made over each cluster with common characteristics. Previous works like [27–33] used similar techniques to solve other physical systems.

This study implements a hybrid intelligent model to make fault detection over the above mentioned type of battery, the LFP. To develop the model, K-Means clustering algorithm was used for making groups of data with the same behaviour. Then, three different regression techniques were tested for each group, to choose the best one based on the lowest Mean Squared Error (MSE) achieved.

The rest of the paper is organized as follow. After this introduction, the case of study section describes the standard employed test and how the dataset was obtained to create the model for making fault detection. Then, the model approach and the tested algorithms taken into account in the research are presented.

The results section shows the best configuration achieved by the hybrid model. After the results, the conclusions and future works are presented.

2   Case of Study: The Capacity Confirmation of the Battery Test

The model has been obtained to make fault detection of a LFP power cell type. To collect the dataset, the standard capacity confirmation test was accomplished, by measuring different variables and obtaining its State Of Charge, defined as the ratio of its current capacity $(Q(t))$ to the nominal capacity (Q_n); $(SOC(t) = \frac{Q(t)}{Q_n})$ [34]. The scheme of the practical implementation to carry out the test is shown on Fig. 1.

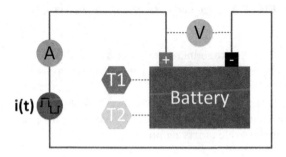

Fig. 1. Scheme of the capacity confirmation test

The developed test measures the device capacity in ampere-hour at a constant current [34]. The first step is to charge the cell to its maximum SOC. After that, the battery is discharged at a constant current up to the discharge voltage limit specified by the manufacturer [34]. Once the cell is recharged to its maximum capacity, the battery capacity and the SOC are calculated at each moment.

The test was done with a battery tester that can charge and discharge the cells at a constant current, and it is able to measure different parameters. These parameters are the voltage provided by the battery, the current flowing to and from the battery, its temperature and the test time.

The test scheme is shown on Fig. 1. On it, it is possible to see different components like a volt-meter *(V)*, an ampere-meter *(A)*, and two temperature sensors *(T1 and T2)* to measure the temperature value at two different places. Also, there is a current source that provides and absorbs the flowing current *(i(t))*.

The cell used during this test was the LiFeBATT X-1P [35]. This power cell is a LFP type, whose nominal capacity is 8000 mAh and its nominal voltage 3.3 V. During the test (shown in Fig. 2), the next steps are carried out:

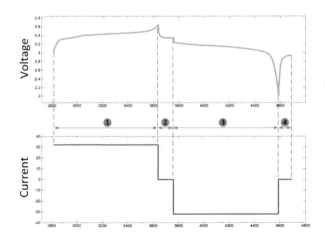

Fig. 2. Voltage and current during one cycle test

(1) Charge: where the voltage increases from 3 to 3.65 V.
(2) Rest after a charging process: where the voltage decreases up to the nominal value of 3.3 V.
(3) Discharge: where the voltage decrease from 3.3 to 2 V.
(4) Rest after discharging process: where the voltage increases to the value of 3 V, and then the cycle starts again.

The analysis of voltage progress for one entire cycle is shown at the top of Fig. 2. The analysis of the current (bottom of Fig. 2) shows that the process carried out was done at a constant value of current. The current is positive when it flows from the source to the battery, and it is negative when it flows from the battery to the source.

With the value of current at each time it is possible to obtain the energy provided or absorbed in ampere-hour. If this energy is represented (top of Fig. 3) it is possible to see how the battery SOC increases during the charging period till 100 % of charge. On the other hand, the SOC of the cell decreases till its minimum value of 0 % during the discharging process.

The measurement of temperatures are done with two sensors located at different places of the battery. These parameters vary cyclically depending on the state of the battery (charge, discharge, rest after charge and rest after discharge) and on its voltage. At the bottom of Fig. 3, it is possible to see the temperature behaviour for each operating region. Highlighting that the temperature at this type of battery is a very good indicator of its state of health [34].

The dataset has been obtained by carrying out the previously mentioned test over the power cell. The current and the voltage were registered to study the state of the battery. Two different temperatures were measured to detect malfunction of the device, if the temperature is far from the predicted one.

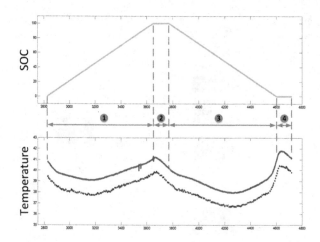

Fig. 3. Energy balance and temperatures during one cycle test

3 Model Approach

The scheme of the model approach is shown in Fig. 4. Taking into account the power cell performance and the test made, it is possible to divide the dataset in N operation ranges. Consequently, N clusters are created and, the regression models (one per output) are implemented for each one. As shown in Fig. 4, the global model has two inputs (the Real Current and the Real Voltage) and two outputs (T1 Predicted and T2 Predicted). The aim of the block selector is to connect the regression models of the chosen cluster (it depends on the Real Current and Voltage values) with the global model outputs. Then, the predicted temperatures are two inputs for the Fault Verification Block. This block allows for the detection of faults by comparing the predicted temperatures provided by the model, with the real values measured in the power cell. The fault existence depends on the deviation range, which is another Fault Verification Block input provided by the user.

3.1 Techniques Used

The techniques tested in the study to achieve the best model are described below.

Data Clustering. The K-Means Algorithm. Clustering is an unsupervised technique of data grouping where similarity is measured [36,37]. Clustering algorithms try to organize unlabeled feature vectors into clusters or groups, in such a way that samples within a cluster are similar to each other [38]. K-Means algorithm is a commonly used partitional clustering algorithm with square-error criterion, which minimizes error function shows in Eq. 1.

$$e = \sum_{k=1}^{C} \sum_{x \epsilon Q_k} \|x - c_k\|^2 \qquad (1)$$

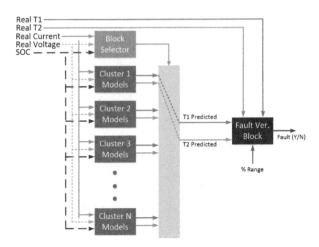

Fig. 4. Model approach

The final clustering will depend on the initial cluster centroids and on the value of K (number of clusters). Choosing K value is the most critical election because it requires certain prior knowledge of the number of clusters present in the data, which is highly doubtful. The K-Means partitional clustering algorithm is computationally effective and works well if the data is close to its cluster, and the cluster is hyperspherical in shape and well-separated in hyperspace.

Polynomial Regression. Generally, a polynomial regression model [39] may also be defined as a linear summation of basis functions. The number of basis functions depends on the number of model inputs, and the degree of the polynomial used.

With a degree 1, the linear summation could be defined as the one shown in Eq. 2. The model becomes more complex as the degree increases, Eq. 3 shows a second polynomial degree for the model.

$$F(x) = a_0 + a_1 x_1 + a_2 x_2 \tag{2}$$

$$F(x) = a_0 + a_1 x_1 + a_2 x_2 + a_3 x_1 x_2 + a_4 x_1^2 + a_5 x_2^2 \tag{3}$$

Artificial Neural Networks (ANN): MultiLayer Perceptron (MLP). A multilayer perceptron is a feedforward artificial neural network [39]. It is one of the most typical ANNs due to its robustness and relatively simple structure. However, the ANN architecture must be well selected to obtain good results.

The MLP is composed by one input layer, one or more hidden layers and one output layer, all of them made of neurons and with pondered connections between the neurons of each layer.

Support Vector Regression (SVR), Least Square Support Vector Regression (LS-SVR). Support Vector Regression (SVR) is based on the algorithm of the Support Vector Machines (SVM) for classification. In SVR the main aim is mapping the data into a high-dimensional feature space F through a nonlinear plotting and doing linear regression in this space [40].

The Least Square algorithm of SVM is called LS-SVM. The solution estimation is obtained by solving a system of linear equations, and it is similar to SVM in terms of performance generalization [41]. The use of LS-SVM algorithm to regression is well-known as LS-SVR [42]. In LS-SVR, the insensitive loss function is replaced by a classical squared loss function, which makes the Lagrangian by solving a linear Karush-Kuhn-Tucker.

3.2 Preprocessing the Dataset

With the aim of achieving a good dataset, it must be taking into account that the battery needs full charging cycles. In order to achieve this fact, some incomplete cycles were discarded. Taking this fact into account, given that the whole data acquisition has twelve cycles, only nine cycles were included to calculate the model. The data was recorded with a sample time of one second, and with the discard data, the dataset was reduced from 18130 to 16369 samples.

4   Results

The first technique applied to the dataset was clustering. To do that, K-means algorithm was applied and four clusters were created. These groups should represent the different states of the cell test.

Each model is obtained from the dataset by using K-Fold cross-validation, and then, the performance of each one was calculated.

The three mentioned regression techniques were trained for the four clusters, one by each output of the model. As an example, the Fig. 5 shows the temperature in sensor 2. The four colors indicate the different clusters, as it was mentioned above.

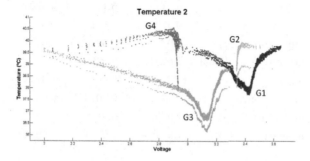

Fig. 5. Temperature 2 vs. battery voltage

K-Means was applied from 2 to 6 for obtaining the clusters, and the best configuration is achieved with 4. Then, the regression techniques were applied for each cluster. That is why, 10 folds has been used for cross validation to ensure a good performance.

The MLP-ANN regression algorithm was trained for different configurations. In all cases the topology uses one hidden layer, whose number of neurons varies from 1 to 15. Its activation function is tan-sigmoid for all tests. However, the output layer neuron has a linear activation function. The used training algorithm was Levenberg-Marquardt with gradient descent, and its performance function was Mean Squared Error (MSE).

The LS-SVR was trained with the self-tuning algorithm developed by KULeuven-ESAT-SCD and implemented in a MatLab toolbox. Due to the fact that there are a lot of samples in some Folds, the above algorithm was performed with 10 % of the samples. With the achieved coefficients, the model was then created, but using all the available samples. The employed kernel was Radial Basis Function, and the type was 'Function Estimation' for regression. The optimization function was 'simplex' and the cost-criterion 'leaveoneoutlssvm' with MSE as a performance function.

For Polynomial regression, the order of the polynomial tested varies from 1st to 10th order.

All the models were compared by using the MSE as the efficiency measurement. The testing data is only used to calculate the MSE, not for training any model.

In Table 1 the lowest MSE achieved appears for each algorithm. Table 2 shows the best regression technique and its configuration for each cluster. Even so, the selection takes the computational cost into account when the MSE for different techniques are close.

Table 1. Best MSE for each regression algorithm

Variable	Cluster	ANN-MLP	LS-SVR	Polynomial
Temperature 1	Global	0.9848	1.0649	7.2484
Temperature 1	(1)	4.2126	4.3306	4.5757
Temperature 1	(2)	4.514e−4	5.194e−4	4.920e−4
Temperature 1	(3)	0.5797	0.5813	0.5983
Temperature 1	(4)	1.931e−4	2.622e−4	0.0057
Temperature 2	Global	2.6294	2.6259	8.6584
Temperature 2	(1)	10.4278	10.8633	11.3793
Temperature 2	(2)	0.0012	0.0013	0.0018
Temperature 2	(3)	2.9655	3.0125	3.0683
Temperature 2	(4)	7.904e−4	0.0011	0.0065

Table 2. Performance measurements for the best methods

Variable	Cluster	Model	MSE	MAE	NMSE
Temperature 1	(1)	ANN-MLP, 14 neurons	4.2126	1.5792	0.0062
Temperature 1	(2)	ANN-MLP, 9 neurons	4.514e−9	0.0161	0.0063
Temperature 1	(3)	ANN-MLP, 14 neurons	0.5797	0.6082	0.0012
Temperature 1	(4)	ANN-MLP, 8 neurons	1.931e−4	0.0111	0.0059
Temperature 2	(1)	ANN-MLP, 15 neurons	10.4278	2.5658	0.0164
Temperature 2	(2)	ANN-MLP, 12 neurons	0.0012	0.0273	0.0191
Temperature 2	(3)	ANN-MLP, 15 neurons	2.9655	1.3599	0.0069
Temperature 2	(4)	ANN-MLP, 12 neurons	7.904e−4	0.0216	0.0297

A validation of the model was carried out. To do that, 100 simulated faults have been created with temperatures out of the right operation range. As operation range, it has been considered the 5 % out of the normal temperature range. All the faults have been detected for the created model.

5   Conclusions

Very good results have been obtained in general terms with the novel approach proposed in this research. The final hybrid intelligent model implemented has different configuration of the ANN-MLP algorithm depending on the cluster used. Despite that the global model has better performance than some clusters, the final proposal is accomplished with local models after having tested a combination of global and local models and demonstrate that combinations had the worst results.

The average MSE obtained with this implementation is 1.1981 for Temperature 1, and 3.3488 for Temperature 2; and the worst MSE is 4.2126 and 10.4278 respectively. The maximum absolute error achieved was nearly 0.2 degrees, and with this accuracy, the minimum steps recommended to set the range of fault detection is 1 %, that should represent approximately 0.3 degrees for real temperature.

It is remarkable that all the fault situations presented in the model was classified correctly as a battery fault; but as the model does not include the dynamics of the process, a bad measure could classify as battery fault too. This problem should be corrected in the next improvement of the model, for example, taking into account that to detect a battery fault not only one measurement should be out of range.

Moreover, in future works more complex testing for batteries should be collected, to ensure that all the possible situations are covered with the fault detection model.

References

1. Chukwuka, C., Folly, K.: Batteries and super-capacitors. In: 2012 IEEE Power Engineering Society Conference and Exposition in Africa (PowerAfrica), pp. 1–6, July 2012

2. Qian, H., Zhang, J., Lai, J.S.: A grid-tie battery energy storage system. In: 2010 IEEE 12th Workshop on Control and Modeling for Power Electronics (COMPEL), pp. 1–5, June 2010

3. Chaturvedi, N., Klein, R., Christensen, J., Ahmed, J., Kojic, A.: Modeling, estimation, and control challenges for lithium-ion batteries. In: Proceedings of the American Control Conference (ACC), pp. 1997–2002, June 2010

4. Vukosavic, S.: Electrical Machines. Power Electronics and Power Systems. Springer, New York (2012)

5. Konig, O., Jakubek, S., Prochart, G.: Battery impedance emulation for hybrid and electric powertrain testing. In: 2012 IEEE Vehicle Power and Propulsion Conference (VPPC), pp. 627–632, October 2012

6. Fernández-Serantes, L.A., Estrada Vázquez, R., Casteleiro-Roca, J.L., Calvo-Rolle, J.L., Corchado, E.: Hybrid intelligent model to predict the SOC of a LFP power cell type. In: Polycarpou, M., de Carvalho, A.C.P.L.F., Pan, J.-S., Woźniak, M., Quintian, H., Corchado, E. (eds.) HAIS 2014. LNCS, vol. 8480, pp. 561–572. Springer, Heidelberg (2014)

7. Casteleiro-Roca, J.L., Quintián, H., Calvo-Rolle, J.L., Corchado, E., del Carmen Meizoso-López, M., Piñón-Pazos, A.: An intelligent fault detection system for a heat pump installation based on a geothermal heat exchanger. J. Appl. Log. (2015, in press)

8. Casteleiro-Roca, J.L., Quintián, H., Calvo-Rolle, J.L., Corchado, E., Meizoso-López, M.C.: Intelligent model for fault detection on geothermal exchanger of a heat pump. In: Herrero, A., et al. (eds.) International Joint Conference SOCO'13-CISIS'13-ICEUTE'13. AISC, vol. 239, pp. 237–247. Springer, Heidelberg (2014)

9. Casteleiro-Roca, J., Calvo-Rolle, J., Meizoso-López, M., Piñón-Pazos, A., Rodríguez-Gómez, B.: Bio-inspired model of ground temperature behavior on the horizontal geothermal exchanger of an installation based on a heat pump. Neurocomputing 150, 90–98 (2015)

10. Zhang, Q., Canova, M.: Fault detection and isolation of automotive air conditioning systems using first principle models. Control Eng. Pract. 43, 49–58 (2015)

11. Farina, M., Osto, E., Perizzato, A., Piroddi, L., Scattolini, R.: Fault detection and isolation of bearings in a drive reducer of a hot steel rolling mill. Control Eng. Pract. 39, 35–44 (2015)

12. Mark, J., Goldberg, M.A.: Multiple regression analysis and mass assessment: a review of the issues. Apprais. J. 56(1), 89 (1988)

13. Jin, R., Cho, K., Hyun, C., Son, M.: MRA-based revised CBR model for cost prediction in the early stage of construction projects. Expert Syst. Appl. 39(5), 5214–5222 (2012)

14. Ho, L.H., Feng, S.Y., Lee, Y.C., Yen, T.M.: Using modified IPA to evaluate suppliers performance: multiple regression analysis and DEMATEL approach. Expert Syst. Appl. 39(8), 7102–7109 (2012)

15. Vilar-Martinez, X.M., Montero-Sousa, J.A., Luis Calvo-Rolle, J., Casteleiro-Roca, J.L.: Expert system development to assist on the verification of TACAN system performance. Dyna 89(1), 112–121 (2014)

16. Cho, Y., Awbi, H.B.: A study of the effect of heat source location in a ventilated room using multiple regression analysis. Build. Environ. **42**(5), 2072–2082 (2007)

17. Casteleiro-Roca, J.L., Pérez, J.A.M., Piñón-Pazos, A.J., Calvo-Rolle, J.L., Corchado, E.: Modeling the Electromyogram (EMG) of Patients Undergoing Anesthesia During Surgery. 10th International Conference on Soft Computing Models in Industrial and Environmental Applications, pp. 273–283. Springer, Switzerland (2015)

18. Casteleiro-Roca, J., Calvo-Rolle, J., Meizoso-Lopez, M., Pin-Pazos, A., Rodrguez-Gmez, B.: New approach for the QCM sensors characterization. Sens. Actuators A Phys. **207**, 1–9 (2014)

19. Reboso, J., Mendez, J., Reboso, H., León, A.: Design and implementation of a closed-loop control system for infusion of propofol guided by bispectral index (BIS). Acta Anaesthesiologica Scandinavica **56**(8), 1032–1041 (2012)

20. Martín-Mateos, I., Méndez Pérez, J., Reboso, J., León, A.: Modelling propofol pharmacodynamics using BIS-guided anaesthesia. Anaesthesia **68**(11), 1132–1140 (2013)

21. Nieves-Acedo, J., Santos-Grueiro, I., Garcia-Bringas, P.: Enhancing the prediction stage of a model predictive control systems through meta-classifiers. Dyna **88**(3), 290–298 (2013)

22. Jang, H., Topal, E.: Optimizing overbreak prediction based on geological parameters comparing multiple regression analysis and artificial neural network. Tunn. Undergr. Space Technol. **38**, 161–169 (2013)

23. Alvarez-Huerta, A., Gonzalez-Miguelez, R., Garcia-Metola, D., Noriega-Gonzalez, A.: Failure detection and prediction in wind turbines by using scada data. Dyna **86**(4), 467–473 (2011)

24. Martínez-Rego, D., Fontenla-Romero, O., Alonso-Betanzos, A.: Efficiency of local models ensembles for time series prediction. Expert Syst. Appl. **38**(6), 6884–6894 (2011)

25. Cherif, A., Cardot, H., Boné, R.: SOM time series clustering and prediction with recurrent neural networks. Neurocomputing **74**(11), 1936–1944 (2011)

26. Ghaseminezhad, M.H., Karami, A.: A novel self-organizing map (SOM) neural network for discrete groups of data clustering. Appl. Soft Comput. **11**(4), 3771–3778 (2011)

27. Crespo-Ramos, M.J., Machón-González, I., López-García, H., Calvo-Rolle, J.L.: Detection of locally relevant variables using SOM-NG algorithm. Eng. Appl. Artif. Intell. **26**(8), 1992–2000 (2013)

28. Calvo-Rolle, J.L., Casteleiro-Roca, J.L., Quintián, H., Meizoso-Lopez, M.C.: A hybrid intelligent system for PID controller using in a steel rolling process. Expert Syst. Appl. **40**(13), 5188–5196 (2013)

29. Quintián, H., Calvo-Rolle, J.L., Corchado, E.: A hybrid regression system based on local models for solar energy prediction. Informatica **25**(2), 265–282 (2014)

30. Rolle, J., Gonzalez, I., Garcia, H.: Neuro-robust controller for non-linear systems. Dyna **86**(3), 308–317 (2011)

31. Osborn, J., Juez, F.J.D.C., Guzman, D., Butterley, T., Myers, R., Guesalaga, A., Laine, J.: Using artificial neural networks for open-loop tomography. Optics express **20**(3), 2420–2434 (2012)

32. Guzmán, D., de Cos Juez, F.J., Myers, R., Guesalaga, A., Lasheras, F.S.: Modeling a mems deformable mirror using non-parametric estimation techniques. Opt. Express **18**(20), 21356–21369 (2010)

33. Moretón, H.A., Rolle, J.C., García, I., Alvarez, A.A.: Formalization and practical implementation of a conceptual model for PID controller tuning. Asian J. Control **13**(6), 773–784 (2011)
34. PNGV Battery Test Manual (2001). http://avt.inl.gov/battery/pdf/pngv_manual_rev3b.pdf (March 2016)
35. LiFeBATT X-1P 8Ah 38123 Cell (2011). http://www.lifebatt.co.uk/documents/LiFeBATTX-1P8Ah38123CellMarch2011.pdf (March 2016)
36. Qin, A., Suganthan, P.: Enhanced neural gas network for prototype-based clustering. Pattern Recogn. **38**(8), 1275–1288 (2005)
37. Ghaseminezhad, M.H., Karami, A.: A novel self-organizing map (SOM) neural network for discrete groups of data clustering. Appl. Soft Comput. **11**(4), 3771–3778 (2011)
38. Kaski, S., Sinkkonen, J., Klami, A.: Discriminative clustering. Neurocomputing **69**(1–3), 18–41 (2005)
39. Bishop, C.M.: Pattern Recognition and Machine Learning (Information Science and Statistics). Springer, New York (2006)
40. Vapnik, V.: The Nature of Statistical Learning Theory. Springer, New York (1995)
41. Kaski, S., Sinkkonen, J., Klami, A.: Discriminative clustering. Neurocomputing **69**(1–3), 18–41 (2005)
42. Li, Y., Shao, X., Cai, W.: A consensus least squares support vector regression (LS-SVR) for analysis of near-infrared spectra of plant samples. Talanta **72**(1), 217–222 (2007)

Author Index

Abelha, António 3
Aguilar-Ruiz, Jesús S. 685, 706
Aguilera, J. 273
Alba, Enrique 225
Almendros-Jiménez, Jesús M. 14
Álvarez, Pablo Morales 549
Analide, César 3
Andruszkiewicz, Piotr 102
Arias-Michel, Rafael 114
Asim, Khawaja M. 634
Ayllón-Terán, María Dolores 451

Bellas, Francisco 659
Blanco, Cecilio 250
Budka, Marcin 27
Burrieza, Alfredo 721

Caamaño, Pilar 659
Calvo-Rolle, José Luis 126, 751
Cano, Alberto 365
Cano, José-Ramón 311
Cárdenas-Montes, Miguel 299, 575
Carmona, Cristobal J. 273
Casteleiro-Roca, José-Luis 126, 751
Cerveny, Jan 402
Charte, David 487
Charte, Francisco 487, 500
Chmielnicki, Wiesław 536
Cho, Sung-Bae 91, 377
Choraś, Michał 441
Cinalli, Daniel 238
Cleofas-Sánchez, L. 524
Cmiel, Vratislav 402
Corchado, Emilio 126, 751
Corral Bobadilla, Marina 609, 621
Crespo-Turrado, Concepción 126
Crişan, Gloria Cerasela 353
Cuzzocrea, Alfredo 14
Cyganek, Bogusław 186, 560

Dahi, Zakaria Abd El Moiz 225
de Cos Juez, Francisco Javier 126
de la Cal, Enrique 261

del Jesus, María José 273, 487, 500
Dinh, Tai 53
Divina, Federico 114
Diz, Lourdes Borrajo 66
Dorado-Moreno, Manuel 451
Duque, Néstor 151
Durán-Rosal, Antonio Manuel 163
Duro, Richard J. 659

Echevarría, Yuviny 250
Enayatifar, Rasul 213
Escribano Garcia, Ruben 621
Ezpeleta, Enaitz 79

Félix, Catarina 332
Fernandez Martinez, Roberto 609, 621
Filipe Santos, Manuel 3
Fischer, Michael 344
Fournier-Viger, Philippe 53
Fuentes-Fernández, Rubén 475

Gabrys, Bogdan 27
Gajić, Jovana 283
Garcia, Ana Cristina Bicharra 238
García, Javier 311
García, Salvador 311, 512
García, Vicente 524
García-Gutiérrez, Jorge 588
García-Heredia, Jose Manuel 694
García-Torres, Miguel 114
Garmendia, Asier 323
Gil-Cumbreras, Francisco Javier 706
Giráldez, Raúl 706
Gomes, Sabino 3
Gómez Hidalgo, José María 79
Gonçalves, Nuno 3
González, Sergio 512
González-Ferreiro, Eduardo 588
Górak, Rafał 730
Graña, Manuel 323
Guerrero, José Miguel 391
Guijarro, María 391, 475
Guijarro-Mata-García, Marta 475

Guimarães, Frederico Gadelha   213
Gutiérrez, Pedro Antonio   427, 451, 597
Gutiérrez-Avilés, David   673
Gutiérrez-Peña, Pedro Antonio   163

Haghnazar Koochaksaraei, Roozbeh   213
Hassan, Fawad   634
Hernández, Emilcy   151
Herrera, Francisco   487, 500, 512, 549
Hervás-Martínez, César   163, 427, 451, 597

Ichise, Ryutaro   40
Iglesias, Eva Lorenzo   66
Ilin, Vladimir   283
Iqbal, Naeem   634

Jankowski, Dariusz   560
Jo, Sang-Muk   91
Jorge, Alípio   332
Julian, Vicente   151, 201

Kanayama, Hiroshi   40
Kasprzak, Andrzej   186
Kepski, Michal   414
Kim, Jun-Ho   377
Kim, Ki-Hoon   377
Kozik, Rafał   441
Ksieniewicz, Paweł   186
Kwolek, Bogdan   414

Lam, Monica   344
Le, Hoai Bac   53
Lin, Jerry Chun-Wei   53
Lopez-Garcia, Pedro   742
Lopez-Guede, Jose Manuel   323
López-Vázquez, José Antonio   126
Lostado Lorza, Ruben   609, 621
Luckner, Marcin   730
Luengo, Julián   549
Luna, J.M.   365

Macedo, Joaquim   3
Machado, José   3
Marqués, Ana I.   524
Martí, Luis   238
Martin Salvador, Manuel   27
Martínez-Álvarez, Francisco   174, 634
Martínez-Ballesteros, María   174, 694
Martínez-Estudillo, Francisco José   163

Matei, Oliviu   353
Mateos-García, Daniel   588
Medina, Alejandro Sánchez   694
Menéndez, Manuel   261
Mezioud, Chaker   225
Montalvo, Martín   391
Montes, Bárbara   575
Muñoz-Velasco, Emilio   721

Nasukawa, Tetsuya   40
Nepomuceno, Juan A.   685
Nepomuceno-Chamorro, Isabel A.   685
Neves, João   3
Neves, José   3

Ojeda-Aciego, Manuel   721
Oliveira, Ruben   3
Onieva, Enrique   742

Padillo, Francisco   365
Palanca, Javier   151, 201
Peláez-Moreno, Carmen   647
Peñaranda, Cristian   201
Perallos, Asier   742
Perez-Castelo, Francisco Javier   751
Pérez-Chacón, Rubén   174
Pérez-Ortiz, María   427, 451, 597
Pichardo, Alberto Gil   694
Pintea, Camelia-M.   353
Pop, Petrică   353
Prieto, Abraham   659
Pulgar, F.   273

Quintián, Héctor   751

Rahoman, Md-Mizanur   40
Ribeiro, Ángela   391
Riquelme, José C.   136
Riquelme-Santos, José C.   588
Rivera, Antonio   487, 500
Rivera-Rivas, Antonio Jesús   273
Romero, Luciano   575
Rubio-Escudero, Cristina   673
Ruiz, Roberto   136

Sáez, Aurora   427
Salgado, Rodrigo   659
Sánchez, José Salvador   524

Sánchez, Luciano   250
Sanchez-Anguix, Victor   151
Sánchez-Lasheras, Fernando   126
Sánchez-Monedero, Javier   427, 597
Sanchez-Pi, Nayat   238
Santorelli, Roberto   575
Schaerer, Christian   114
Sedano, Javier   261
Şerban, Camelia   463
Simić, Dragan   283
Simić, Svetlana   283
Soares, Carlos   332
Somovilla Gomez, Fatima   609, 621
Svirčević, Vasa   283

Talavera-Llames, Ricardo L.   174
Tallón-Ballesteros, Antonio J.   136
Torres-Jiménez, Mercedes   597

Troncoso, Alicia   174, 685
Turecek, Tomas   402

Valero, Soledad   201
Valverde-Albacete, Francisco José   647
Ventura, Sebastián   365
Vergara Gonzalez, Eliseo P.   609
Vergara, Paula   261
Vescan, Andreea   463
Vicente, Henrique   3
Vieira, Adrían Seara   66
Villar, José R.   261
Vlachynska, Alzbeta   402

Walkowiak, Krzysztof   186
Woźniak, Michał   186, 560, 742

Zurutuza, Urko   79

Printed in the United States
By Bookmasters